PHILOSOPHY 2

FURTHER THROUGH THE SUBJECT

EDITED BY

A. C. GRAYLING

OXFORD
UNIVERSITY PRESS

OXFORD
UNIVERSITY PRESS

Great Clarendon Street, Oxford OX2 6DP

Oxford University Press is a department of the University of Oxford.
It furthers the University's objective of excellence in research, scholarship,
and education by publishing worldwide in

Oxford New York

Auckland Bangkok Buenos Aires Cape Town Chennai
Dar es Salaam Delhi Hong Kong Istanbul Karachi Kolkata
Kuala Lumpur Madrid Melbourne Mexico City Mumbai Nairobi
São Paulo Shanghai Taipei Tokyo Toronto

Oxford is a registered trade mark of Oxford University Press
in the UK and in certain other countries

Published in the United States
by Oxford University Press Inc., New York

First published in hardback and paperback 1998
Reprinted in paperback 1999, 2001

This work was originally produced for the use of students
of the External Programme of the University of London

British Library Cataloguing in Publication Data
Data available

Library of Congress Cataloging in Publication Data
Data available

ISBN 0-19-875179-6
ISBN 0-19-875178-8 (Pbk.)

5 7 9 10 8 6

Printed in Great Britain
on acid-free paper by
The Bath Press, Bath

PHILOSOPHY 2

Contents

Notes on the Contributors

NED BLOCK is Professor in the Departments of Philosophy and Psychology at the Center for Neural Science at New York University. Two volumes of his collected papers are forthcoming from MIT Press. He is co-editor of *The Nature of Consciousness: Philosophical Debates*, and is currently writing a book on consciousness.

MICHAEL DUMMETT is Emeritus Professor of Philosophy in the University of Oxford. He was Wykeham Professor of Logic at Oxford 1979–1992, and is an Emeritus Fellow of New College. His publications include *Frege: Philosophy of Language* (Duckworth, 1973), *The Logical Basis of Metaphysics* (Duckworth, 1991), *Frege: Philosophy of Mathematics* (Duckworth, 1991), *Frege and Other Philosophers* (Clarendon Press, 1991), *The Origins of Analytical Philosophy* (Duckworth, 1992), and *The Seas of Language* (Clarendon Press 1993).

SEBASTIAN GARDNER is Lecturer in Modern European Thought at University College, London. His interests lie in Kant, post-Kantian Continental philosophy, aesthetics, and the philosophy of psychoanalysis. He is the author of *Irrationality and the Philosophy of Psychoanalysis* (Cambridge University Press, 1993) and *Kant's 'Critique of Pure Reason'* (Routledge, 1998).

A. C. GRAYLING is Lecturer in Philosophy at Birkbeck College, London and Fellow of St Anne's College, Oxford. His publications include *Wittgenstein* (Oxford University Press, 1988), *Russell* (Oxford University Press, 1996), both in the Past Masters series, *The Refutation of Scepticism* (Duckworth, 1985), *Berkeley: The Central Arguments* (Duckworth, 1986), *An Introduction to Philosophical Logic*, 3rd edn. (Blackwell, 1997), and *Philosophy: A Guide Through the Subject* (Oxford University Press, 1995).

CHRISTOPHER HUGHES (BA, Wesleyan University, Ph.D., University of Pittsburgh) has been a lecturer in philosophy at King's College London since 1984. He works in medieval philosophy, metaphysics, and the philosophy of religion. His publications in medieval philosophy include *On a Complex Theory of a Simple God: An Investigation in Aquinas' Philosophical Theology* and various articles on Aquinas' account of individuation.

DAVID MITCHELL is Departmental Fellow in Philosophy at Birkbeck College, London. His published articles lie mainly in the field of ethics. Besides ancient philosophy, his research interests lie in questions about action, reasons, and reasoning, about which he is currently writing a book.

CHRISTOPHER PEACOCKE is Waynflete Professor of Metaphysical Philosophy in the University of Oxford, and he holds a Leverhulme Personal Research Professorship. He is a Visiting Professor at New York University, and has been a Fellow of the British Academy since 1990. He is the author of *Sense and Content* (Oxford University Press,

1983), *Thoughts: An Essay on Content* (Blackwell, 1986), and *A Study of Concepts* (MIT, 1992). He is currently working on a book on the integration of metaphysics and epistemology.

MICHAEL ROSEN is Fellow and Tutor in Philosophy at Lincoln College, Oxford. His publications include *Hegel's Dialectic and its Criticism* (Cambridge University Press, 1982), and *On Voluntary Servitude: False Consciousness and the Theory of Ideology* (Cambridge University Press, 1996).

DAVID-HILLEL RUBEN is Professor of Philosophy in the Department of Philosophy, Logic and Scientific Method at the London School of Economics. His publications include *Marxism and Materialism* (1979), *The Metaphysics of the Social World* (1985), *Explaining Explanation* (1990), and *Action and Its Explanation* (forthcoming). His research interests include the philosophy of social science, metaphysics, action theory, and epistemology.

ALAN RYAN has taught political theory in most of the English-speaking world since 1963. Until recently he taught at Princeton, and is now Warden of New College, Oxford. His most recent books are *John Dewey and the High Tide of American Liberalism* and an edition of Mill's *On Liberty* and *The Subjection of Women*.

GABRIEL SEGAL is Reader in Philosophy at King's College, London. He is co-author, with Richard Larson, of *Knowledge of Meaning: An Introduction to Semantic Theory* (MIT Press, 1995). His main research interests include the philosophy of psychology and the philosophy of language.

M. W. F. STONE is Lecturer in the Philosophy of Religion at King's College, London. He is the author of the forthcoming *The Subtle Art of Casuistry: An Essay in the History of Moral Reasoning* published by Oxford University Press. His research interests include medieval philosophy, ethics, and the philosophy of religion.

BERNHARD WEISS is Lecturer in the Department of Philosophy at the University of Wales, Lampeter. His research interests include the philosophy of language, logic and mathematics, and analytical philosophy.

PAUL WILLIAMS is Professor of Indian and Tibetan Philosophy and Co-director of the Centre for Buddhist Studies at the University of Bristol. His particular interest lies in Buddhist philosophy, especially the Madhyamaka school in India and Tibet. His publications include *Māhāyana Buddhism: The Doctrinal Foundations* (Routledge, 1989), *The Reflexive Nature of Awareness: A Tibetan Madhyamaka Defence* (Curzon, 1997), and *Altruism and Reality: Studies in the Philosophy of the Bodhicaryāvatāra* (Curzon, 1997).

JOHN WORRALL is Professor of Philosophy of Science at the London School of Economics. He has published numerous essays on topics associated with theory-change in science and is currently completing a book on these topics. His other research interests lie in the foundations and methodology of medicine.

Editor's Introduction

A. C. Grayling

Study is, obviously enough, a progressive enterprise; one masters the introductory stages of a subject in order to proceed to more advanced topics. But advanced topics themselves require some introduction; the student profits from being guided to the central concerns of a given subject and its essential literature, the better to continue independently thereafter. This volume aims to provide just such introductions to most of the important areas of philosophical inquiry beyond the elementary level.

The companion and, by design, precursor to this volume, *Philosophy 1: A Guide through the Subject*, introduces the standard range of core subjects on which this volume builds. It is not of course necessary that *Philosophy 1: A Guide* be the very book read before this one; any good introduction will do, for it is familiarity with the relevant philosphical subject-matter that counts. But such familiarity does indeed count; without some preparatory knowledge of debates in epistemology, metaphysics, and philosophical logic, and an acquaintance with the history of philosophy, most of the following essays will be harder to appreciate, while with it they will be, as they are designed to be, valuable entrances to the advanced subjects they address.

As with its precursor, this volume deals principally with areas of philosophical debate important in 'analytic philosophy'. It is often pointed out that analytic philosophy is not a school of thought, but a style or method of philosophical thinking; in this volume's precursor I described it as 'a style of philosophizing which seeks to be rigorous and careful, which at times makes use of ideas and techniques from logic, and which is aware of what is happening in science. It is, in particular, alert to linguistic considerations, not because of an interest in language for its own sake, but because it is through language that we grasp the concepts we use, and it is by means of language that we express our beliefs and assumptions. One of the principal methods of analytic philosophy is analysis of the concepts we employ in thinking about ourselves and the world: not surprisingly, this is called "conceptual analysis".' Most of the essays that follow—perhaps most especially those on philosophy of language, philosophy of psychology, philosophy of mathematics, philosophy of science, and the work of Frege, Russell, and Wittgenstein—focus on questions essential to the concerns of analytic philosophy.

Analytic philosophy is mainly associated with the contemporary English-speaking world, but it is by no means the only important philosophical tradition. In this volume two other immensely rich and important such traditions are introduced: Indian philosophy, and philosophical thought in Europe from the time of Hegel. Note that if an Indian text on philosophy devoted just one chapter to 'Western philosophy', one would find its vast range, long history, and many contending schools perforce treated with great compression. The same applies in this volume's single-chapter survey of Indian philosophical thought; but as with all the other chapters in this book, the aim is to stimulate readers to find out more on their own account.

The subjects introduced in this volume are various, and each of the chapters is independent of the others. The only unifying theme throughout is the approach: each chapter assumes that its readers have some grounding in the basics of philosophy, and (without attempting to be exhaustive: the bibliographies point the way to further study) offers an account of some of the key questions in the field under discussion. No area of philosophy is entirely free of connections to and overlaps with other areas, however, so it will be found that debate in one chapter throws light on debate in others in a variety of ways—as to which, more below.

Six chapters have as their titles 'The Philosophy of . . .'. In its more advanced regions philosophy often consists in reflection on the assumptions, methods, and claims of an important area of intellectual endeavour. The 'philosophy of' chapters focus on crucial subjects: science, mathematics, social science in general and psychology in particular, language, and religion.

Two chapters extend the study of philosophy's history into periods often neglected in undergraduate study, the 'post-Aristotelian' period of later ancient philosophy, and medieval philosophy. Each is rich in intrinsic interest, and in importance for developments in later philosophy.

The high importance of political philosophy demands that it have a chapter to itself, which it gets here.

I have already mentioned the chapters that respectively survey Indian philosophy and Continental philosophy; as with the others in this volume, they are intended to be prefaces to the further study invited by their bibliographies, but this is a point worth iterating in their case because of their range.

The remaining two chapters discuss the work of individuals. One is devoted to a single individual, Immanuel Kant; the other introduces themes in the thought of three of the principal founders of twentieth-century analytic philosophy: Gottlob Frege, Bertrand Russell, and Ludwig Wittgenstein. The Kant chapter surveys the work of a seminal modern thinker whose views have been influential in epistemology, metaphysics, ethics, and aesthetics across several traditions of philosophical debate. The chapter on Frege, Russell, and

Wittgenstein introduces a number of the most central questions of contemporary philosophy.

It was observed above that no area of philosophy is free of connections to other areas. Although the debates canvassed in the following chapters illuminate one another, this happens in too numerous and sometimes too indirect ways to be detailed here. Nevertheless, it is worth noting that certain chapters naturally group with certain others. The Frege–Russell–Wittgenstein chapter can usefully be read before those on philosophy of language and philosophy of mathematics. The Kant and the Continental philosophy chapters can profitably be read in sequence, in that order. The same applies to the later ancient and medieval philosophy chapters, which, moreover, both relate closely to that on philosophy of religion. And interesting and important comparisons can be drawn between the chapters on the philosophies of science and social science.

Together the essays in this volume constitute an advanced introduction to the further reaches of philosophy. It is not for absolute beginners, but it will thoroughly reward attentive reading by serious students of the subject, not least because many of the contributors are highly distinguished authorities on the subjects they treat.

Again as with its precursor, this volume originated in work done on behalf of the University of London in commissioning material to accompany undergraduate studies in philosophy. Students reading for London University's celebrated single-subject honours degree in philosophy turn, in the later stages of their study, to examine two or three advanced fields of thought (called, in the language of the rubrics, *optional subjects*); the essays in this volume introduce these advanced subjects. They do so robustly, and head-on, but with the needs of progressing students clearly in view. Along with its precursor, this book therefore constitutes, as it is designed to constitute, a major resource for continued philosophical study.

1

THE PHILOSOPHY OF PSYCHOLOGY

Ned Block and Gabriel Segal

INTRODUCTION

Gabriel Segal

Like the philosophy of mind, the philosophy of psychology is a certain type of inquiry into the nature of mind. They differ, however, in that the latter is a branch of the philosophy of science. It is concerned with issues arising from the various branches of the science of psychology. Or, if one has doubts about the scientific nature of psychology, one might say that it is concerned with issues arising from empirical studies of the mind. As such, philosophy of psychology is a very broad subject, including within its scope social psychology, psychoanalysis, and a host of other areas in theoretical, experimental, and developmental psychology. We will examine only a small sample of issues arising in respect of three specific areas of psychology.

The first two sections of what follows are concerned with the branch of psychology called 'cognitive science'. Cognitive science is based on the idea that the mind, or at least some important mental phenomena, can be understood in computational terms. The first section, written by Ned Block, deals with what may be called 'classical computationalism', which takes as its model the digital computer. The second section is concerned with so-called 'connectionism', which takes as its model a special kind of non-digital computer, called a 'parallel distributed processor'.

The third and final section looks at philosophical issues arising in relation to psychoanalytic theory, which was arguably the first scientific theory of mind to be developed in serious depth and detail, and remains one of the most important, interesting, and philosophically significant areas of psychological theorizing.

CLASSICAL COMPUTATIONALISM*

Ned Block

Cognitive scientists often say that the mind is the software of the brain. This section is about what this claim means.

1.1. Machine Intelligence

In this section I will start with an influential attempt to define 'intelligence', and then move to a consideration of how human intelligence is to be

I am indebted to Ken Aizawa, George Boolos, Susan Carey, Willem DeVries, Jerry Fodor, and Steven White for comments on an earlier draft of this part of the chapter. This work was supported by the National Science Foundation (DIR8812559).

*A version of this part of the chapter appeared under the title 'The Mind as the Software of the Brain' in E. E. Smith and D. N. Osherson (eds.), *An Invitation to Cognitive Science*, iii (Cambridge, Mass.: MIT Press).

investigated on the machine model. The last part of the section will discuss the relation between the mental and the biological.

1.1.1. *The Turing Test*

One approach to the mind has been to avoid its mysteries by simply *defining* the mental in terms of the behavioural. This approach has been popular among thinkers who fear that acknowledging mental states that do not reduce to behaviour would make psychology unscientific, because unreduced mental states are not intersubjectively accessible in the manner of the entities of the hard sciences. 'Behaviourism', as the attempt to reduce the mental to the behavioural is called, has often been regarded as refuted, but it periodically reappears in new forms.

Behaviourists don't define the mental in terms of just plain *behaviour*, since after all something can be intelligent even if it has never had the chance to exhibit its intelligence. Behaviourists define the mental not in terms of behaviour, but rather in terms of behavioural *dispositions*, the tendency to exhibit certain behaviours given certain stimuli. It is important that the stimuli and the behaviour be specified non-mentalistically. Thus, intelligence could not be defined in terms of the disposition to give sensible responses to questions, since that would be to define a mental notion in terms of another mental notion (indeed, a closely related one). To see the difficulty of behaviouristic analyses, one has to appreciate how mentalistic our ordinary behavioural descriptions are. Consider, for example, *throwing*. A series of motions that constitute throwing if produced by one mental cause might be a dance to get the ants off if produced by another.

An especially influential behaviourist definition of intelligence was put forward by A. M. Turing (1950). Turing, one of the mathematicians who cracked the German code during the Second World War, formulated the idea of the universal Turing machine, which contains, in mathematical form, the essence of the programmable digital computer. Turing wanted to define intelligence in a way that applied to both men and machines, and indeed, to anything that is intelligent. His version of behaviourism formulates the issue of whether machines could think or be intelligent in terms of whether they could pass the following test: a judge in one room communicates by teletype (this was 1950) with a computer in a second room and a person in a third room for some specified period (let's say an hour). The computer is intelligent if and only if the judge cannot tell the difference between the computer and the person. Turing's definition finessed the difficult problem of specifying non-mentalistically the behavioural dispositions that are characteristic of intelligence by bringing in the discrimination behaviour of a human judge. And the definition generalizes. *Anything* is intelligent just in case it can pass the Turing test.

Turing suggested that we replace the concept of intelligence with the concept of passing the Turing test. But what is the replacement *for*? If the purpose of the replacement is practical, the Turing test is not enormously useful. If one wants to know if a machine does well at playing chess or diagnosing pneumonia or planning football strategy, it is better to see how the machine performs in action than to make it take a Turing test. For one thing, what we care about is that it do well at detecting pneumonia, not that it do it in a way indistinguishable from the way a person would do it. So if it does the job, who cares if it doesn't pass the Turing test?

A second purpose might be utility for theoretical purposes. But machines that can pass the Turing test such as Weizenbaum's ELIZA (see below) have been dead ends in artificial intelligence research, not exciting beginnings. (See 'Mimicry versus Exploration' in Marr 1977; and Shieber 1994.)

A third purpose, the one that comes closest to Turing's intentions, is the purpose of conceptual *clarification*. Turing was famous for having formulated a precise mathematical concept that he offered as a replacement for the vague idea of mechanical computability. The precise concept (computability by a Turing machine) did everything one would want a precise concept of mechanical computability to do. No doubt, Turing hoped that the Turing test conception of intelligence would yield everything one would want from a definition of intelligence without the vagueness of the ordinary concept.

Construed as a proposal about how to make this concept of intelligence precise, there is a gap in Turing's proposal: we are not told how the judge is to be chosen. A judge who was a leading authority on genuinely intelligent machines might know how to tell them apart from people. For example, the expert may know that current intelligent machines get certain problems right that people get wrong. Turing acknowledged this point by jettisoning the claim that being able to pass the Turing test is a necessary condition of intelligence, weakening his claim to: passing the Turing test is a sufficient condition for intelligence. He says, 'May not machines carry out something which ought to be described as thinking but which is very different from what a man does? This objection is a very strong one, but at least we can say that if, nevertheless, a machine can be constructed to play the imitation game satisfactorily, we need not be troubled by this objection' (Turing 1950: 435). In other words, a machine that *does* pass is necessarily intelligent, even if some intelligent machines fail.

But the problem of how to specify the qualities of the judge goes deeper than Turing acknowledges, and compromises the Turing test as a sufficient condition too. A stupid judge, or one who has had no contact with technology, might think that a radio was intelligent. People who are naive about computers are amazingly easy to fool, as was demonstrated in the First Turing Test at the Boston Computer Museum in 1991 (see Shieber 1994). A version of Weizenbaum's ELIZA (described in the next paragraph) was classified as human by five of ten judges. The test was 'restricted' in that the computer programmers were given specific topics that their questions would be restricted to, and the judges were forbidden to ask 'tricky' questions. For example, if the topic were Washington, DC, a judge was not supposed to ask questions like 'Is Washington, DC bigger than a bread-bin?' However, the winning program's topic was 'whimsical conversation', a 'smart-alec' way of interacting that all the judges fell in with immediately, and one that would have had the same effect, even without set topics. Further, the restrictions to non-tricky questions weren't enforced. (I speak as one of the referees who failed to enforce them.) For the most part, the computer-naïve judges didn't really know how to formulate a tricky question. Thus the variant of ELIZA may be regarded as having done well in an unrestricted Turing test. Variants on ELIZA (all written by Joseph Weintraub) were also victorious in the Second and Third Turing Tests. The upshot is that a completely stupid computer program has *already* been shown to pass a reasonable facsimile of a Turing test.

ELIZA is a simple program written by Joseph Weizenbaum that in one version imitates a psychiatrist (see Weizenbaum 1976). It employs a group of simple but effective strategies. For example, it looks for 'key words' on a list supplied by the programmer, e.g. 'I', 'you', 'alike', 'father', and 'everybody'. The words are ordered; for example, 'father' comes before 'everybody', so if you type in 'My father is afraid of everybody', the machine will spit back one of its 'father' responses, such as 'WHAT ELSE COMES TO MIND WHEN YOU THINK OF YOUR FATHER?' If you type in 'Everybody laughed at me', you will get one of its responses to 'everybody', such as 'WHO IN PARTICULAR ARE YOU THINKING OF?' It also has techniques that simultaneously transform 'you' into 'I' and 'me' into 'you' so that if you type in 'You don't agree with me', it can reply: 'WHY DO YOU THINK THAT I DON'T AGREE WITH YOU?' It also stores sentences containing certain key words such as 'my'. If your current input contains no key words, but if you earlier said 'My boyfriend made me come here', the program will say 'DOES THAT HAVE ANYTHING TO DO WITH THE FACT THAT YOUR BOYFRIEND MADE YOU COME HERE?' It also has stock responses to 'Parlez-vous français' (or any other sentence with 'français' in it), for example 'I SPEAK ONLY ENGLISH'. If all else fails, the machine has a list of last-ditch responses such as 'WHO IS THE PSYCHIATRIST HERE, YOU OR ME?'

This type of program is easy to trip up if you know how it works. For example, in the First Turing Test, one judge said 'You're trying to make this difficult for me, aren't you?' and the program's reply included the following: 'WHAT MAKES YOU THINK I AM TRYING TO MAKE THIS DIFFICULT FOR YOU, AREN'T I?' As Shieber points out, the pronoun transposition rules can't handle 'tag questions' that end with, for example, 'aren't you?'

The point that this program illustrates is that a simple program can be extraordinarily successful in activities akin to passing the Turing test. Weizenbaum reports[1] that a computer scientist who knew all about the program sent him a

[1] Personal communication.

computer message while Weizenbaum was taking a nap but had the psychiatrist mode engaged. The colleague was asking Weizenbaum to log off, because Weizenbaum was tying up the computer without using it, and the colleague wanted to use the machine. The colleague's messages were answered by ELIZA, and the conversation might have gone as follows. (I got ELIZA's responses to these questions from a PC version of the program.) 'Joe, will you please log off.' WE WERE DISCUSSING YOU, NOT ME 'I need to use the computer.' DO COMPUTERS WORRY YOU? 'No, computers don't worry me.' WHAT DO YOU THINK MACHINES HAVE TO DO WITH YOUR PROBLEM? 'Come off it.' WHY DO YOU SAY THAT? The colleague, a professional who knew all about ELIZA, had no idea that he wasn't talking to a human, and called Weizenbaum in a rage. Weizenbaum's program is not sophisticated or complex by current standards (there is a PC version that is only 200 lines in BASIC), yet this type of program is better at passing the Turing test than anything else written to date, as is shown by the three victories in a row in the Turing tests mentioned above. Imagine how convincing a program would be produced if the defence budget were devoted to this task for a year! But even if a high-budget government initiative produced a program that was good at passing the Turing test, if the program was just a bundle of tricks like the Weizenbaum program, with question-types all thought of in advance, and canned responses placed in the machine, the machine would not be intelligent.

One way of dealing with the problem of the specification of the judge is to make some sort of characterization of the mental qualities of the judge part of the formulation of the Turing test. For example, one might specify that the judge be moderately knowledgeable about computers and good at thinking, or better, good at thinking about thinking. But including a specification of the mental qualities of the judge in the description of the test will ruin the test as a way of *defining* the concept of intelligence in non-mentalistic terms. Further, if we are going to specify that the judge be good at thinking about thinking, we might just as well give up on having the judge judge which contestants are humans or machines and just have the judge judge which contestants think. And then what the idea of the Turing test would amount to is: a machine thinks if our best thinkers (about thinking) think it thinks. Although this sounds like a platitude, it is actually false. For even our best thinkers are fallible. The most that can be claimed is that if our best thinkers think that something thinks, then it is rational for us to believe that it does.

I've made much of the claim that judges can be fooled by a mindless machine that is just a bag of tricks. 'But', you may object, 'how do we know that *we* are not just a bag of tricks.' Of course, in a sense perhaps we are, but that isn't the sense relevant to what is wrong with the Turing test. To see this point, consider the ultimate in unintelligent Turing test passers, a hypothetical machine that contains all conversations of a given length in which the machine's replies make sense. Let's stipulate that the test lasts one hour. Since there is an upper bound on how fast a human typist can type, and since there are a finite number of keys on a teletype, there is an upper bound on the 'length' of a Turing test conversation. Thus there are a finite (though more than astronomical) number of different Turing test conversations, and there is no contradiction in the idea of listing them all.

Let's call a string of characters that can be typed in an hour or less a 'typable' string. In principle, all typable strings could be generated, and a team of intelligent programmers could throw out all the strings which cannot be interpreted as a conversation in which at least one party (say the second contributor) is making sense. The remaining strings (call them the sensible strings) could be stored in a hypothetical computer (say, with marks separating the contributions of the separate parties), which works as follows. The judge types in something. Then the machine locates a string that starts with the judge's remark, spitting back its next element. The judge then types something else. The machine finds a string that begins with the judge's first contribution, followed by the machine's, followed by the judge's next contribution (the string will be there since all sensible strings are there), and then the machine spits back its fourth element, and so on. (We can eliminate the simplifying assumption that the judge speaks first by recording pairs of strings; this would also allow the judge and the machine to talk at the same time.) Of course, such a machine is only logically possible, not physically possible. The number of strings is too vast to exist, and even if they could exist, they could never be accessed by any sort of machine in anything like real time. But since we are considering a proposed definition of intelligence that is supposed to capture the concept of intelligence, conceptual possibility will do the job. If the concept of intelligence is supposed to be exhausted by the ability to pass the Turing test, then even a universe in which the laws of physics are very different from ours should contain exactly as many unintelligent Turing test passers as married bachelors, namely zero. Note that the choice of one hour as a limit for the Turing test is of no consequence, since the procedure just described works for any finite Turing test.

The following variant of the machine may be easier to grasp. The programmers start by writing down all typable strings, call them $A_1 \ldots A_n$. Then they think of just one sensible response to each of these, which we may call $B_1 \ldots B_n$. (Actually, there will be fewer *B*s than *A*s because some of the *A*s will take up the entire hour.) The programmers may have an easier time of it if they think of themselves as simulating some definite personality, say my Aunt Bubbles, and some definite situation, say Aunt Bubbles being brought into the teletype room by her strange nephew and asked to answer questions for an hour. So each of the *B*s will be the sort of reply Aunt Bubbles would give to the preceding *A*. For example, if *A73* is 'Explain general relativity', *B73* might be 'Ask my nephew, he's the professor'. What about the judge's replies to each of the *B*s? The judge can

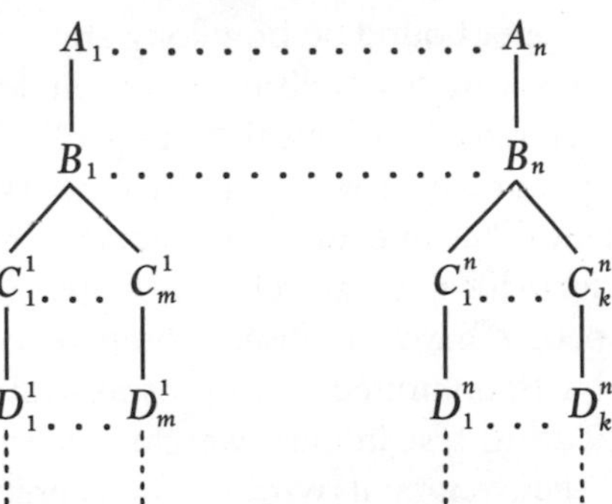

FIG. 1.1. A conversation is any path from the top to the bottom

give any reply up to the remaining length limit, so below each of the *B*s there will sprout a vast number of *C*s (vast, but fewer than the number of *B*s, since the time remaining has decreased). The programmers' next task is to produce just one *D* for each of the *C*s. So if the *B* just mentioned is followed by a *C* which is 'xyxyxyxyxyxyxy!' (remember, the judge doesn't have to make sense), the programmers might make the following *D* 'My nephew warned me that you might type some weird messages'.

Think of conversations as paths downward through a tree, starting with an A_i from the judge, a reply, B_i from the machine, and so on (see Figure 1.1). For each A_i–B_i–C^i_j that is a beginning to a conversation, the programmers must produce a *D* that makes sense given the *A*, *B*, and *C* that precede it. The machine works as follows. The judge goes first. Whatever the judge types in (typos and all) is one of $A_1 \ldots A_n$. The machine locates the particular *A*, say A_{2398}, and then spits back B_{2398}, a reply chosen by the programmers to be appropriate to A_{2398}. The judge types another message, and the machine again finds it in the list of C_s that sprout below B_{2398}, and then spits back the pre-recorded reply (which takes into account what was said in A_{2398} and B_{2398}). And so on. Though the machine can do as well in the one-hour Turing test as Aunt Bubbles, it has the intelligence of a jukebox. Every clever remark it produces was specifically thought of by the programmers as a response to the previous remark of the judge in the context of the previous conversation. Though this machine is too big to exist, there is nothing incoherent or contradictory about its specification, and so it is enough to refute the behaviourist interpretation of the Turing test that I have been talking about.[2]

[2] The Aunt Bubbles machine refutes something stronger than behaviourism, namely the claim that the mental 'supervenes' on the behavioural; that is, that there can be no mental difference without a behavioural difference. (Of course, the behavioural dispositions are finite—see the next paragraph in the text.) I am indebted to Stephen White for pointing out to me that the doctrine of the supervenience of the mental on the behavioural is widespread among thinkers who reject behaviourism, such as Donald Davidson. The Aunt Bubbles machine is described and defended in detail in Block (1978, 1981*a*), and was independently discovered by White (1982).

Note that there is an upper bound on how long any particular Aunt Bubbles machine can go on in a Turing test, a limit set by the length of the strings it has been given. Of course *real people* have their upper limits too, given that real people will eventually quit or die. However, there is a very important difference between the Aunt Bubbles machine and a real person. We can define 'competence' as idealized performance. Then, relative to appropriate idealizations, it may well be that real people have an infinite competence to go on. That is, if humans were provided with unlimited memory and with motivational systems that give passing the Turing test infinite weight, they could go on for ever (at least according to conventional wisdom in cognitive science). This is definitely not the case for the Aunt Bubbles machine. But this difference provides no objection to the Aunt Bubbles machine as a refutation of the Turing test conception of intelligence, because the notion of competence is not behaviouristically acceptable, requiring as it does for its specification a distinction among components of the mind. For example, the mechanisms of thought must be distinguished from the mechanisms of memory and motivation.

'But', you may object, 'isn't it rather chauvinist to assume that a machine must process information in just the way we do to be intelligent?' Answer: Such an assumption would indeed be chauvinist, but I am not assuming it. The point against the Turing test conception of intelligence is not that the Aunt Bubbles machine wouldn't process information the way we do, but rather that the way it does process information is unintelligent despite its performance in the Turing test.

Ultimately, the problem with the Turing test for theoretical purposes is that it focuses on performance rather than on competence. Of course, performance is evidence for competence, but the core of our understanding of the mind lies with mental competence, not behavioural performance. The behaviourist cast of mind that leads to the Turing test conception of intelligence also leads to labelling the sciences of the mind as 'the behavioural sciences'. But as Chomsky (1959) has pointed out, that is like calling physics the science of meter readings.

1.1.2. *Two Kinds of Definition of Intelligence*

We have been talking about an attempt to define intelligence using the resources of the Turing test. However, there is a very different approach to defining intelligence. To explain this approach, it will be useful to contrast two kinds of definition of water. One might be better regarded as a definition of the word 'water'. The word might be defined as the colourless, odourless, tasteless liquid that is found in lakes and oceans. In this sense of 'definition', the definition of 'water' is available to anyone who speaks the language, even someone who knows no science. But one might also define water by saying what water really is, that is, by saying what physico-chemical structure in fact makes something pure water. The answer to this question would involve its chemical constitution: H_2O. Defining a word is something we can do in our armchair, by consulting our linguistic intuitions about hypothetical cases, or, bypassing this process, by simply stipulating a meaning for a word. Defining (or explicating) the thing is an activity that involves empirical investigation into the nature of something in the world.

What we have been discussing so far is the first kind of definition of intelligence, the definition of the word, not the thing. Turing's definition is not the result of an empirical investigation into the components of intelligence of the sort that led to the definition of water as H_2O. Rather, he hoped to avoid muddy thinking about machine intelligence by stipulating that the word 'intelligent' should be used a certain way, at least with regard to machines. Quite a different way of proceeding is to investigate intelligence itself as physical chemists investigate water. We will consider how this might be done in the next section, but first we should note a complication.

There are two kinds (at least) of kind: *structural* kinds such as *water* or *tiger*, and *functional* kinds such as *mousetrap* or *gene*. A structural kind has a 'hidden compositional essence'; in the case of water, the compositional essence is a matter of its molecules consisting of two hydrogen molecules and one oxygen molecule. Functional kinds, by contrast, have no essence that is a matter of composition. A certain sort of function, a causal role, is the key to being a mousetrap or a carburettor. (The full story is quite complex: something can be a mousetrap because it is made to be one even if it doesn't fulfil that function very well.) What makes a bit of DNA a gene is its function with respect to mechanisms that can read the information that it encodes and use this information to make a biological product.

Now the property of being intelligent is no doubt a functional kind, but it still makes sense to investigate it experimentally, just as it makes sense to investigate genes experimentally. One topic of investigation is the role of intelligence in problem-solving, planning, decision-making, etc. Just what functions are involved in a functional kind is often a difficult and important empirical question. The project of Mendelian genetics has been to investigate the function of genes at a level of description that does not involve their molecular realizations. A second topic of investigation is the nature of the realizations that have the function in us, in humans: DNA in the case of genes. Of course, if there are Martians, their genes may not be composed of DNA. Similarly, we can investigate the functional details and physical basis of human intelligence without attention to the fact that our results will not apply to other mechanisms of other hypothetical intelligences.

1.1.3. *Functional Analysis*

Both types of projects just mentioned can be pursued via a common methodology, a methodology sometimes known as *functional analysis*. Think of the human mind as represented by an intelligent being in the head, a 'homunculus'. Think of this homunculus as being composed of smaller and stupider homunculi, and each of these being composed of still smaller and still stupider homunculi until you reach a level of completely mechanical homunculi. (This picture was first articulated in Fodor 1968; see also Dennett 1974 and Cummins 1975.)

Suppose one wants to explain how we understand language. Part of the system will recognize individual words. This word-recognizer might be composed of three components, one of which has the task of fetching each incoming word, one at a time, and passing it to a second component. The second component includes a dictionary, i.e. a list of all the words in the vocabulary, together with syntactic and semantic information about each word. This second component compares the target word with words in the vocabulary (perhaps executing many such comparisons simultaneously) until it gets a match. When it finds a match, it sends a signal to a third component whose job it is to retrieve the syntactic and semantic information stored in the dictionary. This speculation about how a model of language-understanding works is supposed to illustrate how a cognitive competence can be explained by appeal to simpler cognitive competences, in this case the simple mechanical operations of fetching and matching.

The idea of this kind of explanation of intelligence comes from attention to the way computers work. Consider a computer that multiplies m by n by adding m to 0 n times. Here is a program for doing this. Think of m and n as represented in the registers M and N in Figure 1.2. Register A is reserved for the answer, a. First, a representation of 0 is placed in the register A. Second, register N is examined to see if it contains (a representation of) 0. If the answer is yes, the program halts and the correct answer is 0. (If $n = 0$, $m \times n = 0$.) If no, N is decremented by 1 (so register N now contains a representation of $n - 1$), and (a representation of) m is added to the answer register, A. Then, the procedure loops back to the second step: register N is checked once again to see if its value is 0; if not, it is again decremented by 1, and again m is added to the answer register. This procedure continues until N finally has the value 0, at which time m will have been added to the answer register exactly n times. At this point, the answer register contains a representation of the answer.

This program multiplies via a 'decomposition' of multiplication into other processes, namely addition, subtraction of 1, setting a register to 0, and checking a register for 0. Depending on how these things are themselves done, they

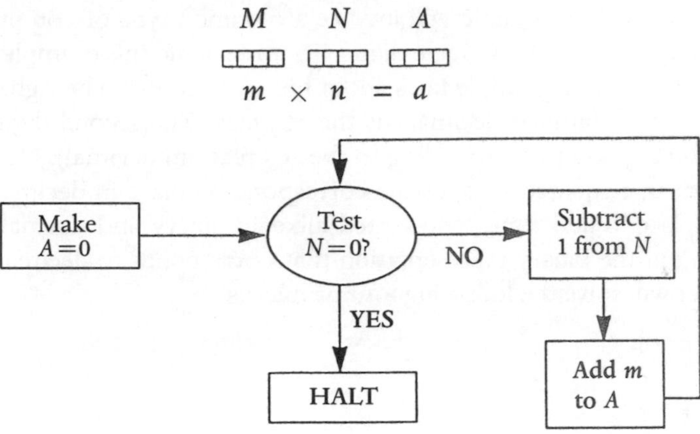

FIG. 1.2. Program for multiplying. One begins the multiplication by putting representations of *m* and *n*, the numbers to be multiplied, in registers *M* and *N*. At the end of the computation, the answer will be found in register *A*. See the text for a description of how the program works

may be further decomposable, or they may be the fundamental bottom-level processes, known as *primitive processes*.

The cognitive science definition or explication of intelligence is analogous to this explication of multiplication. Intelligent capacities are understood via decomposition into a network of less intelligent capacities, ultimately grounded in totally mechanical capacities executed by primitive processors.

The concept of a primitive process is very important; the next section is devoted to it.

1.1.4. *Primitive Processors*

What makes a processor primitive? One answer is that for primitive processors the question 'How does the processor work?' is not a question for cognitive science to answer. The cognitive scientist answers 'How does the multiplier work?' in the case of the multiplier described above by giving the program or the information flow diagram for the multiplier. But if components of the multiplier, say the gates of which the adder is composed, are primitive, then it is not the cognitive scientist's business to answer the question of how such a gate works. The cognitive scientist can say: 'That question belongs in another discipline, electronic circuit theory.' Distinguish the question of how something *works* from the question of what it *does*. (What an adder does is: add.) The question of *what* a primitive processor does is part of cognitive science, but the question of *how* it does it is not.

This idea can be made a bit clearer by looking at how a primitive processor actually works. The example will involve a common type of computer adder, simplified so as to add only single digits. To understand this example, you need to know the following simple facts about binary notation. The rightmost digit in binary—as in familiar decimal—is the 1s place. The second digit from the right is the 2s place (corresponding to the 10s place in decimal). Next is the 4s place (that is, 2 squared), just as the corresponding place in decimal is the 10-squared place. 0 and 1 are represented alike in binary and normal (decimal) notation, but the binary representation that corresponds to decimal '2' is '10'. Our adder will solve the following four problems:

$$0+0=0$$
$$1+0=1$$
$$0+1=1$$
$$1+1=10.$$

The first three equations are true in both binary and decimal, but the last is true only if understood in binary.

The second item of background information is the notion of a gate. An *and* gate is a device that accepts two inputs, and emits a single output. If both inputs are '1's, the output is a '1'; otherwise, the output is a '0'. An *exclusive-or* (either but not both) gate is a 'difference detector': it emits a '0' if its inputs are the same (i.e. '1'/'1' or '0'/'0'), and it emits a '1' if its inputs are different (i.e. '1'/'0' or '0'/'1')

This talk of '1' and '0' is a way of thinking about the 'bistable' states of computer representers. These representers are made so that they are always in one or the other of two states, and only momentarily in between. (This is what it is to be bistable.) The states might be a 4-volt and a 7-volt potential. If one of the two states (say 4 volts) is such that when both inputs are in that state, so is the output, and if every other combination of inputs yields the 7-volt output, then the gate is an *and* gate and the 4-volt state realizes a '1'. (Alternatively, if the 4-volt state is taken to realize '0', the gate is an *inclusive-or* (either or both) gate.) A different type of *and* gate might be made so that the 7-volt state realized '1'. The point is that '1' is conventionally assigned to whatever bistable physical state of an *and* gate it is that has the role mentioned. And all that counts about an *and* gate from a computational point of view is its input–output function, not how it works or whether 4 volts or 7 volts realizes a '1'. Note the terminology I have been using: one speaks of a physical state (4-volt potential) as 'realizing' a computational state (having the value '1'). This distinction between the computational and physical levels of description will be important in what follows, especially in Section 1.3.3.

Here is how the adder works. The two digits to be added are connected both to an *and* gate and to an *exclusive-or* gate as illustrated in Figure 1.3. Let's look at 1.3(*a*) first. The digits to be added are '1' and '0', and they are placed in the input register, which is the top pair of boxes. The *exclusive-or* gate, which, you recall is a difference detector, sees different things, and so outputs a '1' to the rightmost box of the answer register, which is the bottom pair of boxes. The *and* gate outputs a '0' to the left box except when it sees two '1's, and so it outputs a '0'. In this way, the circuit computes '1 + 0 = 1'. For this problem, as for '0 + 1 = 1' and '0 + 0 = 0', the *exclusive-or* gate does all the real work. The role of the *and* gate in this circuit is *carrying*, and that is illustrated in Figure 1.3(*b*). The digits to be added, '1' and '1', are placed in the top register again. Now, both inputs to the *and* gate are '1's, and so the *and* gate outputs a '1' to the leftmost box of the answer (bottom) register. The *exclusive-or* gate puts a '0' in the rightmost box, and so we have the correct answer, '10'.

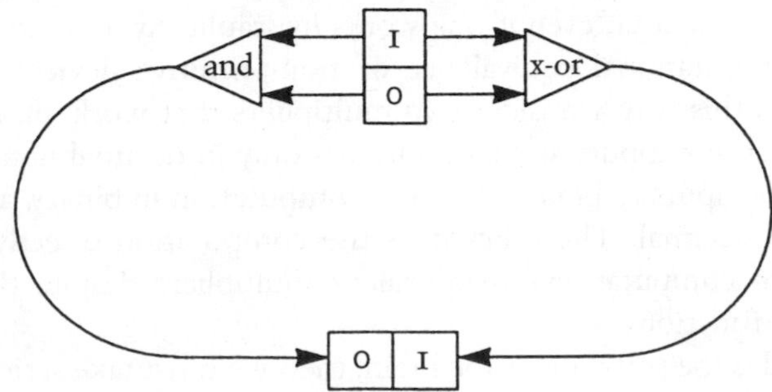

FIG. 1.3. (*a*) Adder doing 1 + 0 = 1

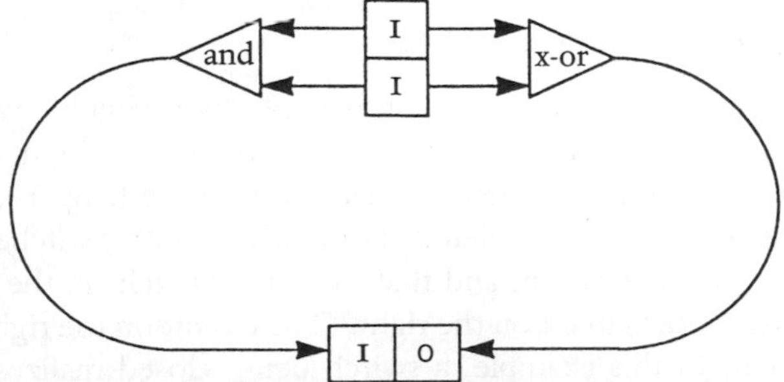

FIG. 1.3. (*b*) Adder doing 1 + 1 = 10

The borders between scientific disciplines are notoriously fuzzy. No one can say *exactly* where chemistry stops and physics begins. Since the line between the upper levels of processors and the level of primitive processors is the same as the line between cognitive science and one of the 'realization' sciences such as electronics or physiology, the boundary between the levels of complex processors and the level of primitive processors will have the same fuzziness. None the less, in this example we should expect that the gates are the primitive processors. If they are made in the usual way, they are the largest components whose operation must be explained, not in terms of cognitive science, but rather in terms of electronics or mechanics or some other realization science. Why the qualification 'If they are made in the usual way'? It would be *possible* to make an adder each of whose gates were whole *computers*, with their own multipliers, adders, and normal gates. It would be silly to waste a whole computer on such a simple task as that of an *and* gate, but it could be done. In that case, the real level of primitives would not be the gates of the original adder, but rather the (normal) gates of the component computers.

Primitive processors are the only computational devices for which behaviourism is *true*. Two primitive processors (such as gates) count as computationally equivalent if they have the same input–output function, i.e. the same actual and potential behaviour, even if one works hydraulically and the other electrically. But computational equivalence of non-primitive devices is not to be understood in this way. Consider two multipliers that work via different programs. Both accept inputs and emit outputs only in decimal notation. One of them converts inputs to binary, does the computation in binary, and then converts back to decimal. The other does the computation directly in decimal. These are not computationally equivalent multipliers despite their identical input–output functions.

If the mind is the software of the brain, then we must take seriously the idea that the functional analysis of human intelligence will bottom out in primitive processors in the brain.

1.1.5. *The Mental and the Biological*

One type of electrical *and* gate consists of two circuits with switches arranged as in Figure 1.4. The switches on the left are the inputs. When only one or neither of the input switches is closed, nothing happens, because the circuit on the left is not completed. Only when both switches are closed does the electromagnet go on, and that pulls the switch on the right closed, thereby turning on the circuit on the right. (The circuit on the right is only partially illustrated.) In this example, a switch being closed realizes '1'; it is the bistable state that obtains as an output if and only if two of them are present as an input.

Another *and* gate is illustrated in Figure 1.5. If neither of the mice on the left are released into the right-hand part of their cages, or if only one of the mice is released, the cat does not strain hard enough to pull the leash. But when both are released, and are thereby visible to the cat, the cat strains enough to lift the third mouse's gate, letting it into the cheesy part of its box. So we have a situation in which a mouse getting cheese is output if and only if two cases of mice getting cheese are input.

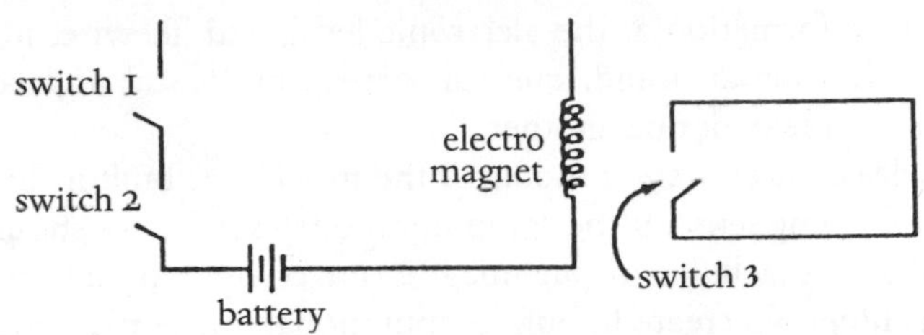

FIG. 1.4. Electrical *and* gate. Open = 0; closed = 1

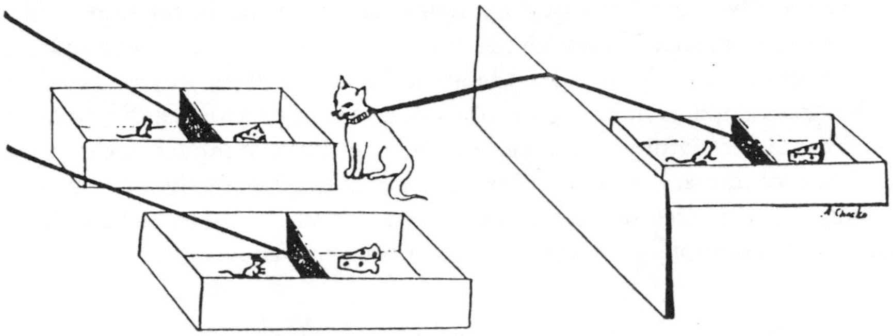

FIG. 1.5. Cat and mouse *and* gate. Hungry mouse = 0; mouse fed = 1

The point illustrated here is the irrelevance of hardware realization to computational description. These gates work in very different ways, but they are none the less computationally equivalent. And, of course, it is possible to think of an indefinite variety of other ways of making a primitive *and* gate. How such gates work is no more part of the domain of cognitive science than is the nature of the buildings that hold computer factories. This reveals a sense in which the computer model of the mind is profoundly *unbiological*. We are beings who *have* a useful and interesting biological level of description, but the computer model of the mind aims for a level of description of the mind that abstracts away from the biological realizations of cognitive structures. As far as the computer model goes, it does not matter whether our gates are realized in grey matter, switches, or cats and mice.

Of course, this is not to say that the computer model is in any way incompatible with a biological approach. Indeed, cooperation between the biological and computational approaches is vital to discovering the program of the brain. Suppose one were presented with a computer of alien design and set the problem of ascertaining its program by any means possible. Only a fool would choose to ignore information to be gained by opening the computer up to see how its circuits work. One would want to put information at the program level together with information at the electronic level, and likewise, in finding the program of the human mind, one can expect biological and cognitive approaches to complement one another.

None the less, the computer model of the mind has a built-in anti-biological bias, in the following sense. If the computer model is right, we should be able to create intelligent machines in our image—our computational image, that is. And the machines we create in our computational image may not be biologically similar to us. If we can create machines in our computational image, we will naturally feel that the most compelling theory of the mind is one that is general enough to apply to both them and us, and this will be a computational theory, not a biological theory. A biological theory of the *human* mind will not apply to these machines, though the biological theory will have a complementary advantage: namely, that such a biological theory will encompass us together with our less intelligent biological cousins, and thus provide a different kind of insight into the nature of human intelligence. Both approaches can accommodate evolutionary considerations, though, in the case of the computational paradigm, evolution is no more relevant to the nature of the mind than the programmer's intentions are to the nature of a computer program.

1.2. Intelligence and Intentionality

Our discussion so far has centred on the computational approach to one aspect of the mind, intelligence. But there is a different aspect of the mind that we have not yet discussed, one that has a very different relation to computational ideas, namely intentionality.

For our purposes, we can take intelligence to be a capacity, a capacity for various intelligent activities such as solving mathematics problems, deciding whether to go to graduate school, and figuring out how spaghetti is made. (Notice that this analysis of intelligence as a capacity to solve, figure out, decide, and the like, is a mentalistic analysis, not a behaviourist analysis.)

Intentionality is aboutness. Intentional states represent the world as being a certain way. The thought that the moon is full and the perceptual state of seeing that the moon is full are both about the moon and they both represent the moon as being full. So both are intentional states. We say that the intentional content of both the thought and the perceptual state is that the moon is full. A single intentional content can have very different behavioural effects, depending on its relation to the person who has the content. For example, the desire that one may be rich may stimulate saving, whereas the belief that one is rich may stimulate spending. (Don't let the spelling mislead you: intending is only one kind of intentional state. Believing and desiring are others.) Intentionality is an important feature of many mental states, but many philosophers believe it is not 'the mark of the mental'. There are bodily sensations, the experience of orgasm, for example, that are genuine mental states but have no intentional content. (Well, maybe there is a bit of intentional content to this experience, e.g. locational content, but the phenomenal content of the experience, what it is like to have it, is clearly not exhausted by that intentional content.)

The features of thought just mentioned are closely related to features of language. Thoughts represent, are about things, and can be true or false; and the same is true of sentences. The sentence 'Bruce Springsteen was born in the USSR' is about Springsteen, represents him as having been born in the Soviet Union, and is false. It would be surprising if the intentional content of thought and of language were independent phenomena, and so it is natural to try to reduce one to the other or to find some common explanation for both. We will pursue this idea below, but before we go any further, let's try to get clearer about just what the difference is between intelligence and intentionality.

One way to get a handle on the distinction between intelligence and intentionality is to note that in the opinion of many writers on this topic, you can have intentionality without intelligence. Thus John McCarthy (the creator of the artificial intelligence language LISP) holds that thermostats have intentional states in virtue of their capacity to represent and control temperature (McCarthy 1980). And there is a school of thought that assigns content to tree rings in virtue of their representing the age of the tree. But no school of thought holds that the tree rings are actually intelligent. An intelligent system must have certain intelligent capacities, capacities to do certain sorts of thing, and tree rings can't do these things. Less controversially, words on a page and images on a television screen have intentionality. For example, my remark earlier in this paragraph to the effect that McCarthy created LISP is about McCarthy. But words on a page have no intelligence. Of course, the intentionality of words on a page is only derived intentionality, not original intentionality (see Searle 1980 and Haugeland 1980). Derived intentional content is inherited from the original intentional contents of intentional systems such as you and me. We have a great deal of freedom in giving symbols their derived intentional content. If we want to, we can decide that 'McCarthy' will now represent Minsky or Chomsky. Original intentional contents are the intentional contents that the representations of an intentional system have for that system. Such intentional contents are not subject to our whim. Words on a page have derived intentionality, but they do not have any kind of intelligence, not even derived intelligence, whatever that would be.

Conversely, there can be intelligence without intentionality. Imagine that an event with negligible (but, importantly, non-zero) probability occurs: in their random movement, particles from the swamp come together and by chance result in a molecule-for-molecule duplicate of your brain. The swamp-brain is arguably intelligent, because it has many of the same capacities that your brain has. If we were to hook it up to the right inputs and outputs and give it an arithmetic problem, we would get an intelligent response. But there are reasons for denying that it has the intentional states that you have, and indeed for denying that it has any intentional states at all. For since we have not hooked it up to input devices, it has never had any information from the world. Suppose your brain and it go through an identical process, a process that in your case is the thinking of the thought that Bernini vandalized the Pantheon. The identical process in the swamp-brain has the phenomenal features of that thought, in the sense of 'phenomenal content' indicated in the discussion of orgasm above. What it is like for you to think the thought is just what it is like for the swamp-brain. But, unlike you, the swamp-brain has no idea who Bernini was, what the Pantheon is, or what vandalizing is. No information about Bernini has made any kind of contact with the swamp-brain; no signals from the Pantheon have reached it either. Had it a mouth, it would merely be mouthing words. So no one should be happy with the idea that the swamp-brain is thinking the thought that Bernini vandalized the Pantheon.

The upshot: what makes a system intelligent is what it can do, what it has the capacity to do. So intelligence is future-orientated. What makes a system an intentional system, by contrast, is in part a matter of its causal history; it must have a history that makes its states represent the world, i.e. have aboutness. Intentionality has a past-orientated requirement. A system can satisfy the future-orientated needs of intelligence while flunking the past-orientated requirement of intentionality. (Philosophers disagree about just how future-orientated intentionality is, whether thinking about something requires the ability to 'track' it; but there should be little disagreement that there is some past-orientated component.)

Now let's see what the difference between intelligence and intentionality has to do with the computer model of the mind. Notice that the method of functional analysis that explains intelligent processes by reducing them to unintelligent mechanical processes does not explain intentionality. The parts of an intentional system can be just as intentional as the whole system (see Fodor 1981). In particular, the component processors of an intentional system can manipulate symbols that are about just the same things that the symbols manipulated by the whole system are about. Recall that the multiplier of Figure 1.2 was explained via a decomposition into devices that add, subtract, and the like. The multiplier's states were intentional in that they were about numbers. The states of the adder, subtractor, etc., are also about numbers and are thus similarly intentional.

There is, however, an important relation between intentionality and functional decomposition which will be explained in the next section. As you will see, though the multiplier's and the adder's states are about numbers, the gate's representational states represent numerals, and in general the subject-matter of representations shift as we cross the divide from complex processors to primitive processors.

1.2.1. *The Brain as a Syntactic Engine: Driving a Semantic Engine*

To see the idea of the brain as a syntactic engine it is important to see the difference between the number 1 and the symbol (in this case, a numeral or digit) '1'. Certainly, the difference between the city Boston and the word 'Boston' is clear enough. The former has bad drivers in it; the latter has no people or cars at all, but does have six letters. No one would confuse a city with a word, but it is less obvious what the difference is between the number 1 and the numeral '1'. The point to keep in mind is that many different symbols, e.g. 'II' (in Roman numerals), and 'two' (in alphabetical writing) denote the same number, and one symbol, e.g. '10', can denote different numbers in different counting systems (as '10' denotes one number in binary and another in decimal).

With this distinction in mind, one can see an important difference between the multiplier and the adder discussed earlier. The algorithm used by the multiplier in Figure 1.2 is notation-*in*dependent: multiply *n* by *m* by adding *n* to zero *m* times works in any notation. And the program described for implementing this algorithm is also notation-independent. As we saw in the description of this program in Section 1.1.3, the program depends on the properties of the numbers represented, not the representations themselves. By contrast, the internal operation of the adder described in Figure 1.3 depends on binary notation, and its description in Section 1.1.4 speaks of numerals (note the quotation marks) rather than numbers. Recall that the adder exploits the fact that an *exclusive-or* gate detects symbol differences, yielding a '1' when its inputs are different digits, and a '0' when its inputs are the same digits. This gate gives the right answer all by itself so long as no carrying is involved. The trick used by the *exclusive-or* gate depends on the fact that whatever two digits of the same type you add together ('1' + '1' or '0' + '0'), the rightmost digit of the answer is the same. This is true in binary, but not in other standard notations. For example, it is not true in familiar decimal notation (1 + 1 = 2, but 0 + 0 = 0).

The inputs and outputs of both the multiplier and the adder must be seen as referring to numbers. One way to see this is to note that otherwise one could not see the multiplier as exploiting an algorithm involving multiplying numbers by adding numbers. What are multiplied and added are numbers. But once we go *inside* the adder, we must see the binary states as referring to symbols *themselves*. For, as just pointed out, the algorithms are notation-dependent. This change of subject-matter is even more dramatic in some computational devices, in which there is a level of processing in which the algorithms operate over parts of decimal numerals. Consider, for example, a calculator, in which the difference between an '8' and a '3' is a matter of two small segments on the left of the '8' being turned off to make a '3'. In calculators, there is a level at which the algorithms concern these segments.

This fact gives us an interesting additional characterization of primitive processors. Typically, as we functionally decompose a computational system, we reach a point where there is a shift of subject-matter from abstractions like numbers or from things in the world to the symbols themselves. The inputs and outputs of the adder and multiplier refer to numbers, but the inputs and outputs of the gates refer to numerals. Typically, this shift occurs when we have reached the level of primitive processors. The operation of the higher-level components such as the multiplier can be explained in terms of a program or algorithm which is manipulating numbers. But the operation of the gates cannot be explained in terms of number manipulation; they must be explained in symbolic terms (or at lower levels, e.g. in terms of electromagnets). At the most basic computational level, computers are symbol-crunchers, and for this reason the computer model of the mind is often described as the symbol manipulation view of the mind.

Seeing the adder as a syntactic engine driving a semantic engine requires noting two functions: one maps numbers onto other numbers, and the other maps symbols onto other symbols. The symbol function is concerned with the numerals as symbols—without attention to their meanings. Here is the symbol function:

'0', '0' → '0'
'0', '1' → '1'
'1', '0' → '1'
'1', '1' → '10'.

The idea is that we interpret something physical in a machine or its outputs as symbols, and some other physical aspect of the machine as indicating that the symbols are inputs or outputs. Then, given that interpretation, the machine's having some symbols as inputs causes the machine to have other symbols as outputs. For example, having the pair '0', '0' as inputs causes having '0' as an output. So the symbol function is a matter of the causal structure of the machine under an interpretation.

This symbol function is mirrored by a function that maps the numbers represented by the numerals on the left onto the numbers represented by the numerals on the right. This function will thus map numbers onto numbers. We can speak of this function that maps numbers onto numbers as the *semantic* function (semantics being the study of meaning), since it is concerned with the meanings of the symbols, not the symbols themselves. (It is important not to confuse the notion of a semantic function in this sense with a function that maps symbols onto what they refer to; the semantic function maps numbers onto numbers, but the function just mentioned which often goes by the same name would map symbols onto numbers.) Here is the semantic function (in decimal notation—you must choose some notation to express a semantic function):

0, 0 → 0
0, 1 → 1
1, 0 → 1
1, 1 → 2.

Notice that the two specifications just given differ in that the first maps quoted entities onto other quoted entities. The second has no quotes. The first function maps symbols onto symbols; the second function maps the numbers referred to by the arguments of the first function onto the numbers referred to by the values of the first function. (A function maps arguments onto values.) Assuming the obvious one–one mapping between the domains of the two functions, the first function is a kind of linguistic 'reflection' of the second. The first function is a kind of linguistic 'reflection' of the second.

The key idea behind the adder is that of an isomorphism between these two functions. The designer has found a machine which has physical aspects that can be interpreted symbolically, and under that symbolic interpretation there are symbolic regularities: some symbols in inputs result in other symbols in outputs. These symbolic regularities are isomorphic to rational relations among the semantic values of the symbols of a sort that are useful to us, in this case the relation of addition. It is the isomorphism between these two *functions* that explains how it is that a device that manipulates symbols manages to add numbers.

Now the idea of the brain as a syntactic engine driving a semantic engine is just a generalization of this picture to a wider class of symbolic activities, namely the symbolic activities of human thought. The idea is that we have symbolic structures in our brains, and that nature (evolution and learning) has seen to it that there are correlations between causal interactions among these structures and useful relations among the meanings of the symbolic structures. To take a crude example: the mechanism by which we avoid swimming in shark-infested water is that the brain symbol structure 'shark' causes the brain symbol structure 'danger'. (What makes 'danger' mean danger will be discussed below.)

The primitive mechanical processors 'know' only the 'syntactic' forms of the symbols they process (e.g. what strings of zeros and ones they see), and not what the symbols mean. None the less, these meaning-blind primitive processors control processes that 'make sense'—processes of decision, problem-solving, and the like. In short, there is a correlation between the meanings of our internal representations and their forms. And this explains how it is that our syntactic engine can drive our semantic engine.[3]

The last paragraph mentioned a correlation between causal interactions among symbolic structures in our brains and rational relations among the meanings of the symbol structures. This way of speaking can be misleading if it encourages the picture of the neuroscientist opening the brain, just seeing the symbols, and then figuring out what they mean. Such a picture inverts the order of discovery, and gives the wrong impression of what makes something a symbol.

The way to discover symbols in the brain is first to map out interesting relations among states of mind, and then identify aspects of these states that can be thought of as symbolic in virtue of their roles in the system. Function, in the sense of role in the system, is what gives a symbol its identity, even the symbols in English orthography, though this can be hard to appreciate because these functions have been rigidified by habit and convention. In reading unfamiliar handwriting, we may notice an unorthodox symbol, someone's weird way of writing a letter of the alphabet. How do we know which letter of the alphabet it is? By its function! Th% function of a symbol is som%thing on% can appr%ciat% by s%%ing how it app%ars in s%nt%nc%s containing familiar words whos% m%anings w% can gu%ss. You will have little trouble figuring out, on this basis, what letter in the last sentence was replaced by '%'.

1.2.2. *Is a Wall a Computer?*

John Searle (1990*a*) argues against the computationalist thesis that the brain is a computer. He does not say that the thesis is false, but rather that it is trivial, because, he suggests, everything is a computer; indeed, everything is *every* computer. In particular, his wall is a computer computing Wordstar. (See also Putnam 1988 for a different argument for a similar conclusion.) The points of the last section allow easy understanding of the motivation for this claim and what is wrong with it. In that section we saw that the key to computation is an isomorphism. We arrange things so that, if certain physical states of a machine are understood as symbols, then causal relations among those symbol-states mirror useful rational relations among the meanings of those symbols. The mirroring is an isomorphism. Searle's claim is that this sort of isomorphism is cheap. We can regard two aspects of the wall at time t as being or corresponding to the symbols '0' and '1', and then we can regard an aspect of the wall at time $t + 1$ as '1', and so the wall just computed $0 + 1 = 1$. Thus, Searle suggests,

[3] The idea described here was first articulated to my knowledge in Fodor (1975, 1980); see also Dennett (1981), to which the terms 'semantic engine' and 'syntactic engine' are due, and Newell (1980). More on this topic can be found in Dennett (1987), index, s.v. 'syntactic engine', 'semantic engine'.

everything (or rather everything that is big or complex enough to have enough states) is every computer, and the claim that the brain is a computer has no bite.

The problem with this reasoning is that the isomorphism that makes a syntactic engine drive a semantic engine is more full-bodied than Searle acknowledges. In particular, the isomorphism has to include not just a particular computation that the machine does perform, but all the computations that the machine *could have* performed. The point can be made clearer by a look at Figure 1.6, a type of *exclusive-or* gate.

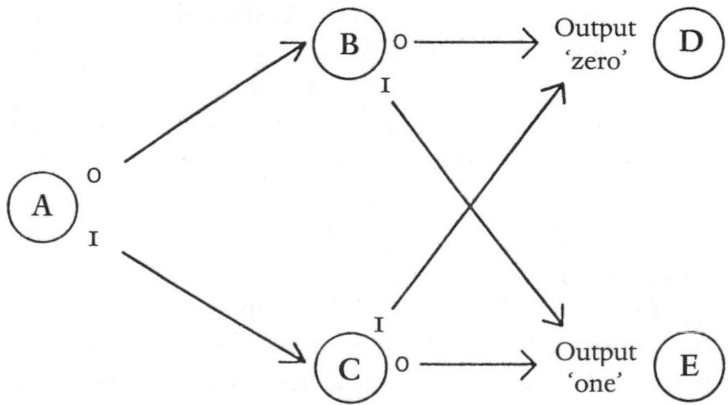

FIG. 1.6. The numerals at the beginning of arrows indicate inputs

The computation of 1 + 0 = 1 is represented by the path A→C→E. The computation of 0 + 1 = 1 is represented by the path A→B→E, and so on. Now here is the point. In order for the wall to be this computer, it isn't enough for it to have states that correspond to '0' and '1' followed by a state that corresponds to '1'. It must also be such that had the '1' input been replaced by a '0' input, the '1' output would have been replaced by the '0' output. In other words, it has to have symbolic states that satisfy not only the actual computation, but also the possible computations that the computer could have performed. And this is non-trivial.

Searle (1992: 209) acknowledges this point, but insists, none the less, that there is no fact of the matter of whether the brain is a specific computer. Whether something is a computer, he argues, depends on whether we decide to interpret its states in a certain way, and that is up to us. 'We can't, on the one hand, say that anything is a digital computer if we can assign a syntax to it, and then suppose there is a factual question intrinsic to its physical operation whether or not a natural system such as the brain is a digital computer.' Searle is right that whether something is a computer and what computer it is is in part up to us. But what the example just given shows is that it is not *totally* up to us.

A rock, for example, is not an *exclusive-or* gate. We have a great deal of freedom as to how to interpret a device, but there are also very important restrictions on this freedom, and that is what makes it a substantive claim that the brain is a computer of a certain sort. Since not everything can be described as an *exclusive-or* gate, it is not totally up to us whether something is an *exclusive-or* gate.

1.3. Functionalism and the Language of Thought

Thus far, we have (1) considered functional analysis, the computer model of the mind's approach to intelligence, (2) distinguished intelligence from intentionality, and (3) considered the idea of the brain as a syntactic engine. The idea of the brain as a syntactic engine explains how it is that symbol-crunching operations can result in a machine 'making sense'. But so far we have encountered nothing that could be considered the computer model's account of intentionality. It is time to admit that although the computer model of the mind has a natural and straightforward account of intelligence, there is no account of intentionality that comes along for free.

We will not survey the field here. Instead, let us examine a view which represents a kind of orthodoxy, not in the sense that most researchers believe it, but in the sense that the other views define themselves in large part by their response to it.

The basic tenet of this orthodoxy is that our intentional contents are simply meanings of our internal representations. As noted earlier, there is something to be said for regarding the content of thought and language as a single phenomenon, and this is a quite direct way of so doing. There is no commitment in this orthodoxy on the issue of whether our internal language, the language in which we think, is the same or different from the language with which we speak. Further, there is no commitment as to a direction of reduction, i.e. as to which is more basic, mental content or meanings of internal symbols.

For concreteness, let us talk in terms of Fodor's (1975) doctrine that the meaning of external language derives from the content of thought, and the content of thought derives from the meaning of elements of the language of thought (see also Harman 1973). According to Fodor, believing or hoping that grass grows is a state of being in one or another computational relation to an internal representation that means that grass grows. This can be summed up in a set of slogans: believing that grass grows is having 'Grass grows' in the Belief Box; desiring that grass grows is having this sentence (or one that means the same) in the Desire Box; etc.

Now if all content and meaning derives from meaning of the elements of the language of thought, we immediately want to know how the mental symbols get their meaning.[4] This is a question that gets wildly different answers from different philosophers, all equally committed to the cognitive science point of view. We will briefly look at two of them. The first point of view, mentioned earlier, takes as a kind of paradigm those cases in which a symbol in the head might be said to covary with states in the world in the way that the number of rings in a tree trunk correlates with the age of the tree (see Dretske 1981; Stampe 1977; Stalnaker 1984; Fodor 1987, 1990). On this view, the meaning of mental symbols is a matter of the correlations between these symbols and the world.

One version of this view (Fodor 1990) says that T is the truth-condition of a mental sentence *M* if and only if: *M* is in the Belief Box if and only if T, in ideal conditions. That is, what it is for 'Grass is green' to have the truth-condition that grass be green is for 'Grass is green' to appear in the Belief Box just in case grass really is green (and conditions are ideal). The idea behind this theory is that there are cognitive mechanisms that are designed to put sentences in the Belief Box when and only when they are true, and if those cognitive mechanisms are working properly and the environment cooperates (no mirages, no Cartesian evil demons), these sentences will appear in the Belief Box when and only when they are true.

One problem with this idea is that even if this theory works for 'observation sentences' such as 'This is yellow', it is hard to see how it could work for 'theoretical sentences'. A person's cognitive mechanisms could be working fine, and the environment could contain no misleading evidence, and still one might not believe that space is Riemannian or that some quarks have charm or that one is in the presence of a magnetic field. For theoretical ideas, it is not enough to have one's nose rubbed in the evidence: you also have to have the right theoretical idea. And if the analysis of ideal conditions includes 'has the right theoretical idea', that would make the analysis circular because having the right theoretical idea amounts to 'comes up with the true theory'. And appealing to truth in an analysis of 'truth' is to move in a very small circle (see Block 1986: 657–60).

The second approach is known as functionalism (actually, 'functional role semantics' in discussions of meaning) in philosophy, and as procedural semantics in cognitive psychology and computer science. Functionalism says that what gives internal symbols (and external symbols too) their meanings is how they function. To maximize the contrast with the view described in the last two paragraphs, it is useful to think of the functionalist approach with respect to a

[4] In one respect, the meanings of mental symbols cannot be semantically more basic than meanings of external symbols. The name 'Aristotle' has the reference it has because of its causal connection (via generations of speakers) to a man who was called by a name that was an ancestor of our external term 'Aristotle'. So the term in the language of thought that corresponds to 'Aristotle' will certainly derive its reference from and thus will be semantically less basic than the public-language word.

symbol that doesn't (on the face of it) have any kind of correlation with states of the world, say the symbol 'and'. Part of what makes 'and' mean what it does is that if we are sure of 'Grass is green and grass grows', we find the inference to 'Grass is green' and also 'Grass grows' compelling. And we find it compelling 'in itself', not because of any other principle (see Peacocke 1993). Or if we are sure that one of the conjuncts is false, we find compelling the inference that the conjunction is false too. What it is to mean *and* by 'and' is to find such inferences compelling in this way, and so we can think of the meaning of 'and' as a matter of its behaviour in these and other inferences. The functionalist view of meaning applies this idea to all words. The picture is that the internal representations in our heads have a function in our deciding, deliberating, problem-solving—indeed in our thought in general—and that is what their meanings consist in.

This picture can be bolstered by a consideration of what happens when one first learns Newtonian mechanics. In my own case, I heard a large number of unfamiliar terms more or less all at once: 'mass', 'force', 'energy', and the like. I never was told definitions of these terms in terms I already knew. (No one has ever come up with definitions of such 'theoretical terms' in observation language.) What I did learn was how to use these terms in solving homework problems, making observations, explaining the behaviour of a pendulum, and the like. In learning how to use the terms in thought and action (and perception as well, though its role there is less obvious), I learned their meanings, and this fits with the functionalist idea that the meaning of a term just is its function in perception, thought, and action. A theory of what meaning is can be expected to fit with a theory of what it is to acquire meanings, and so considerations about acquisition can be relevant to semantics.

An apparent problem arises for such a theory in its application to the meanings of numerals. After all, it is a mathematical fact that truths in the familiar numeral system '1', '2', '3', ... are preserved, even if certain non-standard interpretations of the numerals are adopted (so long as non-standard versions of the operations are adopted too). For example, '1' might be mapped onto 2, '2' onto 4, '3' onto 6, and so on. That is, the numerals, both 'odd' and 'even', might be mapped onto the even numbers. Since '1' and '2' can have the same functional role in different number systems and still designate the very numbers they usually designate in normal arithmetic, how can the functional role of '1' determine whether '1' means 1 or 2? It would seem that all functional role could do is 'cut down' the number of possible interpretations, and if there is still an infinity left after the cutting down, functional role has gained nothing.

A natural functionalist response would be to emphasize the input and output ends of the functional roles. We say 'two cats' when confronted with a pair of cats, not when confronted with one or five cats, and our thoughts involving the symbol '3' affect our actions towards triples in an obvious way in which these thoughts do not affect our actions towards octuples. The functionalist can avoid non-standard interpretations of *internal* functional roles by including in the semantically relevant functional roles external relations involving perception and action (Harman 1973). In this way, the functionalist can incorporate the insight of the view mentioned earlier that meaning has something to do with covariation between symbols and the world.

The emerging picture of how cognitive science can handle intentionality should be becoming clear. Transducers at the periphery and internal primitive processors produce and operate on symbols so as to give them their functional roles. In virtue of their functional roles (both internal and external), these symbols have meanings. The functional role perspective explains the mysterious correlation between the symbols and their meanings. It is the activities of the symbols that give them their meanings, so it is no mystery that a syntax-based system should have rational relations among the meanings of the system's symbols. Intentional states have their relations in virtue of these symbolic activities, and the contents of the intentional states of the system—thinking, wanting, etc.—are inherited from the meanings of the symbols. This is the orthodox account of intentionality for the computer model of the mind. It combines functionalism with a commitment to a language of thought. Both views are controversial, the latter in regard to both its truth and its relevance to intentionality even if true. Note, incidentally, that on this account of intentionality the source of intentionality is computational structure, independently of whether the computational structure is produced by software or hardware. If we think of the computational structure of a computer as coming entirely from a program put into a structureless general-purpose machine, we are very far from the facts about the human brain—which is not such a general-purpose machine.

At the end of this part of the chapter, I will discuss Searle's famous Chinese room argument, which is a direct attack on this theory. The next two sections will be devoted to arguments for and against the language of thought.

1.3.1. *Can there be a Language of Thought?*

Many objections have been raised to the language of thought picture. Let us briefly look at three objections made by Dennett (1975).

The first objection is that we all have an infinity of beliefs (or at any rate a very large number of them). For example, we believe that trees do not light up like fireflies, and that this book is probably closer to your eyes than the US President's left shoe is to the ceiling of the New York Museum of Modern Art gift shop. But how can it be that so many beliefs are all stored in the rather small Belief Box in your head? One line of response to this objection involves making a distinction between the *ordinary* conception of belief and a *scientific* conception of belief towards which one hopes cognitive science is progressing. For scientific purposes, we home in on cases in which our beliefs *cause* us to *do* something, say throw a ball or change our mind, and cases in which beliefs are caused by something, as when perception of a rhinoceros causes us to believe that there is a rhinoceros in the vicinity. Science is concerned with causation and causal explanation, so the proto-scientific conception of belief is the conception of a *causally active* belief. It is only for these beliefs that the language of thought theory is committed to sentences in the head. This idea yields a very simple answer to the infinity objection, namely that on the proto-scientific conception of belief, most of us did not have the belief that trees do not light up like fireflies until they read this paragraph.

Beliefs in the proto-scientific sense are explicit, that is recorded in storage in the brain. For example, you no doubt were once told that the sun is 93 million miles away from the earth. If so, perhaps you have this fact explicitly recorded in your head, available for causal action, even though until reading this paragraph, this belief hadn't been conscious for years. Such explicit beliefs have the potential for causal interaction, and thus must be distinguished from cases of belief in the ordinary sense (if they are beliefs at all), such as the belief that all normal people have that trees do not light up like fireflies

Being explicit is to be distinguished from other properties of mental states, such as being conscious. Theories in cognitive science tell us of mental representations about which no one knows from introspection, such as mental representations of aspects of grammar. If this is right, there is much in the way of mental representation that is explicit but not conscious, and thus the door is opened to the possibility of belief that is explicit but not conscious.

It is important to note that the language of thought theory is not meant to be a theory of all possible believers, but rather only of *us*. The language of thought theory allows creatures who can believe without any explicit representation at all, but the claim of the language of thought theory is that they aren't us. A digital computer consists of a central processing unit (CPU) that reads and writes explicit strings of zeros and ones in storage registers. One can think of this memory as in principle unlimited, but of course any actual machine has a finite memory. Now any computer with a finite amount of explicit storage can be simulated by a machine with a much larger CPU and *no* explicit storage, that is no registers and no tape. The way the simulation works is by using the extra states as a form of implicit memory. So, in principle, we could be simulated by a machine with no explicit memory at all.

Consider, for example, the finite automaton diagrammed in Figure 1.7. The figure shows it as having three states. The states, 'S_1', 'S_2', and 'S_3', are listed across the top. The inputs are listed on the left side. Each box is in a column and a row that specifies what the machine does when it is in the state named at the top of the column, and when the input is the one listed at the side of the row.

The top part of the box names the output, and the bottom part of the box names the next state. This is what the table says: when the machine is in S_1, and it sees a 1, it says '1', and goes to S_2. When it is in S_2, if it sees a '1' it says '2' and goes into the next state, S_3. In that state, if it sees a '1' it says '3' and goes back to S_1. When it sees nothing, it says nothing and stays in the same state. This automaton counts 'modulo' three, that is, you can tell from what it says how many ones it has seen since the last multiple of three. But what the machine diagram makes clear is that this machine need have no memory of the sort that involves writing anything down. It can 'remember' solely by changing state. Some theories based on neural-network models assume that we are such machines.

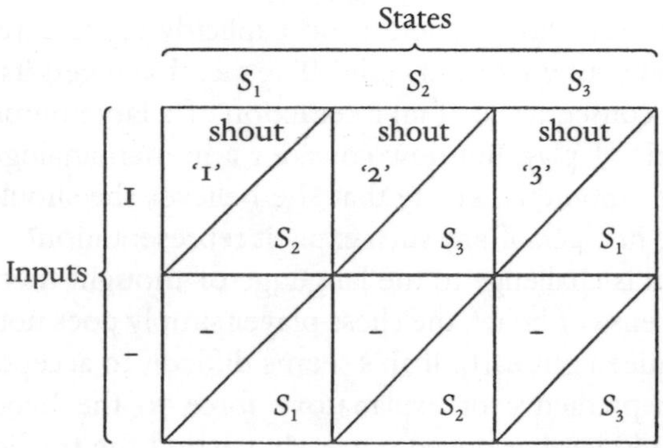

FIG. 1.7. Finite automaton that counts 'modulo' three

Suppose, then, that we are digital computers with explicit repesentations. We could be simulated by finite automata which have many more states and no explicit representations. The simulators will have just the same beliefs as we do, but no explicit repesentations (unless the simulators are just jukeboxes of the type of the Aunt Bubbles machine described in Section 1.1.1). The machine in which remembered items are recorded explicitly has an advantage over a computationally equivalent machine that 'remembers' by changing state, namely that the explicit representations can be part of a combinatorial system. This point will be explained in the next section.

Time to sum up. The objection was that an infinity of beliefs cannot be written down in the head. My response was to distinguish between a loose and ordinary sense of 'belief' in which it may be true that we have an infinity of beliefs, and a proto-scientific sense of 'belief' in which the conception of belief is the conception of a causally active belief. In the latter sense, I claimed, we do not have an infinity of beliefs.

Even if you agree with this response to the infinity objection, you may still feel dissatisfied with the idea that, because the topic has never crossed their minds, most people don't believe that zebras don't wear underwear in the wild. Perhaps it will help to say something about the relation between the proto scientific conception of belief and the ordinary conception. It is natural to want some sort of reconstruction of the ordinary conception in scientific terms, a reconstruction of the sort we have when we define the ordinary conception of the weight of a person as the force exerted on the person by the earth at the earth's surface. To scratch this itch, we can give a first approximation to a definition of a belief in the ordinary sense as anything that is either (1) a belief in the proto-scientific sense, or (2) naturally and easily deduced from a proto-scientific belief.

A second objection to the language of thought theory is provided by Dennett's example of a chess-playing program that 'thinks' it should get its queen out early, even though there is no explicitly represented rule that says anything like 'Get your queen out early'. The fact that it gets its queen out early is an 'emergent' consequence of an interaction of a large number of rules that govern the details of play. But now consider a human analogue of the chess-playing machine. Shouldn't we say that she believes she should get her queen out early despite her lack of any such explicit representation?

The reply to this challenge to the language of thought theory is that in the proto-scientific sense of belief, the chess-player simply does not believe that she should get her queen out early. If this seems difficult to accept, note that there is no additional predictive or explanatory force to the hypothesis that she believes she should get her queen out early beyond the predictive or explanatory force of the explicitly represented strategies from which getting the queen out early emerges. (Though there is no additional predictive force, there may be some additional predictive utility, just as there is utility in navigation to supposing that the sun goes round the earth.) Indeed, the idea that she should get her queen out early can actually conflict with her deeply held chess principles, despite being an emergent property of her usual tactics. We could suppose that if you point out to her that her strategies have the consequence of getting her queen out early, she says, 'Oh no, I'd better revise my usual strategies.' So postulating that she believes that she should get her queen out early could lead to mistaken predictions of her behaviour. In sum, the proto-scientific concept of a causally active belief can be restricted to the strategies that really are explicitly represented.

Perhaps there is a quasi-behaviourist ordinary sense of belief in which it is correct to ascribe the belief that the queen should come out early simply on the basis of the fact that she behaves as if she believes it. Even if we agree to recognize such a belief, it is not one that ever causally affects any other mental states or any behaviour, so it is of little import from a scientific standpoint.

A third objection to the language of thought theory is provided by the 'opposite' of the 'queen out early' case, Dennett's sister in Cleveland case. Suppose that a neurosurgeon operates on someone's Belief Box, inserting the sentence 'I have a sister in Cleveland'. When the patient wakes up, the doctor says, 'Do you have a sister?' 'Yes,' the patient says, 'in Cleveland.' Doctor: 'What's her name?' Patient: 'Gosh, I can't think of it.' Doctor: 'Older or younger?' Patient: 'I don't know, and by golly I'm an only child. I don't know why I'm saying that I have a sister at all.' Finally, the patient concludes that she never really believed she had a sister in Cleveland, but rather was a victim of some sort of compulsion to speak as if she did. The upshot is supposed to be that the language of thought theory is false because you can't produce a belief just by inserting a sentence in the Belief Box.

The objection reveals a misleading aspect of the 'Belief Box' slogan, not a problem with the doctrine that the slogan characterizes. According to the language of thought theory, believing that one has a sister in Cleveland is a computational relation to a sentence, but this computational relation shouldn't be thought of as simply storage. Rather, the computational relation must include some specification of relations to other sentences to which one also has the same computational relation, and in that sense the computational relation must be holistic. This point holds for both the ordinary notion of belief and the proto-scientific notion. It holds for the ordinary notion of belief because we don't count someone as believing just because she mouths words the way our neurosurgery victim mouthed the words 'I have a sister in Cleveland'. And it holds for the proto-scientific notion of belief because the unit of explanation and prediction is much more likely to be groups of coherently related sentences in the brain than single sentences all by themselves. If one is going to retain the 'Belief Box' way of talking, one should say that for a sentence in the Belief Box to count as a belief, it should cohere sufficiently with other sentences so as not to be totally unstable, disappearing on exposure to the light.

1.3.2. *Arguments for the Language of Thought*

So it seems that the language of thought hypothesis can be defended from these a priori objections. But is there any positive reason to believe it? One such reason is that it is part of a reasonably successful research programme. But there are challengers (mainly, some versions of the connectionist programme), so a stronger case will be called for if the challengers' research programmes also end up being successful. (Note that the *type* of success is important to whether connectionism is really a rival to the language of thought point of view.) Connectionist networks have been successful in various pattern recognition tasks, for example discriminating mines from rocks. Of course, even if these networks could be made to do pattern recognition tasks much better than we can, that wouldn't suggest that these networks can provide models of higher cognition. Computers that are programmed to do arithmetic in the classical symbol-crunching mode can do arithmetic much better than we can, but no one would conclude that therefore these computers provide models of higher cognition.

A major rationale for accepting the language of thought has been one or another form of *productivity* argument, stemming from Chomsky's work (see Chomsky 1975). The idea is that people are capable of thinking vast numbers of thoughts that they have not thought before—and indeed that no one may have ever thought before. Consider, for example, the thought mentioned earlier that this book is closer to you than the President's shoe is to the Museum gift shop ceiling. The most obvious explanation of how we can think such new thoughts is the same as the explanation of how we can frame the sentences that express them: namely, via a combinatorial system that we think in. Indeed, abstracting away from limitations on memory, motivation, and length of life, there may be no upper bound on the number of thinkable thoughts. The number of sentences in the English language is certainly infinite. But what does it mean to say that sentences containing millions of words are 'in principle' thinkable?

Those who favour productivity arguments say this: The explanation for the fact that we cannot actually think sentences containing millions of words would have to appeal to such facts as that were we to try to think sufficiently long or complicated thoughts, our attention would flag, or our memory would fail us, or we would die. They think that we can idealize away from these limitations, since the mechanisms of thought themselves are unlimited. But this claim that if we abstract away from memory, mortality, motivation, and the like our thought mechanisms are unlimited, is a doctrine for which there is no direct evidence. The perspective from which this doctrine springs has been fertile, but it is an open question what aspect of the doctrine is responsible for its success.

After all, we might be finite beings, essentially. Not all idealizations are equally correct, and contrary to widespread assumption in cognitive science, the idealization to the unboundedness of thought may be a bad one. Consider a finite automaton naturally described by Figure 1.7. This diagram *could* be used to describe a machine that does have a memory with explicit representation. I say 'naturally described' to indicate that I am thinking of a machine which does not have such a memory, a machine for which Figure 1.7 is an apt and natural description. Its only form of memory is change of state. If you want to get this machine to count to 4 instead of just to 3, you can't just add more memory, you have to give it another state by changing the way the machine is built. Perhaps we are like this machine.

An extension of the productivity argument to deal with this sort of problem was proposed by Fodor (1987) and Fodor and Pylyshyn (1988). Fodor and Pylyshyn point out that it is a fact about humans that if someone can think the thought that Mary loves John, then she can also think the thought that John loves Mary. And likewise for a vast variety of pairs of thoughts that involve the same conceptual constituents but are put together differently. There is a *systematicity* relation among many thoughts that calls for an explanation in terms of a combinatorial system. The conclusion is that human thought operates in a medium of 'movable type'.

However, the most obvious candidate for the elements of such a combinatorial system in many areas are the external symbol systems themselves. Perhaps the most obvious case is arithmetical thoughts. If someone is capable of thinking the thought that 7 + 16 is not 20, then presumably she is capable of thinking the thought that 17 + 6 is not 20. Indeed, someone who has mastered the ten numerals plus other basic symbols of arabic notation and their rules of combination can think any arithmetical thought that is expressible in a representation that he can read. (Note that false propositions can be thinkable—one can think the thought that 2 + 2 = 5, if only to think that it is false.)

One line of a common printed page contains eighty symbols. There are a great many different arithmetical propositions that can be written on such a line—about as many as there are elementary particles in the universe. Though almost all of them are false, all of them are arguably thinkable with some work. Starting a bit smaller, try to entertain the thought that 695,302,222,387,987 + 695,302,222,387,986 = 2. How is it that we have so many possible arithmetical thoughts? The obvious explanation for this is that we can string together—either in our heads or on paper—the symbols (numerals, pluses, etc.) themselves, and simply read the thought off the string of symbols. Of course, this does not show that the systematicity argument is *wrong*. Far from it, since it shows *why* it is right. But this point does threaten the *value* of the systematicity argument considerably. For it highlights the possibility that the systematicity argument may apply only to *conscious* thought, and not to the rest of the iceberg of unconscious thought processes that cognitive science is mainly about. So Fodor and Pylyshyn are right that the systematicity argument shows that there is a language of thought. And they are right that if connectionism is incompatible with a language of thought, so much the worse for connectionism. But where they are wrong is with respect to an unstated assumption: that the systematicity argument shows that language-like representations pervade cognition.

To see this point, note that much of the success in cognitive science has been in our understanding of perceptual and motor modules. The operation of these modules is neither introspectible—accessible to conscious thought—nor directly influenceable by conscious thought. These modules are 'informationally encapsulated' (see Pylyshyn 1984; Fodor 1983). The productivity in conscious thought that is exploited by the systematicity argument certainly does not demonstrate productivity in the processing inside such modules. True, if someone can think that Mary loves John, then he can think that John loves Mary. But we don't have easy access to such facts about pairs of representations of the kind involved in unconscious processes. Distinguish between the conclusion of an argument and the argument itself. The conclusion of the systematicity argument may well be right about unconscious representations. That is, systematicity *itself* may well obtain in these systems. My point is that the systematicity *argument* shows little about encapsulated modules and other unconscious systems.

The weakness of the systematicity argument is that, resting as it does on facts that are so readily available to conscious thought, its application to unconscious processes is more tenuous. None the less, as the reader can easily see by looking at any cognitive science textbook, the symbol manipulation model has been quite successful in explaining aspects of perception, thought, and motor control. So although the systematicity argument is limited in its application to unconscious processes, the model it supports for conscious processes appears to have considerable application to unconscious processes.

To avoid misunderstanding, I should add that the point just made does not challenge all of the thrust of the Fodor and Pylyshyn critique of connectionism. Any neural-network model of the mind will have to accommodate the fact of our use of a systematic combinatorial symbol system in conscious thought. It is hard to see how a neural-network model could do this without being in part an implementation of a standard symbol-crunching model.

In effect, Fodor and Pylyshyn (1988: 44) counter the idea that the systematicity argument depends entirely on conscious symbol manipulation by saying that the systematicity argument applies to animals. For example, they argue that the conditioning literature contains no cases of animals that *can* be trained to pick the red thing rather than the green one, but *cannot* be trained to pick the green thing rather than the red one. This reply has some force, but it is uncomfortably anecdotal. The data a scientist collects depend on his theory. We cannot rely on data collected in animal-conditioning experiments run by behaviourists—who, after all, were notoriously opposed to theorizing about internal states.

Another objection to the systematicity argument derives from the distinction between linguistic and pictorial representation that plays a role in the controversies over mental imagery. Many researchers think that we have two different representational systems, a language-like system—thinking in words—and a pictorial system—thinking in pictures. If an animal that can be trained to pick red instead of green can also be trained to pick green instead of red, that may reflect the properties of an imagery system shared by humans and animals, not a properly language-like system. Suppose Fodor and Pylyshyn are right about the systematicity of thought in animals. That may reflect only a combinatorial pictorial system. If so, it would suggest (though it wouldn't show) that humans have a combinatorial pictorial system too. But the question would still be open whether humans have a language-like combinatorial system that is used in unconscious thought. In sum, the systematicity argument certainly applies to conscious thought, and it is part of a perspective on unconscious thought that has been fertile, but there are difficulties in its application to unconscious thought.

1.3.3. *Explanatory Levels and the Syntactic Theory of the Mind*

In this section, let us assume that the language of thought hypothesis is correct in order to ask another question: should cognitive science explanations appeal only to the syntactic elements in the language of thought (the '0's and '1's and the like), or should they also appeal to the contents of these symbols? Stich (1983) has argued for the 'syntactic theory of mind', a version of the computer model in which the language of thought is construed in terms of uninterpreted symbols, symbols that may have contents, but whose contents are irrelevant for the purposes of cognitive science. I shall put the issue in terms of a critique of a simplified version of the argument of Stich (1983).

Let us begin with Stich's case of Mrs T, a senile old lady who answers the question 'What happened to McKinley?' with 'McKinley was assassinated', but cannot answer questions like 'Where is McKinley now?', 'Is he alive or dead?', and the like. Mrs T's logical faculties are fine, but she has lost most of her memories, and virtually all the concepts that are normally connected to the concept of assassination, such as the concept of death. Stich sketches the case so as to persuade us that though Mrs T may know that something happened to McKinley, she doesn't have any real grasp of the concept of assassination, and thus cannot be said to believe that McKinley was assassinated.

The argument that I will criticize concludes that purely syntactic explanations undermine content explanations because a syntactic account is superior to a content account. There are two respects in which the syntactic approach is superior: first, the syntactic account can handle Mrs T, who has little in the way of intentional content, but plenty of internal representations whose interactions can be used to explain and predict what she does or at least says, just as the interactions of symbol structures in a computer can be used to explain and predict what it does. And the same holds for very young children, people with weird psychiatric disorders, and denizens of exotic cultures. In all these cases, cognitive science can (at least potentially) assign internal syntactic descriptions and use them to predict and explain, but there are problems with content ascriptions (though, in the last case at least, the problem is not that these people have no contents, but just that their contents are so different from ours that we cannot assign contents to them in our terms). In sum, the first type of superiority of the syntactic perspective over the content perspective is that it allows for the psychology of the senile, the very young, the disordered, and the exotic, and thus, it is alleged, the syntactic perspective is far more general than the content perspective.

The second respect in which the syntactic perspective is superior is that it allows more fine-grained predictions and explanations than the content perspective. To take a humdrum example, the content perspective allows us to predict that if someone believes that all men are mortal, and that he is a man, he can conclude that he is mortal. But suppose that the way this person represents the generalization that all men are mortal to himself is via a syntactic form of the type 'All non-mortals are non-men'; then the inference will be harder to draw than if he had represented it without the negations. In general, what inferences are hard rather than easy, and what sorts of mistake are likely, will be more predictable from the syntactic perspective than from the content perspective, in which all the different ways of representing one belief are lumped together.

The upshot of this argument is supposed to be that since the syntactic approach is more general and more fine-grained than the content approach, content explanations are therefore undermined and shown to be defective. So cognitive science would do well to scrap attempts to explain and predict in terms of content in favour of appeals to syntactic form alone.

But there is a fatal flaw in this argument—one that applies to many reductionist arguments. The fact that syntactic explanations are better than content explanations in some respects says nothing about whether content explanations are not also better than syntactic explanations in some respects. A dramatic way of revealing this fact is to note that if the argument against the content level were correct, it would undermine the syntactic approach itself. This point is so simple, fundamental, and widely applicable, that it deserves a name; let's call it the Reductionist-Cruncher. Just as the syntactic objects on paper can be described in molecular terms, for example as structures of carbon molecules, so the syntactic objects in our heads can be described in terms of the viewpoint of chemistry and physics. But a physico-chemical account of the syntactic objects in our head will be more general than the syntactic account in just the same way that the syntactic account is more general than the content account. There are possible beings, such as Mrs T, who are similar to us syntactically but not in intentional contents. Similarly, there are possible beings who are similar to us in physico-chemical respects, but not syntactically. For example, creatures could be like us in physico-chemical respects without having physico-chemical parts that function as syntactic objects—just as Mrs T's syntactic objects don't function so as to confer content upon them. If neural-network models of the sort that anti-language of thought theorists favour could be bio-engineered, they would fit this description. The bio-engineered models would be like us and like Mrs T in physico-chemical respects, but unlike us and unlike Mrs T in syntactic respects. Further, the physico-chemical account will be more fine-grained than the syntactic account, just as the syntactic account is more fine-grained than the content account. Syntactic generalizations will fail under some physico-chemically specifiable circumstances, just as content generalizations fail under some syntactically specifiable circumstances. I mentioned that content generalizations might be compromised if the syntactic realizations include too many syntactic negations. The present point is that syntactic generalizations might fail when syntactic objects interact on the basis of certain physico-chemical properties. To take a slightly silly example, if a token of *s* and a token of $s \rightarrow t$ are both positively charged so that they repel each other, that could prevent logic processors from putting them together to yield a token of *t*.

In sum, if we could refute the content approach by showing that the syntactic approach is more general and fine-grained than the content approach, then we could also refute the syntactic approach by exhibiting the same deficiency in it relative to a still deeper theory. The Reductionist-Cruncher applies even within physics itself. For example, anyone who rejects the explanations of thermodynamics in favour of the explanations of statistical mechanics will be frustrated by the fact that the explanations of statistical mechanics can themselves be 'undermined' in just the same way by quantum mechanics.

The same points can be made in terms of the explanation of how a computer works. Compare two explanations of the behaviour of the computer on my desk, one in terms of the programming language, and the other in terms of what is happening in the computer's circuits. The latter level is certainly more general in that it applies not only to programmed computers, but also to non-programmable computers that are electronically similar to mine, for example certain calculators. Thus the greater generality of the circuit level is like the greater generality of the syntactic perspective. Further, the circuit level is more fine-grained in that it allows us to predict and explain computer failures that have nothing to do with program glitches. Circuits will fail under certain circumstances (for example, overload, excessive heat or humidity) that are not characterizable in the vocabulary of the program level. Thus the greater predictive and explanatory power of the circuit level is like the greater power of the syntactic level to distinguish cases of the same content represented in different syntactic forms that make a difference in processing.

However, the computer analogy reveals a flaw in the argument that the 'upper'-level (the program level in this example) explanations are defective and should be scrapped. The fact that a 'lower' level like the circuit level is superior in some respects does not show that 'higher' levels such as the program levels are not themselves superior in other respects. Thus the upper levels are not shown to be dispensable. The program level has its own type of greater generality, namely it applies to computers that use the same programming language, but are built in different ways, even computers that don't have circuits at all (but, say, work via gears and pulleys). Indeed, there are many predictions and explanations that are simple at the program level, but would be absurdly complicated at the circuit level. Further (and here is the Reductionist-Cruncher again), if the program level could be shown to be defective by the circuit level, then the circuit level could itself be shown to be defective by a deeper theory, for example, the quantum field theory of circuits.

The point here is not that the program level is a convenient fiction. On the contrary, the program level is just as real and explanatory as the circuit level.

Perhaps it will be useful to see the matter in terms of an example from Putnam (1975). Consider a rigid round peg one inch in diameter and a square hole in a rigid board with a one-inch diagonal. The peg won't fit through the hole for reasons that are easy to understand via a little geometry. (The side of the hole is 1 divided by the square root of 2, which is a number substantially less than 1.) Now if we went to the level of description of this apparatus in terms of the molecular structure that makes up a specific solid board, we could explain the rigidity of the materials, and we would have a more fine-grained understanding, including the ability to predict the incredible case where the alignment and motion of the molecules is such as to allow the peg actually to go through the board. But the 'upper'-level account in terms of rigidity and geometry none the less provides correct explanations and predictions, and applies more generally to any rigid peg and board, even one with quite a different sort of molecular constitution, say one made of glass—a supercooled liquid—rather than a solid.

It is tempting to say that the account in terms of rigidity and geometry is only an approximation, the molecular account being the really correct one (see Smolensky 1988 for a dramatic case of yielding to this sort of temptation). But the cure for this temptation is the Reductionist-Cruncher: the reductionist will also have to say that an elementary-particle account shows the molecular account to be only an approximation. And the elementary-particle account itself will be undermined by a still deeper theory. The point of a scientific account is to cut nature at its joints, and nature has real joints at many different levels, each of which requires its own kind of idealization.

Further, what are counted as elementary particles today may be found to be composed of still more elementary particles tomorrow, and so on, ad infinitum. Indeed, contemporary physics allows this possibility of an infinite series of particles within particles (see Dehmelt 1989). If such an infinite series obtains, the reductionist would be committed to saying that there are no genuine explanations because, for any explanation at any given level, there is always a deeper explanation that is more general and more fine-grained that undermines it. But the existence of genuine explanations surely does not depend on this recondite issue in particle physics!

I have been talking as if there is just one content level, but actually there are many. Marr (1977) distinguished among three different levels: the computational level, the level of representation and algorithm, and the level of implementation. At the computational, or formal, level, the multiplier discussed earlier is to be understood as a function from pairs of numbers to their products, for example, from 7,9 to 63. The most abstract characterization at the level of representation and algorithm is simply the algorithm of the multiplier, namely: multiply *n* by *m* by adding *m* to zero *n* times. A less abstract characterization at this middle level is the program described earlier, a sequence of operations including subtracting 1 from the register that initially represents *n* until it is reduced to zero, adding *m* to the answer register each time (see Figure 1.2). Each of these levels is a content level rather than a syntactic level. There are many types of multiplier whose behaviour can be explained (albeit at a somewhat superficial level) simply by reference to the fact that they are multipliers. The algorithm mentioned gives a deeper explanation, and the program—one of many programs that can realize that alogrithm—gives a still deeper explanation. However, when we break the multiplier down into parts, such as the adder of Figure 1.3, we explain its internal operation in terms of gates that operate on syntax, that is in terms of operations on numerals. Now it is crucially important to realize that the mere possibility of a description of a system in a certain vocabulary does not by itself demonstrate the existence of a genuine explanatory level. We are concerned here with cutting nature at its joints, and talking as if there is a joint does not make it so. The fact that it is good methodology to look first for the function, then for the algorithm, then for the implementation does not by itself show that these inquiries are inquiries at different levels, as opposed to different ways of approaching the same level. The crucial issue is whether the different vocabularies correspond to genuinely distinct laws and explanations, and in any given case this question will only be answerable empirically. However, we already have good empirical evidence for the reality of the content levels just mentioned—as well as the syntactic level. The evidence is to be found in this very book, where we see genuine and distinct explanations at the level of function, algorithm, and syntax.

A further point about explanatory levels is that it is legitimate to use different and even incompatible idealizations at different levels (see Putnam 1975). It has been argued that since the brain is analog, the digital computer must be incorrect as a model of the mind. But even digital computers are analog at one level of description. For example, gates of the sort described earlier in which 4 volts realizes '1' and 7 volts realizes '0' are understood from the digital perspective as always representing either '0' or '1'. But an examination at the electronic level shows that values intermediate between 4 and 7 volts appear momentarily when a register switches between them. We abstract from these intermediate values for the purposes of one level of description, but not another.

1.3.4 Searle's Chinese Room Argument

As we have seen, the idea that a certain type of symbol-processing can be what *makes* something an intentional system is fundamental to the computer model of the mind. Let us now turn to a flamboyant frontal attack on this idea by John Searle (1980, 1990b) (see also Churchland and Churchland 1990; the basic idea of this argument stems from Block 1978). Searle's strategy is one of avoiding quibbles about specific programs by imagining that cognitive science of the distant future can come up with the program of an actual person who speaks and understands Chinese, and that this program can be implemented in a machine. Unlike many critics of the computer model, Searle is willing to grant that perhaps this can be done so as to focus on his claim that, even if this can be done, the machine will not have intentional states.

The argument is based on a thought experiment. Imagine yourself given a job in which you work in a room (the Chinese room). You understand only English. Slips of paper with Chinese writing on them are put under the input door, and your job is to write sensible Chinese replies on other slips, and push them out under the output door. How do you do it? You act as the CPU (central processing unit) of a computer, following the computer program mentioned above that describes the symbol-processing in an actual Chinese-speaker's head. The program is printed in English in a library in the room. This is how you follow the program. Suppose the latest input has certain unintelligible (to you) Chinese squiggles on it. There is a blackboard on a wall of the room with a 'state' number written on it; it says '17'. (The CPU of a computer is a device with a finite number of states whose activity is determined solely by its current state and input, and since you are acting as the CPU, your output will be determined by your input and your 'state'. The '17' is on the blackboard to tell you what your 'state' is.) You take book 17 out of the library, and look up these particular squiggles in it. Book 17 tells you to look at what is written on your scratch pad (the computer's internal memory), and given both the input squiggles and the scratch pad marks, you are directed to change what is on the scratch pad in a certain way, write certain other squiggles on your output pad, push the paper under the output door, and finally, change the number on the state board to '193'. As a result of this activity, speakers of Chinese find that the pieces of paper you slip under the output door are sensible replies to the inputs.

But you know nothing of what is being said in Chinese; you are just following instructions (in English) to look in certain books and write certain marks. According to Searle, since you don't understand any Chinese, the system of which you are the CPU is a mere Chinese-simulator, not a real Chinese-understander. Of course, Searle (rightly) rejects the Turing test for understanding Chinese. His argument then is that since the program of a real

Chinese-understander is not sufficient for understanding Chinese, no symbol manipulation theory of Chinese-understanding (or any other intentional state) is correct about what makes something a Chinese-understander. Thus the conclusion of Searle's argument is that the fundamental idea of thought as symbol-processing is wrong even if it allows us to build a machine that can duplicate the symbol-processing of a person and thereby duplicate a person's behaviour.

The best criticisms of the Chinese room argument have focused on what Searle—anticipating the challenge—calls the systems reply. (Searle 1980 is accompanied by more than twenty-five responses; see them and the comment on Searle in Hofstadter and Dennett 1981.) The systems reply has a positive and a negative component. The negative component is that we cannot reason from 'Bill has never sold uranium to North Korea' to 'Bill's company has never sold uranium to North Korea'. Similarly, we cannot reason from 'Bill does not understand Chinese' to 'The system of which Bill is a part does not understand Chinese' (see Copeland 1993*b*). There is a gap in Searle's argument. The positive component goes further, saying that the whole system—man + program + board + paper + input and output doors—does understand Chinese, even though the man who is acting as the CPU does not. If you open up your own computer, looking for the CPU, you will find that it is just one of the many chips and other components on the main circuit board. The systems reply reminds us that the CPUs of the thinking computers we hope to have someday will not *themselves* think—rather, they will be *parts* of thinking systems.

Searle's clever reply (1990*b*) is to imagine the paraphernalia of the 'system' *internalized* as follows. First, instead of having you consult a library, we are to imagine you *memorizing* the whole library. Secondly, instead of writing notes on scratch pads, you are to memorize what you would have written on the pads, and you are to memorize what the state blackboard would say. Finally, instead of looking at notes put under one door and passing notes under another door, you just use your own *body* to listen to Chinese utterances and produce replies. (This version of the Chinese room has the additional advantage of generalizability so as to involve the complete behaviour of a Chinese-speaking system instead of just a Chinese note exchanger.) But as Searle would emphasize, when you seem to Chinese speakers to be conducting a learned discourse with them in Chinese, all you are aware of doing is thinking about what noises the program tells you to make next, given the noises you hear and what you've written on your mental scratch pad.

I argued above that the CPU is just one of many components. If the whole system understands Chinese, that should not lead us to expect the CPU to understand Chinese. The effect of Searle's internalization move—the 'new' Chinese room—is to attempt to destroy the analogy between looking inside the computer and looking inside the Chinese room. If one looks inside the computer, one sees many chips in addition to the CPU. But if one looks inside the 'new' Chinese room, all one sees is *you*, since you have memorized the library and internalized the functions of the scratch pad and the blackboard. But the point to keep in mind is that, although the non-CPU components are no longer easy to see, they are not gone. Rather, they are internalized. If the program requires the contents of one register to be placed in another register, and if you would have done this in the original Chinese room by copying from one piece of scratch paper to another, in the new Chinese room you must copy from one of your mental analogues of a piece of scratch paper to another. You are implementing the system by doing what the CPU would do and at the same time you are simulating the non-CPU components. So if the positive side of the systems reply is correct, the total system that you are implementing does understand Chinese.

'But how can it be', Searle would object, 'that you implement a system that understands Chinese even though *you* don't understand Chinese?' The systems reply rejoinder is that you implement a Chinese-understanding system without yourself understanding Chinese or necessarily even being aware of what you are doing under that description. The systems reply sees the Chinese room (new and old) as an English system implementing a Chinese system. What you are aware of are the thoughts of the English system, for example your following instructions and consulting your internal library. But in virtue of doing this Herculean task, you are also implementing a real intelligent Chinese-speaking system, and so your body houses two genuinely distinct intelligent systems. The Chinese system also thinks, but though you implement this thought, you are not aware of it.

The systems reply can be backed up with an addition to the thought experiment that highlights the division of labour. Imagine that you take on the Chinese-simulating as a nine-to-five job. You come in Monday morning after a weekend of relaxation, and you are paid to follow the program until 5 p.m. When you are working, you concentrate hard on working, and so instead of trying to figure out the meaning of what is said to you, you focus your energies on working out what the program tells you to do in response to each input. As a result, during working hours, you respond to everything just as the program dictates, except for occasional glances at your watch. (The glances at your watch fall under the same category as the noises and heat given off by computers: aspects of their behaviour that are not part of the machine description but are due rather to features of the implementation.) If someone speaks to you in English, you say what the program (which, you recall, describes a real Chinese-speaker) dictates. So if during working hours someone speaks to you in English, you respond with a request in Chinese to speak Chinese, or even an inexpertly pronounced 'No speak English' that was once memorized by the Chinese-speaker being simulated, and which you, the English-speaking system, may even fail to recognize as English because you are so intent on following the program. Then, come 5 p.m., you stop working, and react to Chinese talk the way any monolingual English-speaker would.

Why is it that the English system implements the Chinese system rather than, say, the other way round? Because you (the English system whom I am now addressing) are following the instructions of a program in English to make Chinese noises and not the other way round. If you decide to quit your job to become a magician, the Chinese system disappears. However, if the Chinese system decides to become a magician, he will make plans that he would express in Chinese, but then when 5 p.m. rolls round, you quit for the day, and the Chinese system's plans are on the shelf until you come back to work. And of course you have no commitment to doing whatever the program dictates. If the program dictates that you make a series of movements that leads you to a flight to China, you can drop out of the simulating mode, saying 'I quit!' The Chinese-speaker's existence and the fulfilment of his plans depend on your work schedule and your plans, not the other way round.

Thus, you and the Chinese system cohabit one body. In effect, Searle uses the fact that you are not aware of the Chinese system's thoughts as an argument that it has no thoughts. But this is an invalid argument. Real cases of multiple personalities are often cases in which one personality is unaware of the others.

It is instructive to compare Searle's thought experiment with the string-searching Aunt Bubbles machine described at the outset of this part of the chapter. This machine was used against a behaviourist proposal of a *behavioural conception* of intelligence. But the symbol manipulation view of the mind is not a proposal about our everyday conception. To the extent that we think of the English system as implementing a Chinese system, that will be because we find the symbol manipulation theory of the mind plausible as an empirical theory.

There is one aspect of Searle's case with which I am sympathetic. I have my doubts as to whether there is anything it is like to be the Chinese system, that is, whether the Chinese system is a phenomenally conscious system. My doubts arise from the idea that perhaps consciousness is more a matter of implementation of symbol-processing than of symbol-processing itself. Though surprisingly Searle does not mention this idea in connection with the Chinese room, it can be seen as the argumentative heart of his position. Searle has argued independently of the Chinese room (Searle 1992, ch. 7) that intentionality requires consciousness (see the replies to Searle in *Behavioral and Brain Sciences* 1990). But this doctrine, if correct, can shore up the Chinese room argument. For if the Chinese system is not conscious, then, according to Searle's doctrine, it is not an intentional system either.

Even if I am right about the failure of Searle's argument, it does succeed in sharpening our understanding of the nature of intentionality and its relation to computation and representation.

PARALLEL DISTRIBUTED PROCESSING

Gabriel Segal

2.1. Introduction

A parallel distributed processing system ('PDP system' for short), or, as it is often called, a 'connectionist network', is a particular kind of computer that differs in certain ways from classical computers of the sort discussed in Section 1. It is claimed by some that human cognitive capacities—such as perception, language use, and scientific and general reasoning—could be explained by PDP systems. The basic form of such explanations resembles that of classical computationalist explanations, as discussed in Section 1. The classical computationalist would explain a given cognitive capacity by positing a classical computer, physically realized in the brain, that is responsible for the capacity. For example, the human capacity to see would be explained by positing a classical computer, physically realized by the eyes and visual centres in the brain. This computer mediates the patterns of stimulation on the two retinas and the visual percepts that result from them. It does this by processing representations: the retinal stimulations are construed as representations of patterns of light, and the visual percept is construed as a representation of the shapes, locations, surface markings, and so on of perceived objects in the external world.

Connectionist explanation is just the same in general outline, except that, in place of classical computers, it posits PDP systems. Proponents of connectionist explanation often claim that the account of cognition that results from connectionist explanation is very different from that resulting from classical computationalism. They also claim that connectionism is more likely to provide successful explanations of cognition than classical computationalism. I shall briefly examine the nature of PDP systems, and compare the prospects of connectionist and classical accounts of human cognition.

2.2. What is a PDP System?

Recall from Section 1 that computers can be discussed at three levels of description: hardware, software, and semantic interpretation. To say that something is a PDP system is, in the first instance, to say something about the type of software. Thus, to classify something as a PDP system is to classify it in a very abstract way, a way that directly involves neither any physical description in terms of what the system is made of, nor any semantic description in terms of what the system represents or what problems it is addressing. We begin with the abstract, software description, then move on to some issues about hardware and semantic interpretation.

A PDP system consists in a network of units (sometimes called 'nodes'). Each unit is connected to one or more further units in the network. At any given time, each unit has a specific activation level. The connections allow units to influence one another's activation levels. Each connection connects just two units and is unidirectional, allowing one unit to influence the other. However, two connections can exist between a pair of units, allowing bidirectional influences. Each unit may be connected to many others. Each connection has a specific 'weight', which determines how the activation of one unit affects the other. If the weight is positive, then the higher the activation of the influencing unit, the higher the activation of the unit influenced: such connections are called 'excitatory'. If the weight is negative, then higher activation of the influencing unit causes lower activation of the influenced one: such connections are called 'inhibitory', since activation in one unit inhibits activation in the other. At any given time the state of the network is defined by the pattern of activation at that time (i.e. the level of activation of each unit) and by the connection weights.

Often the units in a network are arranged in so-called 'layers'. There is an input layer, an output layer, and, often, one or more intermediate layers which are termed 'hidden'. One provides inputs to a system by adjusting the activation levels of the input units. Supplying an input will cause activation to spread through the network in a fashion determined by the way the units are connected up. Eventually the network will settle into a steady state in which the activation level of each unit is fixed.

2.3. Hardware

As with classical systems, the nature of a PDP system's hardware is not relevant to the identity of its software. PDP systems could in principle be made out of anything that could instantiate the appropriate abstract patterns of units and connections. However, one important inspiration for parallel distributed processing was its apparent plausibility as neural software. Indeed, PDP systems are sometimes called 'neural networks'. There are certain important respects in which units in a PDP system resemble actual neurones in people's brains. In particular, neurones have firing intensities, and neurones are connected up to one another by excitatory and inhibitory connections, called 'axons' and 'dendrites' (not respectively, a single connection between neurones will involve one dendrite and several axons). Further, a good hypothesis about the physical mechanisms in the brain that underlie learning is that connections between neurones can grow, and existing connections can alter in weight.

The neural plausibility of PDP systems, however, is limited in various respects. There are many properties of the brain that seem to be important to the way it processes information but that are not reflected in PDP systems. One example is the role of neurotransmitters (see Bechtel and Abrahamsen 1991: 285). Secondly, and more importantly, there are features of PDP systems that have no known neural correlate. I will mention two of these.

The first concerns learning. The most often used method of creating a PDP system that succeeds at a particular task—say, recognizing letters of the alphabet or pictures of faces—is called 'back propagation'. Back propagation is a method of 'teaching' or 'training' a network, so that it becomes good at a task. Roughly, the way it works is as follows. The network begins with a random or arbitrary distribution of weights. Inputs are provided and the system settles into a steady state and provides an output. The actual output is then compared to a desired output, and the weights are adjusted according to a specific set of rules. The process is repeated until the actual outputs come to resemble the desired ones. The system is then able to generalize: it produces the correct outputs for previously unencountered inputs. The process of comparing actual outputs to desired ones and then adjusting weights must be carried out by some separate system, which could itself be a classical computer or another PDP network. Now, no process in the brain appears to correspond to back propagation. The problem is that back propagation requires that weights be able to switch polarity, from positive to negative, but connections between neurones never do this.

The second PDP feature that appears to lack a neural correlate relates to a constraint on patterns of neural connectivity. An important feature of many PDP systems is that a given unit can have both excitatory and inhibitory connections radiating from it, enabling it to excite some units while inhibiting others. By contrast, the connections radiating from any neurone are all of the same polarity—either positive or negative. Thus, activity on the part of a given neurone will either excite or inhibit all the other neurones it influences.

Neither of these problems shows conclusively that PDP systems could not be implemented in human brains. There are, in fact, two ways in which connectionists could address the problems of neural implementation. The first involves the crucial notion of 'levels of description', as discussed in Section 1.3. The problems for neural implementation only arise if one supposes that it is single neurones that are the physical realizations of units in the network. But this assumption might be jettisoned. One might suppose that the relation between PDP software and neural wetware is much less direct than that. The software would pertain to a higher and more abstract level of description. A unit in a network might correspond not to a single neurone, but to some more global feature of the brain. Likewise, connections between units in the net would not correspond to connections between individual neurones, but to connections between these global features. If this is right, it is all yet to be discovered: we don't know which global properties of the brain could serve such purposes.

This proposal essentially puts PDP systems and classical systems on a par with respect to neural plausibility: we don't yet know how they might be implemented in the brain, but we have no reason to suppose that such implementation is impossible.

The second possible solution to the problems of neural implementation would be to turn to networks of a different character from those that create the problems. There are methods of training networks other than back propagation. It might be that one of these corresponds to the way in which connections between neurones alter when learning takes place. And that method might prove powerful enough in its own right to allow PDP systems to learn the sorts of thing that human brains learn. So it may be possible to solve the training problem by turning away from back propagation and exploring other training methods.

A similar strategy might apply to the problem of the polarity of connections radiating from individual neurones. There are PDP systems that do not require single units to have outgoing connections of both polarities. Perhaps such systems could be developed to the point at which they were capable of performing the sorts of tasks that are performed by actual human cognition. If so, these nets might enter the explanation of human cognition. (For further discussion, see Churchland 1990.)

2.4. Representation and Processing

Like classical computers, PDP systems are representation processors: they receive representations as inputs and produce representations as outputs. Classical computers also manipulate internal representations. As we shall see, PDP systems may or may not do this. But either way, representation in connectionist networks is very different from representation in classical computers. I shall examine this contrast.

A representation is a physical configuration with a meaning, or semantic interpretation. There are two kinds of semantic interpretation applicable to connectionist systems, called 'localist' and 'distributed'. (Strictly speaking, only distributed systems qualify for the 'D' In 'PDP', but localist systems are important too.) We'll begin with localist systems, then move on to distributed ones.

In a localist system, it is specific, individual units that receive explicit semantic interpretation. Imagine, for example, that a given network is used for the storage and retrieval of information about members of rival criminal gangs—the Jets and the Sharks. (There is in fact such a network; see Bechtel and Abrahamsen 1991 and Clark 1989 for discussion.) There are units representing gang members (Art, Sam, etc.). There are other units representing various of their properties: name, marital status, age, and so on. And there is a pair of units representing gang affiliation: one for the Jets, one for the Sharks. Each gang member unit is connected by mutually excitatory connections to the units representing his properties and affiliation. Nodes representing mutually exclusive properties (e.g. married, single, divorced) are connected by mutually inhibitory connections.

Information is retrievable in a variety of ways. For example, both the 'Art' unit (the unit for Art's name) and the Jet unit are input units, and so can be activated from outside. Stimulation of either unit will increase activation in the other. So one could activate the Jet unit to search for the names of members of the gang, and one would come up with 'Art' as one instance. Or one could stimulate the 'Art' unit to find out more about the individual gang member, and one of the items emerging would be that he is a Jet.

Localist PDP systems differ sharply from classical ones in respect of both the nature of the representations and the kind of processing involved. Classical representations are syntactically structured: complex representations are made up out of atomic ones in fully systematic and determinate ways. If a classical system has the information, say, that Mary swims and John runs, this might be encoded in a representation much like the English sentence 'Mary swims and John runs'. This representation contains three representations as major constituents, corresponding to 'Mary swims', 'and', and 'John runs'. Two of these are themselves complex, containing as constituents 'Mary', 'swims', 'John', and 'runs'. In a localist PDP system, each explicit representation consists in just a single unit with no syntactic constituent structure. Thus, complexity in the semantic interpretation of a representation is not reflected in the structure of the representation itself. If a single unit means that Mary swims and John runs, we might use the English sentence 'Mary swims and John runs' to specify its interpretation. But the syntactic structure then resides only in our description of the representation, and not in the representation itself.

This difference in the nature of the representations brings with it a crucial difference in the nature of processing. In classical systems the syntactic structure of the representations is crucial to the way in which the system operates upon them. The operations are sensitive to the structure, and depend upon it. Thus if the system made an inference from 'Mary swims and John runs' to 'John runs', it would do so precisely because it was responding to the syntactic structure of the first representation. It responds to it as an instance of the general form 'P and Q'. Localist PDP systems obviously cannot work in this way, since their representations do not have syntactic structure. The fundamental account of processing is stated in a different kind of vocabulary altogether: the vocabulary of activation levels and weighted connections. (For discussion, see Fodor and Pylyshyn 1988.)

Considering the Jets and Sharks network, one might get the impression that structured representations are discernible in the system. For example, one could take the excitatory connections between the Art and Jet units to represent the fact that Art is a Jet. Thus we would have two constituent representations, the Art and Jet units, making up a complex one. And indeed, this impression is, in a sense, perfectly correct. There is a great deal of information implicitly present in the network. But the matter is less cut and dried than it seems. For the feature of the system that implicitly contains the information that Art is a Jet does not consist merely in the excitatory connections between the two units. Rather it is the pattern of connectivity across the whole system. Recall that the Art unit and the Jet unit are each connected up to many other units. This means that in spite of the mutually excitatory connections between them, it would be possible in principle for them not to have correlated activations. This is simply because the influence of the other units to which they are connected might overpower their mutually excitatory influences. It is thus the overall pattern of connectivity that maintains the relationship between the two units, not just the connections directly between them. Moreover, this same overall pattern is what carries all the information implicit in the network. The information that Art is single, that Sam is a Jet, that most Jets are single, and so on, all this information is implicit in the overall pattern. There is no real syntactic constituent structure in this kind of information storage.

The information implicit in the Jets and Sharks network is in fact distributed rather than local. In a distributed system, it is not individual units but either states of the whole network, or clusters of units, that are the objects of semantic interpretation.

We turn now more generally to the topic of distributed representation in PDP systems, continuing our focus on points of contrast between classical and distributed connectionist representation. We begin with an example of the former.

Imagine a machine that computes the mathematical function x^3. So, given '3' as input, it produces '27' as output; given '4', it produces '64' etc. Suppose that the machine has three subprocessors, and works as follows. Given an input representing a number, n, one subprocessor computes a representation of n^2. The second subprocessor works in parallel with the first, but has the very simple job of carrying the input, n, forward. Thus, it receives a representation of n as input, and produces a representation of n as output. The outputs from these two subprocessors, representing n^2 and n, then feed into the third subprocessor, which produces a representation of the number you get by multiplying n^2 and n.

In this classical system, the interpretation of the intermediate representations is fixed by their role in computation. The system as a whole is solving a larger problem—computer n^3—by containing subprocessors that solve smaller problems, and combining the results. This kind of hierarchical breakdown is one of the hallmarks of classical computers: a classical computer is usually composed of smaller computers, each of which has its own input and output representations. These further representations, the inputs and outputs of the subprocessors, are interpretable by their role in solving the overall problem. We interpret the internal representations in the example system as representing n^2 and n, because that is part of how we understand the system to be breaking down the problem of computing n^3. Usually, of course, these interpretations will have been predetermined by a human programmer, someone who has actually specified their roles. But even if this were not the case, even if the machine had arisen by some natural means, it would still be true that the internal representations would have to be interpreted as representing n^2 and n, if we were to see the object as a classical system at all. (For related discussion, see Haugeland 1978).

When it comes to interpreting the hidden units in a PDP system, it's all very different. Notice first that the connection weights in a PDP system will normally have been set not by a human programmer, but by a training process, such as back propagation. The roles of the hidden units in processing are thus not specified in advance by a programmer, but arrived at as a result of training. There is therefore no guarantee that the hidden units should be semantically interpretable at all. And, indeed, they may not be. It may be that the only way in which we can understand how the system works is in terms of activation levels, connection weights, and so on. Rather than a neat hierarchical breakdown that reveals how the machine represents aspects of subproblems of its overall problem, we might just find lots and lots of units influencing one another's activation levels.

In other cases, it is possible to interpret activations of hidden units, but not in ways that resemble classical interpretation. Sometimes this is done in terms of so-called 'micro-features'. For example a group of units representing coffee might contain four individual units meaning *hot liquid*, *burnt odour*, *brown liquid contacting porcelain*, and *brown liquid with curved sides and bottom*. The crucial difference between micro-featural distributed representation and classical representation again stems from the fact that the former lacks syntactic structure. The representation may be distributed over a number of units. But it is not the case that these individual units make up syntactic constituents of the representation. The *burnt odour* and *hot liquid* units, for example, are no more syntactic constituents of the distributed coffee representation than 'burn', 'todo', and 'ur' are syntactic constituents of the English expression 'burnt odour'.

The lack of syntactic constituent structure brings with it a lack of a compositional semantics. In a classical system, the meaning of a complex is fully determined by the meanings of its constituents and the way they are put together. This is not so for a distributed representation. This is obviously true in the cases where the component units of a representation have no meaning at all. It is also true (although less obviously) when the component units represent micro-features. There just are no definite rules for determining the meaning of the whole from the meaning of the components. And the interpretation is highly context-relative. In the above example, one takes the units representing *hot liquid, brown liquid contacting porcelain*, and so on to represent *coffee*. But this is because there are other associated units representing such things as *upright container* and *finger-sized handle*. In such a context it makes sense to take the *hot liquid, brown liquid contacting porcelain*, etc. units to mean *coffee*. In a different context the same micro-features might be taken to represent *gravy* or *chocolate sauce*. Moreover, in other contexts a different micro-featural representation of coffee would be appropriate: think, for example, of coffee-grounds in a can and of coffee beans in a paper bag. (See Fodor and Pylyshyn 1988; Smolensky 1988, 1991; and Clark 1989 for discussion.)

2.5. PDP Performance and Psychological Plausibility

Which paradigm is likely to prove more successful as an account of human cognition? The most influential argument that classical, rather than connectionist accounts are likely to succeed is the argument from the systematicity of thought, offered by Fodor (1987) and Fodor and Pylyshyn (1988). Since this was discussed in Section 1.2 I will not discuss it here. Instead I will briefly consider prospects for connectionism, and go on to look at a conciliatory view that leaves room for both classical and connectionist architectures to play important roles in the account of cognition.

PDP systems are better than classical ones when it comes to the recognition of physical shapes and patterns. What is unclear is how far this ability might extend into the domain of cognition. Obviously not all of human cognition can be thought of in terms of recognizing physical shapes. However, it could be that much of human cognition could be brought under the more general rubric of recognition of abstract patterns. The reach of connectionist explanation would thus depend on two things: (1) the extent to which the recognition of abstract patterns is the same sort of process as that of recognizing physical patterns, and (2) how far the notion of abstract-pattern recognition can be extended to cover cognitive activity.

It is, for example, reasonably plausible that chess-playing skills involve the recognition of abstract patterns made by pieces on the board (see Dreyfus and

Dreyfus 1986 for discussion). These patterns aren't in any very obvious sense physical or geometric, involving as they do the roles of specific pieces. a configuration of pieces with a rook in a specific place is obviously different from the same configuration with a knight in the rook's place. However, the relevant difference between a knight and a rook is a difference of how they move on the chessboard, and this, of course, is a geometrical matter. So, in the case of the cognitive capacity of playing chess there is at least a prima-facie case both that the abstract-pattern recognition involved is of the same general ilk as geometric-pattern recognition and, further, that the cognitive skill involved does indeed involve recognizing abstract patterns.

A more difficult case is provided by scientific inductive reasoning. In simple cases such reasoning merely involves generalizing from instances: for example, one notes that all pieces of copper in a given sample set conduct electricity, and goes on to hypothesize that all copper does. Even such an apparently straightforward inference conceals hidden complexity. Suppose the sample set contained six pieces of copper. These six objects all share the property of being made of copper, and it is this property that the scientist picks on as the basis of generalization. However, the six objects in question will also have infinitely many other properties in common. For example, they might also have the complex properties of being long, thin pieces of copper—or of being pieces of metal in the scientist's laboratory—or, for that matter, of being pieces of copper that have been examined prior to the year 2000. The scientist might pick on any of these properties as the basis for generalization. For example, if she picked the last one, she might hypothesize that the only copper objects that conduct electricity are those that have been examined prior to the year 2000. This latter generalization, though compatible with the scientist's evidence, would of course be wrong: even copper objects that haven't been examined before the year 2000 would conduct. (For relevant discussion of generalization in science, see Section 1.7 of Chapter 3 in the companion to this volume, *Philosophy: A Guide through the Subject*.)

What humans in general and scientists in particular seem good at is picking the right properties to generalize from, rather than the wrong ones. Does this cognitive capacity fundamentally involve pattern recognition? If so, in what sense and to what extent? I leave these questions for the reader to consider.

We have now looked briefly at a case for a connectionist account of cognition. Let us move on to consider the possibility of an approach that leaves room for both classical and connectionist theories to play important roles. One obvious move would simply be to allow that connectionism can explain some aspects of cognition, for example those that centrally involve pattern recognition, and that classical computationalism can explain others, for example the systematic ones like the formation of propositional attitudes and the learning and deployment of language. But a second and more interesting possibility adds to that a further role for connectionism. For the fact is that one can implement classical systems in PDP networks. What that means is that classical systems could be made out of connectionist networks.

To see how this works, consider the hierarchic breakdown of a classical system. As we saw above, a large classical system is usually made up of smaller classical systems—subprocessors—that work together. Now consider the subprocessors. These may or may not themselves be made up of even smaller classical systems—subsubprocessors. And these subsubprocessors may or may not be made up of subsubsubprocessors. But, obviously, the hierarchic breakdown must stop somewhere. At some point we will find what were called 'primitive processors' in Section 1.1.4. These, recall, are processors that receive representations as inputs and produce representations as outputs. But the explanation of how they work does not posit further representation processors within them. Rather the explanation must cite something else. One possibility is that they are PDP networks. For PDP networks are indeed representation processors, the representations being realized by the activation patterns of the input and output units. So it might be that both classical and connectionist approaches are correct. One does indeed need to posit classical computational systems to explain systematic aspects of cognition. But the explanation of the workings of these classical systems eventually appeals to connectionist networks.

PSYCHOANALYTIC THEORY

Gabriel Segal

3.1. Introduction

So far we have considered the extent to which mental functioning might be accounted for in computational terms, but I turn now to a very different topic: psychoanalytic theory. Psychoanalytic theory is orthogonal to questions about computation: it is compatible with both classical and connectionist approaches to the mind. (See Cummins 1983 for an argument that psychoanalysis is readily assimilated to a classical computationalist framework.) It is a theory pitched at the semantic, or intentional, level of description, a theory of what kinds of mental state we possess, of what sorts of content they have and the different ways in which they manifest themselves.

The theory was originated and developed in depth by Sigmund Freud. His earliest publications on the subject date from 1895 and Freud altered and

I am most grateful to James Hopkins and Neil Manson for helpful comments on an earlier draft of this section on psychoanalytic theory.

extended the theory in many ways until his death in 1939. Of course he did not work alone; psychoanalytic theory benefited in Freud's own time from the work of many others and has been developed since his death in different ways by various analysts working alone and in groups. However, here I shall focus mainly on the theory as Freud himself presents it, since this is the simplest way to put forward its leading ideas and the philosophical issues they raise.

3.2. Psychoanalysis and Common-Sense Psychology

A good way to embark on an understanding of psychoanalytic theory is to compare it with common-sense psychology, the ordinary, everyday conception of the mind and its workings as accepted by all or most people. Common-sense psychology deploys concepts of propositional attitudes (belief, desire, intention, fear, thinking, and so on) in an explanatory framework. The essence of this framework involves the coordination of two different kinds of property that propositional attitudes possess: representational properties and causal properties. This coordination can be illustrated with a simple example. Suppose that I am cooking a curry. At a certain point I taste the dish, and form the belief that something is lacking. On reflection, I realize that it isn't fragrant enough. I desire to make it more fragrant. I believe that adding ginger to curries makes them more fragrant. I conclude that if I add ginger to the curry I am cooking, it will become more fragrant. So I add ginger.

In this example, there are a number of propositional attitudes: a desire and several beliefs. Each of these attitudes has a specific representational content. For example, the representational content of the desire is that the curry becomes more fragrant. The representational content of the first belief is that the curry is not fragrant enough. And the attitudes have causal properties. Together they cause my body to move in the very specific way required by the action of adding ginger. There is also a certain causal structure in the formation of the attitudes themselves. For example, my belief that adding ginger to curries in general makes them more fragrant causes me to have the further belief that if I add ginger to this specific curry, it will become more fragrant. The causal and the representational properties are coordinated in an obvious way. Here, there is a straightforward logical connection between the contents of the beliefs: the first represents the general case, the second represents a specific instance which follows logically from it. There is also an obvious connection of content between the attitudes and the action that they cause: the action is rational in the light of my desire to make the curry more fragrant and my belief that adding ginger will make it so.

In general, desires and beliefs both cause actions and rationalize them. The representational properties reflect the causal ones, and, in common-sense psychological explanation, we can exploit this connection to explain and (to a degree) predict the formation of attitudes and the performance of actions. (For development of the idea of psychoanalysis as an extension of common-sense psychology, see Hopkins 1988 and Wollheim 1991. For more on the nature of common-sense psychology, see Fodor 1987, ch. 1.)

Psychoanalysis is a scientific extension of the basic explanatory apparatus of common-sense psychology. It retains the core idea that psychological states have representational and causal properties and that the former reflect the latter. But it extends, deepens, and refines the core idea in a number of ways. I consider here some of the most important of these.

The first and most important way in which psychoanalysis extends common sense is by claiming that large tracts of our mental life are unconscious: we are not aware of them by introspection. Common-sense psychology probably leaves room for the idea of unconscious mentality, but it does not accord it a particularly large role. And, as we shall see, the nature and dynamics of the unconscious, as Freud sees them, do not closely resemble those of conscious states recognized by common sense.

Freud's development of the notion of unconscious mentality began with his study of the phenomenon of post-hypnotic suggestion. Subjects are put under hypnosis, and the hypnotist gives them an instruction to be fulfilled after they have been released from the trance. For example, the hypnotist might say, 'When I snap my fingers, open the umbrella'. The subject is released when the hypnotist snaps his fingers, and finds himself opening the umbrella—even though he is indoors and there is no sign of rain. Freud's view was that in these cases a motive is planted in the mind of the subject and remains there although he is quite unaware of it. Nevertheless, its causal potency remains, and it brings about the action that is appropriate in light of its representational content.

Hypnosis, of course, is an unusual phenomenon, but it provides evidence that unconscious mental states do indeed occur. Another kind of example that was important to Freud is provided by obsessional neurotics, who find themselves obsessively performing actions that they cannot account for. To illustrate, I take the case of Freud's patient who is sometimes called 'the tablecloth lady' (Freud 1955–: xvi. 261–4). This lady came to Freud complaining that she would repeatedly go to her dining-room and summon the maid. She had no idea why she did this, and when the maid appeared, would have no task for her to perform. Freud's investigations into her history revealed that on the night of the lady's marriage, she and her husband were staying in a hotel. The husband had been unable to make to love to her and became very worried about this. He was particularly concerned that the next morning the chambermaid would find no blood on the sheets, and become aware of his impotence. He had therefore spilled some red ink on the sheet in order to mislead her. However, he spilled it in the wrong place, and they felt that the ruse would probably fail. It emerged during conversation with the lady that on the tablecloth on her dining-room table there was also a stain. Freud's hypothesis was that the lady was unconsciously distressed by her husband's wedding-night predicament, and that she unconsciously wished a maid to see a stain. This wish manifested itself in her repeatedly summoning her present maid to the dining-room.

The case illustrates an important feature of the unconscious. It is clear that the lady's action is, in a certain sense, irrational. The maid she calls is not the original maid from the hotel and the stain on the tablecloth is not a bloodstain on a sheet, so the action motivated by the unconscious wishes would not in reality alleviate the distress. This shows how unconscious mental states can be isolated from information in the subject's conscious mind. The lady herself is, of course, quite aware of the difference between the two maids, and so on. But the little cluster of unconscious states that lead to her obsessive action continues to operate, quite unaffected by this information. These unconscious motives do not fit with the lady's general aims and goals, and are, in that sense, irrational. The same point also applies to motives caused by hypnotic suggestion. Consider the case of opening an umbrella under post-hypnotic suggestion, mentioned above: it is not a rational thing to do, even by the subject's own lights.

The unconscious is revealed not only in hypnosis and obsessional neurosis, but in a host of other ways. One of the most central to psychoanalytic theory and practice is dreaming. Freud saw dreams as arising from unconscious wishes. I shall use one of Freud's own dreams to illustrate the main points of the general psychoanalytic theory of dreaming. Freud dreamed of one of his patients, Irma. He reports:

> I said to [Irma] 'If you still get pains it's really your own fault.' She replied 'if you only knew what pains I've got now in my throat and stomach and abdomen—it's choking me.' I was alarmed when I looked at her. She looked pale and puffy. I thought to myself that after all I must have been missing some organic trouble . . . Not long ago, when she was feeling unwell, my friend Otto had given her an injection . . . injections of that sort ought not to be made thoughtlessly . . . And probably the syringe had not been clean. (Freud 1955–: iv. 109).

Freud distinguishes between what he calls the 'manifest content' and the 'latent content' of a dream. The manifest content is what is experienced by the dreamer and may be recalled and reported. The quotation above records the manifest content of Freud's dream. The latent content is a cluster of unconscious mental states—thoughts, fears, desires, and so on—that includes in particular the unconscious wish that always, according to Freud, underlies a dream. The latent content is not usually obvious to either subject or psychoanalyst, and further investigations are required to reveal it. Typically these further investigations are arrived at by 'free association': the subject considers various specific aspects of the dream, and sees what associations come to mind.

The key association in this particular case was this: Freud recalled that the day prior to the dream Otto (a friend and colleague) had said of Irma that she was looking better, but not quite well. Freud felt this as a reproof. What this association suggests is that the latent content of the dream includes a wish that he, Freud, was not responsible for any remaining ailment of Irma's. In fact the dream represents Irma's ailments as organically caused. Since Freud was treating her for psychological problems, he would not be responsible for curing organic problems. And it represents Otto, and not Freud, as at fault. This last aspect is an instance of a common feature of unconscious functioning. If someone feels they have an undesirable characteristic, they unconsciously 'project' it (to use the technical term) onto someone else. In his unconscious Freud was saying, 'It is not me who is at fault, but Otto.'

Notice that the explanation of dreams in terms of unconscious wishes does not exactly conform to the pattern of desire–belief explanation in commonsense psychology. The dream is not an action, in the sense of something a person does because she believes that doing so would satisfy some desire. Rather, there is a much more direct relation between the desire or wish and the dream: the dream represents the state of affairs that would fulfil the wish. It is a sort of hallucinatory wish-fulfilment of a kind that is also recognized by commonsense psychology. We are used to seeing certain dreams as wish-fulfilling, just as we are aware that conscious fantasy plays the same role. But Freud's theory of dreams goes beyond common sense in at least three ways. First, he applies the idea of wish-fulfilment far more generally than it is applied in common sense: all dreams, not just some, are held to represent the fulfilment of a wish. Secondly, he goes beyond common sense in the kinds of wish he is prepared to posit. (This point is made in Hopkins 1988.) Freud's wishful projection of fault from himself onto Otto is an infantile and irrational wish. (Irrational because Freud would not actually have wanted Irma to suffer acute pains, or that he himself would have misdiagnosed Irma's complaint, or that his friend should have made a medical mistake.) Finally, he goes beyond common sense in a more deeply theoretical way, when he distinguishes the latent content from the manifest content. Indeed, Freud offered a detailed theory of the ways in which the latent content, the unconscious mental states underlying the dream, is transformed into the manifest content. (Freud deals with dreams at great length in 1955–: iv and v. For briefer and more accessible treatments, see Freud 1955–: xv, sect. 2, and xxii, lect. 29. For discussion, see Wollheim 1991.)

There are many other ways in which the unconscious is manifested, such as slips of the tongue ('Freudian slips', as they are often called), memory lapses and other kinds of errors, and psychological problems of all kinds, such as work problems, anxieties, phobias etc. There is no space to consider these here (for discussion, see Freud 1955–: xv and Wollheim 1991). Rather I shall turn now to the aetiology of unconscious mental states and some criticisms of psychoanalytic theory.

3.3. Repression and the Aetiology of Unconscious Mentality

Freud distinguishes between what he calls the 'pre-conscious' and the 'unconscious'. The former consists in those mental states we are not aware of, but which could easily become conscious. This would include, for example, those things that one can remember but that one happens not to be thinking about at a given time. The unconscious proper consists in mental states that are 'repressed'. These are mental states which the subject would rather not have: she finds them so unbearable that they are banished from awareness. Freud posits a mechanism that is responsible for repressing unbearable thoughts and feelings, which he calls the 'Censor'. Essentially, the Censor is responsible for distinguishing between acceptable and unacceptable thoughts and feelings, and for keeping the latter out of the reach of consciousness.

The existentialist philosopher Jean-Paul Sartre criticized Freud's theory of repression (Sartre 1956). In essence Sartre's criticism was that the Censor would need to be both conscious of and yet at the same time not conscious of the material it was supposed to repress. It would have to be conscious of the material, because it would have to know what exactly it was supposed to repress; but it would have to be unconscious of the material as well, otherwise it would not have successfully repressed it.

A quick response to Sartre's objection would be to point out that the Censor must be distinguished from the subject as a whole. The Censor might therefore remain conscious of the unbearable material, while keeping it out of reach of the subject's conscious mind. The material would then be successfully repressed, since the subject would not be conscious of it, even if the Censor remained aware of it.

However, both Sartre's objection and this quick response to it rest on a misunderstanding of Freud's theory. The Censor is not supposed to be a thoughtful, intelligent being, something like a small, complete mind existing within the larger mind of a human being. It is itself neither conscious nor unconscious of anything. Rather, it is just a mechanism. It is able to identify thoughts which the subject finds unbearable, and either place them in the unconscious (if they are conscious in the first place), or just keep them there (if they originate in the unconscious). In order to do this it need not even recognize or understand the contents of the repressed material. It need only be responsive to the affective quality of the material: that is, it need only be responsive to whether the thought or feeling causes sufficient distress to the subject. Indeed, it is a further important innovation on Freud's part to offer this sort of mechanistic account of aspects of mental functioning. Psychological mechanisms, such as the Censor, are components of the mind in that they perform functions within it, but they are not themselves things which think or reason or feel in anything like the way that the conscious mind does.

To summarize what we have discussed thus far: psychoanalysis extends common-sense psychology in the following ways. (1) It posits a rich domain of unconscious mental life. (2) The unconscious lacks the integration of conscious reasoning. (3) Unconscious mental states are often unpleasant to the subject, infantile, or in other ways of a character not typically recognized by common-sense psychology. (4) The scope of psychological theorizing is extended to cover irrational action (as in obsessional neurosis), dreams, slips of the tongue, as well as a plethora of other phenomena. (5) Unconscious mental states do not always express themselves by rationalizing an action in a common-sense manner. (6) Certain aspects of mental functioning are mechanistic.

3.4. A Methodological Critique of Psychoanalysis

The work of Freud and his followers has attracted considerable critical attention. Some have rejected the psychoanalytic claim to provide causal explanations of the phenomena it deals with (see e.g. Ricœur 1970; Flew 1956). They claim that explanation in terms of motives and reasons is quite distinct from explanation in terms of causes: to explain an action in terms of a motive, on this view, is not to offer a causal explanation at all, but rather to interpret it, to give a meaning. They conclude that psychoanalysis is interesting as an interpretative enterprise, but is guilty of false advertising when it claims to be a science that uncovers hidden causes. There seems to be little in favour of this 'hermeneutic' view of psychoanalysis since, as we have seen, both common-sense psychology and psychoanalysis treat reasons both as meaningful items (in terms of what they represent, how they rationalize actions) and as causes, and, in doing so, offer perfectly cogent modes of explanation.

Others, notably Karl Popper (1963) have rejected its claim to scientific status on the grounds that it is not falsifiable. The basic claim here is that no possible evidence would refute psychoanalytic claims, and that therefore the theory does not have proper scientific credentials.

Finally, some have allowed that psychoanalysis deserves the label of science, and accepted that it is falsifiable. However, they have argued, while it has not yet been falsified, it has also not yet been shown to be true. I focus here on an influential version of this last kind of criticism, due to Adolf Grunbaum (1984: for a short version, see Grunbaum 1986, where it is published along with numerous responses by others).

Grunbaum observes that the overwhelming source of evidence claimed for psychoanalysis comes from clinical work. The evidence consists in what patients say during therapy: the way they describe their symptoms, their reports of dreams, and, crucially, their free associations. But, Grunbaum argues, such clinical evidence does not in fact vindicate the theory, as Freud supposed it did. Grunbaum's critique of psychoanalysis is long and sophisticated. Here I can merely give a very brief sketch of two of his main criticisms, and an indication of how a defender of psychoanalysis might reply to them. The first criticism is that the data arrived at in the clinical situation are themselves suspect. The second is that, even if the data are granted, the reasoning by which Freud attempted to validate his theory is fundamentally flawed. I shall look at these in turn.

Grunbaum's main worry about the clinical evidence is that patients may say things precisely with the aim of verifying the analyst's interpretations, in order to please them and win their approval. For example, the analyst might offer a candidate interpretation of a dream—or the patient may divine what the analyst's favoured interpretation would be—and go on to say something specifically designed to lend confirmation to this interpretation. Let us look at a concrete example.

One of Freud's patient's reported the following dream: 'I wanted to give a supper-party, but I had nothing in the house but a little smoked salmon. I thought I would go out and buy something, but remembered that it was Sunday afternoon and all the shops would be shut. . . . So I had to abandon my wish to give a supper-party' (Freud 1955–: iv. 148). The patient's initial associations included the following. The day before, she had visited a certain friend of hers. She was jealous of the friend because her (the patient's) husband was constantly singing her praises. However, the friend was skinny, and the husband admired a plumper figure. The friend had talked about her wish to grow stouter. She had also said 'When are you going to ask us to another meal? You always feed us so well.'

Freud's interpretation was that the latent wish behind the dream was precisely not to provide supper for her friend. He then asked about the smoked salmon in the dream, and the patient said 'Oh, smoked salmon is my friend's favourite dish.' Freud took this to be further confirmation of his interpretation. However, Grunbaum's worry would be that the patient might have reported that smoked salmon was her friend's favourite dish precisely because she thought that it would confirm Freud's interpretation.

One could put the point like this. Freud would claim that the patient's association of smoked salmon with her friend was caused in part by the same latent thoughts that also caused the dream: these thoughts express themselves once in the dream itself, and again by bringing to the patient's conscious mind the link between smoked salmon and her skinny friend. But Grunbaum offers a competing hypothesis: that the patient reports the link between smoked salmon and her friend because she knows that this would confirm Freud's interpretation, and that is what she wants to do. As long as this remains a possibility, the association does not provide evidence of the truth of Freud's interpretation.

Let us now turn to Grunbaum's second criticism. Grunbaum holds that Freud himself recognized the unreliability of clinical data of the sort we have just considered. And, Grunbaum says, Freud goes on to give a further argument in support of psychoanalysis, one that rests on its therapeutic success. The basic idea behind psychoanalytic therapy is that the analyst can discover the unconscious states that cause a patient's symptoms, and can communicate them to the patient. This can lead to the states becoming conscious, or at least to the patient's achieving greater insight into the workings of her own mind, and this, in turn, leads to alleviation of the symptoms. The essentials of the argument from therapeutic success, as Grunbaum portrays it, are summarized in these two claims:

> (1) Only the psychoanalytic method of interpretation and treatment can yield or mediate for the patient correct insight into the unconscious causes of his neurosis.
>
> (2) The patient's correct insight into the . . . cause of his condition and into the unconscious dynamics of his character is in turn causally necessary for the durable cure of his neurosis. (Clark and Wright 1988: 14)

Grunbaum calls these two claims the 'necessary condition thesis' (NCT), since they state necessary conditions for durable cures of neuroses.

As Grunbaum goes on to argue, NCT is implausible, and may be doubted on a number of grounds. Here are three. First, it is known that neurotics sometimes undergo spontaneous remission: they get better without treatment. Thus, it is certainly false that remission from neurosis only occurs under psychoanalysis. Secondly, patients might get better under psychoanalysis because of a placebo effect. Thus psychoanalytic theory might be quite wrong, and analysts' interpretations might be false, but patients would get better because of their faith in the analyst's power, or for other reasons. Finally, as Freud himself admits, psychoanalysis often does not yield durable cures from neurosis, but only temporary and palliative effects.

It is clear, then, that NCT is in poor shape. And Grunbaum thinks that it is the only serious argument in favour of the use of clinical evidence to vindicate psychoanalysis. He thus concludes: 'Despite the poverty of clinical support, it could conceivably turn out that Freud's brilliant theoretical imagination was actually serendipitously right in some respects. But whereas psychoanalysis may thus be said to be scientifically alive, it is currently hardly well . . .' (Clark and Wright 1988: 30).

Grunbaum's arguments have been subject to a great deal of criticism (see e.g. Hopkins 1988; Wollheim 1991; various of the replies in Grunbaum 1986; Sachs 1991). I shall confine myself to some brief comments. These concern, first, NCT and Grunbaum's criticism of it, and, secondly, the possibility of a different kind of defence of psychoanalysis—one that doesn't depend on therapeutic success.

I begin by noting that the exegesis of Freud is implausible. Although some of Freud's remarks support a version of NCT, it is a much weaker and more plausible one than that specified above. In any event, whatever Freud might have said, it is possible to state a version of NCT which is not vulnerable to any of Grunbaum's objections. It might be put something like this:

(NCT*) Other things being equal, a patient under analysis would not get better unless some of the analyst's interpretations were correct.

The hedge 'other things being equal' allows for the possibility of exceptional cases of improvement caused by such things as spontaneous remission or placebo effect. And the reference to 'durable' cures has been replaced with the more realistic idea of the patient's getting better: some of their symptoms disappearing or lessening.

Of course, the truth of the relatively modest NCT* might be questioned. In assessing this, the key question would be whether alternative explanations of patients' improvements—such as placebo effect or spontaneous remission—can always be made plausible. I will merely point out that there is virtually no theory of the nature of placebo effects nor of the mechanisms by which they work. It is therefore extremely weak as a competing explanation of the alleviation of symptoms. As for spontaneous remission, this seems to be a relatively rare phenomenon outside psychoanalytic treatment. Therefore, the improvement rate is probably better for those in psychoanalysis than those who are not. Given that, the differential effect needs to be explained, and there is room for psychoanalysts to argue that this differential effect is indeed due to the truth of their theory and its application to specific cases.

It seems, then, that Grunbaum's rejection of the evidential value of the apparent curative effects of psychoanalysis is too hasty. What of his view that NCT offers the only serious argument in favour of psychoanalysis? This too is highly questionable. Psychoanalysis offers a structured and detailed theory of the nature and functioning of the unconscious. The theory offers general explanations of neurotic symptoms, dreams, slips of the tongue, and so on. That is, it can say, in general terms, how these phenomena are caused. Further, psychoanalysis has been applied to millions of specific instances: the symptoms, dreams, slips, and so on of thousands of actual patients. In these cases, it offers specific explanations of specific occurrences in the real world. To say that it offers these explanations—both general and specific—is to say that it makes claims which, *if true*, would correctly specify the causes of the phenomena to be explained. Now, all this in itself offers considerable support for psychoanalytic theory. The symptoms, dreams, and so on provide the evidence to which psychoanalysis is answerable. And the extent to which it can offer explanations of these is the extent to which it has evidential support. The extent is therefore considerable.

None of this goes to demonstrate conclusively that the theory is correct and Grunbaum is therefore right to point to the possibility that other things might be the true causes of the phenomena that psychoanalysis seeks to explain; but at the moment there is little by way of serious competition. Psychoanalysis is at least the best explanation that is currently on offer.

BIBLIOGRAPHY

CLASSICAL COMPUTATIONALISM

BEAKELEY, B., and LUDLOW, P. (eds.) (1992), *Philosophy of Mind: Classical Problems/Contemporary Issues* (Cambridge).

Behavioral and Brain Sciences (1990), 13.

BLOCK, N. (1978), 'Troubles with Functionalism', in C. Wade Savage (ed.), *Minnesota Studies in the Philosophy of Science*, ix: *Perception and Cognition* (Minneapolis); repr. in Lycan (1990) and Rosenthal (1991).

——(1980), *Readings in Philosophy of Psychology*, i (Cambridge, Mass.).

——(1981*a*), 'Psychologism and Behaviorism', *Philosophical Review*, 90: 5–43.

——(1981*b*), *Readings in Philosophy of Psychology*, ii (Cambridge, Mass.).

——(1986), 'Advertisement for a Semantics for Psychology', in P. A. French, T. E. Uehling, and H. K. Wettstein (eds.), *Midwest Studies in Philosophy*, x: *Studies in the Philosophy of Mind* (Minneapolis).

——(1990*a*), 'Inverted Earth', in Tomberlin (1990).

——(1990*b*), 'Can the Mind Change the World?', in G. Boolos (ed.), *Meaning and Method: Essays in Honor of Hilary Putnam* (Cambridge).

BURGE, T. (1979), 'Individualism and the Mental', in P. A. French, T. E. Uehling, and H. K. Wettstein (eds.), *Midwest Studies in Philosophy*, iv: *Studies in Metaphysics* (Minneapolis).

——(1986), 'Individualism and Psychology', *Philosophical Review*, 95: 3–45.

CHALMERS, D. (1994), *A Conceptual Foundation for the Study of Cognition*, Washington University Technical Report (Washington).

CHOMSKY, N. (1959), Review of B. F. Skinner, *Verbal Behavior*, *Language*, 35: 26–58.

——(1975), *Reflections on Language* (New York).

CHURCHLAND, P. M. (1981), 'Eliminative Materialism and the Propositional Attitudes', *Journal of Philosophy*, 78: 67–90.

Churchland, P. M., and Churchland P. S. (1990), 'Could a Machine Think?', *Scientific American*, 262: 26–31.

Churchland, P. S. (1986), *Neurophilosophy* (Cambridge).

Clark, A. (1992), *Associative Engines* (Cambridge, Mass.).

Copeland, J. (1993*a*), *Artificial Intelligence: A Philosophical Introduction* (Oxford).

——(1993*b*), 'The Curious Case of the Chinese Gym', *Syntheses*, 95: 173–86.

Cummins, R. (1975), 'Functional Analysis', *Journal of Philosophy*, 72: 741–65; excerpts repr. in Block (1980).

——(1989), *Meaning and Mental Representation* (Cambridge, Mass.).

Davies, M., and Humphreys, G. (1993), *Consciousness* (Oxford).

Dehmelt, H. (1989), 'Triton, . . . Electron, . . . Cosmon, . . . : An Infinite Regression?', *Proceedings of the National Academy of Sciences*, 86: 8618.

Dennett, D. C. (1969), *Content and Consciousness* (London).

——(1974), 'Why the Law of Effect will not Go Away', *Journal of the Theory of Social Behavior*, 5: 169–87.

——(1975), 'Brain Writing and Mind Reading', in K. Gunderson (ed.), *Minnesota Studies in the Philosophy of Science*, vii (Minneapolis).

——(1981), 'Three Kinds of Intentional Psychology', in R. Healy (ed.), *Reduction, Time and Reality* (Cambridge).

——(1987), *The Intentional Stance* (Cambridge, Mass.).

——(1988), 'Quining Qualia', in A. Marcel and E. Bisiach (eds.), *Consciousness in Contemporary Society* (Oxford).

Dretske, F. (1981), *Knowledge and the Flow of Information* (Cambridge, Mass.).

——(1988), *Explaining Behavior: Reasons in a World of Causes* (Cambridge, Mass.).

Dreyfus, H. L. (1979), *What Computers can't Do* (New York).

Field, H. (1978), 'Mental Representation', *Erkenntnis*, 13: 9–61; repr. in Block (1980).

Fodor, J. A. (1968), 'The Appeal to Tacit Knowledge in Psychological Explanation', *Journal of Philosophy*, 65: 627–40.

——(1975), *The Language of Thought* (New York).

——(1980), 'Methodological Solipsism Considered as a Research Strategy in Cognitive Psychology', *Behavioral and Brain Sciences*, 3: 417–24; repr. in Haugeland (1981).

——(1981), 'Three Cheers for Propositional Attitudes', in *RePresentations* (Cambridge, Mass.).

——(1983), *The Modularity of Mind* (Cambridge, Mass.).

——(1985), 'Fodor's Guide to Mental Representation', *Mind*, 94: 76–100.

——(1987), *Psychosemantics: The Problem of Meaning in the Philosophy of Mind* (Cambridge, Mass.).

——(1990), 'Psychosemantics; or, Where do Truth Conditions Come From?', in Lycan (1990).

——and Pylyshyn, Z. W. (1988), 'Connectionism and Cognitive Architecture: A Critical Analysis', *Cognition*, 28: 3–71.

Goldman, A (ed.) (1993), *Readings in Philosophy and Cognitive Science* (Cambridge, Mass.).

Guttenplan, S. (ed.) (1994), *A Companion to Philosophy of Mind* (Oxford).

Harman, G. (1973), *Thought* (Princeton).

——(1990), 'The Intrinsic Quality of Experience', in Tomberlin (1990).

Haugeland, J. C. (1978), 'The Nature and Plausibility of Cognitivism', *Behavioral and Brain Sciences*, 1: 215–26; repr. in Haugeland (1981).

——(1980), 'Programs, Causal Powers and Intentionality', *Behavioral and Brain Sciences*, 3: 432–3.

——(ed.) (1981), *Mind Design* (Cambridge, Mass.).

——(1990), 'The Intentionality All-Stars', in Tomberlin (1990).

Hofstadter, D., and Dennett, D. C. (1981), *The Mind's I: Fantasies and Reflections on Mind and Soul* (New York).

Horwich, P. (1990), *Truth* (Oxford).

Kim, J. (1992), 'Multiple Realization and the Metaphysics of Reduction', *Philosophy and Phenomenological Research*, 52: 177–92.

LePore, E., and Loewer, B. (1987), 'Mind Matters', *Journal of Philosophy*, 84: 630–41.

Lycan, W. (ed.) (1987), *Consciousness* (Cambridge, Mass.).

——(1990), *Mind and Cognition* (Oxford).

McCarthy, J. (1980), 'Beliefs, Machines and Theories', *Behavioral and Brain Sciences*, 3: 435.

Marr, D. (1977), 'Artificial Intelligence—A Personal View', *Artificial Intelligence*, 9: 37–48; repr. in Haugeland (1981).

Millikan, R. G. (1984), *Language, Thought and Other Biological Categories: New Foundations for Realism* (Cambridge, Mass.).

Moor, J. (1987), 'Turing Test', in S. Shapiro (ed.), *Encyclopedia of Artificial Intelligence* (New York).

Newell, A. (1980), 'Physical Symbol Systems', *Cognitive Science*, 4: 135–83.

Papineau, D. (1984), 'Representation and Explanation', *Philosophy of Sciences*, 51: 550–72.

Peacocke, C. (1993), *A Study of Concepts* (Cambridge, Mass.).

Pettit, P., and McDowell, J. (1986), *Subject, Thought, and Context* (Oxford).

Putnam, H. (1975), 'Philosophy and our Mental Life', in *Mind, Language and Reality: Philosophical Papers*, ii (London); repr. in Block (1980) and in somewhat different form in Haugeland (1981); first pub. in *Cognition*, 2 (1973) with a section on IQ that is omitted from all the reprinted versions.

——(1988), *Representation and Reality* (Cambridge, Mass.).

Pylyshyn, Z. W. (1984), *Computation and Cognition: Issues in the Foundations of Cognitive Science* (Cambridge, Mass.).

Ramsey, W., Stich S., and Rumelhart, D. (1991), *Philosophy and Connectionist Theory* (Hillsdale, NJ).

Rosenthal, D. M. (ed.) (1991), *The Nature of Mind* (Oxford).

Schiffer, S. (1987), *Remnants of Meaning* (Cambridge, Mass.).

Schwartz, J. (1988), 'The New Connectionism: Developing Relationships between Neuroscience and Artificial Intelligence', *Daedalus*, 117: 123–42.

Searle, J. R. (1980). 'Minds, Brains, and Programs', *Behavioral and Brain Sciences*, 3: 417–24; repr. in Haugeland (1981).

——(1990*a*), 'Is the Brain a Digital Computer?', *Proceedings and Addresses of the American Philosophical Association*, 64: 21–37.

——(1990*b*), 'Is the Brain's Mind a Computer Program?', *Scientific American*, 262: 20–5.

——(1992), *The Rediscovery of the Mind* (Cambridge, Mass.).

Shieber, S. (1994), 'The First Turing Test', *Proceedings of the ACM*.

Shoemaker, S. (1981), 'The Inverted Spectrum', *Journal of Philosophy*, 74: 357–81.

Smolensky, P. (1988), 'On the Proper Treatment of Connectionism', *Behavioral and Brain Sciences*, 11: 1–23; see also the commentary that follows and the reply by the author.

Stalnaker, R. (1984), *Inquiry* (Cambridge, Mass.).

Stampe, D. W. (1977), 'Toward a Causal Theory of Linguistic Representation', in P. A. French, T. E. Uehling, and H. K. Wettstein (eds.), *Midwest Studies in Philosophy*, ii: *Studies in the Philosophy of Language* (Minneapolis).

Sterelny, K. (1985), Review of Stich, *From Folk Psychology to Cognitive Science: The Case against Belief*, *Australasian Journal of Philosophy*, 63: 510–19.

——(1990), *The Representational Theory of the Mind* (Oxford).

Stich, S. (1983), *From Folk Psychology to Cognitive Science: The Case against Belief* (Cambridge, Mass.).

Tomberlin, J. E. (ed.) (1990), *Philosophical Perspectives*, iv: *Philosophy of Mind and Action Theory* (Atascadero, Calif.).

Turing, A. M. (1950), 'Computing Machinery and Intelligence', *Mind*, 59: 433–60.

Tye, M. (1991), *The Imagery Debate* (Cambridge, Mass.).

Weizenbaum, J. (1976), *Computer Power and Human Reason* (San Francisco).

White, S. (1982), 'Functionalism and Propositional Content', Ph.D. dissertation, University of California, Berkeley.

PARALLEL DISTRIBUTED PROCESSING

Bechtel, W., and Abrahamsen A. (1991), *Connectionism and the Mind: An Introduction to Parallel Processing* (Oxford).

Churchland, P. S. (1990), 'Cognitive Activity in Artificial Neural Networks', in D. Osherson and E. Smith (eds.), An Invitation to Cognitive Science. iii: Thinking (Cambridge, Mass.).

Clark, A. (1989), *Microcognition: Philosophy, Cognitive Science and Parallel Distributed Processing* (Cambridge, Mass.).

Dreyfus, H. L., and Dreyfus, S. E. (1986), *Mind over Machine: The Power of Human Intuition and Expertise in the Era of the Computer* (New York).

Fodor, J. A. (1987), *Psychosemantics: The Problem of Meaning in the Philosophy of Mind* (Cambridge, Mass.).

——and Pylyshyn, Z. W. (1988), 'Connectionism and Cognitive Architecture: A Critical Analysis', *Cognition*, 28: 3–71.

Haugeland, J. C. (1978), 'The Nature and Plausibility of Cognitivism', *Behavioral and Brain Sciences*, 1: 215–26; repr. in Haugeland (1981).

——(ed.) (1981), *Mind Design* (Cambridge, Mass.).

Smolensky, P. (1988), 'On the Proper Treatment of Connectionism', *Behavioral and Brain Sciences*, 11: 1–74.

——(1991), 'Connectionism, Constituency and the Language of Thought', in B. Loewer, and G. Rey (eds.), *Meaning in Mind* (Oxford).

PSYCHOANALYTIC THEORY

CLARK, P., and WRIGHT, C. (1988), *Mind, Psychoanalysis and Science* (Oxford).

CUMMINS, R. (1983), *The Nature of Psychological Explanation* (Cambridge, Mass.).

FLEW, A. (1956), 'Motives and the Unconscious', in Herbert Feigl and Michael Scriven (eds.), *The Foundations of Science and the Concepts of Psychology and Psychoanalysis, Minnesota Studies in the Philosophy of Science*, i (Minneapolis).

FODOR, J. A. (1987), *Psychosemantics: The Problem of Meaning in the Philosophy of Mind* (Cambridge, Mass.).

FREUD, S. (1955–), *The Standard Edition of the Complete Psychological Works*, trans. and ed. J. Strachey, with the assistance of A. Strachey and A. Tyson (London).

GRUNBAUM, A. (1984), *The Foundations of Psychoanalysis: A Philosophical Critique* (Berkeley).

——(1986), 'Précis', *Behavioral and Brain Sciences*, 9, repr. in Clark and Wright (1988).

HOPKINS, J. (1988), 'Epistemology and Depth Psychology: Critical Notes on *The Foundations of Psychoanalysis*', in Clark and Wright (1988).

POPPER, K. (1963), *Conjectures and Refutations* (London).

RICŒUR, P. (1970), *Freud and Philosophy: An Essay on Interpretation*, trans. D. Savage (New Haven).

SACHS, D. (1991), 'In Fairness to Freud: A Critical Notice of *The Foundations of Psychoanalysis* by Adolf Grunbaum', in Jerome Neu (ed.), *The Cambridge Companion to Freud* (Cambridge).

SARTRE, J.-P. (1956), *Being and Nothingness*, trans. H. Barnes (New York).

WOLLHEIM, R. (1991), *Freud*, 2nd ed. (London).

2

THE PHILOSOPHY OF LANGUAGE

Christopher Peacocke

INTRODUCTION

The central concern of the philosophy of language is the nature of linguistic meaning. Because of this concern, the philosophy of language is relevant to virtually all other areas of philosophy. In almost every area of philosophy, questions arise which turn in part on the nature of the meaning of a particular kind of sentence. We may, for instance, be concerned with what can justify us in making statements about the past, or about another person's thoughts, or about the justice of some institution, or about what is necessarily true. In each of these cases, we will be at a loss to defend any particular view of the matter unless we can say something about the meaning of the statement in question. To do so, we must draw upon, or at least presuppose, some position in the theory of meaning. A similar point holds for metaphysical issues about the nature of truth for a given kind of sentence. We will never achieve a clear view of what is involved in the truth of statements of a given kind if we are unclear about their meaning.

From around 1965 to about 1980 the spotlight of research in philosophy was focused on the philosophy of language. It would be fair to say that in the past eighteen years the focus has shifted to the philosophy of mind and psychology. But it would be quite wrong to conclude that, with the focus shifted, the philosophy of language should be of less current interest. On the contrary, many of the most important issues in the philosophy of mind turn on the nature of the content of mental states. Here the content is something evaluable as true or false, in the way in which the content of your belief that the window is closed is evaluable as true or false. Many of the issues which arise about content in the philosophy of mind have direct analogues for linguistic meaning. The theories and discoveries in the philosophy of language are thereby directly relevant to the philosophy of mind. To do the philosophy of mind while neglecting work in the philosophy of language is to risk spending one's time either in reinventing the wheel—or in failing to invent it.

An essay-length exposition and critical discussion of an area as vast and as heterogeneous as the philosophy of language has to be extraordinarily, and painfully, selective. The present discussion is selective both in respect of the range of topics covered, and in the aspects of them which there is room to discuss. Some pointers in the direction of other topics are given in a section of the Bibliography at the end of this essay, where, to avoid a date-peppered

I thank the editor, Anthony Grayling, for advice and comments. The exposition has also been improved by the comments of an anonymous referee for Oxford University Press. I am especially grateful to David Wiggins for much advice, both substantive and pedagogical. The final stages of preparation of this essay were carried out while I was supported by a Leverhulme Personal Research Professorship. Once again, I express my gratitude to the Leverhulme Trust for their support.

main text, virtually all other detailed references to the literature are also to be found.

I have chosen to organize the discussion around an issue whose resolution, it will be agreed by all parties to the discussion, is central to the philosophy of language, the issue of the relation between meaning and truth-conditions. Students wholly new to the subject are warned that this discussion is rather long for reading in one sitting. The major natural break comes between Sections 3 and 4. Any experts reading this may want to know that the main novelties come in the later parts of Sections 2 and 4.

1. THE CLASSICAL TRUTH-CONDITIONAL THESIS

The general view that a sentence's meaning is to be explained somehow in terms of the conditions under which the sentence is true is a view which has been close to centre-stage for the past hundred years. The view was first stated in the context of anything like a developed theory of meaning by Frege, in his *Basic Laws of Arithmetic* (*Grundgesetze der Arithmetik*), the first volume of which was published in 1893. Frege's driving concern was in the philosophy of mathematics. He introduced a formal language, in terms of which he aimed to express arithmetical propositions. His plan was then to derive the true arithmetical propositions, expressed in his formal language, from what he took to be laws of logic.

Frege was inevitably drawn into the theory of meaning. His whole enterprise in the philosophy of mathematics could be satisfactorily carried through only if questions of meaning and truth were addressed. There were two tasks. First, Frege had to show that each sentence of his formal language expressed a thought, had some meaning. He had, secondly, to show that the rules he offered for moving from one set of sentences to another were truth-preserving: that is, if its premisses were all true, so is the conclusion of the rule. Frege made a discovery which simultaneously solved both these problems.

Frege assigned to each basic, atomic expression of his language, such as a name or a predicate, a particular reference. He then went on to give rules which state how the reference of a complex expression of his language is determined from the references of its atomic component expressions. He took the references of some complex expressions—corresponding to indicative sentences—to be truth-values, the value True or the value False. With all of this in place, it could then be determined whether a particular reference rule in his formal language was truth-preserving. The condition for the rule to be truth-preserving was just that whenever all the premisses of the rule are assigned the value True by these rules, the conclusion should be too. In a move of great insight, he also realized that by means of this apparatus which is concerned with the level of reference, he could address the problem of sense or meaning.

The notion of sense has a life in our ordinary, everyday talk about language, but Frege elaborated his use of the notion in a specific way, in terms of potential informational value. The sentence 'Tadpoles are infant frogs' can be highly informative to one who understands it. By contrast, the sentences 'Tadpoles are tadpoles' and 'Infant frogs are infant frogs' are not so potentially informative to one who already understands the language. The expressions 'tadpole' and 'infant frog' have different senses, on the Fregean conception of sense, even though of course they are true of exactly the same things.

This combination of sameness of reference with difference of sense can be present in expressions of any category. Frege originally illustrated the notion of sense with the two proper names 'Hesperus' and 'Phosphorus', to understand which a person must know that the first refers to the evening star, the second to the morning star. The identity 'Hesperus is Phosphorus' is informative, and, on the Fregean conception, the names would have distinct senses. Similarly, 'now', as used by me at 9 a.m., has a different sense from '9 a.m.', since it can be informative to be told what time it is—at 9 a.m., as at any other. The more extreme example of the amnesic shows that 'I' (as used by me) has a different sense from 'Christopher Peacocke'. There is a kind of amnesia in which I understand the first-person pronoun, and I understand the proper name 'Christopher Peacocke'. What I do not know, when suffering from such amnesia, is whether I am Christopher Peacocke.

Frege held a series of theses about sense. They include these principles:

> Thoughts are composed of the senses of individual expressions, built up in sentence-like structures.
>
> Different thinkers can have attitudes to the same thought.
>
> Sense and reference stand in a many–one relation: two expressions differing in sense can have the same reference.
>
> In sentences such as 'John believes that the Communists will return to power in Eastern Europe', the expressions within the 'that . . .' clause refer to their normal senses.

I will refine some of these formulations later.

Even from these very brief introductory remarks it should be clear that sense should not be identified with linguistic meaning (though there is certainly some overlap). A word such as 'here' has a single, constant meaning in English. But if two utterances of 'here' have different references, they must have different senses by the above principles. The same point applies to utterances of 'I' by different speakers, and to utterances of 'now' at different times. For simplicity, though, I will continue to confine my attention to expressions which are not context-sensitive in that way.

Frege's crucial insight was that the sense of an indicative sentence is given by the conditions under which, according to his reference rules, it is true (or, as he would say, denotes the True). In a passage in which, for present purposes, we can read 'name of a truth-value' as 'sentence', he wrote this about the well-formed expressions of his formal language:

> not only a denotation [i.e. reference], but also a sense, appertains to all names correctly formed from our signs. Every such name of a truth-value *expresses* a sense, a *thought*. Namely, by our stipulations it is determined under what conditions the name denotes the True. The sense of this name—the *thought*—is the thought that these conditions are fulfilled. (Frege 1964, §32.)

Frege's insight went further. The sense of a basic, atomic expression is the contribution it makes to the sense of complete sentences in which it occurs. Now the sense of a complete sentence is given by the conditions under which it is true. Those conditions in turn are determined by the references of the component expressions from which the sentence is built up. It follows that a fundamental statement of the conditions for a component expression to have a particular reference can be regarded as a specification also of its sense. Sense does not merely, together with the way the world is, determine reference. Rather, the sense of an expression is individuated by stating the condition which something must meet to be its reference.

The resulting account of sense then has three crucial features. First, it is general, to the extent that it applies to meaningful expressions of any category. Secondly, it is essentially and fundamentally connected with the level of reference. Thirdly, it is componential, in that it gives an explanation of how and why the sense of the complex was fixed from the sense of its parts. This is all explicit in Frege on careful reading; but we owe largely to Dummett its clear extraction and our appreciation of its importance.

The truth-conditional approach to meaning was further developed, in a somewhat idiosyncratic form, in Wittgenstein's *Tractatus Logico-Philosophicus*. It is arguable, though, that Wittgenstein did not appreciate the full power of, and indeed the need for, Frege's notion of sense. Much later, truth-conditional approaches received an influential reformulation and defence in the writings of Davidson. Davidson was able, in ways we shall illustrate, to marshall the techniques developed in Tarski's writings on truth in support of a much more explicit account of what is involved in a truth-conditional theory of meaning. Davidson's approach respects the original Fregean insights in several ways I will discuss later.

Opposed to this truth-conditional approach to meaning is another distinguished tradition. This opposing tradition includes either explicitly or by implication Ramsey, the later Wittgenstein, early—but not later—Strawson, and more recently Harman, the later Field, Block, and Horwich. (As the temporal qualifications in this list indicate, this seems to be an issue on which philosophers change their views, and not always in the same direction.) Many of these writers offer positive accounts of meaning which are represented as being in competition with the truth-conditional account.

There is also a different kind of opposition to the truth-conditional account, one which is sceptical of the possibility of substantial accounts of meaning at all, whether truth-conditional or of any other kind. Schiffer and Johnston are prominent in this camp.

The first step in considering these major debates is to have before us a fuller formulation of the truth-conditional view and its variants. It is to this task that the remainder of this section is devoted.

We need to distinguish between a theory of meaning—a theory of the nature of linguistic meaning in general—and more specific theories which give the meanings of the sentences of one particular language. We can follow Dummett (1991) in calling a theory which gives the meaning of the sentences of a particular language a 'meaning theory'. A meaning theory for a particular language *L* will be a set of principles from which can be derived a statement, for each individual sentence of *L*, of what that sentence means. The nature of meaning theories for particular languages has to dovetail with one's general conception of linguistic meaning—one's theory of meaning. The meaning theory for a particular language should be an instance, for that particular language, of the general form identified in one's theory of meaning.

A corresponding terminology is also helpful in the case of theories of truth. A theory of truth is a general theory of what is involved in an arbitrary sentence, of whatever language, being true. A truth theory for a particular language is a theory which, for each sentence of that language, states the conditions under which it is true. Again, the truth theory for the particular language must conform to one's general theory of truth. With this terminology, we can state one of the most important contributions to the development of the truth-conditional approach to meaning made by Davidson and his followers. Their claim is that a meaning theory for a particular language is to be given by supplying a truth theory for that language. This idea is best conveyed by illustrating it for a very simple language.

We shall consider a language L1 which has just three proper names, three predicates, and three connectives. We suppose the names denote real people. The atomic expressions of L1 are these:

> Names: 'Romeo', 'Juliet', 'Tybalt'
> Predicates: 'loves', 'hates', 'is happy'
> Connectives: 'not-(. . .)', '(. . . or ——)', '(. . . & ——)'.

On the truth-conditional approach, we proceed by giving for each of these atomic expressions a principle which states its contribution to the truth-conditions of sentences containing it. These various axioms are usually called semantic axioms, in that reference plays a crucial role in them. Each axiom either assigns a reference to an expression; or links the truth of simple sentences with the reference of expressions in it; or links truth for complex sentences to the truth of simpler sentences. Thus, for the three proper names in L1 we give these axioms:

(N1) The reference of 'Romeo' = Romeo
(N2) The reference of 'Juliet' = Juliet
(N3) The reference of 'Tybalt' = Tybalt.

For the three predicates, we have

(P1) If α and β are names, then any sentence of the form 'α loves β' is true if and only if the reference of α loves the reference of β.
(P2) If α and β are names, then any sentence of the form 'α hates β' is true if and only if the reference of α hates the reference of β.
(P3) If α is a name, then any sentence of the form 'α is happy' is true if and only if the reference of α is happy.

Finally, for the two connectives, we have

(C1) If *A* is a sentence, then 'not-(*A*)' is true if and only if *A* is not true.
(C2) If *A* and *B* are sentences, then '(*A* or *B*)' is true if and only if either *A* is true or *B* is true.
(C3) If *A* and *B* are sentences, then '(*A* & *B*)' is true if and only if *A* is true and *B* is true.

For the strict-minded, we can add that when we write '(*A* or *B*)' that is just a convenient abbreviation for: the expression consisting of '(', followed by *A*, followed by 'or', followed by *B*, followed by ')'.

These axioms taken together constitute a simple theory. From the axioms of this simple theory we can, using ordinary logic, derive various propositions—the theorems of the theory. It can be shown that for each sentence of L1, there is a theorem of this theory which states the condition under which that sentence of L1 is true. That is, this theory is a truth theory for the language L1. A few simple derivations can illustrate this generalization.

Consider the sentence of L1 'Romeo loves Juliet'. From axiom P1, if we take the name 'Romeo' as the value of the variable 'α', and 'Juliet' as the value of the variable 'β', it follows that

(T1) 'Romeo loves Juliet' is true if and only if the reference of 'Romeo' loves the reference of 'Juliet'.

From T1 and the axioms N1 and N2 it follows that

(T2) 'Romeo loves Juliet' is true if and only if Romeo loves Juliet.

In similar fashion, using axioms N2 and P3, we could derive the theorem

(T3) 'Juliet is happy' is true if and only if Juliet is happy.

From C3 we have that

(T4) '(Romeo loves Juliet and Juliet is happy)' is true if and only if 'Romeo loves Juliet' is true and 'Juliet is happy' is true.

Since we have T2 and T3 as theorems, we can make substitutions following the 'if and only if' in T4 to reach the theorem

(T5) '(Romeo loves Juliet and Juliet is happy)' is true if and only if Romeo loves Juliet and Juliet is happy.

Already in these simple derivations, we have available a striking elaboration of Frege's idea connecting sense with the truth-condition which can be derived from rules which assign references to the atomic components of a sentence. The derivations also make vivid Davidson's idea that a truth theory can be a meaning theory for a language. Intuitively, the sentence 'Romeo loves Juliet' has the sense (expresses the thought) that Romeo loves Juliet. This is just the truth-condition assigned to it in the theorem T2 of this simple theory. This theorem, precisely in accordance with Frege's conception, was derived from a statement of the reference of the atomic components of these sentences.

In saying this, we have to allow that the axioms P1–P3, though they do not strictly assign any entity to each predicate of L1, nevertheless perform the same essential function as Fregean assignments of reference. That is, they say how the truth-value of the whole is determined from the semantic properties of its parts. The same holds for C1–C3.

The above derivation of T5 can be called a *canonical* proof of T5. The derivation proceeds by taking the constituents of the sentence mentioned on the left-hand side of T5, and applying the various semantic axioms of the theory to them. There will be other theorems of the theory, besides T5, which are of the form

'(Romeo loves Juliet and Juliet is happy)' is true iff ——.

For example, the result of replacing the blank here with anything distinct from but truth-functionally equivalent to

Romeo loves Juliet and Juliet is happy

will equally be a theorem. It will not, however, be provable by means of a canonical proof.

Frege implied that the sense of a sentence is the thought that the conditions under which it denotes the True are fulfilled. His idea should be understood as follows. The rules of reference for the atomic components of each sentence *s* determine a condition *p* about the world which does not (in the usual case) make reference to sentences or expressions at all. The major Fregean insight is then this: concerning the condition *p* so determined, what *s* means is that *p*.

It would not be a sympathetic reading of Frege's claim to take it as assigning to each sentence *s* this thought: that the conditions for *s* to be true are fulfilled. That would make the truth-conditions for all the different sentences differ only in which sentence they refer to, and would in any case be quite implausible.

Corresponding to the sympathetic reading of Frege's doctrine is a distinction between two kinds of theorem in the simple theory of truth for L1. T1 and T2 both assign truth-conditions to the sentence 'Romeo loves Juliet'. They are both theorems of the theory. But what follows 'if and only if' in T1 makes reference to expressions and their semantic properties (their references); whereas T2, in fully drawing on the semantic information in the theory about the names 'Romeo' and 'Juliet', assigns to the same sentence a truth-condition which talks only about the non-linguistic world. In terminology introduced by Davidson, we can say that T2 is a T-sentence, while T1 is not. An adequate theory of truth for a particular language is one from whose axioms there are canonical proofs of each sentence of the form

s is true if and only if *p*

where *s* is an indicative sentence of the language in question, and *p* is replaced by a sentence which states the same as *s* states. In other words, an adequate theory of truth is one whose canonically provable T-sentences have on the right-hand side of their biconditionals something which states the same as the sentence mentioned on their left-hand side.

Under this conception, it matters very much how we specify the reference of expressions in a theory of truth which is meant to contribute to a meaning theory for the language in question. Consider the axiom N1*:

(N1*) 'Romeo' denotes the masked teenager attending the dance.

This could be true, and a theory of truth containing it, instead of N1, as an axiom, would have true theorems. But in the resulting variant theory, we would be able to prove only T-sentences such as

(T2*) 'Romeo loves Juliet' is true if and only if the masked teenager attending the dance loves Juliet.

The variant theory would not be an adequate theory of truth. Although T2* is, in the imagined circumstances, a true biconditional, its right-hand side is not what 'Romeo loves Juliet' states. In Dummett's apposite appropriation of a Wittgensteinian distinction, a good axiom in a meaning-giving truth theory *shows* the sense of an expression by *stating* its reference.

The classical conception as expounded so far raises a large number of fundamental questions, including the following.

1. What makes one axiom rather than another the correct axiom for a meaning-giving truth theory for a particular language?

This question can itself be addressed at various different depths. One way of understanding the question is to take for granted the ability of users of a language to employ the concepts expressed in the language, and then to take the question as asking how these users must stand to the expressions of a language for a particular semantic axiom to be correct. There are many genuine issues here, and further subdivisions. There will, for example, be different answers to this question according as the theory of truth is regarded as a theory of a language as employed by a particular person at a particular time, or as a theory of the language of a particular community of speakers (and thus as a semantic theory of an evolving sociolinguistic object with a history, a language). There is also an issue about the correct way to understand the relation between these two notions of a language.

There is also a deeper reading of the question of why one axiom rather than another is correct. At this deeper level, we have to consider what is involved in possessing the concepts expressed by the language in question, for such possession is certainly part of understanding the language. Can there be an account of linguistic understanding which does not take the phenomenon of concept possession for granted? If so, what is it? If there are limitations on the kind of account which can be given in answer to this question, what are they, and what is their source?

2. A second class of questions raised by the classical conception revolves around the notions of knowledge and information. Do ordinary users of a language know what is stated by the axioms of a correct semantic theory for their language? If they have no such knowledge, is there some different relation in which they stand to the information given in the correct axioms?

3. Is the notion of truth really performing essential work in the classical conception, or is it just a device for connecting what is meant by expressions in the language and the expressions themselves? Would other notions serve this purpose equally well? Could we not simply use the notion of meaning itself to effect the connection, thus making any use of the notion of truth redundant?

1–3 are all clusters of central issues in the philosophy of language. The first and third, in particular, are the subject of continuing fundamental debates in the subject. We start with the deeper construal of question (1).

2. WHAT MAKES A SEMANTIC AXIOM CORRECT?

There would be widespread agreement that for a particular axiom of a meaning theory to be correct, it must, in the context of a wider theory about the language and attitudes of the speakers of the language, pull its weight in making the speakers of the language maximally intelligible. Hence we can accept an axiom like P2 for the predicate 'is happy' provided this condition is met:

under the supposition that P2 gives the meaning of 'is happy', the speakers of the language become intelligible, in both their linguistic and their non-linguistic actions, given a theory of the rest of the language, and of the propositional attitudes (beliefs, desires, hopes . . .) possessed by particular speakers. Any axiom not equivalent to P2 would, at some point, make speakers less intelligible. A decrease in intelligibility would, for instance, be present in an interpretation which would assign to a speaker's words a meaning which would make it pointless, or quite unfounded, or irrelevant, to be saying what the interpretation counts him as saying. To make a person's actions intelligible is not necessarily to attribute true beliefs. When a speaker is in misleading natural conditions, or is misled by others, a false belief may be more intelligible than a true belief.

The position stated in the preceding paragraph is one that emerges from an early paper of Grandy, and from Davidson's later writings. Its widespread acceptance coexists with widespread disagreement, explicit and implicit, about the status of the constraint of maximizing intelligibility. Why must a good interpretation maximize intelligibility? Is the constraint derivative from something else, or is it fundamental? If it is fundamental, and not to be derived from anything else, why is it fundamental? What are the comparative consequences of treating it as fundamental, or as derivative?

In rough conformity with previous uses of the term, we label *interpretationism* the thesis that the constraint 'Correct interpretation maximizes intelligibility' is not to be derived from other principles which do not involve the notion of intelligibility. The constraint may, consistently with interpretationism, be explained by other principles which do involve the notion of intelligibility. Indeed, the competent interpretationist will want to explain why he holds his doctrine, and his motivation will have something to do with his view of the nature of the relations between interpretation and intelligibility. So the interpretationist should not be barred from deriving the agreed constraint from general philosophical theses. What the interpretationist should insist upon, as his name implies, is that the application of the notion of intelligibility involved in interpretation cannot be elucidated in other terms that do not, at any point, tacitly involve the notion of intelligibility as exercised when engaging in interpretation.

Modesty is the doctrine that no elucidation is possible of what it is for a thinker to possess the primitive concepts expressed in his language that does not take for granted some understanding of what it is to possess those concepts. Again, this definition does not coincide with all of those used in the recent history of discussion, but I would argue that it isolates the core of what is, and should be, in dispute. The term was employed in roughly this sense by McDowell, and was taken up by Dummett, in his discussions of Davidson and McDowell. The very fundamental issues involved in the correctness of modesty continue to be discussed in the writings of Dummett, McDowell, and others, myself included.

Modesty is intimately and inextricably involved in interpretationism. Interpretationism, when taken together with doctrines which it is very plausible the interpretationist must accept, entails modesty. The argument for this claim runs thus. Suppose the interpretationist is asked for more details of the constraints on the correctness of a particular axiom, such as P2 for 'is happy'. The interpretationist will say such things as this: speakers of the language sincerely apply the predicate to persons in circumstances in which it is intelligible that they should form the belief, concerning the person in question, that he is happy. This kind of elaboration of the constraint, in speaking of the intelligible formation of the belief that the person in question is happy, uses the concept *happy* within the scope of a thinker's propositional attitudes. It simply presupposes our understanding of what it is to possess the concept *happy*, rather than explaining such possession. If intelligibility could, for particular beliefs involving particular concepts, be elucidated in other terms, then perhaps the condition which embeds 'happy' within the scope of the thinker's propositional attitudes could itself be elucidated in other terms, and there would not then be any presupposition of our understanding of what it is to possess the concept *happy*. But such a further account of intelligibility is just what the interpretationist denies. So it does appear that the interpretationist is committed to the doctrine of modesty. The issues raised by interpretationism thus ramify very widely.

There are, among others, three possible motivations for embracing interpretationism. These motivations are in no way exclusive, and some theorists might regard some of the motivations as supporting the others.

(*a*) There may be a metaphysical or constitutive doctrine about what it is for claims of intelligibility to be true. It may be claimed that there is no more to something's being intelligible than that we find it so, in some specified favourable kind of circumstance, or are capable of coming to find it so, in circumstances of the specified kind. The use of 'we find' in this constitutive claim makes this a kind of subjectivism. This constitutive doctrine supports interpretationism, because the explanation of something's being intelligible continues to use the notion of intelligibility, within the notion of finding something intelligible. The doctrine precludes the elaboration of intelligibility in other terms.

(*b*) There may be concerns about the consequences of rejecting modesty. What could an account of possession of a concept which did not presuppose a thinker's possession of concepts possibly be like? Must it not undercut the level of intentional attribution and explanation altogether? If so, one must wonder whether any such level would allow one to reconstruct intentional states of subjects. There may also be doubts about whether any elucidation carried out at the non-intentional level could really support all the features of our intentional scheme. For example, we normally know what people mean by their words, and are entitled to believe that they will apply their words one way rather than another when confronted with a new case. How can there be any assurance of this if intentional states are supposed to be true in virtue of some level of characterization which undercuts the intentional?

(*c*) There would be general agreement that to possess a concept is to be subject to certain norms of correctness when making judgements involving it. It may further be held that we cannot specify what these norms are without using the concept in question, and that the thinker must have some appreciation of these norms, an appreciation the description of which necessarily employs some expression for the concept within the scope of the thinker's propositional attitudes. So again, it may be said, modesty is inevitable.

All of these positions can be developed in further detail, and in more than one way. Though only the third kind of objection explicitly mentions the normative character of content, normativity is in the offing in all of these objections. All the objections are offering theses about the source of, or consequences of, the distinctively normative character of content, and claiming that either interpretationism or modesty (or both) will be required by a proper appreciation of this normative character.

In considering this debate, it is important to distinguish between two kinds of immodesty, which we can call *grand* immodesty and *tempered* immodesty. Grand immodesty attempts to explain concept possession in terms of capacities which undercut the level of content attribution altogether. Grandly immodest theories include not only behaviourism, which no one would hold today, but also other forms with contemporary adherents. Functionalism attempts to say what functional role (in terms of its relations to non-intentional input, output, and other functional states) a given brain state must have to be, or to realize, a given mental state. If functionalism is to be fully general, and so cover mental states with intentional contents, then it will be characterizing states involving concept possession in a vocabulary free of intentional content. To be at all plausible, the functionalism will have to be of the variety called 'long-arm' functionalism, in which inputs and outputs can concern matters in the environment, and not merely happenings at the periphery of the organism.

A very different variety of grandly immodest theory is the constructionist approach to conceptual content outlined in the work of Cussins (1990), who aims to build up an account of conceptual mastery from abilities which do not require possession of the concepts in question. It would be a fair comment that grandly immodest approaches have, to date, been largely programmatic. There has been no elaboration, in grandly immodest terms, of biconditionals of the form 'to possess such-and-such concept is to . . .', where the dots are replaced in the favoured style of theory.

Some of the arguments in favour of interpretationism and modesty are formulated in such a way as to be targeted at grandly immodest theories. This is true of all the arguments which state that there are insurmountable difficulties if we aim at elucidations of conceptual mastery in a vocabulary which undercuts the level of the intentional characterization of mental states and actions. It is a substantive question whether these arguments can be adapted to apply against more moderate versions, which exhibit only tempered immodesty. One example of tempered immodesty would be the theory of concept possession I gave in *A Study of Concepts*. On this approach, a concept is individuated by a true statement of the condition for a thinker to possess the concept, where this statement is subject to certain constraints. The statement will be of the form

> concept *F* is that concept *C* to possess which a thinker must meet condition *A* (*C*).

The possession condition *A* ( ) can, and will, contain propositional-attitude vocabulary, but (on that approach) it must not contain a term for the concept *F*, as the concept *F*, within the scope of the thinker's propositional attitudes. The possession condition can, of course, employ the concept outside the scope of such attitudes. A possession condition would do so if, for example, it required a certain sensitivity of judgements involving the concept to the presence of instances of the concept in the thinker's immediate environment. In effect, a possession condition specifies a designated, canonical role in a thinker's thought—a role at the level of intentional states—which is individuative of that concept. In the case of logical concepts, this will be a role in certain specified inferences. In the case of observational concepts, a role in judgements based on perceptual experience will be an essential part of the possession condition. In other cases, a role in theory may be mentioned. Clearly any properly formulated, correct possession condition does state what it is to possess the concept with which it deals. So the theory is immodest in the technical sense we have identified. But there is no aspiration to grand immodesty, for propositional-attitude vocabulary is pervasive in plausible formulations of possession conditions. It is no accident that propositional attitudes pervade possession conditions. It is quite implausible that one could say what individuates a concept without adverting to certain kinds of reason for accepting or rejecting certain contents involving it.

It is an important issue whether there are further constraints on proper specifications of concepts, constraints relating ultimately to the level of reference and truth, and I will return to this issue in a later section. In exact parallel with the notion of a possession condition for a concept, one can introduce the notion of an understanding condition for a given expression in a particular language, where the notion of an understanding condition is subject to corresponding constraints on its form.

The possibility of tempered immodesty casts a somewhat different light on the landscape surrounding these issues. We are not faced with a choice between modesty and grand immodesty. Other options also emerge as responses to some of the arguments we mentioned that might be used in support of interpretationism and modesty. For instance, an approach to intelligibility emerges which is in competition with the subjectivism mentioned in (*a*). The unintelligibility of an unacceptable interpretation may consist in its assigning attitudes to thinkers in circumstances in which these attributions violate the possession conditions for one or more of the concepts in the contents of the attitudes attributed. Our finding something intelligible may itself be explained in part by its consistency with the possession conditions for the concepts in the attitudes attributed. The intermediate position of tempered immodesty does not, at first blush, involve or require any kind of subjectivism about content and concepts.

What of the epistemological challenge which modesty makes to grand immodesty? Does that challenge equally threaten tempered immodesty? We only briefly alluded to the challenge (in the later part of (*b*) above), and it is worth stating it in more detail. Here is a statement based on McDowell's formulation of the challenge. The Wittgenstein-inspired challenge is that, when we hear or see someone answering the questions 'What is 4 plus 2?', 'What is 6 plus 2?', . . . , it is open to view that they are following the rule *add* 2, rather than some rule which, when they reach 1,000, requires them to answer '1,004' to the question 'What is 1,000 plus 2?' as they understand it. It is not just a hypothesis that they mean plus, rather than meaning some variant which coincides with it over the range so far questioned. This is why we are entitled to judge that the person means addition by 'plus'. But, the challenge continues, it is open to view what they mean only because we can see others as intentionally adding 2, and this description of how we see them involves embedding the concept *adding*, the concept expressed by 'plus', in the intentional description of their actions in a way which would not be permitted on approaches which purport to give accounts of meaning in non-intentional vocabulary (grand immodesty). But, apparently, it would equally not be permitted on *any* non-modest view, including tempered immodesty. Thus runs the extension of the epistemological challenge to the case of tempered immodesty.

A resource to be exploited by non-modest approaches in answering this objection is the nature of the apparently analogous entitlements which exist outside the domain of intentional properties. There are cases in which we have knowledge of some truth, not itself a truth about intentional states, and in which our entitlement cannot be properly explained if we view it as based on a certain kind of evidence. If you walk into a part of your neighbourhood which you have not previously visited, and see houses in the street, you are entitled to your belief, based on your perceptions, that those are houses in the street.

Mere façades would look the same; and there is a sense in which your previous experience is compatible with much of what you have seen having been façades rather than houses. In cases like this, it is tempting to say that there is a social mechanism, operative in your locality, which explains why it is houses, rather than mere façades, which are erected, and your entitlement to judge that these are houses on the newly visited street exists in part because there is such a mechanism. The entitlement exists in part because the mechanism exists, not because you are making hypotheses about the mechanism (for you certainly need not be doing so). For someone who has been there and seen them, it is equally not a hypothesis that these are houses on the newly visited street.

Another, perhaps even sharper, case in which the existence of a mechanism helps to underwrite an entitlement is that of your knowledge of the grammatical structure of someone else's utterances in your native language. There is some evidence that, in learning our first language, we rely on extremely slender evidence before forming correct beliefs about the grammaticality of a new utterance. We can do so because there is a mechanism which ensures that the biological constraints on the grammar learned by the other person are the same as those constraining our learning procedures. It is essential to the nature of our actual entitlement to form beliefs about the grammaticality of another's utterance that we are members of the same species. Because this is so, our entitlement to all knowledge based on testimony—that is, a huge portion of our world-view—rests on the existence of this mechanism. For we attain knowledge from others only if we understand their utterances; and we understand them only if we grasp their grammatical structure.

It is important not only that there is a mechanism which explains why we are right in our judgements about future cases, but also that the mechanism be one which explains why we would be right in counterfactual circumstances which could easily obtain. If in fact there are those who would go on with '1,004' in the Wittgensteinian example—or if indeed there could easily be some—the relevant entitlement lapses. It also lapses in the case of the beliefs about houses, if you live near to Universal Studios, and there are in fact house façades in your neighbourhood. This point has wider repercussions in epistemology. It entails that the knowledgeable status of your belief about some presented object that it has a certain property cannot always depend solely on the relations between you and that object (at whatever level we describe them). It seems that wider environmental conditions, both actual and easily obtaining possibilities, can undermine the status of your belief about the object as knowledge.

It may be wondered how a belief to which one is entitled because of the existence of a mechanism could ever be a rational one. This wondering may be based on a restricted conception of rationality. When there is the right kind of mechanism providing entitlement to a particular belief, then the following counterfactual will be true: if the belief had been false, or if the methods used had been locally unreliable, this would have come to light in evidence available to the thinker. Such counterfactuals are true in the grammatical and semantic cases. When these counterfactuals are true, a thinker with entitlements underwritten by the appropriate mechanisms is not properly described as just judging blindly, or as merely making a stab in the dark. There is a great deal more to be said on these matters, especially on the way in which the existence of a mechanism can be entitling. Those who think that the existence of a mechanism has no role to play at all in the treatment of these examples are invited to attempt to give an alternative epistemology of these cases.

If there are entitlements underwritten by such mechanisms, the theorist of tempered immodesty can appeal to them in answering the envisaged epistemological challenge in the case of meaning, just as a theorist could appeal to them in answering epistemological challenges in the grammatical example. It is only fair to note that the adherent of grand immodesty could appeal to them too, in the event that he becomes able to formulate a theory meeting his grand constraints.

3. SEMANTIC AXIOMS AND THE EXPLANATION OF UNDERSTANDING

An ordinary speaker of English knows that the sentence 'It is raining in Paris at midday on 1 January 1940' is true if and only if it is raining in Paris at midday on 1 January 1940, and knows this simply in virtue of understanding English. That is, he knows what is stated in a T-sentence of a semantic theory of English. Similarly, if our little language L1 were spoken in a community, one who understands it would know, simply by virtue of that understanding, that the sentence 'Juliet is happy' is true if and only if ('iff') Juliet is happy. This claim about knowledge is not made because any speaker of L1 could knowledgeably *say* that the sentence 'Juliet is happy' is true iff Juliet is happy. On the contrary, the little language L1 does not contain the predicate 'is true', and it is far from clear that every conceivable language must contain a truth-predicate. All the same, understanders do know the truth-conditions of the sentences of the fragment of the language they understand. For any sentence of the language which is not too long for them to think about in quotational fashion, they know what is stated by a T-sentence for that sentence.

But do they also have to know what is stated by the semantic axioms for the atomic expressions of their language? Do, for instance, speakers of L1 have to know what is stated by the axiom C2 for alternation in their language? It counts prima facie against the need for any such knowledge that ordinary speakers of English, when studying logic for the first time, have to work out what is the correct truth-table for 'or'. That is, they have to work out, of what C2 states, that it is in fact (also) a correct axiom for English. If they only just acquired that knowledge after working out the correct truth-table, then their understanding of 'or' cannot have relied on that knowledge, since they understood 'or' long before that knowledge was acquired.

The situation has an interesting complexity, however. Students attain a knowledge of the correctness of what is stated in C2 (as applied to English) because they are able to evaluate the truth of sentences of the form '*A* or *B*' in various hypothetical situations, given the truth-values of the constituents *A* and *B*, and so are able to work out each line of a truth-table for alternation. But doesn't this mean that in some sense they must have already grasped that this is the correct truth-table for alternation? Isn't that grasp required in explaining even their knowledge of the truth-value of '*A* or *B*' given a specification of the truth-values of its constituents?

Although we cannot say that understanders have to know what is stated by all the semantic axioms for the expressions they understand, they do in a certain sense possess the information stated in those axioms. Someone who understands an expression draws on the information which is stated in the semantic axiom in coming to understand complete sentences in which the expression occurs. The way in which the information stated in the axiom is drawn upon in the case of linguistic understanding needs some elucidation.

The process of drawing on information which is involved in the explanation of a particular person's understanding an utterance on a particular occasion is a process which is subpersonal, causal, and content-involving. It is subpersonal, because we are concerned here with a level of explanation which does not involve conscious inference, or indeed any transitions at the personal level. At the personal, rational level, the understander simply hears an utterance of 'Juliet is happy' as meaning that Juliet is happy. At the subpersonal level, there is some computation of this meaning from the identity of the constituents of the uttered sentence, their mode of combination, and semantic information about the constituents and this mode of combination. This is a causal claim, about the explanation of the person's hearing the sentence as having that particular meaning. What is explained here is something content-involving. We are not merely explaining the correlation of one sentence with another, or of English sentences with sentences in some system of mental representation whose nature is one day to be discovered by psychology. We are explaining a person's associating, with a particular English sentence, what is stated by a certain 'that . . .' clause, in this case that Juliet is happy.

The claim that someone is drawing upon a certain piece of information in coming to understand sentences containing a certain expression is a claim about the computational explanation of that person's understanding of those sentences, a claim about computation understood in content-involving terms, and not as something merely syntactic or uninterpreted (nor, *a fortiori*, as something merely neurological). The counterfactuals sustained by such explanations are distinctively content-involving. If the person had been drawing on different information about an expression, then the content he would assign to sentences containing it would be correspondingly different.

Under this conception, we can give a natural criterion for a semantic theory for a language to be one that is involved in the explanation of a given person's linguistic understanding—for the semantic theory to be psychologically real for that person, as one says. The criterion is that the semantic axioms of the theory state the information drawn upon by computational processes in the user in producing his understanding of perceived utterances and inscriptions. The information is drawn upon by subpersonal processes which correspond to the inferential principles stated in the theory.

On this approach, the psychological reality of a semantic theory, for a given language-user, involves an intermediate level of description of a computational process. A semantic theory is less specific than an algorithm, which would be a particular set of rules for computing meanings or truth-conditions for complete sentences from semantic information about their constituents. Many different algorithms may draw on the same body of information, and by using the same rules. So the relation between algorithms and semantic theories to which they conform is many–one. On the other hand, a specification of the information drawn upon, and the means used to draw upon it, is much more specific than a description of what is sometimes called (following Russell) a function-in-extension—that is, in the semantic case, a mere list pairing each sentence with its meaning or truth-condition.

Consider that fragment of L1 consisting only of sentences built up using the three names and three predicates, without any connectives. This fragment contains only finitely many sentences—twenty-one to be precise (nine containing 'loves', nine containing 'hates', three containing 'is happy'). As Evans emphasized, we can conceive of someone who has learned these sentences as unstructured idioms. Someone who possesses only this non-compositional capacity will not, in understanding sentences of L1, be drawing on any information about the semantic properties of the parts of the sentences of L1. The theory consisting of the axioms N1–N3, for the names, and P1–P3, for the predicates, is not psychologically real for this envisaged person.

The language or languages which a normal person acquires in childhood, and of which his knowledge may continues to grow in adulthood, are social entities. Languages change, develop, have histories, have different rates of propagation through populations, may merge, may diverge from a common root, and are the vehicles of a community's culture. These points have been emphasized by Dummett and Wiggins. The notion of what is literally said in a particular utterance which is an utterance in a given language is thus correspondingly a social notion. One may indeed introduce the notion of an idiolect, as the language as understood by a particular person at a particular time. Yet a particular person at a particular time aims to make his language conform to the public meaning of the words in the public language (or languages) he is aiming to speak. The notion of an idiolect introduced in the way just indicated may well be no more than someone's conception, at a given time, of the meaning of the words in a public language—which is hardly an alternative to the view of languages as social objects. If we attempt to make the notion of an idiolect primary in the explanation of linguistic meaning, in some way which is not parasitic on the notion of a public language, it is not clear that we will ever be able to make room for the idea of a language in the ordinary sense. Davidson, some of whose writings do seem to emphasize the primacy for meaning of interpretation on a particular occasion, did once reach the conclusion that there is no such thing as a language as that notion is commonly understood. Such a position is by no means required by the truth-conditional conception of meaning, nor by Davidson's insights about the role of rationality and interpretation in the individuation of meaning. The truth-conditional conception, and the Davidsonian insights about rationality and interpretation, can all be happily married to a conception of languages, with their semantic properties, as social entities.

The question now arises of the relation between the account of the psychological reality of a semantic rule, which apparently involved only the individual level, and these latest points, which make language and its semantic properties essentially social matters. If a language is a social entity, can anything more be involved in a semantic axiom's being correct than that it states a rule of the social language? And what, it may be asked, has that to do with computational psychology? Do these points about languages as social objects even make the account of understanding as drawing on information redundant, or at least relegate it to an account of what is required, computationally, for someone to be capable of grasping the rules of a particular language, and not something which would be in a constitutive account of linguistic understanding?

No such consequences ensue. An account of what is involved in understanding a language must be part of a constitutive account of the nature of a language. This point holds no less when the language is conceived (correctly, in my view) as a social object. What is it for you to understand a particular sentence of English? We certainly cannot simply say that it is for that sentence to be a sentence of English, and for English to be your language. There are many expressions of English you (and I, and many others) do not understand. Probably no one person understands all the expression of English. Even the best lexicographer cannot be fully up to date. The condition for a person to understand a particular sentence of English must relate that person to what is stated in the semantic axioms for the constituent expressions composing the sentence in some much more specific psychological relation. The appropriate relation is simply that of the person's drawing on the information given in the rule for the expression in question in his coming to understand sentences containing the expression. Far from being some later, quasi-scientific elaboration of the ('merely') psychological conditions required for grasping a rule of English, this account corresponds to a highly intuitive, constitutive truth about the nature of linguistic understanding. The account is just an elaboration of the idea that a person's understanding of a complex sentence is causally dependent upon his understanding of the expressions from which it is composed. The idea of drawing upon information is in part a spelling-out of the rich web of notions and relations encapsulated in that familiar idea.

A doubt may persist. We have said that the process of drawing on information which is operative in producing understanding of a heard utterance is subpersonal. Yet isn't understanding a particular expression something at the personal level? And if so, is there not a gap between what has been said about understanding and our intuitive notion of the understanding of the constituents explaining understanding of complete sentences? There is a gap, but it can be filled. Understanding an individual word is indeed something at the personal level. When a concept is genuinely expressed by the word, there is an understanding-condition for the word, one derivable from the possession condition for the associated concept. This understanding condition will involve conditions under which the word is rationally applied, and, like other understanding (and possession) conditions, it will itself be formulated at the personal level. It is entirely possible, however, for a state which is individuated at the personal level also to play a role in subpersonal processes. This is what happens when the personal-level state of understanding an expression is implicated in the causal processes leading up to a person's having a perceptual experience as of the occurrence of an utterance meaning that such-and-such. This is a special case of a much more widespread phenomenon. Concepts are individuated at the personal level, in terms of certain reason-giving relations in which they stand. This is entirely consistent with possession of a concept being implicated in subpersonal processes leading up to perception. That is what happens in any case in which we see or hear something as falling under that very concept, as a car, say, or a man.

4. CONCEPTUAL ROLE THEORIES: AUTONOMY AND EXPLANATION

4.1. The Approach Outlined, and Three Choices for the Conceptual Role Theorist

A conceptual role theory of the meaning of an expression is a theory which aims to explain its meaning in terms of

1. certain conditions which lead a person who understands the expression to use it in some specified way, and/or

2. certain consequences for a thinker's other thought and action of his use of the expression in some specified way.

Different sorts of conceptual role theory are generated by different restrictions a theorist may wish to place on the kind of conditions which lead up to or flow from use of the expression in question. Theories may also differ over the kind of use to be distinguished as specially relevant to individuating a particular meaning.

This highly general characterization includes the several distinct approaches explicitly described by their proponents as conceptual role theories, such as those of Sellars, Harman, Field, Block, and Horwich. The general characterization also includes verificationist theories of meaning, which aim to explain the meaning of a sentence in terms of what counts as a verification of it. It covers pragmatist theories too, which claim that the meaning of a sentence is to be given in terms of certain consequences of accepting it. It would even include Wittgenstein's later criterial approach to meaning, on some understandings of that approach. Correlatively with a conceptual role approach to meaning, there can equally be a conceptual role treatment of the identity of a particular concept.

The very way in which the notion of sense is normally introduced makes it highly attractive, indeed almost compulsory, to include at least some conceptual role element in a philosophical account of sense. Two expressions have the same sense if there cannot be circumstances in which a thinker would rationally apply the one expression and not rationally apply the other in the same way. So any difference in sense between two expressions must involve some difference or other in possible circumstances in which a thinker would be willing to apply each of the expressions. This seems to be precisely a difference in conceptual role (here, a role which involves rational application of the expression). If 'Hesperus' and 'Phosphorus' have different senses for a thinker in the commonly alleged situation of the Babylonian astronomer, it seems overwhelmingly plausible that, at some point, we must in our explanation of the difference in sense mention the following facts. The appearance of what is manifestly the last planet to disappear in the morning gives immediate reason for judging 'That's Phosphorus', but does not in itself give immediate reason for judging 'That's Hesperus'. Equally, the appearance of what is manifestly the first planet to appear in the evening gives immediate reason for judging 'That's Hesperus', but does not in itself give immediate reason for judging 'That's Phosphorus'. It is not hard to think of plausible sense-fixing conceptual roles for observational predicates, demonstratives, and logical and theoretical vocabulary. The approach certainly seems to have the generality required of any treatment of meaning.

If meaning is to be exhaustively explained in terms of conceptual role, a meaning-fixing role must satisfy certain restrictions. Suppose we set out to give a conceptual role explanation of the meaning of an expression *E*. If we try to do this by offering a role in inference, or in the acceptance of sentences, which takes for granted the thinker's acceptance of some other sentence containing *E*, understood as having its actual meaning, then we will not (or not thereby) have offered an exhaustively conceptual role theory. So the meaning-fixing role must be specified in a way which meets the conceptual role theorist's goal.

In general, we cannot expect to explain meanings one-by-one. There will very often, perhaps almost always, be families of expressions whose meanings have to be explained in terms of conceptual roles which involve both their relations to one another, as well as their relations to states of the thinker involving other matters. For example, it is plausible that the meanings of the expressions in the two sets {'matter', 'force'}, and {'place', 'time'}, have to be explained simultaneously.

Some theorists have also endeavoured to take conceptual roles as roles of sentences in a language of thought, conceived of as a subpersonal, non-conscious system of mental representations whose nature is discoverable by the techniques of an empirical psychology. These theorists aim to specify the meaning-determining role of an expression in the language of thought by adverting to certain features of states in which the expression is involved, where these states consist in non-intentional relations to expressions in a language of thought. Such a relation might, for instance, be that of storing a sentence in the postulated language of thought in some functionally identified location which is causally influenced by sensory stimulations.

Conceptual role approaches are sometimes developed in that fashion because the conceptual role theory is presented as part of a larger package. The larger package aims to explain how states with intentional content are possible at all. The question of how intentional states are possible evidently needs to be addressed. It is possible, however, to be a conceptual role theorist without insisting on a specification of roles in ultimately non-intentional terms. Indeed, anyone who specifies a role in relation to perceptual experience, taken as having a certain content, is relying on a relation to a content-involving state. The role suggested for the sense of 'Phosphorus' employed by those prior to the discovery of the identity of Hesperus with Phosphorus involves experience in just that way.

A theorist of meaning as conceptual role must also make three other choices.

1. First, the theorist must decide whether or not his conceptual roles involve, as a constitutive matter, a thinker's relations to his environment. In the early 1970s, Putnam invited us to consider a world, twin earth, on which there is a

water-like substance which fills the lakes, and falls from the sky, but whose chemical composition is not H_2O, but (for the sake of brevity in the example) twater, with chemical composition XYZ. You may have a molecule-for-molecule *doppelgänger* on twin earth, Putnam pointed out. But your *doppelgänger's* word 'water' refers to twater, not to water. The point is not confined to the identity of the substance thought about, that is, to the level of reference. It applies to the intentional content of attitudes. Your *doppelgänger* need not have any thoughts to the effect that water is thus-and-so; just as you may not have any to the effect that twater is thus-and-so. Putnam concluded that meaning 'ain't in the head'. Since the internal conceptual role of 'water' will be identical for you and your *doppelgänger*, while the meanings of your and his words 'water' diverge, meaning cannot in general be straightforwardly identical with any kind of internal conceptual role. The nature and wide range of the environmental and social determinants of meaning, which run far beyond natural-kind terms like 'water', were emphasized in a series of papers by Burge.

One reaction to Putnam's cases is to try to split the notion of meaning into two elements. One element is reference, which is agreed to be environmentally determined. The second element is some other component which also contributes to intentional content, and which is allegedly not fixed by anything outside a thinker's head. A conceptual role theorist of meaning may then present his account as a theory of this second element ('narrow content'). However, it is hard, and very likely impossible, to keep environmental relations from entering the proposed non-referential aspects of intentional content. Consider, for instance, a thinker using a demonstrative made available by his perception of (say) a certain car. When he thinks 'That car is illegally parked', his thought is about a certain car, which is presented in his perceptual experience of it as being at a certain distance and direction from him. We should not omit this way in which the car is presented from an account of the intentional content of what he is thinking. It helps determine patterns of informativeness, and so contributes to the determination of the Fregean sense associated in this case with 'That car is illegally parked'. But the prospects must be dim for the possibility of giving an account of what it is to experience something as being at a certain distance from oneself without bringing in the characteristic environmental relations of experiences with such a content. These experiences do, for example, have a special role to play in explaining, in appropriate circumstances, a thinker's moving to a position that distance from his earlier location when something he wants is located there.

The point is a special case of a more general phenomenon. The attitudes a person expresses in his language are capable of explaining a thinker's actions, and the properties of the actions which are so explained are in general relational, environmental properties. The explained properties can include that of moving a particular limb a certain distance and direction; acting in a particular way in relation to particular objects or substances in the environment; or indeed acting in a certain way towards states of affairs picked out in psychological or social terms. The counterfactuals supported by intentional explanations involve the relational properties which they explain, rather than anything having only to do with non-environmental properties. All this gives us good reason to suppose that, outside the special cases of the logical constants and mathematical vocabulary, the conceptual role theorist must appeal to conceptual roles which are not purely internal.

2. A second choice the conceptual role theorist must make is that between the total role, or some more limited canonical, conceptual role as individuating meaning. The latter is virtually obligatory if the theorist is to end up with anything recognizable as meaning. The total conceptual role of an expression, in an individual person's thought, will be dependent upon every belief he has which is linked, directly or indirectly, with his use of that expression. No two thinkers who differ in respect of those associated beliefs will, individually, mean the same by that expression if total role is taken to individuate meaning. To accept that any variation at all in beliefs involving an expression automatically involves variation in the meaning of the expression would be revisionary to the point of destruction of any notion of meaning. It is also quite unclear how the total approach has the resources to explain the notion of what is required for knowing the meaning of an expression in a public language, in cases where we can make sense of such knowledge.

Anyone who distinguishes some aspects of the conceptual role distinctive of a particular meaning as canonical aspects is committed to disagreeing at some point or other with Quine's critique of the distinction between principles constitutive of meaning and principles which are merely obviously true beliefs. The first step for anyone who hopes to make sense of a canonical conceptual role is to set aside those expressions which, in a public language, have only a reference associated with them from those proper understanding of which involves grasp of a certain sense. For the former expressions, it would not be at all surprising—and it appears to be the case—that there is very little a thinker has to accept in order to have mastered the expression in the language. There will be indefinitely many ways of thinking of the reference of the expression. If mastery of the expression involves only knowing of the reference that it is so, this knowledge is something which can be present for many different thinkers each of whom think of the referent in different ways, and for whom different propositions about it would be informative.

When, by contrast, an expression in the public language is associated with a specific sense, the statement of its canonical conceptual role should capture just the following principles or transitions involving the expression: those failure to appreciate which undermines an attribution of understanding.

Certain transitions or principles uncontroversially have this status. For example, anyone who fails to appreciate that '0', '1', '2', . . . refer to things which can count the objects falling under a concept does not understand numerical terms. The theorist will be committed to finding some such principles or transitions for each concept.

3. A third decision for the conceptual role theorist is one concerning the normative character of meaning. Someone who understands a sentence commonly has some appreciation of what would be good reasons for accepting it; and what in turn its acceptance gives good reasons for judging; or indeed for doing. Often these normative links seem to be a matter of the meaning of the sentence. They seem to result from normative characteristics associated with the individual expressions which compose the sentence (together with their mode of combination). So the normative characteristics of the whole sentence have to be componentially explained, as resulting from the normative characteristics of its components. The theorist must say how the normative character of meaning is to be elucidated, in a fashion consistent with its componential character.

A very direct way of capturing the normative dimension of meaning is simply to specify the meaning-fixing conceptual roles of individual expressions in normative terms. Under this approach, for each expression in a language, one would specify its contribution to what constitute good reasons for accepting sentences containing it, and to what sentences containing it give good reason for accepting or doing. This approach dovetails neatly with the Fregean conception of sense as answerable to what can be rationally accepted in particular circumstances.

The approach needs to be developed with some delicacy. It is plain that two thinkers can mean exactly the same by their expressions, whilst differing in their boldness in making judgements. One attractive way to proceed is to place in the meaning-fixing specifications only those normative links which can be seen as suitably related to the truth-condition of the sentence. The nature of the suitable relation then becomes a pivotal issue: is it something fixed independently of conceptual role, or not? In either case, must we not conclude that conceptual role is not in itself an exhaustive account of meaning? We will return to this crux shortly.

A different tactic for accommodating the normative dimension is to keep the specification of canonical conceptual roles non-normative, but then to state the principles according to which norms supervene upon these. The total theory—consisting of conceptual roles plus specific principles of supervenience—would then elucidate the normative dimension. This would also have the advantage of remaining explicit about the descriptive implications of attribution of a particular meaning to an expression in a person's language. The question about the principles of supervenience, and the relations between norms and any truth-conditions attributed to sentences, remains equally pressing on this account too. So let us postpone it no longer.

4.2. What is the Relation between Conceptual Role Theories and the Theory of Truth and Reference for a Language?

As conceptual role theories have been characterized hitherto in this chapter, the relation between conceptual role theories and the theory of reference and truth has been left entirely open. Many prominent proponents of conceptual role theories do, however, present them as alternatives to, indeed as in competition with, substantive truth-conditional theories of meaning. Do conceptual role theories make truth-conditional theories redundant? Or are meaning-fixing conceptual roles themselves required to meet certain constraints drawn from the theory of reference and truth? A pivotal issue in this area is whether a conceptual role theory can or cannot be *autonomous* and *primitive*. An autonomous theory is one according to which meaning-fixing conceptual roles are not answerable to any substantive constraints drawn from the theory of reference and truth. A primitive theory is one which says or entails that a person's conformity in his thought and language to the canonical roles for the expressions is not rationally explained by anything more fundamental. I believe that conceptual role theories can be neither autonomous nor primitive, and will argue for these two claims in that order.

1. Autonomous conceptual role theories are committed to counting as meaningful expressions which, intuitively, have no meaning, and which have no meaning because the specified conceptual role does not fix any contribution to truth-conditions. We can call this 'the problem of spurious meanings'. On the view that conceptual roles are autonomous, any (consistent) conceptual role determines a meaning: there are no other constraints to which meaning-fixing roles are answerable. So on the autonomous view, we should be able to fix a meaning for an operator 'vel' by these specifications of a role:

(*a*) From *A*, it can be inferred that *A vel B*;
(*b*) From *B*, it can be inferred that *A vel B*;
(*c*) From *A vel B*, together with derivations of *C* from *A*, and *C* from *B*, it can be inferred that *C*, provided that *A* contains no logical vocabulary;
(*d*) No rules not derivable from (*a*) to (*c*) are valid for vel.

These rules for 'vel' are consistent, for they are evidently a subset of those for classical alternation. For the theorist of autonomous conceptual role specifications of meaning, they ought to determine a meaning. But intuitively, when considered more closely, they do not determine any meaning at all. What has to be the case for '*A* vel *B*' to be true? It cannot be necessary and sufficient that either *A* or *B* is true. If that were all that is required, then there should be no restriction on the elimination rule (*c*), the restriction that *A* contain no logical vocabulary. So is then '*A* vel *B*' true also in some other case, even when *A* and *B* are both not true, say a case in which some third content *P* is true? But that cannot be right either, for then there should be an additional introduction rule, allowing one to infer '*A* vel *B*' from *P*. (*d*) explicitly rules out that there are any further rules, other than those which are derivable from (*a–c*). The intuitive argument that '*A* vel *B*' has no meaning is in brief simply this: by (*a*) and (*b*) it cannot mean anything stronger than '*A* or *B*'; yet by the restrictions in (*c*) and (*d*), it must mean something stronger. This is a contradiction. The problem, intuitively, is not that the role itself is contradictory (it is not), but that the conditions placed on the role fix inconsistent requirements on the truth-conditions for '*A* vel *B*'.

This statement of the problem of spurious meanings does not have any realistic presumptions. It could be accepted by an anti-realist. Indeed, many anti-realists are not theorists of autonomous conceptual roles in the present sense. The requirement that the specification of a conceptual role fix proof-conditions is itself equally a semantic requirement on legitimate meaning-fixing conceptual roles. 'vel' is, for instance, equally puzzling for a verificationist form of anti-realism. It places inconsistent requirements on the conditions for having a canonical proof of '*A* vel *B*'.

The intuitive argument that 'vel' does not have a meaning arguably tacitly relies on some background presumption that it must make a certain contribution to truth-conditions. This, though, does not make the statement of the problem question-begging. We can put the challenge to the theorist of autonomous conceptual roles thus: if 'vel' has no meaning, how are we to explain why it does not, except by appeal to referential semantics?

The theorist of autonomous conceptual roles might reply that a set of rules like (*a–c*) does not fully determine a meaning if it can be embedded in a larger consistent set of rules. This reply is somewhat *ad hoc*, since the requirement it proposes is not apparently motivated by anything intrinsic to an approach endorsing the autonomy of conceptual roles. The proposed requirement also rules out the possibility of a thinker understanding an expression, and coming to discover that new principles hold for it which do not follow from the principles he previously acknowledged (an example is given further below). If this is a possibility, it must be too strong to say that a set of rules like (*a–c*) does not fully determine a meaning if it can be embedded in a larger consistent set of rules.

A different requirement is that a set of rules like (*a–c*), together with a limiting clause like (*d*), does not determine a meaning if the following condition is met:

the set of rules can be embedded in a larger set for which there is an assignment of a truth-function to the connective which makes all the rules truth-preserving and also makes any limiting clauses like (*d*), but now applied to the larger set, correct.

But to adopt this stronger requirement is to abandon autonomy. This stronger restriction cuts down the class of legitimate meaning-specifying clauses by reference to a requirement having to do with truth. The restriction could not be motivated from within the autonomous conception.

The referential constraint on meaning-specifying conceptual roles in the treatment of this example can be generalized to expressions of any category. The generalization states that a putative meaning-specifying conceptual role genuinely determines a meaning only if there is a semantic value of the appropriate category which, when assigned to the expression, makes the transitions mentioned in the conceptual role always truth-preserving, and makes the belief-forming practices mentioned therein always result in true belief. This is a version of the requirement which, in the terminology of *A Study of Concepts*, I called the requirement of the existence of a determination theory for a conceptual role or proposed possession condition. The conceptual role succeeds in uniquely determining a meaning if there is—possibly together with the way the world is—only one such semantic value. In the case of expressions whose meaning is individuated by the consequences or commitments of accepting sentences containing them, this approach may need to embrace the idea that the semantic value is the weakest semantic value which validates the canonical conceptual role. I will return to that issue.

In any case, however it is developed in detail, a conception which embraces this referential constraint will also respect certain classical theses involving belief and sense. Under such a conception, we can see why it is that in coming to accept sentences on the basis of procedures mentioned in the canonical conceptual roles for its component expressions, we thereby fulfil one of the aims of judgement: that what is judged by true. We also respect the idea that a sense is individuated by the fundamental condition for something to be the sense's semantic value. This fundamental condition is fixed, for a given sense, by its being the one something must satisfy to make the belief-forming procedures mentioned in the possession condition always yield true beliefs.

A second problem for the autonomous conception arises within the class of genuine meanings. Even in the domain of arithmetic and higher-order logic, not every sentence which is true can be derived solely from the principles acceptance of which is required for understanding of the expressions in the sentence. This ought to be an impossible state of affairs if we hold the autonomous conception of meaning as conceptual role. On that conception, there should be no place for a correct (true) arithmetical sentence not establishable as such on the basis of the materials in the canonical conceptual roles of its constituents. But it is arguable that such a state of affairs can be shown to obtain, given Gödel's theorem that for any axiomatizable, consistent system for arithmetic, there will be a true sentence of arithmetic which is unprovable in the system. (For the student with some logical background but new to Gödel's theorem, a full proof is given in Kleene 1971, ch. VIII.)

Understanding universal quantification over the natural numbers 0, 1, 2, . . . requires only that the understander, in accepting such a universal quantification, incur a commitment to arbitrary numerical instances of the first-order predicate which is quantified. It would be too strong to require for understanding that the thinker have a grasp of numerical induction for arbitrary, open-ended properties of the natural numbers. That would be too strong, because we understand these universal quantifications before we learn the validity of numerical induction. Its validity is something which is correct for the meaning of universal quantification over natural numbers which is already grasped, rather than being primitively stipulated. The sentence which Gödel showed to be unprovable in the given system is of the form

> For all natural numbers **n**, **n** is not the Gödel number of a proof of the formula with Gödel number **g**,

where **g** denotes the number of the Gödel sentence in a standard numbering of sentences (the so-called Gödel numbering). Let us abbreviate the Gödel sentence as 'For all **n**, not-Proof(**n**, **g**)'. The standard, and it seems to me, sound reasoning to the truth of this sentence proceeds by first arguing that if the arithmetical system in question is consistent, then each of 'not-Proof(0, **g**)', 'not-Proof(1, **g**)', 'not-Proof(2, **g**)' must be provable in the system. The standard reasoning then continues: each of these provable sentences must be true; and so 'For all **n**, not-Proof(**n**, **g**)' must also be true. We know, however, by Gödel's celebrated reasoning that this universal quantification is unprovable in the system. The question now arises: how can the theorist of autonomous conceptual role explain how universal quantification over the natural numbers has a meaning of such a kind that the Gödel sentence, which is a universal quantification, is *true*?

For the theorist of conceptual role who does not take canonical meaning-fixing roles as autonomous, there is no evident problem. If conceptual roles are regarded as subject to referential constraints, he can say that the truth-condition for any universal numerical quantification is the weakest condition which validates universal elimination inferences. That condition is evidently one for which we can soundly move from the truth of all of the instances of a universal numerical quantification to the truth of that quantification. So the transition we need in arguing for the truth of the Gödel sentence is validated. This validation goes essentially through the theory of truth. It is unavailable to the theorist of autonomous conceptual roles. Though a full discussion of this point would need to go through many more stages, I do not myself see that the theorist of autonomous conceptual roles has the resources to answer this kind of challenge.

2. Now we can turn to the issue of whether a theory of conceptual role should always be primitive or not. Recall that a primitive theory is one which says or entails that a person's conformity in his thought and language to the canonical roles for the expressions is not rationally explained by anything more fundamental. We can be slightly more discriminating in our classifications if we introduce a relativized notion, that of a conceptual role theory's being primitive in respect of a given class of conceptual roles. The theory is primitive with respect to a class just in case it treats the canonical roles in that class as not rationally explained by anything more fundamental. A conceptual role theory can reject autonomy whilst still being primitive in respect of its treatment of a given class of roles. There is no internal incoherence in accepting referential constraints on meaning-determining roles, whilst also holding that a thinker's conformity to meaning-determining conceptual roles is not rationally explained in terms of anything else. (The theory I offered in *A Study of Concepts* implicitly embraced that combination for all canonical conceptual roles, though I would not be so bold as to offer that as a proof that the combination is consistent.) None the less, I have come to think that there is an important case to be made against primitive theories, at least in the case of certain concepts, a case which has ramifications for the theory of rational explanation and for the theory of justification and knowledge.

When an 18-year-old is first taught logic, he has to reflect—no doubt briefly—to appreciate that the rule of or-introduction ('From *A*, it can be inferred that *A or B*') is a sound rule. He already understood the word 'or', and had done so for more than a decade. He was not being introduced to a stipulation governing some newly introduced expression. Rather, the process of reflection leads him to accept that this primitive rule of or-introduction is correct, given his pre-existing understanding of 'or'. It is tempting to say three things of this state of affairs:

(1) His initial understanding of 'or' involves his possession of an underlying conception.
(2) This underlying conception has a semantic content, to the effect that a sentence of the form *A or B* is true just in case either *A* is true or *B* is true.
(3) The process of reflection in which he engaged in coming to accept the primitive rule of or-introduction involves the content of this underlying conception being causally operative, in a non-inferential but nevertheless rationally influential fashion, in his acceptance of the primitive rule.

Suppose, for the sake of argument, that we yield to this temptation to say (1–3). What are the consequences of the resulting view, and how might it be developed?

One may be inclined to dismiss the view on the ground that all that is going on in the reflection which leads to rational acceptance of a primitive inference rule is that the thinker infers that the rule is correct from his knowledge of the contribution to truth-conditions made by the word 'or' in English. Certainly it is true that if asked to offer a justification, a more sophisticated student might come out with something like that. But this cannot be an alternative explanation of the phenomena, for it simply postpones the issue. A thinker can rationally reflect and come to appreciate that or-introduction is sound even if he has not been explicitly taught truth-tables or a truth-theoretic clause. When he has not, what explains his rational appreciation of the correctness of a statement of the contribution 'or' makes to truth-conditions, his appreciation of the correctness of the truth-table? Again, an underlying conception with a semantic content is a candidate explanation.

A theory of underlying conceptions also handles better certain points at which the theorist of primitive conceptions is a little embarrassed. The primitive theorist must agree—for this is familiar to any teacher of elementary logic—that someone who understands 'or', or indeed the existential quantifier, may take some time in coming to appreciate that their respective elimination rules are correct for them. What account is the primitive theorist to give of the reflection which leads to their rational acceptance by the more acute students? He can hardly say that acceptance after a moment's reflection is required generally for understanding, since not all understanders do accept them immediately.

Some theorists of primitive conceptual roles who also accept that canonical conceptual roles are referentially constrained may be inclined to draw on a different resource. They may say that, for example, or-elimination is sound because it is validated by the weakest assignment of semantic value which also makes the or-introduction rule sound, that assignment being the classical truth-function for alternation. (I used to say this myself). One immediate problem with this response is that it is wholly implausible as an account of what goes on in the person whose reflection successfully generates knowledge of the soundness of the or-elimination rule. This person does not need to reflect on his own inferential practice to appreciate that the or-elimination rule is sound. Nor, it seems to me, does he need any information, explicit or tacit, about which assignments of semantic values would validate certain inferential practices, let alone information about the strength or weakness thereof. Rather, his prior understanding of 'or' consists in his associating with it an underlying conception with a semantic content—that '*A* or *B*' is true iff either *A* is true or *B* is true. This underlying conception is operative, when he reflects, in yielding his appreciation that the elimination rule will be sound. As before, some thinkers may articulate a justification, when asked for one, by stating explicitly a semantic rule; and also as before, and for parallel reasons, this cannot be an alternative explanation to the account in terms of underlying conceptions.

This treatment of underlying conceptions is evidently not a view which would have found favour with the later Wittgenstein. None the less, the treatment can be developed in ways which respect some of the most convincing aspects of his discussion of rule-following. First, the account of underlying conceptions can be developed in a way which positively emphasizes something Wittgenstein would have insisted upon, that in basic cases one has no inferential reason for applying an expression in a particular way. The kind of reflection involved in acceptance of a primitive inference rule, or of a primitive semantic rule, is not fundamentally inferential. But still, reflection makes its acceptance rational. It is certainly an item on the agenda in the philosophy of mind to explain how this non-inferential (and of course non-perceptual) rational thought is possible, if it is. It certainly seems to exist, and when it occurs, we seem to be at one of the very interfaces between the personal, rational level and the subpersonal, subrational level.

A second respect in which a theory of underlying conceptions need not contradict some of the insights in Wittgenstein's rule-following arguments is that it need not be any part of the theory of underlying conceptions to deny that in the possession conditions for particular concepts, we should mention what the thinker finds primitively compelling. The problem has been that previous theories have not sufficiently distinguished the cases in which finding something primitively compelling is explained by possession of an underlying conception from those in which it is not. There is apparently no obstacle to developing a theory on which there are constitutive connections between possession of an underlying conception with a semantic content, and finding certain transitions or principles primitively compelling.

In epistemology, the idea of underlying conceptions is a resource available to those accounts of knowledge which aim to emphasize the rationality of procedures which are capable of yielding knowledge. They may also be especially important to those accounts which go further, and say that for knowledge the thinker must have some conception of *why* he is right. Accounts of these two sorts have to say something about the rational acceptance of primitive axioms or inference rules, and to say something which does not involve an abandonment, for these cases, of the standards for knowledge they apply elsewhere. A theory of underlying conceptions can help meet this need for primitive logical rules, and possibly elsewhere. A thinker who has properly reflected in coming to accept a primitive inferential rule, or a primitive semantic rule, is rational in coming to accept it, and correct, and is influenced by what makes it correct; and all this without its acceptance being wholly inferential.

There are not only links with epistemology. There are Platonic aspects of a theory of underlying conceptions. There are also examples of concept attribution which seem to rely on something like a theory of underlying conceptions. One example is the correct ascription of the concept of the limit of a series to Leibniz and Newton, in the face of their completely inadequate explications of the notion, their failure to give its correct definition explicitly. All this suggests that there is more than one motivation for further investigating a theory of underlying conceptions.

5. THE MINIMALIST CHALLENGES

Two forms of minimalism challenge the truth-conditional conception of meaning. The first is minimalism about meaning. It contends that it is a mistake to seek any substantive account of meaning, and that none is necessary. The second form of minimalism is a minimalism about truth. It holds that even if a philosophical account of meaning is possible, the correct philosophical account of truth means that truth-conditions are in principle incapable of bearing the weight of an elucidation of meaning.

5.1. Minimalism about Meaning

Minimalism about meaning we take to be the thesis that no substantive elucidation is possible of the relation 'sentence *s* means in language *L* that *p*'. Whether an account is substantial or not is a matter of degree, and there are varieties of minimalism, differing according to the strength of the possibility they are denying. Accounts will also differ in respect of their positive statement of how we are able to understand attributions of particular meanings to sentences consistently with the denial of the existence of substantive elucidations of the notion. All the varieties of minimalism, must, however, be committed to the thesis that there is equally no possibility of giving a substantive elucidation of the meaning of expressions which compose sentences. For if a substantive account of subsentential meaning were possible, it would surely generate a substantive account of sentential meaning, by way of the principle that the meaning of a sentence is determined by the meaning of its constituents.

Minimalism about meaning is then a double denial, and it is important to separate the two components. A substantive elucidation of 'sentence *s* means in *L* that *p*' might be attempted in either of two ways, and perhaps both. One way is to give an elucidation of the relation of meaning, an elucidation which need not amount to a reduction. That was what was attempted in the programme in the philosophy of language initiated by Grice, and developed by Schiffer (in an earlier phase) and others. In this programme, public language is regarded as a device for the conventional expression of very complex communicative intentions, intentions of a sort which, it is claimed, could in some cases exist outside linguistic practice.

Limitations of space have prevented discussion of the Gricean approach in this essay, but even from this description, it should be clear that the Gricean approach is concentrating on elucidation of the relation *means that*, rather than on the elucidation of the structured content *p*. That is the other way that an elucidation might proceed. Whether or not any elucidation of the relation *means that* is possible, a theorist might still aim to give a substantive theory of what is involved in something's being a structured content that *p*. A truth-conditional account of content is just such a theory. The possibility of developing such a theory is equally denied by the minimalist about meaning. So the classical conception of meaning as truth-conditions which I have been outlining must respond to this second component—the content component—of the challenge, and I will briefly consider what responses are available. The second component must of course equally be addressed by others who believe that non-truth-conditional substantive theories of content are possible, such as pure conceptual role theories, probabilistic theories, or criterial theories.

Before we proceed further, it is worth noting that it is a matter of some delicacy, not always obvious to casual inspection, whether a theorist really is giving the notion of truth a central role in his account of meaning. It is not by itself sufficient that he makes use of the notion of truth in his meaning theory for a particular language *L*. For instance, consider a position according to which we assign meanings to language-users' sentences in a way which makes them maximally intelligible. Now consider the general correlation of sentences *s* and contents *p* fixed by a truth theory θ for the language *L*, that is, the correlation between *s* and *p* given by *it is canonically provable in theory of truth* θ *that s is true iff p*. We can imagine the defender of this position holding that a theory of truth θ for a language is an acceptable theory of meaning if that general correlation, taken as giving the meaning of the sentences, maximizes the intelligibility of the language-users' linguistic and non-linguistic behaviour. Now this position uses a theory of truth; but, given only what has so far been said, the truth-predicate might be functioning for this theorist solely as a means of correlating sentences of the language in question with contents. For such a theorist, an uninterpreted predicate in a theory could equally have served, for all that has been said so far.

Now of course the theorist may also hold the additional thesis that any predicate which performs that correlational function, and does so in a way meeting the interpretational constraints, must in fact be the truth-predicate. This is an attractive position, and is precisely the position of Wiggins, for one. It is important to note that it is that additional thesis which entitles that combination of views to be called a genuinely truth-based approach to meaning, rather than one that is making a merely dispensable use of 'is true' as a correlation device. The general moral is that one can tell whether something is a genuinely truth-based approach to meaning only by looking at a theorist's total position, including his account of what meaning theories of particular languages are answerable to, rather than just the particular form in which a meaning theory for a particular language is presented.

What then might motivate the content component of minimalism about meaning, as applied in particular to truth-conditional theories? I will mention three motivations, though careful readers of the literature will find more.

1. The content component of minimalism about meaning is sometimes motivated by the idea that no kind of grasp of truth theories is required to explain how language-users understand sentences they have never previously encountered. Schiffer has been a vigorous proponent of this source of scepticism about the truth-theoretic approach to content. He considers a thinker who has a structured language of thought ('Mentalese'), and for whom different modes of storage of sentences in that language of thought are correlated systematically with the possession of corresponding beliefs, or desires, or intentions, and so forth. I will use the notation %red% to refer to the expression in the thinker's language of thought which has the same meaning as our word 'red'. Similarly %Mars is red% refers to the sentence of Mentalese which translates our sentence 'Mars is red'. Schiffer envisages the thinker who understands English as making the transition from, for instance, the storage of a Mentalese sentence

%John uttered the sentence 'Not all tomatoes are red'%

to

%John said that not all tomatoes are red%.

Schiffer's point is that the transition from sentences like the first in this pair to sentences like the second is purely syntactic. We can formulate a general and purely syntactic rule for moving from sentences like the first to sentences like the second. We can also suppose our subject to have a perceptual device which, when for instance an English sentence 'Not all tomatoes are red' is uttered in his presence, causes him to store, in the appropriate box, the Mentalese sentence

%John uttered the sentence 'Not all tomatoes are red'%.

If, asks Schiffer, a person has such a perceptual device, and some mechanism which implements the transition from sentences like the first in our pair to sentences like the second, do we not have an explanation of how that person can understand utterances of sentences of English? And if the syntactic operation is described in its proper generality, will the person not have the capacity to understand English sentences he has never heard before? So apparently we have an explanation of understanding which in no way adverts to the understander's grasping or internalizing a theory of truth—or indeed any other form of compositional semantics—for the language.

Defenders of a compositional semantics will be inclined to reply that the capacity of the language-user which needs explanation has to be characterized in content-involving terms. Schiffer's explanation is an explanation of a general capacity described in syntactic terms, at the level of the language of thought. There is indeed a general correlation between the storage of sentences like

%John said that not all tomatoes are red%

and the thinker's perceiving that

John said that not all tomatoes are red.

We have an explanation of the general capacity described in content-involving terms only if we add that for this speaker, %tomato% is true of just the tomatoes, %not *A*% is true iff *A* is not true, and so forth. This supplemented explanation then relies on truths about the meaning of expressions of Mentalese. But further, if the person has some mechanism which maps representations of English expressions to expressions of Mentalese, and these expressions have certain meanings, recursively specifiable, is this not one way of possessing semantic information about the expressions of English? The compositional semanticist should say that having all this is precisely one way the language-understander can draw on the information stated in a theory of truth for the language. Other compositional semanticists will make corresponding remarks.

This is hardly the end of the discussion. What the dialectic so far brings out is that a major part of the debate between the minimalist and his opponent will consist in disputes about what does and does not need explanation. We will have further examples of this state of affairs later. In urging the need for explanation of capacities under their content-involving characterizations, the opponent of minimalism is making a move of a kind that is frequently available. This move involved appealing to the need to explain properties of thinkers which are relationally, and frequently environmentally and socially, individuated. Facts about the linguistic understanding of a speaker are a special case of this phenomenon. Later rounds of the discussion will need to address in greater generality the question of whether or not the minimalist can satisfactorily explain these phenomena. If it is claimed that they can, we will need to know how. If not, there will still be the positive challenge of constructing models and philosophical accounts of better means of explanation.

2. A second motivation for the content component of minimalism is ontological, a concern about what kind of thing the structured entities could be

which are allegedly the senses of complete sentences (and, according to some, the references of 'that . . .' clauses). Such worries had for long exercised Quine. The ontological concerns which motivate this part of minimalism can, though, be stated without the apparent behaviourism and downgrading of the mental found in some of Quine's writings. The worry is that if we look at the various kinds of entity with which structured senses might be identified, the candidates are all in one way or another defective. To summarize briefly the situation: the entities provided by possible-worlds semantics do not seem sufficiently discriminating, however fine we slice; while appeal to sentences themselves seems deeply unexplanatory. The truth-conditional theorist of sense is, though, likely to respond to these concerns by wondering why senses have to be identified with things of some other kind. We are very familiar from the theory of abstract objects more generally of the way in which discourse about natural numbers, or sets, or expression-types, may be given meaning by tying these ontologies to various criteria of identity and individuation. To the theorist who is inclined to individuate senses or concepts by their possession conditions, the parallel is particularly tempting. Just as a natural number is individuated by the fundamental condition for a property to have that number of instances, so a concept is individuated by the condition a thinker must meet to possess it. But the parallel is not restricted to enthusiasts for possession conditions. The more general point is that an ontology can be legitimized by occupying a certain kind of role in a successful theory and continuing practice—in this case the theory of understanding and the practice of the attribution of intentional states. This general point is available to almost all comers.

3. These first two motivations for the content component of minimalism about meaning are directed against any theory of structured intentional contents which endorses, or permits some reconstruction of, the notion of sense. A third possible motivation is more specific to truth-conditional theories. Let us return, it might be suggested, to the account mentioned a few paragraphs back, which used the notion of truth in specifying sentence–content pairings, but which did not really use it in any way in which it could not be replaced by an uninterpreted predicate (and similarly for the relation of satisfaction). Is there anything wrong with the view that truth plays no essential role, and that assignments of content which maximize intelligibility of the language-users is all we need? The truth-conditional theorist should reply that this view will not stand up under detailed examination of what is involved in intelligibility. Rationality must play a large part in it, but large tracts of rationality in thought seem to be best elucidated philosophically by appeal to the relations between the rational thinker and the referential properties of concepts and words. We already noted in an earlier section that the rationality of acceptance of primitive logical principles and axioms was plausibly explained by the thinker's possession of some implicit conception of the semantic properties of the logical constants involved.

This is but one of many cases. Even the humble case of a thinker who moves to obtain a view of an object from another angle to check that it is really as it seems to be is a thinker whose rationality is naturally accounted for by saying that this is a way to check on the properties of the same object as he was thinking about in the original thought. It seems to be doubtful that one could explain rationality and justification of all sorts of belief-forming practices without seeing them as means of verifying or refuting that objects have certain properties or relations, where all of these—objects, properties, and relations—are conceived as being at the level of reference, not the level of sense. One can conjecture that the same holds for the rationality of deductive and of non-conclusive forms of reasoning.

5.2. Minimalism about Truth

The principal claim of the minimal theory of truth—sometimes known as the redundancy or deflationary theory—is that the meaning of 'true', as applied to any sentence '*A*' of the language in which this is written, is exhausted by its conformity to the schema

'*A*' is true iff '*A*'.

The schema just displayed is usually known as the disquotational schema. Some paradoxical instances aside, everyone will agree that all proper instances of the disquotational schema are true, including some of those who disagree with the minimal theory. What is distinctive of the minimal theory is the claim that conformity to the schema is *all* there is to such a sentence's being true.

I have spoken overtly of the meaning of the predicate 'true', but even those who draw back from explicit talk of meanings must somehow capture the notion of exhaustion which is distinctive of the minimal theory. One might, for instance, put the claim of the minimal theory thus: to say that such a sentence '*A*' is true is to say no more than is said in an utterance of *A* itself (modulo the existence of the sentence itself). If that formulation is adopted, 'saying' in some strict sense must be elaborated in such a way as to make it clear that the claim of the minimal theory is going beyond that of the mere general correctness of the disquotational schema.

The minimal theory of truth must, obviously, say something about our application of the predicate 'true' to sentences of other languages. This has been attempted in various ways, which normally involved the notion of translation. Certainly the minimal theorist will want to hold that when some sentence *B* of another language has a translation into English, to say that *B* is true is to say that a translation of *A* is true in the sense already explained by the minimal theory. The minimalist about truth faces the task of showing that we can make sense of translation without any appeal to a notion of truth not explained in minimalist terms. His position would be unacceptable if the only way of elucidating translation is to say that it requires the preservation of truth-conditions in some sense inaccessible to the minimalist position. This is a serious issue, but I will not discuss it here, mainly because it is very plausible that such an objection is good if and only if a truth-conditional theory of meaning is correct. So we lose nothing by staying with that central issue.

There is a straightforward incompatibility between truth-conditional theories of meaning and the minimalist theory of truth. If the meaning of the claim that '*A*' is true is exhausted by its equivalence to *A*, to try to explain the meaning of *A* in terms of its truth-conditions is simply to proceed in a circle. Dummett emphasized this point more than thirty-five years ago, and it has eventually come to be widely accepted.

The incompatibility of the minimalist theory of truth with a truth-conditional theory of meaning cuts both ways. Those who see the truth-conditional approach as the only developed and plausible option for many fragments of natural language will see the incompatibility as evidence against the minimalist theory of truth. Truth-conditional theorists of meaning should also be encouraged by the reflection that many minimalists about truth, such as Horwich and the later Field, propose conceptual role theories of meaning, and it was those theories that were argued above to need constraints drawn from the theory of truth and reference. But however great the weight carried by these general reflections, the claims of the minimalist and their consequences do deserve to be considered more directly.

One important area of contention is the status of instances of the disquotational schema. For the minimalist about truth, these instances, such as

> 'London is noisy' is true iff London is noisy

have the status of primitive axioms—they are part of an implicit definition of 'is true'. For the truth-conditional theorist of meaning, matters stand differently. He will say that this most recently displayed biconditional is something which can be explained. It is explained by these truths: that

> 'London' refers to London,
> 'is noisy' is true of an object just in case it is noisy

and

> A sentence '$F\alpha$' is true iff the predicate F is true of the object referred to by α.

The truth-conditional theorist will say that this is a genuine explanation which supports counterfactuals. If the word 'London' had referred to something else in English, then sentences of English of the form 'London is so-and-so' would have had a different truth-condition. The different truth-condition they would have had would have been determined in part by the then correct referential axiom for 'London' in that counterfactual state of affairs. This claim about explanation applies not just to the explanation of the individual speaker–hearer's understanding of an utterance of the sentence—the issue discussed back in Section 3—but to the sentence of the social language itself. That sentence has the truth-condition it does because of the referential properties of its components.

To say this is not to deny the priority, in one important respect, of sentences in the explanation of meaning. To say that any individual expression has a certain meaning is to say that it makes a certain contribution to the meaning of complete sentences in which it occurs. But that is entirely consistent with the particular contribution made by a specific word contributing to the explanation of the meaning of the complete sentence in which it occurs. Indeed, the general idea in principle of componential explanation of the properties of complete sentences cannot be in principle objectionable to those minimalists about truth who are also conceptual role theorists of meaning. All the plausible conceptual role theories which have been proposed are componential in a corresponding sense. They are committed to the claim that the explanation of the conceptual role of a complete sentence is determined by the conceptual roles of its individual constituent expressions.

There may none the less be a suspicion that the minimalist about truth gives a better account than the truth-conditional theorist of the epistemic status of instances of the disquotational principle, and of such corresponding disquotational ('homophonic') principles as that 'London' denotes London. If these principles are consequences of an implicit definition of truth and reference respectively, it is not surprising that they should have a relatively a priori status, as indeed they appear to do. It would be a mistake, however, to suppose that an explanation of this a priori status is exclusive to the minimalist theory of truth. On the truth-conditional theory too, anyone who understands the name 'London' can know without further information that for any object, 'London' refers to it iff that object is London. Suitable possession of that information is what is involved in understanding the name on the truth-conditional view of meaning. Corresponding points can be made about the status of the other principles invoked to explain why it is true that 'London is noisy' is true iff London is noisy. The upshot is that there is no inconsistency in holding that the instances of the disquotational schema are both explicable, whilst also having an a priori status.

Much else is at stake between the minimalist theory of truth and truth-conditional theories of meaning. I close this section by mentioning two challenges, one for each of the two views. We already noted that referential relations apparently have a role to play in the explanation of what it is for thought to be rationally intelligible. If this is so, then they have a role to play in psychological explanation of thought and action, and it will be a task for the minimalist about truth to see if he can really give a credible description of this role without making use of more substantial notions of reference and truth than is consistent with minimalist views thereof.

The other challenge is for the truth-conditional theorist of meaning. Since the notions of truth and reference used in the meaning theories he gives for particular languages are not to be construed along minimalist lines, we have to say more about what is involved in our understanding of these open-ended notions, which have application to any language. (They apply both to those we understand, those we do not understand, and even those we could never come to understand.) One approach to the task of explaining our understanding of these open-ended notions is to proceed by investigating what properties a truth-predicate must have if a good account of interpretation is to settle its conditions of application to the sentences of a language in use. There is certainly some illumination to be gained from that route, which has been investigated by Wiggins. The properties of truth which arguably emerge from that kind of investigation are not language-specific, but hold of truth in general.

Another kind of approach to the general concept of truth is also possible—indeed the possibility of another approach is already implicit in the first approach just outlined. There must be some answer to the question 'Is there some explanation, deriving from the nature of an open-ended general notion of truth, of *why* it is that a satisfactory account of good interpretation must settle the application specifically of the truth-predicate?' It seems that in the nature of the case this question must be answered by appeal to features of the general concept of truth which speak to more than just its role in interpretation. Indeed, discussions of the nature of the truth-predicate based on its role in interpretation tend to appeal at various points to some prior understanding of a general notion of truth, which is going to need further elucidation.

A plausible conception of the relation between reference and truth on the one hand, and an account of concept mastery on the other, is entirely general, and not restricted to just one particular language. I suggested that concepts have those semantic values (references) which make the belief-forming practices mentioned in their possession conditions yield true beliefs, and to make the inferential principles mentioned therein always truth-preserving. I also suggested that something is a genuine concept only if there is an assignment of semantic value to it meeting these conditions. Now a successful interpretation of a language must say which concepts are expressed by the words of that language. By the preceding points, it must also thereby determine an assignment of references (given the way the world is) and thereby an assignment of truth-conditions.

Many of the distinctive marks of the general notion of truth are directly derivable from these points. One of those marks is that anyone using a meaningful expression must be regardable as aiming at the truth in his sincere utterances involving that expression. For any concept assigned to that expression as its sense, there will be a corresponding account of what has to be the case for something to be its reference, an account which makes truth-yielding the belief-forming procedures mentioned in its possession condition, a possession condition satisfied by a thinker who understands the expression. So necessarily that thinker will be regardable as aiming at the truth in his sincere utterances involving the expression in central cases in which he is judging in accordance with the possession condition. Non-central cases are required to have appropriate rational, truth-directed relations to the central cases.

Similar resources also provide an explanation of the widely accepted point that the correctness of a particular judgement can never consist in the making of that judgement. Even if in certain special cases a judgement cannot be erroneous, that is always because it can be shown that such judgements, perhaps when made for certain reasons, in one way or another guaranteed the holding of the condition for their correctness. A theory of concepts, referentially constrained in the way for which I was arguing earlier, will say that this is so because correctness of a genuine judgement always involves fulfilment of some requirement at the level of reference, some condition on objects, events, properties, and relations.

Limitations of space oblige us to break off here even from this brief outline. I conclude with the expression of the hope that some readers will feel inclined to pursue further these issues about the general notion of truth, and their connections with our general notions of reference and concept possession. These connections are an under-exploited resource not only in the theory of meaning and content, but in epistemology and metaphysics too.

BIBLIOGRAPHY

1. THE CLASSICAL TRUTH-CONDITIONAL THESIS

The first five essays in Davidson's collection *Inquiries into Truth and Interpretation* (1984) outline his conception of the proper form of a truth-conditional meaning theory for a particular language. Davidson (1990) elaborates his conception further in responding to critical discussions. Applications of, and queries about, the Davidsonian approach form the subject-matter of the essays in Evans and McDowell (1976). There are also further developments in Davidson and Harman (1975). A constructive overview of the whole approach, with many applications, is Davies (1981). Tarski's long original essay 'The Concept of Truth in Formalized Languages' (in the collection 1983) also repays study. Platts (1997) is a gentler introduction to the formal aspects of truth theories. Another good introduction is Engel (1991). Blackburn (1984) provides an introduction which ranges more widely. For the serious enthusiast, a reading of §32 of Frege's *Basic Laws of Arithmetic* (*Grundgesetze der Arithmetik*) (1964), and the preceding material in the same book, is illuminating both in itself, and when considered in relation to Frege's views on justification.

Frege's great essay 'Thoughts' ('Der Gedanke: Eine logische Untersuchung') (1977) reads as vividly today as it must have eighty years ago at its publication. 'On Sense and Reference ('Über Sinn, und Bedeutung') (1993) is also highly accessible to those starting out in the subject. There is now an extensive scholarly literature on Frege's notion of sense. Dummett's substantial treatments (1973, 1981) have been focal points of many discussion. Burge (1979*b*, 1990) emphasizes other aspects of Frege's conception of sense. An influential development of the notion of sense, particularly as applied to demonstratives and indexicals, is found in Evans (1982). The best of the interpretative literature on Frege is certainly not only of historical interest. Many of the most interesting and distinctive features of Frege's notion involve aspects of thought and reason of which our present philosophical understanding is extremely patchy.

An approach closely related to, but at crucial points distinct from, truth-theoretic semantics is the situation semantics of Barwise and Perry, which receives an exposition in their joint book (1983).

2. WHAT MAKES A SEMANTIC AXIOM CORRECT?

The significance of the task of considering how we might come to understand a language of which we have no prior knowledge, and for which there are no established translation procedures, was emphasized in Quine (1960). His concern was the construction of a translation manual for the language, rather than a meaning theory. The papers 'Radical Interpretation' and 'Belief and the Basis of Meaning', both in Davidson (1984) summarize Davidson's views on the principles underwriting a meaning theory as correct. A move from a principle of charity to a principle of humanity is recommended in Grandy (1973), and further supported by the considerations in McGinn (1977). Dummett's views on modesty are given in 'What is a Theory of Meaning? (I)', in his collection *The Seas of Language* (1993). McDowell's response 'In Defense of Modesty', together with a reply from Dummett, is in Taylor's collection (1987). McDowell returns to the debate in 'Another Plea for Modesty' (forthcoming); his subjectivism about intentional content is outlined in 'Functionalism and Anomalous Monism' (1986*a*). Tempered immodesty was attempted in Peacocke (1992).

3. SEMANTIC AXIOMS AND THE EXPLANATION OF UNDERSTANDING

Discussions of the relation of a language-understander to the semantic axioms of a correct semantic theory for his language had at least two sources. Thought on these matters was stimulated, first, by the closely related issue of the psychological relation of a thinker to the axioms of a correct syntactic theory for his language. Chomsky claimed that ordinary speakers tacitly know, or at least cognize, these semantic rules. For two amongst many statements of his position, see Chomsky (1980, 1986). Three influential critiques of Chomsky's position are given in Quine (1970), Stich (1971), and Soames (1984). The other stimulus for thought on these matters was the development of

Davidson's truth-theoretic approach to semantic theories. Once one has an explicit, clear conception of a semantic rule, the issue of an understander's relation to what is stated in it is at least sharply formulated. Important contributions towards resolving the question were made by Davies (1981, chs. III and IV; and in his paper 1987) and by Evans (1981). The computational elaboration of this approach was given in Peacocke (1986*a*, 1994). On the importance of language as a social object, see Dummett (1986) and Wiggins (1997). Davidson (1986) defends his very different view, and contains his denial that there is anything which is a language 'if a language is anything like what many philosophers and linguists have supposed' (p. 446).

For a view which does attribute knowledge of the semantic axioms to speakers, see Higginbotham (1991). For the development of a view that semantic theories in no way enter the explanation of linguistic understanding, see Schiffer (1986, 1991), and also the material in Section 5 of the present chapter. For a radically sceptical treatment of the terms of recent discussions of these issues, see Baker and Hacker (1984).

4. CONCEPTUAL ROLE THEORIES: AUTONOMY AND EXPLANATION

A wide variety of conceptual role theories will be on display if the reader looks at Sellars (1974), Harman (1974, 1982), Field (1977, 1994), Block (1986), Horwich (1990), Peacocke (1992), and Brandom (1994). These writers differ radically in the kinds of conceptual role theories developed, and in their views on the relations between conceptual role theories and truth-conditional theories. As noted in the main text, verificationist and criterial theories of content are each special cases of conceptual role theories. Some of the issues in developing them are discussed in Dummett (1976), McDowell (1982), and the essays in Wright (1993) on criteria. For a classical statement of the view that no evidential relations can be isolated as canonical in the individuation of meaning, see Quine (1961, 1976).

Influential examples and statements of anti-individualistic views are given in Putnam (1975), Burge (1979*a*, 1982), McDowell (1986*b*). On the question of the autonomy of conceptual roles, see Peacocke (1993), and, for what is by implication a contrary view, Skorupski (1993). On the issue of whether the sense which is grasped has properties going beyond what is fixed by ordinary understanding, see Burge (1990), Peacocke (1996, forthcoming).

5. THE MINIMALIST CHALLENGES

The theory that there cannot be true, substantive theories of meaning is developed in Schiffer's *Remnants of Meaning* (1987). This book contains detailed critiques of extant theories, written by one who used to be a leading defender of one of those theories. Johnston (1988) also elaborates a minimalist view of meaning; Schiffer (1988) comments on Johnston's position. Schiffer (forthcoming) outlines his most recent views. The redundancy, or, better, minimalist theory of truth has been advocated at various times by Frege (with highly questionable consistency), Ramsey, the later Wittgenstein, Ayer, the early Strawson, Quine, and Field. The most developed and resourceful defences of the minimalist theory of truth are given in Horwich (1990), in which the reader will also find references to the earlier literature, and in Field (1994). The paper by Field locates his version of the minimalist position in a wider deflationary conception of meaning and truth, Since in this critical essay I have clearly been defending a truth-conditional conception of meaning, the reader is strongly urged to read the writings of Horwich and Field for the contrary view. The views of Wiggins are found in his (1991) paper.

FURTHER TOPICS

Naturally the literature on truth-conditional approaches should be read in combination with work on the theory of singular reference. Kripke (1980) and Kaplan (1989) are two of the most celebrated and influential writings since 1945. Critical surveys of the literature to their dates of publication, together with important contributions of their own, are Davies (1981) and Salmon (1986). A thorough critical discussion of work on descriptions is given in Neale's book of that name (1990).

The main discussion above explicitly had to prescind from considering Grice's approach to linguistic meaning. Grice's original paper (1957) is one of the best introductions, and the development of the programme is outlined in Schiffer (1972), before the change of mind reported and explained in his *Remnants of Meaning* (1987). Avramides (1989) provides a sympathetic critical survey of the approach. A rather different approach to linguistic meaning is developed in Searle (1969). An important alternative, an account of linguistic meaning founded in the mechanisms of natural selection, is developed in one of the chapters of Millikan (1984).

Quine (1960) famously claimed that translation is radically indeterminate. Important critical discussions of his reasons are in Chomsky (1969) and Evans (1985). Field (1974) discusses the correct way for a semantic theory to handle indeterminacy, if it does exist.

Kripke's discussion of rule-following (1982), and the arguments of Wittgenstein as they struck Kripke, produced an explosion of interest in the topic. The ramifications of Wittgenstein's thought on this had been explained also by Fogelin (1976) and Wright (1980). The requirements Kripke emphasized, and in particular the normative dimension of meaning, have left a permanent mark in the philosophy of mind and language. Boghossian (1989) provides an original critical discussion of the impact of Kripke's arguments.

The issue of the correct way of conceiving of the relation between thought and language is intertwined with all of the main positions in the theory of meaning discussed above. Rather different views are developed in Davidson (1975) and Dummett (1993*a*). The reader may want to reflect on the bearing of the position of tempered immodesty, outlined in Section 2 of the main text above, on the issue.

An overview of work in pragmatics is given in Davis's reader (1991). Some earlier work is reported in the volume edited by Searle, Kiefer, and Bierwisch (1980). The approach developed in Sperber and Wilson (1995) has also received much attention.

The massive topic of realism would naturally have been the next to be considered had the main text above been continued. Dummett's collection (1978) and book (1991) and Wright's collection (1993) and lectures (1992) outline some anti-realist challenges and approaches. A variety of realist responses—sometimes more than one response from the same author—will be found in McDowell (1976, 1978), Putnam (1978), Peacocke (1986*b*) and Campbell (1994).

REFERENCES

Avramides, A. (1989), *Meaning and Mind: An Examination of a Gricean Account of Meaning* (Cambridge, Mass.: MIT Press).

Baker, G., and Hacker, P. (1984), *Language, Sense and Nonsense* (Oxford: Blackwell).

Barwise, J., and Perry, J. (1983), *Situations and Attitudes* (Cambridge, Mass.: MIT Press).

Blackburn, S. (1984), *Spreading the Word: Groundings in the Philosophy of Language* (Oxford: Oxford University Press).

Block, N. (1986), 'Advertisement for a Semantics for Psychology', in P. A. French, T. E. Uehling, and H. K. Wettstein (eds.), *Midwest Studies in Philosophy*, x: *Studies in the Philosophy of Mind* (Minneapolis: University of Minnesota Press).

Boghossian, P. (1989), 'The Rule-Following Consideration', *Mind*, 98: 507–49.

Brandom, R. (1994), *Making it Explicit: Reasoning, Representing and Discussive Commitment* (Cambridge, Mass.).

Burge, T. (1979*a*), 'Individualism and the Mental', in P. French, T. Uehling, and H. Wettstein (eds.), *Studies in Metaphysics, Midwest Studies in Philosophy*, iv (Minneapolis).

——(1979*b*), 'Sinning against Frege', *Philosophical Review*, 88: 398–432.

——(1982), 'Other Bodies', in A. Woodfield (ed.), *Thought and Object* (Oxford: Oxford University Press).

——(1990), 'Frege on Sense and Linguistic Meaning', in D. Bell, and N. Cooper (eds.), *The Analytic Tradition* (Oxford: Blackwell).

Campbell, J. (1994), *Past, Space and Self* (Cambridge, Mass.: MIT Press).

Chomsky, N. (1969), 'Quine's Empirical Assumptions', in D. Davidson, and J. Hintikka (eds.), *Words and Objections: Essays on the Work of W. V. Quine* (Dordrecht: Reidel).

——(1980), *Rules and Representations* (Oxford: Blackwell).

——(1986), *Knowledge of Language: Its Nature, Origin and Use* (New York: Praeger).

Cussins, A. (1990), 'The Connectionist Construction of Concepts', in M. Boden (ed.), *The Philosophy of Artificial Intelligence* (Oxford).

Davidson, D. (1975), 'Thought and Talk', in S. Guttenplan (ed.), *Mind and Language* (Oxford: Oxford University Press).

——(1984), *Inquiries into Truth and Interpretation* (Oxford: Clarendon Press).

——(1986), 'A Nice Derangement of Epitaphs', in E. LePore (ed.), *Truth and Interpretation: Perspectives on the Philosophy of Donald Davidson* (Oxford: Blackwell).

——(1990), 'The Structure and Content of Truth', *Journal of Philosophy*, 87: 279–328.

——and Harman, G. (eds.) (1975), *The Logic of Grammar* (Encino, Calif.: Dickenson).

Davies, M. (1981), *Meaning, Quantification, Necessity: Themes in Philosophical Logic* (London: Routledge & Kegan Paul).

——(1987), 'Tacit Knowledge and Semantic Theory: Can a Five Per Cent Difference Matter?', *Mind*, 96: 441–62.

Davis, S. (ed.) (1991), *Pragmatics: A Reader* (New York: Oxford University Press).

Dummett, M. (1973), *Frege: Philosophy of Language* (London: Duckworth).

——(1976), 'What is a Theory of Meaning? (II)', in G. Evans, and J. McDowell (eds.), *Truth and Meaning: Essays in Semantic* (Oxford: Oxford University Press).

——(1978), *Truth and Other Enigmas* (London: Duckworth).

——(1981), *The Interpretation of Frege's Philosophy* (London: Duckworth).

——(1986), 'A Nice Derangement of Epitaphs: Some Comments on Davidson and Hacking', in E. LePore (ed.), *Truth and Interpretation: Perspectives on the Philosophy of Donald Davidson* (Oxford: Blackwell).

——(1991), *The Logical Basis of Metaphysics* (Cambridge, Mass.: Harvard University Press).

——(1993*a*), *Origins of Analytical Philosophy* (London: Duckworth).

——(1993*b*), *The Seas of Language* (Oxford: Oxford University Press).

Engel, P. (1991), *The Norm of Truth: An Introduction to the Philosophy of Logic* (Hemel Hempstead: Harvester Wheatsheaf).

Evans, G. (1981), 'Semantic Theory and Tacit Knowledge', in *Wittgenstein: To Follow a Rule* (London: Routledge).

——(1982), *The Varieties of Reference* (Oxford: Oxford University Press).

——(1985), 'Identity and Predication', in *Collected Papers* (Oxford: Oxford University Press).

——and McDowell, J. (eds.) (1976), *Truth and Meaning: Essays in Semantics* (Oxford: Oxford University Press).

Field, H. (1974), 'Quine and the Correspondence Theory', *Philosophical Review*, 85: 200–28.

——(1977), 'Logic, Meaning and Conceptual Role', *Journal of Philosophy*, 74: 347–75.

——(1994), 'Deflationist Views of Meaning and Content', *Mind*, 103: 249–85.

Fogelin, R. (1976), *Wittgenstein* (London: Routledge).

Frege, G. (1964), *The Basic Laws of Arithmetic* (1803–1903), trans. M. Furth (Berkeley, University of California Press).

——(1977), 'Thoughts' (1918), in *Logical Investigations*, ed. P. T. Geach, trans. P. T. Geach and R. Stoothoff (Oxford: Blackwell).

——(1993), 'On Sense and Reference' (1892), in A. Moore (ed.), *Meaning and Reference* (Oxford: Oxford University Press).

Grandy, R. (1973), 'Reference, Meaning and Belief', *Journal of Philosophy*, 70: 439–52.

Grice, H. P. (1957), 'Meaning', *Philosophical Review*, 66: 377–88.

Harman, G. (1974), 'Meaning and Semantics', in M. Munitz, and P. Unger (eds.), *Semantics and Philosophy* (New York: New York University Press).

——(1982), 'Conceptual Role Semantics', *Notre Dame Journal of Formal Logic*, 23: 242–56.

Higginbotham, J. (1991), 'Truth and Understanding', *Iyyun, The Jerusalem Philosophical Quarterly*, 40: 271–88.

Horwich, P. (1990), *Truth* (Oxford: Blackwell).

Johnston, M. (1988), 'The End of the Theory of Meaning', *Mind and Language*, 3: 28–42.

Kaplan, D. (1989), 'Demonstratives', in J. Almog, J. Perry, and H. Wettstein (eds.), *Themes from Kaplan* (New York: Oxford University Press).

Kleene, S. C. (1971), *Introduction to Metamathematics* (Amsterdam: North-Holland).

Kripke, S. (1980), *Naming and Necessity* (Oxford: Blackwell).
——(1982), *Wittgenstein on Rules and Private Language* (Cambridge, Mass.: Harvard University Press).
McDowell, J. (1976), 'Truth Conditions, Bivalence and Verificationism', in J. McDowell, and G. Evans (eds.), *Truth and Meaning: Essays in Semantics* (Oxford: Oxford University Press).
——(1978), 'On "The Reality of the Past"', in C. Hookway, and P. Pettit (eds.), *Action and Interpretation* (Cambridge: Cambridge University Press).
——(1982), 'Criteria, Defeasibility and Knowledge', *Proceedings of the British Academy*, 68: 455–79.
——(1986*a*), 'Functionalism and Anomalous Monism', in E. LePore, and B. McLaughlin (eds.), *Actions and Events: Perspectives on the Philosophy of Donald Davidson* (Oxford: Blackwell).
——(1986*b*), 'Singular Thought and the Extent of Inner Space', in J. McDowell, and P. Pettit (eds.), *Subject, Thought and Context* (Oxford: Oxford University Press).
——(forthcoming), 'Another Plea for Modesty', in his collected papers (Cambridge, Mass.: Harvard University Press).
McGinn, C. (1977), 'Charity, Interpretation and Belief', *Journal of Philosophy*, 74: 521–35.
Millikan, R. (1984), *Language, Thought and Other Biological Categories* (Cambridge, Mass.: MIT Press).
Neale, S. (1990), *Descriptions* (Cambridge, Mass.: MIT Press).
Peacocke, C. (1986*a*), 'Explanation in Computational Psychology: Language, Perception and Level 1.5', *Mind and Language*, 1: 101–23.
——(1986*b*), *Thoughts: An Essay on Content* (Oxford: Blackwell).
——(1992), *A Study of Concepts* (Cambridge, Mass.: MIT Press).
——(1993), 'Proof and Truth', in J. Haldane, and C. Wright (eds.), *Reality: Representation and Projection* (New York: Oxford University Press).
——(1994), 'Content, Computation and Externalism', *Mind and Language*, 9: 303–35.
——(1996), 'Can Possession Conditions Individuate Concepts?', *Philosophy and Phenomenological Research*, 56: 433–60.
——(forthcoming), 'Implicit Conceptions', in E. Villaneuva (ed.), *Philosophical Issues*, ix (Atascadero, Calif.: Ridgeview Publishing).
Platts, M. (1997), *Ways of Meaning: An Introduction to a Philosophy of Language*, 2nd edn. (Cambridge, Mass.).
Putnam, H. (1975), 'The Meaning of "Meaning"', in *Mind, Language and Reality* (Cambridge: Cambridge University Press).
——(1978), *Meaning and the Moral Sciences* (London: Routledge).
Quine, W. V. (1960), *Word and Object* (Cambridge, Mass.: MIT Press).
——(1961), 'Two Dogmas of Empiricism', in *From a Logical Point of View* (Cambridge, Mass.: Harvard University Press).
——(1970), 'Methodological Reflections on Current Linguistic Theory', in D. Davidson, and G. Harman (eds.), *Semantics of Natural Language* (Dordrecht: Reidel).
——(1976), 'Carnap and Logical Truth', in *The Ways of Paradox and Other Essays*, 2nd edn. (Cambridge, Mass.: Harvard University Press).
Salmon, N. (1986), *Frege's Puzzle* (Cambridge, Mass.: MIT Press).

SCHIFFER, S. (1972), *Meaning* (Oxford: Oxford University Press).
——(1986), 'Compositional Semantics and Language Understanding', in R. Grandy, and R. Warner (eds.), *Philosophical Grounds of Rationality: Intentions, Categories, Ends* (Oxford: Oxford University Press).
——(1987), *Remnants of Meaning* (Cambridge, Mass.: MIT Press).
——(1988), 'Reply to Comments', *Mind and Language*, 3: 53–63.
——(1991), 'Does Mentalese Have a Compositional Semantics?', in B. Loewer, and G. Rey (eds.), *Meaning in Mind: Fodor and his Critics* (Oxford: Blackwell).
——(1988), 'Reply to Comments', *Mind and Language* 3: 53–63.
——(forthcoming), 'Meaning and Concepts', *Lingua e Stila*.
SEARLE, J. (1969), *Speech Acts: An Essay in the Philosophy of Language* (Cambridge: Cambridge University Press).
——KIEFER, F., and BIERWISCH, M. (eds.) (1980), *Speech Act Theory and Pragmatics* (Dordrecht: Reidel).
SELLARS, W. (1974), 'Meaning as Functional Classification', *Synthese*, 27: 417–37.
SKORUPSKI, J. (1993), 'Anti-Realism, Inference and the Logical Constants', in J. Haldane, and C. Wright (eds.), *Reality, Representation and Projection* (New York: Oxford University Press).
SOAMES, S. (1984), 'Linguistics and Psychology', *Linguistics and Philosophy*, 7: 155–79.
SPERBER, D., and WILSON, D. (1995), *Relevance: Communication and Cognition* (Oxford: Blackwell).
STICH, S. (1971), 'What Every Speaker Knows', *Philosophical Review*, 80: 476–96.
TARSKI, A. (1983), *Logic, Semantics, Metamathematics: Papers from 1923 to 1938* (Indianapolis: Hackett).
TAYLOR, B. (ed.) (1987), *Michael Dummett: Contributions to Philosophy* (Dordrecht: Nijhoff).
WIGGINS, D. (1991), 'What would be a Substantial Theory of Truth?', in *Needs, Values, Truth*, 2nd edn. (Oxford: Blackwell).
—— (1997), 'Languages as Social Objects', *Philosophy*, 72: 499–524.
WRIGHT, C. (1980), *Wittgenstein on the Foundations of Mathematics* (London: Duckworth).
——(1992), *Truth and Objectivity* (Cambridge, Mass.: Harvard University Press).
——(1993), *Realism, Meaning and Truth* (Oxford: Blackwell).

3

THE PHILOSOPHY OF MATHEMATICS

Michael Dummett

1. WHY IS THERE A PHILOSOPHY OF MATHEMATICS?

Many intellectual disciplines present the philosopher with special problems: there can be a philosophy of biology or of economics. But, from the time of Plato onwards, mathematics has fascinated and challenged philosophers to a quite especial degree. This is due to its unique character. Like philosophy, it appears to be an a priori inquiry; but its methods differ utterly from those of philosophy, as does the definitive character of its results: mathematics makes a steady advance, while philosophy continues to flounder in unending bafflement at the problems it confronted at the outset.

It is this difference between the two subjects that dictates the difference between a study-guide to a branch of the one and a study-guide to a branch of the other. A study-guide to a branch of mathematics will be concerned to convey information about a bit of mathematics. Different authors may choose a different bit of mathematics, or present the same bit in a different way: but all will agree that their aim is to instruct their readers in certain *truths*. A study-guide to a branch of philosophy has no business to attempt any such thing: its aim is to help the readers to arrive at their own conclusions about the truth of the matter. It may instruct them about the views that writers on the subject have taken, the arguments they have advanced, the distinctions they have drawn, and the theorems they have proved: but it ought not to attempt to persuade the readers of the truth of any answer to a philosophical question. For this reason, I will strive to eschew any such attempt. This study-guide will not endorse any philosophical conclusion or pronounce on the validity of any philosophical argument: its purpose is to set you, the reader, on the road to evaluating such arguments and such conclusions.

1.1. What Does One Need in order to Study the Philosophy of Mathematics?

The philosophy of mathematics is a specialized area of philosophy, but not *merely* a specialized area. Many of the questions that arise within it, though by no means all, are particular cases of more general questions that arise elsewhere in philosophy, and occur within the philosophy of mathematics in an especially pure, or especially simplified, form. In an important respect, the subject resembles the philosophy of time. One would hardly attempt to tackle the philosophy of biology without a working knowledge of biology, or the philosophy of economics without a working knowledge of economics. In the same way, it is rash to tackle the philosophy of mathematics unless one has some grounding in mathematics, just as one cannot undertake any full study of the philosophy of time unless one understands how time is handled in the theories of the physicists. In the case of mathematics, there is an additional prerequisite: one ought to have a reasonable knowledge of mathematical logic also, not so much as part of the object of study as serving as a tool of inquiry. Yet some questions that arise in the philosophy of mathematics *can* be fruitfully thought about by one who knows very little mathematics at all, or mathematical logic either, just as holds good for some philosophical problems concerning time. For all that, it is safer to approach such a question with some background of knowledge, even if only to be able to reassure oneself that technical knowledge is not relevant to it, and will not vitiate conclusions arrived at without appeal to it.

If you have little knowledge of mathematical logic, you would be strongly advised to acquire some, because it is relevant to much more than the philosophy of mathematics. But, if you have little knowledge of mathematics, you do not need to remedy that defect before interesting yourself in the philosophy of mathematics. It might be temerarious for you to publish papers on the subject before acquiring greater knowledge of mathematics; but you can very well understand a good deal of the debates on the subject and a good deal of the theories advanced concerning it without an extensive knowledge of its subject-matter. Some acquaintance with the philosophy of mathematics is an essential part of a philosophical education, as acquaintance with the philosophy of economics is not. Of what value, for instance, would anyone's opinions about necessity be if he could say nothing about the necessity of mathematical truths?

1.2. The Fundamental Questions of the Philosophy of Mathematics

The prime question in the philosophy of mathematics therefore concerns the status of the subject. This splits into four subquestions. (1) How do we know that our mathematical theories are true? (2) What is mathematics about? In other words, if a mathematical statement is true, what makes it true? In virtue of what is it true? (3) Are mathematical truths true by necessity, and, if so, what is the source of this necessity? Our answers to these questions can be satisfactory only if they succeed, at the same time, in answering another: (4) how is it possible to *apply* mathematical truths to external reality, and in what does this application consist? It is not, of course, that philosophers of mathematics set about answering these questions separately, one after another. Most usually, they put forward comprehensive theories of the nature of mathematics, which, if correct, will provide answers to all of them.

2. MATHEMATICAL NECESSITY

Most philosophers have considered mathematical truths to be in some sense necessary, at least in the sense that they can be known a priori, that is, in advance of any particular observation of the world. We do not normally consider that the laws of physics *have* to hold; it is just that the universe is such that they do. But consider a fundamental theorem of number theory, that any positive integer can be represented as a product of prime factors in only one way (ignoring the order of the factors). Those who know some mathematics will be aware of domains for the elements of which the unique factorization theorem fails; but it goes against the grain to say that we merely happen to live in a universe in which the theorem holds good *of the positive integers*, and might have lived in one in which *they* could be factorized in two or more essentially different ways. Why? It is not a good answer to say that we cannot imagine a universe in which the theorem was false of the positive integers: there are probably many things that we cannot succeed in imagining which might nevertheless have been so. It goes against the grain because the proposition is a *theorem*, which is to say that it has been proved by rigorous deductive argument. Unless we challenge the principles of reasoning in accordance with which the proof proceeds, we can challenge the conclusion only if we challenge the premisses. The ultimate premisses of the proof are the axioms of number theory. These have not been proved, which is why they are called 'axioms' and not 'theorems'. More exactly, they have not been proved *within number theory*, which starts from them. They can be, and have been, proved in a more general theory thought to embrace number theory; but to invoke such proofs is to tread on dangerous, that is, debatable, ground. But it still goes against the grain to suggest that we happen to live in a universe in which these axioms hold. They do not look like the sort of thing that we could discover was not true; nor do they look like the sort of thing whose truth we have discovered by observing the world about us. They look more like principles that embody what we *mean* by 'number', where the word is used to apply to the *natural* numbers (the whole numbers 0, 1, 2, 3, and so on). This, of course, is not yet an argument, or even a philosophical position: it is merely an expression of our original reluctance to think that a mathematical theorem might have been false if the world were different from the way we find it.

2.1. The Empiricism of John Stuart Mill

Some philosophers have nevertheless maintained that mathematical truths are what we normally take the truths of natural science to be, propositions that register general facts about the world—about how the world happens to be. The most famous of these was John Stuart Mill (1806–73), whose views on the subject are to be found in his *A System of Logic* of 1843 (book II, chapters iv–vii). According to him, mathematics differs from other sciences only in its much greater generality: it is concerned with properties of the physical universe even more general than those investigated by physics.

Mill's 'empiricist' philosophy of mathematics is not dead even yet: there are still philosophers of mathematics who maintain that mathematics is a science like any other. Yet its most striking feature is how *different* it is from other science. Even if all of Mill's views on the matter are accepted, it remains outstandingly different from them. For Mill does not maintain more than that the fundamental concepts of mathematics, such as number, are derived from our perception of external objects, and that the basic principles governing them are generalizations from observed facts involving them: he does not attempt to deny that mathematical theorems are arrived at by deductive reasoning from these first principles. No natural science has this character. It may begin by accepting as its basic concepts those gained from gross observation, and as its first principles governing them generalizations from such observation; but it rapidly refines its concepts and makes more exact observations. It proceeds to construct a theory, as precise as can be achieved, and may then make complex deductions from it; but the scientific purpose of doing so is to arrive at results testable by further observation, whose refutation by such means will demand a revision of the theory. The purpose of deductive argument in mathematics is, by contrast, to establish the truth of the conclusions so reached: they do not normally stand in need of testing by observation to discover if they agree with reality. The empiricist philosophy appears unable to account for the salience of *proof* in mathematics.

It is true, as Imre Lakatos has illustrated in his *Proofs and Refutations*, that a convincing counter-example to a purported theorem may prompt a revision of the first principles of a theory, or, more frequently, the reformulation of a definition; but there is a prominent difference between the mathematical theory and the scientific one. In the mathematical case, it is sufficient, as Wittgenstein observed, that the counter-example be merely conceived or described, whereas a counter-example to an empirical theory must be warranted actually to exist if it is to have any force. This is because the mere *possibility* of a counter-example is enough to refute a mathematical proposition; and what can be refuted by something's merely being possible is what claims, not just to be true as a matter of fact, but to be true of necessity.

2.2. Kant and A Priori Intuition

More than sixty years before Mill wrote, Immanuel Kant (1724–1804), in his *Critique of Pure Reason* of 1781, perhaps the most famous work of philosophy since Aristotle, assigned to mathematical propositions a status intermediate between the empirical and the purely logical. He proposed two different dichotomies for classifying correct judgements, or, as we might prefer to say, true propositions. They could be classified as analytic or synthetic; they could also be classified as made (if judgements) or as knowable (if propositions) a priori or a posteriori. Analytic propositions are those the denial of which leads to contradiction; they are thus sustained by logic alone. Kant conceived of these as having a very restricted form, namely that in which a concept expressed by a predicate is 'contained' in one expressed by the subject; an example would be 'All roses are flowers', because being a flower is part of the concept of being a rose. Analytic propositions are, in Kant's view, trivial, and tell us nothing of substance; analytic judgements do not extend our knowledge. All other propositions are synthetic: their denial will not lead to self-contradiction, and hence to acknowledge them as true is to recognize something factual that genuinely characterizes the world.

A judgement is made a posteriori, or a proposition known a posteriori, if it is made or known on the basis of experience, that is, of observation by means of the senses. A judgement is made, or a proposition known, a priori if it is, or can be, made or known in advance of all experience, or, better, independently of all experience. All analytic judgements are a priori, since they require no experiential basis: they can be recognized as correct by anyone who grasps the concepts, whatever experiences he has or has not had. But not all a priori judgements are analytic: there is also the synthetic a priori. It is to this class, according to Kant, that mathematical judgements belong.

Synthetic a priori judgements are based on what Kant calls pure or a priori intuition. The word 'intuition', in translations of Kant and other German philosophers, does not have its everyday English meaning of 'inspired guess'. It denotes an apprehension of a particular object, or system of objects, by sensory perception or sensory imagination. The notion of an a priori intuition is a very difficult one. Kant thought that we conceive of space, and, equally, of time, as a single all-embracing entity. What makes it possible for us to have an a priori intuition of space and an a priori intuition of time is that we do not merely happen to find ourselves in a universe in which objects are disposed in three-dimensional space and in which they change from one time to another, as if the universe might have been different in either respect. On the contrary, our apprehending things as in space and time is a condition for our apprehending them at all: it is a pre-condition of our having any experience; space and time may accordingly be called *forms* of intuition. We can therefore conceive of space and of time in advance of any particular experience, that is, a priori. What can be grasped as essentially involved in these a priori intuitions of space and time can be known a priori, though it is not analytic, but synthetic: its denial would not result in contradiction, but it would not yield anything we should be capable of imagining, and could be recognized to be incorrect without any investigation of the world as we find it.

In Kant's day, and for long afterwards, mathematics was conventionally characterized as the science of space and of quantity, and accordingly divided into geometry and arithmetic. Kant thought that geometry was founded upon our a priori intuition of space, and arithmetic upon our a priori intuition of time. The truths of both branches of mathematics were therefore, for him, neither analytic nor a posteriori, but synthetic a priori. Time might be thought to enter arithmetic, in the broad sense of 'arithmetic', with the differential calculus, normally introduced by considering rates of change; it remains far less obvious that arithmetic has to do with time than that geometry has to do with space. Indeed, through the geometrical representation of functions of real numbers, originally introduced by Descartes, it was commonplace to think of basic principles of analysis (the theory of real numbers) as resting upon geometrical intuition. In discussing arithmetic, however, Kant confined himself to number theory, that is, the theory of the natural numbers. Indeed, he did not discuss any theorems of number theory, such as the prime factorization theorem mentioned above, but only elementary numerical equations such as '$7+5=12$'. How does time enter number theory? Kant's idea was that the very notion of the totality of positive integers exemplifies the more general notion of a *sequence*: the positive integers are just those elements that can be arrived at by starting with the number 1 and successively adding 1. Few would contest this today, save for preferring to speak of the totality of *natural numbers*, the sequence of which starts with 0 rather than with 1. What is done successively is done in time: first 1 is added to 0 to form the number 1, then 1 is added to it to form the number 2, and so on, each after the preceding one. It was thus exceedingly natural for Kant to believe that the notion of a sequence is essentially temporal; we cannot conceive of a sequence without thinking of it as generated in time. Since the notion of a sequence is integral to that of a positive integer (or of a natural number), even number theory rests upon our a priori intuition of time.

The detail of Kant's theory of a priori intuitions is inessential save for those wishing to espouse or defend it in detail. The important components of his philosophy of mathematics are that our knowledge of mathematical truths does not depend on any observations of what the world happens to be like, but can be attained independently of any such observations or of any awareness of contingent empirical facts; and that such truths are not purely logical in nature, but depend on the general character, known to us a priori, of space and time.

2.3. The Extrusion of Intuition from Arithmetic

Kant's influence on most philosophers was enormous; for many decades, even those who disagreed with him were constrained to express themselves in his terms. But the mathematicians for the most part swam in the opposite direction. The nineteenth century saw a sustained effort on their part to introduce rigour into analysis, that is, the theory of real numbers, rational like $\frac{1}{3}$ or irrational like $\sqrt{2}$ or π. This was desperately needed, owing to the antinomies generated by the preceding century's attempts to found the calculus upon the notion of infinitesimals (infinitely small numbers distinct from 0); but a motive of almost equal strength was to render analysis independent of geometrical notions. This was usually described as freeing it from any appeal to intuition. The earliest to undertake this endeavour was the great Czech mathematician and philosopher Bernard Bolzano (1781–1848). As a philosopher, he was exceptional in being little influenced, indeed little impressed, by Kant. As a mathematician, he was determined to expel intuition from analysis, and to prove from first principles anything that could be proved, no matter how obvious it might seem when thought of in geometrical terms. One reason for this was that what seems obvious may not even be true. If we think of a function continuous throughout an interval (including the end-points) as being represented by a curve on graph paper, it seems obvious that, in the given interval, any such curve must have a determinate slope at all but finitely many points; when, for example, the curve is made up of two straight-line segments at different angles, it will have no slope at the point at which the two lines meet. Bolzano, however, produced the first example of a function continuous throughout an interval but not differentiable at *any* point in that interval. Geometrically expressed, this would be represented by a continuous curve which *nowhere* had a determinate slope; naturally, one cannot draw it, but only a sequence of ever closer approximations to it. (Bolzano's construction was not published; a similar example was published by Weierstrass twenty-three years after Bolzano's death.) Even when what seems obvious is in fact true, however, it remains necessary, on Bolzano's view, to prove it, and to do so without invoking extraneous ideas of space or time: mathematics is concerned, not merely to establish truths, but to determine which truths rest on which others. Thus it is obvious 'to intuition' that, if a continuous curve lies at the beginning of an interval below the x-axis and lies, at the end of the interval, above the x-axis, it must, at some point within the interval, have crossed the x-axis. In purely arithmetical terms this becomes the intermediate value theorem, to the effect that if a continuous function has a negative value at the beginning of an interval and a positive value at the end of the interval, it must have the value 0 somewhere within the interval. In 1817 Bolzano published an attempted proof of this theorem, which, though not without a gap, contributed notably to the programme of freeing analysis from reliance on spatial intuition. In his paper he wrote, 'the concepts of *time* and *motion* are just as alien to general mathematics as the concept of *space*'.

One method of attaining the desired rigour in the theory of real numbers is one that has become salient within mathematics: the axiomatic method. In this case, it would consist in isolating the fundamental features of the system of real numbers, on which all known proofs of theorems about them can be made to rest, much as Euclid did in formulating his axioms and postulates for geometry. These fundamental features can then be assumed as axioms, all that we desire to prove about the real numbers being constrained to be derived from them. A deeper approach is to seek to prove the fundamental principles themselves. To achieve this, it is necessary to attain a precise formulation of what real numbers are: to 'construct' them, as the expression is, from more basic mathematical entities by means of notions assumed to be able to be given in advance.

Since there may be, and indeed certainly are, different methods of constructing the real numbers, the two methods are better represented as complementary rather than as rivals. The axiomatic method shows us what features a system of mathematical entities must have to qualify as a construction of the real numbers; carrying out such a construction guarantees that we do not need to *assume* the existence of a system satisfying the axioms, and so obviates the need for justifying any such assumption.

The two best-known means of constructing the real numbers are those of Georg Cantor (1845–1918), who improved on an earlier construction by Karl Weierstrass (1815–97), and of Richard Dedekind (1831–1916); both were professional mathematicians, although Cantor undertook a good deal of philosophical writing to explain and defend his work on transfinite (infinitely large) numbers. Dedekind, by contrast, made philosophical observations only in passing, from which can be derived no more than a sketchy philosophical position concerning mathematics. He was a staunch supporter of the view that mathematics—or at least its non-geometrical part—relies only on logical notions, and that to appeal to spatial or temporal intuition is to smuggle into it ideas alien to it. Thus at the beginning of the celebrated short treatise of 1872, *Continuity and Irrational Numbers*, in which he propounded his method of constructing the real numbers, he first spoke of the system of real numbers as forming 'a domain of one dimension extending to infinity on two opposite sides', remarking immediately upon his 'use of expressions borrowed from geometrical ideas', and then insisted on the necessity of 'bringing out clearly the corresponding purely arithmetical properties in order to avoid even the appearance that arithmetic is in need of ideas alien to it'.

It is worth while to explain Dedekind's famous construction, in order to give an idea of what a construction of a mathematical system consists in. (In this essay, a set of mathematical objects, with some functions and relations defined upon it, normally known as a 'structure', will be called a 'system', in order to reserve the word 'structure' for the more abstract feature that two systems may have in common.) Dedekind assumes that he may take the rational numbers, comprising integers and fractions of integers such as $\frac{3}{8}$, as given. His construction of the real numbers starts from the thought that an irrational number has a determinate position with respect to the rationals: every rational number is either smaller than or greater than it. He then consider a 'cut' in the rationals. A cut is a partition of all the rationals into two classes, a lower class and an upper class, such that neither class is empty, every rational belongs to one and only one of the classes, a rational number smaller than any given member of the lower class also belongs to the lower class, and one greater than any given member of the upper class also belongs to the upper class. It is of importance that Dedekind considered the notion of a class to be a logical one. One such cut is that which divides the rationals into all those less than or equal to $\frac{8}{5}$ (the lower class) and all those greater than $\frac{8}{5}$ (the upper class). Another is that which divides them into those whose square is less than 2 (the lower class) and those whose square is greater than 2 (the upper class): none is left out, since there is no rational number whose square is 2. It is apparent that a cut must be of one of three types: (1) the lower class has a greatest element, but the upper class has no least element (our first example was of this type); (2) the upper class has a least element, but the lower class has no greatest element; and (3) the lower class has no greatest element, and the upper class has no least element (our second example was an instance of this type).

Although Dedekind believed that arithmetic had no need to call in aid any but logical notions, he did not think that logic by itself would yield arithmetic. He thought, rather, that mathematical objects and structures are 'free creations of the human mind': some creative intellectual activity is needed to arrive at them. This, then, must be shown to play a part in the construction of the real numbers. Hence, having characterized the notion of a cut in the rational 'line' (an unnecessary geometrical metaphor), he says that we can now *create* numbers corresponding to every cut: these are the real numbers. Some will match already existing rational numbers, as with the first of our two examples; others, such as the second of our examples, will not. Frege and Russell both criticized Dedekind heavily for appealing at this point to an act of intellectual creation. Russell took the trouble, which Frege did not, to point out that it was quite unnecessary. Let us first consider only cuts in which the upper class has no least element (this eliminates cuts of the superfluous type 2). We then have no need to create any new numbers corresponding to the cuts: we can, instead, *identify* the real numbers with the cuts, or, even more simply, with, say, the upper classes of such cuts.

3. THE BIRTH OF MODERN LOGIC

Bolzano and his successors had been concerned to expel appeals to intuition from analysis (the theory of real numbers). Kant, however, had argued that such an appeal was integral even to number theory (the theory of natural numbers). The task of extruding intuition from this more basic branch of mathematics was undertaken by Gottlob Frege (1848–1925).

Frege was not a professional philosopher, but a professor of mathematics; yet he has had a profound influence upon modern analytic philosophy. He was the first person in history to devote virtually all his endeavours to logic, both in its formal and in its philosophical aspects, and to the philosophy of mathematics. From very early in his career, he set himself to accomplish a single large task: to devise a definitive foundation for arithmetic (number theory and analysis).

How can it be shown that no appeals to intuition are required for number-theoretic proofs? One requirement is to demonstrate that essential concepts can be defined by purely logical means. The other is to carry out proofs in number theory in such a manner as to preclude any appeals to intuition. That is possible by formalizing the reasoning. In the ordinary informal reasoning in which mathematicians engage, steps—sometimes quite large steps—are taken if they strike us as cogent. There is then a twofold danger. The apparent cogency of a step may be due to some merely intuitive necessity our appeal to which we do not consciously notice: we mistake what in fact relies on intuition for a purely logical argument. But we may make the converse mistake also, believing that we have appealed to intuition when in fact the inferential step we have taken is an uncontaminated instance of logical deduction.

Frege's means of avoiding these twin dangers was to formalize mathematical reasoning. What was needed, first, was a formal language, and then a formal characterization of the only inferential steps to be allowed in a proof carried out in the formal language. The sentences of such a formal language must, for convenience, be composed of symbols, like a mathematical equation, rather than of words. It will have a determinate list of primitive symbols, and precise rules whereby sentences can be formed by putting together these primitive symbols; all its sentences will be built out of the primitive symbols and of other symbols defined in terms of them, so that each sentence could in principle be rewritten in primitive symbols alone. Formal proofs will then be characterized by listing some initial axioms, and by equally precise descriptions, in terms solely of the forms of the sentences, of the allowable inferential transitions by which one sentence can be derived from one or more others. The symbols, and hence the sentences, of such of formal language will have meanings that must be explained; but to check whether a putative formal proof conforms to the rules laid down is a purely mechanical process, which could be carried out without knowing the meanings of any of the sentences making up the lines of the proof. If a formal proof is validated as correct when so checked, we can be certain that the derivation of its conclusion owes nothing to any surreptitious appeal to intuition or any other principle not explicitly stated.

This is what is known as a *formal system*. Frege was the first person ever to have conceived of such a thing and to have devised one. Formal systems play a salient part in modern mathematical logic as objects of study; but Frege intended the formal system he created, not for study, but for use in carrying out proofs of mathematical theorems guaranteed to be without gaps and free of appeals to intuition. The vocabulary and axioms of formal systems may differ according to the mathematical (or scientific) theory being formalized; but the formalization of deductive proof can be common to all, since all employ only logical reasoning. Frege's first task was therefore to formalize logical inference, at least as it occurs in mathematical proofs.

This he did in his first book, published in 1879: a little book, full of unfamiliar symbols, called *Begriffsschrift*, whose title means literally 'Concept-Script'. Frege's *Begriffsschrift* was the first work of modern mathematical logic. Before him, a number of people had been attempting to develop a more systematic theory of logical deduction, in analogy with mathematical theories. The earliest had been George Boole (1815–64); the influential German representative of the school was Ernst Schröder (1841–1902). Frege's formalization of logic owed nothing to the work of these predecessors, and differed from it in two ways. As he repeatedly pointed out, their symbolism at best allowed a particular piece of reasoning to be encoded *ad hoc*, whereas his was a *language*; to express in it statements of any mathematical theory, such as number theory or Euclidean geometry, the most that would be needed would be some additional vocabulary. The structure was already provided, and proofs would then be carried out in accordance with the rules of the logical system.

Secondly, the range of deductive inferences falling in the scope of Frege's logic was immensely wider, covering all that occur in mathematical reasoning. Such reasoning could not be reduced to Aristotelian syllogisms, and Boole and his followers had advanced only a short way beyond that. Frege was able to go far further because he hit on the method by which generality (the notions expressed in natural language by 'everything', 'some', 'there are', and so on) is expressed in modern logic, namely by quantifiers and bound variables. His logical theory in fact comprehended all that is covered by standard modern logical systems; it included a complete formalization of what is known as first-order logic.

By this means, and with this motive, Frege invented modern mathematical logic. The language of mathematical theories lacks a number of features possessed by natural language. It lacks tense, because what holds good in the mathematical realm holds good timelessly. It lacks modality—auxiliary verbs such as 'must', 'may', 'can', and 'might' and adverbs such as 'necessarily' and 'possibly': a mathematical proof need be concerned only with what *is* so, rather than with what may be so, and requires no distinction between what could not be otherwise and what merely happens to be so. Mathematical language is devoid of such verbs as 'believe', 'know', 'wonder', and so on: the states of mind of individuals is not part of the subject-matter of mathematics. It is also devoid of vague expressions, which abound in natural language: mathematicians aim at making the terms they employ absolutely precise. The logic invented by Frege and inherited by logicians after him was incapable of handling these pervasive features of language in general: he invented it to attain an absolutely trustworthy instrument for carrying out mathematical proofs. In more modern times, philosophically minded logicians have sought to extend the scope of formal logic to handle these features of natural language, regrettably with less clear-cut success than Frege's systematization of the logic of mathematics; mathematically minded logicians have preferred to conduct ever more sophisticated investigations of formal theories of mathematics.

3.1. The Completeness of First-Order Logic

First-order logic is distinguished by the fact that it involves generalization (quantification) only over *objects*: second-order logic admits generalization or quantification over *properties* or *kinds* of objects, and over *relations* between them and *functions* defined over them. If I say to someone 'You have something of mine', I am using the word 'something' to generalize over *objects*: I mean that he has some object—a tape recorder, for example—that belongs to me. Suppose, by contrast, that I say to him 'You are something that I am not'; he asks 'What?' and I reply 'An accomplished linguist'. In this case, I was using the word 'something' to generalize over *kinds* of thing or person: I meant that there was something true of him that was not true of me. Likewise, if I say 'You are to her something that I am not', I am using the word 'something' to generalize over *relations*: asked 'What?', I might reply 'A cousin'. A mixed case arises when one person says to another 'You own something that we do not', when the answer to the question 'What?' might be 'A compact disc player'. The statement meant 'You own an object of a certain kind, and we own no object of that kind'. First-order logic concerns those principles of inference that involve only generalization over objects; second-order logic concerns also those principles of inference that involve generalization over properties of, relations between, and functions of objects.

A formalized theory will treat certain entities as its basic objects: for instance, a formal theory of elementary arithmetic will treat the natural numbers as its objects. If it is a first-order theory, only quantification over the natural numbers will be expressible in the formal language: it will be capable of saying things to the effect that all natural numbers have a certain property or that there are some natural numbers that have some other property. It is only in a second-order theory that it will be possible to say that a number has every property satisfying a certain condition, or that it stands to a certain other number in some relation of which some condition holds good, or that there is a function which maps every natural number on to just the numbers of a certain specific kind. Frege made no sharp distinction between first- and second-order logic, and regarded both as equally part of *logic*: the last of the three parts of his *Begriffsschrift* contains far-reaching investigations of second-order logic. Since his day, it has become customary to make a sharp distinction between the stronger and the weaker varieties of logic: so sharp a distinction, indeed, that some question the right of second-order logic to be considered as logic at all.

The reason for this lies in the remark made above, when it was said that Frege's *Begriffsschrift* included a complete formalization of first-order logic. To say that it was complete means that every valid first-order logical inference could be carried out in Frege's formal system; but, to prove that, we need an independent characterization of valid inferences. In view of the way Frege carried out the formalization, a method followed by all subsequent logicians such as David Hilbert (1862–1943) and Bertrand Russell (1872–1970) until Gerhard Gentzen (1909–45), it is sufficient to characterize a valid single formula: but we still need a means of characterizing this otherwise than by appeal to the formalization. Now first-order logic requires the use of *schematic letters*, that is, letters which stand proxy for any actual expression of a given logical type. Standardly, there will be sentence-letters, representing whole sentences, individual constants, representing singular terms, one-place predicate-letters, representing predicates, and two- or more-place predicate-letters, representing relational expressions. A simple law of (classical) first-order logic may then be stated in words as 'Everything either is *F* or is not *F*', in symbols:

$$\forall x\,(Fx \vee \neg Fx).$$

One involving relations is 'If there is something to which everything is *R*, then everything is *R* to something', in symbols:

$$\exists x\,\forall y\,yRx \rightarrow \forall y\,\exists x\,yRx.$$

In the first case '*F*' is a schematic one-place predicate-letter, and in the second '*R*' is a schematic two-place predicate-letter. The validity of the two formulas consists in the fact that, whatever predicate is put in place of '*F*' and whatever two-place relational expression is put in place of '*R*', a true sentence results.

A valid formula is one that is true under every interpretation of its schematic letters; but we shall do well not to define 'interpretation' in terms of substitution by the expressions of any actual language, which might be defective in some crucial way. Rather, the standard notion of an interpretation of a first-order formula is that of one arrived at as follows. First, some non-empty set is specified as the domain over which the individual variables range. Then to each individual constant is assigned some element of that domain, and it is laid down, for each one-place predicate-letter, of which elements it is to be true (under the interpretation); for each two-place predicate-letter it is laid down between which elements it is to hold, and similarly for three- or more-place predicate-letters; and finally, to each unary function-letter is assigned a unary function over the domain (with values in the domain), to each binary function-letter a binary function over the domain, and so on. If the formula contains sentence-letters, truth-values (*true* or *false*) are assigned to them. (Normally, the assignment to a one-place predicate-letter is specified by laying down the subset of the domain consisting of the elements of which it is to be true, that to a two-place predicate-letter the set of pairs of elements between which it is to hold, and so on.) In an obvious way, it is determined whether or not the given formula is true under an interpretation so specified. The formula will be valid if it is true under *every* such interpretation. Likewise, an inference is valid if its conclusion is true under every interpretation under which its premisses are true.

A second-order formula need contain no schematic letters: in this case, an interpretation is specified simply by laying down the domain of the individual variables. The one-place predicate-variables are then normally understood as ranging over *all* properties of elements of the domain (where a property is determined by the set of elements that have it), the two-place predicate-variables as ranging over *all* binary relations between elements, the unary function-variables as ranging over *all* unary functions on those elements, and so on.

We have now arrived at a twofold means of characterizing the intuitive conceptions of a logically true statement and of a correct inference. On the one side is the *proof-theoretic* or *syntactic* characterization, which relies on a formalization of the relevant part of logic: a formula is provable if that formalization admits a proof of it, and the conclusion of an inference is derivable from the premisses if the formalization admits of its derivation from them. On the other side is the *model-theoretic* or *semantic* characterization: a formula is valid if it comes out true under every interpretation and a schematic inference is sound if its conclusion comes out true under every interpretation under which its premisses come out true. This distinction is fundamental. It is one of the basic achievements of modern logic to have drawn it clearly; even Frege, the founder of modern logic, did not have a sharp formulation of it.

The semantic notion stands in judgement on any attempted formulation of the syntactic notion. A formalization of some part of logic, such as first-order logic, is *sound* if every formula provable in it is valid. If it is not sound in this sense, it is plainly erroneous. Given that it is sound, we should prefer that it also be *complete*. It will be complete if every valid formula expressible in its language (e.g. in first-order language) is provable. The completeness of the standard formalizations of first-order logic, including Frege's original one, was first proved by Kurt Gödel (1906–78) in 1930. It is, however, a consequence of his famous theorem on the incompleteness of arithmetic, published in the following year, that second-order logic is incomplete. It is not accidentally incomplete, owing to the omission of one or more necessary principles: it is *essentially* incomplete, in that no complete formalization of it is possible. It is this fact that motivates the strong distinction now customarily drawn between first- and second-order logic.

It is important not to confuse the notion of the completeness of a formalization of a part of logic and that of the completeness of a formalized mathematical theory. Such a theory will have primitive expressions, special to the subject-matter of the particular theory, and axioms, from which the theorems are to be derived in accordance with a formalization of the relevant part of logic. Of a formal theory, we require in the first instance that it be *consistent*: that is, that there be no sentence provable in the theory whose negation is also provable, or, equivalently and more simply, that there be at least one sentence expressed in the language of the theory that is not provable in it. The completeness of a formalization of logic consisted in the coextensiveness of the proof-theoretic notion of provability with the model-theoretic notion of validity. But the completeness of a formal theory is a purely proof-theoretic property: it consists in the fact that, for any sentence expressed in the language of the theory, either it or its negation is provable. Model-theoretic notions can of course be defined for formal theories. To do so, we simply treat the primitive expressions of the theory, which of course have intended interpretations, as if they were schematic letters. A *model* of the theory is then an interpretation (which may be a quite unintended one) under which all its axioms come out true. The model-theoretic notion corresponding to completeness is then that of being *categorical*. A theory is categorical if it has essentially only one model; more exactly, if all its models are isomorphic (or, in mathematicians' jargon, if it has only one model up to isomorphism). A model of a theory consists in a set of objects (the domain), together with particular elements, properties, relations, and functions defined on that set which constitute the interpretations of the terms, predicates, and function-symbols of the theory: it is required that the axioms, and hence the theorems, of the theory come out true in the model. Two models are said to be isomorphic if they have exactly the same abstract structure. More formally, they are isomorphic if there is a mapping ϕ of the domain of one on to the domain of the other which is one–one (it carries distinct elements on to distinct elements) and carries each property, relation, etc., of the one into the corresponding property or relation, etc., of the other. Here a relation R is said to be carried by ϕ into that relation which holds between $\phi(x)$ and $\phi(y)$ iff xRy, and a function f into the function which maps $\phi(x)$ on to $\phi(fx)$. To take a trivial example, suppose we have a formal theory intended to apply to the truth-values T and F; its primitive are τ, intended to denote T, Ω, intended to stand for the relation that T and F have to each other, and a binary operator (function-symbol) &, intended to represent the function defined by the truth-table for conjunction. Another model for such a theory could take the domain as consisting of the numbers 1 and 0, τ as standing for 1, Ω as standing for the relation that 1 and 0 have to each other, and & as denoting multiplication. Then, under the mapping ϕ which takes T on to 1 and F on to 0, ϕ carries T to 1 and the relation of distinctness between truth-values into the relation of distinctness between 1 and 0, while $\phi(u \,\&\, v) = \phi(u) \times \phi(v)$, so that ϕ carries conjunction into multiplication. Thus the intended model is isomorphic to the one whose elements are 1 and 0: they are structurally indistinguishable.

3.2. Induction

How is elementary number theory to be axiomatized? Despite the repeated praise for Euclid's axiomatization of geometry, the idea of axiomatizing arithmetic does not appear to have occurred to anyone before the nineteenth century. Fundamental to the means of doing so is the principle of induction (more specifically, of finite induction), which first became prominent in the seventeenth century. The principle of induction is a method of proving a proposition to hold of every natural number. It consists in first showing the proposition to hold of 0 (the *induction basis*) and then showing that, if it holds of any number k, it must hold also for $k+1$ (the *induction step*). (Since it holds for 0, it must hold for 1; it must therefore hold also for 2, and, by repetition of the argument, for each natural number.) It may be illustrated by proving, by this means, the well-known formula

$$0 + 1 + \ldots + n = n(n+1)/2.$$

When n is put equal to 0, this reduces to

$$0 = (0 \times 1)/2,$$

which is obvious; so the induction basis is easy. Now assume that, for a given number k, the formula holds, so that we have

$$0 + 1 + \ldots + k = k(k+1)/2$$

(the *induction hypothesis*). We wish to show that, on this assumption, the formula will hold good for $n = k+1$. We then have

$$\begin{aligned} 0 + 1 + \ldots + (k+1) &= k(k+1)/2 + (k+1) \\ &= (k+1)(k/2 + 1) \\ &= (k+1)(k+2)/2 \end{aligned}$$

and so the induction step is taken, and the formula thereby proved to hold for all natural numbers.

The principle of induction is not important only as a means of proving statements about all natural numbers: it is important also as serving to say what the natural numbers are. The natural numbers form an infinite sequence—the prototype of the simplest kind of infinite sequence. They are therefore most easily characterized as the terms of such a sequence, the sequence starting with 0 and proceeding, from any term, to its successor (the number one greater than it). How is this characterization to be embodied in a definition? One way is to give a definition with more than one clause, thus:

(1) 0 is a natural number.
(2) The sucessor of any natural number is a natual number.

It may be objected that, while these two clauses enable us to show, of any natural number, that it *is* a natural number, it does not tell us that these are all the natural numbers that there are, or enable us to show, of anything that is not a natural number, that it is not one. Head-on methods of rectifying this deficiency consist in adding a third clause:

(3) Nothing else is a natural number.

or

(3*) Nothing is a natural number unless it follows from clauses (1) and (2) that it is one.

What we have now is what is called an *inductive definition*. Such a 'definition' does not really allow us to do what a definition is supposed to enable us in principle to do, namely to eliminate the defined term, wherever it occurs, by replacing it by the equivalent expression by means of which it has been defined. One of Frege's great discoveries, set out in part III of his *Begriffsschrift*, was how to overcome this difficulty.

Frege's problem was to give a purely logical characterization of a sequence. We saw that Kant considered that the notion of a sequence essentially involves that of time: starting from the initial term, 0 in the case of the natural numbers, we take successive steps from each term to the next, and this can be conceived, Kant thought, only as a temporal process. Frege, however, made use of the principle of induction, and generalized it. Suppose, first, that we want to express the fact that *n* can be reached from *m* by a finite number of steps (0 or more), each going from a number to its successor; the fact, in Frege's terminology, that *n* belongs to the successor-sequence beginning with *m*. First we need the notion of a property's being *hereditary in the successor-sequence*. A property *F* satisfies this condition if the successor of anything that has the property *F* always also has the property *F*. We may then express the fact in question by saying that

> n has every property possessed by m and hereditary in the successor-sequence.

We can then, by specialization, define 'n is a natural number' to mean

> n belongs to the successor-sequence beginning with 0,

that is,

> n has every property possessed by 0 and hereditary in the successor-sequence.

Conversely, we can generalize from the successor relation to any other relation R: a property F may be said to be hereditary in the R-sequence if any object must have the property F if an object having the property F stands in the relation R to it. Then

> y has every property possessed by x and hereditary in the R-sequence

expresses the proposition that y is a term of any sequence whose initial term is x and in which each term is followed by one to which it stands in the relation R. Frege was immensely proud of this definition, which is of course a second-order one, involving as it does quantification over properties. On the one hand, it captured the notion of a sequence by purely logical means, without appeal to temporal or spatial intuition, and provided a basis for proving general propositions concerning sequences, again without recourse to intuition: it was thus a signal victory in the campaign to expel intuition from arithmetic. On the other hand, it made possible a definition of 'natural number' by incorporating the principle of induction into that definition, and thereby falsified the widespread opinion that induction was a method of argument peculiar to number theory.

By far the best-known set of axioms for elementary number theory is that called 'the Peano axioms', having been first published by Giuseppe Peano (1858–1932), although originally formulated by Dedekind. These take as primitive the predicate 'nat(x)', meaning 'x is a natural number', the term '0', and the function-symbol 's(x)', meaning 'the successor of x'. They run as follows:

(1) nat(0)
(2) If nat(x), then nat(s(x))
(3) For every x, s(x) $\neq$ 0
(4) For every x and y, if s(x) = s(y), then $x = y$
(5) For every F, if F(0) and for every x, if F(x), then F(s(x)), then for every x, if nat(x), then F(x).

Axiom (5) of course embodies the principle of induction. Axioms (1) and (2) tell us that the natural numbers comprise all objects in the sequence beginning with

0 and going from each term to its successor. Axiom (5) tells us that every natural number belongs to that sequence. Axiom (3) tells us that the sequence does not go round in a loop, back to its initial term; and axiom (4) tells us that it does not go round in a loop back to some term subsequent to 0. These axioms are categorical: in the sense explained, they have, up to isomorphism, only one model.

Owing to axiom (5), the axioms are also second-order. If we want a first-order formal theory for arithmetic, we must replace the single axiom (5) by an axiom schema with infinitely many instance. Such a schema will take the form

(5*) If A(0) and for every x, if A(x), then A(s(x)), then, for every x, A(x).

Here the letter 'A' is not a symbol of the formal language, but stands proxy for any formula of that language containing a single free variable. It could, for example, be 'for some y, $1 \times y = x$', which may be abbreviated as '1 divides x'; the corresponding instance of (5*) would then be

(5*) If 1 divides 0 and for every x, if 1 divides x, then 1 divides s(x), then, for every x, 1 divides x.

The instances of axiom schema (5*), considered as axioms of a first-order theory, are not collectively as strong as the second-order axiom (5). The latter told us that induction holds good for *every* property of natural numbers; the axiom schema tells us only that it holds for those properties expressible in the theory.

The reason why the conclusion of (5*) omits the qualification 'for every natural number x' is that we may take the variables of the formal theory as ranging only over the natural numbers. Likewise, the symbol denoting the successor function may be tacitly assumed to denote a function taking natural numbers to natural numbers. By this means, the primitive predicate 'nat(x)', together with Peano axioms (1) and (2), may be dropped. On the other hand, since addition and multiplication cannot be defined in a first-order language from 0 and the successor operation, we need to take '+' and '.' (the usual symbol for multiplication, rather than the '×' we have been using so far) as additional primitives. They will be governed by axioms constituting their 'recursion equations', due to Dedekind; these are:

$$x + 0 = x$$
$$x + s(y) = s(x + y)$$
$$x.0 = 0$$
$$x.s(y) = x.y + x$$

The resulting formal system for arithmetic, comprising formalized versions of Peano axioms (3) and (4) and of instances of the axiom schema (5*), together with the two sets of recursion equations, is known as 'Peano arithmetic'.

Gödel's famous theorem of 1931 stated that every consistent formal theory for arithmetic is incomplete. In every such theory, a sentence expressible in the language of the theory can be constructed which is not provable in the theory if that theory is consistent; a slight modification by Rosser of Gödel's original proof shows that it is sufficient to assume the consistency of the theory to show that it is not disprovable, either. The completeness of a first-order theory is equivalent, in view of the completeness theorem for first-order logic, to its categoricity. No consistent first-order formal system for arithmetic can be categorical: it will always admit 'non-standard' models not isomorphic to the intended one, in which the sentence shown by Gödel to be undecidable in that system is false, since the result of adding the negation of the undecidable sentence to the axioms will be consistent, and hence have a model. Gödel's theorem applies just as much to second-order theories; they, too, if consistent, will be incomplete. Since such a theory *is* categorical, it follows that second-order logic is incomplete (in the different sense of 'incomplete' applying to formalizations of logic), and cannot be made complete.

If a first-order formal system for arithmetic is not merely consistent but sound—its axioms and theorems are true under the intended standard interpretation—the undecidable sentence will be palpably true under that interpretation: for it is of the form 'For every x, $B(x)$' where, for each numeral ν, '$B(\nu)$' is provable in the system and hence true. This fact has prompted John Lucas and Roger Penrose to argue that Gödel's theorem establishes that the human mind is more powerful than any computer program, or, at least, that its capacity for recognizing arithmetical truths cannot be represented by any computer program. For a computer program for generating arithmetical truths can be represented by a formal system, consistent if the program is consistent; and a human being who understands what is going on can recognize the truth of the undecidable sentence for that system, which the program will never generate.

You should ponder this argument carefully. In doing so, you should consider the relevance of the following fact. Gödel proved a second incompleteness theorem, to the effect that a consistent formal system for arithmetic cannot prove its own consistency, in the sense that it cannot prove a certain arithmetical statement which is evidently true if and only if the system is consistent (and is said to 'express' its consistency). To do this, he showed how to mimic the entire proof of the first incompleteness theorem within the system, which we may call S. The result will be a provable sentence of S of the form

If Con(S), then U,

where 'Con(S)' is the sentence which expresses the consistency of S, and 'U' is the undecidable sentence for S.

3.3. Logicism

Frege had a slightly different axiomatization of arithmetic; but he was not primarily interested in presenting it as an axiomatic theory. Rather, he concluded that it did not need first principles special to it. He had shown that induction is not a method of reasoning peculiar to arithmetic, but merely an immediate consequence of the correct definition of 'natural number'. He had shown that the notion of a sequence required no appeal to intuition, but could be characterized by purely logical means. He advanced to the position that all arithmetical truths could be derived from logic alone. Arithmetic was simply a branch of logic; the ground of the necessity of arithmetical truths was the same as that of the necessity of logical truths.

This thesis is known as *logicism*. Frege had inherited his general epistemological views from Kant. He accepted from him the trichotomy among knowable propositions of analytic, synthetic a priori, and a posteriori truths, although he could not give the same account as Kant of the synthetic a priori ones, since his philosophy did not allow for Kant's explanation of a priori intuitions. With the trichotomy of knowable truths went a threefold categorization of our sources of knowledge. The a posteriori truths are known by perception, that is, by observation, informed by concepts, by means of the senses. The synthetic a priori truths, such as those of geometry, are known by appeal to a priori intuitions. And, finally, the analytic truths are known by our faculty of reason alone. Frege rejected Kant's view that analytic truths cannot advance knowledge. It was based on a quite inadequate conception of the structure that our sentences may have, and a meagre conception of the scope of logic.

The source of our knowledge determines the scope of the truths we know. What is known by observation holds good only of the world as we find it in experience: it applies only to what is directly or indirectly perceptible. What is known from pure intuition applies only to what is in space or time: it governs not only what we perceive to exist, but all that we can imagine. But truths known by reason alone have the widest scope. They apply to objects of whatever kind, abstract just as much as concrete ones; they hold good of everything that we can conceive intellectually, and can therefore express in words, whether or not we can imagine it. Looked at in this light, arithmetic shares with logic the character of what is derived from unaided reason. Frege was fond of contrasting arithmetic with geometry in this regard. Geometry applies to what is in space; arithmetic holds good in every realm. We can count objects of every kind whatever—not only knives and mountains, but tunes, political theories, and numbers themselves; and the laws of arithmetic hold as inexorably for all these things. Frege assumed geometry to be the science of physical space, and he believed physical space to be Euclidean. He allowed that we can speak intelligibly of a space of more than three dimensions, or of a non-Euclidean space. We can conceive such a thing: all that we are debarred from is to visualize it. But we cannot conceive or speak intelligibly of a world in which the laws of arithmetic fail, any more than we can conceive or speak intelligibly of one in which the laws of logic fail.

Frege's epistemology thus predisposed him to believe the logicist thesis that arithmetical truths are analytic, derived neither from observation nor from intuition of any kind. He first expounded the thesis in a short book called *The Foundations of Arithmetic* (*Die Grundlagen der Arithmetik*), published in 1884, which is essential reading: it is probably the most lucid and the most powerful philosophical treatise of its length ever written. Frege combined his logicism with another view known as *platonism*, which is a combination of two theses. First, mathematical statements are to be taken at face value, that is, as really having the structure that they appear on the surface to have. The statement '7 divides 35' apparently has the same form as the statement 'The moon orbits the earth': both appear to state that a certain object bears a certain relation to another object. The platonist view is that the arithmetical statement really does have this form: when we make mathematical statements, we refer to and quantify over genuine objects and systems of objects, even though these are abstract objects and abstract systems. The second component of platonism is that the abstract objects of which we speak in mathematics exist independently of us, and that the statements we make about them (if true) hold good independently of our knowledge of their truth. Mathematical objects are just as objective as physical objects, or objects of any other kind, and propositions concerning them are objectively true or false just as are propositions about stars or mountains.

It is, at first sight, paradoxical to combine logicism with platonism, for we are disposed to think of logical laws as holding good regardless of what objects exist. Logicism would therefore seem to go more naturally with the view that arithmetical statements are *not* to be understood at face value, but reconstrued so as to involve no reference to or quantification over any objects at all. Frege reconciled the two principles by construing numbers as classes, or, as he preferred to say, as extensions of concepts: classes he viewed as objects, while, in common with all his contemporaries, he took the notion of a class to be a logical one. A logical notion was not, for him, primarily one needed for systematizing deductive inference, but one with a universal application to things of every kind. He chose to speak of objects' falling under a concept rather than of their possessing a property; but he understood concepts extensionally—whatever holds good of a concept must also hold good of any coextensive concept. For him, the notion of a concept was prior to that of a class, which could be conceived only as the extension of a concept; to conceive it otherwise involved taking it to be in some incomprehensible manner *made up out of* its members, whereas the only intelligible explanation of '*x* is a member of *a*' is '*x* falls under some concept of which *a* is the extension'.

3.4. The Application of Mathematics

This is not to say that Frege found it quite unproblematic to justify either the conception of numbers as objects or the existence of the classes with which he identified them. On the contrary, it was for him a central preoccupation; and it ultimately undid him. In *The Foundations of Arithmetic*, he treated the natural numbers as a species of a larger genus, cardinal numbers. Cardinal numbers are those which specify how many things of some given kind (falling under a given concept) there are; Cantor had shown how to develop a theory of transfinite cardinal numbers, those used to specify precisely how many things there are when an imprecise answer is 'infinitely many'. Frege's identification of the natural numbers as the finite cardinal numbers accorded with his view that the principle governing the applications of a mathematical theory is essential to its characterization: 'it is applicability alone', he wrote, 'that raises arithmetic from the rank of a game to that of a science'. The details of any particular application of such a theory will be extraneous to mathematics, which must remain uncontaminated by empirical concepts. But the general principle that makes all its applications possible is intrinsic, and must be embodied in the way in which the objects of the theory are characterized. The most general application of the natural numbers is as cardinals, and hence they must be defined as such. It was for similar reasons that, in his later book, *Basic Laws of Arithmetic* (*Grundgesetze der Arithmetik*), Frege did not follow the same strategy as Cantor and Dedekind, first defining the rational numbers in terms of the natural numbers, and then the real numbers in terms of the rationals, but went straight from the natural numbers to the reals. He argued that the rationals are applied in the same way as the real numbers, namely to specify the magnitude of a quantity, and so must be considered as numbers of the same kind as they.

In *The Foundations of Arithmetic*, Frege recognized the relation of cardinal equivalence as fundamental, and adopted the definition of 'There are just as many *F*s as *G*s' to mean 'There is a one–one map of the *F*s on to the *G*s' which was in process of becoming standard among mathematicians. (The mapping is one–one if it takes distinct *F*s into distinct *G*s; it is 'on to' rather than merely 'into' the Gs if every *G* is the image of some *F*.) In order to construe cardinal numbers as objects, it is then necessary to define the operator 'the number of Φs'. Frege laid down the principle that

The number of *F*s = the number of *G*s
iff
there are just as many *F*s as *G*s.

When this is combined with the definition of 'just as many', it becomes

The number of *F*s = the number of *G*s
iff
there is a one–one map of the *F*s on to the *G*s.

Frege toyed with the idea that this principle could simply be *stipulated* and treated as a definition of the operator 'the number of Φs'. But he rejected it on the ground that it failed to provide a truth-value for a statement equating a number with some object not presented as a number, and hence for a context of the form 'the number of *F*s = *x*' in which a variable stood on one side of the sign of identity. Instead, he treated the principle as a guide to how 'the number of *F*s' should be defined, namely to mean

the class of concepts *G* such that there are just as many *F*s as *G*s;

he then used this definition solely to derive the principle, and, from it, using suitable further definitions (e.g. of '0' and 'successor'), all the basic principles of number theory.

Frege's procedure stands in the sharpest contrast to that of Dedekind, who in 1888 published his own account of the foundations of arithmetic, *Was sind und was sollen die Zahlen?* Dedekind shared with Frege the views that natural numbers should be treated as objects, and that the notion of what he called a 'system' (a class with operations and relations defined on it) is a logical one; but he did not at all view applicability as central. Rather, he wished to characterize the abstract structure of the natural numbers, and did so very effectively; their application as finite cardinals he relegated to the status of a minor corollary. To establish the existence of the natural numbers, he relied on a psychological process in which, strangely in our eyes, many mathematicians and philosophers of the time believed: that of abstraction. Abstraction consists in concentrating upon some features of an object or system of objects and disregarding the rest: it was supposed to have the effect of creating an (abstract) object or system actually devoid of the features disregarded. To obtain the natural numbers in this way, Dedekind believed that he must start with a specific system of objects isomorphic to the natural numbers. By applying the operation of abstraction to it, he believed that we obtained the abstract system of natural numbers, each member of which lacked any property not consequent upon its occupying a particular position in the system. The work of his present-day follower Paul Benacerraf should be studied. Benacerraf, like Dedekind, believes that the natural numbers have no other properties than structural ones. Since, like everyone else nowadays, he disbelieves in the process of psychological abstraction, he concludes that the natural numbers are not specific objects at all, even abstract ones. To talk about 'the' natural numbers is, for him, a figure of speech, like speaking of 'the' eight-element Boolean algebra: we are merely talking about any one of a family of isomorphic systems.

Was Frege right to think that the principle underlying the applications that can be made of a mathematical theory is intrinsic to that theory, and should be embodied in our explanation of the senses of statements of that theory? Or was Dedekind right to think that they are peripheral to the theory, the content of which should be explained in terms of pure structure? Surely Frege was wrong to think that all applications can be provided for in advance? We are often surprised by the fruitful applications of mathematical theories that turn out to be possible: how could we guarantee that such surprises never occur? A Fregean might answer that, when an application is shown to be possible for which we have not provided, we should go back, analyse what made that application possible, and, accordingly, formulate the general principle governing applications of the theory more broadly, and hence characterize the content of the theory in a more general manner. The object is not to guard against *surprise*, which is a mere psychological reaction, but to prevent the applications of mathematics from appearing *miraculous*.

3.5. Russell's Paradox

In *The Foundations of Arithmetic*, Frege had taken the notion of a class (extension of a concept) as requiring no further explanation. When he composed his *magnum opus*, *Basic Laws of Arithmetic* (1893, 1903), he could no longer do this. In the *Basic Laws*, he essayed a formal derivation, within his symbolic notation, of all the fundamental principles of the arithmetic both of natural numbers and of real numbers. The logical system within which the derivation was to be carried out had to be precisely formulated and explained. Frege here generalized the notion of a class to that of a *value-range*: as classes were extensions of concepts, so value-ranges were 'extensions' of functions. This was a generalization, not a mere analogy, because Frege treated the two truth-values, *true* and *false*, as objects within the domain of the individual variables; hence a concept could be taken as a particular case of a function, mapping every object on to one of the truth-values, according to whether, as we should ordinarily say, that object fell under the concept or not. The formal system was that of *Begriffsschrift*, slightly modified, with an abstraction operator added: this operator, applied to any expression for a unary function of objects, was to yield a term standing for an object, namely the value-range of that function.

Frege was aware of the need to justify his logical system, and was much occupied with the problem of warranting the existence of the objects of mathematical theories. In his *Foundations*, he had laid down his celebrated 'context principle', which stated that 'it is only in the context of a sentence that a word refers to anything'. This means that reference to objects—in particular, to abstract objects—is secured if we can determine the truth-conditions of sentences involving reference to them. The problem then is to find a means of specifying those truth-conditions without first laying down the reference of the abstract terms. Frege's specific concern was to warrant the existence of 'logical objects', objects whose existence is certified by logic alone. Numbers of all kinds he regarded as logical objects; and he decided that all logical objects are value-ranges of one sort or another. He therefore wanted to show it legitimate to assume the existence of value-ranges; and he wanted, in particular, to guarantee that every term of his system denoted a unique object and that every sentence possessed a unique truth-value. In accordance with the context principle, the first aim could be secured if the second could be: but in the *Basic Laws* sentences were not allotted so special a theoretical role. A form of context principle still remained in operation, however, since he did not think it necessary to specify the reference of a term of every form *directly*: terms of some type—in his case, the value-range terms—would be certified as having a reference provided that every more complex term containing them was provided with a reference. Although Frege specified the range of the individual variables no more precisely than as containing just the two truth-values and value-ranges corresponding to all terms for them formulable in the system, he believed that he could secure a guarantee of the referentiality of every formal term provided that he could determine a truth-value for every statement of identity; thus his problem reduced to one about the truth-conditions of sentences, even if it no longer started with them. For a statement equating a value-range with a truth-value, it sufficed to identify the truth-values with their own unit classes. For one equating two value-ranges, Frege thought it sufficient to stipulate that

The value-range of $f =$ the value-range of g
iff
for every x, $f(x) = g(x)$,

and embodied this principle in the notorious Axiom V of his formal system.

Alas! it was not sufficient. Frege left *Basic Laws* uncompleted, in the middle of the formal development of the theory of real numbers, as the result of a letter from Bertrand Russell written on 16 June 1902. This announced the possibility of deriving, in the formal system of the book, a contradiction—Russell's paradox. It took Frege four years to recognize that he could not resolve this contradiction in such a way that his proofs would still go through; he then acknowledged that his life's work had failed.

Everyone knows of Russell's paradox of the class of classes that are not members of themselves. It is a member of itself just in case it satisfies its own defining condition, namely that it is not a member of itself. It is more important to grasp how Russell arrived at it, as he himself emphasized. Cantor, investigating transfinite cardinal numbers, had proved that the number of all natural numbers, while the same as that of all rationals, is smaller than the number of all real numbers, in that, while the natural numbers can obviously be mapped one–one into the real numbers, they cannot be mapped *on to* them. The number of real numbers is the same as the number of all sets of natural numbers (or of all extensionally distinct concepts applying to natural numbers); and Cantor had generalized the theorem to one stating that the number of members of any set, finite or infinite, is always smaller than the number of its subsets. Suppose there is a mapping ϕ which carries each natural number into a set of natural numbers: the objective is to show that not every such set is an image under ϕ of some natural number. We form the set K of numbers n such that n is not a member of $\phi(n)$: on pain of contradiction, K cannot be $\phi(k)$ for any natural number k. Equally, if A is a set with more than one element, and ψ maps every element x of A on to a function $\psi[x]$ carrying each element of A into an element of A, there is such a function g not in the range of ψ: we choose distinct elements a and b of A, and set $g(x)=a$ if $\psi[x](x)\neq a$, and $g(x)=b$ if $\psi[x](x)=a$.

Russell wondered about the result of applying this proof to the class of all classes: for all subclasses of that class should be members of it. The result was Russell's paradox. (There cannot therefore be a class of all classes, or one containing all objects.) Frege's great mistake was to overlook questions of cardinality. Whatever the size of the domain in any model of his system, it must, if it contains more than one element, be smaller than the totality of extensionally distinct functions defined over it; but Axiom V says that extensionally distinct functions of objects determine distinct value-ranges, which will themselves belong to the domain. Hence the contradiction.

Russell's paradox was one of a cluster of set-theoretic paradoxes whose discovery troubled the mathematical world around the turn of the century. A closely allied paradox is that of Curry, which is worth explaining as showing that the paradoxes cannot be dispelled by any tampering with negation, such as saying that there are propositions that are neither true nor false, and hence are equivalent to their own negations. Let the set Q be the set of all classes x such that if x is a member of itself, then Queen Elizabeth was a man. We argue as follows. Suppose, first, as a hypothesis, that

(1) Q is a member of Q.

It follows from hypothesis (1) that Q satisfies the condition for membership of Q, i.e. that

(2) If Q is a member of Q, then Queen Elizabeth was a man.

From (1) and (2) it follows that, on the hypothesis (1)

(3) Queen Elizabeth was a man.

Since we have derived (3) from the hypothesis (1), we may assert, independently of the hypothesis, that

(4) If *Q* is a member of *Q*, then Queen Elizabeth was a man.

But (4) is the condition for *Q* to be a member of *Q*, so that we may infer

(5) *Q is* a member of *Q*.

From (4) and (5) together we may conclude

(6) Queen Elizabeth was a man.

Since we could obviously substitute any proposition whatever for 'Queen Elizabeth was a man', we have a paradox.

Russell's paradox was by no means the first member of the cluster to be discovered. That was the paradox published in 1897 by the Italian mathematician Cesare Burali-Forti (1861–1931) concerning ordinal numbers, which is of importance as showing that the paradoxes do not all concern the notion of set or class. Cantor investigated transfinite ordinal numbers simultaneously with transfinite cardinals. Ordinal numbers are most easily explained as the order-types of well-orderings. A well-ordering is a linear ordering with the special property that any non-empty subset of its terms has an element earlier in the ordering than any other element. The natural ordering of the rationals is plainly not a well-ordering, but that of the natural numbers is; so is the ordering in which a natural number n precedes a natural number m if either n is even and m is odd, or n and m have the same parity and n is smaller than m. We suppose that there are correlated to all well-orderings objects called their *order-types*, in such a way that the order-type of one coincides with the order-type of another iff the well-orderings are *similar*. One ordering is similar to another iff there exists a one–one mapping ϱ of the terms of the one on to the terms of the other that preserves the ordering: that is to say, x precedes y in the first ordering iff $\varrho(x)$ precedes $\varrho(y)$ in the second. (The natural ordering of the natural numbers is *not* similar to that defined above, in which all even numbers precede all odd ones.) Now the ordinal numbers have an obvious relation of magnitude between themselves; moreover, this is easily shown to be a well-ordering. Hence there ought to be an ordinal, say Ω, which is the order-type of the well-ordering of all the ordinals. But it can also be shown that the order-type of any segment of the ordinals containing every ordinal smaller than any ordinal it contains is greater than all the ordinals in that segment. Hence Ω is both an ordinal number and greater than every ordinal number: contradiction.

4. AFTER THE PARADOXES

Russell's diagnosis of the set-theoretic paradoxes was that they all concerned concepts with the following property: given any totality of objects falling under that concept, it is possible to define, in terms of that totality, a new object falling under the concept but not belonging to the totality. The disaster that had overtaken Frege was widely held, and still is widely held, to demonstrate the falsity of the logicist thesis. This needs careful thought, which you must give it. It surely does not show that the logicist thesis is wrong from beginning to end: it is very far from evident that the idea that the necessity of arithmetical truths is of the same character as that of logical truths is devoid of substance.

You need, therefore, to ask yourself the question where exactly Frege went wrong. He was aiming at finding an uncontentious method of introducing the domain of a mathematical theory—what we may call a fundamental domain. By a fundamental domain is here meant a domain of mathematical objects that cannot be explained in terms of any already known domain. This means essentially one that forms the prototype of a totality of one or another cardinality. The natural numbers form one such domain, being the prototype of denumerable totalities; if we do not help ourselves to the notion of a set or of an infinite sequence, the real numbers form another fundamental domain, being the prototype of totalities that are non-denumerable in that particular way. Whether such a domain be explained by formal or informal means, it cannot be constructed out of any already understood domain; to stipulate that the domain of a formal theory is to consist of the natural numbers or of the real numbers is simply to duck the problem how it may be explained in a non-question-begging way. Frege attempted to carry out the task once and for all, by introducing the domain of value-ranges; but he failed to devise even a consistent system, let alone one epistemologically unproblematic. How, then, should he have set about the task? In doing so, would he have needed to appeal to more than logic? These are the questions you need to resolve. You are unlikely to come up with clear and compelling answers immediately, for no one can yet be said to have given compelling answers to them; but you should bear the questions continually in mind. They are not merely historical questions about Frege; they are questions that go to the heart of the philosophy of mathematics.

Russell, with his colleague A. N. Whitehead (1861–1947), did not abandon the attempt to establish the logicist thesis, but devoted the three volumes of their massive *Principia Mathematica* (1910–13) to it. That work, which had the same aim as Frege's *Basic Laws*, but a grander scope and a less rigorous logical underpinning, was certainly logicist in intention, but it was no longer whole-heartedly platonist. There was now a necessity to guard against the set-theoretic paradoxes; the means of doing so was the *theory of types*. Frege's logical system had incorporated a hierarchy of logical types. Objects formed the bottom rank: above them came functions of different kinds, unary and binary. The logical type of a function depended upon the number and type of its arguments. On the first level came two types, unary and binary functions of objects; in Frege's system, all functions had objects as their values. Let us for brevity call these types U and B, and take the letter O to designate the type of objects. On the second level came many different types: unary functions with arguments of type U; unary functions with arguments of type B; binary functions with both arguments of type U; binary functions with both arguments of type B; and binary functions with arguments of mixed type—U and B, U and O, or B and O. The hierarchy continued upwards in this way; a variable could range only over one determinate type. But value-ranges did not form a hierarchy in Frege's system. They were all extensions of unary functions of first level, and they were all themselves objects, of zero level; Frege's cardinal numbers were, in *Basic Laws*, classes of equinumerous classes rather than of equinumerous concepts.

Russell and Whitehead concerned themselves, not with functions in general, but with what Frege called 'concepts' and 'relations', and they called 'propositional functions'; and these were arranged in a similar hierarchy. But they dealt with classes in a totally different way. For them, to speak of classes was only a way of speaking of unary propositional functions; and so their classes were necessarily arranged in the same hierarchy as such propositional functions. The bottom rank consisted of 'individuals', and comprised only non-mathematical objects. Above them were classes of individuals (type 1), classes of classes of individuals (type 2), and so on. Cardinal numbers were of type 2, being classes of equinumerous classes. The definition is formally the same as Frege's; but the theory of types gave it in effect an entirely different force. Frege's proof of the infinity of the sequence of natural numbers had turned on their being objects. Given any natural number *n*, the expression '*n* belongs to the successor-sequence beginning with *x*' expresses that *x* is among the natural numbers in the finite sequence 0, 1, … , *n*. Frege showed how to prove formally that the number of terms of this sequence—of objects *x* satisfying the condition just displayed in quotation marks—is the successor of *n* (given that *n* is a natural number), something intuitively clear, since the sequence obviously has $n+1$ terms. But this proof depends absolutely on natural numbers' being objects, since it is objects that are counted: a numerical term of the form 'the number of *F*s' is, for Frege, more explicitly expressed by 'the number of objects *x* each of which is *F*'. If Frege had not taken arithmetical statements at face value, but had treated natural numbers as being of some type other than objects, for instance second-level concepts (concepts under which first-level concepts fall) properly denoted by expressions of the kind 'There are just *n* . . .', the proof that every natural number has a successor would not have been available to him: since it is objects that are counted, natural numbers must be objects if *they* are to be counted.

Russell and Whitehead were in precisely this difficulty. They construed natural numbers as being of type 2, classes of classes. The class of natural numbers from 0 to *n* was then of type 3, and the class of classes equinumerous to it of type 4, and hence unable to serve as the successor of *n*. The difficulty lies in the possibility that there may be only finitely many individuals. Frege could prove that there were infinitely many objects, because cardinal numbers, being classes, counted for him as objects; but for Russell and Whitehead, they were of a higher type than individuals. If there were, say, 4,062 individuals, there would be no class containing 4,063 individuals, and hence no class of classes to serve as the successor of the number 4,062; or, if the null class of classes were reckoned as the successor of 4,062, it would be its own successor, in violation of Peano axiom (4). The authors of *Principia* could therefore do no better than cut the knot by assuming an axiom of infinity to the effect that there are infinitely many individuals. This 'axiom' is *expressible* in logical terms, but its truth is in no way certified by any logical conviction; indeed, since neither numbers nor classes are individuals, it is doubtful whether it is true at all. This was a grave defect in executing the logicist programme.

4.1. The Vicious Circle Principle

The theory of types, as so far described, is only the *simple* theory of types. Owing to the way reference to and quantification over classes is explained in *Principia* in terms of reference to and quantification over propositional functions, classes are categorized in accordance with the simple version of the theory: they are distinguished in terms of the types of their members, a class of type $n+1$ having as members only classes of type *n*. In Russell's *Introduction to Mathematical Philosophy* (1919), another piece of essential reading, it is only the simple theory of types that is explained. But in *Principia* the categorization of propositional functions took a more complex form—what is known as the *ramified* theory of types. According to this, propositional functions are divided into orders, determined by the orders, not only of their arguments, but also of the bound variables occurring in formulas expressing them. A propositional function is of the lowest order higher than variables indicating their arguments and of bound variables in the corresponding formulas. A unary function of individuals expressed by quantification over functions of order 1 (functions of individuals) is therefore of order 2. What was called a 'predicative' function was one of lowest order compatible with its arguments; to speak of classes was construed as speaking of predicative unary functions, which is why they were arranged only in the simple hierarchy.

This led, in *Principia*, to difficulty over the foundations of the theory of real numbers. To secure the completeness of the real numbers, it must be shown (or assumed) that every class *D* of real numbers having an upper bound has a least upper bound. Thus a Dedekind cut in the *real* line always has a real number corresponding to it: there are no gaps in the real line. The normal method of proving this involves quantifying over the members of the class *D*; if, for instance, real numbers are identified with the lower classes of Dedekind cuts in the rational line, the least upper bound of the class *D* is the union of its members. But, since it involves quantification over the real numbers in the class *D*, the propositional function expressing this construction will not be a predicative one; without modification of the theory, it therefore cannot be used to prove the existence of a least upper bound. The solution adopted by Russell and Whitehead was to assume yet another axiom, the axiom of reducibility, which said that, for each propositional function, there exists a coextensive predicative function.

As Russell acknowledged, there is not the slightest direct reason for believing this 'axiom' true; indeed, it conflicts with whatever intuitive reason existed for adopting the ramified theory of types. Russell was reduced to arguing that the axioms of infinity and reducibility were needed in order to derive classical mathematics from logic. On this account, logic no longer serves to provide an epistemological justification for the principles of classical mathematics, that is, to explain why we accept them or how we know them to be true. Rather, we start with two convictions: that classical mathematics is correct; and that it is capable of being derived from assumptions expressible in purely logical terms. We then look to see which assumptions of this kind are required if we are to derive classical mathematics from them: our only reason for accepting certain of these assumptions is that, if they were not true, one or other of our two prior convictions would be unsound. Russell remained a logicist in the attenuated sense of maintaining the second of these convictions; but it is clear that the logicist enterprise had lost its original motivation.

It was pointed out by Frank Ramsey (1903–30) that the simple theory of types suffices to block the set-theoretic paradoxes; the ramified theory might be needed in order to block the semantic paradoxes such as the Liar, as posed by a statement of the form 'This statement is false', but those paradoxes cannot be expressed in the formal language of *Principia* anyway. Russell's reason for adopting the ramified theory was, however, that what he called the *vicious circle principle* required it. This principle, which had been advocated by Henri Poincaré (1854–1912), who was nevertheless opposed to logicism, was seen by Russell as embodying the correct diagnosis of the paradoxes, including the set-theoretic ones: he had hardly any motive for accepting the simple theory of types save that it was implied by a principle which demanded the ramified theory.

The vicious circle principle denied the existence of anything definable only by quantification over some totality to which it belonged. Expressed in this way, it prompts objections appealing to such specifications as 'the tallest man in the room'; and it is then frequently said that the vicious circle principle is false if mathematical objects exist independently of our knowledge of them, and true only if they are constructed by us, that is, created by our thought. This makes it appear that a deep metaphysical question has to be decided in order to determine whether or not the vicious circle principle is sound. What concerned Russell, however, was what means are legitimate, not for picking out particular objects, but for specifying a domain of quantification. Suppose that we have some first-order theory, of which we grasp the intended domain of the variables. We wish to convert it into a second-order theory, involving reference to and quantification over subclasses of the domain. If we believe ourselves to know what is meant by speaking of *all* subclasses of the domain, we may introduce class-variables 'X', 'Y', … , as ranging over such subclasses, together with the symbol '$\in$' for the membership relation, and lay down, as the condition for the existence of classes, the *impredicative comprehension axiom schema*

$$\exists X\ \forall x,\ x \in X \leftrightarrow \mathsf{A}(x).$$

Here '$\mathsf{A}(x)$' represents any formula containing 'x' free, but not containing the variable 'X' free, in the *extended* language containing class-variables. For such a formula must represent a determinate condition, and, since the class-variables range over all subclasses of the domain, there must be a subclass comprising just those elements that satisfy that condition. The axiom schema will not, however, serve to *explain* the domain over which the class-variables range. On pain of circularity, that domain must be presumed to be already known: otherwise a formula '$\mathsf{A}(x)$' containing bound class-variables would *not* represent a determinate condition.

Russell did not suppose himself to grasp the totality of all subclasses of a given class. No one who takes this attitude could accept the impredicative comprehension axiom schema. Rather, if he were in the position of wishing to extend a first-order theory by adding variables ranging over subclasses of the domain, he would adopt a *predicative* comprehension axiom schema of the form

$$\exists X\ \forall x,\ x \in X \leftrightarrow \mathsf{B}(x).$$

Here '$\mathsf{B}(x)$' would represent any formula of the original unextended language that contained 'x' free. More exactly, '$\mathsf{B}(x)$' could be allowed to contain *free* class-variables other than 'X', but no bound class-variables. This comprehension principle *would* serve to explain the intended domain of the new class-variables.

From our understanding of the original language, we know what condition on the elements of the domain is expressed by a formula of that language with one free individual variable: we can therefore take the classes over which the class-variables range to be just those the condition for membership of any of which is given by some such formula.

Indeed, we can now reiterate the step we took. We can now take any formula of the extended language, with bound class-variables, as expressing a determinate condition on the elements of the domain. Hence we can distinguish the class-variables we introduced at the first stage as being of order 1, indicated by a subscript '1', and introduce further class-variables of order 2. We shall now have two predicative comprehension axiom schemas:

$$\exists X_1 \ \forall x, x \in X_1 \leftrightarrow \mathsf{B}(x).$$

and

$$\exists X_2 \ \forall x, x \in X_2 \leftrightarrow \mathsf{C}(x).$$

Here '$\mathsf{B}(x)$' is as before, while '$\mathsf{C}(x)$' represents any formula containing 'x' free and possibly containing free class-variables other than 'X_2' of either order and bound class-variables of order 1, but containing no bound class-variables of order 2. It is obvious that the process can be reiterated indefinitely, so as to obtain an infinite hierarchy of classes. (These, however, will still all be classes of elements of the domain: we are not here concerned with classes of classes.)

The question is therefore not the general one whether (as the platonist believes) mathematical entities exist independently of us, or whether they await our construction of them. It is the more restricted one whether we genuinely always have a determinate conception of the totality of subclasses of any given totality. The supposition that we have such a conception is normally reckoned an item in the platonist creed; this is a further respect in which Russell and Whitehead diverged from platonism.

5. ORDINAL NUMBERS AND CARDINAL NUMBERS

Cardinal numbers specify how many objects of a given kind there are; ordinal numbers specify the place of a term in a well-ordered sequence. Frege identified the natural numbers as finite cardinals; but they serve equally well as finite ordinals. It can indeed be argued that the notion of an ordinal number is the more fundamental of the two. When we count, we necessarily arrange the objects counted in a sequence, by assigning numerals to them in order. The number of the objects we have counted is then given by the greatest number we have assigned to any of them, if we started with 1 as we do in everyday life; or the smallest number we have not assigned to any of them, if we started with 0. Likewise, to discover the (cardinal) number of houses in a street, we have only to discover the highest (ordinal) number assigned to any house in that street. When we want to find No. 37, Cambridge Street, we cannot count up the houses to 37 in any order we like: we must take them in the order in which they have been numbered. But when we want only to discover how many objects of some kind there are, it does not matter in what order we arrange them. This is because any two linear orderings of the same finite set (or of equinumerous finite sets) are similar; it is for this reason that the natural numbers can serve equally well as finite ordinals or as finite cardinals.

The smallest transfinite ordinal is ω; this is the order-type of the natural numbers in order of magnitude. Like every ordinal number, it has a successor, $\omega + 1$. It is far from being the case that all well-orderings of infinite sets are similar; thus $\omega + 1$ is the order-type of the natural numbers so ordered that every positive number precedes 0, while the positive numbers are arranged in order of magnitude. It is of help in grasping what any ordinal number is that each ordinal number is the order-type of all smaller ordinals in order of magnitude. Thus $\omega + 1$ is the order-type of the well-ordered sequence

$$0, 1, 2, \ldots, \omega.$$

$\omega.2$ is the order-type of the natural numbers so ordered that every even number precedes every odd number, and equally of the sequence

$$0, 1, \ldots, \omega, \omega + 1, \omega + 2, \ldots$$

Every ordinal is of one of three kinds: 0, or a successor ordinal such as $\omega + 1$, or a limit ordinal such as ω and $\omega.2$. A limit ordinal is one that is not 0 or a successor, but is the limit of all ordinals smaller than it (the smallest ordinal greater than or equal to any of them). *Transfinite induction* is a method of proving some statement true of all ordinals; it is a generalization of finite induction. To prove that the statement $P(\alpha)$ holds good for every ordinal α, we must show three things:

(1) that $P(0)$;
(2) that, for any ordinal β, if $P(\beta)$, then $P(\beta + 1)$; and
(3) that, if λ is a limit ordinal, and, for every η less than λ, $P(\eta)$, then $P(\lambda)$.

Transfinite induction *up to* some ordinal $\varkappa$ is a means of proving some statement to hold good of every ordinal less than $\varkappa$. Its clauses are like those of unrestricted transfinite induction, save that to (2) must be added the hypothesis that $\beta + 1$ is less than $\varkappa$, and to (3) the hypothesis that λ is less than $\varkappa$. Transfinite induction up to $\varkappa$ can be used for proving some statement $Q(n)$ to be true of all natural numbers, by appeal to a well-ordering of the natural numbers of order-type $\varkappa$; the statement $\mathsf{P}(\alpha)$, for α less than $\varkappa$, is taken to be 'if n is the α-th natural number in the well-ordering, then $\mathsf{Q}(n)$'.

Finite induction may take a different form, sometimes called 'complete induction', from that previously explained; it is useful because the hypothesis of the induction is stronger than that of ordinary finite induction. In this case, only one step is needed: to show that $\mathsf{P}(n)$ holds for every natural number n, we need to show that

for every natural number k, if, for every m less than k, $\mathsf{P}(m)$, then $\mathsf{P}(k)$.

If this holds good, then $\mathsf{P}(0)$, since the hypothesis is vacuously satisfied, there being no numbers less than 0. It follows that $\mathsf{P}(1)$, and hence $\mathsf{P}(2)$, and so on. Ordinary finite induction depends upon the natural numbers having an ordering of order-type ω; but complete induction depends only upon their being well-ordered. It is equivalent to the method of infinite descent, according to which, to show that for all n, $\mathsf{P}(n)$, it suffices to show that, if there were a number k such that not $\mathsf{P}(k)$, then there would be another number m less than k such that not $\mathsf{P}(m)$. For, if there were such a number k, it would follow that, after finitely many applications of the step from k to m, we could show that not $\mathsf{P}(0)$; and then the step could no longer be taken, since there is no number less than 0. The method of infinite descent turns on there being no infinite descending sequence of natural numbers; and to say that there is no infinite descending sequence with respect to an ordering is equivalent to saying that it is a well-ordering. Complete induction may therefore be formulated as a version of transfinite induction; to prove that the statement $\mathsf{P}(\alpha)$ holds good for every ordinal α, it suffices to show that

for every ordinal number $\varkappa$, if, for every μ less than $\varkappa$, $\mathsf{P}(\mu)$, then $\mathsf{P}(\varkappa)$.

However vast the leaps by which a function defined on the ordinals may advance, the slow march of the ordinals will always catch up with it. Let ϕ be a monotonic increasing function whose value for a limit ordinal λ is always the limit of $\phi(\varkappa)$ for $\varkappa$ less than λ. Then, for every ordinal η, ϕ has a fixed point α, greater than η, i.e. an ordinal for which $\phi(\alpha) = \alpha$. The first such fixed point is the limit of the sequence

$$\eta, \phi(\eta), \phi(\phi(\eta)), \ldots$$

Ordinal numbers which are order-types of well-orderings that can be imposed on the natural numbers are called *denumerable ordinals*. After $\omega.2$, $\omega.3$, ... , comes ω^2, which is the order-type of an ordering of the natural numbers in which all prime powers, in order of magnitude, come first, then all numbers with just two distinct prime factors, then all those with just three distinct prime factors, and so on. A sequence of order-type $\omega.2$ may be regarded as a sequence of order-type 2 of sequences of order-type ω, and one of order-type ω^2 ($=\omega.\omega$)

as a sequence of order-type ω of sequences of order-type ω. A sequence of order-type ω^3 is then a sequence of order-type ω of sequences of order-type ω of sequences of order-type ω. The reader may try as an exercise to define an ordering of the natural numbers of order-type ω^3. After ω^2, ω^3, ... , comes ω^ω; a reader who carried out the previous exercise successfully may now try his hand at constructing an ordering of the natural numbers whose order-type is ω^ω. The sequence

$$\omega, \omega^\omega, \omega^{\omega^\omega}, \ldots$$

also has a limit, known as ε_0. This is the smallest ordinal not expressible by means of addition, multiplication, and exponentiation in terms ω and 1; it is also the smallest fixed point of the function ω^ξ. The reader previously unfamiliar with transfinite ordinals may well be feeling dizzy at this point; if so, he will probably not be consoled by being told that ε_0 is considered a relatively small denumerable ordinal.

By no means all ordinal numbers in Cantor's theory are finite or denumerable. The finite and denumerable ordinals themselves form a well-ordered sequence, and so must have an ordinal as their limit, known usually as ω_1, which, being greater than all denumerable ordinals, cannot itself be denumerable. A new reason for thinking that the concept of an ordinal number is more fundamental than that of a cardinal number is that the theory of ordinals forms the substratum of Cantor's theory of cardinals. We have noted two transfinite cardinal numbers: the number of natural numbers, designated by $\aleph_0$ (pronounced 'aleph-nought'), and the larger number of real numbers, or of all sets of natural numbers, commonly designated $2^{\aleph_0}$. The arithmetical operations, applied to cardinal numbers, have a quite different significance from that they possess when applied to ordinals: if $\boldsymbol{m}$ and $\boldsymbol{n}$ are cardinal numbers, $\boldsymbol{n}^{\boldsymbol{m}}$ is the number of functions from a set of cardinality $\boldsymbol{m}$ into one of cardinality $\boldsymbol{n}$. The operation which takes us from $\aleph_0$ to $2^{\aleph_0}$ can of course be indefinitely iterated; but it was not this operation which Cantor treated as fundamental to the theory of transfinite cardinals. The totality of finite and denumerable ordinals forms another non-denumerably infinite set, whose cardinal number Cantor designated by $\aleph_1$: not only is it greater than $\aleph_0$, but it can be shown that there is no cardinal number between them. This, unsurprisingly, is the beginning of another sequence. The totality of all ordinals of cardinality $\aleph_1$ has a limit ω_2, and is of cardinality greater than $\aleph_1$, namely $\aleph_2$; in fact, for every ordinal α, there is an ordinal ω_α, and a corresponding cardinal number $\aleph_\alpha$.

Cantor was very interested to determine the relation between the cardinal number (or 'power') of the continuum (i.e. of the real numbers) and Alephs. He supposed that every set could in principle be well-ordered; it followed that the power of the continuum must be identifiable with one of the Alephs. But very little could, or can, be proved concerning which it is; it cannot, for instance, be

$\aleph_\omega$, but no upper bound for its identification could be found. Cantor made a famous conjecture, called 'the continuum hypothesis', that it was in fact $\aleph_1$. If so, it would follow that any infinite set of real numbers must either be denumerable or equal in cardinality to the set of all real numbers. The continuum hypothesis has proved to be very deep indeed. The results of Gödel and of Cohen have shown that it cannot be either proved or disproved by the resources currently available for proving theorems of set theory.

6. FORMALISM

Full-blooded formalism is the doctrine that mathematics involves nothing but the manipulation of symbols according to certain rules. The symbols have no meaning whatever (and might therefore better be called 'characters'). This philosophy of mathematics evades many hard problems: it need say nothing about mathematical objects, since it denies that there are any, nor about the nature of mathematical truth, since it denies that mathematical formulas express propositions or are apt for assignment of truth-values. It also leaves it unclear what point there is in mathematics.

Formalism is best expressed by use of the concept of a formal system: every mathematical question, according to the formalists, is at root the question whether a certain formula can be derived in a particular formal system. Frege devised the earliest example of a formal system, but he was a resolute opponent of formalism. The best critique of it was contained in a section of his *Basic Laws* translated by Geach and Black in their *Translations from the Philosophical Writings of G. Frege*. Heine and Thomae, the two formalist writers criticized by Frege, did not have the notion of a formal system, and their formulation of the formalist thesis was in consequence clumsy; but neither of Frege's two principal criticisms turns on this fact. He argues, first, that the formalist attempt to empty mathematical questions of meaningful content is doomed to failure. For, even when a particular mathematical theory has been represented by a formal system, the formalist has no means of preventing meaningful questions being posed *about* that formal system—questions other than whether a specific formula is or is not derivable. He draws a contrast between chess and the theory of chess. Positions on a chessboard lack meaningful content; but the theory of chess contains answers to meaningful questions, such as whether it is possible to force mate with a King and two Knights. Likewise, of any formal system we may ask whether it is consistent, or complete, or has this or that other interesting proof-theoretic property; the answers to such questions will be statements with a meaningful content. A cricket umpire can signal that the bowler has bowled a wide, or that the batsman is out, but he cannot signal that the bowler has bowled a wide every over that he was on, or that he has taken the last three wickets. That is because the umpire's signals are not part of a genuine language. Each expresses a very simple sentence; but the umpire lacks any device for transforming the signals into ones expressing more complex sentences. But a statement to the effect that a certain formula is derivable in a particular formal system does belong to a genuine language; that is why no one can be prevented from forming more complex sentences, for instance that every formula of a certain kind is derivable, and asking after their truth.

It could be replied to this criticism that, even if answers to the new question cannot be represented by formulas of the given formal system, another formal system can be constructed within which they can be represented. Ask yourself whether this reply meets the criticism. Has the formalist confused the statement that a mathematical proposition can be shown to be *represented* by a formula of a formal system, in the sense that it is provable just in case that formula can be derived in the system, with the statement that its *whole content* is that the formula is derivable? And has he confused the thesis that, for every question that can be posed within existing mathematics, a formal system can be devised within which it can be represented by some formula, with the thesis that there is a set of formal systems within which every such question can be represented?

Frege's second argument against formalism concerned the application of mathematics. For an uninterpreted formal system to be applied, its symbols must be supplied with an empirical interpretation under which its axioms can be shown to be true and its methods of proof to preserve truth. Whose business is it to certify this? Not, as the formalist views the matter, that of the mathematician, for he is not concerned with truth. But not that of the natural scientist, either, since he is accustomed to take the mathematics as given. On the formalist's view, it falls into the void, Frege argued. Formalism cannot account for the application of mathematics, because it does not allow mathematical statements to have a content; it reduces mathematics to a game, which is not apt for application.

6.1. Hilbert's Philosophy of Geometry

David Hilbert was frequently described in his lifetime as a 'formalist', a designation which is highly misleading as a description of his mature philosophy of mathematics. He had, nevertheless, a strong leaning towards formalism, without ever fully embracing it. His first notable work was the *Foundations of Geometry* (1899 with many subsequent editions). This was a rigorous axiomatization of Euclidean geometry, a great deal more precise than that of Euclid himself. It infuriated Frege because of Hilbert's epistemological attitude to it. Hilbert regarded his axiomatic theory as one open to any interpretation that would bring its axioms out true; it was therefore senseless, in his eyes, to ask whether those axioms were true absolutely, that is, independently of any particular interpretation. The primitive expressions of the theory were thus, in effect, treated as schematic letters with no one specific intended set of meanings; Hilbert compounded this offence by declaring that the axioms jointly determined the meanings of the primitives. For Frege, an axiom was a determinate proposition that we accept as true, but which is too fundamental for us to need, or to be able, to prove it; its component expressions must therefore have definite, unique senses. Hilbert's 'axioms' were not, therefore, axioms at all for him.

On a view such as Hilbert's, all models of a mathematical theory stand on the same level: what models it has, or even whether it has any, is a question extraneous to the theory as such—there is no such thing as the intended model. This is not radical formalism, according to which no symbol is to be recognized as a logical constant, a variable, or a primitive predicate. The sentences of a theory of Hilbert's kind have the structure of real sentences; it is just that the primitives of the theory have no pre-assigned content. The view of mathematics underlying such a procedure is what is now called *structuralism*. This is the currently very popular thesis that what mathematics is about is abstract structure, and nothing more. Structure, whether unique or not, is characterized by a class of mathematical systems closed under isomorphism; and such a class may be circumscribed by means of an axiomatic theory, of whose models it consists.

This is essentially the position of a neo-Dedekindian such as Benacerraf. It makes into the exclusive concern of a mathematical theory what is undoubtedly one of its salient concerns: for axiomatization is among the principal techniques of mathematics, which seeks not merely to prove theorems but to investigate the minimum presuppositions for their proofs, often thereby extending their scope; and it is intrinsic to an axiomatic theory that it serves to characterize only the abstract structure of its models. Frege would have objected that mathematics should be concerned, not only with structure, but with applications, and this is glaringly obvious when the structuralist account is applied, as Dedekind and Benacerraf have applied it, to number theory. The number 4 cannot be characterized solely by its position in a system with the abstract structure delineated by Dedekind, because it has different positions in the system of natural numbers and that of the positive whole numbers, whereas these systems have the very same structure. Whether we are concerned with the natural numbers or the positive integers depends on whether we start with 0 or 1: whether the initial element is 0 or 1 depends solely on the application we make of the elements of the system as finite cardinal numbers.

Hilbert's *Foundations of Geometry* had another feature: the axiomatic theory was purely geometrical. Just as Bolzano and his successors had striven to expel from analysis appeals to geometrical intuition, so Hilbert expelled from geometry all appeal to arithmetic. His axioms made no reference to the real numbers, say as the values of a distance function between points or as a measure of angles. Rather, having developed the theory as quantifying only over points, lines, and planes, he proved a representation theorem, showing that the real numbers could be used to construct a model of the theory. This treatment has inspired Hartry Field, a neo-Hilbertian whose short book *Science without Numbers* is another piece of essential reading. Field is a nominalist: he does not believe that there are any mathematical objects such as numbers or sets. He therefore does not believe that ordinary mathematical theories—which he interprets at face value—are true; his problem is then to explain why, if not true, they have such fruitful applications in science. Hilbert's book on geometry is his prototype for accomplishing such a task. The scientific theories must first be reformulated so as to avoid any appeal to mathematical objects such as real or complex numbers. By means of a representation theorem, it can then be shown that the addition to this reformulated scientific theory of the mathematical theory, say the theory of real numbers, is a conservative extension of it: that is, that anything expressible in the language of the scientific theory that can be derived in the extended theory could have been derived, though perhaps with greater difficulty, in the original unextended theory. If this can be shown, it is explained why the scientist finds it useful to pretend that there are such things as real numbers or other mathematical objects, without having to concede that it is more than a pretence.

6.2. Hilbert's Programme

Hilbert was not a formalist in the proper sense of the term; but he had a very restricted view of the extent of meaningful mathematical statements. He did not think that, when applied to a meaningful predicate, quantification over an infinite totality, such as the totality of natural numbers, would yield a statement with a determinate truth-value. He allowed that such quantification would yield a meaningful expression. But such an expression could be interpreted only as making a claim on the part of the speaker, not as enunciating a proposition, true or false. Existential quantification, as applied to a number-theoretic predicate whose application to any specific number we knew how to judge, expressed an 'incomplete communication'. It made a claim that could be vindicated if, and only if, the speaker could cite a specific number to which the predicate applied: by asserting the existentially quantified sentence, he laid claim to being able to cite a true instance, without vouchsafing what the instance was. Similarly, a universally quantified sentence served to make a general claim, better expressed by a formula in which the variables bound by the quantifier were left free. The claim could be vindicated only by exhibiting a method of proving any of the specific statements that resulted from giving numerical values to the free variables. If an existential quantifier were applied to a free-variable formula, the resulting sentence expressed a claim to be able to cite, not a specific number, but a (calculable) function that would yield an instance of the existentially quantified sentence for any assignment of particular values to the free variables. Further than this Hilbert's interpretation would not go.

To make a claim of any of these kinds was certainly to say something with an objective meaning: the claim might be able to be vindicated to everyone's satisfaction, or the speaker might show himself incapable of indicating it. But to make such a claim was not to express a proposition with determinate truth-conditions: the condition for the truth of a proposition must be independent of the speaker's own cognitive state or capacities. Sometimes, a sentence apparently involving quantification over the infinite totality of natural numbers could be supplemented so as to express a genuine proposition, namely if an upper bound could be set on the value of the bound variable: the quantification was then only over a finite initial segment of the natural numbers, an operation that yielded propositions with definite truth-conditions. But a sentence irresolubly involving quantification over all the natural numbers was not subject to the calculus of truth-functions. It could not be meaningfully negated, or made a clause in a meaningful disjunctive or conditional statement. Since classical number theory allowed unlimited application of the logical operations to its sentences, it could not be considered a meaningful theory in general. Those of its formulas that could be interpreted 'finitistically', that is, as not essentially involving generalization over the infinite totality of all natural numbers, were genuinely meaningful; the rest had only an 'ideal' meaning, that is, were feigned to have a meaning.

Hilbert had a deeply ambivalent attitude towards classical mathematics. On the one hand, his view of the extent to which it consisted of straightforwardly meaningful statements was restricted in the extreme. On the other, he wished to defend it in its entirety (or at least in so far as it did not run foul of the set-theoretical paradoxes). Given the first view, the defence could not be direct, like Frege's: there was no possibility of demonstrating the *truth* of classical mathematics. The defence had of necessity to be indirect. For this purpose, Hilbert invented metamathematics.

Metamathematics is the mathematical study of formal systems. It has long been a commonplace that formalized mathematical theories can themselves be made the subject of mathematical investigation, but, when Hilbert proposed it, it was a novelty. Metamathematics, for Hilbert, was proof theory, not model theory: he could attach no sense to interpretations of the variables of quantification as ranging over the elements of an infinite domain. Moreover, it was to be an unmitigatedly meaningful theory: of the intelligible content of *its* statements no question could be raised. It followed that metamathematical statements must all be finitistic, as must the methods of proof permitted within metamathematics. Such a theory could then be applied, in the first instance, to Peano arithmetic, and subsequently to other formalized theories; its object would be to prove their consistency. That was Hilbert's programme.

For one who accepted the formulas of first-order arithmetic as meaningful, and who recognized classical methods of proof as valid, the project of proving the consistency of arithmetic is absurd: what could be a more convincing demonstration of its consistency than the standard model? But Hilbert did not accept that all first-order arithmetical formulas were meaningful; a finitistic proof of consistency for classical arithmetic was an important but far from trivial aim. It might seem an inadequate vindication merely to prove the theory consistent. But Hilbert regarded classical mathematics as no more than a vast engine for deriving finitistic consequences. It could easily be shown that, if a false finitistic statement were derivable in Peano arithmetic—a free-variable statement that yielded a false instance under some assignment of values to the variables—then Peano arithmetic must be inconsistent. Hence, if it was consistent, any finitistic statement derivable from it must be true: a proof of its consistency was all the vindication required.

As the discovery of Russell's paradox had been a blow to Frege's programme, so Gödel's incompleteness results of 1931 were to Hilbert's. Gödel proved that any consistent formal theory for arithmetic was incomplete: a sentence of the theory could be constructed which was neither provable nor refutable in it. Moreover, since this sentence was manifestly true if it was not provable (in loose language, it 'said of itself' that it was not provable), whoever recognized the theory as consistent must recognize the sentence as true. Indeed, Gödel's second incompleteness theorem turned on the possibility of formalizing the entire reasoning of the first theorem within the formal theory: it followed that no consistent theory for arithmetic could prove its own consistency.

This entailed that the consistency of Peano arithmetic could not be proved by methods all of which could be represented within Peano arithmetic. It did not entail that no finitistic proof of its consistency was possible. Hilbert had never given any precise circumscription of what was to count as finitistic proof; and, after Gödel's result, Gentzen proved the consistency of arithmetic by methods undeniably finitistic except for transfinite induction, applied to free-variable statements only, up to ε_0; it followed from Gödel's second incompleteness theorem that transfinite induction up to ε_0 was not derivable in Peano arithmetic. Since Gentzen also showed that transfinite induction up to any ordinal smaller than ε_0 *was* derivable in Peano arithmetic, his result was the best possible. But, however Gentzen's methods of argument may be judged, Gödel had destroyed the hope of vindicating, by finitistic means, all recognizably valid means of proving even statements of first-order number theory. Kreisel and others have since emphasized the value of partial realizations of Hilbert's programme. The fact remained that, as the underpinning of a comprehensive philosophy of mathematics, it had collapsed.

7. SET THEORY

When the shock of the paradoxes had been absorbed, the task of constructing a consistent theory of sets was undertaken, but in a new spirit. Set theory was no longer seen as part of logic, but simply as a very powerful mathematical theory. The axiomatization that became standard was that devised by Ernst Zermelo (1871–1953), as modified by Adolf Fraenkel (1891–1965). This is a straightforwardly first-order axiomatization: the individual variables range over sets, there are no second-order variables, and the only primitive predicates are '=' for identity and the two-place predicate '∈' meaning 'is a member of'. A fundamental axiom is that of extensionality, stating the identity of sets having the same members; all the other axioms but one assert the existence of sets satisfying various conditions for membership, stated in terms of other elements of the domain; these include an axiom of infinity, stating the existence of a denumerable set (quite different in content from Russell and Whitehead's axiom of infinity). In Zermelo's formulation, there was one axiom schema, that of separation, of the form

$$\forall u \exists y \forall x, x \in y \leftrightarrow x \in u \,\&\, \mathsf{A}(x).$$

This says that, given any set u, we can assert the existence of any subset y of u consisting of those members of u that satisfy a condition expressible by a formula '$\mathsf{A}(x)$' of the theory. A single second-order axiom, allowing any condition, whether so expressible or not, would have expressed more faithfully the intuition on which the axiom of separation was based: if a set lies in the domain of the theory, all its subsets also lie in the domain. But to keep the theory a first-order one, an axiom schema was necessary. Fraenkel's substitute for the axiom schema of separation was based on a more powerful intuition: if a set u is in the domain, then any set with no more members than u is in the domain. This was expressed by the axiom schema of replacement, stated thus

$$\forall x \forall y \forall z[\mathsf{R}(z, x) \,\&\, \mathsf{R}(z, y), \rightarrow x = y \rightarrow \forall u \exists y \forall x[x \in y \leftrightarrow \exists z\, (z \in u \,\&\, \mathsf{R}(z, x))].$$

Here '$\mathsf{R}(z, x)$' represents any formula of the theory with two free variables. The formal theory so axiomatized is known as 'Zermelo–Fraenkel set theory', universally abbreviated to 'ZF set theory'.

7.1.1. *The Cumulative Hierarchy*

The axioms of ZF set theory are not a mere collection of existence principles that do not look as though they threaten inconsistency: they are based on a definite conception of what will constitute a model of the theory, known as the cumulative hierarchy. According to this, the sets have ranks, represented by ordinal numbers: each rank comprises all lower ranks, and the members of any set must be of rank lower than any rank to which it belongs. The elements of rank 0 are those things that have no members. There is only one set of rank 0, the null set ϕ. Other elements of rank 0 are the *Urelemente*, objects that are not sets at all. The most usual version of ZF set theory is that in which all sets are pure. A pure set is one all of whose members are sets, and all the members of the members of which are sets, and so on: in other words, a set all the members of whose transitive closure are sets. The *transitive closure* of a set A is the smallest set C containing all the members of A and also containing all members of any member of C. Pure ZF set theory may therefore adopt an unrestricted version of the axiom of extensionality, stating that $x = y$ if x and y have the same members, without any requirement that x and y be sets: this implies that nothing other than Ø can lack members, so that a model of pure ZF set theory will contain no *Urelemente*. For any ordinal α, the rank $\alpha + 1$ will consist of all subsets of the totality of elements of rank α, together with all elements of rank α; if we are treating of pure set theory, the qualification 'together with all elements of rank α' is redundant, because the sets of rank α will automatically be sets of sets of rank α. Thus, at rank 1 we have all subsets of rank 0: these are just the set {Ø} containing Ø as its sole member, together with Ø itself. At rank 2 we have Ø, {Ø}, {{Ø}}, and {Ø, {Ø}}; and so on. If λ is a limit ordinal, the sets of rank λ are just those of rank η for some η less than λ. Thus the sets of rank ω are all the sets of finite rank, in other words, all the finitary sets (sets every member of whose transitive closure is finite).

Every set A in such a model can be represented by a tree. Below the vertex stand nodes representing the members of A; below each node p stand nodes representing the members of the set represented by p. Sets may be of high infinite cardinality, so that any given node may stand immediately above a great many nodes. But every branch in the tree must be finite, terminating in a node representing an element with no members, a fact expressible by saying that the tree must be well-founded; if the model is of pure set theory, every branch must, after finitely many steps, terminate in a node representing Ø. Let us call the lowest rank to which any set belongs its *degree*, and associate with every node in the tree the degree of the set it represents. Since a set can have as members only sets of lower degree than it, we have associated to any branch of the tree a descending sequence of ordinals; and a descending sequence of ordinals must be finite. There can therefore be no infinite descending sequence of sets (a sequence each set in which is followed by a member of that set).

This fact is expressed by the axiom of foundation, the only axiom other than that of extensionality not embodying an existence assumption. The axiom of foundation says that every non-empty set A has a member whose intersection with it is Ø. We need only select a member E of A of degree no higher than that of any other member of A: then E and A can have no member in common. Conversely, if there were an infinite descending sequence $B_0, B_1, B_2, \ldots$ of sets such that, for each i, $B_{i+1} \in B_i$ (in which the B_i might or might not all be distinct), the set containing just the B_i would violate the axiom of foundation.

There are other axiomatizations of set theory than ZF, notably two-sorted theories in which one sort of variable ranges over *classes*, understood as distinguished from sets. The existence assumptions on classes are much more generous than those governing sets: there will be a universal class, containing all sets, and a class containing all ordinals. Contradiction is avoided because classes are not members, either of sets or of other classes. But ZF set theory remains the standard formal system for set theory.

7.1.2. The Axiom of Choice

The most interesting assumption of all is the axiom of choice. This is not normally regarded as an axiom of ZF; the theory whose axioms are those of ZF together with the axiom of choice is normally designated ZFC. The axiom of choice is most easily formulated in set-theoretic terms, but it is not properly a set-theoretic assumption, but a logical one. It allows us, in the course of a proof, to make infinitely many arbitrary choices. Logic allows us to make a single arbitrary choice, or any finite number of them. Suppose that we wish to prove that some proposition holds of every non-empty set, a proposition that makes no reference to any particular member of that set. We may legitimately start our proof by saying, 'Let A be a non-empty set, and b a member of it', and then proceed to reason to a conclusion that leaves b unmentioned. Logic, in its standard formulation, indeed in any reasonable formulation, validates this way of reasoning. But now suppose that we wished to prove that any non-empty set A which fails to satisfy the axiom of foundation is the initial term of an infinite descending sequence of sets, and argued as follows.

> Set $A_0 = A$. Take A_1 as a member of A. Since we know that A_1 has a member in common with A, we may take A_2 to be such a common member. By repetition of this argument, we shall have formed an infinite descending sequence of sets, starting with A.

We have tacitly made infinitely many arbitrary choices, namely of all the terms of the sequence after A_0. This manœuvre logic, in its standard formulation, does *not* sanction.

It was Zermelo who first perceived that this way of reasoning was not validated by standard logical principles, and who therefore formulated it explicitly as the axiom of choice, believing it to be valid. Previously, it had been tacitly appealed to in mathematical proofs whose authors were not conscious of invoking a novel principle. There are two natural equivalent formulations of the axiom of choice by set-theoretical means. One is:

(1) If D is a set of disjoint non-empty sets, there is a set C which has just one member in common with each member of D.

The other is:

(2) If D is a set of non-empty sets, there is a function f such that $f(x) \in x$ for every $x \in D$.

C in (1) is a *choice* set; f in (2) is a *choice function*. (You may find it a useful exercise to express (1) and (2) symbolically.) When Zermelo first made the principle explicit, there was much debate about its validity. For some, it was obviously true; others objected to asserting the existence of a choice set or of a choice function when no means existed for specifying it. Controversy has now died down, to the extent that few mathematicians jib at appealing to the principle when they need to. They still prefer, however, to avoid appealing to it if they can, and think it best to signal proofs in which they have been unable to avoid it.

The axiom of choice reduces the selection of infinitely many arbitrary representative objects to that of a single arbitrary choice set or choice function. Thus, in the foregoing example, we may take D to be the set of all intersections of members of A with A. For any X, if $X \in A$, let X^* be its intersection with A. We first select a choice function f, and having chosen any member X of A as A_1, we put $A_{i+1} = f(A_i^*)$ for each i.

The axiom of choice has many consequences, some of them highly counterintuitive. It has, in particular, a great many equivalents, some of them apparently remote in subject-matter. Among these equivalents are the statement that every set can be well-ordered, and the statement that any two sets are comparable in cardinality. An important fact, provable without the axiom of choice, is embodied in the Schröder–Bernstein theorem. The cardinality of a set is less than or equal to that of another if the first set can be mapped one–one *into* the other; it is strictly less if it is less than or equal but not equal. The Schröder–Bernstein theorem says that if each of two sets can be mapped one–one *into* the other, either can be mapped one–one *on to* the other. This is equivalent to saying that the relation of magnitude between cardinal numbers is anti-symmetric: if each of two cardinal numbers is less than or equal to the other, they are equal. Without the axiom of choice, however, the possibility lies open that infinite cardinal numbers may simply be incomparable: the continuum problem would then not arise. The axiom of choice guarantees that the relation of magnitude is connected: of any two cardinal numbers, either one is less than the other, or they are equal.

There are also weakened versions of the axiom of choice. We may restrict the set D above to be denumerable; we may also adopt the *axiom of dependent choices*, which permits denumerably many *successive* arbitrary choices. This has the form:

(3) If for every $x \in A$, there exists $y \in A$ such that $R(x, y)$, then, for any $x \in A$, there is an infinite sequence $x_0, x_1, \ldots$ with $x = x_0$ and $R(x_i, x_{i+1})$ for every i.

The axiom of dependent choices is weaker than the general axiom of choice, but stronger than the denumerable axiom of choice: if we wanted to select all the terms of the sequence simultaneously in advance, we might have to make non-denumerably many choices.

The axiom of choice greatly simplifies the arithmetic of cardinal numbers. Russell was fond of an amusing illustration of this. Suppose a millionaire owns denumerably many pairs of shoes and denumerably many pairs of socks: how many individual shoes, and how many individual socks, has he? In the case of the shoes, the answer is what we should expect: denumerably many. By hypothesis, we can enumerate the pairs as pair 0, pair 1, and so on. We can therefore map the number $2n$ on to the left-hand shoe of pair n, and $2n + 1$ on to the right-hand shoe of pair n, for each n. But we cannot prove him to have denumerably many socks by similar means, for we have no way of specifying on to which member of pair n the number $2n$, and on to which the number $2n + 1$, is to be mapped; without the axiom of choice, therefore, we cannot assert that there is such a mapping.

Another example is the following. A set has just n members, for some natural number n, if the natural numbers less than n can be mapped one–one on to it; let us say that a set is *finite* if, for some natural number n, it has just n members, and *infinite* if it is not finite. Dedekind had a different definition, however: according to it, a set is infinite iff it can be mapped one–one on to a proper subset of itself (a subset not containing all its members), as the natural numbers can be mapped on to the even natural numbers. Are these definitions equivalent? It is obvious that a set containing a denumerable subset is infinite in Dedekind's sense; the converse is fairly easily proved (can you prove it?). Now if a set is infinite in Dedekind's sense, it obviously cannot be finite, since no initial segment of the natural numbers is infinite in Dedekind's sense. But how about the converse? We are tempted to argue as follows. Let A be a set that is not finite: we can construct a denumerable sequence $a_0, a_1, \ldots$ of members of it as follows.

Since *A* does not have 0 members, we can choose a member of it to serve as a_0. Now the set consisting of members of *A* other than a_0 cannot be empty, since otherwise the number of members of *A* would be 1; hence we may choose a member of the former set to serve as a_1, and so indefinitely. But here we have made a blatant appeal to the axiom of choice, in its informal version. And in fact our instinct was sound: it cannot be proved that every non-finite set is infinite in Dedekind's sense without appeal to the axiom of choice.

These applications of the axiom of choice support what seems obvious. Impressions of obviousness are to be distrusted in mathematics; but here is a possible way to justify appeal to the axiom of choice in these—by no means in all—contexts. Friedrich Waismann, in an odd book which is nevertheless worth reading, *Introduction to Mathematical Thinking*, argued that the definition of cardinal equivalence in terms of one–one mapping was in effect circular. For, he reasoned, we ought not to say that two sets are equivalent if there actually *is* such a mapping, but only if it is *possible* that there should be. But, he continued, whenever we assert a possibility to obtain, we must specify the respect in which it obtains. We cannot do so in this case without circularity, however. We do not mean merely that it is *logically* possible that there should be such a mapping. It is logically possible that there should be a mapping of the days of the week on to Mrs Blair's children; but that does not imply that she has seven children, but only that it is logically possible that she should have. What we mean, Waismann claims, is that it is possible that there should be a mapping *so far as the number of members of each set is concerned*; and this is circular.

Would it be legitimate, in your view, to meet Waismann's objection by treating the axiom of choice as serving to specify, without circularity, the relevant sense of 'possible'? To say that it is possible that there should be a mapping of one set on to another, so far as the numbers of their members is concerned, is to say that each set has enough members for there to be such a mapping. In such a context, the axiom of choice makes clear what is meant by saying this: there are enough members of a set for there to be a mapping if, were we able to make as many arbitrary choices as necessary, there would be such a mapping. If this is an admissible interpretation of the use of the axiom of choice in such arguments, those uses of the axiom are justified: but you may decide that this entire approach—Waismann's objection together with this rebuttal of it—is misguided.

Gödel proved that, if ZF is consistent, so is the result of adding both the axiom of choice and the continuum hypothesis to its axioms: neither can therefore be disproved in ZF (provided that ZF is consistent). Cohen subsequently showed that, if ZF is consistent, so is the result of adding the negation of the axiom of choice to it, and that if ZFC is consistent (ZF with the axiom of choice), so is the result of adding the negation of the continuum hypothesis to it; other investigators have extended this result by showing the relative consistency of a number of alternatives to the continuum hypothesis. The independence of the axiom of choice from ZF is no surprise; but the inability of ZFC to resolve the continuum hypothesis is a grave defect. The incompleteness of set theory is a quite different phenomenon from the incompleteness of arithmetic. The incompleteness of arithmetic is ineradicable; but we have no reason whatever for supposing there to be non-isomorphic models of arithmetic between which we have no grounds of preference. By contrast, we do not know that the independence of the continuum hypothesis instantiates any persistent feature of formal systems of set theory; but we also do not have the right to speak of a unique intended model of set theory. Gödel believed that reflection will prompt us to adopt new axioms for set theory that will allow us either to prove or to disprove the continuum hypothesis. Models of set theory vary in two respects: their height and their breadth. They vary in height according to the size of the largest ordinal not contained in the model; and additional axioms positing 'large cardinals' (i.e. enormous cardinals), and thereby forcing the height of a model to be very great, abound, without any of them determining the truth-value of the continuum hypothesis. Models vary in breadth according to how many subsets of the totality of sets of any order are to be found at the next order. An axiom used by Gödel in his consistency proof severely restricts the breadth of the model, and also allows a derivation of the continuum hypothesis; but neither Gödel nor anyone else has proposed that we should treat this axiom as true. Is our concept of a set too indeterminate to allow the question 'Is the continuum hypothesis true or false?' to have a definite answer? If not, how are we to attain an adequate characterization of it?

7.2. Skolem's Paradox

Leopold Löwenheim (b. 1878) had proved in 1915 an important theorem, whose content and proof were both subsequently improved by Thoralf Skolem (1887–1963) in papers of 1920 and 1922. The upshot of the Löwenheim–Skolem theorem is that if a set of first-order formulas (with the sign of identity '='), and hence a first-order theory, has a model at all, it has an at most denumerable (finite or denumerable) one. This formal result gives rise to what is known as 'Skolem's paradox'. For many first-order theories have, as their intended models, ones with a non-denumerably infinite domain; set theory is an obvious example. How can it be that we can frame theories whose axioms, on the face of it, demand, for their satisfaction, a domain much larger than the natural numbers, and yet can in fact be satisfied in a denumerable domain (if they can be satisfied at all)? By the completeness theorem for first-order logic, a first-order theory has a model just in case it is consistent. How, then, can it be that, if ZF set theory is consistent, that theory, which contains all Cantor's Alephs, can have a model in the natural numbers?

There have been various answers to Skolem's paradox. Here are two:

1. There are no absolutely non-denumerable totalities: every infinite totality is really denumerable. When we construct a theory that gives the appearance that the domain of a model of it must be non-denumerable, the appearance is due to the fact that there will not be enough mappings *in the model* to map the natural numbers on to the elements of the domain: there will *be* such a mapping in reality, but it will not exist in the model.

2. The existence of a denumerable model for a first-order theory satisfiable by some non-denumerably infinite model is a consequence of the inadequacy of a first-order language to express our grasp of the intended model. Our only reason for believing the theory to be consistent derives from our conception of its intended model; we believe ZF set theory to be consistent, for example, because we intuitively envisage the model given by the cumulative hierarchy, taken through a sufficiently large segment of ordinal numbers (the ordinals less than what is called the first inaccessible ordinal). The proof of the Löwenheim–Skolem theorem does not allow us to form any actual conception of a denumerable model of the theory; we should not believe that it existed if we did not have a conception of the non-denumerable model we are intending the theory to describe.

Which of these two responses do you think is correct? Or do you think that the truth lies somewhere between them? Skolem's paradox is well worth puzzling over: you are strongly recommended to puzzle over it.

7.3. Platonism

Classical mathematics, of which Cantorian set theory is the most extreme example, rests on a platonist conception of what mathematics is. According to this conception, mathematical statements describe objects, and systems of objects, that we are able to conceive but which exist quite independently of us and of what we know or can prove. We do not have to be able to operate effectively upon individual elements of a mathematical system in order to prove facts about it; it is enough that we can conceive of those elements in their totality and say what they are. In just this way, we can prove a great many propositions about the real numbers, even though we are unable even to specify more than a minority of individual real numbers. Just as, on a realist interpretation of empirical statements, those statements are rendered determinately true or false by empirical reality independently of our knowledge or experience, so, on the platonist interpretation of mathematical statements, mathematical reality confers on any such statement possessing a definite sense a determinate value, *true* or *false*, independently of whether we can prove it or disprove it. When the statement belongs to a theory that is intended to apply to different systems of mathematical objects, not all isomorphic to one another, it may not be absolutely true or absolutely false, but, rather, true in some systems that are models of the theory and false in others. Nevertheless, it will be determinately true or false within any one model of the theory, and hence, in proving theorems in the theory, we may reason just as we should if the theory had a unique intended model.

Kurt Gödel, in some celebrated essays on the philosophy of mathematics, advocated a robustly platonistic view. This was not contaminated by logicism, as Frege's version of platonism had been. Gödel believed that we possess a faculty of mathematical intuition, not to be identified with our logical faculty. 'Intuition' in this sense is not the same as Kantian a priori intuition: it is simply a capacity to apprehend an independently existing mathematical reality analogous to the sense-perception by means of which we apprehend physical reality; and it shows itself, according to Gödel, in our ability to propound and recognize as true axioms governing that reality. For Gödel, a belief in the existence of mathematical objects external to us has the same status as our belief in the existence of material objects, and is equally compelling. Both might be said to be postulates; but they are postulates without which we cannot account for our experience—our sensory experience and our mathematical experience—and which cannot therefore be denied.

It is a mistake to decry the importance of sketchy informal conceptions of the mathematical structures which our theories are intended to describe—such a conception as the cumulative hierarchy as a model of ZF set theory. The best way to see the role that such conceptions play is to consider cases in which we have no such conception. One is provided by the system of set theory known as NF or New Foundations, from the title of the article 'New Foundations for Mathematical Logic', in which W. V. O. Quine (1908–) first propounded it. Quine devised the theory in a formalist spirit: he had in mind no model for it, but only a hunch that a certain syntactic constraint on its axioms would serve to ward off contradiction. A set theory based on the simple theory of types is an infinitely many-sorted theory, in which the variables carry subscripts in the form of natural numbers to indicate their type: a formula is well-formed just in case the symbol '$\in$' for set-membership always has on its right a variable of type just one higher than the variable on its left. Quine's NF is a one-sorted first-order theory; it can be axiomatized by an axiom of extensionality and a comprehension axiom schema, giving the conditions for sets to exist. Quine's hunch was that the theory would be consistent provided that the condition for membership of the set asserted by this schema to exist was 'stratified'. A formula is stratified if subscripts could be attached to the variables so as to render it a well-formed formula of simple type theory: the comprehension axiom schema therefore has the form

$$\exists y\, \forall x\, [x \in y \leftrightarrow \mathsf{A}(x)],$$

where '$\mathsf{A}(x)$' represents any stratified formula not containing 'y' free. The sets over which the variables of the theory range are not divided into types; stratification is merely a syntactic device which it is hoped will guard against inconsistency.

The resulting theory is very odd. We can demonstrate in it the existence of a universe set, containing all sets as members, of a set of all unit sets (sets containing only one member), of a set of all unit sets of unit sets, and so on. These prove to be of decreasing cardinality. It follows that we can disprove the axiom of choice, which is incompatible with the existence of an infinite descending sequence of cardinal numbers; that in turn allows us to prove the axiom of infinity, since the axiom of choice would certainly be true if all sets were finite.

Strenuous efforts have failed to devise a model for NF. The nature of the problem is best seen from an observation of Ernst Specker. Suppose we extend the simple theory of types by allowing the variables to carry negative integers as subscripts. The resulting theory is consistent if the simple theory of types is: for in any proof only finitely many variables occur, so that it can be converted into a proof within the simple theory of types by raising every subscript index by the same amount, so that the lowest index that occurs is 0. The theory of (positive and) negative types plainly cannot have a standard model, in which every type is the class of all subsets of the type one below it, since otherwise we should have an infinite descending sequence of cardinal numbers. Specker's remark is that there exists a model for NF just in case there is a model of the theory of negative types in which each type is a copy of the one immediately below it (and therefore of every other type); each type will then be a model for NF.

NF is a living disproof of the formalist contention that all that concerns mathematics is to discover which theorems are derivable from any arbitrarily selected set of axioms. The proof of a theorem within NF is indeed of mathematical interest; but its content is that a certain formula can be derived within the formal theory NF, not that a certain proposition holds of a particular mathematical structure. We do not regard NF as defining a mathematical structure, or a class of mathematical structures, precisely because we have no conception of what a model of it would look like: we regard it simply as a somewhat eccentric formal theory.

Intuitive conceptions of mathematical structures do, therefore, play an important role in mathematics. But are they gained by a special faculty of intellectual apprehension deserving the name of mathematical intuition? Are they prior to their description in words, or are they derived from such descriptions? These are the questions you need to answer in order to decide whether platonism of Gödel's kind is defensible or not.

Quine has defended platonism on quite different grounds. He takes mathematical theories at face value in the sense that the existential quantifiers occurring in them are to be understood in the standard way, and hence regards them as 'postulating' mathematical objects. Such postulation he believes to be indispensable for the use of such theories in scientific applications. Mathematical theories are adjuncts to scientific theories: what is to be evaluated is the composite theory, consisting of both scientific and mathematical components. A theory is vindicated if it has explanatory or predictive power.

8. INTUITIONISM

During the nineteenth century, from Leopold Kronecker (1823–91) onwards, a number of mathematicians, of the tendency known as 'constructivist', felt the platonist conception of mathematics to be alien to them, and wished mathematics not to stand at so great a distance from constructions that human mathematicians can actually make and operations they can actually carry out. The formation of a specific programme for constructive mathematics was the achievement (or one of the achievements) of L. E. J. Brouwer (1881–1966); the school he created is that of the *intuitionists*.

8.1. Intuitionistic Logic

Brouwer took a step that no constructivist had previously taken: he attacked the logic of classical mathematics, what is appropriately called classical, i.e. two-valued, logic. This step is best viewed from Hilbert's finitism as a starting-point. Hilbert held that sentences governed by initial quantifiers whose variables ranged over an infinite domain were meaningful, but could not be construed as expressing propositions with determinate truth-conditions; rather, they serve to make claims, which the speaker might or might not prove able to make good. With this, Brouwer wholly agreed. The truth-value of a sentence involving quantification over an infinite domain, as classically conceived, is the outcome of an infinitary operation: it depends on the truth-values of its infinitely many instances. On Brouwer's view, however, we have no right to presume that every infinitary operation *has* a determinate outcome. An infinite process, *ex vi termini*, is one that never comes to an end, whereas the outcome of a process is what we have obtained when the process has terminated.

So far, then, Brouwer agreed with Hilbert about the only sense that could be given to sentences governed by quantifiers with infinite domains. What he disagreed with was Hilbert's next step, namely to say that sentences expressing claims rather than propositions with definite truth-values were not subject to the standard sentential operators. What we need, rather, is a way of understanding the sentential operators as forming, from sentences expressing claims, more complex sentences expressing other claims. The claim made by one who asserts a mathematical statement is to be able to prove it. We therefore need to explain the logical constants, not by specifying the truth-conditions of complex sentences in terms of those of their constituent subsentences, but by specifying, in terms of proofs of the subsentences, what should constitute the proof of a complex sentence.

The fundamental notion of intuitionistic mathematics is that of a *construction*, that is, the specification, by whatever means, of a mathematical entity or argument. Brouwer himself believed that a construction can never be perfectly communicated by verbal or symbolic language: he therefore conceived of constructions in a solipsistic manner, as processes within the mind of an individual mathematician. You may think, rather, that mathematics is perfectly communicable. An old philosophical thesis was that what can be communicated is structure, not content. The structuralist account of mathematics assigns structure as its sole subject-matter. These two theses together imply that mathematics alone is perfectly communicable. You may well not accept either of the two theses, but may yet think that there is enough truth in them to validate the conclusion that mathematical constructions can be communicated. But, even if an intuitionist is willing to depart this far from Brouwer's solipsistic view, he will not wish to identify a construction with any linguistic item, considered as a physical object. Certainly mathematical constructions cannot be equated with sentences or sequences of sentences in a formal language, whose vocabulary and methods of sentence formation have been circumscribed in advance. Even when expressed linguistically or symbolically, they remain *mental* constructions to the extent that the understanding of them as intended is integral to them; and their means of expression are as unbounded as language itself.

An intuitionistic explanation of a logical constant is, then, effected by specifying when a construction is to count as a proof of a sentence whose principal operator is that constant, taking it as known what counts as proving the immediate subsentences. A proof of "A & B" is, plainly, something that proves A and also proves B. A proof of "A $\vee$ B" is something that either proves A or proves B. A proof of "A $\rightarrow$ B" is an operation of which we can recognize that, applied to any proof of A, it will yield a proof of B. A proof of "$\neg$A" is an operation of which we can recognize that, applied to any proof of A, it will yield a contradiction; it therefore provides a guarantee that we shall never find a proof of A. When the domain is taken as consisting of the natural numbers, the quantifiers are understood essentially in Hilbert's way: a proof of "$\forall x\, \mathsf{A}(x)$" is an operation of which we can recognize that, applied to any natural number n, it will yield a proof of "A(n)"; and a proof of "$\exists x\, \mathsf{A}(x)$" is a natural number n together with a proof of "A(n)". To be warranted in asserting a statement of the form "$\exists x\, \mathsf{A}(x)$", a mathematician is not required actually to cite an actual instance "A(n)"; it is enough for him to exhibit an effective means of finding one. Similarly, one who asserts a disjunctive statement "A $\vee$ B" does not have actually to produce a proof either of A or of B; it is enough that he should indicate an effective procedure which will yield a proof of one or the other. (For instance, he may legitimately assert, of some large number, that it is either prime or composite, even if he does not know which it is, since primality is a decidable property.)

This interpretation of the logical constants validates many of the laws of classical logic, but certainly does not validate them all. Most notoriously, it does not validate the law of excluded middle,

$$p \vee \neg p.$$

The assertion of a statement of the form "A $\vee$ ¬A" will amount to a claim to have an effective method of deciding A, that is, of finding a proof either of A or of "¬A"; it can therefore be warranted only when A is a decidable statement. It must *not* be concluded that intuitionistic logic operates with a threefold classification of propositions into those that are true, those that are false, and those that are neither true nor false. It does not operate with the notions of truth and falsity at all; its semantics does not make use of those notions, but only with that of a construction's being a proof of a statement. The notions of truth and falsity are admissible in intuitionistic mathematics only to the extent that a statement that has been proved may be said to be true and one that has been disproved may be said to be false; that is to say, they may really be regarded as wholly explained by the principle that "It is true that A" is equivalent to A, and "It is false that A" to "¬A". To assume a statement B as a hypothesis, for the purpose of conditional proof, is thus to suppose that we had a proof of B. To say that we cannot in general assume a statement A to be either true or false is therefore simply to say that we do not have an unrestricted right to assert "A $\vee$ ¬A". Conversely, to say that A was neither true nor false would be tantamount to asserting that neither A nor "¬A" was true, that is, to asserting "¬(A $\vee$ ¬A)". This, however, would be a contradiction. In intuitionistic logic, as in classical logic, "¬(B $\vee$ C)" is equivalent to "¬B & ¬C"; "¬(A $\vee$ ¬A)" is therefore equivalent to "¬A & ¬¬A", and this is an outright contradiction. For this reason, although the law of excluded middle is not valid in intuitionistic logic, its double negation,

$$\neg\neg(p \vee \neg p),$$

is.

It is immediately evident from this that the law of double negation,

$$\neg\neg q \rightarrow q,$$

is also intuitionistically invalid; for, if it held, then, by substituting "$p \vee \neg p$" for "q", the law of excluded middle would be immediately forthcoming. The converse,

(*) $q \rightarrow \neg\neg q$,

is evidently valid, since, given a proof of a statement A, we could immediately obtain a contradiction from a proof of "¬A". The double negation "¬¬A" is thus a weaker statement than A. This is in effect to say that a demonstration that we cannot disprove A does not amount to a proof of A. Negation does not indefinitely yield non-equivalent statements, however. Contraposition remains valid: from

$$B \rightarrow C$$

we may derive

$$\neg C \rightarrow \neg B,$$

for, given a proof of "¬C", we could at once derive a contradiction from a proof of B. (The inference from "¬C→¬B" to "B→C" is not valid, however.) Now

$$\neg\neg\neg q \rightarrow \neg q$$

is the contraposition of (*) above, while

$$\neg q \rightarrow \neg\neg\neg q$$

is derivable from (*) by substitution. Triple negation thus reduces to single negation.

The most important failure of a classically valid law of predicate logic is the impossibility of deriving

$$\exists x\, \neg A(x)$$

from

$$\neg\forall x\, A(x).$$

To have shown that a contradiction would be obtainable if we had a method of proving "A(n)" for each natural number n does not provide us with any means of finding a number n such that "A(n)" fails.

8.2. Real Numbers

The use of a divergent underlying logic is the fundamental difference between intuitionistic and classical mathematics, but is far from being the only one. Others appear as soon as we consider the intuitionistic theory of real numbers. As in Cantor's theory of the reals, this is normally developed intuitionistically in terms of infinite sequences of rational numbers; but an infinite sequence is viewed very differently in intuitionistic and in classical mathematics. For the classical mathematician, an infinite sequence is a purely extensional object: it is wholly constituted by which terms it has, irrespective of the way in which it happened to be defined. Moreover, it is an instance of a 'completed infinity': it has determinate properties, depending on the totality of its terms, even though we can cite only finitely many of them. In intuitionistic mathematics, by contrast, every mathematical entity spoken of must be thought of as given to us in a particular way, and its identity is constituted by the way in which it is given. The entities of intuitionistic mathematics are, therefore, intensional ones, and must be so considered even when we are concerned only with their extensional properties. An infinite sequence, for example, may be given by some effective means of calculating its terms; it is not then to be *identified* with a sequence given in some other way, say by a different means of calculating its terms, even if the two sequences should prove to coincide term by term. We can ascribe to a sequence only those properties that can be derived from the way in which it was given (together with some finite number of its terms, more than which we cannot know).

A *real-number generator* is an infinite sequence of rationals satisfying the Cauchy condition, intuitionistically understood: that is to say, for each negative power 2^{-k} of 2, we can find a term of the sequence whose absolute difference from every subsequent term is less than 2^{-k}. We can then identify the real numbers themselves with equivalence classes of real-number generators (ones which converge to the same limit); the equivalence relation is defined as holding between two sequences if, for each negative power 2^{-k} of 2, we can find a number n such that the absolute difference between every pair of corresponding terms of the two sequences after the n-th is less than 2^{-k}. But a real number must always be thought of as given by some specific real-number generator: we have no other way of identifying it.

Real numbers fail to be equal if, considered as equivalence classes, they contain different real-number generators; but a stronger relation may obtain between them, a sort of positive type of distinctness. Two real numbers lie *apart* if the real-number generators by which they are given lie apart; and the real-number generators lie apart if we can find a number n and a negative power 2^{-k} of 2 such that the absolute difference between their corresponding terms after the n-th is always greater than 2^{-k}. This is a good instance of the way in which intuitionistic mathematics allows of finer distinctions than does the classical variety. In intuitionistic mathematics, argument by cases is necessarily rarer than it is classically. For instance, we cannot in general assume, for any real number x, that it is either greater than 0 or less than or equal to 0. We can, however, assume that it is either greater than 0 or less than 1, since one or other can always be determined; and this often serves our purpose.

8.3. The Intuitionistic Axiom of Choice

The most straightforward non-set-theoretic formulation of the axiom of choice is:

$\forall x \exists y \, A(x, y) \rightarrow$
$\exists f \, \forall x \, A(x, f(x))$).

Here 'x' and 'y' may be variables of any sorts, the same or different, while '$A(x, y)$' represents any statement involving those two variables, and 'f' ranges over functions defined on the domain of 'x' with values in the domain of 'y'. Intuitionistically, to assert the existence of a function is always to say that there is an effectively calculable such function. Although a choice function has usually been thought to be a pre-eminently non-constructive thing, indeed one that is not in general independently specifiable, the axiom of choice is, from an intuitionistic standpoint, an obviously true principle. It is true, that is, provided that the quantifiers in the antecedent are understood in their intuitionistic senses: the consequent then follows immediately from those senses. Suppose, for purposes of illustration, that the variables 'x' and 'y' range over the natural numbers. Then a proof of the antecedent will be an effective operation that carries each natural number n into a proof of 'For some y, $A(n, y)$'; and a proof of this latter statement will consist in a natural number m and a proof of '$A(n, m)$'. A proof of the antecedent therefore automatically yields a function that carries any natural number n into a number m satisfying '$A(n, m)$', just as the consequent asserts. Parallel reasoning will apply whatever the ranges of the variables. 'x' and 'y'.

Care needs to be taken in applying the axiom of choice, however, in view of the intensional character of the entities of intuitionistic mathematics. The function f will operate, not upon elements in the domain of the variable 'x', considered extensionally, but upon the way in which they are given. There is therefore no guarantee that it will map extensionally equivalent elements of that domain on to the same element of the domain of 'y'. When 'x' ranges over the natural numbers, there is no problem, regardless of the domain of 'y', since natural numbers can be given in essentially only one way; that is to say, equality between natural numbers is a decidable relation (as equality between real numbers is not). But when 'x' ranges over other domains, say over infinite sequences, there can be no presumption that the values of f for extensionally equal sequences—let alone for equivalent real-number generators—will coincide.

8.4. Choice Sequences

So far, we have reviewed intuitionistic mathematics only so far as it is a version of constructive mathematics. In 1967 the well-known American mathematician Errett Bishop (1928–83) published a book called *Foundations of Constructive Analysis*. In this he announced his conversion to constructivism, and carried the development of mathematics on constructivist principles further than it had been carried by Brouwer and his followers. Although Bishop was not interested in formalizing logic, the logic he accepted was the intuitionistic logic described above (save that he had an unreasonable aversion to any explicit use of negation). In fact, he agreed with all the intuitionistic ideas so far expounded. Since all intuitionistic laws of first-order logic are classically valid, the result is a theory compatible with classical mathematics. It rejects certain methods of proof accepted by classical mathematicians, and makes distinctions between statements which are, by classical standards, equivalent; but it does not propose any principles which would be viewed by a classical mathematician as false.

That is not true of the intuitionism developed by Brouwer. He was not content to identify infinite sequences with those generated by a calculable function of natural numbers. Rather, he allowed that some or all of their terms might be determined by arbitrary choices, unconstrained or subject to effective limitations on what might be chosen. These are the celebrated *choice sequences*. (The exact characterization of choice sequences is problematic, but this sketchy description will serve for present purposes.) Choice sequences may seem at first sight highly non-constructive objects, depending as in general they do upon infinitely many arbitrary choices. They must, however, be thought of constructively, which means that they are not completed infinities. All that can be known of them at any time is a finite initial segment of their terms, together with any law that constrains the choice of those terms (or in special cases determines it); and anything that can be asserted of a choice sequence must be based on such knowledge.

Choice sequences of natural numbers are to be thought of as elements of a *spread*. A spread is what is classically called a tree, whose nodes are finite sequences of natural numbers; what are called the elements of the spread are the paths in the tree, which are all infinite in length, and these are the choice sequences. The null sequence constitutes the vertex; the nodes immediately below any given node (or finite sequence p) are immediate extensions (or descendants) of p, formed by appending a single natural number to the end of p. Each spread is governed by a *spread law*, which is a decidable property of finite sequences of natural numbers; it says whether or not any such finite sequence is admissible in that spread, that is, whether it figures as a node of the tree (and thus as an initial segment of some choice sequence). The spread law is required to recognize the null sequence as admissible; for any admissible finite sequence q, to recognize as admissible each of the finite sequences of which q is an extension; and, for any admissible finite sequence p, to recognize as admissible at least one immediate descendant of p. The spread law thus represents effective restrictions placed in advance on the choice of a term of a choice sequence that is to be an element of the spread.

We of course often need to consider infinite sequences whose terms are not natural numbers, but, say, rational numbers. These are elements of *dressed spreads*. Given a (naked) spread, it can be 'dressed' by an effective correlation law which associates finite sequences of natural numbers admissible in the spread with mathematical objects of the required kind.

The introduction of choice sequences into intuitionistic mathematics is accompanied by the adoption of principles governing them not recognized as holding by constructivists of Bishop's school. These are of two kinds: those that are classically true, and those that are classically false. Of the first kind is the principle of *bar induction*. Suppose that we have a decidable set R of finite sequences of natural numbers admissible in a given spread. Suppose, further, that A is a property of finite sequences (not in general decidable) possessed by every finite sequence in R and hereditary in the following sense: if every admissible immediate descendant of an admissible finite sequence p has the property A, then p itself has the property A. Now we say that the set R *bars* some admissible finite sequence p if every choice sequence of which p is an initial segment has an initial segment in R. (In the terminology of trees, a set R of nodes bars a node p if every path through p goes through some node in R.) On these assumptions, bar induction says that if every element of the spread has an initial segment in R, in other words, if R bars the vertex (the null sequence), then the null sequence has the property A. The induction basis is the fact that every finite sequence in R has the property A; the induction step is that A is hereditary.

The most celebrated application of bar induction is to obtain the *fan theorem*. A *fan* is a finitary spread, that is, one in which each admissible finite sequence has only finitely many admissible immediate extensions. Suppose we are given a fan, and a decidable set R of admissible finite sequences such that every element of the fan has an initial segment in R. Then the fan theorem states that there is a bound m such that every element of the fan has an initial segment in R of length no greater than m.

Both bar induction and the fan theorem are classically true. (The fan theorem is classically equivalent to König's lemma, which says that if there is no finite upper bound to the lengths of the branches of a finitary tree, the tree has at least one infinite branch. The lemma in this form is not intuitionistically provable.) Their classical proofs, however, are not intuitionistically valid. In formalizations of intuitionistic mathematics, bar induction is usually assumed as an axiom; the fan theorem can then be proved from it.

Principles that are far from being classically true are the *continuity principles*, of which we may here describe only the basic case (the next case is controversial). Suppose that we have an *extensional* relation $C(\alpha, n)$ between choice sequences and natural numbers: that is, if $C(\alpha, n)$ holds for given α and n, then $C(\beta, n)$ holds for any β that coincides term by term with α. (We could equally speak of a relation between number-theoretic functions and natural numbers, provided that it was clear that we were including among number-theoretic functions those given by arbitrary choices of their values.) And suppose also that, for any α, we can find n such that $C(\alpha, n)$. Then the continuity principle states that we can find a calculable function e of finite sequences of natural numbers which, for each α, has, for some initial segment of α, a value $n + 1$ such that $C(\alpha, n)$, and has the value 0 for each shorter initial segment of α. The underlying assumption is that if we know that, for any α, we can find n such that $C(\alpha, n)$, and if $C(\alpha, n)$ is an extensional relation, so that n does not depend upon the particular way in which α was given, then we must be able to determine n from some initial segment of α (from finitely many values of α, considered as a function). The effective function e has the value 0 when applied to an initial segment of α that does not give us sufficient information about α for us to be able to determine n, and has the value $n + 1$ as soon as it is applied to an initial segment that does give sufficient information.

The continuity principle allows us to drop the requirement that R be decidable from the fan theorem. It also allows us to replace, in the statement of bar induction, the requirement that R be decidable by the requirement that it be monotonic (any extension of a finite sequence in R is also in R). It does *not* permit all restriction on R to be lifted, however: the result of doing so would be demonstrably false intuitionistically.

Further, the continuity principle allows of the proof of many propositions in conflict with classical mathematics (as well as of some classical theorems that would otherwise be unprovable intuitionistically), particularly by use of the fan theorem. Its power may be judged from a famous result of Brouwer's. First, from the fan theorem may be derived the following corollary. Suppose that, for any element α of a given fan, we can find n satisfying an extensional relation $C(\alpha, n)$. Then there is a number m such that, for every element α of the fan, we can find n such that $C(\beta, n)$ for every element β of the fan agreeing with α on its first m terms.

A real-valued function on the real numbers is a mapping that carries each real-number generator into a real-number generator, and equivalent real-number generators into equivalent real-number generators. Such a function f is *uniformly continuous* in an interval if for every k we can find m such that, for every x and y in the interval, if the absolute difference between x and y is less than 2^{-m}, then the absolute difference between $f(x)$ and $f(y)$ is less than 2^{-k}. We can now use the foregoing corollary of the fan theorem to prove the result, astonishing to the ears of a classical mathematician, that, if a function is defined on every real number in an interval, it is uniformly continuous in that interval.

Frege aimed to justify classical mathematics by directly deriving it from pure logic. Hilbert aimed to justify it indirectly. Brouwer aimed to replace it by a version of mathematics reformed from the ground up, believing that version to be conceptually unproblematic, whereas he regarded classical mathematics as conceptually indefensible. Although he gained some notable converts, he did not succeed in establishing a lasting school; intuitionism has attracted a great deal of attention in recent decades from logicians, but few convinced adherents. Bishop's version of constructivism has had greater success; there is now a respectable body of constructivist mathematicians of his variety in the United States and in Britain, although it looks highly unlikely that they will oust classical mathematicians from their position of dominance.

9. WITTGENSTEIN

Ludwig Wittgenstein (1889–1951), probably the greatest philosopher of the twentieth century, was convinced that he was on the brink of making as substantial a contribution to the philosophy of mathematics as he had done to the more central parts of philosophy. At the same time, he was never satisfied that he had achieved a correct formulation of his views about mathematics. For this reason, although he had planned to devote a considerable section of his posthumously published book *Philosophical Investigations* to the topic, he eventually excised it.

Whether his contribution to the philosophy of mathematics was profound or confused is a controversial question. He retains a small band of utterly committed disciples: for these, of course, Wittgenstein laid bare the true nature of mathematics. By contrast, his writings have made a negligible impact upon most present-day philosophers of mathematics; even those who hold the rest of his work in high regard tend to regard this part of philosophy as one within which a great genius stumbled. How his work is to be assessed is thus a question far more contested than similar questions about the work of any other recent philosopher who concerned himself with mathematics; you will have to form your own opinions about this uncertain matter.

Wittgenstein made a sharp distinction, not drawn by anyone else, between actual mathematics and what he called the 'gas' that surrounds it. Real mathematics is to be observed in the proofs of theorems. If we want to know the actual content of the theorem, we must look to 'see what the proof proves'. It is no business of the philosopher to criticize or call in question actual mathematics. Mathematics and philosophy are two quite different activities, and the philosopher has no right to interfere with the mathematician: he can only observe what the mathematician does, accept it, and describe it.

'Gas', on the other hand, consists of the glosses mathematicians put upon their proofs, attempting to expound what they see as their significance; and this the philosopher is in no way bound to respect. The distinction can be illustrated by (what is usually called) Cantor's proof of the non-denumerability of the continuum. What the proof shows is that, given any enumeration of real numbers, we can define a real number omitted by the enumeration: and that is the genuine mathematics forming the core of the theorem. If, however, we describe this by saying 'Cantor proved that there are non-denumerably many real numbers', we are merely emitting gas. The proof does not assume that there is any such totality as that comprising all real numbers, of which it may be intelligibly asked how large it is. The proof says nothing about the totality of real numbers; to interpret it as proving something about that totality is to envelop the theorem in gas.

Well, then, one might conclude: in this case what the proof shows is that *real number* is an indefinitely extensible concept. An indefinitely extensible concept is one that has the property that Russell saw as the cause of all the set-theoretical paradoxes: given any definite totality of things falling under the concept, we can always define, *in terms of that totality*, something falling under the concept but not belonging to the totality. No! To describe the theorem in this way would be to emit gas as noxious as that consisting in talking about non-denumerable totalities. The argument to the indefinite extensibility of the concept *real number* depends upon assuming every definite totality to be at most denumerable; but the proof of Cantor's theorem says nothing about definite totalities, let alone that they are all finite or denumerable. Cantor's theorem states what the proof proves, and no more: namely that, given any enumeration of real numbers, we can define a real number omitted by the enumeration.

The slogan 'Look to see what the proof proves' is undoubtedly salutary; but a rigid application of Wittgenstein's distinction between genuine mathematics and gas produces a highly puritanical attitude towards mathematics, robbing it, some might think, of much of its interest. Wittgenstein's prohibition on philosophers' interfering with the mathematicians has another strange effect. Mathematicians have argued over numerous general principles: over the axiom of choice, over the legitimacy of impredicative definitions violating the vicious circle principle, over the validity of the law of excluded middle. When he discusses these matters, Wittgenstein always gives the impression of being a very radical constructivist: his arguments against the law of excluded middle, for instance, often closely resemble Brouwer's. But these comments on his part are intended to apply only to the citation of the disputed principles in the course of surrounding mathematical results with 'gas'. Others who have contested one or another principle have believed appeal to that principle in the course of mathematical proof to be illegitimate, and have themselves abstained from making such an appeal. When the appeal is genuinely made in the course of proving a theorem, Wittgenstein, on the other hand, thinks that the philosopher has no right to object: to do so would come under the head of interfering with the mathematicians. We thus have the paradox of a philosopher holding extreme constructivist views, but forbidding criticism on philosophical grounds of even highly non-constructive methods of proof.

It was not only with mathematics that Wittgenstein believed that philosophy ought not to interfere: it must not interfere with natural science or with religion, either; it can only describe. It may be pleaded that none of these subjects or activities is, or can be, as quarantined from philosophy as Wittgenstein supposed and desired. It is not a matter just of prohibiting *philosophers* from interfering: philosophy itself must not intrude, and practitioners of mathematics, of natural science, of religion must refrain from indulging in philosophical considerations. If they do so indulge, then they are engaging in 'gas', of which no notice need be taken. But practitioners of all these subjects have frequently appealed to philosophical considerations; and one motive for their doing so is to decide how they ought to proceed. It is of no use to say to them 'Never mind all that: just carry on as it seems natural to you to do', for they want to make up their minds how they are to carry on. 'The mathematicians', for instance, do not form the monolithic bloc that Wittgenstein's remarks might lead one to expect: they have been, and still are, divided over the legitimacy of one or another mode of mathematical reasoning. To those concerned with such disputes, Wittgenstein's advice is useless.

It can indeed be questioned how ingenuous that advice was: for the line between description and criticism is often blurred. A famous outcry of Hilbert's against the intuitionists' reform of mathematics was 'No one shall drive us out of the paradise that Cantor has opened up for us.' Wittgenstein commented that he had no desire to drive anyone out of a paradise: 'I simply point out to him that it is not a paradise, and then he leaves of his own accord.'

We normally think that a computation routine for a function, or a decision procedure for a property, which can 'in principle' be applied to any number determines in advance the value of the function or the possession of the property. For this reason intuitionists allow the assertion, concerning any natural number, however large, that it is either prime or composite. Wittgenstein rejected this conception of determination in advance. He had no time for what can be done only 'in principle': for him, what determines the sense of a mathematical statement giving the value of the function for a particular argument or saying whether or not a particular number has the property is what we accept *in practice* as the criterion for its truth: and the scope for actually carrying out an effective process is always finite. But Wittgenstein's objection to the conception we find natural was more radical than that. Even within the range in which it could be carried out in practice, he denied that an effective process determined in advance a particular answer in each case. More exactly, he thought that such a claim was admissible only in a *mathematical* sense, as saying that the process would always terminate in an answer, as opposed (say) to one that was so designed as not to terminate in certain cases.

We are now in the difficult region of Wittgenstein's so-called 'rule-following considerations'—so called because exegetes are chary of ascribing to him any statable *thesis* concerning rules. 'What distinguishes a calculation from an experiment?', Wittgenstein repeatedly enquires. His answer is surprising. A natural answer might be that the outcome of the calculation, if correctly performed, is determined a priori, whereas, although the result of the experiment is presumably determined by physical laws, it cannot be discovered in a description of the experiment, but must be revealed by nature to our observation. That is not Wittgenstein's account of the matter. For him, what distinguishes a calculation from an experiment is what happens *after* the calculation has been performed. Given that sufficient care had been taken in carrying out the calculation, we now treat its outcome as a criterion for the subsequent correct carrying out of the same calculation; by contrast, if a repetition of an experiment has a different result, that is no reason for discarding it as incorrect. What makes the calculation a *calculation* is our treating it in this way—our 'putting it in the archives'. And that is therefore also what constitutes the calculation's having the outcome that it does.

Before the calculation is performed, nothing determines what the outcome will be, according to Wittgenstein. The calculation is indeed carried out in accordance with a rule. But, while the rule tells us what is to be done, it does not—cannot—contain any means of determining its own application, that is, of judging whether any attempt to follow it is to count as correct or not. *We* judge the attempt as a genuine or a faulty instance of following the rule; and there is no criterion external to or independent of us to determine whether our judgement is sound or not. The rule has been followed if we judge that it has been followed: that is what constitutes its having been followed.

This applies equally to all mathematical statements, whether the outcome of an effective computation or merely the conclusion of a proof. What makes them true is our judging them to be the outcome of a correct computation or the conclusion of a valid proof. We have rules for determining the validity of a step in a chain of inferences, and hence for deciding the validity of a proof; but, like all rules, these do not determine their outcome in advance. And now we can supply the missing thesis, namely:

> No rule contains the means for determining its own application.

Essentially, then, what renders a mathematical statement true is our accepting it as true and as having been correctly arrived at. And it is our treatment of a mathematical statement that, likewise, confers on it its necessity. There *cannot* be a counter-example to a mathematical theorem, or to the result of a mathematical calculation. Why can there not be? Only because, in accepting the proof of the theorem as valid, or the calculation as having been correctly performed, we thereby 'put it in the archives'; this means that we use it as a standard by which to judge other statements, including empirical ones.

Because it is only our acceptance of it that constitutes the truth of a mathematical statement, it does not possess a truth-value in advance of our accepting it. This has a devastating effect on the assumptions that we ordinarily make—that even constructivists ordinarily make. Consider once more the question whether a given natural number is prime or composite. Even if no one has ever troubled to decide the question, the fact that we have an effective method for deciding it induces in almost everyone the belief that it has a definite answer, even if one as yet unknown to us. God, we may say, knows which the number is, prime or composite. For we think that there must be a true proposition (whose truth is now hidden from us) of the form 'If we were to carry out the decision procedure correctly, it would yield the answer that the number is . . .', where the blank is to be filled either by 'prime' or by 'composite'. But Wittgenstein denied this, even when the decision procedure is practically feasible: 'there is nothing for God to know', he said. There is no proposition, true in advance of our carrying out the decision procedure, about what its outcome *must be* if we do carry it out. *If* someone does carry it out, there will then be the outcome, and the fact (if it is one) that his calculation is generally accepted as having been correctly performed. There will *then* be an answer to the question whether the number is prime or composite, and we shall of course say that this answer already held good before we performed the calculation. But it was only our actually performing it that made it the case that the question had an answer. God cannot know, of every number, whether it is prime or composite, because He does not know what the outcome of a calculation we shall never perform would have been if we had carried it out. He does not know this, not because His omnipotence is limited, but because there are no such true propositions. God must know which numbers *He* would call 'prime' and which 'composite', you may say. Well, God's thoughts are not our thoughts: it is *our* thoughts we have been discussion—the thoughts we express in *our* language.

Do the 'rule-following considerations' confuse epistemology with metaphysics? It is surely true that there is nothing *by which* we judge how to apply a rule; and our normal resource for checking whether someone else has applied a rule correctly is to apply it ourselves. But does this entail that there is nothing whatever, save our judgement, to determine whether or not it has in fact been applied correctly? If it is right to say that there is nothing but our judgement, then it must also be right to say that, in advance of our applying it, there can be nothing that determines what its outcome will be if we do apply it correctly. But is it right to say that? Is there really nothing for God to know?

10. CONCLUSION

This study-guide has not supplied you with any answers: besides giving you some information about what various philosophers and mathematicians have said, and about logical and mathematical results that need to be taken into account, it has merely left you with some very difficult questions. Well, what did you expect? This is philosophy you are studying, not geology.

Let us try, in retrospect, to survey the principal questions. Applied mathematics can borrow concepts from experience, observation, scientific theories, and even economics. It is really the philosophy of pure mathematics that we have been studying. And it is its purity that gives rise to many of the questions we have been puzzling over.

Is pure mathematics merely a series of templates for mathematical applications?

Is there really a problem about the existence of the objects of pure mathematics, or may we leave it to the applications to furnish the objects?

If there is a problem, how can it be solved? By what means can we guarantee the existence of abstract objects, and of such objects in sufficiently large supply?

If there is no problem, how can we justify the applications of pure mathematics? By framing the mathematical theories as not demanding the existence of objects? Or by showing that the assumption of their existence results only in a conservative extension of scientific theories so framed?

Is applicability the *point* of pure mathematics? Or is it an unexpected but inessential bonus? Can we anticipate the applications that will occur? Do we need to?

What is the source of mathematical necessity? Can it be distinguished from logical necessity? If not, why should it have proved so difficult to derive mathematics from pure logic? If so, what other kind of necessity can mathematics have?

In virtue of what is a true mathematical proposition true? Can it be true even though we do not have, and shall never have, any means of proving it? Or does its possession of a proof provide us with the only notion that we have of what constitutes the truth of a mathematical proposition? If the latter, do the methods of argument accepted by classical mathematicians require revision? Or can we carry on using them without needing any further justification of them than their general acceptance?

In the course of reading this study-guide, you will have come across other questions than these: what are listed here are only the most salient ones. Have a go at trying to find answers to them that satisfy you. After all, there is a certain sense in which the philosophy of mathematics is the *easiest* part of philosophy:

if you cannot solve these problems, what philosophical problems can you hope to solve?

BIBLIOGRAPHY

This bibliography was prepared with the valuable help of Marcus Giaquinto and Keith Hossack.

Collections

The most useful collection of readings for this chapter is:

Benacerraf, P., and Putnam, H. (eds.), *Philosophy of Mathematics: Selected Readings* (1st edn. Englewood Cliffs, NJ, 1964; 2nd edn. Cambridge, 1983). Referred to below as B&P. Both edns. are useful.

Other collections of classic papers, more technical than those in B&P, are:

Ewald, W. (ed.), *From Kant to Hilbert: A Source Book in the Foundations of Mathematics*, 2 vols. (Oxford, 1996). Referred to below as *KH*.

Mancosu, P. (ed.), *From Brouwer to Hilbert: The Debate on the Foundations of Mathematics in the 1920s* (Oxford, 1998). Referred to below as *BH*.

van Heijenoort, J. (ed.), *From Frege to Gödel: A Source Book in Mathematical Logic 1879–1931* (Cambridge, Mass., 1967). Referred to below as *FG*.

Mathematics

To bolster your acquaintance with mathematics, you may read:

Allen, R., *Basic Mathematics* (London, 1968).

Courant, R., and Robbins, H., *What is Mathematics?* (Oxford, 1941).

Waismann, F., *Introduction to Mathematical Thinking: The Formation of Concepts in Modern Mathematics* (New York, 1951). This also contains philosophical discussion in the school of Wittgenstein.

A General View

A general survey of the field is provided by the introduction to B&P. Also helpful is:

Parsons, C., 'Foundations of Mathematics', in P. Edwards (ed.), *Encyclopedia of Philosophy* (New York, 1967).

From Plato to Frege

Secondary material is asterisked.

Plato, *Meno*, 82b9–85b7. This famous exchange between Socrates and the slave-boy is essential reading.

Plato, *Phaedo*, 72e–77d.
——*Republic*, 507a–511e, 525d–527c.
*Wedberg, A., *Plato's Philosophy of Mathematics* (Stockholm, 1955).

Aristotle, *Metaphysics* M3.
——*Physics* B2.
*Lear, J., 'Aristotole's Philosophy of Mathematics', *Philosophical Review*, vol. XCI, no. 2 (1982), pp. 161–92.

Stich, S. (ed.), *Innate Ideas* (Berkeley, 1975). Writings by Descartes, Locke, and Leibniz included in this volume bear on the 17th-century debate.

More technical, but of deep interest, is:

*Mancosu, P., *Philosophy of Mathematics and Mathematical Practice in the Seventeenth Century* (Oxford, 1996).

Kant, I., *Critique of Pure Reason* (1781), trans. Norman Kemp Smith (London, 1929). Referred to below as KS. Introduction, sects. iv–vi (KS 49–58), Transcendental Aesthetic (KS 65–91), and 'The Discipline of Pure Reason in its Dogmatic Employment' (KS 576–93).
——*Prolegomena to Any Future Metaphysics that will be Able to Present itself as a Science* (1783), trans. Peter G. Lucas (Manchester, 1953). See first part of the Main, Transcendental Question, 'How is Pure Mathematics Possible?' (Lucas 36–51).
*Parsons, C., 'The Transcendental Aesthetic', in P. Guyer (ed.), *The Cambridge Companion to Kant* (Cambridge, 1992).
*Walker, C. (ed.), *Kant on Pure Reason* (Oxford, 1982). See papers by J. Hopkins, and C. Parsons.

Bolzano, B., 'On the Intermediate Value Theorem', trans. S. B. Russ, from Bolzano, *Rein analytischer Beweis . . .* (Prague, 1817), *Historia Mathematica* (1980), 156–85; repr. in *KH* i. 227–48.
Mill, J. S., *A System of Logic* (1843; repr. London, 1943), II. iv–vii, III. xxiv. 3–9.
Dedekind, R., *Essays on the Theory of Numbers*, trans. W. W. Beman (New York, 1963).
*Kim, J., 'The Role of Perception in A Priori Knowledge', *Philosophical Studies*, vol. 40 (1981), pp. 339–54.

Cantor, G., *Contributions to the Founding of the Theory of Transfinite Numbers*, trans. P. E. B. Jourdain (New York, 1955).
Frege, G., *The Foundations of Arithmetic* (1884), trans. J. L. Austin (Oxford, 1950). Other texts by Frege are given in the next section.
*Dummett, M., *Frege: Philosophy of Mathematics* (London, 1991).
*Resnick, M., *Frege and the Philosophy of Mathematics* (Ithaca, NY, 1980).

The Paradoxes and After

At the end of an entry, (i) signifies an introductory text, (d) a difficult item, and (t) a technical one.

A full statement of all the paradoxes is given in:

Fraenkel, A., and Bar-Hillel, J., 'The Antinomies', in A. Fraenkel *et al.* (eds.), *Foundations of Set Theory* (Amsterdam, 1958). (t)

Logicism

Russell, B., *Introduction to Mathematical Philosophy* (London, 1919). (i) This is a very helpful introduction to logicism in the setting of the simple theory of types, avoiding the complexities of the ramified theory.

Frege

A deeper investigation of Frege's logicism will need to look at:

Frege, G., *Basic Laws of Arithmetic* (i: 1893, ii: 1903), trans. M. Furth (Berkeley, 1982). (t) This gives part 1 of *Basic Laws* from vol. i, and the app. to vol. ii, which is Frege's response to the contradiction. Furth's substantial preface is especially helpful.

——*Translations from the Philosophical Writings*, trans. M. Black, and P. Geach (Oxford, 2nd edn. 1960; 3rd edn. 1980). (i) This contains extracts from the *Basic Laws* not included in the Furth volume. The 3rd edn. omits some items included in the 2nd.

——*Begriffsschrift* ('Conceptual Notation', 1879); repr. in T. W. Bynum (ed.), *Conceptual Notation and Related Articles* (Oxford, 1972) and in *FG* 5–82. (t)

William Demopoulos (ed.), *Frege's Philosophy of Mathematics* (Cambridge, Mass., 1995). (t, d)

Russell

The ramified theory of types is explained in:

Russell, B., 'Mathematical Logic as Based on the Theory of Types' (1908); repr. in *Logic and Knowledge: Essays 1901–1950*, ed. R. Marsh (London, 1988) and in *FG* 152–82. (t, d)

Gödel, K., 'Russell's Mathematical Logic', in B&P. (d)

Ramsey

Ramsey, F. P., 'Foundations of Mathematics', in *Philosophical Papers*, ed. D. H. Mellor (Cambridge, 1980). (d)

Hilbert

The underlying ideas of Hilbert's programme are explained in:

Hilbert, D., 'On the Infinite' (1925); abridged version in B&P, full version in *FG* 369–92.

——'The Foundations of Mathematics' (1927), in *FG* 464–79.

Kreisel's paper in B&P is too technical to count as an exposition of Hilbert's programme: an article that traces a connection between it and Logical Positivism is:

Giaquinto, M., 'Hilbert's Philosophy of Mathematics', *British Journal for the Philosophy of Science*, vol. 34 (1983), pp. 119–32. (i)

Gödel's Incompleteness Theorems

One view of the philosophical bearing of Gödel's incompleteness theorems is given in:

MYHILL, J., 'Some Philosophical Implications of Mathematical Logic', *Review of Metaphysics*, vol. VI (1952), pp. 165–92. (t)

For opposition to the standard view that the incompleteness results sunk Hilbert's programme, see:

DETLEFSEN, M., *Hilbert's Programme* (Dordrecht, 1986).

For a reaction from a constructivist standpoint:

DUMMETT, M., 'The Philosophical Significance of Gödel's Theorem' (1963), in *Truth and Other Enigmas* (London, 1978).

Wittgenstein

WITTGENSTEIN, L., *Remarks on the Foundations of Mathematics*, trans. G. E. M. Anscombe, 3rd edn. (Oxford, 1968).

DIAMOND, C. (ed.), *Wittgenstein's Lectures on the Foundations of Mathematics* (Ithaca, NY, 1976).

DUMMETT, M., 'Wittgenstein on Necessity: Some Reflections' (1990), in *The Seas of Language* (Oxford, 1998).

—— 'Wittgenstein's Philosophy of Mathematics' (1959), in *Truth and Other Enigmas* (London, 1978). (i)

WAISMANN, F., *Lectures on the Philosophy of Mathematics*, ed. W. Grassl (Amsterdam, 1982). Writings by a former disciple of Wittgenstein.

WRIGHT, C., *Wittgenstein on the Foundations of Mathematics* (London, 1980).

Set Theory

The following bear on the question what conception of set we should have, in the light of responses to the paradoxes.

BIGELOW, J., 'Sets are Universals', in A. Irvine (ed.), *Physicalism in Mathematics* (Dordrecht, 1990). (d)

BOOLOS, G., 'The Iterative Conception of Set', in B&P.

HALLETT, M., *Cantorian Set Theory and Limitation of Size* (Oxford, 1984). (d) A comprehensive survey.

LEWIS, D., *Parts of Classes* (London, 1990).

QUINE, W. V., *From a Logical Point of View*, 2nd edn. (Cambridge, Mass., 1961). Contains the article 'New Foundations for Mathematical Logic' (1937), in which Quine expounded his highly deviant set theory NF.

Intuitionism

BROUWER, L. E. J., 'Consciousness, Philosophy and Mathematics' (1949), in B&P.

—— 'Historical Background, Principles and Methods of Intuitionism', *South African Journal of Sciences*, 49 (1952), 139–46.

——'Points and Spaces', *Canadian Journal of Mathematics*, 6 (1954), 1–17.

DUMMETT, M., *Elements of Intuitionism* (Oxford, 1977), introd. and ch. 1.

——'The Philosophical Basis of Intuitionistic Logic' (1973), in B&P. (d)

——'What is Mathematics About?' (1991), in *The Seas of Language* (Oxford, 1993).

HELLMAN, G., 'Never Say "Never": On the Communication Problem between Intuitionism and Classicism', *Philosophical Topics* (Fall, 1989), pp. 47–67.

DETLEFSEN, M., 'Brouwerian Intuitionism', in Detlefsen (ed.), *Proof and Knowledge in Mathematics* (London, 1991). This illuminates the philosophical motivations both of intuitionism and of predicativism.

Predicativism

This is the view that admits only predicative existence assumptions.

POINCARÉ, H., 'The Logic of Infinity', in *Mathematics and Science: Last Essays*, trans. Boldue (New York, 1963).

FOLINA, J., *Poincaré and the Philosophy of Mathematics* (London, 1992).

FEFERMAN, S., 'Foundations of Predicative Analysis', *Journal of Symbolic Logic*, 29 (1964), 1–30. (t)

——'Weyl Vindicated: "Das Kontinuum" 70 Years Later', in *Atti del Congresso Temi e prospcttive della logica e della filosofia della scienza contemporanea* (Bologna, 1988). (t)

CHIHARA, C., *Ontology and the Vicious Circle Principle* (Ithaca, NY, 1973). A defence of predicativism without logicism, with a criticism of Gödel's platonism.

Modern Platonism

Gödel

GÖDEL, K., 'What is Cantor's Continuum Problem?', in B&P. (d) This is essential.

——*Collected Works*, ii (New York, 1990). For those who wish to go further.

WANG, H., *From Mathematics to Philosophy* (London, 1974). This reports Gödel's late views.

Quine

Expressions of Quine's empiricist defence of platonism are scattered throughout his writings. See especially:

QUINE, W. V., 'Posits and Reality', in *The Ways of Paradox and Other Essays* (Cambridge, Mass., 1976).

——'Carnap and Logical Truth', in B&P. This details Quine's break with Logical Positivism.

PARSONS, C., 'Quine's Philosophy of Mathematics', in L. Hahn, and P. Schilpp, *The Philosophy of W. V. O. Quine* (La Salle, Ill., 1987).

QUINE, W. V., 'Reply to Charles Parsons', in the same volume.

Two articles about Quine's indispensability claim are:

MADDY, P., 'Indispensability and Practice', *Journal of Philosophy*, vol. 89 (1992), pp. 275–89.

SOBER, E., 'Mathematics and Indispensability', *Philosophical Review*, vol. 102 (1993), pp. 35–57.

Neo-Fregeans

A version of platonism based on Frege's context principle is advanced in:

WRIGHT, C., *Frege's Conception of Numbers as Objects* (Aberdeen, 1983).

FIELD, H., 'Platonism for Cheap? Crispin Wright on Frege's Context Principle', in *Realism, Mathematics and Modality* (Oxford, 1991). An opposed view.

HALE, B., and WRIGHT, C., 'A *Reductio ad Surdum* . . . ?', *Mind*, vol. 103 (1994), pp. 169–83.

Structuralism

RESNICK, M., 'Mathematics from the Structural Point of View', *Revue Internationale de Philosophie*, vol. 42 (1988), 400–24. Resnick advocates a form of platonism according to which mathematics is the science of structures.

Modern Anti-Platonism

FEFERMAN, S., 'Why a Little Goes a Long Way: Logical Foundations of Scientifically Applicable Mathematics', in *Proceedings of the Philosophy of Science Association*, vol. 2 (1993), pp. 442–55. (t) Feferman maintains that only a small part of mathematics is needed for science.

FIELD, H., *Science without Numbers: A Defence of Nominalism* (Oxford, 1980).

SHAPIRO, S., 'Conservativeness and Incompleteness', *Journal of Philosophy*, vol. 81 (1983), pp. 521–31. (t) A criticism of Field.

PAPINEAU, D., 'Mathematical Fictionalism', in *International Studies in the Philosophy of Science*, vol. 2 (1988), pp. 157–74.

Knowledge of Mathematics

KITCHER, P., *The Nature of Mathematical Knowledge* (Oxford, 1984).

FIELD, H., 'Tarski's Theory of Truth', *Journal of Philosophy*, vol. 69 (1980), pp. 347–75.

GOLDMAN, A., 'A Causal Theory of Knowing', *Journal of Philosophy*, vol. 64 (1967), pp. 357–72.

BENACERRAF, P., 'Mathematical Truth', in B&P. Benacerraf's problem arises if one combines Goldman's view of knowledge with Field's view of truth and reference.

MADDY, P., 'Perception and Mathematical Intuition', *Philosophical Review*, vol. 89 (1980), pp. 163–96. An empiricist account presented as an answer to Benacerraf.

—— *Realism in Mathematics* (Oxford, 1990).

FIELD, H., 'Realism, Mathematics and Modality', in *Realism, Mathematics and Modality* (Oxford, 1991).

CHIHARA, C., *Constructibility and Mathematical Existence* (Oxford, 1991). Chihara criticizes both Maddy's realism and Resnick's structuralism.

LAKATOS, I., *Proofs and Refutations* (Cambridge, 1976). Arguably the most enjoyable of all items listed here: a stimulating exploration of mathematical proof as fallible, and of mathematicians' reactions to proposed counter-examples.

4

PHILOSOPHY AND THE NATURAL SCIENCES

John Worrall

INTRODUCTION

For better or worse (the former in my view), the development of science has had an overwhelming impact on our culture. At the practical level this is obvious enough—space probes, television, personal computers, . . . Add your own favourites to the list. Although some items on the extended list will seem to many mixed blessings at best, even the most technophobic would be hard-pressed to deny that the human condition has been improved by, for example, the increased diagnostic precision afforded by such techniques as computer-assisted tomography or the humbler (only because older) X-ray photograph.

The intellectual impact of the development of science may be less tangible, but is surely of at least equal importance. The modernist, Enlightenment view was that the development of modern science had freed humans from superstition and myth showing them that—amazingly enough—they can discover the innermost secrets of the workings of the universe if they use their intellects appropriately, that is, rationally or scientifically. Everyone knows Alexander Pope's couplet reflecting the eighteenth-century view:

> Nature and Nature's laws lay hid in night,
> God said 'Let Newton be!' and all was light.

But there lies the, more recent, rub. For almost everyone knows Sir John Squire's twentieth-century rejoinder:

> 'Twas not to last, for Devil howling 'Ho,
> Let Einstein be!' restored the status quo.

How exactly can the idea of science as the bastion of objectivity and rationality withstand the impact of the great 'scientific revolutions' brought about, for example, by relativity theory and (perhaps more fundamentally still) by quantum theory? Why do such apparently radical changes in theory occur? Is it for reasons dictated by accumulating observational evidence? If so, according to what precise logic of evidence? If not, if some of the 'reasons' are subjective or social, what differentiates science from other bodies of theoretical claims often thought of as altogether less firmly grounded (such as religious or pseudo-scientific claims)? And what exactly do such revolutionary changes in theory imply about the epistemic status of presently accepted theories in science? Do they, in particular, refute the *scientific realist* view of accepted theories as—perhaps approximate—truths? A nineteenth-century realist would have advocated belief in the approximate truth of the theories then accepted in science. Yet presently accepted theories seem—in fundamentals—radically at odds with these earlier ones: for example, Newtonian theory states that the planets are kept in their (roughly) elliptical paths by action-at-a-distance gravitational forces, yet relativity theory explicitly rejects action-at-a-distance and attributes the planets' orbits to their following geodesics in (curved) spacetime.

Many of the presently central issues in what might be called general philosophy of science concern its 'three Rs': rationality, realism, and revolution. Some of these issues are outlined in Section 1, which includes a brief account of Kuhn's highly influential views, and an outline and critical examination of what is currently the most popular and certainly best-developed *formal* account of rational belief, 'personalist Bayesianism'. (On a number of issues in Section 1, I presuppose—and extend—the treatments given by David Papineau in his chapter 'Methodology: The Elements of the Philosophy of Science' in the earlier companion volume to this book.)

One recent trend in philosophy of science—itself due in part to Kuhn's influence—has been toward the *naturalistic* view that philosophy of science consists simply of descriptions of the way that mature sciences operate. In Section 2, I outline some of these approaches and raise the question whether naturalized philosophy of science can retain normative force or instead must sacrifice the implication that science is genuinely epistemically special.

While there may be reasons to resist the idea that philosophy of science is itself at bottom a science, there can be no doubt that many of its most interesting problems arise in close association with science. Section 3 contains an account of some of these problems: one arising from quantum physics and a couple from evolutionary biology. These problems are more or less randomly selected in an attempt to give some flavour of that important part of philosophy of science concerned, in effect, with analysing and clarifying the logical implications and presuppositions of current scientific theories.

1. RATIONALITY, REVOLUTION, AND REALISM

1.1. Radical Theory Change in Science

Newton's theory (of mechanics plus universal gravitation) is logically inconsistent with Einstein's theory of relativity. The former entails that the universe is infinite; that time is absolute (so that two events simultaneous in one frame of reference are simultaneous in all); that every body acts at a distance on every other body; and that the inertial mass of a given body is a (velocity-independent) constant. Relativity theory contradicts each of these entailments: according to it, the universe may be finite (though unbounded); any two spatially separated events simultaneous relative to one frame of reference are not simultaneous relative to another frame moving with respect to the first; there is no action-at-a-distance; and the inertial mass of a body increases with its velocity. How far 'down' towards the empirically testable consequences of the theory this inconsistency reaches is an issue to which we shall need to return, but at the level of fundamental theory there is simply outright contradiction.

This is no isolated case. Consider, for example, the history of optics: in the seventeenth and eighteenth centuries the most popular theory of the fundamental nature of light was that it consists of tiny material particles; in the early nineteenth century this was displaced by the theory that light consists not of matter but of motion—of periodic motions (waves) transmitted through an all-pervading elastic medium; in the late nineteenth century this theory was in turn replaced by the claim that light consists of vibrations carried, not by a material medium, but by an immaterial electromagnetic field; and finally (so far!) this theory was replaced by the claim that light consists of photons obeying an entirely new quantum mechanics.

Whether such discontinuities are quite as sharp as they have sometimes been made to seem, and whether they pose as severe a threat as is often imagined to the idea that the development of science is a rational process, are questions that remain to be discussed; but the fact that at the level of fundamental theory in science such changes have occurred is surely undeniable.

1.2. The Impact of Kuhn's *The Structure of Scientific Revolutions*

Although Karl Popper had been emphasizing the importance of 'revolutionary' changes in science for many years beforehand, it was Thomas Kuhn's 1962 book *The Structure of Scientific Revolutions* that really brought radical theory change to centre-stage in philosophy of science. Kuhn's views seemed more challenging to older conceptions than Popper's. But just what those views are was an immediate cause of controversy and has remained so ever since. Some of those influenced by Kuhn, encouraged by his talk of 'incommensurability' involving (alleged) total breakdown of communication between scientists in different 'paradigms', of total 'revolutionary' revisions of even the evidential basis of science, and even of the *world* changing as the dominant paradigm does, have seen the book as demolishing the idea that theory change in science is a rational process.

I shall not become embroiled in Kuhnian exegesis here: those who wish to follow the twists and turns of the reinterpretations (or clarifications?) of Kuhn's more outlandish-sounding claims can find references in the bibliography. I shall instead accentuate (what I take to be) the positive. I first explain what seems to me valuable and correct in Kuhn's account and then try to clarify the sharpest challenge to the idea of scientific rationality that these correct and valuable views pose.

1.2.1. *Paradigms versus Theories*

Kuhn insisted that science and its development cannot be analysed satisfactorily in terms of single theories: the unit of scientific commitment is not the theory but the 'paradigm'. This is a notoriously unclear term (a fact that has assisted its subsequent widespread use—or abuse). The main significance of Kuhn's idea is best explained through a simplified and somewhat idealized example from the history of science.

The predominant view about the nature of light in the eighteenth century was that it consists of tiny material particles; these are emitted from sources, such as the sun, and follow paths that are, like those of all other particles, governed by Newton's laws. In particular they travel in straight lines (at constant velocity) unless acted upon by a net external force; and conversely, whenever the particles are bent out of their rectilinear trajectories (as they are, for example, when reflected from a mirror or when refracted on entering a transparent medium like water), there must be some force that accounts for this bending.

Two features should be noted. First, this is a very general set of ideas—in order to make detailed contact with empirical phenomena it must be augmented with specific assumptions *both* about the light-particles themselves (what is it, for example, that differentiates those particles that produce the sensation of blue light from those that produce the sensation of red?) *and* about the forces acting upon them in particular circumstances (how exactly do the 'reflecting force' and the 'refractive force' act, *and* how do they *inter*act?). Secondly, this process of producing specific theories within the general framework supplied by the basic ideas is not a shot in the dark—the process does not consist of a series of 'bold conjectures'. Instead the sorts of particular assumption that might work are indicated by the general framework itself, in conjunction with 'background knowledge'. The general idea was to 'reduce' optics to particle mechanics. Particle mechanics had, through the work of Newton and his successors, already become a highly developed field. Various sorts of candidate for the differentiating features of the light-particles were already available—blue-making particles might, for example, have a different mass from red-making ones, or perhaps a different velocity; and work in other fields supplied ideas about the sorts of force that might do the job in optics. Moreover, the fact that particle mechanics was already a mathematically highly developed theory meant that any specific theory developed within the framework would be mathematically tractable—that is, scientists would be able to deduce what consequences it has at the empirical level.

What existed, then, in the eighteenth century was not a single theory of light, but a general underlying idea (light is *some sort* of particle affected by *some sorts* of force) together with a set of ideas for identifying the particular sorts of particle and the particular sorts of force these might be—a set of ideas provided by previous scientific successes. The problem was to construct specific theories which would account for the phenomena within the general framework supplied by the corpuscular optics 'paradigm'. Paradigms, then, are characterized chiefly by a general theory and a set of ideas for developing that general theory into specific theories that will capture and explain the relevant phenomena. Kuhn refers to this set of ideas as underwriting a 'puzzle-solving tradition', previous successes often supplying 'exemplars' for later developments. Although Kuhn's detailed development of this view—especially his emphasis on inarticulable skills, 'disciplinary matrices', and the like—can be challenged (and certainly stands in need of clarification), he was surely pointing in the direction of an important and then relatively neglected aspect of mature science. Imre Lakatos, with his notion of a research programme complete with 'positive heuristic', and Larry Laudan, with his notion of a research tradition, both later underlined this same point in slightly different (and considerably sharper) ways.

1.2.2. *Anomalies versus Experimental Refutations*

Some phenomena were recognized as presenting special problems for the corpuscular optics paradigm—as especially difficult for any specific theory developed within that paradigm to capture. One such phenomenon was that of partial reflection: if a beam of light in air is incident on the surface of some transparent material, like glass or water, then in general only part of the light is refracted into the material, while the rest is reflected back into the air. The corpuscular optics approach dictated a (repulsive) force of reflection and an (attractive) force of refraction; but why, as partial reflection seemed to indicate, were some of the particles acted on by the reflective force and others by the refractive? In Kuhn's terms this was an experimental *anomaly* for the corpuscular optics paradigm. As Kuhn claims is generally true, the anomaly was regarded, at least initially, as a problem to be solved within the paradigm rather than as a 'falsification' or reason to reject (or even seriously to question) the paradigm.

Once it is recognized that specific theories are generated within general frameworks by the addition of detailed assumptions, the whole debate about anomalies and 'falsifications' (see Lakatos and Musgrave 1970) is remarkably easy to resolve. Sometimes there is a set of detailed assumptions that is privileged in some way—perhaps because the specific theory based on them has been successful with some other phenomena—and that specific theory is actually inconsistent with the anomalous phenomenon (or rather with its description). Sometimes (perhaps more often) specific theories for a certain range of phenomena are in the process of construction—that is, no particular set of more detailed assumptions recommends itself; but it is clear that the anomalous phenomenon is going to be a special difficulty for that construction because any of the obvious or straightforward detailed assumptions suggested by the framework would produce overall theories inconsistent with the phenomenon at issue. It is into this second class that, for example, partial reflection falls.

Neither kind of anomaly, of course, yields any direct reason to give up the general framework theory. When, for example, the initial corpuscular account of what happens when light passes the edge of an opaque object (namely that it proceeds undisturbed in its rectilinear path) turned out to be inconsistent with the phenomenon of 'straight-edge diffraction', corpuscularists simply assumed that there must be a diffracting force (in addition to the already assumed reflective and refractive forces) and proceeded to try to pin down the features of that diffracting force. Kuhn's point about anomalies of this first kind amounts in effect just to the one made long ago by Duhem (1906): deductive logic does not require giving up the general theory underlying the framework in such a case, but only giving up *either* that theory *or* one of the erstwhile preferred specific assumptions. If some observational statement *O* follows not from *T* (the 'general framework' theory) alone but only from *T&S* (where *S* is some set of more detailed assumptions couched within that same framework but not essential to it) then, should *O* turn out to be false empirically, it follows only that so also must be either *T* or at least one of the particular assumptions in *S*.

There is no general reason why a scientist should not hold onto *T* in such a situation and therefore identify the problem as that of finding and replacing the 'faulty' detailed assumption. On the contrary, there is good reason to retain *T*, at least as the initial move. The general theory *T* underpins a whole approach to optics—it sustains in Kuhn's terms a 'puzzle-solving tradition'; hence retaining *T* means retaining a framework that at least to some degree guides the construction of replacement specific theories. The scientist who sees straight-edge diffraction as a 'puzzle' to be solved within the corpuscular optics approach rather than as a reason to reject the whole approach is simply obliged to give up the idea that no force affects the light-particles as they pass the edge of opaque bodies, and is pointed towards postulating a 'diffracting force'—one that may be attractive at some distances and repulsive at others. Once some assumption about the forces is made, the existing mathematics of particle mechanics permits the deduction of logical consequences. A scientist who might instead be inclined to reject *T* on account of this phenomenon would be left—at any rate initially—in an intellectual vacuum.

The second type of anomaly (exemplified in the historical case under consideration by partial reflection) serves, albeit more indirectly, to underline this same methodological lesson. Such an anomaly provides a potential 'Duhem problem' rather than a real one: if any set of available detailed assumptions were added to the general corpuscular view, this would produce a specific theory inconsistent with the facts about partial reflection, but there was in this case no independent reason to prefer any particular set of such detailed assumptions. The whole problem right from the start in such a case was to articulate a specific theory (add a set of detailed assumptions to the core view) that would correctly yield the phenomenon at issue. Partial reflection was an 'anomaly' because it was clear that no set of straightforward assumptions was going to succeed in capturing it. Again it is no wonder that the option of retaining *T* was attractive: taking that option constrains the problem and makes it manageable. One fairly obvious suggestion (investigated by Newton himself) was to give up the idea (always clearly an idealization) that the light consists of point particles and try the idea that they might, as bodies of finite extension, have different properties on different 'sides' (so that the particles arriving at the interface with one side or 'pole' uppermost might be, say, reflected, while those arriving there with the other 'pole' uppermost might be refracted into the glass).

1.2.3. *Revolutions and Reason*

A particular field is, on Kuhn's account, practising *normal science* when there is only one remotely plausible general framework theory available and anomalies are routinely treated as problems for the paradigm to solve rather than as bringing that paradigm into question. As the terminology suggests, this is—in his view—the standard state of a scientific field (at any rate once that field has achieved 'maturity'). Kuhn seems now to have accepted that he initially overdid the 'paradigm monopoly' view—although most eighteenth-century scientists preferred the corpuscular approach to optics there were always significant dissenting voices (one belonged to Euler). Moreover, there are at least some fields of apparently 'mature' science—for example, various fields in contemporary biological sciences—where there are two or more rival general views vying for acceptance. It none the less has sometimes happened, especially in physics and chemistry, that for long periods one general view, one paradigm, has dominated. But there are also periods when the general view is challenged and replaced by one inconsistent with it. Why do these changes occur? It was always Kuhn's views about the process of paradigm *change* or about 'extraordinary' or 'revolutionary' science that provided the chief target for critical fire (Lakatos, for example, claimed that Kuhn's views made theory change in science a matter of 'mob psychology').

The corpuscular approach may not have monopolized optics in the eighteenth century but it does seem to have been easily the most widely accepted approach. In the early decades of the nineteenth century the theory that light consists of periodic disturbances transmitted through a mechanical, elastic medium became dominant. Did this replacement (Kuhn, of course, likes the term 'revolution') occur for good, objective reasons? The account in *The Structure of Scientific Revolutions*—with its talk of a *crisis* of confidence affecting the scientific community, leading some, usually younger scientists, to undergo 'something akin to a religious conversion' to an alternative approach, leading in turn to a 'bandwagon effect' that sees a new community consensus form around the new alternative—seemed to many commentators to amount quite unambiguously to an irrationalist (or arationalist) view of theory change. Although a state of 'crisis' is, on Kuhn's account, always produced by an increase in the number of anomalies and/or by the persistent intractability of certain anomalies, he seemed quite explicit that there were, and could be, no general rules for counting and weighing anomalies and so no threshold beyond which 'crisis' was justified. And Kuhn was similarly explicit that there are no rules for when the shift to a new paradigm becomes rationally dictated and hence continued adherence to the old paradigm irrational: either a new consensus will form around the new basic idea or it will not, that is all there is to the matter.

Most of what his critics found objectionable in Kuhn's account of theory change is reflected in his remarks about 'hold-outs' to 'scientific revolutions'. He claimed that if we look back at any case of a change in fundamental theory in science we shall always find eminent scientists who resisted the switch to the new 'paradigm' long after most of their colleagues shifted. These 'hold-outs'—Priestley's defence of phlogiston against Lavoisierian chemistry is a celebrated example—are often (though not invariably) by elderly scientists who have made significant contributions to the older paradigm. Kuhn added to this interesting but relatively uncontroversial descriptive claim the challenging normative claim that these 'elderly hold-outs' were no less justified than their more fickle contemporaries: not only did they, as a matter of fact, stick to the older paradigm, they were, moreover, not wrong to do so. On Kuhn's view, 'neither proof *nor error* is at issue' in these cases, there being, as he added in a later attempt to clarify his views, 'always some good reasons for every possible choice'—that is, both for switching to the revolutionary new paradigm and for sticking to the old. Hence the hold-outs cannot, on Kuhn's view, be condemned as 'illogical or unscientific'. But neither of course can those, like Lavoisier, who switch to the new paradigm be so condemned. It is this alleged absence of a single 'correct' course of action or single correct set of beliefs for a scientist to adopt that seemed the most threatening aspect of Kuhn's position.

What argument did Kuhn have for this claim? Why, that is, did he hold that those who resist the new paradigm are no less rational than their more mobile colleagues? According to his account in *The Structure of Scientific Revolutions*: 'The source of resistance is the assurance that the older paradigm will ultimately solve all its problems, that nature can be shoved into the box the paradigm supplies' (1962, 151–2). Not only does this feeling of assurance fail to be 'illogical or unscientific', it is that same feeling of assurance that 'makes normal or puzzle-solving science possible'.

But this argument is disappointing. It is of course true that the hold-outs cannot be faulted as 'illogical', if illogicality would require flying in the face of *deductive* logic. Echoing Duhem's point of long ago, the general theories that form the basis of a paradigm have no directly testable deductive consequences of their own, so there must always be *some* auxiliary assumptions that when added to those general theories will entail any given set of evidential statements. To take an example from optics again, although diffraction and interference phenomena are often nowadays taken as direct refutations of the corpuscular approach, this is quite wrong and is certainly not how those phenomena were viewed at the time. Just as Kuhn suggests, the defenders of the corpuscular theory did indeed insist that these phenomena could be shoved into the emissionist 'box'. More interestingly, they actually constructed explanations—at any rate in outline—of how the phenomena could be so 'shoved': by postulating a complicated force of diffraction, for example, or by making interference a physiological phenomenon (the fringes being produced by interference of waves produced in the eye by the light-particles). Such explanations are bound to exist *if all that we require of them is that they deductively yield correct descriptions of the phenomena at issue*. (After all, if this were the only requirement, then the following 'theory' would suffice: light consists of particles subjected to entirely unknown forces emanating from the edges of opaque objects that happen to result in the particles moving along unspecified paths that produce the following patterns of illumination . . . (where we simply fill in the dots on the basis of the known experimental results).)

But are we bound to say that constructing such an explanation automatically balances the evidential scales (at any rate with respect to the phenomena at issue)? Only if we hold that if some evidential statement e is entailed by each of two theories T_1 and T_2 then e confirms both theories to the same extent and so can supply no reason to prefer one of the two theories. But surely no sensible account of confirmation can endorse such a view? All sensible accounts must come to terms with elusive, but clearly important notions like simplicity, unity, and absence of *ad hoc*-ness. No doubt corpuscularists could cobble together a theory that had a correct description of the phenomenon of straight-edge diffraction as a deductive consequence, but this phenomenon may still yield an objective reason to prefer the wave theory if (as is actually the case) it falls out in an entirely natural way from that theory but—so far as we can tell—can only be accounted for in an *ad hoc* way by the corpuscular theory. (The intuitive difference here is often expressed as the difference between explaining a phenomenon (as the wave theory explains diffraction) and merely capturing it *post hoc* (which was the best the corpuscular theory could do).)

Suppose we take it that the principal aim of a theory of scientific rationality is to supply a natural and defensible account of when evidence objectively supports some scientific theory. Suppose further that the claim that the development of science has been by and large a rational process amounts simply to the claim that theory change has always been from theories that are less well supported empirically to theories that are better supported empirically. It follows that Kuhn's points about hold-outs present no threat to the idea of scientific rationality, provided that an account of confirmation or empirical support can be produced that has the following consequence: the support lent to a general theory (or paradigm) by some phenomenon that has been 'shoved' into its 'box' is, in general, less than that lent to that same theory by some phenomenon that 'falls naturally out of its box' (that is, one that is given a 'natural', straightforward explanation within that general theory).

We shall see in Section 1.3.6 whether the approach to empirical support that is currently most popular—personalist Bayesianism—can indeed underwrite such a distinction.

1.2.4. *Kuhn's Later Account of 'Theory Choice'*

In chapter 13 of his (1977) book *The Essential Tension*, Kuhn develops a much more explicit (and, I believe, more challenging) account of the factors underlying what he calls 'theory choice'. He there insists that he never denied that 'reason' in the form of the 'objective factors' from the philosopher's 'traditional list' (including such factors as empirical accuracy and scope, consistency, simplicity, and 'fruitfulness') plays a crucially important role in theory change: 'I agree entirely with the traditional view that [these objective factors] play a vital role when scientists must choose between an established theory and an upstart competitor . . . they provide *the* shared basis for theory choice' (Kuhn 1977: 322). But, these objective factors, Kuhn claims, supply 'no algorithm for theory choice'. At any rate when the choice between rival theories is a live issue in science, these objective factors never dictate a choice. This is for two main reasons. First, single factors often turn out to deliver no unambiguous preference when applied to the theories *as they stood at the time when the choice was being made*. For example, it is often assumed that the Copernican heliostatic theory was empirically more accurate than the Ptolemaic theory. This eventually became true but only as a result of the work of Copernicus, Kepler, Galileo, and others, who had clearly then 'chosen' the Copernican theory for other reasons (if for any *reasons* at all). Secondly, even where single 'objective factors' do point clearly in the direction of one of the rival theories, different factors may point in opposite directions: while simplicity (in a certain sense) favoured Copernican theory, consistency (with other, then accepted theories) undoubtedly favoured the Ptolemaic theory.

Hence, according to Kuhn, the objective factors must always be supplemented by 'subjective' factors in order to deliver a definite preference: 'every individual choice between competing theories depends on a mixture of objective and subjective factors, or of shared and individual criteria' (Kuhn 1977: 325).

Many interesting issues are raised by this later account. Here I give bare outlines of a few of them. (Readers interested in more details should follow up the references supplied in the Bibliography.)

1. Isn't Kuhn's laundry list of 'objective factors' lacking in necessary structure? He presents it as if each of the factors is independent of all the others and that the 'objectivist' could give no reasons for regarding some of the factors as more important than others. In fact many of those philosophers who aim to show that theory choice is an objective affair (Poincaré, Duhem, Lakatos, and many others) would see one of Kuhn's objective virtues—that of predictive (empirical) success—*both* as intimately connected with other virtues (for example, 'fruitfulness') *and* as dominant over others (such as detailed empirical accuracy).

After all, Duhem's point about theory-testing means that scientists always can, in principle, develop detailed theories within a given framework that will capture given known phenomena. What scientists cannot guarantee is that the general framework will be predictively successful. The Copernican who (1) acknowledges that Ptolemaic theory had developed much the more extensive fit with the phenomena (after all it had had several hundred years' start) but who (2) insists that hard work on detailed assumptions within his theory will eventually allow it to match Ptolemaic theory in this regard, and who (3) points to, say, planetary stations and retrogressions as predictive successes for his theory unmatched (and perhaps unmatchable) by the Ptolemaists—such a Copernican is surely winning the objective argument.

Or consider Kuhn's 'objective factor' of consistency with other theories. The suggestion is that because, for example, Copernican theory clashed with accepted Aristotelian cosmology (whereas Ptolemaic theory was consistent with Aristotle), it remained reasonable for those who ranked consistency over, say, predictive success to continue to advocate the Ptolemaic theory. But in fact inconsistency with other accepted theories may surely be reasonably regarded sometimes as a virtue rather than a vice, since it sets an agenda of problems for further research—with, however, the important proviso that there is some independent (empirical) reason for thinking that these problems *can* be satisfactorily solved. Again it seems to be predictive success that supplies that independent reason.

2. Is Kuhn correct that his account diverges comparatively little from that 'currently received' in the philosophy of science? The answer seems to be that because of the essential role it ascribes to 'subjective factors' in supplementing

the always indecisive objective ones, it does indeed sit well with the personalist Bayesian account of rational belief. But it does so on account of the features of personalist Bayesianism that many other philosophers find objectionable (basically, as we shall see later, (alleged) over-reliance on subjective prior probabilities). Although Kuhn advertises his more elaborate account as a decisive rebuttal of the claim that his view makes theory change in science a matter of 'mob psychology', it should be remembered that his account still has the explicit consequence that 'there are always some good reasons for each possible choice (i.e. both for sticking to the "old" theory and for adopting the "new" one)' (Kuhn 1977: 328). And it still has the explicit consequence that the eventual resolution of 'revolutions' is simply a matter of a new consensus happening to emerge around the new paradigm: 'valid' reasons for adherence to the older view run out when and only when the community ceases to take seriously those who subjectively see such reasons.

1.3. The Personalist Bayesian Account of Rational Belief

1.3.1. Probability and Evidence

No amount of evidence can deductively prove a scientific theory (this is 'Hume's problem'); and no amount of evidence can strictly disprove a scientific theory (this might be called 'Duhem's problem'). Some might be tempted to give up on the whole idea that evidence supplies the reason for accepting certain theories over others. But this seems much too quick. Another possible (and, given the undeniable and staggering empirical success of science, surely altogether more plausible) conclusion is that proofs and disproofs were always too much to ask: evidence may establish some theories as at any rate *more* rationally believable than others (indeed some of the less believable theories may be rendered close to incredible by the evidence). An obvious suggestion for trying to make this idea precise is to use the notion of probability. Theories may not be proved by the evidence, but they may be much more probable than any of their rivals in the light of the evidence. Theories may not be disproved by evidence, but they may be made so improbable by it that it hardly makes a difference. There is a long history of attempts to develop these suggestions. These attempts have the great advantage of being able to exploit the simple and mathematically precise theory of probability, which helps make discussion of the issues much sharper than is usual in philosophy.

1.3.2. Carnap and Probabilistic Inductive Logic

Readers who are not already acquainted with the axioms of probability should consult the brief treatment by David Papineau in the companion to this volume or one of the references in the Bibliography. Although initially developed to apply to 'events' (the event of a head coming up on the toss of a coin, the event of a radioactive atom undergoing decay in a given time interval, etc.), the probability calculus can also be interpreted as applying to sentences. The philosopher of science Rudolf Carnap in fact developed the idea that the probability of a sentence S—the chance that S is true—is the proportion of the 'possible worlds' in which S holds compared to all 'possible worlds'. Thus a tautology has probability one since it is true in all possible worlds, and a contradiction has probability zero (false in all possible worlds). The probability of the sentence *either* S *or* S' is the measure of the union of those possible worlds in which S is true and those in which S' is true *minus* the possible worlds in which both are true (otherwise the possibilities in which both are true would be 'counted twice'). So, in accord with the probability axioms,

$$p(S \vee S') = p(S) + p(S') - p(S \& S').$$

An important notion in probability theory is that of the *conditional probability* $p(S \mid S')$, the probability of S conditional on S'. In the case of probabilities of events, we can, for example, ask for the probability that a draw of a single card from a well-shuffled pack has produced a heart, given that the card drawn was a red card. (We may have caught a glimpse of the card and seen that it was red, but not been able to discern whether it was a heart or a diamond.) Intuitively the answer is $\frac{1}{2}$ (whereas the unconditional probability of a heart is of course $\frac{1}{4}$). Similarly, the probability that the card drawn was a spade, given that it was red, is of course 0 (again the unconditional probability being $\frac{1}{4}$).

Provided that $p(S') \neq 0$, then the conditional probability $p(S \mid S')$ is equal to the ratio $p(S \& S')/p(S')$. So, on Carnap's interpretation, $p(S \mid S')$ measures the proportion of possible worlds in which S' holds that are also ones in which S holds. The idea was that the probability calculus, interpreted in this way, would provide a natural extension of deductive logic. The inference from premiss S' to conclusion S is, remember, deductively valid if and only if every interpretation of the language in which these sentences are expressed (every 'possible world') that makes S' true also makes S true. So when S' implies S, S must be true in all the possible worlds in which S' is; and hence the above ratio is 1; that is, $p(S \mid S') = 1$. If there is at least one interpretation in which S' is true and S false, then S' fails to entail S deductively. But Carnap's idea was to give formal sense to such intuitively appealing ideas as that S' may 'almost imply' S, while for other such pairs of sentences S' may 'almost imply' that S is false. In the former case, S would be true in nearly all the possible worlds in which S' is, and so, in the Carnap interpretation, $p(S \mid S') \approx 1$; in the latter case S would be false in nearly all the possible worlds in which S' is true and so $p(S \mid S') \approx 0$.

Carnap's idea was that this extension of the logic of deductive entailment to a logic of partial entailment would underwrite such claims as the following:

although the (total) evidence does not entail any of the available theories $T_1, \ldots, T_n$, it none the less implies one of them, say T_3, to a higher degree (perhaps to a much higher degree) than any of its rivals: $p(T_3 \mid e) >> p(T_i \mid e)$ for any $i \neq 3$; and although the evidence does not entail the falsity of some theory T, it 'almost' does so: $p(T \mid e) \approx 0$. These judgements would be just as objective as the straightforward deductive judgements of which they are natural generalizations.

A successful account of partial entailment between sentences would at the same time be, on this approach, an account of *rational degrees of belief*. Just as a rational person believes tautologies (such as 'either probability theory is hard or it isn't') totally and disbelieves totally contradictions (such as 'probability theory is hard and it isn't'), and just as she must rationally believe that Socrates is mortal, given that she believes that all men are mortal and that Socrates is a man, so she must rationally believe Newton's theory to degree r, if she accepts total evidence e and if $p(\text{Newton} \mid e) = r$. The approach, then, would—it seems—deliver an entirely objective answer to the rational preference problem, for example:

Q: Why is it rational (scientific) to prefer the Darwinian theory of evolution to the creationist account, given all evidence e that we have (about fossils, homologies, etc.)?

A: Because $p(\text{Darwin} \mid e) >> p(\text{creationism} \mid e)$; that is, because e entails Darwinian theory to a much higher degree than it entails creationism, and hence Darwinian theory is (objectively) much more likely to be true, given e, than is creationism.

This is a terrific idea. Unfortunately it doesn't work. It fails for the same reasons that the so-called classical interpretation of probability fails. The fatal flaw lies in the implicit idea that there is always only one way of describing or dividing up the possibilities, so that there is always one answer to the question 'What is the proportion of possible worlds in which S' holds to possible worlds in which both S' and S hold?' The flaw surfaces even in apparently straightforward cases.

Suppose there are three individuals that either possess or do not possess some single property P. We might, for example, be considering a population of three ravens each of which might be black (have the property P) or white (fail to have the property P). We want to know what the probability is that the sentence 'Two of the three ravens are black' is true. What are the possible worlds here? Well, we might say that the proportions of black to non-black ravens are what supply the equal possibilities—that is, one possible world is the one in which all three are black, another possible world is one in which two (*any* two) out of three are black, and so on. It is clear that relative to this account of the possibilities (the possibilities being given here by what Carnap called *structure descriptions*) the sentence 'Two out of three ravens are black' holds in one out of four possible cases (0 black ravens, 1 black raven, ..., 3 black ravens) and so on this account its probability is $\frac{1}{4}$.

On the other hand, we could of course individuate each of the ravens (as their mothers no doubt do) and count 'possible worlds' by looking at each possible *distribution* of the properties black and non-black over all the individual ravens. Given this construal, there is, as before, one 'possible world' in which all the ravens are black, but, unlike before, there are not one, but three, possible worlds in which two ravens out of the three are black (the one in which $raven_1$ is white and the others black, the one in which $raven_2$ is white and the others black, and the one in which $raven_3$ is white and the others black). On this account, using Carnap's terminology, each possible world is characterized by a particular *state description* of the form

$$\pm Pa_1 \,\&\, \pm Pa_2 \,\&\, \pm Pa_3;$$

that is, by any of the threefold conjunctions which either asserts (+) or denies (−) that P holds of each of the a_i. Relative to this reckoning, there are a total of 2^3, i.e. eight, possibilities rather than four, and our particular sentence ('Two of the three ravens are black') holds in three of them. So this way of marking out the possibilities would give that sentence the probability $\frac{3}{8}$ rather than the probability $\frac{1}{4}$.

It is unclear how it could be argued that one of these two ways of counting possibilities is the correct one and the other incorrect. (If you are inclined towards the state description account as somehow clearly the more natural, you might like to reflect that this way of counting possibilities does not permit 'inductive learning'. That is, suppose you have already observed two of the ravens in our three-bird example, and both have turned out to be black. Still the probability, as arrived at through state descriptions, that the third one will also be black given this evidence is just the same (namely, one-half) as it was before any observations were made. This is because there are two state descriptions in which the first two ravens are black and in one of them the third is also black, while in the other the third raven is white. This may not seen *too* counterintuitive, but consider a universe in which there are 1,000 birds and suppose you have observed the first 999 and they were all black; still on the state description measure, the probability that the 1,000th raven is black would be the same as the probability that the 1,000th bird is white, i.e. $\frac{1}{2}$. Of all the $2^{1,000}$ state descriptions in this case, there are again just two in which the first 999 are black, and in one of those the final one is black, while in the other it is white.) Moreover, the problems for Carnap's approach become even more intense when—as will of course standardly be the case in anything like a realistic scientific example—the universe is infinite. (A clear account of these difficulties can be found in Howson and Urbach 1993, chapter 4.)

Although the Carnap programme is long dead, I have outlined it here because its failure sets the agenda for recent concerns. I have no doubt that some readers, when introduced to the more recent probabilistic approach to confirmation of theories, will feel that this approach is 'not objective enough', It is as well to remember, however, that the fully objective probabilistic account has apparently unambiguously failed.

1.3.3. *The Basics of Personalist Bayesianism*

Can probability theory still be used to characterize correct scientific reasoning despite the failure of the Carnap programme? The influential 'Bayesian' school argues that it can.

A Bayesian 'agent' is thought of as having 'degrees of belief' in all the propositions expressible in her language (hence including any truth-functional combination or any logical consequence of any such propositions). Such an agent is 'rational' (scientific) if and only if

(*a*) at any given time, her degrees of belief satisfy the probability calculus (i.e. are formally representable as probabilities); and
(*b*) she *modifies* her beliefs from one time (t_1) to the next (t_2) in the light of the evidence that has accumulated between t_1 and t_2 in a certain way—via the 'principle of conditionalization'.

Concerning (*b*): suppose that all that has happened of epistemic relevance to theory T between time t_1 and time t_2 is that some statement e which was not known to hold at t_1 has now (at time t_2) been accepted (by the agent) as evidence (this is admittedly a rather vague supposition because of the clause about the acquisition of e as evidence being all that happened of epistemic relevance between the two times); the principle of conditionalization then requires that the agent's degree of belief in T at t_2 should be the same as her degree of belief in T at time t_1 conditional on e, that is,

$$p_{t_2}(T) = p_{t_1}(T \mid e).$$

This is sometimes expressed as the requirement that a rational agent's 'posterior' degree of belief in T after evidence e has accrued should be her 'prior' degree of belief of T conditional on e—that is, prior to e's having become evidence.

The approach is called 'Bayesian' simply because probabilities of the form $p(T \mid e)$ are crucial quantities for the approach and these probabilities are evaluated using Bayes's theorem. This theorem (which is a theorem of pure probability theory and hence entirely uncontroversial) in its simplest form states that, provided $p(e) \neq 0$, then:

$$p(T \mid e) = p(e \mid T) \,.\, (p(T)/p(e)).$$

The approach is called 'personalist' because it explicitly eschews Carnap's idea that there is only one correct, 'objective' value of the *prior* probabilities $p(T)$ and $p(e)$ occurring in this expression.

Although this freedom over the priors entails that two equally Bayesian-rational agents may have very different degrees of belief in the same theory in the light of the same evidence, it by no means follows that the approach is entirely subjective, that the approach simply describes the way different people in fact think and reason. Each of the requirements (*a*) and (*b*) imposes objective constraints on degrees of belief that may well not be met by particular real reasoners (indeed some of the constraints provably cannot be met by real reasoners).

For example, since the probability calculus is based on classical logic, the Bayesian requires that an agent is rational only if she is a perfect deductive logician—believing every logical truth absolutely, i.e. to degree 1. (Of course, even the smartest of you would be hard pressed actually to recognize that some complicated sentence involving, say, twenty-seven atomic propositions is in fact a tautology; hence you might not know that your 'real' degree of belief in it, as a Bayesian-rational agent, was in fact one.) Again, Bayesianism dictates that an agent is rational only if her degree of belief in the proposition that 'either the sun will rise tomorrow or blow up overnight'—assuming that she discounts entirely the possibility that it will *both* blow up *and* rise tomorrow—must be the sum of her degrees of belief in the proposition that the sun will rise tomorrow and in the proposition that the sun will explode overnight.

1.3.4. *Bayesianism and Rationality: The Two Main Questions*

The two constraints on 'rational degrees of belief' underlying Bayesianism have, then, some objective bite. The question arises whether an agent needs to satisfy those principles in order to count as rational. That is, would an agent automatically be irrational if her degrees of belief did not satisfy those constraints? A positive answer to this question clearly requires justification of the two Bayesian constraints as necessary conditions for rationality.

Discussion of the first constraint—that an agent's degrees of belief at any given time must be probabilities—has centred around the so-called *Dutch book* argument. The idea is that if an agent's degrees of belief fail to satisfy the probability calculus and hence fail to be probabilities, then she is provably committed to regarding certain bets as fair on which she is bound to lose whatever the real world turns out be like. Extensions of the Dutch book argument have also been developed in an attempt to show that an agent must conditionalize in order to avoid irrationality; while another argument for the principle of conditionalization has been that it is essentially analytic—the fact that your degree of belief in T conditional on e is r simply *means* that your degree of belief in T

would be r if you were to come to know e (but everything else remained the same). There are, however, arguments in the literature against both suggestions and some philosophers regard conditionalization as both substantive and unjustified. References to the interesting literature on these issues can be found in the bibliography.

The second main question about these Bayesian constraints is philosophically more challenging, if less clear-cut, and concerns their *sufficiency*: is an agent whose degrees of belief satisfy the two Bayesian conditions automatically rational (in the intuitive scientific sense)? This seems to come down to the question whether those judgements about correct and incorrect reasoning in science supplied by educated intuition are captured by the Bayesian account. (Of course there is also the possibility that the Bayesian may argue that some particular clash between his principles and educated intuition shows that intuition needs to be *re*-educated.)

There are certain straightforward aspects of scientific reasoning that seem entirely uncontroversial and of which the Bayesian position gives pleasingly neat explications. For example, *theories can be confirmed by observational or experimental evidence and are generally better confirmed by passing 'severe tests'*—that is, by tests the observed outcome of which was implied by the theory but was unlikely in the light of 'background knowledge'. To take a famous example from the history of optics, Fresnel's wave theory of light was confirmed by the discovery that the centre of the shadow of a small opaque disc held in light diverging from a point-source is illuminated. The claim that the centre of the 'geometrical shadow' should be illuminated had been shown to be a consequence of Fresnel's theory (it was Poisson who discovered this logical fact), yet the claim seemed extremely unlikely to be true (so much so, according to the standard story, that Fresnel's contemporaries firmly expected the theory to suffer a major defeat here). In fact, however, when the experiment was performed—by Fresnel himself and his friend Arago—it turned out as predicted by the theory.

The Bayesian account of the evidential confirmation of a theory is simplicity itself: evidence confirms a theory if (and to the extent that) it increases the theory's probability; if, that is, the probability of the theory once that evidence has been established is higher than its probability beforehand. Since the Bayesian principle of conditionalization requires that an agent's 'posterior' degree of belief in theory T—that is, her degree of belief in T once some piece of evidence e has been established (but nothing else of epistemic relevance has happened)—should be her earlier degree of belief in T conditional on e, that is, $p(T \mid e)$, and since $p(T)$ measures her ('absolute') degree of belief in T before e became established, then for a Bayesian

$$e \text{ confirms } T \text{ if and only if } p(T \mid e) > p(T).$$

(Or better, since it is as well to remind ourselves that these are all *personal* probabilities, an agent will see e as confirming T just in case, for her, $p(T|e)$ is higher than $p(T)$.) By Bayes's theorem, assuming $p(e) \neq 0$,

$$p(T|e) = p(e|T).p(T)/p(e).$$

Since in cases of the kind now under consideration, e is entailed by T in conjunction with accepted initial conditions and auxiliaries, it seems reasonable to take $p(e|T) = 1$ (indeed if these accepted initial conditions and auxiliaries are regarded as part of background knowledge, then the Bayesian agent is bound to set the so-called likelihood term at 1). Hence $p(T|e)$ simplifies to $p(T)/p(e)$. This means, in turn, that unless $p(e) = 1$ (that is, unless the agent was completely sure about the outcome of the experiment ahead of time), then e must confirm T on the Bayesian account and moreover the extent of the confirmation—measured by the difference between the posterior degree of belief in T, $p(T|e)$, and the prior, $p(T)$—is greater the smaller is $p(e)$. (Given that $p(e) < 1$, $1/p(e)$ of course becomes larger as $p(e) \rightarrow 0$.)

Does Bayesianism do as well when it comes to other—perhaps rather more subtle and taxing—aspects of reasoning in science? When discussing Kuhn's work earlier, we found that the two most pressing problems that that work poses for the defender of the idea that theory change in science is a 'rational' process were the Duhem problem and the problem of prediction versus accommodation. (Concerning this second problem, the issue arose, remember, of whether a piece of evidence that has been 'shoved' into the 'box' provided by a paradigm might weigh less heavily in that paradigm's favour than evidence that 'falls out' of the paradigm without needing to be shoved.) What can Bayesianism tell us about these two problems?

1.3.5. *Bayesianism and the Duhem Problem*

Duhem pointed out that no assertion that we would naturally think of as a 'single' scientific theory—Newton's theory (of mechanics plus gravitation), the classical wave theory of light, special relativity theory, or whatever—has deductive consequences *of its own* that are directly checkable at the empirical level. In order to deduce from Newton's theory, say, predictions about planetary positions (supposing we take such predictions as directly empirically checkable) we need further independent assumptions—about what other massive bodies exist in the solar system, about the amount of refraction that light undergoes in passing into the earth's atmosphere, and so on. Should the observational consequence be found false, then all that follows deductively is that at least one of the premisses—that is, at least one from the set of assumptions consisting of the 'central' theory under test together with all the background or auxiliary assumptions—must be false. (Let T be the central theory and A the conjunction of the necessary auxiliaries, then if neither T nor A alone but only the conjunction $T\&A$ entails some observational or experimental consequence e, then all we can infer from the observation that e is false is $-(T\&A)$, which is of course equivalent to $-T\vee -A$.) Indeed if the 'central theory under test' itself divides naturally into a 'core' assumption and a set of more specific assumptions (as does 'the' wave theory of light, for example, which consists of the core assumption that light is some sort of wave in some sort of medium together with more specific assumptions about the sorts of wave and the sort of medium), then the situation is one step more complicated. Now the natural formalization of the experimental test involves C (the 'core' assumption), S (the set of still 'central', but more specific, assumptions), and the auxiliaries A. But then again if only the conjunction $C\&S\&A$ entails some evidential statement e, then $-e$ entails only $-(C\&S\&A)$, that is, $-C\vee -S\vee -A$. And, so far as deductive considerations alone go, the scientist now has three options: (1) retain the whole central theory ($C\&S$) and reject an auxiliary; (2) accept the auxiliaries but reject one of the specific assumptions rather than the core assumption (this option will naturally, if rather confusingly, be described as 'modifying' the central theory rather than rejecting it), and finally, (3) reject the core theory.

Scientists, however, do not invariably exploit the freedom left to them by these purely deductive considerations. Sometimes it seems clearly right to reject an auxiliary in the light of an experimental 'anomaly'. A classic and much discussed case concerns the discovery of the planet Neptune. Here there were 'unexplained irregularities' in the observed orbit of the planet Uranus—that is, Newton's theory of mechanics and gravitation, taken together with then accepted auxiliaries and initial conditions, led to predictions about Uranus' orbit that were observably incorrect. Rather than reject the 'central' Newtonian theory, Adams in England and, independently, Leverrier in France suggested that the 'mistake' lay in the auxiliary assumption about the number and masses of other bodies in the universe that had significant gravitational effects on Uranus. Working backwards from the assumption that Newton's theory is true, they were led to postulate the existence of a hitherto unsuspected planet beyond Uranus—a postulate that was subsequently confirmed by astronomical observation. Here the retention of the central theory in the light of an anomaly seems eminently scientifically justified (to the extent that this episode is always counted as one of the great successes of the Newtonian theory).

But defending a cherished theory against apparent counter-evidence by rejecting some less central, specific assumption sometimes seems to be not a great scientific success but the hallmark of *pseudo*-science. Velikovsky's work provides a clear example. The central theory concerned in this case was Velikovsky's claim that a comet had long ago broken away from Jupiter and orbited the earth on a series of occasions producing such notable events as the parting of the Red Sea and the fall of the walls of Jericho. The anomalous evidence was the absence of any records of similar cataclysms to those recorded in the Old Testament in the archives of at least some other record-keeping cultures of the time. Velikovsky pointed out in effect that this is an instance of the Duhem problem: the assertion that records of appropriate cataclysms would have been kept in the cultures concerned can be deduced only by postulating not merely his fundamental cometary hypothesis but also various auxiliary assumptions—for example, the assumption that the culture's scribes would have recorded any cataclysm on the relevant scale if they had witnessed it. (You would indeed think that 'events' on the scale of the parting of the Red Sea would be worth a line or two in anyone's diary.) Just like the Newtonians working back from the assumption of the truth of their central theory, Velikovsky assumed that his comet really did exist and really did perform the complicated dance he postulated, and so he was led to assume that cataclysms had been witnessed in the other cultures and that in fact they had proved so traumatic that 'collective amnesia' had set in. (Of course, Velikovsky postulated that this dread condition had afflicted those and only those cultures who were otherwise keeping records but had no records of appropriate cataclysms.)

It is surely a requirement on any adequate account of scientific rationality that it explain the difference between these two episodes—that it explain Adams and Leverrier's move, but not Velikovsky's, as scientifically reasonable. (Recall that an account that satisfies this condition will avoid many of the problems posed by Kuhn.) Does personalist Bayesianism satisfy the condition?

Colin Howson and Peter Urbach, developing an earlier idea of Jon Dorling's, claim that a straightforward analysis based on personalist Bayesian principles solves the Duhem problem entirely. Consider a case in which some theoretical system can be represented as the conjunction $T\&A$ and in which neither T nor A alone entails any observation statement; and suppose that some experimental consequence of the conjunction has turned out to be false. The situation with respect to deductive logic is symmetric: neither T nor A alone is falsified. But, as Dorling points out, there is no reason why in such cases the effect on T and A should always be symmetric in Bayesian probabilistic terms. The 'posterior probabilities' of T and A are, assuming $p(e) \neq 0$,

$$p(T \mid e) = p(T).p(e \mid T)/p(e), \text{ and}$$
$$p(A \mid e) = p(A).p(e \mid A)/p(e).$$

Plainly, if an agent judges $p(e \mid A)$ to be very close to $p(e)$, while she judges $p(e \mid T)$ to be very much less than $p(e)$, then her posterior probability for A will be very close to its prior while T's posterior will be very much lower than its prior.

Dorling has analysed various historical cases and Howson and Urbach give an especially clear treatment of Prout's hypothesis (that the atomic weights of all elements are integer multiples of the atomic weight of chlorine) facing experimental evidence that seemed to show the element chlorine to have an atomic weight around 35.8. But the idea behind the analysis can be readily illustrated in the case we have cited of Newton's theory and the difficulties with Uranus.

Adams and Leverrier 'held onto' Newton's theory despite the 'recalcitrant' observations of Uranus' orbit, and instead 'laid the blame' on the auxiliary about the number of other planets in the solar system. Let T then be Newton's theory, A the necessary auxiliaries, and e the evidence about Uranus' orbit. Suppose that Adams and Leverrier's belief-states can reasonably be represented (of course in an idealized way) as follows:

(1) $p(A \mid T) = p(T)$ (i.e. T and A are probabilistically independent)
(2) $p(T) = 0.9$
(3) $p(A) = 0.6$
(4) $p(e \mid -T\&A) = p(e \mid -T\&-A) = \frac{1}{2}p(e \mid T\&-A)$.

(The probability $p(e \mid T\&A)$ is of course 0 here since e refutes the conjunction $T \&A$.) That is, these scientists start out having a higher degree of belief in Newton's theory than in the auxiliaries (though these are accepted auxiliaries so their degree of belief in them is none the less substantial); and they think that the observed orbit of Uranus is twice as likely to occur if Newton's theory holds but the auxiliaries are wrong, than, for example, if Newton's theory is false and the auxiliaries are correct.

It follows just by the pure mathematics of the probability calculus that

$$p(T \mid e) = 0.878 \text{ while } p(A \mid e) = 0.073.$$

So a Bayesian agent beginning with the above priors and likelihoods, and conditionalizing on the evidence, would find the credibility of Newton's theory scarcely affected by the 'anomalous' evidence from Uranus, while she would now regard the auxiliaries A, which she had initially regarded as more likely to be true than not ($p(A) = 0.6$), as scarcely credible at all. And the claim is that this analysis reveals the rationale for the markedly asymmetric reaction to this 'anomalous' evidence by Leverrier and Adams: in finding their 'central' (Newtonian) theory scarcely threatened and in 'blaming' the auxiliaries, they were, in effect, operating as rational Bayesian agents.

It is of course by no means clear what would count as an acceptable rational reconstruction of the 'belief dynamics' of some set of scientists. Not even the most committed Bayesian would claim that such accounts are simply descriptive—since no one seriously holds that the historical agents had degrees of belief that are exactly expressed by the numbers used in such Bayesian analyses. No Bayesian to my knowledge has explicitly analysed the Adams–Leverrier case; the numbers used above are taken from Howson and Urbach's treatment of Prout. But similar difficulties seem to arise in all cases. In particular it seems rather difficult to take the likelihood assumptions ((4) above) seriously. Even accepting that no one expects precise numbers, I suspect that one would have got little more than blank stares from Adams and Leverrier if one had asked them what their degree of belief in the evidence about Uranus would be on the assumption that both Newton's theory, and the then accepted auxiliaries, are false.

However, the chief difficulty with this analysis arises once we concede, for the sake of argument, that the above account in terms of personal probabilities does provide a rational reconstruction of the reasoning of Adams and Leverrier. What we set out to find as a solution of the Duhem problem was not simply a reconstruction of the (intuitively correct) reasoning of Adams and Leverrier, but a reconstruction that differentiated that reasoning from the superficially similar, but intuitively highly suspect, reasoning of Velikovsky and followers. The Bayesian analysis fails signally to underwrite this distinction. Nothing is easier than to model Velikovsky's reasoning in Bayesian terms. We just have to make formally the same assumptions about his prior beliefs as in the Adams and Leverrier case. Let T' be Velikovsky's central cometary hypothesis and A' the necessary auxiliaries (including assumptions about the reliability of scribes in various cultures). Then, if his beliefs about these various claims ahead of the evidence (e') of the lack of suitable records in certain cultures are appropriately expressed by

(1′) $p(A' \mid T') = p(T')$ (i.e. T' and A' are probabilistically independent)
(2′) $p(T') = 0.9$
(3′) $p(A') = 0.6$
(4′) $p(e' \mid -T' \,\&\, A') = p(e' \mid -T' \,\&\, -A') = \frac{1}{2} p(e' \mid T' \,\&\, -A')$,

it plainly follows just as before that

$$p(T' \mid e) = 0.878 \text{ while } p(A' \mid e) = 0.073.$$

Hence, as a good Bayesian, Velikovsky will have conditionalized, and so his 'posterior' degree of belief in his central hypothesis will be hardly different from his prior degree of belief, while his degree of belief in the auxiliaries will have been radically reduced. And this indeed captures the way Velikovsky seems to have reacted to this evidence.

Now the Bayesian does not of course condone simply plucking alleged degrees of belief out of the air in order to defend a view favoured for some other (non-epistemic) reason. It may well be that, although Velikovsky could have defended his position as rational on Bayesian principles if he had had the degrees of belief involved, as a matter of fact he did not have (or rather cannot sensibly be idealized as having) the priors and likelihoods cited in (1′–4′). It may well be that he instead made a series of conditionalization errors. But the real Velikovsky's beliefs seem irrelevant to the philosophical point. The Bayesian account seems to be put into deep trouble just by the fact that, according to it, were someone's belief-state to be one that could be appropriately modelled via assumptions (1′) to (4′) then they would be declared perfectly rational in seeing the evidence of no cataclysmic records as barely affecting the credibility of the central cometary hypothesis.

The natural reaction here is of course that some of the priors and likelihoods in (1′–4′) themselves seem intuitively highly suspect. Is it really reasonable, for example, to have a degree of belief as high as 0.9 in Velikovsky's theory of the earth's close encounters with this strange 'comet' ahead of the evidence of no cataclysmic records in some culture *C*? Or is it really reasonable to hold that that evidence is twice as likely on the assumption that Velikovsky's theory is true but that scribes in *C* were inaccurate as it is on the assumption of no close encounters and accurate scribes? However, such questions are *entirely out of place* in the Bayesian scheme which treats such assignments of degrees of belief as 'givens' in the analysis. If you hold that there is an objective difference between the reasoning of, say, Adams and Leverrier and Velikovsky in that the first reasoned scientifically and the second not, then you cannot hold that personalist Bayesian analysis is an accurate and complete account of objective, scientific reasoning.

The criticism that personalist Bayesian analyses are *too* personalist, too dependent on facts about agents' priors, to give an adequate account of the principles underlying correct reasoning in science is one that has often been levelled. There have of course been Bayesian attempts to counter the charge. I shall briefly outline these attempts shortly—after first looking at the Bayesian treatment of our second important methodological issue—that of whether successful predictions are more confirmatory for the theories that make them than are successful accommodations of known facts.

1.3.6. Bayesianism and 'Prediction versus Accommodation'

Kuhn claimed, remember, that one could not fault the hold-outs to revolutions—their belief that some explanation could be given within their paradigm for the allegedly crucial new evidence is demonstrably 'neither illogical nor unscientific'. One straightforward way in which an account of empirical support for scientific theories might counter this claim would be by underwriting a distinction between evidence that was predicted by a theory and evidence that was already known and 'merely' explained by a theory (or accommodated within the theory). Suppose it could be argued that the correct account of empirical support gives, *ceteris paribus*, greater confirmatory weight to a newly predicted fact than to an explained old fact. Suppose a 'revolutionary' new paradigm predicts some hitherto unsuspected phenomenon. Kuhn's hold-outs' belief that the evidential scales could be balanced simply by giving an account of that phenomenon within their old paradigm would then be mistaken—they would, contrary to Kuhn's own claim, be shown to have been unscientific in the sense that they did not weigh evidence according to the correct principles.

So, for example, phlogistonists insisted that the fact that the residue of mercury burned in air weighed more than the initial mercury could be accommodated within their paradigm, despite the fact that it was committed to the idea that something (to wit, phlogiston) was always emitted from substances that burned. They were clearly right: one possibility (that does not in fact seem ever to have been taken seriously) would be to attribute phlogiston 'negative weight' (whatever that might mean); a more plausible possibility would be to hypothesize that the mercury *both* loses phlogiston *and* gains something else, a complex process that happens to result in a net weight increase. But if this were merely an accommodation (that is, if no such suggestion made independently testable predictions) and if accommodations count less than predictions (putting it very roughly) then the hold-outs for phlogiston would indeed be reasoning unscientifically if they counted this as balancing the evidential scales (Lavoisier's oxygen theory having, remember, predicted the result of the mercury experiment).

But does the correct account of empirical support lend a confirmatory premium to new evidence? And, if so, why? This is a long-running issue in philosophy of science. Keynes and Mill are notable representatives of the anti-predictivist side. Keynes wrote (in his *A Treatise on Probability*):

> [the] peculiar value of prediction . . . is altogether imaginary. . . . The question of whether a particular hypothesis happens to be propounded before or after examination of [its empirical consequences] is quite irrelevant.

This echoes John Stuart Mill, who wrote (in his *System of Logic*):

> it seems to be thought that an hypothesis . . . is entitled to a more favourable reception, if, besides accounting for all the facts previously known, it has led to the anticipation and prediction of others which experiment afterwards verified . . . Such predictions and their fulfilment are, indeed, well calculated to impress the ignorant vulgar, whose faith in science rests solely on similar coincidences between its prophecies and what comes to pass. But it is strange that any considerable stress should be laid upon such a coincidence by persons of scientific attainments.

The 'person of scientific attainments' who held this strange view and whom Mill chiefly had in mind was William Whewell. Whewell asserted that successful prediction 'gives a theory a stamp of truth beyond the power of ingenuity to counterfeit'. Similar views were expressed, for example, by Duhem, who held that the 'highest test of [a theory] is to ask it to indicate in advance things which the future alone will reveal' and that if the theory passes such a test, it is especially highly confirmed. (In Duhem's own terms this means that it is likely to be part of a 'natural classification'.) And subsequently by many other philosophers of science.

What does Bayesianism have to say about this contentious issue? The answer is interestingly mixed.

1.3.6.1. *Old Evidence never Confirms (and that's Wrong)* Some analysts—for example, Clark Glymour and, following him, John Earman—have argued that

1. the Bayesian system entails that *only* new evidence ever confirms a theory; and
2. this is completely contrary to intuitively sensible judgements made by scientists.

Glymour holds, in other words, that the answer that would be entailed by the correct account of evidential support is that there is no premium on predictions; and, since he also believes he can demonstrate that Bayesianism entails that only successful predictions count in favour of a theory, it follows that Bayesianism is not the correct account of evidential support.

The issue here has become known as the 'problem of old evidence'. Here is how Glymour argues that Bayesianism entails that only new evidence confirms a theory. If *e* is evidence at time *t*, that is, *e* is already known to hold, then it is part of 'background knowledge' at *t*, and—remembering that all probabilities in the Bayesian scheme are relative to background knowledge—this means that

$$p_t(e) = 1.$$

It is easy to prove that, if so, then no such piece of known evidence *e* can confirm any theory. As we saw earlier, *e* confirms *T* only if $p(T \mid e) > p(T)$. But, by Bayes's theorem, $p(T \mid e) = (p(e \mid T).p(T))/p(e)$. And so if for any old evidence, *e* $p_t(e) = 1$ (which entails $p_t(e \mid T) = 1$), it follows that $p_t(T \mid e) = p_t(T)$. Thus, by conditionalization, once you take *e* into account, your degree of belief in *T* is just the same as it was before—*e* is entirely neutral with respect to *T*, neither confirming nor disconfirming it.

Glymour claims that, to the contrary, there is a whole host of cases from history of science where a theory was not only positively confirmed, but strongly confirmed by some evidence *e* that was already well known. The case that Glymour especially emphasizes is of general relativity theory and the observations of the precession of Mercury's perihelion. The evidence about Mercury was already known when the general theory was formulated, but it provided, in the view of the scientific community, especially compelling evidence for Einstein's theory—more compelling, according to most people's intuitions, than that from newly discovered phenomena such as the Mössbauer effect.

1.3.6.2. *The Garber, Niiniluoto, Jeffrey Attempt to Solve the Old Evidence Problem* Glymour himself suggested a way in which the Bayesian system might be extended to overcome this problem of old evidence. This suggestion was subsequently endorsed and developed by a number of philosophers including Garber, Niiniluoto, and Jeffrey. The suggestion is that the important fact that was unknown in cases like that of general relativity theory and the precession of Mercury's perihelion was not the empirical evidence about Mercury's motion but rather the logical fact that the theory entails the (known) evidence about Mercury's motion. The confirmation arises from the *logical discovery* that the theory entails the evidence.

In order to make this account work a new primitive connective $\Rightarrow$ is introduced. This represents (though one is not formally allowed to recognize it) deductive entailment. It can then be shown that if

(1) an agent has degrees of belief that are probabilities not just in the scientific theories and statements available to her but also in all statements of the form $T \Rightarrow e$, $T_1 \Rightarrow T_2$, and so on; and if
(2) the agent's probability distribution satisfies certain assumptions,

then for some *T*, *e* pairs,

$$p(T \mid T \Rightarrow e) > p(T).$$

Hence although Glymour is right that old evidence in itself cannot Bayesian-confirm any theory, the discovery of the logical fact that the theory entails that old evidence (that is, the discovery that $T \Rightarrow e$) may confirm the theory.

This ingenious suggestion faces certain problems, however. First of all, since a Bayesian agent is supposed to be a perfect (deductive) logician, it is only in virtue of forgetting that $\Rightarrow$ really means deductive entailment and taking it as an undefined primitive that formal contradiction is avoided. And secondly, the intuitive justification seems, on reflection, very doubtful—surely what really confirms the general theory of relativity is empirical evidence about Mercury and not a logical (and therefore analytic) fact about the relationship between the general theory and sentences describing Mercury's motion.

1.3.6.3. *Howson and Urbach's Attempt to Solve the 'Old Evidence Problem'* Some Bayesians—notably Colin Howson and Peter Urbach—have argued that Glymour has it topsy-turvy: it is indeed correct intuitively that old evidence can confirm scientific theories, but the Bayesian position entails exactly this intuitively correct result. The crucial claim behind this particular Bayesian analysis amounts to the following:

> Probabilities are all implicitly relative to background knowledge; but when the impact of evidence *e* on some theory *T* is being weighed, the right probability for *e* is the degree of belief you *would have had* in *e*, were you in the cognitive situation you are in fact in, except that you did not know *e*.

When e is (or was) unknown, this 'correct degree of belief' is just your actual degree of belief at the instant before e becomes evidence for you. However, where e is already known, the relevant degree of belief has a counterfactual character: you pretend that your relevant 'background knowledge' is not B (as it in fact is), but rather, so to speak, '$B - \{e\}$'—what remains when you 'subtract' e from background knowledge B. It follows that $p(e)$ for known e need not be 1, and indeed in general will not be. And so, of course, contrary to Glymour, old evidence may Bayesian-confirm.

Several problems make this suggestion highly problematic. One is the formal problem that the set of sentences '$B-\{e\}$' is not well-defined. Simply 'deleting' e from the (deductively closed) set of B's consequences has no real effect, since e will simply 'reappear' as a consequence of lots of other consequences of B. (Let f be any other consequence of B, then the sentence $e\&f$ will also be a consequence of B.) On the other hand, suppose B is axiomatized in some way and we characterize $B-\{e\}$ as the set of consequences of the axioms with e removed. Since evidential statements like e will not normally be axioms, this operation generally leaves B entirely unaffected. However, suppose $\{B_1 \ldots B_n\}$ are axioms for B, where none of the B_i is the evidential statement e; since e is a consequence of B it is easy to see that the following axiomatization is logically equivalent to the first:

$$\{e, e \rightarrow B_1, e \rightarrow B_2, \ldots, e \rightarrow B_n\}.$$

But now the effect of 'deleting' e from this axiom set will be devastating (the remaining axioms all being relatively weak statements equivalent to sentences of the form 'either not e or B_i').

Howson and Urbach argue that despite these formal difficulties we make good enough intuitive sense of the required idea in many cases. Suppose, for example, a coin has been tossed a single time, and has landed 'heads', we can none the less easily understand the claim that the coin had a probability of one-half of producing tails *on that toss*. But are we not, then, in effect saying 'suppose my background knowledge were as it is except that I didn't know that the coin had turned up heads on this toss, then I would give a probability of one-half to each of the possible outcomes'?

But, whatever may be the case with the coin, it is not at all clear—as John Earman has also suggested—that sense can be made, for example, of what Einstein's cognitive situation would have been in 1915 had he not known about the precession of Mercury's perihelion. Einstein's whole view was so multiply affected by the Mercury anomaly, that it seems hard even to begin to think about what he would have believed had he not known about it. If so, then it is impossible to make any real sense of his degrees of belief in other propositions against this counterfactual background. Similarly, having studied Fresnel's thought and work for many years, I just have no conception of what it might mean to talk of Fresnel's 'background knowledge' *as it would have been* had he not known about, say, the phenomenon of straight-edge diffraction. If this is right, then at least for these particular pieces of known evidence e, the Howson and Urbach counterfactual construal of $p(e)$ fails.

Suppose, however, we go along with this counterfactual suggestion for a while, does it lead to a satisfactory resolution of the predictivism debate? The Bayesian analysis now delivers the (surely correct) implication that known evidence does sometimes confirm. An investigator in 1915, somehow applying the counterfactual interpretation, assigns a probability of (let's assume, considerably) less than one to the statement that Mercury's perihelion precesses in the way it does. Given that the general theory of relativity, R, entails that statement e, then $p(\mathrm{R} \mid e) = p(\mathrm{R})/p(e) >> p(\mathrm{R})$. Hence that investigator, having conditionalized as a good Bayesian, will see R as (strongly) confirmed by e.

However, as is now well known, a classical, non-relativistic account can also be given of Mercury's movements by making entirely *ad hoc* assumptions about the density distribution of the sun (that is, those assumptions about the density are fixed exactly so as to yield the known facts about Mercury and for no other reason). This possibility became known as a result of Dicke's work in the 1960s. Call this classical account C. C also entails e and so again an agent applying the counterfactual construal—say in 1960—will set $p(e) << 1$ and hence will derive $p(C \mid e) >> p(C)$. That is, such an agent will see e as confirming C as well. This in itself need not be problematic: after all we are surely happier with C given that it gets Mercury's motion right than we would have been if (*per impossibile* given the way it was constructed) it had got Mercury's motion wrong. And indeed so long as an agent attributes a very low prior probability (that is, ahead of e) to C, much lower than the prior she assigns to R, then the Bayesian analysis delivers the intuitively correct judgement (or at any rate the one that is firmly entrenched in the scientific community)—that R remains very much more probable than C once the evidence e is taken into account. Indeed, if we measure the support that e lends to theory T by the 'difference measure' ($S(T,e) = p(T \mid e) - p(T)$), then we have, since R entails e and therefore $p(\mathrm{R} \mid e) = p(\mathrm{R})/p(e)$,

$$S(\mathrm{R},e) = p(\mathrm{R} \mid e) - p(\mathrm{R}) = p(\mathrm{R})(1/p(e) - 1).$$

Moreover, since C also entails e,

$$S(C,e) = p(C \mid e) - p(C) = p(C)(1/p(e) - 1).$$

Assuming that $p(e)$ has the same value in both cases and that that value is not one, we obtain the result that

> $S(\mathrm{R},e) > S(C,e)$ (that is, that e supports R more than it supports C) if and only if $p(\mathrm{R}) > p(C)$.

Or, to put the result in its more correct personalist terms: an agent will see *e* as supporting R more strongly than *C* just in case her prior for R is higher than her prior for *C*.

A similar analysis will show that, for example, some piece of evidence (say, some aspect of the fossil record) entailed both by some specific Darwinian theory and by some specific special creationist theory (in the latter case simply by dint of writing the—now alleged—fossil into God's creation) differentially supports the two theories in a way that depends entirely on their prior probabilities ahead of that evidence.

Such a Bayesian agent will make evidential judgements in these cases entirely in accord with the judgements made less formally by the scientific community exactly if she assigns a much higher prior to R than to *C* and a much higher prior to the Darwinian than to the special creationist theory. But what if she is firmly convinced of *C* or of special creation and assigns them much higher priors than their rivals? Then as a good Bayesian she will see the evidence as providing in a sense further support for her views, for she will see her previously favoured theories as the better supported by the evidence at issue. Analogously to the case of the Duhem problem: if you hold that, say, the fossil record should, on the principles of correct scientific reasoning, be seen as favouring Darwinism over special creation whatever one's initial beliefs, then you cannot hold that personalist Bayesianism is a correct and complete account of those principles.

1.3.7. Rejoinders to the Charge of Over-Subjectivism

Bayesians often respond to the charge that their accounts of scientific reasoning are too reliant on merely subjective priors by citing a range of results about the 'swamping' or 'washing-out' of priors. After first advertising the virtue of having a certain amount of 'subjectivism' in one's account of proper scientific reasoning (even in science it would sometimes be unfortunate if all reasoners held the same beliefs), Bayesians then go on to claim that this subjective element does not matter too much because in many situations the subjective element is eventually overwhelmed. In certain situations and subject to certain weak constraints on the priors, all Bayesian agents will tend towards agreement.

For all their formal interest, it is not clear how much philosophical weight these swamping results carry. Priors are only ever fully 'washed out' in the limit, which of course we never really achieve. The fact is that any actual theoretical preference—even the intuitively most bizarre—may be Bayesian rational: provided she began with a sufficiently high prior on her own theory and a sufficiently low prior on the rival evolutionary account, a creationist can have conditionalized away on the accumulating evidence and still have arrived, as of this moment, at an overwhelmingly higher posterior for her scientific creationist theory than for Darwinian theory. The fact that this probability, though overwhelmingly high, is somewhat lower than her prior seems of little consolation; and there seems equally little consolation in the thought that, given certain kinds of future evidence, the sequence of her successive posteriors and that of her erstwhile opponent are destined to converge. If the judgement that a satisfactory theory of proper scientific reasoning ought to deliver is that creationists, Velikovskians, and the rest of the sorry crew are irrational *now*, then personalist Bayesianism is no such theory.

The second type of Bayesian response is that the charge of over-subjectivism is entirely misplaced. The principles of personalist Bayesianism are essentially natural extensions of logical principles. The requirement of coherence (that is, the requirement that one's degrees of belief satisfy the probability calculus) is a natural extension of the requirement of deductive consistency. (Indeed Ramsey—essentially the founder of the position—used the term consistency to cover both the purely deductive and the probabilistic notions.) Moreover, some Bayesians (as we saw earlier) defend the principle of conditionalization as analytic. The imposition of any further requirement (for example constraints on 'sensible' priors) would, however, definitely transcend logic and hence involve substantive assumptions about the world and our ways of comprehending it. But this would raise the awkward question how such assumptions could themselves have any reasoned credentials. How could a synthetic claim that is allegedly constitutive of reason itself be given a reasoned justification without getting involved in an infinite regress? Personalists like Dorling and Howson conclude that any further requirement would be 'arbitrary' and that Ramsey was therefore right to insist that inductive *logic*—personalist Bayesianism—must treat an agent's prior distribution of degrees of belief as simply a given. If this means—as we have seen it does—that a rational Velikovskian, or a rational scientific creationist becomes a possibility, then this must simply be accepted. If Velikovsky started off with some prior for his cometary hypothesis that seems ludicrous to you, then you will of course disagree with him (this simply means that your prior will be different), but so long as he has conditionalized properly on the accumulating evidence, you have no justification for regarding him as non-scientific or irrational—even though he still, even in view of all the evidence, orders the credibilities of the available theories radically differently from the way you do.

This response can itself be attacked in two ways. First, are the principles underlying personalist Bayesianism really 'logical'? Secondly, even if they are logical, wouldn't it simply follow that logic (even in the extended Bayesian sense) is not strong enough on its own to ground an adequate theory of proper scientific reasoning?

1.3.8. *Prediction need not be* Prediction

It seems that, depending on the details of the Bayesian analysis you favour, a Bayesian can endorse either of the possible answers to the old and new evidence problem. But which answer is intuitively the correct one? Does new evidence provide, *ceteris paribus*, more support and, if so, why? The question is still very much an open one—discussions of it have, however, in my view, been obscured by a failure to make the right distinction.

Why on earth should it matter from the point of view of how strongly it supports a theory exactly when some piece of evidence was discovered to be indeed evidence? Why should the fact that the precession of Mercury's perihelion had been well investigated before Einstein articulated the general theory of relativity while the gravitational starshift was discovered only later in itself matter at all? Perhaps it does seem especially impressive, psychologically speaking, when some theory turns out to make a prediction about the outcome of some experiment that no one ever thought of before, and when that experiment is performed it turns out as predicted by the theory. But if this were an essential principle of the way that science has always evaluated empirical support, then we should, I think, simply have to record this as an amazing fact about scientific 'rationality' which itself has no reasonable justification.

However, there is no need to suppose—in order to explain the theoretical decisions they make—that scientists do give extra theory-confirming weight to some piece of evidence just because it was unknown at the time the theory was articulated. There is, I suggest, no epistemically important distinction here beyond that between evidence that 'falls out naturally' from a theory and evidence that has to be 'shoved' into the theory. The important distinction is not that between old and new facts but that between evidence that has, and evidence that has not, been 'written into' or 'accommodated by' the theory—through, for example, fixing the value of some initially free parameter on the basis of the evidence.

For example, the 'scientific creationist' theory merely accommodates the 'fossil' record; by supposing that the creator simply chose to include in the creation some things that happen to look a lot like bones of animals of extinct species and simply chose to scratch patterns in the rocks that happen to look like the imprints of skeletons of such animals. (Indeed the whole creationsit approach is basically an exercise in accommodation: the fundamental theory says that God created the universe much as it presently is; observations reveal how it presently is and those details are then fed into the fundamental theory to create specific creationist theories that unsurprisingly entail the evidence.) On the other hand, Copernicus, for example, needed to make no special assumption in order to explain planetary stations and retrogressions, which were instead an inevitable consequence of the implication of his theory that those planets were being viewed from a moving observatory (attached to the moving earth). Hence even though stations and retrogressions were known long before Copernicus formulated his theory, these phenomena were not accommodated by his theory in the epistemically important sense of the term. Similarly, the general theory of relativity has no free parameters that might be adjusted on the basis of facts about Mercury's perihelion advance, and this is why the theory's success in entailing the right orbit for Mercury counted strongly in its favour.

We can indeed mark this distinction as that between a theory's predicting a result and merely accommodating it *post hoc*, but only if we remember that prediction must be understood in a non-temporal sense that allows the prediction of old facts. This may seem a strange usage—but it is in fact one often adopted both in science and studies of science. The Logical Positivist Moritz Schlick, for example, wrote:

> the confirmation of a prediction means nothing else but the corroboration of a formula for those data which were *not used in setting up the formula*. Whether these data had already been observed or whether they were subsequently ascertained makes no difference at all. (emphasis added)

And French's respected textbook *Newtonian Mechanics* remarks that Newton's theory

> like every other good theory in physics had predictive value; that is, *it could be applied to situations beside the ones from which it was deduced*. Investigating the predictions of a theory may involve looking for hitherto unsuspected phenomena, or it may involve recognizing that an already existing phenomenon must fit into the new framework. (emphasis added)

Despite its many virtues (it is widely and understandably regarded as the best account of confirmation we have at present), the Bayesian system faces many problems, some of which have been examined in this section. It may be the best formal treatment of confirmation we have, but, if so, then even the best, it seems, needs extension and improvement.

1.4. Scientific Revolutions and Scientific Realism

1.4.1. *What is Scientific Realism?*

The state of science at any given time is characterized in part by the theories 'accepted' at that time. Presently accepted theories include the general theory of relativity, the quantum theory, various theories about elementary particles, and, for example, the modern 'synthesis' of Darwin and Mendel, as well as 'lower level' but none the less still theoretical claims, such as that chemical elements have some sort of atomic structure, that electrons are negatively charged, that DNA has a double-helical structure, and so on. These theories talk about, amongst other things, electrons and other elementary particles, a space-time structure with a certain interesting metric, genotypes, species of once living but now extinct animals, and so on.

What exactly is involved in accepting a theory? What should we believe about accepted theories and their associated theoretical terms? The seemingly most straightforward and attractive answers are that (rationally) accepting a theory means (rationally) believing it to be true and hence believing the ontology that the theory postulates is real. Taken at face value, accepted theories (or at any rate many of them) straightforwardly attempt to describe a world of entities 'hidden beneath' the phenomena—entities that function in accordance with certain general laws and as a result produce (in conjunction with the laws governing our own constitution) the phenomena that happen to be manifested to humans. Taken at face value, those theories assert the existence of electrons, spacetime curvatures, genotypes, and the rest. It seems natural to say that 'acceptance' of them implies that it is reasonable to believe that the theories are true and hence that the entities they involve are real (and indeed that no other belief is reasonable).

This amounts to a particularly strong version of 'scientific realism'. Too strong to be sensible: scientific realists do recommend taking accepted theories at face value, but no real realist has any such straightforward view of what is involved in theory acceptance.

First, realist claims are explicitly restricted to accepted theories in 'mature' sciences. Although there is no agreement on a precise characterization of maturity, there is a measure of agreement on individual cases: current physics is definitely mature, and it achieved maturity with Newton at the latest; physics at the time of Aristotle, on the other hand was 'immature', and the same goes for pre-Lavoisierian chemistry, for optics before Newton (or perhaps Fresnel), and for nineteenth-century phrenology, as well as current parapsychology and other cases that may shade off into outright pseudo-science. In all these areas, theories were (or are) accepted in the purely factual, sociological sense of being believed by a group of people, whose research was based on that belief. But the realist will only defend those beliefs as rational when they concern theories from 'mature' sciences. The realist will not, for example, feel any need to defend the phlogiston theory as even approximately true, nor to endorse the entities it postulated—especially phlogiston itself—as real elements of the universe.

Moreover, no relatively sophisticated realist will advocate a uniform attitude towards accepted theories, even within mature sciences. For one thing, not every accepted theory is equally firmly entrenched. A scientist would find it close to incredible that the theory that there are electrons will not be preserved in future science, but would not have the same attitude towards the full quantum theory (indeed the quantum theory is known to require modification, see below). And the attitude of most scientists towards quarks or superstrings, for example, is that they may well exist, that there is a good deal of evidence for them and a good deal that could not be explained without them, but that they none the less retain, for the moment at least, a conjectural quality not shared by electrons. There are, in other words, different grades of 'acceptance': some theories are, at a given time, totally entrenched in that no alternative is being sought or even seriously contemplated; others are accepted in the sense that they are regarded in their field as the only serious contenders so far articulated, as having some degree of support, but as retaining a definitely conjectural character. The realist might, on this account, restrict her realism to accepted theories of the first, very firmly entrenched kind; or, perhaps more plausibly, distinguish between degrees of reasonable belief: the rational belief to have is that all accepted theories have a good probability of being true (or rather, as we shall see, of being 'essentially' or 'approximately true'), the probability reaching, or at any rate approximating, one in the case of the deeply entrenched theories.

A third way in which the notion of acceptance requires refinement is through the recognition that some scientific theories have an *idealizing* character. For some theories (the ideal gas law is the usual example) this is obvious, but many theories reveal elements of idealization, once examined carefully. Newtonian particle mechanics, for example, was certainly a successful theory and was firmly accepted in the eighteenth and nineteenth centuries—yet it was of course recognized that there might be no such thing as a Newtonian particle and that certainly none of the entities to which this theory was (successfully) applied strictly fit that description. The scientific realist is (or should be) in the business of arguing that theoretical science should be taken 'at face value'; but, even at face value, not all accepted scientific theories are intended to be straightforward descriptions of reality; instead, some idealize. Even within a basically realist account, some theoretical notions are to be viewed as connected with reality in rather more complicated ways than through direct reference to real entities.

Finally, the sophisticated realist will realize that 'accepted theoretical science' is invariably internally problematic. For example, it is scarcely controversial that the general theory of relativity and the quantum theory figure in the list of theories currently accepted in science. Yet it is well known that the two theories cannot both be strictly true—not for any philosophical, but for purely scientific, reasons. Basically, quantum theory is not a covariant theory as required by relativity theory; while the fields postulated by general relativity theory are not quantized as required by the quantum theory. It is generally held that a 'synthesis' of the two theories is needed, one that cannot of course (in view of their logical incompatibility) leave both theories fully intact. Quantum field theory is intended to be the required synthesis, but it is not yet known how to articulate this theory fully. This does not mean, however, that the present quantum and relativistic theories are regarded as having an authentically conjectural character. Instead the attitude seems to be that these theories are bound to survive 'in (slightly) modified form' as limiting cases in the future unifying theory; this is why a 'synthesis' is being consciously sought.

For all these reasons, a sophisticated scientific realist is likely to be quite circumspect concerning what it is reasonable to believe about presently accepted theories. Realists do not generally claim that the rational belief is that those theories are true. Instead, as well as restricting their claims to theories in the mature sciences, they perhaps suggest that the rational belief is only that presently accepted theories are approximately true (or perhaps that it is probable to a certain—quite high—degree that they are approximately true).

1.4.2. *Arguments for Scientific Realism*

1.4.2.1. *The 'Miracle Argument'* It would be frivolous to try to deny that science has been strikingly successful at the level of empirical prediction and technological application. Television sets work, and they work, at least in part, because the prediction made by Maxwell's theory of the existence of electromagnetic waves turned out to be correct. Like it or not, atomic bombs work and they work, at least in part, because the predictions of the deep theories about the structure of matter on which they are based panned out at the empirical level. The empirical success of presently accepted theories in mature sciences, like physics, is hugely impressive. Moreover, aside from isolated (and usually soon recaptured) cases of 'Kuhn loss', science has seen a cumulative development at the empirical level: theories accepted now capture all the phenomena that theories accepted earlier did, and then some. How else can we account for this success except by assuming that what our theories say is going on 'beneath' the phenomena is 'essentially' or very largely correct? If, so the argument goes, what the theories say about 'transempirical' reality is true or 'close to the truth', then it is no wonder that those of their consequences that can be empirically checked by direct means turn out to be correct on such an impressive scale. But were those purely theoretical claims not correct (or not even intended to be descriptions of what goes on 'behind' the phenomena), then their empirical success would seem entirely mysterious.

This often rehearsed point can never be more than a plausibility argument—it is, of course, logically possible for a theory to be false and yet have an impressive range of true empirical consequences. (Trivially, every false theory has infinitely many true consequences.) Attempts to formalize the argument as itself a scientific explanation of science's success—for example, as some form of (meta-level) inference to the best explanation—have generally come to grief. Moreover, there is, as van Fraassen has often emphasized, no *need* to explain science's empirical success—the scientific enterprise cannot, on pain of infinite regress, demand that everything be explained; and the weakest claim that would entail (though hardly explain) the empirical success of present scientific theories is, of course, simply that those theories are highly empirically adequate.

The empirical success of present scientific theories none the less seems a strong plausibility consideration in favour of the claim that they have somehow or other 'latched on to' the way things are. The main source of this plausibility is the fact that a significant part of the empirical success of science has been theory-led. As discussed earlier, theoretical frameworks based on different core claims are invariably elastic enough to accommodate known phenomena after the event, but the impressive thing is that many of the empirical laws that are now known were first discovered only as a result of being predicted by theories. Thus, for example, the fact that the centre of the shadow of a small opaque disc is bright was discovered to hold only as a result of its being predicted by Fresnel's wave theory of light. How else could that theory get such a surprising and hitherto unknown result right unless what it says about what is going on behind the phenomena is at least partially correct?

1.4.2.2. *The Argument that Realism is* Heuristically *more Potent* It is has often been suggested—long ago by Feigl and by Popper, for example—that the realist view of theories has proved itself heuristically the more fruitful view: those scientists who have made theoretical breakthroughs are invariably ones who insisted on interpreting present theories as (successful) attempts to describe an underlying reality rather than as merely instrumental frameworks.

One sharp form of this argument goes as follows. Everyone now acknowledges that 'background information' plays a significant role in the development of theoretical science. But when this uncontroversial point is properly thought through it in fact supplies an important argument for realism. Background information includes realistically interpreted assertions about causal relations and theoretical entities that are essential to the way in which that information is used—*both* in underwriting the acceptance of certain theories *and* in developing further theories (sometimes even successor theories). Moreover, the theories arrived at in this way have generally achieved significant instrumental success. We cannot understand the instrumental success of this aspect of scientific procedure unless we assume that the background 'information' relied on is indeed information—that the realist claims about causal connections ineliminably involved in the background information are at least 'essentially' correct and the associated theoretical entities real.

To take one especially simple case, Richard Boyd has argued that background information is used to locate the likely weak spots of proposed theories and hence to guide the construction of severe tests of that theory. What counts as a proper test of a theory about, say, the precise mechanism through which some drug *D* works to destroy bacterium *B* will be indicated by background information that underwrites plausibility judgements about likely alternative hidden mechanisms by which *D* might operate on *B*. These plausibility judgements are, in turn, based on already accepted theories of hidden mechanisms in other pharmacological cases. This method of identifying the proper tests of a theory has, so this argument goes, strikingly often led to the acceptance of theories that have thereafter continued to be empirically reliable. This, then, is one successful aspect of scientific practice which is based on a realist view of theories and theoretical entities and whose success can only be accounted for on the assumption that those background claims have really latched on to the way things are.

1.4.2.3. *The Argument that erstwhile 'Theoretical Entities' may later become 'Observable'* Finally, realists have argued that the distinction between theoretical and observational claims is itself subject to change as science progresses. An entity might start out as explicitly 'theoretical', as explanatory of things or events that can be observed; but, with the advance of technology, it might become observable, at any rate according to the ordinary scientific usage of that term. The bodies in the solar system aside from the earth, for example (understanding the term 'body' to imply that they are constituted of ordinary physical matter), were theoretical entities for a long time (they might after all have been, and were sometimes believed to be, gods or divine fire or whatever), but with the development of space technology they could be observed in a much more direct sense. Photographs and rock samples could be taken, and eventually a few people 'observed' one such body in pretty well as direct a sense as the rest of us observe the earth.

Many similar examples can be drawn from biology: entities like the mitochondria (organelles within the cell nucleus where combustion takes place) were initially introduced as explanatory entities (there had to be something in the cell that produces its energy!), but can now be 'observed' with the help of an electron microscope. (And if that doesn't count as 'real' observation, where, and on what principle, is the line to be drawn? Do I observe through my spectacles, or only—more directly but *very* obscurely—when I take them off?) Examples like these, it is argued, show that there is no principled, fixed distinction to be drawn between 'observable' and 'theoretical' entities; and hence they constitute strong evidence against any philosophy that gives a radically different epistemological status to 'observational' as opposed to 'theoretical' assertions. Anti-realism in its various versions is precisely such a philosophy. It treats observational claims and generalizations as straightforwardly true or false, and their associated entities as unambiguously real, but treats theoretical assertions and their associated ontologies quite differently, usually as codification schemes and useful fictions, respectively.

Van Fraassen has, however, tried to turn this argument around in favour of *anti*-realism, introducing in the process an interesting and much discussed account of what counts as 'observable'. For details refer to van Fraassen (1980).

1.4.3. *Arguments against Scientific Realism*

Several arguments against realism have been based on the philosophical idea that the position is *unnecessarily inflationist*—that it involves metaphysical assumptions that can be, and should be, excluded from science. (This is the main thrust behind van Fraasen's anti-realism, for example.) There is also a series of arguments based on *underdetermination* of theory by data—a methodological phenomenon which is taken by some critics *both* to render realism implausible *and* to remove entirely the force of one of realism's chief supports. (On underdetermination see Papineau's treatment in the earlier companion to this volume.) However, the most telling arguments, in my view, are to do with (1) difficulties concerning the idea of approximate truth and, especially, (2) the problems posed for realism by theory change in science.

1.4.3.1. *The Problems of 'Approximate Truth'* Theories are often accepted despite being known to be in need of modification; and the history of science shows that, often enough, theories that were accepted and *not* initially known to be in need of modification are in fact subsequently modified or rejected outright. Realists claim that it is none the less reasonable to believe that currently accepted theories in the mature sciences are 'essentially' or 'approximately' true. But what exactly does this mean?

Realists generally adopt a Tarskian correspondence notion of truth; and would surely like an account of approximate truth which parallels Tarski's clear and definite analysis. Popper attempted to provide such an account for the weaker notion of one theory's being *closer to the truth* than another.

The basic idea is that one theory *A* (considered as a deductively closed set of statements) is closer to the truth (has 'higher verisimilitude') than another theory *B* if and only if *either A* has more true consequences than *B* without at the same time having more false consequences, *or A* has fewer false consequences than *B* without at the same time having fewer true consequences. Of course, every theory has (denumerably) infinitely many consequences and any false theory has infinitely many true and infinitely many false consequences. The 'more than' relation involved here cannot, then, be defined in terms of set cardinality, for in that sense every false theory has exactly as many false consequences as it has true consequences and exactly as many of both as any other false theory. Popper suggested that—at least for a significant range of cases—the subset relation might be used to better effect to provide the required ordering: *A* being defined as having more true consequences than *B* if the set of true consequences of *B* is a proper subset of the set of true consequences of *A*.

Unfortunately, as Tichy (1974) and Miller (1974) proved independently, it follows from Popper's definition that again any two false statements have the same verisimilitude—no false statement has more Popperian verisimilitude than any other. The proof is straightforward.

Popper's account is that theory *A* has more verisimilitude than theory *B* if either of two conditions holds:

(1) the set of true consequences of *A* properly includes the set of true consequences of *B* while the set of false consequences of *A* is included in the set of false consequences of *B* [intuitively: *A* has (strictly) 'more' true consequences but no more false consequences than *B*]; or
(2) the set of false consequences of *A* is properly included in the set of false consequences of *B* while the set of true consequences of *B* is included in the set of true consequences of *A* [intuitively: *A* has (strictly) 'fewer' false consequences than *B* without paying for this by also having fewer true consequences].

Can condition (1) hold for any pair of false theories *A* and *B*? Well, suppose, in line with the first part of condition (1), that the set of *A*'s true consequences properly includes *B*'s: this means that there is at least one sentence, call it *t*, that (*a*) is true, (*b*) follows from *A*, but (*c*) does not follow from *B*. *A* is false—let *f* be any one of its false consequences. The conjunction $t\&f$ (*a*) is false, (*b*) follows from *A*, and (*c*) does not follow from *B* (if it did then *t* would too, but *t* is by assumption one of the extra true consequences of *A* not shared by *B*). Hence there is at least one false consequence of *A* (namely, $t\&f$) that is not a consequence of *B*; and so the second part of condition (2) cannot hold, if its first part does. Hence condition (1) never holds of any pair of false theories.

How about condition (2)? Suppose, in line with the first part of the condition, that the set of *A*'s false consequences is properly included in *B*'s: this means that there is at least one sentence, call it *g*, that (*a*) is false, (*b*) follows from *B*, and (*c*) does not follow from *A*. (So, intuitively, *g* is one of the sentences that is to show that *A* is 'less false' than *B*.) Let *h* be any false consequence of *A*. The conditional $h \rightarrow g$ (*a*) is true [the truth-table for the conditional gives the truth-value true when both the antecedent and the consequent are false], (*b*) follows from *B* [$h \rightarrow g$ is equivalent to $-h v g$ and *B* entails *g*], but (*c*) does not follow from *A* [if it did then, given that *h* does, so, by *modus ponens*, would *g*; but *g* is, by assumption, not a consequence of *A*]. So, if the first part of this second condition is satisfied (so that *A* lacks a false consequence that *B* has), then *A* must also lack a true consequence that *B* has (namely, $h \rightarrow g$) and so the second part of the condition is not satisfied. Hence, condition (2) also fails to hold for any pair of false theories.

If 'more' and 'fewer' are understood in this set-inclusion sense, then the Tichy–Miller result shows that Popper's idea cannot work because if *A* has more true consequences than *B*, then it cannot have fewer false consequences, while if *A* has fewer false consequences, it cannot have more true ones.

Other definitions of increased verisimilitude and of closeness to the truth have been mooted, but none has won general acceptance (largely because of what seems to many critics an undue dependence of the proposed measure of a theory's verisimilitude on the language in which the theory is expressed). This leaves the sophisticated realist in an unfortunate position; he claims that present theories in the mature sciences are rationally held to be approximately true, but he is unable to give any acceptable precise analysis of what approximate truth means.

1.4.3.2. *The 'Pessimistic Induction'* An eighteenth- or nineteenth-century realist would have claimed that it was reasonable to believe that Newton's theory is 'approximately' or 'essentially' true. Newton's theory involves action-at-a-distance forces of gravity acting across an absolute and infinite space, with a separate, absolute notion of time, according to which any two events simultaneous for one observer are simultaneous for all. A contemporary realist, however, advocates a realist attitude towards a quite different accepted theory—the general theory of relativity. According to the latter, Newton's theory is, of course, a good approximation in a whole range of applications; indeed its predictions, though they always strictly differ from the truth ('the truth' as of course seen by relativity theory), are empirically indistinguishable from it for bodies moving with a sufficiently small velocity compared to that of light. But, good empirical approximation though it undoubtedly is, Newton's basic theoretical claims are simply wrong: there is no action-at-a-distance; instead bodies move along geodesics in a curved spacetime, of which time is an integral, non-separable part, with the consequence that, quite contrary to the absolute classical conception, simultaneity is frame-dependent. It is difficult to see, even intuitively, how Newton's basic theoretical claims could be said even to 'approximate' what relativity theory sees as the truth.

Similarly an early nineteenth-century realist in optics would have held that Fresnel's elastic solid ether theory was at least 'essentially' correct, and hence that something like the elastic solid ether and waves in it exist. Yet, it too was later replaced by theories apparently radically different from it. And unless we stretch the notion of 'something like' to (and beyond) breaking-point, it seems difficult indeed to see Fresnel's fundamental theoretical assumptions, involving as they do an elastic solid medium filling the whole of space, as 'something like' the truth (as of course current theories see it). It is hard to see any ontological resemblance between probability waves in a quantum field and mechanical waves in a material medium.

The 'pessimistic induction' encourages the conclusion that changes of an equally revolutionary kind will, at some time in the future, affect the theories that are presently accepted in science (or at least the conclusion that it is not reasonable to hold that there will definitely not be such changes). How, then, can it be reasonable to hold a realist view of presently accepted theories?

Notice that this argument not only attacks the realist thesis, it also threatens to take all the force from the realist argument from predictive empirical success. The realist asks whether we can really take seriously the possibility that our present theories are as predictively successful as they are if their transempirical claims are 'way off beam'. The argument from scientific revolutions has the effect of simply pointing such a realist towards the history of science, which, allegedly, provides a whole catalogue of theories that were predictively successful, but were none the less quite radically false (or so presently accepted science tells us).

1.4.4. *Realist Rejoinders to these Arguments*

It is difficult to see any explicit response in the writings of leading realists such as Richard Boyd to the difficulties in articulating a precise notion of approximate truth. The implied response seems to be that we have a firm enough intuitive grip on the notion of truth-likeness not to worry about the formal difficulties. Does the realist have a more systematic response to the apparently most telling argument—that from scientific revolutions?

There seem to be three moves that realists could make. First, they could argue that accounts of the 'revolutionary' discontinuities in science have been greatly exaggerated. This might seem a rather desperate measure, but it can be argued with some degree of plausibility at least in some cases. Returning to the example of the elastic solid 'luminiferous ether', one suggestion—advocated, for example, in Kitcher (1992)—is that, although the elastic solid ether was indeed rejected by later theories, it in fact was an essentially idle component of the classical wave theory of light. (No realist should advocate a 'realist attitude' towards all theoretical claims, even theoretical claims within successful theories. Some play no effective role and are, in Kitcher's terminology, 'presuppositional'. Newton's assumption that the centre of mass of the universe is at absolute rest is surely a case in point.) Hardin and Rosenberg (1982), analysing the same ether example, have made the interesting—though I think ultimately unacceptable—suggestion that the elastic solid ether was not in fact rejected in passing to electromagnetic theory; rather Fresnel and other classical wave theorists had (without of course being aware of it) been referring to the electromagnetic field all along when talking about the elastic solid ether.

A second move the realist might make is to restrict his realism to those theories and those theoretical entities for which the history of science provides no basis for the pessimistic induction. This sort of restricted realist (Jon Dorling, for example, appears to favour this position) looks at the history of science and, wherever she believes she can tell a roughly 'continuous' story, advocates a realist attitude to the theory that presently stands at the culmination of the story. Where, however, the discontinuities seem undeniable, such a 'selective realist' admits there is no ground for a realist view. So she might be realist about atoms and electrons, but not about, say, curved spacetime. Aside from issues about what counts as 'continuity' between two different theories, this suggestion seems *ad hoc*: no principled reason is given why some 'revolution' might not in the future occur regarding some item of scientific ontology that has so far had an (allegedly) untroubled history.

A third ploy is to try to argue that even where there have been radical discontinuities at the most basic theoretical level in some science there is a 'level' (below that of the fundamental theories but above the purely empirical) at which there has been continuity or quasi-continuity despite 'scientific revolutions'. Consider again the case of the elastic solid luminiferous ether. Freeze the history of science at the point where Maxwell's electromagnetic theory with its primitive electromagnetic field had been accepted. From that vantage-point, there is an easy explanation of the success of Fresnel's elastic-ether theory of light: from the later point of view, Fresnel clearly misidentified the *nature* of light, but his theory none the less accurately described not just light's observable effects but also its *structure*. There is no elastic solid ether of the kind Fresnel's theory (problematically but none the less importantly) involved; but there is an electromagnetic field. The field is not underpinned by a mechanical ether and in no clear sense 'approximates' it. Similarly there are no 'light waves' in Fresnel's sense, since these were supposed to consist of the motions of material ether-particles. None the less disturbances in Maxwell's field do obey formally similar (in fact, and unusually, mathematically identical) laws to some of those obeyed by the 'materially' entirely different elastic disturbances in a mechanical medium.

Unless—surely very much in the spirit of anti-realism—we think of these theoretical notions as characterized by their observable effects, then we have to allow that Fresnel's most basic ontological claim that the vibrations making up light are vibrations of real material ether-particles subject to elastic restoring forces was entirely wrong. A change in the value of a *sui generis* electric force and a movement of a material particle from its equilibrium position are more 'like chalk and cheese' than are real chalk and cheese. But if Fresnel was as wrong as he could have been about what oscillates, he was right, not just about many optical phenomena, but also that those phenomena depend on the oscillations of something or other at right angles to the light. His theory was more than empirically adequate, but less than true; instead it was *structurally correct*. There is an important 'carry-over' from Fresnel to Maxwell, one at a 'higher' level than the merely empirical, but it is a carry-over of structure rather than content. Both Fresnel's and Maxwell's theories make the passage of light consist of wave forms transmitted from place to place, forms obeying the same mathematics. Hence, although the periodic changes which the two theories postulate are ontologically of radically different sorts—in one material particles change position, in the other field strengths change—there is none the less a structural, mathematical continuity between the two theories.

This third realist response need not be unacceptably 'Whiggish' (Whig history' allows unbridled use of hindsight and sees everything in history as a cumulative progression towards our present state). This response does not assert—indeed it explicitly denies—that Fresnel's theory really amounted to a subtheory of Maxwell's all along, that Fresnel's theory was always about Maxwell's field. Fresnel's theory itself is not a subtheory of Maxwell's, but a structurally identical *facsimile* of Fresnel's theory is. And it is the fact that this facsimile is entailed by the later theory that explains why, from the later vantage-point, the empirical predictive success of Fresnel's theory appeared as no lucky accident.

This account, in terms of the material falsity, but structural correctness, of Fresnel's theory is essentially that given by Poincaré in his *Science and Hypothesis*. The generalization of it—that the structure of earlier theories rather than their content is what is retained through revolutions—might be called 'structural realism'. This may be the most promising line for the realist—though like the other realist responses it certainly faces difficulties and needs much further elaboration. (See the recommended readings for further details.)

2. NATURALIZED PHILOSOPHY OF SCIENCE

What status do the correct principles of scientific methodology (whatever they may turn out to be) have? As indicated above, philosophers have found it hard to agree on *what* these correct principles exactly are; could this be because they have had an incorrect view of the *sorts* of principle they are and hence of how those principles are themselves to be validated? Suppose, for example, we decide that it is a principle of correct scientific, evidential reasoning that *ad hoc* accounts of phenomena weigh less heavily in favour of the theory that provides them than do predictive accounts. What status does this principle have? How might it be justified if it were challenged? Until recently, the almost universally held answer would have been that it needs to be justified as an a priori principle—part of the 'logic of science', not itself dependent on any information provided by science. It is, however, becoming increasingly common for philosophers of science to argue that methodological principles are themselves part of the scientific enterprise and receive *empirical* justification in the same way as scientific theories.

Kuhn, for example, has claimed that

> Rather than being elementary logical or methodological distinctions, which would thus be prior to the analysis of scientific knowledge, [rules of appraisal] now seem integral parts of a traditional set of substantive answers to the very questions upon which they have been deployed. That circularity does not at all invalidate them. But it does make them parts of a theory and, by doing so, subjects them to the same scrutiny regularly applied to theories in other fields. (1962: 9)

Larry Laudan is still more explicit:

> scientific methodology is itself an empirical discipline which cannot dispense with the very methods of inquiry whose validity it investigates. Armchair methodology is as ill-founded as armchair chemistry or physics. (1987: 24)

And Ron Giere explicitly suggests that while the 'endless dispute' about the right account of scientific rationality, the right inductive logic (broadly construed), 'is generally taken to indicate the difficulty of the problem, it . . . may [in fact show] . . . that there is something fundamentally mistaken about the whole enterprise' (Giere 1988: 37). Philosophers should be looking not for a priori principles of 'rationality', but simply for correct *descriptive* accounts of how scientists as a matter of fact operate.

Philosophers of science nowadays tend to be much better informed than their predecessors about the details of the sciences they are philosophizing about, and this, I have no doubt, has led to important improvements in the field. Philip Kitcher asks, 'How could our psychological and biological capacities and limitations fail to be relevant to the study of human knowledge?' The answer is surely that they could not. Similarly, purely descriptive facts about the history of science cannot fail to be relevant to philosophy of science. None the less, it's a big step from 'relevant to' to 'constitutive of'; a big step from 'you won't do good philosophy of science if you don't know about scientific theories and practices' to 'philosophical claims about science are on a par with scientific theories and are to be assessed in the same way'.

Here I shall outline some of the lures that have tempted some philosophers to make this big step; and raise the issue of whether a fully naturalized view of the philosophy of science can in fact be adopted without abandoning the idea that science is epistemically special.

2.1. 'Epistemology Naturalized'

Perhaps the most celebrated advocate of 'epistemology naturalized' in recent times is Quine. Without getting into questions of Quinean scholarship, the picture that most commentators see as emerging from Quine is as follows. We should think of all our knowledge—mathematical, methodological, and logical, as well as scientific—as facing experience as a corporate whole. Some parts of this 'web of belief' may be more firmly entrenched, and so harder to shift, than others, but this is a merely pragmatic issue. All parts—and this includes methodological and logical claims—are basically on a par. The stimuli that the external world provides us sometimes force changes in our webs of belief. There are in principle indefinitely many ways in which we might make such changes—not only do we have the Duhemian choice between modifying either a core theory or an auxiliary one, we also have the option of modifying a logical or methodological principle instead of any 'substantive' one, central or auxiliary. The changes that are in fact made are governed by the attempt to maximize *simplicity*. There is no reason in principle why, given some particular recalcitrant experience, it should not turn out to be simplest to modify our 'analytic' methodological or logical principles rather than our 'synthetic', substantive scientific principles (though there are, no doubt, as a matter of fact rather few cases of this kind compared to cases in which it turns out to be simplest to modify a non-'central', 'synthetic' assumption).

An obvious question arises about this view. Suppose we start off with 'web of belief$_1$'; this is bombarded with some initially recalcitrant experiences, and we switch to web of belief$_2$ as the simplest available modification. Is the criterion of simplicity itself a web-of-belief-dependent notion or does it stand outside the webs as an independent, unjudged judge?

If the former, then, having adopted web of belief$_2$ (complete with simplicity notion$_2$), we shall no doubt be able to justify that web as the simplest available modified system; but that justification is internal—dependent on elements of the web itself. If simplicity is simply simplicity-as-seen-from-within-a-web-of-belief, then of course there is the possibility that some other group of investigators adopting a quite different notion of simplicity might prefer a radically different web of belief$_3$ as replacement for web of belief$_1$. No independent reason to think the majority right and this minority wrong could then be given. This is relativism.

If, on the other hand, we want to claim that there is an objective, independent right and wrong in these cases—that it is, say, objectively simpler to adopt relativity theory than to explain the null result of the Michelson–Morley experiment by sticking to classical physics and adopting the Lorentz–Fitzgerald contraction hypothesis—then we must regard the criterion of simplicity at least as outside the war. *Some part of methodology and logic* must be regarded as privileged (and therefore not on a par with our substantive beliefs) if relativism is to be avoided. And to regard some part of methodology and logic as privileged and so not on a par with our substantive beliefs is exactly to deny (fully fledged) naturalism. It seems that if this Quinean position is fully naturalized, then it entails relativism of standards; and conversely if the position endorses the idea that one scientific shift may be objectively preferrable to alternative shifts, then it is not fully naturalized.

2.2. Scientific 'Reductions' of Philosophy of Science

There are several arguments in the recent literature along the following lines. First, the idea of a special scientific rationality is deeply suspect, if only because so many philosophers have tried to articulate it and have produced so little consensus. Secondly, we should draw the obvious conclusion from this—namely that there is no such defensible notion. Thirdly, this might seem to lead inevitably to historical and community relativism—people, groups who hold beliefs at odds with ours, cannot legitimately be held to have irrational, mistaken beliefs, but merely a different (not in any sense worse) belief system. But, fourthly, this is not in fact so, because science itself supplies us with all sorts of reliable information about how accurately to gather information, how accurately to create knowledge.

One forceful (and admirably clear) representative of this line of argument is Ron Giere. According to Giere (1988), the 'endless dispute' about the right account of scientific rationality 'is generally taken to indicate the difficulty of the problem. But it may also be taken as a basis for suspecting that there is something fundamentally mistaken about the whole enterprise'. This is a conclusion drawn also by social constructivists such as David Bloor; and Giere is quite clear that the constructivists end up in an inescapable and entirely unacceptable relativism, according to which there is no 'objective' preference ordering of scientific theories given the evidence but only different orderings depending on one's social circumstances. However, such relativism is *not* an inevitable consequence for the naturalizer: 'There is [indeed] something important missing from the sociological account. [But t]hat something is not rationality, but causal interaction between scientists and the world. . . . There is a way to avoid relativism without appeal to 'standards' at all. This is to focus on *cognitive processes*, such as those involved in representation and judgment, which are shared by all scientists' (1988: 56). Thus philosophy of science should in fact be pursued as a branch of cognitive science—using our knowledge of the biological and psychological bases of our cognitive processes to explain how science has developed and certain theories have been accepted. On this approach relativism 'is largely [!] avoided, [since w]e know [*sic*] on biological grounds that the processes of representation and judgment are similar for most scientists' (1988: 58).

Several problems for this approach seem to stand out. First, we will surely avoid describing different, conflicting sets of standards for 'good science' on this approach only by heavily (though no doubt implicitly) restricting in advance our choice of who is to count as a genuine scientist. No doubt we could get close to the rough consensus envisaged by Giere (and also arrive at sensible appraisal rules) by studying the 'processes of representation and judgment' of Newton, Maxwell, Einstein, and the like. But what if the list also included the likes of Immanuel Velikovsky, or Duane T. Gish (one of the leading proponents of 'scientific' creationism)? The response that the latter are not 'proper scientists' carries of course normative or evaluative baggage—'not proper' according to which criteria? This suggestion for naturalizing philosophy of science is analogous to the suggestion that we can readily naturalize ethics: to arrive at a correct account of ethical principles simply describe how people as a matter of fact make moral judgements and decisions (though be careful to restrict yourself to the judgements and decisions of moral saints!).

Secondly, there is a slightly less obvious and so perhaps more insidious form of relativism inherent in the approach. Cognitive science, biology, neurophysiology, or whatever naturalists of this stripe recommend we employ to describe the sorts of causal interaction between the scientist and the world that produce knowledge consists, of course, in a set of theories. We do not simply observe the relevant causal interactions: theories tell us about them. These theories are presumably well supported by the evidence (or at any rate better supported than rivals). *Why accept those theories rather than other possible rival ones which would give us different accounts of knowledge?* Again we face a dilemma: *either* the answer to this question is that these theories themselves constitute knowledge in some objective sense—in which case we avoid relativism but only by in effect admitting that underlying this alleged naturalism is a non-naturalized criterion of the traditional philosophical sort; *or* the theories of cognitive science (or whatever) that underpin this account of knowledge have no special status themselves: all we can say is that some people believe them, but if others believe differently and hence give a different cognitive science account of knowledge, then that is equally legitimate. This second horn of the dilemma is again pure relativism.

2.3. Ways into Naturalism via History of Science

A final way into naturalism is based, not on cognitive psychology or any other scientific theory, but instead on the history of science. The background is the Kuhnian claim that even if we restrict ourselves to what most of us think of as good science, we do as a matter of fact find changes in methodological principles from era to era (or paradigm to paradigm). Accepted so-called methodological standards are, historically speaking, no less paradigm-dependent than other more obviously substantive assumptions about the world. This at least makes the claim that methodological principles are a priori unattractive.

If, however, we draw the obvious conclusion that this reflects an absence of such absolute standards, then this seems to open the door to relativism even more explicitly than in the other approaches. If even the standards for judging good science are paradigm-specific, changing with changing paradigm, then nothing stays fixed on the basis of which a judgement of cognitive improvement can be made 'from outside'. If scientists switch, then, of course, having already adopted the new paradigm, they see their new position as an improvement. But if on the contrary they stick with the old paradigm, then they judge—perfectly correctly from the point of view of the standards which they still hold—that the new theory is inferior to the one they already have.

There is a good deal of plausibility in some of Kuhn's examples of 'methodological change', but they all involve taking a very broad view of what counts as a methodological principle. Of course 'methodology' is a very loose term. If we regard any principle that constrains the sort of theory scientists prefer now or have preferred at a given stage in science, then there are undoubtedly changes in methodology. One fairly obvious example is that in the eighteenth century, say, it would have been taken as an implicit requirement on any theory of some range of physical phenomena that it be deterministic, but nowadays, with the success of quantum mechanics, this is no longer so. But such changes in 'big methodology' do not imply that there have been changes in even the basic formal principles of theory preference (such as that inconsistent theories are unacceptable, theories should not be accepted before being tested against plausible rivals, and so on). Indeed the obvious way to explain why science no longer demands deterministic theories is by showing why it is that indeterministic quantum mechanics is such a hugely successful theory—*according to these basic formal principles of theory preference*.

There are, none the less, many interesting defences of 'naturalized' views in the recent literature. Larry Laudan in particular has argued explicitly that the thesis that methodology is part and parcel of science can be defended without either falling into relativism or sacrificing the normative, evaluative role of methodology. And various philosophers, Philip Kitcher as well as some reliabilists, have argued that the circle apparent in the naturalized view—that it takes for granted parts of science as constituting genuine information, while trying to articulate the standards for genuine information—is not a real problem. Readers wishing to know more about this fascinating and still very much open field will find a guide to the relevant literature in the Bibliography.

3. PHILOSOPHICAL PROBLEMS OF CURRENT SCIENCE

Whether or not philosophy of science can be fully 'naturalized', whether or not it can be considered itself as part of science, it is certainly true that some of its most interesting problems involve close consideration of the details of scientific theories. In particular many of the most fascinating problem-areas in current philosophy of science concern foundational issues in current scientific theories. In this final section I shall try to give a flavour of this sort of problem-area. In Section 3.1, I consider in outline the measurement problem in quantum mechanics; in Section 3.2 I consider two particular issues that arise in connection with the (neo-)Darwinian theory of evolution.

3.1. The Measurement Problem in Quantum Mechanics

Is quantum mechanics a coherent theory? Exactly how much of a revolution in our classical ways of thinking is necessitated by acceptance of the theory? Although mastery of a range of demanding technicalities is of course necessary for a full appreciation of the issues here, the most central question can be elucidated using rather little technical machinery.

Stated at its most abstract, quantum theory ascribes to each physical system at any instant a quantum state; and it supplies two rules or laws that govern how that state will evolve over time. One of these—the Schrödinger equation—is entirely deterministic: it dictates that, left to itself and given the forces acting on it and the constraints governing it, the system's state at some later time $t + \Delta t$ is a specific function of its state at time t. The other rule—usually called the projection postulate—is indeterministic: it dictates *probabilities* for the outcome of various possible measurements that might be made on a system that is, at the instant the measurement is made, in a particular quantum state.

If a system happens to be in a special state with respect to some observable, say position, at the time that observable is measured (one of the 'eigenstates' of the operator corresponding to that observable), then the theory entails that the probability is unity that a specific value of the observable (a value characteristic of that eigenstate) will in fact be observed, all other possible values of that variable therefore having zero probability. For any state that is not an eigenstate of the particular operator corresponding to the observable being measured, a range of different possible values of the observable will have non-zero probabilities.

If no measurement is in fact made on the system at time t, then the theory entails that the system's state will continue to evolve in accordance with the Schrödinger equation: the probabilities for various possible outcomes of the observation at t then simply being the probabilities that those outcomes *would* have had if (counterfactually) an observation had been made at t. Suppose, however, a measurement *is* made at t on a system not then in an eigenstate of the corresponding operator. This measurement will produce some particular result—if the system consists of a single electron and the observable is position, then the electron will be detected at some particular position. According to quantum theory, the system will now be in the position-eigenstate corresponding to whatever value of position was in fact measured. This means that if that same position measurement were to be repeated immediately, then it would, with probability one, produce exactly the same result. The system is 'thrown' discontinuously into an eigenstate of the corresponding operator by the initial measurement (this is the so-called 'collapse of the wave packet'). Hence an immediately repeated observation of the same observable would (with probability one) produce the same result.

Can the indeterministic, probabilistic nature of quantum mechanics involved in the projection postulate be regarded as simply a reflection of our ignorance of the true state of the system? Suppose we are experimenting on some single particle, say an electron. Its initial state (dictated by its method of preparation) evolves over time and at some particular time—a time when its state is not an eigenstate of position—we make a position measurement on it. Suppose that the electron is in fact observed at a particular position x. The state of the electron at the time the observation was made specifies a probability (neither zero nor one) that the observation would produce the value x that it has in fact produced. Can we assume that the electron did in reality already have the position x which the measurement simply revealed, the probabilistic element of the quantum state description thus simply coding our ignorance of its detailed position ahead of the measurement?

Unfortunately (at any rate for conceptual conservatives) the answer is definitely 'no'. If quantum mechanics is correct—and masses of striking experimental results support it—then the world is really radically different from the classical picture. We have to get used to the idea that electrons, for example, may—in a perfectly definite sense—be at a given time everywhere and nowhere. One (deservedly) classic illustration of this feature of quantum mechanics is the two-slit experiment.

Suppose electrons are fired in random directions from some point-source at a screen in which there are two small slits symmetrically placed with respect to the source (see Figure 4.1). Quantum mechanics (correctly) implies that if the frequencies with which electrons arrive at the various points on the observation screen are recorded, then the result will be the 'interference pattern' illustrated in the figure, curve 1. This is strange: when the electrons are observed at the observation screen, they are observed as discrete scintillations—as particles with definite positions; if they had definite positions throughout (whether or not *we* knew what those positions were), then each of them must presumably have *either* come through slit 1 *or* come through slit 2 in arriving at the screen from the source; but this seems to entail that if we could first just take the electrons that came through slit 1 alone and record where they arrived at the screen, and *then* could take the electrons that came through slit 2 alone and record where they arrived at the screen, and then simply added the two individual single-slit frequencies, we would get exactly the same total effect as in the original two-slit case. But this process can indeed be realized—by first running the experiment with slit 2 closed and recording the scintillations at the observation screen, and then running the experiment for the same length of time with slit 1 closed (see Fig. 4.1, curves 2). The observed frequencies with which electrons arrive at the various points of the observation screen in this second, two-stage experiment *is* of course the direct sum of the two individual slit frequencies (Fig. 4.1, curve 3); but this is an entirely different result from that obtained when both slits are open at the same time.

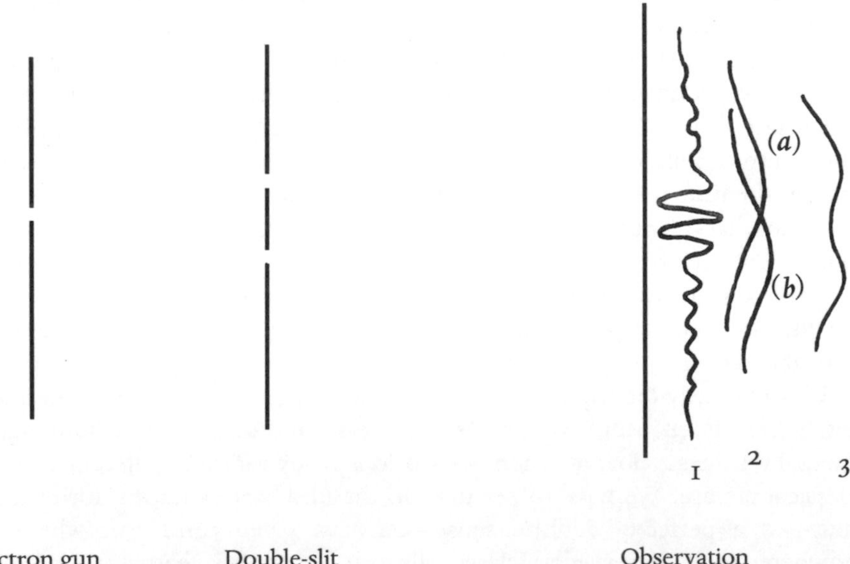

Fig. 4.1. The two-slit experiment with electrons. Curve 1 indicates the frequencies with which electrons are detected at the different points of the observation screen when both slits are open. The curves in 2 indicate those frequencies when (*a*) only the upper slit or (*b*) only the lower slit is open. Curve 3 indicates the frequencies obtained when only slit 1 is open for half the time, then only slit 2 is open for the rest of the time

The electrons in the experiment in which both slits are open cannot, it seems, be said to have arrived at the observation screen by *either* going through slit 1 *or* going through slit 2. Instead the electrons that pass through the double slit are, according to quantum mechanics, in a *superposition* of passing through slit 1 and passing through slit 2; and this superposed state cannot be simply an expression of our ignorance of which slit they 'really' passed through, because the fact that the quantum state is this superposition has real physical effects. (As you would expect from the above, quantum theory implies that if, for example, you set up some recording device for electrons behind each slit, then there would indeed be one electron recorded at one or other of these devices for every electron emitted from the source and eventually recorded at the observation screen, but the introduction of these devices would result in the final outcome being, as in the two-stage single-slit experiment, the direct sum of the two one-slit frequencies. The recording devices 'force' the electrons initially in a superposed state into eigenstates corresponding either to passing through slit 1 or passing through slit 2, and hence destroy the 'interference effects'.)

So, assuming of course that quantum mechanics is correct, we have to get used to the extremely strange idea of superposition. And systems are always in superpositions for some observables. Any quantum system in an eigenstate for one observable—so that the system in that sense has a 'definite value' of that observable (though remember that only means that a measurement of that observable will produce a that value with probability one)—will not at the same time be in an eigenstate for another complementary observable. For example, if an electron's position has been measured, so that it is, momentarily, in the eigenstate corresponding to its measured position, then it is inevitably in a superposition of momentum states. And, again, this superposition cannot be interpreted as meaning that, although the electron has a definite momentum, we do not know what momentum (and therefore what velocity) that is.

Is there any reason, though, why the 'strangeness' of the idea of superposition should mean that quantum theory is incoherent—that it cannot be regarded as a theory that is to be interpreted realistically? After all, science has been in this situation often enough before. The Newtonian idea of gravity as an action-at-a-distance force, for example, was often charged with incoherence when it was introduced (or, at best, as a throwback to pre-scientific, magical ways of thinking). Even Newton himself was unhappy with the notion and hoped eventually to 'reduce' gravity to some sort of mechanistic medium effect. The continued failure to develop an (independently testable) mechanistic explanation of gravity in the end led to the quiet acceptance that this notion could indeed perfectly well be regarded as primitive—a basic feature of the universe not in need of any explanation in terms of an underlying mechanism. And in fact, once scientists had stopped worrying about gravity as action-at-a-distance (not because it got any less 'strange' objectively speaking, but simply because they got used to having the idea around), then further developments in science—notably Coulomb's electrostatic force—were happily based on action-at-a-distance ideas. Similarly, when Maxwell's idea of the electromagnetic field was first introduced, it was assumed—as almost a foregone conclusion (even by Maxwell himself)—that it eventually would have to be explained in terms of the antecedently 'understood' notion of a mechanical ether. That is, it was assumed that the varying electric and magnetic forces at each point in space could not be regarded as *sui generis* (after all, who had thought of such strange ideas before?), but would instead have to be accounted for as the results of some complicated contortions of a mechanical medium that fills space. Again the eventual outcome was that various attempts to 'reduce' the electromagnetic field to the ether failed, and scientists quietly came to regard this as a non-problem: that is, they came to see no obstacle to regarding the field as a primitive, basic notion that requires no further explanation. Is there any reason why familiarity should not eventually engineer a similar fate for quantum superposition?

No reason at all, so I would argue, *if* strangeness were the only problem. The fact that we find certain notions strange just means that they conflict with our previous ideas (ideas that themselves have lost their strangeness only through longevity). But there is an extra problem with quantum theory. *The* problem, the so-called measurement problem, is that, supposing the theory to be generally applicable, its two basic principles seem to be in outright conflict—they have contradictory implications about certain observable situations.

Here's how that comes about. If quantum theory applies generally, then it applies to 'macroscopic' objects as well as to 'microscopic' ones (or, rather, no such distinction is made by the theory). It might seem counter-intuitive to think of, say, cricket balls, no less than electrons, as in superposed states. This would entail, for example, that a cricket ball with a definite position has an 'uncertain' momentum (where this very unfortunate term must be taken to mean, remember, not that the theory cannot predict exactly what the momentum is, but rather that the ball has no definite momentum). But velocity is just momentum divided by mass and surely cricket balls in definite positions do have definite velocities? Well, if quantum theory is generally applicable, then it does unambiguously entail that there is an 'uncertainty' in the momentum, and hence in the velocity, of the cricket ball with a definite position. But the fact that the ball's mass is enormous compared to that of an electron means that, unlike that of the electron, the ball's velocity uncertainty is too small to be observable, and hence means that there is no clash with everyday experience. (Like many things in quantum theory, this is not universally accepted—but it does seem to be the general view.)

But if quantum theory applies to 'macroscopic' systems, if it assigns quantum states to 'macroscopic' objects, then measuring instruments, and, significantly, systems consisting of measuring instruments plus, say, single electrons, have quantum states that evolve in accordance with the laws of the theory. Of course, working out for some particular complex system of measurement device plus electron what quantum state it actually is in, at some given time, would be an enormously complicated, in fact entirely impractical, task. But the argument here is independent of the details of the state and depends only on certain very general features of it and its evolution (general features that the theory guarantees the state and its evolution must have whatever the details).

Suppose we have a pair of 'complementary' observables (this means that any system that is in an eigenstate of the operator corresponding to one observable is necessarily not in an eigenstate of the operator corresponding to the other). To make things as simple as possible, let's avoid position and momentum (each of which can take any of infinitely many values) and choose instead a pair of observables, each of which can take only two possible values. There are such operators according to quantum theory ('spin' for example), but again the details are unimportant. Just in order to have names for them, let's call the observables *wealth* and *age*, the first having the two possible values *rich* and *poor*, the second the two possible values *young* and *old*.

The fact that these are complementary observables entails, remember, that an electron that is, say, *rich* (or, more precisely, is in a state that will produce with probability one a reading of *rich* on a wealth detector) has no age—it is instead in a superposition of *young* and *old*, each of which has (in the simplest case that we shall suppose holds here) a half chance of being produced by an age measurement. Suppose then that we do indeed have a perfect wealth-detector—once again the details are of no significance, all that we need to know is that the detector has, say, two lights, one green, one red, and that if an electron that is in fact *rich* is fed into it, the green light invariably flashes (really 'flashes with probability one', but that wrinkle too won't matter here), while if a *poor* electron is fed into the detector, the red light invariably flashes.

Suppose a rich electron is just about to enter an activated wealth-detector. Whatever the details of the state of the overall system, it must at that instant be an eigenstate of both the operators (machine-)*ready* and (electron-)*rich*; and since quantum theory is empirically adequate and gets results like this right, the dynamics must imply that, once the electron is in the detector, that state has evolved into one that is an eigenstate *both* for *green light* and for *rich*. On the other hand if a poor electron is about to enter the detector, then the evolution is from a state that is an eigenstate for *ready* and *poor* to one that is an eigenstate for *red light* and *poor*.

But now suppose that an electron that we know (because of its preparation) is *old* is fed into that same activated wealth-detecting machine. The initial state Π of the combined system at the instant the electron is about to enter is an eigenstate for *ready* and *old*. What does quantum mechanics say will happen to the combined system's state when the old electron enters the machine? Relative to the wealth observable, the electron is in a superposed state which gives a half chance of it measuring *rich* and a half chance of it measuring *poor*. The initial state of the whole system therefore is a superposition of *ready–rich* and *ready–poor*. In fact

$$\Pi = (1/\sqrt{2})\mu_1 + (1/\sqrt{2})\mu_2$$

where μ_1 is the eigenstate for *ready–rich* and μ_2 that for *ready–poor*.

The first principle of quantum theory—the Schrödinger equation—tells us what will happen to Π as the electron enters the wealth-detector. Again we don't know exactly what state Π is, and therefore there is no question of a full solution of the equation. But we only need one general feature of that equation, namely that it is *linear*. This means that, since $\Pi = (1/\sqrt{2})\mu_1 + (1/\sqrt{2})\mu_2$, and since we already know how μ_1 and μ_2 evolve in the circumstances at issue (namely into eigenstates of *green light–rich* and *red light–poor* respectively), the time evolution of Π *must*, whatever the details, be of the form

$$\Sigma = (1/\sqrt{2})\textit{green light–rich} + (1/\sqrt{2})\textit{red light–poor}.$$

(I am taking lots of liberties with notation here, but I trust the message is clear.) So the Schrödinger equation predicts that Π will, in these circumstances, change into Σ. I shall return to what this means in a moment. The problem, as we shall see next, is that the second principle of quantum theory—the projection postulate—predicts something quite different.

The procedure we have specified, of passing an electron into a wealth-detector, is of course a measurement of the wealth of an electron in state Π. Hence the projection postulate applies and it says that since Π, the initial state here, is no eigenstate of wealth, the measurement effects a discontinuous (and probabilistic) change of the state of the electron and hence of the electron plus measuring device into either the eigenstate *green light–rich* or the eigenstate *red light–poor* (each with probability one-half). This result predicted by the projection postulate is the actual result: that is, on any particular occasion when an old electron is fed into the wealth-detector then in fact either the green light flashes or the red one does and in either case, if the electron's wealth is immediately remeasured, then the same light flashes again; and, moreover, if the experiment is run many times, lots and lots of old electrons being fed into the wealth-detector, then, on average, half the time the green light flashes and half the time the red light flashes.

The state Σ that the overall system must be in according to the Schrödinger equation is, on the contrary, a very strange superposition of green light flashing and red light flashing: for a system in state Σ there is no fact of the matter about whether it is the green or the red light that flashes.

This conflict between the two basic principles of quantum mechanics—the conflict brought about at root by the fact that the projection postulate gives a special role to 'measurements', while the Schrödinger equation applies in principle to all objects including so-called measuring devices—is 'the measurement problem'. It seems to show that quantum mechanics, as it stands, and for all its empirical success, cannot be generally correct.

The problem, as many readers will have recognized, is related to the famous Schrödinger cat problem. But I leave readers to satisfy their curiosity about the cat—and indeed about whether it was curiosity that killed it—via the recommended readings for this section (e.g. Albert 1992; Healey 1989). These also contain discussions of a range of further fascinating logical and foundational issues raised by quantum mechanics.

3.2. Fallacies about Fitness

3.2.1. Is Darwinian Theory Based on a Tautology?

The second area of current science that raises interesting methodological and philosophical issues, some of which I want to outline, is the Darwinian theory of evolution. (This theory is still, of course, very much alive in current biology in the form of the 'neo-Darwinian synthesis'—basically Darwin, plus Mendel, plus lots of more recent modifications and extensions.)

Charles Darwin himself never used the phrase 'survival of the fittest'. This slogan was instead coined by Herbert Spencer. None the less, it is—for good or (mostly) ill—often thought of as capturing Darwin's leading idea. At various stages throughout the career of evolutionary theory, discussion of its credentials has been bedevilled by the charge that the idea is in fact nothing more than a tautology: Darwin claims that it is the fittest organisms that survive; but which organisms *are* the fittest?—those that survive.

An organism's fitness is not about survival as an end in itself but survival as a means of reproduction. But this threatens merely to redefine the difficulty rather than eliminate it: if survival of an organism involves representation in succeeding generations (of the organism's genes rather than of the organism itself, of course) and if the organism's fitness were measured by the number of offspring it leaves, then 'the fittest survive' threatens to reduce to the claim that the organisms that leave the most offspring are the ones that are most heavily represented in succeeding generations.

There are in fact a number of independent reasons why fitness cannot simply be a matter of the actual number of an organism's offspring (or even of the actual number of offspring that themselves reach reproductive age). Consider (to appreciate the most obvious such reason) two monozygotic twin chimpanzees, say, just about to reach sexual maturity, chewing on two opposite ends of the same (long) shoot in the same jungle when lightning strikes one of the chimps dead, while the other survives (a little singed but essentially unscathed) to produce numerous offspring. Same genes, same environment—mere accident that one has many offspring, the other none: it would clearly be absurd to suggest that the surviving chimp had greater fitness than the other. As Mills and Beatty (1979) make clear, Darwinian fitness (if indeed it can properly be applied to individual organisms at all) is a dispositional or probabilistic notion: fitness is to do not with actual, but with *expected*, number of offspring—each of the chimps in this story has the same expected number of offspring, but an external chance event intervenes to make the actual numbers of offspring different.

This consideration, on its own, shows that the claim that the fittest survive cannot be merely analytic. To see this, suppose we have a range of coins with various biases giving them dispositions to produce heads varying from 0.5 (no bias) to 0.9 (heavy bias towards heads). Suppose that all the coins are tossed together some large number of times; the statement 'the coin which produced the largest number of heads was the most strongly biased one' may well be factually false, and so can scarcely be analytically true.

This consideration also shows that evolutionary theory cannot really be committed to the idea that all evolutionary changes are brought about by natural selection. It must (and of course does) allow for the possibility of various chance changes. Nor are chance and natural selection the only possibilities: a trait exhibited by an apparently successful species may be neither an adaptation (that is, a trait that itself yields its bearer greater expected fitness than if it were absent) nor merely present by chance. It might, for example, itself be evolutionarily neutral, but tied (by physico-chemical processes within the organism) to some trait that does have selective value: trait T may be selectively neutral, but the genes that code for trait T' (which does have a selective advantage) may also produce T, as a 'side-effect'.

Darwinian theory is altogether more complex and sophisticated than some of its critics like to acknowledge. But this complexity itself suggests the more challenging and interesting criticism that perhaps underlies the tautology objection. Accepting that fitness is expected reproductive success, how exactly can it be identified independently of observed facts about reproduction? Isn't it too easy to conjecture possible ways in which a trait might prove of selective value? Given that there is an enormous range of possible ways in which a trait might prove of selective value to an organism, and given that Darwinians are by no means committed to regarding every observed trait in an apparently successful species as an adaptation—as itself contributing to greater fitness—aren't they in a position of 'heads I win, tails you lose'? If some particular attempt to explain the presence of some feature of some organism runs into difficulties, there are always lots of other possibilities to hand. In other words, the serious question that underlies the not-so-serious tautology objection is the question of whether Darwinian theory is really *testable.*

3.2.2. *Is Darwinian Theory Empirically Testable?*

This question was raised early in the career of Darwin's theory by his wonderfully named (and quite astute) contemporary Fleeming Jenkin. Jenkin pointed out that the Darwinian, faced with some aspect of natural history for which he has no immediate explanation, will scarcely be nonplussed:

> He can invent trains of ancestors of whose existence there is no evidence; he can marshal hosts of equally imaginary foes; he can call up continents, floods, and peculiar atmospheres, he can dry up oceans, split islands, and parcel out eternity at will; surely with these advantages he must be a dull fellow if he cannot scheme some series of animals and circumstances explaining our assumed difficulty quite naturally. (quoted from Kitcher 1982)

On the particular question of geographical distributions of organisms (why specific kinds of finch are found only on the Galapagos Islands, why marsupials are found only in Australasia, and so on), Jenkin claimed:

> The peculiarities of geographical distribution seem very difficult of explanation on any theory. Darwin calls in alternately, winds, tides, birds, beasts, all animated nature, as the diffusers of species, and then a good many of the same agencies as impenetrable barriers. There are some impenetrable barriers between the Galapagos Islands, but not between New Zealand and South America. Continents are created to join Australia and the Cape of Good Hope, while a sea as broad as the Bristol Channel is elsewhere a valid line of demarcation. With these facilities of hypothesis there seems no particular reason why many theories should not be true. However an animal may have been produced, it must have been produced somewhere, and it must either have spread very widely, or not have spread, and Darwin can give good reason for both results. (quoted from Kitcher 1982)

Not surprisingly, this charge has been seized on by modern critics of Darwinism. The leading 'scientific' creationist Duane T. Gish, for example, remarks:

> the architects of the modern synthetic theory of evolution have so skillfully constructed their theory that it is not capable of falsification. The theory is so plastic that it is capable of explaining anything. (quoted from Kitcher 1982)

Darwin himself, misguidedly, tried to meet this sort of charge by specifying a Popper-style 'potential falsifier' for his theory:

> If it could be demonstrated that any complex organ existed, which could not possibly have been formed by numerous, successive slight modifications, my theory would absolutely break down.

But how could anything so highly theoretical possibly be 'demonstrated'? Every theory is 'falsifiable' if this just means that there are statements that we might come somehow to accept and that are inconsistent with it (the theory's negation would always suffice). The real question concerns how theories come into contact with intersubjectively agreed observation statements: obviously the statement that some complex organ could not possibly have been produced by numerous slight modifications is no such observation statement.

The way properly to meet this 'unfalsifiability' objection is surely as follows. It will remind you of the earlier discussions of Kuhn and of prediction versus accommodation. Again the essential point is the one made long ago by Duhem. Single, 'isolated' scientific theories never have observationally testable consequences of their own but only when incorporated into (usually quite large) theoretical systems that involve a range of further theoretical assumptions. Major scientific achievements are characterized only in part by the central claims they make about the world; they also involve a specification of a set of problems and of patterns of reasoning for addressing those problems.

This is especially true in the case of Darwin's theory—many commentators indeed see the core of the theory as relatively insubstantial. Its power lies in the fact that it provides a framework within which particular explanations of a variety of phenomena have been constructed, explanations many of which are indeed *independently* testable. Contrary to Jenkin's claim, the Darwinian is not free to make any assumption he likes without fear of being proved wrong; assumptions about the movements of land masses, for example, may conflict with independent findings in geology. It is true that, should some particular assumption of this kind not work, there will always be others he can try—but then the crucial question becomes whether Darwinians have been able in some signficant number of cases to score successes by developing particular theories that have independent support. And the answer is overwhelmingly positive. If, for example, Darwinians conjecture that early mammals reached Australasia via Antarctica, then one would expect that appropriate mammalian fossils might be found in Antarctica—and there have indeed been important recent discoveries of such fossils (see the Kitcher references in the Bibliography).

Hundreds of similar examples can be cited. As usual, the classic examples are the most telling. The British biologist H. B. D. Kettlewell studied the peppered moth, *Bison betularia*. The speckled form of this moth was common in Britain before the Industrial Revolution and continues to predominate in rural areas. Melanic variants (with black colouring) became increasingly common in urbanized areas. What explains the change in frequency of the two forms near cities? One possibility is as follows. Industrial pollutants kill the lichens that normally grow on tree trunks; and the peppered moth often rests on tree trunks. (These are of course not simply assumptions plucked out of the air, but are rather themselves independently supported—indeed, parts of 'background knowledge'.) Once the lichens are gone, the tree trunks are uniformly dark. The speckled moths are less visible than the melanic ones against a lichen-covered bark, but the melanic variants are better camouflaged against the uniformly dark trunks. In general, better camouflage is a selective advantage since it lessens the risk of predation. The theory then is that the increased frequency of the melanic form of the moth in industrial areas is explained by its decreased visibility against tree trunks.

Some parts of this account come with independent support, but must the account as a whole be left as a mere possible explanation? Kettlewell performed experiments, capturing moths of both speckled and melanic forms, marking them, and then releasing them in areas with different degrees of industrialization. He later used a night-light trap to capture moths and noted the relative frequencies of the two variants amongst the marked moths that were recaptured. In industrialized areas, a greater proportion of the speckled moths were 'missing, presumed dead'. Rather than leave predation as a mere possibility, Kettlewell watched individual moths through binoculars after release and observed that some of them were indeed eaten, while resting on tree trunks, principally by robins and hedge-sparrows. Moreover, he performed other experiments which gave more support to this specific explanation by undermining alternatives. One alternative possibility, for example, would be that the melanic moths for some reason have greater fertility in industrialized areas. Kettlewell did experiments on the relative fertilities of the two kinds of moth reared in different environments and ruled out this alternative.

The case of Kettlewell's moths is deservedly famous because the evidence is so direct and compelling that it is often presented as a demonstration of natural selection at work. It shows that the way to counter the criticism that Darwin's theory is untestable is not by trying to argue that the basic postulates have experimentally decidable consequences, but instead to show that the basic Darwinian ideas can be, and have been, supplemented by various specific assumptions in such a way that the overall theoretical system thus created has significant independent empirical support.

Other cases are, unsurprisingly, less clear-cut: often there is evidence but it is somewhat less direct; in some cases there are plausible Darwinian accounts but no independent support. Although critics like to latch onto the latter kind of case, there is again nothing special about Darwinian theory in this regard. All theories—in physics as well as biology—face anomalies that they can, at any rate temporarily, account for only in an *ad hoc* way, permitting no independent test. The power of such explanations is simply derivative on the power of other explanations within the same programme or paradigm that do have independent support. So, for example, there is no doubt that the best explanation in the early seventeenth century of the failure to observe stellar parallax (a difference in the relative positions of stars at different times of the year) was the

Copernican one that there must indeed be parallax—the earth revolves around the sun and therefore the angular separation of a given pair of fixed stars will be different depending on where the earth is relative to them—but the distance of the stars from the solar system is so great that, although the parallax is real, it is too small to be detected with available instruments. This explanation is, taken by itself, entirely *ad hoc*—there was no independent evidence about the distance of the stars from the sun; the assumption was made exactly so as to deliver the known fact of no observable parallax within the Copernican system. None the less it was the best available explanation, because the Copernican system was, unlike its Ptolemaic rival, independently testable and independently confirmed by *other* phenomena (such as planetary stations and retrogressions). (And by the seventeenth century the Tychonic third way had dropped out as a serious contender for other reasons.) Theories, having been significantly independently confirmed in various areas, assume the right (temporarily of course) to provide the best available scientific explanation even in other areas where they cannot be independently supported. Darwinian theory, similarly, has been independently confirmed in a striking number of cases, and hence wins the right to supply the best explanations that can presently be provided even in areas where it is not directly and independently testable.

In sum, doubts about the testability of Darwinian theory turn out to be insubstantial.

3.2.3. *Adaptation, Teleology, and Explanation*

The second logical issue that I want to raise about evolutionary theory concerns precisely such 'adaptationist explanations' as the one provided by Kettlewell. Why have melanic moths become more prevalent in industrial areas? Because their colouring provides better camouflage in areas where industrial effluent has killed the lichens on tree barks and hence darkened the trees; and this means that the moth is less susceptible to predation than the original speckled form. It is standard to think of explanations as answers to 'why' questions. The above seems to be a good answer to a 'why' question. It can, it appears, be straightforwardly turned into an explanation of the colouration of melanic moths. Why are these moths black? In order to help avoid predation.

This second explanation accounts for the presence of a trait by stating *what the trait is for*, what value the trait has for its possessor. It therefore seems to be a sharply different form of explanation from anything found in the physical sciences. We would, for example, hardly look for an explanation of light's property of being (partially) reflected when passing from one medium into another in terms of the value this property has for light. Instead, the property is explained by showing that more fundamental laws plus initial conditions entail that light must exhibit the property (the explanation is in terms, if you like, of the property's causal antecedents).

Do, then, adaptationist accounts form an equally legitimate pattern of explanation different from anything found in the 'harder' sciences? Or are such accounts inevitably second-best: temporary place-holders for the real explanations in terms of causes rather than effects that science will eventually uncover?

Suppose that we had a complete theory of the biochemical pathways through which the melanic moths' genetic make-up produces the dark colouring. Suppose that we had a complete historical account of how the mutation that first produced the melanism occurred and of the subsequent mating patterns through to some present population that we are interested in. We should then have, it would seem, a complete account of the causes of the dark colouring of this population of melanic moths. ('These moths have the dark colouring because they have genetic constitution *G* and because *G* plus biochemistry plus the given environment entails the dark colour; moreover, they have genetic constitution *G* because they are related in the following ways to a moth whose genome underwent mutation *M* at time *t* (who in turn was related to a moth whose . . .).') What we would not, however, have—or so some have argued—is an answer to our original 'why' question. We should have a full explanation of the causes of the colouring of the present population of moths in whatever industrialized area we are interested in. But we should not have an explanation of why we are confronted with *that* population of moths, in that particular geographical area: we should have no explanation of why it was melanic moths rather than speckled ones who predominantly survived to reproductive age so as to produce those in the population under study.

Many commentators see this argument as posing a challenge to the idea of a single, unified model of scientific explanation. The challenge is to produce a selectionist explanation for the spread of melanism in moths compared to the earlier speckled form that does not involve the assumption that the gene that produces melanism spread because of the value of the dark-coloured phenotypic trait to the moths in their environment. If the above argument is correct, then the problem cannot be one of incomplete causal information; the problem, it is argued, arises once we have supposed that such complete causal information has been garnered.

What is it that makes some commentators reluctant to allow adaptationist explanation as a legitimate form of explanation, on a par with the more familiar causal form? The outline answer is that such explanations—in terms of the value of a trait to the organism or of the *function* of a trait—are felt to smack of teleology, and it is often thought that the maturity of a scientific discipline can be measured by the extent to which it has eliminated teleological modes of thought.

As with so many terms in philosophy, it is not completely clear what counts as teleology. Plato was, so far as we know, the first philosopher to defend teleological explanations, and he assumed that teleology always involved intelligent design. It was appropriate to explain a trait in terms of the value that trait has for its bearer if and only if the bearer's designer regarded it as good for it to have that trait. Aristotle, on the contrary, defended teleological explanations as independent of considerations of conscious design. For Aristotle trait *T* in organism *O* was explained by identifying what *T* did for *O*, what activity it permitted *O* to perform that contributed significantly to its life.

Adaptationist explanations certainly appear teleological in this Aristotelian sense. And indeed some biologists explicitly endorse teleology as an essential aspect of evolutionary theory. The distinguished biologist Ayala, for example, holds that 'the presence of organs, processes and patterns of behavior can be explained teleologically by exhibiting their contribution to the reproductive fitness of the organisms in which they occur'. (quoted from Rosenberg 1985) And he explicitly characterizes the use of teleological explanation as 'not only acceptable but indeed indispensable' in biology. On the other hand, Darwin is often credited with being the one who finally eliminated teleology from biology: for example, by destroying the argument from design.

The resolution of this difficulty is the recognition that there two senses of teleology that need to be differentiated: an *anthropomorphic* sense, involving human-style intentions and purposes, and another, non-anthropomorphic sense. Darwin eliminated anthropomorphic teleology from biology.

Thanks to Darwin, there is no need in biology to talk of genes, or cells, or whatever exhibiting anything akin to purposeful deliberation. Admittedly, biologists often describe their subject-matter in this anthropomorphic way. Here is a typical short passage from a standard text in biochemistry (cited in this connection by Alex Rosenberg (1985); emphases added): 'These enzymes are highly selective in their *recognition* of the amino acids . . . A much more demanding *task* . . . is to *discriminate* between similar amino acids. . . . How does the synthetase *avoid* hydrolizing isoleucine-AMP, the *desired* intermediate . . . ?' But this and its (many) kin represent simply a manner of speech that can be eliminated without cognitive loss. There is no need for, and every reason to avoid, purposes in biology.

However, the above considerations about adaptationist explanations seem to show that Darwin did introduce explanations into science that are teleological, not in the anthropomorphic sense, but in Aristotle's sense of involving considerations of what is good for the organisms at issue. One suggestion, endorsed by, for example, the eminent Darwinian C. G. Williams, is to introduce the term *teleonomic* for the sort of teleology approved by Darwin, leaving *teleology* to carry the 'bad' connotations.

Other interesting issues about 'functional explanation' in biology can be pursued via the readings listed in the relevant section of the Bibliography.

BIBLIOGRAPHY

1. RATIONALITY, REVOLUTION, AND REALISM

1.1. Radical Theory Change in Science, and 1.2. The Impact of Kuhn's *The Structure of Scientific Revolutions*

Core Reading

DUHEM, P. (1906), *The Aim and Structure of Physical Theory* (Princeton; Eng. trans. of 2nd edn. 1954).

KUHN, T. S. (1962), *The Structure of Scientific Revolutions* (Chicago; 2nd edn. 1970).

——(1977), *The Essential Tension* (Chicago) See especially chapter 13.

LAKATOS, I., and MUSGRAVE, A. E. (eds.) (1970), *Criticism and the Growth of Knowledge* (Cambridge). See especially the article by Kuhn; and that by Lakatos developing his influential methodology of scientific research programmes.

POPPER, K. R. (1963), *Conjectures and Refutations* (London). The first chapter of this book provides an introduction to Popper's falsificationist view of science, especially helpful for those who have not already come across it.

Further Reading

HOYNINGEN-HUENE, P. (1993), *Reconstructing Scientific Revolutions: Thomas S. Kuhn's Philosophy of Science* (Chicago). The only comprehensive study of Kuhn's views and their development.

KITCHER, P. (1993), *The Advancement of Science* (Oxford). In my view the most interesting and sophisticated of recent attempts to account for the development and rationality of science.

SALMON, W. (1990), 'Tom Kuhn meets Tom Bayes', in C. Wade Savage (ed.), *Scientific Theories* (Minneapolis).

WORRALL, J. (1990), 'Scientific Revolutions and Scientific Rationality: The Case of the "Elderly Hold-Out"', in C. Wade Savage (ed.), *Scientific Theories* (Minneapolis).

1.3. The Personalist Bayesian Account of Rational Belief

Core Reading

EARMAN, J. (1992), *Bayes or Bust? A Critical Examination of Bayesian Confirmation Theory* (Cambridge, Mass.). The best recent uncommitted critical analysis of the merits and problems of some of the Bayesian approaches (Earman's view of the Bayesian system of confirmation is essentially the same as Churchill's view of democracy as a political system—that it is the worst system apart from all the rest).

HOWSON, C., and URBACH, P. M. (1993), *Scientific Reasoning: The Bayesian Approach*, 2nd edn. (La Salle, Ill.). The clearest introduction to the personalist Bayesian view and its application to standard problems in philosophy of science. See esp. ch. 2 for an introduction to the theory of probability; and ch. 7 for Bayesian analyses of the Duhem, and other standard methodological, problems.

Further Reading

For Carnap's programme, see:

CARNAP, R. (1947), 'Applications of Inductive Logic', *Philosophy and Phenomenological Research*, 8: 133–48.

——(1950), *Logical Foundations of Probability* (Berkeley).

The Bayesian approach owes a lot to Ramsey's path-breaking work; see:

RAMSEY, F. P. (1931), 'Truth and Probability', in *The Foundations of Mathematics and Other Logical Essays* (London).

On the Bayesian approach to the Duhem problem:

DORLING, J. (1979), 'Bayesian Personalism, the Methodology of Research Programmes, and Duhem's Problem', *Studies in the History and Philosophy of Science*, 10: 177–87.

REDHEAD, M. L. G. (1980), 'A Bayesian Reconstruction of the Methodology of Scientific Research Programmes', *Studies in the History and Philosophy of Science*, 11: 341–7.

On the old evidence problem and prediction and accommodation:

ACHINSTEIN, P. (1990), *Particles and Waves: Historical Essays in the Philosophy of Science* (Oxford). An important rival view on the issue of prediction.

BRUSH, S. J. (1989), 'Prediction and Theory-Evaluation', *Science*, 1124–9.

GLYMOUR, C. (1980), *Theory and Evidence* (Princeton). Ch. 3: the source of the old evidence problem.

HOWSON, C. (1984), 'Bayesianism and Support by Novel Facts', *British Journal for the Philosophy of Science*, 35: 245–51.

——and URBACH, P. M. (1993), *Scientific Reasoning: The Bayesian Approach* (La Salle, Ill.), ch. 11. Also important for the response to the charge of over-subjectivism.

1.4. Scientific Revolutions and Scientific Realism

Core Reading

CHURCHLAND, P. M., and HOOKER, C. A. (eds.) (1985), *Images of Science* (Chicago). Contains a series of critical responses to van Fraassen's position together with very interesting replies from van Fraassen.

HARDIN, C. L., and ROSENBERG, A. (1982), 'In Defence of Convergent Realism', *Philosophy of Science*, 49: 604–15.

LEPLIN, J. (ed.) (1984), *Scientific Realism* (Berkeley). This collection of papers represents a wide range of views on the issue and has a very useful editorial introduction. See esp. the papers by Boyd (defending realism), Laudan (his celebrated 'Confutation of Convergent Realism'—perhaps the most detailed development of the 'pessimistic induction'), Putnam, and van Fraassen.

VAN FRAASSEN, B. (1980), *The Scientific Image* (Oxford). Generally regarded as *the* definitive statement of latter-day 'anti-realism'.

Further Reading

On the notion of verisimilitude and its problems:

MILLER, D. (1974), 'Popper's Qualitative Theory of Verisimilitude', *British Journal for the Philosophy of Science*, 25: 166–77.

NIINILUOTO, I. (1987), *Truthlikeness* (Dordrecht).

ODDIE, G. (1986), *Likeness to Truth* (Dordrecht). Both Oddie's and Niiniluoto's books attempt to develop alternative accounts of verisimilitude that avoid the problems of Popper's.

TICHY, P. (1974), 'On Popper's Definitions of Verisimilitude', *British Journal for the Philosophy of Science*, 155–60.

Works developing alternative or intermediate views between realism and anti-realism:

CARTWRIGHT, N. (1983), *How the Laws of Physics Lie* (Oxford).

FINE, A. (1984), 'The Natural Ontological Attitude', in J. Leplin (ed.), *Scientific Realism* (Berkeley).

HACKING, I. (1983), *Representing and Intervening: Introductory Topics in the Philosophy of Natural Science* (Cambridge).

POINCARÉ, H. (1905), *Science and Hypothesis* (New York).

WORRALL, J. (1989), 'Structural Realism: The Best of Both Worlds?', *Dialectica*, 43: 99–124. This paper explains and examines Poincaré's structural realist view.

2. NATURALIZED PHILOSOPHY OF SCIENCE

Core Reading

GIERE, R. N. (1988), *Explaining Science: A Cognitive Approach* (Chicago).

KITCHER, P. (1992), 'The Naturalists Return', *Philosophical Review*, 101: 53–114.

LAUDAN, L. (1990), 'Normative Naturalism', *Philosophy of Science*, 57: 44–59.

QUINE, W. V. (1969), 'Epistemology Naturalised', in *Ontological Relativity and Other Essays* (New York).

Further Reading

GOLDMAN, A. (1986), *Epistemology and Cognition* (Cambridge, Mass.).

KORNBLITH, H. (ed.) (1985), *Naturalistic Epistemology* (Cambridge, Mass.).

LAUDAN, L. (1984), *Science and Values* (Berkeley).

——(1987), 'Progress or Rationality? The Prospects for Normative Naturalism', *American Philosophical Quarterly*, 24/1: 19–31.

ROSENBERG, A. (1990), 'Normative Naturalism and the Role of Philosophy', *Philosophy of Science*, 57: 34–43.

3. PHILOSOPHICAL PROBLEMS OF CURRENT SCIENCE

3.1. The Measurement Problem in Quantum Mechanics

Core Reading

ALBERT, D. Z. (1992), *Quantum Theory and Experience* (Cambridge, Mass.). This contains the most accessible and lively account of the measurement problem that I know of, and my treatment in the text is indebted to it. (I wish I could be as enthusiastic about Albert's preferred 'many worlds' *solution* to the problem.)

Further references to the extensive literature can be found in Albert's book; for one of many variant treatments, see:

CARTWRIGHT N. (1983), *How the Laws of Physics Lie* (Oxford), essay 9: 'How the Measurement Problem is an Artefact of the Mathematics'.

Further Reading

There are many other fascinating logical and methodological problems in quantum mechanics concerned especially with hidden variables, locality, and the Bell inequalities. The best introduction to these issues (and to the literature on them) is:

REDHEAD, M. L. G. (1987), *Incompleteness, Nonlocality and Realism* (Oxford).

A non-technical account of the problematic nature of the Bell inequalities can be found in:

REDHEAD, M. L. G. (1989), 'The Nature of Reality', *British Journal for the Philosophy of Science*, 40: 429–41.

See also:

HEALEY, R. (1989), *The Philosophy of Quantum Mechanics: An Interactive Interpretation* (Cambridge).

HUGHES, R. I. G. (1992), *The Structure and Interpretation of Quantum Mechanics* (Cambridge, Mass.).

3.2. Fallacies about Fitness

Core Reading

KITCHER, P. (1985), *Vaulting Ambition: Sociobiology and the Quest for Human Nature* (Cambridge, Mass.), chs. 2 and 3.

MILLS, S., and BEATTY, J. (1979), 'The Propensity Interpretation of Fitness', *Philosophy of Science*, 46: 263–86.

Further Reading

HULL D. L. (1974), *The Philosophy of Biological Science* (Englewood Cliffs, NJ). A good introduction to the field.

KITCHER, P. (1982), *Abusing Science* (Cambridge, Mass.).

ROSENBERG, A. (1985), *The Structure of Biological Science* (Cambridge).

SOBER, E. (1984), *The Nature of Selection: Evolutionary Theory in Philosophical Focus* (Cambridge, Mass.).

5

THE PHILOSOPHY OF RELIGION

M. W. F. Stone

INTRODUCTION

In contrast to some areas of philosophical inquiry, such as political philosophy and philosophy of mathematics, the philosophy of religion is not easily demarcated in its scope or point. This might provoke surprise: it may appear uncontroversial that the philosophy of religion is that branch of philosophy which takes the claims of established religions and of religious believers and subjects them to critical scrutiny. While it is true that most contemporary English-speaking philosophers of religion tend to characterize their subject along these lines,[1] it is important that anyone who comes to the study of philosophy of religion for the first time be aware that such a characterization is controversial, if not inaccurate.

The reason for this is historical. The long engagement of 'philosophy' with 'religion' has manifested itself from antiquity to the present day in a wide variety of intellectual inquiries. Thus, contemporary English-speaking philosophers of religion currently address topics and analyse arguments that were earlier conceived as belonging to very different areas of philosophical thought. These topics and arguments once fell under the heads of what ancient Greek philosophers simply called philosophy (*philosophia*), of what patristic and medieval philosophers referred to as revealed teaching or theology (*theologia*), and of what philosophers in the modern period characterize as natural theology or 'natural religion'. In themselves, these titles indicate very different views about how to address the questions that arise from the engagement of philosophy with religion and theology. For this reason it is difficult to sustain the idea that the 'philosophy of religion' has always been a recognizable discipline with an unvarying subject-matter that has spanned the course of Western philosophical history. Any uncritical application of the term 'philosophy of religion' to very different moments and situations in the history of philosophy is open to the charge of anachronism.[2]

I wish to record a debt of thanks to the following individuals for their advice and assistance: David Wiggins, Peter Byrne, and Paul Helm. More particular debts of gratitude, however, are owed to Christopher Hughes for instructive criticism which helped to improve this chapter in innumerable ways, and to the editor of this volume, Anthony Grayling, for advice and encouragement.

[1] See e.g. W. J. Wainwright, *Philosophy of Religion* (Belmont, Calif., 1988), preface, and M. L. Peterson, W. Hasker, B. Reichenbach, D. Basinger, *Reason and Religious Belief* (New York, 1991), 8: 'Philosophy of religion is the attempt to analyse and critically evaluate religious beliefs.' One recent introduction to the subject, however, notes that the task of defining the philosophy of religion is 'perilous'; B. Davies, *Introduction to the Philosophy of Religion* (Oxford, 1993), p. ix. The most comprehensive guide to the subject is P. L. Quinn and C. Taliaferro (eds.), *A Companion to the Philosophy of Religion*, Blackwell Companions to Philosophy (Oxford, 1997).

[2] An important, if slender, history of the subject is to be found in M. J. Charlesworth, *Philosophy of Religion: The Historic Approaches* (New York, 1972). Section 1 of this chapter is indebted to Charlesworth's book. A historically sensitive anthology which might be said to replicate Charlesworth's approach to the subject is P. Sherry (ed.), *Philosophers on Religion* (London, 1987). L. J. Pojman (ed.), *Philosophy of Religion* (Belmont, Calif., 1987, rev. 1994) also reflects the history of the subject.

The term 'philosophy of religion' is itself a modern addition to the philosophical lexicon.[3] Towards the end of the eighteenth century it replaced the earlier phrase 'natural theology'.[4] By this time the content of the subject was taken to consist in a set of rationally discoverable verities both useful to religion and accessible to philosophical inquiry.[5] This conception of the 'philosophy of religion' received lucid exposition in Immanuel Kant's (1724–1804) *Religion within the Limits of Reason Alone* (1793). Building on his demolition of the claims of natural theology in his earlier *Critique of Pure Reason* (1781, revised in 1787), Kant argued in this work that religion was not a matter of theoretical cognition but of moral disposition. Hence religion was to be understood as that 'moral disposition to observe all duties as [God's] commands'. Kant argued further that the practice of religion required the performance of no other duties except those we naturally owe to human beings. The legacy he bequeathed to subsequent philosophers of religion was a model of the subject which guided them in setting out to provide a philosophical answer to the question 'What is religion?'[6]

By the early decades of the nineteenth century, however, the term had already changed its meaning. For philosophers like Friedrich Schleiermacher (1768–1834),[7] 'philosophy of religion' refers to a heavily moralized body of teaching about the nature of the universe. Likewise, in G. W. F. Hegel's (1770–1831) famous *Lectures on the Philosophy of Religion* (1821–1831) the subject is defined as the study of the manner and ways in which God is represented in religious consciousness.[8] In a great deal of nineteenth-century thought,

[3] The earliest use of term that I am aware of is by Ralph Cudworth. In his *True Intellectual System of the Universe* (London, 1678) we find on the thirteenth page of the preface (unpaginated) the following sentence: 'The main thing which the Book pretends to, in the mean time, being the *Philosophy of Religion*' (emphasis added). Further uses of the term can be found in German philosophy of the 1770s. See A. F. Ruckersfelder, *Philosophia de Religione Naturali* (1770). For a discussion of Ruckersfelder and others, see W. Jaeschke, 'Religionsphilosophie', *Historisches Wörterbuch de Philosophie*, 8 (1992), cols. 748–63.

[4] In so far as the term 'natural theology' lends itself to a simple characterization, it might be defined as that approach to philosophical speculation about God which is concerned with the examination of any evidence for the existence of God that can be found in the world of nature. Natural theology is discussed below, Sections 1.1 ff., 2.3, 2.4, 4.2.

[5] For a discussion of the beginnings of the subject, see M. Westphal, 'The Emergence of Modern Philosophy of Religion', in Quinn and Taliaferro (eds.), *Companion to the Philosophy of Religion* and J. Collins, *The Emergence of Philosophy of Religion* (New Haven, 1967).

[6] Kant's philosophy of religion is discussed at length in two books by A. Wood: *Kant's Moral Religion* (Ithaca, NY, 1970) and *Kant's Rational Theology* (Ithaca, NY, 1978). See also J. Bohatec, *Die Religionsphilosophie Kants in der 'Religion innerhalb der Grenzen der blossen Vernunft'* (Hildesheim, 1966) and P. J. Rossi and M. Wren (eds.), *Kant's Philosophy of Religion Reconsidered* (Bloomington, Ind., 1991).

[7] See Schleiermacher's *Religion: Speeches to its Cultured Despisers* (1799), trans. R. Crouter (Cambridge, 1988). A clear introduction to Schleiermacher's work can be found in B. A. Gerrish, 'Schleiermacher', in N. Smart, J. Clayton, P. Sherry, and S. Katz (eds.), *Nineteenth-Century Religious Thought in the West*, i (Cambridge, 1985). The reader might also consult R. B. Brandt, *The Philosophy of Schleiermacher* (New York, 1941; repr. Westport, Conn., 1968), ch. VI.

[8] These lectures have recently been brought together in a new English critical edition edited by P. C. Hodson as *Lectures on the Philosophy of Religion*, 3 vols. (Berkeley, 1984). For a discussion of Hegel's philosophy

'philosophy of religion' is understood in just these terms, as can be witnessed in anglophone works like *Theism* (1876) by Robert Flint[9] and John Caird's *Philosophy of Religion* (1880).[10] Indeed, the Hegelian conception of the subject remained dominant for so long that by the second half of the twentieth century some English-speaking philosophers preferred to distance themselves from it by calling their subject 'philosophical theology' rather than 'philosophy of religion'.[11]

As mentioned above, contemporary English-speaking philosophers of religion are apt to characterize their subject as the critical analysis of certain concepts and issues deemed central to the study of monotheistic Western religions. These concepts and issues are typically, but by no means universally, divided into four main areas of inquiry: (1) *the philosophical or speculative proofs for the existence of God*; or that set of historically enduring arguments in which philosophers have attempted to 'prove' the existence of a deity; (2) *philosophical theology*; or that set of issues concerned with the coherence and description of God's nature; (3) *religious epistemology*; or that set of issues that centre on the question whether or not the belief that 'God exists' can be rationally justified; and (4) *religious language*; or the analysis of the logical character of theological terms.[12] The largest part of this chapter will focus on some main aspects of (1)

of religion, see E. L. Fackenheim, *The Religious Dimension in Hegel's Thought* (Bloomington, Ind., 1967). Also worth consulting are L. Dickie, *Hegel: Religion, Economics and the Politics of Spirit* (New York, 1987) and W. Jaeschke, *Die Vernunft in der Religion: Studien zur Grunglegung der Religionphilosophie Hegels* (Stuttgart, 1986); trans. J. M. Stewart and P. C. Hodgson as *Reason and Religion: The Foundations of Hegel's Philosophy of Religion* (Berkeley, 1990).

[9] Robert Flint (1839–1910); Scottish philosopher, successively Professor of Moral Philosophy at St Andrews (1864–76) and then Professor of Divinity at Edinburgh until 1903. A short discussion of Flint's work can be found in A. P. F. Sell, *The Philosophy of Religion 1875–1980* (London, 1988), 9–12.

[10] John Caird (1835–1908); Scottish philosopher, Professor of Moral Philosophy at Glasgow (1866–93) and then Master of Balliol College, Oxford. For a discussion of Caird's contribution to the philosophy of religion during this period, see Sell, *The Philosophy of Religion*, 19–22.

[11] Here one might compare the approach to the subject taken by J. F. Ross in *Philosophical Theology* (Indianapolis, 1969) with that taken by J. Hick in *Faith and Knowledge*, 2nd edn. (Ithaca, NY, 1966) and later extended in *The Interpretation of Religion* (New Haven, 1989). If one compares these approaches, one finds that Ross's interest might be said to lie in the process of reconstructing distinctively 'scholastic' positions in philosophical theology, while Hick (*The Interpretation of Religion*) is more concerned with what we referred to above as the Kantian legacy, namely, the attempt to provide a philosophical interpretation of religion. An earlier work which attempts to disengage from the Kantian legacy is F. R. Tennant, *Philosophical Theology*, 2 vols. (Cambridge, 1928, 1930).

[12] I am very aware that my selection of the main areas of the philosophy of religion omits other topics which are often studied within the discipline. These are: (*a*) the soul, immortality, and resurrection; (*b*) the relation between religion and science; (*c*) the relation between religion and morality; and (*d*) religious diversity. Those who wish to learn more about these subjects are referred to Peterson *et al.*, *Reason and Religious Belief*, chs. 10–13, and Davies, *An Introduction to the Philosophy of Religion*, chs. 9, 11. A helpful selection of readings which address (*a*)–(*d*) can be found in Peterson, Hasker, Reichenbach, and Basinger (eds.), *Philosophy of Religion* (New York, 1996), pts. 9–12. Also worth consulting is P. Edwards, *Immortality* (New York, 1992). Quinn and Taliaferro (eds.), *Companion to the Philosophy of Religion*, pt. VIII, provides a helpful discussion of many aspects of the relation between theism and modern science.

and (2), although (3) and (4) will also receive attention. By way of introducing these issues, the first section of this chapter provides a survey of the different historical approaches of Western philosophers to the concepts of divinity and religion. The purpose of such a survey is to provide a prolegomenon to the appreciation of contemporary debates, by drawing attention to the fact that these debates have a rich and complex past.

1. HISTORICAL SURVEY

1.1. The Ancient World

Before Socrates (*c.*469–399 BC), philosophers addressed what we would identify as religious matters in three distinct ways. First, some of them criticized what they considered to be implausible or contradictory features of conventional religion. Thus Xenophanes of Colophon (*c.*570–*c.*475 BC) attacked both the immorality and the anthropomorphism of the poets' depiction of the gods.[13] Secondly, other Presocratic philosophers like Democritus of Abdera (fifth century BC) provided mechanistic explanations of the causes of events that were opposed to ideas of divine intention or arguments from design.[14] Thirdly, many Presocratics understood the concept of divinity in terms that were opposed to ordinary experience.[15] The efforts of these philosophers were often caricatured by the public imagination as sublimated instances of impiety. It is therefore unsurprising that Aristophanes, in his play *The Clouds*, depicted philosophers as promoters of irreligion, and Socrates at his trial was accused of being *to parapan atheos*, 'completely godless'.[16]

[13] The targets for Xenophanes' criticism are more often than not Homer and Hesiod, as can be witnessed in the fragment DK B8. For a discussion of Xenophanes' theology, see J. Barnes, *The Presocratic Philosophers*, 2nd edn. (London, 1982), 82–94, and G. S. Kirk, J. E. Raven, and M. Schofield, *The Presocratic Philosophers*, 2nd edn. (Cambridge, 1983), 163–80.

[14] For a discussion of Democritus' mechanistic world-view, see Barnes, *The Presocratic Philosophers*, 342 ff.; and Kirk *et al.*, *The Presocratic Philosophers*, 413 ff.

[15] Examples of this trend can be found in the work of Parmenides (*c.*515? BC) and Anaxagoras (*c.*500–428 BC). For a discussion of their contribution to these issues, see L. P. Gerson, *God and Greek Philosophy: Studies in the Early History of Natural Theology* (London, 1990), 20–8. For a more general discussion of the relation between philosophy and theology in ancient Greece, see the short article by K. Flannery, 'Ancient Philosophical Theology', in Quinn and Taliaferro (eds.), *Companion to the Philosophy of Religion*. These relations are more extensively discussed by D. Wiebe, *The Irony of Theology and the Nature of Religious Thought* (Montreal, 1991), 84–173.

[16] It is important to understand, however, that the Greek term *atheos*, or godless, did not mean exactly the same as our modern term 'atheist'. *Atheos* simply means going against the gods of the city; it does not mean a denial of divine reality. This can be illustrated by appeal to Plato's account of Socrates' trial. There, Meletus accuses Socrates of corrupting the youth of Athens by 'teaching [them] not to believe in the gods in which the city believes, but in other *daimonia* (deities) that are new'. With ease, Socrates then induces Meletus to identify this indictment with a total denial of divine reality: 'This is what I say, that you do not believe in gods at all . . .' 'Do I believe there is no god?' 'You certainly do not, by Zeus, not in any way at all' (Plato, *Apology* 26b–e).

With the work of Plato (427–347 BC) and Aristotle (384–322 BC), these three strategies for addressing the claims of religion were consolidated in ways that did much to determine the direction of subsequent discussion. Plato's Socrates defends traditional mythology and participates in civic rituals. He recounts to the ever attentive Phaedrus the myth about Boreas and Orithyia, and admonishes those who seek to explain its point naturalistically (*Phaedrus* 229b–230a). His famous last words to Crito request that a ritual sacrifice be made on his behalf (*Phaedo* 118a).[17] More formally, however, Plato's dialogues repeatedly turn on a rejection of doubts about the divine. The Athenian in the *Laws* (book 10) provides several arguments against those who deny the existence, nature, or providence of the gods. At the same time, Plato composes his own didactic myths in order to teach the salient differences that exist between the divine considered in itself and quotidian representations of it. Central to his teaching on these issues is the view that human beings in their present life have incomplete knowledge of their own souls and possess even less knowledge of divine matters. The work of philosophy in this context, Plato contends, is to lead souls out of the confines of sensory illusion so that they may begin to commune with the divine reality. His representation of this journey often includes references to various features of divine agency. Plato's most enduring representation of divine action is his account in the *Timaeus* of the divine artisan or demiurge who creates the universe out of a benevolent motive.[18]

In the extant works of Aristotle there are criticisms of popular misconceptions of divinity as well as genuine moments of piety. More important for later philosophical thinking about divine issues, however, are Aristotle's arguments for the existence of a divine prime mover of the universe and his account of that entity. At the end of *Physics* (book 8) and at *Metaphysics* 12, Aristotle argues that the impossibility of an infinite regress in motion requires that there be a fully actualized entity who causes all other motions by being the universal object of desire. In the *Metaphysics* (12.9. $1074^{b}33$–4), Aristotle describes the life of this being as one of 'thinking of thinking' (*noesis noeseos*). Beyond this highly suggestive passage and a few allusions

Socrates eventually goes on to show that this general charge of atheism is absurd since he has sought to live his life in accordance with his *daimon*: 'the god stationed me, as I supposed and assumed, ordering me to live philosophizing and examining myself and others' (ibid. 28e).

[17] For a discussion of Socrates' religious views, see J. Beckman, *The Religious Dimension of Socrates' Thought* (Waterloo, 1979).

[18] The rubrics of Plato's theology are adequately discussed in Gerson, *God and Greek Philosophy*, 33 ff. An older but still useful discussion of the same issues can be found in F. Solmsen, *Plato's Theology* (Ithaca, NY, 1942). Also worth consulting is R. Hackforth, 'Plato's Theism', *Classical Quarterly*, 30 (1939), 4–9; repr. in R. J. Allen (ed.), *Studies in Plato's Metaphysics* (London, 1965). A somewhat different interpretation of these issues is given by M. Despland, *The Education of Desire: Plato and the Philosophy of Religion* (Toronto, 1985). An instructive discussion of Plato's relation to later Christian thinking about God can be found in C. Osborne, *Eros Unveiled: Plato and the God of Love* (Oxford, 1994).

elsewhere, the Aristotelian corpus affords us no explicit description of a divine agent.[19]

After their deaths, followers of Plato and Aristotle widely disseminated their respective theologies throughout ancient world. The disciples of both engaged in a dialogue with some of the teachings of Stoicism.[20] The Stoic analysis of pain and misadventure was facilitated by their doctrine of divine providence. The Stoics were also enthusiastic natural scientists, and this led to their promulgation of many theories about the origin of the universe.[21] Such physical processes, however, were held to be orchestrated by a divine mind, a mind that could perfectly well find expression in the civic gods of traditional religion. These three schools—the Platonic, the Aristotelian, and the Stoic—all disputed at great length with the Epicureans, for whom the gods' interventions in human affairs were nothing but a series of spiteful fictions.[22] What 'gods' the Epicureans did permit were always characterized in terms that made them fully physical and natural, subject to the same laws of generation, corruption, pleasure, and tranquillity that bound human life. An instructive illustration of the dialectic between these competing views, as well as a resistance to Epicurean doctrines, can be found in Cicero's (106–43 BC) *De Natura Deorum* (*On the Nature of the Gods* 1.30 ff.).

1.2. The Patristic and Early Medieval Periods

The course of ancient philosophical speculation about divine matters was dramatically altered as early as the first century AD by the pagan world's contact with Judaism and subsequently Christianity. The intellectual directions of Judaism and Christianity were also shaped as a result of coming into contact with ancient learning. In pagan philosophy, the contact produced a renewed interest in the representation of the divine nature. In Judaism and Christianity,

[19] Aristotle's theology is discussed by Gerson, *God and Greek Philosophy*, 82 ff., and also by J. Owens, *The Doctrine of Being in the Aristotelian 'Metaphysics'* (Toronto, 1963). For further discussions of Aristotle's theology, see W. D. Ross (ed.), *Aristotle's 'Metaphysics'* (Oxford, 1924), introd.; A.-H. Chroust, *Aristotle: New Light on his Lost Works*, 2 vols. (London, 1972), 159–74, 175–93; D. Hamlyn, 'Aristotle's God', in G. J. Hughes (ed.), *The Philosophical Assessment of Theology* (Tunbridge Wells, 1987); M. R. Wright, *Greek Cosmology* (London, 1995), 163 ff.; R. Norman, 'Aristotle's Philosopher-God', *Phronesis*, 14 (1969), 63–74; repr. in J. Barnes, R. Sorabji, and M. Schofield (eds.), *Articles on Aristotle*, iv (London, 1979); and J. De Filippo, 'The "Thinking of Thinking" in *Metaphysics* XII. 9,' *Journal of the History of Philosophy*, 33 (1995), 543–62.

[20] For a general discussion of Stoic theology, see Gerson, *God and Greek Philosophy*, 142–74.

[21] For a consideration of these two issues and their bearing upon natural theology, see M. E. Ressor, 'Necessity and Fate in Stoic Philosophy', in J. M. Rist (ed.), *The Stoics* (Berkeley, 1978); S. Sambursky, *Physics of the Stoics* (London, 1959); D. E. Hahn, *The Origins of Stoic Cosmology* (Columbus, Ohio, 1977).

[22] The Epicureans took their name from the Greek philosopher Epicurus (341–270 BC). Many of Epicurus' ideas were expounded by the Roman poet Lucretius, whose philosophical poem *De Rerum Natura* (*On the Nature of Things*) did much to disseminate Epicurean ideas in antiquity. That part of Lucretius' poem most relevant to the present discussion can be found in book 3.

there is an energetic effort to present the claims of revelation in philosophically articulate ways. The renewed interest among the pagans is most evident in Neoplatonism, a philosophical school that included Plotinus (AD 204–270), Porphyry (AD 232–*c*.305), and Iamblichus (AD *c*.242–*c*.326).[23] Neoplatonism led not only to a rereading of Plato, but also to a series of philosophical defences of the documents and practices of paganism. The new effort of speculation about divine matters can be seen, albeit in a different guise, in Jewish thinkers like Philo Judaeus of Alexandria (*c*.39 BC–AD *c*.45),[24] and among Christian thinkers like Clement of Alexandria (AD 150–215) and Origen (AD 185–255).[25] It led not only to philosophical explorations of Scripture, but also to the development of a view within Christian circles that the 'best' philosophy was to be found in Scripture.

After AD 400 philosophy became subsumed within the three monotheistic religions, Judaism, Christianity, and Islam. The most important thinkers of these three religions carried on teaching and wrote works that substantively engaged with the legacy of ancient thought. But they understood their teaching and their writing not as philosophy *per se*, but as the study of divine law, as an interpretation of divine revelation, or as the codification and clarification of their own religious traditions. Patristic and early medieval thinkers certainly knew what the ancient term *philosophia* signified; for they greatly admired and where possible sought to appropriate the philosophical legacy of the ancient world. Yet they also held that the aims of ancient philosophy had been superseded by divine revelation. To apply the name 'philosophy', let alone 'philosophy of religion', to the writings of these thinkers would be to ignore the concerns and interests they sought to articulate.[26]

[23] For a general discussion of Neoplatonism, see A. C. Lloyd, *The Anatomy of Neoplatonism* (Oxford, 1990), chs. 5–6, and Gerson, *God and Greek Philosophy*, 185–221. For a discussion of the theologies of the individual thinkers named above, see L. P. Gerson, *Plotinus* (London, 1994), 3–22, 203–18; A. Smith, 'Iamblichus' View of the Relationship of Philosophy and Religion in *De Mysteriis*', in H. Blumenthal and E. G. Clark (eds.), *The Divine Iamblichus: Philosopher and Man of Gods* (Bristol, 1993); *Porphyry's Letter to his Wife Marcella concerning the Life of Philosophy and the Ascent to the Gods*, trans. A. Zimmern, with introd. by D. Fideler (Grand Rapids, Mich., 1986). Also worth consulting is R. Sorabji's rich and illuminating discussion of many aspects related to Neoplatonic theology in *Time, Creation and the Continuum* (London, 1983), 157–71, 253 ff.

[24] On Philo's philosophical theology, see H. A. Wolfson, *Philo: Foundations of Religious Philosophy in Judaism, Christianity and Islam*, 2 vols. (Cambridge, Mass., 1947), ii. 73–149. See also H. Chadwick, 'Philo', in A. H. Armstrong (ed.), *The Cambridge History of Later Greek and Early Medieval Philosophy* (Cambridge, 1967).

[25] For a discussion of the relation between the Church Fathers and Neoplatonism, with reference to Origen in particular, see J. Dillon, 'Origen's Doctrine of the Trinity and Some Other Neoplatonist themes', in D. J. O'Meara (ed.), *Neoplatonism and Christian Thought* (Albany, NY, 1982). On Clement, see S. R. C. Lilla, *Clement of Alexandria* (Oxford, 1978), 188–226.

[26] For a further discussion of these issues, see G. L. Prestige, *God in Patristic Thought* (London, 1930); C. Stead, *Philosophy in Christian Antiquity* (Cambridge, 1994); H. Corbin, *History of Islamic Philosophy* (first pub. in French, 1964; London, 1993), pt. 1; H. A. Wolfson, *The Philosophy of the Church Fathers* (Cambridge, Mass., 1956).

1.3. The Medieval World

Throughout the thousand years from the fifth to the fifteenth century, the largest part of speculative talent in the Latin West was devoted to considering questions about God. The body of writing is correspondingly gargantuan.[27] Very few medieval philosophers neglected the issues raised by the confrontation of ancient philosophy with the monotheistic religions. In many works the conversion or ascent of philosophy to faith is the central theme, as can be witnessed in either the *Confessions* of Augustine (354–430) or the *Itinerarium* of Bonaventure (*c*.1217–74). For other medieval thinkers philosophy serves as an intellectual foundation to faith grasped and expressed as theology.[28] In Boethius' (*c*.480–524) *Consolation of Philosophy*, the figure of philosophy reminds Boethius of truths without which his faith cannot be restored. This model is also evident in the work of later writers like Alan of Lille (d. 1203) who present philosophical doctrines as allegories of the Christian faith.[29]

Perhaps the most enduring medieval model of speculative reflection on divine matters was presented by Anselm of Canterbury (1033–1109) in his *Proslogion*.[30] There, Anselm uses the phrase *fides quaerens intellectum*—faith seeking understanding. We need to take this formula seriously to appreciate what many medieval philosophers hoped to accomplish. It is simply untrue that at the start of their philosophical investigations the medievals already knew exactly what they believed.[31] We find them again and again posing the question 'But what do I believe?' In this sense they were not asking what the religious formulas are to which they, as members of a community of faith, had given antecedent assent; they knew them rather well. What they wanted to know was

[27] For a discussion and survey of the Jewish, Christian, and Islamic philosophies of this period, see C. Sirat, *A History of Jewish Philosophy in the Middle Ages* (Cambridge, 1985); H. Davidson, *Proofs for the Eternity, Creation and the Existence of God in Medieval Islamic and Jewish Philosophy* (New York, 1987); L. Milton V. Arrastos, *The Mind of Byzantium* (New York, 1966); O. Leaman, *An Introduction to Medieval Islamic Philosophy* (Cambridge, 1985). For a general history of medieval philosophy, see N. Kretzmann, A. Kenny, and J. Pinborg (eds.), *The Cambridge History of Later Medieval Philosophy* (Cambridge, 1982); F. Copleston, *History of Medieval Philosophy* (London, 1972); J. Marenbon, *Later Medieval Philosophy* (London, 1987). For a more partisan reading of the issues, see É. Gilson, *The Spirit of Medieval Philosophy* (London, 1936).

[28] The relations between philosophy and theology during this period are documented in G. R. Evans, *Philosophy and Theology in the Middle Ages* (London, 1993) and T. J. Holopaninen, *Dialectic and Theology in the Eleventh Century* (Leiden, 1996).

[29] See Evans, *Philosophy and Theology in the Middle Ages*, 3–43. See also her book *Alan of Lille* (Cambridge, 1983), 21–86.

[30] See M. J. Charlesworth's translation and commentary in *St Anselm's 'Proslogion'* (Oxford, 1965). Also worth consulting are G. Schufreider's recent translation and exhaustive commentary on the *Proslogion* in *Confessions of a Rational Mystic* (West Lafayette, Ind., 1994) and G. R. Evans, *Anselm and Talking about God* (Oxford, 1978).

[31] As in Bertrand Russell's unworthy observation in his *History of Western Philosophy* (London, 1946), 484, that medieval philosophers—his example being Aquinas—'lacked the true philosophical spirit' because they sought to find arguments for conclusions given in advance.

what those formulas *meant*; so as *fideles*, people of faith, and as philosophers and theologians, they went in search of understanding.

We can clearly see this strategy at work in Anselm's so-called 'ontological argument' in the *Proslogion* (see Section 2.2.1 below). It can be argued, for instance, that one does much better justice to Anselm's intentions if one views the argument not as a demonstration of the existence of God, but as a systematic investigation into God's mode of existence. As a person seeking understanding (*fidelis quaerens intellectum*), Anselm was not seeking a philosophical proof of God's existence; rather, he was seeking to *understand* God's existence. In this sense, Anselm begins from a faith which constitutes the space or provides the conceptual parameters of his philosophy, and he then attempts to win his way to a better understanding of the divine nature.[32]

In terms loosely contiguous with Anselm's project, other medieval authors clarified the relation between philosophy and theology by insisting that philosophy must be studied thoroughly before proceeding to theology. An example of this tendency can be found in Moses Maimonides' (1135–1204) opening passages of the *Guide of the Perplexed*, in which he rebukes the student for wishing to 'skip' philosophical physics in order to reach the heady heights of theology.[33] In a similar spirit, the Oxford philosopher and natural scientist Roger Bacon (*c*.1220–92) argued that nothing could be known about God without the prior study of languages, mathematics, optics, experiential science, and moral philosophy.[34] As we proceed through the thirteenth century we find various Latin authors so fully appropriating the methods and procedures of ancient philosophy that much of their academic theology is parasitic upon them.[35]

When we arrive at the high point of scholastic speculation on God in the last quarter of the thirteenth and in the first half of the fourteenth century, and acquaint ourselves with the works of Thomas Aquinas (1225–74), John Duns Scotus (*c*.1266–1308), and William of Occam (*c*.1290–1349), we find there a profound illustration of the range and diversity of the engagement of Christian theologians with the Aristotelian inheritance.[36] For Aquinas, theology

[32] For a helpful discussion of these and other matters relating to the interpretation of Anselm, see two articles by M. McCord Adams: '*Fides Quaerens Intellectum*: St Anselm's Method in Philosophical Theology', *Faith and Philosophy*, 9 (1992), 409–35, and 'Praying the *Proslogion*: Anselm's Theological Method', in T. D. Senor (ed.), *The Rationality of Belief and the Plurality of Faith* (Ithaca, NY, 1995).

[33] See the 'Epistle Dedicatory', in the First Part, in Shlomo Pines's translation (Chicago, 1963), i.

[34] See the translated extracts from his *Opus Maius*, in J. Wippel and A. Wolter (eds.), *Medieval Philosophy: From Augustine to Nicholas of Cusa* (New York, 1969), 273–97.

[35] Philosophers who can be mentioned in this connection are Odo Rigald (d. 1275) and Albert the Great (*c*.1200–80).

[36] For a discussion of the medieval reception and interpretation of Aristotle, see B. G. Dod, 'Aristoteles Latinus' and C. H. Lohr, 'The Medieval Interpretation of Aristotle', in Kretzmann *et al.* (eds.), *The Cambridge History of Later Medieval Philosophy*.

(*theologia*) employs, improves, and then perfects the best of ancient philosophy. Aquinas extends great deference to pagan philosophers; he frequently cites Plato, Cicero, and others, extends to Aristotle the honorific title 'the philosopher' (*philosophus*), and then embarks upon a systematic commentary on Aristotle's work.[37] But whenever he speaks in his own voice, Aquinas systematically transforms most of the Aristotelian doctrines he discusses, often in directions quite opposed to Aristotle's original intentions.[38] Duns Scotus, on the other hand, begins by candidly refusing to accommodate Aristotle, but what is called his 'Augustinianism' is nothing but a complex *mélange* of the theological legacy from Augustine, the philosophical deposit of Neoplatonism, Scotus' reaction to the work of his contemporaries (in particular Henry of Ghent; *c.*1217–93) and a model of Aristotelianism derived from reading Aristotle through the filter of Latin Averronism. Scotus typically deploys these sources to address questions that are explicitly theological and which concern our knowledge of the created order and of divine volition.[39] While Occam saw fit to repudiate some of the central features of the 'high' Aristotelianism espoused by his forebears, he repeatedly sought to use Aristotle's work to support his own philosophical views and aspired to be perceived as a faithful Aristotelian.[40]

1.4. The Renaissance and Early Modern Period

The medieval requirement of *fides quaerens intellectum* carried forward into what we now refer to as the Renaissance and early modern period. Yet its legacy was complicated in three distinct ways. First, the Christian reform movements of the Reformation were often sharply critical of the use of philosophy in any discussion of God and his creation. This criticism varied in intensity from one reforming group to another, and often coexisted with much philosophical learning.[41] For example, both Martin Luther (1483–1546) and John Calvin

[37] A helpful discussion of Aquinas' credentials as an Aristotelian commentator can be found in J. Owens's paper 'Aquinas as Aristotelian Commentator', in *St Thomas Aquinas on the Existence of God: The Collected Papers of Joseph Owens*, ed. J. R. Catan (Albany, NY, 1980). For a discussion of Aquinas' philosophical theology, see L. Elders, *The Philosophical Theology of St. Thomas Aquinas* (Leiden, 1990) and N. Kretzmann, *The Metaphysics of Theism* (Oxford, 1997).

[38] An example of this can be found in Aquinas' use of an Aristotelian notion of substance in his defence of transubstantiation. See M. McCord Adams, 'Aristotle and the Sacrament of the Altar: A Crisis in Medieval Aristotelianism', *Canadian Journal of Philosophy*, suppl. vol. 17 (1991), 195–249.

[39] For a discussion of this aspect of Scotus' work, see A. B. Wolter, *The Philosophical Theology of John Duns Scotus* (Ithaca, NY, 1980), 1–27.

[40] M. McCord Adams provides an exhaustive discussion of Occam's philosophical theology in her magisterial *William Ockham*, 2 vols. (Notre Dame, Ind., 1987), vol. ii, pt. v. Also worth consulting is G. Leff, *William of Ockham: The Metamorphosis of Scholastic Discourse* (Manchester, 1975).

[41] This is certainly true of what are now known as the 'Protestant Scholastics'. One such individual was Martin Luther's follower Philip Melanchthon (1497–1565). For a discussion of Melanchthon's debt to scholas-

(1509–64) frequently mock Aristotle, and by implication much of the scholastic tradition of philosophical theology, in favour of experience, and then subordinate both to the gospel.[42] But more commonly the criticisms of philosophy arose from claims about the opposition of philosophy to the gospel, or from a vivid conviction of the impotence of 'sinful' human reason, or from a confidence that God would teach what was needed in human affairs by 'inspiration', and would do so not only for the prince, philosopher, and prelate, but also for the common ploughboy.[43]

The second complication in the relations of philosophy to theological issues arose from fierce disputes over the conclusions of the *nova scientia*, or 'new science'.[44] The condemnation of Galileo (1564–1642) is one well-known example. Opposition to the metaphysical implications of the new science in certain religious quarters made many philosophers cautious in expressing their views. It thus becomes tricky to construe the exact nature of their theological allegiances. On the surface René Descartes's (1596–1650) work, for example, appears to display a scrupulous Catholic orthodoxy accompanied by frequent protestations of obedience to the *magisterium* (or 'teaching authority') of the Roman Church. But Descartes is also extremely reticent and somewhat sheepish about many of his cosmological views, and he continually did his very best to ensure that his publications would not provoke theological controversy.[45] Likewise, Benedictus de Spinoza (1632–77) litters his *Tractatus*

ticism, see S. Kusukawa, *The Transformation of Natural Philosophy: The Case of Philip Melanchthon* (Cambridge, 1995). Those with German are strongly advised to consult the deeply interesting book by G. Frank, *Die theologische Philosophie Philipp Melanchthon (1497–1550)* (Leipzig, 1995). See also J. Platt, *Reformed Thought and Scholasticism: The Arguments for the Existence of God in Dutch Theology 1575–1650* (Leiden, 1982).

[42] See Luther, *Disputation against Scholastic Theology* (1517), in *Luther's Works*, ed. J. Pelikan, and H. T. Lehmann, 55 vols. (St Louis, 1955–75), xxxi. 3–16. Helpful discussion of this and other relevant matters can be found in W. Eckermann, 'Die Aristoteleskritik Luthers. Ihre Bedeutung für seine Theologie', *Catholica*, 32 (1978), 114–30.

[43] An instructive account of the role and place of 'inspiration' within Reformation theology and philosophy, with particular reference to the intellectual history of Scotland, can be found in G. E. Davie, *The Crisis of the Democratic Intellect* (Edinburgh, 1986); see also A. McGrath, *The Intellectual Origins of the Reformation* (Oxford, 1987). Also worth consulting is P. Russell, *Lay Theology in the Reformation* (Cambridge, 1986).

[44] A comprehensive and stimulating discussion of the ways in which certain theological debates were conditioned by the new science can be found in A. Funkenstein, *Theology and the Scientific Imagination: From the Middle Ages to the Seventeenth Century* (Princeton, 1986), chs. 2, 3. Some of the issues first raised by the confrontation of traditional theology with the new science still continue to this day. For a modern-day discussion of these issues, see N. Murphy, *Theology in the Age of Scientific Reasoning* (Ithaca, NY, 1990). That said, it is important to note that the present-day debate between 'science' and 'theology' owes much more to certain 19th-century discussions than to anything which surfaced in the 17th century. See A. Dickson White, *A History of the Warfare of Science with Theology in Christendom* (New York, 1897).

[45] The most striking example of Descartes's deference to the Roman Catholic Church can be found at the end of his *Principles of Philosophy*. There he says: 'Mindful of my own weakness, I make no firm pronouncements, but submit all these opinions to the authority of the Catholic Church, and the judgement of those wiser than myself. And I would not wish anyone to believe anything except what he is convinced of by evident and irrefutable reasoning' *The Philosophical Writings of Descartes*, trans. J. Cottingham, R. Stoothoff,

Theologico-Politicus (anonymously published in 1670) with miscues and misdirections in order to increase the likelihood that the jobbing reader will miss his heterodox interpretation of Scripture.[46] A similar caution in writing about controversial religious matters is manifest in other European philosophers of the period.

The final complication arose from a general impoverishment of traditional philosophical speculation about religious matters. The upshot of this upon the intellectual life of the Roman Church was to be seen in a marked tendency on the part of the hierarchy to legislate upon innumerable points of doctrine. Similar tendencies were also abroad within the Reformed and Lutheran traditions.[47] The effect of such impoverishment not only shrank the scope for unencumbered philosophical speculation upon theological matters, but also reduced much theology to canon law. Theological disputation was consequently reduced to forms of forensic argument: to aggressive demonstrations, to the collection of proof texts, and to extended *ad hominem* arguments against philosophers and theologians from opposing traditions.[48]

By themselves, these complications could by no means undo the ancient engagement of philosophy with speculation about divine matters, nor could they sever the ancient dependence of religious thought upon established modes of philosophical discourse. While the rediscovery of certain ancient texts led to a renewed interest in scepticism in some early modern authors,[49] the overwhelming majority of early modern philosophers affirmed the existence and activity of a God—invariably the so-called 'God of the philosophers' or the *ens realissimum*—and most aligned themselves with one religious denomination or other. This last statement is borne out when we examine the religious beliefs of the influential philosophers of the period. John Locke (1632–1704) and Bishop Berkeley (1685–1753) were both

and D. Murdoch, 2 vols. (Cambridge, 1985), i. 291. However submissive the tone, there is nevertheless something of a sting in the tail here, since if Descartes's own philosophical system is indeed, as he clearly believes it to be, based on 'evident and irrefutable reasoning', then the implication is that any religious doctrine that conflicts with it must be in error.

[46] See Y. Yovel, *Spinoza and Other Heretics*, 2 vols. (Princeton, 1989), i. 3–15, 128–52, ii. 3–26.

[47] Luther frequently explained the nature of faith through law. True knowledge of the law meant the recognition of the total spiritual incapacity of man, namely that man could claim nothing meritorious for himself. The knowledge of the gospel, on the other hand, was to realize that faith in the crucified Christ alone sufficed for salvation. Law was not gospel, but the former was necessary for the true understanding of the latter. See Luther, *The Freedom of a Christian Man* (1520), in *Luther's Works*, xxxi.

[48] An illustration of these techniques on the Roman Catholic side can be found in the *De Fide et Operibus* (1532) of Cardinal Cajetan (1468–1534). In his day, Cajetan was considered to be one of the theological giants of the Counter-Reformation, his work exerted considerable influence on the deliberations of the Council of Trent (1545–63). For a discussion of these and some other matters relevant to a consideration of the period, see H. Oberman, *The Harvest of Medieval Theology* (Cambridge, Mass., 1963), 120 ff.

[49] For a discussion of such scepticism and its relation to religious belief, see R. Popkin, *The History of Scepticism from Erasmus to Spinoza* (Berkeley, 1979) and T. Penelhum, 'Skepticism and Fideism', in M. Burnyeat (ed.), *The Skeptical Tradition* (Berkeley, 1983).

Anglicans.[50] Nicolas Malebranche (1638–1715), Antoine Arnauld (1612–94), and Blaise Pascal (1623–62) all published works which reflected their own distinctive brands of Roman Catholicism.[51] G. W. Leibniz (1646–1716), while a Lutheran, distinguished himself in a period woefully characterized by religious conflict by advancing the case for a sensible ecumenicalism.[52] Jonathan Edwards (1703–58) forcefully expounded the Puritan notion of the utter dependence of all things on God.[53] Of all the philosophers of the period, only Thomas Hobbes (1599–1679), among the so-called 'canonical' figures, appears a tepid theist.[54]

In retrospect, it may be possible to suggest that some of the early modern doctrines about God or religion, and some of the new ways of demarcating religion from science, provided a slow but evident impetus for the intellectual disengagement of philosophy with questions about religion. But one cannot hold that most philosophers of the sixteenth and seventeenth centuries were uninterested in religion or that they did not consider the question of divinity to be one of the central areas of philosophical interest and speculation.

1.5. From the Enlightenment to the Twentieth Century

If many of the central figures of the European Enlightenment were trenchant critics of established religion, they often enough professed views about a divine origin or of a general governance of the created order. This is true of Denis Diderot (1713–84), François-Marie de Arouet, or 'Voltaire' (1694–1778),

[50] A helpful discussion of Locke's religious views and his debt to the scholastic tradition of philosophical theology can be found in R. Ashcraft, 'Faith and Knowledge in Locke's Philosophy', in J. Yolton (ed.), *John Locke: Problems and Perspectives* (Cambridge, 1969). A very general survey of Locke's contribution to the philosophy of religion is provided by N. Wolterstorff, 'Locke's Philosophy of Religion', in V. Chappell (ed.), *The Cambridge Companion to Locke* (Cambridge, 1994). A more extensive, if somewhat questionable, account of Locke's philosophy of religion is to be found in Wolterstorff, *John Locke and the Ethics of Belief* (Cambridge, 1996). A general, but unsympathetic, account of Berkeley's arguments for the existence of God can be found in J. L. Mackie, *The Miracle of Theism* (Oxford, 1982), 64–80.

[51] On Malebranche, see H. Gouhier, *La Philosophie de Malebranche et son expérience religieuse* (Paris, 1948); D. Connell, *The Vision in God: Malebranche's Scholastic Sources* (Paris, 1967); S. Nadler, *Malebranche and Ideas* (New York, 1992), 98–151. On Arnauld, see A. R. Ndiaye, *La Philosophie d'Antione Arnauld* (Paris, 1991) and S. Nadler, *Arnauld and the Cartesian Philosophy of Ideas* (Princeton, 1988). Jan Miel, *Pascal and Theology* (Baltimore, 1969) provides a thorough analysis of Pascal's religiously motivated thought.

[52] Leibniz's theological views are conspicuous in many areas of his philosophical thought. Two recent books which successfully bring out this dimension are R. Adams, *Leibniz: Determinist, Theist, Idealist* (New York, 1994) and D. Rutherford, *Leibniz and the Rational Order of Nature* (New York, 1995).

[53] See Sang Hyuan Lee, *The Philosophical Theology of Jonathan Edwards* (Princeton, 1988).

[54] Hobbes's religious views, however, have been the subject of much scholarly controversy. For a recent contribution to this long debate, a contribution which argues that Hobbes was more religiously orthodox than has often been assumed, see A. P. Martinich, *The Two Gods of Leviathan: Thomas Hobbes on Religion and Politics* (New York, 1992).

and Jean-Jacques Rousseau (1712–78).[55] Perhaps the most important works of this time are David Hume's (1711–76) *Natural History of Religion* (1757) and *Dialogues concerning Natural Religion* (1779, but first written in the 1750s). The former deals with the causes of religion, as it originates in human nature and society, while the latter examines the reasons or putative grounds for believing in a God or gods.[56]

For Hume, the core of what he terms 'natural religion' is what he designates the a priori argument (or a version of the 'cosmological argument' see Sections 2.3ff. below) and the a posteriori argument (or the 'design argument', see sections 2.4ff. below). The former is criticized in the *Treatise concerning Human Nature* (1739–40), the *Enquiry concerning Human Understanding* (1748), and again in part IX of the *Dialogues*. The latter is subjected to a hostile examination in section XI of the *Enquiry* and again throughout the *Dialogues*.[57] The conclusion of Hume's work is that the arguments of natural religion do not establish the existence of any deity which could be the proper object of religious belief. If revelation cannot be authenticated in any way conducive to reason, it might seem that the only answer which can be given to the question 'Why does anyone believe in God or gods?' is that such doxastic practices have natural causes. An investigation of these causes is the subject of the *Natural History of Religion*. Central to Hume's argument in this work is the contention that the origin of a belief in deities is to be found in the numerous human pathologies which derive from a fear of the unknown.

Hume's views have been typically regarded as providing a dialectical framework for modern philosophy of religion. Accordingly, those who adhere to the claims of natural theology and traditional religion are supposed to address his intricate critique of their position, while those enamoured of 'atheism' invariably look to Hume's works as providing a paradigm for how to dispatch the supposed antediluvian claims of religion to philosophical

[55] The concept of 'natural religion' in the Enlightenment and beyond is the subject of an interesting and instructive monograph by P. Byrne, *Natural Religion and the Nature of Religion: The Legacy of Deism* (London, 1989). Also worth consulting is the article by P. Jimack, 'The French Enlightenment II: Deism, Morality and Politics', in S. Brown (ed.), *British Philosophy and the Age of Enlightenment*, Routledge History of Philosophy, v (London, 1996) and P. Harrison, *'Religion' and the Religions in the English Enlightenment* (Cambridge, 1990).

[56] Many of the conclusions Hume advances in the *Dialogues* are anticipated in section XI of the *Enquiry concerning Human Understanding*, where there is also to be found his celebrated onslaught on the credentials of Christian revelation, the chapter 'Of Miracles'.

[57] It is worth noting that one of the principal loci of Hume's attack was the natural theology of the English philosopher Samuel Clarke (1675–1729), especially the second part of Clarke's *Demonstration of the Being and Attributes of God* (London, 1705). The version of the cosmological argument that Hume discusses in part IX of the *Dialogues* strongly resembles that version of the argument favoured by Clarke. Of further note is the fact that the meanings of the terms 'a priori' and 'a posteriori' were different in the early 18th century than they are now. These were not, as they are for us, epistemologically based distinctions, but rather were concerned with whether we are inferring a cause from its effects or vice versa. See J. P. Ferguson, *The Philosophy of Samuel Clarke and its Critics* (New York, 1974), 11–21.

oblivion.[58] As with all suggestive yet rhetorically charged narratives which attempt to establish a point of importance, this view neglects much that is vital to a sober evaluation of Hume's contribution to the philosophy of religion. For while Hume provides an array of sensible arguments which attack the claims of natural theology at source, there is still a sense in which he is very much a part of the tradition whose claims he sought to expose. As we have seen throughout this historical survey, one of the central sources of philosophical speculation about divine matters is the activity of looking at the nature and order of the world and then attempting to present reputable evidence for the existence of a deity who first creates and then sustains that world. Such a strategy can be found in both ancient and medieval philosophical discussions of the concept of divinity.[59] Hume accepted this method as providing the best procedure for subjecting the concept of divinity to philosophical scrutiny. Unlike the natural theologians of antiquity and of medieval times, however, he argued that good evidence could not be produced in order to substantiate the claims of natural theology. In this sense one might refer to Hume as a 'natural *a*theologian'.[60]

The relations of religion and philosophy at the end of the eighteenth and the beginning of the nineteenth century have already been set out. What needs to be added here is that the two principal philosophers of these decades, Kant and Hegel, by no means excluded religious topics or even religious sentiments from their work. What is interesting about their respective projects is the degree that separated their 'philosophical theologies' from conventional religious doctrines. Indeed such was the degree of difference that, despite their best intentions, both their theories eventually lent themselves to forms of anti-theistic scepticism. So, if Kant wishes his reader to pass through a 'critique of all theology based on speculative principles',[61] many of his subsequent readers only took the negative lesson. Likewise, if Hegel accuses Christian theology of misapprehending putative 'higher truths', many of his readers, particularly those on the so-called Hegelian Left, took him to be condemning such theology as a misapprehension.[62] Given this, it is unsurprising that Kant and Hegel are

[58] For examples of these views, see A. J. Ayer, *The Central Questions of Philosophy* (London, 1973); A. Flew, *The Presumption of Atheism* (New York, 1976); K. Nielsen, *Philosophy and Atheism* (Buffalo, NY, 1985). An assessment of Hume's contribution to current philosophy of religion is provided by J. Stout, *Flight from Authority* (Notre Dame, Ind., 1981). Hume's legacy is also the subject of an important study by K. Yandell, *Hume's 'Inexplicable Mystery'* (Philadelphia, 1990).

[59] e.g. Plato's proto-cosmological arguments in the *Timaeus* and *Laws*, and Aquinas' discussion of the 'Five Ways' in the *Summa Theologiae*.

[60] By far the most extensive and interesting discussion of Hume's work in this area can be found in J. C. A. Gaskin, *Hume's Philosophy of Religion*, 2nd edn. (London, 1988).

[61] *Critique of Pure Reason*, ch. III of the Second Division of the Transcendental Dialectic. It is noteworthy that Kant's contemporary Moses Mendelssohn (1729–86) referred to his demolition of the speculative proofs as *Weltzermalmend* or 'world-crushing'.

[62] Other than Marx, these individuals include Ludwig Feuerbach (1804–72), whose account of religion as 'projection' in his *On the Essence of Christianity* (Leipzig, 1841) exerted a profound influence on Marx's thinking.

followed by resolutely anti-theistic philosophers and thinkers, of whom Schopenhauer (1788–1860), Marx (1818–83), Nietzsche (1844–1900), and Freud (1856–1939) are the most prominent.

It is only in the twentieth century that it has become familiar and even culturally acceptable for philosophers in the West to engage with the central concerns of their subject without so much as raising questions about God. The very existence of philosophy of religion as a subfield within the institutional practice of philosophy in Western universities is testimony to this fact. The subfield was created as a safe haven in which philosophical speculation about God and religious topics could continue. Within English-speaking philosophy the demotion of the subject to a subfield had very definite consequences. In the first place, it led to the virtual exclusion of the philosophy of religion from many of the central discussions and debates that typified anglophone philosophy in the early and mid-twentieth century. Many forces contributed to this exclusion, but chief among them was the influence and legacy of Logical Positivism in both Britain and America. The strict empiricism that was the hallmark of positivism launched a wide-ranging critique of traditional philosophical metaphysics by insisting that the subject-matter of philosophy ought to be addressed by scientifically conditioned methods of inquiry. The collective penchant for empiricism in both Britain and America prompted philosophers like Rudolf Carnap (1891–1970) and A. J. Ayer (1910–89) to argue that all religious claims are meaningless.[63] The marginalization of their subject induced many philosophers of religion either to apply the methods of logical empiricism to their own discipline with the consequence that the subject became almost solely preoccupied with the topic of religious language,[64] or else to fight a rearguard action to expose the inadequacies of the positivist critique.[65] Both of these strategies met with paltry success, as they failed to bring the philosophy of religion back within the mainstream of English-speaking philosophy.

With the move away from verificationism and the development of a greater pluralism in so-called 'analytic philosophy', however, philosophers like Alvin Plantinga in the United States[66] and Richard Swinburne in

[63] See Carnap, 'Religious Language is Meaningless', trans. A. Pap, in M. J. Charlesworth (ed.), *The Problem of Religious Language* (Englewood Cliffs, NJ, 1974) and Ayer, *Language, Truth and Logic* (London, 1936). For a brief discussion of these issues, see Section 4 below.

[64] An example of this approach can be found in the work of R. B. Braithwaite, 'An Empiricist's View of the Nature of Religious Belief', in Mitchell (1971). For an illustration of the preoccupation of philosophers of religion of this time with religious language, the reader might consult the above book as well as the earlier collections A. Flew and A. MacIntyre (eds.), *New Essays in Philosophical Theology* (London, 1955) and B. Mitchell (ed.), *Faith and Logic* (London, 1957). See also R. S. Heimbeck, *Theology and Meaning* (Stanford, Calif., 1969).

[65] See J. Hick, 'Theology and Verification', *Theology Today*, 17 (1960), 12–31; repr. in Mitchell, *The Philosophy of Religion*.

[66] Plantinga's works from this period are *God and Other Minds* (Ithaca, NY, 1969), *God, Freedom and Evil* (London, 1974), and *The Nature of Necessity* (Oxford, 1974). Plantinga's achievements are recorded in a celebratory volume of essays edited by J. E. Tomberlin and P. van Inwagen, *Alvin Plantinga: A Profile* (Dordrecht, 1985).

Britain[67] set about the task of applying the rigorous standards of analytic philosophy to the discussion of traditional theological subjects. The effect of their work, particularly when combined with the historical studies of Anthony Kenny,[68] was to increase the institutional profile of the subject in professional philosophy. However, the tremendous growth of the philosophy of religion in the English-speaking world is a very recent phenomenon and is due in part to the establishment of new journals and philosophical societies dedicated to the discipline.[69]

Alongside these developments there has been a growing interest in such subjects as religious pluralism and a greater philosophical attention to the claims of non-Western religious traditions.[70] As part of this general revival of the philosophy of religion, a number of talented philosophers whose main work lies in other areas have been attracted to the discipline. Thus, complex arguments about substance, space and time, epistemic justification, free will, and determinism which might be thought more properly at home in metaphysics, epistemology, philosophical logic, philosophy of mind, and philosophy of science have all been explored with reference to the idea of God. Up to the present moment, the growth in the subject shows no signs of abating. At present, there are efforts to explore cross-cultural philosophies of religion, to articulate feminist challenges to traditional religions, and to consider many practical, moral and social problems from the standpoint of a religiously motivated

[67] Swinburne's reputation was built around his influential trilogy *The Coherence of Theism* (Oxford, 1977; rev. 1993), *The Existence of God* (Oxford, 1979; rev. 1991), and *Faith and Reason* (Oxford, 1981). Swinburne's influence and legacy is discussed in A. G. Padgett (ed.), *Reason and the Christian Religion: Essays in Honour of Richard Swinburne* (Oxford, 1994).

[68] See *The Anatomy of the Soul* (Oxford, 1973), *The God of the Philosophers* (Oxford, 1979), *Faith and Reason* (New York, 1983), and *Reason and Religion: Essays in Philosophical Theology* (Oxford, 1987).

[69] These societies include, in Great Britain, the Society for the Philosophy of Religion and, in the United States, the Society of Christian Philosophers. The major journals for the philosophy of religion in the English-speaking world are *Faith and Philosophy, Religious Studies, International Journal for the Philosophy of Religion*, and *Sophia*. One of the more specific consequences of this revival, particularly for American philosophy of religion, has been the establishment of what can only be termed 'Christian philosophy'. This influential division within American philosophy of religion is concerned with the philosophical project of attempting to clarify and assess issues that have currency for Christian believers such as the Trinity, the Incarnation, and Atonement. For an influential statement of the aims and objectives of this version of Christian philosophy, see A. Plantinga, 'Advice to Christian Philosophers', in M. D. Beaty (ed.), *Christian Theism and the Problems of Philosophy* (Notre Dame, Ind., 1990). Other examples of this same approach are to be found in T. V. Morris (ed.), *Philosophy and the Christian Faith* (Notre Dame, Ind., 1988).

[70] The interest in the topic of pluralism might be said to be one of the intellectual responses within recent philosophy of religion to the widespread phenomenon of religious diversity. The issue has been popularized by authors such as P. F. Knitter, *No Other Name: A Critical Survey of Christian Attitudes toward World Religions* (London, 1985); W. Cantwell Smith, *Towards a World Theology: Faith and the Comparative History of Religion* (London, 1981); Hick, see Hick, *The Interpretation of Religion* and J. Hick and E. S. Metzer, *Three Faiths—One God* (London, 1989). The state of the current debate is the subject of a recent book by P. Byrne, *Prolegomena to Religious Pluralism* (London, 1995). See also J. Hick, ' Religious Pluralism', in Quinn and Taliaferro (eds.), *Companion to the Philosophy of Religion*.

ethics.[71] Further to this, specific issues which are internal to religious traditions are also receiving attention with increased philosophical effort being given to speculation on heaven, hell, the sacraments and the meaning of scripture.[72]

Philosophy of religion, then, might be said to have its place today in English-speaking philosophy not just in the domain of the history of philosophy but also in other areas of philosophical specialization. It is for this reason that the subject presents to the individual already acquainted with the traditional core of Western philosophy, viz. logic, metaphysics, epistemology and ethics, an opportunity to apply their philosophical learning to a set of important questions. One of the reasons for this has, I hope, been made clear in this historical survey; the philosophy of religion, as its history testifies, is nothing more than a rich deposit of questions which have belonged to the central core of subjects that have characterized the concerns of Western philosophers from antiquity onwards. In this sense, to engage with the philosophy of religion is in part to acquaint oneself with many of the questions and subjects of Western philosophy itself. With this in mind, let us examine some of the traditional divisions of the subject as it is presently taught and practised. In what follows, I will consider the philosophical 'proofs' for the existence of God, philosophical theology and religious epistemology, and will conclude with a brief examination of the topic of religious language.

2. THE PHILOSOPHICAL PROOFS FOR THE EXISTENCE OF GOD

2.1. Introduction

The traditional or 'speculative' proofs for the existence of God take the form of either a priori arguments as in the ontological argument, or a posteriori argu-

[71] On the topic of cross-cultural philosophies of religion, see P. J. Griffiths, 'Comparative Philosophy of Religion', in Quinn and Taliaferro (eds.), *Companion to the Philosophy of Religion*; A. Sharma, *A Hindu Perspective on the Philosophy of Religion* (New York, 1990); and the recent book by K. Yandell, *The Epistemology of Religious Experience* (Cambridge, 1993), which examines the nature of religious experience in both Eastern and Western traditions. The subject of feminism in recent philosophy of religion is one of the subjects in M. Daly, *Beyond God the Father: Towards a Philosophy of Women's Liberation* (London, 1985). See also S. Coakley, 'Feminism', in Quinn and Taliaferro (eds.), *Companion to the Philosophy of Religion* and P. S. Anderson, *A Feminist Philosophy of Religion* (Oxford, 1998). The series New Studies in Christian Ethics, edited by R. Gill (Cambridge), is but one example of the effort that some philosophers of religion are currently expending on the analysis of morality. For other examples of such work, see part IX of Quinn and Taliaferro (eds.), *Companion to the Philosophy of Religion*.

[72] Recent examples of this type of work can be found in E. Stump and T. P. Flint (eds.), *Hermes and Athena: Biblical Exegesis and Philosophical Theology* (Notre Dame, Ind., 1993) and E. Stump (ed.), *Reasoned Faith* (Ithaca, NY, 1993). See the contributions by van Inwagen in Stump and Flint (eds.), *Hermes and Athena* and those by Mann, Quinn, and McCord Adams, in Stump (1993). Also worth consulting is part x of Quinn and Taliaferro, (eds.), *Companion to the Philosophy of Religion*.

ments, as in most versions of the cosmological argument and the argument from design.[73] In their many variations, these arguments have been present throughout the history of Western philosophy. Given the extent of historical discussion and contemporary interest in the ontological argument, I shall discuss it in greater detail than the other arguments.

2.2. The Ontological Argument

Put simply, the ontological argument purports to prove, from an analysis of the concept of God, that God's existence cannot be rationally doubted by any individual who entertains the concept of God. It is thus a purely a priori argument, that is to say, it does not make appeal to any facts of experience, but is concerned solely with the implications of concepts, in this case the concept of God as the supreme being.

Like all influential arguments, the history of discussion and comment upon the ontological argument is rich and eventful.[74] Since its first formulation by St Anselm,[75] the argument has long been the object of a fascination among philosophers, and yet few arguments within the history of philosophy have

[73] To these speculative arguments one can add certain moral arguments for the existence of a deity. These are a more recent addition to the class of theistic arguments, and reflect a distinctively modern dissatisfaction with the traditional proofs. Due to the requirements of space these arguments are omitted from discussion. For a discussion of many of the issues relevant to a consideration of the 'moral proofs', see C. Stephen Evans, 'Moral Arguments', in Quinn and Taliaferro (eds.), *Companion to the Philosophy of Religion* and R. M. Adams, *The Virtue of Faith and Other Essays in Philosophical Theology* (New York, 1987), pt. 3. Five recent books written from the opposing standpoints of theism and atheism provide helpful philosophical commentary on most aspects of the proofs for God's existence. These are Mackie, *The Miracle of Theism*; Swinburne, *The Coherence of Theism*; R. Gale, *On the Nature and Existence of God* (New York, 1991); R. Le Poidevin, *Arguing for Atheism: An Introduction to the Philosophy of Religion* (London, 1996); J. J. C. Smart and J. J. Haldane, *Atheism and Theism* (Oxford, 1996) and S. T. Davis, *God, Reason and Theistic Proofs* (Edinburgh, 1997).

[74] An adequate, if somewhat dated, set of guides to the ontological argument can be found in two now standard anthologies: A. Plantinga (ed.), *The Ontological Argument from St. Anselm to Contemporary Philosophers* (New York, 1965) and J. Hick and A. C. McGill (eds.), *The Many Faced Argument* (London, 1968). Also worth consulting is the history of the argument provided by C. Hartshorne in *Anselm's Discovery* (La Salle, Ill., 1965), 137–304. The most complete discussion of the ontological argument to date is G. Oppy, *Ontological Arguments and Belief in God* (New York, 1995); of particular interest is Oppy's exhaustive survey and bibliography at the end of the volume, 'The Literature Notes', pp. 200 ff. The main issues raised by the argument are discussed by C. Dore, 'Ontological Arguments', in Quinn and Taliaferro (eds.), *Companion to the Philosophy of Religion* and P. van Inwagen, *Metaphysics* (New York, 1993), ch. 5.

[75] It is important to note that the attribution of the ontological argument to Anselm is the subject of a great deal of controversy. This is so for two reasons. First, there is good evidence from Hellenistic philosophy that the origins of the ontological argument can be found in certain Stoic texts. The Stoics are thought to have had a 'prototype' of the ontological argument (1) because one the key phrases of Anselm's argument, the famous 'something than which a greater cannot be thought of' (*aliquid quo nihil maius cogitari possit*) is to be found in a number of Stoic texts (see Cicero, *De Natura Deorum*, 2. 18, and Seneca, *Quaestiones Naturales*, 1. 13); and (2) a definite anticipation of the argument has been found in a passage of Sextus Empiricus (*Adversus Mathematicos*, 9. 133–6), which reports an argument elaborated by Diogenes of Babylon. For a discussion of these issues, see the pioneering paper by J.-P. Dumont 'Diogène de Babylone et la preuve ontologique', *Revue philosophique de la France et de l'étranger*, 107 (1982), 389–95. The credentials of Dumont's suggestive thesis are instructively

attracted more opprobrium: some might share Schopenhauer's view that the argument is 'a charming joke' (*eine allerliebste Schnurre*).[76] In order to describe the salient points of the historical and present-day debate about the ontological argument, I discuss it under three heads: (1) the version of St Anselm and its critics; (2) the version of Descartes's and Kant's criticism; and (3) recent versions of the argument.

2.2.1. *St Anselm's* Proslogion *2–3 and its Critics*

Anselm's main arguments are to be found in the second and third chapters of the *Proslogion*.[77] Anselm begins his exposition by a consideration of what God is. His answer is that God is 'something than which a greater cannot be thought of' (*aliquid quo nihil maius cogitari possit*).[78] Next, Anselm considers the view of someone who says that there is no God. Such a person, Anselm says, 'understands what he hears, and what he understands is in his intellect (*in intellectu*)'. From this Anselm concludes that God exists even in the intellect of one denying his existence. Thus, 'Even the Fool (*insipiens*) [of Psalms 13 and 52], then, is forced to agree that something than which a greater cannot be thought can be

examined by J. Brunschwig, 'Did Diogenes of Babylon Invent the Ontological Argument?', in *Papers in Hellenistic Philosophy* (Cambridge, 1994).

Secondly, there is the disputed question whether or not Anselm's argument is indeed an 'ontological argument'. Some of the issues relevant to the question were sketched above (Section 1.3) and will be further examined below. In advance of this examination, however, it is worth pointing out that the very term 'ontological argument' was first coined by Kant in his *Critique of Pure Reason*, 'On the Impossibility of an Ontological Argument for the Existence of God'. There, it is clear that Kant's discussion is directed towards a consideration of the Cartesian rather than the Anselmian version of the argument. For this reason, some scholars have maintained that whatever else might be said of Anselm's *Proslogion* 2–3, it does not contain an 'ontological argument', at least in the sense in which we now understand that term after Kant. This line of interpretation was first advanced by the German scholar Matthias Esser in 'Finden sich Spüren des ontologischen Gottesbeweis vor dem Heiligen Anselm?', *Jahrbücher für Philosophie und spekulative Theologie*, 29 (1910), 293–303. For recent defences of something like the 'Esser view', see G. E. M. Anscombe, 'Why Anselm's Proof in the *Proslogion* is not an Ontological Argument', *Thoreau Quarterly*, 17 (1985), 32–40, and J.-L. Marion, 'Is the Ontological Argument Ontological? The Argument according to Anselm and its Metaphysical Interpretation according to Kant', *Journal of the History of Philosophy*, 30 (1992), 201–18.

[76] See Schopenhauer, *On the Fourfold Root of the Principle of Sufficient Reason* (*Über die vierfache Wurzel des Satzes vom zureichenden Grunde*), II. vii, in *Sämtliche Werke*, i (Wiesbaden, 1948), 10.

[77] Editions of *Proslogion* worth consulting are Charlesworth, *St Anselm's 'Proslogion'* and Schufreider, *Confessions of a Rational Mystic*. Accessible commentaries on Anselm's arguments can be found not only in the above works but also in Mackie, *The Miracle of Theism*, 49 ff.; Gale, *On the Nature and Existence of God*, 205 ff.; J. Barnes, *The Ontological Argument* (London, 1972), 2 ff.; R. A. Herrera, *Anselm's 'Proslogion': An Introduction* (Washington, 1979), 18–25; R. Brecher, *Anselm's Argument: The Logic of Divine Existence* (Brookfield, 1985); G. R. Evans, *Anselm and Talking about God*, ch. 2; Oppy, *Ontological Arguments and Belief in God*, 7–19.

[78] This description of God was probably elaborated by Anselm from similar but not identical descriptions in Augustine; see *De Doctrina Christiana*, I. vii, where Augustine articulates the general notion of God's supremacy as found in the Scriptures. As we saw above (n. 75), the nearest verbal parallel to Anselm's formula is to be found in Cicero and Seneca. For a discussion of Anselm's use of Christian sources, see Dom Francis de Sales Schmitt's introduction to *Sancti Anselmi Opera Omnia*, 6 vols. (Edinburgh, 1945–51), i. 102.

conceived in the intellect, since he understands this when he hears it, and whatever is understood is in the intellect' (*Proslogion*, 2).[79]

This, however, does not provide us with a complete proof for the existence of God as there appears to be nothing exceptional in the observation that God exists in the understanding (*in intellectu*). Surely, if we want God to 'exist' in any tangible sense of that term, we will want God's existence to have much the same 'reality' as other objects in the world. In this sense we will want God to exist not only *in intellectu* but also *in re*; that is, in reality. Anselm is aware of this requirement. He asks, 'Does God exist in any other sense?' His answer to this question is 'yes'. God exists not only in the understanding but also in reality. His reasoning is as follows:

> And surely that than which a greater cannot be thought cannot exist in the mind alone. For if it exists solely in the mind, it can be thought to exist in reality also, which is greater (*quod maius est*). If then, that than which a greater cannot be thought exists in the mind alone, this same that than which a greater cannot be thought is that than which a greater can be thought. But this is clearly impossible (*Sed certe hoc esse non potest*). Therefore, there is absolutely no doubt that something than which a greater cannot be thought exists both in the mind and in reality. (*Proslogion*, 2)[80]

Anselm's point can be summarized as follows: something can be thought as being greater than something existing only in the intellect and that something therefore does not *just* exist in the intellect. In other words, if to think of the concept of 'God' is to entertain the concept 'something than which a greater cannot be thought of', then it follows that God has existence in all spheres; God's greatness necessitates his existing *in re* as well as *in intellectu*.

The argument continues in *Proslogion* 3. Suppose I understand that a certain person, Fred, exists. Then, by Anselm's lights, Fred exists in my intellect, and if Fred exists outside my intellect, then Fred exists both in my intellect and outside it. But Fred is not such that he cannot be thought not to exist. In other words, I can perfectly well acknowledge Fred's existence without supposing that there is no possibility of his not existing. By the same token, Anselm assumes, even if we know that God exists both *in re* and *in intellectu*, it does not follow that there is no possibility of God not existing. If we think that God is such that there is no possibility of him not existing, we need to know more of him than that he exists both in the intellect and outside it. The aim of *Proslogion* 3 is to show that we know this of God.

The obvious retort to this is to ask 'How do we know this of God?' Anselm argues that it can be thought that there is something which cannot be thought not to exist and because God *must* be such a being, God is something than which nothing greater can be thought of. The reason we come to think this way is

[79] Trans. after Charlesworth, *St Anselm's 'Proslogion'*, 117.

[80] Trans. after Charlesworth, ibid.

determined, Anselm argues, by the fact that it can be thought that there exists something that cannot be thought not to exist. If this is so, such a thing would be greater than something which can be thought not to exist. 'For something can be thought to exist that cannot be thought not to exist, and this is greater than that which can be thought not to exist. Thus, if something than which a greater cannot be thought of can be thought not to exist, then something than which a greater cannot be thought of is not that than which a greater cannot be thought of, which is impossible' (*Proslogion*, 3).[81] On these grounds, Anselm claims to have shown that God 'exists' on the basis of analysing what it is to entertain the concept 'God' and then demonstrating what follows from this.

One of the earliest criticisms of the *Proslogion* arguments was put by the monk Gaunilo, a contemporary of Anselm.[82] In his *A Reply to the Foregoing by a Certain Writer on Behalf of the Fool* (*Quid ad haec Respondeat quidam pro Insipiente*), Gaunilo takes issue with Anselm's claims about existence. For Gaunilo, if Anselm is correct, then it is not only God's existence that can be established by the use of the patterns of reasoning defended in the *Proslogion*. The point is illustrated by the famous 'Lost Island' example. Gaunilo writes:

> For example: they say that there is in the ocean somewhere a lost island which, because of the difficulty (or rather the impossibility) of finding that which does not exist, some have called the 'Lost Island'. And the story goes that it is blessed with all manner of priceless riches and delights in abundance . . . and having no owner . . . it is superior everywhere in abundance of riches to all those islands that men inhabit. Now, if anyone should tell me that it is like this, I shall easily understand what is said, since nothing is difficult about it. But if he should then go on to say, as though it were a logical consequence of this: You cannot any more doubt that this island that is more excellent than all other lands exists somewhere in reality than you can doubt that it is in your mind; and since it is more excellent to exist not only in the mind alone but also in reality, therefore that it must needs be that it exists. For if it did not exist, any other land existing in reality would be more excellent than it, and so this island, already thought by you to be more excellent than others, will not be more excellent. If, I say, someone wishes thus to persuade me that this island really exists beyond all doubt, I should either think that he was joking, or I should find it hard to decide which of us I ought to judge the bigger fool. (*Pro Insipiente*, 6)[83]

Gaunilo's point is that if Anselm's arguments were valid, we could prove the existence of this lost island that surpasses the attractions of all inhabited countries, for actual existence is an essential element in any understanding of such superiority. To be fair to Anselm, however, one could say that he is not

[81] Trans. after Charlesworth, ibid.

[82] Not much is known about Gaunilo except that he was a monk of the abbey of Marmoutier near Tours. For a summary of what information there is on Gaunilo's life and career, see ibid. 83–4.

[83] Trans. after Charlesworth, ibid. 163–4.

concerned with the idea of something that is in fact greater than anything else of the same kind. Rather, his point is that God is something than which a greater cannot be thought of; which is to say that whatever the concept 'God' refers to cannot be surpassed in any respect whatsoever. Gaunilo, on the other hand, is concerned with something, an island, which is better than any other island.

The supporter of Gaunilo might accept this point and yet still try to preserve the locus of their complaint. What if, they might say, we construe it as holding that if Anselm's argument is successful, then it is possible to establish the existence not only of the island which is better than all other islands, but also of the island than which no more perfect island can be thought of. This last move has seduced many, but it might be thought to fall short of refuting Anselm. For it crucially depends on the assumption that the concept 'an island than which no more perfect can be thought of' is coherent. Here we run into difficulties, for no matter what description of an island is produced, it is always possible that human imagination can enhance the potential voluptuousness or desirability of the description offered.[84] For this reason, some conclude that Anselm's argument survives Gaunilo's attack.

Gaunilo aside, other lines of criticism surfaced in medieval discussions of Anselm's *Proslogion* arguments. Some philosophers, such as William of Auxerre (d. 1249) and Alexander of Hales (*c.*1185–1245), were prepared to accept the basic insights of Anselm's arguments, while others, such as Duns Scotus and Nicholas of Cusa (1401–64), thought the arguments were in need of further clarification and extension.[85] Of the major scholastics only Aquinas and Occam[86] thought the proof in error. What is interesting about Aquinas' criticisms of what the scholastics referred to as the *ratio Anselmi* is the contrast it invites with modern criticisms of the proof (see Section 2.2.2 below).[87] Aquinas thought Anselm's arguments invalid not for the reason that they treated existence as a predicate, but because the Anselmian formula expressing the concept of God as 'that which nothing greater can be conceived of' does not provide any insight into

[84] For an amusing caveat on this proposal which includes reference to the putative delights of 'dancing-girls' and palm trees, see Plantinga, *God, Freedom and Evil*, 90–1. Other helpful discussions of Gaunilo's argument can be found in Mackie, *The Miracle of Theism*, 53 ff., and Barnes, *The Ontological Argument*, 26–8.

[85] Scholastic interpretations of Anselm's arguments are considered in A. Daniels, *Quellenbeiträge und Untersuchungen zur Geschichte der Gottesbeweise im XIII. Jahrhundert, mit besonderer Beruchsichtigung des Arguments in Proslogion des Hlg. Anselm* (Munster, 1909). A helpful discussion of Scotus' attitude to the proof can be found in J. Doyle, 'Some Thoughts on Duns Scotus and the Ontological Argument', *New Scholasticism*, 53 (1979), 234–41, and Wolter, *The Philosophical Theology of John Duns Scotus*, 254–84.

[86] Occam's views on Anselm's arguments are discussed by P. Streveler, 'Two "New" Critiques of the Ontological Argument', in H. Kohlenberger (ed.), *Analecta Anselmiana*, 5 (1976), 55–64.

[87] Aquinas discusses the *Proslogion* arguments at *Summa Theologiae*, 1a, q. 2, a. 1; *In Primum Librum Sententiarum*, d. 3, q. 1, a. 2, 4 & ad 4; *In Boethi-de Trinitate*, proem, q. 1, a. 3, 6 & ad 6; *Quaestiones Disputatae de Veritate*, q. 10, a. 12, 2 and ad 2; and *Summa contra Gentiles*, 1. 10, 11. For a discussion of Aquinas' criticism of Anselm, see M. Cosgrove, 'Thomas Aquinas on Anselm's Argument', *Review of Metaphysics*, 27 (1974), 513–30.

God's nature. For this reason, Aquinas contends, the formula cannot be self-evidently true. Aquinas' discussion of the *ratio Anselmi* provides a paradigm of an enduring line of criticism of the ontological argument, namely that an a priori argument that attempts to draw conclusions based on the implications of entertaining certain concepts is too thin to prove the existence of a God. As we shall see, a palpable dissatisfaction with a priori reasoning can be said to provide an impetus for many cosmological arguments (see Section 2.3 below).

While Anselm's arguments had its detractors, it also had its supporters. Perhaps the most willing advocate of the *ratio Anselmi* was Bonaventure. At two places[88] Bonaventure quotes and states Anselm's arguments at great length before pointing out that the argument is subject to doubt only if someone has an erroneous notion of God; that is, if one fails to realize that God is that than which nothing greater can be conceived. Bonaventure's defence of the proof reflects an understanding of Anselm's arguments which persisted throughout the medieval and early modern periods.[89] In accordance with the Platonic–Augustinian tradition he so cherished, Bonaventure espied in Anselm's argument a way of preserving an innate conception of the perfect, which can be nothing else but God's imprint on the soul, not in the sense that the soul is perfect, but in the sense that the soul or the mind receives the idea of the perfect through divine illumination. According to this view, we might say the very concept of 'God' affirms the concrete existence of God himself, for it is the presence in the mind of the idea or concept of God that necessarily implies God's existence. We do well to note in advance the resemblance between Bonaventure's enthusiastic defence of the *ratio Anselmi* and Descartes's subsequent ontological argument of the Fifth Meditation.

We can conclude our survey of Anselm's arguments by briefly examining more recent discussions of it. Central to these discussions is the view that Anselm's argument is a modal argument, that is, it attempts to infer God's actuality from his mere possibility. Both defenders and detractors of Anselm's argument have argued for this interpretation.[90] One of the more interesting attempts to expose new fallacies in Anselm's argument which builds upon the modal interpretation is made by David Lewis.[91] Lewis's objection is based on the following thoughts: A crucial step in the argument is the idea that since we

[88] See *The Commentary on the Sentences of Peter Lombard*, I. 8. I. 2, and *De Mysterio Trinitatis*, I. I. 21–4.

[89] For a discussion of Bonaventure's arguments, see J. Doyle, 'Saint Bonaventure and the Ontological Argument', *Modern Schoolman*, 52 (1974), 27–48.

[90] On the side of the defenders one can count N. Malcolm, 'Anselm's Ontological Arguments', *Philosophical Review*, 69 (1960), 41–62; repr. in Plantinga (ed.), *The Ontological Argument from St. Anselm to Contemporary Philosophers*, 136–59; R. M. Adams, 'The Logical Structure of Anselm's Arguments', *Philosophical Review*, 80 (1971), 28–54; repr. in Adams, *The Virture of Faith and Other Essays in Philosophical Theology*, 221–40; C. Hartshorne, 'The Logic of the Ontological Argument', *Journal of Philosophy*, 68 (1961), 471–3. On the side of the detractors one can include D. Lewis, 'Anselm and Actuality', *Nous*, 4 (1971), 175–88, and Gale, *On the Nature and Existence of God*, 201 ff.

[91] See Lewis, 'Anselm and Actuality'.

can conceive of God, God exists in our understanding. Anselm goes on to conclude that God's perfection entails that he exists in reality as well. But, asks Lewis, what does it mean to say that a perfect being exists in the understanding? He offers two answers to this question. It might mean (1) that there is a being in our understanding which is, in some possible world in which it exists, greater than any possible being in any possible world; or (2) that there is a being in our understanding which is, in our actual world, greater than any possible being in any possible world. Lewis argues that if it means (1), the conclusion of Anselm's argument does not follow, but if it means (2), there is no reason to suppose that God exists in our understanding just because we can conceive of him. Thus Anselm's argument is thought to fail.

Despite the interest of Lewis's claims, his analysis of Anselm's argument is nevertheless parasitic upon a modal interpretation. Some commentators have objected to this reading.[92] They argued that even if we choose to understand the word 'can' in the description 'that than which nothing greater can be thought of' in terms of metaphysical possibility, the logic of Anselm's argument itself does not include inferences based on this type of modality. In order to make this point clear some recent commentators argue that it is possible to develop a reading of the *Proslogion* that contains no modal inferences.[93] Rather, the argument is thought to turn on the difference between saying that there is such a thing as *x* and saying that *x* has the property of existence. This new reading, then, attempts to exploit the difference between quantifying over *x* and predicating existence of *x*. Thus, instead of interpreting the argument as having inferred God's actuality from his mere possibility, Anselm is now read as offering a way of inferring God's existence from his mere being. As with all new interpretations, this reading has provoked a further stream of objections. It has also focused criticism on a different part of Anselm's argument.[94]

2.2.2. *Descartes's Argument and Kant's Criticism*

In the Fifth Meditation Descartes presents the following a priori argument for the existence of God.[95] This is to be distinguished from his earlier 'cosmological

[92] See Barnes, *The Ontological Argument*, 18 ff., and P. Oppenheimer and E. Zalta, 'On the Logic of the Ontological Argument', *Philosophical Perspectives*, 5 (1991), 509–29.

[93] See Oppenheimer and Zalta, 'On the Logic of the Ontological Argument' and Edgar Morscher, 'Was Sind und was Sollen die Gottesbeweise? Bermerkungen zu Anselms Gottesbeweis(en)', in F. Ricken (ed.), *Klassische Gottesbeweise in der Sicht der gegenwärtigen Logik und Wissenschaftstheorie* (Stuttgart, 1991).

[94] This line of criticism tends to focus on the so-called second premiss of Anselm's argument, namely his description of God. For one of the pioneering discussions of this line of criticism, see Barnes, *The Ontological Argument*, 67–86.

[95] See *The Philosophical Writings of Descartes*, ii. 44–9. General discussions of this argument can be found in B. A. O. Williams, *Descartes: The Project of Pure Enquiry* (London, 1978), 130–62; A. Kenny, *Descartes: A Study of his Philosophy* (1968; Bristol, 1993), 146–71; J. Cottingham, *Descartes* (Oxford, 1986), 57 ff.; Oppy, *Ontological Arguments and Belief in God*, 20–4. Further commentary is provided by Mackie, *The Miracle of Theism*, 41–9. A

argument' of the Third Meditation (see Sections 2.3ff. below). The Fifth Meditation argument can be paraphrased as follows: Having in mind the idea of a supremely perfect being, or *ens realissimum*, I know with as much clearness and distinctness as any mathematical proof, that such a being must actually and eternally exist, for existence is a perfection. As existence is a perfection, a being that fails to exist would be less than perfect. While essence can be distinguished from existence—that is, a distinction can be made between the question of what the nature of an actual or a possible thing is and the question whether such a thing actually exists—'existence can no more be separated from the essence of God than the idea of a mountain from that of a valley'. Descartes's claim, then, is that it is impossible to conceive a God, or a supremely perfect being, as lacking existence, just as it is impossible to conceive a mountain without a valley.[96]

The first thing to note is that the above argument is very different from the arguments of Anselm's *Proslogion*.[97] Descartes's argument is extraordinarily brief and simple. First, God is defined as a supremely perfect being. Secondly, it is claimed that supreme perfection implies existence. A completely perfect being must, of necessity, possess all perfections, and hence if one were to specify the perfections of God, then existence would have to accompany

discussion of the place of this argument in modern philosophy is provided by D. Henrich, *Der ontologische Gottesbeweis* (Tübingen, 1960).

[96] Spinoza also embraces a version of the ontological argument which is not entirely dissimilar from that of Descartes. He supposes God to be a being such that if God exists at all, he exists by his very nature, not deriving his existence from anything external to himself. Thus conceived, God cannot fail to exist and cannot be thought of as ever coming into existence or ever ceasing to exist. Spinoza, however, identified God, conceived as a necessary and a self-sufficient being, with substance, that is to say with reality itself, maintaining that whatever exists exists only in God and can have no existence apart from God (see *Ethics*, prop. xi of part 1). For a helpful discussion of Spinoza's argument, see D. Garrett, 'Spinoza's "Ontological" Argument', *Philosophical Review*, 88 (1979), 198–223.

Like Spinoza, Leibniz considered the Cartesian form of the argument to be valid. Unlike Spinoza, however, he thought it to be incomplete in so far as it presupposed the possibility of that which it attempted to prove. If the supreme being, as described by Descartes, should be one that could not exist *in re*, then a purely formal proof could not establish its necessary existence. Thus, Leibniz attempted to show that it is possible for such a being to exist given that it then follows from the ontological argument that God does exist. See *New Essays on Human Understanding*, IV. x. For a helpful discussion of Leibniz's attitude to the proof, see D. Blumenfield, 'Leibniz's Ontological and Cosmological Arguments', in N. Jolley (ed.), *The Cambridge Companion to Leibniz* (Cambridge, 1995); Adams, *Leibniz: Determinist, Theist, Idealist*, 136–56; Oppy, *Ontological Arguments and Belief in God*, 24–6; D. Werther, 'Leibniz and the Possibility of God's Existence', *Religious Studies*, 32 (1996), 37–48.

[97] As far as it is presently known, Descartes had no direct acquaintance with Anselm's texts, and it is probable that he may have taken this argument from Aquinas' negative discussion of the *ratio Anselmi* at *Summa Theologiae*, I–I, q. 2, a. 1. Some commentators have also speculated that a further influence on Descartes's characterization of the proof may have been Bonaventure's enthusiastic restatement of it in his *First Book of Commentary on the Sentences of Peter Lombard* and *De Mysteriis*. For a discussion of these matters, see J.-M. Beyssade, 'The Idea of God and the Proofs of his Existence', in J. Cottingham (ed.), *The Cambridge Companion to Descartes* (Cambridge, 1992). Also worth consulting is the classic study by M. Gueroult, *Nouvelles Réflexions sur la preuve ontologique de Descartes* (Paris, 1955).

omniscience and omnipotence (see Sections 3.2.2 and 3.2.3 below). Thus, Descartes concludes, God exists.

'It is necessary', Descartes writes, 'that I attribute all perfections to [the supreme being]. And this necessity plainly guarantees that, when I later realise that existence is a perfection, I am correct in inferring that the supreme being exists.'[98] This would appear to entail that Descartes's argument crucially depends upon the premiss that just as omnipotence and omniscience are perfections, so existence is a perfection. Historically, this premiss has been the major focus of interest for Descartes's critics. It is not difficult to appreciate why such a premiss invites scrutiny. If existence is a perfection, then it must be a property of some kind; yet reflection on this suggests that it would be a rather odd kind of property. For example, if I tell you that my partner is very tall, then you have learned something about her; but, if I simply tell you that she *exists*, this hardly seems to increase your stock of information about her.

This line of criticism was first advanced by Pierre Gassendi (1592–1655) in his 'Objections' to the Fifth Meditation.[99] In reply Descartes says, 'I do not see why existence cannot be said to be a property just like omnipotence—provided of course that we take the word "property" to stand for any attribute, or for whatever can be predicated of a thing.'[100] Are there good reasons for agreeing with Descartes? This question is best answered by confronting head-on the most enduring of modern objections to the ontological argument: Kant's argument that 'existence' is not a predicate.

According to Kant, 'being' or 'existence' is not a determination, or real predicate, hence it cannot serve as an identifying mark which might go to make up the content of some concept. Rather, it is 'merely the positing of a thing, or of certain determinations, as existing in themselves'. When we say 'God is' or 'there is a God', we attach no new predicate to the concept of God, but only posit the subject in itself with all new predicates. On this view, existence is not a reality or a perfection. The point is expressed thus: 'The actual contains no more than the merely possible. A hundred actual dollars do not contain the least bit more than a hundred possible dollars . . . But there is more in my financial position in the case of a hundred actual dollars than in the case of the mere concept (*Begriffe*) of them.'[101]

[98] *The Philosophical Writings of Descartes*, ii. 47. For a recent defence of Descartes's argument, see C. Dore, 'Descartes's Meditation V Proof of God's Existence', in A. J. Freddoso (ed.), *The Existence and Nature of God* (Notre Dame, Ind., 1983).

[99] Gassendi writes: 'existence is not a perfection either in God or in anything else; it is that without which no perfections can be present . . . Hence we do not say that existence 'exists in a thing' in the way perfections do; and if a thing lacks existence, we do not say it is imperfect, or deprived of a perfection, but say instead it is nothing at all' (*The Philosophical Writings of Descartes*, ii. 224–5).

[100] Ibid. 263.

[101] *Critique of Pure Reason*, A598 ff. / B626 ff. Cf. Kant's earlier essay *The One Possible Basis for a Demonstration of the Existence of God* (1762), ed. and trans. G. Treash (Lincoln, Nebr., 1994), 1. i, pp. 57 ff., and *Lectures on Philosophical Theology*, trans. A. Wood and G. Clark (Ithaca, NY, 1978), 59.

Kant's criticism of Descartes's argument depends upon his distinction between two sorts of synthetic proposition: (1) those which 'determine' the subject concept or 'add to' it by predicating some reality or negation of it; and (2) those which 'posit' the concept or the determinations thought in it. In the case of (1), the determinations of 'real predicates' which are applied to a particular thing may serve as the contents of a subject concept. If the predicates 'is' or 'exists' were real predicates, then it could not be denied that the proposition 'God exists' is analytic; but, Kant argues, when we assert that something exists, we do not ascribe any reality to it. We do not determine its concept by anything which could (in another context) constitute the marks by which we identify the content of a subject concept. Since existence is a not a 'real predicate', we are not required to think of it when we entertain the concept of a supremely perfect being or *ens realissimum*, and hence we need not conclude that the existence of such a being is asserted by an analytic proposition. When we assert that 'God exists' we do not add anything to our subject concept, we simply *posit* this concept or the determinations contained in it.[102]

If Kant is right and 'existence' is not a predicate, what might it be? Following the work of Gottlob Frege (1848–1925), many English-speaking philosophers have embraced the view that questions about 'existence' are taken care of by the logical operator known as the 'existential quantifier'. What is said by the phrase 'long-legged mammals exist' is more clearly expressed as 'There are long-legged mammals' and symbolized in logical notation as $\exists x(Lx \,\&\, Mx)$. To construct what philosophers call a 'well-formed' sentence, this quantifier '$\exists$'—pronounced 'There is . . .'—must be attached to the predicate expression, that is, a general expression. What the complete sentence then says is that the collection of features indicated by the predicate expression is instantiated.[103]

Many have thought that the so-called Kant–Frege view delivers a fatal blow to Descartes's ontological argument. For, if existence is simply that which is captured by the existential quantifier, then it is not something that can be said to properly belong, strictly speaking, to an individual at all. It follows from this that existence cannot be a perfection that an individual may possess, or part of an essence, or part of what constitutes the sort of thing something may be. The

[102] Discussion and comment upon Kant's argument can be found in Mackie, *The Miracle of Theism*, 43–9; Barnes, *The Ontological Argument*, 39–66; W. H. Walsh, *Kant's Criticism of Metaphysics* (Edinburgh, 1975), 220–9; S. Morris Engel, 'Kant's "Refutation" of the Ontological Argument', *Philosophy and Phenomenological Research*, 24 (1963–4), 20–35; Wood, *Kant's Rational Theology*, 100 ff.; G. J. Hughes, *The Nature of God* (London, 1995), 19–33; Oppy, *Ontological Arguments and Belief in God*, 29–38.

[103] An example of this type of argument can be found in W. C. Kneale, 'Is Existence a Predicate?', *Proceedings of the Aristotelian Society*, suppl. vol. 15 (1936), 154–74. See also the other contribution to this influential symposium, G. E. Moore, 'Is Existence a Predicate?', repr. in *Philosophical Papers* (London, 1959) and in Plantinga (ed.), *The Ontological Argument from St. Anselm to Contemporary Philosophers*, 71–85. The relation of Kant's thesis to the work of Frege is discussed by J. Hintikka, 'Kant on Existence, Predication and the Ontological Argument', in S. Knuuttila and J. Hintikka (eds.), *The Logic of Being* (Dordrecht, 1986).

Kant–Frege analysis entails, therefore, that existence is not in the correct category to be counted among perfections.

It is important to note, however, that the existential quantifier analysis is by no means the last word on the subject, but has been the subject of much controversy. The analysis concludes that well-formed propositions cannot be expressed by such sentences as 'This zebra exists' or 'God exists' or 'I exist', but only in the form of those types of sentences e.g. 'A zebra exists', 'A god exists', or 'A thinking being exists', which can be easily rendered into the quantifier-plus-predicate-expression form. Against this analysis, it is sometimes argued that in thought as well as in language the term 'exists' seems to be a predicate of individuals. Existing, it is contended, is something that individuals and objects *do*; thereby they ensure the realization of whatever descriptions apply to them, or the instantiation of whatever features they possess.[104]

A tentative conclusion which might be drawn from all this is that Kant's much quoted dictum '"Being" is not a real predicate' (*Sein ist offenbar kein reales Prädikat*), interpreted as the thesis that existence does not belong to individuals but dissolves instead into existential quantification, poses a problem for one standard formulation of the ontological argument. However, further discussion is required before we can accept whether the quantifier analysis itself is acceptable and that the Kant–Frege view accurately reflects Kant's own thinking on this subject.[105]

2.2.3. *Recent Versions of the Argument*

While many recent versions of the ontological argument have taken their cue from the classic statements of Anselm and Descartes, others have been advanced as modal arguments. Both tendencies can be observed in the widely discussed arguments of Norman Malcolm and Alvin Plantinga.[106] Malcolm's

[104] See B. Miller, 'In Defence of the Predicate "Exists"', *Mind*, 84 (1975), 338–54, and N. Salmon, 'Existence', *Philosophical Perspectives*, 1 (1987), 49–108. For a recent defence of the view that existence is not a predicate of individuals, see D. Wiggins, 'The Kant–Frege–Russell View of Existence: Toward the Rehabilitation of the Second-Level View', in W. Sinnott-Armstrong, D. Raffmann, and N. Asher (eds.), *Modality, Morality and Belief: Essays in Honor of Ruth Barcan Marcus* (New York, 1995). Also worth consulting is M. Dummett, 'Existence', in *The Seas of Language* (Oxford, 1993). A helpful overview of these complex issues can be found in Oppy, *Ontological Arguments and Belief in God*, 130–61.

[105] In his remarks on the ontological argument Kant is drawing heavily upon his earlier observations on judgement. The point which he seeks to impress upon his reader is that existential commitment, namely the idea that something exists, is carried by an act of judgement. These observations may well hint at a different reading of the relevant passages, although one needs to add that this reading, should it ever be established, would be at variance with Kant's statements on existence in his pre-Critical writings, e.g. *The One Possible Basis for a Demonstration of the Existence of God*.

[106] See Malcolm, 'Anselm's Ontological Arguments' and Plantinga, *The Nature of Necessity*. Other modal addenda to Anselm's arguments are supplied by Charles Hartshorne, *The Logic of Perfection* (La Salle, Ill., 1962), 3–10; R. Kane, 'The Modal Ontological Argument', *Mind*, 93 (1984), 336–50; T, V. Morris, 'Necessary Beings', *Mind*, 94 (1985), 263–72. The arguments of Kane and Morris are sensibly dispatched by P. J. McGrath, 'The

version attempts to remove the difficulties that have beset the argument in the wake of Kant's criticism. Malcolm grants the force of Kant's objection and says that it can be levelled at Anselm's argument in *Proslogion* 2. However, Malcolm argues that at *Proslogion* 3, Anselm has a version of the ontological argument that does not assume that existence is a perfection. Here, the nub of Anselm's reasoning, Malcolm contends, is that God must exist because the concept of God is the concept of a being whose existence is necessary. God is a being who, if he exists, has the property of necessary existence. Since a being with this property cannot fail to exist, it follows that either God exists (if the concept of God is coherent) or the concept of God is incoherent.

Plantinga argues that Malcolm's version is open to doubt, but he further argues that it can be restated with the assistance of the notion of possible worlds. According to Plantinga our world is a possible world; so too is a world in which there is the merest incremental difference from this world, say, in which I have blond as opposed to brown hair. Working with this conception of possible worlds, Plantinga restates Malcolm's arguments thus:

(1) There is a possible world, *W*, in which there exists a being with maximal greatness.
(2) A being has maximal greatness in a world only if it exists in every world.[107]

This argument establishes that in every world there is a being with maximal greatness. However, says Plantinga, the argument does not establish that there is a God in the actual world; it merely establishes that there is something with maximal greatness. Here Plantinga begins his restatement of the ontological argument. Given his interpretation of Malcolm's argument, it follows, he thinks, that there is a possible world where a being has maximal greatness, which entails that the being exists in every world. Yet this does not entail that in every world the being is greater or more perfect than other inhabitants of those worlds. Plantinga now introduces what he terms 'maximal excellence', which he considers a property connected to maximal greatness. He says 'the property *has maximal greatness* entails the property *has maximal excellence in every possible world. Maximal excellence* entails *omniscience, omnipotence* and *moral perfection*.'[108]

The argument now proceeds as follows: (1) There is a possible world con-

Modal Ontological Argument—A Reply to Kane and Morris', *Mind*, 95 (1986), 373–76. A further attempt to argue for the validity of Anselm's argument is also attempted by S. Makin, 'The Ontological Argument', *Philosophy*, 63 (1988), 83–91. This is criticized by McGrath; see 'The Ontological Argument Revisited', *Philosophy*, 63 (1988), 529–33, and G. Oppy, 'Makin on the Ontological Argument', *Philosophy*, 66 (1991), 106–14. Makin powerfully responds to these objections in 'The Ontological Argument Defended', *Philosophy*, 67 (1992), 247–55. General surveys of the modal version of the ontological argument can be found in Oppy, *Ontological Arguments and Belief in God*, 65–84, and Le Poidevin, *Arguing for Atheism*, 17–31.

[107] Plantinga, *The Nature of Necessity*, 213. [108] Ibid. 214.

taining a being with the property of maximal greatness. (2) Any being with maximal greatness also has the further property of maximal excellence. (3) Any being with maximal excellence is omniscient, omnipotent, and morally perfect. (4) Therefore, in our world there is a being who is omniscient, omnipotent, and morally perfect. Plantinga contends, then, that there actually is a God whose existence follows from his essence and who can be thought to exist *in re* by reasoning that constitutes an ontological argument.[109]

Plantinga's arguments have been the object of much criticism.[110] Discussion has centred on the issue whether or not we are entitled to infer that there is something in our world that is omniscient, omnipotent, and morally perfect from the twin facts that it is possible for there to be something which possesses the attribute of maximal greatness and that our world is a possible world. What appears to make this inference problematic is that there are grounds for doubting whether it really is possible for there to be something with the attribute of maximal greatness if maximal greatness entails maximal greatness in every possible world.[111] A further criticism can be put in the following terms: the very fact that the notion of maximal greatness does not involve any detectable contradiction does not obviously entail that something has that property at some possible world. The point here is that even if maximal greatness has no contradiction, one may not deduce that it is an exemplifiable property. Many have thought that objections of this type pose serious problems for some modal versions of the ontological argument.[112]

2.3. The Cosmological Argument

The cosmological argument is an argument for a cause or reason for the cosmos. It can take either an a priori or an a posteriori form. Many a posteriori versions of this argument begin by reflecting upon the question 'Why is there something rather than nothing?' From there, they seek to make explicit the view that the world or cosmos is not just sufficient of itself but points to a greater reality beyond itself. Unlike the ontological argument, these arguments always contain an existential premiss, their truth being dependent on the claim that something exists.[113]

[109] Plantinga's modal argument is also to be found in his *God, Freedom and Evil*, 108.

[110] Among the better criticisms of Plantinga's argument I would include P. van Inwagen, 'Ontological Arguments', *Nous*, 11 (1977), 375–95; repr. in *God, Knowledge and Mystery* (Ithaca, 1995); Mackie, *The Miracle of Theism* 55–63, to which the above exposition is indebted; P. J. McGrath, 'The Refutation of the Ontological Argument', *Philosophical Quarterly*, 40 (1989), 195–212, and J. E. Tomberlin, 'Plantinga on the Ontological Argument', in Tomberlin and van Inwagen (eds.), *Alvin Plantinga*.

[111] See Mackie, *The Miracle of Theism*, 57–8.

[112] For a discussion of issues relating to these objections, see van Inwagen, 'Ontological Arguments'.

[113] This point is well brought out by W. Rowe, *The Cosmological Argument* (Princeton, 1975), 3. The advantage of Rowe's discussion is its ability to challenge Kant's criticism of the cosmological argument: *Critique of Pure*

A priori versions of the argument can be based on principles like the principle of sufficient reason (see Section, 2.3.1 below). If we possess a strong version of this principle, all we need to get the argument going is the premiss that there might have been contingent things. We get thence to the claim that in some possible world where there are contingent things, there is a necessary being which explains the existence of the *contingentia* at that world: since the being is necessary, it exists in the actual world as well.[114]

Both versions of the cosmological argument possess a long and distinguished history. Their appeal has been impressively broad. At various moments in the history of philosophy both versions have been propounded by ancient Greeks, Jewish and Islamic philosophers and theologians, Christians, and even pantheists. Among their supporters we find many of the greatest philosophers of the West: Plato, Aristotle, Avicenna (980–1037), Maimonides, Aquinas, Descartes, Spinoza, Locke, and Leibniz.[115] In order to bring out the contrast with the ontological argument, I shall consider one version of the a posteriori argument: the third argument of the famous 'five ways' (*quinque viae*) of Aquinas, and I shall also consider Leibniz's 'principle of sufficient reason' argument. Having outlined these arguments, I proceed to examine some standard objections and will conclude with a discussion of a more recent version of the argument by Richard Swinburne.[116]

Reason, Transcendental Dialectic, II. v. There, Kant claimed that the cosmological proof is wrong because it rests on the ontological proof. Since the latter is incorrect, the former, he argues, shares its fate. For further discussion of Kant's objection to the cosmological argument, see Mackie, *The Miracle of Theism*, 82–4, and Wood, *Kant's Rational Theology*, 123–9.

[114] For a recent discussion of the a priori cosmological argument, see van Inwagen, *Metaphysics*, 100–19. For a different version of the a priori argument, see Duns Scotus, *Opus Oxoniense*, I, dist. 2, q. I.

[115] A comprehensive philosophical history of the argument would include not only the above names but also Averröes (1126–98), Gersonides (1288–1344), Bonaventure, Scotus, Suarez (1548–1617), Clarke, and Wolff (1679–1754). Such a history has yet to be written. However, the work of W. Lane Craig provides the best account of the argument's history to date. See his studies *The Kalam Cosmological Argument* (London, 1979) and *The Cosmological Argument from Plato to Leibniz* (London, 1980). The central defect of these works, however, arises from their failure to engage with the a priori versions of the argument. On the Kalam arguments, see also the works by H. A. Wolfson, *The Philosophy of the Kalam* (Cambridge, Mass., 1976) and Davidson, *Proofs for the Eternity, Creation and the Existence of God*. Also worth consulting is the anthology edited by D. R. Burrill, *The Cosmological Arguments: A Spectrum of Opinion* (New York, 1967), which contains many of the relevant extracts from some of the philosophers named above.

[116] For other general surveys of the argument, see W. Rowe, 'Cosmological Arguments', in Quinn and Taliaferro (eds.), *Companion to the Philosophy of Religion*; Mackie, *The Miracle of Theism*, 81–101; Swinburne, *The Existence of God*, 116–32; the ingenious discussion of Gale, *On the Nature and Existence of God*, 238–84; Davies, *An Introduction to the Philosophy of Religion*, 74–93; Rowe, *The Cosmological Argument*; B. Reichenbach, *The Cosmological Argument: A Reassessment*, (Springfield, Ill., 1972); J. J. Shepard, *Experience, Inference and God* (London, 1975); T. F. Torrance, *Divine and Contingent Order* (Totowa, NJ, 1982); D. Braine, *On the Reality of Time and the Existence of God* (Oxford, 1988); C. Dore, *Theism* (Dordrecht, 1984), 14–24; H. A. Meynell, *The Intelligible Universe: A Cosmological Argument* (London, 1982), 7–23; Le Poidevin, *Arguing for Atheism*, 3–15, 33–42; Smart and Haldane, *Atheism and Theism*, 13–15, 16–22, 35–47 (for Smart), 90–139 (for Haldane).

2.3.1. *Aquinas and Leibniz*

Aquinas denies that God's existence is self-evident to us in this life. Thus he eschews all ontological arguments. God's existence can only be established philosophically by reasoning from effect to cause. At *Summa Theologiae*, 1a, q. 2, aa. 3 ff., he presents five arguments in which he argues that God's existence can be proved on the basis of considering certain facts about the world that appear obvious to us.[117] Of these arguments, the third way (*tertia via*) consists of two steps and is concerned with the modal notions of possibility and necessity.[118]

The first step begins with the observation that we experience things that are capable of existence and non-existence and are subject to generation and corruption. It is impossible, Aquinas thinks, that all things that exist are capable of existing and not existing, because for anything that can fail to exist there is a time when it does not exist. If therefore all things are capable of not existing, at some time nothing whatsoever existed, and hence, nothing now would exist. Since not all beings are capable of existing and not existing, there must be a necessary being. Instead of ending the argument there, however, Aquinas adds a second step. He argues as follows: every necessary being has a cause of its necessity from something or else it does not. One cannot regress to infinity with caused necessary beings. Therefore, concludes Aquinas, there must be a necessary being that does not depend on anything else for its necessity and that causes the necessity in everything else. This is a being 'which all name God' (*quod omnes dicunt Deum*).[119]

Leibniz bases his cosmological argument on the famous principle of sufficient reason.[120] In section 32 of the *Monadology* (1714) he expresses this as follows: 'No fact can be real or existent, nor any proposition true, without there being a sufficient reason why it is so rather than otherwise.'[121] His cosmological

[117] The following studies provide useful, if widely diverging, commentaries on Aquinas' arguments: A. Kenny, *The Five Ways: St. Thomas Aquinas' Proofs for God's Existence* (London, 1969); Owens, 'Aquinas as Aristotelian Commentator', 132 ff.; B. Davies, *The Thought of Thomas Aquinas* (Oxford, 1992), 25–31; D. Burrell, *Aquinas: God and Action* (London, 1979), 45 ff.; Elders, *The Philosophical Theology of St. Thomas Aquinas*, ch. 3; Craig, *The Cosmological Argument from Plato to Leibniz*, 158–204; F. van Steenberghen, *Le Problème de l'existence de Dieu dans les écrits de S. Thomas d'Aquin* (Louvain, 1980), 188–201; and F. Copleston, *Aquinas* (London, 1955), 111 ff.

[118] Aquinas' sources for the *tertia via* have been the subject of much debate. Some of its central concepts are to be found in Maimonides. Maimonides offers what appears to be a similar argument to the *tertia via* in *The Guide of the Perplexed*, 2. 1. That said, it can be shown that the *tertia via* is a distinct argument in its own right and not just a restatement of earlier arguments; see van Steenberghen, *Le Problème de l'existence de Dieu*, 53 ff.

[119] For more specific discussion of the *tertia via*, see J. Kansas, 'Necessity in the *Tertia Via*', *New Scholasticism*, 52 (1978), 373–94; Kenny, *The Five Ways*, 46–69; Davies, *The Thought of Thomas Aquinas*, 29–31; Owens, 'Aquinas as Aristotelian Commentator', 142–68; Craig, *The Cosmological Argument from Plato to Leibniz*, 181–98.

[120] All references to Leibniz's works refer to C. I. Gerhardt's edition of *Die philosophischen Schriften von Leibniz*, 7 vols. (Berlin, 1875–90; repr. Hildesheim, 1965); hereafter Gerhardt. All English translations refer to *G. W. Leibniz: Philosophical Papers and Letters*, ed. L. E. Loemker, 2nd edn. (Dordrecht; 1969); hereafter Loemker.

[121] Gerhardt vi. 612: Loemker 646.

argument which appears in his *Ultimate Origination of Things* (1697), and is restated in a shorter form in the *Monadology* (sections 36–8), can be reconstructed thus:

(1) If anything exists, there must be a sufficient reason why it exists.
(2) But this world exists and it is a series of contingent beings.
(3) Therefore, there must be a sufficient reason why this series of contingent beings exists.
(4) Nothing contingent—and, in particular, neither the existing series as a whole nor any of its members—can contain a sufficient reason why this series exists.
(5) A sufficient reason for any existing thing can only be in an existing thing, which is itself either necessary or contingent.
(6) Therefore, a sufficient reason why this series exists must be in a necessary being that lies outside the world.
(7) Therefore, there is a necessary being that lies outside the world.[122]

The arguments of Aquinas and Leibniz have been the object of extensive critical discussion. I begin with Leibniz. Leibniz's argument, as stated here, has been thought open to two separate yet related criticisms. The first questions the need for a principle of sufficient reason by posing the question 'How do we know that everything must have a sufficient reason?'; while the second asks: 'Can there be a necessary being that contains its own sufficient reason?' The criticisms are related because if there is no answer to the second question, it will follow not only that we cannot know that things as a whole can have a sufficient reason, but that such a principle does not exist.[123]

Leibniz thought a reliance upon the principle of sufficient reason (PSR) is implicit in both our theoretical and practical reasoning.[124] He thought that the principle reflects our innate ability to look for and to expect symmetries, continuities, and regularities in the world. On this basis he defined PSR as an a priori principle. However, as Samuel Clarke usefully pointed out in the context of a discussion with Leibniz as to whether or not something like the PSR is implicit in our practical reasoning,[125] even if we have this innate tendency to view the world in certain ways, this does not give us an a priori guarantee that the symmetries, continuities, and regularities that we seek can always be found. In so far as our reliance on such principles as PSR are ever epistemically justifiable, they will be so on grounds that are always a posteriori; that is, by the degree of suc-

[122] Gerhardt vii. 302–3: Loemker 486–7; Gerhardt vi. 612–13: Loemker 646. For helpful commentary on Leibniz's argument, see Adams, *Leibniz: Determinist, Theist, Idealist*, 141 ff.; Rowe, *The Cosmological Argument*, ch. 2; Swinburne, *The Existence of God*, 125–8; Craig, *The Cosmological Argument from Plato to Leibniz*, 257–81.

[123] Cf. Kant's criticism of the cosmological proof. See Wood *Kant's Rational Theology*, 123–9.

[124] See *The Leibniz–Clarke Correspondence*, ed. H. G. Alexander (Manchester, 1976), Leibniz's Second Paper, pp. 15 ff.

[125] Ibid., Clarke's Third and Fifth Replies, pp. 30–5, 97–126.

cess they achieve in interpreting the world. In any case, the counter-argument goes, even if everything in the world had a PSR, or a cause in accordance with some regularity, this would hardly provide us with conclusive grounds for thinking that the world as a whole and its most basic causal laws possess a sufficient reason of a different sort.

PSR expresses an intellectual demand that things in the world should be intelligible objects of knowledge. The reply to the argument on which the principle rests is that there is nothing which can ever justify so stringent a demand, and that there is nothing that provides plausible support for the principle itself. As Clarke recognized, it is difficult to see what conditions could satisfy the principle. The point to note here is that if we reject a version of the cosmological argument which employs the PSR, we are by no means committed to the view that the nature of things is utterly unintelligible. We are simply saying that the methods of inquiry and explanation that we use in our interpretation of the world are not undermined by their inability to make all things in the world intelligible objects of understanding. Although the starting-points of one explanation or inquiry may be clarified and explained by another, this other in turn will have starting-points which are yet unexplained, and so on, however far back we choose to go. The point which the critic of the PSR cosmological argument attempts to press at this stage is that there is no good reason to see this process of explanation and inquiry either as in need of correction, or as unsatisfactory with regard to providing us with reliable, if incomplete, knowledge of the world. The demand that there be an explanation for everything might not be just arbitrary, but might be necessarily unsatisfiable.[126]

This last point is deserving of comment. It has been argued that one of the intellectual advantages of an a posteriori cosmological argument over the ontological argument is that the former is concerned with looking for evidence in the world while the latter is simply concerned with the description of what it is to entertain a certain concept. The reason why an a posteriori cosmological argument has been thought superior is that once sufficient evidence has been gathered and processed and the appropriate conclusion drawn, we are supposed to have a clearer idea of a God 'out there', a God who has not only created the world but sustains it in all its operations.

When we examine the rationale behind Leibniz's arguments, however, we might think that the general philosophical project sustained by his cosmological argument, namely the 'search for evidence', can take us in opposite directions. On the one hand, it can license a concern to explore and interrogate the nature of things in order to search for evidence for the existence of a God. This was certainly the approach of the Kalam philosophers,[127] and it is also implicit in

[126] For a suggestion along this line, see van Inwagen, *Metaphysics*, 104–7. For a different discussion of PSR, see R. Walker, 'Sufficient Reason', *Proceedings of the Aristotelian Society*, 97 (1997), 109–23.

[127] See Craig, *The Kalam Cosmological Argument*, chs. 2–4.

the work of Aquinas. On the other hand, the 'search for evidence' can be a disguise for the expression of an arbitrary demand that there must be an explanation for everything. Such a demand is graphically at work in the Leibnizian PSR, which begins by attending to one of our basic intuitions that because there is something rather than nothing we want to know *why* there is something, and yet concludes with a picture of the universe which might be said to replicate an antecedent intellectual preference for order, harmony, and regularity.

It is important to be aware that Aquinas' cosmological argument of the *tertia via* is concerned with different matters. This argument is based on the simple idea that there is a regress of causes. Although it employs the distinction between things which are contingent (what Aquinas terms *possibilia non esse*) and those which are necessary, it is not content with the conclusion that there is something necessary; for it goes on to argue that there may be many necessary things, and reaches God only once it has established that there is something which has necessity through itself (*per se*).

Traditional lines of criticism to the *tertia via* have usually focused on the second stage of the argument.[128] This part of the argument has been thought invalid for the reason that while it can be argued that we do understand that, if something has an antecedent cause, it depends upon something else, it does not follow that everything (other than God) needs or requires something else, or is dependent on something else in this way. The weakness here, it is claimed, is the requirement that there be a reason for making God the one exception to the supposed need for everything to have something else to depend on. For why should God, rather than anything else, be the only satisfactory termination of the causal regress?[129]

In defence of Aquinas, however, we may well want to give some credence to the view that we do not simply assume that things just happen or that things are just there; we naturally attempt to account for things in terms of something else. To paraphrase a remark made by Peter Geach,[130] if the world is an object, it is certainly pertinent to ask of it causal questions of the sort which would be relevant to a discussion of its parts. If it began to exist, what brought it about? What keeps it from perishing, as some of its parts perish? And what keeps its processes going? In the end someone might simply observe that the universe

[128] The first stage of the argument has also been the object of criticism. This stage is dependent upon the premiss 'what does exist cannot begin to be except through something that is'. This premiss can be identified with the principle that nothing can come from nothing. Some philosophers have thought this premiss problematic. To this end they invoke Hume's point in the *Treatise of Human Nature*, I. iii. 6. There Hume argues against the principle that we can conceive an uncaused beginning-to-be of an object. For a discussion as to whether or not Hume's remarks put the first stage of Aquinas' in jeopardy, see Kenny, *The Five Ways*, 67.

[129] For a clear statement of this argument, see Mackie, *The Miracle of Theism*, 93–4. Cf. Kenny, *The Five Ways*, 47–69.

[130] G. E. M. Anscombe and P. Geach, *The Three Philosophers: Aristotle, Aquinas, Frege* (Oxford, 1961), 112.

goes about its merry way because it is in its nature to continue to exist. But the universe cannot have the nature it has unless it continues to exist, so its continuing to exist can hardly be explained in terms of its nature.[131]

Any final assessment of cosmological arguments like those of Aquinas and Leibniz will turn on the positions that we choose to adopt on the important questions Geach raises. The first is certainly relevant to any determination of the Kalam form of cosmological argument, while the second is certainly relevant to any consideration of Aquinas' *tertia via*. The verdict, if indeed a verdict can be reached, will depend on the outlook we take on the empirical data they provide. In the case of Aquinas, we might conclude that the facts about change and causation upon which his argument is based hold greater promise for grounding a subsequent cosmological proof for God's existence than Leibniz's PSR. It is a further matter, however, whether such a proof could indeed be grounded.

2.3.2. Swinburne's Inductive Cosmological Argument

Richard Swinburne has argued that there is a good inductive variant of the cosmological argument.[132] His account of the existence of a God is linked to a description of inductive or hypothesis-confirming reasoning in general. It might be said that what it means to 'confirm' a certain hypothesis is equivocal. We might think that the confirmation of a hypothesis means (1) that the evidence raises the probability of a certain hypothesis as compared with what it was, or would have been apart from that evidence; or (2) that the evidence increases the verisimilitude of the hypothesis. Swinburne distinguishes what he calls a 'good C-inductive argument', by which he means (1), from a 'good P-inductive argument', by which he means (2).

Swinburne attempts to apply these principles of inductive reasoning to the cosmological argument.[133] He argues that even if the universe has an infinite history in which each event can be causally explained by the conjunction of laws and earlier events, the history of the universe as a whole is still unexplained. The history of the universe might have been different, or else there might not have been a universe at all. Like Leibniz before him, Swinburne argues that no explanation has been offered as to why none of these possibilities was realized. From there, Swinburne suggests that the hypothesis that

[131] Cf. Braine, *On the Reality of Time and the Existence of God*, 10: 'The continuance of the very stuff of the Universe, the fact that it goes on existing, is not self-explanatory. It is incoherent to say that the very stuff of the Universe continues to exist by its very nature since it has to continue to exist in order for this nature to exist or to be operative. Hence, nature presupposes existence.'

[132] Swinburne, *The Existence of God*, 107–32.

[133] Ibid. 130–3. It is important to be aware that Swinburne's version of the cosmological argument as well as his version of the argument from design (see Section 2.4 below) are closely associated with his use of Bayes's theorem. For an exposition of this theorem, see Swinburne, *The Existence of God*, 64–9.

there is a God would help to explain the existence and actual history of the universe.

The crux of Swinburne's argument is to invite us to compare two competing hypotheses that both share the idea that the universe exists: one that there is no further cause or explanation of the complex physical universe, the other that there is a God who created it. Swinburne argues that in relation to our background knowledge—knowledge which can include everything that we know about ourselves and the world—it is more likely that there should be an uncaused God who has created the world than simply an uncaused universe, a universe which is characterized by causal interrelationships but which possesses no further cause for its basic laws being as they are or for its being there at all.

Like other defenders of the cosmological argument, Swinburne's universe is one characterized by order and intelligibility. Unlike his predecessors, he does not go in search of a complete explanation of why the universe exists, such as that provided by a principle of sufficient reason, but rather seeks to limit that part of our picture of the universe which does not lend itself to initial intelligibility. While Swinburne's starting-point is like that of Leibniz, his eventual conclusion is more like that of Aquinas and the Kalam authors, since creation by a person, in this case God, is held to be the most satisfactory explanation of the nature of things. What is to be avoided at all costs is the idea that the universe is simply gratuitous.[134]

2.4. The Argument from Design

This argument has it that the design evident in the world justifies a belief in the existence of a designer. In one version or other, the argument is conspicuous in the work of some Presocratic thinkers, and is to be found in Plato, the Stoics, and Aquinas.[135] However, it is the eighteenth-century version of the argument that Hume and Kant criticized and which early nineteenth-century thinkers like William Paley (1743–1805) defended that has been of most interest to modern philosophers of religion.[136] It is to this version which I shall now turn.

[134] For discussion of Swinburne's argument, see Mackie, *The Miracle of Theism*, 95–101, to which the above is indebted, and Swinburne's reply to Mackie in Swinburne, *The Existence of God*, 293–9; R. W. Prevost, *Probability and Theistic Explanation* (Oxford, 1990). See also Le Poidevin, *Arguing for Atheism*, 33–41.

[135] See Xenophon, *Memorabilia* 1. 4. 4–8; Plato, *Timaeus* 47; Cicero, *De Natura Deorum* 2. 34–5; Aquinas, *Summa Theologiae*, 1a, q. 11, a. 3. A brief history of the argument from design can be found in R. H. Hurlbutt III, *Hume, Newton, and the Design Argument* (Lincoln, Neb., 1965), 95–134. For a discussion of Stoic design arguments, see Gerson, *God and Greek Philosophy*, 154 ff.

[136] See Isaac Newton, *Principia Mathematica*, General Scholium; Bishop Berkeley, *Alciphron*, IV; William Paley, *Natural Theology; or, Evidence of the Existence and Attributes of the Deity Collected from the Appearances of Nature* (London, 1802), 3–12. Other general commentaries on the argument can be found in L. L. Garcia, 'Teleological Arguments and Design Arguments', in Quinn and Taliaferro (eds.), *Companion to the Philosophy*

Near the beginning of part II of his *Dialogues concerning Natural Religion*, Hume presents the design argument through the words of his character Cleanthes. Cleanthes says:

Look around the world: Contemplate the whole and every part of it: You will find it to be nothing but one great machine, subdivided into an infinite number of lesser machines, which again admit subdivisions, to a degree beyond what human senses and faculties can trace and explain. All these various machines, and even their most minute parts, are adjusted to each other with an accuracy, which ravishes into admiration all men, who have ever contemplated them. The curious adapting of means to ends, throughout all nature, resembles exactly, though it much exceeds, the productions of human contrivance; of human design, thought, wisdom, and intelligence. Since therefore the effects resemble each other, we are led to infer, by all the rules of analogy, that the causes also resemble; and that the Author of nature is somewhat similar to the mind of man; though possessed of much larger faculties, proportioned to the grandeur of the work, which he has executed. By this argument *a posteriori*, and by this argument alone, we do prove at once the existence of a Deity, and his similarity to human mind and intelligence.[137]

It is important to note that this is an argument from experience which relies on an analogy. It begins by stating that there is an analogy between a typical feature of nature and a typical feature of what is produced by human contrivance. From this analogy it concludes that the causes of these features are probably similar.

In the *Dialogues* as well as in his *Enquiry concerning Human Understanding*, Hume advances a number of criticisms of the design argument. His first point concerns what we can reliably infer from an effect. When something happens or comes into existence we naturally assume that it was caused, and we proportion the cause to the effect. However, we can only proportion a cause to an effect on the basis of the evidence for doing so. Hume accepts that if the design of the world needs to be explained, then we ought to explain it by appealing to a design-producing being or entity. However, to take a further step and conclude that such a being is 'God' is to go beyond the available evidence.[138]

of Religion; Mackie, *The Miracle of Theism*, 133–49; Swinburne, *The Existence of God*, 133–51; Davies, *An Introduction to the Philosophy of Religion*, 91–119; Dore, *Theism*; T. McPherson, *The Argument from Design* (London, 1972); Le Poidevin, *Arguing for Atheism*, 44–58; and Smart and Haldane, *Atheism and Theism*, 23–7 (for Smart), 121–40 (for Haldane).

[137] David Hume, *Dialogues concerning Natural Religion*, in A. Flew (ed.), *Writings on Religion* (La Salle, Ill., 1992), 203–4. For an extensive discussion of Hume's criticisms of the design argument, see Gaskin, *Hume's Philosophy of Religion*, 11–47.

[138] Hume's first criticism is also echoed by Kant; *Critique of Pure Reason*, A627/B655. There, Kant argues that the argument from design (or what he refers to as 'physico-theological proof') is incapable of establishing the existence of a God who resembles the *ens realissimum* of conventional religion. See Wood, *Kant's Rational Theology*, 130 ff.

Hume's second point is based on the uniqueness of the universe. He says, 'when two species of objects have always been observed to be conjoined together, I can infer . . . the existence of one wherever I see the existence of the other; and I call this an argument from existence'.[139] The problem here, as Hume sees it, is that this inference cannot be used by a defender of the design argument for the following reason: since the universe is unique there is no good reason for inferring that anything like a human designer lies behind its existence. 'To ascertain this reasoning', Hume explains, 'it were requisite, that we had experience of the origin of worlds; and it is not sufficient surely, that we have seen ships and cities arise from human art and contrivance.'[140]

Hume's next argument is directed at the very concept of a designer. He argues that if we posit a designer of the world, we involve ourselves in an infinite regress, for if the actual material world depends upon a similar ideal world, then such an ideal world must depend upon some other world, and so on *ad infinitum*.

To the above arguments Hume adds the following points: (1) that the design argument does not rule out the possibility that the universe was created by 'many designers or gods'; (2) that the universe might easily be a living organism such as a plant, in which case the design argument fails because it depends on the comparison with a machine or artefact; (3) that the putative order in the universe could have come about by simple chance, and (4) that while the universe exudes a degree of order and regularity it also manifests signs of disorder as well.

When Hume's separate objections are brought together they constitute a forceful critique. Recent supporters of the argument such as Swinburne have attempted to meet Hume's objections. Swinburne has it that the argument can be construed as deploying a basic pattern of scientific reasoning to the effect that 'dissimilarities between effects lead the rational man to postulate dissimilarities between causes, and . . . this procedure is basic to inductive inference'.[141] On this basis Swinburne advances his version of the design argument, relying on a notion of temporal order.

For Swinburne, if a deity is to account for the existence of regularities in the universe, then such a being must possess the attributes of freedom, rationality, and power. If the operations of such a being were restricted to one part of the universe, the scientific laws outside his control must operate to ensure that the actions of this being have effects in other parts of the universe. If this were true, Swinburne adds, the postulation that such a being exists would not explain the operations of all scientific laws. Yet, he stresses, to explain the

[139] Flew, Writings on Religion, 210. [140] Ibid.

[141] Swinburne, *The Existence of God*, 149.

operation of all scientific laws is the *point* of postulating the existence of a God. From this, Swinburne concludes that the order of the universe is evidence of the existence of God, first because the occurrence of the universe would be very improbable a priori, and secondly, because of God's character. God has a very good reason for creating an orderly universe if he creates a universe at all.[142]

Swinburne aside, it is important to remember that the argument from design can in most cases be reduced to two components. The first component attempts to show that the world manifests apparent design on analogy with human artefacts. The second step tries to show that the existence of apparent design justifies inference to a designer. In the history of the design argument, philosophers have attempted to justify such an inference in three ways: (1) by appealing to the fact that human artefacts have designers and then by arguing from the analogy; (2) by showing that the design hypothesis is the best explanation of apparent design; and (3) by arguing that the design hypothesis is more probable on the evidence than its rivals.

Labouring under Hume's criticisms, each version of the design argument faces difficulties. Assessment of the claims of the argument hinges upon four things: (1) our assessment of the force of our impression that the world exhibits design, in other words, that the world is like Paley's watch;[143] (2) how we are struck by the differences between the world and human artefacts; (3) the plausibility of competing explanations; and finally (4) our estimate of the competing probabilities of the design hypothesis and its rivals.

By way of conclusion, it is worth remarking that if a version of the design argument proved successful, all it would show is that the world reflects a designer's purposes. As very little would be learned about the nature of the designer's mind, whether, for instance, the designer is omnipotent, omniscient, or perfectly good, one would still have to show that the designer possessed the traditional attributes accorded to God by orthodox Western theology.[144]

[142] Ibid. 146–50. For a helpful discussion of the complex issues raised by Swinburne's argument, see the debate between A. Olding and Swinburne: A. Olding, 'The Argument from Design—A Reply to R. G. Swinburne', *Religious Studies*, 7 (1971), 361–73; Swinburne, 'The Argument from Design—A Reply', *Religious Studies*, 8 (1972), 193–205; Olding, 'Design—A Further Reply', *Religious Studies*, 9 (1973), 229–35. Also worth consulting is Mackie, *The Miracle of Theism*, 146–9, and Olding's later monograph *Modern Biology and Natural Theology* (London, 1991), 131–5, 147–57.

[143] 'When we come to inspect [a] watch we . . . perceive that its parts are framed and put together for a purpose, e.g. that they are so formed and adjusted as to produce motion, and that motion is so regulated as to point out the hour of the day' (*Natural Theology*, 2).

[144] The same point can also be made with equal justice of both versions of the cosmological argument discussed above. This last point serves to show that, in most cases, the God under discussion is the so-called 'God of the philosophers' rather than the God of revelation.

3. PHILOSOPHICAL THEOLOGY

3.1. What is Philosophical Theology?

Philosophical theology is devoted to the study of the concept of God and of the data of revealed theology. Its range of topics traditionally includes the coherence of classical theism, and the claims made about God by the three monotheistic religious traditions: Judaism, Islam, and Christianity. Philosophical theology then proceeds to consider God's relationship to the world.[145] In what follows, I consider what are known as the 'divine attributes', and questions which focus on the relationship of God to the world. Under this head, I shall discuss the so-called problem of evil and conclude with a brief examination of miracles.

3.2. The Divine Attributes

The God of Abraham, Isaac, and Jacob, a God who is recognized and worshipped by Jews, Christians, and Muslims, has been typically described by Western philosophers as possessing distinctive attributes. These attributes have historically been thought by philosophers to 'capture'—in so far as it is ever possible to do this within the purview of imperfect human reason—the essence of God's divinity. Despite great diversity of theological opinion among the different monotheistic traditions of the West, God has traditionally been understood to be: (1) 'simple', or without parts; (2) 'omnipotent', or all powerful; (3) 'omniscient', or all-knowing, and (4) 'perfect', or supremely good. With less than total agreement, God is sometimes held to be 'eternal', 'immutable', and 'timeless'. I consider in turn the first three attributes of God, and then consider eternity, immutability, and timelessness. I conclude with a discussion of divine perfection.[146]

3.2.1. Divine Simplicity

The doctrine of divine simplicity upholds the idea that God has no 'parts', that is, that there are no components to God. On this ground it is held that God has

[145] For a recent introduction to the subject, see T. V. Morris, *Our Idea of God: An Introduction to Philosophical Theology* (Notre Dame, Ind., 1991). A more exacting guide to the subject is provided by Ross, *Philosophical Theology*. Further guides are provided by Kenny, *The God of the Philosophers* and Hughes, *The Nature of God*. Other articles relevant to a wide range of topics within philosophical theology are contained in T. V. Morris (ed.), *The Concept of God* (Oxford, 1987).

[146] A general discussion of the issues pertaining to the attributes of God can be found in W. Mann, 'The Divine Attributes', *American Philosophical Quarterly*, 12 (1975), 151–9, and E. R. Wierenga, *The Nature of God* (Ithaca, NY, 1989).

no properties—God does not contain any property which is either essential or accidental to him. If God has no properties, then God has no spatial extension; so, God cannot be located in any finite space. Further to this, the doctrine holds that God does not have any temporal extension; thus, there is no division of God's life into past or future stages that would imply temporal compositeness.[147] Many supporters of the doctrine of divine simplicity are motivated by the consideration that God is a perfect being, and that, *qua* perfect, God must be independent of all other things to account for his being what he is. God must be sovereign over all other things.[148]

The upshot of the doctrine of divine simplicity is that anyone who holds that God is 'simple' cannot say that God has attributes. For example, one cannot say that God is omnipotent because for God the metaphysical distinction between a substance and its attributes does not apply. As Aquinas famously put it, God *is* his existence, or *is* his omnipotence, or *is* his omniscience, etc., where the 'is' here expresses identity. It follows from this, of course, that the omniscience of God is also the omnipotence of God and vice versa.[149]

Stated thus, divine simplicity appears counter-intuitive, for it seems to involve commitment to the view that there are no distinctions in God. This makes any attribute of God the same as any other attribute; God is identical with each of his actions, and by implication, each of his actions is the same as any other action. A further consequence is that no descriptive predicates can ever be true of God. This is alarming because it appears to rule out not only those benign yet trite ways of talking about God employed by 'piazza preachers' and fundamentalists of all persuasions, but also the traditional attributes of omniscience, omnipotence, perfection, eternity, and immutability. As a result of these difficulties—further compounded by the criticisms of Hume and Kant[150]—simplicity has historically been considered to be one of the more problematic attributes of God.

Recently, however, defences of the traditional doctrine have been

[147] For the *locus classicus* of this view, see John Scotus Eriugena (*c*.800/815–*c*.870), *Periphyseon*, I. 12; and St Anselm, *Monologion*, 21; and *Proslogion*, 20. The doctrine of divine simplicity was also held by Aquinas, see *Summa Theologiae*, 1a, q. 3, a. 7; and *Summa contra Gentiles*, I. 18. Versions of the thesis were also held by Maimonides and Averröes. For a general discussion of this topic, see E. Stump, 'Simplicity', in Quinn and Taliaferro (eds.), *Companion to the Philosophy of Religion*.

[148] A helpful discussion of many issues relating to divine simplicity can be found in A. Plantinga, *Does God Have a Nature?* (Milwaukee, 1980), 28–37. Plantinga's views are criticized by D. Burrell in *Knowing the Unknowable God: Ibn-Sina, Maimonides, Aquinas* (Notre Dame, Ind., 1986), 51–91. A general discussion of the issues can be found in Hughes, *The Nature of God*, 34–63.

[149] For a discussion of Aquinas' doctrine of divine simplicity, see Davies, *The Thought of Thomas Aquinas*, 44–57; Hughes, *The Nature of God*, 34–50; R. M. Burns, 'Divine Simplicity in St. Thomas', *Religious Studies*, 25 (1989), 271–93. The most sophisticated monograph on this subject is by C. Hughes, *On the Complex Theory of a Simple God* (Ithaca, NY, 1989), 3–152.

[150] As we saw in our discussion of the ontological argument (Section 2.2.2 above), Kant thought that it was impossible to provide any sort of link between the notions of absolute necessity and simplicity, while Hume argues that the notion of divine simplicity is vacuous (*Dialogues*, IV).

attempted.[151] One of the more striking contributions to this debate is the work of Christopher Hughes.[152] Hughes argues that if the doctrine is to be restated plausibly, it must detach itself from one of its traditional modes of exposition, the account of divine simplicity offered by Aquinas. The crux of Hughes's case is that we do not have to agree with Aquinas when he claims that 'Nothing distinct from God is a part of God' entails 'God is the same as his intrinsic attributes, essence, and existence', for the reason that the intrinsic attributes, essence, and existence of an individual are all, broadly construed, parts or components of that individual. If we resist this assumption, Hughes argues, there is no good reason why we cannot suppose that God is the same as all his intrinsic attributes etc., since neither they nor anything else are both a part of God and distinct from God. In this way, the idea that God is simple—an idea that Aquinas sought to uphold—can be preserved at the expense of jettisoning Aquinas' compositional account of attribute, essence, and existence.[153]

3.2.2. *Omnipotence*

Western theists have traditionally held that God is 'omnipotent', or all-powerful. As this term has been historically understood, omnipotence is taken to imply that God is able to do anything. What does this mean? This is a difficult question because these same theists are prone to build into their definition the thought that there are many things that God *cannot* do. For example, Augustine claimed that God is unable to die or be deceived,[154] Anselm postulated that 'God cannot be corrupted, or tell lies, or make the true into the false (such as to undo what has been done),'[155] and Aquinas provides a list of things God cannot do such as move, fail, tire, and nullify the past.[156]

[151] See W. Mann, 'Divine Simplicity', *Religious Studies*, 18 (1982), 451–71; T. V. Morris, 'Of God and Mann', *Religious Studies*, 21 (1985), 299–318; repr. in *Anselmian Explorations* (Notre Dame, Ind., 1987); with a reply by Mann, 'Simplicity and Properties', *Religious Studies*, 22 (1986), 343–53; E. Stump and N. Kretzmann, 'Absolute Simplicity', *Faith and Philosophy*, 2 (1985), 353–82; B. Leftow, 'Is God an Abstract Object?', *Nous*, 24 (1990), 581–98; N. Wolterstorff, 'Divine Simplicity', *Philosophical Perspectives*, 5 (1991), 531–52; W. Vallicella, 'Divine Simplicity: A New Defense', *Faith and Philosophy*, 9 (1992), 508–25; R. M. Adams, 'Divine Necessity', *Journal of Philosophy*, 80 (1983), 741–52; repr. in *The Virtue of Faith and Other Essays in Philosophical Theology* (Oxford, 1987), 209–20. For a very helpful historical 'corrective' to recent defences of the doctrine, see K. Rogers, 'The Traditional Doctrine of Divine Simplicity', *Religious Studies*, 32 (1996), 165–86.

[152] Hughes, *On the Complex Theory of a Simple God*, chs. 2, 3.

[153] Ibid., ch. 7 and conclusion. For a discussion of Hughes's thesis, see the review of his book by N. Kretzmann and T. O'Connor, *Faith and Philosophy*, 9 (1992), 526–34. A philosophical discussion of the attributes of the Christian deity can be found in R. G. Swinburne, *The Christian God* (Oxford, 1994).

[154] *De Civitate Dei* ('City of God'), 5. x.

[155] *Proslogion*, 8.

[156] *Summa contra Gentiles*, 1. 2. 25; Cf. *De Potentia*, q. 1, a. 7, where Aquinas argues that God cannot be said to be omnipotent in the sense of being simply able to do everything (*quia omnia possit absolute*). Similar thoughts have also been expressed outside the Christian tradition; see e.g. Moses Maimonides, *Guide of the Perplexed*, 1. 15.

The very diversity of inabilities putatively consistent with being omnipotent may seem to make the task of giving a clear account of the attribute somewhat forlorn. As Peter Geach impatiently remarked:

When people have tried to read into 'God can do anything' a signification not of Pious Intention but of Philosophical Truth, they have only landed themselves in intractable problems and hopeless confusions; no graspable sense has ever been given to this sentence that did not lead to self-contradiction or at least to conclusions manifestly untenable from the Christian point of view.[157]

Geach's disapproval aside, many recent philosophers have offered arguments that attempt to make the concept of omnipotence coherent.[158] One such is that omnipotence can be understood in terms of God's ability to bring about certain states of affairs. This is then specified to mean that God can do all things that are *logically possible*. The idea that any coherent understanding of omnipotence has to be linked to the province of logical possibility is expressed by Aquinas, who says:

God is called omnipotent because he can do all things that are possible absolutely (*omnia possibilia absolute*) . . . For a thing is said to be possible or impossible absolutely when regard is had only to its terms. It is absolutely possible because the predicate is not repugnant to the subject, as that Socrates should sit; and absolutely impossible when the predicate is altogether repugnant to the subject, as for instance, that a man is a donkey (*asinum*).[159]

If, for the purposes of exposition, omnipotence is defined in this way,[160] it is still a matter for discussion whether the concept of the attribute itself is

[157] P. Geach, *Providence and Evil* (Cambridge, 1977), 4. For a more recent argument that omnipotence is impossible to define, see R. LaCroix, 'The Impossibility of Defining "Omnipotence"', *Philosophical Studies*, 32 (1977) 181–90. For other criticisms of the concept, see Kenny, *The God of the Philosophers*, 91–120, and Gale, *On the Nature and Existence of God*, 99–107.

[158] See J. Hoffmann and G. Rosenkrantz, 'Omnipotence', in Quinn and Taliaferro (eds.), *Companion to the Philosophy of Religion*; G. Mavrodes, 'Some Puzzles concerning Omnipotence', *Philosophical Review*, 72 (1963), 221–3; 'Defining Omnipotence', *Philosophical Studies*, 32 (1977), 191–202; Swinburne, *The Coherence of Theism*, ch. 9; G. Rosenkrantz and J. Hoffmann, 'What an Omnipotent Agent Can Do', *International Journal for Philosophy of Religion*, 11 (1980), 1–9; T. Flint and A. Freddoso, 'Maximal Power', in Freddoso (ed.), *The Existence and Nature of God*; S. Davis, *Logic and the Nature of God* (London, 1983), ch. 5; Wierenga, *The Nature of God*, 12–35. An excellent survey of these issues which contains a helpful discussion of the history of the concept as well as much original commentary can be found in Hughes, *The Nature of God*, 114–51.

[159] *Summa Theologiae*, 1a, q. 25, a. 3.

[160] It is important to note that not all theists have accepted this definition of omnipotence. Perhaps the most infamous of this number was the 11th-century scholastic St Peter Damian (1007–72), a. k. a. 'Peter Damian the ridiculous'. In his *De Divina Omnipotentia* ('On Divine Omnipotence'; in J. P. Migne (ed.), *Patrologia Latina*, vol. cxlv, cols. 595 ff.; Eng. trans. in Wippel and Wolter (eds.), *Medieval Philosophy*), Damian argued that God, if he chose to do so, could make a virgin out of a non-virgin. Many of Damian's contemporaries, as well as numerous historians of philosophy, have accused Damian of holding to the doctrine that God can bring about self-contradictory states of affairs. For a discussion of why this accusation is groundless, see Kenny, *The God of the Philosophers*, 200–2. A more comprehensive discussion of Damian's work on this topic can be found in I. M. Resnick, *Divine Power and Possibility in St. Peter Damian's 'De Divina Omnipotentia'* (Leiden, 1992).

coherent. This last point can be illustrated by the famous 'paradox of the stone' as set out by Wade Savage.[161] The paradox can be restated thus:

(1) Either x can create a stone that x cannot lift, or x cannot create a stone that x cannot lift.
(2) If x can create a stone that x cannot lift, then, necessarily, there is at least one task that x cannot perform (namely, lift the stone in question).
(3) If x cannot create a stone that x cannot lift, then, necessarily, there is at least one act that x cannot perform (namely, create the stone in question).
(4) Hence, there is at least one act or task that x cannot perform.
(5) If x is an omnipotent being, then x can perform any task.
(6) Therefore, x is not omnipotent.

Since x could be any being whatsoever, it is advanced that the argument stated in (1–6) proves that the notion of omnipotence discussed above is incoherent.

The first matter to consider when examining the paradox is that, as observed above, some theists have held that there are some things God cannot do. God cannot create free and autonomous beings, with the capacity for choosing between right and wrong, without yielding his complete control over them. Can God make a world he cannot control? Can God limit his own omnipotence? Historically, theologians and philosophers have been divided on this matter. Some have held that God cannot give up omnipotence, for he is essentially omnipotent and doing so would weaken his powers. Others have responded by arguing that a God who can voluntarily limit himself is more powerful than a God who cannot. For these philosophers and theologians, God's omnipotence is non-essential.

How one answers the paradox of the stone will depend upon which of the above two views are accepted. George Mavrodes, for example, accepts the first alternative, arguing that God is essentially omnipotent and so cannot create a stone heavier than he can lift, for the reason that such an act is logically impossible.[162] Yet it might be thought that Mavrodes's solution is question-begging since it presupposes that the statement 'God is omnipotent' is necessarily true.

A second response to the paradox is offered by Harry Frankfurt.[163] Frankfurt argues that if God is able to do one impossible thing, namely make a stone heavier than can he lift, he can also do a second impossible thing and lift that stone. If this is true, Frankfurt argues, then the paradox does not show that the

[161] C. Wade Savage, 'The Paradox of the Stone', *Philosophical Review*, 76 (1967), 74–9. It is important to note that Savage thinks that the argument set out above is fallacious, in that it does not follow from the fact that God cannot create a stone he cannot lift that there is a task God cannot perform.

[162] Mavrodes, 'Some Puzzles concerning Omnipotence' and 'Defining Omnipotence'.

[163] H. G. Frankfurt, 'The Logic of Omnipotence', *Philosophical Review*, 73 (1964), 262–3.

notion of omnipotence is paradoxical. A third response is offered by Swinburne, who argues that God's omnipotence would enable him to create such a stone, but this fact does not diminish God's omnipotence, unless of course God does indeed create such a stone.[164] The point here is that the omnipotence of God at a certain time includes the ability to make himself no longer omnipotent, yet this is an ability which God may or may not choose to exercise. As Swinburne remarks, '[a] person may remain omnipotent forever because he never exercises his power to create stones too heavy to lift, forces too strong to resist, or universes too wayward to control'.[165]

A further difficulty faced by the concept of omnipotence concerns the question whether God's omnipotence affords him licence to sin. In other words, if it is in God's nature to possess the ability to do everything, is it in his nature to sin? Scholastics, such as Aquinas, argued that God's power to do so, if it existed at all, could only be classified as a pseudo-power. Later scholastics, following Occam, argued that God necessarily cannot sin, for the reason that sin is always to be defined as that which is opposed to God's will, and God can never will and oppose his own will, at one and the same time.[166] Recently, Swinburne has argued that an omniscient and perfectly free being cannot sin because sin necessarily involves a failure in reason or freedom.[167] Nelson Pike, on the other hand, has argued that omnipotence includes the ability to sin. In this sense, it is logically possible for God to bring about evil. However, it is unlikely that God will ever sin because he always happens to will the good. Thus, God cannot bring himself to disseminate evil since that would violate a stable feature of his nature.[168]

In summary, then, we might conclude that any characterization and discussion of God's power will always be subject to logical constraints. The characterization of omnipotence will always be limited by the nature and perfections of God, which will include reference to God's goodness. The freedom of finite

[164] Swinburne, *The Coherence of Theism*, 157 ff. Cf. Plantinga, *Does God Have a Nature?*, 95–140.

[165] Swinburne, *The Coherence of Theism*, 161.

[166] It is noteworthy that, unlike Aquinas, Occam did not believe God's omnipotence could be conclusively proved by philosophical argument, but had to be accepted as a tenet of faith. Notwithstanding this proviso, Occam has interesting things to say on omnipotence, which can be found in his *Ordinatio* and *Quodlibeta Septem*. For an exhaustive discussion of Occam's views, see M. McCord Adams, *William Ockham*, ii. 1151 ff. An interesting discussion of scholastic accounts of omnipotence up to Aquinas can be found in L. Moonan, *Divine Power: The Medieval Power Distinction up to its Adoption by Albert, Bonaventure, and Aquinas* (Oxford, 1994). See also C. G. Normore, 'Divine Omniscience, Omnipotence, and Future Contingents: An Overview', in T. Rudavsky, *Divine Omniscience and Omnipotence in Medieval Philosophy: Islamic, Jewish and Christian Perspectives* (Dordrecht, 1985).

[167] Swinburne, *The Coherence of Theism*, 292 ff. Cf. Ross, *Philosophical Theology*, 196–211.

[168] N. Pike, 'Omnipotence and God's Ability to Sin', *American Philosophical Quarterly*, 6 (1969), 208–16. For a different view on these matters which argues that one cannot coherently hold (1) that there is evil; (2) God is all-powerful; and (3) God is all-good, see J. L. Mackie, 'Evil and Omnipotence', in Mitchell (ed.), *The Philosophy of Religion*. It is important to note that Mackie leaves open the idea that omnipotence is coherent.

moral agents may impose a further set of restrictions, but these are best discussed under a different head; see Section 3.3 below.

3.2.3. Omniscience

God's omniscience is taken to mean that God knows everything. For the purposes of discussion we can define 'knowledge' in the following way: We can say that a person knows some proposition *p* when (1) the agent believes *p* is true; (2) *p* is true; and (3) the person has an adequate justification for his belief that *p* is true.[169] On this basis, God's omniscience can be defined thus: For any proposition, God knows whether it is true or false; that is, God's beliefs are justified and true and God holds no false beliefs. Certain questions immediately arise from this definition. For example, some propositional knowledge depends upon experiential knowledge, but experiential knowledge is particular to an individual knower. If I cannot experience how your coffee tastes to you, for example, how can God be said to know our experiences if they are truly ours? Is God's experience of our suffering the same as our actual experience of suffering when he looks within us? And does God need to assume corporeal form in order to experience the kinds of sensations that are peculiar to us?[170]

Historically, discussion of omniscience has been dominated by a specific worry: Is human freedom compatible with divine omniscience? If God knows everything, then God knows everything that is, was, and will be. Therefore, God has foreknowledge of what is going to happen. Is such foreknowledge compatible with human freedom? If God now knows that you will do something in the future, e.g. buy a red car, can you nevertheless be 'free' to do otherwise, e.g. buy a blue car? In the history of discussion of this issue, some have argued that there is no contradiction between human freedom and divine omniscience for the reason that every action is determined, whether or not God knows which action we will perform. Against this view, others have argued that there are significant problems in reconciling the two positions.[171]

[169] I realize that this definition of knowledge is controversial and is open to many famous counter-examples, not least those derived from the work of Edmund Gettier.

[170] For a discussion of these questions as well as a general discussions of omniscience, see G. Mavrodes, 'Omnscience', in Quinn and Taliaferro (eds.), *Companion to the Plilosophy of Religion*; Hughes, *The Nature of God*, 64–113; Wierenga, *The Nature of God*, 36–58; J. Kvanvig, *The Possibility of an All-Knowing God* (London, 1986); Kenny, *The God of the Philosophers*, 15–48; Swinburne, *The Coherence of Theism*, 167–83; A. Prior, 'The Formalities of Omniscience', *Philosophy*, 37 (1962), 119–29; repr. in *Papers on Time and Tense* (Oxford, 1968); N. Wolterstorff, 'God Everlasting', in S. Cahn and D. Shatz (eds.), *Contemporary Philosophy of Religion* (New York, 1982).

[171] The central historical protagonists in this debate—a debate which has its origins in ancient Greek discussions of fatalism—up to the late 16th century include Augustine, Boethius, Aquinas, Occam, and Molina. For a discussion of their individual contributions, see W. Lane Craig, *The Problem of Divine Foreknowledge and Future Contingents from Aristotle to Suarez* (Leiden, 1988). For further discussion of these medieval thinkers, see C. Normore, 'Future Contingents', in Kretzmann *et al.* (eds.), *The Cambridge History of Later Medieval*

It is noteworthy that there is no a priori difficulty in attempting to reconcile knowledge and freedom. Take the following example. In the course of giving a lecture, I may predict that the students will leave the classroom at the end of the lecture. Knowing a good deal about a particular student, say a young man with a penchant for strict time-keeping, I might predict that he will leave the room as soon as the lecture is finished. I am justified in my belief that the student will do this, because he has always done this, and I know that being a stickler for time-keeping he cannot bear to be late for an appointment. Seen from this perspective, we might ordinarily say that I 'know' that the student will rush out of my lecture to his next appointment. The point to note here, however, is that my knowing in no way constrains the student's freedom. One day, for instance, due to the unlikely event of his being stimulated by the topic of my lecture, he might not rush out of the room in order to get to his next appointment but instead might choose to tarry awhile in the classroom and ask me exacting questions about it. Such observations, it is argued, show that if we are really free, our free acts will not depend on whether or not anyone knows what we will do, for in itself, knowledge does not cause actions. My knowing that the student will rush out of the classroom to keep his next appointment has nothing to do with whether or not he is necessitated to do so.

If, in the above example, knowledge and freedom do not conflict, can we not hold that God's foreknowledge in no way causes us to act as we do? Many philosophers such as Augustine and Boethius have argued that we can apply these insights to God because God's knowledge of human actions is *contingent* upon what human beings will do. Thus, God's knowledge is contingent upon the actual choices we make and the actions we in fact perform.[172]

Philosophy, 358–81; Kenny, *The God of the Philosophers*, 51–87; R. Gaskin: 'Conditionals of Freedom and Middle Knowledge', *Philosophical Quarterly*, 43 (1993), 412–30; 'Fatalism, Foreknowledge and the Reality of the Future', *Modern Schoolman*, 71 (1994), 83–113; 'Molina on Divine Foreknowledge and the Principle of Bivalence', *Journal of the History of Philosophy*, 32 (1994), 551–71. Recent contributions to the debate include Kvanvig, *The Possibility of an All-Knowing God*, 72–171; W. Hasker, *God, Time and Knowledge* (Ithaca, 1989); Wierenga, *The Nature of God*, 59–165; J. R. Lucas, *The Future: An Essay on God, Temporality and Truth* (Oxford, 1989); W. Lane Craig, *Divine Foreknowledge and Human Freedom* (Leiden, 1991); L. Zagzebski, *The Dilemma of Freedom and Foreknowledge* (New York, 1991). The most important journal articles on the subject up to 1988 are collected in J. M. Fischer (ed.), *God, Foreknowledge and Freedom* (Stanford, Calif., 1989). More recent articles by R. M. Adams, 'An Anti-Molinist Argument', *Philosophical Perspectives*, 5 (1991), 343–54, and T. Flint, 'Middle Knowledge and the Doctrine of Infallibility', *Philosophical Perspectives*, 5 (1991), 373–94, are also worth consulting. A helpful summary of the central issues is provided by L. Zagzebski, 'Foreknowledge and Human Freedom', in Quinn and Taliaferro (eds.), *Companion to the Philosophy of Religion*.

[172] Augustine, *De Libero Arbitrio* ('On Free Will'), 3. iv, and Boethius, *De Consolatione Philosophiae* ('On the Consolation of Philosophy'), 5. 3. For a discussion of Augustine's arguments, see W. L. Rowe, 'Augustine on Foreknowledge and Free Will', *Review of Metaphysics*, 18 (1964–5), 353–63, and J. Hopkins, 'Augustine on Foreknowledge and Free Will', *International Journal for Philosophy of Religion*, 8 (1977), 111–26; on Boethius, see P. Huber, *De Vereinbarkeit von göttlicher Vorsehung und menschlicher Freiheit in der 'Consolatio Philosophiae' des Boethius* (Zurich, 1976), 12–28, and M. Davies, 'Boethius and Others on Divine Foreknowledge', *Pacific Philosophical Quarterly*, 64 (1983), 313–29. For further discussion, see Craig, *The Problem of Divine Foreknowledge*, 59–98.

Others, however, have objected to the comparison of our knowledge with divine knowledge. They argue that the contingency mentioned above only applies to finite human knowledge. At time *t* I believe that the student will leave the classroom. The student can cause it to be the case that I have a false belief by tarrying after the lecture has finished. God's knowledge, it is held, is not like my contingent knowledge but is *necessary*. In other words, we cannot bring it about by our actions that God believes any falsehoods. If this is true, then we are confronted with a further question: if God, by virtue of his omniscience believes at time *t* that the student will rush out of the classroom at time t_1, how can the student be 'free' to tarry?

The classical position of Augustine, Boethius, and others commits one to the view that at time *t* God believes that the student will rush out of the classroom at t_1, and that it is in the power of the student to refrain from rushing out of the classroom. If this is to act as an answer to the question posed above, then three possibilities present themselves: (1) the student could have brought it about at t_1 that God held a false belief; (2) even though it was in the power of the student to bring it about that God really did not believe that he would rush out of the classroom at t_1 he did hold this belief; or, (3) it was in the power of the student to do something that would have brought it about that any person who believed that he would rush out of the classroom held a false belief and hence was not God.

Since (1–3) seem to contradict both the claims that God is omniscient and that humans act freely, it might be argued that the implications of God's omniscience reveal that it is incompatible with human freedom. We appear to be confronted with the following choice: either we must understand God's omniscience in terms that are at variance with the classical account, or we must be prepared to admit that humans are not really free.[173]

Such a choice might be avoided if we draw a distinction between facts about the past that do not logically include facts about the future and facts about the past that do. The fact that Aquinas travelled from Naples to Paris in the thirteenth century is an example of the first, while the fact that Aquinas died before I completed this chapter is an example of the second. Facts about the past that do not include facts about the future are unalterable. Some facts about the past that include facts about the future, however, are neither unalterable nor necessary in this sense. It may be true that Aquinas died before I finished this chapter and that this is a fact about the past, but the point of importance here is that until I actually complete this chapter, I have the power to bring it about that the fact does not hold.[174]

[173] For a view of this kind, see N. Pike, 'Divine Omniscience and Voluntary Action', *Philosophical Review*, 74 (1965), 27–46; repr. in Fischer, *God, Foreknowledge and Freedom*. Cf. A. Plantinga, 'On Ockham's Way Out', *Faith and Philosophy*, 3 (1986), 235–69; repr. in Morris (ed.), *The Concept of God*.

[174] A helpful discussion of these distinctions can be found in M. McCord Adams, 'Is the Existence of God a "Hard Fact?"', *Philosophical Review*, 76 (1967), 492–503; repr. in Fischer (ed.), *God, Foreknowledge and Freedom*. J. Hoffmann and G. Rosenkrantz, 'Hard and Soft Facts', *Philosophical Review*, 93 (1984), 419–34; repr. in Fischer, *God, Foreknowledge and Freedom*, argue that these distinctions are not so easily drawn.

Many philosophers consider the above line of thought important because they see God's beliefs about the future as facts about the past that logically include facts about the future. But, as noted above, some, if not all, facts about the past that logically include facts about the future *depend* upon the future. God's beliefs about what the student will do might be facts of this kind. If they are, then even though God might believe that the student will rush out of the classroom, and even though God's beliefs might be mistaken, the student has the power to bring it about that God never believed this. The student can rush out of the classroom or he can stay behind. If he rushes out, then God has always believed that he would rush out. If he does not, God has always believed that he would not. Thus, God's beliefs about what the student will do depend upon what in fact the student does. Hence the fact that God's beliefs about the future cannot be mistaken do not reveal that the student's actions are not free. The classical position is retained.

Some, however, question whether this restatement of the classical position is acceptable. They argue that while some facts about the past that logically include facts about the future depend upon the future others do not. For instance, the sentence 'Louis de Bernières finished a certain novel last year' entails 'Louis de Bernières will not be finishing that novel next year'. Thus, the fact that Louis de Bernières finished his novel last year logically includes a fact about the future, yet in this case the future fact depends upon a past fact and not vice versa. Likewise, if God is essentially omnipotent, it is necessarily true that if he has determined that I will bicycle to college tomorrow, then I will bicycle to college. Here a past fact (God's predetermination) logically includes a fact in its future (my bicycling to college), but it does not depend upon it. This shows, the counter-argument says, that the fact that God's foreknowledge logically includes facts about the future is not sufficient to show that it depends upon the future; some facts about the past that include facts about the future depend upon the future and others do not.[175]

It is important to be aware that many of the traditional discussions of divine foreknowledge (here one thinks of the positions of Augustine, Boethius, Aquinas, and Occam, to name the best known) presuppose that there are truths about the future and that if God is omniscient, he must accordingly know them.[176] In more recent discussions of this issue, however, many philosophers have thought that to the extent that the future is open, there aren't 'now' truths about how it will turn out.[177] If this is right, then the very question how can God

[175] See P. Helm, 'Divine Foreknowledge and Facts', *Canadian Journal of Philosophy*, 4 (1974), 305–15. For other significant papers by Helm relating to this and related issues, see 'On Theological Fatalism', *Philosophical Quarterly*, 24 (1974), 360–2; 'Fatalism Once More', *Philosophical Quarterly*, 25 (1975), 289–96; 'Timelessness and Foreknowledge', *Mind*, 84 (1975), 516–27; 'Foreknowledge and Possibility', *Canadian Journal of Philosophy*, 6 (1976), 731–4.

[176] See Normore, 'Divine Omniscience, Omnipotence, and Future Contingents', 10–22.

[177] Many modern discussions of this issue have taken their cue from an interpretation of Aristotle's *De Interpretatione* 9. For discussions of this type, see G. Ryle, *Dilemmas* (Cambridge, 1954), ch. 2; G. E. M.

know future contingents has a false presupposition, namely that there are future contingent propositions to be known.[178]

In conclusion, then, the problem of the relation of divine foreknowledge and human freedom, specified as a problem about the status of God's knowledge of future contingents, has presented two perennial problems in philosophical theology. The first concerns how God knows future contingents, and the second whether God's knowledge of such things is ever compatible with human freedom. The ingenious and subtle arguments offered by recent philosophers testifies to the fact that interest in this most difficult yet fascinating of topics is far from declining.

3.2.4. Eternity, Timelessness, and Immutability

The idea that God is eternal has been traditionally expressed in two separate ways: that God is *timeless*, and that God is *everlasting*.[179] The first idea was widely held by the schoolmen. In scholastic philosophical theology there was a tradition of argument according to which eternity is distinct from time. This tradition was greatly influenced by Neoplatonism.[180] While a defence of eternity can be found in Augustine and Anselm, the idea is lucidly articulated by Boethius in his much quoted axiom *Aeternitas est interminabilis vitae tota simul et perfecta possessio* ('Eternity is the complete and total possession of unending life all at once').[181] The idea here is that God has no beginning or end, no birth or

Anscombe, 'Aristotle and the Sea Battle', *Mind*, 65 (1956), 1–15; R. Sorabji, *Necessity, Cause and Blame: Perspectives on Aristotle's Theory* (London, 1980), pt. II.

[178] This position has been advanced by Arthur Prior. For Prior it is not obvious that if God is omniscient, he knows everything I will do tomorrow. Against the traditional position (here the target is the Occamist) Prior says, 'I think I can attach intelligible senses to the phrases "was *true* yesterday" and "*was the case* yesterday" . . . but I cannot find any such sense for "was *known* yesterday." I can cause a person's guess made yesterday to have been correct by my free choice tomorrow. I can also verify a person's guess right now that the person's guess yesterday was indeed correct. But I don't see how these contingent futures or future-infected pasts can be known. The alleged knowledge would be no more than correct guessing. For there would be *ex hypothesi* nothing that could make it knowledge, no present ground for the guess's correctness which a specially penetrating person might perceive.' See Prior, 'The Formalities of Omniscience', 35–6. For other defences of this view, see R. Thomason, 'Indeterminist Time and Truth-Vale Gaps', *Theoria*, 36 (1970), 264–81; J. Burgess, 'The Unreal Future', *Theoria*, 44 (1978), 157–79. Cf. Lucas, *The Future*, 161 208.

[179] A general survey of these notions can be found in B. Leftow, 'Eternity', in Quinn and Taliaferro (eds.), *Companion to the Philosophy of Religion*. N. Pike, *God and Timelessness* (London, 1970); R. L. Sturch, 'The Problem of Divine Eternity', *Religious Studies*, 10 (1974), 487–93; Kenny, *The God of the Philosophers*, 38–48; Davis, *Logic and the Nature of God*, 9–24; Wierenga, *The Nature of God*, 166–201; Hasker, *God, Time and Knowledge*, 144–85; B. Leftow, *Time and Eternity* (Ithaca, NY, 1990).

[180] Plotinus argues that things subject to time are changing things, which may be contrasted with intelligence (*nous*), which is not subject to time and is eternal. Time, says Plotinus, is 'the life of the soul in a movement of passage from one way of life to another', and eternity is the life of the intelligible world without successiveness; *Enneads* 3. 7. 2.

[181] *De Consolatione Philosophiae*, 5. An interesting discussion of this definition can be found in Sorabji, *Time, Creation and the Continuum*, 115 ff. For a recent and widely discussed defence of the classical position, see E. Stump and N. Kretzmann, 'Eternity', *Journal of Philosophy*, 78 (1981), 429–458; repr. in Morris (ed.), *The Concept of God*. Cf. K. A. Rogers, 'Eternity has no Duration', *Religious Studies*, 30 (1994), 1–16.

death, and that God differs from all other creatures in that his life is unlimited. God does not 'live' a life in time; God has no history.[182]

According to the second idea, 'God is eternal' means that God is sempiternal, or everlasting. This means that God is not outside time. Sempiternality is a twofold thesis claiming: (1) there was no time when God did not exist, and (2) there will be no time when God will not exist. For supporters of sempiternality, (1) and (2) encapsulate what is meant by the divine attribute of eternity.[183]

Until very recently, the scholastic doctrine that God exists in a timeless eternity was considered problematic. The arguments used against it derived from two sources. The first owes itself to W. C. Kneale, who argued that the classical statement of divine eternity is incoherent. If earlier theologians like Boethius understood eternity to mean 'the complete and total possession of eternal life all at once', then, argued Kneale, it was impossible to understand the word 'life' in this context, since life must involve some incidents in time, and if, following Boethius, we are to suppose that the life in question is intelligent, then such a life must involve an awareness of the passage of time.[184]

A second source of opposition to the idea of God's timelessness had their origins in a paper by Prior, who claimed that the notion of timelessness is placed in doubt by the formal requirements of omniscience. He argued that a proposition 'It is raining now' is not equivalent to 'It is raining on Tuesday'. The point here is that an omniscient individual who knew the second proposition would not necessarily know the first, and would necessarily not know it if he were timeless, for the reason that he could not be present on the occasion on which it was raining.[185]

At present, the discussion of these issues is dominated by recent defences of one version or other of the scholastic position. Influential studies by Helm, Leftow, and by Stump and Kretzmann have significantly advanced the debate by clarifying its central issues in contemporary terms.[186] The consequence of these discussions has been to focus interest on the four central concepts of divine eternity: 'life', 'illimitability', 'duration', and 'timelessness'. The discussion and

[182] For a sophisticated defence of this doctrine, see P. Helm, *Eternal God* (Oxford, 1988).

[183] See M. Kneale, 'Eternity and Sempiternity', *Proceedings of the Aristotelian Society*, 69 (1968–9), 223–38; Swinburne, *The Coherence of Theism*, 217–38; Lucas, 'The Future', 211–21.

[184] W. Kneale, 'Time and Eternity in Theology', *Proceedings of the Aristotelian Society*, 61 (1960–1), 87–108. Kneale's arguments were later taken up by J. R. Lucas, *A Treatise on Space and Time* (London, 1973), 300 ff., and by Swinburne, *The Coherence of Theism*, ch. 12.

[185] See Prior, *The Formalities of Omniscience*. Prior's argument has been developed and used by N. Kretzmann, 'Omniscience and Immutability', *Journal of Philosophy*, 63 (1966), 409–21, and Wolterstorff, 'God Everlasting'. The plausibility of this line of argument, however, is denied by H. N. Castaneda, 'Omniscience and Indexical Reference', *Journal of Philosophy*, 64 (1967), 203–10, and by Swinburne, *The Coherence of Theism*, ch. 12. See also the discussion between M. McBeath and P. Helm, 'Omniscience and Eternity', *Proceedings of the Aristotelian Society*, suppl. vol. 63 (1989), 55–87.

[186] See Helm, *Eternal God*; Leftow, *Time and Eternity*; Stump and Kretzmann, 'Eternity'.

further clarification of these concepts draw greatly upon recent work in metaphysics and the philosophy of time.[187]

The concept of immutability is closely related to the doctrines of eternity and timelessness, as it is to divine simplicity. To claim that God is immutable is simply to claim that God cannot change.[188] Immutability can be understood either in a strong or a weak sense. According to the latter, to say of a person that he is immutable is simply to say that he cannot change in character. Thus, to say of God that he is immutable is simply to say that while he continues to exist, *necessarily* he cannot change his character. Traditionally, most philosophers and theologians have understood immutability in a much stronger sense. According to this, to say that God is immutable is to say that he cannot *change at all*. In order to examine whether it is coherent to say that God is immutable in this strong sense, we have first to consider what it is to undergo change.

A much discussed criterion for change is what, following the work of Geach, has become known as 'Cambridge change'.[189] On this criterion a thing *x* changes if some predicate '*p*' applies to it at one time, but not at another. Thus, my suit has changed if it was dry-cleaned yesterday but is not clean today. The point here is that everything which 'changes' in the real sense of that term does seem to change according to the Cambridge criterion but not vice versa. Sometimes '*p*' applies to *x* at one time, but not at another without that thing having undergone change in the ordinary sense of the term. Thus, Socrates may be at one time taller than Plato and at another time Socrates may not be taller than Plato, without Socrates having changed at all, for it can be the case that Plato has grown.

Following this, a number of philosophers have distinguished 'real' change from 'Cambridge' change. Put simply, this distinction exploits the difference between relational and non-relational predicates. A relational predicate is a predicate which expresses a relation to some individual; so, 'opens the window' and 'touches Plato' etc. are relational, whereas, 'thinks', 'is blue', and 'washes' are non-relational. Where we have a relational predicate of the form '. . . *Ry*' (namely, '. . . has relation *R* to *y*'),[190] we might conclude that all that follows from

[187] For a taste of recent discussions in this area, see Leftow, *Time and Eternity*; P. Fritzgerald, 'Stump and Kretzmann on Eternity', *Journal of Philosophy*, 82 (1985), 260–9; H. Nelson, 'Time(s), Eternity and Duration', *International Journal for the Philosophy of Religion*, 22 (1987), 3–19; D. Lewis, 'Eternity, Time and Tenselessness', *Faith and Philosophy*, 5 (1988), 72–86; Hasker, *God, Time and Knowledge*, 169 ff. Stump and Kretzmann reply to their critics in 'Eternity, Awareness and Action', *Faith and Philosophy*, 4 (1992), 463–82.

[188] A general discussion of many of the features and derivative issues that pertain to immutability can be found in R. Creel, 'Immutability and Impassibility', in Quinn and Taliaferro (eds.), *Companion to Philosophy of Religion*; a much more demanding discussion is to be found in Gale, *On the Nature and Existence of God*, 37–97.

[189] See P. Geach, 'What Actually Exists', *Proceedings of the Aristotelian Society*, suppl. vol. 42 (1968), 7–19; repr. in Geach, *God and the Soul* (London, 1969).

[190] Note that the predicate is '—— *R* ——' for '*y*' is one of the subjects of the proposition. I adopt this notation from Swinburne, *The Coherence of Theism*, 220.

x being *Ry* at another time is that either *x* has changed or *y* has changed or both have changed. Therefore, if Plato has not changed, and Socrates is at one time shorter than Plato, and at another and later time not shorter than Plato, then Socrates has changed by growing taller. But—and this is often considered to be the point of importance—a thing does not change simply because it is first an object of thought, and then it is not being thought about. The criterion can only be applied to relational predicates if we already have some understanding of what it is for a thing to change.

If these thoughts help us to illuminate some basic, albeit contentious, ideas about change,[191] what does it mean to say of the God of Western theism that he does not change? If we adhere to the distinctions as expressed above, then certain things appear to be ruled out. For example, these considerations about change appear to cause problems for a conception of divine action: acts occur at particular times and in acting God changes from doing a certain thing to doing some other thing. This is further complicated if we assume with some traditional theists that God's intentions are fixed for all eternity. If we agree with this, we arrive at a conception of God which appears to be at variance with biblical narratives, for, on this view, God is a lifeless entity which does not resemble the biblical God who *reacts* to the various acts and omissions of mankind with expressions of sympathy and anger.[192] A further implication of this stronger conception of immutability is the thesis that God's thoughts would be simply one thought which lasted for ever.[193]

For these reasons, many modern-day philosophers and theologians have resisted the idea that immutability be considered in terms of absolute changelessness and have instead argued that it be recast in terms that convey the idea of steadfastness in character. Recasting immutability in this way is thought to make the attribute consistent with the description of the attributes and activities of God as these are to be found in biblical narratives. In this sense, many recent discussions of immutability in philosophical theology might be said to reveal a strong preference for Jerusalem over Athens.[194]

[191] For a helpful discussion of the shortcomings of the distinction, see T. P. Smith, 'On the Applicability of a Criterion of Change', *Ratio*, 25 (1973), 325–33, and H. Mellor, *Real Time* (Cambridge, 1981), 107–10. Cf. Lucas, *The Future*, 43–7.

[192] The idea that God is not somehow 'moved' to pity or anger or such sentiments and emotions by human acts or omissions is normally referred to as *divine impassibility*. For a recent study of this notion, see R. Creel, *Divine Impassibility: An Essay in Philosophical Theology* (Cambridge, 1986).

[193] For a discussion of this and other related issues, see Kvanvig, *The Possibility of an All-Knowing God*, 150–65, and T. D. Sullivan, 'Omniscience, Immutability and the Divine Mode of Knowing', *Faith and Philosophy*, 8 (1991), 21–35.

[194] Among this number one could include Pike, *God and Timelessness*, 106 ff.; Swinburne, *The Coherence of Theism*, 221–2; Lucas, *The Future*, 214–17. For an interesting juxtaposition of the Thomistic with the current approach to these issues, see Davies, *The Thought of Thomas Aquinas*, 114–17.

3.2.5. Divine Perfection: Goodness and Impeccability

The claim that God is good[195] can be construed in two different ways. According to one, goodness attributes a certain status to God; that is, God's very being is good.[196] The second way might be said to express an ethical judgement: God is morally good or morally perfect; that is, whatever God does is morally perfect.[197] Taken together they express a claim common to theism that God is good. It is important to understand, however, that the claim that God is good can be reduced to two separate yet related theses. The first holds that God is essentially good; that is, it is impossible for God to be other than good or that God be evil. The second thesis claims that God is impeccable. Historically, impeccability has been understood to mean the inability to sin. In recent discussion, the notions that God is essentially good and that God is impeccable have been the object of criticism.

As we saw in our earlier discussion of omnipotence, theists have traditionally argued that God can do no wrong. Nelson Pike has proposed that since omnipotence and perfect goodness are incompatible, we should allow that God must be able to do what is wrong.[198] Some philosophers have argued that Pike's thesis can be taken a step further. W. R. Carter, for instance, has argued that while Pike has shown that omnipotence requires that the person who is God is not essentially morally good, God cannot be accidentally or contingently good either.[199]

A further criticism of the thesis that God is impeccable derives from ideas about the nature of free action. For example, it has been claimed that certain features of free action as articulated by the free-will defence (see Section 3.3 below) can be used to substantiate the claim that God is not essentially morally good.[200] According to the free-will defence, it is possible that God so values creatures who freely choose to do what is right in circumstances in which they are

[195] An excellent general discussion of this concept is by P. Helm, 'Divine Goodness', in Quinn and Taliaferro (eds.), *Companion to the Philosophy of Religion*.

[196] Aquinas, *Summa Theologiae*, 1a, q. 5, a. 1: 'the essence of goodness consists in this, that it is in some way desirable' he adds that a thing 'is desirable only in so far as it is perfect'. At 1a, q. 6, a. 1 ad 2, Aquinas adds that 'to be good belongs pre eminently to God' and that God is the highest good because 'all desired perfections flow from God as their first cause'. For a discussion of this, see N. Kretzmann, 'Goodness, Knowledge, and Indeterminacy in the Philosophy of Thomas Aquinas', *Journal of Philosophy*, 80 (1983), 353–82.

[197] See Swinburne, *The Coherence of Theism*, 179: 'In claiming that God is by nature morally perfectly good, the theist means that God is so constituted that he never does actions which are morally wrong'. A useful collection of recent essays on this topic is edited by S. MacDonald, *Being and Goodness: The Concept of the Good in Metaphysics and Philosophical Theology* (Ithaca, NY, 1991).

[198] Pike, 'Omnipotence and God's Ability to Sin'. Cf. P. Helm, 'God and the Approval of Sin', *Religious Studies*, 20 (1984), 215–22.

[199] W. R. Carter, 'Impeccability', *Analysis*, 42 (1982), 102–5. For a discussion of Carter's thesis, see T. V. Morris, 'Impeccability', *Analysis*, 42 (1983), 106–12. A very different view of the attribute can be found in V. Brümmer, 'Divine Impeccability', *Religious Studies*, 20 (1984), 203–14.

[200] See W. Morriston, 'Is God "Significantly Free"?', *Faith and Philosophy*, 2 (1985), 257–64. The locus of Morriston's criticism is the free-will defence as it is developed by A. Plantinga, *The Nature of Necessity*, 7–64.

significantly free, that he created such creatures even though they would frequently do what is wrong, and, as a result, add moral evil to the world. The argument against impeccability begins by claiming that if God is essentially morally perfect, then God is morally perfect in every possible world. Since moral perfection is incompatible with wrongdoing, there is no possible world in which God can perform a wrong action. Therefore, God's nature is such that it is logically impossible for God to perform a wrong action—God is 'determined' not to perform any wrong act. This entails that God is not significantly free. Since moral goodness presupposes significant freedom, a further implication of this argument is that God cannot be morally good. Facts about freedom, it is claimed, can show that God is not essentially morally good.[201]

3.3. The Problem of Evil

Poor Boethius in his grim prison cell posed the question: *Si quidem deus, est unde mala*? ('If there is a God whence comes evil?')[202] Boethius was certainly right to pose such a question since if God possesses the attributes detailed above, then why should the world be the morally shabby place it so often is? We might rephrase the thought behind Boethius' question in the following terms: If God is omnipotent, then *per definitiones* he could prevent evil if he wanted to. And if God is perfectly good, then *per definitiones* he would surely want to prevent evil if he could. Therefore, if God exists and is both omnipotent and perfectly good, then there exists a being who could prevent evil if he wanted to, and who would want to prevent evil if he could. How then can there be so many evils in the world? In barest outline, this is the traditional theological antinomy known as 'the problem of evil'. Its discussion and attempted resolution have occupied some of the best philosophical minds from antiquity to the present day.[203]

One of the historically enduring lines of response to the problem of evil has been offered by philosophers under the head of *theodicies*.[204] Briefly, a theodicy

[201] Morriston, 'Is God "Significantly Free"?' 258. For a detailed examination of Morriston's argument, see Wierenga, *The Nature of God*, 208–11. Yet a further criticism of impeccability states that God is not worthy of praise for his moral goodness if he is not able to sin; see S. Davis, *Logic and the Nature of God*, 93–5.

[202] *De Consolatione Philosophiae*, I. 4. The question which Boethius posed was much discussed in antiquity: see Epicurus, Fr. 374; Lactantius, *De Ira Dei* 13. 21. Cf. Plato, *Republic* 379a. In *Dialogues concerning Natural Religion*, x, Hume refers to it as 'Epicurus's question'.

[203] Three excellent guides to the subject have recently been published in the form of anthologies: M. McCord Adams and R. M. Adams (eds.), *The Problem of Evil* (Oxford, 1990); M. L. Peterson (ed.), *The Problem of Evil: Selected Readings* (Notre Dame, Ind., 1992); D. Howard-Snyder (ed.), *The Evidential Argument from Evil* (Bloomington, Ind., 1996). Further guides of a general nature are provided by M. L. Petersen, 'The Problem of Evil', in Quinn and Taliaferro (eds.), *Companion to the Philosophy of Religion*; Plantinga, *The Nature of Necessity*, 7–64; Swinburne, *The Existence of God*, 200–25; Mackie, *The Miracle of Theism*, 150–76; Gale, *On the Nature and Existence of God*, 98–178; Hughes, *The Nature of God*, 152–83.

[204] Although the problem is an ancient one, the term 'theodicy' (*theos* god; *dike* justice) was coined by Leibniz. See his letter to the Jesuit Bartholomew Des Bosses, 6 Jan. 1712, in Gerhardt ii. 428.

is a theistically motivated response to questions about whether theism can be true in view of the existence of evils. In the history of discussion of this issue, three theodicies have remained a stimulus to the work of others. These are the responses of Augustine, Aquinas, and Leibniz.

Augustine's solution has come to be known as the free-will defence. The title aptly sums up his case. Human free will is the first cause, or *causa prima*, of evil. The task for theodicy, Augustine contends, consists in properly accounting for the reality of evil in the world in the light of the existence of a God who has bestowed the good of freedom upon human beings. What then is the cause of evil? Augustine answers this question by recourse to his doctrine of privation. Evil is a deficiency in some created good. Human free will, itself a divinely endowed good, is susceptible of such deficiency because, being free, it can be directed away from the good. Thus, the will is corruptible. For Augustine, however, the possibility or even the inevitability that freedom will be abused in no way diminishes the omniscience of God, which includes foreknowledge (see Section 3.2.3 above). Indeed, even the abuse of freedom is subject to the sovereign will of God, who gave humans free will in the first place. Hence it is to be expected that God can bring forth ultimate good out of evil.[205]

What does this mean? In *De Libero Arbitrio* Augustine argues that God can bring forth good from evil by preserving the perfect moral order of the universe. This requires that God ensures that those who are vicious suffer, and those who are virtuous either do not suffer, or suffer in ways that are (in the long run) beneficial to them. Given all this, Augustine thinks he can claim that the world is not as morally shabby a place as one might believe it to be: the appearance of injustice and moral shabbiness arises, at least in part, from a failure to see how much the vicious suffer and also how vicious sufferers are.[206]

For Aquinas all evil is caused accidentally. By this, Aquinas means to convey the idea that evil arises as the by-product of some desired good. On this analysis, it is admissible to conceive of God as the accidental cause of some physical evils without assigning moral culpability to God for the existence of such evil.[207] Aquinas thinks that God permits certain physical evils since they are necessary concomitants to a world with goods of the kind God wills. Yet not all physical evils fit into this analysis. Some are by-products of moral activity, though these

[205] See *De Libero Arbitrio*, I. I, 2. 15–20, 3. 3. For a discussion of Augustine's theodicy, see C. Kirwan, *Augustine* (London, 1989), 60–83. J. Hick, *Evil and the Love of God*, 2nd edn. (London, 1977) criticizes Augustine's approach and commends the work of Irenaeus (AD *c.*130–200) as providing a better foundation for a Christian response to the problem of evil.

[206] *De Libero Arbitrio*, I. I ff.

[207] At *Summa Theologiae*, Ia, q. 49, aa. 2 ff., Aquinas attempts to show how God can be regarded as the accidental cause of natural evils. This passage aside, Aquinas' account of evil can be found at *Summa Theologiae*, qq. 48–9, *Summa contra Gentiles*, qq. 37–9, *Expositio in Job ad Litteram* ('Commentary on the Book of Job'), and in *De Malo* trans. J. and J. Oesterle as *Aquinas, 'On Evil'* (Notre Dame, Ind., 1995).

too are brought about accidentally. The agent here, however, is the human person. Human beings are the *per accidens* cause of all physical evils that are not willed *per accidens* by God. This is so because such evils are themselves by-products of moral evils, all of which are caused *per accidens* by finite human individuals in the exercise of free will. One acts immorally whenever one 'causes evil *per accidens* in [a] quest for good'.[208] Thus, for Aquinas, the efficient cause of all moral evils, and consequently of many natural evils, is the human person. Finite human individuals, not God, are responsible for the existence of all evil acts.

Leibniz's response to the problem of evil in his *Theodicy* can be outlined as follows. A perfect God has the power to create any possible world.[209] Because he is perfect, God would create the very best possible world. No world can be totally perfect, but must contain some evil; so God created a world possessing the optimum balance of good and evil. Since some goods are made possible only by the presence of evil—for instance, compassion is made possible by the witnessing of suffering—God had to calibrate the total value in each of all possible worlds, and actualize the one in which evil contributes to its being the best of all possible worlds.

What distinguishes Leibniz's views from those advanced by Augustine and Aquinas is that Leibniz conceives his theodicy as a defence of God's justice, in particular, the consistency of that justice with God's creation of a world in which some measure of evil is unavoidably present. Central to Leibniz's defence is his representation of God's justice as a corollary of the most plausible account of the world's origin. Thus, for Leibniz, the only intellectually coherent way to account for the existence of the world, as opposed to some other equally possible world, is to regard it as the product of a creative act by a necessarily existing being. Such an act is reasonable in itself, inasmuch as it amounts to the choice of the *best* world from among an infinity of other possible worlds. Herein, Leibniz thinks, lies God's universal justice. God acts justly in creation in so far as he is motivated to select that possible world which his wisdom deems to contain the optimal amount of goodness.[210]

The theodicies of Augustine, Aquinas, and Leibniz give rise to a large number of problems.[211] One recurring theme concerns the question of 'optimality'

[208] *Summa Theologiae*, 1a, q. 49, a. 1; see esp. Thomas's 'Reply to Objection 3'.

[209] G. W. Leibniz, *Theodicy: Essays on the Goodness of God, the Freedom of Man and the Origin of Evil*, ed. A. Farrer, trans. E. M. Huggard (La Salle, Ill., 1985). For the background to this book and its origin as a response to Pierre Bayle, see W. H. Barber, *Leibniz in France from Arnauld to Voltaire: A Study in French Reactions to Leibnizianism* (Oxford, 1955). An illuminating discussion of Leibniz's theodicy can be found in Rutherford, *Leibniz and the Rational Order of Nature*.

[210] See Gerhardt ii. 424–5. Of further relevance to these issues is Leibniz's 1697 essay *The Ultimate Origination of all Things*.

[211] Some of the general issues which arise from classical theodicies are discussed by R. G. Swinburne, 'Some Major Strands of Theodicy', in Howard-Snyder (ed.), *The Evidential Argument from Evil*.

in a consideration of the world God actually created.[212] Some philosophers, for instance, in the context of a discussion of natural evils, have questioned whether it is ever possible to claim that the best possible world might contain no unhappiness at all.[213]

Perhaps the most enduring legacy of earlier theodicies is the Augustinian free-will defence.[214] According to this view, indeterministic free will is a necessary condition of human personhood, a condition which subsequently underwrites our views on such notions as responsibility and accountability. In endowing human beings with free will, and placing them in a world in which evil choices are always possible, God brought it about that he is not responsible for the moral evil in the world. It is a direct consequence of human intentions realized in acts and omissions.[215]

The free-will defence aside, another favoured way of reconciling the indeterministic freedom of human beings with the idea of divine providence is by appeal to middle knowledge (*scientia media*).[216] The idea of middle knowledge was first advanced by the sixteenth-century Jesuit Luis de Molina (1535–1600) in part 4 of his *Concordia*.[217] Molina's thesis, which is more a contribution to the debate on omniscience (see Section 3.2.3 above), maintains that God knows not only what he will do, but what would happen in all possible circumstances in which humans with free will might be placed. It is in the light of this knowledge that God actualizes that possible world which best realizes his purposes. As a solution to the problem of evil, the theory of middle knowledge has been criticized on the grounds that it does not explain why God chose to

[212] For a helpful discussion of this issue, see R. M. Adams, 'Must God Create the Best?', in *The Virtue of Faith*.

[213] One of the more compelling and interesting articles within this class of discussion is R. M. Sainsbury, 'Benevolence and Evil', *Australasian Journal of Philosophy*, 58 (1980), 128–34.

[214] There is an enormous literature on the free-will defence. The modern *locus classicus* is Plantinga, *The Nature of Necessity*. The claim that the free-will defence is Augustinian is disputed by N. Pike, 'Plantinga on Free Will and Evil', *Religious Studies*, 15 (1979), 449–74. Further commentary on these issues is provided by R. M. Adams, 'Plantinga on the Problem of Evil', in Tomberlin and van Inwagen (eds.), *Alvin Plantinga*. Of further interest is Plantinga's reply to Adams, ibid.

[215] For a criticism of this view, see M. Tooley, 'Alvin Plantinga and the Argument from Evil', *Australasian Journal of Philosophy*, 58 (1980), 360–76, and Plantinga, 'Tooley and Evil: A Reply', *Australasian Journal of Philosophy*, 60 (1982), 66–75.

[216] Middle knowledge is part of a tripartite distinction within divine knowledge. First, there is God's *natural knowledge*, by which he knows his own nature and all the things which are possible to him either by his own action or by the action of free possible creatures. Then there is God's *free knowledge*. This is his knowledge of what will actually happen after the free decision has been taken to create free creatures and to place them in certain circumstances. Between the two there is God's *middle knowledge*, which is his knowledge of what any possible creature would do in any possible world.

[217] The full title of Molina's work is *Liberi Arbitrii cum Gratiae Donis, Divina Praescientia, Providentia, Praedestinatione et Reprobatione Concordia*. Part 4 has been translated by A. J. Freddoso, as *Luis de Molina, 'On Divine Foreknowledge'* (Ithaca, NY, 1988). For a helpful discussion of Molina's controversial thesis, see Freddoso's introduction; Craig, *The Problem of Divine Foreknowledge and Future Contingents from Aristotle to Suarez*, 169–206; Gaskin, 'Conditionals of Freedom and Middle Knowledge' and 'Molina on Divine Foreknowledge and the Principle of Bivalence'. A recent defence of the Molinist position has been advanced by Thomas Flint, *Divine Providence* (Ithaca, NY, 1998).

actualize this world with all its faults, and not some other world in which the free will of human beings brings about less moral evil than presently occurs in this world.[218]

A further heading under which the problem of evil occupies the attention of contemporary philosophers of religion concerns what is known as the *evidential argument from evil*.[219] This argument is concerned with the following questions: Is evil evidence against the existence of God? And, even if the existence of God is somehow shown to be 'compatible' with the actuality of evil, does the existence of evil in the world render belief in a God unreasonable? Present discussion of these questions centres on the credentials of two arguments. The first affirms that there is no reason for God to allow certain specific horrors. The content of such horrors is then specified to include the variety and profusion of undeserved sufferings. The second argument asserts that the role and function of the psychological states of pleasure and pain in human and non-human life suggest that non-theistic hypotheses provide a much better explanation of these phenomena. The evidential argument often turns on the ability of theism to provide a convincing rationale for the existence of suffering and misfortune in human and non-human life.[220]

3.4. Miracles

A central claim of all three Western monotheistic traditions is that God reveals himself to his world. One of the mediums in which such revelation is thought to take place is through the occurrence of miracles. A miracle is commonly understood to be a supernaturally induced event whose explanation runs contrary to what is known about or expected of the received set of facts about the world. Hence water is turned into wine and seas are parted.[221]

[218] This and other issues connected to the application of middle knowledge to the problem of evil are discussed by R. M. Adams, 'Middle Knowledge and the Problem of Evil', in Adams and Adams (eds.), *The Problem of Evil*; D. Basinger, 'Middle Knowledge and Human Freedom: Some Clarifications', *Faith and Philosophy*, 4 (1987), 330–6; W. Hasker, 'A Refutation of Middle Knowledge', *Nous*, 20 (1986), 545–57; Gaskin, 'Fatalism, Foreknowledge and the Reality of the Future'; Kenny, *The God of the Philosophers*, 61–71.

[219] For a pioneering discussion of this topic, see R. Richman, 'The Argument from Evil', *Religious Studies*, 4 (1969), 203–11, and A. Plantinga, 'The Probabilistic Argument from Evil', *Philosophical Studies*, 35 (1979), 1–53. All the recent papers of importance on this subject are collected in Howard-Snyder (ed.), *The Evidential Argument*.

[220] On this topic, see W. Rowe, 'The Empirical Argument from Evil', in Audi and Wainwright (eds.), *Rationality, Religious Belief and Moral Commitment*, and 'Evil and Theodicy', *Philosophical Topics*, 16 (188), 119–32. Also worth consulting are M. McCord Adams, 'Horrendous Evils and the Goodness of God', in Adams and Adams (eds.), *The Problem of Evil*, R. Gale, 'Some Difficulties in Theistic Treatments of Evil', and W. Alston, 'The Inductive Argument from Evil and the Human Cognitive Cognition', in Howard-Snyder (ed.), *The Evidential Argument*.

[221] The best companion to this topic is R. G. Swinburne (ed.), *Miracles* (New York, 1989). For a very general discussion of the topic, see G. N. Schlesinger, 'Miracles', in Quinn and Taliaferro (eds.), *Companion to the Philosophy of Religion*.

As in so many areas of contemporary philosophy of religion, the present-day discussion of miracles takes its cue from the powerful criticisms of Hume. In his celebrated discussion of miracles in Section x of *An Enquiry concerning Human Understanding,* Hume advanced an argument which can be reconstructed thus:

(1) One ought to proportion one's belief to the available evidence.
(2) Sense-perception is generally better evidence than testimony, for no other reason than that valid testimony is based on another's sense-experience.
(3) Therefore, whenever there is a conflict between sense-experience and testimony, one ought to base one's belief on sense-perception.
(4) Sense-perception does not reveal any miracles to us but rather the presumption that the laws of nature prevail.
(5) Therefore, we are never justified in believing in miracles, but we are always justified in believing in the naturalness of all events.

The gist of Hume's case is that because we possess good evidence that there is uniformity in nature, every claim that a miracle has occurred must be weighed against that preponderating evidence. This is so even if we believe that we have personally witnessed a miracle. For given the principle that every time we pursue an event far enough we discover it to have a natural cause, we are still not justified in believing the event to be a miracle. Instead, we ought to look further, indeed far enough until we discover the natural cause.[222]

Swinburne takes issue with Hume's conclusion.[223] He argues: (1) that there could be evidence that a law of nature has been violated, and (2) that such a violation can be attributed to the activity of a God. On this basis he then proceeds to detail the kind of evidence we would need in order to believe that a divine being has intervened in our world. To this end, Swinburne distinguishes between situations in which we do and in which we do not have sufficient circumstantial evidence to warrant our attributing an anomalous event to the work of a deity. For Swinburne, the circumstantial evidence must be strong enough before we are ever justified in believing that an anomalous event in nature is a genuine miracle.[224]

Swinburne's interventions aside, it is fair to say that the dominance of empiricism and naturalism in contemporary anglophone philosophy has

[222] For a discussion of Hume's arguments, see Gaskin, *Hume's Philosophy of Religion*, 135–65, and Yandell, *Hume's 'Inexplicable Mystery'*, 315 ff. Many historically important responses to Hume's arguments are collected in S. Tweyman (ed.), *Hume on Miracles* (Bristol, 1996).

[223] See his 'Miracles', *Philosophical Quarterly*, 18 (1968), 320–8; *The Concept of Miracle* (London, 1970); *The Existence of God*, 225–43; *Revelation: From Metaphor to Analogy* (Oxford, 1992), 85–98.

[224] In *Revelation*, 85 ff., Swinburne proceeds to bolster this claim by arguing that since the existence of God is a plausible hypothesis or assumption, it is reasonable to expect that God would reveal himself in human history and will confirm his revelation in the form of miracles.

enabled the letter, and in most instances the spirit, of the Humean critique to survive. The spirit of Hume is conspicuous in the work of the late John Mackie.[225] Mackie's argument against miracles is epistemological rather than logical. That is, while miracles may be logically possible—a fact that Hume was ever mindful not to deny—we can never be justified in believing in them. Even though the concept of a miracle is a coherent one, Mackie argues that it is eventually defeated by the double burden of attempting to show (1) that somehow a naturally anomalous event took place and (2) that the event violated the existing laws of nature. Again the point is Humean. Even if an event occurs for which there is no existing natural explanation, we cannot be led to infer that a natural explanation will never be discovered for its occurrence.[226]

The Humean characterization and refutation of miracles is based on the thought that if miracles exist, they would have to be violations of the laws of nature. An interesting question, however, is whether miracles have to be contra-nomic events. In a recent paper, Christopher Hughes has argued that miracles do not have to be characterized as such but rather can be defined as 'events directly caused by God'.[227] What is suggestive about Hughes's proposal is that it opens the door to the possibility that even if Hume and his heirs are right in supposing we could not be justified in believing in contra-nomic divine interventions, it does not obviously follow that we could not be justified in believing in miracles when these occurrences are defined as events directly caused by God.[228]

4. RELIGIOUS EPISTEMOLOGY

4.1. What is Religious Epistemology?

Religious epistemology is concerned with what has always been one of the central issues in modern philosophy of religion, namely, the rational justification of religious belief. As the subject is currently practised there are five different epistemological approaches which attempt to justify religious belief. These are: (1) natural theology; (2) 'Reformed' epistemology; (3) prudentialist accounts of

[225] See Mackie, *The Miracle of Theism*, 13–29. Cf. M. Curd, 'Miracles as Violations of Laws of Nature', in J. Jordan and D. Howard-Snyder (eds.), *Faith, Freedom and Rationality* (Lanham, Md., 1996), 171–84.

[226] Many of the important recent rejoinders to Mackie from theistically minded philosophers are summarized and evaluated by J. Houston in *Reported Miracles* (Cambridge, 1994), 169 ff. Houston's book also contains a helpful bibliography.

[227] C. Hughes, 'Miracles, Laws of Nature and Causation', *Proceedings of the Aristotelian Society*, suppl. vol. 66 (1992), 179–205.

[228] For an examination of some features of Hughes's argument and other issues relating to the topic, see R. M. Adams, 'Miracles, Laws of Nature and Causation', *Proceedings of the Aristotelian Society*, suppl. vol. 66 (1992), 207–24. A further discussion of miracles which resists the Humean characterization is P. Dietl, 'On Miracles', *American Philosophical Quarterly*, 5 (1968), 130–4.

religious belief; (4) fideistic approaches; and (5) arguments from religious experience. I discuss each in turn.[229]

4.2. Natural Theology

Until recently natural theology was the dominant paradigm in religious epistemology. The substance of natural theology has already been made plain in our earlier discussion of the history of the philosophy of religion (see Sections 1.1ff. above) as well as in connection with a posteriori proofs for the existence of God (namely the cosmological argument and the argument from design; see Sections 2.3 and 2.4 above).[230] Natural theology is principally concerned with the examination of any evidence for the existence of God that can be found in the world of nature. Natural theologians are concerned with the search for evidence in virtue of the view they hold about the status of the belief that 'God exists'. It is argued that this belief is not self-evident. Since any belief which is not self-evident requires evidence to be justified, natural theologians claim that the belief that 'God exists' needs to be justified by appeal to facts about the world. Examples of this approach in the history of philosophy can be seen in the 'five ways' of Aquinas which set about justifying a belief in God's existence by examining certain features of the natural world (see Section 2.3.1 above), as well as in arguments from design such as that advanced by William Paley (see Section 2.4 above), which argue that belief in a God is warranted in virtue of there being overwhelming evidence of intentional order in the universe.[231]

Many arguments given by past and present natural theologians show allegiance, in differing degrees, to the epistemological theory known as foundationalism. Briefly stated, foundationalism holds that some of the propositions we believe are 'basic'—that is, they are not accepted on the basis of any other

[229] By far the best and most helpful companion to the study of religious epistemology is R. D. Geivett and B. Sweetman (eds.), *Contemporary Perspectives on Religious Epistemology* (New York, 1992). This contains most of the important readings as well as an extensive research bibliography. Other introductions to and studies of the subject are A. Kenny, *What is Faith? Essays in the Philosophy of Religion* (Oxford, 1992); T. Penelhum, *Reason and Religious Faith* (Boulder, Colo., 1995); K. J. Clark, *Return to Reason* (Grand Rapids, Mich., 1990), P. Helm, *Belief Policies* (Cambridge, 1994); R. Audi, 'Faith, Belief and Rationality', *Philosophical Perspectives*, 5 (1991), 213–40. Older but still useful discussions of the general issues of religious epistemology can be found in G. Mavrodes, *Belief in God* (New York, 1970); B. Mitchell, *The Justification of Religious Belief* (London, 1973); P. Helm, *The Varieties of Belief* (London, 1973).

[230] A helpful history of natural theology is C. C. J. Webb, *Studies in the History of Natural Theology* (Oxford, 1915). See also Gerson, *God and Greek Philosophy*.

[231] The continuance of natural theology within present-day philosophy is more often than not to be seen in new defences of these a posteriori arguments. For examples of this type of work, see R. G. Swinburne, *The Existence of God*; W. Lane Craig, *The Existence of God and the Beginning of the Universe* (San Bernardino, Calif., 1979) and 'What Place, then, for a Creator?', *British Journal for the Philosophy of Science*, 49 (1990), 473–91; R. M. Adams, 'Flavours, Colors and God', in Adams, *The Virtue of Faith*. A very recent defence of the claims of natural theology which is heavily indebted to the work of Aquinas is Kretzmann, *The Metaphysics of Theism*.

propositions or beliefs—and many of the other propositions we believe are not basic. A basic belief is one that is either self-evident, incorrigible, or known through the senses. Thus, the beliefs 'I see the tree' and that 'all bachelors are unmarried men' can all be held without recourse to any other belief. Whereas, for example, the beliefs that 'cheetahs are faster than leopards' and that 'City are a better team than United' require other beliefs in order for them to be justified. A further stipulation of foundationalism is that non-basic beliefs can be rationally accepted only on the basis of evidence, and this evidence must ultimately be founded upon some set of basic beliefs.

Stated thus, it be might be thought that the credentials of natural theology as a convincing paradigm in religious epistemology are dependent to some degree on the fortunes of one or other version of foundationalism or what is sometimes referred to as *evidentialism*. Those who adhere to foundationalism argue that the proposition 'there is a God' is not basic and that this proposition can only be an object of rational acceptance if some good evidence be found in its support. Given the dependence of natural theology on some form of foundationalism, it is unsurprising that as the influence of foundationalist epistemology has declined, natural theology has been subjected to sustained critical scrutiny.[232]

4.3. 'Reformed' Epistemology

The general questioning of foundationalism in epistemology proper has had definite consequences for religious epistemology. This has led to the development of new approaches to the project of justifying religious belief. One of the more influential of these is known as 'Reformed' epistemology, a movement which gets its name from the theological sympathies of its proponents, who look back to the intellectual resources of the Protestant tradition, especially those connected with Calvinism.[233] Reformed epistemology represents a new approach to the justification of religious belief because it argues that belief in God can be *properly basic*. Thus, the belief that 'God exists' does not require any other belief or proposition for it to be justified.[234]

[232] Two recent works which provide different assessments of this development and its implications for epistemology in general are R. Audi, *The Structure of Justification* (Cambridge, 1993) and S. Haack, *Evidence and Inquiry* (Oxford, 1993). In religious epistemology the implications for the justification of religious belief in the wake of foundationalism's demise are the subject of a study by D. Z. Phillips, *Faith after Foundationalism* (London, 1988). We shall have cause to discuss some of Phillips's views below.

[233] For a general history of this movement, see D. J. Hoitenga, *Faith and Reason from Plato to Plantinga: An Introduction to Reformed Epistemology* (Albany, NY, 1991). It is worth recording that many of the historical remarks made by Hoitenga are open to question. A helpful introduction to the central claims of the Calvinist tradition can be found in P. Helm, *Calvin and the Calvinists* (Edinburgh, 1982).

[234] In many ways, the *locus classicus* of Reformed epistemology is a collection of papers edited by A. Plantinga and N. Wolterstorff, *Faith and Rationality* (Notre Dame, Ind., 1983). Of particular relevance are

A concise statement of Reformed epistemology can be found in Alvin Plantinga's paper 'Is Belief in God Properly Basic?'[235] Plantinga argues that what he terms the 'evidentialist objection' to theistic belief—namely, the idea that belief in God can only be rational if supported by good evidence—is beside the point because the objection is parasitic upon foundationalist epistemology. Since, according to Plantinga, classical foundationalists are unable to provide us with good reasons why we should accept their criteria for what counts as a foundational or basic belief, this standard attempt to criticize theism is poorly grounded.[236]

In contrast, Plantinga argues that belief in God may be properly basic; one is justified in believing in God without basing one's belief on any other beliefs and propositions. By this, he does not mean that there are no justifying circumstances for holding the belief, or that the belief is groundless or gratuitous. Rather, the belief can be justified in another way. Central to this new notion of justification is the idea that the belief 'God exists' is analogous to other properly basic beliefs. When we examine such a belief, Plantinga claims, we always find that there is a circumstance or condition that justifies it. Thus the belief 'I see the tree' is justified by the experience of seeing a tree. In other words, the belief is properly basic because the experience of seeing a tree is what justifies me in holding the belief; it is the *ground* of my justification, and, by extension, the ground of the belief itself. Similar things can be said about belief in God. There are many conditions and circumstances that call forth belief in God. For instance, upon reading a sacred book I may have the impression that God is speaking to me, or upon having erred in my practical affairs, I may form the belief that God disapproves of what I have done. It is the existence of these circumstances that call forth belief in God. Thus, propositions like 'God is speaking to me' and 'God disapproves of what I have done' can, in the *right*

the papers by Plantinga, Wolterstorff, Mavrodes, and Alston. The most complete discussion of the claims of Reformed epistemology to date is M. McLeod, *Rationality and Theistic Belief* (Ithaca, NY, 1993). A helpful introduction to the claims of the movement can be found in A. Plantinga, 'Reformed Epistemology', in Quinn and Taliaferro (eds.), *Companion to the Philosophy of Religion*.

[235] This paper first appeared in *Nous*, 25 (1981), 41–51. Other important papers by Plantinga on this topic include 'On Reformed Epistemology', *Reformed Journal*, 32 (1982), 13–17; 'The Reformed Objection to Natural Theology', *Proceedings of the American Catholic Philosophical Association*, 54 (1980), 49–63; 'On Taking Belief in God as Properly Basic', in J. Runzo and C. K. Ihara (eds.), *Religious Experience and Religious Belief* (Lanham, Md., 1986); 'The Prospects for Natural Theology', *Philosophical Perspectives*, 5 (1991), 287–316. Plantinga's general epistemological position is outlined in his double volume set on the notion of warrant; see *Warrant: The Current Debate* (New York, 1993) and *Warrant and Proper Function* (New York, 1993).

[236] It ought to be remarked upon that Plantinga's broad use of the term 'classical foundationalism' to cover very different moments in the history of epistemology invites close scrutiny. While it can be argued that so-called foundationalists such as Plato, Aquinas, and Descartes share a common approach to the justification of belief, it is a further matter, one requiring much exegesis and argument, to claim that these philosophers all share a common epistemological approach. For a helpful corrective to many of Plantinga's sweeping historical claims, one which focuses on the work of Aquinas, see E. Stump, 'Aquinas on the Foundations of Knowledge', *Canadian Journal of Philosophy*, suppl. vol. 17 (1991), 125–58.

circumstances, be taken as properly basic propositions. Being such, they can be justified without recourse to further evidence. In this way, Plantinga's argument for a new approach to the justification of religious belief begins from a critique of foundationalism and then attempts to show that the class of properly basic beliefs can be extended to include beliefs about God which are formed in appropriate sets of circumstances and conditions.[237]

The critique of foundationalism can be said to complement another important strand in Reformed epistemology, namely its suspicion of the idea that appeals to 'reason' could ever persuade someone to surrender unbelief in favour of belief in God.[238] Such appeals have always been conspicuous in certain quarters of the tradition of natural theology. In this tradition it has often been taken that belief in a God can be made reasonable by appeal to some sort of evidence. Thus, if there is good evidence in the world for the existence of a God, then on pain of irrationality, the reasonable agent ought to accept that evidence as providing grounds for religious belief. Many Reformed epistemologists challenge this analysis. Nicholas Wolterstorff, for one, has argued in favour of Calvin's view that what is operative in many cases of religious unbelief is not so much insufficient awareness of the putative evidence for a God, but rather a resistance to the available evidence brought about by the effects of sin.[239] In this respect, the studies of Wolterstorff and others have contributed to the development of a distinctive outlook on the relationship between faith and reason. This outlook is concerned to uphold the reasonableness of religious faith by making appeal to features that are internal to the believing agent.[240]

[237] In 'Experience, Proper Basicality and Belief in God', *International Journal for Philosophy of Religion*, 27 (1990), 141–99, R. Pargetter attempts first to develop in further detail an account of properly basic belief, in order, secondly, to provide an evaluation of the contention that belief in God can be properly basic. Pargetter concludes that belief in God is properly basic when at least two conditions are realized: (1) that a believer must be reliable and (2) that the believer's doxastic system must cohere with a 'holistic evaluation of rationality'.

[238] See Plantinga, 'Advice to Christian Philosophers', in Beaty (ed.), *Christian Theism and the Problems of Philosophy*; and H. Hart, J. van der Hoeven, and N. Wolterstorff (eds.), *Rationality in the Calvinian Tradition* (Lanham, Md., 1983).

[239] See Wolterstorff, *Reason within the Bounds of Religion* (Grand Rapids, Mich., 1984); 'The Migration of Theistic Argument: From Natural Theology to Evidentialist Apologetics', in Audi and Wainwright (eds.), *Rationality, Religious Belief and Moral Commitment*; 'Is Reason Enough', in Geivett and Sweetman (eds.), *Contemporary Perspectives on Religious Epistemology*.

[240] Wolterstorff and Plantinga aside, other philosophers in this group include Clark, *Return to Reason*; Hoitenga, *Faith and Reason from Plato to Plantinga*; G. Mavrodes, 'Jerusalem and Athens Revisited', in Plantinga and Wolterstorff (eds.), *Faith and Rationality*; K. Konyndyk, 'Faith and Evidentialism', in Audi and Wainwright, *Rationality, Religious Belief and Moral Commitment*. Some writers include William Alston in this group; see McLeod, *Rationality and Theistic Belief*, 11–104. While there is much in common between Alston and those individuals discussed above, particularly in regard to their views on epistemological justification, Alston differs from most Reformed epistemologists in granting some role to natural theology; see *Perceiving God* (Ithaca, NY, 1991), 289. For an illuminating discussion of Alston's work on this issue, see N. Kretzmann, 'Mystical Perception: St Teresa, William Alston and the Broadminded Atheist', in Padgett (ed.), *Reason and the Christian Religion*. Alston's more recent thought on this subject can be found in his essay 'Belief, Acceptance and Religious Faith', in Jordan and Howard-Snyder (eds.), *Faith, Freedom and Rationality*.

In recent years the claims of Reformed epistemology have been repeatedly challenged. One set of objections to Plantinga's work in particular have been advanced by philosophers who adopt 'internalism'. This can be defined by contrasting it with 'externalism'. Briefly, an epistemological theory is internalist to the extent that the conditions for justification—what Plantinga terms 'warrant'—are accessible to the consciousness of the believer. A theory is externalist to the extent that the conditions are not so accessible. As set out above, Plantinga's criterion for justifying a belief is basically externalist, although it is loose enough to cover a multitude of theories and the externalist component is not explicit in his statement of the criterion alone. Plantinga's discussion suggests that the fact that one's belief-forming faculties are working correctly is not something that is typically accessible to the believer's consciousness, although nothing in the criterion excludes such accessibility. The primary difference between Plantinga and those who wish to see a stronger internalist element in the account of warrant is probably less a matter of dispute about the question whether a warranted belief involves properly functioning faculties, than it is a dispute about the extent to which the properly functioning believer is self-reflective.[241]

Another source of objections to Reformed epistemology originates in a concern among some Roman Catholic philosophers of religion to preserve cognitive voluntarism in a discussion of the justification of faith.[242] One of the main reasons for this has to do with the place of Thomism in Roman Catholic philosophy.[243] Both Catholics and Protestants have traditionally held that salvific faith is an endowment from God, but the history and legacy of doctrinal dispute shows that Catholics have assigned a higher degree of voluntary control over belief and the processes leading to belief than have Protestants. For example, Aquinas assigns to the will the function of leading believers to form a belief when the belief is not fully supported by reason.[244] Thus at *De Veritate*, q. 14. a. 2, Aquinas says: 'The will, influenced by the movement of the good contained

[241] A discussion of this and other related matters can be found in the papers by P. Quinn, P. Lee, and J. Greco, in L. Zagzebski (ed.), *Rational Faith: Catholic Responses to Reformed Epistemology* (Notre Dame, Ind., 1993). It is important, however, that one notes an evolution in Plantinga's views. Since the publication of *Faith and Rationality* in 1983 his views have grown more externalist, as can be seen in his two volumes *Warrant: The Current Debate* and *Warrant and Proper Function* from 1993.

[242] See L. J. Pojman, *Religious Belief and the Will* (London, 1986) for a useful discussion of the place of voluntarism within discussion of the justification of religious belief.

[243] For Aquinas, the truths of faith are apparent to us. Faith is an *argumentum*, for faith produces firm adhesion of the intellect to the truth. But faith is also an *argumentum non apparentium*; faith substitutes for evidence. Faith is just a habit of the mind by which eternal life exists inchoately in us, making assent to what is not apparent; see *Summa Theologiae*, 2a-2ae, q. 4, a. 1, c. See J. Barad, 'Aquinas on Faith and the Consent/Assent Distinction', *Journal of the History of Philosophy*, 24 (1986), 311–21.

[244] See S. MacDonald, 'Theory of Knowledge', in N. Kretzmann and E. Stump (eds.), *The Cambridge Companion to Aquinas* (Cambridge, 1993).

in the divine promise, proposes as worthy of assent something not apparent to natural understanding.' Aquinas' suggestion here is that belief-forming mechanisms do permit a function of the will. Furthermore, the ground of the certitude of revelatory beliefs is the will, not the intellect, which in turn suggests that Aquinas was not an evidentialist, at least not as Plantinga characterizes that position.[245]

Further objections to Reformed epistemology take issue with the claim that belief in God can be properly basic.[246] The extent of these as well as the other debates sketched above testifies to the fact that discussion of the claims of the Reformed movement occupies a central place in contemporary English-speaking religious epistemology. Any appraisal of its position has to address not only its critique of foundationalism but also its distinctive theological outlook on the relation between faith and reason.

4.4. Prudentialist Accounts of Religious Belief

A paradigmatic prudentialist argument justifying belief in God is Pascal's famous 'wager' argument. Pascal believed the universe to be religiously ambiguous. This motivated his interest in exploring the possibility that reason could not finally decide whether God exists, for there appears to be evidence both for and against the existence of God. Given this impasse, Pascal believed that one ought to wager one's life on the proposition that God exists; that is, he believed that the existence of God is a 'good bet' and that one ought to organize one's life around it and to act at all times as if it were true. Pascal believed that what one risks in such a bet is trifling, and that the outcome, should one be proved right, would be infinitely good. He thought it more 'rational' to seek to avoid the possibility of an infinite loss; for if one disbelieves in God, and it turns out that God indeed exists, one would have to suffer eternal damnation.[247]

Pascal's wager continues to fascinate philosophers of religion. In recent years

[245] For a discussion of these points as they relate to a criticism of Reformed epistemology, see Stump, 'Aquinas on the Foundations of Knowledge' and T. D. Sullivan, 'Resolute Belief and the Problem of Objectivity', in Zagzebski (ed.), *Rational Faith*. Cf. J. Boyle, J. Hubbard, and T. D. Sullivan, 'The Reformed Objection to Natural Theology: A Catholic Perspective', *Christian Scholar's Review*, 11 (1982), 199–211.

[246] See S. C. Goetz, 'Belief in God is not Properly Basic', *Religious Studies*, 19 (1993), 475–84; R. Grigg, 'The Crucial Disanalogies between Properly Basic Belief and Belief in God', *Religious Studies*, 26 (1990), 389–401; 'Theism and Proper Basicality: A Response to Plantinga', *International Journal for the Philosophy of Religion*, 14 (1983), 389–401. See also A. Kenny, 'Is Natural Theology Possible?', in *What is Faith?*

[247] See Pascal, *Pensées*, in *Œuvres*, ed. L. Brunschvicg (Paris, 1925), sect. III, no. ccxxxiii; trans. into Eng. as *Blaise Pascal, Pensées*, ed. L. Lafuma (London, 1960). A helpful discussion of the wager argument in the context of Pascal's time and theological context can be found in L. Goldmann, *Le Dieu caché* (Paris, 1955) and L. Armour, *'Infini Rien': Pascal's Wager and the Human Paradox* (Carbondale, Ill., 1993).

many have defended it,[248] while others have objected to it.[249] What is interesting about these competing discussions is the degree of disagreement about how it should be reconstructed. For this reason, adjudication of whether this type of prudentialist argument offers a convincing justification for theistic belief depends upon its logical structure. This is one area in which advance in the philosophy of religion is dependent upon other discussions in philosophy.[250]

Another set of prudentialist arguments is found in the work of William James (1842–1910). In 'The Will to Believe'(1896) James argues that in everyday life, where evidence for important propositions is often unclear, we must live by faith or else cease to act.[251] Although we may not make 'leaps of faith' *nolens volens*, practical or prudential considerations often force us to make decisions about propositions whose truth-value is not initially apparent.

Many of the underlying concepts given expression in 'The Will to Believe' first received an airing in James's earlier essay 'The Sentiment of Rationality' (1879).[252] There James defines faith as a 'belief in something concerning which doubt is still theoretically possible; and as the test of belief is willingness to act, one may say that faith is the readiness to act in a cause the prosperous issue of which is not certified in advance'. James illustrates this with a parable about a climber in the Alps. The climber finds himself in a position from which he can only escape by means of one enormous leap. If he tries to calculate the evidence, believing only in sufficient evidence, he will be incapacitated by fear and mistrust and hence will lose all. Without the evidence that he is capable of performing this feat successfully, the climber would be better off getting himself to believe that he can make the leap. James adds that 'in this case . . . the part of wisdom is clearly to believe what one desires; for the belief is one of the indispensable preliminary conditions of the realisation of its object. There are cases where faith creates its own verification.' All this is designed to illustrate the point that religious belief may be such an option for some people, and in this case one has the right to believe the better story rather than the worse.

[248] See T. V. Morris, 'Pascalian Wagering', *Canadian Journal of Philosophy*, 16 (1986), 437–54; repr. in *Making Sense of it All: Pascal and the Meaning of Life* (Notre Dame, Ind., 1992). Another important recent attempt to defend the argument is W. G. Lycan and G. N. Schlesinger, 'You Bet your Life: Pascal's Wager Defended', in J. Feinberg (ed.), *Reason and Responsibility* (Belmont, Calif., 1989).

[249] See J. Cargile, 'Pascal's Wager', in Geivett and Sweetman (eds.), *Contemporary Perspectives on Religious Epistemology*; Mackie, *The Miracle of Theism*, 201 ff.; Gale, *On the Nature and Existence of God*, 345–54; L. Nicholl, 'Pascal's Wager: The Bet is Off', *Philosophy and Phenomenological Research*, 39 (1978), 274–80; M. Martin, 'Pascal's Wager as an Argument for not Believing in God', *Religious Studies*, 19 (1983), 57–64.

[250] For a pioneering attempt to make sense of Pascal's argument, see I. Hacking, 'The Logic of Pascal's Wager', *American Philosophical Quarterly*, 9 (1972), 186–92. A very full study of the logic of the Wager can be found in N. Rescher, *Pascal's Wager* (Notre Dame, Ind., 1985).

[251] *The Will to Believe and Others Essays in Popular Philosophy* (New York, 1897).

[252] Ibid. 63–110.

To do so, one must will to believe what the evidence alone is inadequate to support.[253]

James's proposals raise two sets of questions. The first focuses upon the issue whether it is ever possible to believe in propositions at will. In what sense, if any, can we force ourselves, by an effort of will, to believe propositions for which there is no worthy evidence? Surely, we cannot believe in Ptolemaic astronomy or the claim that there are no prime numbers simply by willing to do so. Further, even if we grant that there might be propositions we can will ourselves to believe, what kind of propositions would they be? For this reason, some philosophers have argued that the prudentialist moves recommended by Pascal and James are psychologically impossible and that to embrace such propositions is an exercise in self-deception.

Yet to be fair to both Pascal and James it appears that the varieties of doxastic voluntarism they recommend are different. In Pascal's case one must will to believe a proposition, discover the best means to get into that state, and act in such a way as to make the acquisition of the belief more likely. Hence Pascal's insistence on the regularity of religious observance once one has embraced the wager. Whereas, for James, one supposes that one can obtain some beliefs simply by fiat of the will. This is legitimate, it is contended, because the truth of the proposition has not yet been decided; the activity of believing the proposition might help to bring about the desired states of affairs, as in the case of the mountaineer.

The second set of questions prompted by James's analysis is connected to what, following the work of W. K. Clifford (1845–79), is referred to as the *ethics of belief*.[254] The central question Clifford addressed is whether it is ever permissible to believe something for which we have no good evidence. His answer is negative. If Clifford is right, the pragmatic justifications offered by James will be nothing more than pale imitations of genuine justifications; they will not command rational assent.

This reintroduces the questions discussed above, concerning the place and status of evidence in the context of justifying religious belief (Sections 4.2 and 4.3). The relevance of evidence to this issue helps illuminate what is often so central to prudentialist arguments; namely, the claim that the authenticity of

[253] A helpful yet unsympathetic account of James's argument can be found in Mackie, *The Miracle of Theism*, 204–10, and Gale, *On the Nature and Existence of God*, 363–87. More sympathetic commentary can be found in H. S. Levinson, *The Religious Interventions of William James* (Chapel Hill, NC, 1981); G. Bird, *William James* (London, 1986), 161–80; W. J. Wainwright, 'James, Rationality and Religious Belief', *Religious Studies*, 27 (1991), 223–38.

[254] W. K. Clifford, *Lectures and Essays* (London, 1879). Clifford's argument is briefly discussed by Gale, *On the Nature and Existence of God*, 354–7. For an illuminating discussion of the consequences of applying Clifford's requirements to our everyday lives, see P. van Inwagen, 'It is Wrong, Everywhere, Always, and for Anyone, to Believe Anything upon Insufficient Evidence', in Jordan and Howard-Snyder (eds.), *Faith, Freedom and Rationality*.

religious faith is rarely based on assent to evidence but rather on some disposition of the heart, or an effort of will. What proponents of prudentialist arguments wish to substantiate, and what their opponents wish to deny, is that religious faith is a particular disposition or sentiment whose integrity need not be based upon matters external to it.[255]

4.5. Fideism

It is perhaps in the context of fideism that the battle between the claims of the heart and the requirements of reason are at their most poignant. Fideism holds that objective reason is inappropriate to the activity of justifying religious belief. Faith does not require reason for its justification; it creates its own justification and possesses its own criteria of internal assessment. In the history of philosophy there have been two formulations of this thesis. The first states that religion is bound to be found lacking if it is judged by the standards of speculative reason. The second holds that religion is a human activity in which the standards of speculative reason are inoperative. The two positions are clearly compatible and have been held by numerous thinkers down the centuries.[256] For instance, the third-century theologian Tertullian committed himself to the view that religious faith was both against, yet transcended, human reason,[257] while many Reformation theologians who embraced the view of *sola fides* held to the second position.[258]

In modern religious epistemology the works of Søren Kierkegaard (1813–55) and Ludwig Wittgenstein (1889–1951) are thought to lend themselves to the fideistic case. For Kierkegaard, faith and not reason is the highest virtue a human being can attain; religious faith is necessary for the fulfilment of our nature. Faith is the soul's deepest yearning and hope, which reason simply cannot fathom. In this respect, even if there were a rational proof for the existence of God, or a method of justifying our religious beliefs, Kierkegaard contends that we ought not to desire one, since theoretical certainty in the guise of a philosophical proof would only diminish the spirit and vivacity of our religious convictions.[259]

[255] For a recent discussion of this issue, see W. J. Wainwright, *Reason and the Heart: A Critique of Passional Reason* (Ithaca, NY, 1995).

[256] For a general introduction to this topic, see T. Penelhum, 'Fideism', in Quinn and Taliaferro (eds.), *Companion to the Philosophy of Religion*.

[257] Certain aspects of Tertullian's views are discussed by B. A. O. Williams in 'Tertullian's Paradox', in Flew and MacIntyre (eds.), *New Essays in Philosophical Theology*.

[258] For a discussion of the philosophical context of this time, see T. Penelhum, *God and Skepticism* (Dordrecht, 1983). Those aspects relating to Reformed thinkers are dealt with by McGrath, *The Intellectual Origins of the Reformation*, chs. 3–6.

[259] See 'Subjectivity is Truth', in *Concluding Unscientific Postscript* (1846). R. M. Adams discusses Kierkegaard's arguments in Adams, *The Virtue of Faith*, 25–41.

Another resource for fideistic arguments emanates from an interpretation of Wittgenstein. This has led to the unhappy label 'Wittgensteinian fideism'.[260] The central figure in this movement is D. Z. Phillips.[261] Phillips and others[262] argue that religion, like science and other areas of human activity, is a form of life (*Lebensform*) which establishes its own internal criteria of meaning and rationality. By these lights, the task of the religious epistemologist is not to engage in the misguided search for 'evidence' or 'justification' for the rationality of religious belief, but rather to describe and make explicit the various practices which constitute the religious form of life and which provide it with its distinctive outlook and value. Such reflections convince Phillips that we need to rethink the relationship between discursive inquiry and religion in order to appreciate more fully that religion is a 'language game' in Wittgenstein's sense. Since a language game can only be meaningfully described and understood by practices internal to it, we cannot bring to bear any external methods of description and assessment, be they reasons or proofs. As a language game, religious belief requires no 'proof'.

A related set of arguments can be found in the work of Norman Malcolm.[263] Malcolm explores the notion of a language game to illustrate the point that in the end language games are ultimately groundless, in the sense of not requiring external justification for their coherence. According to this view, most of the activities that typify our intellectual lives are groundless in the sense Malcolm favours. Thus, the activities of natural science are just as groundless as the practices of religion. Therefore, the religious form of life is as legitimate as any other form of life. Religious belief does not require any further justification to account for its difference from other types of beliefs.

Wittgensteinian fideism has been taken to task by atheist philosophers as well as by the theologically conservative. A common complaint made by both these camps is that the position fails to take account of the meaning of religious language. Thus, those committed to orthodoxy argue that when I express my belief in a set of propositions which proclaim my allegiance to a particular faith,

[260] It is important to phrase matters in this way as it is a matter of conjecture whether Wittgenstein's own views of religion are best represented as fideistic. Wittgenstein wrote precious little on the subject of religious belief, although the subject was clearly of interest to him, and what remains within his *Nachlass* is at best suggestive, lending itself to many competing interpretations. For a sober attempt to work out the implications of Wittgenstein's view for the philosophy of religion, see C. Barrett, *Wittgenstein on Ethics and Religious Belief* (Oxford, 1991). Wittgenstein's own writings on this subject have been collected in a volume entitled *Lectures and Conversations on Aesthetics, Psychology and Religious Belief*, ed. C. Barrett (Oxford, 1966); see 53 ff.

[261] The works of Phillips most relevant to the present discussion are *Faith and Philosophical Enquiry* (London, 1970); *Religion without Explanation* (Oxford, 1976); *Belief, Change and Forms of Life* (London, 1986); *Faith after Foundationalism*.

[262] Among these one could include W. D. Hudson, *Wittgenstein and Religious Belief* (New York, 1975); P. Holmer, *The Grammar of Faith* (New York, 1978); R. F. Holland, 'Religious Discourse and Theological Discourse', *Australasian Journal of Philosophy*, 34 (1956), 147–63.

[263] See Malcolm, 'The Groundlessness of Belief', in *Thought and Knowledge* (Ithaca, NY, 1977) and 'Is it a Religious Belief that God Exists?', in J. Hick (ed.), *Faith and the Philosophers* (London, 1966).

I am making factual claims about the way things are. For example, when reciting the Nicene Creed I am affirming the reality of a God who did this and that and who is part of the nature of things.[264] A similar view of religious language is also held by some atheists. They too contend that utterances of religious belief express a view as to how things are. Their disagreement with the orthodox theist, however, is simply that there is little or no evidence for the truth of such propositions. In this sense, some atheists are of the opinion that Wittgensteinian fideists obscure the nature of religious utterances; the effect of their position is to leave us unclear what constative force, or what truth-value (if any), religious utterances have.[265]

4.6. Arguments from Religious Experience

After being dismissed for many decades in religious epistemology *experientia* arguments for the justification of religious belief have once again attracted philosophical attention. Many reasons contributed to the earlier neglect of religious experience as a source of justification. The principal reason was that many philosophers, influenced by some version or other of evidentialism, thought religious experience too subjective. Given the subjectivity of such experiences, it was argued that a religious experience could never warrant making an existential claim, a claim that an object, namely God, exists outside the experience.[266]

A second factor weighing against *experientia* arguments was a lack of agreement among philosophers as to how religious experience should be described and evaluated. Whenever philosophers thought that religious experience could provide a justification for religious belief they profoundly differed in their accounts of the nature of this justification. Thus, C. D. Broad, in 'The Argument from Religious Experience', and more recently Swinburne and Gary Gutting,[267] argue that the common experience of mystics provides strong evi-

[264] For influential defences of the view, see W. Alston, *Divine Nature and Human Language* (Ithaca, 1989), chs. 1–5, and 'Taking the Curse off Language-Games: A Realist Account of Doxastic Practices', in T. Tessin, and M. van der Ruhr (eds.), *The Philosophy and Grammar of Religious Belief* (London, 1995). Also worth consulting is Swinburne, *The Coherence of Theism*, pt. 1.

[265] This theme is developed in the work of the atheist philosopher Kai Nielsen, who has extensively addressed the claims of Phillips *et al.* See 'Wittgensteinian Fideism', *Philosophy*, 42 (1967), 191–209; 'The Coherence of Wittgensteinian Fideism', *Sophia*, 11 (1972), 4–12; 'The Challenge of Wittgenstein: An Examination of his Picture of Religious Belief', *Studies in Religion*, 3 (1973), 29–49. See also M. Martin's discussion of Phillips in *Atheism: A Philosophical Justification* (Philadelphia, 1990) and Mackie, *The Miracle of Theism*, 217–39.

[266] For arguments of this type, see W. Stace, *Time and Eternity* (Princeton, 1952) and C. B. Martin, *Religious Belief* (Ithaca, 1959). Cf. K. Yandell, 'Religious Experience', in Quinn and Taliaferro (eds.), *Companion to the Philosophy of Religion*, 367–75.

[267] This is reprinted in his collection *Religion, Philosophy, and Psychical Research* (London, 1953). See Swinburne, *The Coherence of Theism*, 244–76, and G. Gutting, *Religious Belief and Religious Scepticism* (Notre Dame, Ind., 1982). For a discussion of Swinburne's and Gutting's arguments, see R. Gale, 'Swinburne's Argument from Religious Experience', in Padgett (ed.), *Reason and the Christian Religion* and L. J. Pojman, 'A Critique of Gutting's Argument from Religious Experience', in Pojman (ed.), *Philosophy of Religion*.

dence for us all that God exists. Others, such as those followers of William James,[268] argue that religious experience can only grant us a weak justification for the existence of a God. The effect of this lack of consensus was to generate uncertainty about the value and prospects for *experientia* arguments.

Recently, however, the situation has changed. This is in part due to important advances in the formulation of arguments of this kind. One of the most thorough and interesting of these recent arguments is William Alston's study *Perceiving God*.[269] Alston's purpose is to show that it is rational for an agent to participate in what he calls Christian mystical practice (CMP) because CMP is a 'socially doxastic practice that is not demonstrably unreliable or otherwise disqualified for rational acceptance'. In other words, we can be rationally justified in holding beliefs about God which emanate from religious experiences.

Alston's argument begins by analysing mystics' reports and arguing that there are no sound arguments against the mystics' claim that they directly perceive God or even against the more common claim among religious believers that they experience God in various ways. Mystical beliefs, Alston claims, are like perceptual beliefs; they are based on experience plus associated background beliefs. Thus, just as my belief that what appears to me as blue is blue requires not only bare perceptual input, but also the ability to use background colour concepts, so a mystic's belief that what appears to him as God is God requires not only a bare mystical input but also the ability to use background theological concepts. Background beliefs are ingredients in, but neither bases for nor interpretations of, perceptual and mystical experience.

The central question for Alston's account is whether mystical practice renders mystical beliefs rationally justified. Alston argues that if beliefs are formed in a reliable practice, they are prima facie justified. Crucially, he claims that only circular arguments can be found to show the reliability of either the common practice of forming perceptual beliefs and practices (PP) or CMP. Save that the former is practically universal and that the latter is limited, they are on an epistemic par in terms of reliability. Moreover, each practice has a system of 'overriders' and checks which weeds out unjustified beliefs when doubts about them arise. Hence, I am justified in believing that the wall before me *is* painted blue unless it is bathed in blue light, or I am colour-blind, so the mystic is justified in believing that what appears to him as God *is* God unless the devil counterfeits the experience, or he is hallucinating.[270]

[268] *The Varieties of Religious Experience* (1902; Glasgow, 1977). A more recent analysis of the phenomenon can be found in W. Proudfoot, *Religious Experience* (Berkeley, 1985). For important philosophical studies of mysticism, see W. J. Wainwright, *Mysticism* (Madison, Wis., 1981) and N. Pike, *Mystic Union: An Essay in the Phenomenology of Mysticism* (Ithaca, NY, 1992).

[269] Alston, *Perceiving God*.

[270] Alston characterizes the overrider system of CMP as follows: 'CMP takes the Bible, the ecumenical councils of the undivided church, Christian experience through the ages, Christian thought, and more generally the Christian tradition as normative sources of its overrider system' (ibid. 193 ff.).

Alston argues that opponents who try to show that participating in CMP is less rational than participating in PP either apply a double standard or engage in 'epistemic imperialism' (i.e. applying the standards from one practice willy-nilly to another). He works to undermine arguments which seek to show that CMP is unreliable. The most obvious one is that CMP should be disqualified because PP is universal and CMP is not. Against this, Alston claims that scientific practice is not universal but is still a paradigm of a reliable epistemic practice. Hence, the fact that a practice is non-universal does not necessarily constitute a good argument against its reliability. If our beliefs are formed in a reliable practice, then they are prima facie justified; CMP has not been shown to be any less reliable than perceptual practice (only less widespread), so the beliefs it forms about God are as prima facie justified as beliefs about the world in perceptual practice.

Alston's argument aims to show that CMP is just as epistemically reliable as any belief derived through sense-perception, and concludes that anyone who subscribes to ordinary perceptual practice cannot consistently criticize CMP, or indeed any other set of mystical practices. Against Alston, some have argued that it is indeed possible to criticize CMP.[271] The central issue is whether Alston has good grounds for his conclusion that mystical practices are really analogous to our ordinary sense-perceptual beliefs. A sense-experience has a cognitive status in that it bestows prima-facie justification upon the objective belief based on it. But for there to be a prima-facie justification there must be a system of background overriders that make it possible for a belief to be epistemically unwarranted or even false. It is argued that there cannot be a convincing analogy here as the systems of overriders in the class of mystical practices is simply too weak for mystical experience to count as cognitive. The reason is that the various extant mystical practices, at least those that find expression in the great faiths of the world, are mutually incompatible, because their respective systems of overriders give incongruous specifications of what counts as spiritual growth or sanctification.[272]

Another set of objections bases itself on the phenomenon of religious diversity. It is argued, for instance, that the account which Alston essays can apply only to one particular system of belief, orthodox Christianity, rather than to any other.[273] Further, it is held that a major requirement of Alston's thesis is that it

[271] See R. Gale, 'Why Alston's Mystical Doxastic Practice is Subjective', in *Book Symposium on 'Perceiving God', by William Alston, Philosophy and Phenomenological Research*, 54 (1994), 869–57. Similar claims are also made in Gale, 'The Overall Argument of Alston's Perceiving God', *Religious Studies*, 30 (1994), 135–49. See also Gale, *On the Nature and Existence of God*, ch. 8, for a more general discussion of arguments from religious experience.

[272] For a related set of criticisms of Alston's idea that there is a good analogy between sense-perception and mystical perception, see G. Pappas, 'Perception and Mystical Experience', *Philosophy and Phenomenological Research*, 54 (1994), 877–83. Cf. R. Audi, 'The Practice Concept of Justification', in Senor (ed.), *The Rationality of Belief and the Plurality of Faith*.

[273] See T. Tilley, 'Religious Pluralism as a Problem for Practical Religious Epistemology', *Religious Studies*, 30 (1994), 161–9, and Alston's reply to Tilley, ibid. 176 ff. See also J. Runzo, *World Views and Perceiving God*

must be shown to offer a successful response to the objection based on pluralism and diversity.[274]

Such objections aside, it is important to remember the modesty of Alston's proposals. This modesty of approach separates Alston's arguments from earlier proposals from earlier arguments from religious experience. Alston is concerned with the justification of beliefs about God, not with what it takes to have knowledge of God. In this sense, all his book can provide is an argument to the effect that beliefs about God which arise out of religious experiences are not irrational. This is noteworthy, as it manifests a shift in recent discussions of religious experience away from attempts to prove the existence of God to the more local activity of providing a way to see the phenomena of religious experiences as rational activities with their own coherence and justification.[275]

5. RELIGIOUS LANGUAGE

5.1. Three Problems of Religious Language

For the sake of simplicity and brevity, the discussion of the subject of religious language in modern philosophy of religion can be said to centre around three kinds of problem.[276] First there is a question about the relation between the sense of religious expressions and the character of the empirical world. For example, it appears to be uncontroversial to say that the sense of the term 'blue' is related to the conditions in which the statement '*x* is blue' is true, whereas it is pertinent to ask whether religious statements are subject to the same conditions. The question is, If such conditions cannot be stated, does it follow that religious language is meaningless?

The second set of questions concerns the term 'God'. Here the pressing questions are: Does this term ever succeed in identifying its referent? What sort of reality does the term pick out? or, What are we referring to? Finally, there is a question about how we ought to understand the terms which we use to predicate certain things of God. Do these terms bear the same sense when used of God and of creatures? And if they do not, how are we to understand their meaning?

(London, 1993), and W. J. Wainwright, 'Religious Language, and Religious Pluralism', in Senor (ed.), *The Rationality of Belief and the Plurality of Faith.*

[274] As well as Alston's reply to Tilley, see his 'Replies' in *Book Symposium on 'Perceiving God' by William Alston, Philosophy and Phenomenological Research*, 54 (1994), 891–9.

[275] For other important discussions of these and related topics, see K. Yandell, *The Epistemology of Religious Experience* (Cambridge, 1993).

[276] Helpful surveys of the main issues connected with the study of religious language can be found in pt. IV of Quinn and Taliaferro (eds.), *Companion to the Philosophy of Religion*; Davies, *An Introduction to the Philosophy of Religion*, 20–31; Peterson *et al.*, *Reason and Religious Belief*, 148 ff. More complex discussions of the issues can be found in Swinburne, *The Coherence of Theism*, 11–98, and Alston, *Divine Nature and Human Language*, 17–120.

Discussion of the first question has in recent times been conditioned by the positivist critique of religious language. This view amounts to the thesis that religious statements only make sense if they are empirically verifiable. Since religious claims do not meet this condition some positivists concluded that they are meaningless.[277] Critics took issue with the positivists in two ways. First they sought to show that the positivist theory of meaning was incorrect. Secondly, some philosophers of religion aimed to show that religious statements could meet the requirement of verification imposed by positivism. What is central to both approaches is the attempt to show a connection between religious discourse and the world. Thus, it is claimed that religious utterances may provide labels for certain patterns that we discern in the empirical world; or it is claimed that religious language provides us with a framework in which we explain the character of our experience; or lastly it is claimed that religious language affords us a means of articulating a constitutive assumption of empirical inquiry.[278]

Consideration of the first question is further developed by reflection on the proposal that, in expressing a religious belief, an individual is simply informing others that he is subscribing to a particular ideal of conduct. This idea of religious language was advanced by R. B. Braithwaite.[279] Braithwaite postulates a twin role for religious language. First, such language serves to express a person's intentions, and secondly, the purpose of religious language in parables and stories is to serve as a stimulus to moral conduct. Against Braithwaite it has been argued that his view simply reduces religious language to the role of a motivator of moral behaviour.[280]

Another response to the first question is offered on behalf of Wittgensteinian fideism (see Section 4.5 above). D. Z. Phillips, for instance, holds that as religious and scientific discourse are to be judged by different standards of meaning and rationality, there is no stronger reason to call into question the meaning or rationality of religious discourse than there is to call into question the meaning or rationality of science.[281] Thus, even accounting for the differences between the language games of science and religion, talk about God is still talk about an *agent*. It is meaningful by its own standards.

[277] See Rudolf Carnap, 'Religious Language is Meaningless'. Cf. Ayer, *Language, Truth and Logic*.

[278] For examples of these separate approaches, see J. Wisdom, 'Gods', *Proceedings of the Aristotelian Society*, 45 (1944–5), 185–206; I. M. Crombie, 'The Possibility of Theological Statements', in Mitchell (ed.), *The Philosophy of Religion*; Hick, 'Theology and Verification'; I. T. Ramsey, *Religious Language: An Empirical Placing of Theological Phrases* (London, 1957); R. M. Hare, 'The University Discussion', in Flew and MacIntyre (eds.), *New Essays in Philosophical Theology*; Heimbeck, *Theology and Meaning*; Mitchell, *The Justification of Religious Belief*; Swinburne, *The Coherence of Theism*; Alston, *Divine Nature and Human Language*, 39–63.

[279] R. B. Braithwaite, 'An Empiricist's View of the Nature of Religious Belief', in Mitchell (ed.), *The Philosophy of Religion*.

[280] See Phillips, *Religion without Explanation*, 139–50.

[281] Ibid. and Phillips, *The Concept of Prayer* (London, 1965). Cf. P. Winch, 'Meaning and Religious Language', in *Trying to Make Sense* (Oxford, 1987).

The second major issue addressed by the topic of religious language concerns the problem of divine predication. Quite simply, this is a problem which arises from reflection upon the question when we use such terms as 'good' and 'wise' of God and of human beings, do we mean the same thing? If the term 'good' means exactly the same when it is used of God as when used of a human, we seem to be faced with two unsatisfactory consequences: (1) an anthropomorphic account of the divine nature; and (2) an inability to locate the religious sense of terms with precision.

This dilemma was recognized by Thomas Aquinas. At *Summa Theologiae*, 1a, q. 13, aa. 5 ff., he proposed that in referring to God there is a middle way between the unappealing options of univocity (sameness of sense) and equivocity (total difference of sense). The intermediate possibility he proposed is *analogy*, where the meaning of a term is stretched in the case of God but is not stretched so far as to lose all connection with its original, human or creaturely sense.[282] Later schoolmen such as Cajetan developed Aquinas' theory of analogy so that it became a commonplace to hold that there are two kinds of analogy: the analogy of attribution and the analogy of proportionality.[283] The difference between them is that in the first case a term applies to just one analogate and in a derivative way to the further analogate by virtue of some relation which it bears to the first analogate. For example, the term 'healthy' is not used in the exact same sense when we are referring to a 'healthy man' and a 'healthy appetite', but at the same time it is not used in totally different senses. In the second case, a term applies to both analogates, but in a different way; as one might speak of a 'loyal partner' and a 'loyal pet', when loyalty in these contexts is proportional to the nature of partner and of pet respectively.[284]

How might these distinctions be applied to the problem of divine predication? The analogy of attribution would suggest that a term which can be applied to an object in the world can also be applied analogically to God, in so far as God is the cause of all created things. This may seem acceptable until we note its implications. For should it be adopted, terms like 'goodness', 'holiness', and 'wisdom' may be used in their most exact sense when referring to the primary analogates, namely creatures in the world, but only derivatively when referring to God. This would appear to conflict with some of the primary commitments of religious believers, who typically wish to say that God is the supreme bearer of such properties as goodness, and it is only creatures who are good and wise etc. in secondary senses of those terms. The analogy of

[282] For a discussion of the development of Aquinas' views on analogy and their relationship to the negative theology of his days, see R. McInerny, *Aquinas on Analogy* (Washington, 1996) and D. Burrell, *Aquinas: God and Action* (London, 1986), 51–70.

[283] Cajetan, *De Nominum Analogia* (1506), trans. E. Bushinski, and H. Koren as *The Analogy of Names* (Pittsburgh, 1953). For a discussion of Cajetan, see McInerny, *Aquinas on Analogy*, ch. 1.

[284] A very helpful discussion of these and other matters related to analogy can be found in J. F. Ross, *Portraying Analogy* (Cambridge, 1981). Cf. H. Palmer, *Analogy* (London, 1973).

proportionality also raises problems, for it suggests that to give sense to a term like 'good' when it is predicated of God, we need to be mindful of the fact that God's goodness is proportional to his nature. This thought, however, provokes the objection that we are caught in a circle: we must possess some notion of what God's nature is like, but we cannot have such a notion without already understanding what terms like 'good' mean when they are predicated of God, for such terms will be basic to our conception of the divine nature.

Analogy, univocity, and equivocity are literal modes of speech. We can also speak of God non-literally, however, by recourse to metaphor. Some philosophers have argued that all talk of God is metaphorical, because the terms we use of God we first learn in relation to creatures, and the properties of God are unlike those we ordinarily assign to living things. Although this is controversial,[285] it nevertheless seems apparent that metaphors indeed have an important role in religious language. Recently, a number of discussions have drawn attention to the importance of metaphors in theology.[286] The effect of these discussions has been twofold. In the first instance, it has been to argue that the metaphorical use of religious language may provide a way of anchoring religious claims in the world, while in the second instance, reflections on the use of metaphor in religious language have led some philosophers to conclude that there are insuperable problems for the view that we can make 'God' a term of literal discourse.

The last of the major problems associated with the study of religious language concerns the problem of reference. In many ways this subject more properly belongs in the philosophy of language, since any advance made in our understanding of the referential function of 'God' will depend upon the theory of reference we choose to adopt.[287] It is unsurprising, therefore, to find this discussion dominated by attempts to apply a particular theory of reference to religious language. Any advance in this area is more likely to come from that direction than through the development of a theory of reference which begins from features of religious language itself.

BIBLIOGRAPHY

Adams, M. McCord, and Adams, R. M., *The Problem of Evil*, (Oxford, 1990).

Adams, R. M., *The Virtue of Faith and Other Essays in Philosophical Theology*, (Oxford, 1987).

[285] See W. Alston, 'Irreducible Metaphors in Theology', in Alston, *Divine Nature and Human Language*.

[286] e.g. J. M. Soskice, *Metaphor and Religious Language* (Oxford, 1985). See Hughes, *The Nature of God*, 62–3, 114, 188, for a discussion of some of these issues.

[287] See Alston, *Divine Nature and Human Language*; Swinburne, *The Coherence of Theism*; Soskice, *Metaphor and Religious Language*.

Alston, W. P., *Divine Nature and Human Language: Essays in Philosophical Theology*, (Ithaca, NY, 1989).

——*Perceiving God: The Epistemology of Religious Experience* (Ithaca, NY, 1991).

Anderson, P. A., *A Feminist Philosophy of Religion* (Oxford, 1998).

Audi, R., and Wainwright, W. (eds.), *Rationality, Religious Belief and Moral Commitment*, (Ithaca, NY, 1986).

Davies, B., *An Introduction to the Philosophy of Religion*, 2nd edn. (1982; repr. Oxford, 1993).

Davis, S. T., *Good, Reason and Theistic Proofs* (Edinburgh, 1997).

Edwards, P. (ed.), *Immortality* (New York, 1992).

Forrest, P., *God without the Supernatural: A Defense of Scientific Theism* (Ithaca, NY, 1996).

Freddoso, A. J. (ed.), *The Existence and Nature of God* (Notre Dame, Ind., 1983).

Gale, R. M., *On the Nature and Existence of God* (Cambridge, 1991).

Geivett, R. D., and Sweetman, B. (eds.), *Contemporary Perspectives on Religious Epistemology* (Oxford, 1992).

Hasker, W., *God, Time and Knowledge* (Ithaca, NY, 1989).

Helm, P., *Eternal God: A Study of God without Time* (Oxford, 1988).

——*Faith and Understanding* (Edinburgh, 1997).

Howard-Snyder, D. (ed.), *The Evidential Argument from Evil* (Bloomington, Ind., 1996).

Hughes, G. J., *The Nature of God* (London, 1995).

Jordan, J., and Howard-Snyder, D. (eds.), *Faith, Freedom and Rationality: Philosophy of Religion Today* (Lanham, Md., 1996).

Kenny, A., *The God of the Philosophers* (Oxford, 1979).

Kretzmann, N., *The Metaphysics of Theism: Aquinas's Natural Theology in 'Summa contra Gentiles' 1* (Oxford, 1997).

Leftow, B., *Time and Eternity* (Ithaca, NY, 1991).

Mackie, J. L., *The Miracle of Theism* (Oxford, 1982).

McLeod, M. S., *Rationality and Theistic Belief: An Essay on Reformed Epistemology* (Ithaca, NY, 1993).

Mitchell, B. (ed.), *The Philosophy of Religion* (Oxford, 1971).

Morris, T. V., *The Logic of God Incarnate* (Ithaca, NY, 1986).

——(ed.), *The Concept of God* (Oxford, 1987).

——(ed.), *Divine and Human Action: Essays in the Metaphysics of Theism* (Ithaca, NY, 1988).

——(ed.), *Philosophy and the Christian Faith* (Notre Dame, Ind., 1988).

Padgett, A. G. (ed.), *Reason and the Christian Religion* (Oxford, 1994).

Peterson, M. L. (ed.), *The Problem of Evil: Selected Readings* (Notre Dame, Ind., 1992).

——Hasker, W., Reichenbach, B., and Basinger, D. (eds.), *Reason and Religious Belief: An Introduction to the Philosophy of Religion* (Oxford, 1991).

————————(eds.), *Philosophy of Religion: Selected Readings* (Oxford, 1996).

Plantinga, A., *God, Freedom and Evil* (London, 1974).

——*The Nature of Necessity* (Oxford, 1974).

——and Wolterstorff, N. (eds.), *Faith and Rationality: Reason and Belief in God* (Notre Dame, Ind., 1983).

Pojman, L. P. (ed.), *Philosophy of Religion: An Anthology* (1987; 2nd edn. Belmont, Calif., 1987; rev. 1994).

Quinn, P. L., and Taliaferro, C., *A Companion to the Philosophy of Religion* (Oxford, 1997).

Senor, T. D. (ed.), *The Rationality of Belief and the Plurality of Faith: Essays in Honor of William Alston* (Ithaca, NY, 1995).

Smart, J. J. C., and Haldane, J. J., *Atheism and Theism* (Oxford, 1996).

Soskice, J. M., *Metaphor and Religious Language* (Oxford, 1985).

Stump, E. (ed.), *Reasoned Faith: Essays in Philosophical Theology in Honor of Norman Kretzmann* (Ithaca, NY, 1993).

Swinburne, R. G., *The Coherence of Theism* (Oxford, 1977; rev. 1993).

—— *The Existence of God* (Oxford, 1979; rev. 1991).

—— *Faith and Reason* (Oxford, 1981).

—— *The Christian God* (Oxford, 1994).

Taliaferro, C., *An Introduction to Contemporary Philosophy of Religion* (Oxford, 1997).

van Inwagen, P., *God, Knowledge and Mystery: Essays in Philosophical Theology* (Ithaca, NY, 1995).

Wainwright, W. J., *Philosophy of Religion* (Belmont, Calif., 1988).

Wierenga, E. R., *The Nature of God: An Inquiry into Divine Attributes* (Ithaca, NY, 1989).

Wolterstorff, N., *Divine Discourse: Philosophical Reflections on the Claim that God Speaks* (Cambridge, 1995).

6

POLITICAL PHILOSOPHY

Alan Ryan

INTRODUCTION

I.1. Political Philosophy: Historical and Conceptual

This introduction consists essentially of some snapshot photographs of parts of a much wider landscape. The principles of selection on which I have assembled these photographs are by no means the only ones that could sensibly be employed, but they are these. I have chosen Plato and Aristotle, Machiavelli, Hobbes, Hegel, and Marx as historical figures to focus on, because they provide contrasting perspectives on politics that are especially apt for the purposes of an introduction. One of these purposes is to illuminate our present concerns by comparing and contrasting them, and the setting in which they arise, with the concerns of our predecessors and the settings in which they arose. Plato and Aristotle write in the context of the Greek *polis*, Machiavelli in the context of the declining Renaissance city-state, Hobbes in the context of the new nation-state, and Hegel and Marx in a political context recognizably like our own. We employ the same word as the Greeks to characterize the way we preserve order, choose leaders, make laws, and organize society, and this raises the question whether we practise 'politics' in any sense that they would have recognized. Hannah Arendt, for one, argued that we do not, and that we have in fact lost touch with the true practice of politics.[1]

Since politics involves, along with much else, the taking of decisions for a whole society, the question whether we have taken such decisions well or badly, and by what means we are to discover the answer, has always been debated. From the beginning of self-conscious thought on the subject, an obvious question has been posed. Why should we put our trust in what we call the *political* process of decision-making? Ought we not rather to trust a wise man or a few wise men? That suggestion raises another question, however. What wisdom should they possess, what sort of knowledge must they have if they are to decide matters for us rather than our deciding for ourselves? Conversely, if we insist that everyone must take part in making political decisions, what must citizens know, if anything? Plato notoriously took away authority from the politician and gave it to the philosopher; so in a different fashion did Hobbes, since Hobbes's insistence that the sovereign's role was simply to lay down the law was itself founded on a philosophical theory of politics that made the ordinary political processes of debate and accommodation look thoroughly irrational. Aristotle on the other hand articulated a practitioner's knowledge that was directed to something other than the pursuit of truth, putting into intellectual currency an argument over the proper analysis of politics that has persisted

[1] Hannah Arendt, *The Human Condition* (Chicago, 1958).

to this day. Today it is sometimes complained that those who defend the right of the 'nine wise men' of the American Supreme Court to override the judgement of Congress display a 'Platonic' contempt for popular judgement, and an equally Platonic confidence in the dictates of an élite.

Thinkers who have wanted to replace politics as it is commonly practised with some other way of making decisions for a society have not always wished to replace politicians with philosophers. Karl Marx's vision of a society in which 'the administration of things replaces the government of men' envisages a world managed by technicians, though his anarchist critic Bakunin denounced it as a 'pedantocracy'. On Marx's analysis, the task of politics had been to secure a general consent—however grudging—to unjust and irrational social and economic conditions. Such a task need no longer be performed in conditions where nobody was exploited or otherwise ill-used, and where resources were employed with the greatest possible efficiency for the good of all. To Marx's mind, Plato's philosopher-kings who discerned the Form of the Good and the True were not needed either. In the absence of social conflict, morality as usually understood would be redundant, so there would be no room for anyone claiming insights into the Good, and in the absence of anyone with a vested interest in obscuring the truth, there would be no need for a specially equipped class of persons claiming insights into the True.

Although other utopian thinkers besides Marx have wanted to replace political rule with expert management, it is sometimes suggested that philosophy is peculiarly inimical to the study of politics in its own terms. One obvious interpretation of this thought is that the task of the philosopher is to analyse, to lay bare conceptual problems, to reach a certain sort of truth, while the task of the political practitioner is to preserve social order, to reconcile the irreconcilable, to stamp his own or his people's mark on the world. A more interesting thought is that because philosophy characteristically aims to reach the right answer to whatever questions are proposed, philosophers necessarily misrepresent the conditions under which politics is practised, conditions where there is neither time to discover 'the right answer', nor any good reason to suppose that there is 'one right answer' to be found. On this view, even contemporary political philosophy, whose practitioners have none of the pretensions of Plato, nevertheless evacuates the political content from the study of politics. As to what would capture the political essence of politics, it is often said that a 'Machiavellian' account of politics—not in the sense of a duplicitous or treacherous account, but in the sense of an account that pays proper attention to the hazards of republican statecraft—would stand us in better stead.[2] Again, it is said that the Machiavellian tradition concentrates more persuasively than modern analytical philosophy has done on the problem of 'dirty hands', or on the place of

[2] As, indeed, by Arendt, ibid.

violence in politics, or on the perennial temptation to do evil today for the sake of good tomorrow—or for the sake of good at some far distant date. Modern moral philosophers certainly discuss conflicting obligations and the difficulty of making rational judgements where incommensurable considerations have to be weighed against one another, but it might be said that it took the vivid descriptive style of Machiavelli and his successors in the same tradition to bring the dilemmas of politics adequately to life.

If Machiavelli's statement of the problem of dirty hands has stood the test of time, then Hobbes's statement of a contractualist theory of politics so clearly sets out the main elements of such a theory and so starkly raises the chief difficulties such a theory encounters that in this respect later contractualists have for three centuries provided footnotes to Hobbes. Today's inheritors of the apparatus first set out by Hobbes in *Leviathan* are Hobbes's equals in intelligence and much his superiors in sophistication, but they escape few of the difficulties evident in his writings. The work of John Rawls, in particular, who derives liberal conclusions from premisses not wholly unlike those from which Hobbes derived authoritarian ones, raises most of the questions that Hobbes's *Leviathan* raised. Similarly, once Hegel and Marx had argued, as nobody had ever done before, that the historicity of our institutions is a central fact about them it became impossible to think about politics ahistorically, without at least a shadow of anxiety. Though Hegel and Marx held very different views about just how it was true that politics was *essentially* conditioned by history, and just what followed from that fact, anyone writing today is acutely aware of the need to frame what they have to say in an appropriate historical context. John Rawls wrote *A Theory of Justice* in something of the same deductive style as Hobbes's *Leviathan*, but whereas Hobbes could write as though he had discovered timeless truths about the nature of political order, Rawls has always been careful to say that he is elucidating political principles appropriate to a modern liberal state.[3] The successors of Hegel and Marx are too numerous to discuss in detail, but I shall later say a little about the impact of Marxism on late twentieth-century political philosophy. The authors discussed here articulate a range of possibilities for political thought and practice that cannot justify, but may partially excuse, the absence of Thomas Aquinas, Rousseau, Locke, the Federalists, Edmund Burke, and Jeremy Bentham, and the appearance of John Stuart Mill among our contemporaries rather than their ancestors.

In discussing contemporary issues in political philosophy, I focus on what have recently been seen as the central problems of liberal political philosophy—problems that focus on the justification of democratic rule, and the analysis of social and political justice.[4] I do so because this is where the great bulk of con-

[3] Thomas Hobbes, *Leviathan*, ed. Richard Tuck (Cambridge, 1996).

[4] Jonathan Wolff, *An Introduction to Political Philosophy* (Oxford, 1996).

temporary work is done, and without prejudging the question whether the liberal consensus is in itself a good thing. If I am allowed a purely personal reflection, it is that the late twentieth-century understanding even of liberalism is thinner than it should be, and that analytical philosophers have been insufficiently willing to engage with the concerns that drive their students into the arms of the disciples of Nietzsche and Heidegger. In the process of tackling the issues I do, I take up some of the concerns of recent jurisprudence, both because much of the most interesting recent work in political theory has emanated from American law schools, and because the connection between constitutional rule and democracy is a contested subject. Although it is true that a broadly liberal perspective dominates recent political theory and political philosophy, there have been two counter-currents that are themselves so much part of the mainstream that they demand some notice here. One is the 'communitarian' critique of liberalism, or more narrowly of the liberal view of the individual, or the liberal concern with justice.[5] This is sometimes, though not always, founded on or associated with an interest in social relations of a rather Hegelian kind. It is also associated with the thought that the liberal conception of freedom, what Isaiah Berlin famously described as 'negative liberty',[6] is not the only kind of liberty that a society should foster. 'Republican' freedom, the positive liberty associated with ideals of self-government, is either to be preferred, or at least to be fostered in conjunction with liberal freedom.[7] The other is a critique from within the (broadly construed) analytical mode of philosophy, and focuses on what might be seen as the unambitious acceptance of something close to the economic and political status quo. Sometimes, as with the work of G. A. Cohen,[8] there has been an attempt to recast the Marxist condemnation of capitalism, and the Marxist theory of its inevitable downfall, in terms that are invulnerable to familiar accusations of incoherence and untestability.[9] Sometimes, as in the work of Brian Barry, the claim is rather that any intellectually sustainable account of justice impugns the existing order and implies redistributive measures of a socialist cast.[10]

I.2. Political Theory and Public Policy

One further topic that I discuss below cuts across these arguments; this is the growth of an interest in the ethics and political theory of public policy. Not all of what is often called 'applied philosophy' is properly a part of political

[5] Michael Sandel, *Liberalism and the Limits of Justice* (Cambridge, 1982).
[6] I. Berlin, 'Two Concepts of Liberty', in *Four Essays on Liberty* (Oxford, 1969).
[7] Michael Sandel, *Democracy's Discontent* (New York, 1995).
[8] G. A. Cohen, *Karl Marx's Theory of History* (Oxford, 1980).
[9] Karl Popper, *The Poverty of Historicism* (London, 1954).
[10] Brian Barry, *A Treatise on Social Justice* (Brighton, 1989–96).

philosophy. The 'problem of abortion', for example, can be understood quite narrowly as a question about the moral permissibility of terminating a pregnancy; but as soon as the question arises of the state's role in regulating the termination of pregnancy, it becomes a question of public policy, and an issue in political philosophy. These themes, lightly treated as they are here, omit a good deal that could properly be considered part of the subject of political philosophy. Neither post-modernist accounts of the politics of identity nor the concerns of recent feminists make more than a passing appearance. Nor does a concern to submit our thinking about international relations to philosophical scrutiny. My hope is only that someone who has a firm grasp of what I do discuss can go on to make their own way through what I do not.

I.3. Timeless Conversation: A Myth?

My first task is to justify the way in which political philosophers characteristically tackle their subject, which is, indeed, the way I do it here. Political philosophy is a branch of philosophy in which, more than in most others, commentators spend their time in the company of the immortal dead. They find it difficult to write about democracy without mentioning Plato's root and branch condemnation of the democratic politics of Athens in *Gorgias* and the *Republic*, to discuss revolution without reference to Aristotle as well as Machiavelli and Marx, and to talk about liberty without mentioning Mill. Two obvious questions cast the habit in a poor light. First, why cannot we think our own thoughts for ourselves? Practitioners of reputable intellectual disciplines such as physics, chemistry, and mathematics largely ignore their ancestors and attend to the problems before them. Why do we not do likewise? It is modern representative liberal democracy that poses the problems that most of us are concerned with; we are not proposing to restore a simulacrum of the Athenian *polis* in Guildford or Exeter (to choose towns whose populations are approximately the right size), so why should we care what Plato had to say against the poets, politicians, and orators of his own day—that is, during the early fourth century BC? This is not a rhetorical question; there have been many philosophers who have wanted to model their philosophical practice on that of natural scientists who may well venerate their ancestors but who do not treat them as having anything to contribute to contemporary science.

It is often said that the conversation we hold with the great dead thinkers who feature in university-level courses in political philosophy is uniquely valuable, either for its own sake, or for the sake of the stimulus it provides us with. These are difficult claims to establish beyond all contradiction. As a pedagogical approach, this continuous recurrence to the discipline's history is exceedingly vulnerable to students who assert flatly that they would rather start somewhere else; if Hobbes uncovers the so-called 'Hobbesian problem of order', why do we not discuss the problem of order rather than Hobbes? Given the linguistic and stylistic gap between the mental habits of the modern student and Plato, can it be true that conversation with the immortal dead is the obvious, let alone the best, way to begin to think about political philosophy? These are pedagogical questions that have been debated for a century and will surely be debated for years to come. There are sharper, more political, objections to the enterprise. Feminist critics and their anti-colonialist allies have lately denounced this historical approach to political thinking as a superstitious communion with Dead White European Males that encourages live white males in their racist and sexist political practices. There is reason to be sceptical about this complaint. The sheer difficulty of reading Plato or Aristotle surely means that their effect on the political prejudices of most students cannot be very great. In any event, the liberal prejudices of most contemporary students are so thoroughly entrenched that they find it difficult to take Aristotle's explanation of the relations that he believed proper to husband and wife or master and slave seriously enough to decide whether the underlying principle—that authority should be allocated by capacity and function—is itself persuasive whatever application Aristotle made of it.[11] In any event, curricular choices may more plausibly be thought to be *symptoms* of our political prejudices than their causes. Someone who thought so could ask some awkward questions: do we study the past in order not to confront the inequities of the present, to evade the moral demands of the misery all around us by changing the subject from *our* politics to that of Aristotle's? Pursuing the argument down that track, however, would take us into the sociological analysis of culture rather than political philosophy.

There is a perhaps more damaging complaint to be made. For the second question is this: is our 'conversation' with the dead not in fact a monologue, and the supposed ideas of the dead our ideas rather than theirs? Do we really understand the long-dead thinkers with whom we habitually wrestle? The society that condemned Socrates to death in 399 BC is so remote from our own, and its habits of thought and feeling so alien to us, that we can have no confidence that we have got thoroughly inside its political ideas and aspirations. Even if it is not impossible to do so, it is anyway an activity at which philosophers are unlikely to be accomplished. To speak with, and listen to, our long-dead predecessors, we must spend a great deal of effort locating them in their own times, uncovering the expectations of their hearers and readers, learning to read and hear them as their contemporaries would have done. To do that with any fluency, we should have to spend so much time becoming adept cultural historians that we should have no time or energy thereafter for philosophical reflection. The dilemma would then be that if we wanted to converse with our long-dead

[11] *The Politics of Aristotle*, ed. Ernest Barker (Oxford, 1949), 32–3.

predecessors, we would have to turn ourselves into historians; so long as we wanted our conversation to be that of philosophers, we should inevitably be confined to talking to our contemporaries.

Only after that problem is somehow dealt with is it worth turning to the problem of the narrow range of those we choose to talk with. If the whole practice is misguided, it cannot be improved by our adding Long-Dead but Non-White and Non-European Women to our reading-lists; for whatever we purport to be doing, what we shall in fact be doing is projecting our own ideas onto the unresisting objects of our fantasies. No doubt some of the ideas thus projected are better than others, but the status of all of them has been undermined once we understand that they are only 'ours' and not 'theirs'. No matter how radical the intentions of those who drew up the reading-lists for a radicalized intellectual history, they would be implicated in the same intellectual disaster as their conservative enemies.

Perennial and Non-Perennial Issues These doubts cannot be dismissed out of hand; indeed, they surely ought to haunt us as we work. Still, they do not show that the mixture of historical interrogation and contemporary reflection that in fact characterizes political philosophy ought not to do so. First, the practice is more or less inescapable. In some traditional societies, the only acceptable answer to the question why the local political order ought to be obeyed was that it always had been; perhaps in some dynastic states, the question of legitimacy was open and shut—the answer to questions about who our lawful rulers were was that this was the ruling family's state, and thus that those who find themselves in the family's territories have found their lawful rulers. But modern nation-states claim a different kind of legitimacy: they are founded upon ideas, and they attribute those ideas to thinkers. That is, a state such as the United Kingdom claims the allegiance of British nationals not simply on the basis of its ability to force most people living within its territory to obey the local rules, but on a principled basis. Upon just what principles the claim to the allegiance of the citizens rests is disputable, but they clearly include the physical safety of the citizen, the availability of the legal arrangements by which he or she can secure their welfare through working, the maintenance of the rule of law, and the securing of the civil rights of individuals, and perhaps the acceptance of some version of the doctrine of government by consent. (One way of thinking about these principles is to imagine a government violating them, and to decide at what point we would think that we no longer owed any allegiance to the government.) But these principles have a history; they were not always and perhaps not at all often discovered by particular writers, but they have often been articulated by them, and it is not to be wondered at that we think about the principles in the formulations offered by these thinkers.

States with written constitutions often have a clearer pedigree still. American politicians who would repudiate any suggestion that they should be 'philosopher-kings' swear fealty to a constitution that was thought up and argued for by James Madison and his friends and allies for reasons he thought he had gleaned from Machiavelli, Hume, Locke, and others; 5,000 miles away, Soviet leaders for seventy-odd years purported to steer the Soviet Union by the very different lights of Marxism-Leninism. Were we to try to burst upon the political scene thinking only our own thoughts, it would be an act of self-destruction. We should be asked how our ideas fitted into or failed to fit into the local traditions of intellectual and political legitimacy, and we would have to find some answer. Even revolutionaries such as Karl Marx make themselves understood by locating themselves in the tradition they wish to overturn. Indeed, Marx himself seems to have understood this very well. His favourite label for his work was 'critique', that is, the criticism of the work of his predecessors and contemporaries in order that a new, more adequate account of society, economy, and polity might be erected on the ruins of other people's errors.

Secondly, it is not obvious that we are impossibly remote from our immortal predecessors. Not all issues in political thinking are 'perennial'—the 'divine right of kings' is a plausible example of a thoroughly dead issue, at any rate in that form, though certainly not in the form of 'charismatic authority'—but a good many are: Plato's complaint that democracies counted heads rather than weighing arguments has lost none of its persuasiveness in two and a half millennia; Aristotle's arguments for trying to create a substantial middle class as a barrier against oligarchical pride and insurrection from below have stood the test of time equally well. Indeed, two of the most distinguished American political scientists of the past fifty years have built two of their most interesting books around just these claims. Robert Dahl's *Democracy and its Critics* argues that the only competitor to liberal democracy is a 'guardian' style of aristocracy. Seymour Martin Lipset's *Political Man* starts from Aristotle's recipe for a stable constitutional polity and reflects on the social and economic conditions necessary to implement that recipe in the twentieth century. There is no reason to think that Plato and Aristotle understood such arguments very differently from ourselves.

Of course, there are many occasions when we cannot think quite what a 'classical' thinker had in mind: Hobbes's views on the nature of science on the one hand and the dependence of justice on contractual relations on the other are two striking examples from a writer whose wonderful clarity and vitality make him otherwise such a pleasure to read. Even then, it is not because Hobbes is irretrievably alien or 'other' that we have such difficulty in working out what he thought on these matters; it is the intrinsic difficulty of knowing how an intelligent and learned man could believe quite what it is that Hobbes seems to say.

Thirdly, it is possible that a person with a sufficiently vivid imagination and a sufficiently fertile intelligence could think up an indefinite number of imaginary interlocutors who would make him or her continuously aware of all the objections that might be levelled against any particular opinion; still, it remains true that history has supplied what the imagination and ingenuity of most of us cannot—critics who differ with us, and thinkers whose intelligence is at least equal to our own, with whom we must come to terms.

Fruitful and Fruitless Comparisons This, then, suggests that we can, to use a mildly derogatory term, exploit the immortal dead for our present intellectual purposes. We must, of course, do our grave-robbing with some delicacy. We shall not get anything out of the dead if we try to recruit them for propaganda purposes or merely to illustrate some favourite thesis of our own. We shall not get anything out of them if we try to exploit them for goals to which their ideas are simply ill-adapted; Hobbes described most intermediate associations as 'worms in the entrails of the body politic', and would be an unlikely source for ideas about the value of voluntary association and the values of civil society; Machiavelli was interested in religion as a social cement and an aid to the inculcation of patriotic and military virtues in the citizenry, and would be an unlikely source for ideas about the Protestant conception of toleration defended by John Locke. Certainly, we must ask *why* Hobbes was so hostile to the pluralist view of the world that later sustained the account of a successful liberal democracy provided by de Tocqueville and Mill, and we must ask whether Machiavelli's toughly pragmatic view of how much religious toleration a society ought to offer might have more to be said for it than a disciple of Locke would admit. But some comparisons make little sense—Plato's views on late capitalism cannot be compared with ours because Plato had none, and he had none because the phenomenon of late capitalism was some two and half thousand years off, and perhaps more importantly, because the most interesting features of late capitalism have too few close analogues in Athenian society to make it useful to speculate about what Plato *would*, *might*, or *must* have thought. We know that he disliked most forms of trade, denied that the accumulation of wealth was good for us, and thought an economy based on money would bring innumerable forms of corruption with it; in that sense, we know that he would have disliked all forms of what the eighteenth century called 'commercial society', of which late capitalism is one variant.[12] All the same, what Plato expresses is a general contempt for the life of trade and money-making, not a usable critique of late capitalism in particular. This is quite different from Plato's critique of democracy, where his views are detailed and vivid and still to a high degree persuasive.

[12] *Republic*, ed. Robert Waterfield (Oxford, 1994), 124 ff.

In what follows, I have tried to bring a very few of the historical figures whose work constitutes something of a 'canon' in political theory into a discussion that observes the strictures just noted: that is, they appear in the interests of illuminating a particular argument or a particular dilemma. There is no attempt to provide more than the barest account of the context of their views, enough only to make their views intelligible. I conclude with a discussion of several issues that have preoccupied political philosophers in Britain and the United States during the past forty years.

1. HISTORICAL FIGURES

1.1. Plato and Aristotle

It is obvious, but important, that Plato and Aristotle wrote about politics in the context of the Greek city-state or *polis*, not in that of the bureaucratic theocracy of ancient Egypt, that of the Persian Empire, or that of the rising Roman Empire. The most important contrast between the Greek *polis* and any modern state— with the exception of Andorra and San Marino perhaps—is that of size. Attica, the countryside over which Athens ruled, and which constituted the territory of the Athenian city-state, was about the size of the English county of Gloucestershire, and somewhat smaller than the smallest American state, Rhode Island. There is no agreement on the size of the population, nor on the proportion of the population that was free or slave, nor on the exact balance of rural and urban population. Most writers suggest about 150,000 for the free population, and thus about 40,000 adult male citizens. Given the vulnerability of the population to plague, poor harvests, and the loss of young adults in war, it probably varied a great deal in the two centuries during which the democratic experiment was tried. Aristotle held that the maximum number of citizens a state should have is some 10,000, the largest number of people who could be expected to have some knowledge of one another and to be easily addressed in a public place.[13]

Athens probably had four times as many citizens as that, one of the things that Aristotle thought had made Athens excessively democratic. The qualifications for citizenship varied greatly from one place to another, but were generally a matter of heredity and wealth in some combination—one had to be able to show citizen descent, to belong to some particular geographical or semi-tribal grouping, and to possess some small amount of property. Athens was more generous with citizenship than most cities, but even in Athens there were large numbers of slaves, resident foreigners, and persons who were free but unqualified for citizenship, among whom free women were the largest single

[13] The principle is laid down in *Politics* 7. 4.

group. One demographic point worth recalling is that, as in all pre-industrial societies, the average age of the population was very low. From childhood onwards, there was steady attrition by disease and injury—quite unlike a modern state where the post-infancy death-rate is very low until people reach their fifties. The presence of so many young people may partly explain the striking propensity of Greek states to embroil themselves in war. For all practical purposes, the Greek city-state came to an end in the late fourth century BC when Philip of Macedon and his son Alexander the Great established their imperial rule throughout the Eastern Mediterranean and Near Asia. That collapse was essentially the result of two centuries of warfare between these tiny states. Among the causes of this continuous intermittent state of war the youthful aggressiveness, not only of the population that went out to fight, but of many of the political leaders who sent them out, has to be borne in mind.

Greek city-states were ruled on a variety of constitutional bases. The most famous, and the most attractive to ourselves, was the popular democracy of Athens. It was unique in Greece, and it was unique in the world until the medieval city-states of Italy. The Roman republic was always a much more oligarchical and overtly class-based political order than the Athenian. It is only in the last century that Athenian democracy has come to seem so attractive. For many centuries before that, Athenian democracy was a by-word for factionalism and self-destructiveness. Until the late nineteenth century few political thinkers were in favour of democratic government, and they especially feared radical, lower-class democracy of the Athenian kind. Even to a modern eye, the Athenian democracy is not attractive in all respects. Among other things, it supported its democratic institutions by exploiting its notional allies in the Delian League; their tribute not only paid for the upkeep of the Athenian navy—a navy that had certainly saved the Greeks from the invading Persians of the early fifth century, and subsequently kept the Aegean free of pirates—but also for the embellishment of the Acropolis and for the payments to sufficient of the Athenian lower classes to enable them to devote some of their time to political activity rather than to earning a living.

Though there was some tendency for democracies to stick together and oligarchies to do likewise, Athens never allowed ideological affinity to override simple self-interest. Unlike modern democracies, which have never gone to war with one another, the Athenian democracy suppressed other democracies when it suited it, and suffered catastrophic defeat late in the Peloponnesian War at the hands of Syracuse, another democratic city-state. This, moreover, omits the single event that ruined the reputation of Athens in the eyes of posterity—at any rate, in the eyes of later philosophers. This was the trial and execution, or forced suicide, of Socrates in the year 399 BC. Socrates was accused of 'corrupting the young' by teaching that there were no gods; the charge that he corrupted the young was obviously absurd inasmuch as Socrates spent his time trying to get his hearers to think more carefully and more passionately about just what their duties to themselves and each other were. While it is true that he denied that the stories about the gods retailed in Greek mythology were true, this was no act of impiety, for he claimed that they must be false because they cast the gods in a poor light.

An idiosyncratic sort of piety seems in fact to have been a particular feature of his make-up. It was this that led him to refuse the court's offer to commute his death sentence: the court offered him the chance to save his life by agreeing not to teach, but he held that the gods had charged him with the task of opening the citizenry's mind to the truth, and that he could not accept his life at the price of silence. Quite what had led the leaders of the democracy to the pitch of dislike that brought about the trial has often puzzled commentators. The plays of Aristophanes were vastly popular, but they were vastly obscene and blasphemous into the bargain. There is therefore a problem about taking the charges at face value. Whatever the cause, it remains a black mark on the Athenian record, and reminds us that it is only in our century that 'democracy' has come to mean 'liberal democracy'. Athenian democracy was non-liberal, and frequently illiberal. It was also politically egalitarian in a fashion almost wholly unknown in the modern world. Not only was the Athenian assembly open to every adult male citizen, the political system had rather little room for the distinction between leaders and led. Its business was largely conducted by committees whose members were chosen by lot; the business of larger committees was managed by smaller committees whose members were once more selected by lot, and they were chaired by individuals who served as chairman only for a day at a time. There were more permanent boards for naval procurement and other purposes, but in general Athens carried to an extreme the idea that nobody should possess any more power than anyone else, and that all officials should be answerable to the whole people.

In a society with very few able-bodied men over 40 years of age, seasoned leaders were at a premium and held office very much more often and for longer periods than pure chance would have allowed. Again, there were positions of great authority that were not strictly political positions—Pericles' position as *strategos*, or commander-in-chief, was one such—and they allowed men of distinction and ability to wield a good deal of personal power. Even then, the assembly had the last word, for good and ill. It had once dismissed Pericles, and it finally destroyed Athens' fighting capacity by choosing the corrupt Alcibiades and the incompetent Cleon as its commanders. Such disasters aside, the system worked extremely well. Even in the Peloponnesian War, Athens survived longer against overwhelming odds than any other state of the time could have done, and characteristically came to grief in the end through a misguided attempt to defeat her enemies through one bold stroke.

It is against this background that one needs to consider Plato's hostility to democracy, and Aristotle's defence of a 'mixed regime' containing at least some democratic features. Plato (*c*.427–347) was Socrates' most accomplished student, and our most important source for Socrates' philosophical views. In the strictest sense, what we have of Plato is not his books, but a series of dramatic renditions of dialogues between Socrates and various interlocutors, many of whom were notable figures in their own day. The early dialogues read particularly convincingly; they show Socrates as a seeker after truth, not as its possessor. They almost never come to a clear-cut conclusion, and Socrates is, if not on a level with the other participants, at least no more than first among equals. The dialogues became increasingly less lifelike, and the *Republic* in particular reads like a real conversation only during the multi-sided discussion of the relationship between justice and convention in book I. Once the body of the argument is reached, the book becomes something close to a monologue by 'Socrates', with little more than admiring interjections and humble requests for further illumination from the rest of the cast.

The first book is best known for Socrates' battle with Thrasymachus, who defends the doctine that 'might is right', or in the alternative that anyone with the strength to commit injustice will do so, and will be well-advised to do so. That these are not the same thought is slowly borne in upon Thrasymachus in the course of the argument. But this dispute follows some earlier skirmishing that tells us a good deal about the difference between Greek and modern conceptions of ethics, and alerts us to some differences between the meaning of the Greek term (*dikē*) translated by 'justice' and the meaning of the modern term. Socrates' interlocutors, one of whom, Cephalus, is a rich, elderly man of conservative inclinations, discuss the benefits of wealth. Cephalus suggests that its greatest value is that it enables a man to die knowing he has paid his debts. Socrates turns the conversation to the definition of justice and asks whether 'paying your debts' is the sum total of justice; he points out that we do not think it good to return a knife we have borrowed to the owner of the knife if he has gone mad in the meantime. It is then suggested that justice consists in doing good to your friends and harm to your enemies. This suggests a striking difference between the Athenian conception of *dikē* and our notion of justice; that is, the concept rendered as 'justice' in all the usual translations of the *Republic* is a wider notion than our own. It also diverges from our own concept inasmuch as Greeks were uninhibited about thinking that a proper ambition of any man of spirit was to make his enemies suffer.

Socrates insists that it can never be good to harm another person. Punishment, for example, is not intended to harm the person punished. It is rather intended to improve the soul of the criminal upon whom it is imposed. Socrates' reason for holding this view is, on the face of it, somewhat odd. Acting justly was, he claimed, the expression of something analogous to a skill. Skills aimed at achieving a goal specific to that skill: potters made pots rather than chairs; doing good could not be productive of harm. A just act could only bring about good. On this basis, he also argued that acting justly must be good for the person who so acted. This is a claim that has never ceased to astonish his readers, and the *Republic* is in large part a treatise on how we are to understand and therefore believe that claim. To the modern eye it seems so obvious that the claims of morality are restraints upon our pursuit of self-interest, instituted so that we can live with one another in tolerable peace and amity, that we find it hard to resist the idea put forward by Glaucon at the beginning of book 2.

Men have agreed to restrain themselves, to forgo behaving unjustly themselves in return for similar forbearance on the part of others. Besides being perhaps the first instance of social contract theorizing in the history of our subject, and a striking anticipation of Hobbes's account of the origins of government, this chimes with the view that the pursuit of self-interest is 'natural' and the restraints of morality 'artificial'. This, too, was a thought that Plato's predecessors had already put into circulation, and one which Aristotle discussed at length.

Before Glaucon puts forward his measured anxieties about Socrates' view of justice, book 1 of the *Republic* ends with one of Plato's most dramatic set-pieces. Thrasymachus denounces Socrates as a child who has been let out without his nursemaid; only a child would think that being just was good for you. Success in life was a matter of doing what you wanted, getting your own way, pure self-aggrandizement. The rest is fairy-tales. Since Plato is in charge of the script, Socrates has little trouble tying Thrasymachus in knots. He does this by means that twentieth-century readers are likely to feel uneasy about. For Thrasymachus is lured into *defining* the practice of justice as 'doing what you please' whereas we are likely to think that he would have done better to argue that terms like 'justice' no doubt *mean* something like 'what is right', but that as a matter of fact most people pass off as what is right whatever they can get away with.

It is some such view as this that animates Glaucon. He represents the view that the ordinary rules of justice represent a kind of compromise. What each of us would most like would be to live in a world where everyone else was willing to observe the usual rules against force and fraud, and the usual injunctions to honesty and fair dealing, but to be able ourselves to get away with breaking those rules whenever it suited us. Glaucon invokes the tale of Gyges, the shepherd who found a ring that could make him invisible, and who used the power this gave him to seduce the king's wife, and then to assassinate the king and to rule in his stead. Glaucon sets Socrates the task of showing that *even if* we had the ring of Gyges, it would still profit us to be just. Glaucon himself takes it that what in fact sustains justice is that we have struck a bargain with everyone else, whose terms are, essentially, that we will obey the rules if they do so, too, and that we will limit our attempts at self-aggrandizement so long as they do so.

It is worth noting that Glaucon's view is not only a precursor of Hobbes's grim account of the fundamental social contract in his *Leviathan*; it is a precursor of the much gentler picture offered by Hume, and even of the account that Mill offers in *Utilitarianism*. All of them take it for granted that if we had no need for the kind of security that the general observance of the rules of justice provides for us all, we would have no motivation to accept the constraints of justice. Hume, for example, claims that if human beings encountered a race of creatures who suffered as we did, but who could do us no harm, they might treat them kindly or cruelly, but would not see themselves as obliged by the rules of justice. Mill distinguishes *justice* from the rest of morality in terms of its greater stringency; but that stringency—the fact that we think the rules of justice bind more tightly than the rest of morality—he explains in terms of the need for security. The rules of justice are those moral requirements that above all keep us secure. Gyges with his ring can take care of himself and has no need of the forbearance of others and therefore no incentive to show them any forbearance.

It has been a common modern view that Socrates ought not to have taken up the challenge he was offered. For that challenge amounts to the demand that he shows that behaving well is in the interests of the person whose conduct is in question. Many modern moral theorists have said that this is simply a mistake. What makes an action right or morally obligatory is something quite other than what makes it prudent or in our interests. To some extent this complaint against Socrates' argument illustrates a difference between modern ideas of morality and classical ethical views. A striking feature of the modern conception of morality, which appears to reflect its Jewish and Christian origins, is the idea of the 'dictates' of morality, as though a system of morality is a system of imperative rules or commands. The nature of a command, as opposed to advice, is that the person commanded must obey, whether he likes it or not. Otherwise, what is offered is advice or entreaty, not a command. If we think of morality on the model of a set of commandments, whether ten or many more than ten, we will easily be moved to think that morality cannot be a matter of our own self-interest. Indeed, we are likely to think immediately that morality stands opposed to self-interest, and that its task is to curb it and control it.

To some degree, however, this opposition has always been softened by another feature of our post-classical view of morality. This is the thought that if the moral law is laid down by a deity who has the welfare of his creation at heart, obedience to the moral law will also do us good. *How* it will do us good has always been problematic; the vulgar suggestion that God will reward us in the hereafter for the sacrifices we make in the here and now has always seemed too like a bribe, while the more refined idea that a person who so internalizes the moral law that he can act on no other motive will find himself truly blessed returns us to the problem that Socrates faces. The Greek conception of ethics took seriously the thought that if the subject-matter of ethics was the study of the good life, that life had to be good for the person whose life it was.

That problem is set up by Socrates himself. He offers to show that the practice of justice is good for its possessor even if in ordinary terms everything goes badly for him. Conversely, the unjust man is to be pitied even if in ordinary terms everything goes well for him. Before we follow Socrates through his account of the way in which the defence of this view embroils us in an account of the good city, the nature of a legitimate ruling class, the education of that class, and finally of the various corruptions of the good city that we are likely to encounter, we ought to pause long enough to notice that the choice before us may not be the one that Socrates offers. That is, we may not have to conclude *either* that justice is good for us under all circumstances *or*, in the alternative, that we are always sacrificing ourselves by behaving well. The third possibility is that *in general* we shall be happier if we behave well: we shall find our dealings with other people go better; we shall not have to practice deception and hypocrisy; we can relax and be open with other people in the knowledge that we are not plotting to exploit them or injure them. But, we may refuse to say that justice has profited us if the only effect of behaving well is to bring about our ruin.

Socrates affects to believe that the nature of justice is more readily perceived on a large scale than on a small scale; this leads him to suggest that we should imagine a properly organized city, in order to understand what justice is in its affairs. The construction leads in a functionalist direction as he imagines that a city will minimally need a labouring class, a warrior class, and a ruling class—the guardians, better known as 'philosopher-kings'. To each class there corresponds a virtue; temperance to the class concerned with material existence, courage to the class concerned with defence, and wisdom to the class concerned with the overall governance of the city. Where, then, is justice? Plato's answer is that it is a property of the whole. Justice is a matter of the proper order of the whole body. In other words, it is a matter of the division of labour. If every element in the society performs its proper task, that is justice. If that is granted, Socrates' view that justice is good for us is impossible to resist. For the opposite of justice is chaos. There is some difficulty in knowing how far Plato's analogies can be pressed. It is easy enough to see how the labouring class might try to take the political power to which Plato supposes it has no title. It is not at all easy to see how, by analogy, the stomach might arrogate to itself the functions of the brain. What is relatively easy to see is that Plato believed that behind the flux of appearance there was an implicit, ideal order in the world, and that in such a world everything had a proper place and a proper function. The ideal for the individual was thus to find his or her proper place in the universe; once this was achieved, each individual would be happy, and the whole society would be perfectly stable. The question, plainly, is why someone might believe that this was a plausible vision of the world, and, secondly, what impact such a belief has on Plato's view of politics.

The simple answer is that we all see the world at least partly in such terms. We are accustomed to making tools that have a function, and whose names imply their functions. A knife has the function of cutting things; something that failed to cut would not be a 'real' knife. Similarly, many of the terms we use for social roles imply a function whose performance is a condition for properly applying the name in the first place. A doctor is so called in virtue of the job he does, or tries to do. A person who merely played at curing people would not be a 'real' doctor. Plato's assumption is that the various political and other occupations that he sketches in his picture of the ideal city have an essence, and that that essence consists in the proper performance of the functions in virtue of which we label them in the first place. If we were to ask why we should want to be a 'real' doctor as opposed to a plausible fake—which is what Socrates accused democratic 'statesmen' of being—we should at a certain point in the argument reach rock bottom once more. If we are naturally fitted to do that job and, on this view, no other, it is irrational to wish to do something else. We would function best by properly functioning as the best kind of person we could be.

There is no space here to follow Plato's argument through such famous cruxes as his account of the knowledge that the philosopher-king enjoys when he steps out of the cave in which all we see are shadows and into the bright sunlight where he sees things as they really are. In any event, the pleasures of reading the *Republic* are such that nobody does well to let somebody else summarize Plato's arguments for her or him. The main thrust of the argument is, however, worth focusing on more sharply. Plato pursues two tasks at once, one to demonstrate that it is always better to suffer injustice than to commit it, the other to show that a city ruled by philosopher-kings would be happy, stable, and possible to create. On the second, he wavers a little. Philosophers in our present, corrupt society certainly seem to be unpractical characters, but that is because they cannot practise the arts of philosophical rulership in a corrupt context. Here, then, they will retire to private life; as he says in a memorable image, they will be like travellers sheltering from the storm under the lee of a wall. They will try to avoid public life. But even now it is possible that some dictator's child might be brought up to virtue and thus combine wisdom with power and goodness. *If* there were an ideal republic, it would tend to remain in existence without deterioration, because it would be so nearly perfect that there would be no corruption. In fact, here too, Plato wavers a little. It is certainly true, according to his account, that there would be little temptation to seek riches or arbitrary power; but he saw clearly enough that the 'succession problem' is one of the central problems of politics. Good men produce sons who lie, cheat, and steal. So one of the driving forces behind his obsession with education was the puzzlement he felt about the difficulty of passing on virtue from father to son. The elaborate system of communal marriage, collective child-rearing, austerity, and a ferociously public-spirited education for the children of the guardians was all aimed at this one problem: how to ensure that virtuous rule endured. It is a problem to which other writers have offered various answers, many of them pragmatic, empirical, and rule of thumb; Plato's answer is at an extreme occupied in the twentieth century by Lenin's account of the role of the Party in instilling scientific knowledge and self-sacrificing—but highly fulfilling—virtue in those who are to form the apparatus of the future.

Plato acknowledged that even his ideal state would be vulnerable to history. The guardians might be unable properly to calculate when to breed future guardians, might admit unqualified men to the ruling élite or shut out the qualified. Slowly, the character of the city would change from perfection to an aristocracy ruled by ideals of honour, then to an oligarchy ruled by greed for money, then to democracy, then to tyranny. These are increasingly disorderly forms of government, ruled more and more by appetite and whim, and less and less by reason and justice. The tyrant plays a peculiar role in the story of decline, because he figures once more in the argument for being just: the tyrant achieves power by becoming an enemy to all the human race, so that whatever he achieves is no compensation for the isolation and fear he feels in his soul. But democracy features more interestingly in the argument about forms of government, because it is the worst form of government but one (that is, according to the view put forward in the *Republic*, though a form of near-democracy is advocated both in *Laws* and *Statesman*). What makes it so deplorable is exactly what many commentators admire—that it is built on freedom. Freedom for Plato is not one of the goals of a good political order, either in the sense of the political independence of the whole state, or in the sense of an individual's immunity to oppressive laws and regulations. He takes it for granted, as the innumerable references to the virtues of the 'auxiliaries' or soldiers of the republic show, that there will be a need to defend the republic against foreign attack. Since it will have no gold, no art works, and nothing worth stealing, there will be less threat of war than was usual in Greek city-states, but Plato knew as well as anyone that Greek city-states often went to war for no other end than to reduce their neighbours to servitude and enhance their own glory thereby. For Plato, the goal of independence has no attractions in its own right, and the freedom of the individual only seemed a cloak for moral disorder and psychic instability. Democracy, therefore, seemed to him to make a goal out of the disorder he deplored, and to be doomed quite naturally to fall into the hands of tyrants who would restore order.

But the tyrant's offer of order is illusory. The tyrant's soul is the most disorderly of all souls, and therefore tyrannical rule the most disorderly of all forms of rule. It is the tyrant who makes Plato's case for the superiority of justice over injustice. His route to the throne alienates him from everyone else in his society; he knows that everyone is an enemy to him and he an enemy to them. He cannot therefore enjoy a moment's peace and security, but must live a life of suspicion and anxiety. Plato's argument is interesting and powerful, even if it does not show what he hoped to show. What he showed is that there are more costs to behaving badly than we are likely to notice at first sight. One of these is the need to dissemble; the old saying that hypocrisy is the tribute that vice pays to virtue has a deep truth to it. The man whose motives are friendly, honest, and built on justice is able to reveal to others just what he is up to; the man whose motives are anti-social and deceptive is enmeshed in a web of lies. Preserving the web of lies is a complicated task that will take most of his psychic energy, and leave him little over for enjoying his successes. To be Stalin or Hitler is not a good bargain if what we seek is a happy life. It follows that behaving justly is on the whole and in general to be recommended as a means to a happy life. It does not follow, and it is not clear that it could be argued, that the man who is accused of a crime he has not committed, who is unjustly tried, condemned, and executed and dies friendless and alone is none the less better off than he would have been profiting from injustice. The Church does not describe martyrs to their faith as 'happy', but rather as 'blessed'. In an appropriate moral and metaphysical framework one might argue that the person who suffers injustice but is pure at heart is 'blessed', and Plato's final recurrence to the myth of Er at the end of the *Republic* suggests that he felt this himself. For there he does argue that we have an immortal soul which will be rewarded for the good we have done on earth. This, however, violates the terms of the argument with which the book begins. There, after all, Socrates offers to show that we are better off being just than unjust, no matter what, and irrespective of consequences. It is that which seems too much for anyone to demonstrate.

After the drama of the *Republic* Aristotle's *Politics* can seem decidedly tame. This was one of its author's intentions. Plato, it is not too much to say, abolishes politics as ordinarily understood. The process of debating what to do, making the best of a bad situation, conciliating losers, trying to square the demands of justice and the demands of social order—all the things that ordinarily make up the political process—are simply obliterated in favour of a high-minded administrative process organized by philosophers who see deep into the nature of the True, the Good, and the Beautiful. Aristotle criticized Plato's utopia in book 2 of the *Politics*, when he complained that Plato's obsessive search for unity ended in the abolition of politics. A *polis* was a *polis* in virtue of including many different sorts of people and activity. Unlike the natural unity of the human body, for instance, that of the *polis* was partly artificial, or rather, was preserved by convention, and by agreement among people whose interests very often differed upon the principles of justice that should reconcile those differences. Human beings governed themselves by principles of justice that they accepted because they were reasonable creatures and able to govern themselves by something better than mere instinct. None the less, this meant that the degree of unity that a state can aim at has a natural boundary; beyond that point, the way it is kept in order ceases to be political, and becomes more nearly that which binds a hive of bees or a herd of cattle. It is, for Aristotle, one of the achievements of human beings, or of the best of them, that is, of the Greeks, that they can form political communities.

Aristotle's idea of the way to study politics has been justly famous for two and a half millennia. We should, he says, look in any inquiry for as much precision as the subject-matter allows, and no more. This is doubtless another criticism of Plato's attempt to reduce politics to a subject of geometrical precision. The suggestion is that politics is a sphere of activity in which we must exercise good judgement; this is not the same thing as accurate calculation in a mathematical sense, but the weighing and balancing of considerations that do not readily—or perhaps ever—yield to precise measurement. The claim relates to Aristotle's suggestion that many virtues lie in a mean between extremes: the brave man does not rush heedless into danger as the merely rash man does, nor does he run away from relatively harmless threats as the coward does. He recognizes danger, but is not so frightened that he cannot control himself; and he has a good sense of what, if anything, will justify his running an appropriate degree of risk. Just as the brave man decides what on the whole is justified by the dangerousness of the situation and the urgency of facing it, without ever being in a situation to say that nobody could possibly hold the opposite view, so the statesman must do what is good for the polity he governs, without supposing that no rational man could hold an opposed view.

Aristotle's influence on subsequent political thinking is all-pervasive. He drew a famous distinction by arguing that whereas 'man is a political animal' for whom political life is natural, all other animals are, at best, 'gregarious'. They swarm together or live in herds, but only by instinct; man alone lives *politically*, that is, by conventions which have to be justified as the dictates of justice. Animals rely on group attraction; we rely on debate and persuasion. What, however, is the political life about? Aristotle has what one might term a two-tier conception of social and political life. *Some* societies practise politics in a special sense. *All* societies hold together in virtue of something like a moral commitment, but only the Greeks practise *politics* in the commendatory sense. Societies that live in too cold a climate and are therefore too impoverished scarcely have a social life at all; societies that live in excessively hot climates submit to despots. The Greeks have the concept of citizenship; citizens hold office in turn, ruling and being ruled, according to constitutional principle.

Although Aristotle really did begin the constitutional tradition that eventuated in modern constitutional states such as the United States—it was he who suggested that a well-run state had a government of laws not of men—he held many views that have not survived so well. Taking it for granted that a society such as Athens could not release citizens from grinding labour unless there were slaves who would perform the manual work required to give their more fortunate superiors the leisure to take part in politics, Aristotle claimed that some people were 'slaves by nature', who were better off working as slaves for a decent master. He admitted that nature often failed to ensure that those who were slaves in fact were also slaves by nature—that non-Greek men with strong bodies and weak intelligences worked for elegant, intelligent Greek masters—and so left room for others to argue that the conditions for acceptable slavery were *never* met. Equally contentiously, he took it for granted that 'nature' had established that men were intended to govern women, and that women had no place in politics. Neither did men who had to spend their lives in 'banausic' activities, earning their living by repetitive manual labour.

What Aristotle left as a permanent legacy was not the detailed, often dismayingly snobbish, ideas that he held about Athenian politics, but the defence of politics against critics who wanted to smooth over social conflict and to tidy up the world by handing over absolute power to some superior person or persons. Against Plato's guardians, this was the argument that the relentless search for social unity would not result in a better *polis* but in something that was not a political enterprise at all. It is, that is to say, essential to politics that people are different, that they have diverse, legitimate interests that they must be able to express, and which it is the job of political leaders to reconcile in a way that promotes the pursuit of a common good. It is characteristic of Aristotle that he differs from some later pluralists in emphasizing the possibility of a common interest, or a common good. The aim of political life, he emphasizes, is not mere life, but a good life, and it is a good life in common that we must try to live. What is common to all good lives is that they suit the people who live them; what is important about the life of citizens is that they live with one another, so that their lives partake of a good that is essentially common.

There is no single thing that constitutes the common good. Aristotle does not suppose that my good fortune is somehow automatically your good fortune, nor that any of us wish for justice to prevail to the exclusion of our own welfare. He certainly was not persuaded by Plato that it was better to suffer injustice than to do it. What we can share, however, is a kind of civic friendship in which your well-being really is one of the things that I wish for, and conversely, and in which we do not want to profit unjustly and at other people's expense. Good governments, of which Aristotle distinguishes three—monarchy, aristocracy, and *politeia*—are rule of one, a few, and many public-spirited men, aiming at the common good. Bad governments, of which again there are three—tyranny, oligarchy, and democracy—are the rule of the one, the few, and the many in their own narrow interest. It is worth noticing that Aristotle thought of democracy as essentially a class-based, and class-interest-driven regime. It was rule by the 'poor many', the *dēmos*, and in that sense rule by one class over everyone else. *Politeia* is hard to characterize. It was Aristotle's preferred form of government, and might be thought of as an expanded form of aristocracy, where anyone of reasonable means, good character, and sufficient maturity to give him good judgement could hope to hold office—to rule and be ruled in turn. But it might also be thought of as a restricted democracy in the modern sense of democracy; since Aristotle did not think in terms of representative government, a fact which explains why he thought a polity could have no more than 10,000 citizens, he wished to restrict effective political power to people whose interests were on average identical with those of the society as a whole. This was why he wanted what amounted to rule by a middle class. He would have been surprised, but certainly pleased, to discover that in countries such as Britain and the United States the nominal equality afforded by universal suffrage is in practice undermined by the fact that the worse off and less educated do not participate in politics in proportion to their numbers, so securing something much closer to rule by the middle ranks.

1.2. Machiavelli

It would be foolish as well as wrong to suggest that political theory in the Greek sense vanished after the death of the autonomous Greek city-state in the late fourth century BC. Roman thinkers influenced by Stoicism thought carefully about the nature of a good republic, and about the duties of man as man and citizen. Cicero, in particular, mined a rich vein of reflection on the connection between private virtue and public duty in his *De Officiis*, a tract on the demands of reason, the nature of justice, and the search for a common good that was part of every well-bred young man's education for many centuries. By the same token, the early Christian Church's antipathy to politics, and its deep conviction that the imminence of the second coming made the affairs of this world utterly unimportant, steadily gave way to the more complicated view that was epitomized in St Augustine's *City of God*. The Christian was a citizen of two worlds. Allegiance to the city of God was undeniably more important than allegiance to the city of man. Still, this world was part of God's creation, and served a purpose of its own. Its obligations were real, even though they were subordinate to those of the heavenly city, and God required us to meet them willingly and loyally. Though all mankind was fallen, and existed in a state of sin, there was a difference between a state and a band of thieves; and that difference was the practice of earthly justice. Take away justice and a state is only a particularly large and persistent robber band.

Yet, it remains true that medieval Christendom saw politics through the prism of a religious faith that almost inevitably reduced the problems of authority and obedience, individual interest and public interest, private good and public good, to questions about the reconciliation of the demands of Christian faith on the one hand with the necessities of political action on the other. This is why Machiavelli, who was in none of the usual senses of the term a philosopher at all, is almost invariably taken to have been the first 'modern', or at any rate post-medieval and probably post-Christian, political philosopher. Best known as he is for the dictum that 'when the means accuse, the end must excuse', the philosophical interest of his work rests rather on his treatment of three other matters.

The doctrine that the end justifies the means is on the one hand banal—for what *could* justify the means if not the end to which it was a means?—and on the other hand neither a complete nor an accurate picture of Machiavelli's views. That is, Machiavelli did not think that absolutely any means, no matter how wicked, was justified in order to achieve whatever political goal we happened to have in mind. Nor did a person who adopted evil and cruel means to his ends escape condemnation; even if justified, he had to live with the fact that he could not be said to be a 'good' man *simpliciter*. Machiavelli had in mind cases where the safety of an entire state or a substantial number of its citizens was at stake. To be deterred from action out of a scruple was in those conditions to behave badly. One might have to lie, cheat, and betray others in acting as the situation demanded; but refusing to do so would leave one no less responsible for the death or misery of those one had failed to save. The reason why Machiavelli is often thought of as a 'post-Christian' philosopher is that he took what one might call the commonsensical view that the answer to Christ's question, 'What shall it profit a man if he gain the whole world and lose his own soul?' is that he would gain the whole world. That is, a man whose primary aim was to preserve his own moral innocence had no business in politics.

The philosophical interest of Machiavelli's work lies in two methodological areas, and in one moral area. So far as method was concerned, Machiavelli believed that he had made a breakthrough in understanding politics; he contrasted his own ability to draw lessons from history with 'the proud indolence of these Christian princes', who took no interest in what history had to teach. Some commentators have credited Machiavelli with a scientific view of politics in a modern sense of that term. The amorality of his masterpiece, *The Prince*, with its advice on how to profit from great crimes and how to avoid suffering the obloquy they naturally attract, has led some commentators to think that Machiavelli was engaged in a dispassionate exercise in extracting from the historical record general principles about what did and what did not work to secure the power of would-be rulers. Since it is commonly thought that science aims to extract general laws from the analysis of factual data, it is easy to conclude that Machiavelli's originality lay in his being the first 'political scientist' in the modern sense. On the whole, however, this is implausible, and not only because it rests on a view of the aims and methods of the natural sciences not shared by anyone in Machiavelli's own day. Machiavelli's method of analysis is interesting and distinctive, and it is unclouded by moral prejudice. None the less, it is not based on extracting general principles from a careful examination of the record.

Rather, what Machiavelli relies on is the thought that success is to be achieved by emulating the best classical practitioners. He contrasted the enthusiasm of his contemporaries for ancient statues dug up in the gardens of Rome with their uninterest in the political successes of their Roman forebears. Yet, he thought, it was obvious enough that the Romans had been even more superior to their successors in the political arts than in the fine arts. A modern prince should model himself on the best classical practice if he was to thrive. Obviously, it was impossible to model oneself *exactly* on predecessors who might have lived anything up to 2,000 years before; it was therefore essential for the political practitioner to know both how to imitate the best practice of an earlier age and when to diverge from it. Machiavelli remarked in a famous discussion of the role of luck, or *fortuna*, in human affairs that nobody could hope wholly to escape the malignity of fate, but that we must none the less try to do so. Fortune was fickle, but not wholly so, and most men came to grief because they could not or would not adapt to changing times. But Machiavelli drew a more surprising moral: as a woman, Fortune favoured bold and impetuous young men who were ready to take her by force, and paradoxically made bold action less risky than caution.

The first large question that this raises is whether politics is a realm in which general principles—either causal laws about how political systems operate or general prescriptions about how to get our own way—are to be looked for. It is painfully true that political science exists as something of a courtesy label rather than an accomplishment; the contrast between the universal laws that physicists and chemists take for granted and the very partial and exception riddled generalizations that political scientists come up with is very obvious. What it implies is another matter. On one view, it could merely be that we have not yet discovered the exceptionless laws that underlie our partial generalizations and prescriptions. The condition of politics might be the same as that of medicine, an often-used analogy for politics; in earlier times all the knowledge that doctors could draw on was a matter of rule of thumb and long experience. Under those conditions, following the methods of known effective practitioners was the path of wisdom, but today our knowledge of physiology, biology, and the underlying physical and chemical principles that govern these sciences allows us to do much more than that. To the objection that progress in politics seems dismayingly slow, one might retort that until seventy-five years ago, doctors were more likely to injure their patients than help them, so it would be unwise to think the comparison had no force.

On the opposed view, the analogy with the growth of scientific knowledge in the sciences that underlie the practice of medicine is misplaced. The understanding of human action, it is sometimes said, is interpretative, and the growth of knowledge is always a matter of our making more complete or less complete sense of particular actions. History is not a resource for the construction of social physics; understanding history is more like understanding a concert or a play, where we are obliged to use our imaginations even in order to imitate our predecessors. On that view, Machiavelli's advice is rather like encouraging a budding pianist to listen so Solomon and Horowitz. Only an ignoramus would think that this was the route to the possession of a set of rules for giving great performances. But an ignoramus who thought that would have failed to see what piano-playing was all about, and would make a fool of himself or herself in performance. If there is to be an analogy with medicine here, it is with the old-fashioned view of medical training that it would hold. Studying with a wise doctor and paying careful attention to each particular patient is the only way to cope with the demands of patients. A well-trained doctor will do well by his or her patients, but infallibility is not to be sought, and the balance that is to be sought between greater scientific knowledge and something closer to an intuitive deftness with patients cannot be laid down in advance. No matter how well one does, bad luck may still bear away the patient; *fortuna* is capricious.

The second large question that Machiavelli raises is what politics is about, if politics is not about something that is readily, or perhaps at all, justified in moral terms. As we have seen, it might be said that Plato's intention was to abolish politics in its ordinary acceptation, in order to have an apolitical, totalitarian regime of pure reason and pure virtue, where the political struggle for power would be absent. To this, Aristotle responded by defending the to-and-fro of debate, the contest for office, and the inevitable dissension of everyday politics as a necessary part of the good life for a social creature such as (at any rate Greek) human beings are. Machiavelli offered no very clear answer to the question of what politics is and why a society needs politics. He may well have been right not to offer one. For part of what he plainly thought the task of the Prince must be was that of preserving some order rather than none, holding things together when everything conspired to blow them apart. This was neither the dictatorship of the wise nor the continued politics of a constitutional regime. On the other hand, the politics of the sort of republic that he described in his *Discourses on Livy*, when he reflected on the early successes and final downfall of classical Rome, were orderly politics. What they sought was freedom on the one hand and glory on the other, though neither freedom nor glory consisted in one thing only. Freedom consisted in part in a state's being firmly in charge of its own affairs and not subject to bullying and interference by its neighbours and rivals. Rome's success in conquering all of Italy and then most of southern Europe gave her freedom in the sense of a freedom of external action. Rome also possessed an internal freedom, which stemmed from its adherence to a constitutional system; all citizens obeyed the law; only those entitled to hold power did so; and tyrants were suppressed until Julius Caesar finally destroyed republican government. Because the Romans were free, justice prevailed too. Indeed, if it had not been the case that security of person and property were so well secured by a free constitution, one can hardly imagine that the Romans would have been so eager to preserve that constitution. None of this implied a taste for a Christian morality. The Romans were fierce, tough, proud, and this-worldly. They did not turn the other cheek, and could have made no sense of the injunction to do so. They might magnanimously refrain from destroying an enemy, even if there was no particular political advantage in so doing; but this would be because it was a magnanimous gesture and reflected well on themselves. Loving-kindness and returning good for evil were not Roman ideals.

The third large issue raised by Machiavelli is that of the relationship between politics and religion. Machiavelli straddles many of the modern world's attitudes to the connection between Church and state, or rather between the religious and the purely secular realms. On the one hand, he plainly has no interest in the state's authority being invoked in order to save the souls of the citizenry; that concern is distinctively Christian, and Machiavelli's concerns are resolutely pagan. The importance of religious belief as a social cement, however, was something Machiavelli insisted on. He was appalled at the ill effects of the papacy's secular role in Italian politics, but did not broaden this into a condemnation of Catholicism. What appalled him was the misuse of the religious authority of the Church for the private ends of the rich families from whom the popes of the fifteenth and sixteenth centuries usually sprang. A pope who united all Italy against the French and Spanish invaders of the day would have been wholly acceptable. This was all of a piece with his view that the Romans had done well to execute soldiers who had insulted the auguries, since that was a mockery that threatened military morale, but that generals who had tampered with the auguries to ensure favourable omens had also done well—it was not a matter of metaphysics, but of social solidarity.

1.3. Hobbes

When the modern age is not said to have begun with Machiavelli, it is often said to have begun with Hobbes. Of Hobbes it is undeniably true that he endeavoured to place politics on a scientific foundation, that he turned his back on any attempt to emulate classical political practices, that he was the first writer to articulate the modern view of the state. He also made a methodological breakthrough of a particularly powerful kind, and turned the notion of the social contract to purposes that twentieth-century thinkers still discuss. Hobbes's life was an exciting one, in spite of his best efforts. Born in 1588, the year of the Armada, he lived through the Civil War of 1641–9, went into exile with the court, but returned to England in 1651 and made his peace with the Commonwealth government of Oliver Cromwell. His masterpiece, *Leviathan*, was indeed written to defend the proposition that we ought to swear allegiance to any government that protected our lives and material interests—and thus that persons like Hobbes were justified in leaving the employment of the exiled royal family and acknowledging the authority of their supplanter.

Leviathan is by some way the greatest work of political theory written in the English language. It is bold, iconoclastic, and simultaneously both persuasive and implausible. There are four things that we can pluck out of the book to illustrate this, and to point us towards Hobbes's successors. The first is Hobbes's insistence that we must begin by imagining mankind in a 'state of nature'. That is, we must imagine away the political structure whose *raison d'être* and structure we are about to explore; only if we can understand what mankind would be like without government can we understand why government is necessary and what a wholly rational political system would be like. In starting from this point, Hobbes rejects not only Aristotle, with his belief that man is an animal born to live in a *polis*, but Machiavelli, with his belief that we should examine past models of political success and then try to emulate them. Aristotle, Hobbes abuses at every turn; and he abuses nothing more fiercely than the teleological assumption that we can understand what human beings are born to do by seeing what they do do under favourable conditions. 'Natural authority' does not exist; and by the same token, there can be no such class of people as 'natural aristocrats'. Politics is artificial through and through, and among the things that are artifices of government our rank, social standing, and entitlement to esteem are three of the most important. They are important because Hobbes ranked pride as one of the greatest threats to political order, and therefore, of course, feared aristocrats who thought they had a natural title to office.

Machiavelli's belief in the utility of history was not directly challenged by Hobbes. He thought that history read properly enforced the morals that he drew from his own scientific analysis of politics, and he wrote *Behemoth*, a decidedly slanted history of the Civil War, to drive home the lessons of *Leviathan*. None the less, Hobbes thought firstly, that most people who claimed to derive their political views from a knowledge of history were really engaged in showing off about their erudition; secondly, that an enthusiasm for classical learning, and for the historically based statesmanship that it was supposed to foster, led too many people to believe dangerous ideas about the virtues of republican institutions and the lawfulness of killing tyrannical rulers; and thirdly, that historical knowledge was essentially piecemeal, partial, and vulnerable to being proved inadequate when the world changed in unexpected ways. Science could achieve what prudence could not. Prudence was useful; science infallible.

The method of science was to start with the basic components of whatever we wished to explain, and then to build up the object or events under investigation from that starting-point. This usually meant a conceptual rather than any actual process of dismantling and rebuilding, but the model was evidently taken from geometry as Hobbes said. Although ultimate success in the analysis of human behaviour would have entailed being able to explain why self-sustaining physical mechanisms such as human beings are must have the psychological dispositions they do, for the purposes of political theory it is enough if we know what those dispositions are. The first chapters of *Leviathan*, then, give an account of science, and of human passion and reason. The object of the argument is always to show what *would* happen if creatures endowed both with reason, and with the human passions Hobbes depicts, were left to their own devices in a world without government.

The 'state of nature' thus constructed is one in which every individual must rely on his or her own resources for survival. Reason does not tell us what to pursue, but only how to draw inferences from what we know about the world. It is essentially hypothetical. Moreover, Hobbes espoused a radical subjectivism about values in these circumstances. 'Good' was not the name of a property that objects and states of affairs possessed independently of human desire. Rather, 'whatsoever every man desireth, that for his part he calleth good'. The key notion was not good or evil, but *calling* good or evil. To call something good or evil was to express a desire for it or a dislike of it, and there was, said Hobbes, no natural coincidence of such desires. Can we know whether something is *really* good or evil? At one level, the question seems to be senseless, since the only sensible question is *who* desires or detests whatever it is. At another, we seem driven to ask it, since otherwise we have no idea whether we are doing as well as we could be doing. From this Hobbes deduces the alarming conclusion that most of us are satisfied not so much by what we have as by the envy of others. If they want what we have, we have what is universally agreed to be good. The consequences are alarming, and are spelled out in a famous paragraph of a chapter entitled 'The Naturall Felicity of Mankind'.

This is the second major Hobbesian theme. Without government, mankind comes to grief. The state of nature is a war of all against all. The argument is compelling. We have no natural tendency to form a group in the way that ants or cows do; gregarious creatures have no idea of their rights, and no wish to exercise authority over one another. We on the contrary would very much wish to be highly regarded rather than the reverse, and in any event resent very much having our rights trampled on. Without artifice, there will be no government, and without government there will be chaos. Against the anarchist who does not see why we could not live tranquil lives, Hobbes argues as follows. Each of us has all sorts of desires we want to satisfy; we are also very anxious, since our reason tells us that what we have today we may not have tomorrow. Above all else, we are anxious not to die. This means that we do not want only an apple for lunch today, but a guarantee that there will be an apple tomorrow; but if we all want this, we shall come into constant conflict, for I shall wish to be able to control your behaviour and you will wish to be able to control mine.

How can we prevent others from attacking us? In the state of nature, the only obvious way is by striking first, and striking fatally. For anything less than a fatal attack leaves our enemy able to retaliate; and failing to strike first is in essence to have left ourselves vulnerable to a first strike by someone else. If we all understand this, as we must, since Hobbes insists on the equality of human understanding, we shall end up fighting one another out of simple fear. It might be thought that persons who understood this would control themselves. Hobbes, however, thought that they would be driven into conflict by competition for scarce resources. In this primitive state the gap between what we wanted and what we could predictably hope to have would be wide. Each of us would represent a threat to everyone else and they to us. We would in a sense be innocent threats to each other; I cannot be expected not to try to feed myself, even if there is too little food to feed both me and you.

The third cause of the war of all against all, however, was less innocent. This was our pride. If we could only think well of ourselves by making others envious of us or by somehow extracting from them the esteem we wanted, this was the way to a war that nothing could prevent. Mutual fear can be cured when a state is instituted, because we cease to have reason to fear each other when we know that a competent government can curb the violence that we fear. It is a small price that I have to pay in not being able to attack you—which I only wished to do in self-defence—especially when I know that you will have no desire to attack me once you know that you need not do so merely to defend yourself. Competition can be coped with under a lawful government, because ordinary economic activity will give us sufficient resources in total to take the edge of the competition for our share. You may eat roast meat three times a week, while I mostly eat bread, but in doing so you do not deprive me of my humbler diet.

Pride is different. The proud person wishes to come first in whatever social competition he finds himself, and he wishes there to be competitions in order to come first. The only point of pride is to edge out all our competitors, and the only position we want is that of the top dog. It is a logical truth, not an unfortunate fact about scarcity, that there can be only one top dog. This, then, is the one element in human nature that cannot be pacified or assuaged by the creation of government, but must be directly controlled. As Hobbes insisted, taking his text from the Book of Job, 'Leviathan is ruler over the children of pride.' Hence Hobbes's reiterated insistence that aristocratic status was merely the gift of the Crown, and that we have no natural title to pre-eminence.

In the state of nature, then, we are compelled to fight each other, out of fear, competition, and pride, or as Hobbes terms them 'competition, diffidence, and glory'. The second central issue that Hobbes tackles is then that of how to create a government that will repress pride, encourage economic activity, and take away the justification for fear and therefore for aggression. The passage from anarchy to government runs in two stages. The first is to set out the laws of nature by which rational persons would *wish* to be governed. Hobbes thinks of these laws as having two faces. On the one side, they were *theorems*, that is logical truths about what mankind would choose if they were set the task of choosing a set of rules to be governed by. To the extent that this is what they are, they are not laws in the strict sense—the strict sense according to Hobbes, that is to say. Laws strictly are commands, general in their application, and addressed by someone who has authority to command to those whose behaviour he is authorized to command. A theorem is a statement of what follows from incontrovertible premisses, and issues commands to nobody. Thus, the first law of nature, according to Hobbes, is that we should seek peace. 'Seek peace' is manifestly a command; 'rational men would observe the injunction to seek peace if they could safely do so' is not an injunction but a theorem. On the other side, however, we may think of the laws of nature as commandments laid down by God, 'who by right commands all things', and so considered they are laws in the strict sense.

The laws of nature number nineteen in all, but the first three are what Hobbes is particularly concerned with. The double-edged nature of the first injunction to seek peace is suggested by its corollary, the right of nature—that where we cannot ensure peace we may use all the helps and advantages of war. The second law of nature requires us to be ready to renounce our rights against other people to the degree that they are ready to renounce theirs against us. In essence, this is the requirement that we should always stand ready to enter into a social contract under which we promise to refrain from theft, violence, and other forms of misbehaviour and to accept a common authority to judge cases in dispute *on condition that* everyone else does likewise. Hobbes follows the statement of this second law with an extensive analysis of the nature of contract, the chief purpose of which is to allow him to say that contracts made under duress are valid in the state of nature—for reasons which we shall soon see. The third law of nature gives teeth to the second, for it simply enjoins that men perform their covenants made. That is, when we make a promise we must carry it out.

This statement of the third law is followed by a lengthy analysis of the concept of justice, since another of Hobbes's purposes is to argue that justice consists entirely in the keeping of covenants. This, too, has a purpose, which we shall soon see, but it is plain that one purpose is to remind us that no matter how we behave in the state of nature we do not act unjustly. But this raises the third issue central to Hobbes and anyone who thinks like him. How do we leave the state of nature, and what are the incentives that lead us out of the war of all against all? It is best to answer this question in reverse order.

Hobbesian man is anxious, and self-centred, hoping for happiness, but above all fearful of death. He or she is not in the modern sense a utility-maximizer; or rather some Hobbesian men are such and hope to do very well, and all of us are at least tempted to measure our success and failure by what they inspire in others by way of envy or mockery; but most of us are 'satisficers', in the sense that we are happy with 'good enough'. If we were not so, we would be in a bad way, because we would find it impossible to keep our promises once we had made them. If we made promises purely as a step towards maximizing our own well-being, we would be obliged to break them as soon as that seemed to be the better path to doing as well as we could. Since we know each other's psychology pretty accurately, we would not trust one another, and promising would become pointless. Hobbesian man is enjoined to regard all others as equal to himself, and can see the point of following that injunction, not because it is likely to maximize his own well-being but in terms of minimizing the risks of social warfare.

Still, in the state of nature, where we are all terrified of each other, what must we do? It cannot be anything that requires us to sacrifice our lives because Hobbes is quite sure that it is an impossibility for us to do that, and that if we were to agree to it we should either be mad or insincere. He distinguishes between obligation *in foro interno*, that is, in the conscience, and *in foro externo*, that is, in external action. Thus we are always obliged to be *willing* to keep our promises, but only when it is safe to keep them are we obliged to act as we have promised. This means that promises will rarely be kept in the state of nature, but not that they can never be. If I promise to exchange a few pears for a few apples, and actually give you the pears, you have no excuse for not handing over the apples and are obliged to do so. It may be wondered why, if that is possible, Hobbes insists that the state of nature is a state of war. The answer is that Hobbes defines as a state of war any condition in which there is not settled peace. It follows that all sovereign states live in a condition that is a war of all against all, even when they are in the ordinary sense at peace. They lack a settled authority with power to enforce peace, and hence in Hobbes's stark opposition of alternatives they are in a state of war. Unlike the ordinary human individual, they are not vulnerable to the kind of extinction that death represents for each of us, and therefore are not under the same pressure to destroy potential enemies before they can be destroyed by them. So the existence of long periods of peace and the existence of commercial relationships across national borders does not mean that anarchy is a safe or stable option for individuals.

So, we can understand that the way to leave the state of nature is by mutually renouncing our rights, and setting up an authority to enforce the rules that pertain to peace and security. We are motivated to do this by the fear of death, and we are motivated to follow the laws of nature because we see they protect us from death, and that we *ought* to observe them if we can. Erecting a sovereign political authority is the obvious way to make it safe to do what we ought to do. Now comes the second stage of the transition to government and the most stunning step in Hobbes's argument. He supposes that we make a covenant 'every man with every man', in which we all promise one another to obey some person or group of persons, who thereby becomes our sovereign. Whether the covenant makes sense is a hotly debated subject. Hobbes supposes that it does because he thinks of our transferring rights as if it happens all at once—so that like the case in which you give me the apples and I give you the pears in the same moment, nobody has to trust anyone else. Once the transfer is effected, there is a sovereign, that is someone whose authority we have all promised to recognize, and we are safe to obey him because everyone else is going to do so, too. The trouble is that the right to receive our obedience is not like apples and pears; it is essentially prospective, that is, when we transfer our right to the sovereign, we say today that we will obey him in the indefinite future. The case for Hobbes is that it is true that so long as everyone else, or a sufficient number of them, does obey the sovereign, we are all safe in doing so, and therefore ought to do so. The case against is that it looks as if a leap of faith, or a willingness to take the first step without a guarantee of its safety, is needed if this process is to get started. But Hobbes is notably unenthusiastic about asking for leaps of faith.

It is worth noticing, since few commentators have paid it enough attention, that Hobbes does not imagine that most sovereigns are 'instituted'. For the most part, we find ourselves in a world in which there is political authority, and the only question before us is whether to acknowledge it or not. Hobbes insists that in this case also we acquire the duty to obey as the result of covenant. But instead of a covenant of all with all, this is a covenant of each one, singly, with the sovereign. And the form of the covenant is alarming. For it amounts to our rulers saying to us that they are entitled to kill us on the spot, if that seems necessary for the sake of security, but that our lives will be spared if we agree to obey them thereafter. Once we have agreed and our lives have been spared, we are obliged to obey them unless and until they either threaten our lives themselves or fail to protect us from imminent death. If that happens, we must, and therefore we may, resort to self-help. Now it becomes clear why Hobbes was so insistent that a promise extracted by force remains a valid promise. Ordinarily, such promises are invalid, as a matter of public policy. In the state of nature they are valid if it is safe to keep them; ordinarily, of course, we would be right to think it unsafe. Inside society, we have good reason to believe it will be safe to obey the sovereign, and therefore safe to keep our promise to do so. Now the point of Hobbes's insistence that injustice only exists where a covenant has been broken becomes clear. In the case of a sovereign by institution, the sovereign is not a party to the covenant, and cannot therefore be bound by it. Nothing the sovereign does can be unjust, therefore. It may be cruel, or imprudent, or maladroit, or much else besides, but it cannot be unjust. Arguing, as he was, against a tradition that held that 'iniusta lex nulla lex est'—that an unjust law is no law at all—and therefore need not be obeyed, Hobbes had to argue, both that law was whatever the sovereign commanded, and that whatever other failings it might exhibit, injustice was not one of them. As to the sovereign by acquisition, who is a party to the covenant with the subject, that covenant is one that the sovereign immediately fulfils by not killing us on the spot. The sovereign having performed, no accusation of injustice will lie thereafter.

Now we come to the third and fourth large issues. What powers and duties does the sovereign have, and given that Hobbes's sovereign is to be absolute and unfettered, what can we expect from him or them? We can tackle both questions quite briefly. The sovereign must have absolute legal authority; otherwise, there will be two or more contending sovereigns and we shall be as badly off as in the state of nature. Hobbes had lived through the Civil War in which king and Parliament quarrelled over who should exercise supreme authority, and thought it essential that there was one and only one source of law. It was obviously no use if the sovereign could not enforce the laws once they were made, and no use if the sovereign could not protect the entire society against foreign attack, so there must be no limits on the sovereign authority to tax and spend, nor on how the laws might be enforced. After a Civil War that had been fought in part over the king's right to levy such imposts as 'ship money', without parliamentary approval, Hobbes was insistent that no such conflicts should again be possible. To a modern eye, none of this looks particularly alarming or surprising, but one matter on which Hobbes was particularly insistent does jar later sensibilities. Hobbes thought it was a central part of the sovereign's duties to judge what doctrines might be publicly taught. It followed from Hobbes's insistence on the omnicompetence of the sovereign authority that the sovereign was legally entitled to regulate spiritual matters, and indeed the unity of Church and state was a central plank in *Leviathan*'s argument. But Hobbes went further; it was one thing to insist that it was lawful for the sovereign to regulate divine worship and all else in Church practice, but another to insist that the sovereign *ought* to exercise that authority.

This, however, brings us to the last point—what a state governed according to Hobbesian principles might be like to live in. The perhaps surprising answer is that under most conditions, it would be a rather liberal state, with substantially *laissez-faire* economic arrangements supported by an adequate welfare state, punctilious observance of the rule of law by police and judiciary, and few restrictions on freedom of speech and opinion. Under the conditions of Hobbes's own day, however, Hobbes wished to insist that none of these things were a matter of natural right, or of rights against the sovereign—since under government there are no rights against the sovereign. Toleration, economic liberty, the rule of law are all excellent things because they conduce to human happiness and security; when they can be had, they should be had. When they cannot be had, a government's first imperative is to secure the authority of the regime. If that goes, the state of nature returns. While this means that Hobbes is not a principled authoritarian, nor a defender of theocracy—the state's business is to secure peace and prosperity, not to save our souls—it means, too, that he is only a fair-weather liberal. Since most liberals are such because they fear that governments will always be inclined to plead the needs of security and order when depriving their subjects of their lives, liberties, and property, they will not think of Hobbes as one of them.

1.4. Locke and Rousseau

Although it is riding roughshod over the subsequent history of political theory to say so, it is at least arguable that with Hobbes the structure of one important argument was fixed. Locke was a better Christian than Hobbes and a better liberal, but added little to the *logic* of contractual theories of government. Indeed, there have been interpreters who have made Locke even more 'Hobbesian' than Hobbes.[14] Locke's *Two Treatises of Government*—or rather the *Second Treatise*, which is all most students will encounter—are apt to strike modern readers as almost too persuasive. When Locke offers us the thought that mankind is born free and equal, owing allegiance to nobody, and having political authority over nobody else, we do not react as his readers would have done in the 1690s. They might have been tempted to respond that we are in fact born as dependent infants, to parents who owe allegiance to the monarch whom God appointed to rule over them, and therefore under the same allegiance. We, however, hear Jefferson's Declaration of Independence in Locke's words, and have no such reaction. Again, Locke's concern to keep government within limits by insisting that its business was with the goods of this earthly life and not with the salvation of its subjects' souls is one we find congenial. We—that is, liberal North Atlantic students—wish to live neither in a theocracy nor in its secular equivalent such as Stalin's Russia. In his own day, Locke's view was a minority view, and globally it still is today. More to the point, however, it is not obvious that a contractual account of government is in itself certain to arrive at a defence of

[14] Richard Cox, *Locke on War and Peace* (Oxford, 1960).

toleration and condemnation of an Established Church. It depends, as modern writers in the same tradition have seen more clearly, on what sort of psychological traits we endow the contracting parties with. Were we to endow them with a passion for religious conviction conjoined to a scepticism about which faith in particular was true, we could well imagine them signing up for a society in which indoctrination was the order of the day.

Of the major historical contract theorists, Rousseau is perhaps the most difficult to place. For Rousseau added the concept of the general will to the permanent vocabulary of politics, but by so doing straddled rather awkwardly the divide between 'individualist' theorists—of whom Hobbes is the archetype—who hold that nothing in politics is explained or justified unless it is explained in terms of the beliefs and desires of individuals and justified in terms of the welfare of those individuals, and 'organic' theorists who hold that society and the state are 'prior to the individuals' as Aristotle said long before. One might think that Rousseau had something of the attitude I have just sketched, that he wanted society to give us a spiritual security that Hobbes and Locke had no concern for, and therefore wished to give the state and its organs a power to mould our souls. It is this strain in Rousseau that has led some commentators to criticize him as a totalitarian theorist.[15] Others have thought that this is far-fetched. The concept of a 'general will' in itself has no very sinister overtones. We may, if we wish, ascribe a corporate will to almost any enterprise that has a common purpose. One might say that the general will of the Liverpool football team is the will to win games, and distinguish that will from the particular will of the team's members, who may be playing for money, for glory, for fun, and many other reasons, but who share—we may hope—a common concern to win. So one might suppose that the general will that animates an entire society is the common intention to promote the welfare of all the members of that society on just and equitable terms. Each of us has all sorts of private and individual ambitions, but we can all commit ourselves to supporting the one institutional arrangement that fosters the well-being of all. As Rousseau pointed out, it must do this by setting up appropriate rules, not by acting directly on particular individuals. No burglar enjoys being caught and sent to jail, but even the most hardened burglar will want there to be rules protecting him against assault, and his legitimately acquired property against theft.

1.5. Hegel

The modern writer who knowingly revived Aristotle's belief in the priority of the whole to its parts was G. W. F. Hegel, and to him and his greatest disciple and critic, Karl Marx, we should now turn. What is most interesting about

[15] J. L. Talmon, *The Rise of Totalitarian Democracy* (Boston, 1961).

Hegel for our purposes, however, is not his restatement of an organic conception of politics. Rather it is where he was decisively modern in his concerns and decidedly un-Aristotelian in his views. It was Hegel who first claimed that political philosophy must take the form of a historical recapitulation of mankind's progress from an unself-conscious and pre-reflective encounter with the world and one another to the developed state of modern, West European humanity, who were capable of governing themselves as free agents under law, and whose success in so doing was one of the goals of history.[16] As might be expected of so sweeping a thesis, it was not encapsulated in one simple statement; Hegel's first book, *The Phenomenology of Spirit*, set out the overall picture on which he relied, but it was two later and in many ways less imaginative works, *The Philosophy of Right* and *The Philosophy of History*, that offered his readers a fairly clear account of human history as a progress towards an adequate understanding of human autonomy and a sketch of how modern political institutions provided a setting for us to lead rational and autonomous existences.

It is the philosophical framework of Hegel's account of politics rather than his view of the nature of the state that is so imaginative. Essentially, he advocated a non-democratic but constitutional state: the people, he said, were to be both respected and despised, their grievances listened to but their views on policy ignored. What was essential was the rule of law, a stable economy based on private property but with sufficient governmental regulation to secure that nobody fell into poverty and that economic fluctuations did not drive anyone out of business. A system of representation was essential, but not by way of universal suffrage; Hegel envisaged a parliamentary system that looked not unlike the Prussian system of his own day, with a lower chamber elected on a 'functional' basis from trade guilds and the like, an upper chamber of large landowners, and representation for the state bureaucracy, or what Hegel termed 'the universal class'. Hegel accepted that this might mean a constitutional monarchy, but was deflationary about what that involved: someone to 'dot the i's and cross the t's of legislation'. Plainly a president would do as well as a king, save that there was a case for having someone in the post who had been chosen by the accident of birth rather than an election.

The way in which Hegel's own preoccupations coloured this picture was by his steadily anti-individualistic stand. In the modern world, people have rights and must have rights; but rights are the product of society and social relations, not the gift of nature and never rights *against* the state. Again, property is, and must be, increasingly understood as private property, held by individuals and something to be bought and sold at will; but not because they had a natural, pre-political right to their property. It was because our kind of society was embarked on a moral and political project that insisted on individuals looking

[16] G. W. F. Hegel, *Philosophy of History*, trans. J. Sibree (New York, 1956).

after themselves, managing their own lives and their own affairs. Their ownership was not 'naturally' free and unencumbered, but had become so as the result of a long evolutionary process. In effect, against the Hobbesian picture of a state created by rational bargainers, Hegel set a picture of a society whose operations went on behind our backs and were understood in retrospect when we looked back at our history in the appropriately philosophical frame of mind. For Hobbes, who played down the role of historical knowledge in forming an adequate understanding of politics, the predicament of men without authority is timeless; for Hegel, on the other hand, authority is a historical and a philosophical phenomenon. What and whom men will consent to obey is something that changes with everything else in their moral and intellectual universe.

1.6. Marx

Hegel's greatest student was his sharpest critic. In Marx's work, what had been a philosophical drama, the unfolding role of Reason in human affairs, became a sociologically explicable drama; the end of the process was not to be found in understanding the world, but in changing it, through a revolutionary upheaval in which the expropriated would expropriate their exploiters. The driving motor of the historical process was the constant struggle between the owners of productive property and those they either enslaved, semi-enslaved, or induced by offering them wages, to work on that property. The dynamic was largely hidden from those whose struggles it reflected, and often enough they fought quite sincerely for religious or national ideals, whose filiation to the underlying causes of social conflict neither Marx nor any subsequent Marxist has traced out to the satisfaction of their critics.

From the standpoint of this chapter, it is not the truth or falsity of Marx's sociological vision that is important; it is the implications of this kind of thinking for political philosophy. In the work of Plato, Aristotle, Machiavelli, and Hobbes—to take the figures I have used to exemplify the most significant different approaches to political thinking—those who have made mistakes in their political thinking are certainly condemned for their folly or chided for their ignorance. Still, they are treated as creatures on, so to speak, level terms with their critics. Plato may have held that the philosophers who are to guide his ideal republic know things that no ordinary layman can understand, but Plato himself does not suggest that he knows anything that could not in principle have been known in any society at any time. Machiavelli and Hobbes accuse those whom they criticize of indolence and self-regard and therefore of wilful ignorance, but they never suggest that the victims of their criticism could not have done better. Hegel and Marx both bracket the thought processes of people in other ages and other societies than their own. They do so for different reasons, but the effect is the same: both thought that political and moral judgements make such sense as they do only within a particular framework, and that the frameworks themselves change under the impulsion of something other than the intellectual efforts of those who work within them.

In the philosophy of science in recent years a similar view has been taken of the way that large bodies of theory structure the experimental work of scientists; scientists, on this view, work within 'paradigms', which tell them what the evidence 'means', which theories to take seriously, when to discount apparent evidence in favour of the dictates of the theory, and when to discard the theory in favour of the contradicting evidence. Both Marx and Hegel emphasized the extent to which political argument takes place within a paradigm—though they never used the term, of course. This means that for both of them the ordinary vocabulary of political argument, such as the language of legitimacy and authority, is at least treated with some reserve. It is thus not true of either of them in any simple fashion that they possessed a 'theory' or even an account of legitimacy, political authority, the scope of state activity, human rights, and so indefinitely on. They both had a great deal that is permanently valuable to say about the fact that modern societies are concerned with rights in a way that classical societies were not; and they both accepted that justice and the demand for rights imposed certain obligations on us. They held different views about this, of course, since Hegel thought that modern forms of private property allowed an important form of individuality to be properly expressed in the world, while Marx thought private property had to be abolished if the workers were to enjoy the fruits of their labour. What they both refused to say was that our conception of any of these things is in any simple way permanent, rooted in the nature of things, or timelessly valid.

1.7. Mill

As a result, they either fit awkwardly into the concerns of political philosophers or else call into question the whole enterprise of political philosophy—or, perhaps, both. Before turning to some modern treatments of the issues raised thus far, it is worth illustrating this point by considering how differently Marx and Mill treated issues of human freedom. Mill's intellectual career was fascinating at the level of human interest, although he did his best to deny this when he wrote his famous *Autobiography*. He was brought up by his father and Bentham to be the white hope of radical reform, but turned away from the aridity of their understanding of utilitarianism and developed an eclectic liberalism that paid something more than lip-service to utilitarianism, but which at the same time imported ideals of aesthetic and spiritual growth from the romantic poets, from Goethe and from von Humboldt. Still, his view of what philosophy could hope to achieve was largely untouched by the currents that carried Hegel and Marx on their revolutionary course. History mattered to Mill, but only because it was absurd to hope that an underdeveloped society, riddled with ignorance and conflict, and unsupplied with the bare necessities of human existence, could sustain liberal institutions. What happened in history determined the practicability of ideals rather than their intelligibility, however, and Mill had no qualms about insisting that the Athenians of Plato's days were more politically alert and more politically intelligent than his own contemporaries. This is the kind of trans-historical and absolutist political judgement that Marx eschewed.

So when Mill came to discuss freedom as he did in his essay *On Liberty*, the freedom he looked for was only partially affected by the fact that he was writing for mid-nineteenth-century Victorian Britons. That is, he defended both a form of 'negative' liberty—the right of individuals to be left to their own devices so long as they did not harm the legitimate interests of other people—and a form of 'positive' liberty—the ideal of being fully the master of one's own thoughts and actions; but it was an ideal that he might have defended with equal intelligibility two centuries earlier. What was distinctively nineteenth century and Victorian was the conviction he had drawn from his own experience and from a reading of de Tocqueville's *Democracy in America*, that democracy posed its own distinctive dangers for freedom. The chief of these was that we might succumb to the wish to be like everyone else, and thus take conformity to public opinion as the highest moral ideal of which we were capable. If we did this, we would conspire against ourselves and become our own oppressors, by shutting down the possibilities of imaginative choice and a new life. This was a distinctive and novel perspective on the question of how much freedom and of what kind we could expect to have in any sort of organized society.

Still, it was very different from what Marx, as a Hegelian heretic, saw as the future form of a free society. It was not exactly that Marx denied what Mill asserted about the conflict between democratic public opinion and the demands of individuality. Marx would have had little difficulty assenting to the view that in a bourgeois society there is a great weight of opinion in favour of maintaining the status quo, and that the average bourgeois will take some care not to think heretical thoughts. Rather, he would have thought it absurd for Mill to ask his contemporaries to behave better, seeing that everything about the society they lived in drove them to behave 'badly' in the way they did; and he would have thought it equally absurd to see the conflict between a stagnant mass opinion and individual vivacity and vitality as embodying some sort of eternal opposition between the natural inclinations of majorities and individuals. Rather, he looked to the day when, as he put it in the *Communist Manifesto*, 'the free development of all is the condition of the free development of each'.

That is to say, he looked forward to a time when the human species had fulfilled its nature as a free and rational species engaged in the common project of turning nature and human nature alike to fulfilling and liberating ends. This was just the sort of project that Mill would have thought it the task of an analytically minded empiricist like himself to undermine by showing that it did not make sense; Mill's essay on 'Nature' considered the natural order as an obstacle to human ends, as a resource for human ends, as a source of beauty, and much else, but Mill could hardly have made sense of the thought that nature might in some fashion be redeemed by the eventual success of the human project. The thought that the tension between individuals and collectivities could simply vanish would have struck Mill as wishful thinking, just as Mill's conviction that it could not would have struck Marx as an instance of a thinker being trapped within a historically limiting framework of which he was unaware.

2. MODERN TREATMENTS

Leaping ahead to the present day is not only an injustice to the writers slighted in this sketch of approaches to political theorizing, but is a prelude to an equally abbreviated and selective account of recent and current arguments. I begin with some staples of recent discussion, turn to some issues in philosophical jurisprudence, then to arguments about 'republican' freedom, and some wider issues raised by a 'Machiavellian' concern with the demands of statecraft, particularly the problem of 'dirty hands' and the supposed necessity for immoral action. I turn back from that to the question of the role of philosophy in discussing the ethics of public policy, and end with a very abbreviated mention of analytical Marxism, and some of the concerns I do not address at all.

For the past fifty years, it has been unfashionable to write against democracy; there have been some curious understandings of democracy, such as 'guided' democracy—otherwise military dictatorship—and 'people's' democracy—otherwise party dictatorship—but very few politicians or theorists have spoken out against democracy in a principled fashion. Yet it is surprisingly hard to defend the uniqueness of the legitimacy of democracy, and even to explain its legitimacy at all. This fact has given much of the discussion of—for instance—'government by consent' a very strained air, as if writers have been over-anxious to reach edifying conclusions, and therefore unwilling to face some of the awkward issues their efforts raise. It is as well to begin by observing that on most understandings of democracy, it makes perfectly good sense to be opposed to it for a variety of reasons, ranging from the tendency of democratic governments to accommodate themselves to the short-term wishes of their electorates and in the process to wreck the environment in which their (non-voting) descendants will live to the tendency of democracy to elevate smooth-talking salesmen to positions of authority that they do not deserve.

2.1. Democracy

Broadly, there are two approaches to explaining and justifying democracy, by which I understand here a system of decision-making in which decisions are made on the basis of a majority vote, or are made by people whose right to make them is acquired as the result of securing a majority in a fair election. One justification is essentially external, and instrumental, and takes the form of an argument to the effect that allowing the mass of people in a society to play a large part in their own government is indispensable if they are to be governed justly. The argument is essentially that the articulate, intelligent, and well-to-do few will exploit the unorganized many unless there are political devices that allow the many to defend themselves. This is not an argument for the *legitimacy* of democracy, which is why I call it an external justification. That is, it is not an argument to the effect that democratic decisions or democratic forms of government have a unique moral authority. To ask whether a form of government is legitimate is to ask why that government's regulations and orders are binding upon me *in conscience*. What I term an 'external' justification is couched in terms that evade that question, and concentrate instead on what the consequences are of constituting government in one way rather than another.

The difference emerges clearly if we contrast the sort of justification I have just offered with one of the commonest 'internal' or legitimizing arguments, the argument from consent. Hobbes, it will be recalled, argued that we were morally obliged to obey even an absolute monarch because we had *promised*, or agreed, or contracted, to do so. Many writers have thought that it was patently obvious that we do not consent to the rule of an absolute monarch, but have thought that democracy really is a form of government by consent. Hard-nosed critics have promptly asked, What do we consent to? On the face of it, most Britons have no choice about being governed in the way they presently are; they have not been asked whether they wish to be governed according to the more or less democratic constitutional arrangements they find in the land of their birth, and if they said they did not wish to be governed in the local fashion, it would do no good. Sometimes it is retorted that we have voted for the government. But this has an obvious drawback; what about those who voted against the government now in power? Nobody suggests that they are exempted from the obligation to obey the law. If we retreat into saying that people who vote against the government none the less support 'the system' by using the electoral system, we are back where Hobbes and Locke tried to take us—for they both held that taking advantage of the system we find ourselves living under is a form of consent.

The instrumental argument for democracy does not try to answer the question of legitimacy in this or any other way. Rather the thought is that democracy is the only system of government likely to secure a measure of economic and other forms of justice; as for our obligation to obey the local laws and regulation, we have a duty to go along with it so long as it is working tolerably effectively. That duty is an extension of a 'natural' rather than a 'political' obligation, namely the duty to help everyone else operate a fair and effective system to promote their welfare. Consider a person caught in a burning cinema; panic is momentarily stilled when a calm, clear-headed usher shouts that we should all stand still and that he will then lead everyone to the nearest exit in good time. Ought we to obey him? Plainly the answer is yes. Is it because he has democratic authority? The answer is plainly no. It is not so much that a decision was reached by democratic means that matters as that we have a general duty to support political arrangements that lead to just outcomes. This external justification is plausible; but it raises one subversive question that the respectable have always answered differently from their radical opponents. If we agree, first that democracy is to be valued only because of its good consequences, and second that it is our individual duty to obey the laws of our own local democracy because that is usually the most effective way of trying to ensure a just society, what is our duty on those occasions when obeying the law appears less likely to achieve a just outcome than taking a short cut? Ought I not to achieve justice more directly, even at the price of breaking the law? To the extent that an answer to this question involves more than an appeal to consequences, as for instance when we argue that *it would not be fair* to expect other people to carry on obeying the rules while we picked and chose which we would obey and when, we go beyond the question of what system best promotes economic and social justice, and appeal to such thoughts as the suggestion that we each have a duty to join with others in some mutually acceptable system of lawful government. This was a claim advanced by Kant, and it begins to move the argument back towards considerations of consent or something like it; for any such argument rests on the idea that it would be unfair to ask other people to enter into a scheme of government in which they were committed to a self-restraint to which we are not committed. That thought can only move us if we are also moved by the thought that a legitimate system of government should be one to which we could plausibly be asked to consent. This is, to be sure, a much slighter claim than Hobbes's claim that *we have in fact* consented, but it perhaps explains the attraction of 'government by consent' as an ideal.

The other route to explicating democracy begins from the considerations just sketched: the view that democracy is uniquely legitimate because it is a uniquely fair or just form of decision-making. This needs some amplification. If

I approach you with a gun in my hand and demand your wallet, you will wish to refuse. If I approach you with a companion and make the same demand, you will be equally eager to refuse. If we say 'We have voted to rob you', you will not be impressed. One writer who has argued that taxation approved by a majority *is* often disguised robbery of this sort is Robert Nozick.[17] It thus follows that majority voting has no *moral* force except in conjunction with a number of constraints upon what we are voting on, and with what intention. If voters vote in their own narrow self-interest, the 'losers' in any vote have no particular reason to go along with the decisions thus arrived at. The behaviour of the Protestant majority in Northern Ireland during the 1930s and 1940s suggests what happens if a permanent majority exploits a permanent minority by using the machinery of government for the purpose. If bare majority rule is neither attractive nor effective in the absence of a just social background, and if it is implemented in an unjust fashion, democracy as practised in liberal societies is at least in aspiration the one system that gives all voices a fair opportunity to be heard. A monarchy gives all the decision-making power to one person; in a democracy, the ideal is that we all share it on terms that all of us can accept. So when the question arises of why I should take any notice of a decision made by democratic means, the reply is that I should be treating other people unfairly if I did not go along with their judgement. All this assumes that democracy in practice is at least a reasonable approximation to the ideal of democracy, and it may not be.

When democracy falls below its own proper standards, there are forms of dissent and disobedience that a democracy makes appropriate that no other form of government would do; our disobedience can be *civil*, because it can appeal to values we share with others. Under an absolute monarch acquiescence or rebellion are likely to be the alternatives available to us. Under democracy, public standards of fairness allow us to appeal to others in the expectation that they wish for our *willing assent*.[18] A reply of this sort explains why democracy is a uniquely legitimate form of government; at any rate it will do so to the satisfaction of individualistic, liberal-minded people who think that there is a real question to be answered. These are, however, considerations that may cut less ice with persons from different cultures. A traditionalist might think that most of us have no business asking why we should obey the rules of those empowered to govern our society; it is enough that we learn the immemorial rules of our own society and obey them. Many religious thinkers have certainly thought that the ruler derives his or her commission from God, and is not further answerable to mortals. Martin Luther, indeed, may be said not only to have subverted the authority of the pope, but to have rendered all authority prob-

[17] Robert Nozick, *Anarchy, State, and Utopia* (New York, 1974).

[18] John Rawls, *A Theory of Justice* (Cambridge, Mass., 1971).

lematic by insisting simultaneously on the duty of all believers to follow their own consciences and on their duty to obey absolutely the powers that be.

2.2. Justice

Both these defences of democracy as a form of government appeal to its connection with justice. But this appeal to justice is different in the 'external' and 'internal' approaches to justifying democracy. Indeed, it may be a different sense of justice altogether that is at stake. That is, an instrumental justification of democracy might be that the power of the poor many secures greater *economic* justice than would any other political arrangement. There might be other equally plausible arguments of an instrumental sort, for instance that the need to account for themselves to a mass audience makes our rulers less warlike and bloodthirsty than traditional aristocracies have been. But, crucially, the goal is related only by cause and effect to the way a democracy is set up. 'One person, one vote' is not a principle of economic justice, but it is one possible definition of democracy. The idea of justice employed in the second kind of argument is essentially a political idea, or perhaps more accurately the political application of an idea of justice. That is, one might think that in economic matters several, or many, different ideals of justice could be applied—that people should be rewarded according to need, or according to contribution, or according to the vagaries of the market-place—and few or none of them would have the simplicity of 'one person, one vote,' but one might well claim that whatever distributive ideal was adopted was the application to politics of a more basic, underlying ideal.

One interpretation of what this ideal is, in societies such as our own, is that of 'justice as fairness', and it has been made famous over the past forty years by the writings of John Rawls.[19] The fundamental idea is not complicated: it starts from the familiar thought that if we have to divide some desirable object such as a cake, where there is not enough to go round, the fairest mode of division is to let someone cut the cake on condition that he or she gets the last slice. Since the cutter will have an incentive to make the last and what they can presume to be the smallest slice as large as possible, they will cut the cake into equal pieces—for selfish reasons they are driven to make a fair division. Applying this reasoning to social affairs, we can see that a plausible conception of justice in both economic and other matters is that the worst-off person should do as well as possible. If we imagine ourselves designing social institutions and not knowing how we will fare under those institutions, the sensible thing to do is to ensure that the worst-off person does as well as possible, since we might turn

[19] This is the conception of justice adopted in *A Theory of Justice; Political Liberalism* (New York, 1992) and is more narrowly concerned with the terms of *political* cooperation.

out to be that worst-off person ourselves. This is often called the 'maximin' theory of justice, in that we *max*imize the *min*imum that anyone receives. In politics, there is no room—or little room—for the argument that one hears in economics to the effect that allowing some people to make large incomes is necessary if the less well-off are to do well at all. This is the argument for 'trickle-down', sometimes phrased as the claim that unless some drive Rolls-Royces nobody will be able to drive Fords. It presupposes that managerial talent, entrepreneurial imagination, and skills of all sorts are unequally distributed in a population, and argues that they will be put to best use if their possessors are entitled to take something like a rent for their use in the shape of high incomes or accumulated wealth.

In politics, it may be true that *some* things, such as the fastidiousness about detail that makes for good administration, are unequally distributed and that there should be a division of labour of the same sort. But no such considerations apply to the idea of having a right to be heard. There is only one just distribution of that right, and it is an equal distribution. This is, evidently, a somewhat time-and-space-bound thought. In many societies, and in Western societies until quite recently, the idea that we each have something like a natural right to have our voice heard in determining our own fate would have seemed either odd or presumptuous. Once it is an ideal, however, it has to be accommodated within anything that could qualify as a theory of justice.

2.3. Rights, Interests, and Justice

Rawls's *Theory of Justice* is an emphatic defence of the idea that individuals have rights. They have a right to be treated justly, and a concern with justice is a concern with rights; rights set limits to what society may demand of or impose on any of its members, no matter what the goods are that society has in mind. Just as your rights as its owner mean that I may not simply take your bicycle even if it is true that I would make better use of it than you will, so no society can treat its members in an 'instrumental' fashion, taking no account of their rights. The fact that taking your income and giving it to some cheerful young person might increase total happiness is of no importance; the government has no right to sacrifice you, even for a good purpose such as increasing human happiness. All the same, Rawls's theory is not one in which rights feature as part of the foundation of the theory of justice. Rawls begins in much the same place as Hobbes, with individuals who are concerned with their own interests and have no pre-existing sense of justice. Unlike Hobbes's anxiety-stricken inhabitants of the state of nature, however, Rawls's protagonists are concerned to secure the benefits of cooperation on terms that preserve what they think of as their vital interests. The innovation in Rawls's theory is his notion of a 'veil of ignorance', which is to say that he asks us to think about what such persons would choose as the rules to govern their cooperation if they *did not know* what abilities they would turn out to have, what tastes they would have, and at what point in time and space they were going to be living.

But for some purposes the crucial point is that Rawls takes interests as the basic building-block of a theory of rights. This is what the Utilitarians whom he criticizes also did. Bentham, Mill, Sidgwick, and every other Utilitarian has always thought that conventionally recognized rights were a vital ingredient of human happiness. Only if we were accorded rights of personal security, allowed the right to choose our occupation, had our property rights secured, and so indefinitely on, would we have any hope of happiness. Without what are generally recognized as rights, insecurity would reign. Mill went further than this, arguing that autonomy and the capacity to conduct one's own life according to one's own ideals were the great goods that a concern for rights protected. Even so, it can properly be said that the basic concepts of Mill's moral and political philosophy are interest-related rather than rights-related. One of John Rawls's sharpest, if most admiring, critics was Robert Nozick, whose *Anarchy, State and Utopia* relied on a theory of rights that itself rested on nothing.

Thus, Nozick's view of rights amounted in essence to the claim that each of us owned himself or herself. We are 'self-owning', and that means that we have over ourselves the rights that people commonly have over their other possessions. Just as I may do whatever I like to my bicycle so long as it does not violate the similar rights of others, so I may do what I choose with myself, my body, and my abilities, so long as it does not violate the same rights in others. The effect is to undermine the legitimacy of many taken-for-granted aspects of the modern welfare state. Even more dramatically than Rawls, Nozick argues that we may not take each other's resources for the sake of some common project or other. Unless we *really* give our consent, that is voluntarily subscribe to whatever project it is that the government, or other people more generally, have in mind, we have been robbed. Taxation in the usual sense is described as forced labour; since we cannot enjoy what we would have enjoyed if we had not paid taxes, the extra work we must engage in to restore our income to the level we want is 'forced'. By the same token, democracy has no particular claim to legitimacy. If rights are inviolable, it does not matter how many people voted to violate my rights; if no one of them had the right to override my own wishes, then no number of them had that right either. Given the closeness of the connection between rights and self-ownership, the claim of a democratic majority to be able to decide what I shall do with myself or my resources amounts to a form of majority slave-holding.

The welfare state is in equally bad shape. If my rights include the right to decide how I shall spend my time, what work I shall do, and how I shall dispose of my income, the welfare state can only exist with my permission. To the thought that the state can decide what good goals to devote society's resources to promoting, the retort is that society has no resources. The only resources that exist are attached to individuals. It thus follows that the usual activities of a welfare state are a form of theft. Consider a national health service. It effectively limits the freedom of doctors and other medical professionals to offer their services to whomever wishes to purchase them, and limits the freedom of patients to choose to seek medical help from whomever they like. It might, of course, be said that a national health service improves the overall health of the society; but just as it might be said that my stealing your bicycle allowed me to use it more fruitfully than you did, without undermining the claim that I really have stolen it, so the fact that good things have been done with the resources taken for the national health service does not undermine the claim that these resources have been stolen. Many of Nozick's readers have been persuaded by these conclusions; others have thought they were so counter-intuitive that they undermine the premisses from which they are derived. Still others have devoted a good deal of effort to arguing that the consequences of 'self-ownership' include a form of socialism rather than the *laissez-faire* minimal state urged in *Anarchy, State and Utopia*.

2.4. Liberalism, Conservatism, Socialism

Talk of rights is common to ideologies other than those that sustain liberal political arrangements, and respect for rights has been fostered by other traditions. Non-liberals understand the argument for rights: anyone can see that arbitrary ill-usage is abominable, and that having whatever rights protect us against it is a good thing. Conservatives in particular have argued that being able to look after our own portion of the world is a source of human happiness, so that private property and membership of stable communities are both valuable. Socialists have argued that human rights include the right to secure and healthy employment, and to the necessary education before a working life and to adequate provision for old age afterwards. The distinctively liberal rendering of such considerations places the thought that human beings are or can be free, autonomous, rational, self-governing agents at the centre of our vision of the political universe. One way of distinguishing between liberal, conservative, and socialist visions not only of rights in particular, but of the political world more generally—not in the hope of finding definitions of these creeds to be carved in stone, nor in the hope of being able to second-guess the self-descriptions of politicians, but in the interests of understanding where some of the lines of cleavage come—is by reflecting on their reactions to the liberal vision of the autonomous individual.

On the whole, conservatives have doubted that human beings could run their lives successfully in the way liberals suppose. The conservative emphasis on tradition, stability, authority, and the like reflects a scepticism about the ability of the man in the street to 'trade upon his individual stock of reason', as Burke put it 200 years ago. Recent, libertarian forms of conservatism have for that very reason been difficult to place in the intellectual landscape, and have often been qualified as neo-conservative or neo-liberal, reflecting that uncertainty about quite what to call them. The crux is not in fact complicated. Many conservatives have felt that both our economic and our social and political arrangements have to be stabilized with the aid of a strong moral authority inhering in society at large but expressed particularly in the religious and educational spheres, and with the help of traditional communal ties. More recently, they have come to think that the economy needs little of such control, but that the remainder of our activities require a lot of it. It is sometimes suggested that there is an incoherence in this view, but it is not at all clear that there is. A strong state plus a largely *laissez-faire* economic system was what Hobbes advocated, and it is a wholly defensible vision. It may be hard to achieve, inasmuch as it may be that *laissez-faire* in the economic sphere tends to weaken the grip of authority elsewhere, but that is a piece of sociological speculation for which there is no conclusive evidence one way or the other. At all events, if libertarians are defined as the advocates of unbridled *laissez-faire* in the moral realm as well as the economic realm, it is clear why they fit awkwardly into the usual categories.

The situation becomes somewhat clearer if we ask whether liberals are obliged to subscribe to *laissez-faire* in economics. If they are, then libertarians are simply consistent liberals, or perhaps simply extreme liberals. The obvious answer is that liberals are concerned with the freedom of individuals; the threats to their freedom that they have historically been concerned to resist have been first the threat to religious liberty presented by a Church backed up by the political authorities, using their power to repress heresy and nonconformity, then second the threat posed by the state itself, whether for malign reasons such as the financial greed or ideological passion of those who control the state, or for benign reasons such as the desire of those who control the state to make sure that their charges live happy, but dependent, existences. By the end of the nineteenth century, the power of large industrial and commercial enterprises had come to seem almost as alarming as the power of the state itself. Hence the twentieth-century phenomenon of liberalism detaching itself from *laissez-faire* and calling in the power of the state to control that of the wielders of economic power. Hence, too, the uncertainty whether, especially in an American context, those who argue for a return to *laissez-faire* are best characterized as neo-liberals or neo-conservatives; one might think that the 'neo' is ill-chosen in the sense that it is an older interpretation of liberalism that is being put forward by neo-liberals, but the point is clear enough.

If this is a plausible interpretation of the distinction at hand, it suggests one classificatory problem. Does it not turn modern liberalism into a form of socialism? There are two responses to that question. The first is to say that just as liberals who believe in economic *laissez-faire* and have some doubts about the success of moral *laissez-faire* are hard to distinguish from conservatives, so some liberals are indeed hard to distinguish from socialists. The more complicated response is to return to first principles. Most socialists are impressed in a way that liberals generally are not with our dependence on one another. They are therefore, but not surprisingly, more akin to conservatives in their moral vision of the world, and there have been a good many cases of conservatives stealing the socialists' clothes in matters of policy. Many of the provisions of the welfare state were put in place by traditional conservatives. But, there is obviously a striking opposition between socialist and conservative views about private property. To the extent that modern conservatism looks to a more or less *laissez-faire* economy as the basis of prosperity and all else, the conflict between conservatives and socialists is acute. It is only at the point where both socialists and conservatives look to some kind of corporate state and the managed capitalism of the 'mixed economy' as the basis of social peace and cooperation between the different social classes that something like a complete collapse of all ideological perspectives into one takes place.

2.5. Communism and Nationalism

The three ideologies just discussed are essentially domestic. They are non-insurrectionary, they take democracy and the search for social justice for granted. By the same token, they will only provide an ideology for a regime that has settled the question of who 'belongs' within the political system in question. It is worth pausing for a moment to consider two of the most visible and dramatic movements of the century to illustrate the contrast between domesticated and undomesticated ideologies. Communism, now dead and apparently buried, proposed to inaugurate a new world of freedom and prosperity, but only after the old ruling class and its agents had been overthrown and destroyed. It was therefore committed to waging a permanent class war until such time as the new world was born. Since new class enemies reappeared as fast as their predecessors were murdered or exiled, the regime lived in a permanent state of siege. It was not that actual regimes were always in such a state: often enough, they settled into a somewhat stagnant and conservative condition. None the less, they were devoted to something other than the consideration of the needs and the protection of the rights of all their citizens. It is in this sense that communism was an ideology that was discontinuous with reformist forms of socialism rather than just an extreme version of them. Getting rid of the obstacles to utopia is not the same kind of activity as managing a state and society whose existence is taken for granted. This is not to deny that the starting-point of communist aspirations is the same as that of most forms of socialism: a sense of outrage at the discrepancy in power, wealth, and well-being between the owners of capital and the actual workers. But at the point where the 'solution' to the problem of a more equitable distribution of the rewards of economic cooperation becomes the destruction of one party to the competition, politics ceases and civil war begins.

2.6. Analytical Marxism

Curiously, the most sophisticated Western varieties of Marxism appeared at almost the moment of dissolution of communism as a half-way viable political system. It had always been a complaint against Marxism that it bore with it too much of its Hegelian origins; Hegel's search for knowledge of the Absolute was, on this view, mirrored in Marx's claim to have discerned the meaning of history. The thought that this expressed was that Marx had in the process passed off as science what was in fact no more than a quasi-religious faith in a historical teleology. The Christian claim that 'the first shall be last, the last shall be first, and the meek shall inherit the earth' seemed all too similar to Marx's faith in the eventual expropriation of the expropriators, and his belief that the propertiless proletariat would inherit the fruits of capitalism once its productive capacities had been unshackled, and communism established. G. A. Cohen's *Karl Marx's Theory of History* was one of several works that set out to rebut the charge that Marx's theories had been unscientific, empirically unsupportable, and essentially metaphysical rather than sociological.

Cohen argued that Marx's belief that social arrangements—'relations of production'—altered so as to foster the growth of productivity—'forces of production'—was the basis of his historical materialism, and could be framed in a way that escaped the usual criticisms levelled against it. To argue this, Cohen also provided an elegant reworking of the idea of functional explanation in the social sciences. 'Functionalism' as an orientation in social science has had a reputation for fostering conservative politics; the reason is not hard to seek—if social phenomena are as they are *because* they serve good, if sometimes obscure, purposes, it suggests that most social institutions and behaviour should continue as they are, for fear that we shall damage society if we alter them precipitately. To rescue Marxism's intellectual respectability by rescuing the respectability of functional explanation is an intellectually bold stroke. Cohen in essence recast '*a* occurs so as to bring about *b*', which is the standard form of a teleological explanation, and captures most of what we mean by saying 'the function of *a* is to produce *b*' as 'the fact that *a* causes *b* causes *a*'.

Interestingly enough, some of Cohen's sharpest critics were other analytical

Marxists. They held that wherever an explanation of the form that Cohen had analysed was plausible, it was because some superior explanation underlay it. Thus, the explanation of our possession of eyes is not that eyes help us to see, but that evolutionary processes have given eye-equipped creatures a competitive edge. Again, where a new productive system comes into existence, that fact is overwhelmingly likely to be explained by some individual having seen and taken the chance to do something new. The persistence of the new arrangements might require any number of explanatory variables, but some combination of their value to individuals who have the ability to make them stick and their use of that ability seems indispensable. Given that approach, functional explanations are redundant. Then the interesting question about revised Marxism is whether it is plausible to suppose that there is always a pressure to improve society's productivity, and that other arrangements in society will always yield to that imperative. Making Marxism philosophically tidier does nothing to make that case more plausible.

2.7. Nationalism

Like communism in power, nationalist regimes are always in danger of turning ordinary politics into civil war—paradoxically, of course, since the integrity of the nation is exactly what nationalists are eager to promote. Nationalism rests on a sentiment that many people have always felt, namely the desire to manage our own affairs in our own way. The interest of nationalism as a doctrine is that it transfers a sentiment that is more or less innate on the scale of a village or a small group, and attaches it to a much larger entity, the nation. Philosophers have always been puzzled by the phenomenon of nationalism, because a 'nation' is a somewhat dubious entity. Human beings have always lived in tribes and families, and have usually settled in villages and towns that possessed some pattern of authority within them. The 'nation' is a modern idea—its medieval origins lie in the allocation of students to different accommodation when they studied in Rome, so that one can assume that the ethnic origins of students mattered long before the idea of a nation-state occurred to anyone. The 'reality' of the nation is in many ways much less apparent than the reality of smaller communities, and our attachment to it therefore more surprising. Yet, today few of us would think of dying for our village while we think it right to be ready to die for our country. What makes nationalistic sentiment surprising, however, is what makes it rather dangerous too. For all nationalisms raise the question of who is and who is not a member of our nation. Is Britain a 'nation-state', one may ask. In some ways it is a paradigmatic nation-state; yet, it seems also to be a multinational state, with members of English, Welsh, and Scottish national or ethnic groups enjoying British citizenship. The 'United' in 'United Kingdom' has cut little ice with many Irish citizens, and not much more with many Scots and some Welsh.

In mainland Britain, these questions will not be settled with the gun. Elsewhere, recent history shows how likely it is that they will be. In fact, in the twentieth century most of the more passionate forms of nationalism have arisen as responses to the experience of being colonized by a more or less distant foreign power. Even where the 'foreign' power was, as it was in what was once Yugoslavia, domestic, the fact that it rode roughshod over the aspirations of what had once been independent states produced the same reactions. Under those conditions, it is easy to feel solidarity with one's 'own' people and to feel intensely the contrast between oneself and the foreigner. After liberation, the question of the basis on which social solidarity is to be re-established as a continuing and reliable basis for everyday social, economic, and political life arises acutely. An emphasis on national unity substitutes for ordinary democratic politics, with its alternation in power of different parties representing different social and economic interests. The fragility of appeals for national unity is evident in the way that so many African countries have succumbed to tribal conflict of one sort and another, and Middle Eastern societies have experienced both religious and more narrowly political conflicts.

Successful societies make a transition from a politics in which national self-assertion bulks large to one in which national identity is taken for granted and is not a salient element in politics. The United States is perhaps the clearest example of such a successful transition, and Britain for the most part another. Even such societies, however, may find themselves shaken by nationalist dissension, as Britain has been by a hundred and more years of demands for a united, independent Ireland, as Canada has been by Quebec separatism, and as France most strikingly was when Algeria sought independence in the 1950s. The philosophical interest of nationalism, other than the puzzle of knowing what makes nations nations, focuses on a large question in moral philosophy whose relevance is a great deal broader than this. This is the question whether particularistic loyalties and attachments can be given a rational but not a universalist basis. It is evident that a universalist moral theory might affirm that it is good on the whole that we have many unthinkingly particular attachments—that we love our own children, look after our own parents, want our team to win, and so on. The explanation is simple enough: our sentiments attach readily to these particular objects, and not readily to objects such as 'humanity at large'. The best indirect means to promote the welfare of humanity at large is for individuals to feel attachments to particular segments of humanity. This might sustain the view that a non-aggressive, non-competitive patriotism is a useful sentiment to inculcate. It will not satisfy the nationalist who really believes that the specialness of Croatia is not only something that Croats should believe in, but is a deep fact about the world.

2.8. The Jurisprudential Turn

A feature of recent political philosophy is that much of it has been generated in the law schools of the major American universities. There is an obvious explanation of this in the active role played by the United States Supreme Court in promoting the civil and political rights of aggrieved groups. That judicial role raises some interesting questions, of which I shall discuss two. The first is what we ought to say about the claims of judges to have *discovered* in the law some right or rights that nobody previously saw there. The second is whether the authority of judges in something like the US Supreme Court is contrary to democratic principles. The first question is raised by the apparent plausibility of what is usually known as 'legal positivism'. This is the theory of law that explains law in terms of, either the commands of a sovereign authority—the view held by Hobbes and Bentham—or rules that are accepted by a particular political society. The most sophisticated recent statement of this view occurs in H. L. A. Hart's *The Concept of Law*. Legal rules are rules with the proper pedigree; they characteristically operate at two rather different levels. Some are rules that impose obligations, for instance regulations forbidding parking, while others are rules about how to change these 'primary' rules, for instance the rules empowering local authorities to make such parking regulations. What makes laws unlike moral 'rules' is that they are alterable by a clear-cut procedure. While it makes no sense at all to suppose that we could decide that from next Tuesday adultery was not wrong, we certainly can decide that from next Tuesday it is illegal to carry a handgun.

Because the validity of law is dependent on pedigree, that is, on its having been made by the proper procedure, there is an interesting question lurking behind this analysis, namely whether law must form a hierarchical system. The answer seems clear enough; it need not. One can imagine a society in which some law gets made by judicial decision and some by statutory enactment, in which there is a convention that clear legislative intention overrides judicial decisions, and yet it remains sometimes unclear which of two prima facie valid laws must give way. So long as conflict occurs infrequently enough it may well be more convenient to accept it than to encumber the legal process with elaborate mechanisms to remove it. The other interesting question concerns the status of what has been called 'the rule of recognition', which is to say the rule setting down the conditions of validity for law. Essentially, Hart's view was that it was a sociological fact that people in such-and-such a society did or did not acknowledge as valid the rules emanating from this source.

It is a consequence of this analysis that the question whether a law is *valid* is quite different from the question whether the law is morally acceptable. It is also a consequence that it leaves it open whether we *ought* to obey any particular law. This view is at the opposite pole from the old natural law dictum that 'iniusta lex nulla lex est', that an unjust law is no law at all. On this view an unjust law may well be valid law; but the good citizen probably ought not to obey it if he or she can safely avoid doing so. To sharpen the argument, consider Nazi law. Most of it was made by the same procedures as had been in force under the Weimar Republic, and most of it was enforced by courts in much the same way as before. Some of it, as for instance the Nuremberg Decrees, was simply disgusting and barbaric. On the positivist view, it was still law. It was made in the way that German society took as the way to make law at that time, and therefore had the status of law.

One recent view has steered a delicate line between the positivist analysis and the natural law view that wicked law simply is not law. Ronald Dworkin has insisted that positivism has unacceptable consequences. One is that when the judges in the famous case of *Brown* v. *Topeka Board of Education* decided that Miss Brown's rights had been violated by the local school board's segregationist policies, what the judges were doing was creating new law, that is, the judges were legislating. This is an unacceptable result for anyone who thinks that the only title to legislate must be a democratic one, that is, that only legislatures may legislate and only in virtue of having been elected by the people to do just that. Since judges have not been elected, and have not been put on the bench to make up new law, it would be intolerable to suppose that they were doing so. The positivist view is that it would indeed be intolerable if judges thought they could legislate as they liked, but that it may not be intolerable if they engage in what is sometimes called interstitial legislation—in effect filling in small gaps left by what is settled law. Dworkin has another argument against even that view, which is that what a person engaging in a lawsuit wishes to know is *what their rights are*, not what the judges have decided they will be. Miss Brown believed that she had rights all along that her local school board had been violating, not that she might persuade the judges to give her some new rights and to penalize the board retroactively. Viewed from the board's perspective, after all, it would have been intolerable to learn that they had been behaving within the law, but now were outside it.

The reason Dworkin's view may be said to steer a delicate line between positivist and natural law accounts of the law is that on his view, the law aims to change our moral obligations—not in the sense that the law can legislate changes in basic moral principles, but in the sense that the law aims to provide us with reasons for doing one thing rather than another that are morally compelling. If the law is to strike us as having a moral claim on us, it must consort with our view of its moral purpose. In the United States at least, these purposes are set out in the US Constitution, and set out in such general terms that judges are clearly required to interpret them for themselves. So when Miss Brown went and demanded her rights, the court was entitled to ask whether segregated education—even 'separate but equal' education, which in practice it never was—was consistent with the constitution's requirements. Previously the court had held that 'separate but equal' provision was permissible; now the court had discovered it was not. On this way, previous justices on the Supreme Court had been wrong about what the law was, and Miss Brown was right to think that her rights had been violated. In contrast with Hart's view, the previous consensus on what the rules governing segregated education were was not decisive as to the status of the law; in contrast with traditional natural law accounts, what entitles judges to apply the particular moral considerations to the validity of the law that they do apply in such cases is the fact that these moral principles are enshrined in the constitution.

Given this analysis, the fear that judicial review of the sort practised in the United States is a 'Platonic' assault on the democratic system can be defused. The argument is not very complicated. As we saw earlier, democracy cannot be explained in terms of the mere weight of numbers possessing a mysterious authority. It must be justified in terms of it providing the nearest approach we can find to a system in which nobody exercises excessive and unchallenged authority over another, in which political and social cooperation occurs on fair terms. It is therefore not a threat to democracy but a safeguard of it to have some arrangement in place for asking the question whether the actual functioning of the political and legal system is consistent with the principles that legitimize it. The mere fact that large numbers of people may have voted in favour of illicit ways of allocating education or anything else does not mean that they are democratically licensed. The attractiveness of this argument is evident if one thinks of the obvious alternative to it as a way of justifying the role of an institution such as the United States Supreme Court. This is to argue that there are two distinct principles at stake. One is what justifies democracy, and it is the argument offered above, that weight of numbers is needed to counteract money, cleverness, and organization in the interest of economic and social justice. The other is the liberal principle that government must be limited in its scope, no matter whether it is democratic, aristocratic, or monarchical . The legislature expresses the first attachment, and the existence of judicial review the second. What makes this view less attractive than Dworkin's is that it exposes judicial decision-making to a sharper scrutiny. Why, it is natural to ask, should unappointed judges have the power to overrule legislatures? One reply, and perhaps the only possible one, is that a society proposing to govern itself by majority rule might well decide that the only terms on which majority rule was tolerable would include some safety mechanism to restrain majority overreaching in particular areas. As to why it would be appropriate to confer that power on judges in particular, the response would be that judges knew more about the law than others, and therefore had qualifications of the right kind to decide whether the government of the day was overstepping its authority as laid down by whatever constitutional principles were at stake.

2.9. Political Science and Political Philosophy

As the past few pages may have suggested, the closer we come to the day-to-day conflicts that animate contemporary politics, the more we are likely to be concerned with the actual sentiments and attachments, and the actual social and economic conflicts, of the day; that is, the more we shall wish to trespass on the terrain of empirical politics, to embroil ourselves with the findings of political scientists. This raises the question whether there is or should be a division of labour between political scientists and political philosophers, such that the former try to tell us how political systems do (or can, or even *must*) function, while the latter elaborate principles according to which they *should* or *ought to* work. In a sense, and up to a point, such a division of labour is taken for granted both in everyday life and in more academic analysis. Someone who believed that strong sentiments of national identity were morally obnoxious, because the only entity to which we ought to feel that kind of allegiance is the entire human race, could not be *shown* to be simply wrong by being shown that most people feel such sentiments only for their own country and not for humanity at large. On the other hand, we might think that if it emerged that it is quite hopeless to urge people to widen their horizons of attachment, we ought to find more attainable ideals. When John Rawls argues in favour of his conception of 'justice as fairness' that it provides the basis for a *stable* social order, he make an argument that invokes both a philosophical analysis of and defence of a particular view of the demands of justice on the one hand, and a hypothesis about what kind of moral consensus people could as a matter of fact develop.

Conversely, when political scientists discuss the functioning of, say, liberal democracies, and seen to be afraid of the effects of the amount of fund-raising that politicians have to engage in in countries such as the United States, it is because they take for granted two things: one that most people believe that democratic government *ought* to be based on a consideration of the public's needs and wants, not on a consideration of how much money a contributor is likely to offer; the second that in a society in which too great a divergence exists between what people think morally reputable and the basis of politics in fact, there will be either apathy as people withdraw from politics or eventually some kind of upheaval as people seek reform. Although political scientists do not have to endorse the public's moral convictions in every respect, they would hardly be able to pursue their discipline at all unless they understood those convictions in some detail. And it is hard to see how they could have such an understanding unless they shared them. In short, there is no risk of political philosophy collapsing into political science or of its being superseded by political science; nor usually is there much risk of political philosophers writing a priori political science in ignorance, or even in contempt, of the facts. But without some sense of what each is doing, neither can prosper.

2.10. Political Theory and Public Policy

One field in which this is particularly obvious is the burgeoning field of what is often called 'applied philosophy'. One part of that field is what is generally taught under the all-purpose heading of 'political theory and public policy', and its purpose is usually to lend some sophistication to the thinking of students who will go into public administration in some form or other. There are two justifications of 'applied philosophy'. One is that it improves the moral judgement of administrators, the other that it sharpens their perception of moral conflict. The first is not an entirely plausible view. In general, students of any age pick up their substantive moral views from other sources than philosophy lectures. Of course, their moral views may change quite drastically when they have time and opportunity to think at some depth about what those views commit them to. That, however, is more nearly an argument of the second sort. The second view provides a genuine rationale for the intervention of philosophers in public debate. Suppose the issue is that of the legal regulation of abortion. Most students will begin by believing that the important issue is to settle the question whether unborn foetuses are 'really' persons, since they assume that there is complete agreement on the principle that we should not kill persons. Not far into the argument, it becomes apparent that most people believe it is quite all right to kill other people in self-defence, and the issue then becomes one of formulating a principle of legitimate self-defence.

Before long, any discussion will certainly be diverted into a discussion of such issues as the ownership of the body—'whose body is it?'—and the limits of a state's rights over our bodies. At some point, the question arises of whether a state *needs* to take any stand on abortion at all, and if so, why. This then becomes a large problem in political ethics, not a matter of the ethics of killing unborn babies, but a matter of what a prudent and well-conducted state must regulate and what it may decently not regulate. And that stretches immediately back into large questions of legitimacy. The value of such discussions for anyone intending to enter government employment is at least that they produce some sophistication about the difference between issues of moral dissension and issues of factual dissension, as well as a decent anxiety about the ease of knowing which it is that faces us on a given occasion. The value for anyone not intending to try to run the country is that such discussions show up the sheer variety of moral visions in the heads of their fellow citizens, and induce, or may induce, some respect for the way other people see the world, and a corresponding willingness to tolerate the complexity of the policy-making process.

This, of course, bears directly on the old problem of dirty hands. The dramatic version of the problem of dirty hands almost always take the form of a politician having to perform some terrible act to save his country. If President Truman had to order the atomic bombing of Hiroshima and Nagasaki in order to save the lives of half a million Americans and five times that number of Japanese who would have been killed in a full-scale invasion of the home islands at the end of the Second World War, then he faced the problem of dirty hands in its most dramatic form. There is no denying that the destruction of those cities was in itself a terrible act—whether more so than the firebombing of Dresden and Tokyo is another question again—and in the absence of some extraordinarily powerful justification would have been mass murder. Some moral philosophers have said that it was indeed mass murder, no matter what Truman thought he was doing. But one might think that Truman was faced with a genuinely tragic dilemma, and was in effect damned whichever way he turned.

That, however, might be said to be the standing condition of all government. For the most part we do not notice because for the most part the damage done is not dramatic or on a large scale, and the good achieved is not dramatic either. But it follows from the nature of government that since it claims authority, it is responsible for its omissions as well as its commissions, and must always be choosing to accept evil in order to do good. A road scheme that saves lives at one place is, given budgetary constraints, a choice to let lives be lost at the other places where improvements might have taken place. Money spent on education improves the minds of the young at the cost of the comforts of the elderly in nursing homes. All choices made by governments might have been made otherwise, and an element of inescapably dirty hands must be part of the moral hazard of acting in politics and government.

2.11. Anti-Politics

With the partial exception of Plato, no representatives have been mentioned of what one might call 'anti-politics'. Plato's contribution to anti-politics was his insistence that political argument, dissension, the assembling of competing groups of people hungry for office, and all the other noisy and fissiparous features of everyday political life must be abolished. The commoner view in the modern world has been anarchism. Not many anarchists have held Plato's views about the omnicompetence of philosophers. Anarchism has come in almost every possible flavour, but there are two or three varieties worth distinguishing. One stems from a hatred of the brute force implicit in the existence of government; a rational society, in which conflict had vanished, would need no government and it could be left to wither away. Many, perhaps most, French socialists of the early nineteenth century belonged in this camp, as did Robert Owen among British thinkers.

A second does not so much detest government as government in its existing forms; it is happy with the thought that there will be government after the present division between rulers and ruled has been abolished, but wants true, genuine self-government. The anarchist strand in Marxism was usually a blend of both these views; Emma Goldman, the American feminist and anarchist, on the other hand, was not in any interesting way a rationalist, and belonged much more nearly to the second. And the French theorist of anarcho-syndicalism, Georges Sorel, with his advocacy of a proletarian insurrection fuelled by the 'myth' of the political general strike, looked forward to a society in which something quite different from rationalism ruled the day—a strong, self-disciplined community attached to an ideal of craftsmanship was to replace capitalism and the dominance of the machine. A last strand is what one might term theoretical anarchist individualism; this is the view that government has no moral authority, and that a person with sufficient moral awareness to run his or her own life will see through the myth of legitimacy. This view was perhaps held by Max Stirner, but in recent years has certainly been defended by R. P. Wolff.[20] It is interesting partly because its practical implications are so unclear. The fact that the government has no moral authority over us stems from the fact that there is only one really conclusive route to the acquisition of authority, and that, as Hobbes insisted, is by contract. Since we do not contract to obey our government, whatever reasons there are for going along with its commands, they are not based on its authority to issue such commands, since it has none. We may none the less behave just like all the other law-abiding citizens of our society, but for our own reasons—essentially that we ought not to make a nuisance of ourselves regardless of the law, and cooperating with what passes for the government where we live is a good way of being cooperative and not being a nuisance.

2.12. Contemporary Feminism

Anarchism is not a very lively creed at present. Of those creeds that are most thoroughly alive, feminism is perhaps the most interesting. I have not commented earlier on the fact that the 'politics' of Plato are sexless; but they are so, in a way that the politics of Aristotle and Machiavelli could not be. Aristotle's

[20] R. P. Wolff, *In Defense of Anarchism* (New York, 1970).

citizen had to be the head of a family, and a soldier, and to be motivated in ways Aristotle thought women were not. Machiavelli took it for granted that some women might have the ambition, the ruthlessness, and the unconcern for private life that the politics he pictured would demand, but he had no need to insist that they would be very few. Whether they would be very much fewer than the men who lived up to Machiavelli's exigent standards one may in fact doubt. But Machiavelli himself surely thought that politics was first cousin to warfare and war was men's business. In a successful Hobbesian state, women could certainly play as large a part in politics as men, supposing that anything one could readily call politics would take place. They could reason about the best laws as well as men, they could give good advice about the best way to organize the churches and the universities, and the needs of the poor, and so on. A state that was running smoothly would not need the rougher and more violent skills that Machiavelli concentrated on. Still, Hobbes clearly had no interest in opening up the political world to women, even if he had no interest in closing it off to them more firmly than to men.

It is, indeed, only when we reach Mill that a 'mainstream', male political thinker places the admission of women to full political rights at the very centre of his writings. William Godwin had taken the equality of women as seriously as the husband of Mary Wollstonecraft ought to have done; but since his concern was to achieve the euthanasia of government, he was a slightly awkward ally of women such as Catherine Macaulay, who wanted to establish a republican regime with a place for women. An interesting feature of recent feminism is that it makes Mill's efforts look very old-fashioned. Recent feminist writers have gone well beyond claiming that a liberal state is committed in principle to opening the way to women's participation in all fields of activity, and therefore that it is high time it made sure that its practice lived up to its principles. Rather, the argument has been that a distinctively feminist perspective on political life reveals much that the tradition here discussed does not mention, and perhaps does not know how to mention. It is for that reason that I have omitted the subject almost entirely rather than trying to shoehorn it in in an inadequate and misleading fashion.

Philosophically, one major division lies between writers who look to a gender-neutral politics, and those who look for a gender-aware politics. Mill was a member of the former class; among recent writers, Catherine MacKinnon is a representative of one tendency among the latter. In essence, a writer of Mill's persuasion can of course agree that if, for instance, Congress had many more women in its ranks, the style of debate, the priorities in policy-making, and the whole 'output' of government would be vastly changed. But he will not think this is of the essence, however benign a result he might think it. What is of the essence is that women should be able to become members of any legislature, government, administrative mechanism on exactly the same terms as men. Knowing when the obstacles to women's participation are as few and as low as they are to men's participation may be difficult; in the educational field, we know that it has proved very much harder than was once expected to recruit women into the bleaker physical sciences, and we may suspect that similar obstacles stand in the way of women's participation in politics. Still, the thought is a simple one: men have overtly and deliberately shut women out of all sorts of professions including politics, and they must stop. When they have stopped doing so, it is up to women to decide what occupations they wish to enter, politics included. Politics is somewhat more special than, say, the law or aircraft design, because it is an occupation whose object is to set down the rules governing all other social practices. But in principle, the equality of the sexes is a matter of women having open access to any occupation or advantage open to men.

The more radical view sees the oppression of women not so much as a breach with liberal principles that are generally honoured, but rather as an intrinsic and perhaps a central part of the operations of a state whose liberalism is a mask for male—and perhaps at the same time for capitalist—domination. Feminism is thus not simply an aspect of a general commitment to equality and justice in social and political relations, but a central plank of analysis. The analogy with Marxism is instructive. A liberal might agree that there is a lot of oppression in the world, and list the various sorts with which he or she is concerned. A Marxist would want to insist that there is one basic exploitative relationship, that which holds between the possessing and the dispossessed classes. All else is either epiphenomenal or a result of it. The most radical feminist analysis replaces this contention with the claim that the decisive relation of subordination is the subordinaton of women to men. *What* follows for the practice of politics as ordinarily understood is not entirely clear. One thing that certainly does, however, is a scepticism about the liberal line between the public and the private. Most liberals would see the family, for instance, as a 'private' sphere in which individuals conduct their lives along mutually agreed lines; radical feminists regard the family as a political institution in which women are socialized into subjection and men into the assumption of authority. Again, some liberal theorists have thought that the division of labour within the family was a private matter, and therefore somehow outside the scope of the kind of theory of justice that John Rawls derived to constrain the way major public, legal arrangements should be constructed. It does not take a very radical critic to notice that this seems to violate the common-sense thought that some families seem to divide the burdens of family life in a thoroughly unjust fashion, and to violate the common-sense thought that perhaps a society's legal arrangements make it either easier or harder to divide up the burdens of family life in a more equitable fashion.

2.13. Communitarianism and Republicanism

One other large contemporary current of thought to which no justice has been done here is communitarianism. It has lately been allied with a revived interest in 'republican' modes of thought, so although there is no necessary connection between them, we may decently look at them together. As one of the many revolts against the liberal consensus that has dominated political life in the West since the end of the Second World War, communitarianism has expressed the widespread sense that there has been too much emphasis on individual rights in liberal societies and too little emphasis on individual duties. Communitarianism is in some ways either not a political theory or something much larger than a political theory, since its focus is on the relationship between individuals and small communities—on our duties to family and friends, to neighbourhood and to co-workers. The connection between an emphasis on community and politics is that recent communitarianism expresses the common feeling that many institutions on which we once relied, and which we tried to escape from as cloying and claustrophobic, have decayed, and that their decay has made the political system ineffective.

For instance, family breakdown has led to a shortage of disciplining authorities in the lives of young boys; they then reach adolescence lacking self-discipline, and with that comes a level of violence and theft that no police force can do much to lessen. Since citizens look to the political system to provide them with physical security of person and security against theft, the state's failure to protect them against both leads to a loss of faith in politics, and a declining willingness to participate in politics, let alone to bear any individual sacrifice for the sake of the public good. Behind this view lies a plausible sociological thought. The formal police power of the state is parasitic on the informal self-discipline of communities; if that is intact, the police power of the state will work efficiently and non-aggressively, but if not, not.

Nor is communitarianism simply repressive or disciplinarian; it also emphasizes that most of us can make sense of our lives only with the aid and reassurance of others who share our view of the world and our goals along with it. Some writers, Charles Taylor perhaps the most prominent of them, treat this as something close to a metaphysical claim. If we did not live in a community of fellow knowers and seekers, we would not live in the world at all; others, such as Robert Bellah and his collaborators, treat it as a more down-to-earth sociological and psychological claim. We need the reassurance of others if we are to live satisfying lives; we cannot do it on our own.

What it means for politics is, however, enigmatic. Nobody has ever denied that we live something other than isolated lives, that we need companionship, that a society of atoms could not be governed, either by brute force or by anything else. The question of what policies will in fact foster stable communities, and whether such policies can be implemented without disastrous side-effects on the economy or an excessive loss of individual liberty all round, is the question that twentieth-century politics has always been about—in those favoured societies that are not asking more fundamental questions about mere survival. De Tocqueville—another omission from this essay—was as emphatic as Edmund Burke that men had to have loyalties to their 'small platoons' if they were to have loyalties to a wider society, and that liberty was not to be had in the absence of connection. The difficult, and as yet unanswered, question is how the balance between attachment and liberty is to be struck. It would be a great mistake to try to pass off one, presently pressing, question as 'the' central question of modern politics, and the one to which philosophers and political scientists ought to be paying attention; but if it were not, that would have as good a claim as any question to be the question of our time.

But it is in conjunction with these doubts that recent forms of 'republican' political thinking have come to the fore. What communitarians and republicans have in common is an anxiety about the readiness of the citizens of modern liberal democracies to sacrifice themselves for the common good, or indeed in any way to acknowledge the claims on them of a common good. This is often expressed as a criticism of liberalism, but perhaps wrongly. It is properly a criticism of a certain kind of consumerist and self-centered individualism that would have been thought by Mill and de Tocqueville to be as inconsistent with liberalism as with any other well-conducted system of government. What makes it non-liberal, perhaps, is its concern to bring to the fore the conception of liberty as self-government that Hobbes so roundly dismissed three and a half centuries ago. Hobbes observed that the city of Lucca wrote the word *libertas* in great letters upon its walls, but went on to point out that nobody could infer from that that a man had more liberty, that is, 'immunity from the service of the republic' in Lucca than in Constantinople. The republican retort is that Hobbes exactly missed the point.

What Lucca had and Constantinople did not was liberty as self-government. The inhabitants of Lucca could assemble and decide their common fate. The subjects of the despotic rulers of Constantinople could do no such thing. Self-government requires more of the citizens than does the sort of society in which self-centred consumers will be satisfied. It requires of them a collective intention to seek a common good and the ability to act to foster it. It does not demand that all their lives should be given over to politics, but just like Aristotle, who thought politics the 'master art' because all the other goods of human life could only be achieved when society was well governed, so modern republicans think that nothing will go well if politics goes badly. What this demands of the citizens is what both Machiavelli and Aristotle, as well as the American Founding Fathers, demanded: citizens must possess a certain form of virtue. This is not to say that they must be 'virtuous' in the somewhat wishy-washy sense that that term usually wears. Machiavelli's account of the political virtue of the Roman citizen included toughness, fierceness, endurance, and courage. Intelligence, energy, and foresight are surely part of it today as they always were; readiness to be led, but not without exercising one's own judgement as to where and what terms is another part of it.

The enemies of republican virtue are comfort, money, and domesticity. It is easy enough to see why. A people whose only interest is in consumption will turn in on itself and turn its back on the public realm. An engaged and active citizenry is an impossibility unless people have the chance to participate in public life in some fashion or other. This is why modern republicanism is more pluralistic than its predecessors; they on the whole saw small-scale private allegiances as competitors for our energies and loyalties, where later writers have followed de Tocqueville in seeing intermediary groups as the nurseries of public spirit. The woman who gets up at a parent–teacher meeting and sticks to her guns is ready to run for the local council or for Parliament, too. The man who gives up his evenings to do the accounts of his local sports club is in good training to run his local Labour Party branch. Hence, of course, the recent enthusiasm for the idea of 'civil society', that space between the purely private and the overtly political within which public spirit can thrive. To what extent the discussion of the conditions of a thriving civil society falls within the scope of political philosophy as opposed to political psychology and political sociology is perhaps the kind of disciplinary question that I can properly end by raising without even suggesting that I can answer it.

BIBLIOGRAPHY

This bibliography follows the pattern of the chapter. First, it lists general introductions and histories, together with several methodological essays; then it lists the work of the authors discussed, together with some commentary; next it lists source material and further reading on the contemporary topics discussed here; and finally, it lists a very little further reading on undiscussed topics.

GENERAL AND HISTORICAL

Klosko, G., *History of Political Theory: An Introduction* (New York, 1995). A sober, lucid, and reliable textbook; vol. i on the classical and medieval period, vol. ii on Machiavelli to Marx.

Plamenatz, J., *Man and Society* (London, 1963). Originally 2 vols., since reissued in 3 vols. with more historical material; a dry, meticulous analysis of thinkers and their thoughts from Machiavelli to Marx.

Sabine, G., *A History of Political Theory* (London, 1937). The staple of political theory courses for sixty years, modestly updated since.

Wolin, S., *Politics and Vision* (London, 1961). A strikingly individual account of selected writers from Plato to Hobbes with a coda on the decline of politics in the past three centuries.

METHODOLOGICAL

Dunn, J., *The History of Political Theory* (Cambridge, 1996).

Skinner, Q., 'Meaning and Understanding in the History of Ideas', *History and Theory*, vol. 8 (1969), 3–53.

Tully, J. (ed.), *Meaning and Context* (Princeton, 1988). Collects five of Skinner's essays on method, with seven critical discussions and a reply by Skinner; between them, they canvass most of the reasons for studying political theory historically and most of the anxieties about our ability to do it intelligently.

AUTHORS AND COMMENTATORS

Thucydides, *History of the Peloponnesian War* (Harmondsworth, 1954).

Plato, *Gorgias* (Harmondsworth, 1956). The classic demolition of the pretensions of the Sophists and democratic orators in a genuine, open-ended dialogue.

——*The Republic*, trans. R. Waterfield (Oxford, 1994). The full-scale demolition of democratic theory and defence of a philosophical dictatorship.

Commentators are legion, but J. Annas, *An Introduction to Plato's 'Republic'* (Oxford, 1981) is one of the very best.

Aristotle, *Politics*, trans. and ed. E. Barker (Oxford, 1948). A massively sensible defence of political common sense against Plato's assault, and correspondingly less exciting to read.

Among commentaries, E. Barker's introduction to his edition above, is very useful. A more modern treatment is R. Mulgan, *Aristotle's Political Theory* (London, 1977).

Machiavelli, Niccolò, *The Prince* (1513).

——*Discourses on Livy* (1526). M. Lerner edited the two works in one vol. (New York, 1940).

Machiavelli has attracted innumerable commentators, who have rarely agreed with one another. Q. Skinner, *Machiavelli* (Oxford, 1981) is an excellent brief introduction.

Hobbes, Thomas, *Leviathan* (1651). Of recent editions, the Penguin (Harmondsworth, 1968) has an interesting introduction by C. B. Macpherson, and the Cambridge edn. (1991), a very different, but equally interesting introduction by R. Tuck.

No single account of Hobbes stands out, but J. W. N. Watkins, *Hobbes's System of Ideas* (London, 1974) does particular justice to the philosophical interest of Hobbes's political theory. T. Sorell (ed.), *A Companion to Hobbes* (Cambridge, 1996) collects essays on all aspects of Hobbes's thinking.

Locke, John, *Two Treatises of Government*. The best edn. remains P. Laslett's magisterial edn. of both treatises (Cambridge, 1991). A useful collection of Locke's work ed. D. Wootton, *Locke: Political Writings* (Harmondsworth, 1993) contains both the *Second Treatise* and the *Essay on Toleration*.

Among commentators, R. Ashcraft, *The Revolutionary Politics of John Locke* (Princeton, 1987) stands out.

ROUSSEAU, JEAN-JACQUES, *The Social Contract* (1762); best read together with his 'Discourses' on the Arts and Sciences, The Origins of Inequality, and Political Economy. The Everyman Library edn. collects all four works in one vol. Rousseau's *Émile* (1762) is second only to Plato's *Republic* in its influence on educational theory. There are many editions.

J. Shklar, *Men and Citizens* (Cambridge, 1969) and R. Masters, *The Political Philosophy of Rousseau* (Princeton, 1968) are among the best commentaries. R. Wokler, *Rousseau* (Oxford, 1996) is a brief and useful mixture of biography and analysis.

HEGEL, G. W. F., *The Phenomenology of Spirit* (1807; Oxford, 1979).
——*The Philosophy of History* (1821; Oxford, 1956).
——*The Philosophy of Right* (1818; Cambridge, 1991).

Surprisingly few readers take advantage of Hegel's own paraphrase of his work, written for the benefit of his own students, but pt. 3 of his *Encyclopedia of the Philosophical Sciences* (1830; Oxford, 1971) is an accessible way into the *Phenomenology* in particular. C. Taylor, *Hegel* (Cambridge, 1974) is both comprehensive and readable. S. Avineri, *Hegel's Theory of the Modern State* (Cambridge, 1972) is excellent on its narrower topic.

MARX, KARL, *Economic and Philosophical Manuscripts* (1844; Buffalo, NY, 1988).
——*Capital*, i (1867; Harmondswoth, 1976).

J. Elster, *An Introduction to Karl Marx* (Cambridge, 1986) and G. A. Cohen, *Karl Marx's Theory of History* (Princeton, 1980) are two recent and very distinguished analytical treatments of Marxism.

MILL, JOHN STUART, *On Liberty* (London, 1858).
——*Considerations on Representative Government* (London, 1862).

F. Berger, *Happiness, Justice, and Freedom* (Berkeley, 1984). The best general account of Mill's political philosophy. J. Skorupski, *Mill* (London, 1991) is much the best account of Mill's larger system.

RECENT WORK

General

QUINTON, A. (ed.), *Political Philosophy* (Oxford, 1967). A collection of essays that has remained valuable for several decades.

HAMPTON J., *Political Philosophy* (Boulder, Colo., 1997).

WOLFF, J., *An Introduction to Political Philosophy* (Oxford, 1996). A useful introduction, both historical and analytical in approach.

PLANT, R., *Modern Political Thought* (Oxford, 1991).

KYMLICKA, W., *Contemporary Political Philosophy: An Introduction* (Oxford, 1990).

BARRY, B., *Political Argument* (London, 1965) did much to revive serious political philosophy as an austere but engaged discipline.

WALZER, M., *Interpretation and Social Criticism* (New York, 1987) defends the thought that 'criticism' is other than, and more useful than, political philosophy.

FEINBERG, J., *Social Philosophy* (Englewood Cliffs, NJ, 1971).

Democracy

SCHUMPETER, J., *Capitalism, Socialism and Democracy* (London, 1942) makes up in (deserved) influence for whatever it lacks in philosophical finesse.

DAHL, R. A., *A Preface to Democratic Theory* (Chicago, 1953) is in the same league.

WOLFF, R. P., *In Defense of Anarchism* (New York, 1969) argues that even universal direct democracy is not a legitimate form of government, and that no legitimate governments exist, therefore.

GUTMANN, A., and THOMPSON, D. F., *Democracy and Disagreement* (Cambridge, Mass., 1995). A defence of 'deliberative democracy'.

Justice

RAWLS, J., *A Theory of Justice* (Cambridge, Mass., 1971) is both the starting-point for most recent academic political thinking and a wonderful compendium of liberal insights. His *Political Liberalism* (Cambridge, Mass., 1991) defends his former politics more strenuously than his economics.

ACKERMAN, B., *Social Justice in the Liberal State* (New Haven, 1980). An alternative view of what a contractualist theory of justice would result in.

NOZICK, R., *Anarchy, State and Utopia* (New York, 1974). A highly readable critique of Rawls's and most other accounts of justice and rights.

BARRY, B., *The Liberal Theory of Justice* (Oxford, 1974). An acerbic and acute critical inspection of Rawls's account.

—— *Theories of Justice* (Oxford, 1987–). Difficult but persuasive defence of 'justice as impartiality'.

WALZER, M., *Spheres of Justice* (New York, 1983) argues that no one account of justice fits all cases.

The Jurisprudential Turn

HART, H. L. A., *The Concept of Law* (Oxford, 1961). The canonical statement of a renovated legal positivism.

DWORKIN, R. M., *Taking Rights Seriously* (London, 1977) states the case against legal positivism; further elaborations come in *A Matter of Principle* (Cambridge Mass., 1985), *Law's Empire* (London, 1986), and *Freedom's Law* (New York, 1996).

RAZ, J., *The Concept of a Legal System* (Oxford, 1973).

Rights, Freedom, and Other Topics

BERLIN, I., *Four Essays on Liberty* (Oxford, 1969) includes 'Two Concepts of Liberty', the most discussed essay on the subject of the past fifty years.

WALDRON, J., *Liberal Rights* (Cambridge, 1991). Brisk, clear essays on a concern for rights and their application in practice.

NICKEL, J., *Making Sense of Human Rights* (Berkeley, 1987).

RAZ, J., *The Morality of Freedom* (Oxford, 1986).

ARENDT, H., *The Human Condition* (Chicago, 1953). The most influential statement of the view that 'politics' is no longer practised in the modern world.

SANDEL, M., *Liberalism and the Limits of Justice* (Cambridge, 1982). The first blow of the communitarians against the liberals.

TAYLOR, C., *The Ethics of Authenticity* (Cambridge, Mass., 1991). A more philosophically nuanced account of the communitarian case.

KYMLICKA, W., *Liberalism, Community and Culture* (Oxford, 1989). A delicately nuanced treatment of the conflict between universal and local allegiances; the argument is developed further in *Multicultural Citizenship* (Oxford, 1995).

GUTMANN, A., and THOMPSON, D. (eds.), *Ethics and Politics*, 2nd edn. (Chicago, 1994). Excellent introduction to the field of ethics and public policy.

JAGGAR, A., *Feminist Politics and Human Nature* (Towota, NJ, 1983).

MACKINNON, C., *Toward a Feminist Theory of the State* (Cambridge, Mass., 1989).

——*Feminism Unmodified* (Cambridge, Mass., 1991).

OKIN, S., *Justice, Gender, and the Family* (New York, 1989) undermines Rawls's view that arguments about justice stop at the family.

YOUNG, I. M., *Justice and the Politics of Difference* (Princeton, NJ, 1990) argues for a conception of justice more sensitive to gender differences.

7

THE PHILOSOPHY OF THE SOCIAL SCIENCES

David-Hillel Ruben

1. KNOWLEDGE OF NATURE AND KNOWLEDGE OF SOCIETY

Philosophers of natural science address questions that arise, in the main, from the practice of natural science itself. These questions or problems may not occur to the natural scientist, but they are concerned with whatever it is that he is doing. Some of the natural sciences, biology and astronomy for example, are about some things that non-scientists talk about too, namely animals and plants, and the stars. But even in those cases, the scientists tell the non-scientist truths about those things that are generally otherwise unavailable to the layperson. And many of the natural sciences are at least sometimes concerned with entities or things entirely unavailable to the unsuspecting layperson: astronomy about black holes, biology about microscopic life forms invisible to the naked eye, and physics about quantum particles, force fields, and so on. In those cases, the truths divulged by natural science are entirely news to the layperson, if indeed he can even grasp them at all.

In this, there is a stark contrast with the activity of the philosophers of social science. To begin with, let us distinguish between concepts and the generalizations which may employ those concepts in their formulation. First, consider the concepts that social scientists use. Most of the things that social science is about, nations, groups, institutions, families, tribes, rules, economic markets, specific sorts of human action or behaviour, and so on, are items that find a place in the discourse of the ordinary layperson. Talk about class, or about purchase and sale, for example, is hardly confined to the social scientist or the philosopher thereof. The man (or woman) on the Clapham omnibus has as good a grasp of common talk about social class and purchase as does the social scientist. Even in those cases in which the social scientist introduces neologisms, for example demand curves or anomie, they seem closely connected to, and sometimes only a refinement of, concepts already grasped by the layperson.

Moreover, the generalizations of social science often have an air of familiarity to the person on that same omnibus that goes beyond simple acquaintance with the concepts used in their formulation. The truths that the social scientist discovers often strike the layperson as things the latter already knew, dressed up in new jargon. This is not always so, and perhaps the layperson underestimates the extent to which the new dressing alters the message, but there is no doubt that many of the generalizations of social science strike the uninitiated in this way. All of this does point to a legitimate contrast between the philosophy of the natural and social sciences. In the philosophy of the social sciences, the issues and problems discussed will have a certain familiarity to any competent speaker of the language, in a way in which this is not true in the philosophy of natural science.

This thought is found in Vico: the idea that society, what it is and how it works, should be transparent to social agents, since society is merely their own creation. One might think of it in this way: philosophers have, since the time of Descartes, often assumed that persons have a special and incorrigible knowledge about the contents of their own minds. If so, and if the very essence of society is to be found in the way in which persons collectively think about things (so, for example, if everyone always believes that something is money, then it is money), then does it not follow that Vico was right, and that persons should be able, by mere reflection, to understand society too? If people know what they believe, and if, in society, (everyone's) believing makes it so, then cannot people, merely by ratiocination, know whether social things are thus-and-so? On the contrary, if society is sometimes opaque to social agents, how can that opacity be accounted for?

Let us call the thought that, as a projection of mind, society must be transparent to social agents 'the transparency thesis'. This thesis has received different, and non-equivalent, formulations. For example, there is the idea that the concepts the social scientist uses to explain, to account for, social reality, must in principle or in practice be available to the social agents themselves.

If the availability of the concepts to the social agents themselves is merely in principle, one will obtain a fairly weak form of the transparency thesis. If one thinks of the social scientific discourse in question as a fragment of a natural language, a fragment which is spoken anyway at least by social scientists, weak availability might, for example, be ensured simply by the intertranslatability in principle of all natural languages, if there be such. The social scientists have, after all, started by speaking a natural language, whether it be one shared with the subjects they are studying or not, and then learned to use this specialist discourse from that linguistic basis. Their scientific discourse is an extension of some natural language, and, as such, it must be translatable into the subjects' language, assuming that all languages intertranslate.

However, if the availability must be actual, then the thesis is significantly stronger. To the extent that the concepts used by the social scientist must be ones he *actually* shares with the agents he studies, they and he must share a 'form of life'. What does that rather vague and over-used expression mean? If a social scientist studies religion, he need not be, like those he observes, a religious believer. But it does mean that he must grasp the concepts they use with the same nuance and comprehension as they do, and this suggests a kind of familiarity with, or even immersion in, that lifestyle, which contrasts with the detachment and objectivity in the relation between the natural scientist and the objects the latter studies.

The argument for this strong thesis is often that, if the social scientist does not use the same concepts that the subjects he studies use, then he has, in some sense, switched the topic of conversation and is not talking about the same things as they are. This argument, baldly stated, seems to presuppose that different concepts cannot be about the same things. Differences in connotation do not entail differences in denotation. Even if the concepts used by scientist and subject differ, it does not follow that what they are speaking about cannot be the same. This distinction is important. Often, writers conclude from the fact that two different speakers use two different conceptual schemes that those speakers inhabit 'different worlds'. No such inference is valid, without the addition of further, and controversial, premisses. There can be different concepts, indeed different conceptual schemes, having the same referents.

Another formulation of the transparency thesis focuses not on concepts but on knowledge of social laws: the idea is that the 'laws' of social science can only be truisms about agents and their psychology that are already available, at least as rough-and-ready generalizations, to the agents themselves. It might be, for instance, that social agents already know partial and incomplete fragments of such laws; the task of the social scientist would be to complete them, perhaps by adding necessary qualifications to render such generalizations exceptionless. So the well-read and informed layperson may know that typically *F*s are *G* (perhaps that revolutionary excesses tend to be followed by counter-revolutionary periods), even though (the layperson knows that) there are exceptions in which this is not so.

The social scientists' job would then be to convert the rough-and-ready generalization into an exceptionless deterministic or stochastic (probabilistic) law.[1] If this were the role of the social scientist, then the laws he formulates must already employ concepts (like *F* and *G*) familiar to the social actors in one of the ways already discussed. But this formulation of the transparency thesis requires more: the generalizations expressed by using those concepts must themselves be already accepted by the layperson, at least in some sort of implicit or incomplete way.

All forms of the transparency thesis tend to downgrade the status of social science, by making whatever the social scientist does continuous with non-scientific modes of understanding. In contrast, the natural scientist often forces us to break with such ordinary ways of understanding the natural world, by introducing radical discontinuity between ordinary and scientific thought about nature. Many writers, Marx being a good example, have rejected the transparency thesis in any significant sense, and found discontinuity between social science and ordinary thought. If there were radical discontinuity between social science and ordinary thought about society, social science certainly would have its work cut out for it. Precisely what is left for the social scientist to do,

[1] A deterministic law has the form: all *F*s without exception are G. A stochastic law has the form: the probability of an *F* being a G is *p*, where *p* measures that probability. Even such a probabilistic law is precise and might be complete, whereas the layperson's rough-and-ready generalization is neither.

assuming the continuity with what we all think about society anyway, will depend on the exact formulation the transparency thesis is given.

Vico's argument for the transparency thesis suggested above (there are others) depended on the assumption that society was merely a projection of mind's contents onto nature. In a way, the very metaphor itself suggests a corrective to the transparency thesis: once mind gets 'embodied' in nature, and since nature is itself outwith the control of agents, there must be some aspects of the social world which need to be discovered simply because of the natural embodiment of mind. Individual and collective action, for example, have unintended consequences, which may not be obvious to the social actors. But a more radical way to challenge the transparency thesis is to question whether it really is true that society, and all its contents, are merely projections of mind. I will turn to this question in the next section.

2. INDIVIDUALISM AND HOLISM IN THE SOCIAL SCIENCES

Historians and social scientists, in the course of their professional activity, explain or investigate at least two sorts of thing: (*a*) those individual human actions which have historical or social significance; (*b*) historical and social events and structures ('large-scale' social phenomena), such as wars, invasions, economic depressions, social customs, the class system, the family, the state, and the crime rate. If the transparency thesis is correct, then (*a*) actions must be transparent in some sense, perhaps because they are merely the projection of the agents' intentions into the world; and (*b*) explanations of these so-called large-scale items can, ultimately, be understood as merely explanations of a large number of individual human actions, that is, as a complex set of explanations of the first kind, (*a*). If social phenomena are merely composed or made up of a great deal of individual human actions, and if actions are transparent to the agent, then society will turn out to be transparent too, as the thesis maintains.

Let me delay addressing the question of the transparency of action. Is it true that social phenomena are merely made up of, or composed of, a great, perhaps indefinite, number of actions of individuals? Such a position has sometimes been called 'individualism', frequently with the unhelpful adjective 'methodological' added in for good measure. Let us call 'holism' any doctrine which simply denies whatever formulation we give to individualism. How precisely should individualism be stated, and is it, in any interesting formulation, true?

Individualism (and hence, holism) in the social sciences comes in at least four broad varieties: (*a*) conceptual, (*b*) metaphysical, (*c*) explanatory, and (*d*) ethical.

Ethical individualism is the view, roughly, that only individual persons are ethical subjects, and that states or groups or corporations etc. can make no legitimate ethical or moral demands of us, or be held morally responsible, except in so far as these demands or responsibilities cash out as the rights of, or obligations owed to, specific individuals. Its slogan might be: only individuals matter morally. Even if conceptual, metaphysical, and explanatory holism were true, ethical individualism might be true. I will not consider (*d*) further.

I will state a version of each of (*a–c*). It is clear, I think, that these three doctrines, each of which is often called 'individualism', are not equivalent. On the other hand, they are not unrelated. I will not attempt to work out the logical relations amongst the three doctrines, other than by way of making a few passing remarks. What logical relations there are amongst them will depend on various matters extraneous to problems specific to the philosophy of the social sciences: a general theory of explanation, the relation between metaphysics and epistemology, and the nature of reduction, to name but three.

Conceptual individualism must begin by distinguishing distinctively social discourse, call it S, and the discourse of individual psychology, call it P. (For good measure, call the discourse about the natural world that excludes any reference to psychology or anything social M.) In S, there will be some concepts, presumably a subset of the non-logical concepts of S, which are specific to S. Call the subset S*. It might not be necessary to include in S* purely theoretical social scientific concepts, introduced by social scientists, but at the very least S* must include all those concepts specific to our ordinary, day-to-day, talk about society.

The claim of conceptual individualism is that *all* such concepts in S* can be 'translated without remainder' into concepts found in P (or perhaps P enriched with M). (Since there is a close connection between concepts and properties, a similar doctrine can be stated in terms of the reduction of social properties to individual psychological properties.) Not too much weight should be placed on understanding the idea of translation here as we normally might. The point of the requirement is that a linkage of some sort with P-concepts needs to be found for all the concepts in S*.

Two of the unclarities in this formulation are: (1) It is not clear what concepts are to be included as belonging to individual psychology. Is the concept of believing that there are institutions, for instance, a concept of individual psychology? It is certainly a psychological concept whose instances are individual persons, since it is persons who believe that there are institutions. In other words, can the concepts of individual psychology have social content? (2) It is not clear what constraints there are on the nature of the linkage required. Is it synonymy, such that each concept in S* is synonymous with some concept(s) in P? Surely that would be too strong. Does the linkage we need require only nomic equivalence or bridge laws, i.e. equivalences underwritten by a law of nature, or true as a matter of nomic necessity? Mere material equivalence would be too weak.

If conceptual individualism were true and required nomic equivalence, it would provide the derivation of discourse about society from, and hence reduction to, individual psychology, via appropriate bridge laws, on at least one standard understanding of what is meant by reduction. In so far as social science itself (as opposed to our ordinary discourse about society) included theoretical neologisms that did not translate in this way, it would simply become otiose.

However, there is no point to talk of derivation of one discourse from another via bridge laws unless both discourses can be formalized, expressed in the canonical form of a formal system. I see no reason to believe that ordinary social discourse or social science are capable of being formalized in such a way that the question of logical derivation can even be significantly posed. Those philosophers who have worked in the unity-of-science tradition have often merely assumed that the social sciences could be formalized, but this seems to me to be itself an assumption on their part.

Even if social discourse or social science on the one hand and individual psychology on the other met the conditions of being formally expressible, there are doubts about the availability of the requisite bridge laws. The bridge laws would have to provide concepts of psychology (say, beliefs and other mental states) which were *necessary and sufficient* for (and thus equivalent to) the ones specific to social discourse (this needs a more precise formulation, but I shall let it pass). There is reason to query if this could even in principle be possible.

Consider the concept of being a mayor. What may be called the argument from variable realization reminds us that there does not appear to be any one set of psychological states held by social actors, or even a finite disjunction of such states, whether beliefs or some other states, necessary for someone to be a mayor. Since what a mayor does is set by human convention and not the laws of nature, it is almost limitless what social actors might believe or expect such a person to do. So even if we obtain nomological sufficiency of the mental for the social (if persons believe various things about a man, then, as a matter of natural law, the latter must be a mayor), equivalence may elude us, on the grounds that the necessity of the mental for the social will be unavailable (if he is a mayor, there is nothing specific that persons must, as a matter of natural law, believe about him, or expect him to do).[2]

Unlike conceptual individualism, metaphysical individualism does not presuppose the translatability or linkage of one set of concepts into those of another set. It is a doctrine couched in the material rather than the formal mode.

[2] They might of course all believe that he is a mayor, but that will hardly be helpful, since it reuses the very social concept that the individualist is trying to eliminate.

It says that what social phenomena *are* are merely (sets of?) individuals in certain psychological states (and who stand in certain relations). This is not equivalent to conceptual individualism, since conceptual individualism could be false and metaphysical individualism true. There might be two discourses, S and P, as indicated above, whose concepts were not translatable in terms of the other, not even nomically equivalent, but yet S and P could in fact be *about* the same things.

Compare formal and material mode views about the relationship between physical objects and sense-data. The formal mode thesis might claim that physical-object statements are translatable without remainder into statements about sense-data. Even if this were false, physical-object statements and sense-data statements might both just *be* about sense-data, or sets thereof. In a similar vein, conceptual individualism might be false, but metaphysical individualism be true.

Metaphysical individualism could be expressed using either identity or composition (or constitution). It is controversial whether the identity relation and the wholly-constituted-by relation are indeed the same relation. In one formulation, metaphysical individualism says that social institutions *are* just individuals standing in certain relations. In the other, metaphysical individualism says that social institutions are wholly constituted by individuals standing in certain relations.

Sometimes, metaphysical individualism is expressed using neither the identity nor the composition relation, but rather by using the relation of a whole to its parts. Although the language of whole–part is a common enough way in which to express metaphysical individualism, I believe that it is misleading. Taken literally, it would make the relation between a society, for example, and the individual members of the society, a mereological relation, characterized by certain axioms, like that of transitivity: if *a* is a part of *b*, and if *b* is a part of *c*, then *a* is a part of *c*. But that is not true of the relation between the members of a social institution and the institution itself. For example, you and I might be members (residents, citizens) of the United Kingdom, and the United Kingdom might be a member of the United Nations, but you and I need not be, in fact are not, members of the United Nations. I take this to show that talk of whole–part, in the context of individuals and social institutions, is at best metaphorical.

Consider the first option, identity: social institutions are identical to the individuals who are their members. Now, the problem with the doctrine is this: the identity sign is flanked on both sides by a name or definite description. So such an identity claim might look like this: 'The United Kingdom = . . .'. 'The United Kingdom' is a name, but what name or definite description is meant to go on the right-hand side of this identity? 'The individuals who are residents or citizens' is not, as it stands, a name or definite description. It does not refer.

Perhaps the referring expression should be: '*the set* of individual residents or citizens'. So some entity or other must be found, whose name or description can flank the right-hand side of the identity sign. And what metaphysical individualism requires is that the entity should be a non-social one, so that a social entity, like the United Kingdom, turns out in the end to be identical to a non-social one.

It seems to me that no social institution could be identical with a set of anything, given the standard understanding of set. For a start, the identity conditions for sets are such that set a = set b if and only if a and b have exactly the same members. But social institutions are typically able to remain numerically one and the same in spite of the addition or deletion of members. Moreover, unlike sets, two different institutions might have exactly the same members: precisely the same crowd of people might be the full membership of two different clubs. So it seems that social institutions cannot be identical to sets. And if not to sets, the challenge that confronts metaphysical individualism is to say exactly to *which* non-social entities social entities like the United Kingdom are identical.

There are similar objections to identifying a social entity like the United Kingdom to a designated land mass, or a designated area. The UK can remain numerically one and the same, and yet the area it occupies numerically differ (qualitative difference is, of course, not relevant here). One problem with my argument is that it in effect treats the identities metaphysical individualism would need as necessary rather than contingent, but it seems to me that this is a valid requirement. I take it that 'the United Kingdom' rigidly designates (that is, holding its meaning constant, it designates the same thing in every possible world in which it designates anything at all). Let 'Land' or 'Set' rigidly designate the area the UK occupies or the set of persons who are its members at some time t. Then, 'The UK = Land' or 'The UK = Set' should be necessary truths, if true at all. But there is no set of persons or land area which would make these necessary truths.

Might the UK be identical to some second-order set, say the set which contains a succession of sets of persons? So, a might be the set containing the citizens of the UK at time t, b might be the set containing the citizens of the UK at t^*, c might be the set containing the citizens of the UK at t^{**}, and so on. Let α be the second-order set whose members are sets a, b, c, and so on. But then 'The UK = α' should be a necessary truth, since both 'the UK' and 'α' rigidly designate. But there is no second-order set, α, such that 'The UK = α' will be a necessary truth, since the UK could remain numerically one and the same even if some set which was a member of α had been different.

More work needs to be done by proponents of metaphysical individualism. Other candidates for the entity identical to a social entity like 'the United Kingdom' might be considered. Groups do not have the same ills as sets for these purposes; a group can remain numerically one and the same in spite of membership change, and two numerically distinct groups might have identical memberships. But the claim that the United Kingdom is identical to the group of people who are citizens or residents does not seem to be a form of metaphysical individualism at all, since groups are, or seem to be, themselves social entities. There might be some advantage to the reduction of nation-states to groups, but amongst those advantages cannot be the reduction of social entities to non-social ones, as we took metaphysical individualism to be proposing. If the composition relation is distinct from identity, the possibility of stating a plausible form of metaphysical individualism using it needs to be considered as well.

I said above: 'In one formulation, metaphysical individualism says that social institutions *are* just individuals standing in certain relations.' Some too easy refutations of metaphysical individualism have assumed that the programme of reductive analysis was to reduce social entities to 'atomic', non-related individuals (this is sometimes called the 'Robinson Crusoe refutation'). In fact, metaphysical individualism can surely help itself to *some* relations between individuals as part of the analysans, at least if the relations to which it helps itself are non-social (spatial or temporal relations, for example). But can it use any relation whatever? Suppose, for instance, that metaphysical individualism used the idea that there are social relations between the individuals to which the social entities (structures etc.) get reduced? There might still be some gain; it would not be trivial to discover that one could eliminate social 'things' in favour of individuals and social relations. But this would not, of course, by itself be a full reduction of the social to the non-social.

Finally, there is explanatory individualism. This is a difficult doctrine to discuss in the abstract, since its virtues or vices will depend very much on what commitments its various proponents make to a general theory of explanation. The central idea, though, is this. (I assume here, without argument, that explanation is always of facts by other facts.) First, a distinction must be drawn between social and non-social (psychological or physical) facts. It may be that the explanation for some social facts is in terms of yet other social facts, and many non-social facts themselves are explained by citing social facts: for example, certain land erosion (a non-social fact) might be explained as the outcome of an inept agricultural policy by the government of the region (a social fact).

Consider the idea of an explanatory chain of facts. Each fact explains (or is part of the explanation of) the fact to its right on the chain, so that each fact on such a chain is explanatorily prior to the one on its right. We are interested in those chains on which there is at least one social fact. The claim by the proponent of explanatory individualism is that *ultimately*, for every explanatory chain containing at least one social fact, as one moves to the left, the chain at some point will become social-fact-free and remains so, no matter how far to the left one travels. That seems to be the cash value of the idea that in the *final analysis* every social fact has an explanation grounded in some facts, not themselves social facts.

One unclarity in this position is the meaning we are to give to 'social fact'. A fact is or is not a social fact intrinsically, and not just in virtue of the sorts of causes or effects it has. Note that there seems to be a difference between social facts and facts of interest to the social sciences. For example, the fact that a certain pattern of land erosion has occurred does *not* itself seem to be a social fact, although it may be of interest to a social scientist (and have a social cause). On the other hand, if it were a fact, the fact that bus-conductors tend to whistle whilst they collect fares would be a social fact (because being a bus-conductor and being a fare are social properties), but not one likely to be of interest or significance to the social scientist (and might not have any social cause or social effect).

First consider only particular facts with the form: object *o* has property S. No doubt a fact is a social fact if the object it is about, *o*, is a social entity (structure, etc.) of some sort. But a fact is social even if *o* is an individual, if 'S' stands for a social property (including of course relational properties). 'S' might stand for a social action property (like, cashing a cheque or dancing a rain dance) or it might stand for the property of being in a certain social state (like being a mayor or a shaman). Consider next general facts, like the fact that whatever has property S has property T. Presumably, a general fact is social if one or both of properties S and T are social. So the question then is: what makes a property a social property?

My own view is that a property S is a social property if and only if (roughly) if it were instantiated, it would follow that some agents had an interlocking and nested set of beliefs and expectations about one another's behaviour. Suppose there are but two agents, *a* and *b*. *a* might expect *b* to do something, and *b* believe that *a* expects him to do this, and *a* believe that *b* believes that he, *a*, has this expectation, and so on, to whatever degree of nesting the agents are psychologically capable. A matching story needs to be told about *b*'s expectations of what *a* will do, and the beliefs that arise therefrom. The idea needs careful elaboration, and further refinements need to be introduced, for this view to be made plausible. Other answers also need to be canvassed. But certainly any plausible form of explanatory individualism will have to come to grips with the question of what makes a fact a social fact, and what makes a property a social property, in order to formulate its explanatory claims.

One problem with explanatory individualism is this. Normally, if someone holds a justified true belief that *p*, part of the explanation for his so believing is that *p* is the case. Suppose, for example, that I truly and justifiably believe that it is raining. Why do I believe this? Partly, the fact that it is raining explains why I believe this. So, to apply this point to the case at hand, if I justifiably and truly believe that *p*, where that *p* is a social fact, then part of the explanation of why I believe that there is this social fact is that there is indeed this social fact.

In most versions of explanatory individualism, the explanation for the social fact that *p* is that certain beliefs prevail in the society ('believing makes it so'). So, on this view of the matter, everyone's (or most people's) believing that *p* explains why *p* (that everyone or almost everyone believes this is money explains why this is money).

Of course, generally it can be true both that social facts are explained by people's beliefs, and in turn that their beliefs are explained by social facts. But, if explanatory individualism is true, this symmetry of social facts both explaining and being explained by individuals' beliefs must ultimately be grounded in a final asymmetry of individuals' beliefs explaining social facts. As we saw, the explanatory chain must eventually become social-fact-free, as one moves to the left on the chain. Without at least this commitment, explanatory individualism would have no content.

Suppose some enthusiastic explanatory individualist tries to convince us that he has located the point on the explanatory chain which contains the 'last' social fact, call it *p*. Further to the left, he says, there are no further social facts, so that ultimately all social facts are explained by non-social ones. Consider just this point on the explanatory chain. We would have a social fact, like the fact that *p*, explained by people's beliefs that *p*. But why would these people believe that *p*; why would they believe that this is money? Following the normal explanatory order described above, if people justifiably and truly believe that this is money, it is at least in part because it is a fact that it *is* money. But, at this point on the explanatory chain, the reply is not available to the explanatory individualist, since, *ex hypothesi*, this is a point on the chain prior to which there are no social facts.

So if people's social beliefs are justified and true, then, at least at one crucial point in the explanatory chain, explanatory individualism gets the direction of explanation wrong. Consider the point *p* at which it is alleged that the explanatory chain becomes social-fact-free. At *p*, there will be only psychological facts about what people believe about various social facts, which psychological facts will be said to explain social facts further along the explanatory chain, after *p*. But what explains those psychological facts about what people believe about various social facts? It cannot be claimed that people's beliefs about these social facts are explained, at least in part, by the obtaining at a point prior to *p*, of those social facts themselves, for that would prevent the chain from becoming social-fact-free at that point. But this seems wrong: people's justified and true beliefs about social facts should be at least in part explained, at every point in the explanatory chain, by the obtaining of those social facts themselves.

Finally, one frequently hears the expression 'methodological individualism'. The expression is ambiguous, and most often what is meant is either conceptual or metaphysical or explanatory individualism. But there is yet another possibility. In discussions of behaviourism about the mental, the distinction has sometimes been drawn between analytic and methodological behaviourism. According to methodological behaviourism, there might well be mental states or events, but since access to them is not intersubjective but rather is available only to a single person, namely the person who is in that mental state, they are 'unscientific' and can be safely omitted from a scientific account of the world. *Pari passu*, methodological individualism might be the idea that whether or not there are irreducible social structures, events, etc. is neither here nor there. Such entities, if such there be, are 'queer' and can be omitted from consideration by the social scientist in his account of social reality. Like mental states, it has sometimes been claimed that social entities are unobservable; all that can be observed are the individuals who are their members.

The unobservability claim is itself mute. No one denies that you can observe an apple, on the grounds that you can only observe its outside but not its inside. One observes a whole apple by observing its surface. One observes a building by observing its front façade. So too, it seems plausible to say that one does observe institutions or groups like the United Nations or the Royal Automobile Club by observing the buildings they occupy or their staff or their representatives.

More importantly, I confess to understanding neither methodological behaviourism nor methodological individualism on this construction. Of course, if there *are* no irreducible mental states or social states and structures, then we can safely ignore both, but then this needs an independent argument; and if there is to be such an argument, either conceptual or methodological or explanatory individualism had better be true. But if there are such things, then how can they be ignored? No scientific account of anything can simply ignore part of what actually exists, if it clearly falls within its field of inquiry.

3. CAUSAL AND NON-CAUSAL EXPLANATIONS IN THE SOCIAL SCIENCES

A causal explanation is an explanation of something in terms of its event-cause(s). (I use 'event' as a term of art, to include states, i.e. unchanges, as well as changes.) Some explanations in science are clearly not causal explanations at all: if one explains a natural law L by citing a higher-level law L*, such that L is a special case of L*, no causal explanation of L is being offered. L* is not the cause of anything, let alone of L, because laws are not things of the sort that can be causes (or effects). But it might be plausible to believe (although it is controversial) that in natural science all explanations of particular facts (as opposed to laws) must cite the causes of those facts.

Would it be plausible to believe this for the case of the social sciences? Some explanations of historical and social events and structures appear not to be causal explanations in this sense. There are two ways in which this appears to happen.

First, we sometimes seem to explain either the origin or continuing existence of a social institution by giving its function or purpose. These explanations are often called functional or teleological explanations. This seems to be an explanation of that thing in terms of its effects rather than by its causes. An explanation of a thing in terms of its effects cannot be a causal explanation of that thing. For example, it might be claimed that an institution like the university system arose or continues to exist *because* of its role in maintaining the class structure of the society. If the institution's origin or continuing existence is the explanandum, and the maintenance of the class structure is the explanans, and yet the institution's existence is the cause of the maintenance of the class structure, we seem to have managed to explain something without reference to its *cause*, but rather by reference to its *effect*.

A number of authors have suggested a way in which to understand functional explanation in social science as a special kind of causal explanation. If the university system's existence is really to be explained by its role in maintaining class structure, then that class structure must itself reinforce the university system in turn by some causal feedback loop. Suppose, for example, that the stronger the class system became, the more it tended to lead to the funding of the university system, which of course in its turn further reinforced the class system. Only if this were to happen could we say that the university system's existence was itself to be explained by the class structure to whose maintenance it also contributed.

It is a distinct question whether or not any explanations in social science meet the causal feedback loop requirement. A plausible speculation is that a few, but only a few, do. Even if there are some legitimate functional explanations in social science, there may not be many. If functionalism were the view that all social institutions can be explained functionally, functionalism would be false; if functionalism only required that some could be so explained, it might be true.

Is the causal feedback loop requirement for functional explanation compelling? One problem is this. Functional explanations are asymmetric: if *X* functionally explains *Y*, then it follows that *Y* does not also functionally explain *X*. But reciprocal causation (for that is what a causal feedback loop entails) is symmetric. In reciprocal causation, *X* causes *Y* and *Y* causes *X* (*X* and *Y* stand, of course, for types and not tokens). Any account that uses a causal feedback loop will need a further condition to introduce the requisite asymmetry into that account. It is not immediately clear what that will be.

The further conditions I discuss below, unintentionality and unrecognizability by the actors, don't appear able to do the job, for the actors might not intend or recognize the causation in either direction. Many accounts add that if *X* functionally explains *Y* (say, in some society *Z*), then *Y* is beneficial for the members of *Z*. So might this introduce the requisite asymmetry? If *Y* (say, social cohesion) is beneficial for the tribe, will or might *X* (say, the rain-dancing) also be beneficial for it? If *Y* is beneficial and *X* causes *Y*, then surely *X* is beneficial too, just in virtue of the fact that it leads to something, *Y*, itself beneficial. So far, no asymmetry. Perhaps some further distinction can be drawn between instrumental and intrinsic beneficiality, as a way of introducing the asymmetry, but I shall not pursue the issue further here.

The causal feedback loop requirement is usually taken to be a necessary but insufficient condition for an explanation to be a functional explanation. It is also common to require (in addition to the beneficiality condition) that, for the explanation to be a functional explanation, the social actors do something intentionally (like rain-dance), while neither being aware of the relevant effects (say, the increase in social cohesion) of what they intentionally do, nor intending what they intentionally do to have those effects. The social cohesion, or whatever, that results from what they do must be happening 'behind their backs', it is often said. In an action explanation, one explains what a person does in terms of his plans, purposes, and projects. The idea here is that functional and action explanation must be kept logically distinct. So if rain-dancing is explained functionally in terms of the contribution it makes to social cohesion, the dancers intentionally dance, but the fact that so doing increases social cohesion can be no part of their plan or purpose.

There seems, at first sight, to be a case for insisting on the lack of intention concerning the relevant effects in a functional explanation, on pain of collapsing the two types of explanation otherwise. On the other hand, one can know that one's action will have certain consequences, without intending that it have those consequences. The argument for ruling out awareness or knowledge of the effects is less obvious, unless it be thought that, once aware of the effects their actions produced, and given that those effects were beneficial, the social actors would be bound to start acting intentionally in order to produce just those effects. But if so, then the no-intentionality condition alone suffices, lack of awareness or of knowledge being important only in so far as it ensures that the behaviour is not intended to produce those effects.

An explanation of an unintended effect of what an agent intentionally does, whether the agent was aware of it or not, is surely just an action explanation with an addition. The agent did such-and-such intentionally, and the effects in question were a causal consequence of his so acting, effects which may have been unintended and of which he might not have been aware. What seems to emerge is that there are a variety of action explanations, some of which incorporate further reference to foreseen but unintended, or unforeseen and unintended, effects of the action. There seems to be no compelling reason to select one or the other of those possibilities as necessary for the explanation to be a functional one. On this account, functional explanations seem merely to be a proper subset of action explanations, namely those which include causal feedback loops.

An alternative proposal for functional explanation sees it as lawlike explanation that explains the existence of some item like a rain dance by the dispositional or conditional fact that if the rain dance did exist, it would produce social cohesion. If, as the Marxist assures us, new production relations would lead to an increase in the forces of production, then new production relations come into existence. If something's beginning to exist or continuing existence were to lead to some (beneficial) effect, then that thing begins or continues to exist.

Such an explanation employs what has been called a consequence law. It is important to see why this proposal would not make functional explanation guilty of the fallacy of affirming the consequent. One commits that fallacy by arguing that if *p*, then *q*, and since *q*, then *p*. The suggestion before us has the following structure: if (if *p*, then *q*), then *p*. Perhaps it is a matter of law that if having long necks would help giraffes reach leaves, then they develop long necks. Similarly, perhaps it is a matter of law that if rain-dancing were to lead to increased social cohesion, rain-dancing occurs.

On this account, functional explanations can be elaborated or filled in by more fine-grained causal mechanisms, explaining how these dispositional facts lead to the items they explain. But even when we are unaware of what those causal mechanisms are, this does not prevent us from offering an explanation for those items, in the way proposed.

The consequence law proposal for functional explanation has at least these two problems that would have to be dealt with before we could accept it. First, there is the problem of functional alternatives. Many items might be such that if they were to exist, they would bring about a certain effect, but only one such item at most, in the typical case at any rate, actually comes into or continues in existence. What privileges that one item? Secondly, there seem to be cases in which if something were to exist, it would bring about beneficial results, but yet it does not exist. For example, no doubt if plants displayed mobility, their chances of survival would be increased, and yet plants have not developed mobility. A dispositional or conditional fact does not appear to be sufficient by itself to explain the existence of an item.

A second example of what appears to be a type of non-causal explanation in the social sciences is this. We sometimes seem to cite social structure as the explanation of something. These are sometimes called structural explanations. For example, it might be claimed that the practice of cousins marrying in a certain society is due to the family structures in that society; that the occurrence of capitalist crises in a society is due to the capitalist structure of that society. Whatever a social structure is, it is not itself an event or a state, and since only (it is often said) events or states can be causes, such a 'structural' explanation does not seem to be a causal explanation.

In contrast to functional explanations, I think that there are a large number of legitimate structural explanations in social science. Introducing a few distinctions may let us appreciate more clearly what a structural explanation involves. Structures are sets of relations. The family structure of the society is the set of family relations that can hold between various individuals: being a father, being a cousin, being a mother. The production relations of a society is the set of production relations that can hold between individuals or between individuals and objects: being a wage labourer, being a slave, being on loan to. Structures, as sets of relations, are, therefore, abstract entities and lack causal powers. But relations, relational properties, have instances: Sam's being a slave of Bill, the car's being on loan to Richard, Blair's being the father of David, Arthur's working on the lathe. These 'instances' are token relational states or events involving two or more things, and these token states or events, either singly or collectively, can exert causal powers.

Understood in this way, structural explanations can count as causal explanations of a sort: they are 'shorthand', in the language of structures, for a causal explanation in 'longhand' terms of indefinite and unspecified token events or states which are instances of the structure. If the capitalist production relations explain the economic crisis, that can only be in virtue of the fact that many token instances of those production relations caused, no doubt indirectly and in a mediated way, specific events which constitute that crisis.

4. ACTION

Whatever else it might also explain, social science explains human actions. In the literature, this is sometimes called intentional (or action) explanation. To be sure, social science is not interested in all human action. But, as I claimed earlier, it is not just interested in social actions either. It is concerned with those human actions, social or non-social, which have some sort of social significance or importance, whatever that might precisely come to. Presumably, social significance has something to do with the effects of that action on largish numbers of people. For example, Brutus' stabbing of Caesar was not a social action as such (because for stabbing to be true of an ordered pair of individuals, it does not follow that there must be a nested set of beliefs and expectations), but it was of enormous social significance, and might be the sort of action a social scientist, a historian for example, would wish to explain. And there may be social actions of such little consequence (for example, my stopping at a pedestrian crossing on such-and-such a day) that they are of no interest to the social scientist at all.

A topic which shall not detain us for long here is that of the identity conditions for actions. We need to make some decisions, simply in order to pose further questions in a clear and perspicuous manner. In broad outline, there are two sorts of theory: austere theories and prolific theories. Suppose I bend my finger, so that, as a result, I release the trigger, shoot you, kill you, and reduce the world's population by one. On the austere theory, these are five different descriptions of one and only one token action, the bending of my finger being a privileged description in the sense that it is basic. On the prolific theory, these are five different token actions, such that the basic action of my bending my finger generates, causally or otherwise, its successor, and the latter its successor, and so on.

In what follows, I adopt the terminology of prolific theory. This decision is not made out of conviction, but from ease of expression. It is simpler to state problems in the language of prolific theory. But I do not believe that any substantive issue in this chapter is thereby affected, and whatever I say should be translatable into the terminology of austere theory.

A question left from before is this. I said that if social phenomena are merely composed or made up of a great deal of individual human actions, and if actions are transparent to the agent, then society will turn out to be transparent too, as the transparency thesis maintained. Are actions transparent to the agents whose actions they are? We must distinguish between basic and non-basic actions. (Recall that we are speaking the language of prolific theory. There is an austere translation of this same point.) Suppose I bend my finger (on the trigger of a gun) and ten months later, as a result, you die. I've killed you. Or, suppose I lift a lever and thereby unknowingly detonate a bomb. I've detonated a bomb. My basic actions are, let us suppose, my movings of parts of my body. If non-basic actions depend on causal consequences or on non-causal 'upshots' of these basic movings,[3] actions certainly are not always transparent, for agents may be unaware of the consequences of what they do, as we saw in the discussion of functional explanation. All basic actions might be transparent to their agents, but certainly not all non-basic actions are.

A basic action is an action an agent does, but not *by* his doing any other action. Basic actions, on some views, are one's moving one's bodily parts; on another view, they are tryings or willings or attemptings. For purposes here, I have adopted the former view. Social actions must be non-basic, since they depend on the causal consequences or non-causal upshots of the basic actions. I have argued that not all non-basic actions are transparent to the agent. But I

[3] My writing a cheque is the upshot of my moving my hand in a certain way over a piece of paper. My writing of the cheque is not caused by my moving my hand, but is a non-causal upshot of the latter.

have not shown that none are. Sometimes I am aware of the consequences of what I do! The social non-basic actions might form a special subset; perhaps they are also transparent. Could I fail to know that I married you when I uttered those fateful words (don't be alarmed, this is only a philosophy example!)? Could I fail to know that I had voted or cashed a cheque when I put the 'X' or signed my name on the paper?

I think the answer to both these questions is in the affirmative. I might find myself in an alien society, and move my bodily parts in such ways that they had, in that society, social consequences of which I was unaware. That is, there could be individual non-transparency. There could also be collective non-transparency. There could be some social rule in virtue of which what I did had just the social upshot it did, although I was unaware of the rule and those aware of the rule were unaware of what I had done.

Still, non-transparency of the social must be parasitic on transparency at some level of the social itself. We could not have complete non-transparency of the social, with transparency only at the basic but non-social level of action. That is, it could not be that no one in the society ever understood their social actions. No one could get married in a society in which every person was unaware of the fact that anyone ever got married at all. (But note that this is not necessarily to accept the reductionist view that believing makes it so.) This marks an important contrast between social non-basic and non-social non-basic action.

Although it is not a question of any special interest to the philosophy of social science, it is interesting to inquire whether it is the case that basic action (all of which must be non-social) is transparent. The transparency claim for basic action is this: whenever an agent acts, he knows (*a*) that he acts; (*b*) assuming that he has acted, what that basic action is.

A person might act, believing that he had not acted. A person might believe falsely that he is unable to move his hand. He is asked to try and move it none the less. He is blindfolded, and his hand is anaesthetized in such a way that he cannot feel where it is. He may then believe that he has failed to move his hand, although he has done so. When the blindfold is removed, he may be surprised to see that he did move his hand after all. If, when he performs some basic action, he does not believe that he has acted at all, *a fortiori* he does not know what his basic action is. The transparency claim even for basic actions seems wrong.

Although some of the discussion of action explanation in social science began life as a distinct literature within the philosophy of history, it has now been absorbed into philosophical action theory more generally. There are a number of questions about action, and action explanation, both generally and as it applies in the social sciences. In this section, I concentrate on questions of action; in the next, on questions about action explanation.

Some of the same distinctions that apply in discussion of individualism and holism apply to actions as well. First, there is a straightforwardly metaphysical question. Consider the distinction between events (like the eruption of Vesuvius, the beating of my heart, the bending of my finger) and actions (like my moving my arm, my bending my finger). Natural science can be thought of (a bit simply) as confined to the investigation of events and the causal relations between them. Can human action be understood within such a naturalist perspective, as merely a special sort of bodily movement or event, perhaps with a distinctive sort of causal history? Perhaps the token action, my bending my finger, is just the token event of my finger's bending, when caused (to avoid further problems: caused in the right sort of way) by my intention that my finger should bend.

One contemporary theory of action is the causal theory of action (CTA). Its main contention is that the speculative question of the last paragraph is indeed to be answered in the affirmative. Actions are bodily movements, caused in the right way by the mental states which rationalize them. The CTA requires *both* causation and rationalization of the bodily movements by the appropriate mental states. The idea of rationalization is that embodied in the idea of the practical syllogism: the action mentioned in the conclusion is shown to be rational in light of the premisses. On the Humean view, the premisses are about a belief and a desire: if a person desires some end, and believes that some action is the only or best way to achieve that end, then the action is the rational thing to do in the circumstances. Alternative accounts of rationalization require intentions, or some other mental state or event, in place of belief and desire pairs. The Humean account fits more easily with examples of instrumental action, action done for some further purpose. It is more difficult to make it work for intrinsic action (if such there be), action done for its own sake, in a way that will preserve the causal role of the belief and desire.

Another naturalistic theory of action identifies actions with a certain subset of movements or events in the brain, those which have a certain consequential history, namely those that successfully end in bodily movements. Let us call this theory the effect theory of action (ETA). Both the CTA and the ETA bring actions 'into' the agent, making them either his bodily or his brain movements. The CTA designates as actions those bodily movements with a certain mental causal antecedent; the ETA designates as actions those brain movements with a certain bodily consequence.

But how could all actions be bodily or brain movements? Don't agents sometimes turn on the lights, flood the valley, damage the environment, and detonate bombs? The valley, the lights, the bomb, and the environment hardly count as bodily parts. On what we called the austere theory of act individuation, all actions are indeed movements of bodily parts (or of the brain), at least under one description. But a single action can be truly described in an indefinitely large number of ways. For example, if I lift a lever to open the floodgates, then my moving my arm is just my flooding the valley. I don't do two things, but one thing describable in two (and more) ways.

On the other hand, on the prolific theory, these really do count as two actions: my moving my arm and my flooding the valley, with a special relation between them. The relation is the relation of causal or non-causal generation: I do one by doing the other, where it is to be understood that the terms of this relation are non-identical particulars. On the prolific view, not all actions are movements of bodily parts, although those actions that are not are only actions in virtue of the agent moving his bodily parts and hence doing them by doing the latter.

An alternative contemporary theory of action, the agent causalist theory (ACT) rejects this naturalistic perspective. For the ACT too, an action is an event, but one caused by an agent (an agent is a person who acts, so 'agent' may be replaced by 'person'). The ACT rejects the idea that only events can be causes and effects. According to it, in bringing about a bodily movement (on purpose), it is the *whole* agent who is the cause, and not just some brain or bodily event or state that involves him. The ACT is not a naturalistic theory, because of its non-naturalistic theory of causation.

A third theory of action might refuse to make the identification of actions as events that the other two theories make, thereby rejecting the claim that an action is an event of any sort. Von Wright defended this view of action. After all, actions might be a distinctive ontological sort of entity, irreducible to any other. In a basic ontology of the world, actions may have to figure in addition to events, substances, and so on. Such a theory owes us an account of what the difference is between actions and events.

The metaphysical theories mentioned so far are about token actions, not about action-types. As far as I can see, they are not committed to any view about the reducibility of action concepts, or in particular to the reducibility of the concept of action to the concept of an event. For example, the CTA (or the ETA) might be true, even if the concept of an action was not the same concept as the concept of an event with such-and-such causal ancestry (or descent). To be clear about this, one would have to have a theory to hand about the identity conditions for concepts. The reducibility of action concepts seems at any rate like an implausibly strong doctrine, and one which it would be wise for any action theorist to avoid.

5. ACTION EXPLANATIONS

A third question, distinct from both the metaphysical and the conceptual question, is a question about action explanation: what kind of explanations are action explanations? The question is distinct, but has connections to the metaphysical question. To begin with, it is not clear that action explanations are causal explanations at all. If (as the joke goes) we want to know why the chicken crossed the road, we might be told: in order to get to the other side. This is a purposive or teleological explanation in terms of a goal, or plan, and it is not clear how goals or plans could be causes, since an agent may act for a goal or plan which he will realize only in the future, or may never even realize at all. A goal realized in the future, if it were to have causal powers, would have to have strange backward ones, if it were to have any, but a goal never brought about, and hence non-existent, could have no causal powers at all.

A standard move to show that these action explanations are causal is to replace the goal by the individual's desire for or beliefs about the goal, or his intention to realize the goal, as the explanans for the action. These mental states, unlike the goal, precede the action. Notice that one could adopt this causal theory of action explanation (CTAE), that an action is causally explained by the prior mental states that rationalize it, without accepting the metaphysical thesis that the action itself could be reduced to or identified with an event of a certain kind, namely one with those mental states as its causes. One might causally explain an irreducible action. That is, the CTAE does not imply the CTA.

Beliefs, desires, and intentions are not events, but states of a person, which endure for periods of time. They are not themselves changes of any sort. Actions, on the other hand, are changes. It seems wrong to think that a state could cause, and hence causally explain, the occurrence of an action. But such explanations, in terms of belief- and desire-states, while not themselves causal, might have whatever explanatory power they have just in so far as they set the parameters within which we can find the change that is the cause, if we wish.

For example, I might explain a car crash as due to the foggy weather. Foggy weather is a state, not an event or change, but mention of foggy weather circumscribes the range of possible causes, and we may be uninterested in finding out which particular cause within that range operated: perhaps it was the driver's not seeing the car ahead of him, or perhaps it was the driver not being seen by the car behind him. Similarly, belief- and desire-states might give the structure which delimits the range of possible causes: perhaps the cause was an increase in his desire from what it had been (the 'onslaught of a desire' as Davidson has it), or an alteration in one of his beliefs to the one he now holds, or perhaps the recognition for the first time on his part that this is what he did really want and believe all along. We may be uninterested in any of this finer tuning, and find the belief and desire explanation sufficient for our purposes, as the foggy weather explanation might be for someone wishing to learn a lesson about the conditions which make it inadvisable to undertake journeys by car. So action explanations in terms of beliefs and desires, or intentions, while not themselves causal explanations, may delimit or set the range of admissible causal explanations there are for the action.

The CTAE is an internalist view, in the sense that, if it were true, all action explanations would cite psychological states of the actor in order to explain his action. Some action explanations appear to cite only facts external to the agent. In the course of engaging in some skilled activity, like swimming across a pool, I engage in many subacts, like lifting my left arm from the water. If I have learned to swim simply by watching someone else, I may have formed no left-arm-involving beliefs. If asked why I lifted my left arm, my reply will be: because that is how one swims, or because doing that is necessary for swimming across the pool. True, this information must of course be hardwired into me, as a result of my watching, but that fact is not part of my explanation, but seems rather to be a presupposition of the explanation. The explanation itself uses what appears to be only 'external' facts about the activity of swimming.

A strong case can be made for an entirely different view of action explanation from the one advanced by the CTAE. On one version of what might be called a hermeneutic or interpretative view, what we do when we explain a person's action is to interpret what he does in a way that makes most sense of him. We narrate a story about him and what he does. We attribute those beliefs and desires, goals and intentions, to him that produce the best story. Explaining action is like reading a text and giving it a coherent interpretation.

Frequently, these theories place emphasis on the social context of action. In the social environment in which action takes place, there are rules or norms that govern the agent's behaviour in the circumstances. The action can only be understood in terms of the rules that make such action intelligible. For example, a person pours liquid from a glass onto the ground. Such an action might be unintelligible to anyone unfamiliar with the religious rules that define and bring into existence the practice of offering libations to the gods.

The CTAE and the hermeneutic or interpretative theory seem in truth to be answering different questions. The CTAE is answering the question: (*a*) *given* that the agent did a token act of type *A*, why did he perform that token act? The hermeneutic theory does not seem to attempt an answer to this question. The hermeneutic theory might be answering either of these two questions: (*b*) did the agent act, or was it only that his body moved? (*c*) assuming only that the agent acted, which action-type did he token?

The social-context variant of the hermeneutic theory of action explanation seems appropriate for (*c*), identifying *which* social action-type the agent tokened when he acted. We may need to refer to the norms or rules of the society in which the action takes place, in order to answer this question. It is only in a social context in which there are religious rules about libations that we can say that what the agent did was to offer a libation to the gods. It may have been clear to us that he acted, but unclear to us what he was doing, until we come to understand the social context as Roman and religious. Then we can see: what he did was to pour a libation.

What of (*b*)? (*b*) is not a question about action explanation at all. The CTAE has no answer to (*b*), since it makes no pretence of being able to specify the difference between action and non-action, but the CTA of course does. Perhaps here the hermeneutic theory competes with the CTA rather than with the CTAE. The former might hold that we decide whether a bodily movement is an action by seeing whether interpreting the movement as an action produces the most coherent story about him overall. A person is driving a car, and approaching a left turn. We see that his hand moves in a characteristic way: interpreting it as giving a signal produces a coherent story, since it fits into a larger story about what he is doing.

If the hermeneutic theory is taken as addressing (*b*), surely it must be wrong. It must be possible for the hand motion to be only the result of a bodily spasm, however much interpreting it as an intentional action better fits with what else he is doing. Surely this is possible: it would have made sense for him to signal a left turn at that moment, but at that moment a spasm occurred and his hand moved in just the way it would have moved, had he been signalling. On (*b*), the CTA is more plausible than the hermeneutic theory. The hand movement is not an action if its cause is a spasm rather than a rationalizing mental state, regardless of whether interpreting it as an action fits in with a coherent story.

A related question about action explanation concerns the role, if any, that generalizations or laws play in action explanation. This question was central at one time in the philosophy of history. A standard empiricist account of explanation, first espoused by J. S. Mill and later developed by Carl Hempel, construes full explanations of token actions or particular occurrences of any sort as (*inter alia*) either deductively valid or inductively strong arguments with at least one law or lawlike generalization as a premiss. This means that part of the full explanation of any action is a law that 'covers' the action (hence, the theory is often called 'the covering law theory of explanation').

Suppose one assumes that laws are strict, i.e. exceptionless. If it is a deterministic law that *F*s are *G*s, then every *F* without exception must be a *G*. If it is a stochastic or probabilistic law that $Pr(G, F) = p$, where $0 < p < 1$, then, for any finite sample *s*, it may well be that the proportion of *F*s in *s* which are *G*s may not be exactly *p*. However, as one examines *F*s indefinitely, the proportion which are found to be *G*s will tend to *p*, and in the limit, the proportion of *F*s which are *G*s will be exactly *p*.

If this is what a law is, laws that might cover actions are not easy to find. Some writers, including Churchland and Ayer, have argued that, with a little ingenuity, such laws can be discovered. Suppose the law of action is alleged to be this: whenever an agent desires goal G and believes that his doing *A* is the only (or best) way in which he can obtain G, and he wants G more than he wants anything else, and there are no undesirable consequences of his doing *A* known to him, then the agent does *A*.

Is such a generalization exceptionlessly true? One particular problem for the view that there are such empirical laws of action is the existence of weakness of the will. If an agent's will is weak, then he may fail to do what he has the most or best reason to do. So a weak-willed agent may falsify the alleged 'law', by not doing *A*, even when the conditions specified in the antecedent hold. If one simply adds the qualification, 'unless his will is weak', we seem to have the no-possible-falsification problem with a vengeance: 'in circumstances *c*, the agent will do *A*, unless his will is weak' seems no better than '. . . unless he doesn't'.

Weakness of the will is a form of irrationality, and adding a premiss that the agent is rational is in line with a suggestion made by Hempel himself, in his account of action explanation. This manoeuvre has difficulties of its own: it smacks of a kind of epistemic circularity. A specification of rationality must at least include taking necessary or best means to achieve one's end, and this must presuppose that a rational agent does not have a weak will. Since weakness of the will is a form of irrationality, we can only know whether the agent is in fact rational *after* he acts and thereby demonstrates that his will is not weak.

Others have argued that the only way in which to ensure exceptionlessness is to render the 'law' analytic or a priori. Ludwig von Mises thought that such generalizations as there were in economics were a priori truths about the nature of action. Still others have claimed that such 'laws' are merely normative claims about the nature of rationality, with prescriptive rather than descriptive force. There is a lot to be said for this view of the matter. Rationality does not describe how people act, but prescribes how they ought to or should act. Acting for what one considers to be the best seems itself to be a goal to which one might aspire. On this view, the 'laws' of social science have more in common with what Hobbes called 'counsels of prudence' than with the laws of natural science. They flesh out in concrete ways the ideal of rationality which empirical agents might seek to realize in their own lives.

One thing seems clearly true: if there are covering laws about actions which are to serve as premisses in an explanatory argument whose conclusion is that such an action has occurred, the vocabulary in which the action is described and the vocabulary of the law must be the same. Deductively valid arguments cannot switch terminology between their premisses and their conclusions. If the covering law is to figure as a major premiss in an explanatory argument and if the action to be explained in the conclusion is someone's *A*-ing, then the law must be about the conditions in which someone *A*s.

Donald Davidson has doubted that there are such laws about action. What will always be true, according to his view, is that there must be a law which 'covers' the action, but such a generalization will be expressible in the language of physics or neurophysiology (since token actions are physical items and hence can also be given descriptions in physical or neurophysiological terms), but not in the terminology of beliefs, desires, and actions. If this is right, it surely rules out the empiricist theory of action explanation with which we began. From only a major premiss that states a law of physics or neurophysiology (suppose, 'All *F*s are *G*') and a minor premiss about the agent's beliefs and desires (suppose, *o* is *P*), no conclusion about the occurrence of an action (suppose, *o* is *Q*) will follow.

One might try to save the empiricist theory of action explanation by supplementing the premiss set with the sort of relevant token identities that Davidson would in any case accept. For example, a further premiss might identify the action to be explained in the conclusion with an item of which the appropriate neurophysiological description mentioned in the law is true (perhaps, *o*'s being *Q* = *o*'s being G). Such a further premiss concerning token identity would bring together the two vocabularies, by linking the neurophysiological and the action descriptions of the token item in question. And similarly for the belief and the desire (perhaps, *o*'s being *P* = *o*'s being *F*). The resulting argument would certainly be valid.

This manoeuvre, however, is fatal to the empiricist theory of action explanation, since the argument now contains unnecessary premisses. The token identity premiss on its own (*o*'s being *Q* = *o*'s being G) trivially entails that the action occurs (*o* is G), which is what is to be explained. No laws would be required at all; from the fact that his acting is identical to his being in some neurophysiological state, it follows at once that that action of his has occurred.

As an alternative to there being laws about actions (*qua* actions), Davidson speaks of rough-and-ready generalizations, expressible in the terminology of action, belief, and desire, which, although not laws because full of ineliminable generous exceptions, escape clauses, and so on, can still serve as a kind of backing in ordinary action explanations. Everyone knows that recent converts to a faith tend to be more zealous than long-time adherents, and that might explain why Torquemada was so beastly to the remaining Spanish Jews, but no one would seriously regard that generalization as a law. How these generalizations, or what Scriven once called 'truisms', gain their explanatory force, and how one distinguishes between such generalizations which are in some sense true in spite of their having exceptions and those which are simply false, is unclear.

Are social scientists interested in explaining the occurrence of action-tokens, or in explaining action-types? What I mean by the latter is this: do they explain why generally tokens of a certain type occur? The answer is that they surely explain both. The historian seems especially concerned with tokens: Napoleon's invasion of Russia, Brutus' stabbing of Caesar, the conversion of Clovis. But economists too sometimes explain tokens: the Crash of 1929 and

Black Monday on the Stock Exchange. But certainly types figure prominently as well. The sociologist is not typically interested in any particular person's suicide, but suicides in a society generally. The economist might be interested in depressions generally, and try to construct a theory thereof, rather than limiting his attention to the Great Depression of the inter-war years.

6. SELF-REFUTING AND SELF-FULFILLING PREDICTIONS

Stock market analysts claim that the stock market will crash. Their predictions cause widespread panic, which leads to a crash. Their predictions have been self-fulfilling. The police announce that they have information that a large number of pickpockets will be operating on such-and-such a day. Their announcement causes the pickpockets to abandon their plans. The police announcement is self-refuting. Self-fulfilling and self-refuting predictions are common enough in the social world. Is this a feature that is special or unique to the social sciences? Does it demonstrate that the human will is free in some contracausal sense?

A subtler case concerns the predictions of pollsters. They predict that candidate McSwindle will win with 53 per cent of the vote. In this sort of example, there will be both a bandwagon and an underdog effect on the original prediction. Some voters, who would not have voted for McSwindle otherwise, will now wish to vote for him since he is the predicted winner. Others, who would have voted for McSwindle otherwise, will now wish to vote for his opponent, out of sympathy for the latter. Can the pollsters make a prediction which will, in advance, take account of these effects and hence be true? Some have argued that this is possible, and have offered a method for doing just this, but their arguments seem to assume that such pollsters do not further make public their strategy of taking the underdog and bandwagon effects into consideration in making their prediction. If they did make their strategy public, there is no reason to believe that their original calculations for the bandwagon and underdog effects would remain stable and unchanged.

Perhaps at least some individual cases of action are in principle unpredictable. How could it be predicted in advance that someone will first invent the corkscrew? If it could be predicted that he will, then would not the predictor have to invent the corkscrew himself, before it was first invented? That thought seems to involve an outright contradiction.

Suppose a predictor predicts what a person will do tomorrow, and the person comes to learn of this prediction. Since deciding what to do is making up one's mind what to do, the person could no longer decide what to do; he would merely know or believe that he will do such-and-such, without ever having decided. So if he does decide, then his deciding seems incompatible with his knowing before his decision what he will do. But if some predictor could predict what he will do, he could come to know this. So, if this argument is sound (but is it?), it seems to follow that prediction and decision-making are incompatible.

Finally, if the person could always learn what he is predicted to do in advance of his doing it, it would seem to be possible for him to alter what he will do, so as to confound the prediction. But then one might ask: could not the predictor take that reaction into account? If the person learns that the predictor has taken his reaction into account and now predicts that he will confound the first prediction, it would seem possible for the person to alter what he will do again, so as to confound the altered prediction. And apparently so on, *ad infinitum*. Such an argument seeks to show that, by the very nature of a prediction being something that must be made in advance of what is *pre*dicted, a person can always react to the prediction (if he learns of it) so that the predictor can never 'catch up' to that reaction in making his prediction.

Notice that this last conclusion is compatible with the idea of determinism: the person's reactions might be completely determined, even if unpredictable. Indeed, it would seem to be possible to build a machine which reacts to predictions in a deterministic way, so that the machine is programmed to confound any prediction made in advance and 'known' to it. If so, unpredictability may not be a phenomenon specific to the human sciences at all; various contrived and perhaps even naturally occurring systems not involving persons at all might display this sort of unpredictability. Nor, of course, does this last argument at least show anything about contracausal freedom of the human will. Suppose both that a person is contracausally free and rational. Many, perhaps most, of his actions would be utterly predictable. If I offer him, no strings attached and he believes that this is so, either £5 or £10, I can predict with total confidence that he will choose the latter. Unpredictability and contracausal freedom of the will seem to be two quite distinct and unrelated ideas.

7. NORMS, RULES, CONVENTIONS, TRADITION

Thus far, mention of norms, rules, and conventions has entered into the discussion only tangentially. This must be rectified, for the importance of these three things in understanding what a society is must be central. There is, in the literature, no generally accepted way of distinguishing between these items; some writers use 'norm' where others use 'rule'. Nor is it clear precisely wherein the difference lies between conventions and sanctionless norms. To some extent, my usage below regarding these matters will be arbitrary.

There are cases both of (*a*) social and (*b*) private (or individual) norms, rules, and conventions. A rule of etiquette is typically a social rule or norm, involving a multiplicity of persons; the rule that a particular person might have, to eat cheese only in the mornings, might be one that he alone has, and hence involve no other person.

Is there a conceptual priority of either case over the other? That is, could it be shown either (*c*) that public rules etc. are merely the sum of each person having the rule for himself, or alternatively (*d*) that individual rules are only possible once there are social rules, so that the former phenomenon is in some sense parasitic on the latter? Arguments have been advanced for both alternatives. In what follows, I will focus only on the social cases, and I will leave open the question of the nature of the relationship between the two cases.

Rules, even restricted to the social variety, are apparently quite diverse: there are rules of language, rules of inductive logic, mathematical rules, rules of a game, and moral and legal rules. There are also a large number of what we might naturally call 'social norms'; these set ways in which various things are to be done in a society. Norms, as I am using the term, include dress codes, standards of etiquette, and tasteful behaviour—ways of interacting with others that do not seem to impinge on the realm of morality at all.

Concerning moral or legal rules and norms, some prohibit or enjoin action of a certain kind, while others are permissive, defining the conditions in which certain action becomes possible (e.g. in order to make a valid will one needs the presence of at least two witnesses). A distinction is frequently drawn between regulative and constitutive rules. A regulative rule is one which regulates a pre-existing type of behaviour; for example, the rule prohibiting murder regulates an activity (murder) whose existence is logically independent of the rule. The rules of chess or the rules of property ownership are constitutive; they make possible activity, playing chess or owning property, which would not be possible apart from some set of rules which define what chess or property ownership is. Both regulative and constitutive rules can be either prohibitive (or obligating) or permissive.

The best work on social rules (and this can be applied to what I have called 'norms' as well) remains H. L. A. Hart's classic *The Concept of Law*. (Laws are a special and important subset of the set of rules of a society.) One way in which to construe Hart's long-standing debate with natural lawyers is over the truth-conditions for statements of the form 'Law *l* is a law of society *s*'. Natural lawyers insisted that, amongst the truth-conditions for statements such as this, there are at least some evaluative statements, and this Hart, following John Austin, the nineteenth-century English philosopher of law, vigorously denied.

What then is the difference between the existence of rules or norms (including laws) and the existence of (merely) regular behaviour in a society? It may be a piece of regular behaviour in certain societies to take baths on Saturday night, or to carry an umbrella when the sky is threatening, or to drink tea at four in the afternoon. But there are no rules or norms enjoining this behaviour. Hart claimed that one of the differences is this: in the case of rules, but not in the case of merely regular behaviour, actors take an 'internal' point of view. They, for example, criticize departures or breaches, or they might encourage compliance. They think of such behaviour normatively, as action that those in relevant circumstances *should* do. The distinction between viewing the behaviour from an internal or an external point of view is crucial, according to this line of thought, in seeing wherein lies the difference between rules and (mere) regular behaviour.

This account, of course, includes no evaluative statements in the truth-conditions for statements that a certain public rule exists in a certain social situation, since statements about what people believe that they and others should do or not do are not themselves evaluative in character. One consequence of this position, little remarked, is that if the truth-conditions for something's being a law or rule are entirely factual, as Hart and the legal positivists maintained, then the fact that something is a law or rule in *s* cannot, by itself, provide anyone with a justifying reason of any strength whatever to engage in the enjoined, or to desist from the prohibited, behaviour. If rules are thought to be essentially action-guiding, to supply justifying reasons for action, then this account does not show how that is possible. But perhaps this is right. Some social rules might be so dreadful, so horrific, that their mere existence provided no one with a justifying reason to do, or refrain from doing, anything. Social actors might believe that the rules do this, but the truth of the matter may be that they do not. And when social rules are action-guiding, as they typically are, it is in virtue of something other than just the fact that they are rules.

The idea of a rule or norm needs also to be distinguished from that of a recommended or suggested way of doing things. It is an awfully good idea to tie double knots in one's shoelaces, and it might be standard practice to do so. When others fail to do it, those who do might criticize those who fail to do so, for showing lack of good sense, and might encourage them to get into the habit of double-knotting their laces. They see the practice from an internal point of view, and believe that the practice is normative for those who care about not tripping when they walk.

But all this seems insufficient to permit talk of rules or norms. If there really were a rule or norm, Hart goes on to claim, there would have to be, at least for the most part, sanctions or punishments for breaches. 'Punishment' is perhaps too strong a word. We must distinguish two cases. Suppose a person has some reasons for doing something, $r_1, r_2, \ldots, r_n$. Now, I might additionally tell the person to do that very thing. In one case, I am reminding the person of the reasons, $r_1, r_2, \ldots, r_n$, that he already has for doing that thing. In the other case, by telling him, I am supplying him with an additional reason, r_{n+1}, for doing that thing. The two cases are quite distinct over the role they allot to the telling. In the former case, the telling is a reminding or suggesting; in the second case, the telling is a putting of additional pressure on him, and hence giving him an additional reason, a prudential reason, to do it.

So a person might rebuke another in one of two ways. In the first way, the rebuke reminds a person about the reasons they already have for doing or not doing something. In the second, the rebuke is meant itself to provide an additional reason for doing or not doing: another reason for doing or not doing is to avoid a subsequent rebuke, or some other form of displeasure on the part of the rebuker. When the rebuke takes the latter form, we can speak of a sanction, and in that case we can begin to speak of rules or norms. In some cases, like that of a law, the sanction is often formally defined, with a specified source for the sanction. In other cases the nature of the sanction is vaguer, with the source of the sanction diffuse and unspecified.

It may be hard to distinguish cases of there being rules or norms from cases of merely recommended behaviour, and there may be borderline cases, in which some people engage in criticism in one spirit and others in the other. But it seems to me that no account of rules or norms can be adequate which omits altogether the idea of a sanction, at least in this weak sense.

A particular situation that calls for the existence of binding norms is known as the prisoners' dilemma. In this situation, two guilty prisoners are interrogated; there is insufficient evidence to convict. They are unable to communicate with one another. Each can either confess or keep silent. If neither confesses, both will be convicted of some minor crime for which there is sufficient evidence, and will be sentenced to a year in prison. If both confess, each will be sentenced to five years in prison. If only one confesses and turns king's evidence, he will be set free and the other will be sentenced to ten years.

It is in each prisoner's rational self-interest to confess, regardless of what the other does. (Confessing dominates not confessing, for each prisoner.) Consider prisoner 1. If prisoner 2 confesses, then prisoner 1 is better off confessing, for he will then receive five years rather than ten. If prisoner 2 does not confess, then prisoner 1 is better off confessing, since he is better off being free than going to prison for a year. Prisoner 2 will reason in the same way. But by so doing, they will both be worse off, since they will both go to prison for five years. They both would have been better off by not confessing and only serving a year in prison. Pursuing rational self-interest is, paradoxically, not in their rational self-interest.

Of course, if the prisoners communicate, they might agree between themselves not to confess. But can they trust their agreement? A new prisoners' dilemma can be set up, with the choices of keeping or breaking the agreement. It would appear to be in the rational self-interest of both prisoners to defect and break the agreement.

Another, arguably related, case is that of free-loading in the case of public goods. Public goods include such things as parks or police protection, street lighting, and defence. My best option seems to be that everyone but me pay for these things. I shall derive the benefits if everyone pays, even when I do not pay, so I have no incentive to pay. But if we both reason in this way and evade payment, there will be no police or public parks, and we shall both be worse off without these things than we would have been had we both paid.

One way, but only one way, out of these dilemmas of rational choice is the introduction of norms. Clearly, norms with sanctions alter the situation, by changing the structure of rewards for each option. If there are laws against tax evasion, draft-dodging, or whatever, backed by stiff penalties, then there is a way out for those who desire the fruits of cooperation and public goods. If our poor prisoners agree in advance to penalize confessing sufficiently, and set up a third party who will exact the penalty, regardless of their own further wishes, neither will confess, since confessing will no longer dominate not confessing. Norms help us, by preventing us from suffering the disabilities of pursuing our unpenalized rational self-interest.

Conventions grow up as rational responses on the part of a large number of people to situations in which there is need to coordinate behaviour, where it does not much matter what is done provided that it fits with what others are doing. These are sometimes called 'coordination problems'. For example, when two people are on the telephone and get cut off, it is undesirable that both try to redial the other, since both would then get a busy signal. If there is a convention, say that the one who first dialled lets the other person redial, they will have found a way to coordinate their behaviour to get the result, the reconnection, they require.

Many social situations take this general form, requiring a convention as the solution to a coordination problem. Coordination does not always demand uniformity; indeed, in the case of the telephone disconnection, coordination provides a way in which two people come to act in a dissimilar way. But many interesting social situations do require uniform behaviour on the part of the social participants: regulation of traffic, etiquette, and the use of a particular legal tender. It does not essentially matter to agents whether they drive on the left or the right, dress with suits or more informally on a certain kind of occasion, use silver or gold as coin. What matters in these cases is simply that they all settle on the same choice, and conventions ensure that this uniform outcome comes about.

The idea of tradition raises different issues from those above. Some societies, or ways of life, are labelled 'traditional' and others 'modern' (or, sometimes, 'liberal'). There are also said to be traditional ways of doing things. Is some activity or way of doing something traditional in virtue of its content, i.e. what is actually done (like arts and crafts rather than assembly-line production), or is a person traditional in virtue of his attitude to what he is doing, whatever that may be? It does not seem to be enough, in order to be traditional, simply to carry on doing things as they have been done, since that is the way most persons act in all societies or in all activities, conforming to a kind of social inertia. Perhaps the traditional attitude is manifested only in a person's reaction to change or criticism.

What is a tradition? Another strand in the idea of tradition is the idea of a continuous tradition over time, like that of a single school of philosophy or some religious way of life. Often, different groups within later generations argue over which, if any, of them is the true descendant of the former generation. Are Popper and Quine part of the positivist tradition? What makes the later Stoics part of the same philosophical tradition as the early Stoics, since the two groups did not hold identical beliefs? Which contemporary Church is the true Church, in line with the authentic traditions set by Jesus and his disciples? Which form of Islam in the modern world constitutes the true faith?

These questions can only be settled by agreeing some identity conditions for traditions. But that may sound easier than it is. The question what constitutes a single line of intellectual, moral, or religious development may be, in W. B. Gallie's memorable turn of phrase, an 'essentially contested' question, unavailable in principle for definitive resolution.

8. RATIONALITY: INDIVIDUAL AND SOCIAL

In Section 4, we spoke about beliefs and desires rationalizing an action, making it the rational thing to do in the circumstances. But what is rationality for the individual? There are at least two modern philosophical traditions about individual rationality, harking back to the Utilitarians and to Kant. The utilitarian idea identifies rationality as maximizing personal utility, or as acting in a personally 'optimific' way. The rational person is the one who attempts to get what he most wants overall and all things considered. He considers his desires and takes that line of action which will yield for him the greatest amount of desire satisfaction.

Many refinements are required to make this idea plausible; for example, since we do not live with any certain knowledge of what will be the consequences of what we do, the idea of probable outcomes must be introduced into any such formulation: the rational person maximizes his expected utility, where his expected utility is itself based on those beliefs about the future that are reasonable for him to hold, in the light of his evidence. We also need to swallow the idea that we can quantify desire satisfaction in some way or other. The classical Utilitarians seemed to think of utility as a definite quantity of something, and therefore treated it cardinally. Four units of desire satisfaction and three units (the units were sometimes called 'utiles') summed to be exactly seven utiles. More modern versions tend to consider utility as an ordinal idea (indeed, they do not often use the word 'utility' at all); there is such a thing as more or less desire satisfaction, but although we can say that eight units of utility is more than four units of utility, it is not plausible to say that it is exactly twice as much.

The Kantian idea considers rationality as a sort of consistency. It is rational to treat relevantly similar cases alike. Kant's insight is deep. There is something irrational about having as a rule that one ought to do *A* to *all Fs* without exception, and then not to do *A* to some particular *F* that one comes across. It is irrational to treat differently two otherwise similar cases or examples. Despite Kant's hope, his idea of rationality, while introducing a necessary element into the idea of rationality, is merely formal, and cannot on its own be what rationality is. What Kant provides for us is an account of rational action, *relative to* some rule or law that one has adopted or that has binding force. But there can be irrational laws or rules, and we often criticize rules or laws precisely on these grounds. Kant does not provide any genuine account of the difference between rational and irrational laws or rules.

But does the utilitarian idea about what rationality is fare any better? The idea of consistency of desires was in fact a part of the utilitarian conception of rationality from the beginning. If a person retains inconsistent wants of similar urgency and acts to realize them, his action plan will be inconsistent too, likely to lead to his getting nothing at all of what he wants. In more modern treatments, the consistency of desires or preferences is specified in terms of the axiom of the transitivity of preferences: if x is preferred to y, and y is preferred to z, then x is preferred to z. Any preference ordering that failed to display transitivity would be inconsistent.

There are reasons to think that, even as so understood, the utilitarian idea of rationality is insufficient. Whereas the Kantian account took laws or rules as fixed or given, the Utilitarians take (any consistent set of) desires or wants as fixed or given, and find rationality in their satisfaction. But just as there can be irrational rules, so too there can be irrational (but consistent sets of) desires or preferences. The desire to wash one's hands repeatedly during the day, whether or not they are dirty, is an example, even if such an odd desire is not actually inconsistent with anything else one desires. Psychotherapists and psychiatrists earn much of their livelihood trying to cure some of us of our less-than-wholly-rational desires.

Many writers have questioned whether this utilitarian idea has room in it for the qualitative evaluation of desires. J. S. Mill tried, unsuccessfully, to introduce a qualitative as well as a quantitative aspect into utilitarian desire evaluation, with his talk of so-called 'higher' and 'lower' pleasures. He thought that all or most who had experienced the pleasures of poetry and pushpin would prefer to obtain pleasure deriving from reading more poetry, however small the amount, rather than pleasure deriving from playing more pushpin, however great the amount, and it was on this basis that the pleasure poetry provided could be designated as higher and that provided by pushpin designated as lower. The theory's mistake is to abstract such questions about pleasure preferences from any context. Imagine a person deprived of pushpin for years, but who has had a surfeit of poetry so that he is mightily sick of the stuff. It is not at all clear that his preferences would be for the pleasure of yet more poetry over that of a decent game of pushpin.

How would the utilitarian account of rationality handle the following sorts of question? What of desires that are base, ignoble, or demeaning? Is there room in such an ideal of rationality for moral commitment or obligation? Can moral commitment or obligation also be understood as just another set of preferences? How shall we account for second-order desires or preferences? I may decide that my preferences are all wrong, and prefer to alter them: I may prefer to smoke rather than not smoke, but I may also, at the same time, prefer to prefer not to smoke rather than to prefer to smoke. As the utilitarian ideal tries to accommodate these criticisms (it always seems ready to do so), it itself changes, and we begin finding that we have a theory vastly different from and much richer than the one with which we started. Nor is it at all clear whether all such criticisms can be absorbed by the theory. How would it accommodate the idea of qualitative evaluation of desire as base, ignoble, or demeaning?

Let's pretend that we understand individual rationality. Further problems about rationality arise for the philosopher of social science in at least two ways: first, there are problems about the rational preferences of an individual when he has to take into account the preferences of another individual: secondly, there are problems about coming to a socially rational decision, given the rational preferences of a number of individuals.

(*a*) Recall the dilemma of our two prisoners, or the free-loaders, described above. What their situation showed us was that two persons may each be deprived of the best outcome for himself by each trying to obtain it. One way out of their situation is the introduction of norms with sanctions: contracts, laws, or whatever. In Ferdinand Tönnies' terminology, their association is a *Gesellschaft*.

But a simpler way out is this: that the two prisoners trust one another. Tönnies contrasts *Gesellschaft* with *Gemeinschaft*. The latter is an association based on relationships which are natural, spontaneous, and affective. Mutual trust is a hallmark of a *Gemeinschaft*. Trust does not alter the structure of payoffs in the way in which the introduction of norms with sanctions did. And it seems patently true that society does not, perhaps cannot, function by curing every prisoners' dilemma with ever more rules or norms with sanctions. A society that attempted this would be a 'Hobbesian' society. It is not at all clear that people could psychologically survive a Hobbesian society, but even if they could survive it, it is neither desirable to be in such a society, nor is it the society we are in.

At some point, people have to trust one another. Empirical evidence suggests that initial trust in a prisoners' dilemma-style situation is quickly reinforced and becomes established if there is no defection; trust breeds trust, as it were, and sooner rather than later. It is fundamental to a society that is in working order that there be a background of trust that binds many or most of its citizenry together much or most of the time, and underpins their collective life. Even disputes and disagreements can become a real possibility only against the background of deeper social agreement. The thought is that the members of a society are engaged, at least some of the time, in some sort of joint or collective enterprise; they are not continually engaging in a war of all against all, mitigated only by a sovereign who can impose a big enough sanction to make it worth each individual's while to behave himself.

It is, of course, perfectly rational, in many situations, for people to trust one another, rational because everyone comes out better in a prisoners' dilemma situation if they do have this trust. But it is hard to see how the utilitarian theory of rationality can accommodate this, for trust is not consistent with the idea of each individual consistently trying to maximize his own pay-offs. That is, indeed, why the situation is referred to as a dilemma: everyone is better off by not trying to make himself best off on each occasion.

(*b*) Suppose one knows the individual preferences of a number of individuals, and a social decision must be taken on this basis. How does one put together individual decisions, in order to arrive at a social decision? If there is anything we know about rational preferences, it is that they are transitive, as I specified above. Some irrational person might prefer *z* over *x*, but his irrationality is evidenced by his lack of a consistent plan of action. He simply cannot act in such a way both to get *x* over *y* and *y* over *z* and also to get *z* over *x*; he will be stymied.

The simple idea of majority rule has long been known to be faulty as a method of amalgamating individual preferences to obtain a social decision, since it breaks this condition of rationality at the social level. Condorcet's voting paradox is a good example. Imagine a society with three people: 1, 2, and 3. Each has to rank ordinally three alternatives: *a*, *b*, and *c*. Person 1 ranks them thus, in descending order of preference: *a*, *b*, *c*. Person 2: *b*, *c*, *a*. Person 3: *c*, *a*, *b*. Two out of three prefer *a* over *b* (persons 1 and 3). Two out of three prefer *b* over *c* (persons 1 and 2). But lo and behold, two out of three prefer *c* over *a* (persons 2 and 3). There is no coherent rational social decision regarding the choice of *c* over *a*, since by transitivity the majority prefer *a* over *c*, and yet also prefer *c* over *a*.

Kenneth Arrow is well known for a result called 'Arrow's impossibility theorem'. It is a generalization on, and refinement of, Condorcet's voting paradox. The theorem states:

> There can be no constitution simultaneously satisfying the conditions of collective rationality, the Pareto principle, the independence of irrelevant alternatives, and non-dictatorship.

Arrow assumes firstly that the social preference is derivable from the individuals' preferences, which includes the idea that both the social and the individuals' preferences must be transitive. Secondly, Arrow imposes a very weak condition on the social preference, which he calls the 'Pareto principle': if there are some alternatives, *x* and *y*, such that every individual prefers *x* to *y*, then the social preference must be for *x* rather than *y*. Thirdly, there is a non-dictatorship condition: there is no individual whose preferences are automatically the social preference, regardless of the preferences of everyone else. Finally, there is a requirement called 'the independence of irrelevant alternatives': the social preference in any situation depends only on the orderings of individuals with respect to the alternatives available in that situation. For example, in voting, the individuals consider only available candidates, and not candidates not available but who might have been available had they put themselves forward. The social preference can depend only on the individuals' preferences so circumscribed to the available alternatives.

Arrow's proof shows that these four assumptions jointly entail a contradiction. For our purposes, what Arrow's proof does is to question the idea of rationality at the social level. One might have thought that there was a simple and straightforward way in which to amalgamate individual rational preferences, in order to produce the rational preference for a society. One might have thought that the social choice function took individual preferences as inputs and could yield an uncontroversially rational social choice as an output. If Arrow's (and Condorcet's) proof is compelling, none of this is so. We do not have a good grasp of what it is for some choice or preference to be rational for a society.

The independence of irrelevant alternatives seems to be the only assumption in Arrow's proof that might be open to dispute. There is a literature on this, to which the reader is directed in the Bibliography.

9. SOCIAL RELATIVISM

Relativism has had some sort of appeal, ever since observers first noticed the facts of various sorts of diversity across people, societies, times, and places. Relativism comes in many different varieties, and they might not stand or fall together as far as their truth is concerned. Forms of relativism are distinguished by their subject-matter. For example, there is conceptual relativism, ethical relativism, linguistic relativism, logical relativism, epistemic relativism, relativism about rationality, and scientific relativism.

Conceptual relativism provides a challenge to our ability to understand 'alien' cultures or societies. It is a fact that anthropologists believe that they can understand the cultures they study. They translate what the natives say, or anyway the anthropologists think that they do so, into their home language. But the sceptical thought suggests itself: perhaps they are merely subjects of a grand, comprehensive illusion. The natives have their own conceptual scheme, somehow incomprehensible to us, and what the anthropologists have done is to foist upon the natives the anthropologists' own conceptual scheme, through the mechanism of that so-called translation. Many who have taken this sort of view have used, or thought that they were using, Quine's work on the indeterminacy of translation.

It may be that nothing can finally dispel this sceptical worry. But short of being able to answer full-blown scepticism, one can cite certain methodological principles and constraints that in fact help to secure accurate and reliable translation for the anthropologist. First, there is what is sometimes called the principle of charity. This methodological principle comes in several versions, one of which is this: translate the natives' speech in such a way as to maximize the number of true things that they say (or, maximize agreement between them and us about what is true). Suppose two different translation manuals of the natives' language are offered us, on the first of which most of what they say comes out as true, on the second of which most of what they say comes out as false. The principle of charity enjoins us to selcct the first manual. (Is there any reason we can give for accepting this principle?)

Another point of non-relative contact seems to be logic. The thought that their, or anyone else's, logic might be radically different from our own soon lapses into incoherence. Suppose they reject 'our' law of non-contradiction. But if that is so, then from their point of view, they might both reject it and not reject it. What on earth could that mean? Similar absurdities can be generated by assuming rules of inference radically different from ours. All translation presupposes the basics of negation, non-contradiction, and simple inference. Armed with the principle of charity and the universality of logic, we should be able to get right the meaning of what the natives say, and hence to understand the conceptual scheme they use, in at least simple and empirically observable situations. As it is sometimes put, we will have constructed for ourselves a 'bridgehead' from which to move to a fuller understanding of their culture.

I listed several different forms of relativism other than conceptual relativism in the opening paragraph of this section. Here are three more examples: ethical relativism is the view that some type of action could be both right when performed by one person and wrong when performed by some other person, there being no relevant differences between the two performances. Scientific relativism is the view that some scientific theory could be warranted for one scientist, but unwarranted for another, when both had precisely the same available evidence for the theory. Relativism about reasons is the view that a reason for doing something could be a good reason if held by one person, but not if held by another, even though their relevant circumstances were otherwise similar. I have, thus far, spoken of relativism about warrantability, reasonableness, and rightness.

Frequently, relativist positions speak of relative truth, i.e. something being true for one person or group but false for another. (There is another sense of relative truth, i.e. limited truth, but this is a different idea and is not open to the same objections.) This formulation seems a non-starter. What is the 'thing' that can be true for one person but false for another? Sentences can *trivially* differ as to their truth-value, if they are ambiguous and can bear two or more different meanings ('Grass is good to smoke' is Newton-Smith's example, whose argument I am borrowing). So using sentences as the 'thing' whose truth can vary will not produce any interesting relativist doctrine. Perhaps the 'thing' whose truth-value can vary is a proposition rather than a sentence. But that cannot be right, for propositions are individuated by their truth-conditions, so there cannot be a single proposition which is both true and false. So there seems to be *nothing* which can be true and false that will provide an interesting thesis in the way relativism is supposed to be.

A better expression of relativism, similarly motivated, would be to dispense with truth altogether, and speak rather of relative warrantability (or assertability), correctness, rightness, and so on. Truth is ineliminably objective; if relativism in any relevant formulation is right, then truth had better be eliminated in favour of something else, like warrantability.

Relativism makes criticism difficult across ethical systems, systems of logic, belief systems, and scientific theories. On some relativist views, this is a welcome consequence of the doctrine. To judge the beliefs, norms, or whatever, of one person, time, or place in terms of the beliefs, norms, or whatever of another seems wrong; each has to be both understood, and judged, only in its own terms. (Many have noticed that there appears to be a strong, non-relative moral message implicit in the preceding sentence.) There is nothing to be said, so the view goes, for imposing alien criteria which are inappropriate. Now, one might swallow this no-valid-criticism consequence to a certain extent. But to what extent? I shall return to this question at the end of this section.

There must be a distinction between ultimate and derived differences, and I tried to incorporate this distinction in my initial formulation of the various forms of relativism. For example, there might be a single norm, enjoining care of the young and the elderly. Different physical or other circumstances might mean that different people, in different times or places, have different ways of fulfilling their obligations under that norm. So some derived way of treating an elderly person might be right for one person, wrong for another. Or, different bodies of evidence warrant different conclusions. The evidence available to one scientist might confer on him epistemic warrant to take that scientific theory as true, but another scientist, at a later time with a different body of evidence, might not be similarly warranted. Or, a person might have a good reason to do something, but, in altered circumstances, it may no longer count as a good reason. Thus, in all these cases, local or derived differences mask deeper similarities: sameness of basic ethical norm, or sameness of criteria for epistemic warrant, or sameness of fundamental reasons for action.

So any interesting form of relativism must be about ultimate differences. It would say that there are or might be ultimate differences such that a theory is warranted for one scientist but not for another, or that an action is right when performed by one person but wrong when performed by another, or that some system of logic might be correct in one time or place but not in another, there being no further *relevant* differences between those times and places, persons, or scientists, etc. that could account for the variable warrant, correctness, rightness, rationality, or whatever. That is, the variability in correctness, warrant, rationality, or rightness would have to be brute, with no further account or explanation available that would show that the variability was only the result of an underlying invariability plus relevant factually different circumstances or conditions. Another way to put the relativist position is this: there may be differences in rightness, or correctness, or reasonableness, or warrantability, such that the *only* explanation for those differences is that they apply to the situations of two different persons, scientists, places, or times. The two formulations of relativism are equivalent, if one assumes that the simple difference of two people, two places, two times, two scientists, etc. *by themselves* do not count as relevant differences.

It is not easy to find any *actual* differences in norms, beliefs, theories, reasons, or whatever that are genuinely ultimate rather than derived, in the way in which the position so formulated requires. Much of the anthropological evidence sometimes adduced for this purpose can be dismissed in the light of this distinction. Of course different societies or people act or think or reason differently, but there are (almost?) always underlying explanations for this, which render the differences local and derived rather than ultimate.

Perhaps the relativist thesis is best put not as one about actuality but rather as one about possibility. It would simply assert, regardless of what the empirical evidence showed, that it was a logical possibility that there be these ultimate differences. Expressed in this modality, some forms of relativism might well be true. Consider, for example, Nelson Goodman's famous new riddle of induction. It can be taken as showing that it is logically possible that there be a group of persons for whom 'grue' and 'bleen' are projectible predicates, because entrenched in their discourse. Or consider the possibility of someone who reasons using counter-induction rather than induction (for however long his short life lasts). If one thinks of these examples as committed to ultimate relativism about inductive logic, as only a logical, rather than an empirical, possibility, the doctrine is not without plausibility.

So far, I have not mentioned 'social relativism'. Social relativism is not a form of relativism as distinguished by subject matter, in the way in which relativism about ethics, language, reason, or science are. Social relativism is a view about that *on which* the correctness, rightness, warrantability (or projectibility) is relative. So far, I have merely spoken of different persons, places, or times. What social relativism asserts is that what these ultimate differences depend on is society: that what is right, correct, projectible, reasonable, or whatever ultimately depends on the *society* in which the action, belief, or whatever is placed.

There is both an unclarity and instability in this view. The unclarity centres around the idea of a society. Every society like Britain is made up of a host of overlapping social groups, individuated by religious or cultural beliefs (the Jews, the Hindus), by national differences (the Welsh, the Scots, the English), by class differences, by occupational differences (the goldsmiths, the insurance brokers, the estate agents), regional cultures (Yorkshire, Devon, Cornwall, Tyneside), even with regard to questions of criminality. How finely are we meant to discriminate societies, for the purposes of relativism?

This unclarity leads to the question of instability. Why make correctness etc. relative to societies under any understanding of that latter term? Between any two persons, there will be apparent differences. Why can there not be ultimate differences in correctness etc. between two persons, just in virtue of their twoness, and in spite of there being no relevant differences between them? Such a move yields not social relativism but individual relativism. What is correct, right, reasonable, etc. for a person ultimately depends on just who he is, and thus something else might be ultimately correct, right, reasonable, etc. for another person, just in virtue of his being a different person.

Nor is there any compelling reason to stop with persons. Why not temporal parts of persons? Why can't some type of action be right for me-at-time-*t* but wrong for me-at-time-*t**, with there being no further difference between the action-tokens at t and *t** save the difference in the temporal parts of me that do them? This thought leads to the absurd position of subindividual relativism, absurd because it makes it impossible for me even to criticize something I did earlier or to evaluate what I should do later. Even if we could swallow the idea that there is no legitimate cross-social or cross-individual criticism, surely it is asking too much to accept that there is no legitimate cross-temporal-person-part criticism. I could never learn lessons from my own past, nor rationally plan my own future.

10. METHODOLOGY: PARADIGMS AND RESEARCH PROGRAMMES

The work of Popper, Lakatos, and Kuhn on scientific methodology has had a strong impact within the social sciences. I will offer a simplified version of the discussion in which they participated, in a rationally reconstructed version. My purpose is not to summarize their thoughts accurately, but to show how the discussion made an impact on the thinking of social scientists. For a fuller account, the reader is directed to A. F. Chalmers's *What is this Thing Called Science*?

Given that we have a body of empirical evidence, what is the theory that that body of evidence justifies us in holding? Suppose that there are two competing theories. Which is the one we ought to prefer? The positivists had an answer. A body of evidence confirms or verifies to a certain degree a theory, and the theory we ought to adopt is the one that is best confirmed or verified by that evidence. On this view, the relationship between evidence and theory is a non-deductive relationship. The idea of confirmation or verification presupposes that inductive inference can be justified. Karl Popper thought that this could not be done. Induction was an unjustifiable practice. Work in confirmation theory seemed to throw up riddles and paradoxes (the ravens paradox, Goodman's new riddle of induction), and hence cast additional doubt on the idea of confirmation itself.

Popper is well known for his proposal for the replacement of the ideas of verifiability and confirmation by that of falsifiability. He claimed that, in one fell swoop, falsifiability dispensed with any reliance on induction, and required only the apparatus of deductive logic. Scientific theories deductively entail predictions. If the predictions do not come out true, then, by simple *modus tollens*, the theory has been falsified. Theories should be put to the test, and the theory which we should accept is the one that has not, at least as yet, been falsified. Any theory which could not be falsified, as a matter of principle, was not science, whatever else it might be.

Popper's proposal had consequences for the social sciences. Popper intended that the criterion of falsifiability would show that Freudian theory and Marxism lacked the credentials of proper science. They seemed to be impaled on the horns of a dilemma. If they were falsifiable, then they have actually been falsified. If they were not falsifiable, then whatever they were, they were not science.

It is true that neither Marxism nor Freudian theory have been notably successful with their predictions. The proletarian revolution failed to materialize in the West; many of Freud's diagnoses did not lead to the improvement, let alone recovery, of the patient. One could always think up yet another manoeuvre for 'protecting' the theory from the apparent falsification. The theory can always be amended in hindsight, to accommodate the apparent falsification. The revolution had not happened in the West because of the super-exploitation of the working classes of the Third World and the appropriation of those surpluses into the metropolitan countries. Or, the diagnosis did not lead to improvement because of the interference of another psychological mechanism by the patient. But these manoeuvres rendered the theories effectively unfalsifiable, since every attempted refutation could be answered from within the theory. So, either falsifiable but falsified, or unfalsifiable so not science.

Popper's criterion of scientificity was not convincing. The work of Duhem, and later Quine, which emphasized the holism of theories and beliefs, showed what was wrong with Popper's simplistic proposal. In order to derive a prediction from a theory, one needs many auxiliary assumptions, about the instruments one is using, about the context in which the occurrence takes place, and so on. Further, statements of initial conditions will be required. No theory by itself entails a prediction. But then if the prediction is false, there is a choice of premisses to hold responsible, whether to say that the theory has been falsified, or to hold that one or more of the auxiliary assumptions is false, or that some of the initial conditions did not after all obtain. One could always exonerate the theory and pin the blame on an auxiliary. Sometimes this will be a perfectly reasonable thing to do. How should one distinguish those cases in which doing so is justified and those in which it is merely an *ad hoc* manoeuvre, used to support a theory that should be discarded?

Lakatos offered an answer. He thought holistically, not of theories but of entire research programmes which might embrace a succession of theories. Lakatos introduced a diachronic element into the debate, since research programmes are by definition extended in time. He tried to distinguish cases in which alterations to a theory are progressive and when they are degenerate, by distinguishing cases in which alterations add and when they fail to add new predictive powers to the theory under discussion (other than the prediction of the anomaly itself). It is true that a research programme can always be altered to accommodate some occurrence, but could the alteration lead to the programme's ability to predict a novel occurrence, at least sometimes?

Lakatos identified the hard core of a research programme, which should be protected against purported falsifications. As long as the research programme remained progressive, it was reasonable to protect the hard core. Lakatos's own view was that Freudian theory and Marxism had ceased to be progressive. They no longer led to the discovery of new phenomena. Since degenerate, they were no longer worthy of protection.

Many 'orthodox' economists seized upon the work of either Popper or

Lakatos. They took one or both of these philosophers to have vindicated economics as a science. There seemed little correlation between the intellectual content of the ideas of Popper and Lakatos on the one hand, and their use by social scientists to justify their disciplines as scientific on the other. It is hard to see any real difference between Marxist and orthodox economics, in terms of the novel predictive power of the two theories. Indeed, it is not easy to discern how either Popper's or Lakatos's ideas could be used to justify the scientific aspirations of any social science, in view of the continuing dismal failure of any social science to predict anything whatever.

Popper and Lakatos were both committed to the view that there is some normative criterion of scientificity or progressiveness or whatever, independent of any theory and hence able to be used to judge the credentials of any theory. Kuhn, in at least some passages, called that view into question. At any time in the history of science, some theory will dominate. It will provide a paradigm within which normal scientific research will be conducted. In the course of that normal scientific activity, various results which provide anomalies for the theory will surface. Such anomalous results will accumulate.

At what point will it be rational, in view of these anomalies with which the theory cannot successfully cope, to abandon the paradigm for another? When does the succession of anomalous results place the theory into intellectual crisis? Of course, there must be some other alternative available. The impact of Kuhn's argument was to call into question the idea that there was some criterion which could show when it was rational to abandon the theory. As a matter of fact, a point is reached when scientists just do, in the face of the anomalies, abandon the theory. A *Gestalt* switch is said to occur. The younger scientists begin seeing the world through the eyes of a new paradigm; older scientists may be stuck and unable to make the switch. This is all a matter of sociological fact rather than rational scientific methodology.

This abandonment of the emphasis on prediction as a key to scientific status should be welcome to the social scientist, in the light of his predictive failures. So far, so good, for the social scientist. However, Kuhn's position has been used to justify a kind of relativism, since it denies any cross-theoretical standards or norms of scientific methodology. It has sometimes been taken to justify a 'what-we-have-got-is-what-we-have-got' attitude. But social scientists do not, I think, believe this. They think that their theories are *better* than their rivals' theories, or that later theories do really *improve* on earlier ones, and it would not be easy to see what could be made of these normative claims, given what appear to be the implications of the Kuhnian 'sociological' account of scientific methodology. What seems to be needed for social science, indeed for science generally, are normative principles of scientific rationality that do not entirely rely on the predictive power of the theories being judged or, if they do, do so in a still more sophisticated way than Lakatos proposed.

11. VALUES IN SOCIAL SCIENCE

A standard topic in the philosophy of the social sciences is the place of values in social science. I confess to finding it a trifle hard sometimes to see just what is at issue here.

To begin with, many of these discussions spend time arguing for or dispensing with certain well-recognized positions-of-straw. Parts of Max Weber's discussion are like this. For example, every science must select some aspect of reality to focus on for its investigations, rather than others. That choice, unless it is simply non-rational, must be made for some reason, and that reason is likely to be that that aspect of reality is important, interesting, has consequences for human welfare, or some such. This all seems trivially true. If this were what was meant by saying that all social science embodies values, the view would be so anodyne as to be of no interest. It would, also, point to no difference between social science and any other area of human investigation like the natural sciences.

Another way that the issue of values in social science has been construed is of more interest. It has often been pointed out that evidence always underdetermines theory choice; for any finite body of evidence, there are always an infinitely large number of theories, however absurd otherwise, that are logically consistent with that evidence. In order to select one theory from that infinitely large number as *the* theory best supported by the evidence, other considerations must be adduced: simplicity, elegance, consistency with other theories. Sometimes these considerations are lumped together as those that confer a 'prior probability' on the theory.

Some have seen a discrepancy here between the natural and the social sciences. In the natural sciences, one might reasonably hold that these prior-probability-making considerations can do their job; that they do select a single theory from all of those logically consistent with the empirical evidence. But in the social sciences, it might be thought, they do not accomplish this. Both orthodox and Marxist economics are (or can be made) consistent with the data, but neither is eliminated by considerations of simplicity, elegance, and so forth. So, ultimately, the argument continues, values play a role in this way: our choice of social theory, after both evidence and prior-probability considerations have been taken into account, is determined by our value commitments in politics, or whatever.

Although interesting, this view makes a number of quite controversial assumptions: (*a*) that we have some theory-independent way in which to spell out these prior-probability-making considerations; (*b*) that these considerations do solve the underdetermination (of theory by evidence) problem for the natural sciences; (*c*) that they do not solve that problem for the social sciences. I have doubts about all three assumptions. Many discussions seek to show that what counts as simplicity etc. is itself relative to the theory at hand. Perhaps more to the point, I can see no reason for thinking that such considerations work differentially. Why should they be able to take up the underdetermination slack in one case but not another? Barring some account of why there should be that difference between the natural and social sciences, the more plausible view would be that they were equally good or bad at solving the underdetermination problem.

Perhaps the standard way to get at the problem of values in social science is via the distinction between factual and evaluative (or normative) statements. It is sometimes alleged that social science contains, in some ineliminible way, evaluative statements as part of the corpus of the science itself. That is, it is not a question of the choice of which factual matters to investigate, nor a question of the choice of theory to explain the facts. Both of those positions, as far as they go, could leave the content of the science itself entirely factual. The more standard view disputes just that; it says that the social sciences themselves contain evaluations (i.e. evaluative statements). Those economists who upheld the idea of 'positive economics' were contesting just that. They believed that they could produce a scientific theory of economics whose theoretical and observational claims were, all of them, entirely factual, containing no normative statements or claims whatever.

In order to pose the question of the value freedom of social science in this way, there needs to be at least a working distinction between two sets of statements: evaluative statements and factual statements (even if the conclusion of the discussion is to be that there is, after all, no logical distinction here at all). It is not at all clear that this condition can be met. One thought is this. It might be that some statements, for example 'This act was just', is evaluative in virtue of its semantic content. But, for the vast majority of the statements which might find a place in social science and which might be suspected of being evaluative, it is not at all clear that their evaluative status, if they are evaluative, derives from semantic content. Rather, it may derive from how they are used, which depends on pragmatic and contextual considerations. For example, 'He is a Jew' might be evaluative if used evaluatively, in a specific context. For statements such as these, one cannot divide statements into two sets, the factual and the evaluative. Rather, any statement, however paradigmatically factual, might acquire an evaluative use on some specific occasion, or in a certain context.

Let's suppose, contrary to the suggestion above, that statements can be divided into two classes after all, the factual and the evaluative. The value freedom of social science thesis (VFSS thesis) could then be put like this: all the statements that comprise social science are factual, and from these statements as premisses, no evaluative conclusions logically follow. This thesis follows the

Humean dictum that insists that 'ought' statements cannot be derived from 'is' statements. It is not disputed that there might be deep psychological connections between the factual and the evaluative: every sane and non-pathological person might take a certain evaluative position regarding some matter described in detail by a social science (for example, the condition of the working class as described by Engels in early nineteenth-century Britain). The VFSS thesis is only committed to there being no logical connection between the factual claims and the evaluations; it can admit any other sort of contingent connection one can dream up.

As a thesis about logical non-derivability of values from (social scientific) facts, the VFSS is clearly wrong. A. N. Prior produced a set of counter-examples to this thesis, although not tied specifically to the case of social science. Here is one: from the statement that there is no man over ten feet tall (factual) it follows logically that there is no man over ten feet tall who ought to sit on a chair (evaluative). Or, from the statement that object *o* is red (factual), it follows that if it is not the case that *o* is red, then object *a* is good (evaluative). The question of logical derivability depends on form alone, and there are valid inferences depending on form that move from factual premisses to evaluative conclusions. None of these counter-examples depend on the meaning of the factual or evaluative statements, on their semantic content.

So if there is a thesis here at all for the VFSS view, it had better be put in terms of meaning. But what would such a view look like? It is not of course disputed that many of the terms we actually use, in social science or more generally, have both factual and evaluative components. It is clear that 'He is a kike' and 'He is sick' typically have a factual and an evaluative component: the first both factually describes a person and negatively evaluates him, the second both provides factual information about a person's condition and negatively evaluates that condition. Of course, no social scientist would employ such terms as these, but think of other examples: alienation, exploitation, harassment, slavery, deprivation, and illness. These terms seem to have both factual and evaluative parts to their conditions of application, and certainly figure in many studies in social science.

So the thesis must then be: it is *logically possible* for there to be a language, which could be used by the social scientist, whose terms had no evaluative components to their conditions of application, and whose statements had no evaluative parts to their truth-conditions. Marx, on one reading of his work, tried to produce a theory of exploitation which was wholly factual. Some theorists in the positivist tradition tried to devise a language suitable for the social scientist that freed various crucial concepts from their evaluative components.

But, on this reading, the VFSS thesis is now anodyne. Of course, it is *logically possible* that there be such a language with which we could speak about social reality. How could it fail to be logically possible? But it seems clear that it would be nothing like the language that we, or social scientists, now use, nor is it at all clear why we should want to have such a language available for social science. Such a language would be dreadfully impoverished, lacking the characteristic richness and nuance with which we speak about the social world. Of course, where values are controversial or in dispute (e.g. the effects of a policy of abortion or capital punishment), it would be worth while to employ terminology that bypasses that specific evaluative dispute.

But whatever the logical possibilities might be, there are some values that all sane and rational people in fact share: that slavery and bondage are bad things, that harassing others for no further purpose ought to be avoided, that deprivation and illness are evils. These are simply not matters of actual controversy. What would the purpose be in constructing a language which allowed us to describe and discuss slavery, disease, alienation, exploitation, harassment, deprivation, and illness in a value-neutral way? It is difficult to state an interesting case for the value-neutrality of the contents of social science that is both true but not anodyne or trivial.

BIBLIOGRAPHY

Armstrong, D., 'The Nature of Tradition', in D. Armstrong, *The Nature of Mind* (Brighton, 1981). A discussion of some of the problems in providing an adequate analysis of the idea of tradition.

Ayer, A. J., 'Man as a Subject for Science', in P. Laslett, and W. G. Runciman (eds.), *Philosophy, Politics and Society*, 3rd ser. (Oxford, 1967). A good discussion of the compatibility of the interpretative and causal approaches to the explanation of human action.

Bishop, J., *Natural Agency* (Cambridge, 1989). In spite of its espousal of a particular point of view, this recommends itself as a superb introduction to the issues and positions in the theory of action.

Chalmers, A. F., *What is this Thing Called Science?* (Milton Keynes, 1980). An excellent introduction to the ideas of Popper, Lakatos, and Kuhn.

Churchland, P. S., 'The Logical Character of Action Explanations', *Philosophical Review*, 79 (1970), 214–36. A spirited defence of the view that there are empirical laws of action.

Cohen, G. A., *Karl Marx's Theory of History: A Defence* (Oxford, 1978). An account of functional explanation as consequence law explanation.

Davidson, D., 'On the Very Idea of a Conceptual Scheme' (1974), repr. in *Truth and Interpretation* (Oxford, 1984).

Dyke, C., *Philosophy of Economics* (Englewood Cliffs, NJ, 1981). A useful if annoyingly written introduction to problems and issues in economics, including Arrow's proof.

Elster, J., *Explaining Technical Change* (Cambridge, 1983). A presentation of the causal feedback loop account of functional explanation, and many other issues as well.

Gallie, W. B., 'Essentially Contested Concepts', *Proceedings of the Aristotelian Society*, 56 (1955–6), 167–98. Introduces the topic of essentially contested concepts into the literature.

Gardiner, P. (ed.), *The Philosophy of History* (Oxford, 1978). A useful collection of the literature in the philosophy of history on the explanation of action. Essays by William Dray, Carl Hempel, and others are included.

Gellner, E., *Cause and Meaning in the Social Sciences* (London, 1973). Essays by Gellner. The essay from which the book takes its title is an interesting discussion and attempted refutation of social relativism.

Goldman, A., *A Theory of Human Action* (Princeton, 1970). Ch. 6 contains an excellent presentation of problems about the predictability of human action.

Hahn, F., and Hollis, M. (eds.), *Philosophy and Economic Theory* (Oxford, 1979). A good collection of papers in the philosophy of economics, including Arrow's paper on the impossibility theorem, an excerpt from Ludwig von Mises' paper on the a priori status of the 'laws' of economics, and a paper by Amartya Sen, 'Rational Fools', which questions some of the basic assumptions of the utilitarian account of rationality.

Hart, H. L. A., *The Concept of Law* (Oxford, 1961). Probably the best discussion of rules there has ever been, specifically tied to the question of legal rules.

Hempel, C., 'The Function of General Laws in History' (1942), repr. in *Aspects of Scientific Explanation* (New York, 1965). A major contribution to the naturalist tradition of action explanation.

——'The Logic of Functional Analysis' (1959), repr. in *Aspects of Scientific Explanation* (New York, 1965). An alternative to the causal feedback loop account of functional explanation.

Hesse, M., 'Theory and Value in Social Science', in C. Hookway and P. Pettit (eds.), *Action and Interpretation* (Cambridge, 1978). Hesse argues from underdetermination to values in the case of social science.

Hollis, M., *The Philosophy of Social Science: An Introduction* (Cambridge, 1994). A very good introduction, and one that pays attention to some of the paradoxes of rational choice.

——and Lukes, S. (eds.), *Rationality and Relativism* (Oxford, 1982). A collection of articles on the question of social relativism. The article by Newton-Smith is particularly helpful.

James, S., *The Content of Social Explanation* (Cambridge, 1984). A good account of the requirements for, and problems of, the reduction of one theory to another.

McKay, A., *Arrow's Theorem: The Paradox of Social Choice* (New Haven, 1980). A full discussion of Arrow's paradox, and his impossibility theorem, and in particular the independence of irrelevant alternatives.

Mill, J. S., *A System of Logic* (London, 1970). A classical statement of the naturalist position.

Oldenquist, A., 'Self-Prediction', in *Encyclopedia of Philosophy*, vol. 7 (New York, 1967). A good summary of some of the main arguments about the predictability of human action.

O'Neill, J. (ed.), *Modes of Individualism and Collectivism* (London, 1973). A good, if somewhat dated, collection of articles on individualism and holism.

Postema, G., 'Coordination and Convention at the Foundations of Law', *Journal of Legal Studies*, II (1982), 165–203. A helpful presentation of coordination problems and conventions.

Prior, A. N., 'The Autonomy of Ethics', *Australasian Journal of Philosophy*, 38 (1960), 199–206. Some interesting alleged counter-examples to Hume's dictum.

Ruben, D.-H., *The Metaphysics of the Social World* (London, 1985). A discussion of the varieties of methodological individualism, and an assessment of their plausibility.

——'Singular Explanation and the Social Sciences', in P. A. French, T. E. Uehling, and H. K. Wettstein (eds.), *Midwest Studies in Philosophy*, xv: *The Philosophy of the Human Sciences* (Notre Dame, Ind., (1990). The volume as a whole is well worth browsing.

Ryan, A., *The Philosophy of Social Explanation* (Oxford, 1973). A somewhat dated but still useful collection of articles on a range of issues about explanation in the social sciences.

Sen, A., and Williams, B. (eds.), *Utilitarianism and Beyond* (Cambridge, 1982).

Taylor, C., 'What is Human Agency?', in T. Mischel (ed.), *The Self: Psychological Issues* (Oxford, 1977). An excellent discussion of the difficulties utilitarian theories of rationality face, regarding the question of the qualitative appraisal of desires.

Ullmann-Margalit, E., *The Emergence of Norms* (Oxford, 1977). A discussion of how rules or norms would be a rational response to three sorts of situation in which persons find themselves.

von Wright, G. H., *Explanation and Understanding* (London, 1971). An insightful discussion of the contrasting merits of the two great traditions of explanation. Unrivalled.

——*Norm and Action: A Logical Enquiry* (London, 1977). A ground-breaking investigation into the analysis of action and the logic of change and action.

Williams, John N., 'Confucius, Mencius, and the Notion of True Succession', *Philosophy East and West*, 38 (1988), 151–71. The only philosophical discussion of which I am aware of the interesting but perplexing problem of the idea of the numerical identity of a tradition over time.

Wilson, B. (ed.), *Rationality* (Oxford, 1973). A useful if somewhat dated collection.

Winch, P., *The Idea of a Social Science* (London, 1958). A well-known statement of the non-naturalistic view of action.

Zeleny, J., *The Logic of Marx* (Oxford, 1980). A defence and elaboration of the method of structural explanation.

8

LATER ANCIENT PHILOSOPHY

David Mitchell

1. PHILOSOPHY IN THE HELLENISTIC PERIOD

1.1. Introduction

The history of ancient philosophy after Aristotle, in which there has been a considerable revival of interest in recent years, extends across almost a millennium. This great span of time is commonly divided by modern historians of philosophy into two periods. These two periods coincide very nearly with the ancient historian's Hellenistic and Imperial periods. The Hellenistic period commences in 323 BC with the death of Alexander the Great of Macedon, whose conquests initiated the Hellenization of the Middle Eastern countries, and continues until 30 BC, when the Imperial period is inaugurated by the ascendancy of Octavian. The corresponding periods in philosophy are distinguished, broadly speaking, by the pre-eminence of different philosophical movements. Platonism and Aristotelianism together dominate one period; but, curiously enough, that is the later period. In the earlier, Hellenistic period, they were outshone by two new schools of thought, Stoicism and Epicureanism.

These two schools rose to vitality in the traditional home of philosophy, Athens. Epicurus established himself as a teacher there in 307, having previously taught for several years near his birthplace, across the Aegean sea in Ionia. Zeno, the founder of Stoicism, came to Athens from his native Cyprus in 312, and, after acquainting himself as a student with, among other philosophical groupings, the Platonic Academy, set up his own school in about 301.

The philosophical outlooks of the two new movements naturally owed much to contemporary and earlier thinkers. Epicureanism, in particular, adopted and developed the views in ethics and physics characteristic of the tradition deriving from the fifth-century thinker Democritus. The affiliations of Stoicism were more various: besides Platonist elements, Zeno's thought contains clear traces of his familiarity with the ethical outlook of the Cynics Diogenes and Crates, and with the logical investigations of Diodorus Cronus and Philo, members of a group known as the Dialecticians. These and other minor philosophical persuasions were not immediately eclipsed by Epicureanism and Stoicism. Likewise, the adherents of the Academy and the Lyceum maintained the Platonic and Aristotelian traditions of theorizing well into the new period. But Aristotelianism gradually lost its impetus, partly as a result of the geographical dispersion of its leading practitioners, and in 273 the Academy abandoned the promotion of Platonic doctrine and adopted a Sceptical orientation (see below, Section 1.4.1). The resulting hegemony of Stoics and Epicureans in constructive philosophy persisted for the next 200 years.

The two schools regarded one another as rivals, and certainly the philosophies they espoused are in many respects mutually antithetical. But there was some common ground. First, Stoics and Epicureans were agreed in their exaltation of the philosopher's way of life. Philosophical reflection is capable of contributing fundamentally to a person's living well. (It is a further question, of course, which are the philosophical conclusions that deliver this result.) In making such claims for the value of philosophy, the Hellenistic schools were not saying anything new; the attitude had numerous precedents. Another shared view, however, was rather distinctive of the period: Epicureans and Stoics agreed upon an empiricist conception of human knowledge. More specifically, they held that all our thought and communication presupposes concepts (or 'preconceptions', to use the customary translation of the technical term *prolēpsis*) which are acquired only as a result of the perception of particular material items by the senses. Some truths are 'evident' to us, thanks to sense-perception; and claims to any further knowledge must be vindicated by reference to these. Similar epistemological views had been propounded before (and Stoic thought in this area appears to be considerably indebted to Aristotle in particular); but their general currency imparts a specific character to the philosophical debates of the Hellenistic period.

The abundant writings in which the Epicurean and Stoic philosophers pursued their debates are almost entirely lost. From the Hellenistic period itself, the only texts which can now be read whole are three expository letters of Epicurus and a short verse hymn by the second head of the Stoic school, Cleanthes. Longer works survive from later centuries: the Roman Epicurean Lucretius' magnificent poem *De Rerum Natura* was written in the middle of the first century BC, and from the next two centuries there are available the Stoic discourses of Seneca, Epictetus, and Marcus Aurelius. Cicero and Plutarch, among others, provide extensive accounts of earlier Stoic and Epicurean thought from an unpersuaded stance. The scholarly reconstruction of Hellenistic debates from the later materials is assisted in the case of Epicureanism by the comparatively low degree of doctrinal innovation in that school; Lucretius is thus a particularly valuable source. The history of Stoicism, by contrast, has several rather distinct phases. The account given below concentrates on the philosophical views of Zeno and his immediate successors, the Old Stoics, among whom Chrysippus, the school's leader in the late third century, is the outstanding figure.

1.2. Epicureanism

1.2.1. *The Use of Epicureanism*

'Just as there is no use in medical expertise if it does not give therapy for bodily diseases, so too there is no use in philosophy if it does not expel the suffering of the soul' (LS 25C).[1] These words of Epicurus express an attitude towards philosophy which was to be characteristic of his school. The Epicureans regarded their philosophy of nature as meeting the therapeutic requirement, in that it could help people to overcome some of their most debilitating fears by providing philosophical arguments to show that these fears are baseless. Such arguments, combined with the inculcation of therapeutic habits, promised to lead the Epicurean to a new and better life.

The promised life was often characterized as a life of tranquillity (*ataraxia*). The Epicurean use of this term has a distinctively strong connotation of *security*: Epicurus' arguments concerning the gods and concerning death imply that human existence is objectively less exposed to invasion by suffering than many people suppose, and the Epicurean, by taking those arguments to heart, acquires a more confident outlook upon life.

The suffering caused to people by their fear of death is to be eliminated by an unequivocal recognition of human mortality. The human psyche is a fragile compound of atoms which does not outlast the life of the human organism. Fear of the gods is to be dispelled by an argument which concludes that there cannot be gods who feel any concern about, or interest in, human affairs. The grounds for these claims in physics and theology will be considered below. But as regards their implications and their psychological effects, doubts can be raised; and in the case of the arguments about death these are of substantial philosophical interest.

Death will be the end of our worries. Does it follow that death should also be the last of our worries? Epicurus is sometimes read as inferring that since nothing can be bad for a dead person, dying is not bad for anyone either, and as concluding thence that we cannot reasonably regret the fact that we are mortal. But this frail-looking line of thought perhaps does not represent Epicurus' considered position. In referring (LS 24C2) to the ideal of a 'complete life', he gives himself room to say that while many people could be benefited by a lengthening of their lives, some could have already lived so well as to have nothing further to gain. As for regretting our mortality, Lucretius at one point appears to suggest that the Epicurean will not be a mourner, but it may be possible to interpret Epicurus as castigating only an excessive distress. Rather than being completely indifferent to the condition of mortality, the Epicurean may cherish life, and hope that death will not come soon. This seems consistent with the main line of Epicurean attack, which is directed against exaggerated and counter-productive apprehensions about death.

1.2.2. *The Best Human Life*

Epicurean ethics is hedonistic. Pleasure is not merely the greatest good, but the only thing good in itself, and the yardstick by which the goodness of all other

[1] LS references are to Long and Sedley; see Bibliography, sect. 1.

things is to be determined. The virtues, for instance, are goods only because they are instrumental to the pleasant life. The Epicurean arguments for hedonism proceed from both phenomenological and behavioural premisses: the value of pleasure is supposed to be indicated both by our feelings and by our observation of the behaviour of every kind of animal. 'He thinks these matters are sensed,' as Cicero puts it (LS 21A2). Thus the judgement that pleasure is something good in itself is thought to articulate what is implicit in our native responses to it. The further judgement that pleasure is the only such good is directly argued for only sketchily in our sources. Some generalizations are offered regarding the role of pleasure in all our motivations, but Epicureans were more concerned to forestall objections arising from errors about what their thesis implied.

What makes the hedonistic ethics of Epicurus distinctive, and perhaps immune to some objections that seem potent against other hedonisms, is a surprising assertion regarding the hedonistic goal of life: 'the complete absence of pain marks the limit of the greatest pleasure' (LS 21A7). This assertion appears to have been designed to distance Epicurean hedonism from the kind of hedonism according to which the best life is a life dominated by processes of desire satisfaction. But it might be thought also to detach the theory from its supposed observational support. What exactly does it mean?

Epicurus is not saying that there is no condition more pleasant than unconsciousness. The context of our reports makes it clear enough that he has in mind the state of a person who is consciously free from all pain. Beyond this, two somewhat divergent readings may be considered. Epicurus may be referring to the pleasure supervenient on a person's normal functioning when no bodily or mental disturbances interfere. Or he may mean that nothing is more pleasant than the consciousness of having attained a lasting security from irruptions of pain into one's life.

In either case, Epicurus disagrees with the Platonic view that all pleasures are processes. He maintains that besides 'kinetic' pleasures there are also static (or 'katastematic') pleasures, both of the body and of the psyche. The greatest pleasure belongs to the static category. Epicurus does say (LS 21L1, Q3) that the good is bound to contain kinetic pleasures afforded by sensory beauty. If that seems difficult to square with his insistence that the value of freedom from pain is unsurpassable, then the latter might be diagnosed as an exaggeration, due to the recoil from vulgar hedonism. Alternatively, Epicurus may just be disregarding as unrealistic the possibility of the best, static condition's arising unaccompanied by enjoyments of sights, sounds, and tastes.

Complete absence of pain is, of course, something Epicureanism cannot pretend to be able to secure. But what is offered is a large step in that direction:

a life secure from serious distress is attainable by anyone who digests the arguments about the groundlessness of humanity's main fears and who acquires Epicurean habits of thought- and desire-management.

1.2.3. Truth and Method

How far should we be guided in our philosophical views by what our senses tell us about the world? Whereas earlier atomists had been chary about the data of the senses, the Epicureans were empiricists: they took sense-perception to be a 'criterion of truth'. Indeed, they maintained that every one of our sense-impressions must be regarded as true.

The Epicureans' grounds for this remarkable thesis are partly pragmatic. Human life becomes unlivable if our judgements do not have some basis in which we place unqualified trust. The argument for trusting all sense-impressions then proceeds by elimination. We cannot reasonably reject any report of the senses unless on the basis of something reasonably regarded as more trustworthy. This cannot be the faculty of reason, 'since all reason depends on the senses' (LS 16B6). But nor can one sense-impression confute another, 'because of their equal validity' (LS 16B4). This phrase, which brings to mind the arguments of the Sceptics (below, Section 1.4.3), can perhaps be understood here as presupposing a binary choice in respect of sense-impressions. Either one trusts a sense-impression or one grants it no evidential value at all; and to respond in the latter way to some but not others of one's sense-impressions looks arbitrary.

But if one trusts all sense-impressions without exception, how can one avoid inconsistent judgements about the world? Epicurus addresses this challenge with the help of an account of what it is for a sense-impression to be true, and hence of what it is to trust a sense-impression. It is worth noting that this account of truth-conditions is not derived from atomist premisses. An impression is true when it is 'like the thing which moves the sense' (LS 16F1), and this mover of the sense, though it is external to the perceiver, is not in general a persisting solid object, but a colour, for instance, or a sound. The fallible attribution of a perceived colour to a distant object is the work of the mind, as distinct from the senses. Epicurus thus holds that if data are not confused with interpretation, and if the senses' objects are correctly identified, trust in the senses does not lead to inconsistency.

The truth of atomism is not evident to the senses. But the Epicureans argue that atomism is not inconsistent with what the senses tell us. For example, that something is not visibly in motion does not entail that it is not invisibly in motion. So far, then, atomism is not at odds with Epicurean epistemology, since accepting everything that the senses report does not require accepting only what the senses report.

But sense-perception is nevertheless 'criterial' for the truth of opinions about the unobserved. The 'self-evident' data of perception provide a secure reference-point, and theories are to be accepted or rejected on the strength of their relations to this. True opinions, then, 'are those attested and those uncontested by self-evidence; false are those contested and those unattested by self-evidence' (LS 18A1). The relevant cases for the evaluation of atomistic theory appear to be contestation and non-contestation, but further interpretation is not straightforward. Sextus' gloss of these two relations between hypothesis and datum as, respectively, 'conflicting with' and 'following from' threatens to render many of the claims of atomism undecidable. Philodemus' defence (LS 18G) of the use of analogies meshes rather more closely with Epicurean practice. Epicurus himself says that a theory must not be insisted upon unless it is 'uniquely consonant with the phenomena' (LS 18C2), and ambitiously claims that the postulation of atomic particles meets this standard. In general, however, Epicurean methodology is not so clear or compelling that it should determine our evaluation of Epicurean method. The arguments for atomism deserve independent assessment.

1.2.4. *Atomism*

Epicurean physics embeds an atomistic account of the constitution of things within an anti-teleological view of nature. Human beings and all other sense-perceptible objects are compounds of invisibly small, indestructible particles in constant rapid motion. And, apart from those things that are the results of human intention or design, nothing in the world has any purpose, or exists for the sake of any goal; nature is not to be understood teleologically.

The Epicureans' arguments against teleology in nature and their arguments in favour of atomism are for the most part independent of each other. Thus, for instance, when Lucretius adduces the flaws and imperfections of the world as evidence against design (LS 13F6), he is not relying on distinctively atomist premisses. Equally, much though not all of the Epicurean account of ultimate physical constituents is untouched by defects in the argument against design.

Epicurean atomism can be expounded in two converging strands of empirically based argument. One strand begins with some evident data of perception. There exist bodies of various densities, and many of them are in motion. Perception suggests that motion requires void: nothing can move unless there is some empty space for it to move into. Movements such as percolation and permeation show that there is void within many of the bodies that we perceive. Given this, variation in density is economically accounted for by saying that part of the volume of any large body is occupied by void, and the remainder is, so to speak, devoid of void. The body's overall density depends on the proportions of such maximally dense body and of void contained.

The more abstract strand of argument begins with the observation of regularity in the causal processes of nature. There could not be such uniform connections as we find among events if it were possible for something to come to be 'out of nothing', or indeed to be 'destroyed into' nothing. There must eternally be something. The uniformity of nature is best explained as due to the behaviour of eternal and in some respects invariant entities. Given the further premiss (LS 5B5) that whatever has independent existence has some three-dimensional extension, the two strands of argument come together in the postulation of atoms, eternal—because voidless—minute bodies which never change in size or shape.

Two further features of Epicurean physics are introduced on logical grounds. The universe is infinitely large (as are the volumes of both void and body). Space is not infinitely divisible. The defence of each thesis is that to deny it leads to self-contradiction.

Epicurean physics becomes explicitly anti-teleological in its explanations of atomic motion and of the properties of compound objects. The colours, odours, and so forth of perceptible objects, the sensations and other affections of perceivers, are 'delivered'—are sufficiently accounted for—by properties of the constituent atoms; and changes in these latter properties are all (with the unique exception of the 'swerve'; see below) mechanically determined. Thus, for instance, that the atoms which compose a particular macroscopic object remain together despite never being stationary is a result of the atoms' shapes: enough of these are irregularly hooked or pitted for 'entanglement' to occur, and to survive some but not all ensuing collisions with other bodies.

Of the specific correlations between events or properties at the macroscopic and at the microscopic levels, the Epicureans give a limited and tentative account. Analogical reasoning is one of the mainstays. Thus a specific macroscopic effect is ascribed to the smoothness of component atoms on the strength of its similarity to the effects of smooth macroscopic objects (LS 12F4). More generally, the way in which qualitative change can be perceived to supervene on quantitative change serves as a model, and the Epicureans emphasize the immense resources of quantitative variation furnished by the infinity of time and space and of the number of atoms, together with the diversity of atomic shapes and sizes.

How objectionable the gaps and guesses in Epicurean physics are depends in part on how strong the arguments against rival approaches are. Epicurean attacks on teleological thought focus on its Platonic and Stoic versions, which infer from the excellence of the cosmos the agency of a divine intelligence which aims at the excellent. Some of the counter-arguments, relating to the world's many flaws and the obscurity of how the divinity can be supposed to produce the cosmos, presuppose little theory, while others presuppose such Epicurean theses as the infinite number of worlds. These arguments are inconclusive; but the case for atomism, as described above, does not entirely depend on them.

Epicurus' own theology is a disputed topic. If we are to be guided by Lucretius, atomically constituted gods enjoy an independent existence in a location conveniently free of the invasion by extraneous atoms which sooner or later destroys all other compounds. The evidence of Cicero (especially LS 23E7), however, suggests a more sophisticated, if in detail no less strange, view that gods exist as objects of thought rather than as solid and everlasting entities. This line of interpretation may seem to be at odds with Epicurus own words: 'for there are gods—the knowledge of them is self-evident' (LS 23B2). But objects of thought, on Epicurus' view, are actually fine films of atoms which can exist independently of particular episodes of thinking, so that if the gods are such, then strictly they are not merely imaginary.

Perhaps, indeed, gods exist in both of the ways described. At all events, the interpreter of Epicurean theology must bear in mind the contemporary discouragements of explicit atheism, as well as the possibility of doctrinal evolution. But one fixed point is that divine interference in our lives is excluded. Epicurus takes it as a datum of perception, in a broad sense of 'perception' which covers mental images, that to be divine is to be blissfully self-sufficient, and to have no more need to get involved in cosmic politics than the happy Epicurean has to engage in the terrestrial variety.

There is thus no risk of divine retribution against us after our deaths. The further conclusion that we do not survive bodily death at all does not follow immediately from the psyche's being an atomic compound. One must add that during the life of the organism the functioning of the psyche shows a very close dependence on that of the body. So, for instance, the comparative mental imbecility associated with infancy and old age suggests that, as and when the body disintegrates, the psyche does so too.

There is one major Epicurean modification of the earlier atomists' picture of our mental lives as entirely determined by the mechanical motions of atoms. In a pioneering discussion, Epicurus contends that such a theory conflicts with our usual conception of our own responsibility for our conduct, and must therefore be revised. These are two distinct points; in principle, one might agree that physics and 'common sense' are in this respect incompatible, but hold that it is the latter which must give way. Epicurus is aware of the distinction, and his arguments are organized accordingly.

The conflict, as formulated by Epicurus, is between saying that everything we do is due to necessity (which the earlier atomists acknowledged was a corollary of their theory) and saying that certain actions are due to us. That being necessitated is incompatible with being chosen is something we understand if we grasp the respective notions at all. This is part of our 'preconception', as the technical term is usually translated, of choice, and as such is something guaranteed ultimately by perception. Epicurus allows that this claim might be overturned if it could be shown that the case is in some way exceptional, but maintains that arguments designed to do this contrive only to change the subject (LS 20C8).

We must choose, then, between accepting the view that all human acts are necessitated (determinism, for short) and continuing to assign to people responsibility for some at least of what they do. The argument for rejecting determinism is in a measure pragmatic. A determinist is vulnerable to perplexity and internal 'conflict', because there are so many ordinary human activities in which a determinist cannot coherently engage. Even to oppose an indeterminist in argument is implicitly to acknowledge that people can be responsible for their views (LS 20C6).

The determinist atomism of Epicurus' precursors must therefore be revised. The favoured revision is as follows. The motion of an unimpeded atom is not at every moment determined by its prior motion: at certain moments an atom may either continue in its previous rectilinear trajectory or shift ('swerve') into an immediately adjacent parallel course. Such a swerve may result in an atomic collision which would not otherwise have occurred, and thus have ramifying consequences. Epicurus appears (e.g. LS 20B6) to envisage human decisions' being capable of determining atomic behaviour in such otherwise undetermined respects, and to salvage thus our responsibility for some of what happens in the world.

1.3. Stoicism

1.3.1. *Logic*

The Stoics describe philosophy as having three parts, namely logic, physics, and ethics. The labels 'logic' and 'physics' are to be understood rather broadly. The subject-matter of physics in the modern sense is included in that of Stoic physics, but so are those of biology and theology. Similarly, Stoic logic is in part concerned with what would now be called epistemological issues, and not merely with those questions regarding consistency and validity, truth and falsity, with which logic is nowadays said to deal.

Logic in this narrower sense is one of the fields in which the work of the Stoics is particularly impressive. The Stoics articulate, in the manner of modern logic, universal laws regarding when an argument is valid and when an individual proposition is true. In stating such laws, one must refer to diverse types of argument and proposition. For this reason, it is essential that the relevant types be accurately identified. Thus classification forms an integral part of the enterprise. So, for example, the Stoics distinguish, and give a canonical form of expression to, the class of 'subconditional' propositions. 'Since it is day, the sun is above the earth' is a subconditional, and as such has its truth-conditions in accordance with the relevant law: a subconditional is true, the Stoics hold, just when its antecedent is true and 'conflicts' with the contradictory of its consequent.

As 'subconditional' identifies a class of propositions, so, for example, 'fifth indemonstrable' identifies a class of arguments, those of the form 'either the first or the second; but not the second; therefore the first'. And every argument thus classifiable is valid.

As the term 'indemonstrable' may suggest, the Stoics follow Aristotle in their method of showing an argument to be valid. A given argument is established as valid, and thus qualifies as a 'syllogism', if it can be reduced to, or analysed into, an instance or instances of any of five types of argument which are taken as indemonstrable—that is, whose validity the procedure does not try to establish. The reduction relies also on certain ground-rules, of which the Stoics give an account more complete than Aristotle's.

The two logics differ greatly, however, in respect of which arguments are ratified as syllogisms. Their divergent choice of arguments to be treated as basic might be thought to account for this. But what most sets the two systems apart is the fact that Stoic syllogisms admit many kinds of proposition which Aristotle's do not admit. (And those which Aristotle does admit are reformulated: 'all men are animals' becomes 'if something is a man, then it is an animal'.)

The Stoics' syllogistic is a chief ancestor of modern propositional logic, as the Aristotelian is of predicate logic. But, contrarily to what these links might suggest, each party regarded the other's system as a rival rather than a complement to their own. Their reasons for this attitude are not easy to determine. On the Stoics' side, the reasons may have included a concern about the implicit ontological commitments of Aristotelian syllogistic, notably in respect of relations among universals (on which see below, Section 1.3.2).

1.3.2. *Ontology*

At Plato, *Sophist* 246–7, the leading participant in the dialogue objects to the view that only what is tangible really exists. He urges that this wrongly denies existence to the psyche, and to virtues such as justice which may belong to a psyche. These, though they cannot be classed as bodies, are real existents, inasmuch as they are capable of having effects on other existents. An alternative mark of existence is therefore proposed: whatever is capable of in any way affecting or being affected by something is itself a real existent.

Stoic ontology embraces this proposal, but with results rather far removed from the proposer's intent. If whatever exists must be capable of acting upon or being acted upon by something, then, the Stoics maintained, everything that exists is corporeal. The immediate ground for this conclusion is that only bodies are capable of such interaction. This view in its turn appears to have rested on the Stoic conviction that it is impossible for entities to interact which are not, directly or indirectly, in contact with each other.

The argument of the *Sophist* appears to have been turned right around. This will not be so, of course, if the Stoics are merely changing the meaning of the term 'body' (*sōma*), so that interacting entities count as bodies by stipulation. But that is not the Stoic position: they subscribe to a definition of body, as 'threefold extension together with resistance' (LS 45F), which does not decide the issue by itself.

Only bodies exist. How restrictive an ontology is this? The Stoics aim to show that it is less restrictive than might be supposed. Virtue, to take Plato's instance, is not barred from existence, at any rate as an attribute of particular persons. To say that virtue can have an effect on something is to say something true, specifically that a person disposed in a certain way can have such an effect. Virtue thus qualifies as a body.

In their subtle discussions of issues similarly raised by modern physicalism, the Stoics make frequent use of phrases which later authors report as technical terms of a list of kinds, or genera, of being, comparable to Aristotle's list of 'categories'. 'Disposed in a certain way', for instance, appears on a list of four Stoic genera in Simplicius (LS 27F). There are reasons for doubting that there was any such express response to Aristotle. Indeed, it is difficult to detect any single principle behind the classification. It is possible that the list derives from Stoic treatments of several obliquely related topics. Among these is the topic of identity over time. The Stoics held that each body has throughout its existence a set of qualities which no other body ever has. This 'identity of indiscernibles' may have been endorsed as being the only way of escaping paradoxes which result from having the continuance of a body depend on the continuance of its constituent matter. It is a view which intersects in interesting ways with other Stoic motifs, such as eternal recurrence (below, Section 1.3.3) and cognitive impressions (Section 1.4.2).

The devices so far considered do somewhat lessen the apparent austerity of this ontology. But a wide range of candidates for existence—space, time, void, universals, fictional entities—remains excluded. The Stoics make room, however, for some further discrimination between, say, the status of space and that of centaurs. They appear, at least, to use a notion of 'subsistence for the mind' (LS 27C) in somewhat this role. The idea may be that one should distinguish among non-existents those which cannot be entirely repudiated if we are to account for the possibility of various kinds of thought. At all events, the conclusion reached is that the incorporeals space, time, and void do 'subsist', whereas universals, such as man and animal, lack even this weakened ontological standing.

Besides space, time, and void, there is one other regularly cited Stoic incorporeal, which appears in a fascinating variety of contexts. This is the 'sayable' (*lekton*). One home of this innovative locution is in semantics, where, as the 'signified', it is distinguished both from the corporeal 'signifier' which is uttered and from another existent—roughly, the object of reference. The sayable is not only what is said when words are significantly used; it is what being true and being false are properly attributed to. Indeed, it is plausible that the Stoics saw their recognition of sayables as essential for any theoretical understanding of false (but significant) utterance.

The premisses and conclusions of arguments count as sayables; and predicates are said to be 'incomplete' sayables. But, as mentioned above, the term is also used outside the context of semantics. It is applied to the objects of several types of conative state, such as desire. It also enters into the analysis of causality. A very common Stoic schema represents causal relations as ternary: one body, by acting, is cause *to* another body *of* a predicate (i.e. of a sayable). It might be wondered whether, if sayables can be effects, they do not meet the Stoic test for corporeality after all. But presumably part of the point of the ternary analysis of causal relations is that effects cannot be identified with what is acted upon, since the latter pre-exists, and is altered by, the cause's acting upon it. The Stoic position seems comparable to a view examined in modern debates about physicalism, that effects are a species of facts.

It will be evident that the Stoic ontology is rather less parsimonious than the slogan 'only bodies exist' at first suggests. Even though the quasi-Aristotelian option of distinguishing different senses of the verb, and saying that facts and propositions do exist, only not in the same sense in which bodies exist, seems to have been resisted, the Stoics did feel the need to specify how, if not by bodily interaction, sayables actually can be related to particular psychological events; but the few surviving testimonies on this point are thoroughly enigmatic (LS 27E, 33F2).

1.3.3. *Cosmology*

'We Stoics look for a primary and universal cause. What is that cause? The answer is "creative reason", that is, god' (Seneca, *Letter* 65. 12). The Stoics are opposed to the Epicureans in rejecting the ideal of, as it might nowadays be put, value-free science. One cannot understand nature without detecting purpose in natural events, that is to say, without seeing in what way they are good. Indeed, Stoic cosmology is not independent of theology, in that its explanations refer to the activity of a divinity.

The Stoics can be aligned in this respect with Platonic and Aristotelian cosmology. They are distinctive, however, in postulating a divine cause not external to but coextensive with the changing cosmos. The Stoic divinity is an all-pervasive presence, and exerts its powers from within nature. The Stoics often compare their god's government of the cosmos with the way in which the individual human organism is governed by the psyche (e.g. LS 44C3), allowing themselves at times an anthropomorphism not so far removed from that of Plato's *Timaeus* (LS 53Y).

The god is one of the two fundamental principles, or starting-points, of the cosmos. The other is a passive principle described as matter. It may be helpful to compare this framework with what is in a sense its counterpart in Epicureanism. That school's two fundamental existents are body and void. Body is capable both of being changed by and of changing other things; it is both active and passive. Void, by contrast, is inactive and impassive: it neither affects, nor is affected by, anything else. (In fact, since an unoccupied portion of space into which a body moves thereby comes to be occupied, the impassivity must be somewhat qualified—whether this second reality is construed strictly as void or instead as space. But the contrast remains broadly as just described.)

The Stoics also distribute such properties among their two fundamentals, but the allocation is different. Matter is the inactive principle which, since it is acted upon by the god, is also passive. The god is active (though not impassive, since some of his action is reflexive). And whereas the Epicureans' body and void are mutually exclusive, the Stoics' god and matter are coextended throughout a voidless cosmos.

Matter is, however, not thought of as eternal. At the destined extinction of the cosmos, matter is entirely consumed by the god, who then exists alone. Indeed, for as long as, thanks to the god's shaping and sustaining activity, the cosmos lasts, neither of the two principles exists in a pure state. Clearly, then, these fundamental existents are far from being discoverable by mere sense-perception. The Stoics postulate them on the strength of arguments purporting to show that they are required if natural phenomena are to be adequately explained.

The surviving arguments for the principles are abundant, though in many cases obviously infirm, and they indicate fairly well just what aspects of the perceived world the Stoics saw as standing in need of explanation. These include the existence and persistence of individuals, the regularity of natural change, and the apparent providence of nature towards the interests of rational beings. One theme to which the arguments often recur is the unity or coherence of the cosmos as a whole, the connectedness of all its parts. It is not easy to fix definitely the sense in which this is intended, but whether the Stoics saw it as corollary or rather as ground of the thesis that the cosmos contains no void spaces, or again of the thesis of determinism, it is at any rate a more theoretical, less observational, premiss than those previously mentioned. It is also worth noting that most of the arguments in question are directed towards just one of the two principles, the deity, as if the existence of an immobile matter entirely lacking in intrinsic qualities were a pre-theoretical datum of experience.

The Stoics proceed, therefore, to develop explanations by reference to the god's rational workings upon matter. The principal guise of the creator within the cosmos is as fire, or as a mixture of fire and air. These apparently earlier and later selections from among the elements conform to common associations with the dynamic and the vital. Chrysippus uses the term 'breath' for the fire–air mixture, different parts of which are in different states of tensional movement.

This tensional movement of the underlying breath plays an explanatory role somewhat comparable to that of the mechanical interactions of constituent atoms in Epicureanism. In each case, different properties of perceptible objects are speculatively correlated with different conditions prevailing at the explanatory level. The Stoics are of course engaged in describing the media of a providential activity, but the specification of the various tensional movements is not in itself such as to declare that this is so.

Another Stoic theme which does not transparently belong in an account of natural events as providentially designed is that of the cosmos' eventual destruction by the divine fire. The middle Stoic Panaetius abandoned this view of his predecessors, and it is plausible that he was moved to do so by doubts about the benefits of conflagration (LS 46P). But the earlier Stoics regarded the conflagration as one episode only of an unending cycle: after an interval given over to his thoughts, the deity turns again to cosmos creation, the cosmos again having a finite duration and fiery end. Since, however, the present cosmos is a perfect specimen of its kind, the deity can hardly wish its successors to be appreciably different. The question thus arises whether an earlier and a later cosmos will be dissimilar at all.

At this point in the Stoics' reasoning, the doctrine of the identity of indiscernibles (above, Section 1.3.2) becomes relevant. According to that doctrine, a cosmos exactly similar in every detail to this present cosmos actually is this cosmos, so that it is not clear that corresponding events in an earlier and a later cosmos can actually be distinct events. Some Stoics, wary perhaps of such logical puzzles, preserve the deity's eternally renewed beneficence by saying that each cosmos differs from each other cosmos in some minute details irrelevant to cosmic excellence. It is conceivable that Chrysippus took a different tack, proposing that time itself is cyclical. As on a line of latitude of a globe each point is both east and west of itself, so in cyclical time each moment is both before and after itself. But if Chrysippus did favour this sophisticated option, that fact is not clearly attested in the surviving reports.

1.3.4. *Nature and Goodness*

The ethics of the Stoics has often been presented, not least by its authors, as stark and uncompromising. This effect can be conveyed by mentioning some of the more celebrated themes: there is nothing good in a life without virtue; there is nothing good in the passions; folly is the keynote of most people's lives. It is worth observing, therefore, that the premisses from which these conclusions are reached are for the most part thoroughly traditional. The Stoics effect a synthesis of themes which are central to the reflections of Plato, Aristotle, and other precursors.

They share, for instance, in the eudaimonistic orthodoxy of the period, taking it for granted that any reflective person will have as their principal goal in life the promotion of their own well-being. They recommend acting constantly upon the guidance of reason. And they advocate with particular emphasis the life in accordance with nature. In combining these themes with each other and with the theme of virtue's incomparable desirability, the Stoics rely especially on their view of nature at large as rationally ordered by a beneficent divinity. In so far as the Stoic synthesis of traditional themes does produce something new in Greek ethics, that is to be attributed in considerable part to the extensive use in their ethical arguments of premisses taken from Stoic physics.

In the bare formula 'one should live in accordance with nature', the reference to 'nature' might be understood in more than one way. It might be nature as a whole which is referred to; or it might rather be the specific nature of human beings. For the interpretation of Stoic ethics, both readings are relevant. Even if individual members of the school make one or other of the two readings primary, the Stoics mostly envisage a way of life which is suitably related both to common or universal nature, i.e. to the workings of the cosmos as a whole, and to specifically human nature.

One can roughly see, even before the phrase 'in accordance with' is given a precise sense, how the Stoics are able to think of a life as being in accordance with both specific and universal nature. The instincts which belong to human nature are implanted in us by universal nature (LS 57A2), so that in following the former's promptings we are not likely to be flouting the latter's purpose. And since the god's creative activity is for the sake of such rational beings as us (LS 54N), living in accordance with universal nature cannot ultimately involve the frustration of human nature.

The notion of living in accordance with human nature seems to be straightforwardly equivalent to the (not itself straightforward) notion of living as it is natural for human beings to live. But what it is to live in accordance with universal nature is not equally clear. The relation in question is also frequently termed 'agreement' (*homologia*). What the Stoics appear to have in mind is in part obedience, but in part also what one might call, in a sense to be explained shortly, assimilation.

The aspect of obedience is particularly prominent in the thought of Cleanthes and of Epictetus. In coming to understand nature, we discover the intentions of the divinity, and being virtuous is a matter of complying with those intentions. This is one way in which the life of virtue is supposed to be a life in agreement with nature.

It may be noticed, however, that if agreement consisted quite simply in obedience to the deity's design, further argument would be needed to show how it is that virtue by itself suffices for well-being, as the Stoics claim it does. There are Stoic arguments which serve this purpose; they adduce the benevolence of the deity and the psychological security of the virtuous person (LS 63B, M, 67S6). But a more immediate connection between well-being and 'living in agreement' becomes apparent if one considers the second aspect of agreement distinguished above, namely assimilation.

According to this line of thought, human nature is developed to its fullest extent only in a way of life which is entirely rational. The 'regularity and . . . harmony of conduct' (LS 59D) which is then achieved is said by the Stoics to have an intrinsic value which nothing else in human life approaches. But this is the same value which is perceived in the cosmos as a whole by the person who appreciates the rationality of its workings. Thus in fulfilling our human nature, we come to resemble cosmic nature; our lives have the kind of value which the divinely ordered world exhibits. Hence, while members of different animal species can be 'perfect in their own kind', those 'which lack reason are perfect only in their own nature, not truly perfect. For that is finally perfect which is perfect in accordance with universal nature, and universal nature is rational' (LS 60H4). The regularity of conduct which constitutes virtue thus confers a kind of perfection on a human life; in this sense, virtue suffices for well-being.

The argument as so far expounded needs to be supplemented at several points. How is it to be established, for instance, that virtue is the culmination of a human being's natural development? The virtuous life, the Stoics may say, is the life guided by reason. But that claim also requires corroboration. What specific habits or activities of the virtuous person are supposed to be particularly expressive of human rationality?

The first of these questions is one which the Stoics in fact address very thoroughly. They wish to show that virtue, while not in any sense native to us, and not attained at all by the majority of people, does nevertheless belong, as last stage, to the same process whose earlier stages every normal human being passes through. What has to be established is that when, as is usual, the process does not continue up to the achievement of virtue, it is better seen as an uncompleted movement towards virtue than as a completed movement towards something less.

The Stoics' account of the earlier stages of an individual's psychosocial development is extremely interesting in its own right. In the early stages of the life of any animal there is to be observed a pattern of behaviour which the Stoics discriminate with the help of a substantially original theoretical notion, *oikeiōsis*. The term is not easy to render satisfactorily into English. Its opposite, *allotriōsis*, has a meaning close to that of 'alienation'. At a psychological level, the relation is one of concern for, or 'identification' with, somebody or something; but the Stoic usage covers also what underlies the behaviour of non-human animals, so that those renderings are perhaps too narrow. Thus the translations 'orientation' and 'appropriation' are also sometimes used. In any case, the relation of *oikeiōsis* is expressed in impulses and attractions, and thence in actual behaviour.

However the relation is to be understood precisely, the animal is related in this way, according to the Stoics, to a gradually widening class of items. In the case of the human being, that class usually comes to embrace the family and the society. The actions towards which we are thus naturally motivated are 'proper functions' of humans; we naturally and rightly ascribe to them a certain kind of value.

At a certain stage in the maturing of a person's powers of understanding or reason, virtue becomes possible. Virtue is a disposition manifested in the consistent selection of what is, in the sense just explained, natural to us. Proper functions are not superseded by virtue; they remain as its raw material, the objects of the virtuous person's selections (LS 59A). Nevertheless, the value of proper functions is altogether transcended by the value of virtue. The actual performance of proper functions is not something good, in the sense in which the disposition of the virtuous person is good; it is merely a 'preferred indifferent' (LS 58A–C).

Stoic virtue, then, is both continuous and discontinuous with more widespread natural tendencies. It expresses itself in the selection of proper functions, and enables us to understand why we have the earlier natural impulses (LS 59D5–6). In this sense, virtue does belong to a process of development which is natural to us, even if as a stage which is rarely reached. But it has a kind of value which belongs to nothing else in human life. To recognize this disparity of value is, the Stoics maintain, essential to being virtuous: a virtuous person, though constant in their selection of proper functions, regards those proper functions only as 'to be preferred', and not as good.

The delicate distinctions implicit in such an outlook are elaborated in varying ways by Stoic writers (LS 58G, K). Their debates about how the virtuous person's judgements of value are most accurately to be described should be viewed in the light of a doctrine to which they are all committed, the doctrine that one is virtuous only if one is completely free of 'passions'. A passion is, or includes, an irrational value-judgement about its object; thus freedom from passion is one of the connotations of calling a virtuous person rational. To have a passion is to regard as good or bad something which is really indifferent (LS 65B). In condemning the passions, therefore, the Stoics are repudiating not feelings merely, but intellectual error. In fact, the Stoics recognize a class of 'good feelings'—joy, kindness, and others—which the virtuous person is likely to have. Their doctrine is less repressive than it initially looks.

The virtuous person's freedom from passion may be compared with the freedom from false belief which is required if a person is to be wise. If one is to have 'scientific knowledge' of any truth, one's grasp on that truth must be so secure as to be 'unchangeable by argument' (LS 41H1). But if one has any false belief, an argument which uses that belief as a premiss could perhaps disturb one's grasp on the truth in question. Wisdom therefore presupposes the complete and assured absence of error. The Stoics thought of the prerequisites of virtue in a similarly holistic way: the virtuous person is utterly consistent, and infallible in his impulses. To fall short of this condition in any way is to be ethically mediocre (*phaulos*), just as any line is crooked which fails, by however little, to be straight.

How comfortably can the Stoics' conviction of the uncommonness of virtue be adjusted to their cosmic optimism? If the cosmos is designed for the sake of rational beings, but the vast majority of humans fails to live the best kind of life, does this not suggest that the design is defective (LS 61N)? The Stoics will not admit this. They contend instead that the existence of some evil is compatible with the perfection of the cosmos as a whole. Chrysippus suggests that the existence of good actually presupposes that there also be evil (LS 54Q1). Cleanthes, in a gesture reminiscent of Heraclitus, speaks obscurely of the god as 'so welding into one all things good and bad that they all share in a single everlasting reason' (LS 54I3).

It might be thought that the Stoics could resolve the difficulty by assigning the blame exclusively to human beings. This would allow them to say that if the cosmos is not altogether perfect, that is no fault of the cosmic designer. But to do this would be to abandon a thesis to which, at least from the time of Chrysippus, the Stoics were very strongly wedded: every detail of what happens in the cosmos is governed by fate, the providential ordering of events which the Stoics readily speak of as identical with the god (LS 55N4, 46B1).

The doctrine of fate is part of what gives rise to a further criticism of Stoic ethics, one which Chrysippus in particular discusses at length. Epicureans (above, Section 1.2.4) and others argue that the all-pervasiveness of fate is incompatible with our being genuinely responsible for any of our conduct. More exactly, Chrysippus' view of fate is alleged to entail that nothing is *eph' hēmin* (up to us, attributable to us, in our power—in advance of interpretation of the arguments, each of these translations of the crucial phrase seems possible).

Before examining Chrysippus' attempted reconciliation of the two theses, it will be helpful to note his grounds for endorsing each of them. One of the chief grounds for saying that everything comes about through fate belongs to Stoic physics; another comes from logic. First, the world would be 'wrenched apart' if there were any uncaused motion (LS 55N2). Here, it is a distinctively Stoic conception of the unity of the cosmos which is relied upon. Secondly, the principle that every proposition is either true or false is held to imply that there is no motion without a cause, 'since anything lacking efficient causes will be neither true nor false . . . The result is that everything that happens happens through fate' (LS 38G). (Epicurus actually agrees about the implication, and therefore rejects the principle; LS 20E.)

The thesis of the all-pervasiveness of fate is often reiterated by the Stoics. And they are equally committed to the second thesis, that all our impulses to action are *eph' hēmin*. The controversial view that in rational animals no impulse occurs without assent serves in particular to support this commitment, which in its turn is taken to license the conclusion that virtue, and thus well-being, is in principle attainable by anyone (LS 62K).

One way of interpreting Chrysippus' approach to the problem is to see him as arguing that to determine need not be to constrain. Reading *eph' hēmin* as 'in our power', one can understand Chrysippus to maintain that although whatever impulses we have are determined by fate, it does not follow that we are forced to have those impulses, in the sense that they result from antecedent causes regardless of whether we assent or not (LS 55S3). Assent does contribute to the generation of behaviour; it is not a mere by-product. This is quite consistent with the Stoic principle that identical circumstances cannot produce contradictory results (LS 38H, 55N3). To say, then, that the virtues are in the power of those who have them is not to imply that it is also in such people's power to be bad (LS 61M).

This interpretation fits much of the surviving evidence well. It perhaps even explains some of the inconcinnities between the sources, as for instance regarding whether or not Chrysippus denies universal necessitation. If to necessitate is merely to determine, he does not deny it; but if it is to constrain, then he does.

However, some of the arguments reported seem ill-adapted to this strategy. It is notable, in the first place, how Chrysippus appears to refrain from saying explicitly that assent is always fated. This would be needless if his only concern were to insist that assent can be efficacious. Further, the above interpretation cannot easily explain why Chrysippus resists the conclusion of the much-debated 'Master Argument', which is that nothing is possible except what is or will be the case. Chrysippus is reported as wishing to say instead that some things which will never be the case are none the less possible (LS 38E3). Again, his elaborate classification of types of cause (e.g. LS 55I), while it could be used to corroborate a denial of constraint, is exploited, according to Cicero's report, to make a point which the above interpretation would not lead one to expect. The fate doctrine implies that everything comes about through 'antecedent' causes. Every impulse, in particular, has as antecedent cause an impression originating from the person's environment. But causes of this kind are not in general sufficient to produce their effects. Otherwise 'it *would* follow that, since these causes were not in our power, impulse would not be in our power either' (LS 62C6). This last remark in particular is hardly in keeping with the approach envisaged above. Perhaps a single, more complex interpretation of Chrysippus' thought can be arrived at. Or perhaps Chrysippus essayed alternative resolutions of the problem on different occasions. Certainly, the libertarian challenge is bound to be an abiding preoccupation for any ethics which asserts as unequivocally as does Stoic ethics both the omnipresence of fate and human beings' responsibility for the lives they live.

1.4. Scepticism

1.4.1. Introduction

The Greek thinkers nowadays known as the Sceptics do not constitute a single philosophical school in the sense in which the Epicureans and the Stoics do so. The term 'Sceptic' is primarily applied to two groups of philosophers. The first group comprises the leading figures of the Platonic Academy during the two centuries following the accession of Arcesilaus to the headship of the school in 273 BC. The most important of the Academic Sceptics besides Arcesilaus is Carneades, who led the school during the middle years of the second century. The Sceptics of the second group, called Pyrrhonists, include most notably the founding figure Aenesidemus (first century BC) and the much later Sextus Empiricus, whose surviving books *Outlines of Pyrrhonism* and *Against the Mathematicians*, written perhaps in the late second century AD, give us plentiful information about contemporary and earlier Sceptical practice.

These two groups of philosophers are historically connected by the fact that Aenesidemus was a member of the Academy who left the institution because of its gradual abandonment of the Sceptical approach to philosophy. The Pyrrhonists' Scepticism differs in some respects from that of Arcesilaus and Carneades, as will be seen. But it shares what are perhaps the two most distinctive characteristics of Academic Scepticism, namely their professed 'suspension of judgement about everything' and the practice of relentless argumentative opposition to the doctrinal commitments of other philosophers.

Scepticism thus conceived was initiated by Arcesilaus. In a looser sense of the term, however, scepticism was nothing new. Indeed, each of the two groups declared their fidelity to the outlook and practice of a philosopher from the past. The Academics professed to be reviving Plato's critical and aporetic approach to philosophy, which his immediate successors had neglected in favour of system construction. Similarly, when Aenesidemus called his own brand of Scepticism 'Pyrrhonist', he was declaring an affiliation to the philosopher Pyrrho of Elis (*c.*360–*c.*270), whose avoidance of theoretical commitment and whose supposed extraordinary tranquillity Aenesidemus took as a philosophical ideal.

Pyrrho resembles some still earlier thinkers such as Xenophanes and

Democritus in his pessimistic estimate of humans' capacities for knowledge. But a closer anticipation of the later sceptics' scruples on the subject of human knowledge is found in the statement of the Democritean Metrodorus that 'we know nothing, nor do we even know just this, that we know nothing'. This statement shows a concern to avoid the charge of implicit inconsistency that might be brought against a claim actually to know that nothing can be known. (The comparable claim, 'All I know is that I know nothing', is sometimes attributed to Socrates. But in Plato's account, at any rate, what Socrates says is rather more nuanced than this; see *Apology* 21d4–6, 23b2–4.) The charge of implicit inconsistency later gave rise to some of the subtlest of the exchanges between the Sceptics and their opponents.

The Greek term *skeptikos*, as applied to a tendency in philosophy, connotes the activity of considering or examining something. Sextus contrasts the Pyrrhonist, who 'persists in his investigations', both with those who cease investigating because they think they have discovered answers and with those who cease investigating because they have come to think discovery impossible (*Outlines of Pyrrhonism* 1.1–3). There is some reason to place the historical Pyrrho, as distinct from the later Pyrrhonists' Pyrrho, in the third of these classes of people, and thus to deny that he was in the strictest sense a Sceptic. However, the technical use of the word *skeptikos* does not appear to have been current before the first century AD. The commonest appellation for the Academic Sceptics was 'those who suspend judgement'. In addition, the Pyrrhonists held that the Academics' position was misdescribed by the Academics themselves. It is perhaps wise, therefore, to suspend judgement about the exact connotation of the label 'Sceptic', and proceed to investigate the philosophical stances of the Academics and Pyrrhonists themselves.

1.4.2. *Scepticism in the Academy*

The Academic Sceptic is devoted to the activity of opposing by argument the doctrines of other philosophers. In principle, this kind of critique was directed at any conclusion advocated by any philosopher. In practice, it was the Stoics who found themselves most of all assailed by Arcesilaus and his successors. The Academics wish to confute their opponents without relying on any alternative philosophical views. For this reason, Academic arguments are typically *ad hominem*, in the sense that their premisses are such as the proponents of the doctrine being attacked cannot well reject. Thus anti-Stoic arguments use, as far as possible, premisses which the Stoics use in their own arguments. Naturally, many of these premisses are expressed in the distinctive technical vocabulary of the Stoics. Likewise, the Academics' replies to Stoic counter-attacks frequently exploit the terms of the Stoics' own epistemology. The study of Academic Scepticism thus cannot be divorced from that of Stoic epistemology.

There is, superficially, a conflict among our reports of the Academics' argumentative procedure. Both Arcesilaus and Carneades are described sometimes as arguing exclusively against theses, sometimes as specializing in argument both for and against a single thesis (LS 68D, L, M; 31OP). The puzzle is perhaps best dissolved by distinguishing between a proposition and the endorsement of that proposition. The Academics argued against, not for, other philosophers' endorsements of propositions; and they did so, frequently, by putting forward both an argument which concludes with the relevant proposition and an argument which concludes with its contradictory. The latter technique is designed to lead the hearer to find that there are reasons of equal weight on the two sides, and consequently to withhold assent from both propositions alike. In many cases, of course, half of the job has already been done before the Sceptic goes to work. This is so in the case of, for instance, debate about the existence of gods (LS 70C) and about whether everything happens through fate (LS 70G). The same pattern is exhibited in what is in some ways the pivotal Stoic–Sceptic debate, regarding the existence of 'cognitive impressions' (though it is perhaps somewhat controversial to say that the Academics suspend judgement about, as opposed to denying, their existence).

The philosophical setting of the dispute about cognitive impressions is, as mentioned above, the epistemology of the Stoics. When a Stoic speaks about a person's 'impressions' (*phantasiai*), what is being referred is how things appear to the person. If one has a visual impression of white, it looks to one as if there is something white that one is seeing. Not all impressions are perceptual: if a certain argument strikes one as fallacious, that is equally a case of one's having an impression. The Stoics insist that to have an impression that something is so is not yet to believe it to be so. For instance, one may find that something which one does not believe to be white nevertheless looks as if it were; one has the impression of white. According to the Stoics, one only has a belief if, in addition to having a certain impression, one assents to that impression. Assents, unlike impressions, are 'in our power' (*eph' hēmin*; see above, Section 1.3.4); so, therefore, are beliefs, together with any consequent impulses to action.

The Stoics rely on this doctrine of assent for their assurance that 'scientific knowledge' (*epistēmē*) is something attainable, despite the apparently exorbitant requirements they impose for its achievement. Having scientific knowledge is incompatible with having any false beliefs at all, since false beliefs undermine the invulnerability to refutation by argument which the wise man must have (see above, Section 1.3.4). But how is the wise man to avoid ever assenting to a false impression? The Sceptics' suggestion, naturally, is that the wise man does so by never assenting to any impressions. The Stoics, however, taking it that the wise man knows, and hence assents to, a whole raft of true propositions about the world, propose as their solution that there exists a 'criterion of truth' on which the wise man relies, namely the 'cognitive' (*katalēptikē*) impression. There is a certain kind of impression, that is to say, which is true in every instance; and human beings have the capacity, given sufficient self-discipline, to avoid assenting to any impressions but these. Cognitive impressions are thus stipulated to be perfectly reliable, and such as can be discriminated by the human mind. And the question which is at issue between the Stoics and the Sceptics is, simply: is there really any such kind of impression?

For the Stoics, it is to be expected that there are such impressions, given the generally providential character of nature (LS 40K6, N3; cf. 57A2). But they do not rely on this general point alone. They describe a type of impression which, they think, can plausibly be regarded as being, in the required way, both infallible and discriminable. Zeno provides the specifics: an impression is cognitive just when (to abbreviate LS 40E3) it corresponds completely to the object which causes it. Cognitive impressions are detailed and striking in a way in which no other impressions are. This is what makes them discriminable, so that the wise man can avoid assenting to any others. It is necessary, however, if cognitive impressions are also to be infallibly true, that the causing object not be misidentified with another of its kind. The impression that one is seeing an egg avoids misidentifying the egg because it does not identify the egg at all. But, as Carneades argued, the impression that one is seeing the same egg one saw a minute ago, and not a second egg instead, is not guaranteed to be correct by the thoroughness with which impressions (and memories of them?) can reproduce the features of eggs unless the Stoics are granted their metaphysical thesis that any two distinct objects can in principle be perceived to be dissimilar. The principle of the identity of indiscernibles (see above, Section 1.3.2) is thus shown by the Academics to be essential to the Stoics' case for the cognitive impression; and it was a principle which the Academics continued to resist.

The Academics do not recognize the Stoic criterion, and they require the Stoics to acknowledge that if there is no criterion, the wise man will never assent, but always suspend judgement. And they themselves purport to suspend judgement about everything; it is not merely a position to which they attempt to commit the Stoics. Their reasons for doing so appear to include some that are in a broad sense ethical, such as the unworthiness of a philosopher' believing anything on authority (LS 68Q). But one might doubt whether it is actually possible for a person constantly to suspend judgement about everything. The commonest form of Stoic counter-attack upon the Academics maintains that total suspension of judgement must result in total inactivity. Carneades responds by describing in detail how, on Stoic premisses, reasonable conduct is possible even if there is no criterion of the Stoic kind. It is a matter of following, without assenting to, impressions of a kind which, in an extremely acute discussion, Carneades classifies as 'convincing, undiverted and thoroughly explored' (LS 69D–E).

Read out of context, this rejoinder of Carneades could be taken for a rather cogent description of how one can live by the guidance of fallible beliefs. Might one suspend judgement, in the Academics' sense, and yet retain beliefs? The suggestion is probably at odds with Carneades' intentions. (It should be noted that the phrase 'suspension of judgement' renders a single word in Greek (*epochē*) which often carries the bare meaning of 'refraining'; that the translation has the separable component 'judgement' is thus somewhat misleading.) But the later Academic Philo of Larissa did incorporate Carneades' classifications into an epistemology which repudiates the cognitive impression but explicitly sanctions beliefs. This was the climate of thought in the Academy just prior to Aenesidemus' founding of Pyrrhonism.

1.4.3. *The Pyrrhonists*

The Pyrrhonist Sceptics, like the Academics, cultivate suspension of judgement, arguing unflaggingly against the doctrines of other philosophers. They differ from their predecessors, however, in at least two ways. First, they link suspension of judgement with the transquillity (*ataraxia*) for which non-Sceptical philosophers vainly search: upon suspension of judgement, they say, tranquillity 'follows like a shadow' (LS 71A3). Secondly, the argumentative method of the Pyrrhonists is shaped to a high degree by systematic methodological reflection, which produced, for instance, the accounts of the diverse 'modes' for suspension of judgement expounded in Sextus and other sources.

These two characteristics of Pyrrhonism both emerge in the work of Aenesidemus, and they appear to be connected: sceptical arguments become sophisticated tools with which to attain and preserve tranquillity. According to Aenesidemus, the celebrated imperturbability of Pyrrho was not a mere quirk of his personality. The Pyrrhonist finds from his own experience that to entertain Sceptical arguments and be forced to suspend judgement does regularly have the welcome consequence of tranquillity. He thus comes to look upon such arguments as tools, or drugs, by which the permanently vulnerable condition of 'dogmatism' can be kept at bay. It is natural, therefore, for the Pyrrhonist to wish to develop his skill in inducing suspension of judgement in others and renewing it in himself. The exhaustive classification of types of Sceptical argument subserves a psychotherapeutic technique.

Sextus defines the Pyrrhonist's skill as follows: 'Scepticism is an ability to set out oppositions among things which appear and are thought of in any way at all, an ability by which, because of the equipollence in the opposed objects and accounts, we come first to suspension of judgement and afterwards to tranquillity' (*Outlines* I. 8). 'Oppositions' may be of various kinds: 'the same wine appears sour to people who have just eaten dates or figs, but it seems to be sweet to people who have consumed nuts or chickpeas' (I. 110); 'against those who seek to establish that there is providence from the orderliness of the heavenly bodies, we oppose the view that often the good do badly while the bad do well' (I. 32). Given such oppositions, the Pyrrhonist finds himself unable either to affirm or to deny that there really is providence, or that the wine is sour, or sweet, in its own nature.

The available kinds of opposition are sorted in numerous ways by our texts. The ten 'modes' probably introduced by Aenesidemus are mainly concerned with the ways things appear to the senses, and distinguish ten sources of variation in the way an object may be perceived. How an object appears depends on the medium in which it is presented, on the condition of the observer, and so forth. In the conflicts engendered by each of these kinds of variation, the Pyrrhonist finds the conflicting appearances 'equipollent', that is, equal in strength. This is ostensibly a mere report: in the Pyrrhonist's experience, once the conflict is exposed, neither of the appearances is 'convincing'. There is no direct appeal to grounds for suspending judgement, no assertion that only the Sceptic's response is justified, or correct. In practice, however, the Pyrrhonist recognizes that frequently the partisan of a given view will not be silenced simply by having a contrary appearance brought to his attention. Thus Sextus will explore the further arguments by which one of the conflicting appearances might be preferred. The five modes attributed to a certain Agrippa assist the Sceptic to formulate a counter-argument, and thereby to restore equipollence. One of these modes exposes circularity in the partisan's argument, another arbitrariness, another infinite regress; there is some overlap with the ten modes mentioned above (I. 164–77).

Most of the examples given in Sextus' exposition of the Pyrrhonist's method concern the supposedly perceptible properties of things. Elsewhere in Sextus' writings, however, where the techniques are actually put to use, the beliefs attacked are generally beliefs peculiar to philosophers and scientists. This fact encourages an interpretation of Pyrrhonism as less radical than it is sometimes thought to be. According to such an interpretation, the Pyrrhonist abjures all theoretical views as to how things are 'in nature', but does not for that reason refrain from 'everyday' beliefs, for instance about how things appear to people.

The interpretation is tempting. The recurrent 'relativity' arguments (e.g. I. 137–40) seem more powerful if directed against claims to a 'pure grasp' of how things are in themselves, 'independently'. Besides, at I. 13, Sextus distinguishes a broader and a narrower way of taking the term 'belief' (*dogma*), and confines his disavowal of belief to the latter, 'the sense in which some say that belief is assent to some unclear object of investigation in the sciences'.

The passage is, however, somewhat exceptional. More usually, Sextus insists on a contrast, even in relation to what 'appears' to the Sceptic at a given moment, between ordinary assertion and the Sceptic's attitude of 'acquiescence' or non-rejection. This contrast is commonly read as equivalent to the earlier-mentioned Stoic contrast (Section 1.4.2) between having and assenting to an impression (the Stoics' 'impression' and the Pyrrhonists' 'appearance' are cognate terms in Greek).

Discussion of the question whether the Pyrrhonist rejects all beliefs should not, of course, proceed as if the notion of belief were itself entirely clear. A thorough investigation of what the ancient Sceptics have to say can hardly avoid raising issues in the philosophy of mind. In this connection, it is notable that Sextus frequently represents the kind of *dogma* which the Pyrrhonist shuns as something active. More fully, the judgements and assertions from which the Pyrrhonist refrains are such as can be accepted or rejected on the strength of reasoning. In respect of other states, however, the person is passive; this is the province of 'appearance'. What is characteristic of the Pyrrhonist is to yield to these appearances. Reasoning never leads him to respond actively to them by way of endorsement or rejection.

To be in this sense consistently passive is not to be inert. In 'following appearance', one is led by hunger, for instance, to eat and by thirst to drink. Pyrrhonism from its beginnings is presented as a viable way of life. Aenesidemus did not accept the stories representing Pyrrho as having been a hopelessly impractical person. There is no reason why the Pyrrhonist should not react adeptly to changes in the appearances.

A potentially more telling objection to this passive way of life concerns the future. If not incapable of action, must not the Pyrrhonist be at least seriously improvident? Might not his circumstances change without warning for the worse? It is difficult not to see Pyrrhonist attitudes as making a person vulnerable—to the risk, if of nothing else, of succumbing in the face of new arguments to dogmatism, with a consequent loss of his prized tranquillity. The presumable answer to this challenge is a characteristic 'perhaps'. The Pyrrhonist will not deny that the future may differ from the past in such a way as to make his present habits unfortunate; but it is a possibility by which he finds himself unconcerned. This answer satisfies those who are already Pyrrhonists, but can hardly render the way of life attractive to others. It is no accident that Sextus says that it is by accident that some philosophers have come to be Pyrrhonists: 'For Sceptics began to do philosophy in order to decide among appearances and to apprehend which are true and which false, so as to become tranquil; but they came upon equipollent dispute, and being unable to decide this they suspended judgement. And when they suspended judgement, tranquillity in matters of opinion followed fortuitously' (i. 25).

2. PHILOSOPHY IN LATER ANTIQUITY

2.1. Introduction

The resurgence of doctrinal Platonism which inaugurated a new phase in ancient philosophy received its first large impetus from Antiochus' refounding of the 'Old Academy' in *c.*87 BC. Later in the same century, the greatly increased dissemination of Aristotle's philosophical work which resulted from the editing of his then little-known 'esoteric', or school, writings by Andronicus of Rhodes similarly revived the appeal of Aristotelianism. The works of both Plato and Aristotle continued to be studied and admired throughout the following six centuries.

Stoicism and Epicureanism retained a substantial independent following until the third century AD. That century may be regarded as a further watershed in the evolution of ancient philosophy, since the movement nowadays known as Neoplatonism originated then in the work of Plotinus (204/5–270), and since at the same time Origen (185–253) made the first major Christian contribution to the philosophers' discipline. These facts have encouraged some historians of philosophy to distinguish a first, 'eclectic' period (Antiochus himself subscribed to a hybrid Platonism, in which a Stoic strain was especially prominent) from a second period dominated by Neoplatonism. However, the thought of Plotinus hardly marks a radical break with the 'Middle Platonism' of Antiochus' successors; and, more importantly, elements of Stoic and, especially, of Aristotelian philosophy lived on as components of the Neoplatonic outlook.

There is thus a substantial continuity in the style of philosophy from the first century BC right through to the sixth century AD. The following are two typifying features: philosophers were disposed to find a high degree of 'harmony' between the outlooks of thinkers who had earlier been regarded as in rivalry with one another; and commentary on earlier philosophical texts became a favoured mode of writing. In addition, differences of religious allegiance became a significant factor in philosophical debate.

The harmony thesis, explicitly advanced as regards Plato and Aristotle by, for instance, Porphyry in the third century, and occurring in more extravagant versions from Antiochus to Proclus (*c*.410–85), was normally combined, as one would expect, with endorsement of the harmonized views. The attitude of respect for the philosophies of distant precursors was not of course entirely new. But what distinguishes the majority of later authors from the Pyrrhonists and Hellenistic thinkers is the inclusiveness of their approbations. Among the Neoplatonists from Porphyry onwards, the conventional form of this attitude took Aristotle's logic and some of his physics to be a vital supplement (in the curriculum of the schools, an appropriate preliminary study) to the ethical and metaphysical truths discoverable from Plato's writings.

The genre of philosophical commentary originated in the first century BC in the writings of Andronicus. His commentary on the *Categories* of Aristotle was particularly widely emulated in the succeeding decades. The *Categories* was to remain a favourite work for commentators, and among Plato's works the *Timaeus* was a comparable focus of interest. Some of the most distinguished later commentaries on Aristotle were written from a specifically Peripatetic viewpoint; an example is the work of Alexander of Aphrodisias (fl. *c*.AD 200). But Aristotle's writings continued to be as much the subject of commentaries as Plato's after the third century, from which time the commentators were all, with the occasional exception such as Themistius in the mid-fourth century, more or less orthodox Neoplatonists. In due course, 'secondary' works, such as

Porphyry's *Introduction* to the *Categories*, were themselves commented upon, as in the particularly influential Latin work of Boethius (*c*.480–524).

Boethius was a Christian Neoplatonist. Many other Christian writers before him had incorporated Neoplatonic ethics and metaphysics into their outlooks. Origen, for example, offered allegorical interpretations of the Christian Scriptures which were thoroughly imbued with Platonism. (The earliest model for this enterprise was the similar treatment of the Hebrew Bible, two centuries earlier, by Philo of Alexandria.) Origen's work was later attacked as heterodox; but an equal approval of Neoplatonist theory is manifest in the less contentious writings of many of his Greek successors, such as Gregory of Nyssa (*c*.331–96). The Latin writer Augustine (354–430) became cooler towards Neoplatonism in later life; but his earlier works represent well the eirenic strand among Christian philosophers, in taking Platonist theology to be not misguided but merely incomplete.

Relations between Christian and pagan writers were of course more polemical in so far as the latter advocated polytheistic beliefs and ritual. This pattern may be illustrated on the Christian side by Origen's *Against Celsus* and on the pagan side by Porphyry's *Against the Christians*. Later Neoplatonists of the Syrian and Athenian schools tended to favour an integration of philosophical activity with pagan religious practices, and the consequent hostility of the Christians led eventually to the emperor Justinian's prohibition of the Academy's teaching activity in 529. The more accommodating school of Alexandria escaped this fate, and appears to have survived, though eventually under Christian leadership, until the city was taken by the Arabs in 640.

One noteworthy example of a philosophical dispute in the context of opposed religious affiliations is associated with the Alexandrian Christian John Philoponus (*c*.490–*c*.575). In his *Against Proclus on the Eternity of the World* and later works, he makes an organized and distinctly original attack on central theses of Aristotelian physics long since adopted by Platonists. As the title just cited indicates, some of Philoponus' arguments concern topics whose Christian resonances are apparent; he also, however, develops anti-Aristotelian positions in dynamics and element theory.

The philosophical views of Plotinus and Augustine are further expounded below. They are selected for special discussion in part because of the great subsequent influence of their writings. But it should be emphasized that in the work of authors such as Alexander, Origen, Boethius, and Philoponus, the period contains many other distinguished contributions to philosophy.

2.2. Plotinus

Among the Greek philosophers of antiquity, there are just two of whom it can be said with confidence that their entire written output has been preserved.

Plato is one of these; the other is Plotinus. The forty-odd treatises posthumously edited as the *Enneads* by his pupil Porphyry were composed between 253 and 270, in the latter part of Plotinus' life, when he lived in Rome as the respected leader of a school of Platonists. Before his move to Rome, Plotinus was for eleven years a disciple of the now obscure philosopher Ammonius in Alexandria; and he may well have been a native of Egypt, though his cultural background was Greek. Valuable information about Plotinus' character and teaching methods is to be found in the *Life* which Porphyry wrote for publication with the *Enneads*.

Plotinus' philosophical work has an elevated purpose. He wishes to elaborate and defend against objections a Platonic conception of reality, with a view to liberating the person from the body and from time. With the help of appropriate intellectual and moral disciplines, one can 'lead back the divine in oneself to the divine in the All'. This compound purpose was shared by the readers for whom Plotinus primarily wrote: his treatises were composed for the benefit of adherents of the school, and their early circulation appears to have been fairly restricted. Individual treatises thus examine specific problems against a background of agreed theory. This procedure does not, however, detract greatly from the philosophical worth of Plotinus' writings, since the treatises collectively deal with a wide range of topics, so that most aspects of the agreed theory are probed for their difficulties and obscurities; and Plotinus addresses these with a high degree of intellectual honesty.

A further reason why the treatises are not organized by a single expository design is that their author viewed them as supplements to an existing body of writing with which his readers were already somewhat familiar. An acquaintance with the works of Plato is obviously of great assistance to the modern reader of Plotinus, not least as indicating how selectively Platonic doctrine is drawn upon by later Platonists. In addition, several of Plotinus' most important themes are actually of Aristotelian rather than Platonic ancestry. A brief outline follows of those among the philosophical views central to Plotinus' thought which would nowadays be regarded as genuinely having been held by either Plato or Aristotle. Many of the views mentioned require a good deal more explanation than they will receive here; but the sense they bear for Plotinus at any rate will become more apparent in the next section.

First, there is the belief in Platonic forms (*eidē*), changeless, non-spatial entities which, though not sense-perceptible, are accessible to thought. Sense-perceptible things are in various ways ontologically inferior to forms, and such understanding as we can have of sense-perceptible things is always by reference to forms. One form, the form of the good, stands in a relation to the other forms somewhat similar to the relation in which forms generally stand to the sense-perceptible. The form of the good is thus the ultimate source of such intelligibility and being as anything else has. The human soul (which is independent of the human body and indeed immortal; thus there is no harm in a Platonist context in rendering the term *psuchē* by 'soul') can enjoy knowledge of the forms to the extent that it is purified and dissociated from the body; and it is philosophy which effects this release into bliss. As the human soul orders and sustains the human organism, so the sense-perceptible world as a whole is ordered and sustained by a soul. And the entire spatio-temporal cosmos, including the world-soul, is the product of the operation of a divine intellect which knows the forms, and is guided in its operation by this knowledge.

Aristotle too uses the term *eidos* very frequently in his philosophical works. Plotinus takes it that some at least of Aristotle's views about forms can be conjoined with Platonic theses. He adopts Aristotelian views in two areas in particular. First, physical objects are compounds of form and matter. So Plotinus distinguishes the sense-perceptible forms which exist 'here' in bodies from the intelligible forms which have an independent, non-spatial existence 'there'. Secondly, Plotinus falls in with certain views about intelligible forms which Aristotle expresses in some difficult passages of *De Anima* 3. 4–6 and *Metaphysics* 12. 7 and 9. There is, according to Aristotle, a species of thought (*noēsis*, intellection) in which the intellect takes on the intelligible form of the object of thought. If the object of thought is something 'without matter' (as a Platonic form would be), the thinking is identical with the activity or actuality (*energeia*) of the object of thought. Furthermore, intellection in humans, or the activity of the human intellect, occurs only thanks to the activity of a distinct and unintermittently active intellect. Finally, Aristotle speaks of his divinity as itself being intellection, and is ready to conclude that, since intellection of something immaterial is identical with its object, the divine thought, which is immaterial, in some sense thinks itself.

In the light of the above appropriations, it is not surprising that according to Plotinus the forms envisaged by Plato are objects of intellection for, and do not exist externally to, the divine intellect. This view had in fact become usual among Platonists well before Plotinus' time; it is expressed, for example, by Philo of Alexandria in the early first century AD. A cardinal theme of Plotinus which is, on the face of it, much more innovative is that intellect and intelligible forms are ontologically secondary to something which is not a form and is not a possible object for intellect. This first principle of Plotinian metaphysics, the One, has somewhat the role of Plato's form of the good; and Plotinus finds his own view adumbrated in discussions of 'the One' in Plato's dialogue *Parmenides*, as well as in Aristotle's account of Plato's ontology (see *Metaphysics* 1. 6). It will become evident, however, from the following exposition that those antecedents were considerably embellished, at least, in Plotinus' articulation of what he took to be the spirit of Plato's thought.

2.2.1. *The Framework*

Plotinus' own philosophical system is most easily explored, and his originality and philosophical acumen best appreciated, if one begins by observing how a small number of highly general views serve as an abiding framework within which arguments on specific topics are pursued. These views regularly furnish Plotinus with premisses in his examinations of philosophical problems. This is not to say that they are merely assumed, but Plotinus' grounds for accepting them are exhibited only piecemeal; for the most part, they are taken not to need further recommendation.

Plotinus' treatments of philosophical issues are guided not only by this framework of theoretical convictions but also by reflection upon his not infrequent mystical experiences. He interpreted these as experiences of ascent to and union with a timeless reality. In his writings, therefore, philosophical reasoning has the double task of resolving difficulties in Platonist metaphysics and of making sense, as far as possible, of a special sort of experience.

A first large theoretical premiss concerns the correlation between the degrees of a number of what one might loosely call positive properties. Being, unity, goodness, power, and self-sufficiency all admit of degrees, in Plotinus' view, and (with a qualification to be mentioned shortly) their degrees are in every instance correlated, in the sense that however one entity stands in comparison with another in respect of one of these scalar properties it also stands comparatively in respect of the others. Whatever is more unified is more self-sufficient; whatever is less powerful is less real; and so forth. (Difference in degree of unity is illustrated, in Ennead 6. 9. 1, by the instances of a chorus, an undivided physical object, and a soul. The notion that being has degrees is more problematic, though of course it is far from being peculiar to Plotinus. There is something to be said, in his case at least, for taking the association of being with goodness, power, and self-sufficiency to be conceptual, so that to say that one item has more being than another in part *means* that it is better and/or more powerful and/or more self-sufficient.)

The correlation principle is not asserted in its full generality by Plotinus. It would perhaps be prudent, therefore, to say only that Plotinus habitually proceeds as if he took it to be assertible; each time he adverts to a subsidiary generalization of the kind just illustrated, he endorses it. The endorsement is sometimes supported by argument; see, besides 6. 9. 1 on unity and goodness, 3. 6. 6 on being and self-sufficiency and 1. 8. 2 on goodness and self-sufficiency.

A second guiding premiss is that there exists something perfectly self-sufficient on which everything else that exists depends: it is not the case that everything, without exception, is dependent on other things, but nor is it the case that more than one thing is entirely independent. From this second premiss, taken together with the above-described correlation between self-sufficiency and unity, it follows that the 'first principle' (*archē*) of everything is entirely 'one'.

Plotinus' theorizing is thus guided by at least four major considerations. There is the correlation between degrees of being, goodness, etc., and the requirement of a first principle which is perfectly self-sufficient. There is the fact that we are presented through perception with a temporally and spatially differentiated world of bodies. And finally there is the discovery that one can have an experience as of union with something timelessly perfect.

2.2.2. *Ontology*

What more can be said about the first principle? From the proposition that it is altogether 'one', Plotinus concludes that it is utterly free of multiplicity. This conclusion perhaps does not rest entirely on the supposition that multiplicity is opposed to unity; there are many indications that Plotinus did not think of that opposition as simply a matter of inverse proportion. A further ground, glimpsed at 5. 1. 9 and 5. 3. 12, is that multiplicity would admit an unsatisfactory contingency to the first principle of everything. Thus Plotinus postulates the non-spatial and non-temporal 'One', which is without parts and without stages. As non-multiple, however, the One must be formless. Agreeing with Plato that it is intelligible forms which are fully real, Plotinus holds that the formless One is therefore 'beyond being', as indeed the form of the good is mysteriously said to be by Plato at *Republic* 509b. (Here is the qualification of the first premiss referred to above: the perfectly real falls short of being perfectly one.)

The *Enneads* distribute the existents posterior to the One into three ontological domains. These are, in order, intellect, soul, and body. Many further discriminations are made, especially in the domain of soul, and the domains overlap in complex ways; but Plotinus adheres to the same broad divisions throughout. The divine intellect, like the One, is timeless. (Plotinus is unprecedentedly explicit in distinguishing the everlasting from the strictly timeless; 3. 7.) Souls, like bodies, have a temporal existence, but are unlike bodies in having no spatial properties.

These several domains are ordered, in Plotinus' view, in respect of the degree of unity of the items they contain. There are, for instance, exclusion relations of various kinds which are said to hold only among bodies. If a body is entirely present at a certain place, then it is absent from other places and other bodies are absent from that place; whereas a soul may be entirely present at more than one place. Temporality imports a kind of multiplicity to the existence of bodies and souls alike: thus a certain condition of the soul excludes, and is liable to be ousted by, another condition. The contents of the divine intellect, by contrast, display no such competitiveness: intellect in some sense is the forms it timelessly contemplates, and all of its contents are 'seen in' each of them. This elusive

Plotinian conception develops from, among other abstract inclusion relations, those of genus and species (4. 9. 2) and of axiom and theorem (4. 3. 2.).

The peculiar combination of unity and multiplicity in the divine intellect helps to make it hospitable also to the individual intellect, and thus to account for the possibility of the individual soul's mystical ascent. Plotinus' conception of the soul appears to vary in some respects between different treatises. He explores a variety of distinctions, in the case of a single person, between souls or parts of souls, in which the 'higher' governs, without being affected by, the 'lower'. A further index of the sophistication of Plotinus' psychological inquiries is provided by his vocabulary: he employs the term *autos* in a manner which invites the translation 'self', and discusses the question what it is that first-person pronouns should strictly be understood to refer to. The mystical experience—a true waking-up, in which one rises 'not with but from' the body (3. 6. 6, line 72)—is presented as a species of self-discovery. Plotinus holds that there is a part of the soul which is 'undescended' from the domain of intellect (4. 8. 8), and when considering in 5. 7 whether there are intelligible forms of individuals he answers in the affirmative: the divine intellect contains not only the form of man but also the form of, for example, Socrates (but consider also the later and apparently more equivocal 6. 2. 22).

2.2.3. Dependence

The items at the different ontological levels are linked by relations of dependence. The less real depend on the more real, but not conversely. The human organism depends on the soul, and the physical world as a whole depends on a soul which Plotinus commonly refers to as 'nature'. All kinds of soul depend upon intellect, and the individual human soul in particular depends on that aspect of the person which remains in the domain of intellect. And intellect as a whole depends on the One. In view of the heterogeneity of these cases, it would not be surprising if Plotinus thought that no more specific characterization could be given of all instances of ontological dependence. He does, however, apply quite uniformly a metaphor of emanation or radiation, in which the higher and lower entities are respectively a light-source and the illumination for which it is responsible. If it can be established what this view comes to in more literal terms, there is the prospect of subjecting the several dependence claims just reported to some sort of critical evaluation.

One suggestion which would presumably not be acceptable to Plotinus is to analyse the assertion of ontological dependence in counterfactual terms. To say that one entity depends on another just if it would not exist if the other did not exist would, apart from other difficulties, fail to capture the asymmetry of the Plotinian relation. This is because the existence of the physical world is regarded by Plotinus as inevitable: the power and goodness of what is timeless is such that there cannot but issue from it a spatio-temporal world of perceptible forms in matter (4. 8. 6). Plotinus might therefore hesitate to say that if the physical world did not exist, the One would nevertheless remain. The counterfactual reading does not sufficiently contrast the One's independence with other things' dependence.

Nor can Plotinus think of lower entities' dependence as consisting in their being caused to come into existence by events at higher levels, since the very lowest of the dependents, matter, is everlasting (4. 3. 9). He does, however, think of bodies, for instance, as receiving being from souls in the sense not of being produced but of being sustained in existence by them. Temporal items in general 'acquire' being continually (3. 7. 4, line 19).

At the heart of Plotinus' non-metaphorical construal of emanation or radiation is the thesis that the higher gives being to the lower by contemplating. Intellect's devotion to contemplative activity has soul as a by-product (*parergon*; 3. 8. 8, line 26), and soul sustains the corporeal in a similar fashion. At each level, the sustained is an image of what sustains it. The image's degree of being is in proportion to the adequacy of the contemplation which gives rise to it, and that in turn is limited by the contemplator's degree of being. At the bottom of this scale of dependence, bodies are incapable of any contemplation and incapable, consequently, of imparting being in this way to anything further. Above this level, the contemplator receives its generative power by being 'turned' towards what is more real. The whole sustaining process thus has as its ultimate source the One.

Fantastical as it might at first appear to be, this hypothesis resembles in some respects Aristotle's account of how the divine intellect teleologically explains celestial motion. Like that account, it promises to show how the changeless can be a cause of the changing, namely, by being an object of thought and of desire. The soul can, after all, be altered by its loving contemplation of the timeless intellect and, mediately, of the One. (As in Aristotle's case, it might be objected that the explanation does not require that the postulated cause actually exist. But if a similar objection could eventually be upheld against Plotinus, it would be his whole system which was damaged thereby, and not this hypothesis about the manner of dependence in particular.)

One model of Plotinus' hypothesis, and his chief resort for the hypothesis's empirical corroboration, is in the field of human action. The soul's thinking in a certain way about a given kind of bodily motion can cause bodily motion of that kind—as when one carries out an intention to wink. Plotinus dwells particularly on the example of artistic production, although the artist's physical handling of the product is one of the features which his extrapolation does not preserve. He attributes a contemplation of the artist's kind to the 'vegetative' soul in us which is responsible for processes of nutrition and growth. In reply to the charge that nature does not consciously reason when producing, Plotinus stoutly replies that this is a mark of the excellence of nature's contemplative activity: nature is not so incompetent as to need to deliberate (4. 3. 18), and we are familiar from our own experience with how some mental activities can be interfered with by our consciousness (*parakolouthia*; the term connotes following alongside) of them (1. 4. 9–10). A modern analogy for Plotinus' approach is supplied by the biologist's notion of genetic instructions or information: the vegetative soul in its contemplation takes on, and propagates, form.

Plotinus accepts that his theory is hardly tenable if the by-products of contemplation are not ascribed some such resemblance to what sustains them as the artist's product has to the content of the artist's creative thoughts (consider, besides the characteristic terms 'image' and 'trace', 3. 8. 5, line 23 and 4. 3. 10, line 35 on 'homogeneity'). Now what appears to make this requirement particularly troublesome is the supposition that the ultimate source of productive power is the One. In so far as it is describable at all, the One is, for the present purpose, disconcertingly simple. By contrast, its first dependant, intellect, comprises all intelligible forms in their surely complex mutual relations. How could it be an image of the One?

Plotinus appears to have two options here. He could, and sometimes does, maintain, in line with the framing presupposition described earlier, that, in respect of degree of goodness, power, and self-sufficiency, intellect has as much affinity to the One as anything distinct from the One can possibly have. Alternatively, he could appeal to the One's ineffability, as ensuring that the general thesis that products are images is at least not refuted by the particular case of intellect's relation to the One. He does frequently insist that it is an error to predicate anything at all of the One: it incorrectly imports plurality to describe the One as self-aware, or even to describe it as one (6. 9. 5)! In a neighbouring passage (6. 9. 3, lines 49–50), however, Plotinus says that to speak of the One specifically as cause is not to predicate something of it in the way he thinks impermissible. It is tempting to wonder whether this difficult remark would be applicable also to the ascriptions of goodness and power to the One about which Plotinus has comparatively few compunctions: it is as the source of other things' goodness and power that the One is surpassingly good and powerful. If this is right, however, circularity threatens. It appears that the ground for holding that intellect derives its perfection and power from contemplation of the One is that the One is surpassingly good and powerful, while the ground (and maybe the whole content) of this latter claim is that it imparts perfection and power to intellect. Perhaps Plotinus would concede that at this point argument needs to be supplemented, if not supplanted, by experience.

2.2.4. *Evil*

Another line of criticism of the view that the spatio-temporal world consists of more or less adequate images of the timeless and perfect, given off by activities of contemplation, concerns apparent evil. The critic asks what, according to this view, is 'responsible for the evils that man does and suffers' (1. 1. 9). Plotinus considers the question in a variety of places, including the treatise on providence (3. 2–3), the treatise (2. 9) against the Gnostics, who refused to regard the maker of this world as good, and several treatises concerning the underlying matter of all perceptible things (2. 4, 3. 6, 1. 8).

Plotinus' conception of matter is in some respects close to that of Aristotelians such as Alexander of Aphrodisias. As that which persists through every change undergone by any kind of body, matter is supposedly 'without qualities'; and this is understood to entail that matter is without size and is not even corporeal (e.g. 2. 4. 8). Plotinus is willing to describe matter as evil, but the main burden of the *Enneads'* discussions is that we are prone for various reasons to overestimate its reality. (Note also that the word translated 'evil' is just the usual Greek contrary of 'good'; we should be somewhat cautious, therefore, of contrasts between the evil and the merely poor or bad.)

Many but not all of Plotinus' observations seem to belong to a line of approach which several points mentioned above might lead one to expect of him. The framing premiss which correlates degrees of being and goodness suggests the specific claim that whatever is to any extent real is also to some extent good. If it is next asked why the world should contain at all some of its least good components, Plotinus has a Platonic precedent for saying that one of the excellences of reality is its 'completeness', its lacking nothing (2. 9. 4; compare *Timaeus* 41b–c). As a consequence of the One's limitless creativity, being is sustained as far as possible in every domain, from the intellect down to matter (5. 2. 2). (And it is supposed to be admirable in the One that it 'cannot leave anything without a share of itself' (4. 8. 6, 16).) Plotinus exploits aesthetic analogies for the claim that the excellence of a whole may be enhanced by its having as a part something whose existence, if considered in isolation, would seem regrettable, though at 3. 2. 14 he allows himself to say, with questionable consistency, that any gain in beauty by a part increases the beauty of the whole.

Taken together, these points invite the conclusion that any removal from nature of its less digestible ingredients would testify against rather than in favour of the power or goodness of the One. However, Plotinus' discussions have in places a different tendency. He attributes many of the facts for which the Gnostics demand an explanation either to the 'audacity' of imperfect beings, notably souls, or to matter itself. The former attribution might be accounted for consistently with the above reading, since audacity may just be part of what lower beings' imperfection comprises. But the latter is less easily assimilated; passages such as 1. 8. 6 seem to assign to matter an explanatory role comparable to that of the Stoics' material principle (above, Section 1.3.3).

It may be that Plotinus has a consistent view. (He himself is alive to the tensions in Plato's own treatment of this topic: 4. 8. 1.) The above description omitted one of the main considerations adduced by Plotinus, namely that embodiment seems to be in many ways bad for the soul. On the whole, however, he resists the Gnostic-style inference to cosmic malefaction. Not only does the embodied soul have the benign role of introducing order and beauty to bodily nature; more to the point, it is possible, if one attends to the task, to govern the body effectively without abandoning the delights of intellection (4. 8. 2). (This is the Plotinian transmutation of the claim that it is possible to be at the same time a good philosopher and a good ruler.)

However one is to interpret the apparently deviant passages, which cluster especially in 1. 8, it seems that Plotinus may have the resources to answer the criticism introduced above, and show that he is not committed to anything from which it would follow that this world is, in respect of value, not an image of the divine. His theory of dependence on intellect and the One requires, however, that likenesses be detectable in other areas too. At this point, one of the *Enneads'* recurrent Platonic themes is relevant: a common source of error in people's conceptions of reality is their tendency crudely to conceive of souls and higher entities on the model of material objects (e.g. 6. 5. 2; compare also Section 2.2.2 above). Plotinus wants to say, for example, that while intellect can be 'present to' soul and soul can be present to body, the relation is not just like one body's presence to another. Again, 'greatness there [in the intelligible world] consists in power, but here in bulk' (2. 9. 17; compare 6. 7. 32). Bulk may therefore be an 'image' of power.

The warning against too narrowly materialistic a conception of the kinds of property that beings may have is a salutary one. The reader of Plotinus must try to settle upon a construal of the '. . . is an image of . . .' relation which is not prejudicially constricted. In general, if the study of the *Enneads* is to be more than a valuable mind-stretching exercise, a middle way must be followed between merely insisting on the commonplace conceptions which Plotinus wishes to overthrow and, on the other hand, interpreting key terms in such a way as tacitly to grant the main claims of Neoplatonist metaphysics. In respect of some parts of Plotinus' system, it is quite clear that this is feasible: his arguments regarding sense-perception, for instance, can be productively evaluated while questions about the universe's first principle are left open. It might be thought more difficult to combine the constructive with the critical when considering the place of mystical experience among Plotinus' grounds for his views. Even in this case, however, reasoned assessment is possible; certainly, Plotinus himself regards the question of how such experience is to be interpreted as suitable material for argument. He presents his metaphysics as answerable, at least implicitly, to widely acknowledged canons of inductive appraisal.

2.3. Augustine

Aurelius Augustinus (354–430), Catholic bishop and saint, was one of the chief agents of the transmutation of the Gospels' religion into the Christianity of the modern era. He was responsible in particular for a considerable strengthening of the Neoplatonic strain in the Catholic thought of the Latin-speaking world, thanks to the voluminous writings composed before and during his tenure of the see at Hippo in his native North Africa.

Augustine was first exposed to, and impressed by, the philosophy of Plotinus and Porphyry at a time when he was, though positively disposed towards Christianity, not yet a believer. This was during his eventful five years in Italy (382–7), at the end of which he was baptized into the Catholic religion of his mother. Augustine mainly relied for his acquaintance with Greek philosophy upon works written in Latin, such as the surveys of Cicero and Varro, and, in the case of Neoplatonism, the translations by the fourth-century philosopher and Christian convert Marius Victorinus.

The earliest of Augustine's published writings date from 386, that is, from a time when, intellectually at any rate, he was already an adherent of Christianity. But we are provided with a detailed account of his thinking in the preceding years in the autobiographical *Confessions* of 397–400. Neoplatonist convictions replaced an earlier allegiance of Augustine's to Manicheism (see below, Section 2.3.2), and then survived abundantly, though with gradually greater modifications, into his Catholic years.

There is a comparable evolution in Augustine's works from the more to the less philosophical: a steadily greater proportion of his output is devoted to scriptural exegesis and pastoral preoccupations. This is not an altogether uniform development; in particular, two large works of the later years, *The Trinity* and *The City of God*, are rich in philosophical discussion. It should be noted that Augustine's own use of the term *philosophia* does not consistently observe the distinction which the above remarks presuppose. But he acknowledges anyway the main methodological point, contrasting arguments which do with those which do not appeal to premisses accepted only by faith, and in practice he often takes care to preserve the demarcation.

Philosophical reasoning is most commonly used by Augustine in the pursuit of 'understanding' of what is accepted by faith. The aim is to progress from believing on authority that *p* towards understanding that *p*. In effect, this is usually a matter of responding to objections to, or difficulties with, articles of faith in terms acceptable to those who raise them. The descriptions below of Augustine's treatments of human freedom and of time exemplify this pattern, and also illustrate how in such a context Augustine's inquiries sometimes develop a momentum of their own. Philosophical argument also serves to situate and defend not just particular beliefs but the Christian's overall attitude of granting primacy to Scripture as a guide to truth. Such arguments belong to epistemology, a field in which, as will be seen, Augustine's work is notably innovative.

2.3.1. *The Justification of Belief*

To what extent, if at all, can the Christian's attitude of faith be vindicated by reasoned reflection? The answer to this question must in part depend, according to Augustine, on how much a person can know independently of authority, and on how defensible it is to suspend judgement on matters inaccessible to such knowledge. If reflection shows that one should be willing to accept some beliefs on authority, one may then debate the further question which authority one should trust.

Augustine was familiar with the account of Academic Scepticism in Cicero's *Academica*, and in his own early *Against the Academics* attempts to show that the requirements for 'cognition', as conceived in the Stoic–Sceptic debate (above, Section 1.4.2), are satisfiable. It is in other works, however, that he anticipates Descartes in bringing forward as prime candidates for knowledge various first-person present-tense statements, among them *sum*, 'I am'. Augustine's claim is that in being certain, or in claiming to know, that I am, I have no need to fear error or deception, since the supposition that a person who has such a belief is mistaken in having it is self-contradictory (*Trinity*, 15. xii. 21; *City of God*, 11. xxvi). Further instances are afforded by 'I know I am' and 'I am alive'. (In the former context, Augustine adds that it is 'impudent' to suggest error in the case of 'I want/will (*volo*) to be happy' and 'I want/will not to be deceived', presumably without meaning to deny that the argument in these cases must be rather more complex.)

The mind knows such truths as these, as it knows arithmetical truths, 'by itself'. Other truths can be known (if in a less stringent sense of 'know'; *Reconsiderations*, 1. xiv) by means of sense-perception. But it would appear that some of the truths most relevant to human happiness are not available to knowledge. Admittedly, *Free (Choice of the) Will* 2. iii. 7–2. xv. 39 advances a proof of the existence of God from the eternal character of arithmetical truths. But the conclusion is described as 'certain though tenuous', and it is not Augustine's settled view that monotheism can be established by reason. In any case, the further saving truths of God's incarnation and resurrection are beyond our knowledge (now). The person who declines to believe anything that cannot be known must agree that he or she may thereby be abandoning the opportunity to achieve beatitude. Indeed, Augustine suggests that refusing to believe anything that cannot be known may result not only in misery but also in wrongdoing (*The Utility of Belief*, 12. xxvi). In general, to decline ever to trust other people's testimony is, Augustine thinks, plainly absurd.

Presented with practical grounds for belief on authority, one might insist that there are some things which cannot be believed in at will. Augustine dismisses this view: it is in our power, thanks to God's gift, to have faith if we will (*The*

Spirit and the Letter, 21. liv). If one avoids the pride by which Augustine saw his own faith as having been delayed, it only remains to consider whom one might believe, and on which questions.

As regards beliefs about the way to happiness, reason is 'not entirely useless' when one is considering which assertions to take as authoritative (*True Religion*, 24. xlv). As before, the findings of reasoning as to the limits of reasoning may be relevant: where the subject is one about which those who wish to persuade us cannot have knowledge, it is less reasonable to trust them if they claim to offer proof than if they do not (*The Utility of Belief*, 9. xxi). This point is made by Augustine in connection with the Manicheans; considerations relevant to whether to regard the Gospel narratives as authoritative include the impossibility of miracles without divine agency and the testimony to the Apostles' good character provided by the their effectiveness in persuasion (*True Religion*, 25. xlvii).

2.3.2. *Evil*

One of the fundamental changes of view which led to Augustine's conversion concerned, in brief, the explanation of evil. He was attracted in his youth to the Manichean solution of the question how to reconcile belief in a good deity with the facts of human experience. The solution was, in effect, to deny the good deity's omnipotence. The Manicheans postulated an evil power (identified with the God of the Old Testament) as responsible for those aspects of the world's workings which would otherwise cast doubt on the goodness of the deity.

The alternative solution which Augustine embraced on becoming a Catholic is most fully expounded in *Free Will*, completed in about 395. Some of the statements in this and contemporary works were to be appealed to by opponents of Augustine in a controversy which occupied much of his energies in his last years. The adherents of the Pelagian heresy who were attacked by Augustine alleged that their own views coincided with views which he had previously expressed but had now abandoned. Augustine repudiated the charge except as regards inessentials; but it is not easy to make of his earlier and later pronouncements a consistent whole.

The evils in view of which it is difficult to understand how, within a Christian perspective, God is not to be regarded as culpable are of two main kinds. In *Free Will*, Augustine refers to these as the evils we suffer and the evils we do. He has in mind first the harm and suffering to which people are subject, and secondly the wrongs that people do. God appears, if not actually to bring such things about, at any rate to permit them to happen. Is this consistent with the Christian conviction that everything God does is good? In order to show that it is, Augustine advances several Plotinian points, such as that the excellence of the creation actually requires that there exist lesser and in various grades corruptible creatures, among whom are human beings (see above, Section 2.2.4).

But he also puts forward an independent argument which concerns divine justice and human freedom.

First, God can be reproached with human suffering only if some of those who suffer are innocent. Those who sin deserve to suffer for their sins, and God's causing or allowing deserved suffering actually testifies to his justice, and thereby to his goodness. Secondly, if God had made it impossible for us to sin, he would thereby have prevented a great good, namely our acting rightly, which requires that we have free choice (*Free Will*, 2. i. 2–3). This is the answer to be given if, in reply to the first point, it is asked why God gave humans the power to sin. (A Plotinian answer can also be provided: such a power is not inappropriate to the less than perfect creatures that there must be in the universe (3. ix. 26).)

If these two points are granted, then the problem of evil is solved if we are indeed free and if among human sufferings there are none which are out of proportion to the sufferer's sins. Do these conditions hold? Augustine examines grounds for doubting each of them. Doubts about human freedom are raised by the doctrine of God's foreknowledge of all human choices: if how one will choose is now (or eternally) known to God, is it not impossible for one to choose otherwise? And if it is impossible, is not the kind of freedom which is required by the above explanation of our being able to sin merely illusory? One of Augustine's replies to this challenge is to assert, in a way which begs the question, that foreknowledge of a free choice is hardly foreknowledge unless the choice genuinely is free. But he also observes that the argument implies that knowledge of the past similarly abolishes freedom, whereas surely 'you apply no compulsion to past events by having them in your memory' (3. iv. 11; compare *City of God*, 5. x).

The second condition, that sufferings not be undeserved, may be thought to fail in view of the widespread suffering of apparently innocent children. Augustine's chief response to this suggestion is to resort to the supposition of original sin, upon which it would be superfluous to comment. It is worth noting, however, that since Augustine does accept the doctrine that all humans sinned in Adam, it is in principle open to him to say that God cannot be convicted of injustice even if many of those who now suffer have not recently added to their guilt. He does not say this. Instead he insists that we are all continually, and of course voluntarily, sinning: without God's assistance, indeed, we would never act well.

This is the location of the Pelagians' dissent. They were concerned that Augustine's view of grace cast doubt on human freedom and ultimately on divine justice. If he holds that human beings are, when left to their own devices, so uniformly sinful, Augustine is at risk, in effect, of undermining his above-described response to the problem of evil. The Pelagians therefore maintained that although the power we have of acting rightly is a gift from God, the use of that power is up to us: we have some chance of acting rightly by our own efforts, and therefore of meriting salvation.

Why did Augustine wish to deny this? A full answer to the question would make reference to several considerations remote from philosophy, such as Church politics and the interpreting of Scripture, notably of the letters of Paul. Besides being actuated by motives of these kinds, Augustine was generally somewhat disposed to go beyond the insistence that nothing evil is to be attributed to God and say that everything good should be attributed to him. To countenance the obtaining of salvation by human merits seemed to him to belittle divine grace. If this were not so, and grace were also given according to our merits, then 'grace would not be grace' (*Predestination of the Saints*, 6. xi). Augustine frequently speaks of human merits as gifts from God (*Sermons*, 191. viii; *Grace and Free Will*, 8. xx); so he was presumably not impressed by the corresponding point that if this were so, then merits would not be merits. A further argument appears at *Manual* xxxii: to say that sometimes a person's own efforts suffice for merit is to say that sometimes 'the mercy of God alone is not sufficient'.

Augustine is well aware of the objection that in making grace so ubiquitously operative in salvation he denies that freedom of humans to act rightly which in the earlier argument helped to justify God's permitting sin. His reply to this is not entirely constant, but perhaps most commonly it is to concede that we are not now free to avoid sinning, since no one is capable of doing so unless or until gratuitously enabled to do so. But grace comes only to some. Thus Augustine's vindication of divine justice by reference to God's having originally given humanity the freedom to act rightly is made still more precarious by the implication of very unequal divine treatment of individuals who are all alike undeserving. Mercy towards some but not all sinners is compatible, in Augustine's opinion, with justice towards the rest.

Augustine's eventual conception of freedom is made more obscure again by passages discussing the future life of the saved, such as *Manual* cv: 'In the future life it shall not be in a man's power to will evil, and yet this will constitute no restriction on the freedom of his will. On the contrary, his will shall be much freer when it shall be wholly impossible for him to be the slave of sin.' The question prompted by such remarks is why, if the great good of freedom can be secured in this way, God instead created humanity with the power to sin. Such passages do appear to favour the Pelagian accusation that Augustine deserts his earlier views for a position which is more vulnerable to objections on the score of justice. But the correct picture of the later evolution of Augustine's thought on these complex issues of justice, freedom, and causality may well be rather less clear-cut.

2.3.3. *Time*

The Christian doctrine that this world was created by God, and is thus finitely old, was a primary target of objections from pagan philosophers both before and during Augustine's lifetime. Two particular allegations which he addressed were that the doctrine imputes to God mutability and arbitrariness. First, if God is thought of as the efficient cause of something's coming into existence, it would appear to follow that God is causally active in the appropriate way at some but not other times; God therefore undergoes change. This reasoning applies also to such post-creative activities as the granting of grace. The second objection pertains specifically to the creation. To express it summarily: if God created the world a particular finite time ago, it may be asked why he did so then. The answer that God had some reason to do so at that time which he did not have earlier can hardly be reconciled with the supposition that only afterwards did anything other than God exist. One must conclude that the timing was arbitrary.

In his treatment of these arguments, Augustine relies on a conception of God's eternity as distinguishable, in the manner of Plotinus, from mere everlastingness. God creates by his eternal word, and it is not required by the causal relation that since the effect comes about a certain time, the word must also be spoken at a certain time (*Confessions*, 11. vii). The imputation of change to God is averted, at the cost of the concession that the operation of God's power 'whereby, being eternal, he is active in temporal events' is 'wonderful' (*City of God*, 22. ix). Likewise, the second argument can be met with the help of the potentially troublesome premiss that time itself is among the eternal deity's creations (*Confessions*, 11. xii). If there was no time before the time when creation actually occurred, it is not true that God might with as much reason have created the world before that time.

In the debates so far considered, Augustine repeats points already made, if less expressly, by Philo of Alexandria. He is more original elsewhere among his many reflections upon time. The intriguing discussion of time and its measurement in *Confessions* 11 contains some elements which recall Ennead 3. 7, but is nevertheless substantially new.

The discussion is propelled by several arguments, first laid out by Aristotle in *Physics* 4. 10, which have the paradoxical conclusion that there cannot be such a thing as a long time. Nothing can be long unless it exists, and whereas the past no longer exists and the future does not yet exist, the only time that is entirely present is an instant which has no length; thus it appears that no time, whether past, present, or future, is of any length. Augustine adds an independent puzzle concerning our measurement of times: a time can be measured only while it is present, but one can hardly tell how long it is until it is over, nor yet when it is over, since it is then no longer present (*Confessions*, 11. xxvii). How, therefore, are we able to determine that, for example, one spoken syllable lasts twice as long as another?

Augustine's proposals for the solution of these puzzles comprise some specific observations about the powers of memory and a general suggestion as to what time itself is. Memory is central to our capacity to measure times. We are able, at least sometimes, to estimate the duration of a past experience just by considering our memory of it. We are also capable of fulfilling an intention regarding the duration of a performed activity by reliance on a memory of a mental rehearsal of that activity. In both cases, we manage to tell, from a memory which remains, the duration of something which passes away.

These acute observations are subsumed by Augustine into an account of time itself as a mental item. We measure times, Augustine says, by measuring mental impressions; 'either, then, this is what time is, or else I do not measure time at all' (11. xxvii). Augustine is willing even to consent to the claim that past and future exist, as long as that is understood to mean that memory and expectation exist. Thus 'a long future is a long expectation of the future, and . . . a long past is a long memory of the past' (11. xxviii).

This solution makes large concessions to the original paradox-engendering arguments: Augustine concedes that only what is present is long, and that whatever we measure must be entirely present when we measure it. Both requirements can be satisfied by memories. Augustine must presuppose that in 'measuring' a memory one is doing something in regard to which the original puzzle about measurement does not recur; and he can at least point out that when one comes to the end of such a measuring, what one was measuring has not passed out of existence. But Augustine's account is open to further and more testing challenges, relating, for example, to the publicity of time. It is unfortunate, and perhaps significant, that the *Confessions*' approach to questions about time is not resumed in subsequent works. But that approach, even if Augustine did abandon it, remains a good example of a philosophical treatment of this topic which is properly sensitive to the phenomenon of time's passage: for human beings, if not for God, time moves ineluctably on.

BIBLIOGRAPHY

GENERAL

Two works which include material on various phases of post-Aristotelian philosophy are:

Armstrong, A. (ed.), *The Cambridge History of Later Greek and Early Medieval Philosophy* (Cambridge, 1967).

Irwin, T., *Classical Thought* (Oxford, 1989), chs. 8–11.

The following wide-ranging volumes are highly recommendable:

Frede, M., *Essays in Ancient Philosophy* (Oxford, 1987).

Sorabji, R., *Matter, Space and Motion* (London, 1988).

—— *Time, Creation and the Continuum* (London, 1983).

The useful series Companions to Ancient Thought contains:

Everson, S. (ed.), *Epistemology* (Cambridge, 1990).

——(ed.), *Language* (Cambridge, 1994).
——(ed.), *Psychology* (Cambridge, 1991).

1. PHILOSOPHY IN THE HELLENISTIC PERIOD

Primary Sources

For Epicureanism, Stoicism, and Scepticism of the Hellenistic period, the outstanding sourcebook, containing translations together with philosophical and historical commentary, is:

Long, A. A., and Sedley, D. N., *The Hellenistic Philosophers*, i (Cambridge, 1987). (LS)

For Sextus Empiricus, there is a translation of *Outlines of Pyrrhonism* by J. Annas and J. Barnes (Cambridge, 1994). Lucretius may be read in the Loeb Classical Library version by W. Rouse and M. Smith (Cambridge, Mass., 1975). There are also Loeb translations of Cicero's *Academica*, *On Ends*, *Tusculan Disputations*, and *The Nature of the Gods*, of Seneca's *Moral Essays* and *Moral Letters*, and of Epictetus' *Discourses* (including the *Manual*).

Further Reading

A good introduction is provided by:

Long, A., *Hellenistic Philosophy*, 2nd edn. (London, 1986).

The proceedings of the triennial Symposia Hellenistica contain many valuable articles. The series comprises, to date:

Barnes, J., and Mignucci, M. (eds.), *Matter and Metaphysics* (Naples, 1987).
——Brunschvig, J., Burnyeat, M., and Schofield, M. (eds.), *Science and Speculation* (Cambridge, 1982).
Brunschvig, J., and Nussbaum, M. (eds.), *Passions and Perceptions* (Cambridge, 1993).
Laks, A., and Schofield, M. (eds.), *Justice and Generosity* (Cambridge, 1995).
Schofield, M., and Striker, G. (eds.), *The Norms of Nature* (Cambridge, 1986).
——Burnyeat, M., and Barnes, J. (eds.), *Doubt and Dogmatism* (Oxford, 1980).

See also:

Long, A. (ed.), *Problems in Stoicism* (London, 1971).
Rist, J. (ed.), *The Stoics* (Berkeley and Los Angeles, 1978).

Recommendable books include:

Annas, J., *Hellenistic Philosophy of Mind* (Berkeley and Los Angeles, 1992).
——*The Morality of Happiness* (Oxford, 1993).
——and Barnes, J., *The Modes of Scepticism* (Cambridge, 1985).
Hankinson, R., *The Sceptics* (London, 1995).
Inwood, B., *Ethics and Human Action in Early Stoicism* (Oxford, 1985).
Nussbaum, M., *The Therapy of Desire* (Princeton, 1994).

2. PHILOSOPHY IN LATER ANTIQUITY

Primary Sources

Plotinus' *Enneads*, together with Porphyry's *The Life of Plotinus and the Order of his Books*, are best read in the Loeb version (7 vols., Cambridge, Mass., 1966–88). For Augustine, a limited selection would include the *Confessions* in the Penguin version (Harmondsworth, 1961), *The Essential Augustine*, edited by V. Bourke (Indianapolis, 1974), J. Burleigh's version of *Earlier Writings* (London, 1953), *On Free Choice of the Will* in the translation by T. Williams (Indianapolis, 1993), and *The City of God* (Harmondsworth, 1972).

The Ancient Commentators on Aristotle is an ongoing sequence of selected commentaries by Philoponus, Simplicius, and others (London, 1987–). A widely illuminating work is Alexander of Aphrodisias' *On Fate*, as translated and edited by R. W. Sharples (London, 1983).

Further Reading

Besides the works mentioned at the beginning of the Bibliography, there are several helpful surveys of parts of the field:

Dillon, J., *The Middle Platonists* (London, 1977).
——and Long, A. (eds.), *The Question of Eclecticism* (Berkeley and Los Angeles, 1988).
Sorabji, R. (ed.), *Aristotle Transformed: The Ancient Commentators and their Influence* (London, 1990).
Wallis, R., *The Neoplatonists* (London, 1972).

On Plotinus, each of the following, and especially the first-mentioned, is a helpful guide:

Emilsson, E., *Plotinus on Sense-Perception* (Cambridge, 1988).
Gerson, L., *Plotinus* (London, 1994).
O'Meara, D., *Plotinus* (Oxford, 1993).

Augustine's philosophical work is discussed in the following books, among which the first-mentioned is particularly reliable:

Kirwan, C., *Augustine* (London, 1989).
O'Daly, G., *Augustine's Philosophy of Mind* (London, 1987).
Rist, J., *Augustine* (Cambridge, 1994).

9

MEDIEVAL PHILOSOPHY

Christopher Hughes

INTRODUCTION

It is sometimes thought that what goes by the name of medieval philosophy is too much the handmaiden of theology to be real philosophy. This view is quite mistaken, but it is true that medieval philosophy is highly theological, and that to enjoy it, one needs a fairly high tolerance for theology. That is not to say that one needs to believe in God; but one does have to have some interest in whether God exists, and what he—and the world—would be like if he did. On the other hand, if one likes theology, but lacks a keen interest in metaphysics and philosophical logic, much of Anselm, or Aquinas, or Scotus, or Occam, will probably seem dull. Also, to profit from the study of medieval philosophy (and in particular scholasticism) one must have a taste for what might be described as logic-chopping and hair-splitting, though I would describe it as arguing carefully and making subtle distinctions. Medieval philosophers were certainly interested in the 'big questions'—the existence of God, mind and body, free will, the nature of right and wrong, and so on—but they were also passionately interested in getting the details of an argument right; only if one shares that passion will medieval philosophy (especially after the year 1000) seem congenial.

In what follows, I cover six philosophers—three pre-scholastics (Augustine, Boethius, and Anselm), and three scholastics (Aquinas, Scotus, and Occam). In order to get an understanding of the major currents in medieval philosophical thought, one need not be especially well acquainted with the thought of all of these philosophers, but it is essential to have a thorough grounding in Augustine, Aquinas, and at least one of the pair <Scotus, Occam>.

1. AUGUSTINE

Augustine was born in what is now Algeria in 354. Though he was raised as a Christian, in his youth he abandoned Christianity, and embraced Manicheism. Under the influence of St Ambrose, and of Neoplatonism, he came to think there was less to be said against, and more to be said for, Christianity than he had supposed. He abandoned Manicheism, was baptized in 387, and ordained not long after. In the years between his (re)conversion to Christianity and his death in 430, Augustine wrote an enormous number of works. Few if any of them could be described as exclusively philosophical, but a great many concern philosophical questions (the rationality of belief in God, the truth of materialism, the nature of evil, the relation of freedom to necessity, the nature of time, the possibility of knowledge, and so on).

I should like to extend many thanks to Martin Stone and Marcia Mayeda.

Chronologically speaking, Augustine is not a medieval philosopher. He is nevertheless a natural starting-point for a course in medieval philosophy, because of his profound influence on its development, and also because in many ways he is a medieval philosopher *ante litteram*. (By contrast, in spite of his enormous influence on medieval philosophy, no one would be tempted to describe Aristotle as a medieval philosopher who happened to be born before the Middle Ages.)

Given the breadth of Augustine's interests in philosophy and philosophical theology, and the limitations on the length of this guide, much of philosophical interest in Augustine will have to be passed over. In particular, I shall not discuss his views on knowledge and scepticism, which in certain ways anticipate Descartes's. (Augustine argued against the Academic Sceptics that I cannot doubt my own existence, because *si fallor, sum* ('if I err, then I exist').) Nor shall I discuss his dualistic account of persons—which, again, resembles Descartes's account more than it does, say, Thomas Aquinas'. (For Aquinas, and other philosophers influenced by the Aristotelian account of persons, a man is essentially constituted of a body and soul: you can no more have a man without a body than you can an automobile without a chassis. As Augustine thinks of it, a man just is a rational soul or mind, causally related in the right sort of way to the right sort of body.) To find out more about Augustine on knowledge and scepticism, a good starting-point would be Augustine's *Contra Academicos* ('Against the Academic Sceptics'); if you want to know more about Augustinian dualism, start with the *De Quantitate Animae* ('On the Quantity of the Soul'). I shall limit myself to discussing Augustine's views on the problem of evil, the way the will fits into the causal structure of the world, and the reality of the past and future.

1.1. God and Evil

De Libero Arbitrio ('On the Free Choice of the Will'), especially book 3; _Confessions, especially book 8; De Gratia et Libero Arbitrio_ ('On Grace and Free Will')

Before his conversion to Christianity, Augustine subscribed to Manicheism, according to which the existence of evil was ultimately to be explained by reference to a first evil principle (conceived of as a material substance), which principle was at war with the principle of goodness (also conceived of as a material substance). Augustine eventually rejected Manicheism on the grounds that the first and highest good could not be a material thing, and on the grounds that the highest good could not be vulnerable to evil in the way implied by Manicheism. But even after he had ceased to be a Manichean, Augustine had great difficulty seeing how Christianity, any more than Manicheism, could provide a satisfactory account of the origin of evil. After all, it seems natural to suppose, if Christianity is true, then all causal chains terminate in the first cause, God. In that case, it seems, evil is ultimately from God. But Augustine thought there was something deeply puzzling about the idea that evil could come from a being who was perfectly good, perfectly powerful, and perfectly knowing. Did evil come into existence, Augustine wondered, because some part of the material from which God made the universe was defective? No; why would a perfectly good and omnipotent God use defective materials? Or was evil just an illusion? No; even if the evils we fear do not exist, our fear of them does, and is evil (see *Confessions*, 5).

The account of the origin of evil Augustine eventually worked out is set out very clearly and in detail in his *De Libero Arbitrio*. It rests crucially on a distinction between two kinds of evil: the evil creatures do (sin, or wickedness), and the evil creatures suffer. The evil creatures suffer comes from God, and consists—for the most part, at least—in (just) punishments for those creatures' sins. For Augustine, if sins went unpunished, evil would violate the just order of things (see *De Libero Arbitrio*, 3. 9). Hence God uses suffering—which is in itself intrinsically bad—to make the world better (more just) than it would otherwise be (if sinners did not suffer). Also, the punishment of sin sometimes produces in the sinner the good of repentance (cf. *De Natura et Gratia* ('On Nature and Grace'), 27).

Although Augustine sometimes makes it sound as though all suffering is just punishment for sins (see e.g. *De Vera Religione* ('On True Religion'), 12) he is aware that innocents (for example, infants) suffer. In such cases, he suggests, God works some good with the suffering, and also brings it about that the innocent sufferer will be—in the long run, at least—as well off as if she had never suffered (*De Libero Arbitrio*, 3. 23).

If God causes suffering (mostly) to punish sins and promote repentance, we don't have a complete explanation of why God causes suffering until we have an explanation of why God causes—or at least allows—sins. Contemporary theodicists sometimes suggest that perhaps it was not within God's power to create free creatures who never sin, and that God allows sins because he deemed a world with both freedom and sins better than a world with neither. Augustine takes a quite different approach. He holds that God actually did create free creatures who (he foreknew) would never sin (*De Libero Arbitrio*, 3. 5). Why then didn't God create only free creatures who he foreknew would never sin? Is it because he judged that some world with sin (and the suffering that follows from it) was better than any sinless world? Not according to Augustine: 'Neither sin nor unhappiness is necessary to the perfection of the universe; rather it is the souls, which, simply because they are souls, are necessary to its perfection. . . . As long as men who do not sin gain happiness, the universe is perfect. When sinners are unhappy, the universe is perfect' (*De Libero Arbitrio*, 3. 9). Augustine's view seems to be that the perfection of the universe requires that virtue and happiness be inseparable, but neither requires nor precludes the existence of sin and unhappiness. So, even though God could have prevented both kinds of evil (sin and unhappiness), he cannot be faulted for not having done so.

This account of why God causes (and allows) evils has a number of interesting features. To cite just one: contemporary theodicies often depend on the idea that if creatures are genuinely free, not even God can guarantee that they will not sin. (A theodicy is an account of why a (perfectly good, perfectly powerful) God would or might cause or allow evils.) Such theodicies presuppose incompatibilism—the view that an act cannot be both free and causally determined. Incompatibilism, in spite of its intuitive appeal, is philosophically controversial. (Moreover, it is controversial whether the assumption that creatures have (indeterministic) freedom is compatible with theism as standardly construed: some philosophers think that we can credit God with omnipotence and omniscience only if there are no undetermined events.) So even an incompatibilist theodicist might want to have, in reserve as it were, an account of why God causes and allows evils which does not depend essentially on the truth of incompatibilism. The Augustinian account just sketched appears not to.

Still, how satisfactory is that account? In thinking about this question, you will find it helpful to distinguish two sorts of objection to Augustine. First, someone might argue that it is very implausible that suffering and sin are as closely linked as Augustine supposes they are. Why should we believe, for example, that evil acts never go unpunished? One might expect Augustine to reply that the illusion of unpunished evils results from not taking the long view (and, in particular, not considering the *post mortem* fate of evildoers). In fact, though, Augustine surprisingly says that there is *never* a time lag between sin and the suffering by which sin is punished (*De Libero Arbitrio*, 3. 15). This suggests that his conception of suffering and unhappiness is rather different from ours, and in particular that, for Augustine, a person's suffering and unhappiness may not be at all manifest to her.

Secondly, someone might claim, Augustine has done more to show that a perfectly *just* God might cause (or allow) evils, than to show that a perfectly *good* God might cause (or allow) evils. If, as Augustine seems to suppose, suffering is always either deserved, or compensated, perhaps a world where free creatures never sin or suffer is no more just than the actual world. But wouldn't such a world be better than the actual world? If it would be, why wouldn't a perfectly good God want to create it, rather than the actual one?

There are also questions about the compatibility of the account of evil in *De Libero Arbitrio* with Augustine's own views on the fall, freedom, and grace. For Augustine, as a result of the fall, men lost the ability to lead good lives (*De Libero Arbitrio*, 3. 18, and *On Grace and Free Will*, 21). The ability to lead good lives is at the opposite end of the spectrum from, say, the ability to ride a bicycle: once the ability ceases to be exercised, it vanishes. Moreover, as Augustine came increasingly to emphasize (in his anti-Pelagian writings), it is only through God's grace that a descendant of Adam can acquire the ability to lead a good life. Augustine seems to hold that grace is not only a necessary, but a (counterfactually) sufficient, condition for a man's leading a good life: it 'is rejected by no hard heart, because it is given for the sake of first taking away hardness of the heart. . . . If God had willed to teach even those to whom the word of the Cross is foolishness to come to Christ, beyond all doubt those also would have come' (*De Praedestinatione Sanctorum* ('On the Predestination of the Saints'), 23 and 24). This is not because grace takes away the sinner's free will: since grace enables one to reacquire freedom, it is compatible with freedom.

So, after the fall, anyone who has the ability to lead a good life has received grace. And anyone who has received grace, actually does lead a good life. This entails that, after the fall, anyone who has the ability to lead a good life does, and that anyone who doesn't lead a good life lacks the ability to do so. In that case, how can suffering consist (in great part) of just punishment for not living a good life? How can someone be justly punished for not doing what it was not within her power to do?

Augustine answers that my failing to do something may be worthy of blame and punishment, even if I am unable to do that thing—if my inability is a result of my previous misuse of free will (*De Libero Arbitrio*, 3. 19). He may be right about this: perhaps I can be blamed and punished for not keeping a promise I could not keep, if I wilfully or negligently put myself into a position where I could not keep it. The difficulty is that, on Augustine's account, Adam's descendants do not do anything to acquire the inability to lead a good life—they are born with it. How can those born in bondage to sin, and not freed by grace, be justly punished for their sins? (Augustine is aware of this difficulty, and makes an interesting suggestion. Perhaps, he says, all souls come from the same sinful soul or souls. How would this supposition help with the problem at issue? Well, suppose a wicked man committed a murder, and then had the left hemisphere of his brain put into one new 'body shell', and the right hemisphere of his brain put into another one. Arguably, neither of the men who existed after the transplants would be the same man as the man who committed the murder; arguably, one or both of the new men would inherit at least some of the murderer's wickedness, and be deserving of punishment, and in need of repentance.)

Augustine's views on the efficacy of grace give rise to a different worry about his account of evil. Suppose you knew that your neighbour was living a wicked life, causing great suffering to himself and, perhaps, to others. Suppose also you knew you could, at no cost to yourself, induce your neighbour to mend his ways, and start living a good life, without in any way interfering with his freedom. If you allowed your neighbour to go on living a wicked life, it seems, you would be unloving, in your indifference to your neighbour's fate, and less than perfectly good. But, according to Augustine, God stands in the same relation to everyone leading a wicked life that, in the story, you stand in to your neighbour. So if God is perfectly loving and perfectly good, why hasn't he already given grace to all sinners? Why don't all men lead good lives? Note that Augustine could not say it would be unjust for God to gives grace to those not living a good life, since that would rule out not just God's giving grace to all, but God's giving grace to any. Nor does it seem he could say that it would be unjust for God to gives grace to those whose wickedness exceeds a certain threshold (and that God give grace to the rest), since he insists against Pelagius that grace is not dispensed according to merit. Augustine would say that God is to be praised for giving grace to some, rather than faulted for not giving grace to all, inasmuch as he owes grace to no one. Again, though, this seems to address the question of whether a perfectly just God could withhold grace, and not whether a perfectly good God could do so.

1.2. The Will

De Libero Arbitrio, book 3; *On Grace and Free Will; On the Predestination of the Saints*

As we have seen, Augustine thinks that the evil we suffer is caused by God. In the *De Libero Arbitrio*, however, he insists the same is not true of the evil we do (*De Libero Arbitrio*, 1. 1). So what is the cause of the latter kind of evil? Augustine says there is no one answer to this question: each wrongdoer causes the wrong he does (*De Libero Arbitrio*, 1. 1, and *Confessions*, 7. 3). For example, Lucifer was the cause of his own fall. Still, we might ask, what caused Lucifer to cause his own fall? Did he (cause his) fall, because of some antecedent defect in his nature, which necessitated his falling? No, Augustine would reply: Lucifer fell of his own free will, and his fall was not necessitated by his nature (*De Libero Arbitrio*, 3. 16). Did Lucifer (cause his) fall because God inclined his will in that direction? No, according to Augustine. Indeed, Augustine seems to think, nothing outside Lucifer's will caused Lucifer to fall: 'A wicked will is the cause of all evil . . . How could it be the root of all evil if you ask for its cause . . . what cause of the will could there be, except the will itself?' (3. 17). 'Sins must be attributed only to a man's will; we need seek no further cause of sins' (3. 22).

These passages, and others like them, suggest that for Augustine no wrongdoing has causes outside the wrongdoer's will. This claim (together with some plausible ancillary assumptions) has the interesting consequence that not all events are caused by other events. To see why this is so, suppose event *e* is the fall of Lucifer, and has no causes outside Lucifer's will. If *e* has an event cause, that cause must consist in Lucifer's will being in a certain (intrinsic) state. Call any event that consists in Lucifer's will being in a certain (intrinsic) state a Luciferian volitional event, or LVE for short. Consider the first LVE in the causal chain terminating in *e* (Lucifer's fall). That event cannot be caused by any other LVE (otherwise it would not be the first LVE in the causal chain). Nor can it be caused by any other kind of event: if it were, its ultimate effect *e* (Lucifer's fall) would have a cause outside Lucifer's will. (I am assuming that the causal relation is transitive.) It follows that the first LVE in the chain terminating in Lucifer's fall is not caused by any other event.

It does not obviously follow that Augustine is committed to the view that some events involving Lucifer's will are uncaused. Some philosophers have thought the causal relation can hold, not just between two events, but between an agent and an act.[1] Such philosophers could say that, although Lucifer's fall was not caused by any other event, it was nevertheless caused by Lucifer himself (who is a substance, not an event). Similarly, it may be Augustine's view that Lucifer's fall has as its only cause Lucifer's will—where that will is conceived of as a non-event (say, a power for opposites, as Scotus would have it).

There are two worries, though, about how Augustine can consistently maintain that wrongdoing has no cause outside the wrongdoer's will. First, he holds that, as a result of sin, the sinner loses the ability to do what is right, even when he sees what is right, and wills to do it (*De Libero Arbitrio*, 3. 18). In such a case, Augustine thinks, the person's failure to do what is right is sinful, because it results from prior misuse of free will (3. 19). So in such cases, it seems Augustine should say, there is a cause of sin outside the will—which, we are supposing, wills *not* to sin. This cause Augustine calls 'the resistance of carnal habit'.

Also, Augustine tells us that there are two sources of sin: unprompted thinking, and persuasion from outside. Unprompted thinking was the source of the Devil's fall, but persuasion was the source of Adam's (*De Libero Arbitrio*, 3. 10). If the Devil's persuasion was a source of Adam's sin, then it seems that the causal history of Adam's fall will include events outside Adam's will (the Devil's blandishments).

To address the first worry: if there is such a thing as willing rightly and acting wrongly, not all wrongdoing is traceable solely to the will. But—at least in his early writings, including the *De Libero Arbitrio*—Augustine seems to be of two minds concerning the interesting question of whether one can sin against one's will. Though he insists it is possible at *De Libero Arbitrio*, 3. 18 and 19, he also says in the first chapter of the first book of that work that sin cannot be imputed to the sinner unless he wills it. Similarly, in *De Vera Religione*, 14, he says that sin is so much a voluntary evil that it is not sin at all unless it is voluntary. Augustine's ambivalence about the possibility of contra-voluntary sins may explain why he

[1] For the classic exposition and defence of this view, see R. M. Chisholm, 'Human Freedom and the Self', in G. Watson (ed.), *Free Will* (Oxford, 1982).

sometimes seems to accept that there are such sins, and at the same time offers an account of the causes of sin inconsistent with their existence.

As for the second worry: if Augustine grants that sins have sources outside the will, how can he deny they have causes outside the will? Perhaps Augustine is tacitly supposing that a cause is something that determines or necessitates its effect. If he did suppose that, he would want to deny that the devil's blandishments caused Adam's fall, on the grounds that they didn't necessitate it. (After all, Augustine would say, Adam could have resisted.) Also, if Augustine thought that causes necessitate their effects, we could see why he says that if sin has a cause outside the agent, then sin is not sin (the thought would be: how could someone be responsible for doing something, if her doing it was determined by external factors?). And we could see why in the *De Libero Arbitrio* Augustine rules out from the outset that God causes sins (the thought would be: what sense would it make to suppose that a perfectly good being compels his creatures to act wickedly?).

If Augustine does identify causation with causal necessitation, this raises a number of interesting questions. First, is he right to do so? Recently the view that one event can cause another, even though the first event could have occurred without the second, has become quite popular. But there are still philosophers who think that if event *e* could perfectly well have happened without event e^*'s occurring, it cannot be true that e^* happened *because e* did. Secondly, there is a question about whether Augustine can consistently identify causation with causal necessitation. We have seen that, on Augustine's account, Lucifer (or his will) caused his fall. So if causation is causal necessitation, you couldn't have Lucifer or his will (the cause) without Lucifer's fall (the effect). But it's hard to believe Augustine could have found this conclusion acceptable, since he insists that Lucifer (and his will) need not have willed to fall. So there seem to be good Augustinian reasons to countenance non-necessitating causes. If we do countenance them, though, it becomes hard to see how the will could be, as Augustine supposes it is, the radical cause of sin.

We have been focusing on the *De Libero Arbitrio* account of the causes of sin. Augustine has more to say about this subject (and much more about the causes of virtuous actions) in his later works—especially *On Nature and Grace*, *On Grace and Free Will*, and *On the Predestination of the Saints*. In these works, there is far more emphasis on God's causal role in creatures' good and evil acts. For example, in *On Grace and Free Will*, 43, Augustine argues that God works in men's hearts to incline their wills as he pleases—either to good deeds (according to his mercy) or to evil ones (according to their deserts). It seems, then, that Augustine comes to hold that God is not only the cause of the evils we suffer, but also (sometimes) the cause of the evils we do (although, Augustine maintains, God never causes evildoing except as a deserved punishment for previous evildoing). It is an interesting and difficult question to what extent Augustine's account of the will in the later works is compatible with the one in the *De Libero Arbitrio*. Judging from his remarks in the *Retractationes* to the *De Libero Arbitrio*, Augustine thought that the two accounts were in the main consistent, in spite of their differing emphases on God's role in our use of the will. Whether he is right about this is not so clear.

1.3. Time and Existence

Confessions, book 11

In the eleventh book of the Confessions, Augustine sets out the following puzzle about time: the past no longer exists, and the future does not yet exist. What no longer exists, or does not yet exist, does not exist. On the other hand, Augustine asks, haven't we all learned as children, and taught our own children, that there are three kinds of time—the past, the present, and the future? Moreover, people remember the past, and foresee the future. How could any of this be true, if the past and future don't exist?

Augustine offers the following solution to this puzzle: whatever we might have learned as children, or say to our own, it is, strictly speaking, false that there are three kinds of time—past, present, and future. Perhaps, though, we can truly say that there are three kinds of time—the present of the past, the present of the present, and the present of the future. All of these things exist, in the present, in our minds. The present of the past exists in (or as) memory, the present of the present in (or as) perception, and the present of the future in (or as) anticipation (*Confessions*, 11. 20). Memory and foreknowledge entail the existence of other times, but not the existence of anything outside the present—memory entails the existence of the present of the past, and foreknowledge entails the existence of the present of the future.

Augustine's starting-point in his discussion of time appears to be what might be called the redundancy theory of presentness. On this theory, *existing now* is a necessary as well as sufficient condition for existing. Consequently, *existing now* and *existing in the present* add nothing to *existing*, in much the way that *actually existing* and *existing in the actual world* add nothing to *existing*. Because Augustine identifies existence and existence now, he does not think of the present as a boundary between different 'parts' or 'regions' of reality, as contemporary philosophers are wont to do. Augustine's discussion of time has the merit of bringing out clearly that the picture of the present as a boundary between different parts of reality does not, on the face of it, mesh with our ordinary (tensed) talk about existence and non-existence.

Whatever the merits of the redundancy theory of presentness, there is a question about whether Augustine could consistently endorse it. For he describes God's (timeless) knowledge in this way: 'God comprehends in a stable and sempiternal gaze all the things that happen in time, whether they are yet to be in the future, or already present, or already over in the past . . . He does not see them in one way, now, in another way before, and in another way afterwards . . . His knowledge of the three times—present, past, and future—does not change as ours does, since in him there is no change' (*De Civitate Dei* ('The City of God'), 11. 21). This passage, and others like it, strongly suggest that God is in direct epistemic contact with past and future events—which in turn seems to entail the reality of those events. It is interesting in this context to compare the passage just cited with *Confessions*, 11. 18. There Augustine insists that when we say someone sees a future event (say, the rising of the sun) we mean only that he sees present causes or signs of that event; we do not mean that he sees the future event itself, because 'the future isn't here yet; if it isn't here yet, it doesn't exist, and if it doesn't exist, it can't be seen'. If future events aren't yet there to be seen, how can even God see them? Augustine would presumably reply that events that are future with respect to us are not future, but present, to God in his eternity (see *Ad Simplicianum*, 2. 2. 2, and *Confessions*, 11. 19). Again, though, how could future events be present to God, if they don't so much as exist?

2. BOETHIUS

Boethius was born in Rome about fifty years after Augustine's death (AD 480). He became consul to Theodoric the Ostrogoth in 510, but was later charged with conspiring against him, imprisoned, and put to death in 524. Boethius has been aptly described by H. F. Stewart and E. K. Rand as 'the last of the Roman philosophers and the first of the Scholastic theologians'. He is an important figure in medieval philosophy for a number of reasons. As the translator of Aristotle's *Categories*, *De Interpretatione*, *Topics*, *Prior* and *Posterior Analytics*, and as the author of commentaries on the *De Interpretatione* and *Categories*, he was the most important channel of Aristotelian ideas to the early Middle Ages. Boethius also applied Aristotelian concepts and distinctions to explicate the doctrines of the Trinity (in his *De Trinitate*) and the Incarnation (in *Contra Eutychen*). He is not, however, simply an interpreter (and defender) of Aristotle. His best-known work, *On the Consolation of Philosophy* (*De Consolatione Philosophiae*), written during his imprisonment, is strongly influenced by Stoicism and Neoplatonism. And his views in the *Quomodo Substantiae* on the relation of an entity (*id quod est*) to its existence (*esse*) are not Aristotelian—though, interestingly, they appear to anticipate Aquinas' views on this issue in certain respects. Boethius made particularly important contributions to subsequent medieval discussions of the problem of universals, and of the compatibility of divine foreknowledge with the contingency of the future.

2.1. Universals

Commentary on Porphyry's 'Isagoge', book 1

In his commentary on Porphyry's *Isagoge*, Boethius notes that Porphyry, in that work, refuses to discuss certain very difficult questions about species and genera—whether they subsist, or instead have existence only in our understanding; whether—if they subsist—they are corporeal or incorporeal; and whether they are separate from sensible things or in those things. Boethius then addresses these questions. He begins by setting out an argument to the effect that genera and species do not subsist. He then sets out an argument purporting to show that if genera and species do not subsist, and exist only in the understanding, then our understanding of species and genera is false and empty (which, Boethius thinks, could not be the case). Boethius then takes issue with each of the two arguments set out, and offers (what he takes to be) the Aristotelian answer to Porphyry's questions: genera and species are incorporeal, and subsist, not by themselves, but 'in sensible things, joined to sensible things'.

The first argument considered by Boethius (the one against the subsistence of species and genera) has a part that in certain ways resembles one found in Plato's *Parmenides*. It has the following structure: if, say, the species *man* or the genus *animal* subsists, it is one thing that is common to many. But this is impossible. For anything that is common is either common by parts (that is, different parts of it belong to different things) or common to different things at different times, or common in such a way that it does not constitute the substance of the things it is common to. But the genus *animal* could not be common in any of those ways: 'it is supposed to be common in such a way that both the whole of it is in all its individuals, and at one time, and also it is able to constitute and form the substance of what it is common to'.

There are various reservations one might have about this argument. If one thought of a species or a genus as a set of individuals, or some other kind of plurality, one might wonder why a species or a genus couldn't be partly in this individual, and partly in that one (there is nothing obviously wrong with saying, for example, that a flock is partly in this sheep, and partly in that one). But this may be less an objection to the argument than an indication that one means something different by 'species' and 'genus' from what is meant in the argument at issue. Alternatively, one might not see why a species or genus couldn't be 'constitutively common to'—wholly present in—different individuals at the same time. It might be objected here that if a species were (wholly) present in two individuals at once, it would have to be (wholly) present in two places at once. Actually, it isn't obvious that if a species is in an individual, it is where that individual is. But suppose it is. Even if no *particular* can be in two places at once, does the same hold for species and genera, if they are universals? Mightn't universals differ from particulars precisely in being able to be wholly present in two places at once?

Boethius, at any rate, does not press this line of objection. Instead, he argues (on what he takes to be Aristotle's behalf) that species and genera can subsist without really having the problematic sort of commonness. Species and genera are universal *in thought*, but are particular in their extra-mental being: 'For genera and species, that is, for singularity and universality, there is one subject. But it is universal in one way, when it is thought, and singular in another, when it is sensed in the things in which it has being' (*Commentary on the 'Isagoge'*, 1). Whatever one thinks of the merits of the argument just sketched, and the merits of Boethius' response to it, both seem to have been very influential. Subsequent medieval discussions of what has come to be known as the problem of universals often took Boethius' commentary on the *Isagoge* as their starting-point. With some exceptions (Remigius of Auxerre, perhaps William of Champeaux, and—much later—Walter Burleigh), medieval philosophers accepted that neither species nor genera (nor anything else) were 'ones in many', wholly present in different individuals at the same time, and that universality could not be a mind-independent distinguishing feature of a special sort of extra-mental thing. (See, for example, Peter Abelard's glosses on the *Isagoge*.)

2.2. Freedom and Foreknowledge

On the Consolation of Philosophy, book 5

In book 5 of *On the Consolation of Philosophy*, Boethius sets out the following argument against the compatibility of human freedom with divine foreknowledge: if God has complete and infallible knowledge of the future, then there is just one way the future could go—the way God foresees it will. In particular, there is just one way I could act—the way God foresees I will. In that case, Boethius concludes, I am not free, and cannot be praised or blamed for what I will do.

As Boethius is aware, someone might offer the following objection: whether or not the occurrence of an event is now inevitable depends on whether there are already in existence necessitating causes of that event; God's knowledge of a future event is not a necessitating cause of that event; so God's knowledge is irrelevant to the contingency or inevitability of future events. Boethius responds that whether or not God's foreknowledge of an event causes that event, that God foreknows an event entails that that event is foreknowable, and no event could be foreknown—that is, foreseen with certainty—unless its futurition is certain—that is, inevitable.

It follows that not even God can have foreknowledge of free acts, or any other not-yet-inevitable events. But, Boethius thinks, it does not follow that we must choose between divine omniscience and freedom and contingency. After all, he says, only temporal beings can have foreknowledge of any kind. God, however, is not in time, but in eternity—an eternity that 'embraces' (though it does not literally include) every moment of time, in such a way that every time is directly present to God. I can have certain knowledge that a man is walking (now), even if his walking is a free act, and came about contingently (i.e. was not inevitable, prior to its occurrence). Just as I have certain knowledge of free acts and other contingent events occurring in my (temporal) present, so, Boethius holds, God has certain knowledge of free acts and other contingent events occurring in his (eternal) present—whether those events take place in our past, present, or future.

Here someone may object: 'we can still ask whether what God eternally sees as occurring in our future is necessarily going to happen or not. If it is, then what God sees won't come about freely or contingently; if it is not, then God's "seeing" isn't a case of (certainly, infallibly) knowing.' Boethius answers that we need to distinguish two kinds of necessity here. If God sees that an event will take place, that event's occurrence is 'conditionally necessary'—necessary in relation to God's knowledge, or on the condition that God knows it. But it is not simply necessary: 'The same future event, when it is related to divine knowledge, is necessary, but when it is considered in its own nature, seems utterly and absolutely free' (*On the Consolation of Philosophy*, 5).

When Boethius says that the future event is necessary when related to divine knowledge, does he simply mean that necessarily, given what God knows, it will take place? Or does he mean that, although the event's occurrence is not now necessary, it is necessary 'when'—at the non-time that—God knows it? Also, what sort of necessity does Boethius take simple necessity to be? You should think hard about just how the distinction between conditional and simple necessity is to be understood, and whether it really will enable Boethius to meet the objection at issue.

There are various other questions about the success of Boethius' attempt to reconcile omniscience with freedom and contingency. One concerns the possibility of timeless existence. Some philosophers think existing just is existing now (in the temporal present). Others think existing just is existing at some time or other. If any of these philosophers are right, nothing could be (timelessly) eternal. Another question about Boethius' attempted solution concerns the possibility of timeless knowledge of temporal events. Such knowledge seems to require causal links between timeless and temporal events or facts—and it is not clear that such links are possible. However that may be, there is no denying the ingenuity of Boethius' approach to the freedom–foreknowledge problem. Moreover, there is at least this much to be said in Boethius' favour: whatever difficulties attend the notion of God's timelessly and infallibly knowing future contingents, God's timelessly (infallibly) knowing that the future will turn out a certain way seems less evidently incompatible with its being open whether or not it will turn out that way than God's *now* (infallibly) knowing that it will turn out that way does.

Book 5 of *On the Consolation of Philosophy* influenced many subsequent medieval treatments of the freedom–foreknowledge problem, among them Anselm's and Aquinas' (see Anselm's *De Concordia*, where he relies on a distinction between antecedent and subsequent necessity very like Boethius' distinction between simple and conditional necessity, and Aquinas' *Summa Theologiae*, 1a. 10, where Aquinas endorses Boethius' definition of eternity, and 1a. 14. 13, where he argues that what is known by God is necessary in relation to God's knowledge, but needn't be necessary in itself, or necessitated by its causes).

3. ANSELM

Anselm was born near Aosta (in what is now Italy) in 1033. At the age of 23, after falling out with his father, he left home, and ended up at the Benedictine abbey of Bec in Normandy. During his thirty years at Bec, Anselm wrote the *Monologion*, *Proslogion*, *De Grammatico*, and the *De Veritate*. In 1093, he became archbishop of Canterbury; in this period he wrote the *Cur Deus Homo* and *De Casu Diaboli*, as well as an unfinished logical treatise (*De Potestate*). He died in 1109.

Anselm's philosophical and theological works are densely written, tightly argued, and unfailingly interesting. Though he often draws on Augustinian ideas, his defence and development of those ideas is highly original. One of the most striking features of Anselm's thought is the way that, in arguing for a claim in philosophical theology, he raises issues of independent logical or metaphysical interest. For example, at chapter 21 of the *Monologion*, Anselm takes himself to have shown that (1) God is without parts of any kind, and (2) God is identical to his life. On the basis of those premisses, he offers the following argument to show that God does not exist in every place or at every time: suppose God were everywhere. Then he would be in different places at the same time. Since nothing can be wholly present in different places at the same time, it would follow that God was partly in one place, and partly in another. And that could not be true unless some part of God were (wholly and solely) in one place, and some part of him were (wholly and solely) in another—which is inconsistent with (1). Now suppose that God were 'everywhen'. It would not immediately follow, Anselm says, that some part of God existed (wholly and solely) at one time, and some part of God existed (wholly and solely) at another: though things cannot be simultaneously wholly present in more than one place, they can be successively wholly present at more than one time. But if 'all of' God existed at two different times, different parts of his life would exist at different times. God's life would be composite, which, given (2), is inconsistent with (1). In Anselm's argument we have an admirably clear formulation of the view—much discussed recently—that substances are not 'spread out' in time in the way they are in space—in other words, that substances do not have temporal parts as well as spatial parts. We also have a very clear formulation of the view that some non-substances—such as the lives of living substances—are spread out in time (have temporal parts).

Anselm wrote a great deal in the area of philosophical logic and the philosophy of language. His work, in its sensitivity to the nuances of ordinary language, reminds one of J. L. Austin's. In the *De Grammatico*, he discusses whether a word like 'grammaticus' (which, in Latin, can function either as an adjective or a noun) picks out a substance or a quality. What emerges from the discussion is an interesting distinction between *significatio* and *appellatio*. These two terms are sometimes translated 'meaning' and 'reference'; though the translation is not ideal, it is probably as good as any other. A term like 'white' signifies just one thing (whiteness), but it 'appellates' (is true of) many white things. Moreover, the thing 'white' signifies it does not 'appellate', since whiteness is not white. Elsewhere, Anselm has interesting things to say about the semantics of the word 'nothing', about the logical interrelations between various kinds of ability statements and possibility statements, and about the various kinds of necessity (see, especially, Anselm's unfinished *De Potestate* and the *De Casu Diaboli*). In these contexts, he often appeals to a distinction between how things are *secundum formam*, or *secundum formam loquendi* (according to our way of speaking), and how things are *secundum rem* (really). For example, when we say that a person is able to be beaten, there is an ability in that person *secundum forman loquendi* but not *secundum rem*; really, the ability is in the person who can do the beating, rather than the person who can be beaten. Again, the term 'blindness' picks out a property of a person *secundum forman* but not *secundum rem*, inasmuch as blindness isn't something real—like sight—but only the absence of something (sight) where that something ought to be.

In spite of his work in the philosophy of language and philosophical logic, Anselm is probably best known nowadays for his contributions to philosophical theology—in particular, his *Proslogion* argument(s) for the existence of God, and his account of why God became man.

3.1. Truth and God

Monologion, especially chapter 18; *De Veritate*; *Proslogion*, especially chapters 2 and 3

In chapter 18 of the *Monologion*, Anselm offers the following argument to show that truth always has existed, and always will exist:

(1) Suppose truth has not always existed.
(2) Then at some time before truth existed, it was true that there was no truth.
(3) But if it was (ever) true that there was no truth, there was truth then.
(4) So there was truth before truth came to be.
(5) Since (4) is a contradiction, (1) must be false. By the same reasoning, truth not only always has existed, but always will exist.

Anselm's attempt to demonstrate a priori that truth always exists has received much less attention than his attempt to demonstrate a priori that God necessarily exists, perhaps because the former argument has a less exciting conclusion than the latter. This comparative neglect is unfortunate because, as we shall see, Anselm's ingenious argument suffers from no evident flaws—except, perhaps, an excess of compression. This compression is evident in the somewhat abrupt passage from (1) to (2) and the absence of support for the crucial premiss (3).

Why does Anselm think (1) entails (2)? He appears to be supposing that, where *P* is a statement, and *t* is a time, only truths are instances of the following schema:

At *t P* if and only if at *t* it is (or was, or will be) true that *P*.

Thus for example, it is true that

(*a*) In 300 BC there were dodos if and only if in 300 BC it was true that there were dodos

and

(*b*) Now there are no dodos if and only if now it is true that there are no dodos and, more to the present point,
(*c*) At the time before truth existed there was no truth if and only if at the time before truth existed it was true that there was no truth.

If (*c*) is true, so is

(*d*) At some time before truth existed there was no truth if and only if at some time before truth existed it was true that there was no truth.

Now if (1) is true, there was a time before truth existed—at which time, naturally, there was no truth. So if (1) is true, so is

(*e*) At some time before truth existed there was no truth.

And (*d*) and (*e*) jointly entail (2).

As I have said, Anselm does not defend premiss (3). But the following defence of (3) seems both natural and Anselmian: it is true that pigs grunt if and only if something that we may call the proposition *pigs grunt* has the property of being true—where we needn't commit ourselves on what properties propositions have, over and above the property of being true (or false). (Anselm clearly does think that truth is a property of propositions; for his account of what property truth is, see the *De Veritate*.) In other words, it is true that pigs grunt if and only if truth is a property of the proposition *pigs grunt*. Now truth could hardly be a property of that proposition, if truth didn't so much as exist. So if it is true (now) that pigs grunt, then truth exists (now). And if it was true (then) that pigs were grunting, truth was (then) a property of the relevant proposition, and accordingly existed then. In just the same way, if it was true at some time before truth existed that there was no truth, then truth was at that time a property of the proposition *there is no truth*, and accordingly existed then. So the supposition that it was true at some time before truth existed that there was no truth entails the absurdity that truth existed even before it had begun to exist.

In the argument just discussed, Anselm attempts to prove a priori that truth always exists by deducing an absurdity from the supposition that it does not (together with some ancillary a priori premisses). He employs the same strategy in the second chapter of the *Proslogion* to argue that God necessarily exists. That argument has the following structure:

(1) God is that than which nothing greater can be conceived.
(2) That than which nothing greater can be conceived exists in the understanding, even if it does not exist in reality.
(3) Suppose that than which nothing greater can be conceived exists only in the understanding.
(4) Then it can be thought to exist not just in the understanding, but in reality—which is greater.
(5) So that than which nothing greater can be conceived is something than which something greater can be conceived.
(6) Since (5) is impossible, than than which nothing greater can be conceived (God) exists in reality, and not just in the understanding.

Anselm's ontological argument (as it has been called since Kant's time) has been the subject of discussion and controversy for almost a millennium. Bonaventure, Scotus, and Leibniz all thought it was on to something, as did Bertrand Russell at one point; Gaunilo, Aquinas, and Kant disagreed. Gaunilo, a contemporary of Anselm, wrote a piece criticizing Anselm's argument, to which Anselm replied: the debate has come down to us, and is well worth reading.

What should we make of the ontological argument? It is often supposed that we needn't worry about the details of Anselm's argument, because it is clear at the outset that nothing like it could work: the denial that a thing exists never entails a contradiction. This (Humean–Kantian) criticism is of doubtful efficacy: as we have seen, it is at least arguable that from 'Truth does not exist', and certain a priori necessary truths, we can deduce a contradiction.

Another objection to Anselm's argument is that it illegitimately presupposes that it makes sense to compare what really exists with what does not really exist. How—the objection goes—can *a* stand in the less-great-than relation to *b*, if there really is no such thing as *a*? But it seems true that the *Millennium Falcon* is faster than any real spaceship, even though the *Millennium Falcon* exists only in the movie *Star Wars*. After all, the speed which, according to the movie *Star Wars*, is the maximum speed of the *Millennium Falcon* is greater than the maximum speed of any real space ship. Notice that this last claim does not—or at any rate, does not obviously—entail that any entity is non-existent and the bearer of a certain relation to something else.

The *Millennium Falcon* doesn't actually exist; but suppose it did. Would it be faster than it in fact is? On the most natural way of construing this (odd) question, it is equivalent to:

> Is the speed which would be the maximum speed of the *Millennium Falcon* (if it actually existed) greater than the speed which in fact, according to the movie *Star Wars*, is the maximum speed of the *Millennium Falcon*?

There is no obvious reason to suppose that the answer to this question is 'yes': why should a real *Millennium Falcon* go faster really than a fictional one goes fictionally?

Now Anselm seems to suppose that if (*a*) that-than-which-no-greater-can-be-conceived doesn't really exist, then (*b*) if it did really exist, it would be greater than it in fact is. And he thinks (*b*) entails an absurdity. It is not clear, though, that someone who accepts (*a*) must accept (*b*). Just as a real *Millennium Falcon* wouldn't have to go any faster really than the one in the story does in the story, someone might say, a real maximally great being wouldn't have to have any more greatness really than the one in my understanding has in my understanding. It might be said here that if that-than-which-no-greater-can-be-conceived doesn't really exist, then, if it did exist, it would have more greatness *really* than it in fact has *really*. This may be true, since it may be that only things that really exist can have greatness (or any other property) really. But does it help Anselm? There is no evident absurdity in supposing that something that has maximal greatness in the understanding has less *real* greatness than something else (if the first thing exists only in the understanding, and the second is real).

In short, although Anselm distinguishes existing in reality from existing in the understanding, he does not draw a corresponding distinction between having a property in reality and having that property in the understanding. It seems we need such a distinction (if for no other reason, because something that really exists can have a property in the understanding, without having it really). Once that distinction is made, it is not clear that Anselm's *Prosologion* argument (or anything much like it) will go through.

Having argued in chapter 2 that God exists, Anselm goes on to argue in chapter 3 that God exists so truly that he cannot be conceived not to exist. Some philosophers have thought that chapter 3 contains a new and better (modal) argument for God's existence than chapter 2; others have thought it merely develops the basic line of reasoning of chapter 2. Be sure to compare chapters 2 and 3 carefully, to see who is right.

3.2. Why did God become Man?

Cur Deus Homo

Early on in Anselm's dialogue *Cur Deus Homo*, Anselm's interlocutor Boso notes that, for Christians, the Word of God became man, suffered, died, and came back from the dead, in order to free us—from our own sins, from the power of the devil, and from the wrath of God. But, Boso goes on to say, unbelievers find this whole story unintelligible. They argue:

> If God was unable to free man from sin, the devil, and his own wrath simply by willing it, he is not omnipotent. If on the other hand God was able to bring about our redemption from sin by a simple act of will, and chose instead to effect it through the suffering and death of his word, he is not wise: 'if for no reason at all, a man were to do with great strain what he could have done effortlessly, he would surely not be judged by anyone to be wise'. (*Cur Deus Homo*, I. 1)

Boso adds that it is no good saying that, had God delivered man from the Devil simply by willing it, he would have dealt with the Devil unjustly; the Devil no more has the right to punish human sinners than one thief has the right to punish another. As Anselm puts Boso's point, even if human sinners ought to be punished by Satan—in the sense that it is a good thing that they be punished by him—Satan ought not punish human sinners—inasmuch as only God has the right to punish anyone.

Boso brings out very clearly that, just as there is a problem of evil for Christians, there is a problem of Christ's passion and death. This may seem strange: since Christ's passion and death is entailed by the Christian story, how can it be a problem for that story? Well, evil constitutes a philosophical problem for Christians because, although Christians affirm that God is all-powerful, and that God is all good, and that there is evil, the first two propositions appear to be in tension with the third. Similarly, although Christians affirm that God is all-powerful, and that he is perfectly wise, and that (the Word of) God suffered and died for our sins, the first two propositions appear to be in tension with the third.

Anselm's attempt to resolve this tension turns on the notion of *satisfaction*. Suppose *a* takes away from, or fails to give, *b* something that belongs to *b*. If *a* subsequently gives *b* what he took from (or failed to give) *b*, and also compensates *b* for (temporarily) not having had that thing, then *a makes satisfaction* to *b* (*Cur Deus Homo*, 1. 11). For Anselm, creatures owe total obedience to God. If creatures sin—that is, disobey God—they fail to give God what they owe him (what belongs to him). If their sin is without subsequent satisfaction, then, Anselm thinks, God ought to punish those sins. Sin that was followed by neither satisfaction nor punishment would dishonour God and upset the moral order of the universe (*Cur Deus Homo*, 1. 15). Unfortunately, creatures are incapable of making satisfaction to God for their sins. This is partly because of the gravity of the sin of disobeying God, and partly because, even before sinning, creatures owe everything to God; once they incur a debt of sin to him, there is no way for them to pay it off. So it looks as though the only way God can preserve his honour and the moral order of the universe is by punishing sinners. But, Anselm thinks, there is an alternative. Though justice requires sins to be followed by either punishment or satisfaction, it does not require that the satisfaction be made by the sinner himself; someone else can make satisfaction on the sinner's behalf. Indeed, according to Anselm, that is just what happened when Christ died for our sins: through his passion and death, the Word of God made satisfaction for us. (Anselm offers various reasons why satisfaction could only have been made by a divine person, but we needn't go into these details here.)

For various reasons, Anselm's account of the point of the Incarnation does not seem to be one that would satisfy the unbelievers Boso has in mind. To start with, when Anselm introduces the concept of making satisfaction, it appears to involve compensating, and hence benefiting, the injured party. Thus someone who injured another person's health makes satisfaction when he not only restores his health, but also compensates him for the health lost (*Cur Deus Homo*, 1. 11). This feature seems absent in the case of the Incarnation: how could the Word's passion and death be any good to God? Inasmuch as the Word of God *is* God, they seem to constitute a further, especially grave injury to God. Anselm says the Word gave the gift of his (supremely valuable) life to God (*Cur Deus Homo*, 2. 11 and 19). But God does not gain the life the Word loses. Perhaps Anselm would say that the Word's death provides God with a kind of benefit, inasmuch as it preserves his honour. Again, though, how could it do any such thing?

A different worry about Anselm's account concerns his view of the requirements of justice. One can see why a stern retributivist might hold that justice demands the punishment of sinners who have failed to make satisfaction. And one can see why someone who thinks that justice does not exclude mercy might hold that justice does not demand the punishment of every sin for which satisfaction has not been made. But, on Anselm's account, justice requires that sins for which satisfaction is not made be punished, without requiring that unsatisfying sinners be punished. This view seems decidedly less attractive than either stern retributivism, or a view on which the right to punishment or satisfaction may be (justly) waived by the injured party. Anselm may at some level be inclined to believe this: in a number of places he appears to endorse the kind of strict retributivism that is inconsistent with his account. (See, for example, *Cur Deus Homo*, I. 13: 'Nothing is tolerated more unjustly than that a creature not repay to God what he removes from him.')

So Anselm's defence of the pointfulness of the Incarnation appears problematic in a number of ways. It is not easy to see, though, how exactly Anselm's account could be modified, to make it satisfying to someone who finds the Incarnation story unintelligible. Indeed, one may come away from the *Cur Deus Homo* with a heightened awareness of just how difficult it is to make sense of the Incarnation.

4. AQUINAS

'The incomparable St. Thomas Aquinas, as great of mind as of heart'[2] was born near Naples in 1225. Against the wishes of his family, he became a Dominican friar at the age of 19. After studying under Albert the Great in Cologne, he was sent by his order to the University of Paris in 1252. In the next seven years he wrote a commentary on Peter Lombard's *Sentences*, the *De Veritate* ('On Truth'), and a pair of monographs on Aristotelian physics and metaphysics, *De Principiis Naturae* ('On the Principles of Nature') and *De Ente et Essentia* ('On Being and Essence'). The monographs are an excellent introduction to the Aristotelian underpinnings of Aquinas' thought. In 1259 Aquinas returned to Italy. There he taught at Orvieto, Rome, and Viterbo, and wrote the *De Potentia* ('On the Power of God'), the *Summa contra Gentiles*, and the first part of his best-known work, the *Summa Theologiae*. The first twenty-seven questions of the first part of the *Summa Theologiae* are perhaps the best introduction to Aquinas' natural theology; later questions concern, *inter alia*, the Trinity, angels, creation, and mind and body. Aquinas returned to Paris in 1268. In his second (less than four-year) stay, he produced a truly awesome amount of work, including commentaries on Aristotle's *De Anima*, *Nicomachean Ethics*, and *Physics*, and the monographs *De Unitate Intellectus* ('On the Unity of the Intellect') and *De Aeternitate Mundi contra Murmurantes* ('On the Eternity of the World against the Mutterers'), as well as the (massive) second part of the *Summa Theologiae*. In his last years, spent in Italy, he completed a commentary on the first twelve books of Aristotle's

[2] Auguste Comte.

Metaphysics, and worked on (though he did not complete) the third and final part of the *Summa Theologiae*. He died around 1276.

If you could have the complete works of just one medieval philosopher with you on a desert island, Aquinas would probably be your best choice. Although he was less influential in the thirteenth and fourteenth centuries than one might have imagined, his subsequent prominence among medieval philosophers is not surprising. Aquinas is more wide-ranging and systematic than any of the figures we have considered so far (in part because he had a better knowledge of Aristotle's whole system than most of his medieval predecessors). At the same time, Aquinas has the sort of interest in distinctions and in the details of arguments that characterize the best contemporary analytic philosophy. As is especially evident in disputed questions such as the *De Veritate* or the *De Potentia*, he has an exceptional ability to foresee the various arguments that might be offered against his views. While one may not always understand, or be satisfied with, the way that Aquinas answers a particular objection, it is *extremely* hard to come up with objections to Aquinas that he hasn't somewhere considered and addressed.

Given the range of Aquinas' interests (metaphysics, philosophical theology, the philosophy of mind, the philosophy of action, ethics . . .) it is impossible to do more than touch on some of them here. I shall concentrate on Aquinas' metaphysics and philosophical theology. But I shall neglect various central areas of Aquinas' philosophy, including his account of the relation of mind and body. The fundamentals of that account—which occupies an intermediate position between Augustinian–Cartesian dualism and contemporary materialism—is set out very clearly at *Summa Theologiae*, 1a, questions 75–7.

4.1. Form, Matter, and Change

De Principiis Naturae ('On the Principles of Nature'); _Summa Theologiae_, 1a. 45. 2, and 76. 4

For Aquinas, change essentially involves both permanence and transience. In an accidental change—say, a birch tree's changing from white to grey—the thing that remains is a substance (the birch), and the things that go out of or come into existence are accidental forms (the birch's whiteness, the birch's greyness). (For Aquinas, the whiteness of this birch is found only in this birch; so it doesn't go on existing (in other birches), when this one ceases to be white.) In a substantial change—say, a bit of air's becoming a bit of water (to use one of Aquinas' examples)—the thing that remains is a bit of matter, and the things that go out of or come into existence are substantial forms (the matter's air-form, the matter's water-form). (See *Summa Theologiae*, 1a. 45. 2, and *De Principiis Naturae*, 1.) Substantial forms differ from accidental forms in a number of ways. First, a substantial form makes a thing the kind(s) of thing it is: for instance, Wilbur's porcine substantial form makes him a pig (and a mammal, and an animal). By contrast, accidental forms make a thing be a certain way: Wilbur's pinkness makes him pink. Secondly, a substantial form makes a thing be *simpliciter* (that is, makes a thing exist), whereas an accidental form only makes a thing be a certain way. ('Substantial form differs from accidental form in that an accidental form does not make a thing be *simpliciter* but rather be a certain way, as heat doesn't make a thing be *simpliciter* but only be hot . . . A substantial form, however, gives being *simpliciter*'; *Summa Theologiae*, 1a. 76. 4.) For this reason, when a substantial form is acquired, generation occurs, and when a substantial form is lost, corruption occurs; the same does not hold for accidental forms.

But how exactly do the subjects of substantial forms (bits of matter) and the subjects of accidental forms (substances) differ? As the careful reader will have noticed, it is not that, for Aquinas, substances are things made of (some particular kind of) stuff, and bits of matter are bits of (some particular kind) of stuff. As Aquinas thinks of it, a bit of water or a bit of air is just as much a substance as a pig or a man. (Aquinas recognizes that in one sense of 'matter', a bit of air may be described as a bit of matter, but *in that sense of matter* a bit of matter is not the subject of substantial change. The matter that is the subject of substantial change is for Aquinas just what would be left of a pig or a man, or a bit of air or water, if you took away that thing's substantial form, and all its accidents; it is, as it were, a thing minus all its forms (and *esse*; see Section 4.3).) Notice that if matter is understood this way, there is no obvious reason to think that only things that are material—in the ordinary sense of the word—have matter. If there are, say, angels or souls, they will certainly be immaterial in the ordinary sense, but it is not immediately evident that 'subtracting' all the accidental or substantial forms from an angel or a soul would leave you with nothing at all. In fact, Aquinas thinks that only things that are material in the ordinary sense of the word have matter. (In this he differs from Bonaventure and various other Franciscans, who thought that everything except God could be 'factored into' matter and forms, so that there was both 'spiritual' and 'corporeal' matter.) But Aquinas finds the thesis that only corporeal things have matter unobvious enough to argue for it at length (see *De Spiritualibus Creaturis*, un. 1, and *Summa Theologiae*, 1a. 75. 5).

If a bit of matter goes from being air-formed to being water-formed, it cannot be essentially or permanently air-formed (or water-formed). Indeed, for Aquinas, the matter that is the subject of substantial change doesn't have any particular substantial form permanently and essentially, although it permanently and essentially has some substantial form or other (compare: a planet isn't always and essentially in any particular place, although it is always and essentially some place or other).

Granted that a bit of matter cannot have essentially any of the substantial forms it has only temporarily, why couldn't matter have some other substantial form permanently and essentially? Why couldn't some or all matter be essentially *x*-formed, where *x* is not fire, or air, or water, or any other *generabile*?

Aquinas would answer that if all matter were (always) *x*-formed, there would be no such thing as generation or corruption. Air would not go out of existence, and water would not come into existence; instead an *x*, or a bit of *x*, would go from being substantially *x*-formed, and accidentally air-formed, to being substantially *x*-formed, and accidentally water-formed (see *Summa Theologiae*, 1a. 76. 4, and *De Spiritualibus Creaturis*, un. 3).

Aquinas seems to have something like this picture in mind: when a bit of matter has acquired a substantial form, what results from the union of these two incomplete beings (matter and form) is a complete individual, or 'being in act', or individual substance. Once this has happened, the only way in which a new substance can be generated from that matter is if the acquired substantial form is replaced by a new substantial form. A substantial form, as it were, 'saturates' its matter—not only enabling it to be the matter of one kind of substance, but also preventing it from being the matter of any other kind. So if a form can be acquired by a thing without prejudice to the substantial form previously had by that thing, then the form in question must be an accidental one (the kind that makes things be a certain way), rather than a substantial form (the kind that makes things be *simpliciter*). From this it follows that if the matter that temporarily acquires the form of water were permanently *x*-formed, the form of water would be accidental, and no new substance would come into existence when the (already *x*-formed) matter acquired the form of water. By the same reasoning, nothing would go out of existence when the (permanently) *x*-formed matter lost the form of air.

This line of reasoning appears unexceptionable, given the premiss that a bit of matter can have only one substantial form at a time. But how do we know that a bit of matter can't have two different substantial forms at once, just as a substance can have many different accidental forms at once? Aquinas might answer as follows: two different accidental forms can (respectively) make the same thing be, say, pale and risible. But two different forms couldn't both make one and the same thing be pale. Similarly, two different forms couldn't both make one and the same thing be *simpliciter*. As we have seen, though, it is proper to any substantial form to make a thing be *simpliciter*. If there could be two substantial forms in the same thing at the same time, they would both make that thing be—which is impossible.

This response presupposes that the thing a substantial form is in (a bit of matter) is the thing the substantial form gives actual being to. But is this so? One might have thought that a substantial form makes a (pre-existing) bit of matter be a certain way (thusly substantially informed), and makes the substance constituted of the matter and the form be *simpliciter*. If this is so, there is no evident impossibility in the idea of one bit of matter's having two substantial forms. The two substantial forms would make the same bit of matter be two different ways (say, x-formed, and y-formed), and would make two different things—the x made of the matter, and the y made of that same matter—be *simpliciter*. The two forms *would not* both make the same thing be the same way, or both make the same thing be. To see how Aquinas might respond to this argument, see his defence of the unicity of substantial form in his disputed question *De Anima*.

4.2. Matter and Individuation

De Ente et Essentia
De Principiis Naturae
De Spiritualibus Creaturis, un. 1

According to Aquinas, matter is the principle of individuation. By this he seems to mean that, for any kind of thing *k* that has or could have more than one member, what makes a certain individual *this k*, as opposed to another one, is its being made of *this* matter as opposed to some other matter. To put the point another way, for any kind of thing *k* that has or could have more than one member, the property *being this k* is necessarily equivalent to the property *being a k made of this matter* (properties are necessarily equivalent when, necessarily, whatever has either property has the other). For example, *being this stone* 'just is' *being a stone made of this matter*, in the sense that nothing could have been this stone without having been made of this matter, and no stone could have been made of this matter without being this stone. Aquinas was happy to accept as a corollary that any two angels were different kinds of angel.

But just how should we understand 'matter' here? As we have already touched upon, Aquinas uses the term 'matter' to refer both to the subject of substantial change, which does not have any particular form essentially or permanently, and to particular bits of some particular kind of stuff (which do): 'Some matter includes a form, like the bronze which is the matter of a statue. Bronze is itself a composite of matter and form. Since it has matter, bronze cannot be called prime matter. Only that matter which is understood without any form or privation, but which is subject to form and privation, is called prime matter' (*De Principiis Naturae*, 2). When Aquinas says that a (non-species-exhausting) thing is individuated by its matter, does he have in mind the kind of matter that is itself constituted of matter and substantial form (as bronze is), or the kind of matter that is what remains of a material thing when all its forms have been abstracted away (that is, the subject of substantial change)? One might think it makes no odds: if say, an amber paperweight is (proximately) individuated by the bit of amber it is made of, and the bit of amber is in turn individuated by its matter, then the amber paperweight will ultimately be individuated by the constituent of it which neither is a form, nor has a form as a part. But this presupposes that whenever a thing is individuated by its 'thick' (form-including) matter, its thick matter will in turn be individuated by its 'thin' (non-form-including) matter. And Aquinas seems to say things inconsistent with this presupposition. Aquinas' favourite example of the individuating matter of a substance is the flesh and bones (or sometimes, the body) of this man (see, for instance, *Summa Theologiae*, ɪa. 75. 4). Flesh is clearly 'thick' matter. Moreover, Aquinas holds, although a man's flesh is always constituted of the same form, it is constituted of different bits of (thin, or prime) matter at different times. ('If we consider flesh . . . according to what is formal in it, the flesh always remains . . . but if we consider flesh according to its matter, it does not remain, but is gradually destroyed and renewed . . .'; *Summa Theologiae*, ɪa. 119. 1.) Aquinas' idea is that in nutrition the (thin) matter that was the matter of the bread I ate for breakfast gradually becomes the (thin) matter of my flesh, replacing the matter that was the (thin) matter of my flesh before I ate breakfast. Similarly, Aquinas thinks, the thick matter that is fire is constituted of different bits of thin matter at different times, as matter that was the (thin) matter of kindling wood becomes the (thin) matter of the fire (ibid. and *Summa contra Gentiles*, 4. 81).

If a man is individuated by his flesh and bones, and if the flesh and bones (and the man having that flesh and those bones) are constituted of this or that bit of thin matter only contingently and temporarily, it would appear that a man is individuated by his thick matter, but not by any bit of thin matter. Now the view that all (non-species-exhausting) things are individuated by their thick matter is on the face of it more defensible than the view that they are individuated by their thin matter, since the former view is compatible with the manifest fact that things undergo compositional change. But there remain some worries about Aquinas' account of individuation. Here are two you may want to think about:

(*a*) If thick matter is the principle of individuation, then no individual substance can be constituted of different bits of thick matter at different times, and no two (distinct) substances of the same kind can be constituted of the same bit of thick matter at different times. Is the consequent of this conditional true?

(*b*) If this man is individuated by flesh and bones that are permanently and essentially constituted of a certain form, and temporarily and contingently constituted of this or that bit of (thin) matter, isn't it at best misleading to say that matter is the principle of individuation? After all, it suggests that matter is prior to form in the individuation of substances, which is not the case, if the thick matter that individuates substances has its form essentially, and its (thin) matter accidentally. If anything, doesn't form have a better claim to be the principle of individuation?

4.3. Essence and Existence

De Ente et Essentia, especially chapter 4; _Summa contra Gentiles_, 2. 54; _Quodlibetum_ 2. 2. 2

In chapter 4 of the *De Ente et Essentia*, Aquinas argues that angels lack composition of matter and form. Nevertheless, he says, they do not lack every form of composition. After all,

> Whatever is extraneous to the understanding of an essence or quiddity comes from without, and enters into composition with that essence . . . But any essence or quiddity can be understood without its existence (*esse*) being understood: I can understand what a man or a phoenix is, without knowing whether it exists in the nature of things. It is evident, then, that existence (*esse*) is different from essence—unless perhaps there is something whose quiddity is its own existence.

Aquinas goes on to argue that there is at most one being whose essence is its own existence, because only beings whose essence is distinct from their existence are, as it were, 'multipliable'. (Notice that this constitutes a different argument for the distinctness of essence and existence in creatures.) Later on in the chapter, and elsewhere (e.g. at *Summa Theologiae*, 1a. 3. 4), he argues that there is at least one being whose essence is its own existence. Putting all this together, we get one of Aquinas' most celebrated (and controversial) theses—that in every substance except God, there is a real distinction and composition of essence and existence. (An essence, for Aquinas, is either a composite of a substantial form and a bit of matter, or a subsistent substantial form, in the case of immaterial substances.)

Although Giles of Rome championed the view that creatures are 'composed' of essence and existence, other contemporaries and successors of Aquinas (including Siger of Brabant and William of Occam) took issue with it. A number of these philosophers were influenced by Averroës' arguments against Avicenna to the effect that a being was not *one* in virtue of an extra-essential accident of unity; instead, it was *one* in virtue of its (one) essence. Similarly, critics of Aquinas and Giles would argue, a substance doesn't exist because it has an extra-essential principle of existence; it exists simply in virtue of (actually) having an essence. Siger of Brabant also appears to endorse the following interesting regress argument, which he attributes to Averroës: if everything that exists exists by virtue of something external to it, then we shall have not just the *esse* in union with a man's essence, but also the *esse* in union with the *esse* in union with the man's essence, and so on *ad infinitum*. If, on the other hand, we say that some things can exist without an 'external existentializer', why not say that an essence is such a thing?

These arguments do not show that it is incoherent to suppose that existence is an extra-essential 'component' or 'principle' of a thing, but they suggest that it is gratuitous. Here is a slightly different way to bring out the same point: as we have seen, for Aquinas, an individual substance—say, a man—does not have a family of decreasingly specific substantial forms. He has just one substantial form, in virtue of which he is a man, a mammal, an animal, and so on (*Summa Theologiae*, 1a. 76. 6 ad 1). If a man's human form makes him not just a man, but also an animal and a living being, why not say it makes him exist, and leave extra-essential *esse* out of it? Isn't such a view in fact suggested by Aquinas' claim that, while an accidental form makes a thing be a certain way, a substantial form makes a thing be *simpliciter*? Aquinas says at *Summa contra Gentiles*, 2. 54, that the substantial form of a thing cannot be its *esse*, because the former is to the latter as potency to act. This seems not so much a consideration in favour of the distinctness of a thing's form from its *esse*, as a consequence thereof.

Of course, none of this addresses Aquinas' arguments for the extra-essentiality of *esse* in the *De Ente et Essentia* and elsewhere. It would be rash to dismiss the thesis that creatures are composed of essence and *esse*, without examining those arguments in detail, and thinking hard about their cogency. It is often said that Aquinas' first argument in chapter 4 of the *De Ente et Essentia* moves illegitimately from a distinction at the level of mental operations (conceiving of a thing, and knowing it exists) to a real distinction at the level of 'components' or 'principles' of a thing. As it stands, though, this criticism is not a refutation of Aquinas' argument but an insistence that it could not work.

4.4. The God of the Philosophers and the Christian God

***Summa Theologiae*, 1a. 3. 27–31, 39–40; 3a. 1–4; *Quodlibetum* 2. 2. 2**

We have seen that, for Aquinas, a material substance is composed of an essence and a set of accidents broadly construed. (Accidents broadly construed include predicamental accidents—that is, the accidents falling under Aristotle's last nine categories—and *esse*.) The essence of a material substance is in turn composed of matter and form. In immaterial creatures, Aquinas thinks, there is composition of the first kind, but not the second: angels are composed of a simple essence (a subsistent form) and accidents broadly construed (for a very clear discussion of the 'metaphysical constitution' of angels, see *Quodlibetum* 2. 2. 2). In God, Aquinas argues, there is neither kind of composition: God's deity and his goodness are not different 'parts' of God, any more than his deity and his existence are. Instead, God's deity, his goodness, and his existence are all just

God. Moreover, Aquinas tries to show, nothing can be composite in any way without having essence–accident and essence–existence composition. So, he concludes, God is absolutely or entirely simple (*omnino simplex*), and whatever is in God is God. (For a compact and clear presentation of Aquinas' varied arguments for God's absolute simplicity, see *Summa Theologiae*, 1a. 3; you may want to compare *Summa contra Gentiles*, chapters 17, 18, 21, and 23, and the disputed question *De Potentia*, 7.) As we have seen, Aquinas supposes that in every change, there is something in the changing subject that remains, and something that passes away. He accordingly concludes that only composite beings can change, and that God's simplicity entails his immutability (*Summa Theologiae*, 1a. 9. 1).

Suppose that Aquinas is right, and God's simplicity and immutability can be established philosophically. Or suppose, more weakly, that it can be established philosophically that should a God exist, he would be simple and immutable. Then, it might seem, it could likewise be established philosophically that there is no such thing as the Christian God. The Christian God is three persons in one nature. Although the three divine persons each *have* the very same nature, it does not seem as though they could *be* that nature: if the three divine persons were all the same as the divine nature, they would all be the same as each other, and there would be one divine person, rather than three. So, it seems, there must be more to the divine persons than just the divine nature: in each person there must be a divine nature (shared with the other persons of the Trinity) and some sort of individuating principle (not so shared). Given the plausible assumption that God is at least as composite as any divine person, we may conclude that divine simplicity is incompatible with the doctrine of the Trinity. In fact, we seem not to need even that assumption. As Aquinas conceives of divine simplicity, it entails not just being incomposite, but also being 'incomponible'—that is, being incapable of being in composition with, or being a component of, anything else (*Summa Theologiae*, 1a. 3. 8). Suppose we tried to square the non-simplicity of the divine persons with divine simplicity, by holding that God was the simple shared divine nature, and the divine persons consisted of God together with some individuating differences. God would then be 'componible' if not composite, and hence, by Aquinas' lights, less than absolutely simple.

Also, the Christian God is a God whose Word was made man. On the face of it, nothing could become—or be—a man, without undergoing change. So if the Word of God is 'true God and true man', it seems to follow that something which is God changes. Hence the Incarnation seems incompatible with divine immutability and divine simplicity. There is also a more direct argument for the incompatibility of the Incarnation with simplicity: since *being a man* entails being composite in various ways, *being a man* and *being God* are both attributes of the Word only if something is both God and composite.

Aquinas did not invent the doctrine of divine simplicity: Anselm, and Augustine before him, identify God with his goodness, essence, and being. Nor was Aquinas the first to see the apparent tension between the doctrine of divine simplicity and Christian orthodoxy: Maimonides thought that the doctrine of the Trinity was obviously incompatible with divine simplicity—and, for that matter, monotheism. But Aquinas sees and formulates the problems in this area with exceptional clarity, and has very worked out (if not obviously successful) ideas on how to solve them.

Aquinas grants that if the persons of the Trinity are in any way composite, divine simplicity is compromised (*Summa Theologiae*, 1a. 40. 2, obj. 1 and ad 1). And he grants that if the divine persons are not different from each other, orthodoxy is compromised (*De Potentia*. 8. 1). He accordingly holds that the divine persons are maximally simple individuals, really distinct from each other, and sharing (numerically) the same (divine) nature. (It is because they share *numerically* the same divine nature that the three persons are one and the same God, rather than three different Gods; three different men have three different human natures; *Summa Theologiae*, 1a. 39. 3.) So, Aquinas thinks, there is in each divine person something in virtue of which he is that person of the Trinity (paternity in the case of the Father, and so on), and something in virtue of which that person is God. Isn't this admission tantamount to giving up the simplicity of the divine persons? Aquinas appears to deny this, on the grounds that the paternity in virtue of which the Father is the Father is not really different (different *secundum rem*) from the deity in virtue of which the Father is God. More generally, he seems to say, the relations that individuate the divine person are not really different from the nature that makes them all the same God (*Summa Theologiae*, 1a. 28. 2).

If this is what Aquinas is saying, then his account appears inconsistent with both the indiscernibility of identicals, and the transitivity of identity. If paternity individuates the Father, it is proper to the Father; if deity is shared by all the divine persons, it is not proper to the Father. So, Aquinas seems committed to saying, two things can be really the same, even though one of them has a property that the other one lacks (namely, propriety). Moreover, if the persons are absolutely simple, and each individuating relation is the divine essence, then the Father is the same as paternity is the same as deity is the same as filiation is the same as the Son. If we are to avoid the heterodox conclusion that the Father is the Son, real identity must not be a transitive relation.

Does this constitute a *reductio* of Aquinas' account of the Trinity? No, Aquinas would say: the view that it does rests on a confusion between what I have been calling 'real identity'—*identitas secundum rem*—and something else called *identitas secundum rationem*. The following arguments are valid:

a is identical *secundum rationem* to *b*.
a is F.

---

b is *F*.

a is identical *secundum rationem* to *b*.
b is identical *secundum rationem* to *c*.

---

a is identical *secundum rationem* to *c*.

If, however, we uniformly substitute 'identical *secundum rem*' for 'identical *secundum rationem*', both arguments become invalid (see *Summa Theologiae*, 1a. 28. 3 *ad* 1, and *De Potentia*, 8. 2 ad 7).

But what exactly does it mean to say that *a* and *b* are identical *secundum rem*, or that *a* and *b* are identical *secundum rationem*? That is not easy to say. There is a fair amount of evidence that, for Aquinas, that *a* is identical *secundum rem* to *b* is true if and only if *a* and *b* are identical. For example, in different passages Aquinas often describes the same pairs of things as identical *secundum rem*, or identical *realiter* (really), or identical [full stop]. And he gives as examples of identical *secundum rem* pairs various pairs of identicals, such as the road from Athens to Thebes, and the road from Thebes to Athens, and the interval between the number 1 and the number 2, and the interval between the number 2 and the number 1. There is also a fair amount of evidence that, for Aquinas, *a* is identical *secundum rationem* to *b* just in case '*a*' and '*b*' not only refer to the same thing, but have the same meaning, or perhaps the same Fregean sense. (Thus the road from Thebes to Athens and the road from Athens to Thebes differ *secundum rationem*, unlike the road from Thebes to Athens and the road from Thebes to Athens.) The difficulty is that if identity *secundum rem* is just identity, then Aquinas is after all committed to denying the transitivity of identity—which looks awfully close to a *reductio* of his account. The only way to avoid this consequence is by treating identity *secundum rem* as some-thing less than identity (whether we then treat identity *secundum rationem* as identity, or treat it as something more than identity). If, however, identity *secundum rem* is something less than identity, it is no longer clear that the absolute simplicity of the divine persons (or of God) is secured by the supposition that whatever is in a divine person (or in God) is the same as that person (or God) *secundum rem*. So it is not clear that Aquinas has reconciled divine simplicity with the doctrine of the Trinity. In fairness, he would not want to claim that a philosophical analysis can render transparent the compossibility of God's simplicity and his trinity, or for that matter the possibility of the Trinity itself.

In thinking about the difficulties Aquinas' account of the Trinity encounters, it is helpful to ask yourself to what extent those difficulties arise from the attempt to harmonize the philosophical doctrine of divine simplicity with the theological doctrine of the Trinity, and to what extent they arise from the doctrine of the Trinity itself.

Aquinas' account of the Incarnation depends crucially on a distinction between a human nature and a human person. A human nature is a particular composed of a bit of matter (a body) and a substantial form (a soul). In every case but one, a created human nature is just the non-accidental part of a created human person. In the Incarnation, however, a created human nature is part of no created human person, because that nature is *assumed* by a divine person. What assumption is is best explained in terms of what it does. As a result of the Word's assuming a human nature, (1) the Word comes to subsist in a human nature, and thus to be (literally and truly) a man (*Summa Theologiae*, 3a. 2. 5); (2) the assumed nature is not a part of the human person who doesn't actually exist, but would have existed, had that nature not been assumed (*Summa Theologiae*, 3a. 4. 2 ad 3); and (3) various things that would have been attributed to the created human person with that nature, had that nature not been assumed, are instead attributed to the Word. For example, we may truly say that the Word was born, died, and the like (*Summa Theologiae*, 3a. 16. 8). Finally, and crucially, assumption is a relation whose holding makes absolutely no difference to the intrinsic (non-relational) properties of the assumer: the Word can accordingly assume a human nature without then (or ever) undergoing any real change. In particular, the Word can assume a human nature while remaining absolutely simple (cf. *Summa Theologiae*, 3a. 2. 4 ad 2).

Could a relation that does everything assumption is said to do be a relation whose holding makes no intrinsic differencc to the assumer? It is hard to see how. (Before assuming a nature, the Word did not have among its parts a human body and a human soul. So, if the Word did not really change in assuming a human nature, after the assumption, the Word did not have among its parts a human body and a human soul. But could anything be *vere et proprie* human, if it wasn't constituted of either a human soul or a body?) Aquinas would agree that we do not understand *how* assumption can both make the Word human, and leave the Word simple; but he would deny that we can know it is *im*possible (see *Summa contra Gentiles*, 4. 39).

4.5. Intellect, Will, and Choice

***Summa Theologiae*, 1a. 80–3; *Summa Theologiae*, 1a 2ae. 9–10**

Aquinas thinks that all things have an 'appetite' for, or inclination towards, the good. In beings without knowledge, this inclination is called *natural appetite*. In beings endowed only with sense knowledge, it is called *animal appetite*, and in beings endowed with reason, it is called *rational appetite*. Another name for rational appetite is 'will' (*Summa contra Gentiles*, 2. 47).

If the will is an inclination towards the good, it might seem impossible to will what is not good. For Aquinas, though, the will does not incline towards things in proportion to their actual goodness, but rather in proportion to their apparent or perceived goodness (*Summa Theologiae*, 1a 2ae. 8. 1). This seems to imply that an agent wills only what she deems all-things-considered best. But, it may be objected, don't agents sometimes will what they consider not all-things-considered best, out of weakness of will? Here Aquinas appeals to an Aristotelian distinction between particular and general judgements. An agent may perform a certain kind of act (e.g. adultery) even though she thinks adultery is not in general a good thing (and not as good as fidelity). But, Aquinas would say, an agent cannot wilfully commit adultery, unless she judges that, here and now, adultery is better than fidelity (*De Veritate*, 24. 2).

Because one and the same good or bad thing may appear good or not, the will may incline towards that thing, or not. This is not to say that the will can will, or not will, anything at all. There are, Aquinas thinks, some things that can only appear good to us, and such things the will wills of necessity. Happiness meets this condition, as does adherence to God, for those who have attained the beatific vision (*Summa Theologiae*, 1a. 82. 1 and 2).

(Incidentally, Aquinas' view that, once God is seen clearly enough, the will cannot but cleave to him raises an interesting question about why God didn't create creatures who, from the first moment of their existence, enjoyed the beatific vision. If something of value would have been lost (a certain kind of freedom, or whatever) why isn't it also lost when creatures attain the beatific vision?)

At any rate, most things do not inevitably impress themselves upon us as good (or bad), and such things can either be willed or 'nilled', depending on how they appear to us. Although the will inclines towards the 'apprehended' good, it does not, on Aquinas' view, decide what is good. The faculty that apprehends things as good or bad is the intellect. This seems to imply that the will is causally dependent in its operation on prior judgements of the intellect. At least some of the time Aquinas appears to accept this consequence: 'Every movement of the will must be preceded by an act of apprehension, whereas not every apprehension is preceded by an act of the will' (*Summa Theologiae*, 1a. 82. 4 ad 3).

It is interesting to compare Aquinas' account of the will (and of wrongdoing) with Augustine's account in the *De Libero Arbitrio*. Like Augustine, Aquinas tells us that 'the root and source of wrongdoing is to be sought in the act of the will' (*Summa contra Gentiles*, 3. 10). But as Aquinas understands this claim, it does not exclude the fact that 'defective' willing is the result of a 'defective' judgement concerning the goodness or badness of a thing—where the defective judgement is not itself sinful, since sin does not take place until the will actually inclines towards that to which it should not incline (see *Summa contra*

Gentiles, 3. 10). For Aquinas, the will is the radical source of (moral) evil in the sense that (moral) evil comes into the world only when, and only because, the will acts defectively. It is not the radical cause of evil in the sense that there is nothing to be said about why the will acts defectively: the will is a secondary agent, moved by the apprehensive power that judges things to be good or bad—which apprehensive power is in turn moved by the thing apprehended (ibid.).

One thing we might find attractive about Aquinas' account (as opposed to Augustine's) is that on it acts of will (including defective ones) are intelligible and explicable. But we might worry whether Aquinas' account leaves enough room for the will to be free. How can the will be free to choose this or that, if it, so to speak, takes its orders from the apprehending intellect?

Aquinas would say this worry stems from a failure to appreciate the interdependence of will and intellect in his account. True, the intellect moves the will—as a formal cause—but the will moves the intellect 'as what changes moves what is changed, and what impels moves what is impelled' (*Summa Theologiae*, 1a. 82. 4). In later works, Aquinas explicates the interdependence of will and intellect in these terms: the will moves the intellect as to its *exercise*, and the intellect moves the will as to its *specification* (*Summa Theologiae*, 1a 2ae. 9. 1). Though it is not entirely clear what he has in mind here, it may be something like this: the will only wills something when the intellect presents that thing to the will as good. By presenting one thing to the will as good, rather than another, the intellect specifies the object of the will. At the same time, the intellect presents something as good—considers it under this or that (good) description—only if the will moves the intellect to consider that thing, and to consider that thing that way. An agent wills something only because she considers it good; but she only considers it at all, because she wills to (*Summa Theologiae*, 1a 2ae. 10. 2). Moreover, if the thing willed is one that can be seen *sub specie boni* or *sub specie mali* (as a good thing, or as a bad thing), the agent focuses on the good aspect rather than the bad one, because she wills to (ibid.).

All this makes it clear that Aquinas' theory of the relation of intellect to will is not a straightforwardly 'unidirectional' one. But it also raises hard questions about how exactly that theory is to be understood. If the intellect's consideration of a thing *sub specie boni* is caused by the will, is the will moved to cause that consideration by a prior judgement to the effect that it would be better to consider it that way than not? If so, a regress impends; and, as we have seen, Aquinas thinks there is no such regress (*Summa Theologiae*, 1a. 82. 4 ad 3). If on the other hand, there is no infinite regress, won't we end up with either an act of apprehension that is not voluntary, or an act of will not 'grounded in'—and not made rational by—a prior apprehension?

5. SCOTUS

Boethius, Anselm, Bonaventure, Aquinas . . . but not *all* the great medieval philosophers and theologians were Italian. John Duns Scotus, for example, was born in Berwickshire (probably) around 1266. He entered the Franciscan order while he was quite young, and was ordained in 1291. He seems to have spent some time in Cambridge, and after his ordination he lectured at Oxford, and subsequently Paris. Some time after 1305, Scotus was sent to Cologne, where he lectured for a short time before his premature death in 1308.

Scotus' lectures on the *Sentences* have come down to us in the form of the *Ordinatio* and the *Reportata*. We also have Scotus' *Quaestiones Quodlibetales* (on various topics in metaphysics and philosophical theology) and the *De Primo Principio* (a short treatise on natural theology). Although not nearly as much of Scotus has been translated into English as, say, Augustine or Aquinas, the Latinless will be happy to know that, thanks to Allan Wolter, both the *Quaestiones Quodlibetales* and the *De Primo Principio* are available in English, as well as some selections from the *Ordinatio* (in Wolter's *Duns Scotus: Philosophical Writings*).

Duns Scotus is not called the *Doctor Subtilis* (Subtle Doctor) for nothing. Unfortunately, the depth and subtlety of his thought are not matched by the clarity of his writing. Because Scotus' prose lacks the immediacy and non-technicality of Augustine's or Anselm's, and the lucidity of Aquinas', you will find it hard going—harder going, probably, than any other philosopher covered in this chapter. But Scotus is well worth the effort. He is an excellent philosopher to read after having read Aquinas. Although he does not usually explicitly criticize Aquinas (one gets the impression he worried much more about Henry of Ghent), Scotus' views often contrast with Aquinas' in interesting and illuminating ways, and involve acute arguments against Thomistic theses. For instance, Scotus argues, *pace* Aquinas, that being is predicated univocally of God and creatures, and of substances and accidents (*Ordinatio*, 1, d. 3, q. 3); that a form of corporeity, distinct from the intellective soul, is required to make a bit of matter a human body; that matter cannot be the ultimate principle of individuation for non-species-exhausting individuals; and that immaterial creatures can differ in number, without differing in species. Of particular interest are Scotus' version of the cosmological argument, and his account of particularity and universality.

5.1. From Creatures to God

De Primo Principio; Ordinatio, 1, d. 2

In both the *Ordinatio* and the *De Primo Principio* Scotus argues for the existence of an infinite being (God). His strategy is indirect. He first tries to establish the lemma that a being with certain relational properties exists, and then argues that only an infinite being could have such relational properties (*Ordinatio*, 1, d. 2, q. 1). In particular, Scotus tries to show, there is a being with a 'threefold primacy'—that is, a being who is first in the orders of efficient causation, final causation, and eminence or perfection.

Scotus has an especially interesting argument for the existence of a first efficient cause (a cause that is itself uncaused and uncausable, whose causality in no way depends on the causality of anything else). Simplifying somewhat (in particular, de-modalizing the first premiss), his argument has the following structure:

> Something is caused. It must be caused by something else, since nothing is self-caused. Call that something else *A*. *A* is either a first efficient cause, or it is caused by something else, *B*. If the latter, *B* is either the first efficient cause, or *B* is caused by something else. Either this causal chain will go back for ever, or it will have a first member—since a circle of causes is impossible. But the causal chain cannot go back for ever; so there is a first efficient cause. (See *Ordinatio*, 1, d. 2, q. 1, and *De Primo Principio*, 3. 8)

Scotus notes that someone might object that the chain of efficient causes might perfectly well go back for ever. He then introduces a distinction between a series of accidentally ordered causes, and a series of essentially ordered causes. In a series of accidentally ordered causes, the posterior members of the series can exercise their causal powers independently of the prior members; in a series of essentially ordered causes, this is impossible. Consequently, in a series of accidentally ordered causes, the prior and posterior members may exist at different times and exercise their causal powers at different times; in a series of essentially ordered causes, all the members must exist and exercise their causal powers simultaneously.

Scotus then offers a battery of arguments to show that a series of essentially ordered causes could not lack a first member. The first one is: suppose that there were an infinity of essentially ordered causes. Then the whole series of caused beings (*universitas causatorum*) would be caused. Since it could not be caused by itself or any of its members, it would have to be caused by something outside the series—a first efficient cause (*Ordinatio*, 1, d. 2, q. 1).

This argument is interesting for a number of reasons. For one thing, it shows an awareness that an infinite series may be bounded by something outside the series. This point may seem trite to those familiar with mathematical analysis, but it is certainly not an obvious point, especially in a language like Latin, where 'infinite' means, literally, 'unbounded'. For another, it brings out that—at least so long as we countenance such entities as series of caused beings—there can be something caused, only if there is something uncaused. (The (finite or infinite) series of caused beings will either be caused by nothing at all, or caused by some being who is caused by nothing at all.) Of course, Scotus wants to show, not just that there is an uncaused being, but that there is an uncaused cause of the whole series of caused beings. To get this conclusion, he needs the following lemma: if each member of a series of essentially ordered causes is dependent, then the whole series of caused beings is dependent. Why does Scotus think he is entitled to this lemma?

Scotus seems to think that (actual) being may be partitioned into the necessary and the caused. (Being taken more broadly, as encompassing the possible as well as the actual, may for Scotus be partitioned into the necessary and the caus*able*.) In other words, any actual being will either exist by the necessity of its nature—in which case it will not need, and could not have, a cause—or it will be (as Wolter aptly puts it) 'essentially indifferent to existence', and exist only because something else is causing it to exist.

If all and only caused beings are contingent, then, it would seem, the series of all caused beings will itself be a contingent being. If the series is contingent, and all contingent beings are caused, then the series will have a cause; and if the series cannot be caused by itself or a part of itself, it will have an uncaused cause—that is, a first efficient cause.

The idea that all contingent beings require a cause for their existence does not originate in Scotus; it figures prominently in Aquinas, *inter alios*. What Scotus sees and shows very clearly is that if we accept this principle (and think that the causal relation is irreflexive and asymmetric, and believe in series) we cannot avoid positing a necessary uncaused being, by supposing that each member of the (infinite) series of contingent beings is caused by some other caused member of that series.

If we accept that (1) all and only contingent beings are caused, and (2) nothing is caused by itself or any of its parts, Scotus' argument will go through. It is not so clear that we should accept the conjunction of (1) and (2), especially if we countenance series of individuals, as well as individuals. Consider the series of all caus*ing* beings. On Scotus' view, this would comprise the necessary first cause, and all the subsequent contingent causes. Since all of the members of this series save one are contingent, it seems that the series itself should be contingent. If it is, the conjunction of (1) and (2) must be false, since the series of *all* causes obviously cannot have a cause that does not belong to that series.

A defender of Scotus might respond here that all Scotus needs for his argument is the principle that a series composed *exclusively* of contingent beings must have a cause. And, she might ask, if we are unhappy with the idea that any particular contingent being 'just exists'—we want to know how it got there—why should we be any happier with the idea that an infinite series of contingent beings 'just exists'? In evaluating Scotus' argument, it would be good to think about how one might answer this last question.

5.2. Common Natures and Individuating Differences

Ordinatio, 2, d. 3, part 1, qq. 1–6

'Equinity itself isn't anything but equinity: it is of itself neither many nor one; neither existent in sensibles, nor in the soul.' So said Avicenna. Scotus took him to mean that it was not part of the definition of equinity either that it existed in the mind, or that it existed in things in the world; nor was it part of the definition of equinity either that it was universal, or that it was particular (*Ordinatio*, 2, d. 3, q. 1). Equinity *as such* is indifferent to mental and extramental existence, to universality and particularity. Equinity as it exists in the mind is a universal, predicable of all its instances; equinity as it exists in a particular horse—say, Seabiscuit—is not a universal, but a particular. Although equinity as such is not universal, it is, on Scotus' account, *common*. What exactly commonness is is not easy to say, but at least some of Scotus' remarks suggest that a thing is common if it is not essentially in just the particular it is actually in. Whatever features a nature has as such, it has in its mode of existence in real things. Scotus accordingly holds that a nature like equinity is not only common as such, but really common.

If equinity is common as such, but not particular as such, Scotus thinks, we cannot explain the fact that the equinity in Seabiscuit is particular, by appeal to the nature of equinity. We must instead posit a different sort of principle or constituent in Seabiscuit that 'particularizes' or 'contracts' the equine nature in Seabiscuit. The relation of a 'contractor' or 'individual difference' to a common nature is in some ways analogous to the relation of the differentia of a species to the genus of that species:

> The reality from which the genus is taken is determinable and able to be contracted or qualified by the reality of the difference. Similarly, in the individual, the specific nature is determinable and able to be contracted by the reality from which the individual difference is taken. There is a positive entity in the same real thing from which the specific nature is taken, and an entity formally other from which the ultimate individual difference is taken—an entity which is totally 'this'. (*Lectura*, n. 171[3])

Scotus characterizes the individual difference primarily in functional and negative terms. Because the difference is what particularizes a nature, and only what is of itself particular can particularize, the individuating difference is of itself particular, and hence non-common. Unlike a specific difference, it is 'non-quidditative'—it is neither matter, nor substantial form, nor accidental form, nor *esse*. It is a simple 'reality' or 'formality', falling under none of the Aristotelian categories, and devoid of any general features whatsoever.

[3] Cited in A. Wolter, 'Scotus' Individuation Theory', in *The Philosophical Theology of John Duns Scotus* (Ithaca, NY, 1990).

On a not unnatural way of understanding Scotus, he is in effect proposing a new form of act–potency composition in creatures, distinct from the familiar compositions of matter and form, subject and accident, and essence and existence. In Seabiscuit, we have a common 'quidditative' component—the 'whatness' of Seabiscuit—and a proper particularizing component—the 'thisness', or *haecceity*, of Seabiscuit. It is important, though, not to be misled by the term 'common'. Scotus does not think that the component in Seabiscuit that is common is literally or numerically identical to the component in another horse—say Secretariat—that is common.

Scotus would not entirely like this way of putting his view, because he thinks that composition, properly speaking, involves things (*res*), whereas the common and particularizing principles of Seabiscuit are not things but 'realities' or 'formalities' (*realitates, formalitates*). Still, it seems that—at least early on—Scotus would have agreed that the common nature and the individual difference are not the same as each other, although they are formalities of the same thing (see *Lectura*, 1, d. 8, pt. 1, q. 3 n. 103). So, early on, when Scotus says that the nature and the individual are 'formally other' or 'formally distinct', he appears to mean that the nature and the difference are distinct formalities in a single thing.

As Marilyn McCord Adams has pointed out, though, Scotus' account of the formal distinction and its relation to composition seems to have changed over time.[4] Scotus thought that the *distinctio formalis* was found not just in creatures, but also in God: in particular, he thought that the personal properties (such as paternity) were formally distinct from the divine nature. If formal distinction entails a composition of formalities in a thing, then the claim that paternity and deity are formally distinct compromises divine simplicity. The Parisian critics of Duns Scotus—who would have presupposed that God was entirely simple—may have objected to Scotus on these grounds. A natural way to meet (or concede) this objection would be to say that the formal distinction held between created formalities like Seabiscuit's nature and his individual difference, but not between the personal properties and the divine nature. In fact, though, Scotus did not take this line. Instead, he seems to have offered a modified account of the formal distinction according to which it does not entail composition of distinct formalities in a thing. On the modified account, the formal distinction is a *distinctio secundum quid* as opposed to a *distinctio simpliciter* (distinction without qualification). Thus to say that this and that are not formally the same does *not* entail that they are not the same *sans phrase*, because 'this and that are formally distinct' is not equivalent to (and does not entail) 'This is a formality, and that is a formality, and this is different from that'.[5]

Scotus' earlier account of the formal distinction may have made the theo-

[4] See her 'Ockham on Identity and Distinction', *Franciscan Studies*, 36 (1976), 5–74.

[5] For a very helpful discussion of these points, see ibid.

logical application of the formal distinction problematic, but the later account makes it much harder to see just what the formal distinction—the relation holding between the common nature and the individuating difference—amounts to. If *a* and *b* can be formally distinct without being distinct formalities, what does their formal distinctness consist in? Scotus tells us that *a* is formally distinct from *b* if *a* and *b* are really the same, but *a* and *b* differ as to the definitions they actually have, or would have were they definable, or *a* and *b* differ as to what they may be predicated of. One can see, though, why Occam would object that *a* and *b* couldn't differ as to their definitions, or as to what they may be predicated of, if they were really the same: that would violate the principle of the indiscernibility of identicals. A defender of Scotus might try to understand how *a* and *b* can be really the same, and formally distinct, in terms of the non-substitutability of the co-referential terms '*a*' and '*b*' in certain referentially opaque contexts involving definitions and predicability. But it is not clear that this is very close to the way Scotus thought about things, and, in any case, it is not at all clear that the contexts with respect to which the relevant terms may not be substituted truth-preservingly really are referentially opaque.

Scotus wants to steer a middle course between the kind of view that Occam would later espouse—according to which natures are individual as such—and the kind of view Burleigh would later champion—according to which natures are universal as such. It is not easy to see, though, just what alternative to those views he has in mind.

6. OCCAM

William of Occam was born some time between 1280 and 1290 in the Surrey village of the same name. Like Scotus, he entered the Franciscan order at a young age, and began the study of theology at Oxford around 1309. Though he spent close to fifteen years there, he never became a *magister actu regens* (holder of a chair in theology), most probably because John Lutterell, ex-chancellor of the University of Oxford, accused him of heresy. In 1323 he was summoned by the Pope to Avignon to defend himself against Lutterell's charges. Occam spent the next four years or so in Avignon. There he completed most of his philosophical writings. (The Commentary on Lombard's *Sentences*, the *Summa Logicae*, and the *Tractatus de Praedestinatione* all seem to have been written before 1328.) The papal court never reached a decision on Lutterell's charges, but while Occam was at Avignon he became involved (some might say, embroiled) in the dispute between the Franciscans and the Pope on poverty. As a result, he left Avignon secretly with Michael of Cesena, and ended up in Munich with Emperor Louis of Bavaria, then engaged in a power struggle with Pope John XXII. Excommunicated by the Pope, Occam sought a reconciliation with the Church after Louis's death in 1347. He died shortly before or after the reconciliation was effected, in Munich, around 1349.

Occam may be the only medieval philosopher to have almost been the central figure in a best-selling novel (Umberto Eco's *The Name of the Rose*). Eco originally intended to make William of Occam the Franciscan detective who solves the crimes, but he changed his mind, because he did not find Occam a likeable enough character. An eminent Occamist—Marilyn McCord Adams—has assured me, however, that there are no grounds for Eco's antipathy to Occam.

Occam is sometimes represented as a destructive rather than constructive thinker. On this view, he is a philosopher who 'unravelled' the thirteenth-century synthesis of Aristotelian reason and Christian faith, leaving us a minimalist natural theology, and the sort of austere metaphysic that best pleases those with a taste for desert landscapes (in Quine's phrase). There are elements of truth in this description. Unlike some of his scholastic predecessors, Occam denied that one could demonstrate philosophically that there was just one God, that he was omnipotent (on a certain construal of omnipotence), and that he created a world with a beginning in time. What can be philosophically demonstrated about God, according to Occam, is less than what can be philosophically demonstrated about him, according to Anselm, or Bonaventure, or Aquinas. It is also true that Occam denied the existence of distinctions in the world, corresponding to distinctions in our concepts, in many cases where (some of) his predecessors affirmed the existence of such distinctions. Thus Occam denies that there is any difference between essence and existence, or common nature and individuating difference, or (material) substance and quantity.

On the other hand, one should not underestimate the continuity between Occam's thought and the thought of the thirteenth century. In natural theology, Occam thinks one can demonstrate the existence of a first conserving cause, endowed with the perfections of will and understanding: he endorses a version of the cosmological argument rather similar to Scotus'. Moreover, Occam's ontology—comprising individual substances and individual accidents—is by no means a radical departure, even if Occam countenances fewer sorts of accident than many of his predecessors or contemporaries.

Occam made contributions to metaphysics, philosophical theology, philosophical logic, epistemology, the philosophy of science, and political philosophy.

6.1. Conditionals and *Consequentiae*

***Summa Logicae*, 2. 31, 3a3ae. 1, and 3a3ae. 38**

Philosophical logicians influenced by Frege often draw a sharp distinction between statements of the form *if A, then B* (or *A only if B*) and statements of the form *A therefore B*. For these philosophers, statements of the first kind—call them *conditionals*—are true unless *A* is true and *B* is false; sentences of the second kind—call them *therefore statements*—are true (or, at least, properly assertible) unless it is possible that *A* is true and *B* is false.

Medieval logicians tended not to draw such a sharp distinction between therefore statements (which they sometimes called *rational propositions*) and conditionals. The medieval term *consequentia* is used by different authors, and not infrequently by the same author, to cover both entailment statements and conditionals. The pseudo-Scotus, for example, suggests that the same *consequentia* may be expressed either by 'If *A* then *B*' or by '*A* therefore *B*' (much as, we would say, the same conditional may be expressed by either 'if *A* then *B*' or '*A* only if *B*'.). Given their tendency to see conditionals and therefore statements as closely linked, it is not surprising that many medievals held that the truth of a conditional required not just the falsity, but also the impossibility, of *A* and not-*B*. For example, both Peter of Spain and Raymond Lull say that for a conditional to be true, it is required that the antecedent cannot be true unless the consequent also is. Similarly, Aquinas says that a conditional with a necessary antecedent and a contingent consequent is false, presumably on the grounds that the antecedent could be true without the consequent's being true (see *Summa Theologiae*, 1a. 14. 13).

Occam also sees therefore statements and conditionals as closely linked: he says that a conditional (*condicionalis*, *propositio condicionalis*) is equivalent to an entailment statement (*consequentia*), so that a conditional is true when and only when its antecedent implies (*infert*) its conclusion (*Summa Logicae*, 2. 31). But Occam's theory is not simply that a conditional is true just in case the corresponding entailment holds just in case it is not possible that the antecedent is true but not the consequent. As we shall see, he distinguishes a number of different kinds of *consequentiae*, and tells us that different rules hold for different *consequentiae*. This suggests—given the equivalence of conditionals and *consequentiae*—that there are a number of different kinds of conditionals.

For Occam, a *consequentia* may be either simple or as-of-now (*ut nunc*). In a simple *consequentia*, there is no time at which the antecedent can be true without the consequent. (Occam uses the term 'antecedent' to cover both what comes between 'if' and 'then' in a conditional, and what comes before 'therefore' in an entailment statement. *Mutatis mutandis*, he uses 'consequent' in the same way.) 'No animal runs; therefore no man runs' is Occam's example of a simple *consequentia*. In an as-of-now *consequentia*, at this time the antecedent cannot be true without the consequent, but the same does not hold for all times. 'Every animal runs; therefore Socrates runs' is Occam's example of an as-of-now *consequentia*: the antecedent cannot be true without the consequent's being true, while Socrates is alive, but it is true without the consequent's being true, when Socrates is dead (*Summa Logicae*, 3a3ae. 1: given that Socrates is dead, and already was dead when Occam wrote the *Summa Logicae*, perhaps 'Every animal runs; therefore Socrates runs' might be better described as an 'as-of-then' *consequentia*).

Secondly, a *consequentia* may hold through 'intrinsic' or 'extrinsic' means. In the former case, the *consequentia* holds in virtue of the truth of a proposition composed of the same terms as the *consequentia* itself. For example, 'Socrates is not running; therefore some man is not running' is a *consequentia* holding through intrinsic means, inasmuch as 'Socrates is a man' is composed of terms figuring in the *consequentia*. When a *consequentia* holds through extrinsic means, it holds in virtue of the truth of a proposition involving terms not figuring in that *consequentia*.

Thirdly, a *consequentia* is *formal* if it holds thanks to an intrinsic or extrinsic means; it is material if it holds just in virtue of the constituents of the *consequentia*. Occam gives as examples of *material consequentiae*: 'If a man runs, God exists' and 'A man is an ass, therefore God does not exist' (ibid.). (Notice that here Occam gives a conditional proposition as an example of a *consequentia*, presumably because he thinks that conditionals and *consequentiae* are equivalent.) You may find Occam's examples puzzling, if you don't bear in mind that, on his account, 'God exists' is necessary, and 'God does not exist' is impossible.

Having drawn various (overlapping) distinctions between kinds of *consequentia*, Occam goes on to discuss the rules for *consequentiae* (*Summa Logicae*, 3a3ae. 38). For example, he tells us that no *consequentia* with a true antecedent and false consequent is a good one; that *consequentiae* are 'contraposable' (if *A therefore B* holds, so does *Not-B therefore not-A*); and so on. Of particular interest for our purposes are the following rules:

> Nothing contingent follows from what is necessary.
> Nothing impossible follows from what is possible.

and

> From the impossible, anything follows.
> What is necessary follows from anything.

Occam notes that the first pair of rules holds for simple *consequentiae*, but not for *ut nunc* ones. And, he says, the second pair of rules is seldom used, because it applies to material *consequentiae*.

It looks, then, as though Occam is saying that whether a certain statement of the form *A therefore B* is a valid *consequentia* depends on what sort of *consequentia* we have in mind: *A* therefore *B* may be unexceptionable as an as-of-now *consequentia*, and defective as a simple *consequentia*. To put this another way, Occam seems to countenance stronger and weaker entailment relations. Again, if conditional statements are equivalent to therefore statements, then Occam recognizes stronger and weaker conditionals. Indeed, Philotheus Boehner has argued that Occam, long before Frege, recognized material conditionals (the ones that are true unless the antecedent is true and the consequent is false).[6] But, although Occam seems not to have simply and straightforwardly identified conditionals with what are nowadays called strict conditionals (the ones that are true unless it is possible that the antecedent is true and the consequent is false), it is not clear that he recognized any conditional as logically weak as the material conditional. For one thing, as we have seen, he characterizes both what it is for an absolute *consequentia* to hold, and what it is for an as-of-now *consequentia* to hold, in modal terms (in the one case, it is always true that the antecedent *cannot* hold without the consequent, in the other, it is true at this time that the antecedent *cannot* hold without the consequent). For another, Boehner does not cite any passages that unambiguously commit Occam to material implication.

In thinking about the adequacy of Occam's account of conditionals, it may be helpful to bear two questions in mind: (1) is there at least one kind of if–then statement whose truth is linked to the truth of the corresponding entailment statement; (2) are all if–then statements such that their truth is linked to the truth of a corresponding entailment statement? Those who construe entailment modally, and take all if–then statements to be material conditionals, would answer both questions negatively. On their view, a conditional of the form *if A, then B* can be true, in the absence of any sort of necessary connection between *A* and *B*: all that is required is that *A* be false, or *B* be true. This position certainly has some unattractive features. To take an example discussed in the literature, suppose that Paul says 'If God does not exist, everything is permitted'. Dorothy answers 'That's not true.' It is hard to believe Dorothy is thereby committed to saying both that God exists, and that not everything is permitted; but it seems this is what she would be committed to, if if–then statements were material conditionals. A theory of conditionals which links them to entailment statements seems to handle this sort of case better: intuitively it seems that what Dorothy is denying is that everything's being permitted *follows from* God's not existing. On the other hand, it is not at all clear that conditionals always pair up with entailment statements, even if we recognize various sorts of entailment. From 'She's on Wimbledon Common or she's in Richmond Park' I may infer 'If she's not on Wimbledon Common, then she's in Richmond Park'; but there doesn't seem to be any necessary connection or entailment relation between her not being on Wimbledon Common and her being in Richmond Park.

[6] See P. Boehner, 'Did Ockham Know of Material Implication?', *Franciscan Studies*, 11 (1951), 203–30.

6.2. Individual Natures and Universal Concepts

Summa Logicae, I, especially chapters 14–16

According to Peter Abelard, William of Champeaux thought that the specific nature of an individual substance was a constituent of that individual wholly present, not just in it, but also in every other member of that individual's species. This view of natures as universals *in re* did not find much favour in the twelfth and thirteenth centuries. As we noted, the lesson many medieval philosophers took from Boethius' and Abelard's commentaries on the *Isagoge*—and from their reading of Aristotle (as more of the Aristotelian corpus became available in Western Europe)—was that one and the same nature couldn't (partially) constitute more than one individual. See, for example, Aquinas, *Summa Theologiae*, 1a. 39. 4 ad 3: 'The unity or commonness of human nature [in different men] is not real but conceptual.' Some historians of medieval philosophy seem to have reached the same conclusion, judging from their use of the grossly tendentious term 'exaggerated realism' to describe the view that natures are literally shared by different individuals.

In the fourteenth century, however, the view Abelard ascribed to William of Champeaux found an able defender in Walter Burleigh, a contemporary of Occam's. For this reason, perhaps, Occam spends a good deal more time than, say, Aquinas or Scotus trying to show that different individuals always have different natures. Some of his arguments are modal. For example, Occam argues that if a specific nature is shared by all the members of the species, this has the unacceptable consequence that God could not annihilate any one member of the species without annihilating all of them, or create any non-initial member of that species. (The presupposition is that it is impossible to annihilate (or create) a thing, without annihilating (or creating) all its parts.) Moreover, Occam says, if the nature is a constituent of many individuals, it could exist without any or all of them—which is absurd. Occam also offers the following non-modal arguments against shared natures: (1) if the same human nature is in Judas and Christ, it is both happy and miserable—which cannot be; (2) if, say, Socrates is composed of a shareable element or elements and particular unshareable ones, he won't be a particular any more than he is a universal—he will be partly particular and partly universal. (For all the above arguments against universals, see *Summa Logicae*, I. 15.)

If the natures in individuals are not universal—as Burleigh has it—could they be 'common' or 'incompletely universal', as Scotus holds? Occam argues that they could not, as follows: since, as Scotus concedes, a thing's nature is not really different from its individuating difference, and since no two things can be discernible unless they are really distinct, the non-commonness of a thing's individual difference entails the non-commonness of its nature. Moreover, if (as Scotus maintains) the human nature in Socrates is numerically distinct from the human nature in Plato, those two natures must differ intrinsically, inasmuch as the distinctness of distinct items always follows upon the intrinsic character of those items. If, however, Plato's and Socrates' human natures differ intrinsically, then *pace* Scotus they do not differ in virtue of being contracted by different individual differences (*Summa Logicae*, I. 16).

How good are these arguments? One can see why Marilyn McCord Adams has suggested that the arguments against Scotus are more effective than those against Burleigh.[7] Take, for example, the argument from creation and annihilation. Though Burleigh does not in fact respond to the argument this way, it seems open to a defender of his view to say that—as long as 'annihilate' means 'destroy every constituent of'—God could no more annihilate Socrates, while leaving Plato intact, than he could annihilate one of a pair of Siamese twins, while leaving the other one (completely) intact. Just as the twins share a particular constituent, she could say, Socrates and Plato share a universal constituent. As for Occam's contention that if Socrates is partly constituted of a universal, he won't be a particular, a defender of Burleigh might say that Socrates is a particular, inasmuch as he (the whole Socrates) cannot be wholly present in two individuals (even if a part of him—the universal that is his human nature—can be). Or she might deny that Socrates is a particular: he might be neither a (pure) particular nor a (pure) universal, in something like the way a being composed of an immaterial mind and a material body would be neither (purely) material, nor (purely) immaterial.

If the natures of individuals are themselves individual, rather than incompletely or completely universal, it might seem that there are no universals, only particulars. Occam would half agree: on his account, there are only particulars, but there are also universals. How can this be?

> The term *particular* has two senses. In the first sense, a particular is that which is one and not many . . . In another sense of the word, we use *particular* to mean that which is one and not many and cannot function as a sign of many . . . in this sense, no universal is a particular . . . A universal is an intention of a particular soul. In so far as it can be predicated of many things . . . it is said to be a universal; in so far as it is a particular form existing in the intellect, it is said to be a particular. (*Summa Logicae*, I. 14)

Occam goes on to distinguish universals by convention (multiply significative words in a spoken or written language) from universals by nature (multiply significative words in a mental language) (ibid.).

For Occam, then, universals (that is, universals by nature) are concepts. But Occam appears to have held two different views about what sort of thing those concepts were. In his earlier work (his commentary on the *Sentences*, and his commentaries on the *Categories* and the *Isagoge*), Occam holds that a universal is

[7] See her 'Universals in the Early Fourteenth Century', in N. Kretzmann, A. Kenny, and J. Pinborg (eds.), *The Cambridge History of Later Medieval Philosophy* (Cambridge, 1982).

neither a substance nor an accident: it is a *fictum*—a non-real being having existence only as the (unreal) object of a (real) act of thought. In Occam's terminology, the universal has *esse objectivum* but no *esse subjectivum*. In his later works (the *Quodlibeta*, the *Quaestiones super Libros Physicorum*, and the *Summa Logicae*), Occam shows a clear preference for an alternative account, on which a universal concept is not the unreal object of a real act of thought, but the real act of thought itself. On this picture, universal concepts are accidents of a mind (see *Summa Logicae*, I. 17 ad 5).

In sum, Occam takes commonness to be the mark of the universal, but he understands this as commonness of predicability, rather than as commonness of inherence: a universal is what is true of many, rather than what is in many. Defenders of Burleigh (or Scotus) might protest that there must be a foundation in the extra-mental world for the fact that, say, *man* may be predicated of both Socrates and Plato. So there is, Occam would reply: what makes it true that *man* may be predicated of both Socrates and Plato is that both Socrates and Plato have a human nature. More generally, the same term may be predicated of different individuals because those individuals resemble each other in certain ways.

Of course, if we think there is no incoherence in one nature's being in many individuals, we might suspect that positing as many natures as there are individuals violates Occam's razor: why posit more natures, when you can explain all the same facts with fewer ones? It is an interesting question whether this suspicion is well-founded. On the one hand, the 'individualist' posits more natures than the universalist. On the other hand, it might be said, the universalist posits two *kinds* of thing (those that can be wholly present in more than one thing, and those that cannot). Also, in order to explain the manifest fact of particularity, the universalist may need to appeal to entities that an individualist like Occam doesn't need—individual differences, haecceities, or the like.

6.3. Bivalence, Contingency, and Foreknowledge

Tractatus de Praedestinatione et de Praescientia Dei et de Futuris Contingentibus ('Predestination, God's foreknowledge, and Future Contingents'); *Summa Logicae*, 3a3ae. 30

Suppose it is genuinely open (not yet settled or inevitable) whether you are ever going to finish reading this paragraph. Is it nevertheless already true, or already false, that you will finish reading it? On Occam's reading of Aristotle, Aristotle thought not (see Occam's commentary on chapter 9 of the *De Interpretatione*, and question I of the *Tractatus de Praedestinatione*). For Occam, Aristotle thought that the law of bivalence (according to which every proposition is either true or false) applied to propositions about what happened in the past, and propositions about what is happening now, but not to propositions about what will (contingently or non-inevitably) happen in the future.

As Occam notes, if future contingent propositions are neither true nor false, there is a quick argument to show that not even God can have knowledge of them: only what is true can be known; future contingents aren't true (or false); so future contingents cannot be known. Notice that this argument for the incompatibility of contingency and divine foreknowledge is different from the one considered by Boethius in book 5 of *On the Consolation of Philosophy*, which does not depend on the denial of bivalence for future contingents.

One of Occam's contemporaries, the Franciscan Peter Aureoli, apparently tried to block the argument from the untruth of future contingents to their unknowability, by denying that God knows only truths. Not surprisingly, Occam finds this denial unintelligible. He accordingly blocks the argument by insisting that bivalence does hold for future contingent propositions. Occam argues as follows: God always knew that Mary would be saved; that Mary would be saved was once a future contingent; so, *contra* Aristotle, some future contingents are known by God, and are *a fortiori* true (*Summa Logicae*, 3a3ae. 30).

These sorts of consideration will no doubt fail to move at least some of the readers of this guide. And, in spite of the fact that most contemporary analytic philosophers side with Occam on whether future contingents have a truth-value, those new to philosophy often side with Aristotle-as-interpreted-by-Occam. (The first time I taught Occam on future contingents, I thought I would have a very hard time getting my students to take the (putatively) Aristotelian view of future contingents seriously; I was surprised to find that only a handful of students found the Occamist alternative nearly as plausible.) People often find it very difficult to see what could make it true *now* that the future will go this way, or that way, if it is genuinely 'up in the air' which way it will go. Occamists reply that what makes it true now is an actual, though not yet inevitable, fact about the future. Champions of the non-bivalence of future contingents—no doubt sincerely—express bafflement about how a proposition could be anything more than something that could *come* true, if it could still turn out to be false.

Someone may suspect that I am giving the non-Occamist too easy a ride. Surely, she will say, we all believe propositions about how the future will go, even when we don't think that the future will inevitable go that way. For example, we all believe that someone will do something, even though he could do something else, and thus won't inevitably do that thing. But to believe a proposition is to believe that that proposition is true. So we must all really be Occamists about the future, even if some of us (inconsistently) repudiate Occamism. This sort of argument will not move the stubborn non-Occamist, who will construe the relevant belief in such a way that it does not entail that the future will actually and non-inevitably turn out a certain way.

The Occamist might have more luck arguing 'backwards' from the truth of a proposition at a later time to its truth at an earlier time. Suppose Tom met Sarah in 1986, and married her in 1990. Looking back now, we can (truly) say that in 1986 Tom met the woman he was going to marry. Suppose further that shortly after introducing Tom to Sarah, William said to Tom 'You've just met the woman you are going to marry.' The Occamist might argue: William said that Tom had just met the woman he was going to marry (we know now that); Tom had just met the woman he was going to marry; so what William said was true—in which case it was already true in 1986 that Tom was going to marry Sarah, even if it was not inevitable in 1986 that he would marry her. More generally, the Occamist could argue from (*a*) the truth of *p* (at a later time), to (*b*) the truth of 'It was to be that *p*' at all earlier times, and thence to (*c*) the truth of 'It was always true that it was to be that *p*' at all earlier times. Actually, this sort of argument won't convince the stubborn non-Occamist either, but I leave it to you to think about why.

Though Occam disagrees with Aristotle about the truth-values of future contingents, he agrees with him that the past and present are settled, and that the future is (at least partially) open. So he still has a problem about how God could know future contingents. Suppose God has always known that *Q*, for an arbitrary proposition *Q*. That God has always known that *Q* is a fact about the past, and hence apparently settled. But if it is settled that God has always known that *Q*, then it is settled that *Q* (since whatever is logically entailed by what is settled is itself settled). In that case, for any proposition *Q*, God's knowing *Q* entails that *Q* is settled. This is just another way of saying that God does not have knowledge of future contingents (either because he is ignorant of them, or because there aren't any to be known).

Someone influenced by the Boethian attempt to reconcile future contingency and divine foreknowledge might say that the above argument illegitimately presupposes that God's having always known that *Q* is a fact about the past. Occam instead stands the argument on its head. Since, for example, it is open whether or not I will be saved, and since nothing settled entails anything open, Occam would say, it is open whether God has always known I would be saved. Either God has always known that I would be saved, or God has always known that I would not be saved—but whichever disjunct is true, it is true only contingently: 'It must be held that God [knows future contingents], but only contingently' (*Tractatus de Praedestinatione*, q. 1, a. 6). In this regard it is interesting to compare Occam with Aquinas. Aquinas considers the argument against the compatibility of divine foreknowledge and future contingency set out above, but responds to it in a quite different way. He argues that, just as God has atemporal and immutable knowledge of temporal and mutable things, he has necessary knowledge of contingent things (*Summa Theologiae*, 1a. 14. 13).

Could it be true at a time that a person knows something, even though it is not yet settled whether she knows it, or is even right about it? If you think the answer is *obviously* no, that may be because you are not distinguishing (*a*) 'It is settled that if a person knows something, then it is true' from (*b*) 'If a person knows something, it is settled that it is true'. Since knowledge entails truth, (*a*) is trivial; but (*b*) isn't. A defender of Occam might say that we can see that a person can know something, before it is settled that she knows it, or is even right about it, once we see that truth does not entail inevitability, and knowledge doesn't entail infallibility. Suppose a person *S* truly believed at a time *t*, and had very good reason to believe, that a certain event would take place, even though its occurrence was not then inevitable. The state of the world at *t*, we may suppose, made it very likely—though not inevitable—that the event would take place, and *S* was aware of this fact. In such a case, it might be argued, we could retrospectively credit *S* with knowledge that the event would take place, once we knew that it had.

Upon reflection, though, it does not seem that this could help us see how God could have knowledge—at least the sort of knowledge that Occam wants to ascribe to him—of future contingents. In the case described above, *S* has at most uncertain and fallible knowledge that a certain event will occur: *S* was right in her belief that the event would take place, and it is no fluke that she was right, but she could have turned out to have been wrong. By contrast, Occam would insist, God's knowledge is certain and infallible.

There is another disanalogy between the case described above and God's contingent knowledge of future contingents as conceived by Occam. In the former case, it is open (at *t*) whether *S* knows that a certain event will take place and open (then) whether *S* doesn't know that that event will take place. We cannot say, though, that at *t* it is open whether *S* knows the event will take place, and open whether *S* knows the event *won't* take place. One the contrary, it is settled at *t* that *S* doesn't know the event won't take place. By contrast, Occam would say, if it is open whether I will be saved, it is open whether God has always known I will be saved, and open whether God has always known I won't be saved. After all, he thinks, it is settled that I will / won't be saved if any only if God has always known I would / has always known I wouldn't be saved. In the human case, *whether S* knows what will happen is open, but not *what* she knows, if she knows. In the divine case, *what* God has always known would happen is open, but not *whether* God has always known what would happen.

How could the facts what God knew—and *judged*—ten thousand years ago depend (counterfactually, if not causally) on now open facts about what will happen ten thousand years hence? A Boethian might answer as follows:

> To say that ten thousand years ago God judged that *P* is just to say that ten thousands years ago it was true that God *timelessly* judges that *P*: the reference to ten thousand years ago is spurious. Moreover, divine timelessness

> resembles the future more than the past in this respect: the facts about how God is timelessly, and in particular about what judgements God timelessly makes, are (partially) open.

Such a Boethian might regard Boethius' and Occam's approaches to the problem of God's knowledge of future contingents as complementary, rather than in competition. The idea would be that Occam is right to suppose that, in order to save the openness of the future, what God knows and judges must be open; and Boethius is right to suppose that divine timelessness is needed to reconcile the facts about what God infallibly knows about the open future with the settledness of the past and the present.

In fact, though, Occam does not appeal to divine timelessness to explain how it can be (now) open whether God certainly and infallibly judges I will be saved, or certainly and infallibly judges I won't be. Instead, he appears to appeal to the idea that the difference between God's knowing (or judging) I will be saved and his knowing (or judging) I won't be is not an intrinsic difference in God. God would be intrinsically just the same, whichever of the two judgements he made, although the future history of the world would of course be different (*Tractatus de Praedestinatione*, q. 2. 4).

Naturally, it is not easy to see what it could be for God to know or judge something, if whether God knows or judges *P* or *not-P* makes absolutely no difference to how God is intrinsically. Occam makes no bones about this: on his account, we cannot say clearly, or clearly understand, *how* it is possible for God to contingently know future contingents, even though we have good reason to suppose *that* it is possible (*Tractatus de Praedestinatione*, q. 1, a. 6).

One last point for you to think about: it is on the face of it a very plausible principle that settled facts are counterfactually independent of open facts. For example, if it is settled that you were in London yesterday, then you were in London yesterday, whether or not you will go to Paris tomorrow. For Occam, the facts about what God knows concerning the open future are open facts. It seems to follow that the facts about what is happening now are counterfactually independent of the facts about what God knows concerning the open future. Could some of God's beliefs about the future be counterfactually—and apparently causally—insulated from the present in this way? (It's a bit as though you knew now that a certain horse would non-inevitably win a race at Epsom; but you could only bet on that horse, if you would have bet on him anyway, even if you hadn't believed he was going to win.) If we do suppose that the present is counterfactually independent of what God knows about the open future, will this leave as much room as Occam would like for divine providence? Will it allow for a satisfactory account of prophecy involving future contingents? Occam thinks so: in thinking about whether he is right, you should look at his remarks on prophecy in the *Tractatus de Praedestinatione*.

BIBLIOGRAPHY

SELECTIONS OF READINGS

BOSLEY, R., and TWEEDALE, M. (eds.), *Basic Issues in Medieval Philosophy* (Peterborough, 1997).

MCKEON, R. (ed.), *Selections from Medieval Philosophers*, 2 vols. (New York, 1957). Volume i would be especially good to get hold of, for its selections from Boethius (and Abelard) on universals.

SPADE, P. (ed.), *Five Texts on the Mediaeval Problem of Universals* (Indianapolis, 1994). Especially useful for the selection from Scotus (incl. the readings for Section 5.2), though it contains other things of interest.

WIPPEL, J., and WOLTER, A. (eds.), *Medieval Philosophy from St. Augustine to Nicholas of Cusa* (New York, 1969).

HISTORIES OF MEDIEVAL PHILOSOPHY

ARMSTRONG, A. H. (ed.), *The Cambridge History of Later Greek and Early Medieval Philosophy* (Cambridge, 1967). The later chapters have some interesting material on Augustine, Boethius, and Anselm.

COPLESTON, F. C., *A History of Mediaeval Philosophy* (London, and New York, 1972). A very sound and clearly written general introduction to medieval philosophy.

KRETZMANN, N., KENNY, A., and PINBORG, J. (eds.), *The Cambridge History of Later Medieval Philosophy* (Cambridge, 1982). A very useful collection of pieces on various aspects of later medieval philosophy. The articles by Adams on universals, Boh on *consequentiae*, Normore on future contingents, and Wippel on essence and existence are especially relevant.

1. AUGUSTINE

Texts

Basic Writings of St. Augustine, ed. W. Oates, 2 vols. (New York, 1948). An excellent collection, containing the *Confessions*, *On Nature and Grace*, *On the Predestination of Saints*, and *On the Immortality of the Soul* (vol. i), and selections from *The City of God* (vol. ii). Vol. i has most of the Augustine you need, but sadly it has only an (admittedly detailed) synopsis of *De Libero Arbitrio*.

Confessions, ed. and trans. H. Chadwick (Oxford, 1991).

Confessions, ed. and trans. M. Boulding (New York, 1997).

On the Free Choice of the Will, trans. A. Benjamin (Indianapolis, 1964).

Secondary Literature

EVANS, G. R., *Augustine on Evil* (Cambridge, 1982). Well-written, sympathetic discussion of the evolution of Augustine's views on God and evil.

KIRWAN, C., *Augustine* (London, 1989). Highly recommended: a careful and philosophically acute discussion of some of the main philosophical themes in Augustine.

Markus, R. A. (ed.), *Augustine: A Collection of Critical Essays* (New York, 1972). Has some interesting pieces, including Rowe and Rist on Augustine on freedom, foreknowledge, and predestination, Matthews on Augustinian epistemology, Lloyd on Augustine on persons, and Jordan and Lacey on time in Augustine.

2. BOETHIUS

Texts

The Theological Tractates and On the Consolation of Philosophy, trans. and ed. H. F. Stewart, E. K. Rand, and S. J. Tester (London, 1918). All the Boethius you'll need except for the commentary on the *Isagoge*, which is in McKeon (see Selections of Readings, above).

Secondary Literature

Davies, M., 'Boethius and Others on Divine Foreknowledge', *Pacific Philosophical Quarterly*, 64 (1983). As much on the others as on Boethius, but a very subtle discussion of the freedom–foreknowledge problem.

Sorabji, R., *Time, Creation and the Continuum* (London, 1983), ch. 8. An intepretation of how Boethius understood the notion of eternity.

Stump, E., and Kretzmann, N., 'Eternity', *Journal of Philosophy*, 78/8 (1981), 429–58. A rival interpretation (and defence) of the Boethian conception of eternity.

3. ANSELM

Texts

Anselm of Canterbury, trans. J. Hopkins and H. Richardson, 3 vols. (Toronto, 1974). Vol. i has the *Monologion*, and the *Proslogion*, together with the debate between Anselm and Gaunilo on the *Proslogion* argument. Vol. ii has the *De Veritate*, and vol. iii has the *Cur Deus Homo*. The *De Veritate* can also be found in McKeon, vol. i (see Selections of Readings, above).

If you have trouble finding this edition, you may be able to find:

St. Anselm: Basic Writings, ed. S. N. Deane (Chicago, 1948), which contains the *Monologion*, *Prologion*, and the debate with Gaunilo (in a less good translation than the Hopkins–Richardson one).

Secondary Literature

Adams, R., 'The Logical Structure of Anselm's Arguments', in *The Virtue of Faith and Other Essays in Philosophical Theology* (Oxford, 1987). Somewhat technical but rewarding discussion of the intricacies of Anselm's argument.

Quinn, P., 'Christian Atonement and Kantian Justification', *Faith and Philosophy*, 3/4 (1986), 440–61. In spite of the title, the first half expounds and discusses the merits of Anselm's account of the Atonement.

St. Anselm's 'Proslogion', trans. M. J. Charlesworth (Oxford, 1965). The extensive introduction has a very good discussion, both of general features of Anselm's thought, and of his ontological argument.

4. AQUINAS

Texts

Aquinas on Spiritual Creatures, ed. M. Fitzpatrick and J. Wellmuth (Milwaukee, 1969). Particularly useful for Aquinas' views on matter and individuation, and his account of mind and body.

Basic Writings of St. Thomas Aquinas, ed. A. Pegis, 2 vols. (New York, 1945). Because it contains the entire first part of the *Summa Theologiae*, excellent for Aquinas' philosophical theology. It also has other slections from the *Summa Theologiae* and *Summa contra Gentiles*.

On Being and Essence, ed. J. Bobik (South Bend, Ind., 1965). A translation of the *De Ente et Essentia* with a detailed and careful commentary.

Quodlibetal Questions I *and* II, ed. S. Edwards (Toronto, 1983). Question 2 is very useful for Aquinas' views on essence and accidents, and essence and existence.

Selected Writings of St. Thomas Aquinas, ed. R. Goodwin (Indianapolis, 1965). A very useful collection for Aquinas' metaphysics: it has the entire *De Ente et Essentia*, and *De Principiis Naturae*.

Summa contra Gentiles, ed. A. Pegis, 4 vols. (South Bend, Ind., 1975). Although it covers much of the same ground as the *Summa Theologiae*, it often covers that ground in interestingly different ways: very good to read in conjunction with the *Summa Theologiae*.

Summa Theologiae, ed. T. Gilby and T. C. O'Brien, 60 vols., Blackfriars Edition (London, 1964–6). This edition has Latin and English on facing pages. Each volume comes with its own introduction, and often with appendices. Though the quality of the commentary varies, it is often very helpful.

Secondary Literature

Copleston, F. C., *Aquinas* (Harmondsworth, 1955; New York, 1976). A readable and reliable general introduction to Aquinas' philosophy.

Geach, P., 'Aquinas', in P. Geach and G. E. M. Anscombe, *Three Philosophers* (Oxford, 1961). An intriguing, if not always textually anchored, discussion of some of the key elements of Aquinas' metaphysics.

Hughes, C., *On a Complex Theory of a Simple God: An Investigation in Aquinas' Philosophical Theology* (Ithaca, NY, 1989). Part I has a detailed exposition and evaluation of Aquinas' arguments for and conception of divine simplicity; part II explores the Thomistic accounts of the Trinity and Incarnation, and their compatibility with Aquinas' natural theology.

Kenny, A., *Aquinas* (New York, 1980). Less complete than Coplestone's introduction, but briskly and clearly written, and a bit more philosophically high-powered.

Korbech, J. B., 'Free Will and Free Choice', in N. Kretzmann, A. Kenny, and

J. Pinborg (eds.), *The Cambridge History of Later Medieval Philosophy* (Cambridge, 1982). A discussion of Aquinas and others on the relation of the will to the intellect.

Kretzmann, N., *The Metaphysics of Theism: Aquinas' Natural Theology in 'Summa contra Gentiles' I* (Oxford, 1997). A very detailed, beautifully written exposition and defence of Aquinas' arguments for God's existence, simplicity, and perfection. A must for any reader interested in Aquinas' philosophical theology.

——'Philosophy of Mind', in N. Kretzmann and E. Stump (eds.), *The Cambridge Companion to Aquinas* (Cambridge, 1993). Very clear exposition of some of the main themes in Aquinas' philosophy of mind. McDonald's piece on Aquinas' theory of knowledge and Wippel's piece on Aquinas' metaphysics are also worth reading.

Wippel, J., 'Aquinas' Route to the Real Distinction: A Note on the *De Ente et Essentia*', *The Thomist*, 43 (1979), 279–95. A very careful discussion of Aquinas' arguments for a real distinction of essence and existence in creatures.

——*Metaphysical Themes in Thomas Aquinas* (Washington, 1984). Contains the article just mentioned, together with various other good pieces on essence and existence, the Thomistic conception of metaphysics, and Aquinas and others on the status of non-actual *possibilia*. Not philosophically adventurous, but textually solid.

5. SCOTUS

Texts

A Treatise on God as First Principle, ed. A. Wolter (Chicago, 1966). A translation of the *De Primo Principio* with a wonderful introduction and commentary: ideal introduction to Scotus' natural theology.

Iohannis Duns Scoti Doctoris Subtilis et Mariani Opera Omnia, ed. P. Balic *et al.* (Vatican, 1950–). If you can read Latin, this is the edition to get hold of (much more reliable than the older Wadding edition).

John Duns Scotus: God and Creatures, The Quodlibetal Questions, ed. A. Wolter (Princeton, 1975). Covers various questions in metaphysics and in philosophical theology.

John Duns Scotus: Philosophical Writings, a Selection, ed. A. Wolter (London, 1965; Indianapolis, 1987). Very nice selection: it includes Scotus on the nature of metaphysics, God's existence, and the relation of body and soul.

Secondary Literature

King, P., 'Duns Scotus on the Common Nature and Individual Differentia', *Philosophical Topics*, 20/2 (1993), 51–76. A rather dense but interesting study of Scotus on individuation.

McCord Adams, M., 'Occam on Identity and Distinction', *Franciscan Studies*, 36 (1976), 5–74. Contains a detailed and extremely helpful discussion of Scotus on the formal distinction. Also highly recommended is her piece 'Universals in the Early Fourteenth Century', in N. Kretzmann, A. Kenny, and J. Pinborg (eds.), *The Cambridge History of Later Medieval Philosophy* (Cambridge, 1982).

Wolter, A., 'The Formal Distinction', 'Scotus' Individuation Theory', and 'The

Realism of Scotus', all in *The Philosophical Theology of John Duns Scotus* (Ithaca, NY, 1990). All three pieces are essential reading for Scotus on particulars and universals. In the same collection, 'Duns Scotus on the Existence and Nature of God' is very helpful, though you won't need to read it if you can get hold of Wolter's edition of the *De Primo Principio* (see above).

6. OCCAM

Texts

Ockham's Theory of Terms: Part 1 of the Summa Logicae, ed. M. Loux (South Bend, Ind., 1974). Excellent for Occam's account of universals, as well as his theory of *suppositio*. The translation is preceded by two essays well worth reading (the first on Occam's ontology, the second on his logic).

Predestination, God's Foreknowledge, and Future Contingents, ed. N. Kretzmann and M. McCord Adams (New York, 1965). Contains not only the *Tractatus De Praedestinatione*, but also related discussions from part 3 of Occam's *Summa Logicae*, and Occam's commentary on book 9 of Aristotle's *De Interpretatione* (where Aristotle talks about the sea-battle). Highly recommended for the introduction, as well as for the readings themselves.

William of Ockham: Philosophical Writings, a Selection, ed. P. Boehner (London, 1957; Indianapolis, 1990). A good selection of Occam's writings in metaphysics, philosophical logic, and philosophical theology.

Secondary Literature

Boehner, P., 'Did Ockham Know of Material Implication?', *Franciscan Studies*, 11 (1951), 203–30. He did, according to Boehner. Worth reading, even if you don't find it ultimately convincing.

McCord Adams, M., *Ockham* (South Bend, Ind., 1988). A very long book on Occam, which goes deeply into his metaphysics and philosophical theology: every page is worth reading. Very helpful on Scotus as well as on Occam.

Normore, C., 'Future Contingents', in N. Kretzmann, A. Kenny, and J. Pinborg (eds.), *The Cambridge History of Later Medieval Philosophy* (Cambridge, 1982). An excellent discussion of Occam and others on future contingents.

Prior, A. N., 'The Formalities of Omniscience', in *Papers on Time and Tense* (Oxford, 1968). Rather more on Aquinas' solution to the problem of God's knowledge of future contingents than on Occam's solution. Still, philosophically first-rate, and definitely worth reading.

10

KANT

Sebastian Gardner

1. KANT'S EPISTEMOLOGY AND METAPHYSICS

Any study of Immanuel Kant's philosophy must start with the *Critique of Pure Reason*,[1] the work that inaugurates Kant's mature, 'Critical' philosophy and stands at the centre of his philosophical system. It has, in the view of some, few close rivals for being considered the greatest philosophical work of any time. It is, however, difficult and demanding, and gaining the necessary familiarity with Kant's complex prose and novel terminology is a lengthy process.

What is intended in this chapter as a whole is a plain statement of Kant's views designed to help with an initial study of his texts, and some indication of the important questions that arise; a thorough and critically informed grasp of Kant's philosophy cannot be attained without some reading of the secondary literature.

This first part of the chapter is organized so as to follow the order of the *CPR*. Each section sketches Kant's main claims and the general direction of his argument, and some of the corresponding exegetical and critical issues; broader critical and interpretative questions concerning Kant's epistemology and metaphysics are indicated in Sections 1.10 and 1.16. At the beginning of each section, references are given to relevant sections from the *CPR*, the *Prolegomena*, and other relevant writings of Kant's, and suggestions for passages from the *CPR* to concentrate on at first reading; at the end, references are given to secondary literature. Regarding the secondary literature, there are a number of exegetically orientated textual commentaries on the *CPR* (listed in the Bibliography) that are likely to prove invaluable, and these should be turned to in the first instance; references to these are not given here, since appropriate sections may be ascertained by consulting their contents pages or index. The secondary literature designated in each section, selected on grounds of critical interest, should be regarded therefore as further reading.

1.1. The Prefaces: Reason, the Copernican Revolution, and Kant's Philosophical Project

CPR, prefaces to the first and second editions, Avii–xxii and Bvii–xliv.[2] See also the introduction, sects. VI–VII, B19–30, The History of Pure Reason, A852–6/B880–4; and *Proleg.*, preface/introduction, 255–64. Passages to concentrate on: Avii–xii, Bxiv–xxii, B21–8.

[1] Kant's texts, and abbreviations used in this chapter, are discussed in the Bibliography.

[2] References in this chapter to the *CPR* refer to the Akademie pagination, cited in the margin of Kemp Smith's translation, from which quotations in this chapter are taken. The 'A' number refers to the first edition and the 'B' number to the second; where only one reference is given, the text appears only in the one edition.

Kant is regarded invariably as the historical successor to rationalism and empiricism, and as having overcome and in a sense synthesized those two philosophical traditions. Kant's philosophy achieves this, however, on the basis of a revolutionary transformation of philosophical method and doctrine, and the best place to start in getting a sense of what this involves is with the problems that Kant was attempting to solve, which are identified clearly in the prefaces.

Kant begins by stressing the contradictory state of metaphysics, which, he says, 'has hitherto been a merely random groping' (Bxii). (The term metaphysics signifies different things for Kant in different contexts; here it is roughly equivalent to philosophy as a whole.) In Kant's view, metaphysics has made no progress and oscillated continually between dogmatism and scepticism, in stark contrast with mathematics and the natural sciences, both of which employ secure procedures. A rejection of metaphysics is, however, not a genuine option, not only because the impulse to metaphysics is a 'natural disposition' of ours (see B21–2), but also because metaphysical inquiry is prima facie justified: metaphysics simply employs, in a pure form, the very same faculty of reason which is employed by common sense and science (see Avii). The contradictions of metaphysics cannot be ignored, for they cast doubt on the legitimacy of reason as a whole and thereby threaten to undermine common sense and science, and even more importantly for Kant, to destroy the metaphysical ideas of freedom, God, and the soul, on which morality, he holds, depends (see Bxxv–xxxv).

With a view to releasing us from this quandary, Kant calls on reason to undertake the task of self-examination—to subject itself to a 'critique'—in order to determine whether or not metaphysics is possible (see Axi–xii). A critique of pure reason is a critical inquiry into the capacity of reason to know things lying beyond the bounds of sense-experience, such as God and the soul. The second half of the *CPR*, the Dialectic, is where Kant subjects metaphysical speculation about such topics to close scrutiny, after its first half, containing the Aesthetic and Analytic, has provided a general account of human cognition.

The self-examination of reason and inquiry into the possibility of metaphysics requires us to determine under what conditions objects can be known by us. The doctrine of transcendental idealism—described by Kant as effecting a 'Copernican revolution' in philosophy (see Bxvi, Bxxii n.)—supplies Kant's answer to this question, and he spells out two of its fundamental components in the second preface:

1. A methodological claim, expressed in Kant's famous statement that, 'Hitherto it has been assumed that all our knowledge must conform to objects', and that we must 'make trial whether we may not have more success in the tasks of metaphysics, if we suppose that objects must conform to our knowledge' (Bxvi).

2. A substantial claim, that the object of our knowledge is 'to be taken *in a twofold sense*, namely as appearance and as thing in itself' (Bxxvii), and that objects are known to us only in the first sense, as appearances (see Bxx, Bxxvi).

An appearance (*Erscheinung*), for Kant, is an object constituted (in a specifically philosophical sense that has yet to be explained in the *CPR*) by the subject; a thing in itself (*Ding an sich*) is an object constituted independently of the subject. (These definitions should be regarded as only rough approximations, the meaning of these terms being inseparable from the controversial question of how Kant's transcendental idealism is to be interpreted.) Claims (1) and (2) are connected thus: in so far as an object is conceived as an appearance, it is conceived as conforming necessarily to our mode of knowledge; in so far as it is conceived as a thing in itself, it is conceived as something which does not conform necessarily to our mode of knowledge, and to which our mode of knowledge must consequently conform.

Because, according to Kant, sense-experience is a necessary component of our mode of knowledge, appearances are necessarily objects given in sense-experience. Transcendental idealism maintains, then, that empirical objects are the only possible objects of knowledge for us: that the limits of knowledge coincide with those of possible experience. Reality in the sense of a realm of objects constituted independently of the subject, a realm consisting of things in themselves, would be transempirical or supersensible, and Kant says that, although this is something that we can (indeed, must) conceive, we can have no knowledge of it.

The verdict of Kant's critique will be, therefore, that reason's claims to knowledge of things within the bounds of experience are legitimate, and its claims to knowledge of things lying outside those bounds illegitimate: metaphysical knowledge is possible in connection with the application of reason to the objects of experience (for example, and paradigmatically, with regard to such propositions as that every event has a cause), and the employment of reason becomes groundless and self-contradictory at the point where it parts company from experience. The metaphysics that Kant attacks, as involving an illegitimate attempt to gain knowledge of things in themselves, are referred to as *transcendent*, or speculative, metaphysics, and those that he defends, as successfully providing us with knowledge of appearances, as immanent metaphysics, or the *metaphysics of experience*.

Because Kant's philosophy restricts knowledge to appearances, it qualifies as a form of idealism. It is called 'Critical' because it is premissed on a prior, reflexive examination of our cognitive powers. Its 'transcendental' dimension stems from the Copernican requirement that objects be considered as standing in conformity with the cognitive constitution of the subject: Kant says that the word 'transcendental' 'does not signify something passing beyond all experience [i.e. transcendent] but something that indeed precedes it a priori, but that is intended simply to make cognition of experience possible' (*Proleg.* 373n.[3]). Transcendental inquiry dictates a special method of philosophical inquiry, which consists in the identification of 'conditions of possible experience' of objects, or transendental conditions, which are held to be necessary if there is to be experience of objects at all. Kant will argue that they include the basic tenets of common-sense metaphysics of experience, such as, that there are substances which persist throughout change, and that every event has a cause. The arguments that identify these conditions are called by Kant *transcendental proofs*, and these, if successful, refute scepticism, such as Hume's, by showing that scepticism incoherently violates the conditions which are necessary for experience to occur. Transcendental concepts and principles are consequently ones that supply us with a priori knowledge of objects.

In addition to legitimizing the metaphysics of experience and, correlatively, common-sense judgements about the empirical world, Kant intends also in the *CPR* to legitimize natural science (specifically, Newtonian physics, regarded by Kant as closely related to the metaphysics of experience), and to explain the grounds of mathematics and geometry. And, although the *Critique* will not provide a theory of morality, Kant claims that it contains an essential preparation for a proper grounding of morality (see Bxxv), which will in turn provide a rational foundation for religion. In this connection, Kant indicates in the prefaces (see Bxxi–ii, Bxxv–xxx)—in anticipation of his ethical theory, and the theory of religion to be based upon it—that reason is able in the practical rather than theoretical sphere of morality to fulfil its interest in the transcendent concepts of freedom, God, and the soul, the reality of which may be affirmed in that context in a restricted sense (see Sections 2.2–2.3).

(The historical background to the *CPR*, and Kant's pre-Critical period, are presented excellently in Beiser 1992; see also Kemp Smith 1923, pp. xxv–xxxiii and app. B; and Wolff 1963, ch. 1. On Kant's conception of reason, see O'Neill 1989, ch. 1; and on Kant's concern to legitimate reason, O'Neill 1992.)

1.2. The Introduction: Synthetic A Priori Judgement

CPR, introduction, A1–16/B1–30. See also A150–3/B189–93; and *Proleg.*, preamble, 265–80. Passages to concentrate on: B1–6, A6–10/B10–14, B14–18.

The introduction aims to establish the existence of a hitherto unrecognized class of judgements which are anomalous for rationalism and empiricism and

[3] References to the *Prolegomena* take the form of either a section number, when preceded by '§', or a page number. Page references follow the Akademie pagination, cited at the top of the page in Beck's translation and in the margin of Ellington's translation. Quotations in this chapter are taken from Ellington's translation.

entail the inadequacy of both rationalist and empiricist epistemology. These are *synthetic a priori* judgements. In this context Kant seeks to provide the philosophical project of the *CPR* with an overarching logical characterization: namely, that of finding a solution to the problem of how synthetic a priori judgements are possible (see B19).

Kant's immediate target is the division, found in Leibniz and Hume, of all our knowledge into two fundamental classes, knowledge that is necessary and a priori, and knowledge that is contingent and a posteriori. Leibniz divides knowledge into (1) truths of reason, derivable from logical principles and so necessary, and (2) truths of fact, contingent propositions known through experience. Metaphysical knowledge falls of course on the side of truths of reason, along with geometry and mathematics. Correspondingly, Hume divides knowledge into (1) relations of ideas, which can be discovered 'by the mere operation of thought' and include geometry and mathematics, and (2) matters of fact, distinguished by the conceivability of their contradictory. Hume bases his critique of causality and general repudiation of metaphysics on the impossibility, he holds, of assigning metaphysical propositions to either class (causal relations are not relation of ideas, since the contradictory of any causal judgement is always conceivable, and necessity is not given in sense-experience). Kant aims to challenge the bipartite picture of knowledge and thereby undermine both Leibniz and Hume's conclusions regarding metaphysics.

Kant begins with the hypothesis that we have a priori knowledge, observing that the fact that all of our knowledge 'begins with' experience does not mean that it all 'arises out of' (derives from) experience (see B1–3). In order to detect the presence of a priori elements in our knowledge, Kant advances two (logically equivalent) criteria (see A1–2, B3–4): (1) 'strict universality', and (2) necessity. A knowledge claim has strict, as opposed to relative, universality if what it predicates is necessarily true of its objects. Kant takes necessity to be a criterion of apriority on the ground that knowledge of necessity cannot derive from experience: experience 'teaches us that a thing is so and so, but not that it cannot be otherwise' (B3).

There are, Kant holds, demonstrable instances of a priori knowledge (B4–6). Mathematical propositions, and the principle that every event must have a cause, are a priori judgements. Two concepts that are a priori and contained in the concept of 'body' are those of spatial extension and substance (Kant's reason for saying this becomes clear later: see Section 1.3). The field in which we aspire to knowledge that is by definition non-empirical and so a priori is of course transcendent metaphysics (see A2–3/B6–7, B21–2), with respect to which Kant formulates the following puzzle: If metaphysical judgements are a priori, how is it possible for them to extend our knowledge, as they are intended to do? Any extension of our knowledge would seem to require experience (Hume's view being that, for that very reason, metaphysics cannot extend our knowledge).

With a view to answering this question, Kant introduces a new distinction, between analytic and synthetic judgements (see A6–8, B10–12). A judgement is *analytic* if the predicate is contained in the concept of the subject, such that the judgement is true by virtue of the principle of contradiction (its negation is self-contradictory). A judgement is *synthetic* if the predicate is connected with, but not contained in, the concept of the subject. Synthetic judgements are true by virtue of something other than the principle of contradiction: there must be some third thing—'something else (X)'—that shows the predicate to be connected with the concept of the subject. Analytic judgements merely explicate concepts by analysing them into their constituents; only synthetic judgements extend our knowledge.

Does the analytic–synthetic distinction correspond to the necessary and a priori–contingent & empirical distinction? Leibniz and Hume would expect all necessary and a priori judgements to be analytic, and all contingent and empirical judgements to be synthetic; their accounts of the sources of knowledge allow of no alternative.

Kant, however, maintains that the two distinctions do not correspond. Metaphysical judgements, whilst being a priori, are not analytic but synthetic. Consider 'every event has a cause' (see A9–10/B13–14). Because it is necessary, it must be a priori. But it is not analytic, for the concept of the predicate is not contained in the concept of the subject: the concept of an event does not contain that of an effect. This makes the judgement synthetic. To say that metaphysical judgements are synthetic a priori is to say that they cannot be derived from either logic (since they are synthetic) or sense-experience (since they are a priori).

That metaphysical judgements are synthetic a priori might seem to return us directly to Hume's conclusion that metaphysics is impossible—were it not that there are other sorts of synthetic a priori judgement which can scarcely be repudiated, namely the propositions of mathematics and geometry (see B14–18). Kant argues that arithmetical judgements such as $7 + 5 = 12$ cannot be regarded as analytic: the concept of the sum of 7 and 5 does not contain the concept of the number 12; a synthesis is required to establish their connection. The same synthetic status is assigned by Kant to geometrical judgements, such as that a straight line is the shortest distance between two points.

We have, therefore, strong reason for thinking that synthetic a priori judgements in general *are possible*, and it follows that in order to account for the possibility of mathematics and geometry, we must reject Leibniz and Hume's division of knowledge into two fundamental types, and install in its place a tripartite division, the third class consisting of synthetic a priori judgements. The

'X' that is responsible for the synthesis grounding synthetic a priori judgements is so far unknown to us, but we may seek to identify it (see B19–20). Metaphysics is not, therefore, derivable from logic, as Leibniz supposed; but nor can Hume have been right to reject it on the basis that it is grounded neither on logic nor on sense-experience.

Kant's account of the analytic–synthetic distinction raises a number of questions. In the first place, the distinction needs to be reformulated so as to give the terms analytic and synthetic application to false judgements and to judgements that are not of subject–predicate form. More importantly, an objection may be raised concerning how it can be known what is and is not contained in a given concept; to which some have added the complaint that Kant's formulation of the criteria for the distinction makes it merely psychological and thus variable between different individuals. And special questions arise regarding Kant's views of arithmetic and geometry, the latter having particular importance for Kant's claims in the Aesthetic.

A widely held view is that the judgements Kant calls synthetic a priori are really analytic judgements, albeit ones of a non-obvious sort, and that they do not form a genuine, unitary class. It is, nevertheless, reasonable to maintain that the notion of synthetic apriority helps to illuminate at least the problem of metaphysics, whatever view is taken of its wider significance.

(Criticizing Kant's conception of synthetic apriority, see Bennett 1966, sects. 2–4; Robinson 1969; and Strawson 1996: 42–4; in its defence, see Allison 1983: 73–8; and Beck 1963. Further discussion may be found in Beck 1969*b*, pt. III.)

1.3. The Transcendental Aesthetic I: Space and Time

CPR, Transcendental Aesthetic, §§1–2, A19–25/B33–40, and §§4–5, A30–2/B46–9. See also *Proleg.*, §§6–13. Passages to concentrate on: A19–25/B33–40.

In the Transcendental Aesthetic, which is concerned with the faculty that Kant calls sensibility, Kant aims to establish the unique status of space and time as 'pure a priori intuitions' that provide the sensible form of experience, and on that basis to explain how geometry is possible and to prove transcendental idealism. (The last is discussed in Section 1.4.)

Kant's discussion of space and time is preceded by his analysis of cognition, which is of fundamental importance for everything that follows in the *CPR* (see §1, A19–22/B33–6; also A15–16/B29–30, A50–2/B74–6). Kant makes a distinction between *intuitions* (*Anschauungen*) and *concepts* (*Begriffe*). Both are species of what Kant calls representations (*Vorstellungen*), a term that encompasses all of the elements of cognition. The distinction between intuitions and concepts is itself based on a more fundamental distinction between two different ways in which our cognitive powers operate: namely, between an object's being *given* to us, and its being *thought* by us. Intuitions are those representations by means of which objects are given to us, and concepts those by means of which we think about objects. The cognitive power, or faculty, that enables objects to be given is *sensibility*, and that which enables objects to be thought is *understanding*. (On Kant's concept of intuition, see Hintikka 1969. Compare Allison 1983: 65–8; Aquila 1983, ch. 2; and Parsons 1992: 63–6.)

Kant fills out the distinction between intuitions and concepts in the following ways: (1) An intuition relates immediately to an object (see A19/33, A320/B377). A concept, by contrast, relates to an object 'by means of a feature which several things may have in common' (A320/B377), and thus only mediately, via intuitions. (2) An intuition is a 'singular representation' (B136n.), a representation of a particular, individual thing. A concept by contrast is inherently general: necessarily, a concept can be applied to more than one particular. (3) Sensibility and understanding are contrasted by Kant in terms of passivity and activity (see A51/B75): sensibility is a capacity of receptivity; for subjects such as ourselves, what is needed for an object to be given is that our minds should be *affected*, the result of which is sensation, which comprises the a posteriori element in cognition. The faculty of understanding, by contrast, is spontaneous.

Kant's analysis has the direct and powerful epistemological implication that neither intuitions nor concepts are individually sufficient for knowledge—'Thoughts without content are empty, intuitions without concepts are blind' (A51/B75)—and that only 'through their union can knowledge arise' (A51/B75–6). Kant therefore concurs with empiricism in rejecting the rationalist claim that metaphysical knowledge can be achieved through concepts alone, and with rationalism in rejecting the empiricist claim that knowledge of matters of fact derives from sense-experience alone. Correlatively, Kant charges rationalism and empiricism with failing to appreciate the difference between intuitions and concepts (see A43–4/B60–2, A271/B327).

Kant's view of our cognitive powers as divided by two heterogeneous, mutually irreducible, and mutually dependent functions may be defended by contrasting human cognition with another kind of which we can form some sort of idea. We can imagine a subject for whom the act of thinking, and being presented with an object, are one and the same. Such a subject would possess *intellectual intuition*, as opposed to the *sensible* intuition that we possess (see B68, B71, A252; also *CJ* 401–3, 406–7). It is evident that we do not have intellectual intuition.

Prefacing Kant's discussion of space and time, and important for an understanding of it, is his doctrine of pure intuition (see A20–2/B34–6). Kant makes a distinction between the *matter* and the *form* of appearances (appearances are understood here simply as objects of sense-experience). Kant argues that whilst the matter of appearances (which is what in appearance corresponds to sensation) is a posteriori, its form must be a priori. Consequently, there must be intuitions that do not contain anything belonging to sensation and provide the form of appearances; these are *pure intuitions*, as opposed to empirical intuitions. The form of appearances is, Kant tells us, space and time. We have therefore pure intuitions of space and time, and Kant claims that pure intuition of space allows it to be explained how geometry is possible: geometry is the synthetic a priori knowledge that we derive from our pure intuition of space (see B40–1). We can study space and grasp geometric truths independently of experience, simply on the basis of mental constructions of lines, triangles, and so on; and from our a priori knowledge of space derives our a priori knowledge of the spatial properties of external objects, which must conform to the principles of geometry. Kant makes a symmetrical claim with regard to principles of Newtonian physics and the pure intuition of time (see B48–9).

A further element in the background to Kant's discussion of space and time—without which it cannot be understood fully—is the opposition between the Newtonian 'absolutist' view and Leibniz's 'relational' view: the Newtonian regards space as an absolutely real, self-subsistent 'container' of physical objects, which would exist even if no physical objects were contained within it; Leibniz regards space and time as logical constructions out of relations between objects. Kant refers to these as the views that space and time are 'real existences' and that they are 'only determinations or relations of things' respectively (A23/B37). Kant's view differs from those of both the Newtonian and Leibniz, which he intends to refute in the Aesthetic.

Kant's arguments that space and time are a priori intuitions are contained in their respective Metaphysical Expositions (§2, A22–5/B37–40; §4, A30–2/B46–8). It is best to concentrate on Kant's discussion of space, of which his discussion of time is largely a reflection. The Metaphysical Exposition of Space is a set of four arguments. The first two are meant to show that space is a priori: (1) Kant argues that the representation of space must be a priori, and not an empirical concept derived from experience of outer objects, because it is presupposed for all experience of outer objects (see A23/B38). My sensations cannot be referred outside me unless I presuppose the representation of space, which must therefore, Kant claims, be a priori. (2) It is impossible, Kant claims, to represent the absence of space (see A24/B38–9). Space is thus a 'necessary', and so a priori, representation. (In this context, note Kant's description of space and time as the forms of inner and outer sense at A22–3/B37: Kant's claim is that we become aware of things distinct from ourselves by representing them as being in space, and of our mental states by representing them as being in time.) The third and fourth arguments are meant to show that space is an intuition: (3) Kant claims that 'we can represent to ourselves only one space', on the grounds that different spaces are 'parts of one and the same space' and contained within it (see A24–5/B39). The relation of space to its parts is unlike that of a concept to its instances, and something of which only one instance can be given must be given in intuition. (4) Space is, Kant claims, 'represented as an infinite given magnitude' (see A25/B39–40), in the sense that it is given to us as unbounded and infinitely divisible, in a way that is asymmetrical with concepts, again making space an intuition.

Two further arguments of Kant's regarding space may be considered. (5) An argument for the intuitive character of space, referred to as the argument from incongruent counterparts—e.g. a left hand and a right hand, identical in all other respects, the difference between which is not relational but intrinsic, a matter of orientation that 'cannot be described discursively'—appears in the *Prolegomena* (285–6). (6) Kant's argument from geometry (see A24, B40–1) is intended to show that space is both a priori and an intuition. Kant argues that *only* if space is an a priori intuition can geometry be accounted for: geometry cannot be based on concepts, since it is synthetic, so it must be based on intuition of space; and it cannot be a posteriori, since it is necessary, so it must be based on a priori intuition of space.

Kant's arguments have elicited extensive commentary. It may be asked, for instance, whether we cannot imagine non-spatial experience of a world, and worlds containing multiple spaces or times, and if Kant's absence of space argument makes anything more than a merely psychological point. Kant is generally regarded as succeeding in showing at least that space and time are markedly different from any other concepts, and that they play a fundamental epistemological role for us in making experience possible, thus making Leibniz's view very hard to defend. But it is not certain that Kant shows them to be a priori: it seems to follow from Kant's arguments that the representation of space must be contemporaneous with, but not that it must be prior to, that of outer objects. Kant may be defended on this score, but doing so involves some interpolation.

(Parsons 1992 reviews all of the issues that arise in the Aesthetic. On Kant's arguments for the apriority and intuitivity of space and time, see Allison 1983: 81–98; Aquila 1983, ch. 3; Horstmann 1976; and Walker 1978, chs. 3–5. Beck 1969*a* discusses Kant's relation to rationalism and empiricism.)

1.4. The Transcendental Aesthetic II: Transcendental Idealism

CPR, Transcendental Aesthetic, §3, B40–5, and §§6–8, A32–49/B49–66, B66–73. See also *Proleg.* 287–94. Later sections in the *CPR* containing sustained discussion of transcendental idealism are: the chapter on Phenomena and Noumena, A235–60/B294–315, the Fourth Paralogism in the first edition, A366–80, and the Antinomy of Pure Reason, sect. 6, A490–507/B518–35. Also helpful to look at is Kant's Letter to Herz, 21

February 1772; and his pre-Critical *Inaugural Dissertation*, sects. II, IV. Passages to concentrate on: B40–5.

Kant's further claim in the Aesthetic is that space and time are *transcendentally ideal*: 'they belong only to the form of intuition, and therefore to the subjective constitution of our minds, apart from which they could not be ascribed to anything whatsoever' (A23/B37–8). From which it follows that all appearances, and thus all objects of our knowledge, are also transcendentally ideal.

To understand the concept of transcendental ideality, it is necessary to look at Kant's distinction of appearances and things in themselves and his discussion of what can be known of each (see A26–7/B42–3), and his claim that transcendental ideality is compatible with empirical reality (see A27–8/B43–4, A35–6/B52–3, A42–3/B59–60).

According to Kant, things are spatial and temporal only under the 'limitation' that they are considered 'from the human standpoint', 'as objects of sensible intuition' (see A26–7/B42–3). To consider things thus is to consider them as appearances; as objects that, in Copernican terms, conform necessarily to our mode of knowledge. Since space and time are the forms of our intuition, appearances can be known to be necessarily spatial and temporal. Space and time, and appearances, are consequently, Kant argues, *empirically real*: the reality from the human standpoint of space and time is guaranteed by the fact that they are the forms of human sensibility and necessary for us to have experience of object; that of appearances is guaranteed by their necessary spatiality and temporality. (The self too is according to Kant known only as appearance, i.e. is transcendentally ideal, since it is known only through inner sense, the form of which is time: see A38/B54–5, B67–9.)

If, however, the limitation of the human standpoint is removed, and things are considered 'without regard to the constitution of our sensibility' (A28/B44), they cannot be considered spatial or temporal. Such a standpoint is occupied in the context of a transcendental inquiry into the conditions under which objects can be known by us (see Section 1.1). The objects of our experience are not real when considered transcendentally, because they are spatial and temporal, and space and time belong only to the form of our intuition. If we had reason to think of space and time as not merely 'special conditions' of our sensibility but 'conditions of the possibility of things' (A27/B43), then the objects of our experience would be real when considered transcendentally; in which case, we would have knowledge of things in themselves. But, Kant argues, we cannot so regard our forms of sensibility. From a transcendental standpoint, therefore, the objects of our knowledge are not real but ideal, i.e. subject-dependent or subject-constituted. And from this it follows that we cannot know anything at all, of a positive or contentful kind, about things in themselves (see A42–3/B59–60).

The full strength of Kant's doctrine of transcendental idealism emerges when it is appreciated that Kant maintains not just that we *cannot* know that things in themselves *are* spatio-temporal, but that we *can* know that things in themselves are *not* spatio-temporal (Kant makes this explicit at A26–8/B42–4, A30/B45). This is again because we can know space and time to belong only to the subjective constitution of our mind, making it impossible for them to belong also to things in themselves. Transcendental idealism is therefore fundamentally distinct from scepticism, which by contrast proclaims uncertainty regarding what we can and cannot know; as it is, for a number of reasons, from Locke's realism (see A45–6/B62–3) and, Kant claims, from Berkeley's idealism (see A29–30/B45, B274; *Proleg.* 288–9).

In sum, transcendental idealism may be defined as the thesis that the objects of our knowledge are empirically real but transcendentally ideal, and so mere appearances, and that things cannot be known as they are in themselves. All other philosophical positions Kant regards as united in supposing that the objects of our knowledge are transcendentally real, and that things can be known as they are in themselves. Accordingly, all pre-Critical philosophy amounts to so many different forms of *transcendental realism* (see A369, A491/B519).

The key to transcendental idealism is thus the claim that space and time belong *only* to the subjective constitution of our mind, and in order to prove this, Kant must rule out even just the bare possibility that space and time belong *both* to our subjective constitution and to things in themselves. Views differ as to where Kant's main argument is to be located. It would seem that Kant appeals at least in part to the results of the Metaphysical Expositions, but four other arguments are advanced explicitly in the Aesthetic in support of transcendental idealism: (1) If the objects of geometry were things in themselves, geometrical necessity would be unaccountable. The objects of geometry are therefore appearances (see A46–9/B64–6). (2) The assumption that space and time are transcendentally real renders them epistemologically inaccessible, and so drives us to reduce the world and the self to mere illusion. Transcendental idealism is therefore necessary if more than mere seemings are to exist (see B70–1). (3) Space and time consist in mere relations, but things in themselves cannot be constitutionally relational (see B66–7). (4) Reality must be conceived as non-spatio-temporal if God is to be conceivable (see B71–2).

On the face of it, the argument from geometry appears the most promising of these four, since the others depend on evidently disputable premisses. Its unsoundness has, however, been established by the subsequent development of non-Euclidean geometries, which shows geometrical truths to be empirical and so contingent. This suggests that a successful reconstruction of the Aesthetic's argument for transcendental idealism would need to base itself on the claim that space and time are a priori intuitions, independently of geometry.

(Key discussions of the Aesthetic's argument for transcendental idealism are Allison 1983: 98–114, to be read in the context of Allison's general reconstruction of Kant's argument in chs. 1–2; and Strawson 1966: 51–62, 68–71. See also Greenwood 1989; and Guyer 1987, ch. 16. Concerning the significance of non-Euclidean geometry for the Aesthetic, see Hopkins 1982; Horstmann 1976; and Strawson 1966, pt. v.)

1.5. The Categories

CPR, Transcendental Logic, from the beginning up to the Transcendental Deduction, A50–95/B74–116. See also _Proleg._, §21, §39. Passages to concentrate on: A55–7/B79–82, A67–70/B92–5, A76–80/B102–6.

The Transcendental Analytic examines the faculty of understanding and specifies the conceptual conditions of human knowledge. Its first task is to identify the fundamental concepts of the understanding on which all other concepts depend. Kant refers to these as the *pure concepts of the understanding* and later, once he has shown which they are and how they are derived, as the *categories*. Kant holds them to be a priori (the proof that there must be such concepts comes in the Transcendental Deduction). Its second task is to justify the application of these a priori concepts to objects of experience, which it attempts to do by showing that they are conceptual presuppositions of an objective world. Kant will claim that among the a priori concepts whose application is justified in this way are the concepts that figure in the metaphysics of experience—above all, those of substance and causality. It is generally thought that the Analytic contains also an argument that it is necessary that there *be* an objective world, and so contains Kant's reply to Hume's scepticism regarding non-transcendent metaphysical concepts. (The manner in which the argument of the Analytic is distributed between its different sections is, however, unclear, which gives rise to different views of what is going on in each section.)

The Analytic is prefaced by an account of what Kant calls *transcendental logic*, which attempts to specify the conditions under which it is possible for thought to relate to objects (see A50–66/B74–91). The contrast is with general logic, which considers merely the relation of thoughts to one another. Since for us thought about objects requires intuition, and our intuition is sensible, transcendental logic is concerned with the relation of thought to objects of sensible intuition. The Analytic comprises one branch of transcendental logic, a 'logic of truth' that specifies the conditions under which thought may succeed in relating to objects; its other branch, a 'logic of illusion', contained in the Dialectic, specifies the conditions under which thought fails, yet falsely seems, to relate to objects.

Kant tells us what the pure concepts of the understanding are in 'The Clue to the Discovery of All Pure Concepts of the Understanding' (A66–83/B91–116), known as the *metaphysical deduction* of the categories. The metaphysical deduction is founded on the supposition that the function of judgement must provide a 'clue' to the pure concepts of the understanding. Judgement consists in the unification of representations, and Kant begins by setting out in the Table of Judgements (see A70/B95) what he takes to be the twelve different 'functions of unity in judgements', or forms of judgement (categorical judgement, hypothetical judgement, and so on). The pure concepts of the understanding, or categories, that correspond to the forms of judgement are set out in the Table of Categories (see A80/B106). For example, corresponding to the logical form of hypothetical judgement there is the category of causality, and corresponding to that of categorical judgement, the category of substance. Kant justifies the transition from formal logic to a priori concepts on the grounds that the only way in which the categories can derive their content is through their having a relation to (pure) intuition. The Table of Categories is thus constructed with a view to identifying a priori concepts that are capable of giving rise to both unity in judgements and unity in intuitions: they both correspond to the logical forms of judgement and play a role in organizing intuition.

Kant's intention in the metaphysical deduction is not fully clear. On a modest interpretation, Kant is merely taking the categories for granted as ones that we actually find ourselves with, and showing of them that they correspond to forms of judgement, and so are strong candidates for categorial status. But the text supports a more ambitious interpretation of Kant as meaning to prove that these categories and no others must be the pure concepts of the understanding. Understood thus, Kant's claims for the derivation of the categories are agreed to fail. For example—quite aside from objections to Kant's classification of the forms of judgement that may be raised in the light of modern propositional and predicate calculus—it is hard to see why the logical function of categorial judgement should yield the rich concept of substance, or why the concept of cause must emerge from hypothetical judgement.

The failure of the metaphysical deduction, if it is one, is not, however, of great importance, since the categories will be vindicated individually later in the Analytic of Principles. What remains important in the metaphysical deduction—and prefigures the Transcendental Deduction—is the suggestion that the categories play a double role, in making judgement and objects of intuition possible simultaneously. The modest reading of the metaphysical deduction is thus all that Kant need lay claim to, and for the duration of the Transcendental Deduction that follows, the question of what particular concepts provide the a priori conditions of knowledge may be suspended.

(For discussion of Kant's broad aim and strategy in the Analytic, including the metaphysical deduction, see Allison 1983, ch. 6; and Strawson 1966: 72–89.

Bird 1962, ch. 7; Guyer 1992*a*: 123–36; and Melnick 1973: 37–42 offer helpful commentary on the metaphysical deduction.)

1.6. The Transcendental Deduction: Synthesis and Apperception

CPR, Transcendental Deduction, A84–95/B116–29, A95–130, B129–69. See also _Proleg._, §§18–22. Passages to concentrate on: A84–95/B116–29, B129–43, B165–9.

The Transcendental Deduction, the centrepiece of the Analytic, traces a wealth of deep and intricate connections between the highly abstract concepts of an object, self-consciousness, judgement, concept application, and experience. It is probably the hardest section of the *CPR*, and keeping sight of a single line of argument when reading it is extremely difficult.

The stated aim of the Deduction is to show that the categories are justified in their application to experience. On the interpretation that is dominant, Kant's strategy is to show that such is a condition of self-consciousness: that I could not be conscious of myself as a subject of thought and experience unless I applied the categories to the objects of my experience. This interpretation is open to challenge—other readings take the Deduction to be concerned with the conditions of empirical knowledge rather than self-consciousness, and so not to have the ambition of refuting scepticism—but in any case, it leaves scope for widely different views of the Deduction's exact premisses, argument, and conclusion. In view of this uncertainty, all that can be expected on a first reading of the Deduction is to gain some familiarity with its central themes and concepts and their interconnections. Some of these are sketched below; assembling them into an argument is a further task, which requires reference to the reconstructions presented in the commentaries.

1. *The problem* (see §13, A84–92/B116–24). A deduction is required to answer a question of rightfulness or justification, as opposed to a question of fact. The justification of the categories cannot be empirical, for an account like that in Locke's *Essay* describes only the manner in which we come to possess concepts, a mere matter of fact. (Appeals to innateness are also to be rejected; see B167–8.) The difficulty of providing a justification emerges when it is reflected that, as yet in Kant's transcendental story, there is no reason to believe that the objects of experience have any relation to the understanding: appearances might 'be so constituted that the understanding should not find them to be in accordance with' its own conditions (see A90/B123). For example, everything in the series of appearances 'might be in such confusion' that nothing presented itself answering to the concept of cause and effect. The Deduction will try to show that this possibility is not genuine, but Kant's point is that nothing said so far in the *CPR* excludes it.

2. *The solution in outline* (see §14, A92–5/B124–9). The categories can be justified—under Copernican assumptions (see A92–3/B124–6, B166–7)—if they can be shown to be transcendental conditions: 'If we can prove that by their means alone [i.e. of the categories] an object can be thought, this will be a sufficient deduction of them, and will justify their objective validity' (A96–7). Specifically, Kant focuses on the concept of an object in general, which is an a priori presupposition of all experience (see A93/B126).

3. *Synthesis* (see A97–103, B150–2). The manifold (multiplicity of elements) given to us in intuition must be combined into a unity, if it is to be thought as giving an object. This combination cannot come to us through the senses and must be the a priori work of the understanding (see §15, B129–31). Thus objects of experience presuppose synthesis, the function that gives unity to representations. Kant gives (different) accounts of the multi-level structure of synthesis at A97–105 and B150–2. Synthesis guarantees that objects of experience conform to our mode of cognition.

4. *The transcendental object* (see A104–6, A109). Kant employs the term 'synthetic unity' to denote the fundamental unity of an object that precedes even the application of the categories. Synthetic unity involves application of the concept of the transcendental object, the pure concept of 'something in general = *x*' (A104), which is required if we are to conceive of objects as 'corresponding to, and consequently also distinct from' our representations. The transcendental object is a mere '*x*' without content because, whilst giving unity to the manifold of intuition, it 'cannot itself be intuited by us' (A109): it is the same whatever object is synthesized, and in view of its emptiness, all that it can refer to is 'that unity which must be met with in any manifold of knowledge'. This means that for us objects cannot consist in anything more than representations systematically interconnected according to rules.

5. *Apperception* (see A106–8, A116–18, B131–7, B153–6, B157–9). For any object to be thought, the subject must be self-conscious in the specific sense that it must be aware of itself *as* the self-identical subject of all of its thoughts and experiences: 'It must be possible for the "I think" to accompany all my representations; for otherwise something would be represented in me which could not be thought at all, and that is equivalent to saying that the representation would be impossible, or at least would be nothing to me' (B131–2). Consciousness of self-identity cannot be empirical, because no 'fixed and abiding self can present itself in this flux of inner appearances' (A107; see also A133), and so must be a priori. The a priori unity of consciousness Kant calls *transcendental unity of apperception*—a 'pure original unchangeable consciousness' (A107) of self, without which the empirical self-consciousness of inner sense would not be possible (see B134). Kant emphasizes that transcendental apperception does not amount to knowledge of anything: it is mere, formal consciousness of oneself as thinking.

Kant claims that transcendental apperception imposes a condition on experience, namely that it form a systematic unity. The transcendental unity of apperception plays the same role with respect to the understanding as space and time do with respect to sensibility (see A107, B136): it makes objects thinkable in the same way that space and time make them intuitable, and in fact counts as the 'highest principle in the whole sphere of human knowledge' (B135). The unity of apperception is, Kant suggests, the source of the synthetic unity of objects (see A105, A109–10, B137). Complementarily, synthesis of objects is a condition of the unity of apperception (see A108, A112, B133).

6. *The justification of the categories* (see A111–13, A119, A128; §20, B143; B150–1; §26, B159–65). On the grounds that synthesis must satisfy the requirements of apperception, that apperception is tied to the function of judgement, and that the categories are derived from the forms of judgement, Kant claims the application of the categories to objects of experience to be justified. (The internal connection of apperception with judgement is established by Kant on the basis of a distinction between the subjective (contingent) and objective (necessary) unity of consciousness, and a claim that the latter implicates (objectively valid) judgement: see §§18–19, B139–42.)

Kant claims it not only as a condition of the success of the Deduction but also as a consequence of its argument (on the grounds that the requirements of apperception could not otherwise be fulfilled) that the objects of experience are transcendentally ideal with respect to how they are conceptualized (see A114, A125–30): 'the order and regularity in the appearances, that we entitle nature, we ourselves introduce'; the understanding is the 'lawgiver of nature'. A further crucial implication claimed by Kant for the Deduction is that the objective validity of the categories is restricted strictly to objects of possible experience (see §§22–3, B146–9).

Because the identity of the argument of the Deduction is so uncertain, the job of evaluating it critically merges with that of giving a correct exegesis of it, in which context complex issues arise, including: the relation between the Deductions in each edition; the significance of Kant's distinction between 'subjective' and 'objective' deductions (see Axvi–xvii, A97); and the relation between the Deduction in the *CPR* and the *Prolegomena*'s reworking of this part of Kant's argument in terms of a distinction between 'judgements of perception' and 'judgements of experience' (see *Proleg.*, §§17–20, §21a).

Some (of the many) pertinent questions to be asked of any reconstruction of the Deduction are the following: (1) In the first place, is the question that Kant sets himself to answer in the Deduction a good one: is Kant right that empiricism cannot answer it, and does it in any case allow of some other answer than that which Kant seeks to supply? (2) In view of the evident undesirability of having to conclude that any one section of the *CPR* makes any other redundant, how is the task of the Deduction to be distinguished from that of other sections, in particular the metaphysical deduction and the Refutation of Idealism? (3) What senses of 'object' are involved in the premisses and conclusions of the Deduction, and is its argument free from equivocation in this respect? (A weak sense of 'object of judgement' and a strong sense of 'spatio-temporal objective particular' may both be detected in Kant's text, and it has been objected that Kant slides illicitly from the first to the second.) (4) Regarding the Deduction's fundamental, anti-empiricist thesis that experience is not independent of concepts, does Kant mean to claim that there cannot *be* experiences independently of the categories—or only that experience in so far as it provides the basis for judgement presupposes the categories? (In this context, see Kant's remarks at A112, A120, B131–2.) If the first, how does Kant avoid the (absurd) implication that dreams, hallucinations, and other 'extra-categorial' experience is impossible? (5) Is Kant justified in describing the conditions of apperception as constituting the objects of experience, rather than as simply restricting the conditions under which objects can be experienced? On this depends Kant's claim to have advanced the argument for transcendental idealism in the Deduction. (The status of the Deduction as a transcendental argument leads to general questions about the nature of such arguments; see Section 1.10.)

Though it cannot of course be assumed that a reconstruction of the Deduction that represents its argument as invalid must have given an incorrect exegesis of it, any with a claim to our interest must reveal Kant to have answers of some sort to these questions.

(On a more basic exegetical front, Ewing 1938, ch. 3, is useful. Henrich 1982 discusses more complex exegetical issues. Detailed reconstructions and criticism of the Deduction's argument may be found in Allison 1983, ch. 7, 1996, chs. 2–3; Bennett 1966, chs. 8–9; Bird 1962, chs. 8–9; Guyer 1992*a*, at greater length in Guyer 1987, pt. II; Henrich 1982, 1989, 1994, ch. 4; Schwyzer 1990, esp. chs. 4–5; Strawson 1966: 89–117; Wolff 1967*a*, at greater length in Wolff 1963: 78–202, and the papers in Förster 1989, pt. I. Familiarity with Strawson's reconstruction is presupposed in much writing on the Deduction. Ameriks 1978 and Walker 1978, ch. 6, offer views of the Deduction's argument that differ from the standard one. The line of objection to Kant stemming from dreams etc. is discussed in Beck 1978, ch. 3. Ameriks 1982*b*: 11–19 reviews helpfully a variety of different reconstructions. Regarding specific concepts that appear in the Deduction, see Bermúdez 1994 and Henrich 1989 on the transcendental unity of apperception, and Allison 1968 on the transcendental object.)

1.7. The Analogies: Substance and Causality

***CPR*, Analytic of Principles, A130–235/B169–294, of which the most important sections are the Schematism of the Pure Concepts of Understanding, A137–47/B176–87, the Analogies of Experience,**

A176–218/B218–65, and the Refutation of Idealism (discussed in Section 1.8). See also *Proleg.*, §§14–17, §§23–9, §36. Passages to concentrate on: A137–47/B176–87, A182–211/B224–56.

In the Analogies of Experience Kant seeks to legitimize the concepts of substance and causality by showing them to be conditions of objectivity, thereby refuting Hume's scepticism regarding these key concepts in the metaphysics of experience. (The Analogies are intended also, in the view of some, to legitimize principles of Newtonian physics that Kant regards as synthetic a priori.)

The concepts of substance and causality that Kant deals with in the Analogies of Experience are not the original categories of the Table of Categories, but *schematized* versions of these, a notion that Kant explains in the brief but concentrated Schematism of the Pure Concepts of Understanding (A137–47/B176–87). Kant considers that the Transcendental Deduction leaves behind it a problem concerning the application of a priori concepts to appearances, which arises because the subsumption of any object under a concept requires concept and object to be 'homogeneous', and the categories as they stand are 'quite heterogeneous' from sensible intuition (see A137/B176). The solution is to assume 'some third thing', homogeneous with both the categories and intuition, by means of which the categories may gain application to appearances (see A138/B177). This 'mediating representation', in one respect intellectual and in another sensible, Kant calls a *schema*. Schematism, a function of the imagination, is the process by which schemata are generated (see A140/B179), and Kant argues that time provides its key (see A138–9/B177–8). The twelve categories are accordingly reinterpreted in *temporal* terms: for instance, the pure logical concept of substance ('something that can be thought only as subject') becomes the concept of 'permanence of the real in time' (see A143/B183); and the pure logical concept of causality (the relation of ground to consequent) becomes the concept of 'the real upon which, whenever posited, something else always follows' in accordance with a rule (see A144/B183).

Time plays a central role in the Analogies (A176–218/B218–65), where substance and causality are argued to be conditions for an objective temporal order. Two key premisses of the argument of the Analogies are: that the unity of apperception requires a 'necessary connection of perceptions' and the synthetic unity of appearances in a single time (see A176–8/B218–21), and that time 'cannot itself be perceived', which entails that we cannot locate appearances in time simply by observing their relation to the temporal framework, as if the latter were some sort of object (see B219, B225, A215/B262). This raises the question how it is possible to discriminate between the subjective temporal order of our representations and the objective temporal order of objects, as required for the constitution of an objective world (see B219).

In the first analogy (A182–9/B224–32) Kant claims that discrimination of an objective time order presupposes the principle that all appearances 'contain the permanent (substance) as the object itself, and the transitory as its mere determination, that is, as a way the object exists' (A182). Kant argues (see A182–4/B224–7): (1) The time in which appearances are thought must *itself* remain the same: 'change does not affect time itself, but only appearances in time' (A183/B226). As Kant puts it, time is the 'substratum' of appearances (B225). (2) Time cannot itself be perceived (B225). (3) Something must consequently be found in the realm of the objects of perception, that is, in appearances, that 'represents' (B225) or 'expresses' (A183/B226) time in general by playing the role of an unchanging substratum of appearances. (4) This something cannot be subjective, because there is nothing permanent in our apprehension of the manifold of appearances (A182/B225). (5) It must therefore be objective: that is, there must be something permanent, that remains the same throughout change, in appearances, and this (by definition of the category) is *substance*. Kant reformulates the conclusion by saying that all change (*Wechsel*) must be regarded as alteration (*Veränderung*), i.e. change occurring *in* substances (see B232–3).

The second analogy (A189–211/B232–56) aims to establish the principle of causality, that 'all alterations take place in conformity with the law of the connection of cause and effect' (B232): (1) In order for change to be regarded as alteration, as the first analogy shows to be required, the relation of succession in appearances must be thought of as objective; otherwise we have only a 'play of representations, relating to no object' (A194/B239). (2) In order to be thought of as objective, the relation of succession must be 'determined', i.e. necessary and irreversible (see A198–9/B243–4). To explain this point, Kant contrasts a case of a merely subjective succession that represents objectively coexistent parts—viewing a house, where experience changes while the object remains unaltered—with a case of a subjective succession that represents an objective succession—watching a ship move downstream, where change in experience derives from alteration in the object (see A190–3/B235–8). What is needed, Kant argues, to make it so much as thinkable that the two cases differ is the concept of a rule, applying in the case of the ship but not that of the house, which renders the temporal order of perceptions necessary and irreversible. (3). The concept of a necessary and irreversible succession is the concept of the relation of *cause and effect*.

The third analogy (A211–15/B256–62) adds to the second that coexistent substances must be regarded as capable of causal interaction (community or reciprocity). The Analogies show, therefore, that experience of an objective world requires that objects be represented as interacting substances whose alterations are causally necessitated.

Kant's general thought that substance and causality are conditions of objectivity is persuasive. Questions arise, however, regarding the strength of the conclusions to which Kant is entitled. It may be wondered whether the first analogy proves that permanence must be absolute rather than relative, and so, as Kant claims, whether it renders it inconceivable that substance should come into being or pass away. Regarding the second analogy, it needs to be asked if Kant proves that all events, as opposed to just a sufficient number of them, must be subject to the principle of causality; and if he establishes that causality is itself a relation of necessitation, rather than just the necessity of there being causal relations (in other words, whether Kant's legitimate conclusion is incompatible with a Humean analysis of causality). In addition questions arise, due to the abstractness of the conclusions of the analogies, as to how the first analogy's conclusion regarding substance (in the singular) is related to the individuation of substances (in the plural) and to the concept of matter; and how the second analogy's conclusion regarding the principle of causality is related to knowledge of particular causal laws.

(On the Schematism, see Allison 1983, ch. 8; Bennett 1966, ch. 10; Guyer 1987, ch. 6; Schwyzer 1990, ch. 2; and Walker 1978: 87–94. Bell 1987 relates the Schematism to the topic of judgement in general.

On the Analogies, see Allison 1983, chs. 9–10; Beck 1978, ch. 8; Bennett 1966, chs. 11, 13, 15; Bird 1962, ch. 10; Buchdahl 1992, ch. 9; Guyer 1987, chs. 8–11; Melnick 1973, chs. 2–3; Strawson 1966: 118–52; Walker 1978: 98–105; and Walsh 1969. Harper and Meerbote 1984 is a collection of papers devoted largely to the second analogy. Melnick 1973: 7–30 relates the view of space and time in the Analytic with the seemingly different view in the Aesthetic.)

1.8. The Refutation of Idealism: Berkeleian Idealism and Cartesian Scepticism

The Refutation of Idealism, which was added to the second edition of the *CPR*, occupies only four pages, B274–9, of the Postulates of Empirical Thought in General. It is amplified in the long footnote in the preface to the second edition, Bxxxix–xli n. See also B69–71, the Fourth Paralogism in the first edition, A366–80; and *Proleg.* 288–94, §§26–30, §49, 374–5. Passages to concentrate on: B274–9, A369–76.

The Refutation of Idealism is the final part of the extended argument in the Analytic concerning the need for experience to be of an objective world: it is Kant's attempt to prove that we have experience of outer objects in space and thus to refute scepticism about the external world (the continued existence of which Kant describes as a 'scandal to philosophy and to human reason in general'; Bxxxix).

Kant prefaces the Refutation with a brief discussion of the different forms of idealism (see B274–5). Kant employs here the term 'material idealism' to refer to the forms of idealism that contrast with transcendental idealism (which is a 'formal idealism' B519n., or 'Critical idealism', *Proleg.* 294). Material idealism divides into two sorts: (1) The 'dogmatic' idealism of Berkeley ('mystical and visionary idealism'; *Proleg.* 293), which holds the existence of an external world to be 'false and impossible'. It is dogmatic because it claims that we can know there to be no external world. (2) The 'problematic' idealism of Descartes ('sceptical idealism'; A377), which asserts the existence of an external world to be possible but 'doubtful and indemonstrable', on account of the insecure inference from inner states that claims to knowledge of it involve (see A367–8).

Kant's reason for grouping together Berkeleian idealism and Cartesian scepticism under the single heading of material idealism is that both assume that the immediate objects of knowledge are exclusively subjective, private, mental items, and that knowledge of external objects would require inference. Of course, neither Berkeley nor Descartes means to reduce the world to illusion or affirm solipsism, but on Kant's view, they cannot avoid doing so, for the assumption that only inner objects are known immediately allows no inferential route to empirical reality (see A368).

Kant in the first edition (Fourth Paralogism, A366–80) argues against idealism that since external objects are nothing but a species of my representations, and my representations are known immediately, so therefore are external objects. This strategy led to the charge—strongly repudiated by Kant—that his position on the reality of the external world was essentially no different from that of Berkeley, and in the second edition he sought to undo this impression.

In the second edition Kant does not appeal to any identification of external objects with representations and instead offers the following argument (see B275–6; it is restated at Bxxxix-xli n.): (1) 'I am conscious of my own existence as determined in time', i.e. have empirical self-consciousness. (2) 'All determination of time presupposes something *permanent* in perception' (the lesson of the first analogy). (3) 'This permanent cannot, however, be something in me', since all that I intuit in inner sense are my representations (Kant rejects Descartes's *res cogitans* as a candidate for the permanent). (4) Therefore the necessary 'perception of this permanent is possible only through a *thing* outside me and not through the mere *representation* of a thing outside me'. (5) Therefore, 'the consciousness of my existence is at the same time an immediate consciousness of the existence of other things outside me'.

Kant's intention is thus to defeat scepticism by showing that 'inner experience, which for Descartes is indubitable, is possible only on the assumption of outer experience' (B275), obviating any problematic inference from inner to outer experience. Because the argument works by showing that the conclusion of the sceptic's argument contradicts a presupposition of its premiss (as Kant puts it, 'the game played by idealism has been turned against itself'; B276), the

Refutation is often cited as the paradigm of a transcendental argument (see Section 1.10).

Aside from issues concerning the interpretation of its highly condensed argument (particularly premiss 1), and its relation to the Deduction, the principal question that arises regarding the Refutation is the following. Does the crucial move at 4 to '*thing* outside me' depend upon a transcendental idealist conception of things, even though the doctrine does not figure explicitly in the argument's premisses—or is it independent of that doctrine? If the latter, then the Refutation is an argument that can be employed by transcendental realists. (The general question raised here of the relation of transcendental arguments to transcendental idealism is discussed in Section 1.10.)

(Kant's various discussions of non-transcendental idealism are helpfully charted in Kemp Smith 1923: 298–321. On the Refutation, see Allison 1983, ch. 14; Aquila 1979a; Bennett 1966, ch. 14; Gram 1982; Guyer 1987, pt. IV; and Strawson 1966: 125–8.)

1.9. Things in Themselves and Noumena

CPR, The Ground of the Distinction of all Objects in General into Phenomena and Noumena, A235–60/B294–315, and Amphiboly of Concepts of Reflection, A260–92/B316–49. See also *Proleg.*, §30, §32, §34, §36, §45, §§57–9. Passages to concentrate on: A248–53, B305–9, A254–60/B309–15, A279–80/B335–6, A285–9/B341–6.

Having completed his positive account of knowledge, and before embarking on the negative task of the *CPR*, Kant discusses the new concept of noumenon. Kant's intention in the chapter on phenomena and noumena, which provides a bridge from the Analytic to the Dialectic, is to sharpen our understanding of what is involved in any attempt to think beyond the limits of the 'land of truth' (A235 / B294) defined by the Analytic.

Kant begins by discussing in general terms the conditions of employment of the categories (see A235–48 / B294–305), and affirms that they 'can *never* admit of *transcendental* but *always* only of *empirical* employment' (A246 / B303)—the transcendental employment of a concept being 'its application to *things in general and in themselves*', and empirical employment 'its application *merely to appearances*' (A238–9 / B298). The categories are, therefore, 'not of themselves adequate to the knowledge of things in themselves' (A287 / B343). The further question that arises is whether the categories taken apart from sensibility have any meaning at all. Kant is clear that apart from sensibility (i.e. unschematized) the categories do not have determinate meaning or objective reality (see A244–5); what is less clear is whether, as mere 'logical functions', they are altogether without meaning (see Kant's remarks at e.g. A244–6, A239–41 / B298–300,

A248/B305, B308; *Proleg.*, §30, §33). The view that Kant requires, in any case, for his further claims regarding the existence of things in themselves, and his ethical theory, which demands that the categories be applied to things in themselves in the context of practical reason (see *CPracR* 54–7, 134–41), is undoubtedly that some sort of meaning and potential for application remains when relation to sensibility is subtracted from a category; more controversial is whether Kant is entitled to that position.

Kant then introduces the epistemological concept of a *noumenon*, an object of understanding 'which, nevertheless, can be given as such to an intuition, although not to one that is sensible', i.e. to intellectual intuition (see A248–9, B306). A noumenon is thus a purely intelligible entity. Objects considered thus are 'represented *as they are*', not '*as they appear*' (A249–50), i.e. are things in themselves. The contrast is with *phenomena*, sensible entities which are objects of sensible intuition and so identical with appearances.

Kant then shows that our thought about noumena is subject to two opposing pressures.

On the one hand, noumena are logically possible, since the concept of an object of intellectual intuition is not contradictory (see B310). Furthermore, Kant holds that the very concept of appearance points to that of a noumenal ground: appearance 'can be nothing by itself, outside our mode of representation', and 'something which is not in itself appearance must correspond to it' (A251). This leads us to divide 'the world into a world of the senses and a world of the understanding' (A249). Kant's endorsement of the line of thought that leads to the grounding of appearances in things in themselves is clear in numerous contexts (see Bxx, Bxxvi–vii, B308–9, A695–6/B723–4; *Proleg.*, §57); and it would seem that Kant's doctrine of sensibility as involving 'affection' (see A19/B33, A68/B93, B207, B129, B309, A494/B522; *Proleg.*, §32, §36) requires that appearances be considered the result of our being affected by things in themselves.

On the other hand, the impossibility of assuming the possibility of non-sensible intuition, of which we have no knowledge or even contentful idea (B308), conjoined with the impossibility of transcendental employment of the categories, would seem to entail that the concept of noumenon cannot be held to have objective reality.

Kant's solution is to suppose that the opposing pressures force apart two senses of the concept of noumenon: the *negative*, indeterminate concept of a thing in so far as it is *not* an object of our sensible intuition, which Kant's 'doctrine of sensibility' does give us grounds for employing; and the *positive*, determinate concept of a thing in so far as it is an object of *non-sensible* (intellectual) intuition, which we have no grounds for employing (see B307). (In the first edition, A250–3, this distinction appears to be expressed in the alternative terms of a distinction between the concept of the transcendental object and that of noumenon.) The necessity of our taking appearances to point to things in themselves is thereby reconciled with the impossibility of transcendental employment of the categories or assuming the existence of intellectual intuition.

Since the possibility of non-sensible intuition can be neither proved nor disproved, the existence of noumena as objects of such intuition must remain an 'open question' (A252). The concept of noumenon is thus 'problematic'—it is a 'representation of a thing of which we can say neither that it is possible nor that it is impossible'—but it is employed legitimately as a 'merely *limiting concept*' that is necessary 'to prevent sensible intuition from being extended to things in themselves' (see A254–6/B310–12, A286–8/342–4).

As indicated, Kant's right to affirm the existence of things in themselves, in view of the epistemology of the Analytic, is disputable, and a number of commentators claim that in doing so Kant violates basic principles of Critical philosophy.

(Kant's account of things in themselves is a central issue in transcendental idealism; see Section 1.10 below and the references given there.)

1.10. Transcendental Idealism: Critical and Interpretative Issues

The end of the Analytic is an appropriate point at which to take up the topic of transcendental idealism as a whole. Any assessment of the overall significance and coherence of transcendental idealism must engage with a number of interconnected issues simultaneously. The following distinction of issues is consequently somewhat artificial, and considerable overlap will be found between the secondary literature referred to under each heading.

1. *Kant's case for transcendental idealism.* Obviously, any assessment of transcendental idealism must consider whether Kant succeeds, not merely in articulating it as a coherent philosophical position, but in proving the doctrine. There are three sections of the *CPR* to be considered. The Aesthetic and Analytic share a single broad form of argument for transcendental idealism: both are concerned with the necessary formal features of experience, from consideration of which Kant seeks to extract the subject-constitutedness of its objects. In the Antinomy of Pure Reason Kant advances a quite distinct argument for transcendental idealism, an 'indirect proof' of it that proceeds by way of a demonstration that transcendental realism is contradictory (see Section 1.13). (For completeness' sake, Kant's intimation in *CPracR* 6 of a moral proof of transcendental idealism with regard to the self should also be mentioned.)

Views that have been taken of this issue are the following (there are of course many varieties of each): (1) that Kant succeeds in establishing his strong thesis that things cannot be known as they are in themselves; (2) that Kant establishes that we cannot know that our knowledge is of things in themselves but not the impossibility of its being so; and (3) that Kant does nothing to shake the naive realist conviction that the objects of our knowledge are things in themselves, and even that the *CPR* supplies materials for defending that view.

As said in Section 1.4, Kant's arguments in the Aesthetic, as they are explicitly stated, may well appear to fall short of establishing transcendental idealism, and the same holds for the arguments in the Analytic and Antinomy. A proper evaluation of the case for transcendental idealism, however, must take into account the methodological or metaphilosophical dimension of Kant's Copernican revolution, and the question of whether transcendental realism is in a relatively stronger position than transcendental idealism as regards such problems as the possibility of knowledge and refutation of scepticism.

(For commentary on the argument for transcendental idealism in the Aesthetic, see the references in Section 1.4, and on that in the Antinomy, Section 1.13. On the argument for transcendental idealism in the Analytic, see Guyer 1992*b*, ch. 17. On the case for transcendental idealism as a whole, see Allison 1976*a*, 1983, chs. 1–2, 1996, ch. 1; Guyer 1987, pt. v; Melnick 1973, ch. 4; Strawson 1966, pt. IV; and Walker 1978, ch. 9. Ameriks 1992*b* is an incisive commentary on recent discussions of transcendental idealism.)

2. *Transcendental idealism and things in themselves*. It is with respect to the concept of things in themselves and Kant's affirmation of their existence that the sharpest opposition, and some of the most intricate issues in the interpretation and evaluation of transcendental idealism, arise. Very roughly, the field may be divided into those who support the 'two-object' and those who support the 'two-conception' interpretation of things in themselves. The two-object interpretation regards the distinction of appearances and things in themselves as concerning two distinct sets of objects, composing two distinct 'worlds'; the two-conception interpretation takes it to concern a single set of (empirical) objects considered in two different ways or from two different standpoints. (There is textual evidence for both: suggesting two objects, see e.g. B308–9, A287–8/B344; suggesting two conceptions, see e.g. Bxviii-xixn., A38/B55, B69.)

By and large, though not exclusively, those who adopt the two-conception interpretation defend transcendental idealism as at least coherent, whereas those who take the two-object view go on to declare transcendental idealism incoherent, on account of difficulties allegedly involved in the application of the categories outside space and time and the notion of transcendental affection. (Special issues also arise in this context regarding the claim that the self is transcendentally ideal: see Section 1.12.)

(Strawson 1966: 38–42 and pt. IV is a lucid statement of the two-object interpretation and its difficulties. A classic statement of the two-conception interpretation is Prauss 1974; it is also advanced in Allison 1976*b* and 1983, ch. 11; and, in different terms, in Matthews 1982 and Melnick 1973, sect. 21. See also, on transcendental idealism and things in themselves, Aquila 1979*b* or 1983, ch. 4; Bird 1962, chs. 1 2, 5, and 1982, Buchdahl 1992, chs. 4–6; Gram 1976; Schrader 1967; and the papers in Beck 1974, pt. VI; Ameriks 1982*b*: 1–11 provides a helpful overview of the literature. One way of approaching the issue is by examining the fate of the thing in itself in post-Kantian idealism, where it is, on the one hand, eliminated in the idealism of Fichte and Hegel and, on the other, claimed by Schopenhauer to be identical with the will: see Fichte 1794–1802: i. 480–91, Hegel 1817–27, §44; Schelling 1856–61: 100–2; and Schopenhauer 1819–44: i. 435–7, 501–7, ii. ch. 18.)

3. *The strength of Kant's empirical realism*. Though it is Kant's claim that transcendental idealism is compatible with, and indeed provides the only way of establishing, empirical realism, the question arises as to whether Kant's doctrine does genuinely secure the reality of the world as common sense conceives it (as containing objects that exist unperceived and so on); or whether Kant's view of the reality of tables and chairs does not ultimately resemble more closely that of Berkeley than that of Locke—contrary to Kant's explicit intentions. Three questions may be collected under this heading:

What does Kant mean by appearance? The difficulty concerns the relation of appearances to representations. Appearance is defined in the Aesthetic as an 'undetermined object of an empirical intuition' (A20/B34), but Kant also describes appearances as 'nothing but representations' (A250): as 'the mere play of our representations' that 'in the end reduce to determinations of inner sense' (A101) (see also A104, A189–91/B234–6, A370–2, A384–7, A563/B591; the tendency is particularly pronounced in the first edition, though not confined to it). So we seem to have one sense of appearance which makes them *objects* of representations, and another in which they are themselves *representations* (of, it is natural to then think, things in themselves). The original Copernican definition of appearances as objects conforming necessarily to our mode of knowledge merely contrasts them with things in themselves and does not help to settle the issue.

Aside from the question of consistency, this issue has importance in so far as Kant's identification of empirical objects with appearances, and of appearances with representations, appears to reduce empirical objects to 'determinations' of the subject—which, it has been held, collapses Kant's idealism into that of Berkeley. To forestall this impression, it is necessary to underline the strictly transcendental status of Kant's identification of appearances with representations (see A29–30/B45).

How close is Kant to phenomenalism? A parallel difficulty arises in the context of determining Kant's relation to phenomenalism—the doctrine articulated by, for example, J. S. Mill and A. J. Ayer, and generally attributed to Berkeley, that physical objects are constructions out of, and hence reducible to, sense-experience, in opposition to realist theories of perception, such as that of Locke. The fact that Kant calls empirical objects appearances and at times says that they are identical with representations, as just noted, and that he talks of concepts as rules for the synthesis of representations and of nature as a set of systematically connected representations, strongly invites an attribution of phenomenalism. (Passages that may be thought particularly phenomenalistic are those in which Kant discusses objects distant from us in space and time; A492–6/B521–4.)

There are, however, countervailing reasons for saying that if Kant is a phenomenalist, then his phenomenalism is of an unusually sophisticated kind: as usually understood, phenomenalism presupposes a level of awareness of raw sense-experience that is ruled out by Kant's doctrine of synthesis; it also presupposes the independence of subjective states from outer objects, which is explicitly rejected in the Refutation of Idealism. It may also be doubted that Kant intends to reduce '*X* exists unperceived' to 'There is a possible *X*-experience', rather than simply regarding the truth of the latter as a consequence of the truth of the former.

Does Kant's idealism differ significantly from that of Berkeley? As indicated, if a certain view is taken of Kant's concept of appearance and relation to phenomenalism, then the distance between Kant and Berkeley is narrowed considerably. Furthermore, it has been argued that the central anti-realist arguments of Kant and Berkeley are fundamentally similar.

Nevertheless, the following differences are crucial and should not be lost sight of: Berkeley has no notion of the mind as making an a priori contribution to objects, which makes the sense in which objects depend upon the subject for Berkeley profoundly different from that in which they do so for Kant; and Berkeley is, in Kant's terms, a transcendental realist, as well as being a material idealist, since he supposes that we know things as they are in themselves. (Kant distinguishes Berkeley's idealism from his own at B69–71, B274; *Proleg.* 293–4, 374–5; passages discussed in Section 1.8.)

(Kant's concept of appearance is discussed in Bird 1962, ch. 1. Advancing the phenomenalist interpretation of Kant—which may be called the 'standard picture'—see Bennett 1966, sects. 8, 32; and Strawson 1966: 257–63. Bird 1962, chs. 1–4, resists it persuasively, as does Allison 1983: 3–10, 30–4. On this issue, see also Aquila 1983, ch. 4. On Kant's relation to Berkeley, see Allison 1973; Justin 1974; Turbayne 1969; Walker 1985; and Wilson 1971; these and other writings on the subject are collected in Walker 1988.)

4. *Transcendental idealism and transcendental arguments.* Some, above all Strawson, have taken the view that there are two quite distinct strands in the *CPR*, the independence of which Kant may be thought to have failed to appreciate: on the one hand, the metaphysic of transcendental idealism, and on the other, Kant's employment of what have come to be known in analytical philosophy as transcendental arguments. Transcendental arguments are ones

that work back from a premiss *Q*—concerning some matter as incontrovertible as that I am self-conscious, or a subject of thought and experience, or have experience of time, denial of any of which would be unintelligible—to a presupposition *P* which expresses a philosophically contentful claim about the world or our conceptual scheme, for example, concerning causal order; thereby showing scepticism about *P* to be self-refuting. The Deduction, Analogies, and Refutation of Idealism may all be thought to conform to this pattern, and it may also appear to correspond to Kant's definition of a 'transcendental proof' at A783/B811 (Kant discusses the method of proof of transcendental propositions at A216–17/B263–4, A736–7/B764–5, A782–94/B810–22). Transcendental arguments, it is further claimed, are independent of transcendental idealism, and employment of them to the end of displaying our conceptual scheme and refuting scepticism does not in itself commit one to any metaphysical doctrine, and so is compatible with (transcendental) realism.

The exegetical question whether there really are two distinct strands in Kant's thought cannot be separated from that of whether transcendental argumentation has the independent potential that its proponents claim for it. A standard line of criticism has been that, without tacit idealist or verificationist assumptions, transcendental arguments deliver at best conclusions about how we must think, not about how things must be; leaving scepticism untouched. If so, then Kant's insistence that the conditions of possibility identified by transcendental proofs are valid only with respect to appearances would seem fully justified (see A92–3/B124–6, A114, A125–30, B163–5, A180–1/B223–4; *Proleg.*, §§26–30).

(Strawson's 1966 'analytic' perspective on Kant is summarized on pp. 15–24. The literature on transcendental arguments is extensive, some of it being independent of Kant's philosophy: an excellent selection of papers, many bearing on Kant, is contained in Bieri *et al.* 1979; see also Schaper and Vossenkuhl 1989, pt. II. Stroud 1982 and Körner 1969 are two key papers critical of transcendental arguments; Brueckner 1983 and 1984 criticize Strawson's and others' attempts to construct anti-sceptical arguments along Kantian lines. On transcendental arguments in Kant, including their relation to transcendental idealism, see Cassam 1987; Guyer 1987: 417–28; Harrison 1982; Hintikka 1972; Walker 1978, chs. 2, 9; and the papers in Schaper and Vossenkuhl 1989, pt. I.)

I.11. The Dialectic: Ideas of Reason, Transcendental Illusion, and Regulative Employment

CPR, Transcendental Dialectic, from the beginning up to the Paralogisms, A293–340/B349–98, and appendix, A642–704/B670–732. Sections of the Analytic particularly relevant to the Dialectic's critique of transcendent

metaphysics are the discussion of modal concepts in the Postulates, the chapter on Phenomena and Noumena (discussed in Section 1.9), and the systematic critique of the principles of Leibniz's philosophy in the Amphiboly. See also *Proleg.*, §31, §33, §35, §§40–5, §§56–60, 365–71. Passages to concentrate on: A293–311/B349–68, A321–40/B377–98, A642–8/B670–6, A663–82/B691–710.

Before approaching Kant's analyses of the specific ideas of pure reason in the three central sections of the Transcendental Dialectic—which is a considerably more straightforward, though no less original, section of the *CPR* than the Analytic—it is necessary to grasp Kant's general conception of reason and its ideas, given at its beginning (introduction and book 1) and end (appendix).

The Dialectic returns to the consideration adduced in the prefaces as launching the critique of pure reason—the failure of metaphysics to make good its claims to knowledge of supersensible reality. The result of reason's self-examination has already been announced in the Analytic: outside the bounds of possible experience, thought is possible, but knowledge is impossible. The principal task of the Dialectic is to work out the implications of this verdict: to diagnose the specific errors of transcendent metaphysics, and offer explanations of what goes wrong when thought parts company with experience in each particular sphere of metaphysical speculation. Whereas the Analytic argued against the empiricist's conception of experience, the Dialectic is pitched against the rationalist's conception of reason as capable of grasping non-sensible reality through its own resources.

Though pure reason cannot know any objects, the Dialectic will show that thought outside the bounds of possible experience is nevertheless necessary: the ideas that reason forms have an indispensable role to play in guiding our thought about empirical reality. They are also essential for morality, in which context, Kant holds, pure reason finds fulfilment (see Sections 2.2–2.3). The Dialectic therefore treads a line between the legitimate empirical and illegitimate transcendent employment of reason: it shows that there is more to be said than is said in the Analytic, but not as much as is supposed in transcendent metaphysics. In the conclusion of the *Prolegomena* (350–65) Kant relates the Dialectic explicitly to transcendental idealism and Critical philosophy, describing its treatment of transcendent metaphysics as providing 'positive cognition' (361) of the exact bounds of experience and knowledge.

The framework of the Dialectic may be organized under the following headings:

1. *Transcendental illusion* (see A293–8/B349–55). Dialectic, the 'logic of illusion', is the second branch of transcendental logic, and Kant uses the term to refer to both the pseudo-logic that our reason follows when fallen prey to transcendental illusion, and the corresponding philosophical study of such pseudo-

reasoning. Transcendental illusion, as distinct from empirical and logical illusion, is what results when principles not meant for use outside experience are nevertheless employed as if they were. It is natural and inevitable. (See Kant's optical analogy for transcendental illusion, A644–5/B672–3.)

The grounds of transcendental illusion in general are twofold: (1) Given that the pure concepts of the understanding do not arise from experience, it is natural that they should appear to be 'applicable to things in themselves' (*Proleg.*, §33) independently from experience (a point made already in the Analytic: see A60–4/B85–8, A146–7/B186–7). (2) It is also natural, Kant claims, that reason should move from considering experiences singly, in doing which it remains within the domain of experience, to considering experience as a whole, the 'collective unity' or 'absolute totality of all possible experiences' (*Proleg.* 328), which is of course not *itself* an object of experience, making any thought about such an 'object' transcendent.

2. *The faculty of reason* (see A298–309/B355–66). Transcendental illusion arises from reason. Earlier in the *CPR* Kant uses reason to include the understanding, but here it refers to a distinct faculty. The faculty of reason has the logical function of syllogistic inference, and this, Kant claims, explains its interest in absolute totality: because syllogistic reasoning is concerned with identifying conditions for the truth of judgements, reason forms the idea of the *totality of conditions* for any given judgement and thus of the *unconditioned*, and it adopts the principle that 'if the *conditioned is given, the entire sum of conditions, and consequently the absolutely unconditioned* (through which alone the conditioned has been possible) *is also given*' (A409/B436; see also A307–8/B364, A417/B445n.).

3. *The ideas of reason (transcendental ideas)* (see A310–38/B366–96). Identification of the pure ideas (*Ideen*) of reason, like that of the pure concepts of the understanding, is relatively straightforward. Kant offers several specifications of reason's system of transcendental ideas (see A322–3/B379–80, A333–5/B390–2, A396–7, A405–6/B432–3; *Proleg.*, §43), showing them to be different formulations of the idea of the unconditioned, and identical with the transcendent metaphysician's ideas of the soul, the world, and God—the topics of rational psychology, cosmology, and theology. That the transcendental ideas can be derived a priori from our subjective mode of cognition does not of course entail that they have objective reality, and Kant goes on to define dialectical inference as reasoning the conclusion of which asserts their objective reality (see A338–40/B396–8). The three central sections of the Dialectic—the Paralogisms, Antinomy, and Ideal of Pure Reason—expose the dialectical inferences that lead to claims about the self, world, and God respectively.

4. *Regulative employment of the ideas of reason* (see A642–704/B670–732). Though no deduction of the kind given for the categories is possible for the transcendental ideas of reason, since they are not conditions of possibility of experience (see A336/B393)—making their status, like that of the concept of

noumenon, 'problematic' (see A338–9/B396–7)—they none the less have a legitimate use, which is *regulative* rather than constitutive (constitutive employment of concepts is the prerogative of the understanding). This is to unify, simplify, and systematize the understanding through the provision of 'maxims'—methodologically significant precepts that direct it towards an ideal 'whole of knowledge' (A645/B673), of the kind to which scientific theory aspires. Kant adds that in the context of regulative employment the ideas of transcendent metaphysics may receive a deduction of an oblique sort: we should proceed in empirical inquiry *as if* the appearances of inner sense were of a soul, the series of appearances endless, and nature the product of an intelligent being (see A669–75/B697–703).

(Bennett 1974 works through the Dialectic in detail: chs. 1, 12 discuss the above general themes. On the regulative employment of reason and its role in science, see Buchdahl 1992, ch. 7; Friedman 1991; Neiman 1994, ch. 2; and Wartenburg 1992.)

1.12. The Paralogisms: The Self and Self-Knowledge

CPR*, Paralogisms of Pure Reason, A341–405, B399–432. See also *Proleg.*, §§46–9. Passages to concentrate on: A341–8/B399–406, A348–51, B406–32.

Kant's target in the Paralogisms is rational (or pure) psychology, which attempts to establish a body of knowledge concerning the self through the transcendent use of reason. The rational psychologist (Descartes) claims to be able to infer that the self is an indivisible substance, in the permanence of which personal identity consists, and that can exist independently of the material world. Thus arises the traditional view of the soul as immaterial, spiritual, incorruptible, and so on (see A345/B403).

Kant stresses that 'I think' (transcendental apperception) is 'the sole text of rational psychology, and from it the whole of its teaching has to be developed' (A343/B401). Four paralogisms (fallacious syllogisms) are attributed to the rational psychologist. (1) The first paralogism concludes from the fact that the 'I' is always the subject of thought and never a predicate, that I am a *substance* (see A348–9, B407). (2) The second infers the *simplicity* (indivisibility, non-composity) of the 'I' that thinks from the necessary unity of thought, on the grounds that the several representations contained in a single thought cannot be thought by different subjects (see A351–2, B407). (3) In the third paralogism it is inferred, from the consideration that self-consciousness implies consciousness of self-identity, that the self is a *person*, i.e. a substance that has consciousness of its numerical identity over time and throughout change (see A361–2, B408). (4) The fourth paralogism is different in each edition. In the first (see A366–9, also B417–18), its conclusion is that outer objects are *ideal*, on the grounds that, whereas the existence of the 'I' with its perceptions is known immediately and with certainty, that of outer objects requires inference and is doubtful (see Section 1.8). In the second (see B409), it is concluded that the existence of the 'I' is *independent* of that of outer objects, including my body, on the familiar Cartesian grounds that consciousness of myself is possible without that of things outside me.

Kant's criticisms of these inferences are detailed (see A349–51, A352–61, A362–6, A369–80, B407–9), and reveal a fundamental error in rational psychology. This may be identified simply with the inference in the first paralogism, on which all the others depend, and which Kant shows involves a crucial equivocation between a logical and a non-logical (intuition-involving) sense of 'subject' (see B410–13) (similarly regarding 'thought': see B411–12 n.). Alternatively it may be identified with a common pattern of argument exemplified in all four paralogisms, in which the categories of substance, simplicity, and so on are employed transcendentally in the major premisses, but empirically in the minor premisses and conclusions (see A402–3); a confusion that is reflected in the way in which each paralogism attempts to derive a synthetic judgement from analytic premisses, which is not possible (see B416–20).

The upshot of Kant's criticisms is that the question 'What is the constitution of a thing that thinks?' has no a priori answer (A398). The rational psychologist has mistaken, under the influence of an entirely natural and non-arbitrary transcendental illusion (analysed by Kant at A396–402 and B426–7), the formal condition of apperception for knowledge of an actual existent, a *res cogitans* (see Kant's summary of the relation of Descartes's *cogito* to the 'I think' at B422–3 n.). The only knowledge that can be gained of the self is therefore empirical and thus of the self *qua* mere appearance: it can amount to only a '*physiology* of inner sense, capable perhaps of explaining the appearances' of the self (A347/B405). Only in the practical context of morality, Kant intimates, may any further knowledge of the self be possible (see B430–2).

On the basis of his critique of rational psychology, supplemented by appeal to the doctrine of transcendental idealism, Kant claims to be able to resolve some connected philosophical disputes, which exhibit the contradictions into which reason falls inevitably when employed transcendentally: (1) the problem of dualism versus materialism, with regard to which Kant claims that the self cannot be known to be material any more than it can be known to be immaterial (see A356–60, B420); (2) the problem of interaction of mind and body, which Kant argues to be dissolved in the perspective of transcendental idealism (see A384–93, B427–8); and (3) the question of personal immortality, the theoretical possibility of which has been protected, and justification of belief in which may be found in the context of morality (see A383–4, A393–4, B413–15, B421, B424–6).

Kant's own account of the self and self-knowledge raises questions and requires independent discussion (Kant recapitulates its central elements at B428–30). The outstanding interest of Kant's account, as it emerges from the Paralogisms, is that Kant would seem to succeed in going between Descartes's view of the self and that of Hume, salvaging what is true in their respective accounts but avoiding their weaknesses. It has been objected, however, that Kant's central claim that the self is known only as appearance is incoherent, on the grounds that Kant has no intelligible account of the relation of phenomenal to noumenal selves or of the self's 'self-affection', and that Kant cannot avoid commitment to the claim that we have knowledge of the self as a thing in itself. Any adequate solution to these difficulties, which otherwise create a deep problem for the doctrine of transcendental idealism, and perhaps refute it, will involve a careful examination of Kant's distinction between apperception and inner sense.

(Ameriks 1982*a* and Powell 1990 are detailed studies of the topic as a whole. On Kant's critique of rational psychology, see Allison 1973: 278–86; Ameriks 1982*a*, chs. 2–6; Bennett 1974, chs. 4–6; and Strawson 1966: 162–9. On Kant's own account of the self and its transcendental ideality, see Allison 1973, chs. 12–13; Ameriks 1982*a*, ch. 7; Strawson 1966: 38–9, 169–74, 247–9; Walker 1978: 131–4; and Walsh 1982.)

1.13. The Antinomy: The World, and the Contradictions of Pure Reason

CPR, Antinomy of Pure Reason, A405–567/B432–595. See also _Proleg._, §§50–4. Passages to concentrate on: A405–61/B432–89, A497–507/B525–35.

The Antinomy of Pure Reason deals with the contradictions of reason in their most acute form, as they emerge from reason's attempts to employ the transcendental idea of the cosmos, of the world as a totality that provides an unconditioned unity of appearance. Kant aims to show that every transcendent claim about the cosmos—every *thesis*—is counterposed by an opposing claim—an *antithesis*—which enjoys an equal degree of justification in the eyes of pure reason, with the result that pairs of contradictory propositions—called by Kant *antinomies*—are formed. Because reason's endeavour to know the world as a totality necessarily results in contradictions, its attempt at constitutive employment of the transcendental idea of the world must be declared illegitimate. The Antinomy also contains (even more importantly, in view of their implications) a further proof of transcendental idealism, and Kant's solution to the problem of human freedom.

Cosmological ideas are formed, Kant explains, in the following way (see sect. 1, A408–20/B435–48). Whereas the starting-point of rational psychology is purely intellectual ('I think'), that of rational cosmology is empirical. Because every appearance is conditioned, and so implies a corresponding series of conditions, reason forms the idea of an absolute totality of the conditions for any given conditioned. This is at the same time the idea of an absolutely complete series and an absolutely complete synthesis of appearances. In addition to the general idea of the cosmos or 'world-whole' to which this gives rise, reason forms four specific ideas of totality with respect to each of the different fundamental aspects of appearances: of the world as an absolute totality of appearances in space and time; of the product of a complete division of material objects; of an absolute totality of causal conditions; and of the totality of the conditions of existence.

There are four antinomies, one corresponding to each cosmological idea (see sect. 2, A420–60/B448–88): (1) The thesis of the first antinomy is that the world has a beginning in time and is limited in space; its antithesis, that the world is infinite in both respects. (2) The thesis of the second antinomy is that every composite substance is composed of simple parts; its antithesis, that everything that exists is infinitely divisible. (3) The thesis of the third antinomy is that there is, in addition to causality according to the laws of nature, a distinct causality of freedom; its antithesis, that there is no causality of freedom and that everything takes place according to the laws of nature. (4) The thesis of the fourth antinomy is that there exists a being that is absolutely necessary and belongs to the world; its antithesis, that no such being exists. (The third and fourth antinomies are discussed in Sections 1.14 and 1.15 respectively.)

As the Observations that follow the expositions of the antinomies make clear, Kant regards each thesis and antithesis as constituting a valid proof. The theses represent legitimate demands of reason, and the antitheses express legitimate requirements of the understanding.

Having demonstrated their inescapability, Kant proceeds to argue that we are not allowed to conclude that the questions of cosmology are simply 'undecidable'; the antinomies *must* be resolved (see sect. 4, A476–84/B504–12; *Proleg.*, §56). Furthermore, their solution cannot be 'dogmatic', i.e. refer to 'the constitution of the object in itself', since any attempt to provide an answer of such a (transcendental realist) sort will simply 'cast us from one inconceivability into another' (see sect. 5, A485–90/B513–18). The only possible solution of the antinomies is therefore Critical: the questions of cosmology must be turned around so that they become instead questions about our cognition. We must accordingly adopt what Kant calls the 'sceptical method' (not to be confused with scepticism) of identifying, from the position of an impartial umpire, the 'point of misunderstanding' which gives rise to the disputes (see A422–5/B450–3). Kant identifies the assumption responsible for forcing us into the contradictions of cosmology as the assumption that one or the other of the thesis and antithesis of each antinomy 'must be in the right' (see sect. 7, A497–507/B525–35). Transcendental realism makes this assumption mandatory, Kant argues, but transcendental idealism releases us from it. According to transcendental idealism, 'the world does not exist in itself', and so, to take the case of the first antinomy, 'exists *in itself* neither as an *infinite* whole nor as a *finite* whole' (A505/B533). The cosmological disputes are dissolved once the common presupposition of both sides, that the world of appearances exists in itself and has a determinate magnitude, is denied. In the case of the first and second antinomies, which Kant calls 'mathematical', both thesis and antithesis may simply be declared false. The appropriate form of solution for the third and fourth, 'dynamical' antinomies, Kant argues, is, however, more complex (see Sections 1.14 and 1.15).

The legitimate employment of reason in the cosmological sphere, Kant explains in the detailed Solutions to each antinomy, is exclusively regulative: reason directs the understanding to proceed according to the rule of always seeking further conditions for each appearance (see sects. 8–9, A508–67/B536–95).

Now, if all of this is correct, Kant has shown not just that cosmology presupposes transcendental realism, but that transcendental realism *implies* the contradictions of cosmology. (If the world exists in itself, it must exist in itself as either a finite whole or an infinite whole; similarly for the other antinomies.) Transcendental realism therefore entails contradictions, and from its falsity, the truth of transcendental idealism may be inferred. The Antinomy thus constitutes an 'indirect proof' of transcendental idealism, independent from any given earlier in the *CPR* (see A506–7/B534–5).

Kant's reasoning throughout the Antinomy may be challenged at a number of points, starting with the question of the soundness of the proofs of the theses and antitheses, into which Kant may be thought to have inserted premisses that are non-obligatory or reflect doctrines of his own. Also disputable is Kant's claim that cosmological questions cannot be answered by empirical means. And in order for Kant's indirect proof of transcendental idealism to succeed, it needs to be shown in any case that Kant's strategy does not presuppose (as it may seem to do) an identification of empirical truth with empirical decidability, i.e. a strong (and unproven) verificationism.

(On the antinomies, and the Antinomy's proof of transcendental idealism, see Allison 1983, ch. 3; Bennett 1974, chs. 7–9; Gram 1969; Guyer 1987, ch. 18; Strawson 1966: 175–206; and Walsh 1975, sects. 34–5. Al-Azm 1972 examines the antinomies in a historical perspective. Moore 1988 discusses the associated theme of the infinite in Kant's philosophy.)

1.14. The Third Antinomy: Freedom

CPR, Third Antinomy, A444–51/B472–9, and its Solution, A532–58/B560–86. See also the Concluding Note and Preliminary Observation, A528–32/B556–60, the Canon of Pure Reason, sect. 1, A797–804/B825–32; and _Proleg._, §53, Passages to concentrate on: A444–51/B472–9, A532–58/B560–86.

The third antinomy is concerned in the first instance with the cosmological problem of whether there is a 'first beginning' to the causal series that requires a causality of freedom or 'original causality', or whether natural causality is the only kind of causality (see A444–51/B472–9, A532–5/B560–3). The thesis, reflecting the demands of reason, says that without assuming a causality of freedom, the causal series cannot be complete, contradicting the principle that everything that happens has a sufficient cause. The antithesis, reflecting the requirements of the understanding, says that such a causality would violate the laws of nature and in any case is not an object of possible experience.

As Kant indicates in the Observation on the Thesis (see A448/B476), the problem of human freedom arises in this cosmological context because the relation of an original causality to nature (of God to the world, as we may think of it) may be likened to that of a human agent to their freely performed action: in both cases, something empirically undetermined has empirical effects. Both exemplify what Kant calls *transcendental freedom* (see A446/B474), the power of bringing into existence an empirical causal series independently of empirical causes. Kant tries to show the necessity of assuming the existence of transcendental freedom by arguing that it is presupposed by what he calls *practical freedom*, which is the power of rational agency—of acting according to judgements of what ought to be done, evidencing a causality of reason—that we attribute to human beings and not to animals (see A533–4/B561–2, A547–8/B575–6, A801–2/B829–30). Transcendental freedom is what provides 'the real stumbling-block' (A448/B476) in philosophical consideration of the problem of human freedom and renders compatibilist solutions to it inadequate.

Now, if the third antinomy were to be resolved on the pattern of the first and second, the thesis as much as the antithesis would have to be declared false, and human freedom non-existent. It is, however, Kant argues, for complex reasons, not necessary that the dynamical antinomies be resolved in the same manner as the mathematical: the theses and antitheses of the former may '*both* alike be *true*' and 'the suit may be settled to the satisfaction of both parties' (see A528–32/B556–60; *Proleg.*, 343).

It is transcendental idealism that uniquely makes such a resolution possible (see A535–57/B563–85). If empirical objects are not things in themselves but appearances, then it is possible for a conditioned event (a human action, such as my standing up) to be caused by something which is not itself an appearance *as well as* being caused by antecedent appearances: one and the same event may arise from both freedom and nature. Because transcendental idealism takes the object of knowledge in a 'twofold sense', it allows events to be conceived as the effects of both an intelligible causality, by virtue of which they are free, and an empirical causality, by virtue of which they are empirically determined. So conceived, as the products of both transcendental freedom and natural causality, human actions fall under two sets of causal laws, one deriving from the agent's *intelligible character* and the other from its *empirical character* (see A539/B567). When an action is related to intelligible character, it is not viewed as following from it in a temporal sense, since intelligible character and intelligible causality are not in time: rather it is related to a condition of reason outside the series of appearances (see A551–2/B579–80). A subject's intelligible character cannot be known therefore, since it is not appearance; but it may be thought, as in some way mirroring or analogous to its empirical character.

That such a structure is coherent, and its application to human beings has some prima-facie warrant, is shown by independent considerations: (1) transcendental idealism in any case maintains that appearances, as mere representations, 'must themselves have grounds which are not appearances' (see A537–9/B565–7); (2) we know ourselves to be subjects of apperception, which is not empirically conditioned, and to possess faculties that are not objects of sensible intuition, namely understanding and reason (see A546–7/B574–5); and (3) our reason has a causality of its own independent of that of nature, or rather—since scepticism about this matter is, Kant wishes to acknowledge, possible in the present theoretical context (see A803/B851)—we at least represent it to ourselves in such terms (see A547–8/B575–6).

To suppose that none of this is possible—that events must be *either* free *or* caused by laws of nature, that freedom and determinism according to the laws of nature are exclusive, as is assumed to the detriment of human freedom in the proof of the antithesis—is to think in line with the assumptions of transcendental realism, which does indeed, Kant affirms, eliminate human freedom (see A535–6/B563–4). Freedom can exist alongside natural causality only on the condition of transcendental idealism.

What Kant has shown is not that human freedom exists, only that 'freedom is at least *not incompatible with* nature' (see A557–8/B585–6). (The incompatibility of freedom and nature is a transcendental illusion engendered by transcendental realism.) Kant has shown that a causality of freedom is in general thinkable, so that, although we cannot know that we are free, equally we cannot know that we are not (symmetrically with Kant's conclusions regarding personal immortality and, Section 1.15 will show, the existence of God). This leaves open the possibility of human freedom, a possibility which, Kant will attempt to show, may be exploited to the advantage of morality when we turn from the perspective of theoretical reason to that of practical reason (Kant sketches how things will go here at A550–6/B578–84 and B825–32/A797–804).

Kant's ultimate view of the thesis and antithesis of the third antinomy is, then, that they are false as they stand, in so far as they illegitimately affirm and deny respectively the reality of freedom. But with modification both may emerge as true: the thesis contains the truth that freedom is conceivable, and the antithesis is right that everything takes place according to the laws of nature.

Kant's account of freedom raises many questions. That our ordinary concepts of freedom and rational agency do assume transcendental freedom is a controversial point and one that compatibilists such as Hume will dispute. Also open to dispute is whether Kant is within his rights to propose to resolve the dynamical antinomies on a different model from the mathematical. The deepest and most complex issue, however, is whether the notions of intelligible causality and intelligible character make sense; consideration of which raises again the question of the coherence of supposing that appearances are grounded in things in themselves, but with added complications created by the relation between empirical and intelligible character and the concept of timeless agency.

(On the third antinomy, see Al-Azm 1972, ch. 3; Allison 1983, ch. 15, and 1990, pt. 1; Bennett 1974, ch. 10; Bird 1962, ch. 12; Körner 1967; Meerbote 1984; Rosen 1989; and Wood 1984*a*.)

1.15. The Ideal of Pure Reason: God

CPR, Fourth Antinomy, A452–61/B480–9, its Solution, A559–65/B587–93, and the Ideal of Pure Reason, A567–642/B595–670. See also _Proleg._, §55, 355–60. Passages to concentrate on: A452–61/B480–9, A559–65/B587–93, A590–614/B618–42, A620–30/B648–58.

The Ideal of Pure Reason contains Kant's critique of theology. In the background to it is Kant's discussion in the fourth antinomy (A452–61/B480–9) of reason's idea of an absolutely necessary being, which is of importance for theology in so far as it is, though not equivalent to our concept of God, an essential component of it. The thesis of the fourth antinomy says that the series of appearances, which exists merely contingently, requires that an absolutely necessary being belonging to the world be assumed to exist; its antithesis, that the requirements of causality entail that no such being can exist. Kant's Critical solution to this antinomy (A559–65/B587–93) is symmetrical with his solution to the third: transcendental idealism allows both thesis and antithesis to be true when 'taken in different connections' (A560/B588). It may be true that everything in experience is contingent and empirically conditioned, and yet also true that the series of empirical conditions has an empirically unconditioned, *intelligible* condition. This does not establish the existence of an absolutely necessary being, but it shows that the antithesis is wrong to claim knowledge of its non-existence (A562–3/B590–1).

The Ideal takes up first the question of the transcendental origin of the concept of God, of what in reason gives rise to it. Kant's account (sect. 2, A571–83/B599–611) is difficult and introduces an entirely new set of concepts. Kant argues that because every thing must be conceived as susceptible to a 'complete determination' (a specification of all the predicates belonging to it), thought about things presupposes the idea of the 'sum-total of all possibilities'—that which contains the 'material *for all possibility*' and 'the data *for the particular possibility* of each and every thing' (see A571–3/B599–601). Kant argues that this sum-total may itself be conceived as an individual being, and that, as such, it qualifies as the *ideal* of pure reason (a notion explained in sect. 1, A567–71/B595–9). This ideal Kant then shows to be identical with the concept of something that contains all reality (*omnitudo realitatis*) and has the highest degree of reality (*ens realissimum*) (see A573–9/B601–7). The ideal of pure reason thus supplies the transcendental idea of theology, which 'hypostatizes' it under the influence of dialectical illusion (see A581–3/B609–11), reinforced by reason's interest in discovering something satisfying the description of an absolutely necessary being (see A583–7/B611–15).

The three traditional arguments for the existence of God that Kant attacks are, he claims, the only ones that can be given (see A590–1/B618–19). (1) The ontological argument is based on a priori concepts, by means of which alone it infers the existence of a being with the highest degree of reality, namely God. (2) The cosmological argument is based on experience in general (of contingent existents), from which it infers the existence of an absolutely necessary being, which it then identifies with God. (3) The 'physico-theological' argument (argument from design) is based on the determinate experience of the world as having an (orderly) constitution, from which it infers, through causal reasoning, the existence of an 'author of nature', which is again then identified with God. Our concept of God is, Kant believes, a composite of the concepts of an *ens realissimum*, an absolutely necessary being, and an author of nature, with supplementary features of moral personality (see *Proleg*., 355–60).

The ontological argument (sect. 4, A592–603/B620–30) is rejected on the grounds that existence is not, as the argument assumes, a 'real' predicate (positive attribute), and so not analytically contained in the concept of a being containing all reality (see A597–602/B625–30).

The cosmological argument (sect. 5, A603–20/B631–48) is attacked at two points. Its inference to the existence of an absolutely necessary being reposes, Kant claims, on a 'whole nest of dialectical assumptions' (see A609–10/B637–8). But more importantly, even if the inference is granted, it follows that *God* exists only if the existence of an absolutely necessary being entails that of an *ens realissimum*; and Kant points out that if that were so, then the converse would also hold, i.e. the concept of an *ens realissimum* would contain that of necessary existence—which is precisely the (refuted) claim of the ontological argument; so the cosmological argument fails without the ontological argument, which, if it succeeded, would render the cosmological argument redundant (see A606–9/B634–7).

Despite its enormous intuitive force, which Kant acknowledges, the argument from design (sect. 6, A620–30/B648–58) cannot be accepted, for the reason that whatever it may prove by way of the existence of a cause of order in nature falls far short of proving the existence of an *ens realissimum*; a defect that could be remedied only by returning to the a priori reasoning of the cosmological and ontological arguments—both of which have already been refuted (see A626–30/B645–8).

It must be recognized that it is not Kant's intention to destroy or in any way to weaken religious belief, but rather to free it from dogmatism and render it consistent with natural science and empirical knowledge; hence Kant's claim to have 'found it necessary to deny *knowledge*, in order to make room for *faith*' (Bxxx). The Ideal shows atheism to be every bit as unjustified as theoretical claims to knowledge of God's existence (see A640–1/B668–9), and prepares the way for Kant's provision of an alternative, 'moral' theology that grounds religion on practical rather than theoretical reason (see Section 2.3).

Whilst Kant's reconstruction of the origin of the concept of God has often been dismissed, as a reversion to rationalist modes of philosophizing, Kant's critique of the traditional arguments for the existence of God has been widely approved and appealed to. Many of those who have done so, however, have neither sympathized with Kant's own metaphysics nor shared his interest in erecting a moral theology, and it is important to appreciate that Kant is prepared to grant a good deal more to theology than would now generally be allowed—above all, the intrinsic coherence and rational necessity of the concept of God. Kant's critique of the theological arguments for God's existence turns ultimately on the claim that existence is not a real predicate, and though Kant's conclusion regarding existence and predication is widely accepted, his own defence of it is open to challenge, and it is less than certain that Kant shows the contrary view of the rationalist theologian to involve any strict incoherence.

(Wood 1978 is a detailed study of Kant's treatment of theology. On Kant's account of the ideal of pure reason, see Strawson 1966: 221–3; Walsh 1975, sect. 37; and Wood 1978: 25–63. On Kant's critique of theology as a whole, see Strawson 1966: 223–31; and Walsh 1975, sect. 38. On the ontological argument specifically, see Bennett 1974, sects. 72–4; Engel 1967; Plantinga 1966; Schaffer 1969; and Wood 1978: 100–23; on the fourth antinomy and cosmological argument, Al-Azm 1972, ch. 4; Baumer 1969; Bennett 1974, sects. 75–80; Remnant 1969; Strawson 1966: 207–21; and Wood 1978: 123–30; and on the argument from design, Bennett 1974, sect. 81; Walker 1978, ch. 12; and Wood 1978: 130–45.)

1.16. Kant's Critique of Transcendent Metaphysics

It would be hard to deny that, at a minimum, and whatever is made of transcendental idealism and Kant's own accounts of such topics as the self and human freedom, Kant demonstrates the inadequacy of the foundation provided by rationalism for the enterprise of transcendent metaphysical speculation, and that its defence would require either a wholesale reconstruction of rationalist philosophical methodology (a challenge that Kant issues at A638–9/B666–7),or a wholly different foundation.

It should be emphasized, however, that Kant's intention is not by any means to eliminate metaphysical thought as meaningless; his ethical writings show his unequivocal commitment to its indispensability. A question to be considered at the end of the Dialectic, though, concerns the balance struck by Kant between criticism and affirmation of the possibility of metaphysics. To what extent does Kant successfully harmonize the demands of pure reason with the empirical conditions on thought and meaning? The history of philosophy shows Kant's critique of transcendent metaphysics being regarded, from opposing quarters, as not having gone far enough. On the one side, it has been held that Kant's doctrine of the unknowability of reality as it is in itself results from an insufficiently rigorous idealism, and that when idealism is carried through to its proper conclusion, the claim that absolute reality can be grasped non-empirically through the intellect may be renewed. On the other, it has been thought that Kant's mistake lies in failing to carry through his critique of metaphysics to its proper, wholly anti-metaphysical and positivistic conclusion.

(Ameriks 1992*a* and Walsh 1975, sect. 16, discuss the question of Kant's success in dismantling traditional metaphysics, Ameriks suggesting that Kant's intentions here are limited. Hegel 1817–27, sects. 45–52, criticizes Kant's resolution of metaphysical problems in the Dialectic.)

2. KANT'S ETHICS

Reason, on Kant's view, is practical as much as theoretical: it places demands on our actions as much as it does on our beliefs. It is the task of the *Groundwork of the Metaphysics of Morals* and the *Critique of Practical Reason* to show what practical reason requires, and this, on Kant's account, is above all morality. These two works contain, therefore, the core of Kant's ethical theory (though not the theory in full, for which *the Metaphysics of Morals* is required in addition).

The highly abstract character of Kant's ethical theory makes it considerably harder to grasp than those of Aristotle, Hume, or Mill, and this reflects Kant's wholly original view of the nature of morality. Kant holds that although ordinary persons have a firm grasp of right and wrong, the nature of morality has been radically misunderstood: the accounts that philosophers have given of morality obscure its fundamentally a priori character. Kant's attempt to uncover the true, a priori foundation of morality exemplifies the Critical method of the *CPR*: by abstracting from everything empirical, Kant seeks to trace morality to its source in the subject's powers, from which it may be seen to derive its validity. Morality emerges as an objective, universal, and necessary structure, symmetrical with the metaphysics of experience, grounded on our nature as rational beings, and dependent neither on empirical fact, including facts of human psychology, nor on the supersensible reality of transcendent metaphysics, as in theological ethics.

The idea of a pure ethics is unfamiliar, so it is worth highlighting at the outset the two central considerations that Kant adduces in support of his conception of ethical theory. (1) The first is stated in the *CPR* at A547–50 / B575–8. A moral judgement is a judgement that something *ought* to be done, and such judgements are heterogeneous with empirical judgements, which say merely what in nature *is* the case: 'When we have the course of nature alone in view, "*ought*" has no meaning whatsoever. It is just as absurd to ask what ought to happen in the natural world as it is to ask what properties a circle ought to have' (A547 / B575). If 'ought' is not contained in the empirical world, then the foundation of morality cannot be a posteriori. (2) The second is a theme developed in the *Groundwork*. We recognize morality as making claims on us of a higher order from those of desire and custom, which are required to cede to morality: moral judgements exhibit, as Kant puts it, absolute *necessity*. Both considerations indicate that morality derives from an order of reason, not an order of nature.

Kant's ethical theory has an importance in his philosophical system quite equal to that of his epistemology and metaphysics. They are, indeed, not ultimately independent of one another. Kant holds that in the context of morality, the ideas of pure reason attain the objective reality that is denied them in the theoretical sphere, reflecting the fact that the ultimate purpose of reason is practical rather than theoretical (see *CPR*, Canon of Pure Reason, A795–831 / B823–59); and this transcendence of the bounds of sensibility by practical reason depends in turn on Kant's metaphysics, which removes obstacles that would otherwise stand in its way (see Bxxv–ix).

Kant's ethical theory may be divided into (1) an *analysis* of morality, and (2) a *justification* of morality. Kant's analysis of morality starts with ordinary moral thought—the legitimacy of which Kant assumes provisionally or at least does not question—and seeks to determine its ultimate presuppositions, to arrive at the 'supreme principle of morality', as Kant puts it.

Kant's analysis of morality tells us what has to be assumed if morality is to be justified, but it does not on its own provide morality with a justification. In order to justify morality, Kant starts at the other end, with certain claims of transcendental philosophy regarding freedom and reason, and seeks to show how these imply, and thereby justify, morality as ordinarily conceived. The analysis of morality is undertaken in *Groundwork* I and II,[4] and recapitulated, in

[4] Roman numerals following *Groundwork* refer to chapters (sections). Arabic numerals following *Gr.* refer to the Akademie pagination, cited in the text in square brackets in Beck's translation and in the margin in other translations. Page references to the *CPracR* refer also to the Akademie pagination, cited in Beck's translation both at the top of the page and in the text, and in the margin in Gregor's translation. Quotations in this chapter are taken from Gregor's translation of the *Groundwork* and the *CPracR*.

similar terms but with significant additions, in the *CPracR*. The justification of morality is presented, in one form, in *Groundwork* III, and again, in terms that are importantly different, in the *CPracR*.

2.1. Kant's Analysis of Morality in *Groundwork* I and II

2.1.1. *Moral Goodness: The Good Will and Duty*

Kant's analysis of morality begins with the claim that the fundamental form of moral goodness is what Kant calls a *good will*—the will of an agent who is morally worthy. A good will, Kant argues, is the only thing that can be conceived as possessing unconditional value (see *Gr.* 393–4). It is also what is exemplified in our ordinary concept of dutiful action (see *Gr.* 397): the concept of duty is that of a good will operating under the conditions of human sensibility, that is, in an agent whose will is also susceptible to being determined by inclination (inclination is Kant's broad term, roughly equivalent to desire, for any motive to action supplied by our empirical as opposed to purely rational natures). Kant contrasts a human with a 'holy will', which is incapable of departing from the moral law: a holy will cannot experience the moral law as obligating or constraining in the way that it is experienced by human beings (see *Gr.* 414).

An action is dutiful if it is not merely in conformity with a rule, but performed with a certain motive, namely for the sake of duty. This entails, Kant maintains, the following (see *Gr.* 397–401): (1) In order to have moral worth an action must be motivated independently of inclination. This is shown, Kant claims, by four examples that he gives of cases where one and the same action may have either duty or inclination as its motive. (2) The moral worth of an action derives from the principle on which an agent acts, and not from the results intended by the agent or attained by the action. Since this principle must exclude inclination, it must be, as Kant puts it, 'formal' and a priori. (3) The motive of duty consists in respect (or reverence: *Achtung*) for the moral law, as possessing a value surpassing the satisfaction of inclination.

(On the good will, see Aune 1979: 3–9; Höffe 1994, sect. 8.1; Korsgaard 1996, ch. 9; and Paton 1946, ch. 2. On Kant's account of duty, see Allison 1990, ch. 6; Aune 1979: 9–12, 20–8; Dietrichson 1967; Korsgaard 1996, ch. 2; and Paton 1946, chs. 3–6.)

Kant's analysis of moral goodness rules out any consequentialist, utilitarian, or Aristotelian foundation for morality, since these assign priority to merely conditional goods: desirable states of affairs, happiness, and qualities of character such as moderation and self-control are good only on condition that they are related to a good will (the happiness of the wicked is not a good, self-control is not good when in the service of a bad will, and so on). More generally, it follows from Kant's argument that morality cannot be either analysed or justified in terms of any concept drawn from experience, since no a posteriori concept of 'the nature of the human being' or 'the circumstances of the world in which he is placed' (*Gr.* 389)—or of moral sentiment deriving from these—can account for the good will. The foundation of morality must be therefore wholly a priori (see *Gr.* 388–91, 408), and since the only possible source of a priori motivation is reason, the foundation of morality must lie in reason: ethical theory must take the form of a 'metaphysics of morals' (see *Gr.* 388).

Kant has, however, a second (formally distinct though closely related) argument for his conclusion regarding the foundation of morality. Kant declares that the moral law holds with 'absolute necessity': it directs us to act in certain ways even when all of our desires are opposed to doing so. If it does this, Kant claims, then it must extend to all rational beings, not just to all human beings (see *Gr.* 389, 408, 425); and since a law that is valid for all rational beings cannot be based on conditions that are specific to the constitution of a human agent, the moral law must be based on the condition of pure rational agency, i.e. on reason alone.

2.1.2. *The Moral Law: The Categorical Imperative*

Kant has claimed that our ordinary concept of dutiful action presupposes a will determined by a principle that is formal and a priori. To identify this principle is to identify the supreme principle of morality. Now, Kant maintains, it follows from the fact that the moral law holds for all rational beings that the supreme principle of morality can be derived from the concept of a rational being in general (see *Gr.* 412): it must be possible to extract the supreme principle of morality by purely analytical means from the bare concept of rational agency.

Kant's claim, in *Groundwork* II, is that the supreme principle of morality is the *principle of autonomy*: a rational agent is one who acts autonomously, i.e. on laws that it can regard as having prescribed to itself. Thus stated, the principle of autonomy is descriptive: it says what a perfectly rational agent *would* do. To a human agent, whose rationality is imperfect, the principle appears in a prescriptive form: it says what a human agent *ought* to do; namely, determine its will in such a way that it can regard itself as autonomous. (Kant's subordination of the concept of the good, traditionally the fundamental concept of ethical theory, to that of autonomy may be regarded as constituting a 'Copernican revolution' in ethics: see Silber 1967.)

Kant's account in *Groundwork* II of why autonomy comprises the essence of morality is complex. The argument begins with an intricate analysis of practical reason, out of which emerges Kant's key claim that the moral law takes the form of what he calls a categorical imperative (see *Gr.* 412–20).

Kant defines will, or the faculty of practical reason (Kant identifies the two), as the ability to act according to a *conception* of law. The contrast is with nature, which exemplifies simply action in accordance with law. Kant expresses the role of a conception of law by saying that all actions involve *maxims*. Maxims are *subjective* principles of action. On Kant's account, a rational agent necessarily determines her actions in accordance with maxims, analogously to the way in which the objects of theoretical judgement are necessarily brought under concepts. This is the fundamental point at which Kant departs from empiricist accounts of agency such as Hume's, to which he is standardly opposed (see Korsgaard 1996, ch. 11): Kant holds that *all* action involves committing oneself to a general rule of some sort, and thereby denies that action can ever be regarded as simply caused by desire.

A maxim is a personal or private rule: it is regarded as applying merely to oneself. If it is to be rational, it must be based on what Kant calls an *objective* principle. An objective principle defines how maxims should be formed: it is impersonal and regarded as applicable to all rational agents. An example of a maxim or subjective principle would be Smith's maxim 'When I am thirsty, let me drink'; an example of an objective principle, 'When one is thirsty, one ought to drink'. (Accounts of Kant's terminology here differ slightly: see Allison 1990: 86–94; Aune 1979: 12–20; and Paton 1948: 59–60.)

Kant then introduces the concept of an imperative, and a distinction between different kinds of imperatives (see *Gr.* 412–20). Whereas maxims are principles that an agent does actually act on, objective principles are ones that a human agent—not being perfectly rational—ought to, but may not in fact, act on. Consequently, objective principles take, for human agents, the form of *imperatives*: they are grasped as 'necessitating' or commanding. Imperatives are expressed in the form of a judgement that something *ought* to be done: 'ought' expresses the relation between an objective principle and a subjective constitution that may be, but is not necessarily, determined by it. (No question of 'ought' arises, therefore, for a holy will.)

Some objective principles are conditioned by an end, or purpose. This may be one that an agent takes an interest in contingently, or one that it must take an interest in by its very nature (for human beings, this necessary end is happiness, according to Kant). Principles that are conditioned by ends give rise to *hypothetical* imperatives. A hypothetical imperative enjoins us to perform an action because of its effects: the action is represented as *good as a means* to an independently specified end. Such are the imperatives of prudence.

But there are other objective principles, Kant supposes, which are not conditioned by any end and so represent actions as 'objectively necessary'. This subset of objective principles Kant calls *practical laws*. Practical laws give rise to *categorical* imperatives. A categorical imperative represents an action as *good in itself*—as to be performed for its own sake, because of the principle that it embodies. (Note that Kant's distinction between hypothetical and categorical imperatives concerns their grounds and has nothing to do with their grammatical form; Kant might have called them instead conditional and unconditional imperatives, which is indeed how he describes them at *Gr.* 432–3. On the distinction of kinds of imperative, see Hill 1992, ch. 1.)

Now it is clear that a categorical imperative is identical with the moral law, since the concept of a practical law coincides with that of a principle that determines a good will, and with that of a law that is absolutely necessary. Out of Kant's analysis of practical reason emerges, then, the claim that morality takes the form of a categorical imperative, and the task of formulating the supreme principle of morality can now be recast as that of discovering what is contained in a categorical imperative. Kant's argument for the identification of the supreme principle of morality with the principle of autonomy proceeds by way of successive formulations of the categorical imperative.

1. *The formula of universal law* (see *Gr.* 402–3, 420–5). Kant gives the first formula of the categorical imperative, the formula of universal law (FUL), in *Groundwork* I:

> I ought never to act except in such a way that I could also will that my maxim should become a universal law. (*Gr.* 402–3)

FUL is restated in *Groundwork* II, in positive terms, as:

> act only in accordance with that maxim through which you can at the same time will that it become a universal law. (*Gr.* 421)

With regard to FUL, as to each of the later formulas, Kant must show two things: (1) that what it commands is what is required for a categorical imperative, and (2) that moral requirements follow from it.

Kant's argument that suitability as universal law is required for a categorical imperative is stated very briefly, and somewhat obscurely, on two occasions and in different terms (first at *Gr.* 402, then again at *Gr.* 420–1). First, Kant argues that since the principle of a good will is not derived from any particular subjective end, nothing is left as a principle of a good will but 'the conformity of actions as such with universal law' (*Gr.* 402). Secondly, Kant argues that since a categorical or unconditional imperative can contain 'beyond the law, only the necessity that the maxim be in conformity with this law', this law can contain nothing but 'the universality of law as such' (*Gr.* 420–1). Kant's claim is that only a law that is valid universally (that it is rational for all beings to adopt) can give rise to an unconditionally good will or command unconditionally: the possibility of being followed by any rational being is the only possible ground that such a law can have. The universality of the moral law is, then, the source of the impartiality and objectivity that characterizes ordinary moral thinking.

Kant gives a subsidiary formulation of FUL in terms of the concept of a law of nature (FULN):

> act as if the maxim of your action were to become by your will a universal law of nature. (*Gr.* 421)

FULN is required because reference to laws of nature is essential for the application of FUL by sensible beings in the empirical realm: in order to determine what can be willed universally, it needs to be considered what the effects of acting on a given principle would be in our actual world, which requires consideration of the specific laws of nature that obtain in it. In so doing, we consider ourselves not just as beings with reason but also as subject to natural necessity, and, teleologically, as having certain inherent natural purposes. (Kant explains the necessity of applying FUL through FULN in *CPracR* 67–71, where natural law is said to serve as the 'type', or model, of the moral law.)

FULN is sometimes regarded as a second formula of the categorical imperative, rather than a subsidiary formulation of the first; commentators count the formulas differently, reflecting different views of how they are related to one another (compare Paton 1946: 129 with Sullivan 1989: 149–50 or 1994: 29). This raises the general question of what Kant is doing in offering different formulas of the categorical imperative. It would seem that the sequence of formulas is intended to form an unbroken chain of argument, but Kant says also that the formulas are equivalent (*Gr.* 436). By this he means not that they are identical in meaning—if so, there would be no point in multiplying them—but that they have the same ultimate ground and determine the same extension of duties. Complex issues arise in considering the interrelations of the formulas, but Kant's general purpose in rearticulating the categorical imperative is to demonstrate its richness and show that the purely formal FUL may be re-expressed in more intuitively resonant terms (see *Gr.* 436–7). (On the relations between the formulas, see Aune 1979: 111–20; O'Neill 1989, ch. 7; Paton 1946, ch. 13; and Williams 1968, ch. 3.)

Also to be noted, regarding the term categorical imperative, is the distinction—which Kant does not make explicit but is shown by the context of his use—between *the* categorical imperative, or Categorical Imperative, which is what is formulated in FUL and FULN, and of which Kant is speaking when he says that there is 'only one'; and particular categorical imperatives such as 'keep your promises' or 'keep your promise to Smith', of which there can be indefinitely many.

To show that moral requirements follow from FUL, Kant gives first the example of someone who is tempted to make a promise without the intention of keeping it (see *Gr.* 402–3). Such an action can of course be willed when considered from the perspective of self-interest, but not when considered from the perspective of universal law, for to will the law that promises be made without the intention of being kept is to render the very concept of a promise incoherent. In *Groundwork* II. 421–3, Kant gives a fuller set of examples of duties that, he claims, follow from FUL: (1) self-preservation, (2) promise-keeping, (3) the cultivation of one's talents (self-perfection), and (4) beneficence. These are intended as illustrations and by no means as exhaustive (Kant's comprehensive and systematic statement of what morality requires is reserved for his *Metaphysics of Morals*).

In deriving these duties, Kant employs a test of contradiction for maxims (see *Gr.* 424). Kant's underlying idea is that the requirement of consistency or avoidance of contradiction which is constitutive of reason may be applied, with appropriate modification, in the practical sphere: rationality requires that an agent's maxims be self-consistent, and consistent with one another. The test of contradiction comes in two parts, *contradiction in concept* and *contradiction in will*. In applying the first, we consider whether the universalization of the maxim of an action would result in conceptual incoherence (as in the case of false promising). Maxims that pass this test must also pass the second, in which we consider whether the universalization of the maxim of an action would result in incoherent willing, i.e. the simultaneous willing and not willing of some end. This test is less straightforward, but well illustrated by Kant's derivation of the duty of beneficence (see *Gr.* 423): I cannot will that I should not help another in need when able to do so, for I must will the means to the fulfilment of my own ends, and these often presuppose the cooperation of others; a principle of exclusive self-interest or egoism, considered as universal law, would contradict itself, since it would result in my simultaneously willing an end, my interest, and not willing the necessary means to it, namely the voluntary assistance of others.

The test of contradiction functions negatively: if a maxim fails the test, actions in conformity with that maxim are ones that we ought *not* to perform. (It does not follow, note, that maxims that do pass the test of contradiction—e.g. 'to walk at a brisk pace'—are ones that we are morally obliged to perform: rather they are ones that it is morally permissible to perform.) Since some of the things that we ought not to do are themselves negative—e.g. 'not helping others'—the test is able to generate broad, positive duties of indefinite scope such as beneficence, as well as narrow, negative duties such as promise-keeping.

(On FUL and the test of contradiction, see Aune 1979: 28–69; Korsgaard 1996, chs. 2–3; Nell 1975, ch. 5; O'Neill 1989, chs. 5 and 7; Paton 1946, ch. 14; Sullivan 1989, chs. 11–12 or 1994, ch. 3. On FULN as the 'type' of FUL and the teleology associated with it, see Dietrichson 1964; Paton 1946, ch. 15; and Sullivan 1989, ch. 13.)

2. *The formula of ends* (see *Gr.* 427–30). The second formula of the categorical imperative (FEnds) is:

> So act that you always treat humanity, whether in your own person or in the person of any other, always at the same time as an end, never merely as a means. (*Gr.* 429)

(See also the version at *Gr.* 436, where rational beings are described as limiting conditions on our choice of ends.)

Kant establishes the necessity of treating persons as ends as follows. If there is to be a categorical imperative, it must incorporate an end, since all willing presupposes an end. And yet it must abstract from all subjective ends, i.e. all ends given by inclination. It follows that there can be a categorical imperative only if there is an *objective end*, something that can be taken as an end for all rational beings, and is given by reason alone. This requires 'something the *existence of which in itself* has an absolute worth', '*an end in itself*' (*Gr.* 428). Now the only candidate for such an end is 'rational nature', i.e. rational beings in general (persons). Thus a categorical imperative is possible only on the assumption that rational nature 'exists as an end in itself' (*Gr.* 429). (This is in any case an assumption—Kant claims in what is in effect a second and independent argument for FEnds at *Gr.* 429—that is forced on rational beings by virtue of their self-conception.) Rational nature is known to us only in the form of human beings, and FEnds is referred to also as the formula of humanity.

Kant then shows (see *Gr.* 429–30) that the same illustrative set of four duties can be derived from FEnds as from FUL: to promise falsely is forbidden because it is to use an other merely as a means; to promote the happiness of others (the duty of beneficence) is necessary in order that humanity be treated as an end in a positive sense; and so on.

Kant later develops the thought that persons are ends by introducing the claim that persons have *dignity*, as opposed to mere 'price' (see *Gr.* 434–5): rational beings have a value, deriving from their capacity for bearing a good will, that sets them beyond comparison with anything else and renders them irreplaceable.

(On FEnds, see Aune 1979: 70–83; Guyer 1993*b*: 58–63; Hill 1992, ch. 2; Korsgaard 1996, ch. 4; O'Neill 1989, ch. 7; Paton 1946, ch. 16; and Sullivan 1989, ch. 14 or 1994, ch. 4.)

3. *The formula of autonomy* (see *Gr.* 430–4, 440–4). The third formula of the categorical imperative (FAut) enjoins us to act only

> so that the will could regard itself as at the same time giving universal law through its maxim. (*Gr.* 434)

What FAut adds to FUL is the idea that we *make*, as well as will, universal law. The implication of FAut is that we are subject to the law *because* we make it—that a will that obeys the moral law is subject to it for the sole reason that the moral law is the product of its own self-legislation. The importance of FAut is then that it refers to the *ground* of our acknowledgement of the validity of the moral law: it brings out the independence of the moral law from any interest (see *Gr.* 432). It also suggests a critical connection of morality with freedom, which *Groundwork* III will elaborate.

The introduction of the new concept of autonomy allows Kant to restate his objection to ethical theories that fail to provide morality with an a priori foundation (that is, all theories other than his own): these derive morality from some interest and misconstrue its imperatives as hypothetical. They consequently misrepresent morality as a form of *heteronomy*, a condition in which the will is given its law by something other than itself (see *Gr.* 432–3). Kant concludes *Groundwork* II with an examination of the various species of moral theory (empiricist and rationalist) that misconstrue morality as heteronomous (see *Gr.* 441–4).

FAut follows from FUL and FEnds. Kant suggests several routes of derivation: FAut is implicit in FUL (see *Gr.* 434), and in FEnds (see *Gr.* 434, 435), and it can be formed by combining FUL with FEnds (see *Gr.* 431). It is unnecessary for Kant to show that FAut is capable of generating duties, since the earlier formulas from which it derives have already been shown to do so.

The pre-eminence of FAut in formulating the supreme principle of morality becomes clear in *CPracR*, where it is described as the 'fundamental law of pure practical reason' (*CPracR* 30) and so takes the place occupied in the *Groundwork* by FUL.

(On FAut and Kant's concept of autonomy, see Allison 1990: 94–106; Aune 1979: 83–94; Hill 1992, ch. 5; Paton 1946, ch. 17; Sullivan 1989, ch. 12; and Williams 1968, ch. 3.)

4. *The formula of the kingdom of ends* (see *Gr.* 433–6, 438–9). This formula (FKEnds) reads:

> A rational being must always regard himself as lawgiving in a kingdom [or realm: *Reich*] of ends possible through freedom of the will. (*Gr.* 434)

(Note also the version at *Gr.* 436, in which a teleological view of nature is incorporated.) The point of this most comprehensive formula—which, Kant says, brings the categorical imperative 'closer to intuition (by a certain analogy) and thereby to feeling' (*Gr.* 436)—is to present us with a vision of what can be realized through the moral law: namely an ideal community in which all make and obey the same law, elaborated in a system of laws, and in which all ends are harmonized systematically with one another; in a kingdom of ends the private ends of individuals are pursued only within the limitations imposed by the condition that rational beings be treated as ends. The notion of a kingdom of ends suggests a form of civil society or political order, and also points towards the idea of an intelligible world that Kant will introduce in *Groundwork* III.

Again this formula is derivable from its predecessors, by combining FAut with FEnds (see *Gr.* 433), and, as with FAut, it is unnecessary for Kant to show that it entails duties.

(On FKEnds, see Aune 1979: 104–11; Hill 1992, ch. 3; Paton 1946, ch. 18; and Sullivan 1989, ch. 15 or 1994, ch. 5.)

2.2. Kant's Justification of Morality

Kant's analysis, if correct, identifies the supreme principle of morality, but to do this is not to provide morality with a justification (see *Gr.* 444–5): Kant grants that it remains perfectly possible that morality is a mere 'phantom'.

Kant formulates the problem of justifying morality in terms of the question, How is a categorical imperative possible? (see *Gr.* 417–20). There is no difficulty in seeing how hypothetical imperatives are possible, for it is analytic that if one wills a certain end, then one wills also the means to that end, and particular hypothetical imperatives can be derived simply by applying this principle to particular given ends. But there *is* difficulty in seeing how a categorical imperative is possible: here by contrast no end is presupposed, so the imperative cannot be validated by pointing out that the action that it commands constitutes the means to any end.

In logical terms, the problem is that a categorical imperative is a further instance of a synthetic a priori judgement. A categorical imperative declares an action to be necessary, and necessity entails a priority; at the same time, it combines the concept of a rational being with that of obligation, and the concept of a rational being does not contain that of obligation, so it must be synthetic (see *Gr.* 440). A transcendental deduction is required therefore: a third term, synthesizing subject and predicate, needs to be found. Only then will it be shown that what a human agent ought to do is what a perfectly rational being would necessarily do.

2.2.1. *The Justification of Morality in* Groundwork III

The task of justifying morality is undertaken first in *Groundwork* III. Here Kant argues that the third term that provides the justification of morality is reason's idea of *freedom*. (Note that it is transcendental, not mere practical, freedom that is in question in Kant's ethics.) Kant's strategy is to argue that the moral law is justified if we are free, and that the presupposition of freedom is justified; so morality is justified.

The connection of morality with freedom is straightforward and merely requires further analysis (see *Gr.* 446–7). (On this early part of the argument, see Allison 1990, ch. 10; and Paton 1946, ch. 20.) To conceive the will of a rational agent as unconditioned by natural causes is to conceive it as free in a merely *negative* sense. This is, however, an incomplete conception of a free will. A will is a kind of causality, and causality implies law (at least, the will of a rational being cannot be *lawless*). *Ex hypothesi*, the laws of a rational will cannot be laws of nature. So the only laws that can determine a rational will are ones that it has imposed on itself. Thus the concept of the will of a rational being leads to the concept of a will that is free in a *positive* sense equivalent to that of *autonomy*.

Given that the principle of autonomy supplies the supreme principle of morality, it follows that 'a free will and a will under moral laws are one and the same' (*Gr.* 447).

Kant's identification of freedom with morality may appear to entail that immoral action cannot be free—paradoxically making it impossible for the wicked to be blamed. Thus Sidgwick (1907) argues that Kant faces a dilemma, reflecting a systematic equivocation in his theory between two senses of freedom: either freedom is the unique preserve of morality, and we are not responsible for our evil actions; or freedom is exhibited in immoral action, in which case its identity with morality dissolves. Kant meets this objection with the aid of a distinction between what he calls *Willkür*, the capacity for exercising choice in relation to action, and *Wille*, the capacity for acting in accordance with practical laws. *Wille* is associated with the 'ought' of practical reason and with autonomy. (The distinction is clearest in Kant's *Metaphysics of Morals*, 213–14; it is discussed in Allison 1990: 129–36; Beck 1960: 176–81; and Caygill 1995: 413–15.) Immoral agents are free in the sense of *Willkür*, which is sufficient for moral responsibility, and so are blameworthy.

To show that freedom in the positive sense is presupposed by morality does nothing, however, to justify morality. And unless the presupposition of freedom is justified, morality is no more secure now than it was before its connection with freedom was demonstrated. The third antinomy may have showed that reason's idea of transcendental freedom is neither self-contradictory nor excluded by the nature of experience, but at the same time it showed that claims to theoretical *knowledge* of freedom are illegitimate (see Section 1.14). As Kant observes, we seem to be caught in a circle: we need to prove the reality of freedom in order to justify the moral law; but we are unable to refer, it seems, to anything but the moral law as a ground for assuming the reality of freedom (see *Gr.* 448–50).

The further argument of *Groundwork* III, in which Kant appears to attempt to meet the challenge of justifying freedom independently of morality, is particularly dense. There is no difficulty in identifying its two central themes and general thrust: Kant means to show that the reality of freedom and our membership of the intelligible world are legitimate assumptions from the practical point of view. What is not clear is how exactly the pieces fit together.

1. *The practical point of view* (see *Gr.* 447–50). First Kant asserts the necessity of assuming freedom for practical purposes, and makes the striking claim that rational agents must be assumed to be 'really free in a practical respect' (*Gr.* 448): 'the same laws hold for a being that cannot act otherwise than under the idea of its own freedom as would bind a being that was actually free' (*Gr.* 448 n.).

In support of the claim that the idea of freedom is inescapable, Kant argues that reason in general must regard itself as free (see *Gr.* 448): even when it is employed to theoretical ends, reason must regard itself as self-determining, for it is implicit in the very concept of making a judgement that one is determined by reason, and not by natural causes.

The significance of this is not to justify directly the moral law—Kant acknowledges that the necessity of presupposing freedom from the practical point of view does not explain why morality should be regarded as binding (see *Gr.* 449–50)—but to circumvent the difficulty presented by the impossibility of theoretical knowledge of freedom: Kant claims that an argument that restricts itself to establishing freedom from a practical point of view escapes from the onus of having to prove freedom from a theoretical point of view (see *Gr.* 448n.).

2. *Membership of the intelligible world* (see *Gr.* 450–8). Recognizing that more is needed, Kant turns to the resources of transcendental idealism, hitherto absent from his ethical theory. As the *CPR* showed, there are two points of view that may be taken on all objects, our selves included: they may be considered either as appearances or as things in themselves. Specifically, as the third antinomy showed, our actions, considered as the effects of our intelligible characters rather than as events in nature, may be regarded as the effects of an intelligible causality, and so regarded, are free.

To bring the metaphysics of the intelligible world to bear in the context of morality, Kant refers again to our knowledge of ourselves as possessed of the power of reason. He claims that the pure 'spontaneity' of reason—its independence from and power of transcending sensibility, as exhibited in its forming the idea of an intelligible world distinct from the sensible—shows that we must consider ourselves as belonging, *qua* intelligences, to the intelligible world (see *Gr.* 452; and Paton 1946, ch. 23). This is again not a claim to knowledge, but it provides, Kant supposes, a sufficient defence of the presupposition of freedom and thereby removes the overhanging threat of circularity (see *Gr.* 453). In confirmation of the claim that the idea of an intelligible world is implicated in morality, Kant offers the thought that we refer ('transfer') ourselves implicitly to the intelligible world whenever we wish that we were free of inclination and morally worthy (see *Gr.* 454–5).

This, if sound, completes the justification of morality: it is justified by the necessity of presupposing freedom from a practical point of view together with our entitlement to conceive ourselves as members of the intelligible world.

It remains only for Kant to emphasize the coherence of his account. Kant points out (1) that morality can be justified only on the condition of transcendental idealism, without which freedom cannot be defended against the claims of natural necessity (theoretical philosophy proves here essential for practical philosophy, by disposing of theoretical obstacles to the affirmation of freedom) (see *Gr.* 455–6); (2) that his account remains consistent with the doctrines of the *CPR* that we can have no knowledge of the intelligible world and that freedom cannot be explained (see *Gr.* 458); and (3) that it follows from his account that moral interest neither needs nor is capable of receiving any explanation (see *Gr.* 459–60); the fact that we take the interest we do in morality is an ultimate limit of practical knowledge, on a par and bound up with the limits of theoretical knowledge.

(Differing accounts of the argument of *Groundwork* III may be found in Allison 1990, ch. 12; Hill 1992, ch. 6; Korsgaard 1996, ch. 6; O'Neill 1989, ch. 3; Paton 1946, chs. 21–4; and Sullivan 1989, ch. 7 or 1994, ch. 10.)

2.2.2. *The Justification of Morality in the* Critique of Practical Reason

The solution to the problem of justifying freedom that Kant offers in the *CPracR* differs from that in the *Groundwork*. In the *CPracR* Kant seems to acknowledge that the justification of morality presented in *Groundwork* III does not succeed (for reasons given in Section 2.3 below) and abandons the attempt to provide freedom with an independent justification. The justification of freedom is allowed instead to depend on morality.

The *CPracR* formulates the problem of justification in terms of the question 'whether pure reason of itself alone suffices to determine the will or whether it can be a determining ground of the will only as empirically conditioned' (*CPracR* 15). The possibility of pure practical reason is the possibility that reason can motivate action on its own, independently of empirical conditions, as opposed to just taking up the empirical motives supplied by inclination.

Kant's answer goes directly to the given fact of our moral consciousness, which Kant calls a 'fact of reason' (see *CPracR* 29–31, and the chapter entitled 'Of the Deduction of the Principles of Pure Practical Reason', 42–50). Knowledge of morality precedes, Kant affirms, knowledge of freedom: it is the moral law which '*first* offers itself to us' and 'leads directly to the concept of freedom'. What is given to us is the fact of our actual capacity to recognize a law that is absolutely necessary and to act out of respect for it—that is, the possibility of pure practical reason. Freedom is the ground of the moral law, but our moral consciousness may be regarded as the ground of our *knowledge* of freedom. Accordingly, Kant says that 'the objective reality of the moral law cannot be proved by any deduction', and that, instead, the moral principle 'itself serves as the principle of the deduction' of our freedom.

(On the fact of reason and justification of morality in the *CPracR*, see Allison 1989 and 1990, ch. 13; Beck 1960, ch. 10; Henrich 1994, ch. 2; Herman 1989; Höffe 1994, sect. 8.4; Rawls 1989, sect. 4; and Sullivan 1989: 88–90. Locating Kant's justification of morality in the context of his general (re)conception of reason, see Neiman 1994, ch. 3; O'Neill 1989, ch. 1; and Velkley 1989, ch. 1.)

2.3. Kant's Moral Theology

Though rarely highlighted, it is important to recognize, for an accurate picture of Kant's philosophy as a whole, that Kant regarded religious belief as an essential component of morality (see *CPracR*, Dialectic; the argument is stated earlier in the *CPR* at A633–4/B661–2 and A804–47/B832–47, and discussed later in the *CJ* at §§85–91).

Kant's is not the familiar claim of theological ethics, that we are obliged to obey the moral law because it is the will of God—which makes the justification of morality rest on God and requires God's existence to be proven independently of morality (as the *CPR* says cannot be done; see Section 1.15). Kant's claim is that the requirements of morality require us to 'postulate' the existence of God and the immortality of the soul: morality gives rise to a 'pure rational' and 'pure practical' faith that provides the proper foundation of religion, thereby reversing the order of theological ethics.

Kant's argument turns on his conception of what he calls the 'highest good'. The highest good has two components: (1) virtue, which constitutes worthiness to be happy, and (2) happiness proportional to virtue (see *CPracR* 108–11). The highest good is a 'necessary object' of a moral will, Kant claims: without hope of being able to achieve the highest good, practical reason would be caught in an antinomy, and the moral law would generate a practical absurdity and forsake its validity (see *CPracR* 111–14). Now the conditions of each part of the highest good are, respectively, immortality (to make it possible for us to progress to a condition of complete virtue, as our finite empirical existence does not) and the existence of God (to distribute happiness proportionately to virtue, as nature does not) (see *CPracR* 122–5). Since the moral law commands unconditionally, and hope of attaining the highest good is necessary for us to fulfil it, practical reason is warranted in enjoining our assent to belief in God and immortality—such belief arises 'from the moral disposition'.

It may be asked how practical reason can ascribe objective reality to ideas that theoretical reason cannot affirm as having objects without descending into dogmatism. Kant claims that the warrant for the postulates lies in what he calls the 'primacy of pure practical reason' over speculative reason (behind which lies Kant's thesis of the unity of reason: see *Gr.* 391; *CPracR* 89, 91, 121). According to this doctrine, in cases where theoretical reason has nothing to say against a need of practical reason's, the interests of the latter legitimately take precedence: we may, indeed must, go ahead and believe (see *CPracR* 119–21). Kant emphasizes that the postulates constitute knowledge 'only *for practical purposes*'; we cannot go on to assume the objective reality of God or the soul in theoretical contexts (see *CPracR* 133–8).

(Kant's philosophy of religion is set out at length in his *Religion within the Boundaries of Mere Reason*. On the antinomy of practical reason, highest good, postulates of practical reason, and Kant's moral theology in general, see Beck 1960, chs. 13–14; Buchdahl 1992, ch. 15; Neiman 1994, ch. 4; Sullivan 1989: 139–44, 218–26; and Wood 1992; Wood 1970 is a detailed study of the topic. On the primacy of practical reason, see Sullivan 1989, ch. 8.)

2.4. Central Critical Issues

The issues thrown up by Kant's ethical theory are numerous and intricate. Among the most important, and most intensively discussed in the commentaries, are the following.

1. An important initial difficulty arises with respect to Kant's account of what is necessary for an action to have moral worth. Kant's exclusion of inclination encompasses acts performed from sympathy (see *Gr.* 398), and to deny such actions moral worth has struck many as counter-intuitive, if not perverse. Defences of Kant on this score proceed by noting that Kant requires not the absence or elimination of motives other than duty, only that the motive of duty in some appropriate sense preponderates. (Dealing with this criticism, see Allison 1990, ch. 6; Dietrichson 1967; Herman 1993, ch. 1; and Paton 1946, ch. 3.)

2. Objections to Kant's account of the categorical imperative tend to focus in the first instance on the formulation in terms of universal law and test of contradiction. (Overviews of the various criticisms that have been made of the categorical imperative may be found in Broad 1930, ch. 5; Norman 1983, ch. 6; and Walker 1978: 152–9. In more detail, see Aune 1979: 120–30; Dietrichson 1964; Ebbinghaus 1967; J. Harrison 1967; Herman 1993, chs. 4–5; Kemp 1967; Korsgaard 1996, ch. 3; and Nell 1975, chs. 2–3, 5–7.)

It has been objected that (1) the plain fact of immorality is sufficient to show that immoral action can be conceived and willed, refuting Kant's test of contradiction; (2) FUL allows an agent to will whatever principles reflect her own preferences and values, plunging the moral law into subjectivism or relativism; (3) the categorical imperative, by virtue of its appeal to future or possible undesirable states of affairs consequent upon the universal adoption of a principle, rests on a covert appeal to egoistic motivation (see Schopenhauer 1841, ch. 2, §7).

These objections may be argued to rest on misunderstandings. The first Kant deals with at *Gr.* 424: when we violate our duty, we do not will the maxim of our action as universal law, rather we will that an *exception* be made to universal law for ourselves. The possibility of willing immoral actions in this sense—from a *partial*, inclination-dependent point of view—does nothing to show that they can be willed in the *impartial*, inclination-independent sense of the categorical imperative. The first objection thus reflects a misunderstanding of what is meant by being 'able to will' a maxim as universal law. The second objection repeats this mistake, and is again met by saying that the perspective of willing as universal law presupposes that one abstracts from one's contingent preferences and any conception of the good that one may hold. The third objection confuses the reasoning required by the categorical imperative with prudential reasoning: the categorical imperative requires us to consider the effects of actions solely with respect to the formal requirement of non-contradiction—it does not appeal in any way to the *desirability* of the consequences of the universal adoption of a rule (see Sullivan 1989: 163–4).

Other common objections identify semi-technical difficulties in the application of the categorical imperative. One such is the problem of relevant descriptions. The problem is that with little ingenuity *some* description can be found for every individual action under which it can be willed universally: for instance, it can be described in terms so minimal that it becomes morally innocuous. If it cannot be determined what counts as *the* maxim of a given action then, whatever constraint FUL may set on choice of maxims, FUL fails to effect any constraint on choice of action. To solve this problem, it is necessary to show that restrictions can be put on the descriptions of actions that are relevant to determining whether they can be willed universally. Opinions vary as to how easily this can be done, but it is plausible to maintain that this difficulty, and others of a similar order, may be overcome. (On the problem of relevant descriptions, see Nell 1975, chs. 2–3; and Sullivan 1989: 160–2.)

The most frequently voiced objection to the categorical imperative—one that goes to the heart of Kant's theory and is not so easily met—is that even if Kant is justified in saying that the moral law requires universality, this condition, being completely formal, is at the same time and as a consequence completely empty.

Hegel puts this objection. According to Hegel, Kant's minimal conception of duty as 'the absence of contradiction' makes 'the transition to the specification of particular duties' impossible, such that 'any wrong or immoral line of conduct may be justified' by means of FUL. In order to condemn theft or murder, for example, material must be 'brought in from outside': it is necessary to establish on independent grounds 'that property and human life are to exist and to be respected'. A 'contradiction must be a contradiction of something, i.e. of some content presupposed from the start'. Duty must be willed, therefore, not for duty's sake, but 'for the sake of some content' (1821, sect. 135). (Hegel's critique of Kant's ethics is found in Hegel 1821, Second Part, 'Morality', sects. 105–41. On Hegel's critique of Kant's ethics, see Wood 1990, chs. 8–9. Bradley 1876, ch. 4, restates eloquently Hegel's criticisms.)

Mill similarly charges Kant with being unable to make the transition from form to content: 'But when he [Kant] begins to deduce from this precept any of the actual duties of morality, he fails, almost grotesquely, to show that there would be any contradiction, any logical (not to say physical) impossibility, in the adoption by all rational beings of the most outrageously immoral rules of conduct' (1863: 4).

To neutralize the charge of emptiness, a more explicit account of the relation between the highly abstract categorical imperative and concrete moral judgement is needed. Two lines of response have been particularly prominent.

To some commentators it has seemed profitable to divert attention away from FUL towards the other, apparently more contentful formulas. Thus one might look for a criterion of action to FULN, as the *CPracR* arguably encourages; or to FEnds, where the idea of rational nature as an end in itself may seem to provide a definite content to direct practical thought (see Hill 1992, ch. 2; and Murphy 1970, chs. 2–3); or to FKEnds, with its conception of an ideal legislative vantage-point (see Hill 1992, ch. 3). But here again it may be doubted—in view of the indefiniteness of the teleological conception of human beings presupposed by FULN, and the open-endedness of the notions of treating something as an end, and of legislating for a kingdom of ends—that significantly more definite moral instructions can be derived from the other formulas than from FUL.

Whether or not the later formulas have more to offer than FUL, a second line of response that has been explored is to question the assumption of Hegel, Mill, and many others that Kant does indeed intend the categorical imperative to provide direct and determinate moral guidance. Kant's true intention may have been only to indicate the basis on which genuinely moral thinking precedes and its general direction. Since the categorical imperative is described as providing a test for the morality of maxims, not of individual actions, Kant may be read as regarding the test of contradiction as yielding only a basic set of maxims whose application to individual cases cannot be determined mechanically by a set of rules, and requires a further exercise of judgement. In which case, it is inappropriate to expect the categorical imperative to yield a moral 'decision procedure' for individual actions—its practical value consists rather in its circumscribing, by means of its clarification of the essential nature of morality, the attitude of will or standpoint constitutive of moral consciousness. (For this reading of Kant, see Paton 1946, ch. 14; and, more explicitly, Williams 1968, chs. 4 and 9. Arguing that the categorical imperative can establish only 'deliberative presumptions', see Herman 1993, ch. 7. Compare O'Neill's extended defence of the capacity of the categorical imperative to provide moral guidance, in Nell 1975 and O'Neill 1989, chs. 5 and 7.)

A further issue that arises in the context of Kant's analysis of morality is Kant's 'rigorism' or absolutism, his view that moral principles are such that it is never permissible to violate them, whatever the circumstances. This is Kant's avowed position, but most sympathetic commentators regard this doctrine as due to an excess of enthusiasm for morality on Kant's part, rather than a strict implication (and thus, arguably, a *reductio*) of his ethical theory (see Sullivan 1989: 170–7).

Kant's analysis of morality confronts difficulties and elicits sharp disagreement, but some of its difficulties are common to other ethical theories, and there is some degree of consensus that, whatever its limitations, Kant's analysis is roughly on the right track, at least as regards a central component of our moral thought. Its enduring significance is shown not least in the way that contemporary liberal political theory draws heavily on Kant's ideas, pre-eminently in the influential work of Rawls. (See Rawls 1971, sect. 40; and 1980. Kant's own legal and political philosophy may be found in the Doctrine of Right in *The Metaphysics of Morals*, and in Kant, *Political Writings*. It is discussed in Aune 1979, ch. 5; Höffe 1994, ch. 9; Kersting 1992; Murphy 1970, ch. 4; O'Neill 1989, ch. 2; and Sullivan 1989, chs. 16–17, or 1994, ch. 1.)

3. Kant's justification of morality, by contrast, meets widespread rejection. In part this registers its dependence on the controversial metaphysic of transcendental idealism, from which many defendants of Kant's ethical theory attempt to prise it apart. Dependence on transcendental idealism can hardly be regarded in Kant's own terms as a weakness, however, and the first question that needs to be asked in evaluating his justification of morality is whether Kant succeeds in showing that we have a grasp of freedom sufficient to underpin morality, consistently with his denial in the *CPR* that we can have knowledge of freedom.

Undoubtedly, *Groundwork* III suffers from an inherent weakness when considered as attempting a *deduction* of morality, if this is taken to mean a proof of morality from non-moral premisses, addressed to the moral sceptic or 'amoralist', to the effect that any doubt or denial regarding the existence of moral obligation contradicts a principle of practical reason which all rational agents must accept and so refutes itself. A deduction of morality in that sense would require an assurance of our reality as members of the intelligible world independently of morality. But this is something that Kant does not supply in *Groundwork* III: the spontaneity of reason that Kant refers to may well show that we are free in a *negative* sense, but it does not establish that we are free in the *positive* sense of belonging to an intelligible world conceived as having objective reality, as required for a deduction of morality (see Allison 1990: 227–8). Kant has not proven that we are free in that positive sense, for the considerations that he cites leave it open that we are agents whose wills are never merely empirically determined but also never empirically unconditioned (pure); it may be that we are agents who are not determined by inclination but who are equally incapable of autonomy in Kant's sense. The sense of freedom that we are entitled to credit ourselves with, and the sense of freedom required for morality, come apart. In the terms of the *CPracR*, the problem is that, as Kant himself says, we do not understand *how* pure reason can be practical (see *Gr.* 461), and there is nothing that can be appealed to, independently of morality, that will show its possibility. (On the failure of *Groundwork* III considered in such terms, see Allison 1990, ch. 12; Ameriks 1982*a*, ch. 6; Henrich 1994: 72–82, 104–7; and Paton 1946, ch. 24.)

The *CPracR*, by reversing the order of argument, avoids these pitfalls, and it is a delicate question whether it does not succeed, in the terms of Kant's philosophical system, and on the condition of transcendental idealism. (See Allison 1989; Ameriks 1982*a*, ch. 6; Beck 1960, ch. 10; Guyer 1993*a*; Henrich 1994: 82–7, 107–13; and Herman 1989. For a blunt repudiation of Kant's alleged fact of reason, see Schopenhauer 1841, ch. 2, sect. 6.)

4. Kant's derivation of the postulates of practical reason is vulnerable to the objection that—even though the idea that religious belief is somehow the natural fulfilment of moral consciousness may be far from absurd—Kant fails to make it clear why the highest good must be willed, and so in what sense a will without hope of attaining it would be rationally paralysed and unable to do its duty. (Criticizing Kant's account of the postulates, see Broad 1930: 139–42; Walker 1978: 136–41; and Walsh 1975, sects. 39–40; in partial defence, see Buchdahl 1992: 354–62; and Sullivan 1989: 226–9.) The upshot of rejecting the postulates is to damage Kant's moral theology whilst leaving the rest of his ethical theory intact.

3. KANT'S AESTHETICS

Kant's aesthetic theory in the Critique of Aesthetic Judgement (which comprises part I of the *Critique of Judgement*) addresses in the first instance the question of whether aesthetic judgement—the paradigm of which is, for Kant, a judgement of the beauty of a natural object—is susceptible to any kind of justification.

The problem that Kant attempts to resolve had given rise in the eighteenth century to many conflicting theories and is known as the problem of taste. (On the historical background to Kant's aesthetics, see Pluhar 1987, sect. 4.) It is that a judgement that an object is beautiful involves an exercise of taste, and seems to rest on nothing but a subjective feeling. This would appear to mean that there should be no more disputing about matters of taste than there is about personal, arbitrary likes and dislikes, and yet aesthetic judgements are commonly regarded as intended to command agreement and treated as fit objects of contention, as if, like empirical judgement, and moral judgement, and unlike mere private avowals of feeling, they could attain objectivity. There is in this a sort of paradox. Expressed in Kant's terms, it is that aesthetic judgements appear to lay claim to objectivity whilst precluding the necessary conditions of objective validity: they are, it would seem, too remote from rules and concepts for their claim to agreement to be justified in the way that empirical judgements are justified in the *CPR*, and too dependent on subjective feeling to receive anything similar to Kant's justification of moral judgements in terms of pure practical reason.

That transcendental philosophy can encompass aesthetic judgement was not always Kant's view. In the *CPR*, Kant had dismissed as 'abortive' the attempt of the rationalist philosopher Baumgarten to construct a science of the rational principles underlying beauty, on the grounds that the 'said rules or criteria' of beauty are 'merely empirical' and that our judgements of taste cannot be directed by a priori principles (see A21n./B35n.). (Kant had in fact himself undertaken a kind of empirical anthropology of aesthetic preference in his pre-Critical *Observations on the Feeling of the Beautiful and the Sublime*.) In the *CJ* Kant reverses this position, first by providing an analysis, more acute than those of his predecessors, of judgements of taste and the problem they set, designed to show that judgements of taste, symmetrically with empirical and moral judgement, presuppose an a priori foundation; and, secondly, by arguing that Critical philosophy has the resources to provide such a foundation and solve the problem of taste. (Kant may be read as if responding to and seeking to improve on, in particular, Hume's (1757) treatment of the problem of taste: see Mothersill 1984, chs. 7–8; Savile 1993, ch. 4; and Schaper 1983.)

Kant's aesthetic theory may be divided into an analytical and a justificatory part. The former is contained in the Analytic of the Beautiful, the latter in the Deduction of Pure Aesthetic Judgement and the Dialectic of Aesthetic Judgement.

3.1. Kant's Analysis of Judgements of Taste

Whereas the term 'aesthetic' now denotes matters having to do with art and beauty, Kant uses the term in a technical sense to refer to any judgement whose basis is wholly subjective. The contrast is with what Kant calls logical judgement (of which there are two species, the theoretical and the practical). On Kant's account, the only judgements that are aesthetic are ones that are grounded in feeling. There are three species of aesthetic judgement: (1) *judgements of the agreeable*, that an object is pleasant; (2) *judgements of taste*, that an object is beautiful; and (3) *judgements of the sublime*, that an object is sublime. The Analytic of the Beautiful analyses judgements of taste, a separate and later analytic being reserved for the sublime. Note that the concept we express by 'aesthetic judgement' therefore has no precise counterpart in Kant's theory, since his use of that term is broader than ours, and what he means by judgements of taste comprise only one species of what we now call aesthetic judgement. The most fundamental questions raised by aesthetic judgement (in our sense) are, however, treated in Kant's account of judgements of taste.

The Analytic of the Beautiful is broken up into four 'moments', each of which presents and defends a different formula concerning beauty. Like the formulas of the categorical imperative, they may be regarded in two ways, as forming an argumentative chain in which each claim follows from its predecessors, and as a set of partial definitions and explications of beauty. Kant's analysis, if successful, shows what are the necessary and sufficient conditions for a subject to have made a judgement of taste, and what is contained in the concept of beauty. What also emerges in the course of the Analytic of the Beautiful is Kant's theory of aesthetic response, his account of what is involved in experiencing an object in a way that leads us to judge it beautiful.

(Discussing the central claims of the Analytic of the Beautiful as a whole, see Crowther 1989: 51–60; Guyer 1979: 120–33; Kemal 1992: 23–33; McCloskey 1987, ch. 4; Pluhar 1987, sect. 5; Savile 1987, ch. 4; Schaper 1979, ch. 3; and Zimmerman 1967.)

3.1.1. *The First Moment: Disinterestedness*

The first moment identifies two features of judgements of taste: their *aesthetic* (in Kant's sense) character, and their *disinterestedness*.

1. That a judgement of taste presupposes pleasure Kant regards as self-evident (see §1[5]). Pleasure, like pain, is on Kant's view a representation that must be 'referred to the subject': it cannot be regarded as representing the object, only as registering how the subject is affected by the object (more precisely, by their representation of the object). That is why pleasure is a feeling. Consequently, judgements of taste, like all aesthetic judgements, cannot be regarded as cognitive.

2. Kant's doctrine of the disinterestedness of judgements of taste (see §§2–5), which has given rise to many later theories of the aesthetic attitude, employs a technical sense of interest, closely related to that involved in Kant's discussion of moral interest. Interest is defined by Kant in the *CJ* as pleasure taken in the representation of an object as really existing, and involves the object's having a role in relation to desire (will or inclination). Judgements of taste are merely contemplative; they do not presuppose the existence of their objects and do not relate their objects to desires. The first moment thus asserts that in a judgement of taste the object is judged beautiful on the basis of a disinterested feeling of pleasure.

Kant considers it self-evident that judgements of taste must be disinterested, in much the same way as it is self-evident that they presuppose a feeling of

[5] References to the *Critique of Judgement* take the form of either a section number, when preceded by '§', or a page number. Page references follow the Akademie pagination, cited in the margin of Pluhar's translation, from which quotations in this chapter are taken.

pleasure, observing that, in reply to the question of whether I find a palace beautiful, certain answers are irrelevant, namely any that make reference, explicitly or implicitly, to the fact of its existence—such as that I do not approve of such exhibitions of personal vanity, or have no need of such a habitation (see §2); judgements of taste influenced by such considerations are defective. The only kind of answer that is relevant is one that refers exclusively to the subject's liking: all that is at issue is 'what I do with this presentation within myself'.

To bring out the disinterested character of judgements of taste, Kant contrasts them with the two other species of judgement that express likings for their objects, judgements of the agreeable and judgements of the good. A judgement of the agreeable—such as, that an object is 'graceful, lovely, delightful, gladdening etc.'—is based on what the senses like in sensation (see §3). Judgements of the agreeable give rise to inclination, so are interested. In the case of a judgement of the good—that something is either good as a means, or morally good—the object is liked 'through its mere concept', and the concept of the good contains that of a purpose: if an object or action is judged good, the subject judges that they have reason to cause it to exist, rendering judgements of the good also interested (see §4).

There are two other respects in which judgements of taste are differentiated from judgements of the agreeable and the good (Kant refers to these also in the first moment, although the main arguments for them are given later). Laying these out gives a sense of where Kant's analysis is heading.

In addition to the distinction between interested and disinterested judgements, Kant distinguishes between judgements that presuppose the application of a *determinate concept* and those that do not, and between judgements that presuppose *reflection* and those that do not. Judgements of the agreeable, e.g. an expression of liking for a wine, are interested, and presuppose neither a determinate concept nor reflection; the mere sensing of the object is all that is involved. Judgements of the good, e.g. that an action is a matter of duty, are interested, and presuppose both a determinate concept and reflection. Judgements of taste, e.g. that a rose is beautiful, are disinterested and presuppose no determinate concept; but they do presuppose reflection, and therefore in some sense involve cognitive activity, unlike judgements of the agreeable.

The central thrust of the Analytic of the Beautiful is to show that judgements of taste stand mid-way between judgements of the good and judgements of the agreeable: they incorporate the rationality, universality, and necessity of the former, with the sense-dependence, subjectivity, and conditioned character of the latter. It follows that the experience of beauty is possible only for human beings, beings that are both animal and rational: animals, lacking reason, are restricted to experience of the agreeable; and purely rational beings, lacking sensibility, cannot experience beauty. (Note the analogy with consciousness of obligation, which is similarly unavailable to non-rational beings and purely rational beings.)

(On the first moment, see Crawford 1974, ch. 2; Guyer 1979, ch. 5; Kemal 1992: 33–7; and McCloskey 1987, chs. 5–6.)

3.1.2. The Second Moment: Universality

The second moment aims to show that judgements of taste are *universal* (valid for everyone, or at least regarded as such) and that this universality is *subjective*.

1. Kant has two arguments for the claim to universality. The first (see §6) maintains that the universality of judgements of taste follows from their disinterestedness: if the subject is conscious of his liking as not resting on any interest, 'then he cannot help judging that it must contain a basis for being liked [that holds] for everyone', and so 'must believe that he is justified in requiring a similar liking from everyone'. The subject must suppose this, because he 'cannot discover, underlying this liking, any private conditions, on which only he might be dependent, so that he must regard it as based on what he can presuppose in everyone else as well'.

This is arguably too quick, however, for it may be that judgements of taste rest on idiosyncrasies of sensibility, albeit ones that have nothing to do with desire—perhaps we just all happen to vary arbitrarily in the way that we respond to objects.

Kant's second argument (see §7 and 213–14) is stronger. It maintains that the universality of judgements of taste is shown by the way in which they, as opposed to judgements of the agreeable, are regarded as having a justification, one that necessarily excludes reference to the personal constitution of the subject. A judgement that an object is beautiful cannot be justified by reference to some fact about one's personal self, as may of course be done for judgements of the agreeable. This is reflected in the fact that the very concept of taste is destroyed (the beautiful collapses into the agreeable) if taste is regarded as something that cannot be shared, as would be implied if we were to speak of each as having 'his own particular taste' or of an object as 'beautiful for me'. Kant puts this by saying that judgements of the agreeable are 'private' and judgements of taste 'public'. (Note the obvious analogy with Kant's ethics: both judgements of taste and moral judgements involve abstracting from one's contingent features, and thereby attaining the impartiality that is needed to ground a claim to universality.)

2. The next question is what grounds this claim to universality (see §6). The universality of a judgement of taste could only be grounded on a concept, if that concept were connected necessarily with a feeling of pleasure. But there is no necessary connection between applying a concept and having a feeling of

pleasure: 'from concepts there is no transition from concepts to the feeling of pleasure or displeasure'. (Morality is an exception: we are rationally bound to feel pleasure at an action that we judge to be morally worthy. A judgement of taste is, however, disinterested, unlike a judgement of the good, so pleasure in beauty cannot arise through a concept in the same manner as pleasure in the good.) If the universality of judgements of taste does not arise from concepts, its ground cannot be objective. So it must be subjective. Judgements of taste involve therefore a claim to *subjective universality*. The second moment thus asserts that an object judged beautiful is an object of universal liking (219).

Kant's argument for the subjective universality of judgements of taste comprehends, therefore, an argument for the claim that a judgement of taste presupposes no determinate concept of its object. Judgements of taste resemble in this respect judgements of the agreeable, and contrast with judgements of the good, which do presuppose determinate concepts of their objects. Here then is a further sense in which judgements of taste stand mid-way between judgements of the good and judgements of the agreeable: they incorporate the universality of the former with the independence from determinate concepts of the latter.

Kant has two other, independent arguments in support of his claim that judgements of taste are independent of any determinate concept: an argument based on the fact that, at least in certain paradigmatic cases, it is unnecessary to have any concept of the object judged beautiful (see 207); and an argument based on the impossibility of aesthetic generalizations (e.g. 'all roses are beautiful'), which Kant takes to show that it is the non-conceptual particularity of an object that is in question in a judgement of taste (see 215, 285).

That the universality of judgements of taste is not based on a concept creates a problem, effectively the same as the problem of taste described earlier. Kant emphasizes the strangeness of the fact that we should so much as have the concept of an aesthetic judgement that possesses universality; in other words, that we should bother to discriminate, as we do, between matters of the agreeable and matters of taste (see §8). It is not, after all, as if judgements of taste enjoyed a convergence not enjoyed by judgements of the agreeable; so it is not experience that inclines us to make the distinction. Yet the difficulty of agreeing on matters of taste never disposes us to think that judgements of taste are not possible.

What Kant's analysis shows is that a *universal voice*, concerning a 'liking unmediated by concepts', is postulated in judgements of taste (216). All that is postulated with regard to such a universal voice is its *possibility*, not its actuality, for a judgement of taste does not postulate that everyone *will* agree, only that everyone is required (*ought*) to agree. The universal voice is therefore 'only an idea'. It may not in fact be realized, since one who makes a judgement of taste may not in fact be speaking with a universal voice, i.e. may be wrong in supposing that others ought to agree, but it is nevertheless an idea that is invoked simply by virtue of intending to make a judgement of taste—the use of the term 'beautiful' establishes that commitment.

(On §§6–8 of the second moment, see Guyer 1979: 133–47; Kemal 1992: 38–53; McCloskey 1987, ch. 7; and Savile 1993, ch. 1.)

An important point that emerges is that, on Kant's account, beauty is not a property of objects: for Kant it is more accurate to speak of objects as *judged* beautiful than as *being* beautiful. Judgements of taste are indeed expressed in a form that makes it seem as if they ascribe beauty as a property to objects, and gives them the superficial appearance of being cognitive (as some, especially rationalist, aestheticians mistakenly assume them to be). But this, Kant suggests (see §6), is explained by their sharing a claim to universality with logical judgements. Because a judgement of taste is a judgement, it must combine a subject with a predicate, but its subject is the singular representation of the object, and its predicate is not, as in logical judgement, a concept, but, as in all aesthetic judgement, a feeling of pleasure; more precisely, a feeling of pleasure *judged to be universally valid* (see §37). The point of predicating beauty of the object in a judgement of taste—rather than merely predicating pleasure of oneself—is therefore to relate the object to a feeling of pleasure *in all others*.

The presumption to universality of judgements of taste is of course, for Kant, evidence of a priori conditions, and so argues in favour of the need for a transcendental account of judgements of taste. Kant is now poised to begin his account of how judgements of taste are possible and of how the problem of taste may be resolved, and in §9 introduces his theory of aesthetic response.

This begins with a general point concerning the relation between pleasure and judgement in a judgement of taste, to the effect that the pleasure in such a judgement must rest upon a *preceding* activity of judging. This is because a judgement of taste claims universality, and universality cannot derive directly from the subject's feeling of pleasure, since pleasure, considered for itself, cannot be universal. It follows that the pleasure must be grounded on another state of mind, one that is universal. Now the only universal states of mind are ones that have to do with cognition. Because the powers exercised in cognition are imagination and understanding, judgements of taste must have to do with imagination and understanding. But since judgements of taste are not themselves cognitions, somehow the powers of cognition must be involved without applying a determinate concept to the object. The state of mind in question consists, Kant proposes, in the *relation* between imagination and understanding that is involved in *cognition in general*; a relation that is subjective, since it concerns merely the relation of cognitive powers to one another in the subject and not their relation to an object, but at the same time universal, since it is presupposed for all empirical cognition and so must be the same for all subjects. Kant describes this relation as one of 'reciprocal harmony' and 'proportioned attunement' of imagination and understanding. Furthermore, since in a judgement of taste no determinate concept is involved, imagination and understanding are not bound to the goal of determinate cognition: they are, as Kant puts it, in 'free play'. Because the feeling of pleasure involved in a judgement of taste is, Kant declares, a feeling *of* the harmony and free play of imagination and understanding—a universal state of mind—it too must be universal. An object is deemed beautiful, in sum, when the subject is conscious of it as effecting a state of harmony and free play of imagination and understanding, and thus as itself harmonizing with the universal conditions of cognition. To be beautiful *is* to be so related to our cognitive powers.

To avoid confusion, it is important to note that not one but two judgements are involved in a judgement of taste: (1) a 'judging of the object' that *precedes* the subject's feeling of pleasure, and consists in a recognition that the object engenders a harmony of imagination and understanding; (2) the judgement of taste itself that *follows* the subject's feeling of pleasure, and declares it to be universally valid.

Kant's theory of aesthetic response thus explains how judgements of taste—like judgements of the good, but unlike judgements of the agreeable—can presuppose reflection. That judging must precede pleasure and pleasure be based on judging, Kant calls the 'key to the critique of taste'.

(On §9 of the second moment, see Guyer 1979, ch. 3 and pp. 151–60, and 1982; Henrich 1992, ch. 2; Kemal 1992: 53–6; and McCloskey 1987: 69–71.

3.1.3. *The Third Moment: Purposiveness*

In the third moment Kant endeavours to say what it is about an object that gives rise to a feeling of pleasure in the subject in the context of taste.

Kant begins with a distinction between particular, determinate purposes (*Zwecke*), and what he calls *purposiveness* (*Zweckmäßigkeit*, also translated as 'finality'). The important point is that it is possible to have purposiveness without purpose: purposiveness is exemplified when an object is recognized as purposeful but no particular, determinate purpose is ascribed to it (see §10).

Kant then analyses beauty in terms of this distinction (see §§10–11, §15). A judgement of taste, since it is disinterested, cannot be based on a judgement that its object has a 'subjective purpose' (a purpose for the subject, such as that of providing pleasure). Nor can it be based on an 'objective purpose', since that would presuppose a determinate concept of the object. (Kant therefore rejects the rationalist conception of beauty as a kind of perfection, on the grounds that perfection presupposes an objective purpose: see §15.) Objects of judgements of taste can be considered, then, only in terms of purposiveness. But they cannot have objective purposiveness, for again that would imply bringing the object under a determinate concept. Therefore, all that can be presupposed by a judgement of taste is the *subjective purposiveness* of the object, its 'mere form of purposiveness': meaning that the object is purposive by virtue of its form alone and only relative to the subject. Later Kant tells us more precisely in what the subjective purposiveness of an object judged beautiful consists: as his theory of aesthetic response in §9 implies, the object is recognized as being unified and organized in a way that *allows it to be judged*, as being suitable or *fit* for the application of a concept (although we do not go on to apply any concept to the object) (see 279 and §38). The third moment thus asserts that an object judged beautiful is discerned as exhibiting purposiveness in its form without any representation of purpose (236).

Kant relates this account of beauty in terms of purposiveness to the pleasure involved in a judgement of taste by *identifying* the feeling of pleasure with consciousness of the object's subjective purposiveness (see §§12–13). This makes it a priori that objects that are subjectively purposive for our faculties should be experienced with pleasure, and so explains why beauty should involve pleasure necessarily.

Kant's claim that it is the *form* of an object alone, i.e. its spatio-temporal features, that is involved in a judgement of taste allows him to distinguish judgements of taste that are *pure* from those that are not. Judgements of taste forsake purity when they incorporate, in addition to form, either features of sensation or a concept of the object. Sensational features may add 'charm' or emotional appeal to the object, and judging an object in terms of a concept may give rise (when the object is perfect in terms of that concept) to what Kant calls 'accessory' or dependent (as opposed to free) beauty, which usefully allows taste to become fixed and united with reason; but both forms of impurity interfere with the universality of judgements of taste, and neither actually increases the beauty of an object (see §§13–14, §16).

(On the third moment, see Crawford 1974, sect. 5.1; Guyer 1979, ch. 6; Kemal 1992: 57–62; and McCloskey 1987, ch. 8.)

3.1.4. The Fourth Moment: Necessity

In the fourth moment, Kant attempts to identify what needs to be presupposed in order for judgements of taste to possess universality. This leads to the notion of what Kant calls a 'common sense', a universally shared subjective basis for judgement that incorporates a principle operating by means of feeling rather than concepts.

Judgements of taste presuppose a *necessary connection* between the representation of the object and the pleasure felt towards it (see §18). This is evidenced by the fact that a judgement of taste asserts that all others *ought* to feel pleasure in contemplating the object—the aesthetic ought, like the moral ought, implies necessity. The fourth moment thus asserts that an object judged beautiful pleases necessarily, independently of concepts (240).

The necessity of taste is not of the same kind as that found in other contexts: it is of course not empirical; it is not theoretical, since it concerns what ought to happen rather than what does happen; and it is not practical, since it is not derived from reason. The only sense in which judgements of taste can be necessary is in what Kant calls an *exemplary* sense: the claim that they embody is that a particular object is an example of something that conforms to a rule (the standard of taste), for which reason it ought to be apprehended with pleasure—even though we cannot state the rule, and can communicate it only by pointing to examples of objects that conform to it.

The necessity of judgements of taste is, as well as being exemplary, also *subjective*, since it concerns a feeling of pleasure, and it is *conditioned*, since it does not rest, as does morality, on any objective principle (see §19). The condition of a judgement of taste is that all others share the same subjective basis as myself, and that I have correctly 'subsumed' the object under it.

However, Kant argues, judgements of taste must presuppose *some* principle, or it would not occur to us to claim necessity for them, and they would not be distinguished from judgements of the agreeable. (According to the *CPR*, necessity presupposes rules or principles of judgement.) So judgements of taste must presuppose a *subjective principle*, one that determines judgement on the basis of *feeling* rather than concepts, and yet possesses universality. Kant calls this subjective principle a *common sense*—a way of responding to empirical objects that is the same in all subjects (see §20, §40). A common sense functions as an 'indeterminate norm'. It is in fact the same as what Kant described earlier as the 'universal voice' implicated in a judgement of taste.

Is the presupposition of a common sense legitimate? Kant returns to his theory of aesthetic response and once again gives an argument based on cognition in general (see §21). Cognition presupposes, as said in §9, an 'attunement of the cognitive powers'. Now there must be, Kant claims, one attunement that is *optimal*, in the sense of being most conducive to the mutual quickening of the imagination and the understanding. Only feeling can determine which attunement is optimal. Both the optimal attunement, and the feeling of it, must be universally communicable. Kant therefore identifies a common sense with *the capacity to feel this optimal attunement*. The general conditions for cognition thus legitimate the idea of a common sense.

(On the fourth moment, see Crawford 1974, sect. 6.1; Guyer 1979: 160–6; Kemal 1992: 62–72; McCloskey 1987: 57–9; and Savile 1993, ch. 2.)

3.2. Kant's Justification of Judgements of Taste

The Deduction of Pure Aesthetic Judgements is Kant's attempt to justify judgements of taste. Kant explains that a deduction is needed whenever a judgement lays claim to universality and necessity, and an a priori principle is consequently involved; this applies as much to judgements whose necessity is subjective as it does to objectively necessary judgements (see §§30–1, §§36–7). Judgements of taste, like moral judgements, present us with a further instance of the general problem of synthetic a priori judgement: a judgement of taste is a priori, because the pleasure is imputed universally, and it is synthetic, because it connects a representation of an object with a feeling of pleasure (see §36). The question is what makes this synthesis possible.

1. *The Deduction.* The deduction of judgements of taste in §38 assembles points made already in the Analytic of the Beautiful: (1) The only thing that can be judged in a judgement of taste is 'the subjective conditions for our employment of the power of judgement as such'. (2) These conditions of judgement can be assumed to be the same in everyone. (3) We are entitled to assume, of any object that pleases solely through the engagement of its form with our power of judgement, that it will engage similarly with the powers of everyone else. Thus the pleasure that I feel in these circumstances has universal validity. (4) So I am entitled to require this pleasure from everyone. This argument is transcendental in character, like those in the Analytic of the *CPR*, for it says that the possibility of judgements of taste is derivable from the conditions of cognition in general.

Kant remarks that what makes the deduction 'so easy is that it does not need to justify the objective reality of a concept': because beauty is not a concept of an object and judgements of taste are not cognitive, they do not require justification in the same manner as logical judgements. Kant's solution to the problem of taste is therefore to grant that judgements of taste cannot have *objective* validity—for which they would need to be logical judgements—but to affirm that they partake of the *universal* validity of objectively valid judgements (see 214–15). This explains why they may seem to contain a paradoxical and unfulfillable aspiration to objectivity; and why the demand that they be shown to be objective in order for them to be regarded as justified is inappropriate.

The completeness of the deduction at this point is put in doubt, however, by the fact that Kant goes on to discuss the idea of an *interest* in beauty, the significance of which would be, he says, that if such a thing could be assumed, 'we could explain how it is that we require from everyone as a duty, as it were, the feeling [contained] in a judgement of taste' (296): which seems to imply that the aesthetic ought still needs to be subsumed under the moral ought, and would involve a further task. By way of an approach to that idea, Kant argues in §§41–2 that, although the grounds of a judgement of taste must of course be disinterested, there is no barrier to combining taste with an interest in beauty, and indeed that the existence of a moral interest in beauty is testified by the consideration that it is part of our common lore that the appreciation of natural beauty (though not of art) is bound up with moral goodness. Kant will explain later what the link of beauty and morality consists in; the conclusion so far is just that *if* an interest in beauty does derive from its link with morality, it will justify the aesthetic ought.

2. *The Dialectic.* Next—in the Dialectic of Aesthetic Judgement—Kant formulates an 'antinomy of taste', intended to show that 'conflicting concepts arise naturally and inevitably' when we think about taste, casting doubt on the very possibility of judgements of taste (see §55). The antinomy is in effect a reformulation of the original problem of taste.

There are, Kant says, two 'commonplaces' about taste: (1) 'Everyone has his own taste', and (2) 'There is no disputing about taste' (see §56). These may seem compatible, but Kant shows that they are not. The first implies that disagreement over matters of taste is impossible. The second says that matters of taste are ones that we cannot come to agreement over by means of proof—implying that there *is* something over which we disagree. So we have an antinomy of principles concerning taste: a *thesis* asserting that a judgement of taste is not based on concepts, for otherwise matters of taste could be decided by means of proof; and an *antithesis* asserting that a judgement of taste is based on concepts, for otherwise matters of taste could not be subject to disagreement.

Kant accepts that, as the antithesis says, judgements of taste must refer to *some* concept—otherwise they could not lay claim to universality—and that, as the thesis says, they are not provable from a concept. Since neither of these claims can be rejected, some way must be found of reconciling them. Kant's solution is given is §57: the concept to which judgements of taste refer must be, Kant claims, one that is intrinsically indeterminate and 'inadequate for cognition'. It must be, therefore, an idea of reason: specifically, the concept of the 'indeterminate idea of the supersensible in us', the 'supersensible substrate of humanity'. This concept does not provide an objective principle that would allow judgements of taste to be proved, but it does provide a subjective principle for judgements of taste, making it possible for judgements of taste to possess universality.

The antinomy is resolved formally, then, by identifying different senses of 'concept' in the thesis and the antithesis. The thesis is true in so far as judgements of taste are *not* based on *determinate* concepts. The antithesis is true in so far as judgements of taste *are* based on an *indeterminate* concept. The reformulated thesis and antithesis are both true and consistent. (On the antinomy, see Crawford 1974, sect. 3.3; Guyer 1979: 331–45; and Savile 1993, ch. 3.)

The antinomy has introduced transcendental idealism, for the first time, into Kant's aesthetic theory, and shown it to be necessary for the legitimacy of judgements of taste, since the concept of taste otherwise falls into contradiction.

Further, as transpires in the final sections of the Critique of Aesthetic Judgement (§§59–60), the new notion that judgements of taste implicate the supersensible allows Kant to extend the justification of judgements of taste by combining taste with moral interest. This final part of the argument is condensed into a passage occurring in the middle of §59 at 353 and the very last paragraph of §60 at 356. Here Kant may be interpreted as arguing that various points of analogy between beauty and morality, concerning the similarity of the 'mental attunement' involved in each (beauty is, Kant says, the 'symbol of the morally good'), mean that taste can be demanded as a duty: for we have an obligation to cultivate dispositions that are favourable to the good will, and taste increases moral feeling. In this way, it becomes possible to identify the supersensible invoked by judgements of taste with the supersensible (intelligible world) invoked by moral judgements; and the creation of a community of taste becomes, like the demand that we create a kingdom of ends, a demand of reason. (Crawford 1974, ch. 7, and Elliott 1968 advance this reading of Kant. Cohen 1982 offers an elucidation of the symbolization of morality by beauty.)

(On the Deduction and Kant's justification of judgements of taste, see Crawford 1974, *passim*; Crowther 1989: 51–60; Elliott 1968; Guyer 1979, chs. 7–11; Kemal 1986, chs. 1, 5–6, and 1992, chs. 5–6; McCloskey 1987, ch. 9; Pluhar 1987, sects. 6–7; and Savile 1987, chs. 5–6. Kemal 1992: 103–15 collates usefully the views of several different commentators. The question of when the deduction is completed is, however, controversial, as discussed below in Section 3.4.)

3.3. The Sublime, Art, Teleology, and Judgement

The following further topics are essential for a full understanding of Kant's aesthetic theory.

1. *The sublime.* The third species of aesthetic judgement is that of the sublime, and in the Analytic of the Sublime Kant gives it an extended treatment, that in part mirrors and in part contrasts with his treatment of beauty.

In contrast with objects of taste, sublime objects are distinguished by their formlessness—nature strikes us as possessing either incomparable magnitude (the 'mathematical sublime') or matchless might (the 'dynamical sublime')—and emotion is integral to the sublime (see §23). Despite these differences, judgements of the sublime share the central features of judgements of taste: disinterestedness, universality, subjective purposiveness, and necessity (see §24). Whereas Kant's theory of aesthetic response for beauty concerns imagination and understanding, his theory of aesthetic response for the sublime concerns imagination and *reason* (see §§25–9). In experience of the sublime, Kant claims, we become aware of ourselves, in so far as we possess reason, as surpassing nature: our pleasure consists in consciousness of the purposiveness of the process whereby a prospect in nature experienced as immeasurable or terrifying leads us to recognize ourselves, *qua* rational beings, as transcending nature. The 'mental attunement' that constitutes the sublime is in fact the same as that produced in us by the moral law, which is defined similarly by awareness of the superiority of reason over sensibility, and Kant declares that the respect that we feel for the sublime object is in fact respect for our own moral vocation (see 257). The sublime prepares us for moral sacrifice, and judgements of the sublime can be regarded, like judgements of taste, as commanding agreement on moral grounds (see 265, 292). The sublime presupposes only a capacity for moral feeling, and a deduction of judgements of the sublime is not needed (see §30).

(On Kant's theory of the sublime, see Crowther 1989, chs. 4–6; McCloskey 1987, ch. 10; and Pluhar 1987, sect. 9.)

2. *Art.* Kant's theory of art is contained in §§43–54 of the Deduction. Works of art contrast with the natural objects that lie at the centre of Kant's account of taste in several respects: they fall under concepts and conform to rules, and they are purposive products of the artist's intention. Nevertheless, Kant holds that it is possible for a work of art to be an object of a judgement of taste on the condition that, even though we are conscious that it is art, it 'looks to us like nature' (see §45).

This tends to suggest that nature is the measure of beauty in art, and that art can offer only mediate experience of what nature provides immediately. When it is also recalled that Kant reserves for nature and denies to art a direct connection with morality, it can come to seem that Kant rates art as inferior to nature, and that the sections on art are a mere digression.

This view is certainly too crude. Art has, on Kant's account, a distinctive value that derives from the fact that works of art exhibit *genius* (see §§46–7, §49). Genius is the ability to express what Kant calls *aesthetic ideas*, these being sensible products of the imagination that cannot be encapsulated by means of concepts (see §49, and Comment I to §57). A work of art presupposes both taste and genius: works that are beautiful without exhibiting genius are merely inoffensive, and works of genius undisciplined by taste nonsensical (§48, §50). What emerges from Kant's discussion then is a view of art as different in kind from natural beauty.

(On Kant's theory of art and genius, see Gadamer 1989: 42–60; Gotshalk 1967; Kemal 1986, pt. I; McCloskey 1987, chs. 11–14; Pluhar 1987, sect. 8; Savile 1993, chs. 5–6; Schaper 1979, ch. 4; and the papers in Cohen and Guyer 1982, pt. II.)

3. *Teleology and judgement.* The Critique of Teleological Judgement, part II of the *CJ*, is Kant's attempt to resolve the philosophical problem associated with the application of concepts of purpose to nature, as in the explanation of the

parts of biological organisms in terms of their functions. The problem that Kant addresses is that, whilst the need for teleological explanation cannot be doubted, its ground is obscure: the concept of natural purpose cannot be legitimized on empirical grounds, and nor can it be validated, like the category of causality, as a condition of the possibility of experience; nor of course can appeal be made to divine causality. There is, furthermore, an apparent conflict between the teleological principle and the law of (mechanical) causality shown in the Second Analogy to have unrestricted validity with respect to nature (see Section 1.7). To get some idea of Kant's view of the problem and the regulative solution that he offers, without reading the whole of part II of the *CJ*, see §61, §§70–1, §78. (On the Critique of Teleological Judgement, see Höffe 1994, sect. 12.3; and Pluhar 1987, sects. 10–13.)

Why does Kant include in a single volume an aesthetic theory alongside what is in effect an extension of his theory of natural science? At one level, the connection is that the concept of purpose discussed intensively in part II figures also in the analysis of beauty (part I deals with the subjective purposiveness of objects, part II with their objective purposiveness), and that both judgements of taste and teleological judgements are forms of what Kant calls 'reflective' judgement (in which judgement is presented with a particular and must discover a rule or concept under which to bring it).

There is, however, a deeper rationale for Kant's yoking the two subjects together, which concerns the further end that Kant has in view in the *CJ*. This is discovered by turning to the preface and introduction. (The latter comes in two versions: the original, known as the First Introduction, is printed after the text of the *CJ* in Pluhar's edition; it is lengthier but more closely related to issues in aesthetics.) The power of judgement, although it is needed for the employment of theoretical and practical reason, is not analysed in either of the first two *Critiques*. The third *Critique* is intended to make good this omission, and it identifies judgement as that which mediates between understanding and reason, and so between theoretical and practical reason. The special interest of aesthetic judgement for a critique of judgement is, Kant argues, that beautiful objects exemplify the conformity of nature to cognition: judgements of taste display our a priori assumption of the agreement of nature with our cognitive powers, which is presupposed for teleological and indeed for *all* judgement. Taste takes us to that which makes judgement as such possible and casts a bridge over the gulf that otherwise separates the domains of theoretical and practical reason, unifying our conception of the supersensible and giving us insight into the unity of reason. The *CJ* thus unifies the two earlier *Critiques* and Kant's philosophical system as a whole.

(On the theme of judgement and the unity of the *CJ*, see Bell 1987; Cassirer 1981, ch. 6; Gotshalk 1967; Guyer 1987, ch. 2; Kemal 1992: 152–65; Pluhar 1987, sects. 0, 14–15; and the papers in Förster 1989, pt. III.)

3.4. Central Critical Issues

On the whole criticism has tended to accept that Kant is right in detecting in judgements of taste an aspiration to universality (though it may be wondered if Kant does not misconstrue or exaggerate the strength of the claim made by a judgement of taste; see Mothersill 1984: 211–18; and Savile 1987: 127–8), and in regarding their justification as a central and difficult philosophical task; for which reason the *CJ* remains a foundational text for contemporary aesthetics.

This is not to deny, of course, that there is room for disputing Kant's aesthetic theory on a number of fundamental scores—in particular, the methodological priority that Kant assigns to nature over art, his arguable 'intellectualization' of aesthetic experience and arbitrary exclusion of emotion, the adequacy of his treatment of art and alleged devaluation of art in favour of nature, and his formalism (see Walker 1978: 145–6). Such general criticisms, however, tend to presuppose (if they are to have force) an independently articulated rival aesthetic theory, and it is the internal problems of Kant's aesthetic theory that need to be focused on in the first instance. Some of the most frequently discussed are the following (a further selection may be found in Mothersill 1984, ch. 8).

1. A first set of issues arises regarding the order of Kant's argument. In particular, there is a difficulty concerning disinterestedness, which Kant presents as the most basic element in his analysis. On examination, Kant's claim that judgements of taste must be devoid of interest may seem undersupported and the very concept of disinterestedness unclear (see Guyer 1979, ch. 5), which may seem to put in jeopardy the argument of the Analytic of the Beautiful. Consequently, some commentators propose modifying the order of Kant's argument and deriving the first moment from later claims.

2. A second set of issues surrounds the criteria for judgements of taste. How is it to be *known* that one's pleasure is disinterested and consists in consciousness of the harmony and free play of imagination and understanding? The first and third moments are presumably supposed to provide the criteria for a judgement of taste. Kant is, however, prepared to grant our fallibility regarding the ground of our pleasure (see e.g. 216, 237), just as we may mistake the motives for our actions, so the question arises of how we may ever justifiably take ourselves to be warranted in demanding the agreement of others. It may be thought that this problem is solved by Kant's identifying pleasure in beauty as a unique sort of pleasure (see Aquila 1982), a claim that is, however, open to objections (see Guyer 1979: 202–4); alternatively, that Kant's answer lies in the dimension of communication and intersubjective confirmation (see Kemal 1992: 87–102).

3. Evaluation of Kant's justification of judgements of taste is greatly complicated by an exegetical issue: where does the deduction begin and where does it end? The evidence is contradictory. On the one hand, Kant's official statement

of the deduction in §38 seems merely to amplify points from the Analytic of the Beautiful, which makes it seem as if the Analytic must show implicitly the legitimacy of judgements of taste in the course of unpacking their content and presuppositions. On the other hand, as indicated, there is strong reason for thinking that the deduction is not in fact complete until the link of beauty with morality is made towards the end of the Dialectic: Kant seems to say that the justification of judgements of taste requires an interest in beauty, and in any case the Dialectic seems to declare that judgements of taste are not justified until the antinomy has been solved with the aid of the supersensible.

In an effort to solve this puzzle, one might attempt to distinguish between either different claims receiving justification, or different senses or degrees of justification provided at different points in the text. At issue in discussion of this question is the dependence of Kant's justification of judgements of taste on his ethical theory and metaphysics: some commentators endorse this dependence, whilst others regard Kant's analysis of cognition as offering a more secure ground for the justification of judgements of taste, and consign the link of beauty with morality to the supplementary task of explicating the 'deeper meaning' of beauty.

4. An issue with crucial importance for Kant's deduction arises in connection with his theory of aesthetic response. It is essential for Kant that the mental state involved in aesthetic response should be a special, heightened condition, not realized in empirical cognition, for otherwise his analysis will carry the implication that all empirical cognition involves pleasure and that all empirical objects are beautiful. At the same time, this mental state must be one that I can know to be universal—I must have some reason to think that the representations that engender pleasurable mental harmony in me will do the same in you, that our mental attunements are the same in all contexts; failing which, scepticism intervenes quite reasonably. How, though, can this be known? That we have reason to believe in a cognitive common sense does not mean that we have reason to believe in an aesthetic common sense. Because aesthetic response is on Kant's account constituted by freedom from determinate cognition, a gap opens up between the universality of cognition, which can be known, and that of aesthetic response, which, it would seem, cannot.

By tying judgements of taste so closely to the conditions of empirical cognition, Kant's theory either risks passing on the implications of judgements of taste to empirical judgements, leading to the absurdities just mentioned; or avoids doing so only at the cost of inserting into the account of taste an extra condition that may succeed in accounting for the difference between aesthetic response and empirical cognition, but the universality of which cannot be guaranteed by the universality of the conditions of empirical cognition. (See Crowther 1989: 62–5; Guyer 1979: 294–7, 318–24; Meerbote 1982: 80–6; and Savile 1987: 141–6; and, by way of a reply, Henrich 1992, ch. 2.)

This problem must be resolved by those who seek to ground Kant's justification of judgements of taste solely on his analysis of cognition and theory of aesthetic response; otherwise the link with morality will seem to offer the only prospect of saving the deduction.

(For criticism of Kant's justification of judgements of taste, see the works referred to in Section 3.2. Crawford, Elliott, and Kemal affirm its dependence on morality; Guyer and McCloskey deny it. Guyer 1979, ch. 11, argues in detail against the link with morality.)

5. Finally, it should be noted that, in order to maintain that Kant's aesthetic theory stands independently from transcendental idealism as well as from morality, as many seek to do, it is essential to argue, against Kant, either that there is no genuine antinomy of taste, or that it can be solved without invoking the idea of the supersensible. (Guyer 1979, ch. 10, argues accordingly that the concept of the harmony of the faculties may play the required role; see also Savile 1993, ch. 3.)

BIBLIOGRAPHY

General recommendations for reading are given below, and references for specific issues in the text. An extensive bibliography of writings on all aspects of Kant's philosophy may be found in Guyer (1992*b*), and a thematic bibliography on the *CPR* in Walker (1982).

The following books covering Kant's philosophy as a whole are recommended: Cassirer (1981); Höffe (1994); Kemp (1968); Körner (1955); Scruton (1982); and Walker (1978). Guyer (1992*b*) contains excellent papers on all aspects of Kant's philosophy, of which the introduction provides a brief overview. A reference work that is of some use for grasping the core meanings of Kant's terms is Caygill (1995).

KANT'S MAIN TEXTS

The works of Immanuel Kant's to concentrate on, and that are discussed in this chapter, are the following (in chronological order, with abbreviations employed in the text):

CPR	*Critique of Pure Reason* (1781; 2nd edn. 1787).
Proleg.	*Prolegomena to Any Future Metaphysics* (1783).
Gr.	*Groundwork of the Metaphysics of Morals* (1785).
CPracR	*Critique of Practical Reason* (1788).
CJ	*Critique of Judgement* (1790).

The *Critique of Pure Reason* ('first *Critique*') is Kant's principal work of epistemology and metaphysics. There are extensive and significant differences between the first and second editions of the work, which are interlaced in the translation by N. Kemp Smith (2nd edn. London, 1933). In the years between the two editions of the *CPR*, Kant published a short work intended to improve its exposition and allow it to be grasped as a whole, his *Prolegomena to Any Future Metaphysics*; recommended translations are those of L. W. Beck (Indianapolis, 1950) and J. Ellington (Indianapolis, 1977).

Kant's ethics are found in two texts, the *Groundwork* ('Foundations' / 'Grounding') *of the Metaphysics of Morals* and the *Critique of Practical Reason* ('second *Critique*'). Both are contained, with his other ethical writings, in Kant, *Practical Philosophy*, trans. and ed. M. Gregor, introd. A. Wood (Cambridge, 1996). Other recommended translations are those of L. W. Beck, and Paton's translation of the *Groundwork* in his (London, 1948) *The Moral Law*, which contains a section-by-section commentary.

Part I of the *Critique of Judgement* ('third *Critique*'), the Critique of Aesthetic Judgement, contains Kant's aesthetic theory. Recommended for its surrounding scholarly apparatus is the translation by W. Pluhar (Indianapolis, 1987).

The standard edition of Kant's works in German, referred to as the Akademie or Prussian Academy edition, is *Kants gesammelte Schriften*, ed. Königlich Preußischen Akademie der Wissenschaften (Berlin, 1990–). References in the secondary literature to this edition standardly take the form *Ak.* followed by volume number and page number, e.g. *Ak.* VI. 251.

KANT'S OTHER TEXTS

A selection of Kant's earlier ('pre-Critical') writings, referred to in many commentaries, are collected in Kant, *Theoretical Philosophy 1755–1770*, trans. and ed. D. Walford and R. Meerbote (Cambridge, 1992), and in Kant, *Selected Pre-Critical Writings and Correspondence with Beck*, trans. G. Kerford and D. Walford (Manchester, 1968). The latter contains an important selection from Kant's philosophical correspondence, which is found in full in Kant, *Philosophical Correspondence 1759–1799*, ed. and trans. A. Zweig (Chicago, 1967).

A third text of Kant's on ethics that may be consulted is *The Metaphysics of Morals* (1797), trans. M. Gregor (Cambridge, 1991) (included in Kant, *Practical Philosophy*). It is divided into two parts, the Doctrine of Right and the Doctrine of Virtue, which may also be found published separately.

Though not discussed in this chapter, it should be noted that Kant wrote extensively in his Critical period also on natural science, politics, and religion. Kant's *Metaphysical Foundations of Natural Science* (1786), trans. J. Ellington (Indianapolis, 1970) is concerned with the foundations of physics. Kant's essays on subjects in political philosophy are collected in Kant, *Political Writings*, trans. H. Nisbet, ed. H. Reiss (2nd edn. Cambridge, 1991). Kant's philosophy of religion is set out in *Religion within the Boundaries of Mere Reason* (1793), in Kant, *Religion and Rational Theology*, trans. and ed. A. Wood and G. di Giovanni (Cambridge, 1996).

A selection from Kant's manuscripts left incomplete at the time of his death, fragmentary in form but of interest, is published as *Opus Postumum*, trans. E. Förster and M. Rosen, ed. E. Förster (Cambridge, 1993).

1. KANT'S EPISTEMOLOGY AND METAPHYSICS

A first reading of the *Critique of Pure Reason* is a difficult task, in which it makes sense to refer to commentaries for elucidation (but always with awareness that what any commentary offers is most often open to question in some respect), and to concentrate on specific passages in Kant's text. A second work of Kant's that may usefully be read alongside or after the *CPR* is the *Prolegomena*. Before you embark on the *CPR*, Scruton (1982), a succinct overview of Kant's philosophy, may helpfully be read.

There are a number of exegetically orientated works containing textual commentary on the *CPR* to choose from, that differ widely in their detail and complexity, in the balance of exegesis and criticism that they contain, and in their overall interpretation and estimate of Kant's project. Which commentary is suitable will depend partly on individual preference (and availability, many of the older commentaries being out of print). When first reading the *CPR*, it is reasonable to restrict oneself to one or two of these, and for this purpose, Broad (1978), Ewing (1938), Höffe (1994, pt. II), Körner (1995, chs. 1–5), and Walsh (1975) are recommended. Ewing and Körner are plain and predominantly expository, Broad and Walsh more critical; Höffe is helpfully attentive to historical and architectonic matters. Alternatives are Weldon (1945, pt. II); Wilkerson (1976); and Wolff (1963).

Two classics of Kant scholarship, which just about equal the *Critique* in length, should also be mentioned. Paton (1936) is a two-volume work covering the first half of the *CPR* that offers clear and judicious consideration of Kant's meaning, and may be turned to for elucidation of particular sections of the text. Kemp Smith (1923) is another illuminating work of classic status that examines the text closely, taking a firmer and more critical interpretative line than Paton.

Having got an overall impression of the *CPR*, and with a view to going into particular topics in depth, you may approach studies of Kant's epistemology and metaphysics containing more detailed scholarship and critical discussion, and some reading of these is necessary in order to build up a critical perspective on Kant. Here Allison (1983), though not straightforward, is most strongly recommended. Also highly recommended is Strawson (1966). Strawson and Allison together form a stimulating contrast: Strawson's work is a classic of reconstructive analytic studies in the history of philosophy, that distinguishes sharply Kant's transcendental arguments from the allegedly superfluous and incoherent idealist side of the *Critique*; Allison defends and attempts to elucidate precisely those contentious metaphysical aspects of Kant that Strawson rejects.

Other recommended critical studies at this level are: Bennett (1966, 1974), containing detailed criticism of Kant's arguments; Bird (1962), a carefully constructed account of the Analytic and non-phenomenalist interpretation of transcendental idealism; Guyer (1987), subjecting the text to close scrutiny and, like Strawson, rejecting Kant's idealism but defending some of the central theses of the Analytic; Melnick (1973), concentrating on the Analogies; and Walker (1978), a strongly critical but challenging study of Kant's philosophy as a whole.

Collections that may be consulted are Beck (1969*b*, 1974); Guyer (1992*b*); Harper and Meerbote (1984); Penelhum and MacIntosh (1969); Schaper and Vossenkuhl (1989); Walker (1982); Wolff (1967*b*); and Wood (1984*b*).

An additional selection of recent studies of Kant's epistemology and metaphysics of interest would include Ameriks (1982*a*); Aquila (1983); Bencivenga (1987); Buchdahl (1992); Henrich (1994, chs. 1, 4); Kitcher (1990); Neiman (1994, chs. 1–2, 5); Powell (1990); Schwyzer (1990); and Waxman (1991).

2. KANT'S ETHICS

The *Groundwork* needs to be read first. The textual commentary ('Analysis of the Argument') prefacing Paton's edition (1948) is helpful, and may be supplemented by Paton (1946), which discusses the most important exegetical points whilst remaining extremely clear. The *Critique of Practical Reason* should be read next. It is divided into an Analytic and a Dialectic. The Analytic covers material presented in the *Groundwork*, but also contains (in the chapter entitled 'Of the Deduction of the Principles of Pure Practical Reason') Kant's revised view of the justification of morality. In the Dialectic Kant introduces the postulates of practical reason. To accompany a reading of the *Critique of Practical Reason*, Beck's (1960) commentary is detailed and helpful.

For a comprehensive, succinct overview of Kant's ethical theory, see Schneewind (1992). For a brief account of the *Groundwork*, see the introduction to Hill (1992). Other chapter-length accounts of Kant's ethics may be found in Cassirer (1981, ch. 5); Höffe (1994, ch. 8); Kemp (1968, ch. 3); Körner (1955, chs. 6–7); Korsgaard (1996, ch. 1); Scruton (1982, ch. 5); and Walker (1978, ch. 11). A brief and elementary introductory book is Acton (1970); Sullivan (1994) provides a more substantial introduction (complementing his detailed study 1989). For an outstanding account of the overall conception and underlying motivation of Kant's ethical theory, see Henrich (1992, ch. 1; 1994, ch. 2).

For detailed discussion of Kant's analysis of morality, see Aune (1979, chs. 1–4); Korsgaard (1996, chs. 2–3); Nell (1975); Paton (1946, books I–III); Sullivan (1989, pts. II–III); Williams (1968); and Wolff (1967*b*, pt. II).

Kant's justification of morality is discussed in Allison (1990, pt. III); Beck (1960, ch. 10); Förster (1989, pt. II); Guyer (1993*b*); Henrich (1994, chs. 2–3); Korsgaard (1996, ch. 6); Paton (1946, book IV); and Sullivan (1989, ch. 7).

Further recommended discussion of Kant's ethical theory, tending to presuppose an understanding of it, may be found in Henrich (1994, ch. 3); Herman (1993); Neiman (1994, ch. 3); O'Neill (1989); and Velkley (1989).

3. KANT'S AESTHETICS

Regarding Kant's own writings on aesthetics, it is necessary to read only part I of the *Critique of Judgement*, the Critique of Aesthetic Judgement. The preface and introduction may be read afterwards in order to gain an understanding of the place of Kant's aesthetic theory in the context of the third *Critique*.

Schaper (1992) brings out the central issues in Kant's aesthetic theory. Pluhar's introduction to his translation of the *CJ*, sects. 4–9, serves the same purpose. Zimmerman (1967) usefully sets out Kant's main claims regarding aesthetic experience and judgement in analytical terms. There are also chapter-length accounts of Kant's aesthetics in Höffe (1994, sect. 12.2); Kemp (1968, ch. 4); Körner (1955, ch. 8); and Scruton (1982, ch. 6).

Recommended for the purpose of accompanying a first reading of the text is Kemal (1992), which combines clear exegesis with some good critical discussion. McCloskey (1987) also contains a relatively straightforward commentary on the text, but with the accent on relating Kant to issues in contemporary analytical aesthetics.

For more advanced discussion, having worked through Kant's text, see the papers in Cohen and Guyer (1982, esp. pts. I and III); Crawford (1974), offering detailed exegesis and reconstructing Kant's argument in terms of a Deduction in several 'Stages' (summarized on pp. 66–9); Elliott (1968); Förster (1989, pt. III); Gadamer (1989, pt. I, ch. 2), a historical perspective; Guyer (1979), a lengthy and highly detailed study (Guyer 1982 presents some of his claims more briefly), extended in Guyer (1993*a*); Henrich (1992, ch. 2); Kemal (1986), a complex account of Kant's aesthetic theory that highlights the importance of art; Savile (1987), a reconstruction of Kant's main argument, resumed in Savile (1993); and Schaper (1979), discussing themes in Kant's aesthetic theory in relation to the epistemology of the *CPR*.

REFERENCES

Acton, H. B. (1970), *Kant's Moral Philosophy* (London).

Al-Azm, S. (1972), *The Origins of Kant's Arguments in the Antinomies* (Oxford).

Allison, H. (1968), 'Kant's Concept of the Transcendental Object', *Kant-Studien*, 59: 165–86.

——(1973), 'Kant's Critique of Berkeley', *Journal of the History of Philosophy*, 11: 43–63.

——(1976*a*), 'Kant's Refutation of Realism', *Dialectica*, 30: 223–53.

——(1976*b*), 'The Non-Spatiality of Things in Themselves for Kant', *Journal of the History of Philosophy*, 14: 313–21.

——(1983), *Kant's Transcendental Idealism: An Interpretation and Defense* (New Haven).

——(1989), 'Justification and Freedom in the *Critique of Practical Reason*', in Förster (1989).

——(1990), *Kant's Theory of Freedom* (Cambridge).

——(1996), *Idealism and Freedom: Essays on Kant's Theoretical and Practical Philosophy* (Cambridge).

Ameriks, K. (1978), 'Kant's Transcendental Deduction as a Regressive Argument', *Kant-Studien*, 69: 273–87.

——(1982*a*), *Kant's Theory of Mind: An Analysis of the Paralogisms of Pure Reason* (Oxford).

——(1982*b*), 'Recent Work on Kant's Theoretical Philosophy', *American Philosophical Quarterly*, 19: 1–24.

——(1992*a*), 'The Critique of Metaphysics: Kant and Traditional Ontology', in Guyer (1992*b*).

——(1992*b*), 'Kantian Idealism Today', *History of Philosophy Quarterly*, 9: 329–42.

Aquila, R. (1979*a*), 'Personal Identity and Kant's "Refutation of Idealism"', *Kant-Studien*, 70: 259–78.

——(1979*b*), 'Things in Themselves and Appearances: Intentionality and Reality in Kant', *Archiv für Geschichte der Philosophie*, 61: 293–308.

——(1982), 'A New Look at Kant's Aesthetic Judgements', in Cohen and Guyer (1982).

——(1983), *Representational Mind: A Study of Kant's Theory of Knowledge* (Bloomington, Ind.).

Aune, B. (1979), *Kant's Theory of Morals* (Princeton).

Baumer, W. (1969), 'Kant on Cosmological Arguments', in Beck (1969).

Beck, L. W. (1960), *A Commentary on Kant's 'Critique of Practical Reason'* (Chicago).

——(1963), 'Can Kant's Synthetic Judgements be Made Analytic?', in Wolff (1967*b*).

——(1969*a*), 'Kant's Strategy', in Penelhum and Mackintosh (1969).

Beck, L. W. (ed.) (1969*b*), *Kant Studies Today* (La Salle, Ill.).
——(ed.) (1974), *Kant's Theory of Knowledge* (Dordrecht).
——(1978), *Essays on Kant and Hume* (New Haven).
Beiser, F. (1992), 'Kant's Intellectual Development: 1746–1781', in Guyer (1992*b*).
Bell, D. (1987), 'The Art of Judgement', *Mind*, 96: 221–44.
Bencivenga, E. (1987), *Kant's Copernican Revolution* (Oxford).
Bennett, J. (1966), *Kant's Analytic* (Cambridge).
——(1974), *Kant's Dialectic* (Cambridge).
Bermúdez, J. L. (1994), 'The Unity of Apperception in the *Critique of Pure Reason*', *European Journal of Philosophy*, 2: 213–40.
Bieri, P., Horstmann, R.-P., and Krüger, L. (eds.) (1979), *Transcendental Arguments and Science: Essays in Epistemology* (Dordrecht).
Bird, G. (1962), *Kant's Theory of Knowledge: An Outline of One Central Argument in the 'Critique of Pure Reason'* (London).
——(1982), 'Kant's Transcendental Idealism', in Vesey (1982).
Bradley, F. H. (1876), *Ethical Studies* (Oxford, 1962).
Broad, C. D. (1930), *Five Types of Ethical Theory* (London).
——(1978), *Kant: An Introduction*, ed. C. Lewy (Cambridge).
Brueckner, A. (1983), 'Transcendental Arguments I', *Nous*, 17: 551–75.
——(1984), 'Transcendental Arguments II', *Nous*, 18: 197–225.
Buchdahl, G. (1992), *Kant and the Dynamics of Reason: Essays on the Structure of Kant's Philosophy* (Oxford).
Cassam, Q. (1987), 'Transcendental Arguments, Transcendental Synthesis and Transcendental Idealism', *Philosophical Quarterly*, 37: 355–78.
Cassirer, E. (1981), *Kant's Life and Thought*, trans. J. Haden (New Haven).
Caygill, H. (1995), *A Kant Dictionary* (Oxford).
Cohen, T. (1982), 'Why Beauty is a Symbol of Morality', in Cohen and Guyer (1982).
——and Guyer, P. (eds.) (1982), *Essays in Kant's Aesthetics* (Chicago).
Crawford, D. (1974), *Kant's Aesthetic Theory* (Madison, Wis.).
Crowther, P. (1989), *Kant's Sublime: From Morality to Art* (Oxford).
Dietrichson, P. (1964), 'When is a Maxim Fully Universalisable?', *Kant-Studien*, 55: 143–70.
——(1967), 'What does Kant Mean by "Acting from Duty"?', in Wolff (1967*b*).
Ebbinghaus, J. (1967), 'Interpretation and Misinterpretation of the Categorical Imperative', in Wolff (1967*b*).
Elliott, R. (1968), 'The Unity of Kant's *Critique of Judgement*', *British Journal of Aesthetics*, 8: 244–59.
Engel, S. M. (1967), 'Kant's "Rufutation" of the Ontological Argument', in Wolff (1967*b*).
Ewing, A. C. (1938), *A Short Commentary on Kant's 'Critique of Pure Reason'* (Chicago).
Fichte, J. G. (1794–1802), *The Science of Knowledge*, trans. P. Heath and J. Lachs (Cambridge, 1982).
Förster, E. (ed.) (1989), *Kant's Transcendental Deductions: The Three 'Critiques' and the 'Opus Postumum'* (Stanford, Calif.).

Friedman, M. (1991), 'Regulative and Constitutive', *Southern Journal of Philosophy*, 30, suppl., 73–102.

Gadamer, H.-G. (1989), *Truth and Method*, trans. J. Weinsheimer and D. Marshall, 2nd edn. (London).

Gotshalk, D. (1967), 'Form and Expression in Kant's Aesthetics', *British Journal of Aesthetics*, 7: 250–60.

Gram, M. (1969), 'Kant's First Antinomy', in Beck (1969*b*).

——(1976), 'How to Dispense with Things in Themselves (I), (II)', *Ratio*, 18: 1–16, 107–23.

——(1982), 'What Kant Really Did to Idealism', in J. N. Mohanty and R. Shahan (eds.), *Essays on Kant's 'Critique of Pure Reason'* (Norman, Okla.).

Greenwood, T. (1989), 'Kant on the Modalities of Space', in Schaper and Vossenkuhl (1989).

Guyer, P. (1979), *Kant and the Claims of Taste* (Cambridge, Mass.).

——(1982), 'Pleasure and Society in Kant's Theory of Taste', in Cohen and Guyer (1982).

——(1987), *Kant and the Claims of Knowledge* (Cambridge).

——(1992*a*), 'The Transcendental Deduction of the Categories', in Guyer (1992*b*).

——(1992*b*), *The Cambridge Companion to Kant* (Cambridge).

——(1993*a*), *Kant and The Experience of Freedom* (Cambridge).

——(1993*b*), 'Kant's Morality of Law and Morality of Freedom', in R. M. Dancy (ed.), *Kant and Critique* (Dordrecht).

Harper, W., and Meerbote, R. (eds.) (1984), *Kant on Causality, Freedom, and Objectivity* (Minneapolis).

Harrison, J. (1967), 'Kant's Examples of the First Formulation of the Categorical Imperative', in Wolff (1967*b*).

Harrison, R. (1982), 'Transcendental Arguments and Idealism', in Vesey (1982).

Hegel, G. W. F. (1817–27), *Logic*, trans. W. Wallace (Oxford, 1975).

——(1821), *Philosophy of Right*, trans. T. M. Knox (Oxford, 1952).

Henrich, D. (1982), 'The Proof-Structure of Kant's Transcendental Deduction', in Walker (1982).

——(1989), 'The Identity of the Subject in the Transcendental Deduction', in Schaper and Vossenkuhl (1989).

——(1992), *Aesthetic Judgement and the Moral Image of the World: Studies in Kant* (Stanford, Calif.).

——(1994), *The Unity of Reason: Essays on Kant's Philosophy*, ed. and introd. R. Velkley (Cambridge, Mass.).

Herman, B. (1989), 'Justification and Objectivity: Comments on Rawls and Allison', in Förster (1989).

——(1993), *The Practice of Moral Judgement* (Cambridge, Mass.).

Hill, T. (1992), *Dignity and Practical Reason in Kant's Moral Theory* (Ithaca, NY).

Hintikka, J. (1969), 'On Kant's Notion of Intuition (Anschauung)', in Penelhum and MacIntosh (1969).

——(1972), 'Transcendental Arguments: Genuine and Spurious', *Nous*, 6: 274–81.

Höffe, O. (1994), *Immanuel Kant* (New York).

Hopkins, J. (1982), 'Kant's Visual Geometry', in Walker (1982).

Horstmann, R. (1976), 'Space as Intuition and Geometry', *Ratio*, 18: 17–30.

——(1989), 'Transcendental Idealism and the Representation of Space', in Schaper and Vossenkuhl (1989).

Hume, D. (1757), 'Of the Standard of Taste', in *'Of the Standard of Taste' and Other Essays* (Indianapolis, 1965).

Justin, G. (1974), 'On Kant's Analysis of Berkeley', *Kant-Studien*, 65: 20–32.

Kemal, S. (1986), *Kant and Fine Art: An Essay on Kant and the Philosophy of Fine Art and Culture* (Oxford).

——(1992), *Kant's Aesthetic Theory: An Introduction* (London).

Kemp, J. (1967), 'Kant's Examples of the Categorical Imperative', in Wolff (1967*b*).

——(1968), *The Philosophy of Kant* (Oxford).

Kemp Smith, N. (1923), *A Commentary to Kant's 'Critique of Pure Reason'*, 2nd edn. (London).

Kersting, W. (1992), 'Politics, Freedom, and Order: Kant's Political Philosophy', in Guyer (1992*b*).

Kitcher, P. (1990), *Kant's Transcendental Psychology* (Oxford).

Körner, S. (1955), *Kant* (Harmondsworth).

——(1967), 'Kant's Conception of Freedom', *Proceedings of the British Academy*, 53: 193–217.

——(1969), 'The Impossibility of Transcendental Deductions', in Beck (1969*b*).

Korsgaard, C. (1996), *Creating the Kingdom of Ends* (Cambridge).

McCloskey, M. (1987), *Kant's Aesthetic* (London).

Matthews, H. E. (1982), 'Strawson on Transcendental Idealism', in Walker (1982).

Meerbote, R. (1982), 'Reflection on Beauty', in Cohen and Guyer (1982).

——(1984), 'Kant on the Nondeterminate Character of Human Actions', in Harper and Meerbote (1984).

Melnick, A. (1973), *Kant's Analogies of Experience* (Chicago).

Mill, J. S. (1863), *Utilitarianism* (London, 1972).

Moore, A. W. (1988), 'Aspects of the Infinite in Kant', *Mind*, 97: 205–23.

Mothersill, M. (1984), *Beauty Restored* (London).

Murphy, J. (1970), *Kant: The Philosophy of Right* (London).

Neiman, S. (1994), *The Unity of Reason: Rereading Kant* (Oxford).

Nell (O'Neill), O. (1975), *Acting on Principle: An Essay on Kantian Ethics* (New York).

Norman, R. (1983), *The Moral Philosophers: An Introduction to Ethics* (Oxford).

O'Neill, O. (1989), *Constructions of Reason: Explorations of Kant's Practical Philosophy* (Cambridge).

——(1992), 'Vindicating Reason', in Guyer (1992*b*).

Parsons, C. (1992), 'The Transcendental Aesthetic', in Guyer (1992*b*).

Paton, H. J. (1936), *Kant's Metaphysics of Experience: A Commentary on the First Half of the 'Kritik der reinen Vernunft'*, 2 vols. (London).

——(1946), *The Categorical Imperative: A Study in Kant's Moral Philosophy* (London).

——(1948), *The Moral Law* (London).

Penelhum, T., and MacIntosh, J. J. (eds.) (1969), *The First Critique: Reflections on Kant's 'Critique of Pure Reason'* (Belmont, Calif.).

PLANTINGA, A. (1966), 'Kant's Objection to the Ontological Argument', *Journal of Philosophy*, 63: 537–46.

PLUHAR, W. (1987), Translator's Introduction to Kant, *Critique of Judgement* (Indianapolis).

POWELL, C. THOMAS (1990), *Kant's Theory of Self-Consciousness* (Oxford).

PRAUSS, G. (1974), *Kant und das Problem der Dinge an Sich* (Bonn).

RAWLS, J. (1971), *A Theory of Justice* (Cambridge, Mass.).

——(1980), 'Kantian Constructivism in Moral Theory' (Dewey Lectures 1980), *Journal of Philosophy*, 77: 515–72.

——(1989), 'Themes in Kant's Moral Philosophy', in Förster (1989).

REMNANT, P. (1969), 'Kant and the Cosmological Argument', in Penelhum and MacIntosh (1969).

ROBINSON, R. (1969), 'Necessary Propositions', in Penelhum and MacIntosh (1969).

ROSEN, M. (1989), 'Kant's Anti-Determinism', *Proceedings of the Aristotelian Society*, 89: 125–41.

SAVILE, A. (1987), *Aesthetic Reconstructions: The Seminal Writings of Lessing, Kant and Schiller* (Oxford).

——(1993), *Kantian Aesthetics Pursued* (Edinburgh).

SCHAFFER, J. (1969), 'Existence, Predication, and the Ontological Argument', in Penelhum and MacIntosh (1969).

SCHAPER, E. (1979), *Studies in Kant's Aesthetics* (Edinburgh).

——(1983), 'The Pleasures of Taste', in Schaper (ed.), *Pleasure, Preference and Value* (Cambridge).

——(1992), 'Taste, Sublimity, and Genius: The Aesthetics of Nature and Art', in Guyer (1992*b*).

——and VOSSENKUHL, W. (eds.) (1989), *Reading Kant: New Perspectives on Transcendental Arguments and Critical Philosophy* (Oxford).

SCHELLING, F. W. J. von (1856–61), *On the History of Modern Philosophy*, trans. A. Bowie (Cambridge, 1994).

SCHNEEWIND, J. B. (1992), 'Autonomy, Obligation, and Virtue: An Overview of Kant's Moral Philosophy', in Guyer (1992*b*).

SCHOPENHAUER, A. (1819–44), *The World as Will and Representation*, trans. E. F. J. Payne, 2 vols. (New York, 1966).

——(1841), *On the Basis of Morality*, trans. E. F. J. Payne (Indianapolis, 1965).

SCHRADER, G. (1967), 'The Thing in Itself in Kantian Philosophy', in Wolff (1967*b*).

SCHWYZER, H. (1990), *The Unity of Understanding: A Study in Kantian Problems* (Oxford).

SCRUTON, R. (1982), *Kant* (Oxford).

SIDGWICK, H. (1907), 'The Kantian Conception of Free Will', app. to *The Methods of Ethics*, 7th edn. (London).

SILBER, J. (1967), 'The Copernican Revolution in Ethics: The Good Reexamined', in Wolff (1967*b*).

STRAWSON, P. F. (1966), *The Bounds of Sense: An Essay on Kant's 'Critique of Pure Reason'* (London).

STROUD, B. (1982), 'Transcendental Arguments', in Walker (1982).

SULLIVAN, R. (1989), *Immanuel Kant's Moral Theory* (Cambridge).

Sullivan, R. (1994), *An Introduction to Kant's Ethics* (Cambridge).

Turbayne, C. (1969), 'Kant's Relation to Berkeley', in Beck (1969*b*).

Velkley, R. (1989), *Freedom and the Ends of Reason: On the Moral Foundation of Kant's Critical Philosophy* (Chicago).

Vesey, G. (ed.) (1982), *Idealism Past and Present* (Cambridge).

Walker, R. (1978), *Kant* (London).

——(ed.) (1982), *Kant on Pure Reason* (Oxford).

——(1985), 'Idealism: Kant and Berkeley', in J. Foster and H. Robinson (eds.), *Essays on Berkeley* (Oxford).

——(ed.) (1988), *The Real in the Ideal: Berkeley's Relation to Kant* (New York).

Walsh, W. H. (1969), 'Kant on the Perception of Time', in Beck (1969*b*).

——(1975), *Kant's Criticism of Metaphysics* (Edinburgh).

——(1982), 'Self-Knowledge', in Walker (1982).

Wartenburg, T. (1992), 'Reason and the Practice of Science', in Guyer (1992*b*).

Waxman, W. (1991), *Kant's Model of the Mind: A New Interpretation of Transcendental Idealism* (Oxford).

Weldon, T. D. (1945), *Introduction to Kant's 'Critique of Pure Reason'* (Oxford).

Wilkerson, T. E. (1976), *Kant's 'Critique of Pure Reason': A Commentary for Students* (Oxford).

Williams, T. C. (1968), *The Concept of the Categorical Imperative* (Oxford).

Wilson, M. (1971), 'Kant and "The *Dogmatic* Idealism of Berkeley"', *Journal of the History of Philosophy*, 9: 459–75.

Wolff, R. P. (1963), *Kant's Theory of Mental Activity: A Commentary on the Transcendental Analytic of the 'Critique of Pure Reason'* (Cambridge, Mass.).

——(1967*a*), 'A Reconstruction of the Argument of the Subjective Deduction', in Wolff (1967*b*).

——(ed.) (1967*b*), *Kant: A Collection of Critical Essays* (London).

Wood, A. (1970), *Kant's Moral Religion* (Ithaca, NY).

——(1978), *Kant's Rational Theology* (Ithaca, NY).

——(1984*a*), 'Kant's Compatibilism', in Wood (1984*b*).

——(ed.) (1984*b*), *Self and Nature in Kant's Philosophy* (Ithaca, NY).

——(1990), *Hegel's Ethical Thought* (Cambridge).

——(1992), 'Rational Faith, Moral Theology, and Religion', in Guyer (1992*b*).

Zimmerman, R. (1967), 'Kant: The Aesthetic Judgement', in Wolff (1967*b*).

11

CONTINENTAL PHILOSOPHY FROM HEGEL

Michael Rosen

1. THE CONTINENTAL TRADITION

Historians of philosophy writing in English typically construct their narratives as if the authors whom they are discussing were all taking part in a single argument—an argument that is conducted in terms of those problems that we now recognize to be relevant. This appears to leave no place for those who do not share our current assumptions regarding the nature of the issues—who lie outside what we think of as 'our tradition'.[1] Yet what is the alternative? Unless we can situate the authors whom we study in relation to our own concerns, what *philosophical* value (rather than value of a historical, biographical, or sociological kind) is there in engaging with them?

Fortunately, this apparent dilemma rests on a misunderstanding. Philosophy is not a discipline carried on according to rules and assumptions fixed once and for all. On the contrary, it has always involved an attempt to examine and call into question ideas and commitments that are otherwise taken for granted. Thus we do not need to share assumptions with the authors whom we study (or, worse, pretend that we share them when we do not) in order to include them in our discussion. Indeed, it may be the very fact that authors proceed from an underlying position very different from our own that makes studying them valuable: the difference challenges us to reflect on commitments that we would otherwise not even realize that we had. The problem is to explain the distinctiveness of the authors' own concerns in sufficient detail to make them intelligible and to find enough common ground to make the challenge that they represent a productive one. That is the purpose of this chapter.

The authors to be dealt with fall within the tradition that is known as 'Continental' philosophy, in contrast to the 'analytic' tradition that dominates in the English-speaking world. Both labels are, however, potentially misleading. Although the authors discussed (Hegel, Schopenhauer, Nietzsche, Husserl, and Heidegger) did indeed live and work in the countries of Continental Europe, so too did many other philosophers who are not counted as part of that tradition. Two groups in particular are, by convention, excluded: Marxists and those, principally Austrian, thinkers known as 'positivists' and 'Logical Positivists'. While it is true that these two groups are intellectually distinctive, it should be remembered that they were an important part of the intellectual environment within which Continental authors were writing.

[1] One of the most trenchant critics of the way in which conventional approaches to the history of philosophy neglect and distort the context within which authors write has been the Cambridge historian of political thought, Quentin Skinner. His views are presented and discussed critically in J. Tully (ed.), *Meaning and Context* (Cambridge, 1988). A collection of essays on the history of philosophy written by a variety of authors who share similar misgivings is: R. Rorty, J. B. Schneewind, and Q. Skinner (eds.), *Philosophy in History* (Cambridge, 1984).

The term 'analytic' is misleading for another reason. It suggests that those authors to whom the label is applied share a common commitment to a single philosophical method: analysis. But this is plainly untrue. Not only have very different ideas as to what analysis might amount to been put forward in the course of time (Bertrand Russell's conception is quite different from J. L. Austin's) but many of the most distinguished members of the analytic tradition do not seem to be practising analysis in any very distinctive sense at all. In the face of this, the difference between analytic and Continental philosophy is sometimes characterized—by analytic philosophers in particular—as merely one of style: analytic philosophy is careful and rigorous, paying attention to the nuances of language, and Continental philosophy is—what? Loose and careless? Put like this, the contrast is hardly very flattering to Continental philosophy: the difference seems to be simply that analytic philosophers are good ones and Continental philosophers aren't!

A more sympathetic way to try to characterize the Continental tradition is in terms of the kinds of answer that it gives to certain problems whose force we (whether we agree with those answers or not) can recognize and appreciate. It will be helpful, I suggest, to start by identifying four recurrent issues which in one way or another have concerned almost all of the philosophers in the Continental tradition.

1. The first is the question of philosophy itself. Is philosophy possible at all? And, if so, how—what is its method?

2. A second question concerns the relationship between philosophy and the natural sciences. Where does science end and philosophy begin? Is there a sharp dividing-line at all between the two disciplines?

3. Thirdly, there is the relationship between philosophy and history. Is the fact that philosophy is part of a process of historical change itself a fact of philosophical significance?

4. The final issue concerns the unity of theory and practice. If philosophy is something other than a form of science (if it is, instead, an exercise in self-knowledge, for example) it seems reasonable to suppose that it will affect one's attitudes and practices in a more direct way than the discovery of some new scientific fact.

Clearly, these issues interact. If the truth about the physical world can be discovered only via the experimental method of the natural sciences then does not that make philosophy redundant—at least insofar as philosophy's objective is the traditional one of 'metaphysics', to discover the ultimate nature of reality? Either philosophy must find some other objective (and a corresponding method to suit) or it must accept that it will find itself time and again sitting like King Canute on the beach, watching its claims being refuted by the incoming tide of scientific progress.

The idea of history, too, poses a challenge to philosophy. Let us suppose (as seems reasonable) that a 'post-metaphysical' philosophy takes as at least part of its subject-matter the study of those fundamental concepts through which the human mind comes to perceive and understand the world. Now, what if it is also true (as it again seems reasonable to suppose) that those concepts vary in the course of history and from society to society? Philosophy would appear to be limited in consequence to the articulation and exploration of one limited point of view; it would no longer possess the vantage-point from which it could claim to have universal validity.

These are troubling issues—and not just for Continental philosophers, of course. But Continental philosophers have tended to see their significance in a particular way, partly because of the historical context which has shaped their approach to them. Another term which is often applied to the Continental tradition is 'post-Kantian' philosophy, and this label gives us an important insight into the way in which almost all the thinkers under consideration here viewed their place within the history of philosophy: they saw themselves as continuing, but at the same time critical of, the work of Kant. Let us then orientate ourselves in relation to Kant's successors by examining first Kant's own attitude towards these four issues.

As Kant describes it in the *Critique of Pure Reason*, the task of philosophy is to set up what he calls a 'court-house which will assure to reason its lawful claims'.[2] The metaphor carries important implications for the way in which the task of philosophy is conceived. First, it implies that philosophy is a *normative* discipline. Like a court, its objective is to adjudicate disputes that are brought before it. Philosophical disputes are neither to be decided *dogmatically*—in response to some authority whose legitimacy consists solely in its established power—nor to be by-passed *sceptically*. Philosophers are engaged in a kind of philosophical jurisprudence, allowing as admissible only what it is open to reason to determine. This is why Kant, his thinking interwoven as ever with the political vision of the Enlightenment, compares philosophy's role in bringing peace to the 'battlefield of metaphysics' with the political order established with the foundation of civil society.[3]

But what is the extent of reason's competence? What method can it use for its critique? To answer this question Kant employs another, even more famous, metaphor: philosophy is to carry out a *Copernican revolution*. Philosophical disputes would not be capable of rational resolution were the issues involved questions about the ultimate structure of reality, independent of the human mind. But they are not. Philosophical questions, for Kant, concern the relationship between the human mind and a reality which has been, in some partial sense,

[2] Immanuel Kant, *The Critique of Pure Reason*, trans. N. Kemp Smith (London, 1970), Axi.
[3] Ibid. A753/B781.

produced by the mind—a reality whose features have been 'synthesized' by the activity of a non-empirical agency, the *transcendental subject*. What we have made (or 'constituted') in this sense we can know—not because the subject's transcendental activity is accessible to us introspectively, just by our own awareness of our own thinking, but because its effects can be determined by a process of philosophical argument. It is this idea—that philosophy should give its attention first and foremost to experience—that, for Continental philosophers, is the significance of Kant's 'Copernican revolution'.

Kant's normative conception of philosophy was presented in the form of a deliberate contrast to that of his empiricist predecessors, Locke in particular. Although Locke in the *Essay concerning Human Understanding* had also set out to draw boundaries and justify knowledge claims (its object, he wrote, was to 'inquire into the original, certainty and extent of human knowledge'[4]) the method that he used was, in the eyes of Kant and his successors, merely psychological and descriptive: Kant refers to Locke's philosophy as 'physiological'.[5] Whatever their reservations about Kant's own philosophy, Kant's successors in the Continental tradition can, almost without exception, be said to endorse (and, indeed, extend) Kant's negative view of this kind of enterprise. While there has been a great deal of sympathetic interest among analytic philosophers in the idea that philosophy should be continuous in method and subject-matter with the natural sciences—what is commonly referred to as 'positivism'—Continental philosophy has generally dismissed such ideas as no more than a reversion to a pre-Kantian conception of the philosophical enterprise.[6] For similar reasons, Continental philosophy has also been hostile to what it calls 'psychologism', another unfortunately slightly elastic term, that is generally used to denote the attempt to substitute a description of mental phenomena of the kind to be found in psychology for a philosophical account of such phenomena as knowledge, judgement, and meaning.[7] Thus there has been a certain symmetry in the relationship between the two traditions: just as analytic philosophers fail to take Continental philosophy seriously, Continental philosophers are inclined to dismiss analytic philosophy as simply a reprise of an 'Enlightenment project' whose limitations are essentially the same as those criticized by Kant and the German Idealists in the late eighteenth and early nineteenth centuries.

[4] John Locke, *An Essay concerning Human Understanding* (Oxford, 1975), I. i. 2.

[5] *The Critique of Pure Reason*, A87/B119.

[6] An interesting and fair-minded account of positivist philosophy written from a point of view sympathetic to Continental philosophy is L. Kolakowski, *Positivist Philosophy* (Harmondsworth, 1972). A famous (or notorious) clash between positivism and Continental philosophy is recorded in T. W. Adorno (ed.), *The Positivist Dispute in German Sociology*, trans. G. Adey and D. Frisby (London, 1976).

[7] See the discussion of Husserl below. We may note that this is a point of agreement between Continental philosophy and one important strand of analytic philosophy. Many analytic philosophers influenced by Wittgenstein also regard the opposition to 'psychologism' as a central issue for the philosophy of mind. John McDowell is one contemporary author who has pursued this line of argument with particular vigour.

So far, we have concentrated on those aspects of Kant's *Critique of Pure Reason* with which Continental philosophers have in general agreed. We shall, of course, deal with specific disagreements in the course of the discussion of individual authors, but, again, it is worth outlining some widely held reservations, all of which can be found in at least one of the authors to be discussed, as well as being raised elsewhere in the Continental tradition.

The first set of reservations relate to one of the *Critique of Pure Reason*'s central features: its dualistic conception of experience and the (closely connected) doctrine of transcendental agency implicit in the idea of 'synthesis'. According to Kant, our encounter with reality (insofar as that encounter amounts to experience and is capable of being a matter for judgement and reflection) takes place through the joint operation of *intuitions* and *concepts*. Intuitions and concepts are species of 'representation' (*Vorstellung*—Kant's generic word for mental items) each of which is associated with a mental power or 'faculty'—*sensibility* and *understanding* respectively. Concepts, Kant says, guide the process by which we synthesize what is given to us through the senses into the everyday reality of objects and events. Yet Kant, many of his immediate critics objected, gave no satisfactory answer to the question how these two faculties related to one another. Indeed there was, they argued, little advance over Descartes. Kant, it is true, had got rid of Descartes's dualistic division between extended substance and thinking substance, but he had merely replaced it with a no less problematic doctrine in the form of a contrast between two radically different aspects of the human mind.

Dissatisfaction with Kant's 'faculty psychology' is by no means confined to the Continental tradition. What is striking, however, is that, while this criticism has led analytical philosophers (for example, P. F. Strawson, in *The Bounds of Sense*) to try to reconstruct Kant's theory purged of the idea of a synthesizing subject altogether, Kant's most immediate critics, the German Idealists, reinterpreted the transcendental subject as something more than just a psychological capacity on the part of the individual agent to give form to what is given to it from outside. As one commentator very pithily puts it: in German Idealism after Kant, 'the place of transcendental processes of determination is taken by transcendental processes of generation'.[8]

The Continental philosophers' disagreements with Kant are not confined to the *Critique of Pure Reason*. As well as the *Critique of Pure Reason*, Kant wrote two other *Critiques*: the *Critique of Practical Reason* and the *Critique of Judgement*. In the former Kant envisages a more ambitious role for reason. Human beings, insofar as they are the subjects of action—of moral action, in particular—can, he argued, be treated as part of a higher realm, a world not just of appearances but of things in themselves. Human beings are free to the extent that they are

[8] Karl-Heinz Haag, *Philosophischer Idealismus* (Frankfurt, 1967), 31.

subject to a self-given law and reason is capable of developing such a law: the categorical imperative. It is fair to say that criticism of this aspect of Kant's thought in the Continental tradition has gone in two completely opposite directions. For the German Idealists (represented here by Hegel) Kant's categorical imperative is a major insight that Kant himself does not take far enough. In particular, they believe, it demonstrates the capacity of reason to generate content a priori—an important discovery with implications that go far beyond the realm of ethics. For Schopenhauer and Nietzsche, on the other hand, Kant's belief in an unconditionally necessary 'moral reason' is precisely where he goes wrong: there is, they maintain, no such thing.

The *Critique of Judgement* deals with two further topics that might seem to us nowadays to be only very remotely related to one another: the nature of beauty and aesthetic judgement, on the one hand, and the understanding of nature insofar as it is systematic or purposive on the other. In each case, however, Kant is dealing with a phenomenon that threatens to contradict the carefully set-out hierarchy of faculties presented in the first *Critique*. According to the definition of objects given there, the concept of an object embodies a kind of universal rule in subordination to which particular elements of experience are organized. But beautiful objects appear to contradict this picture. It seems to be characteristic of them that there is an inherent appropriateness in the way in which their particular elements express universal characteristics. As it is sometimes said, beautiful objects *embody* the universal in the particular, rather than having concepts imposed indifferently on the raw material subsumed under it.

Similarly, organic nature may appear to conflict with Kant's confident definition of nature as 'the existence of things so far as it is determined according to universal laws'.[9] The *organized* character of organic beings—the purposive adaptation of parts to whole, and their capacity for developmental growth, self-maintenance, and self-reproduction—seemed to the eighteenth century, at least, not to be capable of being explained according to deductively structured bodies of physical law. There would never be, Kant asserted, a 'Newton of a blade of grass'.[10]

Kant's response, both in the field of aesthetics and in his account of organic nature, was not to deny the existence of such phenomena altogether, but to deny that they fell within the domain of objective explanation. For his successors and critics, however, this restriction represented a regrettable failure of nerve on Kant's part. On the contrary, they argued, art and organic nature give the lie to the simplistic division of experience between sense and understanding of the first *Critique* and Kant's reductive definition of nature in terms of universal laws. The subject-matter of the third *Critique*, or so the German Idealists

[9] I. Kant, *Prolegomena to Any Future Metaphysics* (Indianapolis, 1950), 42.

[10] I. Kant, *Critique of Judgement*, trans. J. H. Bernard (New York, 1968), 248.

would argue, shows that, Kant's own views to the contrary, the highest faculty—reason itself or the 'Idea'—does, in certain cases, play an objective or constitutive role in experience, helping to reconcile intuitions and concepts by a kind of 'intuitive understanding'.

Versions of this appealing (if highly obscure) position are advanced, as we shall see, by such otherwise opposed thinkers as Hegel and Schopenhauer. For the moment let us note merely its most general consequence. It gives aesthetic experience a central philosophical importance: art is an epistemologically distinctive realm where the otherwise harsh antitheses of human experience are mediated, an alternative to the technocratic and instrumental conception of nature that is, supposedly, characteristic of a scientific civilization. This is, of course, a theme that came to occupy a central position in Western culture at the time of Romanticism—and has retained it ever since.

Although Kant presents a highly original answer to the question of what the method of philosophy should be, one which separates his enterprise both from traditional metaphysics and from the empirical parts of the natural sciences, his conception of philosophy is in one respect quite traditional. Kant, no less than Descartes or Spinoza or Leibniz, wants philosophy to give objective answers to questions that are general in scope. If follows then that, for Kant, philosophy is not in any sense a historical discipline: philosophers aim, at least, to settle things once and for all: 'When, therefore, someone announces a system of philosophy as his own creation, he is in effect saying that there has been no other philosophy prior to his. For, were he to admit that there is another (and true) philosophy, then he would be admitting that there are two different philosophies concerning the same thing, and that would be self-contradictory.'[11]

Yet while, for Kant, philosophy tries to rise above history, it is easy to see how certain aspects of Kant's ideas can be given a quite different twist. Kant believes that the fundamental concepts through which we experience the world—the categories—are the same for all human beings. Indeed (notoriously) he tries to deduce their necessity from the structure of logic. What if the categories are historically and culturally variable, however? If that is so, then concentrating on the concepts through which we come to appropriate the world will give us something much more specific: an understanding, insofar as that is possible, of our own particular perspective. It follows from this that philosophy is a different kind of activity from the investigation of empirical truths about the world. To discover that one sees the world in a certain way (for instance, partially, refracted through a certain matrix of concepts) is to discover that one approaches the world within a certain kind of structure of pre-understanding.

This brings us to the final contrast between the analytic and the Continental traditions that should be borne in mind: the concern to be found in the

[11] I. Kant, *The Metaphysical Elements of Justice* (Indianapolis, 1965), 6.

Continental tradition for the relationship between life and philosophy. Analytic philosophers, as we have noted, have most commonly adopted a conception of the task of philosophy that ties it closely with science (clearing the ground for scientific theory, for example, or providing its own quasi-scientific account of the nature of thought and language). Where they have not (for instance, in so-called 'ordinary language' philosophy) the analytic philosophers' account of the practical role of philosophy has been primarily negative, as a 'therapy' for the illusions endemic within philosophy itself. Kant's conception of philosophy combines elements of both these views.

Post-Kantian Continental philosophy, by contrast, has most frequently taken a view of the relationship between theory and practice much closer to that of the great progenitor of the tradition of Western philosophy, Plato. For Plato, in coming to *know* a truth human reason would have to make that truth its own—*appropriate* it, as we might say—so philosophical knowledge is supposed to transform both our understanding and the way in which we live our lives. The question in dispute in the Continental tradition has been not so much whether this aspiration towards the unity of theory and practice is intrinsic to philosophy, but whether it is capable of fulfilling it. For those who deny that it is (a position that is most obviously associated with Marx but is to be found in this chapter represented by Nietzsche) philosophy as traditionally conceived is not so much a means to the good life as one of the obstacles in the way of achieving it, 'another form and mode of human alienation',[12] as Marx puts it.

2. HEGEL

Hegel—Georg Wilhelm Friedrich Hegel, to give him his full name—was born in 1770, the son of an official in the service of the Duke of Baden-Württemberg. He studied from 1788–93 at the Tübinger Stift, a higher-education seminary that specialized in training candidates for state service. There he formed friendships with two fellow students who would also make very significant contributions to intellectual life in Germany, the great poet Friedrich Hölderlin and the philosopher Friedrich Schelling. The three young men were extremely close during the 1790s and shared a common outlook in relation to politics, art, and philosophy. Like many others, they were inspired by the early years of the French Revolution and hoped for a corresponding political regeneration to transform the patchwork of absolutist states into which Germany was then divided. Culturally, they contrasted the fragmentation of contemporary art and religion unfavourably with the harmony, as they saw it, of Greek life. Only in philosophy did they consider Germany to be a leading force, thanks to the work of Kant. Yet here again they were by no means uncritical. Hölderlin compared

[12] Karl Marx, *Early Writings*, trans. R. Livingstone and G. Benton (Harmondsworth, 1975), 381.

Kant's significance to Moses. Like Moses, that is, he had led his people out of bondage; someone else must be found to enable them to enter the Promised Land.

These sorts of idea are apparent in a remarkable short piece written in 1797, known as the *Oldest System-Programme of German Idealism*.[13] Until recently the author of the *System-Programme* was generally believed to have been Hegel himself, but there is now evidence that points strongly towards Hölderlin. In any case, there is no doubt that Hegel endorsed the piece since it is in his handwriting. The author of the *System-Programme* articulates, albeit very cryptically, a programme for a radically new kind of philosophy, one in which philosophy will become continuous with art: 'The philosopher must have as much aesthetic power as the poet.'[14] Like J. G. Fichte, whose philosophy had come to prominence in Germany in the early 1790s, the author of the *Oldest System-Programme* takes the fact that human beings are capable of a distinctive kind of moral rationality to be of central metaphysical significance. The starting-point for philosophy, the author writes, must be the conception of the individual as an 'absolutely free' moral being. The key idea here is the Kantian one that freedom consists in subjection to a law, but a law given to the individual from within him- or herself. The fact that human reason is capable of generating such a law (and of having insight into its validity) is held to be a sign that—in direct contradiction to Kant's own view—reason need not be limited to a purely regulative role. Reason, the faculty of Ideas, can break Kant's restriction of knowledge to the mere application of concepts to intuitions. The question by which philosophy should be guided is thus, according to the *Oldest System-Programme*: 'How must a world be ordered for a moral being?'[15] The answer to that question, the author claims, will be a vision of the world as a system of Ideas (understood in a sense that combines both Kant and Plato) something that he supposes to have implications in two directions.

First, the Ideas are to give philosophy the capacity to animate physics—to 'give wings' to what would otherwise remain a 'slow and plodding' experimental science.[16] Secondly, they form the basis for a revolutionary critique of the state: 'I wish to show that there is no *Idea* of the state, because the state is something mechanical, as little as there is an Idea of a machine. Only what is an object of freedom can be called 'Idea'. So we must go beyond the state! For every state must treat free men as mechanical gear-cogs.' The role of philosophy as it is envisaged in the *Oldest System-Programme* is to provide the symbolic foundations for a future egalitarian society, based on the 'absolute freedom of

[13] *Oldest System-Programme of German Idealism*, trans. Taylor Cowan, *European Journal of Philosophy*, 3/2 (Aug. 1995), 199–200.

[14] Ibid. 199.

[15] Ibid.

[16] Ibid.

all minds (*Geister*) that carry the intellectual world within themselves and seek neither God nor immortality outside'.[17]

Thus it is apparent that, at the outset of his career, Hegel saw philosophy as part of a movement of radical political transformation. His first publication, a defence of his friend Schelling against Fichte, called *The Difference between the Fichtean and the Schellingean Systems of Philosophy* (1801) takes up a similar theme. Hegel there locates the origin of philosophical systems in the need to re-establish unity in human life: 'Division (*Entzweiung*) is the source of the need for philosophy . . .'.[18]

The very existence of philosophical systems, he claims, is a product of the fact that 'that which is a form of appearance of the Absolute has isolated itself from the Absolute and become fixed as something independent'.[19] According to Hegel at this stage of his intellectual development, philosophy is the symptom of a divided culture as well as a remedy for it: philosophy is a theory whose practical function is to restore the unity of theory and practice. The idea that philosophy is both a kind of disease and an attempt to cure it is familiar enough to analytic philosophers from the writings of Wittgenstein, but there is an important difference that should be noted. Hegel, unlikc Wittgenstein, does not suppose that when the cure is completed philosophy itself will become redundant. Rather, thought based upon the understanding will lose its hegemony, giving place to (and becoming integrated as a subordinate part within) a new, higher, speculative form of thought.

As we shall see, this theme of the supersession of the understanding by speculative reason will continue throughout Hegel's philosophical career. But by the time of the *Phenomenology of Spirit* (1807) Hegel's view of the place of philosophy had become far more conservative. Instead of being part of a movement of social and political transformation, its role was now to bring to consciousness a cultural development which had already been achieved, implicitly, by the agency that Hegel calls *Geist*, that common intellect in which, he claims, all human beings, as individual intelligences, participate.[20] (*Geist*—pronounced to rhyme with 'spiced'—is most frequently translated into English as 'Spirit', but sometimes also as 'mind'; to avoid confusion, I shall leave it untranslated.)

The *Phenomenology* has always been the most admired of Hegel's works.

[17] Ibid.

[18] *The Difference between the Fichtean and the Schellingean Systems of Philosophy*, in R. Bubner (ed.), *German Idealist Philosophy* (Harmondsworth, 1997), 262.

[19] Ibid.

[20] 'This past existence is an already attained possession of the universal *Geist*, which is the substance of the individual and so, although it appears as external to him, constitutes his non-organic nature. *Bildung*, in this respect, seen from the side of the individual, consists in acquiring what is thus present, absorbing his non-organic nature into himself, and taking possession of it' (*Phenomenology of Spirit*, trans. A. V. Miller (Oxford, 1977), 16).

Though difficult, it has a breadth and grandeur of presentation that carry the reader through its complexities. On one level, the starting-point for the *Phenomenology* lies in the rejection of Kant's dualistic conception of experience. According to Hegel, Kant's philosophy makes use of a model—of the mind imposing its form on an essentially non-mental reality—that is psychological, not philosophical, in origin. The idea that we could discover the necessary structures of experience by somehow standing outside the knowing process and taking a 'sideways view' of our mental activity misconceives the mind as if it were an instrument or medium, Hegel argues in the Introduction to the *Phenomenology*. Moreover, Hegel explicitly rejects Kant's account of concepts as simply 'functions of unity among our representations',[21] given by the faculty of understanding. On the contrary, *Begriff* (Kant's German word for 'concept') for Hegel must be understood in a quite different, speculative sense (for this reason, Hegel's use of the term is most often translated as 'notion'). As Hegel remarks rather loftily in the *Encyclopedia of the Philosophical Sciences*: 'The concept (*der Begriff*) in the speculative sense is to be distinguished from what is commonly called concept. It is in this latter, one-sided sense that the assertion has been made, repeated countless times and turned into a common prejudice that the infinite cannot be grasped by concepts.'[22]

And yet, although it rejects the Kantian conception of experience, the *Phenomenology* is, at another level, profoundly Kantian. Hegel, like Kant, aims to disclose the fundamental structures underlying experience. Now, for the reasons just given, Hegel cannot proceed by trying to isolate the form of experience and treating it as something to be analysed independently of its content. Instead, he adopts an approach which traces the forms which *Geist*'s relation to the world takes at each stage of historical development. Thus human beings' political and cultural relations (which, from *Geist*'s point of view, are simply forms of its own self-relation) are just as much part of the *Phenomenology*'s subject-matter as the traditional questions of body and mind.

An obvious objection presents itself. The traditional goal of philosophy is not just the mapping of thought but its justification: the demonstration that certain structures do indeed underlie reality (or, at least, reality insofar as it is thinkable for us). Simply to record the historical forms of human experience is to show only how something has come to be. In that case the *Phenomenology* would be, at best, an exercise in historical psychology or a piece of cultural history. But that is far from the limit of Hegel's ambition. Instead, he claims that, however it may seem (or once have seemed) as an actual historical process, the development from one form to another is a necessary one. Each transition has, to use Hegel's terminology, a *logical* force, in the sense that each succeeding stage is a

[21] *Critique of Pure Reason*, A68/B93.

[22] *Encyclopedia of the Philosophical Sciences*, vol. i, trans. William Wallace (Oxford, 1975), para. 9.

completion of the one that preceded it and to that extent the final form of thought can be seen to be justified.

Of course, it is easy enough to show that a feature was not present in that former stage, but it is something else again to show that this is an inadequacy or deficiency of the earlier stage and that the new feature is in some way a completion of what went before. We must be able to see the resulting stage as a completion or fulfilment of the preceding stage, a development from that earlier stage and not a mere replacement of it. Hegel describes the way in which one form of thought gives place to another as follows: 'it is only when it is taken as a result of that from which it emerges that it is, in fact, the true result; in that case it is itself a *determinate* nothingness, one which has a *content*'.[23] This idea of 'determinate negation' is essential to what Hegel means by the term 'dialectic'. The *Phenomenology* assumes that we, its readers, are capable of comprehending the forms of thought from a developmental vantage-point, seeing each one as the completion of its predecessor. But this assumption is itself, surely, not something everyone would accept: from a certain metaphysical position such a claim seems contrary to common sense. It appears, then, as though the *Phenomenology* presupposes its own result: it assumes a form of philosophical reasoning that it is its duty to justify.

Hegel does not regard the objection of apparent circularity as fatal; he actually makes the point himself. As he puts it, 'a knowledge which makes this one-sidedness its very essence [i.e. which fails to see new forms as *developments*] is itself one of the patterns of incomplete consciousness which occurs on the road itself'.[24] The *Phenomenology* presupposes that consciousness has *already reached* the stage at which 'Science' (in Hegel's sense) is possible. The development leading to the 'standpoint of Science' has, Hegel writes, 'already been *implicitly* accomplished; the content is already the actuality reduced to a possibility, its immediacy overcome, and the embodied shape reduced to abbreviated, simple determinations of thought'.[25]

Thus the *Phenomenology* draws on a conception of philosophy that reminds one strongly of Plato's idea that philosophy is recollection. Our mind has certain structures, in Hegel's view, but it is not aware that it has those structures. As he puts it in a crucial phrase in the Preface: *Was bekannt, darum nicht erkannt*, which we might translate as: what we are acquainted with, we do not therefore know. But while, for Plato, the dialectic by which we aim to restore ourselves to the realm of reason is a matter of pure, timeless argument, for Hegel, it is a matter of tracing through the forms of thought as they were to be found in history. If Hegel is right, then history has reached a point at which consciousness can retrace its own forms so that it sees in each one a *determinate negation*. To

[23] *Phenomenology of Spirit*, 51.

[24] Ibid.

[25] Ibid. 17.

start with, it has this capacity merely practically, implicitly—it does not know *that it has the capacity*. It comes to acquire this knowledge through the practical exercise of the capacity itself, in the process of following the course of the *Phenomenology*.

As we trace through the development of *Geist*, it becomes apparent, according to Hegel, that *Geist* is more than just a psychological or epistemological structure which *human beings* happen to have in common. On the contrary, at the highest point of *Geist*'s development, which Hegel calls Absolute Knowledge, the individual, he claims, becomes aware that *Geist*'s structure permeates all of reality, nature as well as history. The opposition between *Geist* and external reality is, in Hegel's famous technical term, *aufgehoben*—raised up, removed, and preserved. With this, the development of *Geist* has reached a point of completion. History has, in some sense, ended, and the stage is set for a study that will present the forms of thought in complete a priori purity: the *Science of Logic*.

While the *Phenomenology* traces the appearance of philosophical 'science', the *Science of Logic* is to present 'the system of pure reason, as the realm of pure Thought'.[26] The term that Hegel uses here, Thought (*Denken*) is an important technical one. For Kant, the generic term for the contents of the mind is *Vorstellung*, conventionally translated as 'representation'. Thus, according to Kant, intuitions, concepts and even Ideas are all species of 'representation'.[27] For Hegel, however, the realm of representations is characteristic of thought limited to the understanding. It is to be contrasted with the higher, speculative nature of Thought, the true method of philosophy. He puts the point very explicitly in the *Encyclopaedia of the Philosophical Sciences*: 'The difference between *Vorstellung* and Thought is of special importance because philosophy may be said to do nothing but transform *Vorstellungen* into Thoughts.'[28]

The *Science of Logic* presupposes that the reader has attained the capacity to carry through metaphysical reasoning in the pure realm of Thought—that was the conclusion of the *Phenomenology*. What is presented in the *Science of Logic* is a self-developing system of categories that incorporate, in true Platonic fashion, the necessary, ultimate structure of reality—'the presentation of God, as He is in His eternal being before the creation of nature and of a finite spirit', as Hegel puts it at one point.[29]

The *Logic*, then, is the very centre of Hegel's mature philosophy, but Hegel's interests are by no means confined to it. On the contrary, his later writings include extensive works on art, religion, history, politics, the history of philosophy, and the philosophy of nature. In each case, Hegel is concerned to discover

[26] G. W. F. Hegel, *The Science of Logic*, trans. A. V. Miller (Oxford, 1969), 50.

[27] This use of terminology becomes somewhat more comprehensible when we appreciate that *Vorstellung* was the German translation for the term 'idea' as used by Locke and the British Empiricists.

[28] *Encyclopedia of the Philosophical Sciences*, vol. i, para. 20.

[29] *The Science of Logic*, 50.

and make explicit a conceptual structure within the diverse empirical material that he is dealing with. Philosophy, then, articulates a priori structures within the realm of the empirical sciences and, in so doing, he believes, gives them an extra kind of necessity:

Philosophy, then, owing its development to the empirical sciences, gives their content in return that most essential form, the freedom of Thought: an *a priori* character. These contents are now warranted as necessary instead of depending on the evidence of facts merely as found and experienced. The fact becomes a presentation and a copy of the original and entirely independent activity of Thought.[30]

It is obviously not possible here to follow through in detail how Hegel imagines that this programme is to be realized. Suffice it, in conclusion, for us to review Hegel's position in relation to the four issues that we identified in the previous section.

1. Hegel's conception of philosophy is affirmative and rationalist. It represents a rejection of Kant, to the extent that Kant denied that philosophy was capable of giving a priori knowledge of the ultimate structure of reality. Hegel's use of the term 'speculation' is significant in this respect. While, for Kant, this is a pejorative term, characteristic of the 'dogmatic' metaphysics that he claims to have superseded, Hegel affirms the speculative nature of philosophical truth.

2. For Hegel, the method of philosophy is not the same as that of the natural sciences. But it is not, for that reason, to be seen as subordinate to or dependent on the sciences. On the contrary, philosophy is supposed to be at least as rigorous as the sciences and, in articulating the categorial structure that is implicit within the explanatory frameworks of scientific knowledge, it has a foundational and justificatory role to play in relation to the latter.

3. Hegel's account of philosophy is historical in a way that subordinates history to philosophy rather than the other way round. In other words, instead of philosophy being threatened with contingency by having its categories shown to be merely the product of some particular time and place, Hegel's grand ambition is to show that each apparently accidental manifestation of *Geist* is in fact a part of the process of *Geist*'s coming to self-knowledge: a process that can be seen from a rigorous and timeless point of view (even if that vantage-point is one that can only be attained by human reason in retrospect).

4. Finally, for Hegel, philosophical understanding, in bringing the individual to an awareness of what *Geist* has achieved, is supposed to reconcile him or her to existing reality. Philosophy articulates the rationality and necessity that are the governing structures of the world, and, in this sense, as Hegel puts it in the *Philosophy of History*, it contains the true 'theodicy': the justification of God's works to mankind.[31]

[30] *Encyclopedia of the Philosophical Sciences*, vol. i, para. 20.

[31] G. W. F. Hegel, *The Philosophy of History*, trans. J. Sibree (New York, 1956), 15.

3. SCHOPENHAUER

Arthur Schopenhauer was born in 1788, in Danzig (the Hanseatic city now known in Polish as Gdańsk) and he died in 1860, in Frankfurt. He studied philosophy in Göttingen and Berlin and originally hoped to pursue a university career as a philosopher. That was not to be, however. The famous story is told of how, when he was given the right to teach at the university in Berlin, Schopenhauer scheduled his lectures in direct competition with those of Hegel, the principal professor of philosophy. The result was humiliating. Whilst Hegel's audience was in the hundreds, only a very few attended Schopenhauer's course. Schopenhauer (who had an independent income, inherited from his businessman father) withdrew into private life. In his writings, however, he never misses an opportunity to pour scorn on professors of philosophy in general and on Hegel in particular, for whom Schopenhauer always retained a vivid loathing.

Wounded vanity apart, Schopenhauer's objection to the German philosophers of his day lay in his belief that they had perverted Kant's legacy and that only he, Schopenhauer, was capable of understanding Kant's thought and taking it further. The very title of his masterpiece, *The World as Will and Representation*, published in 1819, echoes two of Kant's central terms. Representation (*Vorstellung*) is crucial for Schopenhauer, as it is for Hegel. But the two thinkers differ quite fundamentally in their attitudes towards it. Hegel, as we have seen, thinks that the task of speculative philosophy is to raise everyday thought to a vantage-point beyond the dualism of subject and object. Schopenhauer denies that this is possible, in agreement with Kant's doctrine that objective knowledge must remain limited to the world of representation. Schopenhauer's account of the division between sensibility, understanding, and reason and the role that they play in perception and knowledge is very similar to Kant's. According to Schopenhauer, sensibility and understanding between them give us a world with three fundamental intellectual characteristics: position (in time), location (in space), and a kind of immediate awareness of causal necessity. Reflection and the application of concepts, on the other hand, are a matter of the faculty of reason and so do not enter into the world as we find it to be given to us. (There is a contrast here with Kant, who thought that the categories were concepts applied unconsciously within experience by the understanding.)

Like Kant, Schopenhauer thought that the twin doctrines of transcendental idealism—that objects cannot be given except in relation to some subject, and that the content of experience is not produced by the subject alone—point inevitably to a further question: What is the nature of reality independent of the activity of the subject? This question, the question of the 'thing in itself', is, according to Kant, both inescapable and unanswerable. To answer it satisfactorily we would have to be able to transcend the dualism of subject and object, the basic condition of knowledge itself. Yet Schopenhauer, although he too accepts this Kantian premiss, claims nevertheless to be able to say something philosophical about the thing in itself: its nature is, he says, *will*. What does Schopenhauer mean by this claim and how does he justify it?

The best place to start in understanding the claim is with Schopenhauer's account of causality. According to Schopenhauer, our experience of causality is of the existence of a law-governed, necessary connection holding between items (Schopenhauer says between 'changes') such that when one occurs another always follows. What we do not have in the normal case, however, is any understanding of the *kind* of connection that there is between cause and effect. We know the *that* of causality, one might say, but not the *how* or the *why*. Now, on a certain view of causality—what might be called a *phenomenalist* view—that is all that there is to understand. Yet Schopenhauer disagrees, for in one particular case, he claims, we can understand the causal process not just from the outside but from the inside as well. That is the case in which we both observe and exercise our own will. When we will, the relationship between our mental state and the bodily state that follows is not just part of a universal sequence: it is also intelligible. Although, according to Schopenhauer, 'For the purely knowing subject as such this body is a representation like any other, an object among objects', the movements and actions of the body are 'unravelled for [the subject] in an entirely different way'.[32] Not that we can give an account in discursive terms of what it is in which our willing consists, but we are aware of that willing none the less as a kind of amorphous and purposeless driving and striving beyond the fixed determinacy of the 'principle of individuation'. This then, according to Schopenhauer, is a paradigm of what we discover when we penetrate beyond the dualism of subject and object.

Many commentators have objected that Schopenhauer's argument does not entitle him to the much stronger claim that he now goes on to make: that will is the thing in itself. Even if Schopenhauer is right in saying that the key to the inner nature of human action is the directionless striving of the will, why should we think that that is true of reality as a whole? Many people would argue that it is irrational to universalize on the basis of only one instance. Schopenhauer, on the other hand, clearly believes that this generalization is perfectly reasonable, even rationally compelling:

> The reader who with me has gained this conviction, [namely, that will is the inner nature of human action] will find that of itself it will become the key to the knowledge of the innermost being of the whole of nature, since he now transfers it to all those

[32] A. Schopenhauer, *The World as Will and Representation*, trans. E. F. J. Payne (New York, 1969), vol. i, sect. 18, p. 99.

phenomena that are given to him, not like his own phenomenon both in direct and indirect knowledge, but in the latter solely, and hence merely in a one-sided way, as *representation* alone. He will recognize it not only in those phenomena that are quite similar to his own, in men and animals, as their innermost nature, but continued reflection will lead him to recognize the force that shoots and vegetates in the plant, indeed the force by which the crystal is formed, the force that turns the magnet to the North Pole, the force whose shock he encounters from the contact of metals of different kinds, the force that appears in the elective affinities of matter as repulsion and attraction, separation and union, and finally even gravitation, which acts so powerfully in all matter, pulling the stone to earth and the earth to the sun; all these he will recognize as different only in the phenomenon, but the same according to their inner nature. He will recognize them all as that which is immediately known to him so intimately and better than everything else, and where it appears most distinctly is called *will*.[33]

Reading this passage, it is hard to escape the conclusion that the merciless critic of the pretensions of Hegelianism was rather prone to jump to sweeping metaphysical conclusions himself. There is, I think, no way of giving further arguments in support of Schopenhauer's claim that, in understanding human agency, he had discovered the 'key to the innermost being of the whole of nature' (to be fair, he himself is clear that it depends upon an intuitive analogy) but it is, at least, possible to put it into its intellectual context. We can see in Schopenhauer's thought at this point another post-Kantian reprise of the tension in Kant's own thought between the *Critique of Pure Reason* and the rest of the Critical Philosophy.

The *Critique of Pure Reason* had restricted objective knowledge to the mathematical laws governing the sequence of events in space and time. Yet, as Kant himself recognized, this excluded from the sphere of objective knowledge those aspects of nature which gave it an *organized* character. Schopenhauer was enough of a Romantic philosopher of nature (he had collaborated with Goethe on the latter's researches into colour) to find such a restriction intolerably reductive. To do justice to the richness of nature he adopts a version of Platonism. Between the will as thing in itself—the ultimate source of everything—and the ordered necessity of the world of phenomena there exists, he asserts, a realm of Ideas: transcendental entities that act as a kind of governing focus for natural processes. Of course, by assumption, we cannot have direct access to these entities, but it is thanks to them, Schopenhauer claims, that things in the natural world (and organic processes in particular) take the forms that they do. 'For us', says Schopenhauer, 'the will is the *thing-in-itself*, and the *Idea* is the immediate objectivity of that will at a definite grade.'[34]

It is not just the organic realm, for Schopenhauer, that points us beyond the world of phenomena. Art, too, can be properly understood only from the point

[33] A.Schopenhauer, *The World as Will and Representation*, sect. 21, pp. 109–110.

[34] Ibid., sect. 31, p. 170.

of view of the duality between the world of phenomena and the thing in itself as will. Art offers us two things. In the first place, in the form of music, it allows us a grasp of reality beyond the 'principle of individuation'. Music, like the empirical world itself, Schopenhauer claims, is an '*immediate* . . . objectification and copy of the whole *will*', but one whose form is quite unlike the differentiated and individuated realm of phenomena.[35] Furthermore, the contemplative beauty of art—the 'disinterested pleasure' that Kant had identified as characteristic of the aesthetic realm—gives human beings a chance to escape, if only briefly, from the remorseless striving of the will and the suffering that that entails. Thus art appears in Schopenhauer's thought as both metaphysically dignified—it gives access to the transcendent realm in a way that mere empirical investigation or logical reasoning cannot—and of the highest human value. It is not perhaps surprising that Schopenhauer's philosophy has proved congenial to many very distinguished artists over the years (one might mention, amongst others, Wagner, Mahler, Richard Strauss, Hardy, Proust, and Thomas Mann).

Schopenhauer was one of the earliest West European philosophers to write from an explicitly atheistic standpoint (a-theistic in the strict sense: the Eastern religions that he admired and to some extent endorsed were, he believed, religions without God) and he adopts a position regarding the nature of evil that is quite different from those which are to be found in the tradition of Judaeo-Christian monotheism. Three main accounts of the nature of evil have been used in the Judaeo-Christian tradition to reconcile the existence of evil with an ultimately benevolent Creator. The first is that evil is a deserved punishment, visited on mankind for its sinfulness in eating the forbidden fruit in the Garden of Eden. This is the most orthodox Christian doctrine, associated in particular with St Augustine. The second is that what human beings see as evil is not really so. What is apparently evil is really good when properly understood in terms of the overall benevolent purpose that it helps to realize. This idea can be found in the early modern period in Locke, Leibniz, and, most strikingly, Hegel. Finally, there is the idea that evil is really human in origin: that the so-called 'natural' evils—death and disease—are not true evils, while other evils are a direct result of the abuse of human freedom, something for which man, not God, should be counted responsible. Perhaps the best-known expression of this view is to be found in the 'theological' section of Rousseau's *Émile*, known as the 'Confession of Faith of a Savoyard Vicar'.

These three accounts are all forms of 'optimism'—attempts to show that reality is part of an ultimately benevolent order. Optimism, Schopenhauer says, 'seems to me to be not merely an absurd, but also a really *wicked*, way of thinking, a bitter mockery of the unspeakable sufferings of mankind.'[36] The ultimate

[35] Ibid., sect. 52, p. 257. [36] Ibid., sect. 59, p. 326.

character of reality is impersonal, not personal, he believes, and, insofar as the striving of the will is the source of intrinsically meaningless suffering, the nature of the world is bad, not good.

One final aspect of Schopenhauer's philosophy deserves mention, for it seems to have been quite unjustly ignored: his views on ethics. Schopenhauer's highly original position comes from playing off against one another two aspects of Kant's ethical thought (as Schopenhauer understands them). Kant, famously, maintains that the only thing that can be thought of as good 'without restriction' (as he puts it at the beginning of the *Groundwork to the Metaphysics of Morals*) is a good will. Thus the will, and the responsible action associated with it, form the starting-point for Kant's ethical system from which all its value-judgements can, in principle, be derived. Well and good, says Schopenhauer. But has Kant not demonstrated in the *Critique of Pure Reason* that free will in the sense required for full ethical responsibility is an illusion; that there is freedom not in the world of phenomena but only at the level of the thing in itself? Since human beings decide and act in accordance with the characters they have in the phenomenal world, it follows, Schopenhauer believes, that, from the standpoint of human agency, determinism is true. Schopenhauer rejects the 'soft determinist' strategy of trying to find a sense for human freedom while accepting the overall truth of determinism. When we act, we cannot but act according to our characters, Schopenhauer believes, and so, since these are as subject to fixed laws as any other natural processes, we are simply not free in the way that an ethical system based on the notion of responsibility would require.

There have, of course, been many determinists in the history of philosophy, but for the most part they have been subjectivists in some form: emotivists or ethical sceptics of one kind or another who deny the possibility of ethical objectivity. What is unusual about Schopenhauer is that, while he rejects the ideas of freedom and responsibility, he retains Kant's conviction that objectivity is essential to ethics. That objectivity, however, lies not, as it does for Kant, in the existence of an objective principle to guide moral reasoning, but in an emotion which has impartiality built into it: sympathy. In acting on sympathy, Schopenhauer claims, we are moved, not by some kind of rational recognition of the justice of the claims that others make upon us, but by a perception of the ultimate artificiality of the distinction between their welfare (or, rather, from the Schopenhauerian perspective, their suffering) and our own (those familiar with current writing in ethics might see some similarities here between Schopenhauer's position and ideas to be found in the writings of the contemporary Oxford philosopher, Derek Parfit). In ethical action, according to Schopenhauer, the individual transcends his or her own individuality. It is striking that a man who, from what one can tell, seems to have been particularly narrow and self-centred in his dealings with others, should have been inspired by such a generous ethical vision.

4. NIETZSCHE

In one guise, Nietzsche is an anti-philosopher: an unsparing critic of the aspirations and procedures of philosophy, prepared to attack his targets by whatever means he feels will be effective—sarcasm and parody as well as critical argument. He does philosophy (as he puts it in the subtitle to his *Twilight of the Idols*) 'with a hammer'. Yet, behind all his jokes and aphorisms, Nietzsche is also committed to distinctive and trenchant positions regarding Continental philosophy's central preoccupations. Thus Nietzsche occupies a position both outside and within philosophy: outside it, to the extent that he believes that the implication of his position is to deny philosophy's right to exist as an independent discipline; within it, because his position is a sceptical one that challenges philosophy to defend itself.

The scepticism with which philosophers are most familiar is scepticism about our knowledge of the external world, the idea that perhaps there is nothing objective corresponding to what is given to us in consciousness. But Nietzsche's scepticism is aimed at a different target. He challenges received ideas of truth and knowledge by denying our capacity to find a unique, objective vantage-point from which to know the world. The term that Nietzsche himself uses for his position is 'perspective'. What Nietzsche means by perspective amounts, in effect, to a variation of Kantian epistemology. The traditional knowing subject, Nietzsche claims, is like a perspectiveless eye, 'an eye that is completely unthinkable, an eye turned in no particular direction, in which the active and interpreting forces, through which alone seeing becomes seeing *something*, are supposed to be lacking'.[37] Like Kant, however, Nietzsche believes that our encounter with reality is always mediated by the character of the cognitive apparatus through which we come to apprehend it. We can never escape from the shaping, limiting influence of our own interpretations. Thus we are condemned to see the world from one particular perspective: 'There is *only* a perspective seeing, *only* a perspective knowing; and the *more* affects we allow to speak about one thing, the *more* eyes, different eyes, we can use to observe one thing, the more complete will our "concept" of this thing, our "objectivity", be.'[38]

In advancing this view, Nietzsche, it should be noted, has not simply denied the truth of traditional philosophical treatments of the problem of knowledge; he has asserted a position of his own (to deny perspective, he says, 'means standing truth on her head'[39]). Yet how can he claim that perspectivism is true? Two objections present themselves. In order to establish the truth of

[37] *On the Genealogy of Morals*, in *On the Genealogy of Morals and Ecce Homo*, trans. R. J. Hollingdale and W. Kaufmann (New York, 1969), III. 12.

[38] Ibid.

[39] *Beyond Good and Evil*, trans. R. J. Hollingdale (Harmondsworth, 1973) preface, p. 14.

perspectivism, would we not require some vantage-point from which we could determine that ours is only one perspective amongst many? But, beyond that, is it even meaningful for Nietzsche to talk about 'truth' in relation to a philosophical position? If all our assertions are just assertions made from a particular perspective, does that not undermine the force of the concept of truth itself (which implies, one might think, that the content of our assertion corresponds to the way that reality, determinately, is)? In many passages Nietzsche himself does not appear to shirk this consequence:

> What is truth? A mobile army of metaphors, metonymies, anthropomorphisms—in short, a sum of human relations which, poetically and rhetorically intensified, become transposed and adorned and which, after long usage by a people, seem fixed, canonical and binding on them. Truths are illusions which one has forgotten *are* illusions, worn-out metaphors which have become powerless to affect the sense, coins which have their obverse effaced and are now no longer of account as coins but merely as metal.[40]

Yet can any scepticism consistently go so far? It may seem that a scepticism so radical as to call into question the concept of truth itself must be self-undermining. Arthur Danto expresses the apparent dilemma forcefully:

> was it [Nietzsche's] intention, in saying that nothing is true, to say something true? If he succeeded, then of course he failed, for if it is true that nothing is true then something is true after all. If it is false, then something again is true. If, again, what he says is as arbitrary as he has said, critically, that all of philosophy is, why should we accept him if we are to reject the others?[41]

It is possible, however, to reconstruct Nietzsche's position in such a way that it is at least not corrosively paradoxical. To explain how, let us start by noting that when we say of a proposition that it is true we mean (at least) two different things. (1) We are, in the first place, *commending* the proposition in question: it is the sort of thing that it is good to believe. But, more than that, (2) we are also conveying to our hearer something about the reason why it is a good thing to believe—namely, because it expresses the way that the world is.

Now Nietzsche's fundamental claim is that (2) is mistaken. Since, according to perspectivism, we do not have access to the way that the world ultimately is, it follows that it could not possibly be the ground according to which we establish the validity of beliefs. But this does not mean that the concept of truth has been entirely abandoned: that one belief is simply as good as another in Nietzsche's view. Nietzsche can still retain the concept of the true as what it is 'good to believe' whilst disputing the traditional interpretation of why it is good to believe it. The Oxford philosopher, John Mackie, in his book *Ethics: Inventing Right and Wrong*,[42] famously puts forward what he calls an 'error theory' of

[40] 'On Truth and Lie in an Extra-Moral Sense', in *Friedrich Nietzsche: Werke*, ed. K. Schlechta (Frankfurt, n.d.), iii. 314.

[41] A. Danto, *Nietzsche as Philosopher* (New York, 1980), 230.

[42] (Harmondsworth, 1977).

morality. According to him, we naturally (but falsely) believe that moral properties are a part of objective reality, when, in fact, they are subjective. In a similar spirit, we might say that Nietzsche has an 'error theory' of truth: when we say of a proposition that it is true we naturally, but falsely, believe that its value consists in its articulating the nature of the one true world. There is nothing inconsistent in this position.

Somewhat confusingly, however, Nietzsche sometimes chooses to make this point the other way round: retaining the concept of truth as correspondence to the world, but denying that this is what it is good to believe. Thus when he writes: 'The falseness of a judgement is to us not necessarily an objection to it: it is here that our new language perhaps sounds strangest'[43] we can interpret him as follows. A proposition may be worth believing (it may embody that part of the concept of truth) *even if* it cannot meet the standard of representing the world as it really is (it is, in that sense, false). Nevertheless, that cannot be the end of the matter, for when he describes perspectivism as true, however, it seems clear that Nietzsche is straightforwardly commending it.

What, then, for Nietzsche, makes a proposition good to believe, if not the simple fact that it corresponds to the way that the world is? The answer to this has, in my view, two parts. The first, and most familiar, is that we should ask of any proposition (as, indeed, of other products of our minds): What is its value for those who hold it?, noting that, for Nietzsche, that value is not to be confused with the utilitarian goal of maximizing pleasure or minimizing pain (a reduced conception of the human good for which Nietzsche felt loathing and contempt). Nietzsche's second idea, however, on my reading of him, is that beliefs that he claims to be true in the sense that he claims that perspectivism is true are (although he himself would not have used the word) rational beliefs, beliefs which there are good—impersonally good—reasons to hold. This interpretation will strike many readers of Nietzsche as very odd, not least because, if beliefs are not justified by being shown to correspond to the way that things are, what other kind of good reasons could there be in their favour?

To answer this sort of objection let us turn to the discussion in the third essay of *On the Genealogy of Morals* of the relationship between what Nietzsche calls the 'ascetic ideal' and the 'will to truth'. The 'ascetic ideal' embodies, he maintains, the mental impulse behind the Judaeo-Christian tradition; it represents an attempt to escape from the world by turning away from it and denying its value. Many similar accounts of Christianity are to be found elsewhere in Nietzsche's works, but in this case he turns the discussion towards some of Christianity's (apparently) most vigorous opponents: contemporary scientific materialists. Are these 'last idealists left among philosophers and scholars . . . the desired *opponents* of the ascetic ideal, the *counteridealists*?',[44] he asks. They are not, he

[43] *Beyond Good and Evil*, sect. 4, p. 17. [44] *Genealogy of Morals*, III. 24.

replies, for, so far from being free from all ideals, the scientific materialists themselves adhere to a form of the ascetic ideal: they '*still have faith in truth.*'[45] Appearances to the contrary, the will to truth is not opposed to the religious impulse that, on the face of it, would-be scientific materialism contradicts:

Everywhere [except in Nietzsche's own thought] that the spirit is strong, mighty, and at work without counterfeit today, it does without ideals of any kind—the popular expression for this abstinence is 'atheism'—*except for its will to truth*. But this will, this *remnant* of an ideal, is, if you will believe me, this [ascetic] ideal itself in its strictest, most spiritual formulation, esoteric through and through, with all external additions abolished, and thus not so much its remnant as its kernel.[46]

Nietzsche characterizes the ascetic faith in truth in various ways. It is a desire to be honest, a desire not to be deceived, to stand on solid ground, a search for foundations, for sufficient reasons; in modern terms, we might say, it is a commitment to critical rationality. Whilst Nietzsche criticizes its asceticism, he also plainly admires the faith in truth. His faith in truth makes the philosopher 'more rigid and unconditional than anyone', he writes.[47] But the value of the will to truth for Nietzsche depends upon its honesty ('All honour to the ascetic ideal *insofar as it is honest!* so long as it believes in itself and does not play tricks on us!'[48]) and the final test of that is its willingness to apply its critical standards to itself. It was its own impulse towards truthfulness that undermined the credibility of Christianity; and it is nothing but the will to truth that will lead to the overcoming of Christianity's philosophical legacy, the belief in a firm, unique foundation to our knowledge: 'All great things bring about their own destruction through an act of self-overcoming . . . After Christian morality has drawn one inference after another, it must end by drawing its *most striking inference*, its inference *against* itself; this will happen, however, when it poses the question "*what is the meaning of all will to truth?*" '[49]

Nietzsche's thought at this point embodies a form of what the Frankfurt School authors, Adorno and Horkheimer, were to describe as the 'dialectic of the Enlightenment'. Initially, Enlightenment, in the form of philosophy, turns its standards of rationality against the world of myth and finds the latter wanting. Yet it is found to be reluctant to turn those standards on itself: the philosophers 'are all oblivious of how much the will to truth itself requires justification'.[50] When we see that the will to truth cannot meet its own central requirement Enlightenment is exposed as being itself a form of myth and a new question arises, according to Nietzsche, 'that of the *value* of truth'.[51]

Thus an important part of what makes something 'truthful' for Nietzsche, in the sense of being good to believe, is that it should be able to withstand the probing, critical activity of the will to truth. Yet philosophy, as traditionally

[45] *Genealogy of Morals*, III. 24. [46] Ibid. 27. [47] Ibid. 24.
[48] Ibid. 27. [49] Ibid. [50] Ibid. 24. [51] Ibid.

practised, fails its own test. Insofar as what is believed is the philosophical theory that beliefs are true if they can be established on a firm foundation then that belief itself falls to the force of criticism: the traditional concept of truth is, to that extent, untrue.

With this in mind, let us now return to what Nietzsche has to say about perspectivism. If Nietzsche is commending it by calling it 'true' (as he surely is) then this cannot be because it is something established from just the kind of vantage-point whose existence the doctrine denies. Nietzsche makes this point himself in a section of *The Gay Science* that he titles 'Our new "infinite"':

> Whether . . . all existence is not essentially actively engaged in *interpretation*—that cannot be decided even by the most industrious and most scrupulously conscientious analysis and self-examination of the intellect; for in the course of this analysis the human intellect cannot avoid seeing itself in its own perspective and *only* in these. We cannot look around our own corner: it is a hopeless curiosity that wants to know what other kinds of intellects and perspectives there *might* be; for example, whether some beings might be able to experience time backward, or alternately forward and backward (which would involve another direction of life and another concept of cause and effect).

It seems, rather, that Nietzsche believes that the grounds for the acceptance of perspectivism have something to do with the situation of modern man:

> But I should think that today we are at least far from the ridiculous immodesty that would be involved in decreeing from our corner that perspectives are permitted only from this corner. Rather has the world become 'infinite' for us all over again, inasmuch as we cannot reject the possibility that *it may include infinite interpretations*.[52]

In the light of what has been argued above, we may interpret this as follows: what makes perspectivism reasonable for us now is that the contrary view, the idea of 'perspectiveless seeing', has become a piece of 'ridiculous immodesty', shown to be unsustainable by philosophy's own critical standards, the 'will to truth'.

So far, we have discussed Nietzsche's view of philosophy as seen 'from the inside'. But this is only a part of his enterprise. Nietzsche is also concerned to place philosophy in context, to diagnose its place within the wider systems of human life and culture. These two aspects of Nietzsche's undertaking are not opposed to one another. On the contrary, the one leads to the other, in Nietzsche's view, since it is only from the wider point of view that we can answer the question which, according to Nietzsche, is raised by the internal development of philosophy: the question of the value of truth.

One of the clearest presentations of Nietzsche's views regarding the nature of the search for truth is to be found in his first book, *The Birth of Tragedy*. The book deals with its main subject, the nature of Greek tragedy, in the context of

[52] *The Gay Science* (New York, 1974), sect. 374, p. 336.

a remarkable diagnosis of the human condition. Nietzsche sees human culture as faced with an overriding standing problem: how to deal with the perennial fact of death and suffering (it is apparent here how much Nietzsche owed to Schopenhauer). Among the ancient Greeks Nietzsche identifies two kinds of response to suffering which he calls, famously, Dionysian and Apollonian. Put very briefly, they involve either intoxication or fantasy; self-abandonment or the imagination of another world. Nietzsche sees classic Greek tragedy as drawing on both these elements. Yet for our purposes it is a third impulse, the impulse which Nietzsche calls 'Socratism', which is significant. This, too, Nietzsche identifies as a response to suffering, one which is, indeed, powerful enough to undermine the Dionysian and Apollonian alternatives. It consists in the search for reasons: the desire to find an explanation for *this world*.

It is easy to see how Socratism provides a response to suffering when we see it in the context of Christianity (or other forms of monotheism). If we can explain that suffering, death and other apparent evils have their origin in the will of an omnipotent (and benevolent) being then, of course, we have given a reason to accept that suffering. But Nietzsche's point is more radical. It is not just explanations that relate events back to a benevolent being that are consoling; even impersonal explanations can console us by at least making the world appear to be governed by a comprehensible necessity. Thus 'stoicism'—the desire to understand the anonymous necessity of the universe and to submit oneself to it—is, for Nietzsche, an important form of the Socratic impulse. Although he was later to criticize some of the specific positions that he adopted in *The Birth of Tragedy*, his account of Socratism as a response to suffering is plainly the ancestor of his later account of the ascetic ideal and the will to truth. Thus he writes at the end of the third essay of *The Genealogy of Morals*:

> Apart from the ascetic ideal, man, the human *animal*, had no meaning so far . . . Man, the bravest of animals and the one most accustomed to suffering, does *not* repudiate suffering as such; he *desires* it, he even seeks it out, provided he is shown a meaning for it, a purpose of suffering. The meaninglessness of suffering, not suffering itself, was the curse that lay over mankind so far—and the ascetic ideal offered man meaning![53]

In *The Birth of Tragedy* Nietzsche diagnosed the end of Socratism as having been brought about by its own corrosive internal momentum. Specifically, he attributes to Kant and Schopenhauer the philosophical achievement of having shown Socratism's limitations. In its place, he announces a 'rebirth of tragedy' which will, he hopes, move beyond the limitations of the purely theoretical attitude which had dominated European culture in the two millennia since Socrates. Later, Nietzsche was to regard this view as hopelessly naive. Yet the cultural problem, as he sees it, remains essentially the same: how to deal with the fact that the will to truth—the ascetic ideal—has reached its limits.

[53] *Genealogy of Morals*, III. 28.

Nietzsche is haunted by the idea that, with the demise of the ascetic ideal, Western culture may collapse into a kind of paralysed melancholia which he calls 'nihilism': The ascetic ideal 'was the only meaning offered so far; any meaning is better than none at all . . . In it, suffering was *interpreted*; the tremendous void seemed to have been filled; the door was closed to any kind of suicidal nihilism.'[54] It is in this context that we should see the point of many of the most striking aspects of his writing: his rhetorical presentation of himself as the lonely prophet, the Anti-Christ, Zarathustra, the advocate of the Eternal Return, the revaluer of all values. In each case, we may say, Nietzsche is trying to provide an alternative to the demoralizing effects of the collapse of Christianity—to the loss of cogency of the drive that lies behind established religious institutions and which, appearances to the contrary, also animates the apparently 'secular' and 'scientific' alternatives to Christianity.

In conclusion, then, we may say that Nietzsche's appropriation of Kant leads him to a radical critique of philosophy and its relation to society. Philosophy, when pushed to its limit, undermines itself to the extent that it can no longer continue to exist as an independent discipline, aiming at objective knowledge. What the critique of philosophy calls into question—our belief that knowledge of the world can be given a firm and determinate foundation—is just as central to the natural sciences, however, so, their own self-understanding to the contrary, the sciences do not represent a real alternative to the discredited world-views of religion and metaphysics. To recognize that philosophy is incapable of providing timeless, objective knowledge is to recognize its embeddedness in history. But this is not to establish history as the master discipline that can offer us a perspective-free vantage-point; our grasp of history is always itself only interpretation from a perspective. Finally, we must understand that philosophy, even (indeed, especially) when it pretends to be objective and impersonal, is part of a drive to make sense of the world, to give it value for individuals. Even if we accept that the philosophical strategy of giving meaning to the world by making it intelligible has come to an end, Nietzsche believes, the need to give value to the world remains.

5. HUSSERL

We have characterized the Continental tradition in philosophy as 'post-Kantian' in the sense that its leading figures are best understood in terms of a legacy of issues inherited from Kant's critical philosophy. Edmund Husserl represents a partial exception to this. The reasons lie in Husserl's philosophical background. Husserl came to philosophy late, having originally studied mathematics, and his

[54] Ibid.

training in philosophy took place under Franz Brentano, an important and original thinker but one whose approach was at odds with the dominant trends in the German philosophy of his day.

Husserl's first writings were concerned with two issues which are, in fact, more closely associated with the analytic tradition than the Continental: the nature of a priori knowledge (and of mathematical knowledge in particular) and the possibility of giving a philosophical account of the structure of judgement. These issues were also preoccupying the acknowledged founder of analytic philosophy, Husserl's near-contemporary, Gottlob Frege (indeed, it seems that Frege's sharp criticisms of Husserl's early views of mathematics were important in pushing the latter towards his mature position). Both philosophers believed that any adequate account of thought must draw a clear distinction between the content of thought, on the one hand, and the process of thinking, on the other, and that, whilst the former was the proper concern of philosophy, the latter was a matter for psychology. To fail to make such a distinction was to commit the error of 'psychologism'.

But, despite their agreement on this important point, the difference between Husserl and Frege remains fundamental. Frege believes, first, that language is primarily a public institution, and, secondly, that language is prior to (in the sense that it gives significance to) thought. From which it follows, for Frege, that the private character of thought—the fact that it takes place for each of us individually, 'in our heads'—is actually its least interesting or philosophically important feature. For Husserl, on the other hand, philosophy itself consists in a certain 'turn inwards', a reflexive self-examination on the part of the thinker, but one which focuses on those aspects of thought that are necessary and structural to the exclusion of those which are merely contingent.

It could be said that all of Husserl's voluminous writings are nothing but a repeated series of attempts to explicate and defend the idea of phenomenology (the title, incidentally, of one of his books) and so it is here that we shall start. The word 'phenomenology' itself had been used in a number of senses prior to Husserl, all of which denote in one way or another a study based on appearances (thus, according to Hegel, the *Phenomenology of Spirit* is supposed to present the forms of appearance of consciousness that lead to the emergence of philosophical science). Husserl makes two important statements regarding his own conception of phenomenology: first of all, that it is 'descriptive' and, secondly, that it involves a suspension of judgement, a 'bracketing' of the empirical beliefs that we hold (either explicitly or tacitly) about the world.

An immediate objection presents itself. If phenomenology simply describes the contents of consciousness—the way that the world is given—it would appear to exclude from the outset the most philosophically important questions: for example, whether we have any warrant for believing that something exists outside our consciousness or whether it is possible to provide any justifications for our claims to knowledge. In which case, the great ambitions that Husserl has for phenomenology—that it should embody a revolution in philosophical method which will establish the status of philosophy as a science—appear quite unjustified. Phenomenology, if one follows this objection, is no more than an exercise in empirical psychological description.

We may present Husserl's response to this objection in two stages. First of all, he would argue, we must not misunderstand what he means by 'description'. On a certain conception of things (which to philosophers of an empiricist bent may seem to be no more than 'common sense') to describe is simply to record whatever happens to be there; it carries no further implication regarding what there might or must be. This does indeed seem to be a fair account of our empirical practice of describing the world. But it would be a mistake, according to Husserl (one form of the mistake of 'psychologism', in fact) to assume that descriptions of our mental life must have the same character. Insofar as descriptions are descriptions of features of thought that have general or relational characteristics, they can indeed be necessary and structural, in Husserl's view.

What sorts of thing form the subject-matter of such descriptions? This question brings us to the second stage of the response that we might attribute to Husserl, his rejection of a picture of mental life (a picture derived in part from the legacy of empiricist philosophy, in part from the attempt to apply the methods of physics to psychology) that he considers to be fundamentally misguided. According to this received view, the basic constituents of the mind are a collection of independent mental items. Although each of these mental items ('ideas', as they are usually called in the empiricist tradition) is intrinsically particular, it has the power of being associated with other items, whether by being 'bundled together' to form single complex objects, or by being ordered into sequences according to laws. The contents of consciousness have no existence outside consciousness on this view: their being consists simply in their presence to consciousness. Consciousness itself is conceived as a kind of invisible screen, something to which contents are given but which is itself without content.

This sketch of the received view is, of course, a caricature. Nevertheless, it has value in providing us with a sharply contrasting background against which to focus Husserl's own view of the mind. Husserl can be said to reject the received view at five crucial points.

1. *Simplicity versus relation*. On the received view, the fundamental constituents of the mind are like atoms: individual and not further divisible. Against this, Husserl believes that the 'objects' that phenomenology describes are complex, in the sense that, although they have internal structures, they are not capable of being analytically decomposed into self-subsistent elements.

2. *Particularity versus generality*. Similarly, the received view supposes that the contents of the mind are particular. Husserl, by contrast, claims that phenomenological objects are, as he calls it, 'eidetic'; that is, that they have essences—ones that they are capable of revealing when subjected to philosophical inspection.

3. *Immediacy versus intentionality*. For the received view, as we have described it, consciousness is a kind of screen whose sole function is to be that *to which* items are given. For Husserl, on the other hand, consciousness is active and this activity has a structure which (following Brentano) Husserl calls 'intentionality'. Intentionality, Husserl claims, is 'the unique peculiarity of experience to be "the consciousness *of* something" '.[55] In other words, mental life does not simply consist in a series of self-contained events; those events have *content*.

4. *Givenness versus reflection*. Any reasonable picture of the mind must be able to account for the fact that we do not just have experiences; we also have thoughts about those experiences—and, indeed, thoughts about our thoughts. Notoriously, however, the received view finds it difficult to give an account of such reflexive thoughts. For Husserl, on the other hand, it is intrinsic to the nature of our mental acts that we should be capable of becoming conscious of them, and that this becoming conscious should itself be a possible subject for further consciousness.

5. *Transparency versus differential givenness*. For Husserl, as for the received view, to experience is to be conscious. But there is also an important difference. On the received view, if an item is given to consciousness then the thinker is aware of it, just as it is. Husserl's view, on the other hand, is that not everything that is perceivable in principle is, in fact, perceived at any one time:

> We see that *it is the intrinsic nature of experience to be perceivable through reflection*. Things also are *perceivable*, on principle, and in perception they are apprehended as things of the world that surround me. Thus they too belong to this world without being perceived, they are thus *there for the Ego even then*.[56]

Thus consciousness, for Husserl, is a matter of light and shade rather than perfect self-transparency (although that does, indeed, remain the ideal).

From this background we can assess the objectives that Husserl sets for phenomenology and the methods by which he hopes to achieve them. Phenomenology, in Husserl's view, is to be an a priori science, directed towards what is essential in our thinking. 'Essence' here, it should be noted, does not signify (as one would normally suppose) simply what our different thoughts have in common. The *eidos* of a thought is, Husserl says, its *meaning*: whatever it is that makes that thought the thought that it is.

As for the method of phenomenology, it depends, Husserl believes, on a special kind of insight or intuition, an ability to grasp 'eidetic truth', as he calls it.

[55] E. Husserl, *Ideas*, trans. W. R. Boyce Gibson (New York, 1962), 223. [56] Ibid. 129.

Although this capacity is not something with which only a few, privileged individuals are endowed, its significance has not been appreciated until now. The reason, Husserl argues, is that the importance of phenomenological understanding has been obscured by the domination over our intellectual life of two other powerful paradigms of knowledge: the formal methods of mathematics and the observationally based practices of the natural sciences.

What is necessary in order to engage in phenomenology is a kind of ground-clearing that will enable us to focus directly on what is at issue. Husserl calls this process the 'phenomenological reduction' and it is, by common consent, one of the most obscure features of his work. The basic thought is this. The subject-matter of phenomenology, according to Husserl, is the object 'in the manner of its givenness', and to attend to this requires that we should examine our thoughts without reference either to the state of the world or to the particular psychological states or attitudes of the thinker who thinks them. We are supposed to 'bracket' or 'suspend' those aspects of our thoughts that involve commitments regarding the nature of empirical reality; this suspension

> is not a transformation of the thesis into its antithesis; of positive into negative; it is also not a transformation into presumption, suggestion, indecision, doubt (in one or another sense of the word) . . . And yet the thesis undergoes a modification—whilst remaining in itself what it is, *we set it as it were 'out of action'*, we *'disconnect it'*, *'bracket it'* . . . We can also say: The thesis is experienced as lived (*Erlebnis*), *but we make no use of it.*[57]

Thus purged, the essential aspects of the thought in question will 'emerge' in response to the phenomenologist's investigation.

But there is a very serious problem with this idea. It is easy enough, of course, to suspend some particular belief about the world. Husserl, however, wants us to suspend *all* our beliefs about the world while at the same time maintaining the content of our thought. There are very strong reasons for thinking that this is impossible. On the most plausible view, the very content of many of our thoughts depends on beliefs about the world, in such a way that if we were to suspend those beliefs then we would alter the content of the thoughts in question. Consider the following. When I look out of my window I see my next-door neighbours' house. I see it *as* my neighbours' house; that is, I don't just have a mental image. I see it as something that is made of bricks and stone, is suitable for being lived in, has its kitchen at the back, is lived in by Ros and David, and so on. These are all beliefs about the world that go into my understanding of the house as I see it. How could I 'bracket' those beliefs and still go on seeing it in the way that I do? The only way for that to be possible would be if I were able to make a distinction and say that these beliefs are not *part of* what I see but beliefs *about* what I see. But then what would remain that I could be

[57] Ibid. 97–8.

said to see? The only answer seems to be that what I would see would be some kind of perceptual image, bare of all the judgements and pre-conceptions associated with it. Yet that cannot be Husserl's view, for that would return phenomenology to just the kind of empiricist picture of the mind that he so vehemently rejects—the idea that what is given to us in experience is a series of bare sensible particulars. Husserl might be thought to recognize this problem when he claims in the passage quoted above that 'the thesis [that is, our beliefs about the reality that we experience] is experienced as lived, *but we make no use of it*'. Yet (as is typical of his writing) this is not so much a counter-argument on Husserl's part as an assertion—and a wholly implausible one at that: surely it is simply wrong to say that when I see the Houses of Parliament as the Houses of Parliament I am 'making no use' of my belief that what is in front of me is the building in which Parliament meets.

Phenomenology faces many other difficulties and objections. Husserl, especially in his earlier writings, describes the objective of phenomenology to be the study of 'logic' and 'meaning'. Later, he starts to use Kantian terminology and to speak of this as the study of 'transcendental logic' and of revealing the 'constituting' function of consciousness in the origin of meaning. Analytical philosophers will object that the study of meaning is senseless except as part of the study of a social institution: language. Even those who are not committed to this view might still doubt how helpful it is to think of meaning as having its origin in some constituting process. It seems as though Husserl is thereby raising again all of the most acute difficulties of the Kantian doctrine without allowing himself even Kant's own (admittedly dubious) solution: the transcendental-psychological doctrine of synthesis. To this objection the phenomenologist can, of course, always reply that those who doubt phenomenology's ability to give an account of transcendental processes are merely expressing their own inability to attain the level of phenomenological reflection. But this reply, common though it is, is by no means satisfactory—it reminds one all too much of the tailors' reply to those who objected that they could not see the emperor's new clothes. Even if we are too unintelligent to see them ourselves, we would still like to have some good reason to believe that they are there.

Yet, in conclusion, it is not right to dwell on the objectionable features of Husserl's philosophy in assessing his importance. While Husserl's philosophy now has only a few devotees (who make up in zeal for what they lack in numbers) his influence on the tradition of Continental philosophy has been much broader. It can be seen, I suggest, in three main ways.

1. *The anti-empiricist view of the mind*. Whilst the empiricist conception of the mind as a collection of discrete items, pushed together and pulled apart by a kind of mental gravity, still haunts analytic philosophy, Husserl and Brentano can be said to have laid it to rest in the Continental tradition. If anything, it is the

opposite doctrine—the idea of the mind as an independent self-knower—that has been made into an unquestioned dogma, particularly amongst German philosophers.

2. *Anti-positivism*. Closely associated with this empiricist view, have been a series of attempts (going back all the way to the seventeenth-century distinction between primary and secondary qualities) to distinguish between 'real' and only 'apparently objective' aspects of what we experience. The basis for such a distinction, Continental philosophers argue, following Husserl, always comes back to the superimposition on the experienced 'life-world' of an account based upon the natural sciences and the claim that it is only those features that figure in that latter account that have the highest degree of reality. This dogma they most vehemently reject.

3. *A priori knowledge*. Finally, and perhaps most seductively, there is Husserl's claim that it is possible to develop philosophical knowledge that is both (in some sense) necessary and, at the same time, derived from the world as it is experienced. To philosophers brought up in a tradition saturated with empiricist and positivist assumptions such a claim will, no doubt, seem bizarre. On this view, it seems evident that what is given to the senses is particular; if there are 'necessary connections' in the world, these are discovered and tested by the investigations of science, not the reflections of the philosopher. But, against this, the Continental philosopher will argue that what we are dealing with here is the life-world, and it is simply a positivist prejudice to assume that what is true of the world as described for us by science is also true of the world as we live it. If that is so, then it may be possible to find internal connections between parts of our experience purely by philosophical reflection on the way that that experience presents itself to us.

6. HEIDEGGER

Heidegger was Husserl's chosen successor: his most brilliant pupil and later his colleague at Freiburg. Indeed, *Being and Time*, Heidegger's masterpiece, is dedicated to Husserl 'in friendship and admiration'. Yet by the time that Husserl died his attitude towards Heidegger was one of bitter disappointment. There are two reasons for this. The first is personal and political. When the Nazis came to power, Heidegger identified himself closely with the new regime: he became the Rector of Freiburg University and joined the Nazi Party. At the same time, he broke off relations with Husserl who, in consequence of his Jewish background, had been forbidden to teach at the university and was subject to monstrous harassment. But the rift between the two men also had an intellectual aspect. At the start of his career, Heidegger was evidently reluctant to allow the depth of his philosophical disagreements with Husserl to become apparent. He presented *Being and Time,* at least superficially, as a continuation and application of phenomenology. Thus in the Introduction to *Being and Time* Heidegger writes at one point: 'Only as phenomenology is ontology possible.'[58] But a careful reader will soon see that this is rather misleading. Had Heidegger been less concerned to preserve good relations with Husserl, he might have put it the other way around; 'only as ontology is phenomenology possible' would be a better expression of his position. Ontology, as Heidegger understands it, is intended to displace phenomenology as advocated by Husserl.

What is ontology? For traditional philosophy, the answer is rather simple: it is the study of what there is. The sort of questions that ontology addresses are: Are there universals? Are numbers real? and so on. In modern philosophy, ontology has been seen as a branch of philosophy subordinate to epistemology—for how could we settle questions about what there is without having previously settled the question of what we can know? Yet Heidegger, so far from accepting ontology's subordinate role, believes that the revival of ontology and its associated question, the question of Being (*Seinsfrage*) is the key to the renewal of philosophy. Ontology is, Heidegger goes so far as to claim, 'more primordial' than the empirical sciences themselves.[59] Clearly, his conception of ontology must be very different from the received view. If we understand that conception and the critique of the received view that it contains we will have the key to the understanding of *Being and Time*—indeed, of Heidegger's philosophy as a whole.

Traditional ontology, in Heidegger's view, rests on a mistake. At least since the Presocratics, philosophers have approached the ontological question as if it were a form of the question: What sorts of things are there? In Heidegger's famous expression, the question of Being has been reduced to the question of what there is. Thus whatever philosophers have come up with as ultimately real—substances, matter, atoms, events, universals, modes, entities, categories, classes, even consciousness, representations, or ideas—are tacitly assumed to have this positive, thinglike nature. Even if, like Plato's Ideas, the entities in question are supposed to be outside time, they are conceived of as being in some way 'present': 'Entities are grasped in their Being as "presence"; this means that they are understood with regard to a definite mode of time—the "Present"'.[60]

Like Plato (and Hegel and Wittgenstein, for that matter) Heidegger sees philosophy as an exercise in bringing to awareness something that is, in a sense, already known. A grasp of the 'Being of what there is' (*das Sein des Seienden*) is sedimented, Heidegger claims, in our language and is implicit in the attitudes we take up towards the world. And yet philosophical understanding is made dif-

[58] M. Heidegger, *Being and Time*, trans. J. Macquarrie and E. Robinson (Oxford, 1967), 60.
[59] Ibid. 31. [60] Ibid. 47.

ficult because this 'ontological' comprehension has been consistently misconstrued. A kind of preconception has become overlaid on the understanding of Being, and Being is thereby made into something objectified and thinglike. This is what makes the task of renewing ontology so pressing: 'The very fact that we already live in an understanding of Being and that the meaning of Being is still veiled in darkness proves that it is necessary in principle to raise this question again.'[61]

The mistake is built into our language. The very word 'what' in the apparently innocuous question: What is there? reaches out for the wrong kind of answer. So long as ontology is a matter of 'what there is', it will appear to be no more than an extension of the scientific enterprise of identifying and classifying reality—an attempt, like the sciences, to say what reality is composed of, but simply carried out at a higher level of abstraction and generality. Yet, for Heidegger, this sort of classifying activity is not ontological but 'ontic' and the two must not under any circumstances be confused.

For Heidegger, the confusion of the ontological and the ontic is itself a consequence of ontological misunderstanding: the fact that we impose a single ontological model on reality, thereby distorting its character. When I look at the pen on my desk, I classify it in certain ways: it is blue, cylindrical, spatiotemporally extended, an artefact, a tool for writing. Yet, Heidegger believes, the knowledge of the pen that I have on the basis of observation is different from my ontological pre-understanding; indeed, the former always takes place informed by the latter. But when (to use Heidegger's own language) the Being of an entity is itself made into an entity (that is, when we think of the entity's ontological character as if it were simply a further category under which to classify the object) we lose sight in consequence of the distinctiveness of ontological understanding.

Bearing this in mind, several of the most striking features of Heidegger's philosophy become more comprehensible. There is the fact, for instance (apparent to even the most casual reader), that *Being and Time* makes use of a philosophical vocabulary largely of Heidegger's own invention. But this is not just wilful obscurity (or megalomania) on Heidegger's part. The inherited vocabulary of philosophy is, he believes, so saturated with ontological misunderstanding that the only alternative is to start again, as far as possible. Nor is it just in its vocabulary that Heidegger's philosophy is different from traditional philosophical discourse. If Being is not to be reified into an entity, it must, Heidegger says, 'be exhibited in a way of its own'.[62] Any attempt to express insight into the nature of Being in conventional propositional form risks distorting it: 'Whenever a phenomenological concept is drawn from primordial sources there is a possibility that it may degenerate if communicated in the form of an assertion.'[63]

[61] Ibid. 23. [62] Ibid. 26. [63] Ibid. 60–1.

We can see too why *Being and Time* at once resembles and differs from a traditional exercise in ontology. To the extent that *Being and Time* is attempting to provide a comprehensive account of the structure of reality it resembles traditional ontology. Where the traditional ontologist sought to divide Being into 'categories', Heidegger, correspondingly, tries to identify structures that he calls 'existentials'. On the other hand, Heidegger's conception of ontology's status is very unconventional. Whilst the traditional ontologist had thought of ontology as an exercise in transcending the limits of the human understanding to attain the truth about a timeless realm of 'Being in itself', Heidegger regards this way of conceiving the enterprise as misguided. Heideggerian ontology is directed towards the understanding of Being possessed by the thinking first person—Dasein, in Heidegger's technical language. Dasein is concerned with the nature of Being not just because it (like everything else) 'has' Being. Dasein is distinguished: 'by the fact that in its very Being, that *Being* is an issue for it . . . Dasein is actually distinctive in that it *is* ontological.'[64] Yet the fact that Being is always Being-for-Dasein should not be understood as implying that, for Heidegger, the study of ontology is something that is only limited and subjective. On the contrary, Heidegger would argue, the idea of 'subjectivity' as something that only gives us a partial view of a wider, subject-independent truth is itself a typical example of how false ontologies pervert philosophical understanding.

The ontological mode that, according to Heidegger, lies behind much of our ontological misunderstanding is what he calls 'Vorhandenheit'—translated as 'presence-at-hand'. This is, of course, a Heideggerian term of art, but it carries important resonances. There is, in particular, a close affinity with the Kantian (and Hegelian and Schopenhauerian) term 'Vorstellung' (representation): *Vorstellungen* are what are 'placed before' the mind; *Vorhandenheit* is the quality of being present-in-front-of. The idea of presence-at-hand is very closely connected to the conventional notion of an object in space; things that are present-at-hand are salient, unified, objective occupiers of a single location. Now it should be noted that presence-at-hand, for Heidegger, is not simply an illusion: it is one of the existentials that form the structure of Being. What is to be criticized is an ontological preconception that extends presence-at-hand beyond its proper scope and uses it as a model for the nature of reality in general.

In allowing the present-at-hand to dominate, we neglect, according to Heidegger, another way in which we have access to the world, an attitude towards reality in which things are not just salient objects and do not present themselves as differentiated spatial items. This is the mode that Heidegger calls *Zuhandenheit*—translated as 'ready-to-handness'; what we have access to in this way are not 'objects' but what he calls 'equipment' (*Zeug*). Equipment is not a different kind of thing but, we might say, things encountered in a different way:

[64] M. Heidegger, *Being and Time*, 32.

'In our dealings we come across equipment for writing, sewing, working, transportation, measurement.'[65] When we are concerned with things in this way, our engagement does not allow for the traditional differentiation of subject and object: our attitude towards them is (to use words that Heidegger certainly would not) immediate and unreflective. For those who hold traditional views of ontology, such things are, at best, ontologically secondary—this table, for instance, they might say, is 'really' a piece of wood. But Heidegger would reject this as a concealed piece of prejudice (why should we consider that whatever accounts for something's physical make-up is what it 'really' is?). Indeed, there is a sense in which, for Heidegger, the ready-to-hand has priority over the present-at-hand, for it is only when the immediate engagement characteristic of the ready-to-hand is in some way broken or disrupted that the present-at-hand comes on the scene: 'But the ready-to-hand is not thereby just *observed* and stared at as something present-at-hand; the presence-at-hand which makes itself known is still bound up in the readiness-to-hand of equipment.'[66]

Conceiving objects as solely present-at-hand leads to important further consequences, however. In the first place, in Heidegger's view, it goes together with a misleading, simplistic conception of knowledge. Heidegger claims that the Greeks had two words for knowing: *legein*—the word for 'know' in a sentence like 'I know that the train will be late'—and *noein*, a kind of knowing which takes a direct accusative, as in 'I know Jones'.[67] According to Heidegger, it is this latter conception of knowledge that has, perniciously, come to dominate our view of the relationship between mind and world, with the effect that knowing is thought of on the analogy with mental vision: 'Under the unbroken ascendance of the traditional ontology, the way to get a genuine grasp of what really is has been decided in advance: it lies in *noein*—intuition in the widest sense.'[68] Putting the two prejudices together—the conception of the world as present-at-hand and the idea of knowing as *noein*—leads, Heidegger asserts, to a flattened conception of knowledge and perception. On the contrary, he maintains, all perception has an interpretative quality (what Husserl would have called 'intentionality') to which accounts of knowledge based on the traditional ontology cannot do justice.

Finally, the traditional ontology leads, in Heidegger's view, to a misconception of the self itself. Insofar as it is supposed to be the function of the self to intuit ('be conscious of') present-at-hand things, Dasein itself comes to be thought of as presence-at-hand, a characterization that is, Heidegger says, 'essentially inappropriate to entities of Dasein's character'.[69] Not surprisingly perhaps, for Heidegger, the prime example of this way of conceiving the mind

[65] Ibid. 97. [66] Ibid. 104.

[67] Many experts believe that this philological claim of Heidegger's is, in fact, highly dubious. *Legein*, they point out, means 'say' or 'tell', rather than 'know'.

[68] Ibid. 129. [69] Ibid. 67.

is Descartes: 'With the "*cogito sum*" Descartes had claimed that he was putting philosophy on a new and firm footing. But what he left undetermined when he began in the "radical" way, was the kind of Being which belongs to the *res cogitans*, or—more precisely—the meaning of the Being of the "*sum*" '.[70] Descartes is most commonly represented as a revolutionary whose ideas mark a radical break in the history of philosophy. But for Heidegger it is the continuity that he finds in Descartes with the traditional, received conception of the ontological primacy of the present-at-hand that is the most significant feature of Descartes's philosophy.

I have explained that, for Heidegger, ontology has priority over epistemology, rather than the other way round. We are now in a better position to understand the reasons why he takes this view. In short, it is because he rejects the epistemological project. Heidegger believes that, as they are commonly conceived, the problems that epistemology sets for itself are incapable of solution (or lead to wholly implausible philosophical doctrines) because the terms in which they are posed themselves contain misguided ontological commitments. Thus Heidegger does not set out to answer the questions of epistemology in their own terms but to reveal, criticize, and disarm the motivations which lie behind them.

It is easy to see how the standard epistemological difficulties regarding the relationship between mind and the world arise. If we grant that we only have direct knowledge of what is given to us in consciousness then it seems that we are facing an alternative: either our knowledge of objects is indirect or (all natural belief to the contrary) what we call 'objects' are really just items in our consciousness. One way of challenging this way of looking at things is particularly associated with Kant. In the Refutation of Idealism of the *Critique of Pure Reason*, Kant calls into question the contrast between the 'direct' knowledge that we have of our own mental states and the 'indirect' knowledge that we have of non-mental reality. He then goes on to argue that, since knowledge of our own mental states in fact depends on our knowledge of non-mental reality, there is no reason to think that the latter is in some sense secondary or derivative. But Heidegger is dissatisfied with Kant's solution: 'It seems at first as if Kant has given up the Cartesian approach of positing a subject one can come across in isolation. But only in semblance. That Kant demands any proof at all for the "existence of things outside of me" shows already that he takes the subject—the "in me"—as the starting-point for this problematic.'[71]

Kant writes of the 'scandal' that philosophy still does not have a proof of the existence of the external world. For Heidegger, however, the scandal 'is not that this proof has yet to be given, but that *such proofs are expected and attempted again and again*.'[72] Such attempts, according to Heidegger: 'arise from

[70] M. Heidegger, *Being and Time*, 46.
[71] Ibid. 248. [72] Ibid. 249.

ontologically inadequate ways of starting with *something* of such a character that independently *of it* and "outside" *of it* a "world" is to be proved as present-at-hand'.[73]

But what is Heidegger's alternative? The best way to present his view is as a radicalization of Kant's doctrine of Transcendental Idealism. Kant had believed that objects cannot be given except in relation to some subject—all of the objects that we know are, he says, 'appearances'. Space and time, the forms of sense, are also, he says, 'in us'. Yet this does not mean, Kant claims, that we have to deny our ordinary beliefs about objects existing unperceived, for the sense in which space and time are said to be in us is a transcendental one. Transcendental idealism, for Kant, is thus quite compatible with empirical realism. Although the language that he uses is very different, Heidegger, to the extent that he believes that Being is always Being-for-Dasein, could be said to endorse this position. Where he parts company sharply with Kant, however, is in rejecting the fact that Kant associates transcendental idealism with an account of the way in which we perceive—the picture of the mind imposing its own order on whatever is given to it through the senses. To include such doctrines, Heidegger believes, is to contaminate philosophy with concerns that are, ultimately, psychological. It is when idealism is interpreted in this latter way that it leads to paradoxical claims (for example, the idea that the world is 'in our heads'): 'As compared with realism, *idealism*, no matter how contrary and untenable it may be in its results, has an advantage in principle, provided that it does not misunderstand itself as "psychological" idealism.'[74] In interpreting idealism in a 'non-psychological' way, however, Heidegger at the same time distances himself from the concerns of epistemology as most commonly understood. Such questions as: What form does the connection take between the mind and external reality? and: To what extent is the order that we find in our experience itself a product of our own activity? are not properly the concern of philosophy, in Heidegger's view. Thus we might say that Heidegger endorses idealism only in a rather negative sense; it is not so much an affirmative account of the nature of the relationship between mind and world as the negation of a certain (in Heidegger's view, misguided) view of it. To say that the world is 'ideal' means only that it is, essentially, *our world*, the world of experience, and that it is, as such, open to understanding.

It would be hard to exaggerate the significance that Heidegger has had—and continues to have—for modern Continental philosophy, in France, Germany, and elsewhere (his writings are extremely influential in the formerly Communist countries of Eastern Europe, Poland, and the Czech Republic in particular). Above all, his conception of the nature and scope of philosophy itself has proved to be of lasting importance. For Heidegger, the philosophical enterprise is not to be wound up or 'transcended' completely, as Nietzsche, for

[73] Ibid. [74] Ibid. 251.

example, or Marx appear to want. Yet nor does Heidegger believe that it is possible to attain the kind of timeless vantage-point and impersonal objectivity embodied in the traditional philosophical ideal. Philosophy takes as its subject-matter the world as we live in it—not some reduced description that corresponds to the account of the world that is given to us by science—and its most important sister disciplines are history and the study of literature rather than logic and the natural sciences. It is this view of philosophy as, broadly speaking, an exercise in historically limited cultural self-understanding that has become (if anything is) the orthodoxy amongst Continental philosophers in the late twentieth century.

BIBLIOGRAPHY

1. BACKGROUND

Richard Rorty, *Philosophy and the Mirror of Nature* (Princeton, 1979), Edward Craig, *The Mind of God and the Works of Man* (Oxford, 1987), and Ian Hacking, *Why does Language Matter to Philosophy?* (Cambridge, 1975) are three historical works that present philosophy—both analytical and Continental—not just as a self-contained argument but as incorporating ideas and assumptions from elsewhere in society. Each could serve as a useful introduction linking the two traditions. Julian Roberts, *German Philosophy: An Introduction* (Cambridge, 1988) is an excellent introduction to the main authors. The treatment of Kant is especially good. Frederick Beiser, *The Fate of Reason* (Cambridge, Mass., 1987), a study of the immediate responses in Germany to the *Critique of Pure Reason*, helps to explain why German Idealist philosophy came to take the form that it did. Jürgen Habermas, *Knowledge and Human Interests* (London, 1972) contains a highly influential neo-Marxist account of the development of Continental philosophy.

2. HEGEL

There is an excellent collection of short extracts from the writings of the German Idealists (Kant, Fichte, Schelling, Hegel) edited by Rüdiger Bubner, *German Idealist Philosophy* (Harmondsworth, 1997). Almost all of Hegel's major works are available complete in English translations. The 'Encyclopedia' Logic (*Hegel's Logic* (3rd edn. 1830), trans. William Wallace (Oxford, 1975)) is a good starting-point. Although Wallace makes rather freer with Hegel's words than would be considered acceptable nowadays, the result is splendidly readable. The translation of the *Phenomenology of Spirit* (1807) by A. V. Miller (Oxford, 1977) is extremely good, as is the same translator's version of the *Science of Logic* (1812–16; Oxford, 1969). The *Lectures on the History of Philosophy* is another of Hegel's more accessible works, but the translation (by E. Haldane and F. Simpson (London, 1892–6)) is now very hard to find. The introduction and prefaces to *The Lectures on the Philosophy of World History* and *The Philosophy of Right* (1821) (both trans. H. B. Nisbet (Cambridge, 1981 and 1990)) also contain important material on wider philosophical issues.

Charles Taylor's *Hegel* (Cambridge, 1975) remains the best comprehensive English-language treatment of Hegel. Frederick Beiser (ed.), *The Cambridge Companion to Hegel* (Cambridge, 1993) is an outstanding collection with an excellent bibliography. Studies that provide a counterpoint to Taylor include Robert Pippin, *Hegel's Idealism* (Cambridge, 1988), Michael Rosen, *Hegel's Dialectic and its Criticism* (Cambridge, 1982), and Robert Stern, *Hegel, Kant and the Structure of the Object* (London, 1990).

3. SCHOPENHAUER

Schopenhauer's major work is *The World as Will and Representation* (1818; trans. E. F. J. Payne (New York: Dover, 1969)). Schopenhauer himself claimed that *On the Fourfold Root of the Principle of Sufficient Reason* (1813; trans. E. F. J. Payne (La Salle, Ill., 1974)) was essential to its understanding.

Amongst the secondary literature, two books by Christopher Janaway stand out. *Schopenhauer*, in the Past Masters series (Oxford, 1994) is a model of what a short introduction to a philosopher should be: perceptive, authoritative, and beautifully written. *Self and World in Schopenhauer's Philosophy* (Oxford, 1989) deals with these central themes in greater depth but with equal clarity. Also recommended is John Atwell, *Schopenhauer on the Character of the World: The Metaphysics of the Will* (Berkeley, 1995).

4. NIETZSCHE

Most of Nietzsche's works are now available in English translations. The majority (including *The Birth of Tragedy* (1872), *The Gay Science* (1882; 2nd edn. 1887), *Beyond Good and Evil* (1886), *On the Genealogy of Morals* (1887), and the posthumous collection entitled *The Will to Power*) are published by Vintage Books, New York, in translations by Walter Kaufmann or by Kaufmann and R. J. Hollingdale. Others (including *Thus Spake Zarathustra* (1883–92) and *Twilight of the Idols* (1889)) are Penguin Classics, while *Human, All Too Human* (1878; 2nd edn. 1886) and *Daybreak* (1881; 2nd edn. 1886) are available from Cambridge University Press. *The Gay Science, Beyond Good and Evil*, and *On the Genealogy of Morals* would be a good starting-point for a philosophical study of Nietzsche. A translation of the important little essay 'On Truth and Lie in an Extramoral Sense' is to be found in *Philosophy and Truth: Selections from Nietzsche's Notebooks of the Early Seventies*, ed. D. Breazeale (Atlantic Highlands, NJ, 1979).

The Nietzsche literature in English is now extensive. Its quality, however, is variable. The following is a very brief selection. Alexander Nehamas, *Nietzsche: Life as Literature* (Cambridge, Mass., 1986) is the best recent book. Arthur Danto, *Nietzsche as Philosopher*, 2nd edn. (New York, 1980) is another excellent book. Maudemarie Clark, *Nietzsche on Truth and Philosophy* (Cambridge, 1990) is a significant attempt to give a general account of Nietzsche's view of truth. Henry Staten, *Nietzsche's Voice* (Ithaca, NY, 1990) takes a distinctive approach to understanding Nietzsche's writing from the inside.

5. HUSSERL

Husserl was an extremely prolific (not to say rather repetitious) writer. From the point of view of the present chapter his most important writings are the *Ideas* (1913; trans. W. R. Boyce Gibson (New York, 1962)) and *The Crisis of European Sciences and Transcendental Philosophy* (1936; trans. David Carr (Chicago, 1970)). The first is Husserl's most sustained presentation of what phenomenology might be, whilst the latter tries to use phenomenology to reflect on the intellectual situation of Europe in the 1930s. R. Solomon (ed.), *Phenomenology and Existentialism* (New York, 1972), a collection of extracts from Husserl and others, does an excellent job of presenting the main strands of the phenomenological tradition.

The best book on Husserl in English is David Bell, *Husserl* (London, 1989), an unusually clear, philosophically sophisticated, and outward-looking work. It is also highly critical. *The Cambridge Companion to Husserl*, edited by Barry Smith and David Woodruff Smith (Cambridge, 1995) is a collection of articles that are much more sympathetic to Husserl. It contains an extensive guide to the literature.

6. HEIDEGGER

Heidegger's masterpiece remains *Being and Time* (1927; trans. John Macquarrie and Edward Robinson (Oxford, 1967)). Many people find it helpful to read *The Basic Problems of Phenomenology* (1927; trans. Albert Hofstadter (Bloomington, Ind., 1982)) alongside *Being and Time*. These are lectures given by Heidegger in the 1920s and in some cases provide a more accessible treatment of topics to be found there. Of the later works, perhaps *What is Called Thinking?* (New York, 1968) is the most interesting for showing the development of Heidegger's thought after *Being and Time*. The collection edited by Solomon, mentioned in the previous section, is also recommended.

Arne Naess gives a sympathetic introduction to Heidegger in *Four Modern Philosophers* (Chicago, 1969). John Richardson, *Existential Epistemology* (Oxford, 1986) is an exceptionally lucid attempt to relate Heidegger to contemporary Anglo-American philosophy. Hubert Dreyfus, *Being-in-the-World* (Cambridge, Mass., 1991) is a helpful commentary on Division 1 of *Being and Time*. Michael Murray (ed.), *Heidegger and Modern Philosophy* (New Haven, 1978) is a very good collection of essays with a most helpful bibliography.

12

FREGE, RUSSELL, AND WITTGENSTEIN

A. C. Grayling and Bernhard Weiss

INTRODUCTION

Philosophical inquiry has developed in two dramatic ways during the last hundred years: more people are systematically studying the problems of philosophy than ever before, and they are doing so with greater technical expertise than ever before. These developments are particularly spectacular in 'analytic philosophy', the dominant philosophical tradition of the anglophone world. Among those who contributed to this tradition, three have been especially significant. They are Gottlob Frege, Bertrand Russell, and Ludwig Wittgenstein.

What follows introduces the principal ideas of these three thinkers. We assume that readers already have some grounding in philosophy in general, and in logic and philosophical logic in particular (as given, for example, by Mark Sainsbury's 'Philosophical Logic' in the companion to this volume, *Philosophy: A Guide through the Subject*). That is, we expect readers have already encountered some discussion of Frege, Russell, and Wittgenstein, and have at least a preliminary idea of their contributions to philosophy. Our aim here is to build on this acquaintance and to provide a more advanced introduction to their work.

The sections on Frege begin with his arguments against psychologism, and continue with a discussion of his *Begriffsschrift* and his essay 'Function and Concept'. This is followed by an examination of his ideas in *Die Grundlagen der Arithmetik* ('The Foundations of Arithmetic'), and the essay 'On Sense and Reference'. Frege's work is important for its technical innovations, and especially for its novel way of approaching epistemological and ontological problems through questions of meaning.

Russell, like Frege, attempted a 'logicist' philosophy of mathematics. But despite this similarity there are deep differences between them. Russell's celebrated paper 'On Denoting' is taken as pivotal to understanding his position. The background to it is examined in the metaphysics of his *Principles of Mathematics*, and we continue by discussing his theory of incomplete symbols (an instance of which is the Theory of Descriptions) in his Multiple Relations Theory of Judgement and his *Philosophy of Logical Atomism*.

This last topic introduces Wittgenstein. Discussion begins with his 'picture theory' of meaning in the *Tractatus Logico-Philosophicus*, and is followed by a look at the work of his middle period, in which Wittgenstein rejected the *Tractatus* and began to develop his later philosophy. This latter is primarily conveyed by his *Philosophical Investigations*, in examining which we pay particular attention to questions about meaning and understanding, rule-following, and the possibility of private language.

1. FREGE

1.1. Introduction

Frege's contribution to philosophy is embodied in work whose principal aim seems, at first, remote from traditional philosophical concerns—namely, to show that mathematics rests on logical foundations. Prior to Frege's day, styles of mathematical proof, although believed to confer certainty on their conclusions (indeed, a degree of certainty unattainable in any other science), could not be said to justify this belief, because they were *informal* in character, involving short cuts and steps whose justification is unexplicit. Mathematicians' willingness to rest content with this situation was, it seems, prompted by the belief that proof relies on 'intuition' (in Kant's sense of 'experience'). This implies that proof depends on the structure of the mind—that is, on psychological facts about us—rather than on the nature of mathematical truth, which we otherwise take to be objective. Frege pointed out that although we indeed have access to objective mathematical truths, we therefore do not understand how.

It was the endeavour to carry out the 'logicist' project of basing mathematics firmly on logic that led Frege to a number of important insights both in logic and philosophy. He rejected the notion, central to Kant's views, that logic and mathematics reflect facts about the constitution of our minds—such a view is known as 'psychologism'—and he devised a new logical language (his *Begriffsschrift*, or 'Concept Script') which increased the power and range of logic. In the process, he developed a number of seminal philosophical ideas.

1.2. Frege's Anti-Psychologism

Psychologism is the view that the content, meaning, or nature of any concept can be explained by reference to the underlying psychological states and processes in the minds of possessors of that concept. Frege's opposition to this view was trenchant and unrelenting: the preface to *Begriffsschrift*, his first major work, sets out an anti-psychologistic manifesto, and his late essay 'Thoughts' continues the attack on psychologism. His anti-psychologism is one of the three guiding principles of his programme in *The Foundations of Arithmetic*.

Nevertheless, it is not easy to find in Frege's writings a definitive encapsulation of his reasons for rejecting psychologism. There is instead a linked set of considerations spread variously about his writings. His underlying concern is the threat posed to objectivity by subjectivism; but the kind of objectivity he had in view differs from one place to another. Among his chief reasons for rejecting psychologism, however, are the following.

1.2.1. *Classification of Truths*

Near the beginning of *Begriffsschrift* Frege considers whether truths should be classified according to how they are known or how they are proved. If we dwell exclusively on the psychological preconditions of knowledge it will, he says, seem that experience is always essential to knowledge. But truth is objective; it cannot depend on how we come by our knowledge of it. Therefore we should concentrate on questions about methods of proof and verification of truths. On this basis truths will be classified according to whether their verification follows from logical considerations alone, or whether experience is required in addition. This underlies Frege's sharp insistence on holding apart questions about the truth of a proposition from the question whether anyone has grounds for taking the proposition to be true.

1.2.2. *Explanatory Inadequacy*

The inadequacy of psychologism is shown by the fact that even if we had a psychologistic account of concept possession, it would not explain our employment of given concepts. An explanation of a given concept should encapsulate what is known, or what capacity is exercised, by one who grasps the concept. If we have such an account we can use it as a guide to employing the concept. But a psychologistic account fails to satisfy this requirement: one could understand the psychological mechanism underlying possession of a certain concept, yet still be unable to *use* it.

1.2.3. *Ideational Views of Meaning*

Psychologism seems attractive because it opposes behaviourism. Most people find it hard to believe that linguistic meaning is merely the outcome of responses (sounds and marks) to stimuli (a crucial subset of which are sounds and marks produced by others). It is therefore tempting and natural to see the significance of words as grounded in a mental basis for verbal behaviour: words mean, on this view, in virtue of their correlation with mental items—namely, ideas. We understand each other by interpreting each other's words, that is, by finding the correct correlation of another's words with ideas. So psychologism seems to be a consequence of, or to lead naturally to, an ideational theory of meaning. In this view word meaning is primary: words have meaning through their correlation with ideas, and sentences have meaning as complexes of (independently) meaningful words. (We shall see Frege rejecting this view in *The Foundations of Arithmetic*.)

1.2.4. *Communication*

But an ideational theory of meaning cannot satisfactorily account for communication. On the basis of the fact that communication consists in the sharing of thoughts, Frege gives two arguments (a stronger and a weaker—he does not explicitly distinguish them) to show this. The weaker argument goes as follows: Thoughts and meanings can be shared. Ideas are had. What can be had cannot be known to be shared. So if thoughts and meanings are ideas, they cannot be known to be shared. Therefore, we cannot know that we communicate.

The stronger argument goes as follows: Thoughts and meanings can be shared. Ideas are had. What can be had cannot be shared. So thoughts and meanings are not ideas (that is: if thoughts and meanings are ideas, we cannot communicate).

1.2.5. *The Objectivity of Truth*

If the content of a sentence, or the nature of a concept, is determined by its psychological basis, then—since truth-value depends on content and the way the world is—truth will in part be a product of psychological factors. So it is possible that the truth-value of a sentence might change with changing psychology—with, say, the evolution of the brain. But this, according to Frege, is absurd; truths are timeless.

One would miss Frege's point if one replied that a changed psychological state simply constitutes a change in meaning (and thus, unsurprisingly, a change in truth-value). His objection rests on the absurdity of supposing that changes in meaning can rest solely on psychological change. (Where change in psychology prompts change in usage, it is the latter fact that constitutes change of meaning.) This shows that one of Frege's aims is to preserve the objectivity of meaning.

But Frege is also concerned that psychologism makes the truth of propositions depend on their being *thought* in a particular way. This contradicts what he takes to be an obvious truth: that a proposition, if true, is true independently of the ways it is thought, or even whether it is thought at all.

1.2.6. *Laws of Truth*

Frege wished to explain the laws of truth. If we correctly characterize the laws of truth we thereby secure a theory of the laws of thought—that is, a theory stating ideal standards of rationality (to which we aspire even if we often fall short). The laws of truth are responsible to the nature of the world, and in that sense are descriptive; but, because thought *aims* at truth, a theory of truth will tell us how we should reason, and is also therefore a normative theory. But now it is clear that such a theory is not responsible to the way we *actually* reason, so it is not responsible to psychologistic accounts of thinking.

1.3. The *Begriffsschrift*

Frege invented a 'concept script' (*Begriffsschrift*) as a language free of all 'intuition', using this term in its Kantian sense to mean '(possible) representations of objects in the minds of subjects of experience'. Such a language is required because, as the foregoing shows, a theory resting in part on the supposed contributions of intuition cannot be properly objective. Frege designed the *Begriffsschrift* to help attain complete rigour in mathematics, and at the same time to reveal the nature of its central concepts.

In Frege's view, as we saw, traditional uses of mathematical proof are problematic because informal; they rest on the idea that proof in some way involves the nature of the mind rather than depending solely on objective mathematical truth. This, Frege held, cannot be right. He was not sceptical about mathematical knowledge; we do indeed, he says, have access to mathematical truths; what these considerations show is that we do not know how we gain that access. To judge—without appeal to intuition—whether arithmetical truths are provable, we need a means of representing proofs in which every step is explicit. Only then can we detect whether a gap in an informal proof is merely apparent, or genuine in the sense that it involves appeal to intuition. The *Begriffsschrift* supplies the essential technical apparatus for displaying proofs perspicuously. Frege's *Grundlagen* puts that apparatus to work in demonstrating that the truths of arithmetic are guaranteed by logic alone.

There is nothing new in Frege's aims. Like Kant and other predecessors he was interested in the epistemology of mathematics, wishing to show that mathematical knowledge is secure. He also wished to clarify the concepts of mathematics. What is novel is his means of pursuing these aims by means of a specially devised *Begriffsschrift*. In ambition the *Begriffsschrift* is approached only by Leibniz's idea of a 'universal language' in which everything can be expressed with complete clarity and univocality; and the nearest that anything had come to it was Boole's logical calculus—which is much less powerful, and anyway was invented to serve less ambitious ends (Boole sought to capture formal aspects of reasoning, whereas Frege aimed for a language that reveals content).

Moreover, the *Begriffsschrift* offers a theory of the laws of thought in a normative sense: it is a theory of how we *should* think, not an empirically based *description* of thinking. It appeals to the laws of truth rather than of psychology.

Function and Object A major innovation in *Begriffsschrift* is its abandonment of the subject–predicate analysis of propositions in favour of a 'function–object' analysis. Traditionally logic taught that a proposition contains a subject of which something is predicated: in *Socrates is wise* wisdom is predicated of Socrates. Frege instead employs the mathematical notion of a function. A function takes one object (the *argument*) and assigns to it another object (which is the *value* of the function for that argument). So, for instance, multiplying by two is a function which takes 0 to 0, 1 to 2, 2 to 4, and so on. Similarly, in natural language 'the mother of' stands for a function which takes Rembrandt to Cornelia van Zuytbrouck, Mozart to Anna Maria Pertl, and so on again.

Frege describes functions as 'incomplete' because they require completion by an object. This can be elucidated as follows. Competence in using a function to take arguments to values can be explained as grasp of a 'gapped' expression: '$(\ )\times 2$' or 'The mother of ( )'. Similarly, eliminating the name of some object from a complex name yields a function—for example, eliminating 2 from $(2+3)\times 7$ gives the function $((\ )+3)\times 7$. Note that these remarks involve mention of names and expressions, that is, linguistic items; Frege takes ontological categories (categories of things in the world) to be mirrored by linguistic (syntactic) categories.

Concepts Functions whose values are truth-values are called *concepts*.

The value for any argument of the function $(\ )+3=5$ is a *truth-value*. In Frege's terminology, '$1+3=5$' refers to the False, '$2+3=5$' refers to the True. Similarly for the elimination of names from sentences: eliminating 'Rembrandt' from 'Rembrandt was a painter' yields '( ) was a painter', which refers to the True when Rembrandt is the argument and to the False when Mozart is the argument.

The picture is as follows:

Language		World
names or singular terms	↔	objects
functional expressions	↔	functions
sentences	↔	truth-values

Quantification One feature to recommend the function–object analysis is the fact that it does not invariably analyse such sentences as 'England beat France' and 'France was beaten by England' as standing for different propositions. The subject–predicate theory has to treat these as standing for different propositions, for in the first England is the subject and in the second France is the subject.

But its great advantage is the elegant and powerful account of quantification it makes possible.

Consider the sentence 'All fish have fins'. On the subject–predicate theory, this sentence predicates fin-possession of all fish. But what sort of object is *all fish*? If *all fish* is an object of some kind, why not represent the sentence's negation as 'All fish do not have fins' (rather than 'Some fish do not have fins')?

Consider 'Everyone loves someone'. If 'everyone' and 'someone' each stand for certain things (the subject and object respectively), it is difficult to see why the sentence is ambiguous between 'There is someone (one lucky person) whom everyone loves' and 'Everyone loves someone (possibly a different person in each case)'.

Frege's theory handles such cases beautifully. Consider 'There is a black swan', which contains the function expression '( ) is a black swan'. Normally the function is completed by insertion of an object, but we now see it as completed by a function of functions, expressed by 'There is an *x* such that ( )*x*'. This gives 'There is an *x* such that *x* is a black swan'.

For 'All fish have fins' consider the function expression '( ) is a fish implies ( ) has fins'. Then take the function of functions expressed by 'For all *x*, ( )*x*'. Now we get 'For all *x*, if *x* is a fish then *x* has fins'. To negate 'All fish have fins' we get 'Not all fish have fins', that is, 'Some fish do not have fins'.

'Everyone loves someone' can be seen as built up from the function expression '( ) loves . . .' in two ways. First: we can use 'For all *x*, ( )*x*' on the first gap to get 'For all *x*, *x* loves . . .'. Now use 'There is a *y* such that ( )*y*' to get 'There is a *y* such that for all *x*, *x* loves *y*'. Secondly: we can use 'There is a *y* such that ( )*y*' on the second gap to get 'There is a *y* such that ( ) loves *y*'. Now use 'For all *x*, ( )*x*' on the first gap to get 'For all *x* there is a *y* such that *x* loves *y*'.

So the ambiguity can be resolved by noting how the sentence is constructed. This determines which function of function expression has largest *scope*. This is an important new concept; it means that we do not see sentences as mere concatenations of syntactic units.

1.4. The Foundations of Arithmetic

Frege set out his project for the philosophy of mathematics in *Grundlagen*. The foregoing sections have sketched Frege's formal system and his reasons for thinking that examination of the foundations of mathematics requires such a system; so it comes as a surprise to find that the arguments of *Grundlagen* are informally presented. However, the conceptual framework established in the *Begriffsschrift* is fundamental to Frege's positive proposals in *Grundlagen*. The full realization of that proposal—its implementation in the formal system of

Begriffsschrift—Frege carried out later in *Die Grundgesetze der Arithmetik* ('The Basic Laws of Arithmetic').

1.4.1. *Frege's Three Maxims*

In the introduction to *Grundlagen* Frege adopts three principles: always separate sharply the psychological from the logical and the subjective from the objective; never ask for the meaning of a word in isolation, but only in the context of a proposition; and never lose sight of the distinction between concept and object.

The first and third are self-explanatory. The second has come to be known as the Context Principle. Despite the fact that it has been widely endorsed (by, among others Wittgenstein, both early and late) it is controversial. There is also controversy over whether Frege still held to this principle in *Grundgesetze*, in which Frege seems to abolish the distinction between names and sentences, thereby undercutting the Context Principle.

Frege offers no argument for the Context Principle. It is, however, possible to see a motivation for it in his anti-psychologism. Psychologism and an ideational theory of meaning are natural allies. The latter states that words mean by standing for ideas, which implies that words have meaning in isolation. This violates the Context Principle. Now, it is hard to see what, in the ideational view, explains how ideas join into complexes, and in particular what explains the meanings of whole sentences. If we adopt the Context Principle, however, we see the meaning of a word as derivative—its meaning is the contribution it makes to the meaning of a sentence. If the meaning of a sentence is objective (for example: is the condition for its truth), then the meaning of a word is objective too. Accepting the Context Principle therefore seems integral to an anti-psychologistic view.

1.4.2. *Logicism and Rigour*

Frege offered *Grundlagen* as a contribution to making mathematics more rigorous, which in his view meant using secure and explicit methods of proofs in conjunction with clear and explicit definitions. He therefore took his project to involve clarification of the most basic of mathematical concepts, namely, the concept of number. His chief aim was to clarify the grounds of mathematical assertions; he was not primarily concerned with quelling doubts about the truth of mathematics, but with revealing 'the dependence of truths on one another'.

The terminus of his investigation is logicism, the thesis that mathematics is logic. This view is, for Frege, easily established: since mathematics is unrestrictedly applicable, it cannot be the product of any special science, and must therefore be, or be reducible to, a branch of the only wholly general science, namely, logic.

1.4.3. *Arithmetical Propositions*

Frege first turns his attention to the status of arithmetical formulae. These include the simplest sort of statements, for example, 713 + 286 = 999. He examines the theories of various writers to learn from their mistakes.

Kant claims that such formulae as 713 + 286 = 999 are not provable because they are synthetic, and they are not self-evident axioms because there is an infinite number of them. Instead each has to be seen as the product of intuition. This, Frege claims, is absurd: we do not have intuitions of large numbers, and if we did, their truth would be immediately evident, which it is not (one has to work the calculation 713 + 286 = 999 to see whether it is true). Kant seems to have been misled by focusing only on relatively small numbers. But since there is no sharp boundary between small and large numbers, this cannot provide even the basis for arithmetical knowledge. So arithmetical truths have to be provable.

Leibniz claimed that arithmetical formulae are provable from the definitions of each number given in terms of its predecessor. So, for instance, to prove 2 + 2 = 4,

(1) 1 + 1 = 2	(def)
(2) 1 + 2 = 3	(def)
(3) 1 + 3 = 4	(def)
(4) 1 + 1 + 2 = 4	from (2) and (3), by substitution of identicals
therefore	
(5) 2 + 2 = 4	from (1) and (4), by substitution of identicals

But Frege points out that this is not, as it stands, a proof, because it fails to appeal to the associative law, (a + (b + c) = (a + b) + c), on which it depends. The associative law is a general arithmetical law and we thus need an account of our knowledge of *general* arithmetical truths. But Frege agreed with Leibniz that arithmetic formulae are provable and that the numbers are to be defined as the successors of their predecessors.

Mill endorsed Leibniz's definition but denied that it states logical facts. Rather, it states facts of the sort that an aggregate which impresses our senses thus: ∴ can be rearranged thus: . . .

If this were correct, Frege argued, we could not count such entities as ideas or the number of solutions to an equation. As with Leibniz, Mill fails to see the need for the associative law, and so cannot explain *general* mathematical truths. Again, each definition states what is particular to the number being defined, so it cannot be encompassed in a general law; yet it is absurd to suppose we could observe what is particular to each individual number. Nor, said Frege, can Mill account for *zero* in these terms. If he tried to explain it as a manner of using a given symbol, then why not say the same of all numbers? And finally, Mill shares Kant's problem with large numbers; he cannot claim that we begin with small numbers and construct the others from them, because there is no sharp boundary between large and small numbers.

1.4.4. *Arithmetical Laws*

Frege thus argues that numerical formulae are provable from definitions together with some general laws, and that they neither assert nor presuppose observable facts.

Mill had claimed that arithmetical laws are inductively known from empirical truths; addition consists in forming one aggregate from other aggregates, and we generalize laws about addition from many observations of this physical process. Frege argues that Mill confuses the meaning of a proposition with particular applications of it. A particular use of an arithmetical proposition can lead to empirical truths. To take this as revealing the meaning of the proposition is to give the mathematical proposition empirical content, and this, according to Frege, is Mill's mistake. Frege is not impugning the applicability of mathematics; indeed he held that mathematics would be a mere game were it not applicable. But what matters is *all possible* applications, not particular ones.

Secondly, Frege questions the supposed inductive base. It cannot consist of numerical formulae (observed to be true), because, if so, we lose the point of defining numbers (that point being, remember, to facilitate proofs of numerical formulae). Moreover, there is no uniformity in the inductive base. Each number occupies its place in the series *essentially*; its place is essential to its properties. Lastly, if we think that the numbers can be brought under some concept (for example, 'following in the series beginning with 0 and produced by increasing by one') that is because we think that their properties *follow from* its creation by this process; that is, the properties of each number follow from its definition, so general laws follow from what is common to their generation.

The conclusion of these thoughts is that arithmetical truths are known a priori.

1.4.5. *Is Arithmetic Analytic or Synthetic A Priori?*

If arithmetic is synthetic a priori—in Kant's sense of 'applying to experience but not learned from experience'—it is because it requires a faculty of intuition to know arithmetical truths. But this cannot be the ground of our knowledge of arithmetical laws—that is, general truths about numbers—for we cannot know in advance in what ways a given number can resemble, and therefore represent, all numbers.

Also, and this repeats an earlier point about Frege's logicism, the universal applicability of arithmetic shows that its truths cannot be grounded in intuition, and therefore that arithmetic is a branch of logic. But the real aim of *Grundlagen* is to show, by reducing arithmetic to logic, that its truths are independent of intuition. Kant and his followers believed that mathematics must be synthetic because it yields substantive knowledge. Frege sought to show that its substantive character is differently based.

Are Numbers Properties of External Things? So far it has been established that numbers are defined in terms of 1 and the successor function. Arithmetical formulae are provable from these definitions together with certain general laws about numbers. These laws, in turn, are proved not just from the definitions but from the concept of number. Frege now turns his attention to a direct examination of this concept.

In contexts other than arithmetical calculation we chiefly use numbers adjectivally as in *the three wise men*. It is therefore tempting to see 'three' as functioning in the same way as 'wise', in the sense of denoting a property we ascribe to the aggregate. In other words, number is a property of external things which are, in themselves, pluralities. This model is obviously misleading; we talk about *the wise men* just when each man in the aggregate is wise but when we talk of *the three men* you cannot infer that each man in the aggregate is three.

Perhaps this problem can be circumvented by noting that it is acceptable to describe the contents of a bag of sweets as 'those multicoloured sweets' where each sweet is uniform in colour. Frege does not discuss this possibility. He has other worries. We use numbers in answer to the question 'How many?' but we cannot simply point at an aggregate and ask 'How many?' without inviting the query 'How many what?' For example, one pile of cards may be two packs, or eight complete suits, or . . . Clearly, if number were a property of an aggregate it would have contrary properties. So what number belongs to an aggregate depends on how we choose to regard the aggregate.

Recall that we are trying to explain how we acquire the concept of number. The thought is that number is a property of external things and that we get the concept of it by *abstracting* from aggregates which are relevantly similar. Frege rejects this approach; how, he asks, could abstraction yield a universally applicable concept? How could we abstract from the properties of certain concrete entities to arrive at a concept which is applicable also to the abstract and subjective realms?

Is Number Subjective? It might seem that our idea of number is a function of the way we regard aggregates. This suggests that number is subjective, inviting a psychologistic investigation. Frege, predictably, rejects this. He argues that although the designation of our words is the product of convention and reflects our interests, the objectivity of facts about what our words designate is not thereby impugned. He further argues that the objectivity of number does not imply its concrete existence in space and time. So we do not need to see number as a property of external things in order to see it as usable in reporting objective facts. A fact is objective, for Frege, if we can share knowledge of it. This means that it should be free from contributions of imagination, intuition, and sensation, but not of rationality. So an objective feature can be a product of thought. Frege points out that subjective experience is a precondition for mastery of colour words, but this does not mean that the content of colour judgements is subjective. On the contrary, such words record objective distinctions.

The distinction between what is subjective (private and unshareable) and what is fully objective is a sharp one for Frege; he ignores or overlooks the possibility of intersubjectivity. So, for him, if numbers are ideas they must be private. But if they are private, your number three is different from mine; there would be no guarantee that our arithmetics coincide; they might deal with different objects, and therefore we might fail to communicate arithmetically.

The conclusion therefore is that numbers are not properties of external things, nor are they subjective. They are non-sensible and objective.

Frege next raises the question whether numbers are particular sets or multitudes. The problem with this is that it gives no account of 0 and 1; we need an account of what the sets contain. Clearly they cannot contain ordinary particular objects, so the temptation is to say they contain units. But what, Frege asks, are units?

Unity and One Is *one* a property of objects? An affirmative answer is encouraged by talk of (for example) 'one dog', where 'one' seems to function adjectivally. But if 'one dog' is modelled on 'furry dog' it would make as much sense to say 'Fido is one' as it does to say 'Fido is furry'—which it does not. Also if *one* were a property of objects it would apply to every object and so would be vacuous.

Is the concept of oneness the same as the concept of an individual, undivided and isolated? Frege notes that animals have a concept of individuals, as demonstrated by the attributability to them of beliefs and desires essentially involving such a concept; but we cannot attribute possession to them of the concept *one*; a dog cannot be said to grasp what is common between raising one paw and biting one postman.

It might be tempting to look for ultimate units, that is, things which are incapable of dissection and which therefore cannot be regarded as many. What would these be? If they exist, we have to regard as mistaken our frequent ordinary practice of counting dissectable objects as one thing. If we try to salvage the practice by saying that we are thinking of these objects as undissectable, we are misleading ourselves.

Are units identical with one another? When we come to make assignments of number we disregard the properties that distinguish objects. Does this mean we treat them as identical? If so, it would seem that either we take a subjective view, or we rely on a falsehood. If, on the other hand, we abstract from the peculiarities of the objects concerned, we simply reach the general concept under which they all fall, and this is not many but one. So there seems to be no point in attempting reduction to units, for it risks eliminating the diversity essential to plurality.

Are units distinct from each other? Each number is an aggregate of units. If they are distinct we need to distinguish them in our symbolism. So for 5 we would have $1' + 1'' + 1''' + 1'''' + 1'''''$. The trouble is that we get an infinity of distinct number threes ($1' + 1'' + 1'''$, $1' + 1''' + 1''''$, ...)—and so for the rest. Although we may have abstracted from the grounds of distinction between objects, this tactic retains distinctness, which is enough to resurrect the same problems one would have in remaining with the original objects. So numbers cannot be seen as agglomerations of things because these latter need to be distinct (in order to have multiplicity), yet we cannot have an infinity of distinct number ones, twos, threes, and the rest.

Time and space might provide a solution, for points in space and moments in time are intrinsically indistinguishable yet are distinguishable as part of the total intuition. However, in many cases of counting, the grounds of distinction are neither spatial nor temporal. The fact that counting takes time is a merely psychological fact; the grounds of distinction between objects is not a matter of temporal succession. So this cannot be part of the content of number either.

Finally, Frege considers Jevons's view that we abstract 'from the character of the difference from which plurality arises, retaining merely the fact'. But, as noted, the fact of the difference is enough to generate multiple numbers. Also for 1 and 0 there is no fact of difference to be the product of abstraction. Admittedly, 0 and 1 are, in some sense, special, but why should we be forced to make this distinction by a philosophical account of number?

1.5. Frege's Account of Number

From his survey of the available suggestions Frege concludes that number is not a property of external things, nor is it abstracted from the properties of things (as, say, colour might be); and that they are neither physical nor subjective. None of the theories satisfactorily explain what number is asserted of. And those theories that attempt to define number in terms of sets fail to explain the notion of units—which anyway seems a contradictory notion, because units have to be both identical and distinguishable.

Having rejected all versions of abstractionism, Frege presents us with his own account. First he notes that in asserting 'Here are sixty grapes' after asserting 'Here are two bunches of grapes', we do not imply that anything external has changed. There is a change of terminology, which indicates a change of *concept*. So number is asserted of concepts. In fact, if we recall Frege's *Begriffsschrift* system, this result seems obvious. Take the expression 'The number of ( ) is *n*'. Clearly this is incomplete. To determine what sort of function it expresses we need to know what can fill the argument place. Could an object be the argument? No; 'The number of Matisse is *n*' does not make sense. Try the next possible substitution, a function (of objects), 'The number of *x*s such that the mother of *x* is *n*'. Again, this is nonsense. Therefore, try a concept: 'The number of *x*s such that *x* is a grape is *n*'. This, at last, makes sense. So the original expression 'The number of ( ) is *n*' expresses a concept of concepts; 'The number of ( )' is a function of concepts.

Why, given that this result is so easily achieved in Frege's system, does he make such an effort to dismiss alternative views, some of them obviously implausible? A chief reason is that reviewing theories of number reveals the various difficulties any adequate theory needs to resolve, which offers a good test. Frege claims his theory passes that test. It is instructive to note how.

First, zero presents no problem for Frege's view; it is treated in the same way as other numbers. 'The number of *x*s such that *x* is a grape is 0' simply means that there are no grapes, that is, that no object satisfies the concept '( ) is a grape'.

Secondly, the account does not make number subjective. The ascription of number indeed changes according to how we regard a plurality, but this is not a subjective phenomenon, for each ascription reports an objective fact about different concepts. It only appears to be subjective if we forget that the abstract realm is thoroughly objective. Frege points out that the temptation to think otherwise is a product of neglecting the Context Principle, doing which might tempt one to an ideational account of meaning.

Thirdly, we now see why ascriptions of number, although depending on diversity, are unifying; they encompass the multitude as a whole. We unify the objects to be enumerated under some general concept. Not all concepts are fit for attributions of number; we cannot, for instance, talk simply of 'The number of blue things', because we have to know what *sort* of thing we are considering. Concepts which, in themselves, carry information about the sorts they collect are called 'sortal' concepts, for example *cat, table, nation-state, sentence*. The point about sortals is that understanding them does not just require that we can apply them to the right things, but that we can distinguish those things from each other and can recognize them as the same again—in other words, they involve criteria of individuation and identity.

Fourthly, Frege's theory explains the universal applicability of numbers. Since number is attributed to concepts it makes no difference whether or not the objects falling under the concept are abstract or concrete, provided only that the concept itself is a sortal.

1.5.1. *Platonism*

Frege's view is that numbers are objects, and that *number* is itself a sortal concept. In the expression 'The number of *F*s is *n*' the number term, '*n*', appears as a component. It does not itself name a property of *F*. In fact it names an object (objects can be constituents of functions). Frege gives his reasons for thinking that numbers are objects rather briefly: he says that we speak of *the* number 1 (etc.) where use of the definite article serves to show that we are using a singular term, so numbers are the referents of singular terms—that is, are objects; and he adds that in mathematics we make such assertions as that $2 + 3 = 5$ in which the numbers are treated as objects (for instance, they flank the identity sign); and that we count numbers (for example, there are four primes between 0 and 10).

Matters are not, however, so simple, for we also use numbers adjectivally—'There are six shopping days to Christmas'. Frege appears to have two responses: first, that science and mathematics take priority, and secondly, that all adjectival uses can be paraphrased as statements of identity—so the above becomes 'The number of shopping days until Christmas is six'. The problem with these claims is that it is not clear which mode of analysis should take priority. We can define numerically definite quantifiers as follows:

> There are just 0 *F*s iff for all *x*, not *Fx*.
>
> There are just $n + 1$ *F*s iff for some *x*, *x* is an *F* and there are just *n* *F*s distinct from *x*.

But these definitions only work if we assume that there exists an infinite number of objects.

1.5.2. *The Definition of Number*

At section 62 of *Grundlagen* a remarkable thing happens. Frege asks, 'How are numbers given to us?' and immediately invokes the Context Principle to change this question into one about the meaning of sentences in which number terms occur. Claiming that he has already settled that numbers are objects, he says, 'If we are to use the symbol *a* to signify an object, we must have a criterion for deciding in all cases whether *b* is the same as *a*, even if it is not always in our power to apply this criterion.'

The section is remarkable because in it Frege transforms a difficult question about the nature of number into a question about meaning. It is often cited as the first instance of the 'linguistic turn'. Moreover, Frege immediately draws from this observation the notion of a criterion of identity: we can only grasp talk of a range of objects if we have established what it is to recognize those objects as the same again.

So the first step in defining number is the specification of identity conditions. Frege (following Hume) adopts the following definition of numerical identity:

> The number of *F*s = the number of *G*s iff there is a one–one correlation of *F*s to *G*s.

This is often (inaccurately) described as Frege's contextual definition of number. Frege questions it; should we instead derive the criterion of identity for numbers from a general grasp of identity (from, say, Leibniz's views) and the concept of number? But in Frege's view we should proceed in the opposite direction: we state conditions of numerical identity in order to clarify the concept of number. He compares this to the case of directions and parallelism. Here we have

> The direction of *a* = the direction of *b* iff *a* is parallel to *b*.

The equivalence explains the concept of direction. The meaning in other contexts is defined so as to preserve intersubstitutability of identical directions as thus characterized.

At this point Frege raises a famous objection. We have only been given an account of identity in restricted contexts; in particular, we do not know whether 'The direction of *a* is Julius Caesar'. The definition is obviously inadequate.

We can't say 'Julius Caesar is a direction iff there is some line, *b*, such that Julius Caesar is the direction of *b*', for this is circular. Nor can we say that Julius Caesar is a direction iff it is introduced according to the definition, for this makes the definition a property of an object. Once introduced, the definition can be seen as an assertion about the object, but then it is on the same level as all other assertions about it. Moreover, the usefulness of identity statements lies in our ability to identify things when they are presented to us in different ways. The current proposal makes manner of presentation intrinsic to the identity of the object, and therefore threatens the utility of identity statements.

Another way of noting the inadequacy of this 'definition' is to see that specifying a criterion of identity does not uniquely pick out which object is the number of apples on the tree (say). For it is clear that the same criterion of identity will hold for the following:

The number of *F*s + 1 = The number of *G*s + 1.

The moral seems to be that we do not succeed in specifying a range of objects if we only supply a set of singular terms and a criterion of identity applicable to them. The question, therefore, is: what more is required?

1.5.3. *The Explicit Definition of Number*

The comparison between number terms and terms for directions prompts Frege to form an explicit definition of number based on 'definition by (logical) abstraction', a procedure dear to mathematicians. One begins with a domain of objects (for example, lines). The objects can be related to each other in various ways; it may be that some of these relations are 'equivalence relations', which exhaustively partition the domain into a number of disjoint (non-overlapping) subdomains. The following properties of equivalence relations account for this: they are reflexive—that is, for any x we have xRx; they are symmetrical—that is, if xRy then yRx; and they are transitive—that is, if xRy and yRz then xRz. Call *the equivalence class* of an object, m, the set of all the objects m is R-related to, that is, all x such that mRx. Each object is then in some equivalence class, for each object is R-related at least to itself. So the equivalence classes exhaust the original domain. And each pair of equivalence classes either overlaps completely (they are identical) or not at all. We can now treat these equivalence classes as ('new') objects with the criterion of identity given by the equivalence relation defined on the original objects. So, in the case of lines, 'being parallel to' is an equivalence relation: the direction of two lines is identical just when they are parallel. We can *identify* dirctions with equivalence classes of lines:

> The direction of *a* is the extension of the concept *parallel to a*, that is, is the equivalence class of *a* under the relation *being parallel to*.

Similarly, for numbers we get,

> The number of *F*s is the extension of the concept *equinumerous with F*, that is, is the equivalence class of *F* under the relation (between concepts) of equinumerosity.

So now we know what, in general, a (cardinal) number is. We know that a number is an extension of a concept of concepts. *If*, in particular, we know that Julius Caesar is not an extension (and therefore not an extension of a concept of concepts), then we know, reassuringly, that Julius Caesar is not a number. So, it would seem that we have (at least partially) solved the 'Julius Caesar' problem. But we still require a systematic way of generating definitions of each number in the number sequence. From those and a definition of the successor function, together with logic, we can derive the axioms of arithmetic (as given by Peano).

Frege has given a definition of number in terms of extensions of concepts. The notion of a concept's extension *might* be a logical notion. If it can be shown to be so, and if we can derive the axioms of arithmetic from the definitions, then we shall have, as Frege promised, an arithmetic based solely on logic. We therefore need to explain 'the extension of a concept'.

1.5.4. *The Definition of the Individual Numbers*

Let us begin with 0. The number of *F*s is 0 just in case there are no *F*s. So to define 0 we need a concept which is guaranteed to apply to no object whatever. Since every object is self-identical the concept of being non-self-identical, although meaningful, is guaranteed to have nothing falling under it. So,

> 0 is the extension of the concept 'equinumerous with the concept *not identical with itself*'.

Now to define 1 we need a concept which is guaranteed to have just one object falling under it. Use the concept of being identical with 0 to give

> 1 is the extension of the concept 'equinumerous with the concept *identical with 0*'.

In general, if we have defined *n*, then:

> n' is the extension of the concept 'equinumerous with the concept *member of the series of natural numbers ending with n*'.

Since we start with 0 this concept clearly applies to $n + 1$ objects. This definition is not immediate; Frege has first to define the notion of 'being a member of the series of natural numbers ending with *n*', and then to define the notion of 'following in the series of natural numbers immediately after *n*'. Finally he has to show that the number following in the series of natural numbers immediately after *n* is indeed the extension of the concept 'equinumerous with the concept *member of the series of natural numbers ending with n*'. He does this in sections 76 to 83.

1.5.5. *The Extension of a Concept*

Frege says little in *Grundlagen* about what an extension is. Later, in *Grundgesetze*, extensions clearly figure as objects. Frege supplies a criterion of identity for them (his Axiom V):

> The extension of $F =$ the extension of G iff (x) $(Fx$ iff $Gx)$.

But this is all he says; and it will not suffice, for his procedure here is exactly analogous to what in *Grundlagen* he had found inadequate as a definition of number. The Julius Caesar problem reappears, this time for extensions—and this proved disastrous, as shown by Russell's later discovery that Axiom V leads to contradiction.

Given that extensions are objects, they can fill the argument space of a function. In particular we might have either *F*(the extension of *F*) or not-*F*(the extension of *F*), for any function *F*. Define the function G where G holds of *x* just in case there is a concept *F* such that *x* is the extension of *F* and not-*Fx*, i.e.

> *Gx* iff (∃*F*)(*x* = the extension of *F* and not-*Fx*)
> Let *g* be the extension of *G*.

So, using this definition, we have,

> If not-*Gg* then (*F*)(if *g* = the extension of *F* then *Fg*).

But,

> If (*F*)(if *g* = the extension of *F* then *Fg*) then (if *g* = the extension of G then *Gg*).

So,

> If not-*Gg* then *Gg*.

So,

> *Gg*.

From the definition of G we get,

> (∃*F*) (*g* = the extension of *F* and not-*Fg*).

Let *F* be such a concept, i.e.

> *g* = the extension of *F* and not-*Fg*.

Then by Axiom V (going from left to right)

> (*x*)(*Gx* iff *Fx*).

Since we have not-*Fg* we must thus have not-*Gg*. But this contradicts our proof that *Gg*.

This meant the end of Frege's attempt to carry out his logicist programme. We see below how Russell attempted to cope with this problem.

1.5.6. The Context Principle

Frege encounters problems because he gives an explicit definition of number in terms of extensions. Crispin Wright tries to salvage Frege's project by showing that he could have contented himself with the contextual definition, so avoiding the need to introduce extensions. Wright, moreover, claims that all that is needed to support this view is a plausible interpretation of the Context Principle.

In Wright's view the Context Principle embodies what he calls a 'syntactic priority thesis', namely, that syntactic categories are prior to ontological ones. For Frege, objects are the referents of singular terms; but by the Context Principle we can ask for the meaning of a word only in the context of a sentence, not in isolation; so if we wish to determine the reference of a singular term we must ask whether it occurs (appropriately embedded) in true sentences. There is therefore no direct means of settling ontological disputes, no means of settling what there is by direct inspection. Rather, if we have ontological questions we must first settle the syntactic category of the relevant class of terms, and then ask whether sentences containing them are true. Questions about reference are thus secondary to questions about truth.

Viewing ontological questions in this way is integral to Frege's argument for Platonism about mathematical objects. Once we have settled that number terms are genuine singular terms, we need only ask whether or not they occur (appropriately) in true sentences. Because we are convinced that many arithmetical formulae are true, that amounts to a conviction that numbers exist. This Platonism is epistemologically congenial because, by making reference subservient to truth, it removes any need to postulate a mysterious perception-like access to numbers. We are required only to give an account of how we know mathematical sentences to be true—and in Frege's logicism such knowledge is the yield of deductive inference.

'Syntactic criteria for singular termhood' are not strictly syntactical, because they turn on an appeal to inferences of the sort sustained by sentences containing singular terms. This is a complicated matter, but one can briefly say that a term qualifies as a singular term only if it has a relevant criterion of identity associated with it, sustains inferences to existential generalization—that is, from Fa deduce $(\exists x)Fx$ (other modes of inference are also important in fully specifying the criterion)—and is 'negation asymmetrical' (given any function, F, we can form its negation, not-F, which applies to just those objects which are not F; but given any object, say, Socrates, we cannot necessarily form an object which possesses just those properties which are not possessed by Socrates).

Now Wright's point is that the Context Principle (interpreted, as above, as a principle about reference) entitles us to rest content with a not fully explicit definition—that is, we do not need a definition of number which takes the form 'The number of *F*s is . . .', but only an *explanation* which can be given to characterize the use of number terms. Having achieved this much, the Context Principle shows us that there can be no further question about whether we have succeeded in specifying a range of objects.

There are two kinds of objection to Wright's suggestions. The first arises from ontological reductionism and is a challenge to his interpretation of the Context Principle. The second questions any attempt to justify contextual definitions.

1.5.7. Ontological Reductionism

Consider again the criterion of identity for directions given by parallelism of lines,

Da = *Db* iff *a* is parallel to *b* (where '*Da*' is 'the direction of *a*').

Wright wishes to say that once we know that terms for directions are singular terms, that there is a criterion of identity for them, and that they appear in true sentences (flanking the identity sign), there can be no further significant question about whether directions exist. So the equivalence guarantees the existence of directions.

Not everyone would accept this. An ontological reductionist would interpret the equivalence as showing precisely that directions are *not* bona fide objects. He would point out that we do not learn the truth of identity statements for directions by picking out (in some direct way) the referents of direction terms. Rather we learn their truth indirectly by learning the truth of a statement about given lines being parallel. So, although we may think we are talking about directions, we are really only talking about lines and relations between them. The equivalence reveals this to us.

Ontological reduction has its attractions. When we seem to be talking about a range of puzzling entities, a reductionist might argue that we are taking too seriously the surface structure of our sentences, and that investigation shows we are *really* talking about some range of other (innocuous or unproblematic) objects. The motive for reductionism might be epistemological (there is no obvious epistemology for such troublesome objects as directions or numbers), or a desire for metaphysical economy as in the principle of Occam's Razor—'do not multiply entities without need'.

But reductionism raises the vexed question of ontological commitment. What features of our use of a set of sentences, or our adoption of a theory, commit us to accepting the existence of given entities? Call Wright's preferred interpretation of the equivalence 'the robust reading' to distinguish it from reductionism. He argues that it is not enough for the reductionist to mention the mere possibility of his interpretation. The reductionist says that the left-hand side of '*Da* = *Db* iff *a* is parallel to *b*' appears to refer to certain objects, but the right-hand side takes priority, showing that this is merely apparent reference. The robust view questions why the right-hand side should take priority, for we can equally well read the right-hand side as making a reference to directions. Both parties agree that the right-hand side has *epistemological* priority; we learn about directions through relations between lines (we learn about numbers through correlations between concepts). But the robust view questions why ontological priority should follow epistemological priority. Moreover, it claims that a reduction prompted by epistemological worries is misplaced, because both sides can adopt the reductionist epistemology—which shows, by the robust view's lights, that there is no problem about our epistemological access to *truths* about directions and numbers.

The question now is whether we should always adopt the reductionist ontology when in this position with regard to numbers and directions. Wright argues that desire for ontological economy is not only largely unmotivated but, very probably, ill-motivated—for it is likely that the ontological economist will question our commitment even to ordinary middle-sized objects.

1.5.8. Contextual Definition

Dummett doubts whether Wright's reconstruction of Frege is either Fregean or coherent. Recall that Wright sought to rescue Frege from contradiction by resisting the need to give an explicit definition of number. Dummett observes that Wright's procedure for defining number is analogous to Frege's for defining extensions. Since that led to contradiction, we cannot take it that such procedures are invariably legitimate.

Secondly, Wright supports his view by invoking the Context Principle which, he claims, means that we do not always have to give explicit definitions. (This implies that Frege failed to appreciate the full import of his own view.) Dummett resists this move. Explicit definition is not inconsistent with the Context Principle (we are, after all, giving the meaning of *sentences* of the form 'The number of *F*s is . . .'). Frege is always fully aware of the Context Principle, which he cites just before giving the criterion of identity for numbers. It is not that he first thought the Principle would justify contextual definition, only to discover the Julius Caesar problem and therefore give it up. Rather, Frege took 'contextual definition' to be inadequate because it fails to determine a meaning for all possible sentences containing number terms. His point is that an adequate definition should succeed in doing this, and, moreover, *by the Context Principle* any definition which both achieves this and complies with the criterion of identity is adequate. Frege's argument is, therefore, that his final definition is justified because it yields the correct criterion of identity. This argument makes essential appeal to the Context Principle.

Lastly, Wright is left with a Julius Caesar problem which he solves by saying that two objects are distinct if they are subsumed under different criteria of identity. This seems 'un-Fregean' in that it appears to make an object's manner of presentation essential to it. It also subverts Frege's attempt to give an explicit definition of number: is the criterion of identity for numbers that given by Frege or is it the criterion of identity for extensions (since numbers *are* extensions)? Answers to this last question seem to depend upon the order in which the definitions are given.

1.6. Frege's Notion of Sense

The *Begriffsschrift*, considered earlier, presented the outline of a semantic theory, that is, a theory of the way language relates to the world. Although the theory is useful both in the sense that it supplies the framework for Frege's reconstruction of arithmetic (in *Grundgesetze*) and because it points us in the right direction for an analysis of language, it does not provide a theory of *meaning*. Why not?

1.6.1. *Arguments for the Notion of Sense*

Can one give the meaning of every expression of a language by saying, first, what its primitive expressions denote and, secondly, how the references of its complex expressions are determined by their structure and the references of their constituents? Consider the fact that identity statements can be informative. Bassanio would have acted differently had he known that Balthazar is Portia. Bassanio was sure of the trivial truth that Balthazar is Balthazar, so the information conveyed by 'Balthazar is Balthazar' differs importantly from the information conveyed by 'Balthazar is Portia'. How is this to be explained?

In considering the general form of identity statements '$a = b$' Frege asks himself what the identity relation relates. If it relates what the names 'a' and 'b' stand for, it is just not clear why '$a = b$' differs from '$a = a$'. In both cases we would be talking about a relation which a bears to itself alone. If meaning is given by what an expression stands for, the only alternative is to suppose that the relation holds between the names. But this will not do, because either the identity statement is plainly false (the names are different) or it has to be treated as a stipulation or convention. So the picture of meaning sketched in the first sentence of this section blocks an account of informative identity statements.

To solve the difficulty we need a notion of how expressions relate to the world which is not simply a matter of arbitrary convention but, instead, is a function both of the way the world is and of how we pick things out in the world. So to each expression Frege assigns a *sense*. The sense of an expression is the mode of presentation of its referent. What mode of presentation we associate with an expression is a conventional matter, but which *referent* is associated with a given mode of presentation is not conventional; it is determined by the way the world is. So, returning to Bassanio's predicament, the sense of

'Balthazar' might be given by (something like) 'the cleverest young lawyer in Italy' and that of 'Portia' by 'the heiress of the caskets'. Bassanio then learns something about the world when he learns that 'Balthazar is Portia' is true, for he learns that these *two* senses pick out the same object.

Frege's way of stating the problem is not entirely happy, for it seems to turn solely on considerations of identity. If that were so, then, because identity only (in Frege's view) relates objects, we would have no more than an argument for the sense of names and singular terms. But Frege thinks *all* expressions have sense. Moreover, if Frege is merely concerned about the relata of identity statements, introducing a notion of sense does not help because in informative identity statements the sense of each name differs.

Dummett considers the notion of sense from the perspective of linguistic understanding. He points out that we cannot, in general, credit speakers with *as much as* a grasp of the reference of any expression, nor can we, in general, credit speakers with *as little as* a grasp merely of reference. He concludes that grasp of the reference of an expression is not, in general, an ingredient of understanding. On the other hand, grasp of sense *is* an ingredient of understanding.

Why not 'as much as a grasp of reference'? The answer is that if understanding always involves a grasp of reference, we would need to know a name's bearer in order to understand it; so when two names have the same bearer we would already, just in virtue of understanding the names, know that the relevant identity statement is true. Moreover, understanding a concept expression would likewise involve knowing its reference, and thus would involve knowing which objects it takes to which truth-values. So given an understanding of the name and the concept expression in a simple sentence, we would thereby know what its truth-value is. But this is absurd.

Why not 'as little as a grasp of reference'? If understanding consisted simply in grasp of reference, we would be unable to explain why sentences which contain co-referring terms convey different information (have different 'cognitive values'). We should be unable to explain why 'Portia is Balthazar' differs from 'Portia is Portia', and why 'Matisse is a creature with a heart' differs from 'Matisse is a creature with a kidney'.

There is another problem here, this time concerning the substitution of co-referential terms in opaque contexts. Suppose Bassanio wonders whether Balthazar is Portia. But now, since Balthazar is Portia, and since we should always be able to intersubstitute identicals without altering the truth-value of their embedding sentences, we should be able to conclude that Bassanio wonders whether Portia is Portia. But clearly we do not wish to attribute that level of confusion to him. So we cannot always intersubstitute identicals; co-referential terms are not always intersubstitutable. How is this to be explained?

Frege solves the problem by further exploiting the notion of sense. He claims that in such contexts ('opaque' contexts; examples are the propositional attitudes—*believing that, wondering whether, hoping that*—and modal contexts) the reference of the expression shifts; its reference is no longer what it refers to in transparent contexts, but *its customary sense*. So, for Frege, senses are included in the realm of reference.

1.6.2. *Properties of Sense*

To grasp an expression thus includes grasping its sense; but it might involve grasp of more than just its sense. Grasp of sense is an *ingredient* of understanding. To see what aspect of understanding falls under the heading 'grasp of sense', we need to note something more—for so far we only have the somewhat metaphorical description of sense as a 'mode of presentation of the referent'.

To grasp the sense of an expression is to grasp a way of *determining* its reference. So grasp of sense consists in knowing what is relevant to determining reference.

Note that this need not constitute a complete grasp of meaning, for Frege allows that there may be other aspects of meaning—for example, what he calls the 'colour' and 'tone' of expressions—which are excluded. For instance, 'dog' and 'cur' have the same sense (we do precisely the same to check whether an object is a cur or a dog), but they clearly differ in tone.

As to the relation of sense to reference, we can uncontroversially say that it is 'many–one': a given reference can be picked out by (indefinitely) many senses, but a sense can have at most one reference. More controversially, we might argue that there can be referenceless senses: we may grasp a condition that picks out at most one object, for example, *the president of Britain*, but the world might fail to supply an object satisfying that condition. Frege viewed this as an inadequacy of natural language. It is anyway not clear that the notion of a mode of presentation which presents nothing is even intelligible. Nor is it clear whether *any* sense can lack a referent, or whether there is a species of sense in which each is *guaranteed* a reference.

One can summarize some of the properties of sense as follows. Sense is an ingredient of meaning (reference is not); all expressions have sense; grasp of sense is grasp of a way of determining reference; the sense–reference relation is many–one; an expression can have sense without reference; and, senses exist in the realm of reference.

1.7. Summary

A graphic representation of Frege's view looks like this:

Language		The World
Name / Singular term	Sense of name	Object
Concept expression	Sense of concept expression	Concept
Sentence	Thought	Truth-value

Note that the truth-values of sentences are overdetermined. One can either proceed from the senses of a sentence's constituents to determining their references, and from there to the truth-value of the sentence; or one can determine the thought from the senses of the sentence's constituents, and then directly determine its truth-value. (This point becomes relevant below.)

1.7.1. *The Context Principle Revisited*

We must return briefly to consideration of the Context Principle, for although Frege distinguished between sense and reference *after* having written *Grundlagen*, we are faced with the question whether the Context Principle applies at the level of reference, or sense, or both.

Recall that, in using the principle in his argument that numbers are contextually defined objects, Wright is committed to interpreting it as a principle, at least in part, about reference. We also saw that Dummett doubts whether this approach is Fregean.

Recall Wright's argument against the ontological reductionist, to which he contrasts his preferred 'robust reading' of the equivalences. He has to do this because a reductionist reading offers a counter-example to his interpretation of the Context Principle. Dummett favours an intermediate position which he calls 'tolerant' reductionism, in which we can assert the existence of numbers without thereby committing ourselves to full-blooded mathematical realism.

Dummett's 'tolerant reductionist' points out that realism about a given subject-matter consists in adopting a particular semantic theory for its associated language. A semantic theory is not just a theory of logical categories together with a specification of what they relate to in the world. If this were so, all language would (for a Fregean) admit of the same semantic theory. Rather, a semantic theory also states how the references of expressions are determined; it provides the framework of a theory of sense. A fully realist semantic theory assumes that we understand a thought by understanding its construction and its constituent senses. We determine truth-values by determining the references of constituent senses. In particular, we have to determine the reference of names prior to determining the truth-value of sentences.

A departure from realism will have us grasp thoughts (most likely, as above, by grasping their construction and constituent senses), but will then have us determine the truth-value of thoughts directly. We might do *that* by using equivalences of just the sort that Frege gives between directions and lines or numbers and concepts. We determine the truth-value of statements about numbers without determining the reference of number terms; so we are justified in taking a less than realist view of numbers.

The question of ontological commitment, accordingly, appears far more substantial than on Wright's reading (where it reduces into questions about syntax and truth). This implies that the Context Principle is not in a strong sense a principle about reference. It anyway seems wrong to interpret Frege in Wright's way, for in *Grundgesetze* he does not repudiate the Context Principle, but abolishes the distinction between names and sentences and explicitly rejects the notion of contextual definition. So it seems more plausible to interpret the Context Principle as a principle about sense—in fact, as a principle about the compositionality of meaning.

Frege rejects the idea of any *direct* correlation of words with meanings (assuming otherwise, he says, is a mistake that leads to psychologism). Instead he starts with *thoughts*, by which he means *the meanings of complete sentences*. But if we take the meanings of sentences as primary—that is, if we take the meaning of a word to be its contribution to the meaning of sentences in which it occurs—we require an explanation of how we come to understand new sentences by understanding their construction and the words they contain. There is a position intermediate between taking either single words or whole sentences as the basic unit of meaning. This is to say that the meaning of a word is determined by its contribution to the meanings of certain simple sentences in which it occurs—enough sentences to comprise, in Dummett's words, a complete language but which, in fact, is only a fragment of language. We then understand complex sentences by knowing the systematic contribution made by the meanings of the words it contains to the meaning of the whole sentence. In this way the Context Principle figures as an insistence on a compositional theory of meaning which is not atomic (word-meaning based) but molecular (it respects the idea that word-meaning is a function of contributions to sentence-meaning).

2. RUSSELL

2.1. The Early Russell

Both Russell and Frege were *logicists*, that is, they believed that mathematics is reducible to logic. But they saw logicism as serving different ends. For Frege it was primarily a corrective to Kant. He did not dispute the idea of a 'synthetic a priori', but thought that no theory of arithmetic based on intuition could explain its universality. In contrast, Russell saw logicism as part of a rejection of Kantian and idealist views. The difference between the two emerges in their accounts of geometry and the paradoxes

Although Frege disagreed with Kant's view of arithmetic, he agreed with him about geometry. Russell took geometry to be in one sense logical and in another empirical. The process of constructing a geometrical theory is purely logical; axioms are laid down and theorems deduced from them. But to *apply* geometry we need to know whether the axioms are true of actual space. This is an empirical matter, in which no 'synthetic a priori' is involved.

The emergence of the paradoxes destroyed Frege's logicist project: he became convinced that the notion of an extension of a concept is not a logical one. In his last years he developed a thoroughly Kantian philosophy of mathematics. This was not the lesson of the paradoxes for Russell. He maintained that they are paradoxes in *logic*, and cannot be resolved by changing our account of mathematics. He set himself the immense task of developing a natural system of logic free of paradox and capable of serving as the basis of mathematics. This endeavour began with *The Principles of Mathematics* and culminated in *Principia Mathematica*, which Russell wrote jointly with A. N. Whitehead.

2.1.1. The Principles of Mathematics *(1903)*

A study of Frege's views is not the best preparation for reading Russell's first major work, for although he had read some Frege, and even included an appendix on Frege's logical system, Russell reversed many of the lessons Frege taught. He takes it that whatever can be talked about—whatever can be the subject of a proposition—is a *term*, and anything can be the subject of a proposition (even the denial of its status as such makes it one) and hence a term.

Propositions are formed by predicating something of a term (note the contrast with Frege's functional analysis). 'Term' applies to the broadest ontological category, because it picks out whatever can be talked about. The category of terms is divided into *things* and *concepts*. Things can only occur as subjects of propositions. Concepts, however, have a dual nature; they may appear either as terms or as what is predicated of terms. So Socrates is a thing, wisdom is a concept: Socrates occurs only as a subject, but wisdom occurs both as predicate and as term, as in *Wisdom is desirable*.

Again note the difference from Frege. Whereas for Frege syntactic categories reflect ontological categories, this is not so for Russell. 'Wisdom' and 'is wise' both stand for the same thing despite their difference in syntax. This means that Russell avoids certain difficulties that faced Frege, but thereby acquires a problem in accounting for the unity of a proposition, that is, in distinguishing the proposition *Socrates is wise* from the list *Socrates wisdom*.

Russell gives the following argument for not distinguishing the entities picked out by 'is wise' and 'wisdom'. If there is a difference between what these expressions denote, we should be able to assert it—we should have the proposition '*Wise* differs from *wisdom*'. But here *wise* occurs as a term, so the sentence is false unless there is a difference over and above the fact that *wise* is a predicate and *wisdom* a term. However, the supposition is that *wisdom* differs from *wise* precisely in being a term rather than a predicate.[1] Russell has to say that this is because the concept is being used as a predicate, or, as he later says, it is the result of 'the relation appearing as the relating relation'. But what this latter formulation implies is unclear, for Russell wished the term–predicate distinction to be a logical and not a psychological one.

Russell's view is that meaning must be understood on the model of the name-bearer relation: expressions 'stand for' entities. This is complicated by the fact that some expressions stand for entities that have a dual nature. We understand a proposition through acquaintance with its constituents and their mode of combination. Russell is not interested in word-meaning as such (see p. 47); rather, he is interested in the nature of complexity—in particular, in propositional complexes—and in how we grasp these latter. Logic is concerned with the structure of complexes, the epistemology of logic with grasp of complexes.

A comment about truth is required here. Suppose we accept that the world consists of terms formed into complexes, some of which are propositions, and that these are determinately either true or false. Truth and falsity are thus properties of propositions. But note that for Russell a true proposition has exactly the same ontological status as a false one. Truth is accordingly a *primitive* property that inexplicably attaches to some propositions and not others. We therefore have no account of why truth serves as a regulative ideal (why we aim at it rather than falsity). Russell replies by saying that truth-seeking is an 'ethically ultimate' demand; which is not an adequate response.

2.1.2. *Denoting Concepts*

To every concept, for example *dog*, there corresponds a set of denoting concepts, for example *all dogs*, *every dog*, *any dog*, *a dog*, *some dog*, *the dog*. These for Russell are complexes which are especially useful, but especially troublesome to understand. They are useful because they exhibit the only *logical* relation of meaning. When they occur in subject position in a proposition, the proposition is not about the denoting concept but about *what the denoting concept denotes*. So, to take Russell's example, when I say 'I met a man' I do not intend to be interpreted as saying anything about the denoting concept *a man*, but about the man I met. The usefulness of the denoting relation lies in its explaining how we can

[1] See *The Principles of Mathematics*, 2nd edn. (London, 1956), 46.

entertain and even, on occasion, know propositions that are about entities we are unacquainted with. You are able to understand my proposition about the man I met, and know that I met him, without knowing (being acquainted with) the man himself. We similarly understand propositions about, for example, the centre of mass of the solar system and the tallest tree in the world. A notion of denoting is crucial to Russell's account of our grasp of propositions. But despite its importance, he gives no account of the mechanism of denoting, contenting himself with a catalogue of different cases (see *Principles*, 59).

Note here another departure from Frege. Frege does not distinguish *All Fs are G; Every F is G; Any F is G* because they are all analysed as *For all x, if x is an F then x is a* G. Also Russell explicitly rejects identifying *All Fs are* G with *For all x, if x is an F then x is a* G, because in his view the former makes an assertion about a certain class (the denotation of *all Fs*) whereas the latter holds unrestrictedly.

2.1.3. *Comparison of Senses and Denoting Concepts*

In Frege's account, one grasps a sentence by grasping the thought it expresses. For Russell the same feat is accomplished by grasping the proposition expressed. In this sense Frege's thoughts and Russell's propositions are alike. But there the similarities end. The constituents of Fregean thoughts are senses, the constituents of Russellian propositions are entities. Consider the sentence 'Mt Everest is snow-capped'; Russell says that the corresponding proposition contains the object Mt Everest itself, while for Frege the thought only contains the sense of the name 'Mt Everest'.

Now consider the sentence 'The highest mountain is snow-capped'. Given what we know about the world we can agree that this sentence is about the mountain which is, in fact, Mt Everest. Frege accounts for this by saying the sentence is about the referent of the sense of 'The highest mountain' (which is Mt Everest), and Russell says that the sentence is about the denotation of the denoting concept 'The highest mountain' (which is, again, Mt Everest). Terminology aside, it seems we are being told formally identical stories. Indeed Russell himself seems to have believed this because he claimed that his theory of denoting concepts was a theory of sense for these expressions.

But there are several differences. First, Fregean sense attaches to all linguistic expressions. In Russell's theory only denoting phrases have associated denoting concepts. Secondly, sense is explained as the sense of a linguistic expression, while for Russell denoting concepts can exist independently of language. Thirdly, the denoting relation is closely linked to the notion of 'aboutness'—an obscure notion meant to elucidate 'being the subject of a proposition'. This last feature limits Russell's account to particular expressions only. Frege instead appeals to the notion of *cognitive value* and so gives a perfectly general argument. The notion of aboutness becomes more obscure when we move away from definite descriptions to other phrases. Is 'All men are mortal' really about *all men*? Recall that this provides Russell's reason for rejecting the Fregean analysis.

None the less, the three-stage analysis is common to both for, at least, a certain class of expressions. And both Frege and Russell see senses and denoting concepts respectively as objective entities in the world. Again, any entity may be denoted by indefinitely many denoting concepts (Russell) or be the referent of indefinitely many senses (Frege)—in other words, both relations are many–one.

2.1.4. Russell's Abandonment of 'Denoting Concepts'

By the time he wrote 'On Denoting' (1905) Russell was dissatisfied with the theory of denoting concepts. He came to think he had an argument which refuted both it and Frege's theory of sense. The argument is difficult and disputed but, because it marks an important departure in Russell's thought and might provide a telling criticism of Frege, it is worth examining.

The argument can be reconstructed as follows. Russell's *Principles* tells us that a denoting concept is logically related (given the way the world is) to its actual denotation. To give an account of the logical relation of denoting we must specify the entity at each end of the denoting relation, that is, the denotation and the denoting concept. There is no problem about the first; we simply use the denoting concept. But how do we specify the denoting concept itself? The following diagram illustrates the predicament:

Language	**The World**
	The denotation of *C*
C	
	Denoting concept of *C*

We need to explain the bottom right-hand corner. Remember that when a denoting phrase is used, the resulting expression is not about the denoting concept but its denotation. So the expression 'the denoting concept of *C*' is about the denoting concept of the entity named in the top right-hand corner—which is not what we are seeking. Normally we would mark this distinction by some such device as quotation marks. So how about 'the denoting concept of "C"'? But we cannot assume that this does the trick, for it makes the relation of denoting 'purely linguistic through the phrase', and so the *logical* relation of denoting eludes us. To see why, note that 'the denoting concept of "*C*"' is itself a denoting phrase. The corresponding denoting concept must include constituents which account for its ability *logically* to pick out the thing named in the bottom right-hand corner. But what could it be? If we think that the denoting concept is itself one of the constituents, we are supposing that this, combined with other constituents, enables us to 'work back' from the denotation to the denoting concept. (This is because whenever the denoting concept is a constituent, we are talking about the denotation.) But we cannot 'work back' in this way because the denotation can be denoted by indefinitely many denoting concepts (the relation is many–one). On the other hand, if the denoting concept is not itself a constituent, it is mysterious how the right denotation is effected. Indeed since we would require some explanation of *this* denoting relation in turn, we are in danger of regress. Russell therefore concluded that the theory of denoting is fundamentally confused.

The following five premisses are crucial:

(1) When a denoting concept is a constituent of a complex the complex is about the denoting concept's denotation, not about the denoting concept itself.
(2) Given the way the world is, it is intrinsic to a denoting concept to have the denotation it actually has.
(3) The denoting concept is determined by its composition.
(4) Denoting concepts must be specifiable.
(5) The relation of denoting concept to denotation is many–one.

2.2. Russell's Theory of Descriptions

2.2.1. *Indefinite Descriptions*

Russell took it that denoting is an important notion for explaining our grasp of propositions about entities we are unacquainted with. Note that his emphasis is on denoting *phrases*, in the form of both definite and indefinite descriptions. He first gave a theory of the latter. For any concept, *F*, we get five indefinite descriptions: all *F*s, every *F*, any *F*, an *F*, some *F*. In *The Principles* Russell was careful to distinguish among these; later he identified 'all *F*s' and 'every *F*'; 'an *F*' and 'some *F*' ('any' is different from 'all' but its use does not give rise to the assertion of a definite proposition).

Some examples show how Russell's theory of indefinite descriptions works:

> 'Everything is drifting in a haze' becomes '"*x* is drifting in a haze" is always true' (or 'For all *x*, *x* is drifting in a haze').
>
> 'Something is rotten in the state of Denmark' becomes 'It is false that ("*x* is rotten in the state of Denmark" is false) is always true' (or 'It is not the case that for all *x*, *x* is not-(rotten in the state of Denmark)').

Russell takes an equivalent of the universal quantifier, namely, '"*C*(*x*)" is always true', as primitive, and defines 'everything', 'something', and 'nothing' in terms of it.

The actual definitions are as follows:

> 'C(everything)' means '"$C(x)$" is always true' (or 'For all x, $C(x)$').
> 'C(nothing)' means '"($C(x)$) is false" is always true' (or 'For all x, not-C(x)').
> 'C(something)' means 'It is false that ("$C(x)$" is false) is always true' (or 'It is not the case that for all x, not-$C(x)$').

He also proposes that, for example, 'C(all dogs)' means '"If x is a dog then $C(x)$" is always true'.

Note that this analysis is close to the Fregean view Russell had previously rejected, thinking that 'C(all dogs)' was about *all dogs* whereas '"If x is a dog then $C(x)$" is always true' is simply true unrestrictedly. Here he is saying that although the sentence *appears* to be about a certain subject, we may discover this to be an illusion: grammar is not an infallible guide to logical form.

2.2.2. *Definite Descriptions*

Definite descriptions prompt a number of difficulties. Some arise from the fact that they seem to function as names (they pick out individuals); but if they are treated as names we cannot account for their role in certain inferences. For instance, we can infer from *the black dog is asleep* that *something black is asleep*. But how do we account for this if the semantic role of the expression is simply that of denoting an individual? We can only account for the validity of the inference if we discern some structure in the description, which, if we treat it as a name, we prevent ourselves from doing.

But definite descriptions also share some of the problems of names. What truth-value do we assign to sentences containing empty singular terms? If 'The president of France is bald' is meaningful (at time of writing it is true), then 'The president of Britain is bald' is also meaningful. But if the latter is meaningful, it succeeds in determining a definite condition for its truth. So is it, as the world stands, true or false? At time of writing it is not true. But equally it cannot be false, for if it is, then 'The president of Britain is not bald', being the negation of the original sentence, would be true. But at time of writing it is also not true. Moreover, it seems that to account for the meaningfulness of 'The president of Britain is bald' we need to assume an entity which is the president of Britain: the sentence is true just in case this entity is bald, false otherwise. If this entity does not exist, it must (in some sense) subsist. But if we grant that, we seem obliged to grant also the subsistence of—say—the golden mountain (an unlikely object), and even the round square (an impossible object).

This last problem is a familiar one. Russell's version of it is as follows. George IV wished to know whether Scott is the author of *Waverley*. Scott is indeed the author of *Waverley*. So, on the principle that we should be able to intersubstitute co-referential terms without altering truth-values, we should be able to infer that George IV wished to know whether Scott is Scott. But, as Russell remarks, 'an interest in the law of identity can hardly be attributed to the first gentleman of Europe'.

It is worth wondering whether Frege's notion of sense helps resolve these difficulties. Russell did not think so. He therefore required a solution consistent with the argument against sense and denoting concepts. His solution is as follows. Consider again the sentence 'The president of Britain is bald'. What does it take for this sentence to be true? Surely the following three conditions are necessary and sufficient:

(1) There is something which is president of Britain.
(2) There is at most one thing which is president of Britain.
(3) That thing (which is president of Britain) is bald.

Just when these conditions are fulfilled the original sentence is true. Russell takes it that the conjunction of these three sentences *gives the meaning* of the original sentence:

> 'The president of Britain is bald' means 'There is something which is president of Britain; anything which is president of Britain is identical with that thing; and that thing is bald'

or, semi-formally,

> $(\exists x)(Px \,\&\, (y)\,(Py \rightarrow y = x) \,\&\, Bx)$, where '$Px$' is '$x$ is president of Britain' and 'Bx' is 'x is bald'.

In general we have:

> 'C(the F)' means '$(\exists x)(Fx \,\&\, (y)(Fy \rightarrow y = x) \,\&\, Cx)$'.

How does this help with our problems? Consider 'The black dog is asleep'. This becomes $(\exists x)(Bx \,\&\, Dx \,\&\, (y)(By \,\&\, Dy \rightarrow y = x) \,\&\, Sx)$, from which we easily deduce $(\exists x)(Bx \,\&\, Sx)$ (just by eliminating the second and third conjuncts from the existential statement).

What about the truth-value of 'The president of Britain is bald'? Well: what is the truth-value of '$(\exists x)(Px \,\&\, (y)(Py \rightarrow y = x) \,\&\, Bx)$'? Clearly it is false, for there is no entity that satisfies these conditions. Does this commit us to the truth of 'The president of Britain is not bald'? No. What we are committed to is the truth of

(1) 'not-$(\exists x)(Px \,\&\, (y)(Py \rightarrow y = x) \,\&\, Bx)$',

that is, to the truth of 'It is not the case that the president of Britain is bald'. This is clearly a different statement from 'The president of Britain is not bald', for, according to the theory of descriptions, the latter means

(2) $(\exists x)(Px \& (y)(Py \rightarrow y = x) \& \text{not-}Bx)$.

(1) denies an existential claim, whereas (2) asserts one.

An important and general philosophical moral is suggested here. We often need to distinguish between the relative scopes of certain sentential operators (for example, quantifiers and negations). In (1) the *negation* has 'wide' scope—that is, applies to the whole proposition; in (2) the *existential quantifier* has wide scope. The operator with widest scope determines the sort of statement that is being made. Because, in this case, the negation has two possible scopes, we need to uncover the logical form of the original sentence. Only when that has been done can we know that, for instance, (1) is the negation of the original sentence, whereas (2) is not.

Note also that the sentence's logical form does not commit us to the being or subsistence of a president of Britain merely to account for its meaningfulness; only the *truth* of the sentence commits us to the existence of such a thing.

Finally, consider opaque contexts, as exemplified in the case of George IV and the law of identity.

> George IV wished to know whether Scott is the author of *Waverley*.

That is, according to the theory of descriptions,

> George IV wished to know whether $(\exists x)(Wx \& (y)(Wy \rightarrow y = x) \& x = \text{Scott})$.

Note that there is now no second term in the sentence for which one could substitute 'Scott', thereby rendering George IV's curiosity trivial.

Russell distinguished between a primary and a secondary occurrence of a description. This again is a matter of scope. In the above case the description has secondary occurrence because it falls within the scope of George IV's wish to know. The description might have primary occurrence thus,

> $(\exists x)(Wx \& (y)(Wy \rightarrow y = x) \&$ George IV wished to know whether $x = \text{Scott})$.

That is, George IV wished to know *of* the author of *Waverley*, whether he is Scott. Here the description is not part of the content of George IV's thought; rather, it provides *our* means of specifying which object George IV is thinking about when he wonders whether Scott is the author of *Waverley*. In this case we could infer that, since Scott is the author of *Waverley*, George IV wished to know *of* Scott whether he is Scott. And notice that this is not an absurd report of George IV's musings.

Two questions worth asking at this juncture are these: Russell's method of analysis consists in finding a sentence logically equivalent to the description-containing sentence under consideration. He *assumes* that the former gives the meaning of the latter. Given that this is clearly not always the case, what justifies the method?

The problems noted in connection with opacity and empty singular terms infect both names and definite descriptions. Russell's solution applies only to descriptions. How should he solve the same problems for names?

2.2.3. *Incomplete Symbols*

Both Russell and Frege use the term 'incompleteness', but in quite different ways. For Frege incompleteness is *unsaturatedness*; incomplete items require complementation. For Russell, incomplete *symbols* (only linguistic items are incomplete) are *eliminable* symbols.

Consider how the above definitions work. We are not told what, for instance, 'The *F*' stands for; that is, we are not given a definition of the form 'The *F* = such-and-such'. Instead we are told what any sentence of the form '*C*(the *F*)' means: such terms are *contextually* defined. Given any sentence involving a description, we can rewrite that sentence as one which contains no term corresponding to the descriptive phrase. The descriptive phrase has been eliminated and a sentence with an apparently different logical structure emerges. Russell describes this by saying that such phrases have no meaning in isolation; they only have meaning as a contribution to the meaning of a sentence. Although this seems reminiscent of Frege's Context Principle, the underlying thought is different. Russell, recall, took it that the meaning of an expression is what it stands for: words are labels for things. In this sense incomplete symbols have no meaning; they occur in sentences which are meaningful because their meanings are given by other, more basic, sentences, the meanings of whose parts are the things they denote; and no separable part corresponds to the original descriptive phrase.

The invention of the notion of incomplete symbols was important to Russell's philosophical development. It enabled him to recognize that a sentence is meaningful without having to presuppose that an entity corresponds to a phrase occupying the subject position. Because a phrase *might* be incomplete, one is now faced with the task of deciding whether certain expressions should be contextually defined and so treated as incomplete. The *ontological* question of whether a given class of entities must be assumed to exist becomes a question of how we are to introduce symbols for those entities, whether or not such symbols are incomplete. We decide that question by giving the correct logical form for sentences containing the appropriate symbols. So ontological questions are linked closely with questions of logic and the whole enterprise is driven by an effort to provide a correct analysis of language. (Note that many questions about what counts as a 'correct' analysis of language, and what is the 'correct' logical form of a sentence, remain undecided; more below.)

2.3. Russell's Logical Atomism

The theory of descriptions is a neat technical solution to certain logical problems. But it is, at least for Russell, far more than that. If one accepts the theory, one has also to accept the notion of an incomplete symbol—a symbol which has meaning in the context of a sentence but which is eliminable by analysis. Consequently, one has also to accept that the surface grammar of a sentence can obscure the logical form of the proposition it expresses. So, whereas in the *Principles* Russell had been happy to accept grammar as a guide to logical form, he now rejected that view. The question is, what replaces grammar as a guide to the correct analysis of a sentence?

Here one must anticipate later discussion. Russell held that natural language is, from the viewpoint of logic, imperfect because it relies on expressions (for example, the definite article) that mask underlying logical form. Moreover, it leads us to construct sentences based on confusions about logical form, rendering them nonsensical. Prime examples are sentences that lead to paradox. For philosophical purposes natural language should therefore be replaced by a logically perfect language. (The language of *Principia Mathematica*, Russell claims, is one such.) So another way of asking our question about what makes for a correct analysis of a sentence is to ask what makes a language logically perfect.

2.3.1. *Knowledge by Acquaintance and Knowledge by Description*

Problems about denoting are both epistemological and logical. The epistemological dimension is present because we wish to account for our ability to have thoughts and (on occasion) knowledge about entities with which we are unacquainted. There are *logical* problems in accounting for the role of descriptions in certain inferences, in opaque contexts, and whenever descriptions are empty. The logical and epistemological problems are closely linked. Indeed it seems that the logical problems arise because of our epistemological predicament: it is *because* we grasp propositions about entities which fall outside our range of acquaintance that we risk using empty descriptions; it is because we lack acquaintance with the entity that we need a means of specifying it—which then becomes part of the informational content of the proposition, relevant to its use in both opaque contexts and inferences.

Epistemology and logic are therefore closely linked in Russell's view. The connection is made explicit by his adoption of the Principle of Acquaintance:

'every proposition which we understand must be composed wholly of constituents with which we are acquainted'. The puzzle which the Theory of Descriptions aims to resolve is how we can obey this principle yet still show how we grasp propositions *about* entities lying outside our range of acquaintance. In the idiom of analysis this is put by saying that a sentence is problematic until we can analyse it into (usually) a logically equivalent sentence expressing a proposition whose constituents are objects of acquaintance.

What are we acquainted with? Russell's answer is: universals and particulars. The latter are, in *Principles* terminology, things: they are entities which can only be named. Universals are the concepts of the *Principles*—properties, and relations between particulars. Thus: if I know that this patch is red, I must be acquainted with this patch (a particular) and with redness (a universal).

Many of the problems affecting definite descriptions affect names also: names can be empty, and substitution of one co-referential name for another in opaque contexts does not necessarily preserve truth-value. Russell's solution is simple and economical. Names susceptible to these problems are not *logically proper names*, but disguised definite descriptions. 'Logically proper names'—names immune to these problems—are logically simple, are guaranteed to refer whenever used, and are such that their users are always acquainted with their referents. (And if I use two logically proper names to co-refer, this must be immediately apparent to me.) For Russell, one can only, properly speaking, *name* one's present experience, that is, an existing sense-datum. The paradigm names are 'this' and 'that'. Sense-data are therefore the only particulars.

2.3.2. *The Multiple Relations Theory of Judgement*

A feature of the emerging picture is that its account of linguistic meaning has become complicated: we cannot adopt the labelling model for the meaning of many expressions. And remember that Russell had a problem with truth: if we regard sentences as names of propositions, then a sentence is meaningful only if it stands for a proposition—but then we have no account of the difference between true and false propositions.

The thesis about sentences is similar to that of (logically proper) names. On the earlier view we had to suppose that, to be meaningful, a name must name something. The theory of descriptions shows that this is a confusion. Russell now attempts a similar solution for sentences. But the difficulty of applying the theory of incomplete symbols to sentences is that names, *unlike* sentences, have an obvious context of use, namely: the sentences in which they occur. But if sentences are themselves context-free, self-standing devices, this seems only to defer the problem. So Russell rejects this view of sentences, arguing instead that sentences and propositions only have a use in the contexts of 'attitudes' such as judging, believing, supposing, and the like. If we can account for the attitudes without assuming the existence of propositions, then we shall be able to say that a sentence is meaningful without having to assume that it expresses an independently existing proposition. We can then say that a sentence is true if it corresponds to a fact, false otherwise.

The core of Russell's theory of judgement is that it is a relation of the judging subject not to a proposition but to a set of entities: judging is a multiple relation. *S*'s judgement that '*a* is similar to *b*' is symbolized *J*(*S*, *a*, *b*, similarity). No proposition corresponds to the sentence '*a* is similar to *b*', so it is an incomplete symbol. If it is a fact that *a* is similar to *b*, '*a* is similar to *b*' is true and '*a* is not similar to *b*' false. So truth is explained as a relation of a judgement to a fact, and because *two* judgements correspond to each fact (one by being true and the other false) the relation is not one of naming or labelling: meaning attaches to sentences and names in different ways.

This view contains difficulties. All we have been told is that judging is a multiple relation between a subject and certain entities. A minimal constraint on a theory of judgement is that it allows us to judge all and only what is meaningful. It is not enough to list possible constituents of a judgement; we need to know how they are related so as to yield meaningful judgements. We need, in short, to be able to represent the judgement's logical form.

In judging that *a* is similar to *b* we make a two-place relational judgement. The only way Russell can express its form is as a fact. Moreover, this fact must have no constituents (it might otherwise fail to occur, rendering such judgements impossible). So he expresses the form by the completely general fact that something is related to something. With this symbolized *R*(*x*, *y*), the judgement becomes *J*(*S*, *a*, *b*, similarity, *R*(*x*, *y*)). Russell assumes that we have self-evident acquaintance with logical forms, presupposed in our understanding of sentences.

There are sketches of the theory dating from about 1906, and Russell is still hinting at it in the 'Lectures on Logical Atomism' of 1918; but his chief attempt occurs in the *Theory of Knowledge* manuscript of 1913. That project, designed to provide the epistemological basis for his logical doctrines, was interrupted by Wittgenstein's criticisms. Wittgenstein claimed that Russell's theory failed to meet the minimal constraint, mentioned above, that a theory of judgement must allow us to judge all and only what is meaningful. The reason for its failure is the oddity of the relation of judgement. Because we can make all sorts of judgements, the argument places of the judging relation can be filled by anything: they are not selective. Accordingly, a meaningful judgement is possible only if the entities filling the argument places are of the right sort *relative to each other*. But we have no way of guaranteeing that this will always happen. Russell's use of logical form, which should have dealt with the problem of ill-formedness, cannot help because it simply becomes one more value of an argument place. These considerations were an important stimulus in Wittgenstein's development of a different notion of logical form in his *Tractatus*.

2.3.3. *Logical Atomism*

According to Russell's logical atomism the world consists of distinct objects—atoms—possessing properties and standing in various relations. The atoms are not those of science: they are logical atoms, revealed by analysis of language or, alternatively, by considering what is named in a logically perfect language. It has already been noted that, on Russell's view of logically proper names, sense-data are the only logical atoms. Anything else we are able to think about is a 'logical construction' out of sense-data.

Because sense-data cannot be shared, a logically perfect language must be private to an individual. Speakers succeed in communicating if their sentences are about the same thing or have the same truth-conditions. There is some unclarity here; when we talk about external objects or other minds we are really, says Russell, talking about logical constructions of sense-data; but he also says we do not know whether such things exist. His point might be that the object or mind cannot be known to exist as we ordinarily suppose (to this extent he accepts scepticism), but we can substitute a rigorous logical point of view for our ordinary conceptions without doing violence to our usual practice. And because we *can* dispense with these ordinary conceptions we *should*, by Occam's Razor, do so.

2.3.4. *Monism*

Logical atomism, although pluralistic, rejects mind–matter dualism in favour of a monism of sense-data. Sense-data should not, according to Russell, be conceived as 'in the head'. Rather, they are objective constituents of the world; they are, literally, all there is. But sense-data are not the subject-matter of physics. Instead sense-data underlie both physics and psychology, constituting external objects—the subject-matter of physics—or segments of a subject's experience—the subject-matter of psychology—depending upon the point of view from which they are considered.

2.3.5. *Summary*

Russell developed a view in which analysis of language assumes great philosophical importance. Philosophy's role is to dispel confusions created by taking the surface forms of language too seriously, and by assuming that we can give a uniform account of meaning. Our guide in analysis is the Principle of Acquaintance combined with Occam's Razor. These generate a theory of meaning associated with a monism of sense-data. But Russell faces great difficulty, first, in giving an account of logical form and, secondly, in showing that his logically perfect language is indeed adequate. So far he has only sketched its form.

2.4. Russell's Resolution of the Paradoxes

Russell's reaction to his discovery of the paradoxes was very different from Frege's. Frege abandoned the logicist programme because of them, but Russell saw the paradoxes as infecting *logic*, so he drew no pessimistic conclusions about logicism's viability. One reason was that he thought the class paradox shared the same form as the 'Liar' and the paradox of heterologicality. (A version of the liar is: 'This proposition is false'. As to the heterologicality paradox: a property is heterological if it does not apply to itself. Now ask yourself whether the property of heterologicality is heterological.) The point about these paradoxes is that they do not arise from any specifically mathematical assumptions—for instance, about the nature of infinity. Rather there seems to be a *logical* problem arising from their self-referential nature. To solve them, said Russell, we need to change some of our assumptions.

2.4.1. *The Vicious Circle Principle*

Russell held that the clue to diagnosing the source of the paradoxes is the fact that each involves a vicious circle. But what exactly is vicious circularity? Each paradox involves the specification or definition of a certain sort of entity: a proposition, or a propositional function, a property, or a class. The problem, Russell argued, is that we attempt to define that entity by reference to a totality which, were it to exist, would include that very entity. The process is circular because, since the totality presupposes its members, it cannot be used to define one of its members. Therefore the solution to the paradoxes is to outlaw that kind of definition—or equivalently, to outlaw the assumption that such totalities exist (that is, totalities which contain members definable only in terms of the totality itself). This is the Vicious Circle Principle (VCP).

It may not be obvious that the paradoxes violate the VCP, so note the following. The class of 'non-self-membered classes' is the class of *all those classes* which do not contain themselves as members. 'This proposition is false' says (according to Russell) '*There is a proposition* which I am now affirming and which is false'. Heterologicality is that property which applies to *all properties* which do not apply to themselves.

The VCP is not entirely clear as Russell states it. 'Presupposition' is left unexplained, for one thing; and for another, it is not obvious that the existence of an entity depends on our ability to define it in a particular way. As Gödel pointed out, if the entities and totalities are supposed to exist mind-independently, what does it matter that in *specifying* the entity *we* are forced to refer to the totality?

To clarify matters we must examine how Russell explains and uses the VCP. The first point to note is that, although contravention of the VCP is the source of the paradoxes, obeying it cannot be the solution, because this would itself contravene the VCP. The VCP rules out certain modes of definition, but we cannot develop a paradox-free logic by restricting definitions to those that respect the VCP, for in doing so we would be endorsing talk of, say, all classes by reserving this to talk of all classes except those defined in terms of all classes. But this itself illegitimately involves talk of all classes. So what we require of a solution is an argument for a logical system naturally constrained so as not to contravene the VCP.

2.4.2. *Incomplete Symbols*

Russell's first step is to treat class terms as incomplete symbols. He gives an account of class talk without assuming the existence of classes, by providing a way of giving the meaning of sentences involving classes in terms that make no reference to classes. In short, he defines them contextually.

Russell provides a reduction of classes to *propositional functions*. These are functions that yield propositions as values when their argument places are filled (they are the analogues of Frege's 'concepts'). To define classes contextually Russell needs to explain in class-free terms what it is to assert something of a class. His solution is to treat such an assertion as being about the propositional function defining the class. The problem with this is that assertions made of propositional functions are not *extensional*—two propositional functions might have differing properties despite the fact that they are coextensive (true of the same objects). Classes, on the other hand, are identical when their members are the same. Russell therefore needs a way of restricting attention to extensional properties of propositional functions, that is, properties which apply uniformly to coextensive propositional functions. Assume that we have a class given by a propositional function *f*. We wish to fix the truth-conditions of f applied to the class of *f*s. Russell does this as follows: f applies to the class of *f*s just in case there is a propositional function *j* which is coextensive with *f* such that f applies to *j*. Note that if *z* is coextensive with *f* then f will either apply or fail to apply to both since the truth-values of the relevant sentences will depend on whether f applies to some function *j* which is coextensive with each of *f* and *z*. So, in virtue of this definition, any function of a class will be extensional.

The effect of this reduction of classes to propositional functions is to reduce the class paradox to that of propositional functions: a class is a candidate for membership of itself only if a propositional function can be applied to itself. Thus if we explain why propositional functions cannot be applied to themselves we will have solved both paradoxes. Alternatively, we need to motivate the VCP as applied to propositional functions from considerations relating to propositional functions.

2.4.3. *Propositional Functions*

Russell now explains the VCP, or, as he claims, the most fundamental instance of the VCP, as a consequence of the nature of propositional functions. His point is that a propositional function is an ambiguity standing in a relation to the values of the function. We appreciate the nature of this relation once we realize that in asserting a propositional function we do not assert anything definite; rather, we assert *any* (recall that Russell distinguishes 'any' from 'all') value of the function. For example, when I assert 'x is wise' I assert any value of the function, that is, I ambiguously assert 'Socrates is wise', 'Aristotle is wise', and so on. (Note that this is not to say, absurdly, that I assert all of these propositions.) So a propositional function *ambiguously denotes* any of its values. Moreover, this role is exhaustively distinctive of propositional functions (no other sort of entity has this role and propositional functions that coincide in what they ambiguously denote are identical). Russell concludes that a propositional function is only definite once its values are definite; that is, the values of a propositional function cannot presuppose the propositional function itself. So the VCP is a consequence of the (metaphysical) nature of propositional functions.

The effect this point has on our system is, first, that no propositional function can take itself as argument: Russell's paradox of classes and the analogue for propositional functions are thus avoided. Secondly, we are now forced to see propositional functions as belonging to a hierarchy. The possible arguments of a propositional function must, in some sense, be prior to the function. The possible arguments of a propositional function, its *range of significance*, is a *type*. Thus, at the lowest level, we have individuals and functions applicable to them; then we have functions applicable to functions of individuals; then we have functions applicable to functions applicable to functions of individuals; and so on. But a hierarchy of this form is still too simple because we need to admit propositional functions which are capable of having more than one argument. We can form propositional functions of fewer arguments from these by *quantifying over* one or more of the argument places. For instance, consider the propositional function $F(x, j)$. This function presupposes the domain of individuals and that of propositional functions of individuals. We can quantify over the latter to form, for example, $(\exists j)F(x, j)$, which is itself a propositional function of individuals. It would contravene this VCP if this were in the same domain as that of the variable *j*. So this function must be of a different *order*. The VCP thus imposes a 'ramified' hierarchy of propositional functions.

One problem is that the contextual definition of classes given above no longer works. That definition says that f applies to the class of *f*s just in case *there is* a coextensive propositional function *j* such that f applies to *j*. This involves quantifying over the domain of propositional functions which apply to a given type. But we have just learned that this is an illegitimate totality; we can only quantify over propositional functions of a given order, and propositional functions applying to a given type occur at all orders of the hierarchy. Russell thus uses a modified definition in which he confines the quantification to what he calls 'predicative propositional functions' (that is, propositional functions which are of order one higher than their arguments). The problem with this is that given some non-predicative propositional function, *f*, there is no guarantee that there is a coextensive *predicative* propositional function—indeed, it seems there may be none. (In this case the existential claim would always be false, no matter what f is. This, in turn, means that f would be false of the class of *f*s *and* similarly not-f would be false of the class of *f*s: an absurdity.) Russell's solution is *ad hoc*; he adopts this assumption—the assumption that for any propositional function there is a coextensive predicative propositional function—as an axiom, which he calls 'the Axiom of Reducibility'. He simply recommends that we adopt it because it gives us what we need and, since it is implied by the assumption that classes exist, is weaker than that assumption.

There is something suspect about the VCP. The system it generates is very complicated, and it is incoherent unless supplemented by the Axiom of Reducibility, which is not only doubtful in its own right but, in effect, runs counter to the spirit of the VCP because it says that for the needs of mathematics (that is, for extensional concerns) we can effectively ignore features of a propositional function (the bound variables it includes) which the VCP insists we respect. But it is worth noting that the VCP is detachable from Russell's view of classes, which neatly explains our grasp of infinite classes (we do so intensionally) and the many–oneness of classes (the unity is given by the defining function, the plurality by the many objects that function holds of). The big question remaining is: how are we to solve the mysterious problem underlying the reasoning that leads to paradox?

3. WITTGENSTEIN

Wittgenstein is credited with having made two contributions to philosophy, the first in his *Tractatus Logico-Philosophicus* (1921) and the second in his *Philosophical Investigations* (together with other writings associated with it in time and subject-matter). Here the principal theses of both are sketched, with a note on the transition between them. Despite the many and significant differences between his 'early' and 'late' views, there is a link between them, which is Wittgenstein's conviction that philosophical problems arise because we 'misunderstand the workings of our language'. His views about how language works changed radically between his early and late philosophies; these competing views are the subject of what follows.

3.1. The *Tractatus*: Facts, Objects, and Pictures

In the *Tractatus* Wittgenstein attempts to understand the way language and thought are related to the world. The inquiry aims to explain how thoughts can be representational and language meaningful, thus setting a limit to significant uses of language. The theory has metaphysical implications: for representation to be possible, the world has to have a certain structure.

The seven main propositions of the *Tractatus* are:

1. The world is all that is the case.
2. What is the case—the fact—is the existence of states of affairs.
3. A logical picture of facts is a thought.
4. A thought is a proposition with a sense.
5. A proposition is a truth-function of elementary propositions. (An elementary proposition is a truth-function of itself.)
6. The general form of a truth-function is $[\bar{p}, \bar{\xi}, N(\bar{\xi})]$. This is the general form of a proposition.
7. What we cannot speak about we must pass over in silence.

The *Tractatus* consists of comment, elaboration, and defence of these main propositions, each with a dependent number, for example '1.1', '2.0121'.

The 1s present us with an abstract, metaphysical picture of the world's structure. The 2s elaborate this picture, introducing and explaining the notions of 'fact', 'states of affairs', and 'objects', which are then used to explain what Wittgenstein calls the 'picturing relation' between language and the world. The notion of a picture is deployed in the 3s to explain representation in both thought and language, where we are also introduced to the concept of a 'sign'. The 4s give an account of meaning, aimed at showing where the limits of meaning lie.

The 5s explore the logic of language. Some problems inherited from Frege and Russell are resolved, the nature of the logical constants is described, and in 6 we are told the 'general form' of the proposition. Wittgenstein then considers whether the 'propositions' of various regions of discourse (logic itself; the laws of natural science; ethics; and philosophy) can be said to have this form. The inquiry attempts to show that some apparent propositions are vacuous, and that others are meaningless. In neither case does this diminish their importance—indeed, they constitute 'the more important unwritten half' of the *Tractatus*—but one must not to be misled into thinking that they succeed in saying something. This thought leads to the overall conclusion that figures as 7.

3.1.1. The Metaphysics of the Tractatus

The *Tractatus* view is often described as a version of logical atomism. But whereas Russell's atomism premisses the claim that the world is constituted of independently existing things, Wittgenstein denies this: the world is the totality of facts (*Tatsachen*), not of things (*Dinge*) (1.1.). Another difference is that the notion of possibility plays a central role in the *Tractatus*. Neither Frege nor Russell favoured talking of how things 'might have been otherwise', and therefore both characterize logic as ultimately *general*. Wittgenstein, by contrast, says:

> 1.21. Each item can be the case or not while everything else remains the same.

Facts are independent of each other and, given any fact, it might not have been the case. The world is all that is the case, so the world is all the facts that exist. Once we know which facts exist *and* that they are *all* the facts, we know which facts do not exist; for the totality of facts, both existing and non-existing, is unchangeable.

Having anatomized the world in terms of facts, Wittgenstein proceeds to anatomize facts in terms of objects.

> 2. What is the case—the fact—is the existence of states of affairs (*Sachverhalten*).

This is followed, first, by a definition of states of affairs in terms of objects, then an account of objects, and then, in 2.04–2.063, a set of propositions which echo the 1s but with 'existing state of affairs' substituted for 'fact'. It seems that the 2.0s are thus an argument for 2 from the definition of states of affairs.

States of affairs are combinations of objects (*Gegenstanden*). Each object is associated with a set of possible states of affairs, in each of which it is a constituent. This is an *essential* property of an object. To know the object one needs to know all its internal properties, but not its external properties; so one needs to know all its possibilities of combination, but not which among them actually exist. Objects are constituents of possible states of affairs, and cannot be imagined in isolation. (So even if the world were reducible to objects or combinations of them, we could not say that the world is the totality of objects since that would be to think of objects in abstraction from possible combinations.)

2.03. Objects are simple.

Objects make up the substance of the world, and therefore cannot be complex. Complexes, consisting of components in combination, are analysable, and not therefore ultimate. But the bottom-most level of analysis is not itself analysable; it is simple. It is what constitutes the substance of the world.

2.0211. If the world has no substance, then whether a proposition had sense would depend on whether another proposition was true.
2.0212. In that case we could not sketch a picture of the world (true or false).

Wittgenstein is gesturing at a regress which would make representation impossible. The point is made in 2.0201: propositions about complexes are resolvable into propositions about their parts and arrangement. If there were no simple objects, then we are forced (again by 2.0201) to describe the parts. But since we know the parts exist, the propositions describing them would have to be *true*. So 2.0211 follows: the sense of a proposition would always require the truth of a distinct proposition.

Objects constitute the 'unalterable form' of all possible worlds. They combine to form states of affairs, some of which are actualized. The world is the totality of existing states of affairs, and states of affairs are independent of each other. A fact—'what is the case'—is an existing state of affairs.

3.1.2. The Picture Theory: Essentials

The notion of a picture is introduced in 2.1. Pictures represent possible states of affairs. The elements of a picture each represent an object. The elements of a picture stand in determinate relations to each other, which is what constitutes its form. A picture represents a possible state of affairs by representing the possibility that the objects for which their elements stand are related as are the elements of the picture. The picture can thus always be compared to reality, since the objects it represents are guaranteed to exist.

There are just two possibilities: either the objects are related as in the picture (the pictured situation exists), or not (the pictured situation does not exist). Pictures are themselves facts, and so are inherently structured. This is Wittgenstein's way of solving the problem of the form of representations. Russell's programme foundered precisely here, and Frege was driven to invent the notion of incompleteness. Wittgenstein begins (and ends) with facts.

Pictures must share the form of what they represent. For example, in a painting one might use a certain patch of colour to represent the sea, the patch representing the sea as similarly coloured. The form is provided by the colour spectrum, as the set of possibilities for both patch and sea. What is shared is 'logical form':

2.182. Every picture is *at the same time* a logical one. (On the other hand, not every picture is, for example, a spatial one.)

A picture and what it depicts do not have to share external properties: the picture exists while what it depicts may not. This allows the picture to be 'true' or correct, or otherwise—we have two mutually exclusive alternatives. The picture is 'outside' the pictured but cannot be 'outside' its own representational form, and therefore cannot depict its own representational form. But it can *show* it. (And note that since all pictures are logical pictures, there can be no picture of logical form.)

Thoughts, Propositions, Signs, and Symbols By the end of the 2s Wittgenstein has set out his ontology and his picture theory. His task in the 3s is to use these resources to develop an account of thought and its expression. He says:

3. A logical picture of facts is a thought.

A thought is itself a fact (it is a picture) and as such must have constituents. Wittgenstein does not say what they are, because that is an empirical, not a philosophical, question. But certain properties of thoughts immediately follow from their being picture': (i) they all have a logical form, so illogical thought is impossible; (ii) they can picture the world correctly or incorrectly, so no genuine thought is true or false a priori.

For the expression of thought a perceptible sign (*Zeichen*) of some kind is required: 'In a proposition a thought finds . . . expression' (3.1). Wittgenstein does not mean that the *proposition* is the perceptible sign; what is perceptible is a written or spoken sentence, say. Wittgenstein writes: 'What constitutes a propositional sign is that in it its elements (the words) stand in a determinate relation to one another. A propositional sign is a fact' (3.14).

As a fact, a propositional sign has a certain form. It can therefore be projected onto the world. For this, each name must be correlated with an object. Logic dictates that these objects are constituents of possible states of affairs. The possible arrangements of objects are mirrored by the possible arrangements of names in propositional signs. A given propositional sign together with a method of projection thus determines a possible state of affairs (which may or may not exist). So 'a proposition is a propositional sign in its projective relation to the world' (3.12).

Note that Wittgenstein, in contrast to both Russell and Frege, links his notion of a proposition with its expression in language. Russell simply saw propositions as certain sorts of complex existing independently of language, and independently graspable also, while for Frege thoughts (the closest analogue of propositions) are the senses of sentences, which although explained *as* the senses of sentences, exist independently of them. For Wittgenstein a proposition is a *method of projection of a sign*: 'Instead of, "The complex sign '*a*R*b*' says that *a* stands to *b* in the relation R", we ought to put, "*That* '*a*' stands to '*b*' in a certain relation says *that a*R*b*"' (3.1432).

Because the signs '*a*' and '*b*' are arranged a certain way in a fact (the former is to the left of the sign '*R*', the latter to the right) we can say (if we project appropriately) that *aRb*. But this plausible account conceals a danger: it masks the fact that the sign '*R*' does not function in the same way as '*a*' and '*b*'; not all signs stand for an entity in the world. So an explanation is required of how these entities are combined in a complex with a specific form, and of how the sign relates to just *that* complex. Wittgenstein's account is that the sign '*R*' means in a different way, it is part of the *form* of the fact which is the sign. So it restricts possible projections of the complex sign.

The Sense of a Proposition In the *Tractatus* Wittgenstein uses both *Sinn* and *Bedeutung*, Frege's terms for sense and reference respectively. But Wittgenstein has it that only propositions have sense; names do not. This is partly because he thought both (the early) Russell and Frege were mistaken in modelling sentences on names. (For Russell, sentences are names of propositions; for Frege they are names of truth-values.) In his view, whereas a name merely picks out an object, a proposition has sense; it is directed, pointing towards what makes it true and away from what makes it false. In more contemporary terminology: a name picks out an object in possible worlds, whereas a proposition divides the set of all possible worlds into two, those in which it is true and those in which it is false.

Is the sense of a proposition, in Wittgenstein's view, anything like a Fregean sense? He gives hints in 3.11 (a proposition is 'a projection of a possible situation') and 3.13, which make 'projection' seem like Frege's mode of presentation—except that what is being presented is the *sense* of the proposition. So sense appears to be a species of reference (*Bedeutung*). This is encouraged by later remarks to the effect that sense is external to the proposition.

Wittgenstein's view is clearer if not seen through Fregean spectacles. Paragraph 3.11 says that the projected possible situation is the proposition's sense. It fixes just what has to be the case if the proposition is true; so it is the proposition's truth-condition.

Wittgenstein thus offers an analysis of language in four components: sign, method of projection, truth-condition, truth-value. Frege's notion of sense identifies the two middle components. He often characterizes sense as 'mode of presentation', 'cognitive value', 'informational content', or 'method of determining reference'. But he also treats sense as that which, given the way the world is, determines reference, so making the sense of a sentence its truth-condition. The two notions come apart when we look at Frege's view of mathematics, in which sentences have the same truth-conditions (they are true in all circumstances) but have differing senses determined by the senses of their constituents (important for Frege's account of mathematics' utility). Wittgenstein separates the two notions, and takes the notion of truth-conditions to be primary; which prompts a very different account of logic and mathematics.

Signs and Symbols A sign is a written, spoken, or mental mark. (Note that Wittgenstein says that 'A' is the same sign as 'A', so signs are *types* of marks, not tokens.) Complexes of signs are articulated facts, which allows them to represent by means of the picturing relation. The use of signs to represent is accomplished by setting up a method of projection: the sign so used is a symbol. Signs and symbols must be sharply distinguished.

Objects can only be named, facts can only be pictured, complexes can only be described. Wittgenstein accepted Russell's theory of descriptions for complexes, which are not guaranteed to exist. Terms for complexes may be contracted (by definition), so we get a class of pseudo-names. To reveal the logical form of a proposition one must effect an analysis yielding a proposition containing only genuine names. This process must yield a unique proposition; the existence of alternatives would show that further analysis is possible.

> 3.3. Only propositions have sense; only in the nexus of a proposition does a name have meaning.

So propositions mean in a way different from other expressions. The second half of 3.3 looks like Frege's Context Principle. A name can only mean when it is included in an expression having form, namely a proposition. Propositions are thus the primary bearers of meaning. But notice the interdependence: a proposition has its meaning determined compositionally by its constituents, but any subpropositional expression (symbol) has meaning only in the context of a proposition and, in fact, 'presupposes the forms of all the propositions in which it can occur' (3.311). So although language is articulated into propositions, each with its own structure, the sense of each proposition presupposes the possibility of other propositions, which is to say: the rest of language. (This mirrors Wittgenstein's ontology, which is based on the existence of independent states of affairs. These consist of objects each of which contains the form of all the states of affairs in which it is included. So states of affairs exist in logical space as a whole.)

We have the following picture: the symbol (the sign with a significant use) presupposes the logical form of those propositions in which it can occur. Our choice of sign is conventional (at least for simple signs) and the choice of a use for a particular sign is conventional. But certain things follow from the construction of the symbol: it is meaningful only in propositions of a certain form, in each of which it makes a specific contribution to determination of sense. So any system of notation must be constructed by making a set of arbitrary decisions embedding the signs in a context of possible uses, once and for all.

3.1.3. Ordinary Language, Philosophy, and Formal Concepts

In the 4s Wittgenstein turns to ordinary language. Although he has given an account of thought and the proposition, it is not yet linked to use of language, because the picturing relation depends on correlating elements of the picture with objects, and objects remain mysterious. Two themes emerge from Wittgenstein's focus on ordinary language: one is an account of the nature of philosophy, and the other concerns nonsense.

Ordinary Language Wittgenstein attributes to Russell the insight that the logical form of ordinary language is hidden (a consequence of the theory of descriptions is that the logical form of sentences containing descriptions is that of existential generalizations). The logical form of language is opaque because the meanings of many expressions are opaque. We learn language by being inducted into complex conventions governing the use of language. These conventions establish correlations between words and objects (or complexes of objects) without speakers having to know precisely what they are. Because of tacit conventions governing, for instance, contractions and ellipsis, the true logical form of a sentence may escape us: we are ignorant about which are the logically proper names in our language.

This view makes language the primary focus of philosophy. Thc *activity* of philosophy consists in providing the correct analysis of language, especially in showing how relevant parts of language represent reality. Analysis of language enables us to see certain aspects of reality aright: this is revealed in the logical form of the analysed language. But it also changes our conception of traditional philosophical problems, which now appear to arise from confusions about the nature of our language. When we free ourselves from linguistic confusions, philosophical problems are revealed as pseudo-problems. (See 4.003.) This theme persists into Wittgenstein's later philosophy.

Understanding Granted that aspects of meaning might escape us, what do we understand when we understand a language? Wittgenstein holds a compositional, truth-conditional account of understanding; he thinks that we understand a proposition when we understand what has to be the case for it to be true, and that we achieve that by understanding the expressions constituting the proposition. A proposition says that a possible state of affairs obtains; knowing this is what is required to understand it—we do not need to know that the state of affairs actually obtains. Note that though Wittgenstein allows, even insists, that there may be something fugitive about what *words* mean, this is not the case at the level of *propositions*: to understand a proposition we need to know just which possible situation it asserts to obtain.

Wittgenstein is committed to bivalence: every proposition asserts that a certain situation obtains, so every genuine proposition is either true or false depending on whether the situation obtains or not. Both alternatives must be possibilities and must exhaust all possibilities.

Truth and the Logical Constants An important aspect of the independence of the sense of a proposition from the facts is that this explains our grasp of a proposition before we know whether it is true. It also provides an account of truth. Because a proposition asserts the existence of a certain situation, and asserts this independently of whether that situation exists, we can say that it is true just when that situation exists. But if we reject this we would have to explain the meaning of a proposition by way of existing situations. In this case *p* and not-*p* would apparently express the same thing, the former in the true (false) way and the latter in the false (true) way. (See 4.061.)

This helps explain what Wittgenstein regarded as fundamental, namely that 'the "logical constants" are not representatives (*nicht vertreten*); that there can be no representatives of the *logic* of facts' (4.0312). This also pinpoints where Wittgenstein departs from both Frege and Russell. For the two latter, a sentence picks out a thought or proposition (respectively) which is capable of being true or false. Therefore, we can specify a thought or proposition and then discover (or, perhaps, decide) what truth is. Only then will we have determined the sense of the sentence. On this view one would think that *p* and *not-p* picked out different propositions *determined by their different constituents*, with the constraint that when one is true the other is false. But this view is fraught with difficulty. What are the constituents? What explains the interdependence of truth-values? What does truth consist in? (Consider 4.063.)

Wittgenstein's propositions, by contrast, do not pick out things; they have a sense, that is, they assert that such-and-such a situation obtains. So *not-p* asserts the existence of a situation which is different from that asserted by *p*, but is determined by *p*; it asserts the existence of a situation in which the situation asserted to exist by *p* does not exist. Accordingly, the logical constant 'not' does not *represent* (it picks out no constituent of reality), but instead determines a manner of representation, the form of the picture.

All propositions have logical form, and represent reality in virtue of sharing the logical form of reality. No picture can represent its form. It cannot be *said*, only *shown*.

Formal Concepts Recall that objects are 'colourless'; they have no properties besides their possibilities of combination, and these they possess *essentially*. A state of affairs, likewise, is *essentially* a combination of objects. Wittgenstein calls such properties 'formal' or 'internal'. We can never assert (or deny) that some formal property is exhibited in a situation; any attempt to say anything about it is (literally) nonsensical. But in representing the situation we thereby *show* its formal properties.

It makes no sense to assert 'x is an object', for if x is an object it is *necessarily* one. That x is an object is shown by our use of a name to refer to it. That something falls under a certain formal concept is shown by our method of symbolizing it. So, on Wittgenstein's view, Frege is forced to say, paradoxically, that the concept *horse* is not a concept because he is treating a formal concept as an ordinary one: he is trying to say what can only be shown.

The only way of 'expressing' a formal concept is by means of variable expressions, which *say* nothing but *show* form. Thus the variable name x 'represents' the formal concept *object*, and the variable expression $f(x)$ 'represents' the formal concept *one-place function*. Above we have talked about objects, states of affairs, facts, and propositions, and number, all of them formal concepts. On Wittgenstein's view, all such talk is nonsense.

3.1.4. *Propositions*

Elementary propositions assert the existence of states of affairs. Given, say, three states of affairs there are eight possibilities, determined by whether each exists or not. Where p, q, r are elementary propositions corresponding to the states of affairs, the possibilities can be represented as follows:

p	q	r
T	T	T
T	T	F
T	F	T
T	F	F
F	T	T
F	T	F
F	F	T
F	F	F

We might then want a way of describing the situations in which, say, any of the first three possibilities or the last hold. Given a convention for how to write the table we can symbolize this simply as (T, T, T, –, –, –, –, T) (p, q, r). For each line of the table there are two possibilities so, here, 2^8 such expressions. Each expression is an expression for a proposition: a proposition is a truth-function of elementary propositions (an elementary proposition is a truth-function of itself, see 5).

This account needs a little refinement. A proposition is a picture, and therefore to know its truth-value one has to compare it to reality. Consider the signs (T, T, T, T, T, T, T, T) (p, q, r) and (–, –, –, –, –, –, –, –) (p, q, r). The first is guaranteed to be true in any circumstance and the latter false. The first is a tautology, the latter a contradiction; both say nothing. But they are products of the symbolism, and as such are not *nonsensical* (*unsinnig*) but *senseless* (*sinnlos*), that is, they do not determine truth-conditions. (See 4.466, 4.4661.)

3.1.5. Logical Consequence, Generality, the General Form of the Proposition

The concept of a proposition as a truth-function of elementary propositions can now be used to explain logical relations between propositions—in particular, the relation of logical consequence. First, however, a lacuna needs to be filled. The account so far given is easily applied to finite sets of propositions, and so can be adapted equally easily to explain the propositional connectives. But it is not obvious how it explains general propositions. Wittgenstein's main aim is to characterize the general form of the proposition because this gives the 'essence of description' and hence the essence of the world.

Logical Consequence Once there is a convention for writing out the table of possibilities of truth and falsity for elementary propositions, we can express a proposition in symbols of the form (T, T, T, –, –, –, –, –) (p, q, r) (label this example S). Wittgenstein calls the possibilities that make a proposition true its 'truth-grounds'. Now for any two propositions one of the following three possibilities must hold:

(1) the truth-grounds of one include the truth-grounds of the other;
(2) the truth-grounds overlap;
(3) the truth-grounds exclude each other.

Examples of each case for S (to simplify matters, we consider only propositions with the same truth-arguments, i.e. propositions which are truth-functions of the same elementary propositions):

(1) (–, T, T, –, –, –, –, –) (p, q, r) (T)
(2) (–, –, T, –, –, T, T, –) (p, q, r) (U)
(3) (–, –, –, –, –, T, –, T) (p, q, r) (V)

The truth-grounds of S contain the truth-grounds of T, so S follows from T (if one of T's truth-grounds is satisfied, then one of S's must be). In the second case neither S nor U follows from the other. We can, however, give the probability of U given that S: there are three ways that S can be true and only one of those ways is a way for U to be true, so the probability is $\frac{1}{3}$. Finally, S and V cannot both be true; they are contraries.

Note also that T is a consequence of S and (–, T, T, T, T, –, –, T) (p, q, r) (label this W), because the truth-grounds common to both S and W (i.e. the truth-grounds that would succeed in making both true) are the truth-grounds of T.

Operations All we so far have, however, is a description of propositions as expressions of a certain form. This is not enough for Wittgenstein, for clearly there is an underlying form common to all propositions, and he wished to make it explicit. He therefore needed to show how propositions are generated from elementary propositions. This looks difficult, given the potential infinity of propositions. The problem of infinity arises in connection with formal concepts since an essentially infinite sequence of objects is given by a formal concept such as *number*. Such a sequence combines a starting-point of the sequence with a method for generating, from a given member, the next member of the sequence. (The relation of each element to its successor is formal, that is, internal.) So in the account of the natural numbers one gives the general form as $(0, x, S(x))$, where 0 gives the first member of the sequence and the next two elements of the trio show how the successor of any element is generated from it.

This approach can be adapted to the case of propositions. At first sight a problem seems to be that there is no *single* operation (comparable to the successor operation) that generates propositions from some base. But there is indeed one: the operation of joint negation, N. N(p) is not-p; N(p, q) is not-p and not-q; and, in general, N applied to a set of propositions is the conjunction of their negations. Recall that all the propositional connectives can be defined in terms of 'not' and 'or', and note that not-p is N(p) and p or q is N(N(p, q)). So the operation N suffices to generate all propositions from the base of elementary propositions.

The difference between this case and that of the natural numbers is that here the base is not a single element but the set of elementary propositions, and the operation applies to sets of propositions. Wittgenstein symbolizes the fact that his variables represent sets of entities by overlining them. So the general form of a proposition is: $[\bar{p}, \bar{\chi}, N(\bar{\chi})]$.

An operation is not a function; it is a way of producing an item from other items. Its product can be fed back into the operation to produce yet more items. (This allows us to characterize infinite sequences by means of operations.) Operations are not 'things', for they can vanish; for instance, N(p) is not-p, but N(N(p)) is p. Propositions are truth-functions of elementary propositions, generated by truth-operations. The base of a truth-operation is a truth-function (of elementary propositions) and it produces a truth-function (of elementary propositions).

Generality How is one to explain the general propositions $(x)F(x)$ and $(\exists x)F(x)$? There seems to be a dilemma here. Consider '$(x)F(x)$'. One might say that $(x)F(x)$ means ($F(a)$ and $F(b)$ and $F(c)$ and …), running through the names for all the objects there are. This makes $(x)F(x)$ the logical product of all propositions of the form $F(x)$. The benefit of this method is that it explains why it is valid to infer, say, $F(a)$ from it. The drawback is that $(x)F(x)$ is only logically equivalent to the logical product if we can ensure that $a, b, c, \ldots$ exhaust all the objects there are. So to ensure logical equivalence (a necessary condition for shared meaning) we would need a clause saying that there does not exist an x distinct from $a, b, c, \ldots$. But that itself is a general proposition, so one cannot *explain* generality this way (see 5.521).

The second horn of the dilemma is this. If one follows Frege and treats quantifiers as functions of functions, it becomes obscure why $F(a)$ follows from $(x)F(x)$, that is, why, if a certain function holds of F, we are entitled to infer that F holds of a. One might be able to introduce the notion of generality this way, but doing so loses the connection with logical product.

Can both ideas be kept together? For Wittgenstein the notion of generality is captured in the variable. Replacing a by x in $F(a)$ gives a propositional variable $F(x)$, which shows the form common to all propositions $F(a), F(b), \ldots$. So $F(x)$ is a way of specifying all and only the propositions in that set. Now recall that the proposition-forming operator N applies to sets of propositions. We can connect this with the general mode of generating propositions: N $(\overline{F(\chi)})$ is not-$(\exists x)F(x)$ (see 5.52). So the variable gives the notion of generality by specifying just the set of propositions in which we are interested; the proposition-forming operator acts on this set (no matter whether it is infinite) to produce quantificational propositions; *and* these are seen to have the general form of propositions.

Logic Wittgenstein gives an account of the nature of logic in the early 6s, but the conceptual resources for it occur in the 5s. Tautologies and contradictions do not fix truth-conditions; they are senseless. Logically equivalent propositions fix the same truth-conditions, so they have the same sense. This means that what matters in determining the identity of a proposition is what truth-function of elementary propositions it is: two signs expressing the same truth-function express the same proposition. '*p*' and 'not-not-*p*' express the same proposition; as do 'not-(not-*p* and not-*q*)' and '*p* or *q*'. So the sense of an expression is not determined by the sense of its logical constituents, for there are no such constituents. This illustrates Wittgenstein's 'fundamental idea' that there are no logical objects, that logical expressions are not representational.

If logical truths are tautologies and *say* nothing—are senseless—why is logic important? The answer is that they *show* something. Consider 'not-(not-*p* and not-*q*) iff *p* or *q*'. The fact that this is a tautology shows that from 'not-(not-*p* and not-*q*)' we can infer '*p* or *q*', and vice versa. Demonstrating that an expression is tautologous shows the validity or otherwise of certain inferences.

This view of logic differs from Frege's and Russell's, who both took logic to be distinguished from the special sciences by its ultimate generality, universality, and concomitant lack of a special domain of its own. Wittgenstein rejected this view; a discipline could be universally applicable, yet not be logic; what is essential to logic, he held, is that its truths are tautologous.

The Analysis of Language Propositions picture the world. Picturing is an 'all or nothing' relation, so propositions must be in perfect logical order. Ordinary language cannot therefore be, as Frege and Russell thought, logically imperfect and in need of reconstruction.

The analysis of language must, of course, show that all propositions are truth-functions of elementary propositions. What, then, are elementary propositions? The response (5.55) is that elementary propositions consist of names. But because we cannot give all the names with their different meanings (we do not know what objects there are) we cannot give the composition of elementary propositions.

This in turn means that we cannot construct language from the elements upwards by means of truth-operations. Instead we have to begin with language as it is, and analyse it in accordance with logic (for the only essential relations between propositions are logical). But that means we need some access to *logic* itself.

> 5.552. The 'experience' that we need in order to understand logic is not that something or other is the state of things, but that something *is*: that, however, is *not* an experience.
>
> Logic is *prior* to every experience—that something *is so*.
>
> It is prior to the question 'How?', not prior to the question 'What?'
>
> 5.5521. And if this were not so, how could we apply logic? We might put it this way: if there would be a logic even if there were no world, how then could there be a logic given that there is a world?

Wittgenstein appears to be attacking Russell-like notions of logic according to which we have self-evident acquaintance with logical forms. Even if this is *self-evident* access to logic, it is still an experience that things are a particular way. So logic would not be prior to certain 'hows'. Logic is prior to any comparison with the world, so it is prior to 'How?', but it is not prior to the possibility of representing. This possibility requires something, an answer to 'What?' The second remark is illuminating: logic for Wittgenstein is not *in* the world, since if it were it could be represented (thus 6.13: 'Logic is transcendental'). But logic is not separable from the world: it is the form of language and of the world. If logic were independent of the world it would be utterly mysterious how it relates to the world; one would not know how to apply it. So logic is prior to every experience; although not independent of the world, it must be given a priori.

3.1.6. Solipsism and Science

Knowing the general logical form of the proposition, Wittgenstein claims, gives us the essence of description and the essence of the world. These may seem large claims, but in the context of the *Tractatus* their meaning is clear. To know the general form of a proposition is to know how all propositions are produced (as joint negations of elementary propositions). Given that representation depends on the picturing relation, this has clear metaphysical implications: the world is the totality of states of affairs—what elementary propositions picture—in logical space. Since we know the form an expression must have for it to be able to express a sense, we can see the limits of expressibility (and thus recognize nonsense).

Limits to expression occur in two main ways. Proposition-like expressions might be meaningless because they attempt to say what can only be shown. Such expressions are nonsensical. Prime examples are those that treat formal concepts as substantive. Other propositions—the propositions of logic—are not nonsensical but senseless. Although well-formed, and thus capable of showing the logic of the world, they have no truth-conditions because their truth-value can be judged a priori.

Solipsism It is useful to inspect an example of important nonsense, and Wittgenstein's attempt to reconcile science with his view of sense.

On Wittgenstein's account, 'Logic pervades the world: the limits of the world are also its limits' (5.61; compare with 5.5521). If I can show that language is *my* language, the world will be *my* world. And this will show what is right about solipsism. Yet so far Wittgenstein has talked of logic and language in a wholly objective manner. How does it turn out that language is subjective?

The argument goes as follows. The limits of sense are revealed by propositions whose truth-value can be known a priori. But then *I* know the proposition *I am here now* to be true a priori. Moreover, I am the only subject who can know that proposition to be true a priori. So, since the language I speak is characterized by its a priori knowable propositions, only I can speak the language I speak. So language is *my* language.

An objector might say that this is an artefact of the way terms like 'I' (indexicals) operate, and that such terms do not (should not) figure in a properly scientific language. But this, in itself, does not help. If I am NN and you are MM then I have a special relation to propositions about NN (and not to those about MM) and vice versa for you. This would again show that my language is peculiar to me.

Wittgenstein does not think we can *state* solipsism: 'it cannot be *said*, but makes itself manifest' (5.62). His reason is that solipsism asserts the existence of the subject alone, and there is, for Wittgenstein, no subject: 'The subject does not belong to the world: rather, it is a limit of the world' (5.632).

This point is considered shortly. First it is appropriate to assess the solipsistic argument in the light of Wittgenstein's denial of the existence of the subject. The problem is a general feature of the *Tractatus'* eventual position: how are we to accept 'arguments' whose conclusions imply that the arguments themselves are nonsensical? The answer is perhaps this: I cannot give a *general argument* for solipsism; I have to *show* what is true about it. We do this by showing how my language could not be spoken by another. I do this by pointing out instances of, say, 'propositions' which have an a priori status for me alone. Once we see the world aright these examples show us the truth in solipsism. It follows that the subject is not found in the world, but is revealed as a limit to the world (that is, to language).

If the subject were in the world there would be a priori experiences (5.634). The impossibility of these shows that there is no subject. But this means that the subject is only a limit of the world: we cannot set the world over against the subject. So solipsism coincides with realism.

Wittgenstein denies that there is a psychological self, that is, a subject who thinks, hopes, remembers, and the rest. The metaphysical self has a place in philosophy as the limit of the world. There is another argument for solipsism at 5.542–5.5421, where Wittgenstein addresses an apparent counter-example to his account of the proposition's general form, namely, belief and thought ascriptions—propositions of the form *A believes that p*. These have typically been analysed as a relation between an object *A* and a complex *p*, so the proposition occurs as something other than an argument to a truth-function. Wittgenstein counters by saying that belief ascriptions should be analysed as *'p' says p*, that is, a complex sign pictures a certain situation as obtaining. This shows that there is no subject because the putative subject *A* has vanished and has been replaced by a complex *'p'*—and a subject cannot be a complex.

Science, Ethics, and the Tractatus Wittgenstein says that the totality of propositions is language and the totality of true propositions is science. This is unproblematic when we think of scientific reports of particular and general facts; but what of scientific laws?

The problem here is that for Wittgenstein all relations between propositions are logical, so everything subject to a law lies in the province of logic and everything outside logic is contingent (see 6.3). Where do the laws of nature stand? These seem to *require* that the world be a certain way—for example, the law of gravity requires that bodies are massive. Because a law requires certain things it is used as an explanation of why those things occur. Wittgenstein seems to have left no room to account for the explanatory power of nomic necessities.

His response is to say that it is an illusion to suppose that laws of nature are explanatory. When we discover a 'law of nature' we don't discover a uniformity that *governs* natural phenomena, rather, laws of nature are (in part) summations of regularities in our experience. So the law that all masses attract each other is, in part, a report that all observed masses have attracted each other. The problem is that the law applies to *all* masses, not just to those observed; and this is why it is tempting to say that the law explains the observations and therefore applies in cases yet to be observed.

Scientific laws might accordingly have to be seen as products of observation together with (amongst possible others) the laws of causality and induction. This prompts questions about their status. The principle that every event has a cause is not a law of nature because we cannot conceive having to revise it. Wittgenstein remarks,

> 6.36. if there were a law of causality, it might be put in the following way: There are laws of nature.
>
> But of course that cannot be said: it makes itself manifest.

Wittgenstein's point seems to be that to say there are laws of nature is not to say anything about the world. The claim is a priori because it governs our attempts to describe natural phenomena, not natural phenomena themselves.

Neither is inductive validity a law of nature; induction says that we should accept 'the simplest law that can be reconciled with our experiences', which, again, is a feature of our attempts to describe the world.

There is a characteristic similarity of approach in Wittgenstein's views about ethics. He says, 'All propositions are of equal value' (6.4).

This implies that we cannot find value *in* the world. If something had value, it would have to have it, in Wittgenstein's view, essentially; but if anything in the world were valuable, what gives it value would be accidental. But something accidental cannot determine something essential. So value is not in the world. Rather it is a condition or limit of the world.

These views on science and ethics illustrate and confirm the thesis towards which the *Tractatus* works, and is already clear in the theory of the proposition:

> 6.54. My propositions serve as elucidations in the following way: anyone who understands me eventually recognizes them as nonsensical, when he has used them—as steps—to climb up beyond them. (He must, so to speak, throw away the ladder after he has climbed up it.)
>
> He must transcend these propositions, and then he will see the world aright.
>
> 7. What we cannot speak about we must pass over in silence.

3.2. Wittgenstein's Middle Period

3.2.1. *Strains in the* Tractatus *System*

One might make, among others, three points about the programme of the *Tractatus*, each prompting unease. First, Wittgenstein followed Frege in rejecting psychologism. He is primarily interested in the language–world relation, which he takes to be the objective basis of meaning. He allows a place for the mental activity of understanding, but having invoked it to establish, in some unexplained way, the projective correlation between language and world, he drops mind from his account, and relegates questions about understanding to psychology.

Secondly, the account is wholly programmatic. Wittgenstein believes himself 'to have found, *on all essential points*, the final solution of the problems' of philosophy. But the actual solution awaits the full implementation of the *Tractatus* programme. In particular, the nature of elementary propositions, states of affairs, and objects will be revealed only when a successful analysis of language is achieved.

Thirdly, the fundamental picturing relation seems to depend on the logical independence of elementary propositions. An elementary proposition represents a state of affairs when it mirrors its internal properties. These are, on the one hand, the logical connections between the state of affairs and other (complex) facts—the state of affairs in logical space—and, on the other, the logical relations between the elementary proposition and other propositions—the logic of language. A consequence of the picture theory, as noted, is that all necessity is logical necessity. So necessary connections in language must be shown in the logic of language. No formal (logical) connections are exhibited between elementary propositions; they are logically independent of each other.

3.2.2. *The Colour Exclusion Problem*

Nothing can, simultaneously, be both red and green all over, although something can, simultaneously, be both red and smooth all over (see 6.3751). These seem to be conceptually necessary statements; no empirical explanation suffices for them. But they are identical in form, so it seems that they are not (respectively) purely logically impossible and possible. The *Tractatus* is committed to there being only logical possibility and impossibility, so Wittgenstein has to say that despite appearances there is indeed a logical difference between them. He seems to suppose that *on analysis* we will discover '*x* is red all over at *t*' to have the form (say) *s.t.u* and '*x* is green all over at *t*' to have the form (say) *q.r.~s* from which we can see that their conjunction is a contradiction.

In 1929 Wittgenstein returned to this problem in a short paper entitled 'Some Remarks on Logical Form', which begins by inquiring into the form of elementary propositions, and goes on to claim that only analysis can provide an answer. But Wittgenstein soon tells us that numbers can appear in elementary propositions. The colour exclusion and related problems provide the reason; such problems occur when we have propositions making use of a scale. In these cases an assertion that an object has a property measured by some degree of the scale automatically excludes the possibility that it has a property given by a different degree; for example, to say something is *x* metres tall automatically excludes the possibility that it is any other height. We cannot analyse such propositions in terms of units.

Wittgenstein's solution is to acknowledge a departure from the strict Tractarian system. Propositions using a scale to make assertions occur in interconnected systems. '*x* is red at *t*' is of the form *Rxt*; eliminating *R* gives us ( )*xt*. Wittgenstein's point is that the gap can only be filled by one colour term: the form of colour means that distinct colours exclude each other. Note that this means that *Rxt* and *Gxt exclude* each other, they do not contradict each other: *Rxt* & *Gxt* is not a contradiction but nonsense. So the usual truth-table for two propositions has to be amended. Instead of

p	*q*		*Rxt*	*Gxt*
T	T		—	—
T	F	we get	T	F
F	T		F	T
F	F		F	F

That is, instead of the normal four possibilities the sense of the propositions determines that there are only three possibilities.

Where does this leave the picture theory? The unit of comparison in the original theory was the proposition, because we could guarantee that its logical possibilities of truth and falsity matched those of the existence or non-existence of a state of affairs, *irrespective of anything else*. This is no longer the case; the unit of comparison is now the proposition in a specific system of propositions; we need such a system, with appropriately restricted possibilities, to represent specific aspects of reality. These restrictions Wittgenstein hopes to capture in the syntax of the symbolism. He remarks, 'Such rules cannot be laid down until we have actually reached the ultimate analysis of the phenomena in question. This, as we all know, has not yet been achieved.'[2]

[2] 'Some Remarks on Logical Form' (1929), 171.

3.2.3. The Problem Solved?

The system of the *Tractatus* in effect yielded a hostage to fortune. It explained elementary propositions in terms of states of affairs and objects. But these are left unexplained. So the form of elementary propositions is an a posteriori question, to be resolved by the process of analysis. However unsatisfying this position is, at least the goal of analysis is clear, because elementary propositions are logically independent of each other. But now, on Wittgenstein's account of the colour exclusion problem, it is not simply that the structure of elementary propositions is an a posteriori matter, but the rules governing the use of logical connectives also only emerge after analysis. This calls fundamental features of the *Tractatus* view into question.

Logic occupies a pivotal position in the *Tractatus*: the picturing relation depends on shared logical form ('every picture is *at the same time* a logical picture'), and analysis proceeds in accordance with logic. These views are plausible just so long as logic is given. If logic itself is determined (in part) by the nature of the phenomena, it is no longer clear in what sense it permeates all representation, or how analysis is to be effected. All the fundamental notions of the *Tractatus* lose definition.

3.2.4. Developments in Wittgenstein's Thought

The disintegration of the *Tractatus* view prompted—but by evolutionary means—radical changes in Wittgenstein's thought, eventually encapsulated in the *Philosophical Investigations*.

Wittgenstein adhered throughout his philosophical life to the *Tractatus* view that

> 4.111. Philosophy is not one of the natural sciences. . . .
>
> 4.112. Philosophy aims at the logical clarification of thoughts.
>
> Philosophy is not a body of doctrine but an activity.
>
> A philosophical work consists essentially of elucidations.
>
> Philosophy does not result in 'philosophical propositions', but rather in the clarification of propositions. . . .

But he became disillusioned with the way it is there implemented. The *Tractatus* is wholly scientific in approach, and the result is paradoxical. In it Wittgenstein constructed an edifice of *apparent* propositions which, among other things, assert a theory of meaning entailing their own meaninglessness. The paradox is supposedly resolved by seeing that these pseudo-propositions provide elucidations enabling us to see the world aright, after which they can be jettisoned. But the air of paradox persists.

Moreover, the *Tractatus* advances the ultimate theory of language, the world, and their relation. Its success is manifestable by its ability to explain the phenomena. But the ambition to explain is very unclear: what is a philosophical explanation? Unlike a scientific theory, a philosophical theory is not explanatory because of empirical success in, say, predicting observations. So how does one test it?

Wittgenstein became convinced that these problems infect all attempts at purely philosophical explanation. Philosophy, he therefore claimed, must restrict itself to description.

3.3. The *Philosophical Investigations*

3.3.1. The Augustinian View

Wittgenstein begins the *Investigations* with a quotation from Augustine setting out what seems a natural account of our introduction to language. Wittgenstein uses it as the basis of his investigation into the nature of understanding—which has become the chief concern for him, marking a change from the Tractarian focus upon the relation of language to the world.

Wittgenstein takes Augustine's description to embody a specific view about the *essence* of language, which is that every word has a meaning, and that its meaning is the object for which it stands. In other words, the name–bearer relation is taken to be the paradigm of meaning: when we ask 'What is the meaning of *x*?' we are asking about an entity to which *x* is correlated by the meaning relation. Accordingly, one understands the language when one grasps (by whatever means) these correlations. In practice, the correlations are set up by ostensive definition.

A number of questions press. Does the account deal adequately with all kinds of expressions? Is ostensive definition apt for its assigned role? Wittgenstein immediately points out that the picture deforms our thinking about meaning because it unwarrantedly generalizes from a concern with the relation of certain nouns to what they stand for. His aim is to probe views about meaning whose foundations lie in the Augustinian view, notably those of Frege and the *Tractatus*. Recall that in Frege's semantics it is crucial to recognize that signs fall into different categories: names stand for objects, function expressions for functions. The different uses of the expressions are explained in terms of the different entities they denote. Similarly, in the *Tractatus* expressions have different logical roles: names name objects, concatenations of names (elementary propositions) display possible combinations of objects. In each case the nature of the thing denoted by the expression dictates its grammatical role, thereby establishing a harmony between language and the world. In rejecting this kind of conception Wittgenstein is not simply claiming that words have different roles—but that to understand meaning we must look at the role of the expression, that is, at its use.

1. But what is the meaning of the word 'five'?—No such thing was in question here, only how the word 'five' is used.

Wittgenstein approaches meaning by way of understanding, on the grounds that to understand an expression is to know what it means, where 'knowing the meaning' is not acquaintance with an entity. There is no special philosophical method for this; Wittgenstein's assumption is that we can clarify understanding by considering what we regard as criteria for ascription of understanding.

What seems deeply mistaken about Augustinian views, on this tack, is that explanation and use seem to be related to understanding merely externally. That is, it seems to be a happy accident that the explanations we give secure the correct (or, even, any) meanings to our terms. And one has further to explain how a particular meaning determines a use. These are themes that repeatedly recur in different contexts throughout the *Investigations*.

This does not signal a return to psychologism by Wittgenstein. His project is, rather, concerned with criteria governing our use of language. This concern has two aspects. Wittgenstein wishes to clarify the criteria used in making ascriptions of understanding. These are not sensitive to internal psychological features of speakers but to capacities that can be publicly exercised. And secondly, he wishes to clarify what constitutes grasp of criteria for the use of particular terms. Our ordinary explanations of terms are important because they specify criteria for their use, and (fallibly) enable speakers to learn their meanings; and when produced by a speaker they (fallibly) function as a criterion for ascribing understanding to him.

3.3.2. Language Games

Wittgenstein employs a notion of 'language games' to illuminate how language works; later he seems to suggest that our language is a complex of language games. In the language game (sect. 2) of Wittgenstein's builders the only words are names for different objects ('pillar', 'brick' . . .). One builder calls out a name and the other brings something named by it. Wittgenstein asks what it is to learn such a language. Augustine suggested that a form of ostension is the basis; but although Wittgenstein admits that ostension has a role (he distinguishes ostensive teaching from ostensive definition because the latter occurs within, and so presupposes, language; see below), he argues that establishing word–object connections is only possible in the context of already established linguistic practices. This point turns out to be crucial in clearing the way for a new approach to language understanding.

Wittgenstein complicates the builders' language by including words for numbers and places—'three' and 'here'. The correct way to understand these words, he says, is to look at their use in the language game; one should not look for an underlying unity in their functioning—there is no such thing, any more than there is an 'underlying unity' among the tools in a toolbox.

Neither the first nor the second builder's language games make assertions about the world. Each consists entirely of commands. This shows that description is not the *essence* of language. (Recall that in the *Tractatus* the general form of the proposition is 'This is how things are'.) We cannot explain this situation by saying that these language games are incomplete, and that a complete language must include assertions which, philosophically speaking, have a certain priority. In what sense are these games incomplete? We cannot do in these languages what we can in ours. But then is our language complete? When did it become so? (Is only the language of 'completed science' complete?)

In sections 19–20 Wittgenstein uses the example of the first language to reflect on the relation of language use to thinking. When the builder says 'Slab!' he wishes his colleague to bring him a slab. That is what is normally meant by 'Bring me a slab!' Does the builder's utterance consist of one word, or is it really *four* words as ours is? (For that matter, is our sentence 'really' one word or four?) One might say that our sentence must be four words because we also use sentences such as: 'Lend me a slab'; 'Bring me three slabs'; 'Bring me a pillar'. But what shows that, when the builder utters his sentence, he means it as one word whereas we mean it as four? The phenomenology of understanding inclines us to think that there is an answer to this question. Our lack of an adequate response shows that the phenomenology of understanding is not essential to understanding. Moreover, the form of the sentence appears not to be dictated by the proposition we are expressing but, perhaps, only by the character of propositions we are capable of expressing, that is, by the *practice* in which our utterance is embedded.

We are capable of using language to issue questions, commands, assertions, etc. We are tempted to think that we can isolate a content which can be asserted, questioned, and so on; in Frege's terminology, we think we can distinguish sense from force. Wittgenstein is pointing to the multiplicity of language uses to shake our confidence that there is an underlying systematicity waiting to be described.

3.3.3. *Ostensive Definition*

In seems natural to suppose that explanations of meaning are of just two kinds: purely verbal definition and ostensive definition, with the latter serving as the basis of language because it picks out an object *as the meaning* of an expression, thus forging a language–world connection. The Augustinian view suggests this picture.

Wittgenstein's examination of ostensive definition is not intended to show that it fails to explain the meanings of words—for it does—but that it does not play the *foundational* role demanded of it by empiricist theories like logical atomism.

Ostensive definitions typically take the form 'This' (with the object pointed at) 'is *x*'. We suppose that use of the demonstrative succeeds in picking out an object which, if he understands what is happening, the learner therefore comes to call *x*. Wittgenstein notes, first, that ostensive definitions can be used to define expressions for many *sorts* of object: general nouns ('dog'), names of shapes, names of colours, proper names, and so on. But the problem is that an ostensive definition can never be definitive. If, pointing in the direction of a tennis-ball, I say 'This is pulo', you only know what 'pulo' means if you know whether I am pointing to its shape, its colour, its material composition—or the ball itself. No explanation is proof against a misunderstanding.

It is a considerable conceptual feat to know the *kind* of thing being defined ostensively. It demands an ability to discriminate among kinds of objects and to be able to reidentify them. So ostensive definition, in the absence of a considerable background competence, is impotent. It therefore cannot be foundational.

32. Augustine describes the learning of human language as if the child came into a strange country and did not understand the language of the country; that is, as if it already had a language, only not this one. Or again: as if the child could already *think*, only not yet speak. And 'think' would here mean something like 'talk to itself'.

3.3.4. *Family Resemblance*

The Augustinian view implies that the only successful explanation of meaning is: specification of the necessary and sufficient conditions for a given item to be the denotatum of some word. These are called *merkmal* definitions. In many cases we do not or cannot give merkmal definitions, which makes it seem that ordinary uses of language are inadequate: that explanations of meaning leave learners to guess the essential point, or that language is at fault and a philosophical project is needed to reconstruct it. Wittgenstein's account of ostension is a repudiation of this view. 'Family resemblance' is another challenge to the philosophical prejudice in favour of merkmal definitions.

At section 65, after his examination of ostensive definition and his stress on the variety of language games, Wittgenstein's interlocutor challenges him to specify the essence of language. But Wittgenstein questions the legitimacy of this challenge by pointing out that many concepts are introduced on the basis of similarities between objects; there are no necessary and sufficient conditions determining the set of objects a given concept collects. It collects those objects because resemblances among them are of the kind that evidence the kinship among members of a family.

Consider the example of games—tennis, chess, athletics, hopscotch. Wittgenstein asks why we suppose that there must be a set of properties shared by all games and definitive of 'game'.

> 66. Don't say: 'There *must* be something common, or they would not be called "games" '—but *look and see* whether there is anything common to them all,—for if you look at them you will not see something that is common to all, but similarities, relationships, and a whole series of them at that . . . 'games' form a family.

This applies equally to the concepts that especially exercise philosophers, such as knowledge, meaning, language, and truth. If we wish to clarify them we need to look at our practice—for example, at the criteria used to ascribe knowledge, understanding, and the rest, to competent speakers.

3.3.5. Meaning and Understanding

Sections 81 to 137 contain a series of pronouncements about analysis and the nature of philosophy. Much of this recapitulates the *Blue Book*, and comments on the *Tractatus*. At 138 begins an investigation into the nature of understanding. Is it a mental process, an experience, a state of mind?

It seems that we invest signs with meaning, and that this process is a distinctively *mindful* occupation—a mental activity of some kind; perhaps the correlation of a word with a mental image. There are familiar difficulties with this view. First, it is unclear how an image is supposed to represent both the general and the particular (how, for instance, are we to imagine a general triangle which is distinct from all particular triangles). Secondly, images need interpretation. Wittgenstein poses the problem of how a picture of a man walking up a hill is to be distinguished from that of a man sliding down a hill. So an image cannot dictate how a word is to be used since it does not by itself tell us. Thirdly, on this model understanding 'red' would be a matter of having, say, an image of redness in one's mind. So obeying the order 'Pick a red flower' would, in some sense, involve comparing the colour of the flower with one's image (if we cannot give content to this comparison it is difficult to see how the image could be linked to use). But then obeying the order 'Have an image of red' would involve comparing one's image of red with one's (standard) image of red. But the sense in which the one image is a standard and determines the correctness of the other is unclear. This example throws into doubt the sense in which the sample as image is an advance on the physical sample.

Finally, it seems clear that possession of an image is neither necessary nor sufficient for ascriptions of understanding. Someone might be credited with understanding in virtue of their ability to use a term correctly, yet have no image, or have one that we might think irrelevant or incorrect; while someone else might possess the right image but be unable to use the term correctly.

There is a disanalogy between talk of activities and talk of understanding. An activity is clockable; it has a beginning, middle, and end. One can talk of bringing an image before one's mind at a certain time. But one does not say one understands an expression at a certain time; one does not ask '*When* do you know the meaning of "red"?'

Is Understanding a Mental State? Understanding might best be conceived as an ability—specifically, a disposition to use a term correctly. This links understanding to use without collapsing either into the other, for one might have an appropriate disposition but, on occasion, fail to implement it correctly; and the nature of one's dispositions will not be exhausted by a finite sample of uses.

It is uncontroversial to say that someone possessing a certain disposition is in a certain state. We might even call this a mental state, but if we do we should beware possible confusions. First, understanding should not be assimilated to such other kinds of mental states as depression, excitement, and pain. These are all temporally well-defined: a pain comes on, can be interrupted by analgesics or sleep, and might recur. Understanding is not like this. One might of course say 'I didn't understand *x* until you mentioned *y*', but understanding does not have a specific duration and a degree of intensity, and it is not available to introspection.

Further confusions are prompted by reductionism. To understand a word is to be able to use it correctly. Speakers are generally able to apply a word when the criteria for its use are fulfilled. Given this, we must explain what gives a speaker this ability. Two lines of investigation suggest themselves: we could undertake a psychological investigation into the physiological basis of our ability to use language; or we could look for a mental mechanism (in a specifically mental medium) underlying linguistic ability. The first is a scientific investigation, the second a philosophical one. Wittgenstein issues two warnings, the first against the assumption that there *must* be a reductive explanation, the second against the idea that linguistic ability is to be identified with what instantiates it.

Take the second point first. It is obviously a fallacy to identify the ground of an ability with that ability itself. Consider an example: a plant's ability to photosynthesize depends on the presence of chlorophyll in its cells. Chlorophyll can be dissolved in a solution, but one cannot thus dissolve the *ability to photosynthesize* that the chlorophyll gives the plant. Accordingly, linguistic ability might rest on brain or mental structure and processes, but understanding is not thereby shown to be a brain or mental process or structure. The moral is: do not assume we can identify an ability (or disposition) with what 'carries' it—its vehicle.

If we insist on specifying vehicles for abilities, philosophical clarification of understanding is incomplete until its underlying vehicle has been found. Wittgenstein rejects this project, arguing that the idea of a mental mechanism as the vehicle of understanding is a myth. To say that someone who understands a word establishes a correlation of it with a meaning is unenlightening, because our criterion for when someone has done this is his ability to use the word correctly—that is, understand it.

Ascriptions of understanding are made on the basis of a speaker's use of language. They are defeasible: if we credit a speaker with understanding a word, but he later applies it abnormally, we rescind the ascription. This makes it seem that use is merely *good evidence* of understanding. Were this so, attributions of understanding would only ever be hypotheses, and mutual understanding would itself be an hypothesis. This is not Wittgenstein's view. He holds that, first, attributions of understanding are only possible in an established practice, requiring a background of agreement. It is not possible that we all might misunderstand one another. True, the practice might disintegrate, but then we would not be able to attribute understanding, and so could not hypothesize mutual *mis*understanding.

Secondly, the correct use of a term *in a practice* is a *criterion* for understanding; it does not merely provide evidence of it. A criterion for understanding is internally linked to the concept of understanding, whereas evidence is what has been discovered to be good grounds for application of a concept. The status of something as evidence demands that we have a more direct means (available in principle) for determining whether a concept applies. In the case of understanding, nothing provides more direct grounds than use.

3.3.6. *Wittgenstein on Following a Rule*

In sections 143 to 242 Wittgenstein undertakes a detailed examination of rule-following, with the aim of clarifying the nature of meaning and understanding. Whatever meaning is, however we account for it, it must determine (must be internally related) to use. If it is correct to use two expressions in the same circumstances, then they must have the same meaning; if their uses diverge, so must their meanings. Therefore, to understand an expression is to grasp what determines correct use. And this means that understanding an expression is an ability to follow a rule for its correct use.

But the notion of following a rule is not unproblematic. When I am able to follow a rule I can be said to be in a certain state (a state of understanding). This view is encouraged by the manner in which we often seem to understand an expression 'in a flash'. But how can any state determine a use which is indefinitely extended over time, and extended to an indefinite variety of circumstances? The question is: how does a rule determine its application? How, for example, does grasp of a rule for applying a term determine how to apply it?

Kripke's Exposition Wittgenstein's views on this matter are not clear, and have therefore been variously interpreted. One interpretation, owing to Kripke, has been especially influential in the debate, providing a good place to start.

When asked to perform an addition never encountered before, for example 254 + 857, we assume that there is an answer we should give if we are faithful to the meanings of our terms. But Kripke asks us to imagine a sceptic who asks why we should not give the answer, say, '5'. That is, the sceptic asks for a justification of our *present* use of '+'. He is not asking us for a justification of our concept of addition by recommending some novel variant. His point is that, given the way we have used '+' in the past, we *should* now be responding with the answer '5'. So, in so far as the concept is determined by the history of our usage (and what else could it be determined by?), we *should* be responding other than the way we are inclined. The challenge is to point to a fact which justifies our actual inclination as correct.

The dialectic is as follows. Asked for the answer to 254 + 857, I respond with '1111' because by '+' I mean 'plus'. The sceptic responds by saying that if I intend to be faithful to the way I meant '+' in the past I should respond with '5', for in the past I meant 'quus' by '+' (where 'quus' agrees with 'plus' for numbers less than 250, say).

The point of putting matters this way is that the sceptic does not challenge what we presently mean by '+', so we are able to converse with him. But if we cannot answer the sceptic about what we meant in the past, then there is no fact of the matter about what we meant in the past. But if that is so, there is no fact of the matter about what we mean now. So we are left with the self-refuting conclusion that there is nothing we mean by our words.

There are two questions to be answered. Is there a fact of the matter about whether we mean 'plus' or 'quus'? Why are we confident that we should answer '1111' rather than '5'?

Another important point is that the sceptic grants us full (epistemic) access to facts about our past uses, and our mental and behavioural histories. We thus have access to all the facts that could conceivably constrain the way we should now use our terms. So the resultant scepticism is *not* epistemological scepticism. The conclusion is not that *for all I know* I should say '5' rather than '1111'. Rather, it is that there is no fact of the matter whether I should say '5' or '1111'—and therefore putative constraints provided by meaning are vacuous, and meaning is a fiction.

This argument, if right, is highly consequential, and merits scrutiny, as follows.

No matter how absorbed our past lives have been in arithmetic, we will have performed only a finite number of additions. When we come across a new sum we have to reconcile that finite base with infinitely many alternative responses; and a finite sample of past uses cannot (on its own) determine what we should say. But in most cases we do not learn an expression simply by exposure to samples. We are given—and, often, when we understand an expression we can ourselves give—an explanation of its meaning. So, ideally, we learn an expression by internalizing the rule for its use. For example, we learn how to add two numbers, *a* and *b*, by an explanation of counting a set consisting of two disjoint parts which have *a* and *b* many members. But clearly this only succeeds if we can guarantee that a rule for the correct use of 'counting' has been established. But the sceptic will repeat a version of his challenge at just this point; so we either enter a regress, or have to appeal to the problematic notion of a self-intimating rule.

The point is this: we are concerned to understand '+', and the explanation gives us an interpretation. An interpretation will only succeed if its terms are already understood—which begs the sceptic's question. 'An interpretation', says Wittgenstein, 'hangs in the air together with what it interprets.' Kripke agrees with Wittgenstein that 'justifications come to an end', and says that use is, at some point, 'an unjustified stab in the dark'; which he takes to be the sceptical conclusion.

Dispositions The problem in answering the sceptic is that the range of facts to which we can appeal is too narrow to rebut his challenge. A way of widening this range is to invoke dispositions. The thought is that if I were asked for the sum of 254 and 857 I would be justified in saying '1111' because this present use accords with my past meaning since, in the past, I would have been disposed to give this answer.

There are, however, numerous objections to the dispositional view. For one thing, dispositions cannot, ultimately, provide a *justification* for use because they themselves require justification in terms of grasp of meaning. For another, how can one's present use be justified by a hypothesis about one's past dispositions? I know I now have a certain disposition, but how do I know that I then had the same disposition—and how would this knowledge justify my present use unless I knew that this was the correct disposition to have anyway?

Again, use is supposed to be *guided* by grasp of meaning, but it is difficult to see how it could be guided by an hypothesis about past dispositions: how do I know what these were? If, on the other hand, past and present dispositions are assumed (at least in the absence of contrary evidence) to coincide, there will be no constraints on present use: 'whatever seems right to me will be right'—which destroys the notion of rightness. Collapsing the ability to follow a rule into possession of dispositions ignores the *normativity* of rule-following.

The point of introducing dispositions was to widen the base from actual use. But dispositions are also finite, and therefore provide no solution.

There are two problems here. One is that dispositions (which include dispositions to error) do not explain the normativity of meaning; the other is that they are finite. The problems are linked; if we could invoke an infinite set of dispositions we could say that all future uses are anticipated in past dispositions, and that conformity with past dispositions constitutes correctness. But this move is not available. Nor, on inspection, are moves which try to objectify dispositions by hedging them with *ceteris paribus* clauses, or which otherwise try to bolster appeal to them; the attempts fail because they misconstrue the relation of meaning and intending to future action as *descriptive*, whereas it is in fact *prescriptive*.

This discussion exploits Kripke's derivation of a sceptical paradox from Wittgenstein's remarks about rule-following. The paradox comes to a head in Section 201:

> This was our paradox: no course of action could be determined by a rule, because every course of action can be made out to accord with the rule. The answer was: if everything can be made out to accord with the rule, then it can be made out to conflict with it. And so there could be neither accord nor conflict here.

The question is, are we led to this paradox only because of misconceptions about the nature of meaning and understanding, or is meaning-scepticism inevitable?

Kripke's Sceptical Solution The conclusion of the sceptical argument is intolerable, so Kripke has a hard task in persuading us that it is unanswerable. In his view, the sceptic shows that one sort of justification for ordinary practice is unavailable, but he argues that we can nevertheless show our practice has value and inevitability. If we view meaning in (quasi-)contractual terms we come to see use as normatively unconstrained—thus, as meaningless; but this does not mean that we cannot explain the illusion of constraint, and the usefulness of ascriptions of meaning and understanding.

Kripke helpfully draws an analogy with Hume, who argued that our unreflective talk of causation treats it as a substantial relation between token events, although it is nothing more than regular conjunctions of tokens of certain event-types. Hume did not wish to revise our ordinary talk of causation; his naturalism shows that is unavoidable, and explains why. Kripke applies the insight to Wittgenstein in the following way.

The problem with rule-following is that grasp of a rule is supposed to constrain one's use *normatively* (and not causally). So grasp of a rule cannot be equated with one's (fallible) application of it. The temptation is to think of the rule as distinct from applications of it—which invites sceptical challenge because we then need interpretations to mediate rules and their application. This triggers regress, or prompts the myth of self-intimating rules.

Here is where Kripke offers a solution on Hume's model. The notion of a cause appears vacuous when we concentrate on the relations between token events. But once we widen our view to type events the notion acquires substance—not of the kind sought by a causal realist, but enough to explain causal talk. Kripke, on Wittgenstein's behalf, claims that scepticism shows that if we focus on the individual, no sense can be made of following a rule; but if we focus on the individual's use *within a practice of communal use* we can give an account on the following lines.

The first step is to reject the truth-conditional approach. On that view the meaning of a sentence is the condition under which it is true (so asserting the sentence is asserting that this condition obtains). The truth-condition of the sentence is determined by the reference (or, more neutrally, semantic values) of its components. So, once we have established the referential relations of the primitive terms of our language, the truth-conditions of all sentences are determined. Thus a pattern for their correct use is determined, without further contribution from us. Kripke says that the rule-following considerations demolish this approach, and that what is required is an *assertibility conditions* account, in which one is warranted in asserting a sentence just in case one can secure communal agreement with one's assertion. This is intended to exploit the platitude that no one is obliged to withdraw an assertion if he can get the rest of the community to agree with his right to make it.

Despite the separation of the community's use from individual use, warranted assertibility is not a static criterion of correctness separate from use itself; it is not a strict guide-line to which we hold our use responsible. Individuals attempt to bring their usage into accord with that of the community, which is itself under no constraints. The basis of language is agreement brought about by training, not by rational convergence. Agreement is contingent—but although important, it is not philosophy's business to describe its basis. The sceptic forces us into difficulties by continually requesting a justification of our use as the employment of a rule. But as justifications must come to an end, at some point we act blindly—although, as Kripke (following Wittgenstein) notes, not without right. At this point we simply rely on the fact that we agree; we say '*This* is what we do'. Language ultimately is grounded in action—in *human* action, that is, in a form of life.

Kripke claims that Wittgenstein is not saying that to apply a rule in the same way as fellow speakers *means* to apply it as the community does. This would be to revert to fixing truth-conditions for assertions. Instead we should content ourselves with the truistic claim that we *say* that someone is applying a rule in the same way as us when their application agrees with ours:

241. 'So you are saying that human agreement decides what is true and what false?'—It is what human beings *say* that is true and false; and they agree in the language they use. That is not agreement in opinions but in forms of life.

To agree that grass is green is not what makes 'grass is green' true, nor does it entail that 'grass is green' means that we agree in asserting 'grass is green'. The point is that the conditions in which *we* take 'grass is green' to be warrantedly assertible determine the content of that sentence; so we agree in our language, not necessarily in our opinions. If you wish to clarify the content of 'grass is green' you need do no more than look to its assertibility conditions.

Kripke's solution to the sceptical paradox entails that attributions of correctness—and hence of meaningful language use—depend upon the persistence of a communal practice. His solution therefore precludes the possibility of private language. We revert to this point shortly. In Section 202 Wittgenstein infers (from 201 quoted above),

And hence also 'obeying a rule' is a practice. And to *think* one is obeying a rule is not to obey a rule. Hence it is not possible to obey a rule 'privately': otherwise thinking one was obeying a rule would be the same thing as obeying it.

Problems with the Sceptical Solution Whatever the intrinsic merits of his approach, has Kripke got Wittgenstein right? For one thing it is odd, given Wittgenstein's philosophical method, to attribute scepticism to him. Wittgenstein claims that philosophy cannot advance theses; that it leaves everything as it is; that the philosophical method is purely descriptive. A number of commentators argue that Wittgenstein is not advancing a *sceptical* paradox, but identifying one that arises from mistaking *grasp of a rule* for *possession of an interpretation*. Note section 201:

It can be seen that there is a misunderstanding here from the mere fact that in the course of our argument we give one interpretation after another . . . What this shews is that there is a way of grasping a rule which is *not* an *interpretation* . . .

This is an exegetical query. More fundamental is a query about whether the assertibility conditions thesis solves the problem in hand. The thesis has it that the assertion conditions of a sentence are those under which it is *correctly* assertible. So construed, they look suspiciously like standards with which use must accord. And they involve the problematic notion of correctness. A slimmer notion of assertibility conditions would be one in which they merely report patterns of use. But why should generalizing from the individual to the community produce meaning? How, if each member of a community considered in isolation is simply a babbler, does the sum of babblings become meaningful? How is a crowd of babblers transformed into a community of speakers?

Wittgenstein on Rules: Against the Sceptical Reading Given these reasons for wariness about the sceptical reading of Wittgenstein on rule-following, it is worth considering an alternative account, which takes section 201 seriously by noting that its sceptical first paragraph is followed by one that locates paradox in misconceptions about rule-following.

Note, to begin with, why understanding appears such a queer phenomenon. On the one hand, one's use of a term is supposed to flow from one's understanding of it, but not *causally*. Rather, one's understanding determines what counts as the *correct* use, which actual use need only approximate. But, on the other hand, it seems as if understanding is a state (we talk of understanding something 'in a flash', of 'coming to understand' something). It seems irresistible to think that use of a term is somehow 'contained in' understanding of it. What could this containment be other than grasp of a correct interpretation of a rule? Yet once we accept this, the sceptical considerations apply.

Note that this is just the view which Russell and the *Tractatus* adopted. According to them, language is meaningful because of correlations between words and objects. Such correlation *of itself* determines future applications. So Wittgenstein is attempting to dispel illusions which arise from *philosophical* misunderstandings about meaning.

195. 'But I don't mean that what I do now (in grasping a sense) determines the future use *causally* and as a matter of experience, but that in a *queer* way, the use is in some sense present.'—But of course it is, 'in *some* sense'! Really the only thing wrong with what you say is the expression 'in a *queer* way'.

Wittgenstein agrees with his imagined interlocutor that the relation between understanding and use is not an external relation, but he opposes mystifying it. He suggests instead that it is 'criterial'. The apparent metaphysical conundrum is to be dissolved by getting clear about the grammar of our language.

Justifications Come to an End The sceptic persistently asks for justification of our use of an expression. Because justifications do not come to an end in something self-validating, the sceptic concludes that our use is ultimately a 'stab in the dark'. This is the conclusion urged by Kripke. Wittgenstein, however, says,

211. How can he *know* how he is to continue a pattern by himself—whatever instructions you give him?—Well how do I know?—If that means 'Have I reasons?' the answer is: my reasons will soon give out. And then I shall act, without reasons.

Wittgenstein says that rule-following is not governed by reasons. We simply do it. This is not to say that we act *un*reasonably or *ir*rationally, for that would be to imply that we could offer a reason for our patterns of use, whereas we cannot. Wittgenstein's point is that a doubt is in many cases inappropriate (or even impossible), so requests for justification are inappropriate. Merely to lack a reason is not to be in doubt. The sceptic, who mistakenly conflates grasping a rule with knowing an interpretation, misdescribes the situation. Because a finite segment of use is reconcilable with various alternative interpretations, the sceptic supposes that one has *chosen* one interpretation from among the others. The question then would be what justifies (or governs) that choice. But in Wittgenstein's view the question of choice simply does not arise: 'I obey the rule *blindly*' (section 219).

His point is that it is a philosophical illusion to think that the *possibility* of raising a doubt suffices to demolish certainty. So, in this case, the philosophical misconception that there is a mysterious relation between understanding and use makes it seem that use unsupported by reason is suspect.

In contrast to the Augustinian picture, we cannot, on Wittgenstein's view, see learning a language as rationally forming hypotheses about meanings. To grasp the meaning of a word is to acquire the ability to use it correctly. This is an ability acquired in the *practice* of using the word—a kind of training. Because learning a language is acquiring an ability to engage in certain practices, it only *makes sense* to talk of obeying a rule in the context of a practice: there can be no singular applications of a rule. Thus understanding determines use, not in a queer way and not causally, but because understanding *is* the ability to participate in a practice.

Normativity and the Role of Agreement Kripke is alert to questions about norms. His sceptical solution entails that it is correct to use a term just when one can secure communal assent to one's use. This means that communal agreement is a precondition for the meaningful use of signs. In the alternative interpretation, obeying a rule depends on the persistence of a practice, itself in turn dependent on communal agreement. An accusation often levelled at Kripke's account is that it only makes space for a surrogate of normativity, giving only the illusion of being guided by a rule. This contrast repays attention.

Any theory that equates the following sentences is at least controversial:

(1) *x* is red.
(2) *x* would be called 'red' by (most) English speakers.

Kripke, as noted, tries to avoid committing himself to their equation; he argues that the meaning of a sentence is determined by its assertibility conditions and, platitudinously, a sentence will be assertible just when we can secure agreement. The idea then is to characterize the meaning of a sentence in terms of its assertibility conditions, while noting that it does not state that its assertibility conditions are fulfilled. Thus (1) does not state that (2) holds; (1) states that *x* is red. So, it is supposed, we can allow that (1) and (2) have different content.

The problem is that (1) and (2) have precisely the same assertibility conditions (and, arguably, the same defeating conditions). On Kripke's account, this gives

(1) and (2) the same meaning. Even if this is not an irresistible consequence of the view, we have no explanation why we distinguish between the two sentences, nor why we have a use for sentences of the form (1).

McDowell sees Wittgenstein as positing a dilemma: either there is no substance to meaning, or we have to appeal to the myth of self-intimating rules. Kripke accepts the first option, supplementing it by the community view. But in McDowell's reading, Wittgenstein uses the notion of a practice to reject the dilemma altogether, by rejecting the premiss that generates it: the premiss, namely, that understanding consists in grasp of an interpretation. McDowell and Kripke agree on the role of practice, and agree that justifications come to an end. But, whereas Kripke uses the community to account for correctness, McDowell confines understanding wholly within practice, thus warning us against 'digging below bedrock'. Below bedrock are phenomena that can be described in norm-free terms (and which might or might not coincide across the community). The coincidence of these phenomena are a precondition for the existence of the practice, and so for talk of correctness; but they do not *constitute* correctness. Indeed, Wittgenstein is alerting us to the dangers of attempting to characterize meaning in non-normative terms.

3.3.7. A Private Language?

In section 202 Wittgenstein notes that one cannot obey a rule 'privately', for merely thinking that one is doing so is no guarantee of success. At section 243 he asks whether there could be a language created exclusively for private use, that is, a language in which reference is made to objects available only to the speaker (for example, pains and tickles). This question invites two interpretations. One is that Wittgenstein means to argue that no speaker can infallibly determine whether he is following a rule because rule-following is an ability whose exercise is not accompanied by an experience of 'being right' when it is right. This accords with section 202; but it does not—according to those who give this interpretation—by itself render incoherent the notion of a solitary practice, which is why the 243 consideration about private reference is needed.

The other interpretation is that the rule-following considerations by themselves succeed in establishing that there cannot be private language, because language is a practice and a practice cannot be solitary; so the later concern with reference to private objects is not the centre-piece of a campaign against private language, but answers a counter-example to his thesis, the counter-example being that sensation language must be unshareable.

To evaluate these interpretations it is appropriate to look at Wittgenstein's examination of sensation language. His discussion bears on such traditional problems as reference, knowledge of other minds, and the character of the mental.

What is a Private Language? Wittgenstein's question in sections 243 and 244 is: how does the private linguist give himself an ostensive definition to which he alone is privy? One who believes that there can be private language holds that we can recognize a private object which is, at most, linked contingently with any publicly observable phenomenon. So, for example, someone might have an itch which is linked only contingently with the usual causes of itchiness and with the usual responses to itchiness: he might feel an itch for no apparent cause, and might not scratch it. (And likewise for pain, tiredness, and the like.) I recognize my private objects in a way unavailable to you; you have only contingent links between observable causes and behaviour and the inner objects whose possible existence you therefrom—unreliably—infer. But if you are to confirm these contingent links you have to observe a regular connection; and you can do this only in your own case, not in mine.

The familiar 'argument from analogy' tries to show that from acquaintance with my own case and observation of yours I can conclude that you have a mind. The argument is weak; it is an induction with a base class of one, and therefore vulnerable to scepticism. It remains a coherent conjecture that one is the only creature with a mind in a community of automata.

Behaviourists attempt to reduce mental to behavioural phenomena: to be in a certain mental state is just to have certain behavioural dispositions. The inference from behaviour to mental state is accordingly unproblematic—but is made so at the cost of rendering mysterious the unmediated, non-inferential access we have to our own mental states.

Private Ostensive Definition The private linguist tries to establish the meaning of a word by linking it to a given private object. To do this he must identify the referent. But how? Ostensive definition in the private realm is no different from ordinary uses of ostension, which Wittgenstein has already shown cannot be linguistically basic. In the private linguist's case it is supposed that he 'points' simply by focusing attention on the immediately given private object. But the mere utterance of the word in conjunction with such a 'pointing' cannot confer a meaning on the word unless something counts as using the world *correctly* in line with this correlation:

> 258. . . . But 'I impress it on myself' can only mean: this process brings it about that I remember the connexion *right* in the future. But in the present case I have no criterion of correctness. One would like to say: whatever is going to seem right to me is right. And that only means that we can't talk about 'right'.

Reference to an inner object is thus an illusion.

This result seems paradoxical, because nothing seems clearer than that we have incorrigible knowledge of our own mental states. My statement that I am in pain is, provided that I am sincere and understand the sentence, guaranteed to be true. I cannot be in pain but be oblivious of it; I cannot feel that I am in pain and be wrong. But Wittgenstein argues that this peculiar security of avowals shows them *not* to be statements of knowledge. He does not wish to say that 'I know I am in pain' is senseless, because one can imagine certain uses of that expression. His point is that it is not used as an expression of a doubt resolved: there is no practice of doubting whether one is in pain or not. Therefore, we are mistaken to say that one is *certain* about *one's own* mental states, but merely has *beliefs* about those of *others*.

We are tempted to construe 'I am in pain' as fact-stating, and to interpret the absence of doubt as evidence of a uniquely secure relation of knowledge. But Wittgenstein rejects this, arguing that we treat such avowals as factive because of a philosophical prejudice to the effect that language has one basic function. The absence of doubt does not reveal certainty, but shows the inapplicability of the concept of knowledge. (This thesis is developed further in Wittgenstein's last work, *On Certainty*.)

Wittgenstein and Behaviourism In section 307 Wittgenstein asks himself whether he is a behaviourist in disguise. He responds by saying that he is not fictionalizing our mental life but speaking of a *grammatical* fiction, the tendency to mistake the functioning of language and, in this instance, to see talk of sensations as functioning on the model of object and designation. He is not criticizing ordinary linguistic practice, but diagnosing 'illusions' generated by misconceptions of its nature. In the case of sensations we apply the model of ordinary fact-stating discourse, which prompts the myth of a transparent inner realm only contingently connected with behaviour. Wittgenstein argues that, so construed, the objects to which sensation terms putatively refer vanish.

But this refusal to countenance private objects does not entail behaviourism. Both behaviourism and Cartesianism stem from a similar pilosophical hankering for objects and processes underlying talk of the mental. Behaviourists are impressed by the problems that beset Cartesianism and so try to reduce mental phenomena to behaviour. But Wittgenstein's methodology in philosophy is equally at odds with this behaviourist programme. His aim is restricted to giving an account of the use of sentences involving sensation terms. A successful account must maintain the connection with behaviour and allow for the incorrigibility of avowals—but neither, he says, require a metaphysical underpinning.

4. CONCLUSION

The foregoing sets out some of the chief ideas of Frege, Russell, and Wittgenstein, but it is by no means an exhaustive account of their views. We do not discuss Russell's repeated attempts to work out an epistemological theory aimed at demonstrating the empirical foundations of science, nor Wittgenstein's many notes (since edited and published by his literary executors) on questions in the philosophies of mathematics and psychology, and in epistemology. A full appreciation of their work of course requires a study of these too. But the themes presented here are central, not just to their work but to the subsequent development of ideas in analytic philosophy, especially in the philosophies of language, mathematics, and logic.

The influence of the work of these three thinkers stems from the questions they asked and the ways they attempted to answer them. It might be asked why their work is accorded such importance given that Frege abandoned his project in despair upon the discovery of the paradoxes, that Russell's solutions to them involve *ad hoc* manoeuvres, and that Wittgenstein repudiated most of his earlier thinking, coming to believe that systematic theorizing is not the way to solve problems because (in his—rather questionable—view) it is theorizing that generates them in the first place. The answer is that the contributions of all three thinkers have been immensely fertile in opening the way to more than could have been conceived without them, showing once again that—as the saying has it—the journey is as important as the arrival. All three, but Frege and Russell especially, took philosophical inquiry far beyond the point at which they found it, forging ideas and techniques which are now permanent possessions in the history of philosophy. Anyone making a serious study of contemporary analytic philosophy must have a good knowledge of their contributions; the foregoing maps a path towards acquiring it.

BIBLIOGRAPHY

FREGE

Texts

Begriffsschrift (1879), in *From Frege to Gödel*, ed. and trans. J. van Heijenoort (Cambridge, Mass., 1967); excerpts also in Geach and Black (next item). An exposition of Frege's logical system. Inevitably it is mostly technical, but the introduction provides some good clues to Frege's underlying motivations.

Translations from the Philosophical Writings, ed. and trans. P. Geach and M. Black (Oxford, 1980). An excellent collection including the three crucial papers 'On Sense and Meaning' (1892), 'On Concept and Object' (1892), and 'Function and Concept' (1891).

Logical Investigations, trans. P. Geach and R. Stoothoff (Oxford, 1977). A collection of three late papers which find Frege in his most reflective, philosophical mood, including 'Thoughts'.

The Foundations of Arithmetic (1884), trans. of *Die Grundlagen der Arithmetik* by J. L. Austin (Oxford, 1980). Frege's presentation of the core of his philosophy of arithmetic.

Dummett hails it as 'unquestionably the most brilliant sustained performance of its length in the entire history of philosophy'.

The Basic Laws of Arithmetic (1893–1903), trans. of *Die Grundgesetze der Arithmetik* by M. Furth (Berkeley, 1964). Frege's attempt to implement the programme outlined in *Grundlagen*. The introduction (at least) is essential reading for anyone with a serious interest in Frege.

Posthumous Writings, ed. Hermes, Kambartel, and Kaulbach (Oxford, 1979). This book is comprised mainly of snippets and plans. They often provide invaluable insights into Frege's precoccupations.

Secondary Literature

BEANEY, M., *Frege: Making Sense* (London, 1996). An excellent dissection of Frege's notion of sense.

BELL, D., *Frege's Theory of Judgement* (Oxford, 1979). Thoughtfully explains and criticizes Frege's account of content, providing a link with Wittgenstein's thought in the *Tractatus*.

BENACERRAF, P., 'Frege: The Last Logicist', in Demopoulos (ed.), *Frege's Philosophy of Mathematics* (below). Downgrades Frege's philosophical motivations in favour of the mathematical search for rigour.

CURRIE, G., *Frege: An Introduction to his Philosophy* (Brighton, 1982). A clear exposition of Frege's corpus.

DEMOPOULOS, W. (ed.), *Frege's Philosophy of Mathematics* (Cambridge, Mass., 1996). An important collection of papers discussing the more technical aspects of Frege's foundational work in mathematics.

DIAMOND, C., *The Realistic Spirit* (Cambridge, Mass., 1995), chs. 2–5. A set of papers discussing the nature and limits of Frege's analysis of language.

DUMMETT, M., *Frege: Philosophy of Language* (London, 1973). An immense and important book. Much of Dummett's own philosophy emerges from this thorough engagement with his subject.

——*Frege: The Interpretation of Frege's Philosophy* (London, 1981). A 600-page sequel to the previous book.

——*Frege: Philosophy of Mathematics* (London, 1991). Briefer and more organized than the previous books. Dummett gives penetrating exegesis of Frege and argues for his contemporary relevance.

EVANS, G., *The Varieties of Reference* (Oxford, 1982), ch. 1. Tackles the question of whether Frege's theory of sense adequately accounts for empty singular terms.

HAAPARANTA, L., and HINTIKKA, J. (eds.), *Frege Synthesized* (1986). An excellent collection of papers on all aspects of Frege.

KLEMKE, E., *Essays on Frege* (Chicago, 1968).

PARSONS, C., 'Frege's Theory of Number', in Black (ed.), *Philosophy in America* (Ithaca, 1965) and Demopoulos (ed.), *Frege's Philosophy of Mathematics* (above). An influential and detailed study of Frege's account of number.

RESNIK, M., *Frege's Philosophy of Mathematics* (Ithaca, NY, 1980). Concentrating mainly on the *Grundlagen*, this book gives a clear presentation and critique of Frege's views.

SCHIRN, M., *Studien zu Frege*, 3 vols. (1976). An exhaustive collection. Some papers are in German. See especially those by Dummett, Parsons, Wiggins, Resnik, and Dudman.

Sluga, H., *Gottlob Frege*, The Arguments of the Philosophers (London, 1980). An attempt to reorientate thinking about Frege by placing him in historical perspective.

Weiner, J., *Frege in Perspective* (Ithaca, NY, 1990). Weiner constructs a thought-provoking reading of Frege by placing his interest in the foundations of mathematics at the centre of things.

Wright, C., *Frege's Conception of Numbers as Objects* (Aberdeen, 1983). Neo-Fregean Platonism and logicism are vigorously defended, a major source of much contemporary debate about Frege and the philosophy of mathematics.

——(ed.), *Frege: Tradition and Influence* (Oxford, 1984). A useful collection. See especially the papers by McDowell, Weiner, and Wiggins.

RUSSELL

Texts

The Principles of Mathematics (1903), chs. 1, 4, and 5 (sects. 56–8).

——'On Denoting' (1905), repr. in *Logic and Knowledge* and *Essays in Analysis* (below). A 'classic' of analytical philosophy: essential reading.

——'Knowledge by Acquaintance and Knowledge by Description', in *Mysticism and Logic and Other Essays* and in *Propositions and Attitudes* (Salmon and Soames eds.)

——'Mathematical Logic as Based on the Theory of Types', in *Logic and Knowledge* (below). Russell's first systematic statement and justification of the theory of types.

——*Principia Mathematica to *56* (Cambridge, 1962), introd. Contains Russell's considered explanation of the system.

——'The Philosophy of Logical Atomism', in *Logic and Knowledge* (below) and in *Russell's Logical Atomism*, Pears ed. (Especially first four lectures.) The conversational style and the inclusion of questions and responses make this an engaging exposition of the main lines of logical atomistic thought.

——'Logical Atomism', in *Logic and Knowledge* (below). Concise but less accessible than the previous item.

Logic and Knowledge. Essays 1901–1950 (London, 1956; repr. London, 1992).

Essays in Analysis, ed. D. Lackey (London, 1973).

Secondary Literature

Ayer, A. J., *Russell, Moore, and the Analytical Heritage* (London, 1971), chs. 3–5.

Blackburn, S., and Code, A., 'The Power of Russell's Criticism of Frege', *Analysis* (1978). A clear, though controversial reading of Russell's obscure argument.

Donnellan, K., 'Reference and Definite Descriptions', in *Philosophical Review*, 75 (1966), repr. in Harnish (ed.), *Basic Topics in the Philosophy of Language* (Brighton, 1994). Argues that not all uses of descriptions can be accounted for on Russell's model. An influential piece.

Evans, G., *The Varieties of Reference* (Oxford, 1982), ch. 2. A focused discussion of Russell's views on denoting.

Grayling, A., *Russell* (Oxford, 1996). A short critical introduction and overview.

Hylton, P., *Russell, Idealism and the Emergence of Analytical Philosophy* (Oxford, 1990), chs. 5 (for the more robust) and 6. A detailed and at times penetrating study of Russell.

Irvine, A., and Wedeking, G., *Russell and Analytic Philosophy* (Toronto, 1993). A good collection of recent scholarly papers.

Kripke, S., *Naming and Necessity* (Oxford, 1980). A seminal book attacking both Frege and Russell whose difficulty and depth is masked by its easy style.

——'Speaker's Reference and Semantic Reference', in *Contemporary Perspectives in the Philosophy of Language* (1989).

McCulloch, G., *The Game of the Name* (Oxford, 1989), chs. 2 and 3 (and, relatedly, 4). Uses Frege and Russell to animate a complex of philosophical issues to do with language.

Neale, S., *Descriptions* (Cambridge, Mass., 1990). A vigorous contemporary defence of Russell's theory of descriptions.

Sainsbury, M., *Russell*, The Arguments of the Philosophers (London 1979). Lucidly engages with the whole range of Russell's most important philosophy.

Savage, C. W., and Anderson, C. A., (eds.), Rereading Russell, *Minnesota Studies in the Philosophy of Science*, xii: (Minneapolis, 1988).

Searle, J. R., 'Russell's Objection to Frege's Theory of Sense and Reference', *Analysis* (1958).

Strawson, P., 'On Referring', in *Logico-Linguistic Papers* (London, 1971). A seminal paper and an important response to Russell's account of a Theory of Descriptions.

WITTGENSTEIN

Major Works

EARLY

Notebooks 1914–1916, ed. G. H. von Wright and G. E. M. Anscombe, trans. G. E. M. Anscombe (Oxford, 1961).

Tractatus Logico-Philosophicus (1921), trans. C. K. Ogden (London, 1922); trans. D. F. Pears and B. F. McGuinness (London, 1961; rev. 1974).

MIDDLE

The Blue and Brown Books (Oxford, 1958).

Philosophical Grammar, ed. R. Rhees, trans. A. Kenny (Oxford, 1974).

Philosophical Remarks, ed. R. Rhees, trans. R. Hargreaves and R. White (Oxford, 1975).

LATE

Philosophicla Investigations, trans. G. E. M. Anscombe (Oxford, 1958).

Zettel, ed. G. E. M. Anscombe and G. H. von Wright, trans. G. E. M. Anscombe (Oxford, 1967).

On Certainty, ed. G. E. M. Anscombe and G. H. von Wright, trans. D. Paul and G. E. M. Anscombe (Oxford, 1969).

Remarks on the Foundations of Mathematics, ed. G. H. von Wright, R. Rhees, and G. E. M. Anscombe, trans. G. E. M. Anscombe, 3rd edn. (Oxford, 1978).

Remarks on the Philosophy of Psychology, ed. G. E. M. Anscombe and G. H. von Wright, trans. G. E. M. Anscombe (Oxford, 1980), i.

Secondary Literature

Anscombe, G. E. M., *An Introduction to Wittgenstein's Tractatus*, 3rd edn. (London, 1967). This exposition is both elegant and insightful, though it is demanding.

Baker, G. P., and Hacker, P. M. S., *Scepticism, Rules and Language* (Oxford, 1984). Applies a similar line to the next piece to attack and supplant Kripke's account.

——— *Understanding and Meaning* (Oxford, 1983). Presents a reading of Wittgenstein as disabusing us of misconceptions which arise out of certain philosophical preconceptions.

Black, M., *A Companion to Wittgenstein's 'Tractatus'*, (Cambridge, 1964). A compendious blow-by-blow commentary. Worth consulting about particularly perplexing stages.

Boghossian, P., 'The Rule Following Considerations', *Mind*, 98 (1989). An immensely helpful survey of this now voluminous and difficult debate.

Bolton, D., *An Approach to Wittgenstein's Philosophy* (London, 1979). A particularly thoughtful overview.

Budd, M., *Wittgenstein's Philosophy of Psychology* (London, 1989). A perceptive study highlighting the originality of Wittgenstein's view of the mental.

Diamond, C., *The Realistic Spirit* (Cambridge, Mass., 1991), introd. and chs. 6–9. In ch. 6 Diamond constructs an impressive reading of the *Tractatus* by contrasting Frege's view of logic as the ultimately general science with Wittgenstein's view that logic is formal and so unsayable. The other pieces present aspects of the later work, emphasizing Wittgenstein's philosophical method.

Grayling, A., *Wittgenstein* (Oxford, 1988). A short critical introduction and overview.

Hacker, P. M. S., *Insight and Illusion*, rev. edn. (Oxford, 1986). An overview of Wittgenstein's philosophy which places his differing views of philosophy itself at centre-stage.

Kenny, A., *Wittgenstein* (Harmondsworth, 1973). Concise but exhaustive; an engaging overview.

Kripke, S., *Wittgenstein on Rules and Private Language* (Oxford, 1982). A *tour de force* which has galvanized discussions both of Wittgenstein's thought and of the nature of meaning.

McDowell, J., 'Wittgenstein on Following a Rule', *Synthese*, 58 (1984). McDowell rejects imputations that Wittgenstein was a sceptic and instead argues for a non-reductive view of norms.

McGinn, C., *Wittgenstein on Meaning* (Oxford, 1984). In a reaction to Kripke's book McGinn offers exposition and critical appraisal of Wittgenstein's views on meaning and understanding.

McGinn, M., *Wittgenstein and the 'Philosophical Investigations'* (London, 1997). An introductory survey.

Malcolm, N., *Nothing is Hidden: Wittgenstein's Criticism of his Early Thought* (Oxford, 1986). Shows how the later work grows out of Wittgenstein's questioning of assumptions underpinning the early work.

Mounce, H., *Wittgenstein's 'Tractatus': An Introduction* (Oxford, 1981). A good starting-point: clear and helpful.

Pears, D., *The False Prison* (Oxford, 1987). Vol. i: Draws out the Schopenhauerian background to Wittgenstein's early work. Vol. ii shows how, despite some continuity in

Wittgenstein's concerns, the later thought develops a distinctive philosophical method.

Stenius, E., *Wittgenstein's 'Tractatus': A Critical Exposition of its Main Lines of Thought* (Oxford, 1960). Concentrates on the metaphysics and the picture theory on meaning. Combines some useful exposition with provocative evaluations.

Wright, C., *Wittgenstein on the Foundations of Mathematics* (London, 1980). Despite the title this is also an important contribution to understanding Wittgenstein's thought in the philosophy of language. Focuses on the implications of the rule-following considerations and discusses the relationship between Wittgenstein's views and contemporary anti-realism.

Collections

Block, I. (ed.), *Perspectives on the Philosophy of Wittgenstein* (Oxford, 1981).

Griffiths, A. Philips (ed.), *Wittgenstein Centenary Essays* (Cambridge, 1992).

Holtzman, S., and Leich, C. (eds.), *Wittgenstein: To Follow a Rule* (London, 1981).

Pitcher, G. (ed.), *Wittgenstein: The Philosophical Investigations* (New York, 1966).

13

INDIAN PHILOSOPHY

Paul Williams

INTRODUCTION

Indian philosophy is as diverse as European philosophy and can only with distortion be characterized in a few simple expressions. The all-too-common slogans that 'Indian philosophy is mystical', or 'spiritual', or 'Indian philosophy is intuitive', or 'non-rational' (and therefore is not really philosophy at all, as Westerners understand the term), are, as characterizations of Indian philosophy, simply nonsense. They betray a gross ignorance of the vast critical analytic writing produced in India covering the nature of knowledge, perception, causation, truth, the nature of valid inference, consciousness, word and referent, ontology, and so many other clearly philosophical issues. The religious basis of much (but by no means all) of Indian philosophy is no different from that of medieval philosophy in the West, and to study Indian theories of truth through the eyes of analytic philosophy is no different from—and has the same problems as—studying medieval theories this way. It can be done, and it can be done profitably—but it must also be done sensitively.

Indian philosophy usually occurs in *darśanas*, systems which aim to be complete explanations of all that is necessary to attain the supreme goal of humanity as posited and understood by that system. Broadly speaking, systems can be divided into 'orthodox' (*āstika*) and 'heterodox' (*nāstika*), a division traditionally based on whether or not the system accepts as the final source of spiritual authority at least the ideal of the primordial Hindu Scriptures, the Vedas. Thus orthodox systems are what we would call 'Hindu'; heterodox are systems related to religions like Buddhism and Jainism, or the Cārvāka–Lokāyata approach of anti-religious scepticism and materialism. In general Indian philosophy in classical times consists in explanations of how things actually are, commonly integrated into path structures leading to *seeing* things this way. Indian philosophy consists also in debate between rival systems, arguing for the position of one's own system and defending it in minute detail against all possible or actual criticisms, and positing one's own system through criticisms of the positions of others. The basis for such debate, however, is agreed canons of inference and agreement on what is to count as grounds for knowledge claims. Thus epistemology and logic—an informal inductive-type logic arising out of the practical context of debate, rather than the formal deductive Aristotelian logic which never really developed in India—were integral to the Indian philosophical enterprise.

I shall not be concerned here with material which is incidentally of a philosophical nature but appears within the context of such texts as Vedic hymns to the gods, or spiritual teachings such as the Upaniṣads, or the teachings of the Buddha or Mahāvīra. These were the original inspirations for religious developments which issued in systems and eventually philosophy. In this chapter I look at a range of topics chosen for their importance and because they are topics on which there is interesting contemporary scholarship; secondly, because they illustrate the nature of Indian philosophy; but most of all because they might appeal to those interested in what is known in Western academic discourse as 'philosophy'. In Section 1, on Hindu thought, I shall examine some issues in three of the great classical *darśanas*, Sāṃkhya, Vaiśeṣika, and Nyāya, particularly the linked Nyāya–Vaiśeṣika perspective, the orthodox tradition most associated with developments in logic and epistemology which were honed through centuries of debate particularly with the Buddhists, notably the tradition of the Buddhist epistemologists Diṅnāga (Dignāga) and Dharmakīrti. I shall then look at the theory of language and semantics put forward by the great grammarian-philosopher Bhartṛhari. In Section 2 there will be a survey of the main schools of Buddhist philosophy, a look at some aspects of Jain thought, and consideration of what might almost be called India's 'Logical Positivists', the Cārvāka–Lokāyata tradition.

Unfortunately the critical philosophical study of Indian philosophy is still very much in its infancy and there are no completely adequate surveys of the field. However, for those who wish to read further I have mentioned in the Bibliography a few books which are relatively up to date and written by scholars who are not just philologists but also philosophically aware.

It is as impossible to write a short study guide to Indian philosophy as it would be to write one on European philosophy, and this chapter is highly selective. Many important figures have had to be omitted. There will be nothing on the famous Hindu thinker and religious figure Śaṅkara, for example, who, for all his historical and enduring importance to Hindu thought, is not so interesting as a creative philosopher. Nevertheless, in reading this chapter, and perhaps some of the recommended further reading, you should gain a good initial introduction to Indian philosophy, and I hope a love and fascination for what is a rather neglected field for Western philosophers.

1. SOME ORTHODOX (*ĀSTIKA*) PHILOSOPHIES

1.1. Sāṃkhya

1.1.1. *Ontology*

In origins, Sāṃkhya thought is possibly the earliest systematic school of Indian philosophy and its historical development is still very hazily understood. Sāṃkhya is a soteriological philosophy (one modern Indian scholar has called it 'a grand system of speculative metaphysics'), aiming for liberation from all suffering through complete and final freedom from the mundane world and thus from continued transmigration (*saṃsāra*). This liberation lies in realizing the eternally uninvolved isolation of the True Self. In looking at Sāṃkhya thought—which I shall do through the picture of classical Sāṃkhya given in a text known as the *Sāṃkhyakārikā* by Īśvarakṛṣṇa (third or fourth century CE)—it may be interesting to bear in mind as a suggestive social analogy the Indian religious and social renunciate (the 'holy man'), one who has wandered forth from his village to seek the final, liberative truth. Seated at the root of a tree, he looks back at the village from which he is now irrevocably separated, liberated.

Sāṃkhya thought is based on a radical and uncompromising dualism, a dualism between the True Self (called *puruṣa*—e.g. our renunciate seated beneath his tree), which is pure consciousness and alone is consciousness, and everything else which is the totality of everything (e.g. the village seen in the distance) minus consciousness. This 'everything else' is essentially not-consciousness, and is known as matter, or nature (*prakṛti* or *pradhāna*). The dualism is of types, orders of reality, not entities since for Sāṃkhya True Selves are *infinite* although there is only one *prakṛti*. Unlike certain Western ontological dualisms, however, this is a dualism between the essentially transcendent True Self (bare consciousness as such, not any particular instance of consciousness) and not-consciousness, not a dualism between mind and body. Clearly mind, or what we might call the mental, is not identifiable solely with bare consciousness.

Prakṛti is itself not a unitary entity, but is made up of three ever mobile constituents called *guṇas*. Descriptions of these *guṇas* are in terms of moral, physical, and psychological properties, which makes it very difficult to encapsulate them in brief formulas. The first constituent is called *sattva*—illumination, clarity, lightness, perhaps even purity, characteristics which are culturally positive. *Rajas* is activity, stimulating, moving. *Tamas* is restriction, heavy and enveloping. It is also dullness and lethargy. When these three constituents are in a state of balance and equilibrium *prakṛti* is, as it were, self-contained, and the cosmos (i.e. everything apart from *puruṣa*, True Self) is in what is thought of as a state of dissolution ('implosion'), a kind of latency. When the balance of the *guṇas* is upset a process of sequentially ordered cosmic unfolding ('evolution') takes place which eventually issues in the world as we know it. The sequence of this evolutionary unfolding of *prakṛti* is, in order, (1) will or intellect (manifesting under the predominance of *sattva*); (2) egoity; (3–13) mind, and the 'capacities' of hearing, touching, seeing, tasting, smelling, speaking, grasping, walking, excreting, and procreating (all manifesting under a predominance of *sattva* in the egoity); (14–18) the five 'subtle elements' of sound, touch, form, taste, and smell (manifesting under a predominance of *tamas* in the egoity); and (19–23) the five gross elements of space (or 'ether', *ākāśa*), wind or air, fire, water, and earth, which emerge out of the five subtle elements and then, in various combinations, make up through a secondary evolution the gross objects of our physical world. Including *prakṛti* itself, and *puruṣa*, this makes the twenty-five 'principles' (*tattva*) of the Sāṃkhya system.[1] On the common Hindu model, this evolution–devolution process takes an immense amount of time, but is nevertheless a regular cyclic event throughout all eternity. Note that in this form of classical Sāṃkhya there is not thought to be any need for a God in order to explain all this. There is, however, a very real problem in explaining why exactly an imbalance in the *guṇas* should take place. The usual answer is one of the proximity to *prakṛti* and reflection in *prakṛti* of *puruṣa*. *Puruṣa*, however, is a completely different order of reality from *prakṛti*, and such an explanation would seem to suggest more problems than it solves.

We see, crucially, that among the evolutes of *prakṛti* are factors such as will or intellect (*buddhi*), egoity (*ahaṃkāra*), and the mind (*manas*), which in the West we have tended to separate out as 'mental' and therefore distinct from the 'physical'. The Sāṃkhya dualism places the ontological division at consciousness versus everything else. Thus *anything at all* other than consciousness comes under *prakṛti*. Therefore, Sāṃkhya is saying that fundamentally, ontologically, anything other than consciousness is of the same primordial 'stuff' ('matter', 'nature') and on a direct continuum. Consciousness, on the other hand, is a completely different order of reality, and that is our True Self. To know this is spiritually (and morally?) liberating, final fulfilment.

Because consciousness is a completely different order of reality from not consciousness (*prakṛti*) it is crucial to Sāṃkhya that, in spite of appearances, consciousness really is completely uninvolved in *prakṛti*. How could one order of reality in a radical dualism implicate or involve another? (Compare Descartes's problems in relating body and mind.) This point is always extremely difficult for those new to Sāṃkhya to grasp. *Puruṣa* is not, and never was or will be, involved in *prakṛti* or bound by *prakṛti*. The process of liberation in Sāṃkhya lies *not* in freeing the True Self from a *prakṛti* within which it is bound, but rather in realizing that *puruṣa* never was bound by *prakṛti*: *freedom for Sāṃkhya lies in realizing that one always was free.* That is why freedom is unconditioned and permanent. Indian soteriologies are commonly gnostic systems—freedom lies in *knowing* something about which we were previously ignorant. Thus although Sāṃkhya talks sometimes as if *puruṣa* made a mistake, confused itself, with *prakṛti* and was bound, actually this is only an 'as if' in order to bring one to the here and now, the starting-point of understanding. The bondage never happened. One never was bound. It is very important not in any way to compromise this point in understanding Sāṃkhya.[2]

[1] I have listed the evolutionary principles. Of course, making sense of all of this is quite a different thing. For attempts, see the reading mentioned in n. 2.

[2] For additional reading, see Larson (1969: 7–16 (summary), 166–9, 173–94 (you can continue to p. 213 if you particularly want the details of the evolutionary schema), 213–27). A more recent and detailed account of the

1.1.2. *Causation:* satkāryavāda

Indian philosophy was very interested in the topic of causation, perhaps precisely because of its relevance to a spiritual path which was felt to involve a sequential move from the conditioned and perhaps largely determined everyday world to an unconditioned state or realm of freedom. The Sāṃkhya system is the classical exponent in Indian philosophy of an approach or perspective known as *satkāryavāda*. The name *satkāryavāda* refers to the doctrine (*vāda*) of the existent (*sat*) effect (*kārya*). The doctrine appears to mean that the effect is present in latent form in some way within the cause prior to the effect's actual production. In the classical Sāṃkhya version the effect is thus a manifestation or transformation of the cause rather than a creation *ex nihilo*.

The *satkāryavāda* is always spoken of as the Sāṃkhya theory of causation, but it is not clear whether Sāṃkhya teachers were really thinking in terms of a universal general theory of the nature of cause and effect. What we appear to have here is a theory of the transformation of a material substance (the 'cause') into something else (the 'effect'), and this would seem to be perhaps a particular example of causation occurring rather than a philosophical theory of causation. Clearly, as a theory of causation there are numerous everyday examples which would not fit the *satkāryavāda* explanation.

In fact, what Sāṃkhya is thinking of—and the reason why *satkāryavāda* is so important to it—is the precise context of the transformation of *prakṛti* into its evolutes. At least one Sāṃkhya commentator (Vācaspatimiśra; late tenth century CE) specifically states that it is *satkāryavāda* alone which will enable one to infer back from the given to unevolved *prakṛti* as the final material cause. Thus the Sāṃkhya approach to causality is tailored to fit a particular metaphysic.

The reasons urged by Sāṃkhya on behalf of *satkāryavāda* are as follows (*Sāṃkhyakārikā* 9):

(1) There does not occur the bringing into existence of that which does not exist.
(2) There is recourse to the material basis.
(3) There does not occur origination from everything [i.e. as the commentator says, we get gold from gold-ore, not silver, grass, dust, sand, etc.].
(4) There is the potentiality for effecting only that which the cause is able to effect.
(5) The effect is of the nature of the cause [i.e. barley comes from barley, rice from rice].

Actually in the Sanskrit there are two possible interpretations of reason (1): (*a*) One cannot cause that which is non-existent; or (*b*) A non-existent thing cannot

whole Sāṃkhya system, also by Larson, can be found in Larson and Bhattacharya (1987: 31–2, 43–103). This volume also includes detailed summaries of all the Sāṃkhya texts, and is invaluable for detailed research.

cause anything (or something cannot arise from nothing). I incline towards interpreting the reason (1) with interpretation (*a*). As it is understood by the commentator Gauḍapāda (perhaps early eighth century CE) reason (1) is precisely distinct from reason (2) in that (1) states that 'There does not occur the bringing into existence of that which does not exist'. Thus the argument here (critically expounded by the rival scholar Śrīdhara of the Vaiśeṣika school (late tenth century CE) in his *Nyāyakandalī*) is that causality involves a relationship between cause and effect, where the cause acts on the effect. There can be no relationship, however—certainly, it is claimed, no relationship like causality where one thing acts on another—if one terminus of that relationship does not exist. Thus if the effect does not exist already it could not have a relationship with its cause. Śrīdhara's critical response is that the causal relationship *is* a relationship, but not a relationship with a completely non-existent thing as it would be if the effect were, say, a square circle (he uses the common Indian example of a 'sky-flower', which does not distinguish between unexampled terms and logical contradictories). In the case of causation the effect both exists and does not exist. This is possible in such cases because, Śrīdhara says, the effect does not exist at time *t*, before the causal operation has occured, and does exist at $t+1$, after the causal operation has taken place. As it stands, Śrīdhara is perhaps begging the question, but there are certainly alternative means of escape here from the Sāṃkhya conclusion that the effect must exist prior to its causation in order to be related to, i.e. acted upon, in being causally produced.

Reason (2) is that, as Potter (1963) puts it, 'you can't get water from a stone', but of course the fact that it is not possible to obtain an effect from something which is not its cause cannot be taken to entail as a general theory of causation that somehow the effect is already present, contained, in the cause. My seeing a butterfly is (in part) caused by my having functioning eyes, but one could scarcely claim that seeing the butterfly is already existent, contained within my functioning eyes, prior to its occurrence.

A common Indian criticism of *satkāryavāda* is that if the effect already exists, then there is no need to produce it. Thus causation itself would be destroyed on such a theory. Of course, what Sāṃkhya is actually saying is not that *x* produces *x*, but that *x* in form *y* transforms into *x* in form *z*. Apart from the fact that this transformation is a very particular example of change occurring, and would seem to *require* an explanation of causality, rather than serve as an explanation itself, if we represent by $x(y)$ '*x* in form *y*' and by $x(z)$ '*x* in form *z*', then it is at least arguable that inasmuch as with a causal relationship between $x(y)$ and $x(z)$ *x* is the same in both cases, there can be no causal relationship at all as concerns *x*. Thus the causal relationship (the relationship that needs explaining) is between the two forms *y* and *z*. Since these are clearly different, inasmuch as causation occurs at all the cause and effect are different and *satkāryavāda* taken as a general theory of cause and effect consequently collapses.[3]

1.1.3. *Consciousness*

Sāṃkhya philosophy is often thought of as fairly unsophisticated by Indian standards, and it has been ignored by those interested and trained in Western philosophy even more than other areas of Indian philosophical thought. One of the only Western-trained philosophers to look constructively at Sāṃkhya has been Pratima Bowes, in a little-known and much-neglected study (1971). Bowes's discussion of the meaning and role of consciousness in the Sāṃkhya system is a reasonably accessible critical attempt to derive from the Sāṃkhya perspective material of interest to contemporary philosophical debate, and I summarize here her main points:

1. For Bowes what is particularly significant about the Sāṃkhya dualism is the distinction made between consciousness (the Self), 'the being of which lies solely in its function of manifestation', and the mind, which is part of *prakṛti* and is 'conceived as intelligent activity based on a capacity (unconscious) for discrimination, sensory, intellectual and volitional' (1971: 168). Mental functions are thus material functions, but we are more than just the material, the physical, for we also have consciousness, which is a quite different and underived 'principle of subjectivity as such' (p. 169).

2. Consciousness here is not to be confused with a particular instance or instances of consciousness. It is that *of which* such instances are instances. The function of consciousness as such is manifestation of an object as well as itself in the very same act (p. 169: i.e. consciousness is uniquely characterized by reflexivity). The Sāṃkhya claim is that it is also possible to experience in 'transcendental self-experience' consciousness as such distinct from consciousness of objects (p. 170).

3. Bowes argues that it is in everyday life perfectly possible to have activity we would call 'mental', i.e. a particular sophisticated level of activity which is 'purposeful, discriminative and so on' without it involving conscious awareness (p. 171). This could hypothetically be explained in neurophysiological terms. Computers, for example, can be seen to be intelligent: 'it is not necessary for a man to be conscious in order to behave intelligently' (p. 173). But with consciousness another dimension comes into the picture. Consciousness is represented not by intelligent behaviour but by knowing *that p*, and this cannot be reduced to neurophysiological terms. Computers are intelligent, but do not (as yet—see later) know that.[4]

[3] On the *satkāryavāda*, see Larson (1969: 177–81) and Potter (1963: 106–11, 150–3).

[4] Note that Bowes relates this discussion to Sartre's treatment of consciousness, a point also developed by Larson.

4. Thus, Bowes wants to say, inspired through her reading of Sāṃkhya plus a background in Sartrean phenomenology, 'the distinction between the mental and the conscious is this, mental is a state apt for the production of discriminative behaviour, conscious is the awareness of this state as this state' (p. 174). Knowing that requires not just an awareness of the object but also self-manifestation in the very same act, and this is precisely and solely what it is to be consciousness. There are no *states* of consciousness. Manifestation as such has no states (p. 174). A metaphorical way of speaking (common in India and Tibet) might be to say that consciousness is that very luminous quality which makes experiences *experiences* (knowing-thats; p. 175). This luminous quality is irreducible to anything else (i.e., it is argued, it could not be explained in neurophysiological terms). Hence Sāṃkhya dualism.

5. Bowes sees a problem, however, in identifying the *self* with consciousness understood as the function of manifestation. If we are referring here to the empirical self, the being in society that I normally think of as me, then it is simply false that my self is consciousness as understood by Sāṃkhya, and also false that as an empirical subject I am actually an absolute and my consciousness of an object is not dependent upon the environment and so on (pp. 182–3). However, since Sāṃkhya is a dualism and real interaction between *puruṣa* and *prakṛti* is denied, Sāṃkhya naturally wants to identify the self with consciousness, and explain the empirical self as a mistake, a confusion. Thus we have a *True* Self, consciousness, distinguished from the confused empirical self. Knowing that this is the True Self for Sāṃkhya bestows freedom, for such a Self is free by nature.

6. Bowes's problem, however, is that even if this were true it would still not explain freedom as it applies to the *empirical* individual (i.e. how *you and me* could be free; p. 184). Moreover, since for Sāṃkhya the principle of freedom is a wholly transcendent and *essentially inactive* consciousness, it is difficult to see how a free *act* can take place, and therefore how we can ever transcend, as it were, our state of bound unenlightenment and 'become' liberated.

7. One final interesting point Bowes also wants to add, however, is that if we hold that consciousness in Sāṃkhya interacts with the mind–body system when the latter is at a sufficient level of complexity, then there is nothing a priori to prevent the suggestion that, on Sāṃkhya principles, in the future consciousness could interact with (be reflected in) the mind–body system of robots. From the Sāṃkhya perspective, as seen by Bowes, robots are not now (as far as we know) conscious like human beings, but there is no intrinsic reason why they could not become so (pp. 194–7).[5]

[5] See Bowes (1971, pp. xvii–xx, 168–97). Cf. also Larson (1969: 228–38) and Larson and Bhattacharya (1987: 73–83).

1.2. Vaiśeṣika

1.2.1. *Introductory*

The ontology of the linked Nyāya–Vaiśeṣika schools is sometimes spoken of as an attempt to construct an ontology of 'common sense' (whatever that may be), issuing in a form of pluralistic realism. The fact that some of its hypotheses—such as, relations are separate realities from their relata, or wholes are different and separate realities from parts—seem scarcely to be intuitively obvious to the 'person in the street' may indicate the problems which arise when trying to carry through the construction of a 'common-sense metaphysics'. The starting-point of (Nyāya-)Vaiśeṣika lies in its saying, *astitva jñeyatva abhidheyatva*, 'existence (*astitva*) is knowability and nameability'. However, knowability and nameability seem not to be given in Vaiśeṣika in any simplistic way as a *criterion* for existence. In its influential use in Praśastapāda's *Padārthadharmasaṃgraha* (fifth or sixth century CE) the slogan would appear to be used not as a definition or criterion of 'existence' ('isness', *astitva*), but simply to characterize the common features of the six (later seven) categories (*padārthas*)—the categories of 'primary existents'—recognized by Nyāya–Vaiśeṣika.

Central to Nyāya–Vaiśeṣika thought is what might be called the substratum–property model. Commonly this is referred to as a model of *dharmin* (substratum) and *dharma* (property), where the *dharma* is said to reside in the *dharmin* by the relationship *x*. The rephrasing of natural language statements in *dharmadharmin* language is frequent in Nyāya–Vaiśeṣika (particularly in the later Navya– or new Nyāya), and there is no doubt that there was a feeling in these circles that property–substratum relationship language reflected much better the requirements of ontological precision. Even a name like 'cat' could be unpacked in the technical language with reference to the occurrence of catness (a universal) in the locus *x* (a substance) by an inherent relationship (see below). It is interesting to reflect on how far the structure and flexibility of the Sanskrit language facilitated this tendency. Anyway, it is not surprising that looking out at the world and wishing to categorize the given into broad types, Vaiśeṣika thinkers initially responded with a framework of substance, quality, and motion, mirroring a simple Sanskrit sentence structure: e.g. '[The] righteous brahmin sacrifices.' However, once we start to unpack such a simple sentence in a way which can easily be done in Sanskrit using the substratum–quality relationship model, employing the Sanskrit locative for the substratum as well as the easy ability of Sanskrit to compound and create endless degrees of abstraction, we are likely very soon to be tempted into introducing further categories, categories including universals and relationships such as inherence, as independent realities.

Substance, quality, and motion are the first three Vaiśeṣika categories. Note that the Sanskrit term *padārtha* (category) has the etymological meaning of referent (*artha*) of a word (*pada*). These first three categories are given a primary ontological status even among the categories themselves. The highest universal, *sattā* (being, or 'existence' (Matilal), but cf. *astitva*) is applied in Praśastapāda's all-important text to the first three categories alone. All six categories, however, including in addition universals, individuators, and inherence (*samavāya*), are indeed *padārthas* and have therefore *astitva*, 'isness' (as well as knowability and nameability). They are thus realities, and indeed realities which are objective—hence discovered, rather than mentally created—and separately distinguishable. Nevertheless, as Matilal (1985) points out, if a category like that of universal actually had existence or being (*sattā*) as well as reality, then, since existence is itself a universal, there would be the danger of an infinite regress. A later view which would include absences (*abhāva*) under the categories (an absence is a negative intentional referent which is discovered, not mentally created) would thus be willing to refer to even absences as independent realities. Absences, however, are to be distinguished from non-entities (like the proverbial 'sky-flower'), which are simple and complete fictions, cannot therefore be negated, and will thus require a form of unpacking if their expression is to be rescued by Nyāya–Vaiśeṣika from sheer nonsense ('some outrageous perversion', as one Naiyāyika referred to it).[6]

1.2.2. *Categories* (padārthas)

I shall look in more detail at some of the categories below. The full list of seven Vaiśeṣika categories consists of substance, 'quality' (actually 'quality instances'; see Matilal 1986: 357–8), motion, or action-moments (moments of movements of objects in space), universals, individuators, inherence, and absences (which are, after all, knowable and nameable). There are nine substances: earth, water, fire, air, *ākāśa* ('ether'), time, place, self, and mind or 'internal organ' (*manas*). According to the finally accepted system there are twenty-four qualities: colour, taste, smell, touch, number, contact, disjunction, farness, nearness, dimension, separateness, knowledge, pleasure, frustration, desire, hatred, effort, weight, fluidity, viscosity, dispositional tendency, merit, demerit, and sound. And according to the *Vaiśeṣikasūtras* (*c.*CE 50–150) there are five types of action or motion: throwing upwards, throwing downwards, contracting, expanding, and going (see Potter 1977).

Note that some qualities uniquely characterize certain substances (i.e. the five elements of earth, water, fire, air, and *ākāśa* ('ether'), plus the Self). Thus smell uniquely characterizes earth; colour fire; taste, fluidity, and viscosity

[6] For further reading, see Potter (1977: 47–50); Matilal (1985: 269–76, top). For more demanding reading, Bhaduri (1947/1975, ch. 1) is good. The Vaiśeṣika school was in classical times very closely linked with that of Nyāya. Thus the separation between this and the next main topic is really only notional.

water; touch air; sound *ākāśa*, and so on. The Self is uniquely characterized by knowledge, pleasure, frustration, desire, hatred, and so on. It is also very important to note that in Nyāya Vaiśeṣika qualities (such as colour) are to be distinguished absolutely not only from substances but also from universals. Thus red is a quality (in fact as such a quality instance, a trope), but redness is a universal, coming under quite a different category. The universal 'redness' is to be understood as a property the possession of which demarcates membership of the class of red things. The quality red will relate to a substance as its substratum, but redness here will relate to the quality red as its substratum. There is also a hierarchy of universals, including such universals as substanceness, with the highest universal that of *sattā*, being or existence. Note also that among qualities are included knowledge or cognition (*jñāna*), a quality which occurs in the Self as its substratum—the Self, a substance, *has* knowledge; in itself it is therefore not-knowledge, not consciousness—and also contact (*saṃyoga*), a relationship which, as a quality, has to be related to its relata by a further relationship, inherence. Inherence is a different category altogether and does not require a further relationship itself in order to relate the inherence to its substrata.

The category of individuator (*viśeṣa*, from which the Vaiśeṣikas get their name) is necessary in order to distinguish things which would otherwise be completely identical. The Vaiśeṣika system accepts the existence of material atoms. The individuator pertains to final things such as atoms of the same type as, for example, two earth atoms. It would normally not be possible to distinguish two earth atoms by their different spatial locations (as in the case of, for example, two pots), since atoms are not thought to be in time and space as are pots (note that with the earth atoms, time and place are themselves different substances). Thus each earth atom is distinguished by an individuator, the function of which is solely to distinguish such things. As to the question what distinguishes individuators from each other, in order to avoid an infinite regress the reply has to be that they are self-distinguishing. Given the Vaiśeṣika premisses this is perhaps not as absurd as it might seem, since *if* an individuator is just that which serves to distinguish, say, one atom from another of the same type, then it must *ipso facto* distinguish itself from another individuator.[7]

*1.2.3. Substance (*dravya*)*

Substances can be divided into permanent and impermanent. All the atoms in the case of the four elements which ultimately have atomic form, i.e. earth, water, fire, and air, plus all the other types of substance, are permanent.

[7] For the categories, see Hiriyanna (1932: 228–38)—a straightforward general survey—and Matilal (1986: 357–9), much more philosophically aware and interesting. For the detailed lists, see Potter (1977)

Impermanent substances are those things of intermediate size which are made out of atoms. Another way of dividing substances is by size. The elemental atoms plus the internal organ ('mind', *manas*) are partless and infinitesimal, impermanent substances like pots and pans have parts and are of intermediate size, while *ākāśa* (more or less), space, time, and Selves are partless and infinite in size. Selves, however, while infinite are constricted by their associated physical organisms. Yet another way of dividing substances is into material or immaterial substances (see Potter 1977: 73 for details).

As examples of some of the rather strange positions which the supposedly 'common-sense' Nyāya–Vaiśeṣika tradition finds itself adopting, we should note the view that the animal body is made entirely of earth atoms and therefore is an entity which is simply in contact (contact is itself a quality) with its bodily fluids. Also note that the physical animal body is thought not to include the sense-organs, for which it is simply the locus. The sense-organs operate *through* the relevant parts of the body, but are not identical with them. This can be seen if we notice, for example, that the organ of taste is composed according to Vaiśeṣika entirely of the water element, but the physical body is entirely of the earth element. The sense-organs themselves are composed each of the relevant element of earth, water, air, fire, and *ākāśa*. Because each element has an association with a different sense it is held the different resultant sensations of smell, taste, touch, sight, and hearing respectively can actually take place. This is no doubt helped by the fact that sense-data are qualities (see Potter 1977: 113), which as such must occur in their corresponding elements which are their substantial substrata (ibid. 88–9). The physical body, which might be thought to be directly connected in some way with the sensation of touch, is made of earth atoms which are in fact associated with smell. It is the element air which is associated with touch.

The element of *ākāśa* is not itself space, but what fills space, and is necessary in order for the quality of sound to have a substratum to inhere in. Due to the fact that the Vaiśeṣika sees space and time as objective, infinite, partless realities, it has been common to portray them as absolute containers within which temporal and spatial divisions are made for convenience. Potter (1977), however, portrays space and time as relational, or rather 'the necessary relating principles among physical things which enables those things to be related by [spatial and temporal] relations' (p. 91; cf. Hiriyanna 1932: 229). One infers space and time from spatial and temporal relational judgements which connect pairs of objects, 'space and time are continua of relations potentially available to relate any objects "anywhere" and "anywhen"' (Potter 1977: 93).

The internal organ (*manas*) seems to serve some sort of coordinating function, and links the data received through the senses to the Self as the subject of experience. It is eternal and atomic, and migrates from life to life in association with the 'subtle body'. The existence or otherwise of the Self was a central topic during centuries of intense debate with the Buddhists, debates which led to significant refinement of the Nyāya–Vaiśeṣika position. Since knowledge or cognition is held to be a quality ('I see the book' can be partially unpacked as 'There is an incidence of seeing in the locus referred to by "I"'), it follows of course that there must be a Self as the substratum for cognitive acts. For Nyāya–Vaiśeṣika psychological events are distinct qualities not to be confused with physical qualities. These psychological acts are transitory events possessed by a constant Self which can be spoken of as their agent. It is worth considering, incidentally, how far the common Sanskrit linguistic model of verbs requiring agents who *do* the actions, and must therefore be distinguished from the actions themselves, may have determined a 'natural' ontology here.

1.2.4. *Wholes and Parts*

The Nyāya–Vaiśeṣika view is that the whole is a different entity from the parts, and the whole inheres in each of the parts. Note the correct way round to express this. To think that the parts such as the threads in relationship to the cloth should inhere in the whole is still to think of the whole as somehow the totality of the parts, or made up out of the parts, and to miss what Nyāya–Vaiśeṣika is saying when it asserts the whole to be a completely different (albeit closely linked) reality from the parts. *The whole is not simply an aggregate of 'its' parts*, although the parts are held to be among the causal factors which produce the whole.

This theory may well be particularly important when looking at atoms, since atoms are partless and infinitesimally small and it is arguable that no amount of aggregation would produce gross objects unless something new is produced over and above the minute atomic parts (see next section). The whole is one, it is unitary, and it occurs in each of the parts. Thus by seeing a part of something we may consider as we often do that we have directly seen the thing itself, and for Nyāya–Vaiśeṣika we are correct to do so.

Mohanty 1970 (and Matilal 1986: 266–75 too) relates the Nyāya–Vaiśeṣika discussion of wholes to the claim by some philosophers in both West and East that we never really see the unity we think we see, say the tree, but rather we have to infer the tree from perception of, for example, the tree's parts such as this side of the trunk, some of the branches, or phenomena such as sense-data. The tree as a perceptual object is the result of an inference or logical construction. Against this, the Nyāya–Vaiśeṣika view is that to see a tree is to see a unity, a whole, which is not understandable on the basis of inferential or logical construction from more basic data. Rather, our experience tells us that seeing a tree is perceptually and indeed logically prior and we may or may not subsequently attend to seeing other associated factors such as the parts.

If on the view of the opponent the tree is simply a collection of its parts, and we do indeed see directly some of those parts, then clearly all we actually infer are the unseen parts. We do not thus infer, the Nyāya–Vaiśeṣika points out, a *tree*. If on the other hand the tree is more than the sum (a heap) of its parts, then how could inferring the unseen parts lead to inferring the tree, when there has never been seen independently a tree alongside the parts? Why should we ever infer a tree? Of course, we could not construct a tree if we had never seen a tree. But what, under such circumstances, could the parts then be parts *of*? The Nyāya–Vaiśeṣika from its side wants to hold (1) that a physical object is more than just the assemblage of its parts, and (2) that to perceive the whole does not require perception of the totality of the parts. For example, the final parts of the tree are its infinitesimal unperceivable atoms. If perceiving the tree required perceiving the atoms, the tree would always remain unperceived. Moreover, we all know from our own experience that to perceive a tree is not to perceive a collection of things, but is rather to perceive something which has a clear given unity (Mohanty 1970: 185–6).

To the question from the Buddhist whether the parts are in the whole (would each part be in the entire whole or just part of the whole?) or the whole in the parts, and if the latter does the whole in its entirety or only in part reside in any one part (the Buddhist would want to draw unwelcome conclusions in either case), the Nyāya–Vaiśeṣika simply responds that the Buddhist has missed the point. Of course, the parts do not reside in the whole. The Buddhist still does not understand the unitary nature of a whole. The whole does not have parts; it is not that sort of thing. Actually the whole resides in each part, but we are not required to answer the question whether the whole in its entirety or in part resides in any one part. These concepts do not apply in the case of a whole. Rather the whole is present in each of the parts and in the totality of the parts (Mohanty 1970: 188–9). Since the whole is present in each of the parts, it follows that it is not necessary to perceive all the parts in order to perceive the whole (although we know from our experience that it does not follow that in perceiving a part we *necessarily* perceive the whole). In other words, it is not necessary to perceive all the parts of the tree, or infer the unseen parts, in order to perceive the tree. In fact we normally perceive the tree in looking at the tree, and we might if we so wish *subsequently* attend to our perception of one or more parts. Perception of the tree is prior also to inferring (if we wish) the unseen parts. This understanding, the Nyāya–Vaiśeṣika would maintain, is free of paradox and corresponds to our actual experience of perceiving a tree. It is [a clarification of] common sense.

Of course, Mohanty (1970) points out, unclarities remain. Not all coming together of things produces a whole. What are the criteria for judging the production of a whole, rather than a mere aggregate? Could not the entire world be seen as a whole? The Nyāya–Vaiśeṣika response appears to be one of experience—in our experience certain things just do manifest ('call for') wholes, others do not—and it is not clear to me that this is an unsatisfactory answer.[8]

1.2.5. Atoms

Atoms are eternal, indivisible, the terminating point of physical division. As such, atoms must be without dimension, that is, without any size at all. That there are atoms is inferred from their effects, gross objects, and the fact that the division of gross objects has to have an end. That terminating point to division must by definition be indivisible, and therefore must have no parts. A common Indian counter-argument to atoms (found in the Buddhist scholar Vasubandhu, for example) is that if two atoms met, then they would either touch only partially or they would have to coalesce. If they touched partially, then it could not be true that the atoms have no parts. If on the other hand they truly do have no parts, then the two atoms could only coalesce. Under such circumstances no matter how many atoms met there could still be no aggregation, for the result would be no larger than the original dimensionless atom. One Vaiśeṣika *reductio ad absurdum* reply—that without atoms matter would be infinitely divisible and therefore there would be no gross objects—would be quite acceptable to at least some Buddhist opponents, who want to maintain that there is something radically skewed in our common-sense assumption of objective reality. For the Vaiśeṣika, on the other hand, contact between atoms (which are in themselves outside time and space) simply does lead to something larger being produced, since it is impossible for two material substances to coalesce, even if the material substances are infinitesimal and partless. Once we grant that atoms can aggregate, then the process of aggregation is thought to occur through two atoms making a dyad, three dyads a minimum perceptible, and so on. Of course the aggregation of atoms will bring about not just an aggregation but also a new whole, with its own properties.

An interesting topic which caused considerable controversy was the phenomenon of cooking. What this amounts to on the Vaiśeṣika explanation is that in the example of baking a pot change occurs at the level of individual atoms. What seems to follow from this is that the heat of cooking destroys the contact of the atoms making up the pot (as well as their colour); the whole which was the unbaked pot therefore ceases, and it is replaced by the whole which is the baked pot. Change occurs through the cessation of the thing itself and its replacement by another thing. Since it is admitted by the Vaiśeṣika that at the level of gross objects change is occurring all the time, if the Vaiśeṣika is not careful this theory will be indistinguishable from the Buddhist theory of con-

[8] Some extremely interesting philosophical work has been done on this topic of Nyāya–Vaiśeṣika thought. See Potter (1977: 74–9); Matilal (1971: 52–9; 1986: 266–75). Mohanty (1970: 184–97) is an outstanding paper on the subject.

tinual flux, with no continuing (gross) objects at all, a theory which seems very unlike that of 'common sense' and vehemently opposed by Nyāya–Vaiśeṣika. On this issue the Vaiśeṣika is also attacked by the follower of Nyāya (the Naiyāyika), who simply refuses to accept that change needs to occur at the level of the individual atoms themselves and that therefore there is an unbaked pot whole which ceases and is replaced by a different baked pot whole.[9]

1.2.6. *Inherence (*samavāya*)*

The relationship of inherence, as an objective relationship between inseparables which is a category in its own right, is a uniquely Nyāya–Vaiśeṣika concept. It is seen as essential in order to link those objectively distinct realities such as substance and qualities recognized by Nyāya–Vaiśeṣika which are nevertheless in normal everyday experience taken as in some sense to form one unity. Thus inherence is the relationship, a distinct reality itself, which links substance and qualities, substance and motions, particular things and their universals, ultimate things and their individuators, and whole and parts. Inherence can be distinguished from the other important relationship, contact (*saṃyoga*), which is a quality. In contrast with contact, inherence is a much, much stronger type of relationship, the sort of relationship which will not allow for the separation of the relata. If the inherent relationship between the two relata were to be broken (supposing it is breakable), the breakage would necessarily involve the destruction of at least one of the relata. Thus, for example, there can be no qualities separating themselves from their substances and, as it were, floating by themselves substanceless. The relationship of contact is itself a quality relating two substances where at least one of the substances must be material. Therefore contact is held actually to require inherence in order to relate it to its relata.

The Buddhist wanted to know whether inherence too requires a further inherence to relate it to its relata, with the threat of an infinite regress. From a Nyāya–Vaiseṣika standpoint the very fact that this would lead to an absurd infinite regress is a perfectly valid reason for denying it and adopting another strategy which is not likely to be so vicious. Inherence is a self-linking connector (*svarūpasambandha*; Potter 1977: 53). *If* it relates its relata, then it follows that it does not require a further relationship to relate itself to its relata. To think that inherence might require further inherences to relate it to its relata rests on visualizing the inherent relationship on the model of an adventitious variable relationship like contact, which as a quality does indeed require some further relationship—inherence to be precise—in order to relate it to its relata. That inherence should be understood on the model of contact simply does not

[9] For further reading, see Potter (1977: 79–86); Hiriyanna (1932: 238–42); Matilal (1986: 261–3).

follow, and if the inherent relationship actually occurs, then what more needs to be said?

Inherence is one only and eternal. More than one inherence is felt to be unnecessary, and if there were more than one inherence, then there would be problems with universals (inherenceness) and individuators which would need to be related to inherence with an inherent relationship. Thus we end up of course with an inherent relationship between inseparables as an independent reality which can survive the destruction of both its relata, again an apparent challenge to 'common sense'.[10]

1.3. Nyāya

1.3.1. *Causation:* asatkāryavāda

The Nyāya–Vaiśeṣika approach to causation is with the question what it is to be a cause and effect, rather than (as with Sāṃkhya) that of wrestling with the metaphysics of the exact relationship between them. Fundamental to being an effect in a cause–effect relationship is that the effect should be newly existent, that is, the effect could not have existed in any way prior to its production. Thus the Nyāya–Vaiśeṣika position on causation is one of *asatkāryavāda*—the doctrine of the effect which is non-existent (*asat*, i.e. prior to its production)—and in that respect contrasts with the Sāṃkhya *satkāryavāda*.

We can summarize the main points of the Nyāya–Vaiseṣika treatment of causation as follows (I rely on a very handy statement contained in a late Nyāya manual the *Tarkasaṃgraha* of Annambhaṭṭa (*c*.1575/1600?), and its commentaries):

1. The *Tarkasaṃgraha* defines cause as 'that which is an invariable antecedent to its effect'. It is not simply antecedent, because then you would have to include, for example, the potter's donkey as a cause of the pot. It must, nevertheless, be antecedent, because otherwise you would have to include the effect itself as a cause. Note, however, problems involved in treating causation this way. For example, even granted invariability, how long before the appearance of the effect can a cause occur? If there is any time gap at all, it is always possible for something to prevent the effect. Alternatively, one has to include the entire universe at time t as a cause of the effect at $t + 1$, and that would make repetition and therefore an empirical account of the discovery of causes impossible (a point made elsewhere by Russell).

2. The commentaries to Annambhaṭṭa's text improve the definition some-

[10] See Potter (1963: 118–29; 1977: 50–2); Hiriyanna (1932: 235–7); Matilal (1968: 37–41, top). An excellent, more detailed critical study of inherence made with particular reference to the Buddhist attack is Shastri (1964, ch. 10). Note that Hiriyanna's reference to redness as a colour on p. 236 must be an all-too-easy slip. As we have seen, red is the colour, a quality particular. Redness is a universal, quite a different thing.

what by adding, 'providing it is not too remote from the effect'. There are said to be three types of remote antecedence (*anyathāsiddha*), or irrelevance.

(*a*) If x is prior to z by virtue of an association with y, x is a remote antecedent of z; for example, in the case of threads the colour of the threads, or threadness, in relationship to the cloth.

This type of remote antecedence refers specifically to factors which *inhere* in the cause. Take the case of the cloth, which is, of course, a new whole brought into existence over and above the threads. While we number the threads among its causes we do not number among the causes of the *cloth* (cf. the colour of the cloth under 'inherent cause' below) the colour of the threads, or the universal threadness, both of which inhere in the threads.

(*b*) If x is known to be antecedent to y, which is antecedent to z, x is a remote antecedent of z; as in the case of ether (*ākāśa*) in relationship to a pot, when ether has antecedence to the vocalized sound 'pot' when uttered as a prior cause of the pot itself.

Someone announces that he is to make a pot. Sounds were thought to inhere in the ether. Thus although the sound 'pot' requires the ether in order to occur, we cannot include the ether here among the causes of the pot.

(*c*) Whatever is associated with the cause, inasmuch as it has invariable antecedence, is a remote antecedent; for example, as in the case of the prior non-existence of the colour in relationship to the smell produced by cooking.

The prior non-existence of the colour of the cooked item is associated with the cooked item itself as an invariable antecedent. And the cooked item is among the causes of the smell produced by cooking. But the invariable antecedence possessed by the prior non-existence of the colour could not be taken as a cause of the smell itself.

Different texts have different classifications of remote antecedents (the above was taken from the *Tarkadīpikā* commentary), but either way this category indicates the wish of Nyāya–Vaiśeṣika to remain in touch with 'common sense' in its treatment of causality. Nevertheless, a Buddhist for example—always the great rivals of Nyāya–Vaiśeṣika—might want to argue that ruling out certain things as causes can only be arbitrary. In the last analysis everything is interconnected. On what *grounds* can one say that the potter's father is not a cause of the pot?[11]

3. The effect is defined as the 'counterpositive of a prior non-existence'. A

[11] For more on remote antecedence, see Potter's discussion of *ananyathāsiddha* (1977: 67) and Hiriyanna (1932: 244).

commentary (*Nyāyabodhinī*) explains that prior to the production of a pot we hold that 'a pot will be here'. That non-existence is called the 'prior non-existence'. The counterpositive of that is the effect itself, i.e. the pot.

4. There are three types of cause: inherent, non-inherent, and efficient. (*a*) The inherent cause is that *in which* the effect inheres. For example, the threads in relationship to the newly produced whole which is the cloth. That is, the cloth inheres in the threads, and the threads are therefore its inherent cause. (*b*) The non-inherent causes are additional factors closely connected to either the effect or the inherent cause yet not inhered in by the effect. For example, the conjunction of the threads inheres in the threads (the inherent cause of the cloth), and the cloth also inheres in the threads. Thus the conjunction of the threads is the non-inherent cause of the cloth. They have a common locus, the threads. Or the colour of the threads inheres in the threads, the threads are the inherent cause of the cloth, the cloth is the inherent cause of the colour of the cloth, and the colour of the threads is thus a non-inherent cause of the colour of the cloth. Therefore, the colour of the threads inheres in the same substratum (the threads) as does the cloth, which is itself the inherent cause of the colour of the cloth, the effect. Thus the colour of the threads is the non-inherent cause of the colour of the cloth. (*c*) The efficient or instrumental cause is anything else (examples commonly given are the shuttle and loom), but subject always to the strictures of *ananyathāsiddha* (not being a remote antecedent) mentioned above.

According to the great Nyāya scholar Udayana (eleventh century?), causation can be seen as actually a relationship between universals (see Potter 1977: 55). This is perhaps rather obscure. Take, for example, the causal relationship between clay and a pot. To *be*, for example, clay in Nyāya–Vaiśeṣika is unpacked as (among other things) an incidence of clayness occurring in the locus *x*. Thus the causal relationship between clay and pot can be partially unpacked as a relationship between an incidence of clayness in the locus *x*, and an incidence of potness in the locus *y*.[12]

[12] See Potter (1977: 54–9, 65 (middle)–68); Hiriyanna (1932: 238–40, 243–4). For a fuller account, there is Bhaduri (1947/1975, ch. 12). Potter includes also the Nyāya–Vaiśeṣika critical response to the *satkāryavāda* of Sāṃkhya. See also pp. 59–65, which treats criticisms of Buddhists and the Mīmāṃsā school (on *jātisaṃkara* (p. 65), see pp. 135–6). Potter relies for his account on the perhaps misleading descriptions of the Buddhist position contained in Nyāya–Vaiśeṣika sources, and his account is also rather compressed (he is similarly rather misleading in his treatment of the Buddhist position; pp. 66–7. Cf. Shastri 1964, ch. 7). When Potter talks about 'causation as a relation between individuals, not solely between events' (1977: 54) he means by 'individuals' any entity belonging to one of the categories (p. 49). There is, however, a misprint on p. 56. Potter has repeated the definition given for the *laghvī* non-inherence cause in his account of the *bṛhatī* version. Since he is following the scholar Vyomaśiva (mid-tenth century), we can see from the summary on p. 438 that p. 56 should read: '(*b*) "big" (*bṛhatī*), where the noninherence cause inheres in the same substance as the inherence cause of the effect'. In the summary of Vyomaśiva on p. 438, on the other hand, under the *laghvī* definition one should substitute 'the noninherence cause' for 'the inherence cause'.

1.3.2. *Epistemology*

The Means of Knowing (pramāṇas) A number of Sanskrit epistemological terms are based on the root *mā* + *pra* (to measure out), of which *pramāṇa*, the means or instrument of true knowledge, is perhaps the most important. It is commonly held in Indian philosophy that a discussion of what is to count as a means of knowledge is the first prerequisite to the construction of an epistemology. In Nyāya–Vaiśeṣika the *pramāṇas* are perception, inference, comparison, and verbal testimony. Their great rivals, the Buddhists of the tradition associated with the scholars Diṅnāga and Dharmakīrti, reduced these acceptable means of knowledge to just perception and inference. Dharmakīrti (seventh century CE) also argued for the *pramāṇa* as the actual knowledge episode (*jñāna*) itself. In other words, for Dharmakīrti the *pramāṇa* properly speaking ceases to be the means of knowledge and becomes the knowledge itself (cf. the ambiguity of 'cognition' in English). Gautama (possibly second century CE), in the root-text for Nyāya thought, the *Nyāya Sūtras*, also speaks of the perception *pramāṇa* as a *jñāna* (see next section). One problem which arises in addition to that of what is to count as a means of knowledge is one of wherein lies the validity of a particular *pramāṇa* or a particular knowledge episode.

A special difficulty associated with the *pramāṇas* was put forward by the Buddhist scholar Nāgārjuna (also probably second century CE). This is that of the criteria by which we can claim to know the *pramāṇas* themselves. In other words, what validates the means of knowledge, the very means of validation themselves? If I claim to know that *x* is the case through perception, what validates perception as a means of knowing? What means of knowledge do I use when I assert that perception in general, or a particular case of perception, are valid means of knowledge? The danger is one of an infinite regress. (Were Nāgārjuna to meet Descartes he would point out that among the things Descartes failed to doubt was the validity and processes of reasoning itself.) An opponent might argue that *pramāṇas* do not actually need to be validated because they validate themselves in the very act of validating their referents—as lamplight illuminates itself in the very act of illuminating its objects. But Nāgārjuna's response to this is that if we can make any sense at all of using expressions like 'lamplight illuminates itself', then it must be meaningful to speak of lamplight first being unilluminated, and that is absurd.[13] Basically Nāgārjuna appears to want to argue that the establishment of *pramāṇas* as a

[13] For a discussion of the Nyāya attempt to unravel where Nāgārjuna has gone wrong in this response, see Matilal (1986: 49 ff.). Note that Matilal points out that the standard Nyāya view does not itself hold to the thesis that knowledge events are actually self-illuminating (*svaprakāśa*) a view which is indeed held by, say, Diṅnāga and Dharmakīrti.

critically grounded epistemological foundation for the construction of the edifice of a true philosophical system cannot get started. It is not clear, however, whether Nāgārjuna thought that there could be no actual *pramāṇas* at all—no generally agreed pragmatic everyday valid inference, for example, in opposition to the *pramāṇa* of inference as a critically established category within the context of abstract philosophical system-building—even within the everyday commonly agreed transactional pragmatic context, where Nāgārjuna could also place his own critique. Nāgārjuna's tradition of Buddhist philosophy, known as Madhyamaka, will be treated at the appropriate point in Section 2 below.[14]

*Perception (*pratyakṣa*)* Gautama defines perception in *Nyāya Sūtra* 1. 1. 4 as 'a knowledge event (*jñānam*) produced from sense–object connection (*indriyārthasannikarṣotpannam*) which is non-verbal (*avyapadeśyam*), non-deviant (*avyabhicāri*), and of a certain (i.e. definite) nature (*vyavasāyātmakam*)'. The basic Nyāya epistemological starting-point appears to be that perception itself is obvious and requires no justification, and its referents are known in perception just as they are. In framing a suitable definition, Gautama seeks to do justice to our 'common-sense' intuitions. Perception is the knowledge event which is the result of sense–object contact. The qualifiers in the definition were added in order to rule out the fault of overextension of the definition to include, for example, knowledge of the object which is not perceptual but comes through language—the testimony of a witness—percetual error, and doubt.

The term 'perception', however, can refer (among other things) to the cognitive event itself, or to the means by which (the faculty within which?) perceptual events occur. For classical Nyāya, perception as a *pramāṇa* is a *means* of knowing. Gautama, on the other hand, refers to perception as the knowledge event itself. A knowledge event (*jñāna*) is an impermanent quality of the Self in Nyāya–Vaiśeṣika. This contradiction within the tradition of the school was mercilessly criticized by the Buddhist Diṅnāga (or Dignāga; fifth or sixth centuries CE), and later Jayanta Bhaṭṭa, Vācaspatimiśra (both *c.*ninth–tenth century), and others urged the addition of 'by which' (*yataḥ*) to the definition so that perception becomes the instrument of cognition rather than the cognition itself (see Shastri 1964: 426 ff.).

Note that in this definition there is no distinction made between indeterminate (*nirvikalpa*), or non-propositional, and determinate (*savikalpa*), or propositional, perception. This distinction between the first vague moment of a perceptual act and its subsequent conceptualization—judgemental qualificative determination—which has become standard in later Nyāya, appears to have

[14] See Potter (1977: 153–60); Matilal (1986: 5–8, 21–30, 35–41, 49–65). For further reading there are also the other sections from the beginning of Matilal (1986, up to p. 68). They are readable and exciting. See also Mohanty (1992: 227–68).

been clearly introduced by Vācaspatimiśra or perhaps his teacher Trilocana. It may have been influenced by the centrality of this distinction for their Buddhist rivals like Diṅnāga. Vācaspatimiśra's reading involves taking *avyapadeśyam* (non-verbal) as referring to the *nirvikalpa* stage, and *vyavasāyātmakam* (of a determined or definite nature) the *savikalpa* stage, and portraying these as two different stages of perception. This sits very uneasily with the syntax of Gautama's definition. Unlike for the Buddhist, as we shall see, the *savikalpa* stage of perception for Nyāya is a genuine perception which truly cognizes what is really the case. It is not a stage of conceptual falsification. Things really are like that—cows really are qualified by their attributes, universals, and so on, as they are apprehended by full *savikalpa* perception. Essential to this Nyāya perspective is of course the reality of universals, a point completely opposed by Diṅnāga and Dharmakīrti, for whom a determinate conceptualized perception as involving universals apparently 'out there' must therefore involve a level of falsification.

According to Vācaspatimiśra, what happens is that, for example, the cow and its cowness, apprehended separately in the *nirvikalpa* ('without mental construction') stage, are related quite correctly as substratum and its universal at the *savikalpa* (lit. 'with mental construction') stage. For Udayana (probably eleventh century) on the other hand, in the *nirvikalpa* stage the cow is seen, but not its cowness. Perhaps he means it is seen, but not seen as *cow*. For Jayanta, in the *nirvikalpa* stage the perception is correct but vague and indefinite because there has been no verbalization, that is, no conceptualization. For the Navya-Nyāya scholar Gaṅgeśa (thirteenth or fourteenth century), the *nirvikalpa* stage seems to be beyond consciousness altogether. (That is, Gaṅgeśa might be thinking that the first non-propositional, preconceptual stage of a perceptual act cannot be spoken of as a *knowing that*).

Diṅnāga maintains that the qualifiers 'non-verbal', 'non-deviant', and 'of a certain nature' are unnecessary in defining perception, since a perceptual cognition cannot be verbalized, cannot be erroneous, and cannot be determinate (he takes this as 'conceptual'), since all these additional factors require subsequent and different mental acts in addition to perception. These have not yet come into play at the level of sense-perception itself. Diṅnāga also objects that there are problems involved in the model (is it actually a metaphor?) of sense–object *connection* (or contact). How under such circumstances, for example, could we perceive something which is at a distance from the eye, or exceeds the eye in size? Moreover, Diṅnāga points out, why is there no mention of the mind (*manas*) in the definition? The mind is commonly treated in Indian thought as a sixth sense, the faculty by which pleasure, pain, and so on are perceived. Gautama's definition is clearly framed solely with the fivefold sensory perception in mind. In fact Gautama himself had already taken notice of an objector who pointed out that the mind must nevertheless be necessary in order for even ordinary sense-perceptions to take place, yet there is no mention of the mind in the definition. Gautama's response is simply to deny that it is necessary to mention *all* the causal factors involved in a perceptual act in order to define perception.[15]

Error and Illusion Although our concern is with the Nyāya–Vaiśeṣika treatment of perceptual error, known as *anyathākhyāti*, the 'misplacement' (Matilal) theory, Nyāya scholars themselves position their treatment in opposition to their understanding of a number of rival theories. These theories are two attributed by Nyāya–Vaiśeṣika to the Buddhists—those of *asatkhyāti* ('revelation of the non-existent') and *ātmakhyāti* ('revelation of the awareness itself')—the theory of the school of Advaita Vedānta known as *anirvacanīyakhyāti* ('revelation of the inexplicable or ineffable'), and a theory called *akhyāti* ('no illusion') espoused by the Prābhākara Mīmāṃsā school. According to the first, as represented by its Nyāya critics, error lies in taking what does not exist as existent. The second holds that error involves the perception as external of something actually internal to consciousness. The third argues that in an erroneous perception the object cannot be held not to exist since it is given, and yet it is not real. Thus it is inexplicable as either existent or non-existent. In the final view all perceptual judgements are true, and error only occurs through failing to distinguish two perceptual judgements which in themselves are therefore both true. For example, when I see a shell and take it to be silver I am simply failing to distinguish between two genuine perceptual judgements, the one involving seeing a shell and the other seeing a piece of silver.

The Nyāya view might be represented as the positive counterpart to that of the Prābhākara Mīmāṃsā. Instead of failing to apprehend a difference, error lies in the positive apprehension of an identity. Matilal (1986: 180–1) wants to distinguish between what he calls a 'simple awareness' which deals with just one object, and a 'non-simple awareness' which takes more than one object. Perceptual awareness is mostly non-simple and it is with non-simple awarenesses that error and illusion can occur. Basically, what is entailed in the Nyāya view of *anyathākhyāti* is that what is seen in the non-simple awareness which is a perceptual illusion (the snake, for example, in the standard Indian example of mistaking in the half-light a rope for a snake) is a real existent object in the 'external' world. The illusion lies not in what is seen as such but in the misplacement of our experience of a snake, which genuinely does or did exist elsewhere and has been genuinely perceived elsewhere, onto the perception of the rope which is actually here. This misplacement occurs due to the similarity

[15] For further study, see first the short account of definition in Potter (1963: 86–7). Then Potter (1977: 160–9) (note that I shall treat perceptual error separately as the next topic); Matilal (1971: 21–6, 77–91; 1986: 223–9). See also the rest of Matilal (1971, paper 1). Shastri (1964, ch. 12) is very detailed and very good on this topic; especially useful are pp. 426–33 and 438–41. For Diṅnāga's detailed criticisms, see Hattori (1968, sect. 3).

between a rope and a snake generating a memory of the snake seen elsewhere. Note that for Nyāya the snake seen in an illusion is not some sort of mental existent or image but a genuine snake, albeit a snake which exists (or existed) elsewhere. Thus there can be no such thing as an illusion involving a non-simple awareness of an object the component parts of which could not be analysed into experiences of actual existents actually experienced elsewhere.

A corollary of this is that it would make no sense to speak of *all* things being an illusion. If there could be no simple or indeed non-simple awarenesses of actual existents, there could be no non-simple illusory awarenesses. Thus what we find in the Nyāya–Vaiśeṣika theory of *anyathākhyāti* is a theory which will preserve as far as possible the actual objective existence of what is seen in perceptual illusion. Since perceptual objects are usually complex (substrata, qualities, universals, inherences, and so on), the Nyāya–Vaiśeṣika can analyse the complex perceptual object and find the mistaken component in perceptual illusion embedded in a complex the rest of which is quite genuine (cf. also the discussion of Navya-Nyāya and Truth below).[16]

Logic and Inference In India discussions of logic and inference originated within the context of formal and often public debate, and never really left behind the very practical requirements of debate. This explains the importance of empirical examples in reasoning, and the relative lack of clear awareness of and interest in issues of formal deductive inference. Logical reasoning is held in Nyāya to arise in uncertainty and doubt, and aim at understanding. As the scholar Uddyotakara (550–625 CE) put it, this has the purpose of achieving happiness and avoiding unhappiness. Thus reasoning is from the beginning pragmatic, embedded in human projects and psychology, and in the classical Indian context it is therefore usually embedded within a wider framework which is broadly religious.

The structure of Indian logic and argumentation is employed constantly in commentarial writing. Incidentally the intensive study of logic and an intriguing version of the Buddhist practice of public debate going back to Diṅnāga and Dharmakīrti is also still employed in the large Tibetan monasteries and it is not difficult to see Tibetan debate either on television or by visiting some of the Tibetan refugee monasteries in India.

The classical Nyāya inferential schemata ('syllogism') has five members. In abstract terms, the significance of each of these members has been expressed by Matilal (1986: 78) as follows:

(1) statement of the position;
(2) citing of the evidence;

[16] See Potter (1977: 165–7); Matilal (1986: 180–220). There is also a reasonable discussion in Potter (1963, esp. 200–10).

(3) invoking the general principle with an example;
(4) subsuming the present case under the general rule;
(5) statement of the position as proved thereby.

Thus can be illustrated, as does Matilal, by using a classic Nyāya example:

(1) There is fire on that hill.
(2) For there is smoke there.
(3) Wherever there is smoke there is fire, as in the kitchen.
(4) There is smoke on that hill 'accordingly' (=*tathā*).
(5) Therefore, there is fire there (to be sure).

Thus the position, or hypothesis (*pratijñā*), is stated, and supported with a reason (*hetu*), and an example (*dṛṣṭānta*) to illustrate the general principle. Sometimes a negative example is also given, such as 'unlike in the case of a lake'. This is then all applied to the present case, and the conclusion drawn as well-founded. The inference has five terms:

'That mountain' is the *pakṣa*, the subject.
'Fire-possessing' is the *sādhya*, that which is to be proved.
'Smoke-possessing' is the *hetu* (not to be confused with the use of *hetu* above for the reason), the ground.
'Kitchen' is the *sapakṣa*, the positive example. 'Lake' would be the *vipakṣa*, the negative example.

In a valid inference the subject is said to be 'pervaded' (*vyāpti*) by that which is (was) to be proved. In other words, all the members of the class 'that mountain' are members of the class 'fire-possessing'. In order to establish the valid inference, in the Indian context there were finally developed and accepted five rules (Potter 1963): (*a*) All terms must be exemplified. There can be no null class. (*b*) The class offered as the positive example must overlap both the class of the ground and the class of that which is to be proved. In other words there must be at least one individual offered as a positive example who is also a member of both other classes. There must be at least one kitchen which is both a member of the class of smoke-possessors and a member of the class of fire-possessors. (*c*) The class offered as the negative example must fall completely outside both the class of the ground and the class of that which is to be proved. There must be no members in common between the class of lakes and the class of smoke-possessors and the class of fire-possessors. (*d*) The subject must fall completely within the ground. That is, all members of the class 'that mountain' must fall completely within (be pervaded by) the class of smoke-possessors. And finally, (*e*) the ground must fall completely within that which is to be proved. All members of the class of smoke-possessors must be pervaded by the class of fire-possessors.

It can be seen that as far as this discussion is concerned reasoning in the Indian context is not concerned with formal deductive inference, but rather with drawing well-founded conclusions in debate from observational data. As Potter (1963) points out, in listing fallacies Indian thinkers give not only the various ways in which the above rules may be broken but also such fallacies as 'proving what has already been accepted', and other fallacies which amount to wasting time and clearly stem fom the practical context of debate.[17]

1.3.3. Word and Referent

If the word 'cow' refers to an individual, the individual cow, then it would become an equivalent of, say, 'this cow here'. Thus the word 'cow' could become a proper name, and it would be impossible to use the word except for a specific individual. The alternative, that the one word 'cow' refers to more than one individual, can only make sense, it is argued, if it refers to what all cows have in common such that we use the one word to refer to them. In other words, 'cow' must refer to the universal property cowness. Then in saying, for example, 'Milk [the] cow' (Sanskrit lacks the definite article) we would appear to be asking for the universal property cowness to be milked. To try and explain the exact relationship here between the universal as the referent of a name, and individuals which bear the universal, is no easy matter. These two rival views were associated from antiquity with the names of the grammarians Vyāḍi and Vājapyāyana respectively.

The Nyāya response to this problem is to suggest that the referent of a naming term is the thing itself (as Matilal 1982: 76 puts it, the 'lump'), but the thing as qualified by its universal. Thus the term is used to refer to this individual here, but because it is the individual as qualified by its universal the term can

[17] For further reading try first Matilal (1986: 69–93). Then Potter (1963: 59–84), Matilal (1990: 156–66), followed by Potter (1977: 179–208). The material from Matilal (1986) is a fairly general and readable discussion of the role of reasoning and debate in Indian philosophy, particularly what Matilal calls 'the Nyāya method'. On the nature and role of reasoning in India see also Mohanty (1992: 100–32). Potter (1963) provides a well-known and reasonably clear short and systematic introduction to Indian logic, including practical exercises (pp. 89–91). Note that Potter is not only treating Nyāya logic, and he devotes a good discussion to Diṅnāga's important *hetucakra* (pp. 68–71). Potter (1977) is more closely related to issues of Nyāya logic, but because of their centuries of rivalry and mutually influenced development it is impossible really to separate a discussion of Nyāya from that of Buddhist logic. Potter (1977: 207) is perhaps less clear than he could be. With reference to *tarka*, 'first one takes the opponent's pervasion, which seems to be a pervasion because of the presence of an *upādhi*'. It is not that the *upādhi* is apparently making it a pervasion. Quite the reverse. The *upādhi* is making it not a pervasion at all, but merely a similitude of a pervasion. The stress here should be on the word 'seems', i.e. the opponent's pervasion is fallacious: it is merely an apparent pervasion and not a true pervasion. Although a short discussion, Matilal (1990) is very good on key points in Diṅnāga's logic and the Nyāya response to them. In Potter (1977: 191–5) there is a useful discussion of the *trairūpya*, also associated with Diṅnāga, although Diṅnāga was by no means the only epistemologist to contribute to this central concept in Indian logic. On Tibetan debate, for a book and a video on the subject see the Bibliography under Perdue.

also be used quite justifiably to refer to other individuals qualified by that universal. (Actually, the earliest Nyāya view is that the referent is the individual as a lump with shape or configuration (*ākṛti*) qualified by its universal. Thus it is also possible to use the word 'cow' to refer to a model of a cow. The later Navya-Nyāya ('New Nyāya') saw no problem here in speaking of the referent as simply the individual qualified by its universal.)

Among other interesting topics relating to Nyāya discussions of word and referent, we can note the claim for a parallel structure of the knowledge event (*jñāna*, cognition) in a *savikalpa* (determinate, propositional) perception with its linguistic representation. The full *savikalpa* perception thus becomes a 'propositional judgement', and it was thought that the minimal qualifier–relation–qualified structure of the proposition exactly mirrors a minimal ontology of substratum, inherent relationship, and quality, and so on. Thus by analysing the structure of the proposition one is held to be analysing both a knowledge event and also the ontological situation to which knowledge event and proposition refer. Moreover, since, for example, the cognition of a cow can be unpacked with reference to the ontology of the inherence of cowness in the cow particular *x*, so even a word such as 'cow' can be unpacked as a sentence, a 'minimal propositon' (Potter 1977): 'Cowness inheres in *x*'. This is one reason why in Nyāya the primacy in meaning-bearing is given to the individual words which make up the sentence, rather than the sentence itself.[18]

It is unfortunate that in secondary-source writing on Indian semantic theories there tends to be so very little sensitivity to the distinction drawn by Frege, Strawson, and others between meaning and reference. The situation is complicated by the fact that Sanskrit has just one word, *artha*, which is often translated as either 'meaning' or 'referent'. In general an *artha* is that which is aimed for. In a philosophical or psychological context it is best understood as that which is intended, the intentional referent. In psychology the *artha* is, for example, the object of a sense-organ. Thus in the light of the Frege–Strawson distinction it seems to me to be rather misleading for modern writers on Indian thought, as is even now so very common, to refer without discussion to the *artha*, the linguistic *referent*, as a word's *meaning*. This is notwithstanding the fact that in some contexts it may sometimes make sense to speak of linguistic meaning. One should not think that Indian philosophers actually held the rather antiquated view that the meaning of, say, a noun is its referent. The theory that the meaning of a name is its referent appears to be a false semantic theory. In Sanskrit it is of course tautologously true to say that the *artha* of a noun is its

[18] See *abhihitānvayavāda* and *anvitābhidhānavāda* in Potter (1977: 151). In this connection, cf. also Bhartṛhari's theory of *sphoṭa* below.

artha (and the *artha* of 'cow' is what the word refers to—individual, universal, or whatever that might be). Linguistic *meaning* is a different issue.[19]

1.3.4. *Universals*

Broadly speaking, a universal in Nyāya is a property which demarcates class membership. Thus the possession of cowness by *x* is possession of the property which demarcates *x*'s membership of the class 'cows'. The universal property is, however, *universal*, i.e. cowness is one only. Each cow instantiates this one unitary property of cowness. That is precisely how it is we can identify them all as members of the *same* class. Remember that, according to the Nyāya–Vaiśeṣika categories, a universal such as blueness is not at all the same as a quality such as blue. The blue of a particular pot is a trope, a quality specific to that pot as its substratum, and is destructible. The universal blueness inheres in the *blue* (not the pot), which latter then itself inheres in the pot.

The Nyāya universal is real, each universal is one only, a universal is ontologically independent of those realities (such as substances or qualities) which might be thought to manifest or perhaps instantiate them. The universal is timeless and indeed ubiquitous, although—in opposition to the Buddhist objection that cowness should then occur in horses—cowness can only be manifested or instantiated by cows. These timeless realities, however, should not be thought of as occupants of some other more real world, as are the universals of Plato. The Nyāya universals are timeless simply because a universal is not the sort of entity which could be born and die.

Nyāya does not want to maintain that absolutely everything which gives rise to the concept of class membership is a universal. For example, transitory class membership is excluded. There is no universal 'inhabitant of Londonness', or 'cookness' possessed by all those who cook. Such pseudo-universals are called *upādhis*, 'imposed properties', and a great deal of effort was taken by Nyāya writers to provide criteria for distinguishing a genuine universal from an *upādhi*. Rather as with remote antecedents in our discussion of the Nyāya treatment of causation, sometimes these attempts can tend to look rather arbitrary, but it is worth remembering that Nyāya–Vaiśeṣika takes as its starting-point the priority of our everyday world and is attempting philosophically to do justice to that starting-point in as consistent a manner as possible. From such a perspective it may sometimes be legitimate to say 'that is just how it must be'.

[19] I am not aware of any easily available and adequate comprehensive discussion of the Nyāya treatment of language and reference. For a tolerable brief general survey of issues in Indian philosophy of language, read Coward and Kunjunni Raja (1990: 5–12, and then pp. 26–7). This can be followed with Potter (1977: 147–53) and Matilal (1982: 72–90). Some of the issues with reference to the early grammarian-philosophers (particularly Vyāḍi and Vājapyāyana) are dealt with in a philosophically sophisticated and interesting way in Matilal (1971: 97–122).

Note also the feature of what has been called the 'nesting' of universals. Universals can be placed in a hierarchy. Cowness is a lower universal than that of, say, the highest universal, existence (*sattā*), although both universals are possessed by the same individual cow. There is no problem with this providing the lower universal is entirely nested within the higher. In other words, as Matilal (1971: 75) puts it, 'the class of individuals having the first generic property [universal] is only a subclass of, and hence completely included in, the class of individuals having the second generic property'. Where this is not the case then occurs what is called 'cross-division' or 'cross-connection' (*saṃkara*) and both are then usually held to be pseudo-universals. Potter (1977: 136) cites the case of elementhood and materiality. Neither is a genuine universal because in the case of a particular individual they would not nest but rather would overlap.[20]

1.3.5. Navya-Nyāya and Truth

Navya-Nyāya (New Nyāya) is that highly sophisticated and refined form of Nyāya using a very elaborate technical vocabulary which began to flourish from the time of Gaṅgeśa (probably mid- to late thirteenth century CE), and continues to the present day.[21] A brilliant and influential discussion of the Navya-Nyāya treatment of truth and allied topics can be found in Matilal (1968), and the following are some of his main relevant points:

1. I begin from a consideration of the nature and role in Nyāya epistemology of the cognition particular, or knowledge event (*jñāna*). There is held to be a parallel structure between the *jñāna* in a determinate (judgemental, qualificative, *savikalpa*) cognition and its linguistic representation. All *savikalpa* cognitions can be correlated to some linguistic form, and in analysing that linguistic form in terms of its logical structure Nyāya considers that it is uncovering the structure of the corresponding *jñāna*.

2. The determinate qualificative (*savikalpa*) cognition is what can be said to be true or false (doubtful cognitions count as false). In a qualificative cognition a locus or substratum—the qualificand—appears as qualified by various qualifiers. Note that the cognition of a pot, which could be represented linguistically just by '[A] pot', is more precisely represented by uncovering as its concealed structure 'There is an occurrence of potness in the locus *x*' (where *x* is, for example, the object in front of me). Thus Nyāya creates the foundation for a second-order language which will, for example, translate 'The pot is blue'

[20] For background to this issue of cross-connection, see Potter (1977: 118). For a brief statement of the Nyāya treatment of universals, see Hiriyanna (1932: 233–4). See also Potter (1977: 133–46), Matilal (1971: 50–2, 71–91; 1986: 379–86, 417–25). For more detail the whole of the chapter in Matilal (1986) is interesting and useful. Shastri (1964: 319–42) are very clear and useful and go into greater detail on the controversy with the Buddhists.

[21] Perhaps the most important single volume on Navya-Nyāya is now Potter and Bhattacharyya (1992), which contains detailed summaries of all the important primary sources.

into something like 'There is an occurrence of potness in the locus *x*, and an occurrence of blueness in the locus *y* [blue colour], and *y* qualifies [here "inheres in"] *x*.' In this case, of course, both the pot (a substance) and blue colour (a quality) are in different ways qualificands, with the substance the chief qualificand.

3. Whatever appears in a determinate qualificative cognition must appear as *something*, i.e. it must be qualified by its universal (unless it is a connector—a relationship—like inherence). The universal itself, however, does not have to be qualified by its own universal *ad infinitium*, since only those elements given in the linguistic representation of the *jñāna* are actually cognized as something and therefore require mention of their universals in the second-order language expansion. Thus in the cognition 'A pot', *x* is cognized *as a pot*, i.e. potness must be cognized. But here there is no determinate qualificative cognition of potness *as potness*, and thus the analysis of 'A pot' does not require mention of potness-ness. It follows that the cognition 'This is a pot' is revealed in the second-order language as *not* equivalent to the cognition 'This has potness'.

4. A *jñāna* is true if and only if it agrees with reality. The ultimate or primary constituents of the content of a *jñāna* are always real things. Navya-Nyāya speaks of the 'contentness' (*viṣayatā*) of a cognition as broadly that situation of qualificands, qualifiers, and relationships referred to by the cognition. To simplify Matilal's rather elaborate discussion, the cognition 'A pot' might be said to have a simple contentness ('occurrence of potness in *x*'), but in a complex cognition ('The pot is blue') which happens to be true there is both a complex contentness representing the whole situation (contentness$_1$) and also a contentness (contentness$_2$) which is merely the aggregate combination of the simple contentnesses (e.g. 'occurrence of potness in *x*', 'occurrence of blueness in *y*', 'occurrence of *y* in *x*'). In the case of a false cognition there is no contentness which represents the whole situation (contentness$_1$). As for contentness$_2$, which is a combination of simple contentnesses, the simple contentnesses are true but are resident in different objects (it really is a pot, and thus *x* really is qualified by potness, the blue colour *y* really is qualified by blueness—and really does occur elsewhere in, for example, the blue lotus—but the pot is actually yellow, i.e. *x* is really qualified by *z* [yellow] rather than *y*). Thus although Matilal prefers to speak of the contentness in the case of a false cognition as based on 'conditioning' rather than qualifying, it is only the actual qualification of the pot by blue colour which is false here and is thus a case of conditioning rather than qualification. There are still substantial elements of genuine qualifying occurring even in a false cognition. We are of course back here with the Nyāya–Vaiśeṣika theory of error, the *anyathākhyāti* which we examined earlier.[22]

[22] See Matilal (1968: 6–30, omitting if necessary the sections concerning Nyāya linguistic theory, sects. 2.11, and 3.2–3.5 inclusive). For further important discussion, particularly with reference to the Navya-Nyāya treatment of truth, Mohanty (1966: 24–79) is extremely good, and there is also Mohanty (1992: 133–49).

1.4. Bhartṛhari: The Philosophy of the Grammarians

Matilal (1986) speaks of the approach of the great grammarian-philosopher Bhartṛhari as one of 'holistic monism' and 'psychological nominalism'. In reality, underlying everything (spoken of here as the duality of signifier, *vācaka*, and signified, *vācya*) there is only a seamless imperishable Whole referred to by Bhartṛhari as '*Śabda*-Brahman', Word-[or 'Language']-Brahman, which is of the nature of consciousness. Thus non-dual consciousness is the only reality, a seamless whole artificially divided into signifier and signified. This *Śabda*-Brahman is the only real substance in the system and therefore the only real, final referent of all words. Just as in grammar individual words are abstractions torn out of the sentence and sentence composites (discourse) which are for us the actual meaning-bearing units, concepts are also abstractions torn by language out of the actual seamless reality.

All actual everyday significant experience is concept-laden, and those concepts are verbal. Thus all actual everyday significant experience is through and through intrinsically language-laden, language-embedded. What this means is that effectively for Bhartṛhari there is no significant pre-linguistic given. The referent of a naming term is conceptually reified by that term, that is, it is created by that term (it is endowed with *upacārasattā*, 'metaphorical existence'). Thus language creates reified conceptual entities as its own referents, and for Bhartṛhari the linguistic referent is therefore in reality effectively indistinguishable from the term itself. All everyday conventional 'things' are concepts, and all concepts are words. Note here that the linguistically elitist Sanskrit grammarians are actually only considering the *Sanskrit* names for things as identical with their referents. This is reflected in Brāhmanical *mantra* theory where the correct Sanskrit names can therefore be used to magically manipulate things themselves. Kashmiri Śaivite scholars such as Utpaladeva and Abhinavagupta (tenth century CE), who also made significant contributions to the philosophy of grammar in India, were significantly followers of Tantric practices where the employment of *mantras* is particularly important.

However, even in everyday usage, for Bhartṛhari, the actual word is not the audible sound (*nāda*). Rather the audible and sequential sounds c, o, w, reveal the true word 'cow', a whole, a seamless and non-sequential unity which is grasped, intuited, when hearing the sequence of phonemes c, o, w. After all, by the time 'w' is heard, 'c' and 'o' have ceased, yet we say we hear one word, 'cow'. Never are all three phonemes given together. What, therefore, is the one word 'cow' which we think we hear? Inasmuch as words are meaning-bearing units, actually we intuit the 'real word' (Matilal), the real meaning-bearing unit, the unitary and invariant word-*sphoṭa* revealed by the audible sequence of phonemes. This *sphoṭa* is also the principal cause which makes the audible sequence as *articulated word* possible. Note that the *sphoṭa* is held to be *revealed*, it is intersubjectively common rather than only a privately accessible psychological event. In fact, at this level the *sphoṭa* must be *what is said* as meaningful, what is intersubjectively revealed as common when, for example, the word 'cow' is pronounced in six different accents (would our elitist Sanskrit grammarians want to say that the same *sphoṭa* is revealed when 'cow' is said not in Sanskrit but in different languages?). It would appear that in reality, however, finally, for Bhartṛhari there is beyond all conceptual reification only one seamless unitary meaning-bearing unit. There is really only one *sphoṭa* which is of course *Śabda*-Brahman itself.[23]

2. SOME HETERODOX (*NĀSTIKA*) PHILOSOPHIES

2.1. Buddhism

2.1.1. *The Buddhist Orientation: Not-Self*

Whereas other systems search for a permanent, unchanging, and therefore true, Reality which underlies all change—a Reality eventually called the Self (*ātman*) or Brahman—it was the discovery of the Buddha (Buddhists claim) that the truth is that there is no such thing. The final cessation of grasping craving, which otherwise leads to continued rebirth and therefore continued frustration and suffering in *saṃsāra*, lies in a rather deep and complete sort of letting-go. Inasmuch as the search for the permanent had led to the Self, a grasping after a True Reality to serve as the unchanging referent for the personal pronoun, the great insight the Buddha claimed is that there is in reality no such Self at all. Really we are an everchanging causally connected flow of psychophysical factors. These psychophysical factors were early classified into the five aggregates (Sanskrit: *skandhas*; Pāli: *khandhas*) of physical matter, sensations, conceptions, mental contents such as volitions and so on, and consciousness. This everchanging flow is all there is. There is nothing more to us, and the sooner we realize this the better.

The hallmark of much of Buddhist philosophy in India lies in a rigorous critical analysis, a reduction of the world given to us as consisting of relatively stable subjects and objects into the flow of components which, it is claimed, is what is *really* there. 'Coming to see things the way they really are' is the

[23] See Matilal (1968: 29–34, 109–13; 1986: 386–98; 1990: 120–41). For a detailed discussion of the defence of the *sphoṭa* theory by the scholar Maṇḍana Miśra (9th century CE) against the Mīmāṃsaka teacher Kumārila Bhaṭṭa (previous century), see Coward and Kunjunni Raja (1990: 66–80). This book also contains useful summaries of all the relevant texts. Most important is Bhartṛhari's *Vākyapadīya*. Although as far as I know no one has yet done so, there should be an interesting area for comparative research in a detailed comparison of the *sphoṭa* with the Stoic *lekton*.

path which leads to enlightenment. Thus a form of reductive philosophical analysis was from the very beginning built into the Buddhist soteriological project. Buddhist thought naturally analyses wholes into parts, and the relatively static into a flow of processes. Buddhist thought therefore contains implicitly from its very beginning a distinction between appearance and reality (but not an unchanging Reality), referred to in Buddhist philosophy as a distinction between conventional truth (or reality—*saṃvṛtisatya*, sometimes called 'worldly' (*laukika*) or 'transactional' (*vyavahārika*) truth) and the ultimate truth (*paramārthasatya*), how things actually are.

The Buddhist project is one of knowing and letting-go—knowing the conventional *as conventional*—but it does not appear to be one of wholesale linguistic revisionism, for example. The Buddhist seeks to uncover the 'merely transactional, merely conventional linguistic usage' of the personal pronoun, not to ban its use. On the level of how things really are, however, what is really there beyond all fabrication (i.e. ultimate truth), there is just the causal flow of impersonal elements (Sanskrit: *dharmas*; Pāli: *dhammas*), not a Self.

Problems associated with *reconstructing* the everyday given from its reduced elements and processes, for example how to explain rebirth (or 'reincarnation') without a Self, and how to explain personal identity in a sense sufficiently strong enough for the moral law of *karma* over not just one life but infinite lives, from early times provided Buddhist thinkers with some very real and sophisticated philosophical problems.[24]

2.1.2. *Abhidharma*

Originally the term 'Abhidharma' referred to a section of the Buddhist scriptures which aimed to give a more precise description of 'how things really are'. In time it came to refer to the development of that approach to Buddhist philosophy.

The basic Buddhist project is one of some sort of reductionism, and the Abhidharma represents an attempt to create lists of classes of elements (*dharmas*) into which things can be reduced. So all Buddhist philosophy occurs within an Abhidharmic framework even where details and whole aspects of the Abhidharma project were criticized by some Buddhists themselves. Central to understanding Abhidharma and indeed much later Buddhist thought is the distinction expressed in the Vaibhāṣika school's approach to Abhidharma as that between substantial or 'primary' existence (*dravyasat*) and conceptual or 'secondary' derived existence (*prajñaptisat*). This distinction corresponds here to

[24] See Collins (1982: 3 (bottom)–5, 20–6, 78–84, 95–115, 177–95); Williams (1989: 1–6). On some of the problems of reconstruction and personal identity, see in particular Collins, and also references for the next section. Note Collins's brief reference to the important contemporary work of Derek Parfit. Parfit himself seems to have read Collins's book and has noticed the apparent Buddhist parallels.

that between ultimate and conventional truth mentioned previously. For Vaibhāṣika these are two types of genuine existence, based on whether or not it is possible to analytically reduce or fragment *x* into component parts. Tables and persons, for example (secondary existents, constructs) are *not* said here to be merely subjective fictions, unreal or illusory, but they can be reduced to components and are therefore the results of a causal process of synthetic composition and conceptual reification which means that they are unreal as uniquely qualified *things in their own right*.

Those (usually impermanent, momentary) components which cannot be analytically reduced are clearly not the results of aggregation and thus actually do exist in their own right in that sense. They are said to possess their own uniquely defining characteristic (to be *sasvalakṣaṇa* or *sasvabhāva*). They are primary substantial existents, and are the components of all things. They are also known as *dharmas*, and *dharmas* are the ultimate truths in Abhidharma. Note the plural here ('ultimate truth*s*'). Each *dharma* is an ultimate truth in Abhidharma because it is that *into which* conventional things can be analysed as their ultimate components. Each *dharma* is in itself unique (although it is of a type which can be classified into the list of classes of *dharmas*), and nearly all *dharmas* are radically impermanent, forming a causal series. Thus all things are either primary existents, *dharmas*, or secondary existents composed out of *dharmas*. Since they are the results of composition from impermanent elements, 'everyday' objects are thought by nature to be themselves impermanent, and the intended result of Abhidharma is thus renunciation—'letting-go'.

It is sometimes said that for Vaibhāṣika Abhidharma language about secondary existents is *true* not through correspondence but as 'a function of the linguistic and cultural conventions which make it possible' (Griffiths 1986: 50). However, if this is an appeal for something other than a referential correspondence theory of truth when applied to propositions about secondary existents (a pragmatic theory? a coherence theory?), then it does not follow from the distinction between primary and secondary existents as such, for this would be to ignore the Vaibhāṣika point that the difference between primary and secondary existents lies not in existence, but in what it is to exist, what the precise ontological status of *x* is *qua* existent. Secondary existents exist. There is thus no reason to think that language about secondary existents ('The cat sat on the mat') is not true, if true, through correspondence. The fact that cats and mats are secondary existents analytically reducible to primary existents in a causal flow is another issue.[25]

[25] Collins (1982: 234–47) (some Theravāda Abhidhamma discussions); Griffiths (1986: 43–58) (good on the Vaibhāṣika orientation); Matilal (1986: 240–54) (perception and Vaibhāṣika, based on the scholar Vasubandhu's 'Treasury of Metaphysics', *Abhidharmakośa*; perhaps 4th century CE); Skorupski (1987: 333 (from 'Technical usages')–338 (on the *dharma* lists); Williams (1989: 13–16) (brief overview).

2.1.3. Madhyamaka

The basic ontological vision of the Madhyamaka school is that all things without exception, no matter how elevated, can be demonstrated to be nothing more than secondary existents. When searched for under critical analysis—derived from the Abhidharma way for seeking ultimate truths, primary existents—nothing can be found (i.e. everything is found to be incoherent in the light of reason). The rest of Madhyamaka flows from this. In Abhidharma terms to be a secondary existent is to be a causal construct, constructed through a process of aggregation out of more fundamental constituents, while to be a primary existent is to have uniquely determined existence, to have a unique and simple (non-compounded) identity. For Madhyamaka this must amount to having independent, i.e. intrinsic, existence (having a *svabhāva*, understood now as inherent existence). However, nothing, not even the Abhidharma primary existents, can claim to have that sort of existence. Nothing in fact has *inherent*, causally independent, existence. This would be to have necessary existence, whereas all things which exist without exception are contingent. All things are relative, in some way or another the intersecting points (and for Madhyamaka *only* the intersecting points) of causal conditions. Thus in reality there are no primary existents—all existence is secondary existence, all existence is the existence of reified conceptually created entities (*prajñaptisat*).

Madhyamaka can best be understood as a move within the Abhidharma framework, as an Abhidharma project which sees something significantly incomplete in the Abhidharma ontology. Even *dharmas* are finally no different ontologically from tables, chairs, or persons. Soteriologically, ultimately everything must be let go. All things, no matter what, are empty (*śūnya*) of inherent existence (i.e. they are *niḥsvabhāva*) because all things are dependently originated (*pratītyasamutpanna*). Emptiness, as Madhyamaka writers ceaselessly tell us, is the same as (better, a corollary of) dependent origination, the causal flow. Far from the accusation of ontological and therefore moral nihilism hurled at them, emptiness is thus thought by Mādhyamikas (followers of Madhyamaka) like Nāgārjuna to be an implication of existence—of course existence seen now as it really is, as merely contingent secondary existence. Things have to originate through causes and conditions in order to be empty. Buddhist rivals of Madhyamaka, however, found something very strange (an incoherent intellectual sleight of hand?) in claiming that *all* things could be secondary existents—all things are constructs with consequently nothing for them to be constructed from. If there is (are) no primary existent(s) this must, they wanted to point out, reduce to nihilism. And they would simply deny that primary existence understood properly as uncompounded existence—independent of causation only in the sense of independent of the process (conceptual or actual) of aggregation or compounding—entailed necessary existence.

For the Mādhyamika the ultimate truth is that there simply are no ultimate truths (i.e. primary existents). On the level of ultimate truth (*paramārthasatya*)—that is, where ultimate truths like the Abhidharma *dharmas* would be—there is nothing. That level is indeed one of emptiness (*śūnyatā*)—essentially *not* because emptiness is found there as itself an ultimate truth or Reality, but because nothing is found there on that level at all. It is ultimately true that all things (including of course emptiness itself) are empty of ultimate truth (primary, i.e. inherent, existence), because all things are one way or another the results of causal forces and conceptual construction. Note here that Madhyamaka therefore uses 'ultimate truth' in two senses: (1) *an* ultimate truth, i.e. a primary existent, something found under an investigative analysis of its existence, and therefore found as having inherent existence; and (2) the ultimate way of things (the *dharmatā*). For Madhyamaka the ultimate truth in sense (2) is that there is nothing having ultimate truth in sense (1). Ultimate truth in sense (2) is demonstrated by the Madhyamaka, inasmuch as it is demonstrated (to those who hold otherwise) that this is indeed how things must be.

Seeing the conventional as fictitious (a mere concession to unenlightenment), and the move to enlightenment as a move *from* conventional *to* ultimate truth, would, however, be quite the wrong model for understanding Madhyamaka. Since the ultimate truth in Madhyamaka is emptiness, if the move were simply towards ultimate truth, then as emptiness is in itself merely an absence (the absence of inherent existence) the move would be from this world (*saṃsāra*) to a state of simple nothingness (thus postulated in this context as *nirvāṇa*). The concern of Buddhism, however, is with gnosis, knowing how things really are. The concern of Madhyamaka therefore is not with moving from the conventional to the ultimate truth, but rather with enlightenment as understanding how (it is claimed) things really are and thus cutting the forces which lead to frustration, suffering, and rebirth (*saṃsāra*). Madhyamaka is saying that all things are really the results of causal forces *and nothing more*. This is the 'ultimate truth' (*paramārthasatya*) of things, a truth which shows them up as not ultimates but merely conventionalities (*saṃvṛtimātra*), secondary existents (*prajñaptimātra* = *niḥsvabhāva* = *śūnya*). Thus for a Mādhyamika emptiness (*śūnyatā*), the ultimate truth, is a property of things and therefore things remain as they actually are, but no longer the subject of grasping craving. The move is actually the move of gnosis; it is a move in understanding, from seeing things as ultimates to seeing them as conventionalities.[26]

[26] For a more extensive discussion, see Williams (1989: 37–76) (including some of the Mahāyāna religious background). For quite a different approach to Madhyamaka to the one adopted here, there is Huntington (1989: 25–67). Huntington's book is philosophically sophisticated and stimulating, adopting a reading of Madhyamaka which owes a great deal to Wittgenstein and Rorty. On why I disagree with it, see Williams (1991).

2.1.4. *Yogācāra*

As far as the Yogācāra school is concerned, the idea that all things without exception must be secondary existents is incoherent. In fact it amounts to ontological nihilism. To be a secondary existent requires that there is a primary existent (it is part of the meaning of 'secondary existent' that there is a primary existent). If there is no primary existent, then nothing would exist at all. Thus in opposing as nihilism the Madhyamaka universality of secondary existents, Yogācāra is required to postulate at least one primary existent as a substratum for secondary existents. That primary existent is the non-dual stream of consciousness (*citta*). Hence it is *cittamātra*, 'mind-only'.

It is no doubt true that in its origin Yogācāra scholars were perhaps mainly interested in meditation experience rather than ontology. Nevertheless, classical Yogācāra certainly is an ontology, and in spite of a view held by some contemporary interpreters of Yogācāra, it seems to me that its ontology is very different from that of Madhyamaka. There has also been some allied discussion in relatively recent scholarship about whether Yogācāra can properly be understood as a form of idealism or not. In one sense the answer is that 'it all depends what is meant by "idealism"'. On the other hand it seems clear that Yogācāra does teach that there is one, non-dual, primary existent and that that primary existent is in some sense mentalistic. The word *citta* is used for it. Moreover, as Matilal points out, the arguments for Yogācāra *cittamātra* are classically 'idealist' arguments. Thus, although there may be certain apologetic reasons in some circles for avoiding the term 'idealism', I do not think I would be sufficiently bothered to object to the term 'idealism'.

The key to understanding *cittamātra* lies in the Three Aspects (*trisvabhāva*). The first of the Three Aspects is the 'constructed aspect' (*parikalpitasvabhāva*), the realm of subject–object duality, the world as seen by the unenlightened and also the realm of linguistic operation. This polarization into intrinsically separate subject and object is actually false; that is not how things really are. The second aspect is the 'dependent aspect' (*paratantrasvabhāva*). It is the flow, a dependently originated continuum, of cognitive experiences (*vijñapti*). It is the substratum, that *which* is erroneously polarized into subjects and objects. All the world of objects, and we who confront those objects, are nothing more than a series of experiences. As a flow of experiences this flow must, of course, be mentalistic in nature. The 'perfected aspect' (*pariniṣpannasvabhāva*) is the true way of things, which has to be seen in meditation. It is also said to be emptiness. As with Madhyamaka, 'emptiness' (*śūnyatā*) is still predicated universally in Yogācāra, but this time 'emptiness' is redefined to equal 'non-duality'. A substratum which is held as therefore (really) existing is empty not of its own inherent existence (i.e. in Abhidharma terms it is a primary not a secondary existent), but it is empty rather of duality. The model is that of '*x* is empty of *y*', where *x* is therefore found in the analytic investigation which searches for primary existents and thus remains in emptiness.

One should *not* assume that because the perfected aspect is in some sense the highest of the Three Aspects, it refers to the non-dual flow of consciousness itself. Although there are some forms of Yogācāra which do seem to veer towards this interpretation (perhaps the Yogācāra of the Indian missionary Paramārtha (499–569) in China would be an example), the view of the mainstream of classical Yogācāra in India is that the perfected aspect is emptiness, i.e. *the absence of the constructed aspect in the dependent aspect.* That is, the perfected aspect is the fact of the absence of reified subject–object duality in the consciousness flow, the flow of perceptions or experiences. It is what has to be known in order for liberation to occur, for knowing this is what cuts grasping craving for subjects and objects. Therefore, by extension the perfected aspect is sometimes also spoken of as the way things are seen by enlightened beings. One should not assume that 'highest' in Indian philosophy always means *ontologically* the highest, the most Real. Here as so often in Buddhism 'highest' refers rather to what is soteriologically highest, that is, what is to be known or seen for enlightenment. The 'ontologically highest', what for classical *cittamātra* is the most Real, the primary existent, is actually in terms of the Three Aspects the dependent aspect.[27]

Certain Yogācāra texts, such as Vasubandhu's *Viṃśatikā*, also give arguments to counter any objections to the idea that all is simply experience, that there are no (subjects and) objects external to consciousness, all is one primary existent (*ekadravya*). For example, the existence of spatio-temporal determination can be explained on the model of dream experiences where we experience spatio-temporal difference. The fact that, unlike in the case of a hallucination, many experience the same thing can be explained on the model of a common collective hallucination. Also it is difficult to explain the actual existence of 'external' objects, since things cannot be wholes in their own right because they are not experienced that way. Nor can they be constructs out of minute 'atoms', since an atom as the smallest possible piece of matter, indivisible and therefore without spatial extension, which is then capable of aggregation into spatially extended gross objects, is thought to be paradoxical in the extreme. Thus there can be no explanation of the world of matter. Yet clearly there is *something*. Since there is no matter (*rūpa*), but nevertheless there must be something, that something must itself be mentalistic (*citta*). The dependent aspect as a flow of experiences is the base, the substratum, which becomes the 'ultimate reality' in Yogācāra.

[27] In order to compare this with a form of Buddhist thought which might be protrayed as representing the soteriologically highest as also ontologically the highest, see the Buddha-nature (*tathāgatagarbha*) teachings in Williams (1989: 96–115). For further reading on Yogācāra, see Williams (1989: 77–95); Griffiths (1986: 76–104); Matilal (1974: 139–58) (plus the translated material for the arguments in more detail).

2.1.5. Diṅnāga and Dharmakīrti

Momentariness Some writers of the Diṅnāga–Dharmakīrti tradition in late Indian Buddhism took to producing short but very technical monographs intended to establish particular philosophical tenets. The scholar Ratnakīrti (eleventh century) wrote two such works intended to prove momentariness, the thesis that if something exists it could exist for one moment only. The moment is simply the time it takes to have causal efficacy. Existence is so short in duration that it is simply the time it takes to make the difference between existing and not existing, in terms of causing the next momentary existent. This time must be infinitesimal. These momentary entities, the ultimate particulars, are therefore the only existents (i.e. primary existents), self-characterized (*svalakṣaṇa*) and therefore self-defined. Since language must operate with universals, these ultimate particulars are strictly beyond language.

Existence for the Diṅnāga–Dharmakīrti tradition *is* causal efficacy (*arthakriyākāritva*; on this crucial concept, see Mookerjee 1978: 6 ff.). Let us look at the structure of an argument found in a monograph by Ratnakīrti aiming to prove that whatever is non-momentary is non-existent (the contraposed version of 'Whatever is existent is momentary'):

X exists for either
- (1) one moment; or
- (2) more than one moment.

If (1), then *x* is momentary. QED.

If (2), then
- (*a*) *x* produces all its effects in the first moment; or
- (*b*) *x* produces its effects successively.

If (*a*), then since existence = causal efficacy, we have momentariness. QED.

If (*b*), then this successive production of effects is either
- (A) due to factors internal to *x* (the cause); or
- (B) due to factors external to *x*.

If A, then the internal factors for successive production are either
- (i) due to a change in *x*; or
- (ii) due to an internal disposition within *x* to do this.

If A(i), then *x* would have to change from moment to moment (since existence equals causal efficacy). But since each moment produces a different effect, each moment must be a different entity. Therefore, we have momentariness. QED.

If A(ii), then either
- (*a*) there is an internal disposition to produce the effects, pure and simple; or

(*b*) there is an internal disposition to produce different effects at different times.

If A(ii)(*a*), then all effects would be produced in the first moment, and therefore there would be momentariness. QED.

If A(ii)(*b*), then this is incoherent. If the cause is a unitary permanent entity, either there is a capacity to produce the effect, pure and simple, in which case we have momentariness, or there is no such capacity, in which case the cause could not exist at all. That is, it makes no sense to talk of a unitary cause producing effects all by itself *at different times*.

If B, then the external factors would be the cause of the effect and not *x*. Thus *x* would not exist.

Ratnakīrti does not discuss here whether successive production could be due to both internal and external factors, but he would have held that this is simply incoherent. One cannot talk about an internal disposition in the cause to produce effects successively (it is the *nature* of the cause to do this), where production of the effects will not occur without a series of further extraneous factors. Ratnakīrti's arguments to prove momentariness can of course be directed against any hypothetical non-momentary entity, and therefore in the cosmological context they can and were used by Buddhists in order to construct a disproof of the existence of a permanent and unchanging creator God.[28]

Epistemology Here there are only two *pramāṇas*, perception (*pratyakṣa*) and inference (*anumāṇa*). The *pramāṇas* lead to right cognition (or, for this tradition, *are* right cognition), and right cognition is 'knowledge not contradicted by experience' (Dharmottara; *c.* late eighth century CE). The reason there are only two *pramāṇas* is succinctly expressed by Diṅnāga in his *Pramāṇasamuccaya* I. 2 (Hattori 1968). Cognitive objects such as whatever is given to us in our everyday experience have only two aspects, those of particular and universal. Perception cognizes the particular. Inference cognizes the universal.

Diṅnāga's ontology does not include the real existence of universals. Thus perception and perception alone actually cognizes directly what is really there. It also follows that if things are momentary only the very first moment of a perceptual act cognizes objective reality, since after that moment the object has ceased to exist. Thus (sense-)perception as a *pramāṇa* is actually restricted to the

[28] For further reading I suggest, in the following order, Warder (1970: 447–62); Jackson (1993: 117–26); McDermott (1969, p. 41, para. 83.20–p. 43, para. 84.17, and associated notes at the back of the book); Mookerjee (1975: 1–19). In addition there is also Jackson (1993)'s short chs. 8–9, 12. Stcherbatsky (1962: 79–118) is dated but famous.

very first moment of what we normally call 'the perceptual act'. Subsequent moments of the perceptual act are correllated to subsequent momentary *svalakṣaṇas* which are of the same type (in the same causal series) as the original perceptual object but are, nevertheless, absolutely different from it (although one wonders how there can really be similarity, 'same type', between absolutely distinct particulars).

The Diṅnāga–Dharmakīrti tradition refers to the first moment of the sensory perceptual act as *nirvikalpa*, 'without construction'. The subsequent stages of perception, which involve the construction of a non-momentary entity, are called *savikalpa*, 'with construction'. However, since reality is momentary, it follows that, inasmuch as the *savikalpa* stages involve the construction (apparently through linguistic reification) of a non-momentary entity, they are constructing what does not exist, what is actually therefore a universal. Those stages cannot thus be stages of *perception*. Perception properly speaking can only be *nirvikalpa*. Nevertheless, the *savikalpa* stages can still come under *pramāṇa* since they do lead to correct action and are therefore not contradicted by experience. This is because they are *based on* correct perception of a *svalakṣaṇa* in the *nirvikalpa* stage. Since for Diṅnāga definition involves demarcating that which is to be defined from what it is not, we therefore end up with Diṅnāga's famous definition of perception as simply being 'free from conceptual construction' (*Pramāṇasamuccaya* I. 3), although Dharmakīrti felt constrained controversially to add to this definition 'and non-erroneous (*abhrānta*)'. For Diṅnāga all error results from mental activity and therefore cannot apply to the *nirvikalpa* perception but only to the *savikalpa* stages.

The Diṅnāga–Dharmakīrti tradition speaks of four types of perception: (1) sense-perception; (2) mental perception; (3) extra-sensory 'yogic perception'; and (4) reflexivity, or 'self-awareness'. There is some dispute among scholars as to whether Diṅnāga himself thought there are four or only three types, excluding self-awareness as an actual type of perception.

On (2), it seems possible that *one* reason for mental perception is that in order for the linguistic association necessary for conceptual construction to take place, there has first of all to be a momentary 'reception' by the mind. This mental reception which is the very next moment after sense–object contact must also be *nirvikalpa* and therefore fits the definition of perception. However, the problem is that the momentary object of the sense–object contact has ceased. Therefore, the moment of mental perception (if it is to be a perception) must take as its object another completely different *svalakṣaṇa*, the very next moment in the 'object series'. Thus, rather strangely, mental perception must take a completely different object from sense-perception, yet both are for Diṅnāga correct and are the first two stages of what in everyday terms is one 'perceptual act'.

On (4), self-awareness (*svasaṃvedana*) was strongly criticized by a number of other Buddhist traditions, such as the Madhyamaka.[29] What it amounts to is that in all awareness there is not just a knowing of *x*, but also a knowing that one knows *x*. An argument used for this position is that in memory we not only remember, say, blue but we also remember that we experienced blue. Thus in the original experience there must have been an awareness not only of blue but also of the awareness of blue. We cannot remember what we did not experience.

There is a problem in isolating exactly what the *svalakṣaṇa*, the momentary entity, is supposed to be. Stcherbatsky and those influenced by him see it as the infinitely small spatio-temporal minimum, the 'point-instant'. There are very good arguments for this interpretation. It would certainly fit with the idea of the *svalakṣaṇa* as completely beyond all language. However, the concept of a *spatial* minimum may not always fit with the texts, and indeed under such circumstances there could be a problem in explaining construction, particularly the construction of a common 'lived world'. 'Dharmakīrti's experiment' in which he advocated concentrating very hard and cutting all distractions as a way of gaining some understanding of the pure non conceptual sensation of the *svalakṣaṇa* could at the most be a (perhaps misleading) analogy, since it is not possible even through strong concentration to isolate a *spatio-temporal* minimum. A *patch* of blue would not fit the bill. Diṅnāga's own reference to the Abhidharma 'seeing of blue but not seeing it as "blue"' will still not give us a *spatio*-temporal minimum. The alternative might be to take the *svalakṣaṇa* in some way as a minimal temporal segment but with nevertheless spatial extension. On the other hand, it is arguable that any spatially extended object would already show a degree of construction which would not be acceptable to Diṅnāga and Dharmakīrti. Once we start to talk of simples prior to construction it is difficult to know where or how the process of reduction is to end.[30]

Logic and Inference Several topics of Indian logic were particularly discussed and developed in an extremely influential way by the Diṅnāga–Dharmakīrti tradition:

1. It was perhaps Diṅnāga who first clarified the *trairūpya*, the 'triple characteristic of a valid reason' (Mookerjee 1978), whereby for a correct inference the reason (*hetu*) must be (*a*) present in the subject concerned (*pakṣa*), (*b*) present in the positive (*sapakṣa*) example, and (*c*) always absent in the negative (*vipakṣa*) example. (*a*) is the actual instantiation of the *hetu* in the subject, while (*b*) and (*c*) are then thought to guarantee the pervasion or 'universal concomitance'

[29] Matilal (1986) devotes a whole chapter to it.

[30] See Matilal (1971: 34–9; 1986: 110–2, 133–5, 148–53, 288, 309–21, 324–9); Hattori (1968, sect. 1 and nn.); Mookerjee (1975: 273–99, 311–27, 337–45). Again, Stcherbatsky (1962: 146–69) on this topic is particularly famous although marred (I think) by its Kantian tendency.

(*vyāpti*) between that which is to be proved (*sādhya*) and the reason (see Matilal 1982: 138–9). The sign (*liṅga*) which provides the reason is said to be the pervaded (*vyāpya*), and that which is to be proved is the signified (*liṅgin*), which is the pervader (*vyāpaka*; ibid. 135). Note, therefore, that the smoke which serves as a sign for the presence of fire is the pervad*ed*; the fire is the pervader. Fire pervades smoke, not the other way round. Thus in the case of 'fire on the mountain because there is smoke', smoke (the *liṅga–vyāpya*) must actually be on the mountain, and also present in the kitchen (where there is a fire, the *liṅgin–vyāpaka*), and never present in the lake (where there is never a fire). It appears to be Diṅnāga who first clarified that there can be established a pervasion between the presence of smoke and that of fire (whereby the class of things possessing fire is said to pervade the class of things possessing smoke) which will enable the inference of fire on the mountain from the presence of smoke.

2. For Diṅnāga *what* exactly is inferred (the *anumeya*) in an inference is 'the present property-possessor (*dharmin*)—viz., the mountain—possessing the property, fire', a view which was not felt to be completely satisfactory by his opponents (see Matilal 1985: 61).

3. Dharmakīrti developed a theory of the only three possible types of *hetu* (reason): (*a*) the *hetu* identical with that which is to be proved (*tadātmya* or *svabhāvahetu*); (*b*) the *hetu* which is a result of that which is to be proved; and (*c*) non-perception (*anupalabdhi*) as a *hetu*. Thus (*a*) occurs when the class of the *hetu* (e.g. oak) is identical with or contained within the class of that which is to be proved (e.g. tree); (*b*) occurs when the *hetu* (e.g. smoke) is the result of that which is to be proved (e.g. fire); (*c*) occurs when all factors necessary for the perception of *x* are present, *x* could and would be perceived, and yet it is not. We can thus use the non-perception of *x* as a *hetu* for its absence.[31]

4. We can make mention also of Diṅnāga's famous *hetucakra* ('wheel of logical reasons'), which given the reason (*hetu*), the positive example (*sapakṣa*), and the negative example (*vipakṣa*) of the *trairūpya* took the nine mathematically possible resultant relationships between them and indicated the only two that would yield a valid inference, and the nature of the invalidity in the cases of the other seven.[32]

5. Considerable attention was given to the nature of pervasion, and why it was thought that pervasion entails the drawing of the inference. *Vyāpti*, or at least its nature and significance, appears to have been first noticed by Diṅnāga. Particularly worthy of note is the debate over *antarvyāpti* ('internal concomitance': Mookerjee 1975) versus its opposite, *bahirvyāpti*. If one accepts *antarvyāpti*, then the pervasion relationship is held to be in some sense natural, intrinsic, presumably a necessary relationship. The inferential sign *could not*

[31] Matilal (1982: 141) points out the connection between (*a*) and the *antarvyāpti* (see below).

[32] There is a useful summary of the *hetucakra* in Vidyabhusana (1971: 283–6) and a summary discussion including other fallacies of the *hetu* (pp. 293–5).

occur without the signified: smoke could not occur without fire. One infers the signified from the contradictory nature of the occurrence of the sign without the signified (for example, to use Ratnakīrti's case, one infers momentariness from the contradictory nature of existence without momentariness). *Antarvyāpti* appears to have been formulated originally by Jaina logicians, and opposed by Buddhists since if it is true it is arguable that the *trairūpya* in order to guarantee pervasion is unnecessary, and therefore from the point of view of logic (in opposition to the psychology of persuasion) the examples are unnecessary. It seems that later Buddhist logicians such as Ratnakīrti and his pupil Ratnākaraśānti (eleventh century) were prepared to adopt *antarvyāpti*. This topic also relates to a general discussion which took place in India concerning the nature, role, and dispensability or otherwise of various members of the inferential schemata, the so-called 'syllogism'.[33]

*Language (*apohavāda*)* A naming term like 'cow', for example, cannot refer as such to a cow since if the cow is a momentary entity the learning of the word would, as it were, exhaust the referent and the word could never actually be used. Moreover, the word could not refer to an identical universal which can be repeatedly instantiated, since momentariness shows that there are no universals. On the other hand if all words lack association with referents (*artha*) altogether, they are *meaningless* (*anartha*). What Diṅnāga wants to say, therefore, is that although a naming term cannot directly refer to an actual reality, it can have a negative use. The word 'cow' can capture a momentary referent through ruling out the referent's membership of the class of non-cows. *Apoha* is exclusion; to refer is only to negate.

Satkari Mookerjee (1975) has argued for three phases of the *apoha* doctrine in India. Diṅnāga seems to have been severely criticized for what was taken as a suggestion that the referent of naming terms is simply a negation. Opponents such as Kumārila Bhaṭṭa wanted to argue that the negation 'not non-cow' (or not not cow) is conceptually parasitic upon the positive 'cow', and thus we cannot explain 'cow' as a naming term through 'not non-cow'. Clearly, substitution of 'not non-cow' for 'cow' would lead to an infinite regress. The Buddhist philosopher Śāntarakṣita (eighth century CE) appears to have responded by suggesting that the direct referent of the naming term is indeed a positive entity—the 'mental representation' (Matilal 1986: 400)—but that mental representation is explicable in terms of its logical formation through *apoha*, as ruling out membership of the contradictory class (Matilal's 'exclusion class'). In response to further criticisms Ratnakīrti (if I understand him correctly)

[33] Mookerjee (1975: 346–400); Matilal (1982: 133–6, 138–44, 148–51; 1985: 58–76, 128–30). See also discussions of Diṅnāga's logic (particularly *trairūpya* and *hetucakra*) in the reading mentioned above, n. 17. Further material especially on *trairūpya*, and fallacies and the *hetucakra*, can be found in Stcherbatsky (1962: 242–5, 248–50, 320–40). Stcherbatsky adds to his Kantianism an all-too-ready use of Aristotelian terminology and interpretations.

appears to want to hold that the referent of naming terms is both positive and negative, as a mental representation which *is* the ruling out of membership of the contradictory class. Some of this seems philosophically obscure, and logical and psychological (as well as linguistic) issues appear to be rather confused.[34]

It is not clear whether the *apoha* doctrine is a nominalism, a conceptualism, both or neither. Matilal (1982) seems sure that it is a nominalism, since for Diṅnāga's tradition universals simply do not exist and there is thus in linguistic reference only names (which are themselves really momentary, as is nearly everything else). Names cannot refer to concepts, for there are no universal concepts, and concepts as referents which are themselves momentary individuals would not explain anything. The problem for Matilal's interpretation here is that in everyday life 'cow' can indeed refer. It can refer to [a] cow. The question is, therefore, what exactly *is* a cow as an everyday given object? An everyday given cow for Diṅnāga is in fact an entity hypostasized through mental construction and reification. For Diṅnāga it is not an individual but, as it were, a concealed universal. If conceptualization is recognizing *x* as a member of the class '*x*s', then this hypostasization seems to involve conceptualization. Thus the everyday given object named 'cow' is a member of the class 'cows', and this class membership is equivalent to being a conceptual construct. The *process* of conceptualization for Diṅnāga seems to be through *apoha*. To be a member of the class 'cows' is actually explicable in terms of not being a member of the contradictory class. That linguistic referents taken as positive entities (rather than merely negative exclusions) are for Diṅnāga universals and therefore ontological fictions does not mean that they are not the referents in the fiction of our unenlightened perception. Everyday naming terms refer to everyday conceptual constructs. The *formation* of everyday constructs and indeed their ontological status is, I suggest, another matter. I am not sure whether what we have here is actually conceptualism or not.[35]

2.2. Jainism, and Cārvāka–Lokāyata

*2.2.1. Manifoldness (*anekāntavāda*) and 'From a Certain Point of View' (*syādvāda*)*

Central to Jainism as a religion and an ethical system is non-violence or non-harming, and it is plausible to see the doctrines of *anekānta* and *syāt* as non-

[34] Mookerjee (1975) is useful for the way in which he outlines the Indian arguments (following mainly the 8th-century *Tattvasaṃgraha* of Śāntarakṣita and its *Pañjikā* by Kamalaśīla), but unfortunately Mookerjee's writing is philosophically extremely unsophisticated and a certain amount of philosophical probing and clarification is necessary. Apart from 'meaning' for *artha*, as far as I can tell, Mookerjee (*pace* Mill) seems also to use 'connote–connotation' and 'denote–denotation' as equivalents.

[35] See Matilal (1971: 39 (ignore the reference to Nāgārjuna's 'absolute')–46; 1982: 91–112; 1986: 398–403; 1990: 37–9); and Mookerjee (1975: 107–39).

harming extended into the areas of philosophy. *Anekāntavāda* is the doctrine of manifoldness, that reality is actually infinitely complex. Reality, and any existent, has infinite facets. Thus any attempt to capture things in formulas as being simply (exclusively) *x*, or simply not *x*, etc. is going to be only partially true at the most. Looked at another way, alternative formulas would be equally true. Hence *syādvāda*—the doctrine of its being the case 'from a certain point of view'. Note here that the Jaina approach is *in*clusivist, each perspective is *true*, but only true from a certain point of view. Thus in the *anekānta* approach to causality, for example, there is an accepting from a certain point of view of *satkāryavāda*, and from a certain point of view of *asatkāryavāda*. The Jaina treatment of substance draws on and yet contrasts with Vaiśeṣika on the one hand and Buddhism on the other. For the Jain, the follower of Jainism, substance has all three characteristics of origination, decay, *and* stability or persistence. Becoming implies being and vice versa. Impermanence is true 'from a certain point of view', and stability of substance is also true 'from a certain point of view'. The whole can also be accepted from a certain point of view. Those traditions which hold exclusively to one facet or another of an infinitely complex and manifold reality are 'one-sided' (*ekānta*), extremist.

There are seven possible standpoints (*nayas*), and the *syādvāda* involves a sevenfold predication. Thus:

(1) From a certain point of view *x* (e.g. substance) is.
(2) From a certain point of view *x* is not.
(3) From a certain point of view *x* is, and from another point of view *x* is not.
(4) From a certain point of view *x* is inexpressible.
(5) From a certain point of view *x* both is, and is inexpressible.
(6) From a certain point of view *x* both is not, and is inexpressible.
(7) From a certain point of view *x* is, is not, and is inexpressible.

The category of 'inexpressible' (4) is appropriate when there is a simultaneous joint application as one unitary predication of the contradictory 'is' and 'is not'. Thus the distinction between the third predication ('From a certain point of view *x* is, and from another point of view *x* is not') and the fourth predication ('From a certain point of view *x* is inexpressible') is the distinction between sequentially predicating '*x* is' and '*x* is not' as true of something, and predicating the two in a simultaneous and combined manner. Where they are simultaneously predicated, there is no formula which can be used to express this precisely and so it is called 'inexpressible'. (5) occurs when we say that *x* is, and yet if we simultaneously apply 'is' and 'is not' it becomes inexpressible. And so on.

In considering objections to the Jaina position on all of this we can note in particular the observation of the Nyāya–Vaiśeṣika philosopher Vyomaśiva (*c.*CE 950) that if for an accurate picture the *syādvāda* should be applied to all propositions, then it should be applied to the *anekāntavāda* and *syādvāda* themselves. Thus the *anekāntavāda* which is the very starting-point of Jaina thought will itself not be really (absolutely) true of the way things are. Matilal (1981, 1985) suggests the application here of Nāgārjuna's approach in dealing with a similar objection against emptiness: 'If all is empty, then your own words are also empty.' What this amounts to is that the Jain could accept that the position of *anekāntavāda* is true only from a certain point of view while at the same time seeing this as a vindication rather than a refutation of *anekāntavāda* and *syādvāda*. *Anekāntavāda* is true only from a certain point of view precisely *because* all propositions are true only from a certain point of view.[36]

Perhaps it would also help here to make a Tarskian distinction between first-order philosophical propositions which should be subject to the *syādvāda* because of the complex nature of reality, and the second-order metastatements of *anekāntavāda* and *syādvāda* themselves. If the latter are taken as first-order propositions, then *anekāntavāda* and *syādvāda* would of course apply to them too. This is because the Jain has stated (second-order) that *all* first-order philosophical propositions are subject to *anekāntavāda* and *syādvāda*. Thus the application to *anekāntavāda* and *syādvāda* of itself is precisely the result of the acceptance of the second-order metastatements of *anekāntavāda* and *syādvāda*. So long as we make the distinction between first- and second-order there need be no problem, no contradiction, and no infinite regress here.[37]

2.2.2. *Cārvāka–Lokāyata*

With the exception of the slightly problematic case of the *Tattvopaplavasiṃha*, we know of the ideas of the school known alternatively as Cārvāka or Lokāyata only from the expositions and attacks by their opponents. In India it was widely held that 'nihilism'—what the Buddhists call the doctrine of annihilation (*ucchedavāda*)—the view that there is no life after death, *must* entail appalling immorality. It is quite possible that it was critics of Cārvāka epistemology and the materialist approach to consciousness who derived from that approach as a necessary corollary the egoistic and hedonistic amoralism attributed to the school.[38]

Traditional Cārvāka–Lokāyata appears to have encompassed philosophically

[36] See Mookerjee (1978: 153 ff.); Matilal (1981: 57–8; 1985: 310–11). I am not entirely clear that I understand Mookerjee on this, but I think it must end up like Matilal's strategy.

[37] For an overview of Jaina philosophy, see Jaini (1979: 89–106); Matilal (1981: 1–6, 19–29, 32–61; 1985: 279–84, 294–314). In Matilal (1985) he repeats much of the material in perhaps a rather more philosophically mature and crisp manner. Mookerjee (1978) gives a comprehensive account of Jaina theories and critics in the traditional way.

[38] Note, incidentally, that *pace* Riepe (1961: 75) it is not obvious that a form of hedonism based on materialism would be incompatible with moral virtues like compassion. The Egoistic Utilitarian Jeremy Bentham was also a most humane and compassionate man because, as he said, compassion gave him pleasure.

a form of radical empiricism (the only *pramāṇa* is sense-perception) and consequential anti-religious materialism, particularly with reference to consciousness and *post mortem* survival.[39] The *reasons* given for rejecting inference as a *pramāṇa* were connected mainly with the problem of establishing the all-important pervasion inductively, particularly given an emphatic rejection of universals. Of course one can raise the question here of whether it is contradictory to use reason in order to argue that inference cannot lead to truth.[40] Franco (1983, 1987) suggests that it was indeed the further difficulty of establishing sense-perception as a *pramāṇa* once inference had been denied which turned Jayarāśi in the direction of a complete scepticism. Other followers of Cārvāka–Lokāyata adopted an alternative strategy of admitting a limited use of inference for everyday purposes, while denying that inference could possibly establish supersensible entities like God, or *post mortem* existence.

Jayarāśi in his *Tattvopaplavasiṃha* traces his intellectual ancestry to the mythical originator of the Cārvāka perspective Bṛhaspati, and appears to have adopted a Cārvāka–Lokāyata approach. Epistemologically, however, Jayarāśi does not adopt the (older?) Cārvāka strategy of denying the validity of all the *pramāṇas* except sense-perception as means of establishing truth. Rather, he is a straight epistemological sceptic. For Jayarāśi, sense-perception too cannot be accepted as a *pramāṇa* and he is highly critical of attempts by other schools to do so. Thus to be consistent the so-called Cārvāka tenets as a school (such as that the Scriptures are false, there is no God, there is no such thing as the 'law of *karma*', and consciousness is simply a by-product of material forces) ought not to be acceptable to Jayarāśi as discovered truth-statements, for they could not be proved. It appears, however, that he is not consistent here, for he does indeed appear to hold with Bṛhaspati that consciousness is a by-product of physical processes, and there is therefore no life after death.[41] In his study of Jayarāśi Eli Franco attempts an interesting defence of Jayarāśi's scepticism. But it is of course one thing to be able to defend scepticism as a plausible and not inconsistent philosophical strategy, and another to explain how it is that a complete sceptic like Jayarāśi can claim to *know* that consciousness is a by-product of material processes and that there is no after life.

One of the good reasons for looking at Cārvāka–Lokāyata in a brief introduction to Indian philosophy is that not only does it show that not all Indian philosophy is 'mystical' and religious (demonstrating that the rich and complex history of Indian philosophy refreshingly produced also empiricists, materialists, and rigorous sceptics), and not only do we meet here some remarkably

[39] For an opponent's argument that memory should suggest that consciousness is not simply a by-product of material processes, and the Cārvāka reply, see Bhattacharyya (1990: 456–8).

[40] On this issue, see e.g. Bhattacharyya (1990: 455–6), and Franco (1987: 35 ff.).

[41] See Franco (1987: 46–7). On how we are to assess Jayarāśi's inconsistencies, see Franco (1987, and also 1984: 127 ff.).

modern perspectives and arguments, but inasmuch as considering critically the arguments of the sceptic is a common entry into philosophy, it is here in particular that we can think of engaging critically with our Indian material.[42] But in looking at Indian philosophy as a whole, this is something we should have been doing all along.

BIBLIOGRAPHY

BASIC READING

Although it is not possible to recommend one or two books as completely adequate surveys of the material, for limited further study it may just about be possible to get by with this short chapter plus the following works.

For the Hindu schools, early Buddhism, Jainism, and Cārvāka there is Hiriyanna (1932). Williams (1989) can be used for the Mahāyāna Buddhist schools, and there is Matilal (1986) for many of the issues of epistemology, logic, and semantics as well as his philosophical approach. Radhakrishnan and Moore (1957) provides a rich selection of primary-source material for some further reading.

HIRIYANNA, M. (1932), *Outlines of Indian Philosophy* (London). Many reprints recently by Motilal Banarsidass (Delhi, 1993). Perhaps the best of the old-fashioned general surveys. It has dated much less, and is less idiosyncratic and opinionated, than many. Hiriyanna's *Essentials of Indian Philosophy* is an abridged version of the same work.

MATILAL, B. K. (1986), *Perception: An Essay on Classical Indian Theories of Knowledge* (Oxford). A brilliant book—the best—by the leading scholar in the field of the critical philosophical study of Indian philosophy, and immensely respected in India. Matilal had a mission to show philosophers that India produced serious analytic philosophy as worthy of study and as rewarding as, say, Greek philosophy. Sadly Matilal died while still relatively young. This book was written for and is dedicated to his friends Peter Strawson and Michael Dummett. Given the book's scope and complexity it is unfortunately marred by a very inadequate index.

RADHAKRISHNAN, S., and MOORE, C. A. (1957), *A Sourcebook in Indian Philosophy* (Princeton). Reprinted many times. By far the best general sourcebook for texts. Very good value indeed. Use really to come to grips with some primary texts in translation.

WILLIAMS, P. (1989), *Mahāyāna Buddhism: The Doctrinal Foundations* (London). An up-to-date survey reflecting recent research, which covers Mahāyāna religious ideas as well as philosophy.

[42] For general studies of Cārvāka, see Riepe (1961: 53–78); Bhattacharyya (1990: 452–73). On Jayarāśi and the *Tattvopaplavasiṃha*, see Franco (1983, 1984: 127–33). Franco (1987: 1–8, 15–53) covers some of the same ground as his (1983) paper but more fully, and has a very useful discussion of Jayarāśi as a sceptic.

FURTHER READING

BHADURI, S. (1947/1975), *Studies in Nyāya–Vaiśeṣika Metaphysics* (Poona). A comprehensive study in the traditional manner of the categories, and allied problems such as wholes and parts, and causality. An important source for Potter (1977).

BHATTACHARYYA, A. K. (1990), 'Cārvāka Darśana', in D. Chattopadhyaya, *Cārvāka/Lokāyata* (New Delhi). Translated from the Bengali. A survey in traditional style by one who is not himself a follower of Cārvāka, but remarkably clear and sympathetically written. The whole Chattopadhyaya book is a very comprehensive source of material on Cārvāka, useful for further research.

BOWES, P. (1971), *Consciousness and Freedom: Three Views* (London). From India, Bowes taught in the United Kingdom and originally worked in Western philosophy. Here she thinks through some issues in the philosophy of mind with reference to materialism, phenomenology, and two Indian views, Sāṃkhya and Vedānta. An interesting discussion by a rather neglected philosopher.

COLLINS, S. (1982), *Selfless Persons: Imagery and Thought in Theravāda Buddhism* (Cambridge). A sophisticated study of the Buddhist not-Self doctrine in its cultural and intellectual context, by one with a philosophical training and an interest in cultural anthropology. By far the best study of its subject.

COWARD, H. G., and KUNJUNNI RAJA, K. (1990), *Encyclopedia of Indian Philosophies: The Philosophy of the Grammarians* (Delhi and Princeton). Given that the material cries out for philosophically sensitive and sophisticated treatment, this is a disappointing book. However, there is not very much easily available on the Indian philosophy of grammar, and the book is particularly valuable for its summaries of texts.

FRANCO, E. (1983), 'Studies in the *Tattvopaplavasiṃha* I: The Criterion of Truth', *Journal of Indian Philosophy*, 11: 147–66.

——(1984), 'Studies in the *Tattvopaplavasiṃha* II: The Theory of Error', *Journal of Indian Philosophy*, 12: 105–37. Two papers on epistemology by the foremost contemporary scholar of Jayarāśi. The first paper is more accessible.

——(1987), *Perception, Knowledge and Disbelief: A Study of Jayarāśi's Scepticism* (Stuttgart). To date the only book-length survey of its subject, with a fully annotated edition of the Sanskrit text and translation of the *Tattvopaplavasiṃha*. A good introduction which repeats some of the material from Franco's previous papers and defends Jayarāśi's scepticism.

GRIFFITHS, P. J. (1986), *On Being Mindless: Buddhist Meditation and the Mind-Body Problem* (La Salle, III.). Actually a study of certain philosophical problems which arise through a meditative achievement called *nirodhasamāpatti*, the 'attainment of cessation' when mental activity is apparently supposed to stop, but the book also contains good general discussions of Theravāda, Vaibhāṣika, and Yogācāra thought with particular reference to philosophical psychology.

HATTORI, M. (1968), *Dignāga: On Perception* (Cambridge, Mass.). An edition of the Tibetan texts of the opening sections of the *Pramāṇasamuccaya*, with Sanskrit reconstruction, translation, and extensive notes. Contains Diṅnāga's exposition of his own position on perception, together with his criticisms of rival views. Difficult material at times, but this is a standard work which well repays reading.

HUNTINGTON, C. W., Jr. (1989), *The Emptiness of Emptiness* (Hawaii). By far the best attempt to develop a Wittgensteinian reading of Madhyamaka. An intelligent book but I happen to consider this approach quite mistaken. Contains a translation from the Tibetan of Candrakīrti's *Madhyamakāvatāra*, but the translation has been done in the light of Huntington's interpretation and is therefore sometimes problematic.

Jackson, R. R. (1993), *Is Enlightenment Possible? Dharmakīrti and rGyal tshab rje on Knowledge, Rebirth, No-Self and Liberation* (Ithaca, NY). A translation of part of a commentary by the the Tibetan rGyal tshab rje (1364–1462) to Dharmakīrti's *Pramāṇavārttika*, giving *inter alia* an attempted proof of rebirth, but with a long introduction on the background to Buddhist epistemology (and particularly its spiritual role), and Dharmakīrti and rGyal tshab rje. Note that the views of rGyal tshab rje and his dGe lugs tradition on Dharmakīrti's thought were controversial even in Tibet and should be taken as one *possible* reading of Dharmakīrti.

Jaini, P. S. (1979), *The Jaina Path of Purification* (Berkeley and New Delhi). An authoritative and highly respected survey of most aspects of Jainism by a scholar who is also very familiar with Buddhism.

Larson, G. J. (1969), *Classical Sāṃkhya: An Interpretation of its History and Meaning* (Delhi). A sympathetic attempt to rethink Sāṃkhya philosophically, based on a close reading of the *Sāṃkhyakārikā*, which is also translated.

——and Bhattacharya, R. S. (1987), *Encyclopedia of Indian Philosophies*, iv: *Sāṃkhya: A Dualist Tradition in Indian Philosophy* (Princeton and Delhi). An important study, including detailed summaries of all the primary sources.

McDermott, A. C. S. (1969), *An Eleventh-Century Buddhist Logic of 'Exists': Ratnakīrti's Kṣaṇabhaṅgasiddhiḥ Vyatirekātmakā* (Dordrecht). Edition of the Sanskrit text, translation, with extensive commentarial notes, of a late Indian treatise from the Diṅnāga–Dharmakīrti tradition, aiming to establish the contraposed version of the thesis of momentariness: 'Whatever is non-momentary is non-existent'. The need to cite as an example a completely non-momentary and therefore fictitious entity gives rise to peculiar problems in Indian logic. McDermott had previously worked in medieval Western logic.

Matilal, B. K. (1968), *The Navya-Nyāya Doctrine of Negation: The Semantics and Ontology of Negative Statements in Navya-Nyāya Philosophy* (Cambridge, Mass.). Matilal's doctoral thesis, which attempts to explain systematically in a philosophically meaningful way how Navya-Nyāya epistemology *works*, and why Nyāya philosophy is as it is. Acclaimed when it first appeared as possibly the best work on Indian philosophy ever written in a European language. Not an easy piece of writing at first reading (partly because Matilal is easily sidetracked, particularly by Western philosophy), but it well repays rereading. Extremely influential. N.B. It is rumoured that the publishers Motilal Banarsidass in Delhi are reprinting all Matilal's works. Banarsidass's books are not difficult to obtain in the West.

——(1971), *Epistemology, Logic and Grammar in Indian Philosophical Analysis* (The Hague). A collection of Matilal's early papers. Better written and clearer than some of his later articles, with many of the same themes (on a personal note, the book which awakened me from my 'dogmatic slumbers' to the real possibilities of Indian philosophy).

——(1974), 'A Critique of Buddhist Idealism', in L. Cousins, A. Kunst, and K. R. Norman (eds.), *Buddhist Studies in Honour of I. B. Horner* (Dordrecht). On the nature of Buddhist 'idealism', and criticisms from its mainly Hindu opponents. Includes translated material. Generally it seems that the papers Matilal published in the West appear to be more organized, better finished, than those published in India.

——(1981), *The Central Philosophy of Jainism (Anekānta-Vāda)* (Ahmedabad). Matilal's work is always interesting but he was a poor lecturer. This book is a series of lectures on Jainism which he gave in India in 1975 and it tries to cover too much, at times rather superficially. I suspect the lectures were largely unrevised. Still, there is not so much available on Jain philosophy. Better versions of the philosophically more interesting material can be found in Matilal (1985).

——(1982), *Logical and Ethical Issues of Religious Belief* (Calcutta). A series of lectures delivered in 1978. Variable in quality, and although Matilal argues that they are all interconnected, the lectures do not hang together terribly well. Still, a much more interesting series than Matilal (1981), including an Indian perspective on some stock topics in the philosophy of religion, such as suffering, the problem of evil, and ineffability.

——(1985), *Logic, Language and Reality: An Introduction to Indian Philosophical Studies* (New Delhi). In spite of the subtitle, this is yet another collection of Matilal's papers treating mainly issues of logic, epistemology, and philosophical semantics. Some of the papers show the author moving towards positions he adopted in Matilal (1986). Much better overal quality than Matilal (1981, 1982), but although Matilal attempted to organize the material under general headings, the book's limited scope and lack of systematic treatment mean that it cannot really serve as a much-needed single-volume 'Introduction to Indian Philosophy'.

——(1990), *The Word and the World: India's Contribution to the Study of Language* (New Delhi). A short book written after the onset of Matilal's terminal illness. Treats many of the themes relating to language, perception, universals, etc. which concerned Matilal throughout his career, and particularly useful for its discussion of Bhartṛhari and his successors. Appendices include a paper on mysticism and ineffability, and an excellent short introduction to Indian logic and debate.

MOHANTY, J. N. (1966), *Gaṅgeśa's Theory of Truth* (Santiniketan). A translation of the *Pramāṇya (jñapti) vāda* section of Gaṅgeśa's *Tattvacintāmaṇi*, with a very valuable introductory essay. An extremely important predecessor and complement to Matilal (1968).

——(1970), 'Reflections on the Nyāya Theory of *Avayavipratyakṣa*', in *Phenomenology and Ontology* (The Hague). Mohanty's brilliant paper on the Nyāya theory of the Whole in the light of comparative philosophy. This volume of Mohanty's papers contains mainly papers on Western philosophy—including phenomenology, Hartmann, Ryle, and Moore—but also has a paper on the Nyāya treatment of doubt.

——(1992), *Reason and Tradition in Indian Thought: An Essay on the Nature of Indian Philosophical Thinking* (Oxford).

MOOKERJEE, S. (1975), *The Buddhist Philosophy of Universal Flux: An Exposition of the Philosophy of Critical Realism as Expounded by the School of Dignāga* (Calcutta, 1935; Delhi). A standard work on its subject. Mookerjee writes in the traditional manner, following the Sanskrit texts closely and in detail. Since there is very little by way of general surveys of Diṅnāga's thought—or Jaina philosophy—the fact that Mookerjee tends not to impose in any obvious way his own philosophical ideas on the material (in the way Stcherbatsky does) is a definite advantage. Note that a great deal of the Diṅnāga–Dharmakīrti material is lost in Sanskrit and survives only in Tibetan. The fact that (like Matilal, but unlike Stcherbatsky) Mookerjee was unable to use Tibetan meant that he often had to rely on critical expositions of Buddhism by its opponents.

MOOKERJEE, S. (1978), *The Jaina Philosophy of Non-Absolutism: A Critical Study of Anekāntavāda* (Calcutta, 1944; Delhi). A standard detailed study covering much more Jaina philosophy than simply *anekāntavāda* (for example, universals).

PARFIT, D. (1984), *Reasons and Persons* (Oxford).

PERDUE, D. E. (1992), *Debate in Tibetan Tradition* (Ithaca, NY). A very detailed study of the sophisticated and complex system of logic and debate as it is practised to the present day in dGe lugs Tibetan monasteries. A fascinating subject, although while Perdue is clearly very knowledgeable of the Tibetan tradition and material, the book is not very philosophically aware. For a video on Tibetan debate, see *Debate in the Tibetan Tradition*, Tibet Foundation Films, 3 Heathcock Court, Strand, London WC2R 0PA.

POTTER, K. H. (1963), *Presuppositions of India's Philosophies* (Englewood Cliffs, NJ). A clever attempt to rethink how to present Indian philosophy in terms of paths to freedom. Critical, philosophically aware, and very variable in quality. Excellent in presenting Indian logic, but not always very reliable, to say the least, on (for example) Buddhist thought. Still worth consulting, although a great deal of significant work has been done since this book first appeared.

——(1977), *Encyclopedia of Indian Philosophies*, i: *Indian Metaphysics and Epistemology: The Tradition of Nyāya–Vaiśeṣika up to Gaṅgeśa* (Princeton and Delhi). The first volume of the multi-volume *Encyclopedia of Indian Philosophies* (apart from the Bibliography volume), and arguably still the best. The series continues. A long, up-to-date, and generally reliable introduction by Potter, followed by detailed summaries by a team of international scholars of many important texts, keyed to standard editions of the Sanskrit. It is very useful indeed to have all this material in one place, and this is an extremely valuable work.

——and BHATTACHARYYA, S. (1992), *Encyclopedia of Indian Philosophies*, vi: *Indian Philosophical Analysis: Nyāya–Vaiśeṣika from Gaṅgeśa to Raghunātha Śiromaṇi* (Princeton and Delhi).

RIEPE, D. (1961), *The Naturalistic Tradition in Indian Thought* (Delhi). A rather dated book now, and it is not clear whether Riepe reads any oriental languages. Tends to set Indian views alongside Western views drawn piecemeal and out of context from the whole range of Western philosophy. But the book still has its uses as an accessible survey of otherwise rather neglected 'naturalistic' trends in Indian thought.

SHASTRI, D. N. (1964), *Critique of Indian Realism: A Study of the Conflict between the Nyāya–Vaiśeṣika and the Buddhist Dignāga School* (Agra); repr. as *The Philosophy of Nyāya–Vaiśeṣika and its Conflict with the Buddhist Dignāga School* (Delhi, 1976). Although Shastri is unable to use the Tibetan sources, this is a comprehensive and critical survey—particularly as regards the Nyāya–Vaiśeṣika—with a number of new perspectives. Clear and very useful.

Skorupski, T. (1987), 'Dharma: Buddhist Dharma and Dharmas', in M. Eliade, *The Encyclopedia of Religion* (New York). A handy survey of the lists, relating mainly to the Vaibhāṣika *dharma* system.

Stcherbatsky, T. (1962), *Buddhist Logic*, 2 vols. (Leningrad, *c*.1930; New York). For long the standard work in English on the Diṅnāga–Dharmakīrti tradition (written under the materialist eye of Stalin). Stcherbatsky was an excellent scholar in Sanskrit and Tibetan with a comprehensive knowledge of Western philosophy and a particular admiration for Kant. A pioneering and very influential, if rather long-winded, work with considerable insight, although Stcherbatsky's interpretations are often nowadays thought questionable. The second volume contains *inter alia* a translation of Dharmakīrti's *Nyāyabindu* with Dharmottara's commentary. A book that it is impossible to ignore.

Vidyabhusana, S. C. (1971), *A History of Indian Logic* (first pub. 1920; Delhi). A pioneering work by a scholar who was also important in the study of Tibet and Tibetan. Summaries of texts, it is really a reference work which is more like a glorified bibliography at times. Still useful though.

Warder, A. K. (1970), *Indian Buddhism* (Delhi). A comprehensive and useful survey which makes good use of the primary texts.

Williams, P. (1991), 'On the Interpretation of Madhyamaka Thought', *Journal of Indian Philosophy*, 19: 191–218. Review article of Huntington (1989).

Index